DICTIONARY

Edited by
NEIL MORRIS
ROSWITHA MORRIS

Based on
The Oxford German Minidictionary
Gunhild Prowe
Jill Schneider

Based on The Oxford German Minidictionary
© Oxford University Press 1993.
This abridged edition published 1995 by
Parragon Book Services and Magpie Books,
an imprint of Robinson Publishing Ltd.,
by arrangement with Oxford University Press.

Oxford is a trade mark of Oxford University Press

ISBN 0–75250–037–6

Printed and bound in the United Kingdom by
HarperCollins Manufacturing

Typeset by Latimer Trend & Co. Ltd.

Contents

Introduction

A swung dash ~ represents the headword or that part of the headword preceding a vertical bar |. The initial letter of a German headword is given to show whether or not it is a capital.

The vertical bar | follows the part of the headword which is not repeated in compounds or derivatives.

Square brackets [ ] are used for optional material.

Angled brackets ⟨ ⟩ are used after a verb translation to indicate the object; before a verb translation to indicate the subject; before an adjective to indicate a typical noun which it qualifies.

Round brackets ( ) are used for field or style labels (see list on page vi) and for explanatory matter.

A box □ indicates a new part of speech within an entry.

od (oder) and *or* denote that words or portions of a phrase are synonymous. An oblique stroke / is used where there is a difference in usage or meaning.

≈ is used where no exact equivalent exists in the other language.

A dagger † indicates that a German verb is irregular and that the parts can be found in the verb table on page 499. Compound verbs are not listed there as they follow the pattern of the basic verb.

The stressed vowel is marked in a German headword by – (long) or · (short). A phonetic transcription is only given for words which do not follow the normal rules of pronunciation. These rules can be found on page 497.

In English headwords and derivatives, stress marks for pronunciation are given where these are felt to be helpful.

German headword nouns are followed by the gender and, with the exception of compound nouns, by the genitive and plural. These are only given if they present some difficulty. In the case of compound nouns if they present some difficulty. Otherwise the user should refer to the final element.

Nouns that decline like adjectives are entered as follows: **-e(r)** *m/f,* **-e(s)** *nt.*

Adjectives which have no undeclined form are entered in the feminine form with the masculine and neuter in brackets **-e(r,s).**

The reflexive pronoun **sich** is accusative unless marked (*dat*).

Proprietary terms

This dictionary includes some words which are, or are asserted to be, proprietary names or trade marks. Their inclusion does not imply that they have acquired for legal purposes a non-proprietary or general significance, nor is any other judgement implied concerning their legal status. In cases where the editor has some evidence that a word is used as a proprietary name or trade mark this is indicated by the letter (P), but no judgement concerning the legal status of such words is made or implied thereby.

Abbreviations/Abkürzungen

adjective	a	Adjektiv
abbreviation	abbr	Abkürzung
accusative	acc	Akkusativ
Administration	Admin	Administration
adverb	adv	Adverb
American	Amer	amerikanisch
Anatomy	Anat	Anatomie
Archaeology	Archaeol	Archäologie
Architecture	Archit	Architektur
Astronomy	Astr	Astronomie
attributive	attrib	attributiv
Austrian	Aust	österreichisch
Motor vehicles	Auto	Automobil
Aviation	Aviat	Luftfahrt
Biology	Biol	Biologie
Botany	Bot	Botanik
Chemistry	Chem	Chemie
collective	coll	Kollektivum
Commerce	Comm	Handel
conjunction	conj	Konjunktion
Cookery.	Culin	Kochkunst
dative	dat	Dativ
definite article	def art	bestimmter Artikel
demonstrative	dem	Demonstrativ-
dialect	dial	Dialekt
Electricity	Electr	Elektrizität
something	etw	etwas
feminine	f	Femininum
familiar	fam	familiär
figurative	fig	figurativ
genitive	gen	Genitiv
Geography	Geog	Geographie
Geology	Geol	Geologie
Geometry	Geom	Geometrie

Grammar	Gram	Grammatik
Horticulture	Hort	Gartenbau
impersonal	impers	unpersönlich
indefinite article	indef art	unbestimmter Artikel
inseparable	insep	untrennbar
interjection	int	Interjektion
invariable	inv	unveränderlich
irregular	irreg	unregelmäßig
someone	jd	jemand
someone	jdm	jemandem
someone	jdn	jemanden
someone's	jds	jemandes
Journalism	Journ	Journalismus
Law	Jur	Jura
Language	Lang	Sprache
literary	liter	dichterisch
masculine	m	Maskulinum
Mathematics	Math	Mathematik
Medicine	Med	Medizin
Meteorology	Meteorol	Meteorologie
Military	Mil	Militär
Mineralogy	Miner	Mineralogie
Music	Mus	Musik
noun	n	Substantiv
Nautical	Naut	nautisch
North German	N Ger	Norddeutsch
nominative	nom	Nominativ
neuter	nt	Neutrum
or	od	oder
Proprietary term	P	Warenzeichen
pejorative	pej	abwertend
Photography	Phot	Fotografie
Physics	Phys	Physik
plural	pl	Plural
Politics	Pol	Politik
possessive	poss	Possessiv-

past participle	pp	zweites Partizip
predicative	pred	prädikativ
prefix	pref	Präfix
preposition	prep	Präposition
present	pres	Präsens
present participle	pres p	erstes Partizip
pronoun	pron	Pronomen
Psychology	Psych	Psychologie
past tense	pt	Präteritum
Railway	Rail	Eisenbahn
reflexive	refl	reflexiv
regular	reg	regelmäßig
relative	rel	Relativ-
Religion	Relig	Religion
see	s.	siehe
School	Sch	Schule
separable	sep	trennbar
singular	sg	Singular
South German	S Ger	Süddeutsch
slang	sl	Slang
someone	s.o.	jemand
something	sth	etwas
Technical	Techn	Technik
Telephone	Teleph	Telefon
Textiles	Tex	Textilien
Theatre	Theat	Theater
Television	TV	Fernsehen
Typography	Typ	Typographie
University	Univ	Universität
auxiliary verb	v aux	Hilfsverb
intransitive verb	vi	intransitives Verb
reflexive verb	vr	reflexives Verb
transitive verb	vt	transitives Verb
vulgar	vulg	vulgär
Zoology	Zool	Zoologie

A

Aal m -[e]s,-e eel

Aas nt -es carrion; (sl) swine

ab prep (+ dat) from □adv off; (weg) away; (auf Fahrplan) departs; **ab und zu** now and then; **auf und ab** up and down

abändern vt sep alter

Abbau m dismantling; (Kohlen-) mining. **a~en** vt sep dismantle; mine ⟨Kohle⟩

abbeißen† vt sep bite off

abbeizen vt sep strip

abberufen† vt sep recall

abbestellen vt sep cancel; **jdn a~** put s.o. off

abbiegen† vi sep (sein) turn off; **[nach] links a~** turn left

Abbildung f -,-en illustration

abblättern vi sep (sein) flake off

abblend|en vt/i sep (haben) **[die Scheinwerfer] a~en** dip one's headlights. **a~licht** nt dipped headlights pl

abbrechen† v sep break of

abbrennen† v sep □vt burn off; (niederbrennen) burn down □vi (sein) burn down

abbringen† vt sep dissuade (von from)

Abbruch m demolition; (Beenden) breaking off

abbuchen vt sep debit

abbürsten vt sep brush down; (entfernen) brush off

abdanken vi sep (haben) resign; ⟨Herrscher:⟩ abdicate

abdecken vt sep uncover; (abnehmen) take off; (zudecken) cover

abdichten vt sep seal

abdrehen vt sep turn off

Abdruck m (pl ¨e) impression. **a~en** vt sep print

abdrücken vt/i sep (haben) fire; **sich a~** leave an impression

Abend m -s,-e evening. **a~** adv **heute a~** this evening, tonight; **gestern a~** yesterday evening, last night. **A~brot** nt supper. **A~essen** nt dinner; (einfacher) supper. **A~mahl** nt (Relig) [Holy] Communion. **a~s** adv in the evening

Abenteuer nt -s,- adventure. **a~lich** a fantastic

aber conj but; **oder a~** or else □adv (wirklich) really

Aber|glaube m superstition. **a~gläubisch** a superstitious

abfahr|en† v sep □vi (sein) leave □vt take away; (entlangfahren) drive along; use ⟨Fahrkarte⟩; **abgefahrene Reifen** worn tyres. **A~t** f departure; (Piste) run

Abfall m refuse, rubbish; (auf der Straße) litter; (Industrie-) waste. **A~eimer** m rubbish-bin

abfallen† vi sep (sein) drop, fall; (übrigbleiben) be left (für for); (sich neigen) slope away

abfallig a disparaging

abfangen† vt sep intercept

abfassen vt sep draft

abfertigen vt sep attend to; (zollamtlich) clear; **jdn kurz a~** (fam) give s.o. short shrift

abfeuern vt sep fire

abfind|en† vt sep pay off; (entschädigen) compensate; **sich a~en mit** come to terms with. **A~ung** f -,-en compensation

abfliegen† vi sep (sein) fly off; (Aviat) take off

abfließen† vi sep (sein) drain

Abflug m (Aviat) departure

Abfluß m drainage; (Öffnung) drain. **A~rohr** nt drain-pipe

abfragen vt sep jdn od jdm Vokabeln a~ test s.o. on vocabulary

Abfuhr f - removal; (fig) rebuff

abführ|en vt sep take away. **A~mittel** nt laxative

abfüllen vt sep **auf** od **in Flaschen a~** bottle

Abgase ntpl exhaust fumes

abgeben† vt sep hand in; (abliefern) deliver; (verkaufen) sell; (zur Aufbewahrung) leave; (Fußball) pass; (verlauten lassen) give; cast (Stimme); **jdm etw a~** give s.o. a share of sth

abgedroschen a hackneyed

abgehen† v sep ◇ vi (sein) leave; (Theat) exit; (sich lösen) come off; (abgezogen werden) be deducted ◇ vt walk along

abgehetzt a harassed. **abgelegen** a remote. **abgeneigt** a **etw** (dat) **nicht abgeneigt sein** not be averse to sth. **Abgeordnete(r)** m/f (Pol) Member of Parliament. **abgepackt** a pre-packed.

abgeschlossen a (fig) complete; (Wohnung) self-contained. **abgesehen** prep apart (from **von**). **abgespannt** a exhausted. **abgestanden** a stale. **abgestorben** a dead; (Glied) numb. **abgetragen** a worn. **abgewetzt** a threadbare

abgewöhnen vt sep **jdm/sich das Rauchen a~** cure s.o. of/ give up smoking

abgießen† vt sep pour off; drain (Gemüse)

abgleiten† vi sep (sein) slip

Abgott m idol

abgöttisch adv **a~ lieben** idolize

abgrenzen vt sep divide off; (fig) define. **A~ung** f - demarcation

Abgrund m abyss; (fig) depths pl

Abguß m cast

abhaken vt sep tick off

abhalten† vt sep keep off; (hindern) keep, prevent (**von** from)

Abhandlung f treatise

Abhang m slope

abhäng|en¹ vt sep (reg) take down; (abkuppeln) uncouple

abhäng|en²† vi sep (haben) depend (**von** on). **a~ig** a dependent (**von** on). **A~igkeit** f - dependence

abhärten vt sep toughen up

abheben† v sep ◇ vt take off; (vom Konto) withdraw; **sich a~** stand out (**gegen** against) ◇ vi (haben) (Cards) cut [the cards]; (Aviat) take off; (Rakete:) lift off

abheften vt sep file

abhelfen† vi sep (+ dat) remedy

Abhilfe f remedy

abholen vt sep collect

abhorchen vt sep (Med) sound

abhör|en vt sep listen to; (überwachen) tap; **jdn** od **jdm Vokabeln a~en** test s.o. on vocabulary. **A~gerät** nt bugging device

Abitur nt -s ≈ A levels pl

abkaufen vt sep buy (dat from)

abklingen† vi sep (sein) die away; (nachlassen) subside

abkochen vt sep boil

abkommen† vi sep (sein) **a~ von** stray from; (aufgeben) give up. **A~** nt -s,- agreement

Abkömmling m -s,-e descendant

abkratzen vt sep scrape off

abkühlen vt/i sep (sein) cool; **sich a~** cool [down]

Abkunft f - origin

abkuppeln vt sep uncouple

abkürz|en vt sep shorten; abbreviate (Wort). **A~ung** f short cut; (Wort) abbreviation

abladen† vt sep unload

Ablage f shelf; (für Akten) tray

ablager|n vt sep deposit. **A~ung** f -,-en deposit

ablassen† *vt sep* drain [off]; let out ⟨*Dampf*⟩

Ablauf *m* drain; (*Verlauf*) course; (*Ende*) end; (*einer Frist*) expiry. **a~en**† *v sep* □*vi* (*sein*) run or drain off; (*verlaufen*) go off; (*enden*) expire; ⟨*Zeit:*⟩ run out; ⟨*Uhrwerk:*⟩ run down □*vt* walk along

ablegen *vt sep* put down; discard ⟨*Karte*⟩; (*abheften*) file; (*ausziehen*) take off; sit, take ⟨*Prüfung*⟩. **abgelegte Kleidung** cast-offs *pl*.

Ableger *m* **-s,-** (*Bot*) cutting; (*Schößling*) shoot

ablehnen *vt sep* refuse; (*mißbilligen*) reject. **A~ung** *f* refusal; rejection

ableiten *vt sep* divert; **sich a~en** be derived (**von/aus** from). **A~ung** *f* derivation; (*Wort*) derivative

ablenken *vt sep* deflect; divert. **A~ung** *f* -,-en distraction

ablichten *vt sep* photocopy. **A~ung** *f* photocopy

abliefern *vt sep* deliver

ablösen *vt sep* detach; (*sich abwechseln*) take turns

abmachen *vt sep* remove; (*ausmachen*) arrange; (*vereinbaren*) agree. **A~ung** *f* -,-en agreement

abmagern *vi sep* (*sein*) lose weight. **A~ungskur** *f* slimming diet

abmelden *vt sep* cancel; (*im Hotel*) check out

abmessen† *vt sep* measure

abmühen (sich) *vr sep* struggle

abnehmen† *v sep* □*vt* take off, remove; pick up ⟨*Hörer*⟩; **jdm etw a~en** take/(*kaufen*) buy sth from s.o. □*vi* (*haben*) decrease; (*nachlassen*) decline; ⟨*Person:*⟩ lose weight; ⟨*Mond:*⟩ wane. **A~er** *m* **-s,-** buyer

Abneigung *f* dislike (**gegen** of)

abnorm *a* abnormal, *adv* -ly

abnutzen *vt sep* wear out. **A~ung** *f* - wear [and tear]

Abonnement /abonə'mã:/ *nt* **-s,-s** subscription. **A~nent** *m* **-en,-en** subscriber. **a~nieren** *vt* take out a subscription to

Abordnung *f* -,-en deputation

abpassen *vt sep* wait for; **gut a~** time well

abraten† *vi sep* (*haben*) **jdm von etw a~** advise s.o. against sth

abräumen *vt/i* (*haben*) clear away; clear ⟨*Tisch*⟩

abrechnen *v sep* □*vt* deduct □*vi* (*haben*) settle up. **A~ung** *f* settlement; (*Rechnung*) account

Abreise *f* departure. **a~n** *vi sep* (*sein*) leave

abreißen† *v sep* □*vt* tear off □*vi* (*sein*) come off

abrichten *vt sep* train

abrufen† *vt sep* call away; (*Computer*) retrieve

abrunden *vt sep* round off

abrupt *a* abrupt

abrüsten *vi sep* (*haben*) disarm. **A~ung** *f* disarmament

abrutschen *vi sep* (*sein*) slip

Absage *f* -,-n cancellation; (*Ablehnung*) refusal. **a~n** *v sep* □*vt* cancel □*vi* (*haben*) [**jdm**] cancel an appointment [with s.o.]; refuse [s.o.'s invitation]

Absatz *m* heel; (*Abschnitt*) paragraph; (*Verkauf*) sale

abschaffen *vt sep* abolish; get rid of ⟨*Auto, Hund*⟩

abschalten *vt/i sep* (*haben*) switch off

abscheulich *a* revolting; (*fam*) horrible

abschicken *vt sep* send off

Abschied *m* **-[e]s,-e** farewell; (*Trennung*) parting. **A~ nehmen** say goodbye (**von** to)

abschießen† *vt sep* shoot down; (*abfeuern*) fire; launch ⟨*Rakete*⟩

abschirmen *vt sep* shield

abschlagen† *vt sep* knock off; (*verweigern*) refuse

Abschlepp|dienst m breakdown service. **a~en** vt sep tow away. **A~seil** nt tow-rope

abschließen† v sep □vt lock; (beenden) conclude; make (Wette); balance (Bücher) □vi (haben) lock up; (enden) end

Abschluß m conclusion. **A~-prüfung** f final examination. **A~zeugnis** nt diploma

abschmecken vt sep season

abschmieren vt sep lubricate

abschneiden† v sep □vt cut off □vi (haben) **gut/schlecht a~** do well/badly

Abschnitt m section; (Stadium) stage; (Absatz) paragraph

abschöpfen vt sep skim off

abschrauben vt sep unscrew

abschreck|en vt sep deter; (Culin) put in cold water (Ei). **a~end** a repulsive. **A~ungsmittel** nt deterrent

abschreib|en† v sep □vt copy; (Comm & fig) write off □vi (haben) copy. **A~ung** f (Comm) depreciation

Abschrift f copy

Abschuß m shooting down; (Abfeuern) firing; (Raketen-) launch

abschüssig a sloping; (steil) steep

abschwellen† vi sep (sein) go down

absehbar a in a~barer Zeit in the foreseeable future. **a~en†** vt/i sep (haben) copy; (voraussehen) foresee; **a~en von** disregard; (aufgeben) refrain from

abseits adv apart; (Sport) offside □prep (+gen) away from. **A~** nt (Sport) offside

absend|en† vt sep send off. **A~er** m sender

absetzen v sep □vt put or set down; (ablagern) deposit; (abnehmen) take off; (abbrechen) stop; (verkaufen) sell; (abziehen) deduct □vi (haben) pause

Absicht f -,-en intention; **mit A~** intentionally, on purpose

absichtlich a intentional

absolut a absolute, adv -ly

absolvieren vt complete; (bestehen) pass

absonder|n vt sep separate; (ausscheiden) secrete. **A~ung** f -,-en secretion

absorbieren vt absorb

abspeisen vt sep fob off (mit with)

absperr|en vt sep cordon off; (SGer) lock. **A~ung** f -,-en barrier

abspielen vt sep play; **sich a~** take place

Absprache f agreement

absprechen† vt sep arrange; **sich a~** agree

abspringen† vi sep (sein) jump off; (mit Fallschirm) parachute; (abgehen) come off

Absprung m jump

abspülen vt sep rinse

abstamm|en vi sep (haben) be descended (von from). **A~ung** f -,-en descent

Abstand m distance; (zeitlich) interval; **A~ halten** keep one's distance

abstatten vt sep **jdm einen Besuch a~** pay s.o. a visit

Abstecher m -s,- detour

absteig|en† vi sep (sein) dismount; (niedersteigen) descend; (Fußball) be relegated

abstell|en vt sep put down; (lagern) store; (parken) park; (abschalten) turn off. **A~gleis** nt siding. **A~raum** m box-room

absterben† vi sep (sein) die; (gefühllos werden) go numb

Abstieg m -[e]s,-e descent; (Fußball) relegation

abstimm|en v sep □vi (haben) vote (über+acc on); (koordinate) coordinate (auf+acc with). **A~ung** f vote

Abstinenzler m -s,- teetotaller

abstoßen† vt sep knock off; (verkaufen) sell. **a ~ d** a repulsive

abstrakt /-st-/ a abstract

abstreiten† vt sep deny

Abstrich m (Med) smear; (Kürzung) cut

abstufen vt sep grade

Absturz m fall; (Aviat) crash

abstürzen vi sep (sein) fall; (Aviat) crash

absuchen vt sep search

absurd a absurd

Abszeß m -sses,-sse abscess

Abt m -[e]s,ˬe abbot

abtasten vt sep feel; (Techn) scan

abtauen vt/i sep (sein) thaw; (entfrosten) defrost

Abtei f -,-en abbey

Abteil nt compartment

Abteilung f -,-en section; (Admin, Comm) department

abtragen† vt sep clear; (einebnen) level; (abnutzen) wear out

abtreib|en† vt sep (Naut) drive off course; **ein Kind a ~ en lassen** have an abortion. **A ~ ung** f -,-en abortion

abtrennen vt sep detach

Abtreter m -s,- doormat

abtrocknen vt/i sep (haben) dry; **sich a ~** dry oneself

abtropfen vi sep (sein) drain

abtun† vt sep (fig) dismiss

abwägen† vt sep (fig) weigh

abwandeln vt sep modify

abwarten vt sep ˈ wait for ˈ vi (haben) wait [and see]

abwärts adv down[wards]

Abwasch m -s washing-up; (Geschirr) dirty dishes pl. **a ~ en**† vt sep ˈ vt wash; wash up (Geschirr); (entfernen) wash off ˈ vi (haben) wash up. **A ~ lappen** m dishcloth

Abwasser nt -s,ˬ sewage. **A ~ kanal** m sewer

abwechseln vi/r sep (haben) [sich] a ~ alternate; (Personen:) take turns. **a ~ d** a alternate

Abwechslung f -,-en change; **zur A ~** for a change

abwegig a absurd

Abwehr f - defence; (Widerstand) resistance; (Pol) counter-espionage. **a ~ en** vt sep ward off. **A ~ system** nt immune system

abweich|en† vi sep (sein) deviate; (von Regel) depart (von from); (sich unterscheiden) differ (von from). **A ~ ung** f -,-en deviation

abweisen† vt sep turn down; turn away (Person). **a ~ end** a unfriendly. **A ~ ung** f rejection

abwenden† vt sep turn away; (verhindern) avert

abwerfen† vt sep throw off; throw (Reiter); (Aviat) drop; (Kartenspiel) discard; shed (Haut, Blätter); yield (Gewinn)

abwert|en vt sep devalue. **A ~ ung** f devaluation. **a ~ end** a pejorative

Abwesenheit f - absence; absent-mindedness

abwickeln vt sep unwind; (erledigen) settle

abwischen vt sep wipe

abzahlen vt sep pay off

abzählen vt sep count

Abzahlung f instalment

Abzeichen nt badge

Abzieh|bild nt transfer. **a ~ en**† v sep ˈ vt pull off; take off (Laken); strip (Bett); (häuten) skin; (Phot) print; run off (Kopien); (zurückziehen) withdraw; ˈ (abrechnen) deduct ˈ vi (sein) go away; (Rauch:) escape

Abzug m withdrawal; (Abrechnung) deduction; (Phot) print; (Korrektur-) proof; (am Gewehr) trigger; (A ~ söffnung) vent; **A ~ e** pl deductions

abzüglich prep (+ gen) less

Abzugshaube f (cooker) hood

abzweig|en v sep ˈ vi (sein) branch off ˈ vt divert. **A ~ ung** f -,-en junction; (Gabelung) fork

ach int oh; **a ~ je!** oh dear! **a ~ so** I see

Achse f -,-n axis; (Rad-) axle

Achsel f -,-n shoulder; **die A ~ n zucken** shrug one's shoulders. **A ~ höhle** f armpit

acht¹ inv a, **A ~** f -,-en eight

acht² außer a ~ lassen disregard; **sich in a ~ nehmen** be careful

achte(e)(r,s) a eighth. **a ~ eckig** a octagonal. **A ~ el** nt -s,- eighth

achten vt respect □ vi (haben) **a ~ auf** (+ acc) pay attention to; (auf-passen) look after

Achter|bahn f roller-coaster

achtgeben† vi sep (haben) be careful; **a ~ auf** (+ acc) look after

achtlos a careless

achtsam a careful

Achtung f - respect (**vor** + dat for); **A ~ !** look out!

acht|zehn inv a eighteen. **a ~ zehnte(r,s)** a eighteenth. **a ~ zig** a inv eighty. **a ~ zig-ste(r,s)** a eightieth

Acker m -s,- field. **A ~ bau** m agriculture

addieren vt/i (haben) add

Addition /-'tsio:n/ f -,-en addition

ade int goodbye

Adel m -s nobility

Ader f -,-n vein

Adjektiv nt -s,-e adjective

adlig a noble. **A ~ e(r)** m nobleman

Administration /-'tsio:n/ f - administration

Admiral m -s,-e admiral

adop|tieren vt adopt. **A ~ tion** /-'tsio:n/ f -,-en adoption. **A ~ tiv-eltern** pl adoptive parents. **A ~ tivkind** nt adopted child

Adrenalin nt -s adrenalin

Adres|se f -,-n address. **a ~ sie-ren** vt address

Adria f - Adriatic

Adverb nt -s,-ien /-jən/ adverb

Affäre f -,-n affair

Affe m -n,-n monkey

affektiert a affected

affig a affected; (eitel) vain

Afrika nt -s Africa

Afrikan|er(in) m -s,- (f -,-nen) African. **a ~ isch** a African

After m -s,- anus

Agentur f -,-en agency

Aggression f -,-en aggression. **a ~ siv** a aggressive

Ägypten /ɛ'gʏptən/ nt -s Egypt. **Ä ~ er(in)** m -s,- (f -,-nen) Egyptian. **ä ~ isch** a Egyptian

ähneln vi (haben) (+ dat) resemble; **sich ä ~** be alike

ahnen vt have a presentiment of; (vermuten) suspect

Ahnen mpl ancestors. **A ~ for-schung** f genealogy

ähnlich a similar, adv -ly; **jdm ä ~ sehen** resemble s.o. **Ä ~ keit** f -,-en similarity; resemblance

Ahnung f -,-en premonition; (Ver-mutung) idea, hunch

Ahorn m -s,-e maple

Ähre f -,-n ear [of corn]

Aids /e:ts/ nt - Aids

Akademie f -,-n academy

Akadem|iker(in) m -s,- (f -,-nen) university graduate. **a ~ isch** a academic

akklimatisieren (sich) vr become acclimatized

Akkord m -[e]s,-e (Mus) chord. **A ~ arbeit** f piece-work

Akkordeon nt -s,-s accordion

Akkumulator m -s,-en /-'to:rən/ (Electr) accumulator

Akkusativ m -s,-e accusative. **A ~ objekt** nt direct object

Akrobat(in) m -en,-en (f -,-nen) acrobat. **a ~ isch** a acrobatic

Akt m -[e]s,-e act; (Kunst) nude

Akte f -,-n file; **A ~ n** documents. **A ~ ntasche** f briefcase

Aktie /'aktsiə/ f -,-n (Comm) share. **A ~ ngesellschaft** f joint-stock company

Aktion /ak'tsjo:n/ f -,-en action.
A~är m -s,-e shareholder
aktiv a active
aktuell a topical; (*gegenwärtig*)
current
Akupunktur f- acupuncture
Akustik f- acoustics pl.
Akzent m -[e]s,-e accent
akzept|abel a acceptable. **a~ie-
ren** vt accept
Alarm m -s alarm; (*Mil*) alert.
a~ieren vt alert; (*beunruhigen*)
alarm
albern a silly □adv in a silly way
Album nt -s,-ben album
Algebra f - algebra
Algen fpl algae
Algerien /-iən/ nt -s Algeria
Alibi nt -s,-s alibi
Alimente pl maintenance sg
Alkohol m -s alcohol. **A~frei** a
non-alcoholic
Alkohol|iker(in) m -s,- (f-,-nen)
alcoholic. **a~isch** a alcoholic
all inv pron **all das/mein Geld** all
the/my money; **all dies** all this
All nt -s universe
alle pred a finished
all|e(r,s) pron all; (*jeder*) every;
a~es everything, all; (*alle Leute*)
everyone; **a~e** pl all; **a~e beide**
both; **a~e Tage** every day; **a~e
drei Jahre** every three years;
ohne a~en Grund without any
reason; **vor a~em** above all;
a~es in a~em all in all; **a~es
aussteigen!** all change!
Allee f -,-n avenue
allein adv alone; (*nur*) only; **a~
der Gedanke** the mere thought;
von a~[e] of its/⟨*Person*⟩ one's
own accord; (*automatisch*) automatically □conj but. **A~erzie-
hende(r)** m/f single parent.
a~ig a sole. **a~stehend** a
single; **A~stehende** pl single
people

allemal adv every time; (*gewiß*)
certainly; **ein für a~** once and
for all
aller|beste(r,s) a very best; **am
a~besten** best of all. **a~dings**
adv indeed; (*zwar*) admittedly.
a~erste(r,s) a very first
Allergie f -,-n allergy
allergisch a allergic (**gegen** to)
Aller|heiligen nt -s All Saints
Day. **a~höchstens** adv at the
very most. **a~lei** inv a all sorts of
□pron all sorts of things.
a~letzte(r,s) a very last.
a~liebste(r,s) a favourite □adv
am a~liebsten for preference;
am a~liebsten haben like best
of all. **a~meiste(r,s)** a most
□adv **am a~meisten** most of all.
A~seelen nt -s All Souls Day.
a~wenigste(r,s) a very least
□adv **am a~wenigsten** least of
all
allgemein a general. **A~heit** f-
community; (*Öffentlichkeit*) general public
Allianz f -,-en alliance
Alligator m -s,-en /-'to:rən/ alligator
alliiert a allied; **die A~en** pl the
Allies
alljährlich a annual
Alltag m working day; **der A~**
(*fig*) everyday life
alltäglich a daily; (*gewöhnlich*)
everyday; ⟨*Mensch*⟩ ordinary
alltags adv on weekdays
allzu adv [far] too; **a~vorsichtig**
over-cautious. **a~oft** adv all too
often
Alm f -,-en alpine pasture
Almosen ntpl alms
Alpdruck m nightmare
Alpen pl Alps
Alphabet nt -[e]s,-e alphabet
Alptraum m nightmare
als conj as; (*zeitlich*) when; (*mit
Komparativ*) than; **nichts als** nothing but; **als ob** as if or though

also *adv & conj* so; **a~ gut** all right then

alt *a* (älter, ältest) old; (*gebraucht*) second-hand; (*ehemalig*) former; **alt werden** grow old

Alt *m* -s (*Mus*) contralto

Altar *m* -s,-e altar

Alt|e(r) *m/f* old man/woman; **die A~en** old people. **A~eisen** *nt* scrap iron. **A~enheim** *nt* old people's home

Alter *nt* -s,- age; (*Bejahrtheit*) old age

älter *a* older; **mein ä~er Bruder** my elder brother

altern *vi* (sein) age

Alters|grenze *f* age limit. **A~heim** *nt* old people's home. **A~rente** *f* old-age pension. **a~schwach** *a* old and infirm. **A~tum** *nt* -s,-er antiquity. **a~tümlich** *a* old; (*altmodisch*) old-fashioned

altklug *a* precocious, *adv* -ly

alt|modisch *a* old-fashioned. **A~papier** *nt* waste paper. **A~warenhändler** *m* second-hand dealer

Alufolie *f* [aluminium] foil

Aluminium *nt* -s aluminium, (*Amer*) aluminum

am *prep* = **an dem**; **am Montag** on Monday; **am Morgen** in the morning; **am besten** [the] best

Amateur /-'tø:ɐ/ *m* -s,-e amateur

Ambition /-'tsjo:n/ *f* -,-en ambition

Amboß *m* -sses,-sse anvil

ambulan|t *a* outpatient ... *adv* **a~t behandeln** treat as an out-patient. **A~z** *f* -,-en out-patients' department

Ameise *f* -,-n ant

amen *int*, **A~** *nt* -s amen

Amerika *nt* -s America

Amerikan|er(in) *m* -s,- (*f* -,-nen) American. **a~isch** *a* American

Ammoniak *nt* -s ammonia

Amnestie *f* -,-n amnesty

amoralisch *a* amoral

Ampel *f* -,-n traffic lights *pl*

Amphitheater *nt* amphitheatre

Amput|ation /-'tsjo:n/ *f* -,-en amputation. **a~ieren** *vt* amputate

Amsel *f* -,-n blackbird

Amt *nt* -[e]s,-er office; (*Aufgabe*) task; (*Teleph*) exchange. **a~ieren** *vi* (haben) hold office. **a~lich** *a* official. **A~szeichen** *nt* dialling tone

Amulett *nt* -[e]s,-e [lucky] charm

amüs|ant *a* amusing. **a~ieren** *vt* amuse; **sich a~ieren** be amused (über + *acc* at); (*sich vergnügen*) enjoy oneself

an *prep* (+ *dat/acc*) at; (*haftend, berührend*) on; (*gegen*) against; (+ *acc*) (schicken) to; **an dem Tag** on that day; **an [und für] sich** actually; **die Arbeit an sich** the work as such (*angeschaltet*) on; (*auf Fahrplan*) arriving; **an die zwanzig Mark** about twenty marks; **von heute an** from today

analog *a* analogous; (*Computer*) analog. **A~ie** *f* -,-n analogy

Analphabet *m* -en,-en illiterate person. **A~entum** *nt* -s illiteracy

Analy|se *f* -,-n analysis. **a~sieren** *vt* analyse. **A~tiker** *m* -s,- analyst

Anämie *f* - anaemia

Ananas *f* -,-[se] pineapple

Anat|omie *f* - anatomy. **a~omisch** *a* anatomical, *adv* -ly

Anbau *m* cultivation; (*Gebäude*) extension. **a~en** *vt sep* build on; (*anpflanzen*) cultivate, grow

anbei *adv* enclosed

anbeißen† *vt sep* take a bite of □ *vi* (haben) ⟨Fisch:⟩ bite

anbeten *vt sep* worship

Anbetracht *m* **in A~** (+ *gen*) in view of

anbieten† *vt sep* offer; **sich a~** offer (zu to)

anbinden† *vt sep* tie up

Anblick m sight. **a ∼ en** vt sep look at

anbrechen† v sep vt start on; break into ⟨Vorräte⟩ □vi (sein) begin; ⟨Tag:⟩ break; ⟨Nacht:⟩ fall

anbrennen† vt sep vi light □vi (sein) burn

anbringen† vt sep bring [along]; (befestigen) fix

Anbruch m (fig) dawn; **A ∼ des Tages/der Nacht** daybreak/nightfall

Andacht f -,-en reverence; (Gottesdienst) prayers pl

andächtig a reverent, adv -ly; (fig) rapt, adv -ly

andauern vi sep (haben) last; (anhalten) continue. **a ∼ d** a persistent; (ständig) constant

Andenken nt -s,- memory; (Souvenir) souvenir

ander|e(r,s) a other; (verschieden) different; (nächste) next; **ein a ∼ er, eine a ∼ e** another □pron **der a ∼ e/die a ∼ en** the other/others; **ein a ∼ er** another [one]; (Person) someone else; **kein a ∼ er** no one else; **einer nach dem a ∼ en** one after the other; **alles a ∼ e/nichts a ∼ es** everything/nothing else; **unter a ∼ em** among other things. **a ∼ enfalls** adv otherwise. **a ∼ erseits** adv on the other hand. **a ∼ mal** adv **ein a ∼ mal** another time

ändern vt alter; (wechseln) change; **sich ä ∼** change

andernfalls adv otherwise

anders pred a different; **a ∼ werden** change □adv differently; ⟨riechen, schmecken⟩ different; (sonst) else; **jemand** someone else

anderseits adv on the other hand

andersherum adv the other way round

anderthalb inv a one and a half; **a ∼ Stunden** an hour and a half

Änderung f -,-en alteration; (Wechsel) change

andeuten vt sep indicate; (anspielen) hint at. **A ∼ ung** f -,-en indication; hint

Andrang m rush (nach for); (Gedränge) crush

androhen vt sep jdm etw a ∼ threaten s.o. with sth

aneignen vt sep sich (dat) a ∼ appropriate; (lernen) learn

aneinander adv & pref together; ⟨denken⟩ of one another; **a ∼ vorbei** past one another

Anekdote f -,-n anecdote

anerkannt a acknowledged

anerkenn|en† vt sep acknowledge, recognize; (würdigen) appreciate. **a ∼ end** a approving. **A ∼ ung** f - acknowledgement, recognition; appreciation

anfahren† v sep □vt deliver; (streifen) hit; (schimpfen) snap at □vi (sein) start

Anfall m fit, attack. **a ∼ en†** v sep □vt attack □vi (sein) arise; ⟨Zinsen:⟩ accrue

anfällig a susceptible (für to). **A ∼ keit** f - susceptibility

Anfang m -s,-e beginning, start; **zu od am A ∼** at the beginning. **a ∼ en†** v sep (haben) begin, start; (tun) do

Anfänger(in) m -s,- (f -,-nen) beginner

anfangs adv at first. **A ∼ buchstabe** m initial letter. **A ∼ gehalt** nt starting salary

anfassen vt sep touch; (behandeln) treat; tackle ⟨Arbeit⟩; **sich a ∼** hold hands

anfechten† vt sep contest

anfeuchten vt sep moisten

anflehen vt sep implore, beg

Anflug m (Aviat) approach

anforder|n vt sep demand; (Comm) order. **A ∼ ung** f demand

Anfrage f -,-en enquiry. **a ∼ n** vi sep (haben) enquire, ask

anfreunden (sich) *vr sep* make friends **(mit** with)

anfügen *vt sep* add

anfühlen *vt sep* feel; **sich weich a ~** feel soft

anführ|en *vt sep* lead; *(zitieren)* quote; *(angeben)* give. **A ~ er** *m* leader. **A ~ ungszeichen** *ntpl* quotation marks

Angabe *f* statement; *(Anweisung)* instruction; *(Tennis)* service; **nähere A ~ n** particulars

angeb|en *v sep* ▢ *vt* state; give *(Namen, Grund)* *(anzeigen)* indicate; set *(Tempo)* ▢ *vi (haben)* *(Tennis)* serve; *(fam: protzen)* show off. **A ~ er(in)** *m -s, - (f -,-nen)* *(fam)* show off. **A ~ erei** *f -(fam)* showing-off

angeblich *a* alleged, *adv* -ly

angeboren *a* innate; *(Med)* congenital

Angebot *nt* offer; *(Auswahl)* range; **A ~ und Nachfrage** supply and demand

angebracht *a* appropriate

angeheiratet *a* ⟨*Onkel, Tante*⟩ by marriage

angeheitert *a (fam)* tipsy

angeh|en *v sep* ▢ *vi (sein)* begin; ⟨*Licht*⟩ come on; **a ~ gegen** fight ▢ *vt* attack; tackle ⟨*Arbeit*⟩; *(bitten)* ask **(um** for); *(betreffen)* concern

angehör|en *vi sep (haben)* (+ *dat*) belong to. **A ~ ige(r)** *m/f* relative

Angeklagte(r) *m/f* accused

Angel *f -,-n* fishing rod; *(Tür-)* hinge

Angelegenheit *f* matter

Angel|haken *m* fish-hook. **a ~ n** *vi (haben)* fish **(nach** for) ▢ *vt (fangen)* catch. **A ~ rute** *f* fishing-rod

angelsächsisch *a* Anglo-Saxon

angenehm *a* pleasant; *(bei Vorstellung)* **a ~ !** delighted to meet you!

angeregt *a* animated

angesehen *a* respected; ⟨*Firma*⟩ reputable

angesichts *prep* (+ *gen*) in view of

angespannt *a* intent, *adv* -ly; ⟨*Lage*⟩ tense

Angestellte(r) *m/f* employee

angewandt *a* applied

angewiesen *a* dependent **(auf** + *acc* on); **auf sich selbst a ~** on one's own

angewöhnen *vt sep* jdm etw a ~ get s.o. used to sth; **sich** *(dat)* **etw a ~** get into the habit of doing sth

Angewohnheit *f* habit

Angina *f* - tonsillitis

angleichen† *vt sep* adjust *(dat* to)

anglikanisch *a* Anglican

Anglistik *f* - English

Angorakatze *f* Persian cat

angreif|en† *vt sep* attack; tackle ⟨*Arbeit*⟩; *(schädigen)* damage. **A ~ er** *m -s,-* attacker; *(Pol)* aggressor

angrenzen *vi sep (haben)* adjoin **(an etw** *acc* sth). **a ~ d** *a* adjoining

Angriff *m* attack; **in A ~ nehmen** tackle. **a ~ slustig** *a* aggressive

Angst *f -,-̈e* fear; *(Psych)* anxiety; *(Sorge)* worry **(um** about); **a ~ haben** be afraid **(vor** + *dat* of); *(sich sorgen)* be worried **(um** about)

ängstigen *vt* frighten; *(Sorge machen)* worry; **sich a ~** be frightened; be worried **(um** about)

ängstlich *a* nervous; *(scheu)* timid; *(verängstigt)* frightened, scared; *(besorgt)* anxious

angstvoll *a* anxious

angurten (sich) *vr sep* fasten one's seat-belt

anhaben† *vt sep* have on

anhalt|en† *v sep* ▢ *vt* stop; hold ⟨*Atem*⟩; **jdn zur Arbeit a ~** en urge s.o. to work ▢ *vi (haben)* stop; *(andauern)* continue. **A ~ er(in)** *m -s,- (f -,-nen)* hitch-hiker; **per A ~ er fahren** hitch-hike

anhand prep (+ gen) with the aid of

Anhang m appendix

anhäng|en† vi (haben) be a follower of. **A~er** m -s,- follower; (Auto) trailer; (Schild) [tie-on] label; (Schmuck) pendant. **A~erschaft** f - following, followers pl. **a~lich** a affectionate

anhäufen vt sep pile up

anheben† vt sep lift; (erhöhen) raise

Anhieb m auf A~ straight away

Anhöhe f hill

anhören vt sep listen to; **sich gut a~** sound good

animieren vt encourage (zu to)

Anis m -es aniseed

Anker m -s,- anchor; **vor A~ gehen** drop anchor. **a~n** vi (haben) anchor; (liegen) be anchored

anketten vt sep chain up

Anklage f accusation; (Jur) charge; (Ankläger) prosecution. **A~bank** f dock. **a~n** vt sep accuse (gen of); (Jur) charge (gen with)

Ankläger m accuser; (Jur) prosecutor

anklammern vt sep clip on; **sich a~** cling (an + acc to)

ankleben v sep □vt stick on □vi (sein) stick (an + dat to)

anklopfen vi sep (haben) knock

anknipsen vt sep (fam) switch on

ankommen† vi sep (sein) arrive; (sich nähern) approach; **nicht a~ gegen** (fig) be no match for; **a~ auf** (+ acc) depend on

ankreuzen vt sep mark with a cross

ankündig|en vt sep announce. **A~ung** f announcement

Ankunft f - arrival

anlächeln vt sep smile at

Anlage f -,-n installation; (Industrie-) plant; (Komplex) complex; (Geld-) investment; (Plan) layout;

(Beilage) enclosure; (Veranlagung) aptitude; (Neigung) predisposition; **[öffentliche] A~n** [public] gardens; **als A~** enclosed

Anlaß m -sses,-̈sse reason; (Gelegenheit) occasion; **A~ geben zu** give cause for

anlass|en† vt sep (Auto) start. **A~er** m -s,- starter

anläßlich prep (+ gen) on the occasion of

Anlauf m (Sport) run-up; (fig) attempt. **a~en**† v sep □vi (sein) start; (beschlagen) mist up; (Metall:) tarnish; **rot a~en** blush □vt (Naut) call at

anlegen v sep □vt put (an + acc against); put on (Verband); lay back (Ohren); aim (Gewehr); (investieren) invest; (ausgeben) spend (für on); draw up (Liste); **[mit] Hand a~** lend a hand; **es darauf a~** (fig) aim (zu to) □vi (haben) (Schiff:) moor

anlehnen vt sep lean (an + acc against); **sich a~** lean (an + acc on)

Anleihe f -,-n loan

anleit|en vt sep instruct. **A~ung** f instructions pl

anlernen vt sep train

Anliegen nt -s,- request; (Wunsch) desire

anlieg|en† vi sep (haben) [eng] **a~en** fit closely; [eng] **a~end** close-fitting. **A~er** mpl residents; **'A~er frei'** 'access for residents only'

anlügen† vt sep lie to

anmachen vt sep (fam) fix; (anschalten) turn on; dress (Salat)

anmalen vt sep paint

Anmarsch m (Mil) approach

anmeld|en vt sep announce; (Admin) register; **sich a~en** (Admin) register; (Sch) enrol; (im Hotel) check in; (beim Arzt) make an appointment. **A~ung** f announcement; (*Admin*) registration; (*Sch*) enrolment; (*Termin*) appointment

anmerk|en vt sep mark. **A~ung** f -,-en note

Anmut f grace; (*Charme*) charm

anmutig a graceful

annähen vt sep sew on

annäher|nd a approximate. **A~ungsversuche** mpl advances

Annahme f -,-n acceptance; (*Adoption*) adoption; (*Vermutung*) assumption

annehm|bar a acceptable. **a~en†** vt sep accept; (*adoptieren*) adopt; acquire (*Gewohnheit*); **sich a~en** (+ *gen*) take care of; **angenommen, daß** assuming that. **A~lichkeiten** fpl comforts

Anno adv **A~ 1920** in the year 1920

Annon|ce /aˈnõːsə/ f -,-n advertisement. **a~cieren** /-ˈsiː-/ vt/i (*haben*) advertise

annullieren vt annul; cancel

Anomalie f -,-n anomaly

anonym a anonymous

Anorak m -s,-s anorak

anordn|en vt sep arrange; (*befehlen*) order. **A~ung** f arrangement; order

anorganisch a inorganic

anormal a abnormal

anpass|en vt sep try on; (*angleichen*) adapt (*dat* to); sich a~ adapt (*dat* to). **a~ungsfähig** a adaptable. **A~ungsfähigkeit** f adaptability

Anpfiff m (*Sport*) kick-off

Anprall m -[e]s impact. **a~en** vi sep (*sein*) strike (**an etw** *acc* sth)

anpreisen† vt sep commend

Anprobe f fitting. **a~ieren** vt sep try on

anrechnen vt sep count (**als** as); (*berechnen*) charge for; (*verrechnen*) allow (*Summe*)

Anrecht nt right (**auf** + *acc* to)

Anrede f [form of] address. **a~n** vt sep address; (*ansprechen*) speak to

anreg|en vt sep stimulate; (*ermuntern*) encourage (**zu** to). **A~ung** f stimulation; (*Vorschlag*) suggestion

Anreise f journey; (*Ankunft*) arrival. **a~n** vi sep (*sein*) arrive

Anreiz m incentive

Anrichte f -,-n sideboard. **a~n** vt sep (*Culin*) prepare; (*garnieren*) garnish (**mit** with)

anrüchig a disreputable

Anruf m call. **A~beantworter** m -s,- answering machine. **a~en†** vt sep □vt call to; (*bitten*) call on (**um** for); (*Teleph*) ring □vi (*haben*) ring (**bei jdm** s.o.)

anrühren vt sep touch; (*verrühren*) mix

Ansage f announcement. **a~n** vt sep announce

ansammeln vt sep collect; (*anhäufen*) accumulate; **sich a~eln** collect; (*sich häufen*) accumulate; (*Leute*) gather. **A~lung** f collection; (*Menschen*) crowd

ansässig a resident

Ansatz m beginning; (*Versuch*) attempt

anschaff|en vt sep [**sich** *dat*] etw **a~en** acquire/(*kaufen*) buy sth

anschalten vt sep switch on

anschau|en vt sep look at. **a~lich** a vivid. **A~ung** f -,-en (*fig*) view

Anschein m appearance; **den A~ haben** seem. **a~end** adv apparently

anschirren vt sep harness

Anschlag m notice; (*Vor-*) estimate; (*Überfall*) attack (**auf** + *acc* on); (*Mus*) touch; (*Techn*) stop.

a~en† *v sep* □*vt* put up ⟨*Aushang*⟩; strike ⟨*Note, Taste*⟩; cast on ⟨*Masche*⟩; (*beschädigen*) chip □*vi* (*haben*) strike/(*stoßen*) knock (**an**+*acc* against) □*vi* (*sein*) knock (**an**+*acc* against)

anschließen† *v sep* □*vt* connect (**an**+*acc* to); (*zufügen*) add; **sich a~ an** (+*acc*) adjoin; (*folgen*) follow; **sich jdm a~** join s.o. □*vi* (*haben*) **a~ an** (+*acc*) adjoin; (*folgen*) follow. **a~d** *a* adjoining; (*zeitlich*) following □*adv* afterwards

Anschluß *m* connection; (*Kontakt*) contact; **A~ finden** make friends; **im A~ an** (+*acc*) after

anschnallen *vt sep* strap on; **sich a~** fasten one's seat-belt

anschneiden† *vt sep* cut into; broach ⟨*Thema*⟩

anschreiben† *vt sep* write (**an**+*acc* on); (*Comm*) put on s.o.'s account; (*sich anmelden*) write to

Anschrift *f* address

anschuldig|en *vt sep* accuse. **A~ung** *f* -,-en accusation

anschwellen† *vi sep* (*sein*) swell

ansehen† *vt sep* look at; (*einschätzen*) regard ⟨*als* as⟩; **jdn etw a~** look at sth; (*TV*) watch sth. **A~** *nt* -s respect; (*Ruf*) reputation

ansehnlich *a* considerable

ansetzen *vt sep* join (**an**+*acc* to); (*veranschlagen*) estimate

Ansicht *f* view; **meiner A~ nach** in my view; **zur A~** (*Comm*) on approval. **A~s[post]karte** *f* picture postcard. **A~ssache** *f* matter of opinion

ansiedeln (sich) *vr sep* settle

ansonsten *adv* apart from that

anspannen *vt sep* hitch up; (*anstrengen*) strain; tense ⟨*Muskel*⟩

Anspielung *f* allusion; hint

Anspitzer *m* -s,- pencil-sharpener

Ansprache *f* address

ansprechen *v sep* □*vt* speak to; (*fig*) appeal to □*vi* (*haben*) respond (**auf**+*acc* to)

anspringen *v sep* □*vt* jump at □*vi* (*sein*) ⟨*Auto*⟩ start

Anspruch *m* claim/(*Recht*) right (**auf**+*acc* to); **A~ haben** be entitled (**auf**+*acc* to); **in A~ nehmen** make use of; (*erfordern*) demand; take up ⟨*Zeit*⟩; occupy ⟨*Person*⟩. **a~slos** *a* undemanding; **a~svoll** *a* demanding; (*kritisch*) discriminating; (*vornehm*) up-market

anspucken *vt sep* spit at

anstacheln *vt sep* (*fig*) spur on

Anstalt *f* -,-en institution

Anstand *m* decency; (*Benehmen*) [good] manners *pl*

anständig *a* decent; (*ehrbar*) respectable; (*richtig*) proper

anstandslos *adv* without any trouble

anstarren *vt sep* stare at

anstatt *conj & prep* (+*gen*) instead of

ansteck|en *v sep* □*vt* pin (**an**+*acc* to/on); put on ⟨*Ring*⟩; (*anzünden*) light; (*in Brand stecken*) set fire to; (*Med*) infect; **sich a~en** catch an infection (**bei** from) □*vi* (*haben*) be infectious. **a~end** *a* infectious, (*fam*) catching. **A~ung** *f* -,-en infection

anstehen† *vi sep* (*haben*) queue

anstelle *prep* (+*gen*) instead of

anstell|en *vt sep* put, stand (**an**+*acc* against); (*einstellen*) employ; (*anschalten*) turn on; (*tun*) do; **sich a~en** queue [up]. **A~ung** *f* employment; (*Stelle*) job

Anstieg *m* -[e]s,-e climb; (*fig*) rise

anstiften *vt sep* cause; (*anzetteln*) instigate

Anstoß *m* (*Anregung*) impetus; (*Stoß*) knock; (*Fußball*) kick-off; **A~ erregen** give offence (**an**+*dat* at). **a~en**† *v sep* □*vt* knock;

(mit dem Ellbogen) nudge □vi (sein) knock (an+acc against) □vi (haben) a~en clink glasses; a~en auf (+acc) drink to; mit der Zunge a~en lisp

anstößig a offensive

anstrahlen vt sep floodlight

anstreichen† vt sep paint; (anmerken) mark

anstrengen vt sep strain; (ermüden) tire; **sich a~en** exert oneself; (sich bemühen) make an effort (zu to). **a~end** a strenuous; (ermüdend) tiring. **A~ung** f -,-en strain; (Mühe) effort

Anstrich m coat [of paint]

Ansturm m rush; (Mil) assault

Ansuchen nt -s,- request

Antarktis f - Antarctic

Anteil m share; (fig) interest (an+dat in). **A~nahme** f - interest (an+dat in); (Mitgefühl) sympathy

Antenne f -,-n aerial

Anthologie f -,-n anthology

Anti|**alkoholiker** m teetotaller. **A~biotikum** nt -s,-ka antibiotic

antik a antique. **A~e** f - [classical] antiquity

Antikörper m antibody

Antilope f -,-n antelope

Antipathie f - antipathy

Antiquariat nt -[e]s,-e antiquarian bookshop

Antiquitäten fpl antiques. **A~händler** m antique dealer

Antrag m -[e]s,"-e proposal; (Pol) motion; (Gesuch) application. **A~steller** m -s,- applicant

antreffen† vt sep find

antreiben† v sep □vt start; take up ⟨Amt⟩ □vi (sein) line up

Antrieb m urge; (Techn) drive; **aus eigenem A~** of one's own accord

Antritt m start; **bei A~** eines **Amtes** when taking office

antun† vt sep jdm etw a~ do sth to s.o.; **sich** (dat) **etwas a~** take one's own life

Antwort f -,-en answer, reply (auf+acc to). **a~en** vt/i (haben) answer (jdm s.o.)

anvertrauen vt sep entrust/(mitteilen) confide (jdm to s.o.)

Anwalt m -[e]s,"-e, **Anwältin** f -,-nen lawyer; (vor Gericht) counsel

Anwandlung f -,-en fit (von of)

Anwärter(in) m(f) candidate

anweisen† vt sep assign (dat to); (beauftragen) instruct. **A~ung** f instruction; (Geld-) money order

anwenden† vt sep apply (auf +acc to); (gebrauchen) use. **A~ung** f application; use

anwerben† vt sep recruit

Anwesen nt -s,- property

anwesend a present (bei at); **die A~den** those present. **A~heit** f - presence

anwidern vt sep disgust

Anwohner mpl residents

Anzahl f number

anzahlen vt sep pay a deposit on. **A~ung** f deposit

anzapfen vt sep tap

Anzeichen nt sign

Anzeige f -,-n announcement; (Inserat) advertisement; **A~ erstatten gegen jdn** report s.o. to the police. **a~n** vt sep announce; (inserieren) advertise; (melden) report; (angeben) indicate

anziehen† vt sep attract; (festziehen) tighten; put on ⟨Kleider, Bremse⟩; (ankleiden) dress; **sich a~en** get dressed; **a~end** a attractive. **A~ungskraft** f attraction; (Phys) gravity

Anzug m suit

anzüglich a suggestive

anzünden vt sep light; (in Brand stecken) set fire to

anzweifeln vt sep question

apart a striking

apathisch *a* apathetic
Aperitif *m* -s,-s aperitif
Apfel *m* -s,- apple
Apfelsine *f* -,-n orange
Apostel *m* -s,- apostle
Apostroph *m* -s,-e apostrophe
Apotheke *f* -,-n pharmacy.
A~er(in) *m* -s,- (*f* -,-nen) pharmacist, [dispensing] chemist
Apparat *m* -[e]s,-e device; (*Phot*) camera; (*Radio, TV*) set; (*Teleph*) telephone; **am A~!** speaking!
Appell *m* -s,-e appeal; (*Mil*) roll-call. **a~ieren** *vi* (haben) appeal (**an** + *acc*)
Appetit *m* -s appetite; **guten A~!** enjoy your meal! **a~lich** *a* appetizing, *adv* -ly
Applaus *m* -es applause
Aprikose *f* -,-n apricot
April *m* -[s] April
Aquarell *nt* -s,-e water-colour
Aquarium *nt* -s,-ien aquarium
Äquator *m* -s equator
Ära *f* - era
Araber(in) *m* -s,- (*f* -,-nen) Arab
arabisch *a* Arab; (*Geog*) Arabian; ⟨*Ziffer*⟩ Arabic
Arbeit *f* -,-en work; (*Anstellung*) employment, job; (*Aufgabe*) task; (*Sch*) [written] test; (*Abhandlung*) treatise; (*Qualität*) workmanship; **an die A~ gehen** set to work; **sich** (*dat*) **viel A~ machen** go to a lot of trouble. **a~en** *v sep □vi* (haben) work (**an** + *dat* on) □ *vt* make. **A~er(in)** *m* -s,- (*f* -,-nen) worker; (*Land-, Hilfs-*) labourer. **A~erklasse** *f* working class
Arbeitgeber *m* -s,- employer.
A~nehmer *m* -s,- employee
Arbeitsamt *nt* employment exchange. **A~erlaubnis, A~genehmigung** *f* work permit. **a~los** *a* unemployed; **a~los sein** be out of work. **A~lose(r)** *m/f* unemployed person; **die A~losen** the unemployed *pl*.
A~losenunterstützung *f* unemployment benefit. **A~losigkeit** *f* unemployment
arbeitsparend *a* labour-saving
Arbeitsplatz *m* job
Archäologe *m* -n,-n archaeologist. **A~logie** *f* archaeology
Architekt(in) *m* -en,-en (*f* -,-nen) architect. **a~tonisch** *a* architectural. **A~tur** *f* - architecture
Archiv *nt* -s,-e archives *pl*
Arena *f* -,-nen arena
Argentinien *nt* -s Argentina. **A~ier(in)** *m* -s,- (*f* -,-nen) / -,-nen Argentinian. **a~isch** *a* Argentinian
Ärger *m* -s annoyance; (*Unannehmlichkeit*) trouble. **ä~lich** *a* annoyed; (*leidig*) annoying. **ä~n** *vt* annoy; (*necken*) tease; **sich ä~n** get annoyed (**über** jdn/etw with s.o./ about sth). **Ä~nis** *nt* -ses, -se annoyance; **öffentliches Ä~nis** public nuisance
Arglist *f* - malice
arglos *a* unsuspecting
Argument *nt* -[e]s,-e argument. **a~ieren** *vi* (haben) argue (**daß** that)
Arie /ˈaːrjə/ *f* -,-n aria
Aristokrat *m* -en,-en aristocrat. **A~kratie** *f* - aristocracy. **a~kratisch** *a* aristocratic
Arktis *f* - Arctic. **a~isch** *a* Arctic
arm *a* poor
Arm *m* -[e]s,-e arm; **jdn auf den Arm nehmen** (*fam*) pull s.o.'s leg
Armaturenbrett *nt* instrument panel; (*Auto*) dashboard
Armband *nt* (*pl* -bänder) bracelet. **A~uhr** *f* wrist-watch
Arme(r) *m/f* poor man/woman; **die A~en** the poor *pl*
Armee *f* -,-n army
Ärmel *m* -s,- sleeve. **A~kanal** *m* [English] Channel. **a~los** *a* sleeveless

Arm|lehne f arm. **A~leuchter** m candelabra

ärmlich a poor; (*elend*) miserable

armselig a miserable

Armut f - poverty

Arran|gement /arãʒə'mã:/ nt -s,-s arrangement. **a~gieren** /-'ʒi:rən/ vt arrange

arrogant a arrogant

Arsch m -[e]s,ᵉe (*vulg*) arse

Arsen nt -s arsenic

Art f -,-en manner; (*Weise*) way; (*Natur*) nature; (*Sorte*) kind; (*Biol*) species; **auf diese Art in this way**

Arterie /-jə/ f -,-n artery

Arthritis f - arthritis

artig a well-behaved

Artikel m -s,- article

Artillerie f - artillery

Artischocke f -,-n artichoke

Arznei f -,-en medicine

Arzt m -[e]s,ᵉe doctor

Ärzt|in f -,-nen [woman] doctor. **ä~lich** a medical

As nt -ses,-se ace

Asbest m -[e]s asbestos

Asche f - ash. **A~nbecher** m ashtray. **A~rmittwoch** m Ash Wednesday

Asiat|(in) m -en,-en (f -,-nen) Asian. **a~isch** a Asian

Asien /'a:zjən/ nt -s Asia

asozial a antisocial

Asphalt m -[e]s asphalt. **a~ie-ren** vt asphalt

Assistent|(in) m -en,-en (f -,-nen) assistant

Ast m -[e]s,ᵉe branch

ästhetisch a aesthetic

Asthma nt -s asthma.

Astro|loge m -n,-n astrologer. **A~logie** f - astrology. **A~naut** m -en,-en astronaut. **A~nomie** f - astronomy

Asyl nt -s,-e home; (*Pol*) asylum. **A~ant** m -en,-en asylum-seeker

Atelier /-'lje:/ nt -s,-s studio

Atem m -s breath. **A~los** a breathless

Äther m -s ether

Äthiopien /-jən/ nt -s Ethiopia

Athlet|(in) m -en,-en (f -,-nen) athlete. **a~isch** a athletic

Atlant|ik m -s Atlantic. **a~isch** a Atlantic; **der A~ische Ozean the Atlantic Ocean**

Atlas m -lasses,-lanten atlas

atmen vt/i (*haben*) breathe

Atmosphäre f -,-n atmosphere

Atmung f - breathing

Atom nt -s,-e atom. **A~bombe** f atom bomb. **A~krieg** m nuclear war

Atten|tat nt -[e]s,-e assassination attempt. **A~täter** m assassin

Attest nt -[e]s,-e certificate

Attrak|tion /-'tsjo:n/ f -,-en attrac-tion. **a~tiv** a attractive

Attribut nt -[e]s,-e attribute

ätzen vt corrode; (*Med*) cauterize; (*Kunst*) etch. **ä~d** a corrosive

au int ouch; **au fein!** oh good!

auch adv & conj also, too; (*außer-dem*) what's more; (*selbst*) even; **a~ wenn even if; sie weiß es a~ nicht she doesn't know either; wer/wie/was a~ immer whoever/however/whatever**

Audienz f -,-en audience

audiovisuell a audio-visual

Auditorium nt -s,-ien (*Univ*) lec-ture hall

auf prep (+ dat) on; (+ acc) on [to]; (*bis*) until, till; (*Proportion*) to; **auf deutsch/englisch** in Ger-man/English; **auf einer/eine Party** at/to a party; **auf die Straße** in the street; **auf einem Ohr taub** deaf in one ear; **auf die Toilette gehen** go to the toilet; **auf ein paar Tage verreisen** go away for a few days; **auf 10 Kilometer zu sehen** visible for 10 kilometres □adv open; (*in die Höhe*) up; **auf und ab** up and down; **sich auf und davon machen** make off; **Tür auf!** open the door!

aufatmen *vi sep* ⟨haben⟩ heave a sigh of relief

aufbahren *vt sep* lay out

Aufbau *m* construction; (*Struktur*) structure. **a~en** *vt* construct, build; (*errichten*) erect; (*schaffen*) build up; (*arrangieren*) arrange; **sich a~en** (*fig*) be based (**auf**+*dat on*) ○ *vi* ⟨haben⟩ be based (**auf**+*dat on*)

aufbauschen *vt sep* puff out; (*fig*) exaggerate

aufbekommen† *vt sep* get open; (*Sch*) be given [as homework]

aufbessern *vt sep* improve; (*erhöhen*) increase

aufbewahr|en *vt sep* keep; (*lagern*) store. **A~ung** *f* - safe keeping; storage; (*Gepäck-*) left-luggage office

aufblas|bar *a* inflatable. **a~en†** *vt sep* inflate

aufbleiben† *vi sep* ⟨sein⟩ stay open; (*Person:*) stay up

aufblenden *vt/i sep* ⟨haben⟩ (*Auto*) switch to full beam

aufbocken *vt sep* jack up

aufbrauchen *vt sep* use up

aufbrechen† *v sep* ○ *vt* break open ○ *vi* ⟨sein⟩ (*Knospe:*) open; (*sich aufmachen*) set out, start

aufbringen† *vt sep* raise ⟨Geld⟩; find ⟨Kraft⟩

Aufbruch *m* start, departure

aufbrühen *vt sep* make ⟨Tee⟩

aufbürden *vt sep* **jdm etw a~** (*fig*) burden s.o. with sth

aufdecken *vt sep* (*auflegen*) put on; (*abdecken*) uncover; (*fig*) expose

aufdrehen *vt sep* turn on

aufdringlich *a* persistent

aufeinander *adv* one on top of the other; ⟨schießen⟩ at each other;

⟨warten⟩ for each other. **a~folgend** *a* successive; ⟨Tage⟩ consecutive

Aufenthalt *m* stay; **10 Minuten A~ haben** ⟨Zug:⟩ stop for 10 minutes. **A~serlaubnis, A~sgenehmigung** *f* residence permit. **A~sraum** *m* recreation room; (*im Hotel*) lounge

Auferstehung *f* - resurrection

aufessen† *vt sep* eat up

auffahr|en† *vi sep* ⟨sein⟩ drive up; (*aufprallen*) crash, run (**auf**+*acc* into). **A~t** *f* drive; (*Autobahn-*) slip road; (*Bergfahrt*) ascent

auffallen† *vi sep* be conspicuous; **unangenehm a~** make a bad impression

auffällig *a* conspicuous

Auffassung *f* understanding; (*Ansicht*) view.

auffordern *vt sep* ask; (*einladen*) invite. **A~ung** *f* request; invitation

auffrischen *vt sep* freshen up; revive ⟨Erinnerung⟩; **seine Englischkenntnisse a~** brush up one's English

aufführ|en *vt sep* perform; (*angeben*) list. **A~ung** *f* performance

auffüllen *vt sep* fill up

Aufgabe *f* task; (*Rechen-*) problem; (*Verzicht*) giving up

Aufgang *m* way up; (*Treppe*) stairs *pl*; (*Astr*) rise

aufgeben† *v sep* ○ *vt* give up; post ⟨Brief⟩; send ⟨Telegramm⟩; place ⟨Bestellung⟩; register ⟨Gepäck⟩; put in the paper ⟨Annonce⟩; **jdm eine Aufgabe a~** set s.o. a task; **jdm Suppe a~** serve s.o. with soup ○ *vi* ⟨haben⟩ give up

Aufgebot *nt* contingent (**an**+*dat* of); (*Relig*) banns *pl*

aufgedunsen *a* bloated

aufgehen† *vi sep* ⟨sein⟩ open; (*sich lösen*) come undone; ⟨Teig, Sonne:⟩ rise; ⟨Saat:⟩ come up;

(Math) come out exactly; **in Flammen a ~** go up in flames

aufgelegt *a* **gut/schlecht a ~ sein** be in a good/bad mood

aufgeregt *a* excited; *(erregt)* agitated

aufgeschlossen *a (fig)* openminded

aufgeweckt *a (fig)* bright

aufgießen† *vt sep* pour on; *(aufbrühen)* make ⟨Tee⟩

aufgreifen† *vt sep* pick up; take up ⟨Vorschlag, Thema⟩

aufgrund *prep* (+*gen*) on the strength of

Aufguß *m* infusion

aufhaben† *v sep* □*vt* have on; **den Mund a ~** have one's mouth open; **viel a ~** *(Sch)* have a lot of homework □*vi (haben)* be open

aufhalten† *vt sep* hold up; *(anhalten)* stop; *(abhalten)* keep, detain; *(offenhalten)* hold open; hold out ⟨Hand⟩; **sich a ~** stay

aufhäng|en *vt/i sep (haben)* hang up; *(henken)* hang; **sich a~en** hang oneself. **A~er** *m* -s,- loop

aufheben† *vt sep* pick up; *(hochheben)* raise; *(aufbewahren)* keep; *(beenden)* end; *(rückgängig machen)* lift; *(abschaffen)* abolish; *(Jur)* quash ⟨Urteil⟩; repeal ⟨Gesetz⟩; *(ausgleichen)* cancel out; **gut aufgehoben sein** be well looked after

aufheitern *vt sep* cheer up; **sich a~** ⟨Wetter:⟩ brighten up

aufhellen *vt sep* lighten; **sich a~** ⟨Himmel:⟩ brighten

aufhetzen *vt sep* incite

aufholen *v sep* □*vt* make up □*vi (haben)* catch up; *(zeitlich)* make up time

aufhören *vi sep (haben)* stop

aufklappen *vt/i sep (haben)* open

aufklär|en *vt sep* solve; **jdn a~en** enlighten s.o.; **sich a~en** be solved; ⟨Wetter:⟩ clear up.

A~ung *f* solution; enlightenment; *(Mil)* reconnaissance; **sexuelle A~ung** sex education

aufkleb|en *vt sep* stick on. **A~er** *m* -s,- sticker

aufknöpfen *vt sep* unbutton

aufkochen *v sep* □*vt* bring to the boil □*vi (sein)* come to the boil

aufkommen† *vi sep (sein)* start; ⟨Wind:⟩ spring up

aufkrempeln *vt sep* roll up

aufladen† *vt sep* load; *(Electr)* charge

Auflage *f* impression; *(Ausgabe)* edition; *(Zeitungs-)* circulation

auflassen† *vt sep* leave open; leave on ⟨Hut⟩

Auflauf *m* crowd; *(Culin)* ≈ soufflé

auflegen *v sep* □*vt* apply *(auf* + *acc* to); put down ⟨Hörer⟩; **neu a~** reprint □*vi (haben)* ring off

auflehn|en (sich) *vr sep (fig)* rebel. **A~ung** *f -* rebellion

auflesen† *vt sep* pick up

aufleuchten *vi sep (haben)* light up

auflös|en *vt sep* dissolve; close ⟨Konto⟩; **sich a~en** dissolve; ⟨Nebel:⟩ clear. **A~ung** *f* dissolution; *(Lösung)* solution

aufmach|en *v sep* □*vt* open; *(lösen)* undo; **sich a~en** set out *(nach* for) □*vi (haben)* open. **A~ung** *f -,-en* get-up

aufmerksam *a* attentive; **a~ werden auf** (+*acc*) notice; **jdn a~ machen auf** (+*acc*) draw s.o.'s attention to. **A~keit** *f -,-en* attention; *(Höflichkeit)* courtesy

aufmuntern *vt sep* cheer up

Aufnahme *f -,-n* acceptance; *(Empfang)* reception; *(in Klub, Krankenhaus)* admission; *(Einbeziehung)* inclusion; *(Beginn)* start; *(Foto)* photograph; *(Film-)* shot; *(Mus)* recording; *(Band-)* tape recording. **a~fähig** *a* receptive.

A~prüfung f entrance examination

aufnehmen† vt sep pick up; (absorbieren) absorb; take (Nahrung, Foto); (fassen) hold; (aufnehmen) accept; (leihen) borrow; (empfangen) receive; (in Klub, Krankenhaus) admit; (beherbergen, geistig erfassen) take in; (einbeziehen) include; (beginnen) take up; (niederschreiben) take down; (filmen) film, shoot; (Mus) record; **auf Band a~** tape

aufopfer|n vt sep sacrifice; **sich a~n** sacrifice oneself. **A~ung** f self-sacrifice

aufpassen vi sep (haben) pay attention; (Sch vorsehen) take care; **a~ auf** (+ acc) look after

Aufprall m -[e]s impact. **a~en** vi sep (sein) **a~en auf** (+ acc) hit

aufpumpen vt sep pump up, inflate

aufputsch|en vt sep incite. **A~mittel** nt stimulant

aufquellen† vi sep (sein) swell

aufraffen vt sep pick up; (fig) pick oneself up; (fig) pull oneself together

aufragen vi sep (sein) rise [up]

aufräumen vt/i sep (haben) tidy up; (wegräumen) put away

aufrecht a & adv upright. **a~erhalten**† vt sep (fig) maintain

aufreg|en vt sep (beunruhigen) upset; (ärgern) annoy; **sich a~en** get excited; (sich erregen) get worked up. **a~end** a exciting. **A~ung** f excitement

aufreiben† vt sep chafe; (fig) wear down

aufreißen† v sep ▢vt tear open; dig up (Straße); open wide (Augen, Mund) ▢vi sep (sein) split open

aufrichtig a sincere. **A~keit** f sincerity

aufrollen vt sep roll up; (entrollen) unroll

aufrücken vi sep (sein) move up; (fig) be promoted

Aufruf m appeal (**an** + dat to). **a~en**† vt sep call out (Namen); **jdn a~en** call s.o.'s name

Aufruhr m -s,-e turmoil; (Empörung) revolt

aufrühr|en vt sep stir up. **A~er** m -s,-, rebel. **a~erisch** a inflammatory; (rebellisch) rebellious

aufrunden vt sep round up

aufrüsten vi sep (haben) arm

aufsagen vt sep recite

aufsässig a rebellious

Aufsatz m top; (Sch) essay

aufsaugen† vt sep soak up

aufschichten vt sep stack up

aufschieben† vt sep slide open; (verschieben) put off, postpone

Aufschlag m impact; (Tennis) service; (Hosen-) turn-up; (Comm) surcharge. **a~en**† v sep ▢vt open; crack (Ei); (hochschlagen) turn up; (erhöhen) increase; cast on (Masche); **sich** (dat) **das Knie a~en** cut (open) one's knee ▢vi (haben) hit (**auf etw** acc/dat sth); (Tennis) serve; (teurer werden) go up

aufschließen† v sep ▢vt unlock ▢vi (haben) unlock the door

aufschlußreich a revealing; (lehrreich) informative

aufschneiden† vt sep cut open; (in Scheiben) slice

Aufschnitt m sliced sausage, cold meat [and cheese]

aufschrauben vt sep screw on; (abschrauben) unscrew

Aufschrei m [sudden] cry

aufschreiben† vt sep write down; **jdn a~** (Polizist:) book s.o.

Aufschrift f inscription; (Etikett) label

Aufschub m delay; (Frist) grace

aufschürfen vt sep **sich** (dat) **das Knie a~** graze one's knee

aufschwingen† (sich) vr sep find the energy (**zu** for)

Aufschwung m (fig) upturn

aufsehen† vi sep (haben) look up (zu at/(fig) to). **A~** nt -s **A~ erregen** cause a sensation. **a~erregend** a sensational

Aufseher(in) m -s, (f -,-nen) supervisor; (Gefängnis-) warder

aufsein† vi sep (sein) be open; (Person:) be up

aufsetzen vt sep put on; (verfassen) draw up; (entwerfen) draft; **sich a~** sit up

Aufsicht f supervision; (Person) supervisor. **A~srat** m board of directors

aufsperren vt sep open wide

aufspielen v sep □vi (haben) play □vr **sich a~** show off

aufspießen vt sep spear

aufspringen† vi sep (sein) jump up; (aufprallen) bounce; (sich öffnen) burst open

aufspüren vt sep track down

aufstacheln vt sep incite

Aufstand m uprising, rebellion

aufständisch a rebellious

aufstehen† vi sep (sein) get up; (offen sein) be open; (fig) rise up

aufsteigen† vi sep (sein) get on; (Reiter:) mount; (Bergsteiger:) climb up; (hochsteigen) rise up; (Sport) be promoted

aufstellen vt sep put up; (postieren) post; (in einer Reihe) line up; (nominieren) nominate; (Sport) select (Mannschaft); make out (Liste); lay down (Regel); make (Behauptung); set up (Rekord). **A~ung** f nomination; (Liste) list

Aufstieg m ascent; (fig) rise; (Sport) promotion

Aufstoßen nt -s burping

aufstrebend a (fig) ambitious

Aufstrich m [sandwich] spread

aufstützen vt sep rest (auf+acc on); **sich a~** lean (auf+acc on)

Auftakt m (fig) start

auftauchen vi sep (sein) emerge; (fig) turn up; (Frage:) crop up

auftauen vt/i sep (sein) thaw

aufteilen vt sep divide [up]. **A~ung** f division

auftischen vt sep serve [up]

Auftrag m -[e]s, ⁓e task; (Kunst) commission; (Comm) order; **im A~** (+gen) on behalf of. **a~en†** vt sep apply; (servieren) serve; **jdm a~en** instruct s.o. (zu to). **A~geber** m -s,- client

auftrennen vt sep unpick, undo

auftreten† vi sep (sein) tread; (sich benehmen) behave, act; (Theat) appear; (die Bühne betreten) enter; (vorkommen) occur

Auftrieb m buoyancy; (fig) boost

Auftritt m (Theat) appearance; (auf die Bühne) entrance; (Szene) scene

aufwachen vi sep (sein) wake up

aufwachsen† vi sep (sein) grow up

Aufwand m -[e]s expenditure; (Luxus) extravagance; (Mühe) trouble; **A~ treiben** be extravagant

aufwärmen vt sep heat up; **sich a~** warm oneself; (Sport) warm up

Aufwartefrau f cleaner

aufwärts adv upwards; (bergauf) uphill. **a~gehen†** vi sep (sein) es **geht a~** mit jdm s.o. is improving

Aufwartung f - cleaner

aufwecken vt sep wake up

aufweichen v sep □vt soften □vi (sein) become soft

aufweisen† vt sep have, show

aufwenden† vt sep spend; **Mühe a~en** take pains. **a~ig** a lavish; (teuer) expensive

aufwerfen† vt sep (fig) raise

aufwerten vt sep revalue. **A~ung** f revaluation

aufwickeln vt sep roll up

aufwiegeln vt sep stir up

Aufwiegler m -s,- agitator

aufwisch|en vt sep wipe up; wash ⟨*Fußboden*⟩. **A~lappen** m floor-cloth

aufwühlen vt sep churn up; (fig) stir up

aufzähl|en vt sep enumerate, list. **A~ung** f list

aufzeichn|en vt sep record; (zeichnen) draw. **A~ung** f recording; **A~ungen** notes

aufziehen† vt sep pull up; hoist ⟨*Segel*⟩; (öffnen) open; draw ⟨*Vorhang*⟩; (großziehen) bring up; rear ⟨*Tier*⟩; mount ⟨*Bild*⟩; thread ⟨*Perlen*⟩; wind up ⟨*Uhr*⟩; (fam: necken) tease

Aufzug m hoist; (Fahrstuhl) lift; (Prozession) procession; (Theat) act

Augapfel m eyeball

Auge nt -s,-n eye; (Punkt) spot; **vier A~n werfen** throw a four; **unter vier A~n** in private; **im A~ behalten** keep in sight; (fig) bear in mind

Augenblick m moment; **A~!** just a moment! **a~lich** a immediate; (derzeitig) present □ adv immediately; (derzeit) at present

Augen|braue f eyebrow. **A~höhle** f eye socket. **A~licht** nt sight. **A~lid** nt eyelid

August m -[s] August

Auktion /-ˈtsi̯oːn/ f -,-en auction

Aula f -,-len (Sch) [assembly] hall

Au-pair-Mädchen /oˈpɛːr-/ nt au-pair

aus prep (+ dat) out of; (von) from; (bestehend) [made] of; **aus Angst** from or out of fear; **aus Spaß** for fun □ adv out; ⟨*Licht, Radio*⟩ off; **aus und ein** in and out; **von sich aus** of one's own accord; **von mir aus** as far as I'm concerned

ausarbeiten vt sep work out

ausarten vi sep (sein) degenerate (**in** + acc into)

ausatmen vt/i sep (haben) breathe out

ausbauen vt sep remove; (vergrößern) extend; (fig) expand

ausbedingen vt sep sich (dat) **a~** insist on; (zur Bedingung machen) stipulate

ausbessern vt sep mend, repair. **A~ung** f repair

ausbeulen vt sep remove the dents from; (dehnen) make baggy

ausbilden vt sep train; (formen) form; (entwickeln) develop; sich **a~en** train (als/zu as); (entstehen) develop. **A~er** m -s,- instructor. **A~ung** f training; (Sch) education

ausblasen† vt sep blow out

ausbleiben† vi sep (sein) fail to appear⟨(Erfolg:⟩ materialize; **es konnte nicht a~** it was inevitable. **A~** nt -s absence

Ausblick m view

ausbrechen† vi sep (sein) break out; ⟨*Vulkan:*⟩ erupt; (fliehen) escape; **in Tränen a~en** burst into tears. **A~er** m runaway

ausbreiten vt sep spread [out]; sich **a~** spread

Ausbruch m outbreak; ⟨*Vulkan-*⟩ eruption; ⟨*Wut-*⟩ outburst; ⟨*Flucht*⟩ escape, break-out

ausbrüten vt sep hatch

ausbürsten vt sep brush

Ausdauer f perseverance; (körperlich) stamina. **a~nd** a persevering; (unermüdlich) untiring; (Bot) perennial □ adv with perseverance; untiringly

ausdehnen vt sep (fig) extend; sich **a~** stretch; (Phys) expand

ausdenken† vt sep sich (dat) **a~** think up; (sich vorstellen) imagine

Ausdruck m expression; ⟨*Fach-*⟩ term; (Computer) printout. **a~en** vt sep print

ausdrücken vt sep squeeze out; squeeze ⟨*Zitrone*⟩; stub out ⟨*Zigarette*⟩; (äußern) express

ausdrucks|**los** *a* expressionless. **a ~ voll** *a* expressive

auseinander *adv* apart; (*entzwei*) in pieces. **a ~ falten** *vt sep* unfold. **a ~ gehen**† *vi sep* (*sein*) part; ⟨*Linien, Meinungen:*⟩ diverge; ⟨*Ehe:*⟩ break up; **a ~ halten**† *vt sep* tell apart. **a ~ nehmen**† *vt sep* take apart *or* to pieces. **a ~ setzen** *vt sep* explain (jdm to s.o.). **A ~ setzung** *f* -,-en discussion; (*Streit*) argument

auserlesen *a* select, choice

Ausfahrt *f* drive; (*Autobahn-, Garagen-*) exit

Ausfall *m* failure; (*Absage*) cancellation; (*Comm*) loss. **a ~ en**† *vi sep* (*sein*) fall out; (*versagen*) fail; (*abgesagt werden*) be cancelled; **gut/schlecht a ~ en** turn out to be good/poor

ausfallend, ausfällig *a* abusive

ausfertig|**en** *vt sep* make out. **A ~ ung** *f* -,-en **in doppelter A ~ ung** in duplicate

ausfindig *a* **a ~ machen** find

Ausflug *m* excursion, outing

Ausflügler *m* -s,- [day-]tripper

Ausfluß *m* outlet; (*Abfluß*) drain; (*Med*) discharge

ausfragen *vt sep* question

Ausfuhr *f* -,-en (*Comm*) export

ausführ|**en** *vt sep* take out; (*Comm*) export. **a ~ lich** *a* detailed □*adv* in detail. **A ~ ung** *f* execution; (*Comm*) version; (*äußere*) finish; (*Qualität*) workmanship; (*Erklärung*) explanation

Ausgabe *f* issue; (*Buch-*) edition

Ausgang *m* way out, exit; (*Flugsteig*) gate; (*Ende*) end; (*Ergebnis*) outcome. **A ~ spunkt** *m* starting-point. **A ~ ssperre** *f* curfew

ausgeben† *vt sep* hand out; issue ⟨*Fahrkarten*⟩; spend ⟨*Geld*⟩; **sich a ~ als** pretend to be

ausgebildet *a* trained

ausgebucht *a* fully booked; ⟨*Vorstellung*⟩ sold out

ausgefallen *a* unusual

ausgefranst *a* frayed

ausgeglichen *a* [well-]balanced

ausgeh|**en**† *vi sep* (*sein*) go out; ⟨*Haare:*⟩ fall out; ⟨*Vorräte, Geld:*⟩ run out; (*verblassen*) fade; **gut/ schlecht a ~ en** end well/badly; **leer a ~ en** come away empty-handed; **davon a ~ en, daß** assume that. **A ~ verbot** *nt* curfew

ausgelassen *a* high-spirited

ausgelernt *a* [fully] trained

ausgemacht *a* agreed

ausgenommen *conj* except; **a ~ wenn** unless

ausgeprägt *a* marked

ausgeschlossen *pred a* out of the question

ausgeschnitten *a* low-cut

ausgesprochen *a* marked □*adv* decidedly

ausgestorben *a* extinct; **[wie] a ~** ⟨*Straße:*⟩ deserted

Ausgestoßene(r) *m/f* outcast

ausgewogen *a* [well-]balanced

ausgezeichnet *a* excellent

ausgiebig *a* extensive; (*ausgedehnt*) long; **a ~ Gebrauch machen von** make full use of

ausgießen† *vt sep* pour out

Ausgleich *m* -[e]s balance; (*Entschädigung*) compensation. **a ~ en**† *v sep* □*vt* balance; even out ⟨*Höhe*⟩; (*wettmachen*) compensate for; **sich a ~ en** balance out □*vi* (*haben*) (*Sport*) equalize. **A ~ streffer** *m* equalizer

ausgrab|**en**† *vt sep* dig up; (*Archaeol*) excavate. **A ~ ung** *f* -,-en excavation

Ausguß *m* [kitchen] sink

aushaben† *vt sep* have finished ⟨*Buch*⟩

aushalten† *vt sep* bear, stand; hold ⟨*Note*⟩; (*Unterhalt zahlen für*) keep; **nicht auszuhalten, nicht zum A ~** unbearable

aushändigen vt sep hand over

Aushang m [public] notice

aushängen[1] vt sep (reg) display; take off its hinges 〈Tür〉

aushängen[2] vi sep (haben) be displayed. **A~eschild** nt sign

ausheben† vt sep excavate

aushecken vt sep (fig) hatch

aushelfen† vi sep (haben) help out (jdm s.o.)

Aushilfe f [temporary] assistant; **zur A~e** to help out. **A~skraft** f temporary worker. **a~sweise** adv temporarily

aushöhlen vt sep hollow out

auskennen† (sich) vr sep know one's way around; **sich mit/in etw** 〈dat〉 ~ know all about sth

auskleiden vt sep undress; (Techn) line; **sich** ~ undress

auskommen† vi sep (sein) manage (mit/ohne with/without); (sich vertragen) get on (gut well)

auskosten vt sep enjoy

auskugeln vt sep **sich** 〈dat〉 **den Arm** ~ dislocate one's shoulder

auskühlen vt/i sep (sein) cool

auskundschaften vt sep spy out

Auskunft f -,⁀e information; (A~sstelle) information desk; (Teleph) enquiries pl; **eine A~** a piece of information

auslachen vt sep laugh at

Auslage f [window] display; **A~n** expenses

Ausland nt im/ins A~ abroad

Ausländer(in) m -s,- (f -,-nen) foreigner. **a~isch** a foreign

Auslandsgespräch nt international call

auslass|en† vt sep let out; let down 〈Saum〉; (weglassen) leave out; (Culin) melt; (fig) vent 〈Ärger〉 (**an**+dat on). **A~ungszeichen** nt apostrophe

Auslauf m -[e]s vi sep (sein) run out; 〈Farbe:〉 run; 〈Naut〉 put to sea; 〈Modell:〉 be discontinued

ausleeren vt sep empty [out]

ausleg|en vt sep lay out; display 〈Waren〉; (bedecken) cover/ (auskleiden) line (mit with); (bezahlen) pay; (deuten) interpret. **A~ung** f -,-en interpretation

ausleihen† vt sep lend; **sich** 〈dat〉 **a** ~ borrow

auslernen vi sep (haben) finish one's training

Auslese f - selection; (fig) pick; 〈Elite〉 elite

ausliefer|n vt sep hand over; 〈Jur〉 extradite. **A~ung** f handing over; 〈Jur〉 extradition; 〈Comm〉 distribution

auslosen vt sep draw lots for

auslös|en vt sep set off, trigger; (fig) cause; arouse 〈Begeisterung〉; (einlösen) redeem; pay a ransom for 〈Gefangene〉. **A~er** m -s,- trigger; 〈Phot〉 shutter release

Auslösung f draw

auslüften vt/i sep (haben) air

ausmachen vt sep put out; (abschalten) turn off; (abmachen) arrange; (erkennen) make out; (betragen) amount to; (wichtig sein) matter; **das macht mir nichts aus** I don't mind

ausmalen vt sep paint; describe; **sich** 〈dat〉 **a** ~ imagine

Ausmaß nt extent; **A~e** dimensions

Ausnahme f -,-n exception. **A~zustand** m state of emergency. **a~slos** adv without exception. **a~sweise** adv as an exception

ausnehmen† vt sep take out; gut 〈Fisch〉; **sich gut a** ~ look good. **a~d** adv exceptionally

ausnutzen, ausnützen vt sep exploit. **A~ung** f exploitation

auspacken vt sep unpack; (auswickeln) unwrap

auspfeifen† vt sep whistle and boo

ausplaudern vt sep let out, blab

ausprobieren *vt sep* try out

Auspuff *m* -s exhaust (system).
A~gase *ntpl* exhaust fumes

auspusten *vt sep* blow out

ausradieren *vt sep* rub out

ausrauben *vt sep* rob

ausräuchern *vt sep* smoke out;
fumigate ⟨Zimmer⟩

ausräumen *vt sep* clear out

ausrechnen *vt sep* work out

Ausrede *f* excuse

ausreichen *vi sep* (haben) be
enough; **a~** **mit** have enough.
a~d *a* adequate; ⟨Sch⟩ *a* pass

Ausreise *f* departure. **A~n** *vi sep*
(sein) leave the country. **A~vi-
sum** *nt* exit visa

ausreißen† *v sep* □*vt* pull *or* tear
out □*vi* (sein) ⟨fam⟩ run away

ausrenken *vt sep* dislocate

ausrichten *vt sep* align; ⟨bestel-
len⟩ deliver; ⟨erreichen⟩ achieve;
jdm **a~** tell s.o. (daß that); **kann
ich etwas a~?** can I take a message? **ich soll Ihnen Grüße von
X a~** X sends [you] his regards

ausrotten *vt sep* exterminate;
⟨fig⟩ eradicate

Ausruf *m* exclamation. **a~en†** *vt
sep* exclaim; call out ⟨Namen⟩;
⟨verkünden⟩ proclaim; call
⟨Streik⟩; jdn **a~en** lassen have
s.o. paged. **A~zeichen** *nt* exclamation mark

ausruhen *vt/i sep* (haben) rest;
sich a~ have a rest

ausrüst|en *vt sep* equip. **A~ung**
f equipment; ⟨Mil⟩ kit

ausrutschen *vi sep* (sein) slip

Aussage *f* -,-n statement; ⟨Jur⟩
testimony. **a~n** *vt/i sep* (haben)
state; ⟨Jur⟩ give evidence, testify

ausschachten *vt sep* excavate

ausschalten *vt sep* switch off

Ausschank *m* sale of alcoholic
drinks; ⟨Bar⟩ bar

Ausschau *f* - **A~ halten nach**
look out for

ausscheiden† *v sep* □*vi* (sein) leave;
⟨Sport⟩ drop out; ⟨nicht in Frage
kommen⟩ be excluded; **aus dem
Dienst a~** retire

ausschenken *vt sep* pour out

ausscheren *vi sep* (sein) ⟨Auto⟩
pull out

ausschildern *vt sep* signpost

ausschlafen† *v sep* □*vi/r* (haben)
[sich] **a~** get enough sleep; ⟨mor-
gens⟩ sleep late □*vt* sleep off
⟨Rausch⟩

Ausschlag *m* ⟨Med⟩ rash; **den
A~ geben** ⟨fig⟩ tip the balance.
a~gebend *a* decisive

ausschließen† *vt sep* lock out;
⟨fig⟩ exclude; ⟨entfernen⟩ expel.
a~lich *a* exclusive

ausschlüpfen *vi sep* (sein) hatch

Ausschluß *m* exclusion; expulsion; **unter A~ der Öffentlichkeit** in camera

ausschneiden† *vt sep* cut out

Ausschnitt *m* excerpt, extract

ausschöpfen *vt sep* ladle out;
⟨Naut⟩ bail out; exhaust ⟨Mög-
lichkeiten⟩

ausschreiben† *vt sep* write out;
⟨ausstellen⟩ make out; ⟨bekannt-
geben⟩ announce; put out to tender ⟨Auftrag⟩

Ausschreitungen *fpl* riots; ⟨Ex-
zesse⟩ excesses

Ausschuß *m* committee; ⟨Comm⟩
rejects *pl*

ausschütten *vt sep* tip out; ⟨ver-
schütten⟩ spill; ⟨leeren⟩ empty

aussehen† *vi sep* (haben) look; **es
sieht nach Regen aus** it looks
like rain. **A~** *nt* -s appearance

aussein† *vi sep* (sein) be out;
⟨Licht, Radio:⟩ be off; ⟨zu Ende
sein⟩ be over; **a~ auf** (+ *acc*) be
after

außen *adv* [on the] outside; **nach
a~** outwards. **A~bordmotor**
m outboard motor. **A~handel** *m*
foreign trade. **A~minister** *m*
Foreign Minister. **A~politik** *f*

foreign policy. **A~seite** f outside. **A~seiter** m **-s,-** outsider; (fig) misfit. **A~stände** mpl outstanding debts

außer prep (+dat) except [for], apart from; (außerhalb) out of; **a~ sich** (fig) beside oneself □conj except; **a~ wenn** unless. **a~dem** adv in addition, as well □conj moreover

äußer|e(r,s) a external; (Teil, Schicht) outer. **Ä~e(s)** nt exterior; (Aussehen) appearance

außer|ehelich a extramarital. **ä~gewöhnlich** a exceptional. **a~halb** prep (+gen) outside □adv **a~halb wohnen** live outside town

äußer|lich a external; (fig) outward. **ä~n** vt express; **sich ä~n** manifest itself

außerordentlich a extraordinary

äußerst adv extremely

äußerste(r,s) a outermost; (weiteste) furthest; (höchste) utmost; (letzte) last; (schlimmste) worst. **Ä~(s)** nt das **Ä~** the limit; (Schlimmste) the worst

Äußerung f -,-en comment; (Bemerkung) remark

aussetzen v sep □vt expose (dat to); abandon (Kind); launch (Boot); offer (Belohnung); **etwas auszusetzen haben an** (+dat) find fault with □vi (haben) stop; (Motor:) cut out

Aussicht f -,-en view; (fig) prospect (auf+acc of); **weitere A~en** (Meteorol) further outlook sg. **a~slos** a hopeless

ausspannen v sep □vt spread out; unhitch (Pferd) □vi (haben) rest. **A~ung** f rest

aussperren vt sep lock out

ausspielen v sep □vt play (Karte); (fig) play off (gegen against) □vi (haben) (Kartenspiel) lead

Aussprache f pronunciation; (Gespräch) talk

aussprechen† vt sep pronounce; (äußern) express; **sich a~** talk; come out (für/gegen in favour of/against)

Ausspruch m saying

ausspucken v sep □vt spit out□vi (haben) spit

ausspülen vt sep rinse out

ausstatt|en vt sep equip. **A~ung** f -,-en equipment; (Innen-) furnishings pl; (Theat) scenery and costumes pl

ausstehen† v sep □vt suffer; **Angst a~** be frightened; **ich kann sie nicht a~** I can't stand her □vi (haben) be outstanding

aussteigen† vi sep (sein) get out; (aus Bus, Zug) get off; **alles a~!** all change!

ausstell|en vt sep exhibit; (Comm) display; (ausfertigen) make out; issue (Paß). **A~ung** f exhibition; (Comm) display

aussterben† vi sep (sein) die out; (Biol) become extinct

Aussteuer f trousseau

Ausstieg m -[e]s,-e exit

ausstopfen vt sep stuff

ausstoßen† vt sep emit (Fluch); heave (Seufzer); (ausschließen) expel

ausstrahl|en vt sep (sein) radiate, emit; (Radio, TV) broadcast. **A~ung** f radiation

ausstrecken vt sep stretch out; put out (Hand)

ausstreichen† vt sep cross out

ausströmen v sep □vi (sein) pour out; (entweichen) escape □vt emit; (ausstrahlen) radiate

aussuchen vt sep pick, choose

Austausch m exchange. **a~bar** a interchangeable. **a~en** vt sep exchange; (auswechseln) replace

austeilen vt sep distribute; (ausgeben) hand out

Auster f -,-n oyster

austragen† vt sep deliver; hold ⟨Wettkampf⟩; play ⟨Spiel⟩

Austral|ien /-ịən/ nt -s Australia. **A∼ier(in)** m -s,- (f -,-nen) Australian. **a∼isch** a Australian

austreiben† v sep ▢vt drive out ▢vi (haben) (Bot) sprout

austreten† v sep ▢vt stamp out; (abnutzen) wear down ▢vi (sein) come out; (ausscheiden) leave (aus etw sth); (Mil) be excused

austrinken† vt/i sep (haben) drink up; (leeren) drain

Austritt m resignation

austrocknen vt/i sep (sein) dry out

ausüben vt sep practise; carry on ⟨Handwerk⟩; exercise ⟨Recht⟩; exert ⟨Druck, Einfluß⟩

Ausverkauf m [clearance] sale. **a∼t** a sold out

Auswahl f choice, selection

auswählen vt sep choose, select

Auswander|er m emigrant. **a∼n** vi sep (sein) emigrate. **A∼ung** f emigration

auswärt|ig a non-local; (ausländisch) foreign. **a∼s** adv outwards; (Sport) away. **A∼sspiel** nt away game

auswechseln vt sep change; (ersetzen) replace; (Sport) substitute

Ausweg m (fig) way out

ausweichen† vi sep (sein) get out of the way; **jdm/etw a∼en** avoid/ (sich entziehen) evade sb/sth

Ausweis m -es,-e pass; (Mitglieds-) card. **a∼en†** vt sep deport; **sich a∼en** prove one's identity. **A∼papiere** ntpl identification papers. **A∼ung** f deportation

auswendig adv by heart

auswerten vt sep evaluate

auswickeln vt sep unwrap

auswirk|en (sich) vr sep have an effect (**auf** +acc on). **A∼ung** f effect; (Folge) consequence

auswringen vt sep wring out

auszahlen vt sep pay out; (entlohnen) pay off; (abfinden) buy out; **sich a∼** (fig) pay off

auszählen vt sep count; (Boxen) count out

Auszahlung f payment

auszeichn|en vt sep (Comm) price; (ehren) honour; (mit einem Preis) award a prize to; (Mil) decorate; **sich a∼en** distinguish oneself. **A∼ung** f honour; (Preis) award; (Mil) decoration; (Sch) distinction

ausziehen† v sep ▢vt pull out; (auskleiden) undress; take off ⟨Mantel, Schuhe⟩ ▢vi (sein) move out; (sich aufmachen) set out

Auszug m departure; (Umzug) move; (Ausschnitt) extract, excerpt; (Bank-) statement

Auto nt -s,-s car. **A∼ fahren** drive; (mitfahren) go in the car. **A∼bahn** f motorway

Auto|bus m bus. **A∼fähre** f car ferry. **A∼fahrer(in)** m(f) driver, motorist

Autogramm nt -s,-e autograph

Automat m -en,-en machine; (Münz-) slot-machine; (Verkaufs-) vending-machine; (Techn) robot. **A∼ik** f automatic mechanism; (Auto) automatic transmission

automatisch a automatic

Autonummer f registration number

Autopsie f -,-n autopsy

Autor m -s,-en /-'to:rən/ author

Auto|reisezug m Motorail. **A∼rennen** nt motor race

Autorin f -,-nen author[ess]

Autori|sation /-tsjo:n/ f authorization. **A∼tät** f -,-en authority

Auto|schlosser m motor mechanic. **A∼skooter** /-sku:tɐ/ m -s,-dodgem. **A∼stopp** m -s per

A ~ stopp fahren hitch-hike.
A ~ verleih *m* car hire [firm].
A ~ waschanlage *f* car wash
autsch *int* ouch
Axt *f* -,-̈e axe

B

B, b /be:/ *nt* - (*Mus*) B flat
Baby /'be:bi/ *nt* -s,-s baby.
  B ~ ausstattung *f* layette
Bach *m* -[e]s,-̈e stream
Backbord *nt* -[e]s port [side]
Backe *f* -,-n cheek
backen *vt/i* † (*haben*) bake; (*braten*) fry
Backenzahn *m* molar
Bäcker *m* -s,- baker. B ~ ei *f* -,-en,
  B ~ laden *m* baker's shop
Back|obst *nt* dried fruit. B ~ ofen
m oven. B ~ pfeife *f* slap in the
face. B ~ pflaume *f* prune. B ~ -
pulver *nt* baking-powder
Bad *nt* -[e]s,-̈er bath;(*Zimmer*)
bathroom; (*Ort*) spa
Bade|anstalt *f* swimming baths
pl. B ~ anzug *m* swim-suit.
B ~ hose *f* swimming trunks *pl*.
B ~ mantel *m* bathrobe. b ~ n
vi (*haben*) have a bath; (*im Meer*)
bathe □ *vt* bath; (*waschen*) bathe.
B ~ ort *m* seaside resort.
B ~ tuch *nt* bath-towel.
Bagger *m* -s,- excavator; (*Naß*)
dredger. B ~ see *m* flooded gravel-pit
Bahn *f* -,-en path; (*Astr*) orbit;
(*Sport*) track; (*einzelne*) lane;
(*Rodel-*) run; (*Stoff-*) width; (*Eisen-*)
railway; (*Zug*) train;
(*Straßen-*) tram. b ~ brechend *a*
(*fig*) pioneering. B ~ hof *m* [railway] station. B ~ steig *m* -[e]s,-e
platform. B ~ übergang *m* level
crossing
Bahre *f* -,-n stretcher; bier
Baiser /bε'ze:/ *nt* -s,-s meringue
Bake *f* -,-n (*Naut, Aviat*) beacon

Bakterien /-jan/ *fpl* bacteria
Balanc|e /ba'lã:sǝ/ *f* - balance.
b ~ ieren *vt/i* (*haben/sein*) balance
bald *adv* soon; (*fast*) almost
Baldachin /-xi:n/ *m* -s,-e canopy
bald|ig *a* early; (*Besserung*)
speedy. b ~ möglichst *adv* as
soon as possible
Balg *nt & m* -[e]s,-̈er (*fam*) brat
Balkan *m* -s Balkans *pl*
Balken *m* -s,- beam
Balkon /bal'kõ:/ *m* -s,-s balcony;
(*Theat*) circle
Ball[1] *m* -[e]s,-̈e ball
Ball[2] *m* -[e]s,-̈e (*Tanz*) ball
Ballade *f* -,-n ballad
Ballast *m* -[e]s ballast. B ~ stoffe
mpl roughage *sg*
Ballen *m* -s,- bale; (*Anat*) ball of
the hand(*Fuß-*) foot; (*Med*) bunion
Ballerina *f* -,-nen ballerina
Ballett *nt* -s,-e ballet
Ballon /ba'lõ:/ *m* -s,-s balloon
Balt|ikum *nt* -s Baltic States *pl*.
b ~ isch *a* Baltic
Bambus *m* -ses,-se bamboo
banal *a* banal. B ~ ität *f* -,-en
banality
Banane *f* -,-n banana
Banause *m* -n,-n philistine
Band[1] *nt* -[e]s,-̈er ribbon; (*Naht-,
Ton-, Ziel-*) tape; (*Anat*) ligament;
laufendes B ~ conveyor belt; am
laufenden B ~ (*fam*) non-stop
Band[2] *m* -[e]s,-̈e volume
Band[3] *nt* -[e]s,-e (*fig*) bond
Bandage /ban'da:ʒǝ/ *f* -,-n bandage. b ~ ieren *vt* bandage
Bande *f* -,-n gang
bändigen *vt* control, restrain;
(*zähmen*) tame
Bandit *m* -en,-en bandit
Band|maß *nt* tape measure.
B ~ scheibe *f* disc

bang[e] *a* anxious; **jdm b~e ma-chen** frighten s.o. **b~en** *vi* (*haben*) fear (**um für**)

Banjo *nt* -s,-s banjo

Bank¹ *f* -,-e bench

Bank² *f* -,-en (*Comm*) bank. **B~einzug** *m* direct debit

Bankett *nt* -s,-e banquet

Bankier /baŋ'kje:/ *m* -s,-s banker

Bankrott *m* -s,-e bankruptcy. **b~** *a* bankrupt

Bann *m* -[e]s,-e (*fig*) spell. **b~en** *vt* exorcize; (*abwenden*) avert

Banner *nt* -s,- banner

bar *a* (*rein*) sheer; (*Gold*) pure; **b~es Geld** cash; **[in] bar bezah-len** pay cash

Bar¹ *f* -,-s bar

Bär *m* -en,-en bear

Baracke *f* -,-n (*Mil*) hut

Barbar *m* -en,-en barbarian. **b~arisch** *a* barbaric

barfuß *adv* barefoot. **B~geld** *nt* cash

barmherzig *a* merciful. **B~keit** *f* - mercy

barock *a* baroque

Barometer *nt* -s,- barometer

Baron *m* -s,-e baron. **B~in** *f* -,-nen baroness

Barren *m* -s,- (*Gold-*) bar, ingot; (*Sport*) parallel bars *pl*. **B~gold** *nt* gold bullion

Barriere *f* -,-n barrier

Barrikade *f* -,-n barricade

barsch *a* gruff

Barsch *m* -[e]s,-e (*Zool*) perch

Bart *m* -[e]s,-e beard; (*der Katze*) whiskers *pl*

bärtig *a* bearded

Barzahlung *f* cash payment

Basar *m* -s,-e bazaar

Base *f* -,-n (*female*) cousin

Basel *nt* -s Basle

basieren *vi* (*haben*) be based (**auf** + *dat* on)

Basilikum *nt* -s basil

Basis *f* -,Basen base; (*fig*) basis

basisch *a* (*Chem*) alkaline

Baskenmütze *f* beret. **b~isch** *a* Basque

Baß *m* -sses,-sse bass

Bassin /ba'sɛ̃:/ *nt* -s,-s pond; (*Brunnen-*) basin

Bassist *m* -en,-en bass player

Bast *m* -[e]s raffia

basteln *vt* make □*vi* (*haben*) do handicrafts

Batterie *f* -,-n battery

Bau¹ *m* -[e]s,-e burrow; (*Fuchs-*) earth

Bau² *m* -[e]s,-ten construction; (*Gebäude*) building; (*Körper-*) build; (*B~stelle*) building site. **B~arbeiten** *fpl* building work *sg*. **B~art** *f* design; (*Stil*) style

Bauch *m* -[e]s, Bäuche abdomen, belly; (*Magen*) stomach; (*Bauchung*) bulge. **B~nabel** *m* navel. **B~redner** *m* ventriloquist. **B~schmerzen** *mpl* stomach-ache *sg.* **B~speicheldrüse** *f* pancreas

bauen *vt* build; construct □*vi* (*haben*) rely on (**auf** + *acc*) (*fig*) rely on

Bauer¹ *m* -n,-n farmer; (*Schach*) pawn

Bauer² *nt* -s,- [bird]cage

bäuerlich *a* rustic

Bauernhaus *nt* farmhouse

baufällig *a* dilapidated. **B~ge-nehmigung** *f* planning permission. **B~gerüst** *nt* scaffolding. **B~jahr** *nt* year of construction. **B~kunst** *f* architecture. **b~lich** *a* structural

Baum *m* -[e]s, Bäume tree

baumeln *vi* (*haben*) dangle

bäumen (sich) *vr* rear [up]

Baumwolle *f* cotton

Bauplatz *m* building plot

Bausch *m* -[e]s, Bäusche wad; **in B~ und Bogen** (*fig*) wholesale. **b~en** *vt* puff out

Bausparkasse *f* building society. **B~stein** *m* building brick. **B~stelle** *f* building site; (*Stra-*

ßen-) roadworks pl. **B~werk** nt building. **B~zaun** m hoarding

Bayer(in) m -s,-n (f -,-nen) Bavarian. **B~n** nt -s Bavaria

bay[e]risch a Bavarian

Bazillus m -,-len bacillus

beabsichtigen vt intend. **b~t** a intended; (absichtlich) intentional

beacht|en vt take notice of; (einhalten) observe; (folgen) follow; **nicht b~en** ignore. **b~lich** a considerable. **B~ung** f - observance; **etw** (dat) **keine B~ung schenken** take no notice of sth

Beamte(r) m, **Beamtin** f -,-nen official; (Staats-) civil servant; (Schalter-) clerk

beanspruchen vt claim; (erfordern) demand

beanstand|en vt find fault with; (Comm) make a complaint about. **B~ung** f -,-en complaint

beantragen vt apply for

beantworten vt answer

bearbeiten vt work; process; (behandeln) treat (mit with); (Admin) deal with; (redigieren) edit; (Theat) adapt; (Mus) arrange

Beatmungsgerät nt ventilator

beaufsichtig|en vt supervise. **B~ung** f - supervision

beauftrag|en vt instruct; commission ⟨Künstler⟩

bebauen vt build on; (bestellen) cultivate

beben vi (haben) tremble

Becher m -s,- beaker; (Henkel-) mug; (Joghurt-, Sahne-) carton

Becken nt -s,- basin; (Mus) cymbals pl; (Anat) pelvis

bedacht a careful; **darauf b~ anxious (zu** to)

bedanken (sich) vr thank

Bedarf m -s need/(Comm) demand (**an** + dat for); **bei B~** if required. **B~shaltestelle** f request stop

bedauer|lich a regrettable. **b~licherweise** adv unfortunately. **b~n** vt regret; (bemitleiden) feel sorry for; **bedaure!** sorry! **B~n** nt -s regret; (Mitgefühl) sympathy. **b~nswert** a pitiful; (bedauerlich) regrettable

bedeck|en vt cover; **b~t** a covered; (Himmel) overcast

bedenk|en† vt consider; (überlegen) think over. **B~** pl misgivings; **ohne B~** without hesitation

bedenklich a doubtful; (verdächtig) dubious

bedeut|en vi (haben) mean. **b~end** a important; (beträchtlich) considerable. **B~ung** f -,-en meaning; (Wichtigkeit) importance. **b~ungslos** a meaningless; (unwichtig) unimportant. **b~ungsvoll** a significant; (vielsagend) meaningful

bedien|en vt serve; (betätigen) operate; **sich [selbst] b~en** help oneself. **B~ung** f -,-en service; (Betätigung) operation; (Kellner) waiter. **B~ungsgeld** nt service charge

Bedingung f -,-en condition; **B~en** conditions; (Comm) terms. **b~slos** a unconditional

bedroh|en vt threaten. **b~lich** a threatening. **B~ung** f threat

bedrücken vt depress

bedruckt a printed

bedürf|en† vt (haben) (+gen) need. **B~nis** nt -ses,-se need. **B~nisanstalt** f public convenience. **b~tig** a needy

Beefsteak /ˈbiːfsteːk/ nt -s,-s steak; **deutsches B~** hamburger

beeilen (sich) vr hurry; hasten

beeindrucken vt impress

beeinflussen vt influence

beengen vt restrict

beerdig|en vt bury. **B~ung** f -,-en funeral

Beere f -,-n berry

Beet nt -[e]s,-e (Hort) bed

Beete f -,-n rote B~ beetroot

befähigen vt enable; (qualifizieren) qualify. B~ung f -qualification; (Fähigkeit) ability

befahrbar a passable

befallen† vt attack; ⟨Angst:⟩ seize

befangen a shy; self-conscious; (Jur) biased. B~heit f - shyness; self-consciousness; bias

befassen (sich) vr concern oneself/(behandeln) deal (mit with)

Befehl m -[e]s,-e order; (Leitung) command (über + acc of). b~en† vt jdm etw b~en order s.o. to do sth □ vi (haben) give the orders. B~sform f (Gram) imperative. B~shaber m -s,- commander

befestigen vt fasten (an + dat to); (Mil) fortify

befeuchten vt moisten

befinden† (sich) vr be. B~ nt -s [state of] health

beflecken vt stain

befolgen vt follow

befördern vt transport; (im Rang) promote

befragen vt question

befreien vt free; (räumen) clear (von of); (freistellen) exempt (von from); sich b~en free oneself. B~er m -s,- liberator. B~ung f -liberation; exemption

befreunden (sich) vr make friends

befriedigen vt satisfy. b~end a satisfying. B~ung f - satisfaction

befruchten vt fertilize. B~ung f - fertilization; künstliche B~ung artificial insemination

Befugnis f -,-se authority

Befund m result

befürchten vt fear. B~ung f -,-en fear

befürworten vt support

begabt a gifted. B~ung f -,-en gift, talent

begeben† (sich) vr go; sich in Gefahr b~ expose oneself to danger

begegnen vi (sein) jdm/etw b~en meet s.o./sth. B~ung f -,-en meeting

begehren vt desire

begeister|n vt jdn b~n arouse s.o.'s enthusiasm. b~t a enthusiastic; (eifrig) keen. B~ung f - enthusiasm

Begierde f -,-n desire

Beginn m -s beginning. b~en† vt/i (haben) start, begin

beglaubigen vt authenticate

begleichen† vt settle

begleit|en vt accompany. B~er m -s,- companion; (Mus) accompanist. B~ung f -,-en company; (Mus) accompaniment

beglück|en vt make happy. b~wünschen vt congratulate (zu on)

begnadigen vt (Jur) pardon. B~ung f -,-en (Jur) pardon

begraben† vt bury

Begräbnis n -ses,-se burial; (Feier) funeral

begreif|en† vt understand; nicht zu b~en incomprehensible. b~lich a understandable

begrenz|en vt form the boundary of; (beschränken) restrict. b~t a limited. B~ung f -,-en restriction; (Grenze) boundary

Begriff m -[e]s,-e concept; (Ausdruck) term; (Vorstellung) idea; im B~ sein be about (zu to)

begründ|en vt give one's reason for. b~et a justified. B~ung f -,-en reason

begrüß|en vt greet; (billigen) welcome. b~enswert a desirable. B~ung f - greeting; welcome

begünstigen vt favour

begütert a wealthy

behaart a hairy

behäbig a portly

behag|en *vi* (haben) please (jdm s.o.). **B~en** *nt* **-s** contentment. **b~lich** *a* comfortable. **B~lichkeit** *f* comfort

behalten† *vt* keep; (sich merken) remember

Behälter *m* **-s,-** container

behand|eln *vt* treat; (sich befassen) deal with. **B~lung** *f* treatment

beharr|en *vi* (haben) persist (auf + dat in). **b~lich** *a* persistent; (hartnäckig) dogged

behaupt|en *vt* maintain; (vorgeben) claim; (sagen) say; sich **b~en** hold one's own. **B~ung** *f* **-,-en** assertion; claim; (Äußerung) statement

beheben† *vt* remedy

behelf|en (sich) *vr* make do (mit with). **b~smäßig** *a* makeshift □ *adv* provisionally

beherbergen *vt* put up

beherrsch|en *vt* rule over; (dominieren) dominate; (meistern) control; (können) know. **b~t** *a* self-controlled. **B~ung** *f* control

beherzigen *vt* heed

behilflich *a* jdm **b~** sein help s.o.

behinder|n *vt* hinder; (blockieren) obstruct. **b~t** *a* handicapped; (schwer) disabled. **B~te(r)** *m/f* handicapped/(schwer) disabled person. **B~ung** *f* **-,-en** obstruction; (Med) handicap; disability

Behörde *f* **-,-n** [public] authority

behüten *vt* protect

behutsam *a* careful; (zart) gentle

bei *prep* (+ dat) near; (dicht) by; at ⟨Firma, Veranstaltung⟩; **bei sich haben** have with one; **bei mir** at my place; (in meinem Fall) in my case; **Herr X bei Meyer** Mr X c/o Meyer; **bei Regen** when/(falls) if it rains; **bei Feuer** in case of fire; **bei guter Gesundheit** in good health

beibehalten† *vt sep* keep

beibringen† *vt sep* jdm etw **b~** teach s.o. sth; (mitteilen) break sth to s.o.; (zufügen) inflict sth on s.o.

Beichte *f* **-,-n** confession. **b~en** *vt/i* (haben) confess. **B~stuhl** *m* confessional

beide *a & pron* both; (dreißig) **b~** (Tennis) thirty all. **b~rseitig** *a* mutual. **B~rseits** *adv & prep* (+ gen) on both sides (of)

beieinander *adv* together

Beifahrer(in) *m(f)* passenger; (Motorrad) pillion passenger

Beifall *m* **-[e]s** applause; (Billigung) approval; **B~ klatschen** applaud

beifügen *vt sep add*; (beilegen) enclose

beige /beːʒ/ *inv a* beige

beigeben† *vt sep* add

Beihilfe *f* financial aid; (Studien-) grant; (Jur) aiding and abetting

Beil *nt* **-[e]s,-e** hatchet, axe

Beilage *f* supplement; (Gemüse-) vegetable

beiläufig *a* casual

beilegen *vt sep* enclose; (schlichten) settle

Beileid *nt* condolences *pl.* **B~sbrief** *m* letter of condolence

beiliegend *a* enclosed

beim *prep* = bei dem; **b~ Militär** in the army

Bein *nt* **-[e]s,-e** leg; jdm ein **B~ stellen** trip s.o. up

beinah[e] *adv* nearly, almost

Beiname *m* epithet

beipflichten *vi sep* (haben) agree (dat with)

Beirat *m* advisory committee

beisammen *adv* together

Beisein *nt* presence

beiseite *adv* aside; (abseits) apart; **b~ legen** put aside; (sparen) put by

beisetz|en *vt sep* bury. **B~ung** *f* **-,-en** funeral

Beispiel *nt* example; **zum B~** for example. **b~sweise** *adv* for example

beißen† *vt & i (haben)* bite; *(brennen)* sting; **sich b~en** *(Farben:)* clash. **B~end** *a (fig)* biting. **B~zange** *f* pliers *pl*

Bei|stand *m* -[e]s help. **b~stehen**† *vi sep (haben)* jdm **b~stehen** help s.o.

beistimmen *vi sep (haben)* agree

Beistrich *m* comma

Beitrag *m* -[e]s,-̈e contribution; *(Mitglieds-)* subscription; *(Versicherungs-)* premium; *(Zeitungs-)* article. **b~en**† *vt/i sep (haben)* contribute

bei|treten† *vi sep (sein)* (+ *dat*) join. **B~tritt** *m* joining

Beize *f* -,-n *(Holz-)* stain; *(Culin)* marinade

beizeiten *adv* in good time

beizen *vt* stain *(Holz)*

bejahen *vt* answer in the affirmative; *(billigen)* approve of

bejahrt *a* aged, old

bekämpfen *vt* fight. **B~ung** *f* -fight *(gen* against)

bekannt *a* well-known; *(vertraut)* familiar; jdn **b~ machen** introduce s.o. **B~e(r)** *m/f* acquaintance; *(Freund)* friend. **B~gabe** *f* announcement. **b~geben**† *vt sep* announce. **B~lich** *adv* as is well known. **b~machen** *vt sep* announce. **B~machung** *f* -,-en announcement; *(Anschlag)* notice. **B~schaft** *f* - acquaintance; *(Leute)* acquaintances *pl*; *(Freunde)* friends *pl*

bekehr|en *vt* convert. **B~ung** *f* -,-en conversion

bekenn|en† *vt* confess; profess *(Glauben)*; **sich [für] schuldig b~en** admit one's guilt. **B~tnis** *nt* -ses,-se confession; *(Konfession)* denomination

beklag|en *vt* lament; *(bedauern)* deplore; **sich b~en** complain.

b~enswert *a* unfortunate.

b~te(r) *m/f (Jur)* defendant

bekleid|en *vt* hold *(Amt)*. **B~ung** *f* clothing

Beklemmung *f* -,-en feeling of oppression

bekommen† *vt* get; have *(Baby)*; catch *(Erkältung)* ◦ *vi (sein)* jdm **gut b~** do s.o. good; *(Essen:)* agree with s.o.

bekömmlich *a* digestible

beköstig|en *vt* feed. **B~ung** *f* - board; *(Essen)* food

bekreuzigen (sich) *vr* cross oneself

bekümmert *a* troubled; *(besorgt)* worried

bekunden *vt* show

Belag *m* -[e]s,-̈e coating; *(Fußboden-)* covering; *(Brot-)* topping; *(Zahn-)* tartar; *(Brems-)* lining

Belagerung *f* -,-en siege

Belang *m* **von B~** of importance. **B~e** *pl* interests. **b~los** *a* irrelevant; *(unwichtig)* trivial. **B~losigkeit** *f* -,-en triviality

belassen† *vt* leave

belast|en *vt* load; *(fig)* burden; *(beanspruchen)* put a strain on; *(Comm)* debit; *(Jur)* incriminate

belästigen *vt* bother; *(bedrängen)* pester; *(unsittlich)* molest

Belastung *f* -,-en load; *(fig)* strain; *(Comm)* debit. **B~smaterial** *nt* incriminating evidence. **B~szeuge** *m* prosecution witness

belaufen (sich) *vr* amount

belauschen *vt* eavesdrop on

beleb|en *vt (fig)* revive; *(lebhaft machen)* enliven. **b~t** *a* lively; *(Straße)* busy

Beleg *m* -[e]s,-e evidence; *(Beispiel)* instance (**für** of); *(Quittung)* receipt. **b~en** *vt* cover; *(garnieren)* garnish *(mit* with); *(besetzen)* reserve; *(Univ)* enrol for; *(nachweisen)* provide evidence for; **den ersten Platz b~en**

(*Sport*) take first place.
B~**schaft** *f* -,-en work-force.
b~t *a* occupied; (*Zunge*) coated;
b~te Brote open sandwiches

belehren *vt* instruct

beleidig|en *vt* offend; (*absichtlich*) insult. **B~ung** *f* -,-en insult

belesen *a* well-read

beleucht|en *vt* light; (*anleuchten*) illuminate. **B~ung** *f* -,-en illumination

Belg|ien *|-jən| nt* -s Belgium. **B~ier(in)** *m* -s,- (*f* -,-nen) Belgian. **b~isch** *a* Belgian

belichten *vt* (*Phot*) expose

Belieb|en *nt* -s **nach B~en** [just] as one likes. **b~ig** *a* **eine b~ige Zahl** any number you like □ *adv* **b~ig lange** as long as one likes. **b~t** *a* popular

bellen *vi* (*haben*) bark

belohn|en *vt* reward. **B~ung** *f* -,-en reward

belustig|en *vt* amuse. **B~ung** *f* -,-en amusement

bemalen *vt* paint

bemängeln *vt* criticize

bemannt *a* manned

bemerk|bar *a* **sich b~bar machen** attract attention. **b~en** *vt* notice; (*äußern*) remark. **b~enswert** *a* remarkable. **B~ung** *f* -,-en remark

bemitleiden *vt* pity

bemüh|en *vt* trouble; **sich b~en** try (**zu** to; **um etw** to get sth); (*sich kümmern*) attend (**um** to); **b~t sein** endeavour (**zu** to). **B~ung** *f* -,-en effort

bemuttern *vt* mother

benachbart *a* neighbouring

benachrichtig|en *vt* inform; (*amtlich*) notify

benachteilig|en *vt* discriminate against; treat unfairly. **B~ung** *f* -,-en discrimination

benehmen† (*sich*) *vr.* behave.
B~ *nt* -s behaviour

beneiden *vt* envy (**um etw** sth)

Bengel *m* -s,- boy; (*Rüpel*) lout

benötigen *vt* need

benutz|en, benütz|en (*SGer*) *vt* use; take (*Bahn*). **B~ung** *f* use

Benzin *nt* -s petrol

beobacht|en *vt* observe. **B~er** *m* -s,- observer. **B~ung** *f* -,-en observation

bequem *a* comfortable; (*mühelos*) easy; (*faul*) lazy. **b~en** *vr* sich deign (**zu** to). **B~lichkeit** *f* -,-en comfort; (*Faulheit*) laziness

berat|en† *vt* advise; (*überlegen*) discuss; **sich b~en** confer □ *vi* (*haben*) discuss (**über etw** *acc* sth); (*beratschlagen*) confer. **B~er** *m* -s,- adviser. **B~ung** *f* -,-en guidance; (*Rat*) advice; (*Besprechung*) discussion; (*Med, Jur*) consultation

berechn|en *vt* calculate; (*anrechnen*) charge for; (*abfordern*) charge. **B~ung** *f* calculation

berechtig|en *vt* entitle; (*befugen*) authorize; (*fig*) justify. **b~t** *a* justified, justifiable. **B~ung** *f* -,-en authorization; (*Recht*) right; (*Rechtmäßigkeit*) justification

bered|en *vt* talk about; (*klatschen*) gossip about. **B~samkeit** *f* - eloquence

beredt *a* eloquent, *adv* -ly

Bereich *m* -[e]s,-e area; (*fig*) realm; (*Fach-*) field

bereichern *vi* enrich

bereit *a* ready. **b~en** *vt* prepare; (*verursachen*) cause; give (*Überraschung*). **b~halten†** *vt* have/(*ständig*) keep ready. **b~legen** *vt sep* put out [ready]. **b~machen** *vt sep* get ready. **b~s** *adv* already

Bereitschaft *f* -,-en readiness; (*Einheit*) squad. **B~sdienst** *m* **B~ haben** *vt* be on call. **B~spolizei** *f* riot police

bereit|stehen† *vi sep* (*haben*) be ready. **b~stellen** *vt sep* put out

bereitwillig ready; (*verfügbar machen*) make available. **b~willig** a willing

bereuen vt regret

Berg m -[e]s,-e mountain; (*Anhöhe*) hill. **b~ab** adv downhill. **b~an** adv uphill. **B~arbeiter** m miner.- **b~auf** adv uphill. **B~bau** m -[e]s mining

bergen† vt recover; (*Naut*) salvage; (*retten*) rescue

Berg|führer m mountain guide. **b~ig** a mountainous. **B~kette** f mountain range. **B~mann** m (pl -leute) miner. **B~steiger** m -s,- mountaineer, climber

Bergung f - recovery; (*Naut*) salvage; (*Rettung*) rescue

Berg|wacht f mountain rescue service. **B~werk** nt mine

Bericht m -[e]s,-e report; (*Reise*-) account. **b~en** vt/i (haben) report; (*erzählen*) tell (von of). **B~erstatter** m -s,- reporter

berichtigen vt correct

berieseln vt irrigate. **B~ungsanlage** f sprinkler system

Berlin nt -s Berlin. **B~er** m -s,- Berliner; (*Culin*) doughnut

Bernhardiner m -s,- St Bernard

Bernstein m amber

berüchtigt a notorious

berücksichtig|en vt take into consideration. **B~ung** f - consideration

Beruf m profession; (*Tätigkeit*) occupation; (*Handwerk*) trade. **b~en†** vt appoint; **sich b~en** refer (**auf**+acc to); **b~en sein** be destined (**zu** to). **b~lich** a professional; (*Ausbildung*) vocational; **b~lich tätig sein** work, have a job. **B~sberatung** f vocational guidance. **b~smäßig** adv professionally. **B~sschule** f vocational school. **B~ssoldat** m regular soldier. **b~stätig** a working; **b~stätig sein** work. **B~ung** f -,-en appointment;

(*Bestimmung*) vocation; (*Jur*) appeal; **B~ung einlegen** appeal. **B~ungsgericht** nt appeal court

beruhen vi (haben) be based (**auf**+dat on)

beruhig|en vt calm [down]; (*zuversichtlich machen*) reassure; **b~end** a calming; (*tröstend*) reassuring; (*Med*) sedative. **B~ung** f - calming; reassurance; (*Med*) sedation. **B~ungsmittel** nt sedative; (*bei Psychosen*) tranquillizer

berühmt a famous. **B~heit** f -,-en fame; (*Person*) celebrity

berühr|en vt touch; (*erwähnen*) touch on. **B~ung** f -,-en touch; (*Kontakt*) contact

besagen vt say; (*bedeuten*) mean

Besatz m -es,-e trimming

Besatzung f -,-en crew; (*Mil*) occupying force

beschädig|en vt damage. **B~ung** f -,-en damage

beschaffen vt obtain, get □ a **so b~ sein, daß** be such that. **B~heit** f - consistency

beschäftig|en vt occupy; (*Arbeitgeber:*) employ; **sich b~en** occupy oneself. **b~t** a busy; (*angestellt*) employed (**bei** at). **B~ung** f -,-en occupation; (*Anstellung*) employment

beschatten vt shade; (*überwachen*) shadow

Bescheid m -[e]s information; **jdm B~ sagen** od **geben** let s.o. know; **B~ wissen** know

bescheiden a modest. **B~heit** f - modesty

bescheinen† vt shine on; **von der Sonne beschienen** sunlit

bescheinig|en vt certify. **B~ung** f -,-en [written] confirmation; (*Schein*) certificate

beschenken vt give a present/ presents to

Bescherung f -,-en distribution of Christmas presents

beschießen† vt fire at; (mit Artillerie) shell, bombard

beschildern vt signpost

beschimpf|en vt abuse, swear at. **B~ung** f -,-en abuse

beschirmen vt protect

Beschlag m in **B~ nehmen**, monopolize. **b~en**† vt shoe □vi (sein) steam or mist up □a steamed or misted up. **B~nahme** f -,-n confiscation; (Jur) seizure. **b~nahmen** vt confiscate; (Jur) seize

beschleunig|en vt hasten; (schneller machen) speed up ⟨Schritt⟩; **sich b~en** speed up □vi (haben) accelerate. **B~ung** f - acceleration

beschließen† vt decide □vi (haben) decide (über + acc about)

Beschluß m decision

beschmutzen vt make dirty

beschneid|en† vt trim; (Hort) prune; (Relig) circumcise

beschnüffeln vt sniff at

beschönigen vt (fig) gloss over

beschränken vt limit; **sich b~ auf** (+ acc) confine oneself to

beschrankt a ⟨Bahnübergang⟩ with barrier[s]

beschränkt a limited; (geistig) dull-witted. **B~ung** f -,-en limitation, restriction

beschreib|en† vt describe. **B~ung** f -,-en description

beschuldig|en vt accuse. **B~ung** f -,-en accusation

beschummeln vt (fam) cheat

Beschuß m -sses (Mil) fire; (Artillerie) shelling

beschütz|en vt protect. **B~er** m -s,- protector

Beschwer|de f -,-n complaint; **B~den** (Med) trouble sg. **B~en**† vt weight down; **sich b~en** complain. **b~lich** a difficult

beschwindeln vt cheat (um out of); (belügen) lie to

beschwipst a (fam) tipsy

beseitig|en vt remove. **B~ung** f - removal

Besen m -s,- broom

besessen a obsessed (von by)

besetz|en vt occupy; fill ⟨Posten⟩; (Theat) cast ⟨Rolle⟩; (verzieren) trim (mit with). **b~t** a occupied; ⟨Toilette, Leitung⟩ engaged; ⟨Zug, Bus⟩ full up; **der Platz ist b~t** this seat is taken. **B~tzeichen** nt engaged tone. **B~ung** f -,-en occupation; (Theat) cast

besichtig|en vt look round ⟨Stadt⟩; (prüfen) inspect; (besuchen) visit. **B~ung** f -,-en visit; (Prüfung) inspection; (Stadt-) sightseeing

besiedelt a **dünn/dicht b~** sparsely/densely populated

besiegen vt defeat

besinn|en† (sich) vr think, reflect; (sich erinnern) remember (auf jdn/etw s.o./sth). **B~ung** f - reflection; (Bewußtsein) consciousness; **bei/ohne B~ung** conscious/unconscious. **b~ungslos** a unconscious

Besitz m possession; (Land-) property; (Gut) estate. **b~anzeigend** a (Gram) possessive. **b~en**† vt own, possess; (haben) have. **B~er(in)** m -s,- (f -,-nen) owner; (Comm) proprietor

besoffen a (sl) drunken; **b~ sein** be drunk

besonder|e(r,s) a special; (bestimmt) particular; (gesondert) separate. **b~s** adv [e]specially, particularly; (gesondert) separately

besorg|en vt get; (kaufen) buy; (erledigen) attend to; (versorgen) look after. **b~t** a worried/(bedacht) concerned (um about). **B~ung** f -,-en errand; **B~ungen machen** do shopping

bespitzeln vt spy on

besprech|en† vt discuss; (rezensieren) review. **B~ung** f -,-en discussion; review; ⟨*Konferenz*⟩ meeting

besser *a & adv* better. **b~n** *vt* improve; **sich b~n** get better. **B~ung** *f* - improvement; **gute B~ung!** get well soon!

Bestand *m* -[e]s,˙-e existence; ⟨*Vorrat*⟩ stock (**an**+*dat* of)

beständig *a* constant; ⟨*Wetter*⟩ settled; **b~ gegen** resistant to

Bestand|saufnahme *f* stock-taking. **B~teil** *m* part

bestätigen *vt* confirm; acknowledge ⟨*Empfang*⟩. **B~ung** *f* -,-en confirmation

bestatt|en *vt* bury. **B~ung** *f* -,-en funeral. **B~ungsinstitut** *nt* [firm of] undertakers *pl*

Bestäubung *f* - pollination

bestaunen *vt* gaze at in amazement; ⟨*bewundern*⟩ admire

best|e(r,s) *a* best; **b~en Dank!** many thanks! **B~e(r,s)** *m/f/nt* best

bestech|en† *vt* bribe; ⟨*bezaubern*⟩ captivate. **b~end** *a* captivating. **b~lich** *a* corruptible. **B~ung** *f* - bribery. **B~ungsgeld** *nt* bribe

Besteck *nt* -[e]s,-e [set of] knife, fork and spoon; ⟨*coll*⟩ cutlery

bestehen† *vi* (haben) exist; ⟨*fortdauern*⟩ last; ⟨*bei Prüfung*⟩ pass; **b~ aus** consist/(gemacht sein) be made of; **b~ auf** (+*dat*) insist on □ *vt* pass ⟨*Prüfung*⟩

besteig|en† *vt* climb; ⟨*aufsteigen*⟩ mount; ascend ⟨*Thron*⟩. **B~ung** *f* ascent

bestell|en *vt* order; ⟨*vor-*⟩ book; ⟨*ernennen*⟩ appoint; ⟨*ausrichten*⟩ tell; cultivate ⟨*ausrichten*⟩ tell; **zu sich b~en** send for; **b~t sein** have an appointment; **kann ich etwas b~en?** can I take a message? **B~schein** *m* order form. **B~ung** *f* order; ⟨*Botschaft*⟩ message; ⟨*Bebauung*⟩ cultivation

besten|falls *adv* at best. **b~s** *adv* very well

besteuer|n *vt* tax. **B~ung** *f* - taxation

Bestie /ˈbɛstiə/ *f* -,-n beast

bestimm|en *vt* fix; ⟨*entscheiden*⟩ decide; ⟨*vorsehen*⟩ intend; ⟨*ernennen*⟩ appoint; ⟨*ermitteln*⟩ determine; ⟨*definieren*⟩ define; ⟨*Gram*⟩ qualify □ *vi* (haben) be in charge (**über**+*acc* of). **b~t** *a* definite; ⟨*gewiß*⟩ certain; ⟨*fest*⟩ firm. **B~theit** *f* - firmness; **mit B~theit** for certain. **B~ung** *f* fixing; ⟨*Vorschrift*⟩ regulation; ⟨*Ermittlung*⟩ determination; ⟨*Definition*⟩ definition; ⟨*Zweck*⟩ purpose; ⟨*Schicksal*⟩ destiny

Bestleistung *f* ⟨*Sport*⟩ record

bestraf|en *vt* punish. **B~ung** *f* -,-en punishment

Bestrahlung *f* radiotherapy

Bestreb|en *nt* -s endeavour; ⟨*Absicht*⟩ aim. **B~ung** *f* -,-en effort

bestreiten† *vt* dispute; ⟨*leugnen*⟩ deny; ⟨*bezahlen*⟩ pay for

bestürz|t *a* dismayed; ⟨*erschüttert*⟩ stunned. **B~ung** *f* - dismay

Bestzeit *f* ⟨*Sport*⟩ record [time]

Besuch *m* -[e]s,-e visit; ⟨*kurz*⟩ call; ⟨*Schul-*⟩ attendance; ⟨*Gast*⟩ visitor; ⟨*Gäste*⟩ visitors *pl*; **B~ haben** have a visitor/visitors; **bei jdm zu od auf B~ sein** be staying with s.o. **b~en** *vt* visit; ⟨*kurz*⟩ call on; ⟨*teilnehmen*⟩ attend; go to ⟨*Schule*⟩. **B~er(in)** *m* -s,- (*f* -,-nen) visitor; caller. **B~szeit** *f* visiting hours *pl*

betagt *a* aged, old

betäub|en *vt* stun; ⟨*Lärm:*⟩ deafen; ⟨*Med*⟩ anaesthetize; ⟨*lindern*⟩ ease ⟨*Schmerz*⟩; **wie b~t** *a* dazed. **B~ung** *f* - daze; ⟨*Med*⟩ anaesthesia; **unter örtlicher B~ung** under local anaesthetic. **B~ungsmittel** *nt* anaesthetic

Bete *f* -,-n **rote B~** beetroot

beteilig|en *vt* give a share to; **sich b~en** take part (**an** + *dat* in); (*beitragen*) contribute (**an** + *dat* to). **b~t a b~t sein** take part/(*an Unfall*) be involved/(*Comm*) have a share (**an** + *dat* in); **alle B~ten** all those involved. **B~ung** *f* -,-en participation; involvement; (*Anteil*) share

beten *vi* (*haben*) pray

Beton /be'tɔŋ/ *m* -s concrete

betonen *vt* stress, emphasize

beton|t *a* stressed; (*fig*) pointed. **B~ung** *f* -,-en stress

betr., **Betr.** *abbr* (**betreffs**) re

Betracht *m* in **B~ ziehen** consider; **außer B~ lassen** disregard; **nicht in B~ kommen** be out of the question. **b~en** *vt* look at; (*fig*) regard (**als** as)

beträchtlich *a* considerable

Betrachtung *f* -,-en contemplation; (*Überlegung*) reflection

Betrag *m* -[e]s,:-e amount. **b~en†** *vt* amount to; **sich b~en** behave. **B~en** *nt* -s behaviour; (*Sch*) conduct

betreff|en† *vt* affect; (*angehen*) concern. **b~end** *a* relevant. **b~s** *prep* (+ *gen*) concerning

betreib|en† *vt* (*leiten*) run; (*ausüben*) carry on

betreten† *vt* step on; (*eintreten*) enter; **'B~ verboten** 'no entry'; (*bei Rasen*) 'keep off [the grass]'

betreu|en *vt* look after. **B~er(in)** *m* -s,- (*f* -,-nen) helper; (*Kranken-*) nurse. **B~ung** *f* -care

Betrieb *m* business; (*Firma*) firm; (*Treiben*) activity; (*Verkehr*) traffic; **außer B~** not in use; (*defekt*) out of order

Betriebs|anleitung *f* operating instructions *pl*. **B~anweisung** *f* operating instructions *pl*. **B~ferien** *pl* firm's holiday. **B~leitung** *f* management. **B~rat** *m* works committee. **B~störung** *f* breakdown

betrinken† (**sich**) *vr* get drunk

betroffen *a* disconcerted; **b~ sein** be affected (**von** by)

betrüb|en *vt* sadden. **b~t a** *a* sad

Betrug *m* -[e]s deception; (*Jur*) fraud

betrüg|en† *vt* cheat, swindle; (*Jur*) defraud; (*in der Ehe*) be unfaithful to. **B~er(in)** *m* -s,- (*f* -,-nen) swindler. **B~erei** *f* -,-en fraud

betrunken *a* drunken; **b~ sein** be drunk. **b~e(r)** *m* drunk

Bett *nt* -[e]s,-en bed. **B~couch** *f* sofa-bed. **B~decke** *f* blanket; (*Tages-*) bedspread

Bettel|ei *f* - begging. **b~n** *vi* (*haben*) beg

Bettler(in) *m* -s,- (*f* -,-nen) beggar

Bettpfanne *f* bedpan

Betttuch *nt* sheet

Bettwäsche *f* bed linen. **B~zeug** *nt* bedding

betupfen *vt* dab (**mit** with)

beug|en *vt* bend; (*Gram*) decline; conjugate ⟨*Verb*⟩; **sich b~en** bend; (*lehnen*) lean; (*sich fügen*) submit (**dat** to). **B~ung** *f* -,-en (*Gram*) declension; conjugation

Beule *f* -,-n bump; (*Delle*) dent

beunruhig|en *vt* worry; **sich b~en** worry. **B~ung** *f* - worry

beurlauben *vt* give leave to

beurteil|en *vt* judge. **B~ung** *f* -,-en judgement; (*Ansicht*) opinion

Beute *f* - booty, haul; (*Jagd-*) bag; (*eines Raubtiers*) prey

Beutel *m* -s,- bag. **B~tier** *nt* marsupial

Bevölkerung *f* -,-en population

bevollmächtig|en *vt* authorize. **B~te(r)** *m/f* [authorized] agent

bevor *conj* before; **b~ nicht** until

bevormunden *vt* treat like a child

bevorstehen† *vi sep* (*haben*) approach; (*unmittelbar*) be imminent. **b~d** *a* approaching, forthcoming; **unmittelbar b~d** imminent

bevorzug|en vt prefer; ⟨begünstigen⟩ favour. **b~t** a privileged; ⟨Behandlung⟩ preferential

bewachen vt guard

bewachsen a covered (mit with)

Bewachung f - guard

bewaffn|en vt arm. **b~et** a armed. **B~ung** f - armament; ⟨Waffen⟩ arms pl

bewahren vt protect ⟨vor + dat from⟩; ⟨behalten⟩ keep; **die Ruhe b~** keep calm

bewähren (sich) vr prove one's/⟨Ding:⟩ its worth; ⟨erfolgreich sein⟩ prove a success

bewähr|t a reliable; ⟨erprobt⟩ proven. **B~ung** f - ⟨Jur⟩ probation. **B~ungsfrist** f [period of] probation. **B~ungsprobe** f ⟨fig⟩ test

bewältigen vt cope with; ⟨überwinden⟩ overcome; ⟨schaffen⟩ manage

bewandert a knowledgeable

bewässer|n vt irrigate. **B~ung** f - irrigation

bewegen vt ⟨reg⟩ move; **sich b~** move; ⟨körperlich⟩ take exercise

Beweg|grund m motive. **b~lich** a movable, mobile; ⟨wendig⟩ agile. **B~lichkeit** f - mobility; agility. **B~ung** f -,-en movement; ⟨Phys⟩ motion; ⟨Rührung⟩ emotion; ⟨Gruppe⟩ movement; **körperliche B~ung** physical exercise. **b~ungslos** a motionless

Beweis m -es,-e proof; ⟨Zeichen⟩ token. **B~e** evidence sg. **b~en†** vt prove; ⟨zeigen⟩ show; **sich b~en** prove oneself/⟨Ding:⟩ itself. **B~material** nt evidence

bewerb|en† (sich) vr apply (um for; bei to). **B~er(in)** m -s,- ⟨f -,-nen⟩ applicant. **B~ung** f -,-en application

bewerten vt value; ⟨einschätzen⟩ rate; ⟨Sch⟩ mark, grade

bewilligen vt grant

bewirken vt cause; ⟨herbeiführen⟩ bring about

bewirt|en vt entertain. **B~ung** f - hospitality

bewohn|bar a habitable. **b~en** vt inhabit, live in. **B~er(in)** m -s,- ⟨f -,-nen⟩ resident, occupant; ⟨Einwohner⟩ inhabitant

bewölk|en (sich) vr cloud over; **b~t** cloudy. **B~ung** f - clouds pl

bewunder|n vt admire. **b~nswert** a admirable. **B~ung** f - admiration

bewußt a conscious ⟨gen of⟩; ⟨absichtlich⟩ deliberate. **b~los** a unconscious. **B~losigkeit** f - unconsciousness. **B~sein** n -s consciousness; ⟨Gewißheit⟩ awareness; **bei B~sein** conscious

bez. abbr ⟨bezahlt⟩ paid

bezahl|en vt/i ⟨haben⟩ pay; pay for ⟨Ware, Essen⟩. **B~ung** f - payment; ⟨Lohn⟩ pay

bezaubern vt enchant

bezeichn|en vt mark; ⟨bedeuten⟩ denote; ⟨beschreiben, nennen⟩ describe (**als** as). **b~end** a typical. **B~ung** f marking; ⟨Beschreibung⟩ description (**als** as); ⟨Ausdruck⟩ term; ⟨Name⟩ name

bezeugen vt testify to

bezichtigen vt accuse ⟨gen of⟩

bezieh|en† vt cover; ⟨einziehen⟩ move into; ⟨beschaffen⟩ obtain; ⟨erhalten⟩ get; **sich b~en** ⟨bewölken⟩ cloud over; **sich b~en auf** (+ acc) refer to; **das Bett frisch b~en** put clean sheets on the bed. **B~ung** f -,-en relation; ⟨Verhältnis⟩ relationship; ⟨Bezug⟩ respect; **B~ungen haben** have [good] connections. **b~ungsweise** adv respectively; ⟨vielmehr⟩ or rather

Bezirk m -[e]s,-e district

Bezug m cover; ⟨Kissen-⟩ case; ⟨Beschaffung⟩ obtaining; ⟨Kauf⟩ purchase; ⟨Zusammenhang⟩ reference; **B~e** pl earnings; **B~**

nehmen .refer (**auf** + *acc* to); in b~ **auf** (+*acc*) regarding

bezüglich *prep* (+ *gen*) regarding □*a* relating (**auf** + *acc* to)

bezwecken *vt* (*fig*) aim at

bezweifeln *vt* doubt

BH /be:'ha:/ *m* -[s],-[s] bra

Bibel *f* -,-n Bible

Biber *m* -s,- beaver

Bibliothek *f* -,-en library. B~**thekar(in)** *m* -s,- (*f* -,-nen) librarian

biblisch *a* biblical

bieg|**en**† *vt* bend; **sich b~en** bend □*vi* (*sein*) curve (**nach** to); **um die Ecke b~en** turn the corner. b~**sam** *a* flexible, supple. B~**ung** *f* -,-en bend

Biene *f* -,-n bee. B~**nstock** *m* beehive. B~**nwabe** *f* honey-comb

Bier *nt* -s,-e beer. B~**deckel** *m* beer-mat. B~**krug** *m* beer-mug

Biest *nt* -[e]s,-er (*fam*) beast

bieten† *vt* offer; (*bei Auktion*) bid

Bifokalbrille *f* bifocals *pl*

Bigamie *f* bigamy

bigott *a* over-pious

Bikini *m* -s,-s bikini

Bilanz *f* -,-en balance sheet; (*fig*) result; **die B~ ziehen** (*fig*) draw conclusions (**aus** from)

Bild *nt* -[e]s,-er picture; (*Theat*) scene

bild|**en** *vt* form; (*sein*) be; (*erziehen*) educate

Bild|**erbuch** *nt* picture-book. B~**fläche** *f* screen. B~**hauer** *m* -s,- sculptor. b~**lich** *a* pictorial; (*figurativ*) figurative. B~**nis** *nt* -ses,-se portrait. B~**schirm** *m* (*TV*) screen. B~**schirmgerät** *nt* visual display unit, VDU. b~**schön** *a* very beautiful

Bildung *f* - formation; (*Erziehung*) education; (*Kultur*) culture

Billard /'bɪljart/ *nt* -s billiards *sg*. B~**tisch** *m* billiard table

Billett /bɪl'jɛt/ *nt* -[e]s,-e & -s ticket

Billiarde *f* -,-n thousand million million

billig *a* cheap; (*dürftig*) poor; **recht und b~** right and proper. b~**en** *vt* approve. B~**ung** *f* - approval

Billion /bɪl'jo:n/ *f* -,-en million million, billion

Bimsstein *m* pumice stone

Binde *f* -,-n band; (*Verband*) bandage; (*Damen-*) sanitary towel. B~**hautentzündung** *f* conjunctivitis. b~**n**† *vt* tie (**an** + *acc* to); make (*Strauß*); bind (*Buch*); (*fesseln*) tie up; (*Culin*) thicken; **sich b~n** commit oneself. B~**strich** *m* hyphen. B~**wort** *nt* (*pl* -wörter) (*Gram*) conjunction

Bind|**faden** *m* string. B~**ung** *f* -,-en (*fig*) tie, bond; (*Beziehung*) relationship; (*Verpflichtung*) commitment; (*Ski-*) binding; (*Tex*) weave

Binnenhandel *m* home trade

Binse *f* -,-n (*Bot*) rush

Bio- *pref* organic

Bio|**chemie** *f* biochemistry. b~**dynamisch** *m* organic. B~**graphie** *f* -,-n biography

Bio|**hof** *m* organic farm. B~**laden** *m* health-food store

Biologe *m* -n,-n biologist. B~**ie** *f* - biology. b~**isch** *a* biological; b~**ischer Anbau** organic farming; b~**isch angebaut** organically grown

Birke *f* -,-n birch [tree]

Birma *nt* -s Burma. b~**anisch** *a* Burmese

Birn|**baum** *m* pear-tree. B~**e** *f* -,-n pear; (*Electr*) bulb

bis *prep* (+*acc*) as far as, [up] to; (*zeitlich*) until, till; (*spätestens*) by; **bis zu** up to; **bis auf** (+*acc*) (*einschließlich*) [down] to; (*ausgenommen*) except [for]; **drei bis**

vier Mark three to four marks; **bis morgen!** see you tomorrow! □*conj* until

Bischof *m* -s,-̈e bishop

bisher *adv* so far, up to now

Biskuit rolle /bis'kvi:t-/ *f* Swiss roll. **B~teig** *m* sponge mixture

Biß *m* -sses,-sse bite

bißchen *inv pron* **ein b~** a bit, a little

Bissen *m* -s,- bite, mouthful. **b~ig** *a* vicious; *(fig)* caustic

bisweilen *adv* from time to time

bitt|**e** *adv* please; *(nach Klopfen)* come in; *(als Antwort auf 'danke')* don't mention it, you're welcome; **wie b~?** pardon? *(empört)* I beg your pardon? **B~e** *f* -,-n request; *(dringend)* plea *(um* for). **b~en†** *vt/i (haben)* ask/*(dringend)* beg *(um* for); *(einladen)* invite, ask. **b~end** *a* pleading

bitter *a* bitter. **B~keit** *f* -bitterness. **b~lich** *adv* bitterly

Bittschrift *f* petition

bizarr *a* bizarre

bläh|**en** *vt* swell; ⟨*Vorhang, Segel:*⟩ billow □*vi (haben)* cause flatulence. **B~ungen** *fpl* flatulence *sg*, *(fam)* wind *sg*

Blamage /bla'ma:ʒə/ *f* -,-n humiliation; *(Schande)* disgrace

blamieren *vt* disgrace; **sich b~** disgrace oneself; *(sich lächerlich machen)* make a fool of oneself

blanchieren /blã'ʃi:rən/ *vt* (*Culin*) blanch

blank *a* shiny. **B~oscheck** *m* blank cheque

Blase *f* -,-n bubble; *(Med)* blister; *(Anat)* bladder. **B~balg** *m* -[e]s,-̈e bellows *pl*. **b~n†** *vt/i (haben)* blow; play ⟨*Flöte*⟩. **B~nentzündung** *f* cystitis

Bläser *m* -s,- *(Mus)* wind player; **die B~** the wind section *sg*

Blaskapelle *f* brass band

blaß *a* pale

Blässe *f* - pallor

Blatt *nt* -[e]s,-̈er *(Bot)* leaf; *(Papier)* sheet; *(Zeitung)* paper

Blätterteig *m* puff pastry

Blattlaus *f* greenfly

blau *a*, **B~** *nt* -s; blue; **b~er Fleck** bruise; **b~es Auge** black eye; **b~ sein** *(fam)* be tight; **Fahrt ins B~e** mystery tour. **B~beere** *f* bilberry. **B~licht** *nt* blue flashing light

Blech *nt* -[e]s,-e sheet metal; *(Weiß)* tin; *(Platte)* metal sheet; *(Back-)* baking sheet; *(Mus)* brass; *(fam: Unsinn)* rubbish. **B~schaden** *m* (*Auto*) damage to the bodywork

Blei *nt* -[e]s lead

Bleibe *f* - place to stay. **b~n†** *vi (sein)* remain, stay; *(übrig-)* be left; **ruhig b~** keep calm; **bei etw b~** *(fig)* stick to sth; **b~n Sie am Apparat** hold the line. **b~nd** *a* permanent; *(anhaltend)* lasting

bleich *a* pale. **b~en†** *vi (sein)* bleach; *(ver-)* fade □*vt (reg)* bleach. **B~mittel** *nt* bleach

blei|**ern** *a* leaden. **b~frei** *a* unleaded. **B~stift** *m* pencil. **B~stiftspitzer** *m* -s,- pencil-sharpener

Blende *f* -,-n shade, shield; *(Phot)* diaphragm; *(Öffnung)* aperture; *(an Kleid)* facing. **b~n** *vt* dazzle, blind

Blick *m* -[e]s,-e look; *(kurz)* glance; *(Aussicht)* view; **auf den ersten B~** at first sight. **b~en** *vi (haben)* look/*(kurz)* glance *(auf* + *acc* at)

blind *a* blind; *(trübe)* dull; **b~er Alarm** false alarm; **b~er Passagier** stowaway. **B~darm** *m* appendix. **B~darmentzündung** *f* appendicitis. **B~e(r)** *m/f* blind man/woman; **die B~en** the blind *pl*. **B~enhund** *m* guide-dog. **B~enschrift** *f* braille.

B~**gänger** m -s, (Mil) dud.
B~**heit** f blindness

blink|en vi (haben) flash; (funkeln) gleam; (Auto) indicate.
B~**er** m -s, (Auto) indicator.
B~**licht** nt flashing light

blinzeln vi (haben) blink

Blitz m -[e]s,-e [flash of] lightning; (Phot) flash. B~**ableiter** m lightning-conductor. b~**artig** a lightning . . . □ adv like lightning. b~**en** vi (haben) flash; (funkeln) sparkle; **es hat geblitzt** there was a flash of lightning. B~**gerät** nt flash. B~**licht** nt (Phot) flash. b~**sauber** a spick and span. b~**schnell** a lightning . . . □ adv like lightning

Block m -[e]s, block -[e]s,-s & -e pad; (Häuser-) block

Blockade f -,-n blockade

Blockflöte f recorder

blockieren vt block; (Mil) blockade

Blockschrift f block letters pl

blöd[e] a feeble-minded; (dumm) stupid

Blödsinn m -[e]s idiocy; (Unsinn) nonsense

blöken vi (haben) bleat

blond a fair-haired; (Haar) fair

bloß a (alleinig) mere □ adv only, just

bloß|legen vt sep uncover. b~**stellen** vt sep compromise

Bluff m -s,-s bluff. b~**en** vi (haben) bluff

blühen vi (haben) flower; (fig) flourish. b~**d** a flowering; (fig) flourishing, thriving

Blume f -,-n flower; (vom Wein) bouquet. B~**ngeschäft** nt flower-shop, florist's. B~**nkohl** m cauliflower. B~**nmuster** nt floral design. B~**ntopf** m flowerpot; (Pflanze) pot plant. B~**nzwiebel** f bulb

blumig a (fig) flowery

Bluse f -,-n blouse

Blut nt -[e]s blood. b~**arm** a anaemic. B~**bahn** f bloodstream. B~**bild** nt blood count. B~**druck** m blood pressure. b~**dürstig** a bloodthirsty

Blüte f -,-n flower, bloom; (vom Baum) blossom; (B~zeit) flowering period; (Baum-) blossom time; (Höhepunkt) peak, prime

Blutegel m -s,- leech. b~**en** vi (haben) bleed

Blüten|blatt nt petal. B~**staub** m pollen

Bluter m -s,- haemophiliac. B~**erguß** m bruise. B~**gefäß** nt blood-vessel. B~**gruppe** f blood group. b~**ig** a bloody. B~**körperchen** nt -s,- corpuscle. B~**probe** f blood test. B~**rünstig** a (fig) bloody, gory. B~**schande** f incest. B~**spender** m blood donor. B~**sturz** m haemorrhage. B~**transfusion**, B~**übertragung** f blood transfusion. B~**ung** f -,-en bleeding; (Med) haemorrhage; (Regel-) period. b~**unterlaufen** a bruised; (Auge) bloodshot. B~**vergiftung** f blood-poisoning. B~**wurst** f black pudding

Bö f -,-en gust; (Regen-) squall

Bob m -s,-s bob[-sleigh]

Bock m -[e]s,-e buck; (Ziege) billy goat; (Schaf) ram; (Gestell) support. b~**ig** a (fam) stubborn. B~**springen** nt leap-frog

Boden m -s,- ground; (Erde) soil; (Fuß-) floor; (Grundfläche) bottom; (Dach-) loft, attic. B~**satz** m sediment. B~**schätze** mpl mineral deposits. B~**see** (der) Lake Constance

Bogen m -s,- & - curve; (Geom) arc; (beim Skilauf) turn; (Archit) arch; (Waffe, Geigen-) bow; (Papier) sheet; **einen großen B~um jdn/etw machen** (fam) give

s.o./sth a wide berth. **B~gang** *m*
arcade

Bohle *f*-,-n [thick] plank

Böhm|en *nt* -s Bohemia. **b~isch**
a Bohemian

Bohne *f*-,-n bean

bohner|n *vt* polish. **B~wachs** *nt*
floor-polish

bohr|en *vt/i* (haben) drill (nach
for); drive 〈Tunnel〉; sink 〈Brun-
nen〉; 〈Insekt:〉 bore. **B~er** *m* -s,-
drill. **B~insel** *f* drilling rig.
B~turm *m* derrick

Boje *f*-,-n buoy

Böllerschuß *m* gun salute

Bolzen *m* -s,- bolt; (Stift) pin

bombardieren *vt* bomb; (fig)
bombard (mit with)

Bombe *f*-,-n bomb. **B~nangriff**
m bombing raid. **B~nerfolg** *m*
huge success

Bon /bɔŋ/ *m* -s,-s voucher; (Kas-
sen-) receipt

Bonbon /bɔŋˈbɔŋ/ *m & nt* -s,-s
sweet

Boot *nt* -[e]s,-e boat. **B~ssteg** *m*
landing-stage

Bord[1] *m* (Naut) **an B~** aboard, on
board; **über B~** overboard.
B~buch *nt* log[-book]

Bord[2] *nt* -[e]s,-e shelf

Bordell *nt* -s,-e brothel

Bordkarte *f* boarding-pass

borgen *v* borrow; **jdm etw b~**
lend s.o. sth

Borke *f*-,-n bark

Börse *f*-,-n purse; (Comm) stock
exchange. **B~nmakler** *m* stock-
broker

Borste *f*-,-n bristle

Borte *f*-,-n braid

bösartig *a* vicious; (Med) malignant

böse *a* wicked, evil; (unartig)
naughty; (schlimm) bad; (zornig)
cross; **jdm b~ sein** be cross with
s.o.

bos|**haft** *a* malicious; (gehässig)
spiteful. **B~heit** *f*-,-en malice;

spite; (Handlung) spiteful act-
|(Bemerkung) remark

böswillig *a* malicious

Botanik *f* - botany. **B~ker(in)**
m -s,- (f-,-nen) botanist

Bot|**e** *m* -n,-n messenger. **B~en-
gang** *m* errand. **B~schaft** *f*
-,-en message; (Pol) embassy.
B~schafter *m* -s,- ambassador

Bouillon /bʊlˈjɔŋ/ *f*-,-s clear soup.
B~würfel *m* stock cube

Bowle /ˈboːlə/ *f*-,-n punch

box|**en** *vi* (haben) box □*vt* punch.
B~en *nt* -s boxing. **B~er** *m* -s,-
boxer

brachliegen† *vi sep* (haben) lie
fallow

Branche /ˈbrɑ̃ːʃə/ *f*-,-n [line of]
business. **B~nverzeichnis** *nt*
(Teleph) classified directory

Brand *m* -[e]s,ˬe fire; (Med) gangrene; (Bot) blight; **in B~ geraten** catch fire; **in B~ setzen** *od*
stecken set on fire. **B~bombe** *f*
incendiary bomb

Brand|**stifter** *m* arsonist.
B~stiftung *f* arson

Brandung *f* - surf

Brand|**wunde** *f* burn. **B~zei-
chen** *nt* brand

Branntwein *m* spirit; (coll) spirits *pl.* **B~brennerei** *f* distillery

bras|**ilianisch** *a* Brazilian. **B~i-
lien** /-jən/ *nt* -s Brazil

Brat|**apfel** *m* baked apple.
b~en† *vt/i* (haben) roast; (in der
Pfanne) fry. **B~en** *m* -s,- roast;
(B~stück) joint. **b~fertig** *a*
oven-ready. **B~hähnchen** *nt*
roast chicken. **B~kartoffeln**
fpl fried potatoes. **B~pfanne** *f*
frying-pan

Bratsche *f*-,-n (Mus) viola

Bratspieß *m* spit

Brauch *m* -[e]s,ˬe custom.
b~bar *a* usable; (nützlich) useful. **b~en** *vt* need; (ge-, verbrauchen) use; take 〈Zeit〉; **er b~t es
nur zu sagen** he only has to say

Braue f -,-n eyebrow

brau|en vt brew. **B~er** m -s,- brewer. **B~erei** f -,-en brewery

braun a, **B~** nt -s,- brown; **b~ werden** (Person:) get a tan

Bräune f - [sun-]tan. **b~n** vt/i (haben) brown; (in der Sonne) tan

braungebrannt a [sun-]tanned

Braunschweig nt -s Brunswick

Brause f -,-n (Dusche) shower; (an Gießkanne) rose; (B~limonade) fizzy drink

Braut f -,-e bride; (Verlobte) fiancée

Bräutigam m -s,-e bridegroom; (Verlobter) fiancé

Brautkleid nt wedding dress

Brautpaar nt bridal couple; (Verlobte) engaged couple

brav a good; (redlich) honest □ adv dutifully; (redlich) honestly

bravo int bravo!

BRD abbr (**Bundesrepublik Deutschland**) FRG

Brech|eisen nt jemmy. **b~en†** vt break; (Phys) refract (Licht); (erbrechen) vomit; **sich b~en** (Wellen:) break; (Licht:) be refracted; **sich** (dat) **den Arm b~en** break one's arm □ vi (sein) break □ vi (haben) vomit, be sick. **B~reiz** m nausea. **B~stange** f crowbar

Brei m -[e]s,-e paste; (Culin) purée; (Hafer-) porridge

breit a wide; (Schultern:) broad. **B~e** f -,-n width; breadth; (Geog) latitude. **b~en** vt spread (über + acc over). **B~engrad** m [degree of] latitude. **B~enkreis** m parallel

Bremse[1] f -,-n horsefly

Bremse[2] f -,-n brake. **b~n** vt slow down; (fig) restrain □ vi (haben) brake

Bremslicht nt brake-light

brenn|bar a combustible; **leicht b~bar** highly [in]flammable. **b~en†** vi (haben) burn; (Licht:) be on; (Zigarette:) be alight; (weh

tun) smart, sting □ vt burn; (rösten) roast; (im Brennofen) fire; (destillieren) distil. **b~end** a burning; (angezündet) lighted; (fig) fervent. **B~erei** f -,-en distillery

Brennessel f -,-n stinging nettle

Brenn|holz nt firewood. **B~ofen** m kiln. **B~punkt** m (Phys) focus. **B~spiritus** m methylated spirits. **B~stoff** m fuel

Bretagne /breˈtanjə/ (die) - Brittany

Brett nt -[e]s,-er board; (im Regal) shelf; **schwarzes B~** notice board. **B~spiel** nt board game

Brezel f -,-n pretzel

Bridge /brɪtʃ/ nt - (Spiel) bridge

Brief m -[e]s,-e letter. **B~beschwerer** m -s,- paperweight. **B~freund(in)** m(f) pen-friend. **B~kasten** m letter-box. **B~kopf** m letter-head. **b~lich** a & adv by letter. **B~marke** f [postage] stamp. **B~öffner** m paper-knife. **B~papier** nt note-paper. **B~tasche** f wallet. **B~träger** m postman. **B~umschlag** m envelope. **B~wahl** f postal vote. **B~wechsel** m correspondence

Brikett nt -s,-s briquette

Brillant /brɪlˈjant/ m -en,-en [cut] diamond

Brille f -,-n glasses pl, spectacles pl; (Schutz-) goggles pl; (Klosett-) toilet seat

bringen† vt bring; (fort-) take; (ein-) yield; (veröffentlichen) publish; (im Radio) broadcast; show (Film); **ins Bett b~** put to bed; **jdn nach Hause b~** take (begleiten) see s.o. home; **um etw b~** deprive of sth; **jdn dazu b~, etw zu tun** get s.o. to do sth; **es weit b~** (fig) go far

Brise f -,-n breeze

Brit|e m -n,-n, **B~in** f -,-nen Briton. **b~isch** a British

Bröck|chen *nt* -s,- *(Culin)* crouton. **b~elig** *a* crumbly; *(Gestein)* friable

Brocken *m* -s,- chunk; *(Erde, Kohle)* lump

Brokkoli *pl* broccoli *sg*

Brombeere *f* blackberry

Bronchitis *f* bronchitis

Bronze /ˈbrõːsə/ *f* -,-n bronze

Brosch|e *f* -,-n brooch. **b~iert** *a* paperback. **B~üre** *f* -,-n brochure; *(Heft)* booklet

Brösel *mpl* *(Culin)* breadcrumbs

Brot *n* -[e]s,-e bread; **ein B~** a loaf [of bread]; *(Scheibe)* a slice of bread

Brötchen *n* -s,- [bread] roll

Brotkrümel *m* breadcrumb

Bruch *m* -[e]s,꞊e break; *(Brechen)* breaking; *(Rohr-)* burst; *(Med)* fracture; *(Eingeweide-)* rupture, hernia; *(Math)* fraction; *(in Beziehung)* break-up

brüchig *a* brittle

Bruch|landung *f* crash-landing. **B~rechnung** *f* fractions *pl.* **B~stück** *nt* fragment. **B~teil** *m* fraction

Brücke *f* -,-n bridge; *(Teppich)* rug

Bruder *m* -s,꞊ brother

brüderlich *a* brotherly, fraternal

Brügge *nt* -s Bruges

Brüh|e *f* -,-n broth; *(Knochen-)* stock. **B~würfel** *m* stock cube

brüllen *vt/i (haben)* roar

brumm|eln *vt/i (haben)* mumble. **b~en** *vi (haben)* *(Insekt:)* buzz; *(Bär:)* growl; *(Motor:)* hum; *(murren)* grumble

brünett *a* dark-haired

Brunnen *m* -s,- well; *(Spring-)* fountain; *(Heil-)* spa water

brüsk *a* brusque

Brüssel *nt* -s Brussels

Brust *f* -,꞊e chest; *(weibliche, Culin: B~stück)* breast. **B~bein** *nt* breastbone

brüsten (sich) *vr* boast

Brust|fellentzündung *f* pleurisy. **B~schwimmen** *nt* breaststroke

Brüstung *f* -,-en parapet

Brustwarze *f* nipple

brutal *a* brutal

brüten *vi (haben)* sit *(on eggs)*; *(fig)* ponder *(über + dat over)*

Brutkasten *m (Med)* incubator

brutto *adv*, **B~-** *pref* gross

Bub *m* -en,-en *(SGer)* boy. **B~e** *m* -n,-n *(Karte)* jack, knave

Buch *nt* -[e]s,꞊er book; **B~ führen** keep a record *(über + acc of)*; **die B~er führen** keep the accounts

Buche *f* -,-n beech

buchen *vt* book; *(Comm)* enter

Bücherei *f* -,-en library. **B~regal** *nt* bookcase, bookshelves *pl.* **B~schrank** *m* bookcase

Buchfink *m* chaffinch

Buch|führung *f* bookkeeping. **B~halter(in)** *m* -s,- *(f* -,-nen) bookkeeper, accountant. **B~haltung** *f* bookkeeping; *(Abteilung)* accounts department. **B~handlung** *f* bookshop

Büchse *f* -,-n box; *(Konserven-)* tin, can

Buch|stabe *m* -n,-n letter. **b~stabieren** *vt* spell [out]. **b~stäblich** *adv* literally

Bucht *f* -,-en *(Geog)* bay

Buchung *f* -,-en booking, reservation; *(Comm)* entry

Buckel *m* -s,- hump; *(Beule)* bump; *(Hügel)* hillock

bücken (sich) *vr* bend down

bucklig *a* hunchbacked. **B~e(r)** *m/f* hunchback

Bückling *m* -s,-e smoked herring

Buddhis|mus *m* - Buddhism. **B~t(in)** *m* -en,-en *(f* -,-nen) Buddhist. **b~tisch** *a* Buddhist

Bude *f* -,-n hut; *(Kiosk)* kiosk

Budget /byˈdʒeː/ *nt* -s,-s budget

Büfett nt -[e]s,-e sideboard; (Theke) bar; **kaltes B**~ cold buffet

Büffel m -s,- buffalo

Bügel m -s,- frame; (Kleider-) coathanger; (Steig-) stirrup; (Brillen-) sidepiece. **B~brett** nt ironing-board. **B~eisen** nt iron. **B~falte** f crease. **b~frei** a non-iron. **b~n** vt/i (haben) iron

Bühne f -,-n stage. **B~nbild** nt set. **B~neingang** m stage door

Buhrufe mpl boos

Bukett nt -[e]s,-e bouquet

Bulgarien /-jən/ nt -s Bulgaria

Bull|**auge** nt (Naut) porthole. **B~dogge** f bulldog. **B~dozer** /-do:zɐ/ m -s,- bulldozer. **B~e m -n,-n** bull; (sl: Polizist) cop

Bummel m -s,- (fam) stroll. **B~lei** f - (fam) dawdling

bummel|**ig** a (fam) slow; (nachlässig) careless. **b~n** vi (sein) (fam) stroll □vi (haben) (fam) dawdle. **B~streik** m go-slow. **B~zug** m (fam) slow train

Bums m -es,-e (fam) bump

Bund[1] nt -[e]s,-e bunch

Bund[2] m -[e]s,-e association; (Bündnis) alliance; (Pol) federation; (Rock-, Hosen-) waistband; **der B**~ the Federal Government

Bündel nt -s,- bundle. **b~n** vt bundle [up]

Bundes- pref Federal. **B~genosse** m ally. **B~kanzler** m Federal Chancellor. **B~land** nt state; (Aust) province. **B~liga** f German national league. **B~rat** m Upper House of Parliament. **B~republik** f die **B~republik Deutschland** the Federal Republic of Germany. **B~tag** m Lower House of Parliament. **B~wehr** f Army

bünd|**ig** a & adv kurz und b~ig short and to the point. **B~nis** nt -sses,-sse alliance

Bunker m -s,- bunker; (Luftschutz-) shelter

bunt a coloured; (farbenfroh) colourful; (grell) gaudy; (gemischt) varied; (wirr) confused. **b~e Platte** assorted cold meats. **B~stift** m crayon

Bürde f -,-n (fig) burden

Burg f -,-en castle

Bürge m -n,-n guarantor. **b~n** vi (haben) **b~n für** vouch for; (fig) guarantee

Bürger|**(in)** m -s,- (f -,-nen) citizen. **B~krieg** m civil war. **b~lich** a civil; (Pflicht) civic; (mittelständisch) middle-class; **B~liche(r)** m/f commoner. **B~meister** m mayor. **B~rechte** npl civil rights. **B~steig** m -[e]s,-e pavement

Burggraben m moat

Burgunder m -s,- (Wein) Burgundy

Büro nt -s,-s office. **B~angestellte(r)** m/f office-worker. **B~klammer** f paper-clip. **B~kratie** f -,-n bureaucracy. **b~kratisch** a bureaucratic

Bursche m -n,-n lad, youth

Bürste f -,-n brush. **b~n** vt brush. **B~nschnitt** m crew cut

Busch m -[e]s,-e bush

Büschel nt -s,- tuft

buschig a bushy

Busen m -s,- bosom

Bussard m -s,-e buzzard

Buße f -,-n penance; (Jur) fine

Bußgeld nt (Jur) fine

Büste f -,-n bust; (Schneider-) dummy. **B~nhalter** m -s,- bra

Butter f - butter. **B~blume** f buttercup. **B~brot** nt slice of bread and butter. **B~faß** nt churn. **b~n** vt butter

b.w. abbr (bitte wenden) P.T.O.

C

ca. *abbr* (**circa**) about

Café /ka'fe:/ *nt* -s,-s café

camp|**en** /'kɛmpən/ *vi* (**haben**) go camping. **C~ing** *nt* -s camping. **C~ingplatz** *m* campsite

Caravan /'ka:|ravan/ *m* -s,-s (*Auto*) caravan; (*Kombi*) estate car

CD /tse:'de:/ *f* -,-s compact disc, CD

Cell|**ist(in)** /tʃɛ'lɪst(ɪn)/ *m* -en,-en (*f* -,-nen) cellist. **C~o** /'tʃɛlo/ *nt* -,-los & -li cello

Celsius /'tsɛlzjʊs/ *inv* Celsius, centigrade

Champagner /ʃam'panjɐ/ *m* -s champagne

Champignon /'ʃampɪnjɔn/ *m* -s,-s (*field*) mushroom

Chance /'ʃã:sə/ *f* -,-n chance

Chaos /'ka:ɔs/ *nt* - chaos

Charakter /ka'raktɐ/ *m* -s,-e /-'te:rə/ character. **c~isieren** *vt* characterize. **c~istisch** *a* characteristic (**für** *of*), *adv* -ally

charm|**ant** /ʃar'mant/ *a* charming, *adv* -ly. **C~e** /ʃarm/ *m* -s charm

Charter|**flug** /'tʃ-, 'ʃarte-/ *m* charter flight. **c~n** *vt* charter

Chassis /ʃa'si:/ *nt* -,- /-'si:[s], 'si:s/ chassis

Chauffeur /ʃɔ'fø:ɐ/ *m* -s,-e chauffeur; (*Taxi-*) driver

Chef /ʃɛf/ *m* -s,-s head; (*fam*) boss

Chem|**ie** /çe'mi:/ *f* - chemistry. **C~ikalien** /-jən/ *fpl* chemicals

Chem|**iker(in)** /'çe:-/ *m* -s,- (*f* -,-nen) chemist. **c~isch** *a* chemical; **c~ische Reinigung** drycleaning; (*Geschäft*) drycleaner's

Chiffre /'ʃɪfrə, 'ʃɪfrɐ/ *f* -,-n cipher; (*bei Annonce*) box number

Chile /'çi:le/ *nt* -s Chile

China /'çi:na/ *nt* -s China. **C~ese** *m* -n,-n, **C~esin** *f* -,-nen Chinese. **c~esisch** *a* Chinese. **C~esisch** *nt* -[s] (*Lang*) Chinese

Chip /tʃɪp/ *m* -s,-s [micro]chip. **C~s** *pl* crisps

Chirurg /çi'rʊrk/ *m* -en,-en surgeon. **C~ie** /-'gi:/ *f* - surgery

Chlor /klo:ɐ/ *nt* -s chlorine

Choke /tʃo:k/ *m* -s,-s (*Auto*) choke

Cholera /'ko:lera/ *f* - cholera

cholerisch /ko'le:rɪʃ/ *a* irascible

Cholesterin /ço-, koles'te:ri:n/ *nt* -s cholesterol

Chor /ko:ɐ/ *m* -[e]s,"-e choir

Choreographie /koreogra'fi:/ *f* -,-n choreography

Christ /krɪst/ *m* -en,-en Christian. **C~baum** *m* Christmas tree. **C~entum** *nt* -s Christianity. **C~in** *f* -,-nen Christian. **c~lich** *a* Christian

Christus /'krɪstʊs/ *m* -ti Christ

Chrom /kro:m/ *nt* -s chromium

Chromosom /kromo'zo:m/ *nt* -s,-en chromosome

Chronik /'kro:nɪk/ *f* -,-en chronicle

Chrysantheme /kryzan'te:mə/ *f* -,-n chrysanthemum

circa /'tsɪrka/ *adv* about

Clou /klu:/ *m* -s,-s highlight

Clown /klaʊn/ *m* -s,-s clown. **c~en** *vi* (**haben**) clown

Club /klʊp/ *m* -s,-s club

Cocktail /'kɔkte:l/ *m* -s,-s cocktail

Comic-Heft /'kɔmɪk-/ *nt* comic

Computer /kɔm'pju:tɐ/ *m* -s,- computer. **c~isieren** *vt* computerize

Conférencier /kõferã'sje:/ *m* -s,-s compère

Cord /kɔrt/ *m* -s, **C~samt** *m* corduroy

Couch /kaʊtʃ/ *f* -,-es settee

Cousin /ku'zɛ̃:/ *m* -s,-s [male] cousin. **C~e** /-'zi:nə/ *f* -,-n [female] cousin

Creme /kreːm/ f -s,-s cream; (Speise) cream dessert

Curry /ˈkari, ˈkœri/ nt & m -s curry powder □nt -s,-s (Gericht) curry

D

da adv there; (hier) here; (zeitlich) then; (in dem Fall) in that case; **von da an** from then on □conj as, since

dabei (emphatic: **dabei**) adv nearby; (daran) with it; (eingeschlossen) included; (hinsichtlich) about it; (währenddem) during this; (gleichzeitig) at the same time; (doch) and yet; **dicht d~** close by. **d~sein†** vi sep (sein) be present; (mitmachen) be involved; **d~sein, etw zu tun** be just doing sth

Dach nt -[e]s,¨er roof. **D~boden** m loft. **D~luke** f skylight. **D~rinne** f gutter

Dachs m -es,-e badger

Dachsparren m -s,- rafter

Dackel m -s,- dachshund

dadurch (emphatic: **dadurch**) adv through it/them; (Ursache) by it; (deshalb) because of that; **d~, daß** because

dafür (emphatic: **dafür**) adv for it/them; (anstatt) instead; (als Ausgleich) but [on the other hand]; **d~, daß** considering that

dagegen (emphatic: **dagegen**) adv against it/them; (Mittel, Tausch) for it; (verglichen damit) by comparison; (jedoch) however; **hast du was d~?** do you mind?

daheim adv at home

daher (emphatic: **daher**) adv from there; (deshalb) for that reason; **das kommt d~, weil** that's because □conj that is why

dahin (emphatic: **dahin**) adv there; **bis d~** up to there; (bis dann) until/(Zukunft) by then; **jdn d~ bringen, daß er etw tut** get s.o. to do sth

dahinten adv back there

dahinter (emphatic: **dahinter**) adv behind it/them. **d~kommen†** vi sep (sein) (fig) get to the bottom of it

Dahlie /-jə/ f -,-n dahlia

dalassen† vt sep leave there

daliegen† vi sep (sein) lie there

damalig a at that time; **der d~e Minister** the then minister

damals adv at that time

Damast m -es,-e damask

Dame f -,-n lady; (Karte, Schach) queen; (D~spiel) draughts sg. **d~nhaft** a ladylike

damit (emphatic: **damit**) adv with it/them; (dadurch) by it; **hör auf d~!** stop it! □conj so that

Damm m -[e]s,¨e dam

dämmerig a dim. **D~licht** nt twilight. **D~n** vi (haben) ⟨Morgen:⟩ dawn; **es d~t** it is getting light/(abends) dark. **D~ung** f -,-en ⟨des Morgens⟩ dawn; (Abend-) dusk

Dämon m -s,-en /-ˈmoːnən/ demon

Dampf m -es,¨e steam; (Chem) vapour. **d~en** vi (haben) steam

dämpfen vt (Culin) steam; (fig) muffle ⟨Ton⟩; lower ⟨Stimme⟩

Dampfer m -s,- steamer. **D~kochtopf** m pressure-cooker. **D~maschine** f steam engine. **D~walze** f steamroller

danach (emphatic: **danach**) adv after it/them; (suchen) for it/them; ⟨riechen⟩ of it; (später) afterwards; (entsprechend) accordingly; **es sieht d~ aus** it looks like it

Däne m -n,-n Dane

daneben (emphatic: **daneben**) adv beside it/them; (außerdem) in addition; (verglichen damit) by comparison

Dän|emark *nt* **-s** Denmark.
D~in *f* **-,-nen** Dane. **d~isch** *a*
Danish

Dank *m* **-es** thanks *pl*; **vielen D~**!
thank you very much! **d~** *prep*
(+ *dat or gen*) thanks to. **d~bar** *a*
grateful; (*erleichtert*) thankful.
D~barkeit *f* - gratitude. **d~e**
adv **d~e** [**schön** *od* **sehr**]! thank
you [very much!] **d~en** *vi* (*ha-*
ben) thank (**jdm** s.o.); (*ablehnen*)
decline; **nichts zu d~en**! don't
mention it!

dann *adv* then

daran (*emphatic*: **daran**) *adv* on
it/them; (*denken*) of it; **nahe d~** at the point; (*etw zu*
tun of doing sth); **d~setzen** *vt*
sep **alles d~setzen** do one's utmost (**zu** to)

darauf (*emphatic*: **darauf**) *adv*
on it/them; (*warten*) for it; (*ant-*
worten) to it; (*danach*) after that;
(*d~hin*) as a result. **d~hin** *adv*
as a result

daraus (*emphatic*: **daraus**) *adv*
out of *or* from it/them; **er macht**
sich nichts d~ he doesn't care
for it

darlegen *vt sep* expound; (*erklä-*
ren) explain

Darlehen *nt* **-s,-** loan

Darm *m* **-[e]s,~e** intestine

darstell|en *vt sep* represent;
(*bildlich*) portray; (*spielen*) play;
(*schildern*) describe. **D~er** *m* **-s,-**
actor. **D~erin** *f* **-,-nen** actress.
D~ung *f* representation; interpretation; description

darüber (*emphatic*: **darüber**) *adv*
over it/them; (*höher*) above
it/them; (*sprechen, lachen, sich*
freuen) about it; (*mehr*) more

darum (*emphatic*: **darum**) *adv*
round it/them; (*bitten, kämpfen*)
for it; (*deshalb*) that is why

darunter (*emphatic*: **darunter**)
adv under it/them; (*tiefer*) below

it/them; (*weniger*) less; (*dazwi-*
schen) among them

das *def art & pron* s. **der**

dasein† *vi sep* (*sein*) be there/
(*hier*) here; **noch nie dagewesen**
unprecedented. **D~** *nt* **-s** existence

daß *conj* that

dasselbe *pron* s. **derselbe**

Daten|sichtgerät *nt* visual dis-
play unit, VDU. **D~verarbei-**
tung *f* data processing

datieren *vt/i* (*haben*) date

Dativ *m* **-s,-e** dative. **D~objekt** *nt*
indirect object

Dattel *f* **-,-n** date

Datum *nt* **-s,-ten** date; **Daten** (*An-*
gaben) data

Dauer *f* - duration, length; (*Jur*)
term; **auf die D~** in the long run.
D~auftrag *m* standing order.
d~haft *a* lasting; (*fest*) durable.
D~karte *f* season ticket.
D~milch *f* long-life milk. **d~n** *vi*
(*haben*) last; **lange d~n** take a
long time. **d~nd** *a* lasting; (*stän-*
dig) constant. **D~welle** *f* perm

Daumen *m* **-s,-** thumb; **jdm den**
D~ drücken *od* **halten** keep
one's fingers crossed for s.o.

Daunen *fpl* down *sg*. **D~decke** *f*
[down-filled] duvet

davon (*emphatic*: **davon**) *adv*
from it/them; (*dadurch*) by it;
(*damit*) with it/them; (*darüber*)
about it; (*Menge*) of it; **das**
kommt d~! it serves you right! **das**
d~kommen† *vi sep* (*sein*) escape. **d~laufen†** *vi sep* (*sein*) run
away. **d~tragen†** *vt sep* carry
off; (*erleiden*) suffer; (*gewinnen*)
win

davor (*emphatic*: **davor**) *adv* in
front of it/them; (*sich fürchten*)
of it; (*zeitlich*) before it/them

dazu (*emphatic*: **dazu**) *adv* to it/
them; (*damit*) with it/them; (*da-*
für) for it; **noch d~** in addition to
that; **jdn d~bringen**, **etw zu tun**

get s.o. to do sth; **ich kam nicht
d ~** I didn't get round to [doing] it.
d ~ kommen† vi sep (sein) arrive
[on the scene]; (hinzukommen) be
added; **d ~ rechnen** vt sep add to
it/them
dazwischen (emphatic: **dazwischen**) adv between them, in between; (darunter) among them.
d ~ kommen† vi sep (sein) crop up; **wenn nichts d ~ kommt**
if all goes well
Debatte f -,-n debate; **zur D ~
stehen** be at issue. **d ~ tieren** vt/i
(haben) debate
Debüt /de'by:/ nt -s,-s début
Deck nt -[e]s,-s (Naut) deck; **an
D ~** on deck. **D ~ bett** nt duvet
Decke f -,-n cover; (Tisch-) table-
cloth; (Bett-) blanket; (Reise-) rug;
(Zimmer-) ceiling; **unter einer
D ~ stecken** (fam) be in league
Deckel m -s,- lid; (Flaschen-) top;
(Buch-) cover
decken vt cover; tile (Dach); lay
(Tisch); (schützen) shield; (Sport)
mark; meet (Bedarf); (fig) cover up for s.o.; **sich d ~**
(fig) cover oneself (gegen
against); (übereinstimmen) coincide
Deckname m pseudonym
Deckung f (Mil) cover; (Sport)
defence; (Mann-) marking; (Boxen) guard; (Sicherheit) security;
in D ~ gehen take cover
defensiv a defensive. **D ~ e** f -,-n
defensive
definieren vt define. **D ~ ition**
/-'tsio:n/ f -,-en definition
Defizit nt -s,-e deficit
deformiert a deformed
deftig a (fam) (Mahlzeit) hearty;
(Witz) coarse
Degen m -s,- sword; (Fecht-) épée
degradieren vt (Mil) demote; (fig)
degrade

dehn|bar a elastic. **d ~ en** vt
stretch; lengthen (Vokal); **sich
d ~ en** stretch
Deich m -[e]s,-e dike
dein poss pron your. **d ~ e(r,s)**
poss pron yours; **die d ~ en** pl
your family sg. **d ~ erseits** adv
for your part. **d ~ etwegen** adv
for your sake; (wegen dir) because
of you, on your account. **D ~ etwillen** adv **um d ~ etwillen** for
your sake. **d ~ ige** poss pron der/
die/das **d ~ ige** yours. **d ~ s** poss
pron yours
Dekagramm nt (Aust) 10 grams;
10 D ~ 100 grams
Dekan m -s,-e dean
Deklin|ation /-'tsio:n/ f -,-en de-
clension. **d ~ ieren** vt decline
Dekolleté /dekɔl'te:/ nt -s,-s low
neckline
Dekor m & nt -s decoration. **D ~ a-
teur** /-'tø:ɐ/ m -s,-e interior decorator; (Schaufenster-) window-
dresser. **D ~ ation** /-'tsio:n/ f -,-en
decoration; (Schaufenster-) win-
dow-dressing; (Auslage) display.
d ~ ativ a decorative. **d ~ ieren** vt
decorate; dress (Schaufenster)
Delegation /-'tsio:n/ f -,-en delegation. **d ~ ieren** vt delegate
delikat a delicate; (lecker) delicious. **D ~ essengeschäft** nt delicatessen
Delikt nt -[e]s,-e offence
Delinquent m -en,-en offender
Delirium nt -s delirium
Delle f -,-n dent
Delphin m -s,-e dolphin
Delta nt -s,-s delta
dem def art & pron s. der
dementieren vt deny
dem|entsprechend a corres-
ponding; (passend) appropriate
□ adv accordingly; (passend) appropriately. **d ~ nächst** adv soon;
(in Kürze) shortly

Demokrat *m* -en,-en democrat.
D~ie *f* -,-n democracy. **d~isch** *a*
democratic
demolieren *vt* wreck
Demonstr|ant *m* -en,-en demonstrator. **D~ation** /-'tsjo:n/ *f* -,-en
demonstration
demontieren *vt* dismantle
Demoskopie *f* - opinion research
Demut *f* - humility
den *def art & pron s.* der. **d~en**
pron s. der
denk|bar *a* conceivable. **d~en†**
vt|i (haben) think (an+*acc of*);
(*sich erinnern*) remember (an etw
acc sth); **das kann ich mir d~en**
I can imagine [that]; **ich d~e
nicht daran** I have no intention
of doing it; **d~t daran!** don't forget! **D~mal** *nt* memorial; (*Monument*) monument
denn *conj* for; besser/mehr **d~**
je better/more than ever □*adv*
wie/wo d~? but how/where? **es
sei d~** [, daß] unless
dennoch *adv* nevertheless
Denunz|iant *m* -en,-en informer.
d~ieren *vt* denounce
Deodorant *nt* -s,-s deodorant
deplaciert /-'tsi:ɐt/ *a* (*fig*) out of
place
Deponie *f* -,-n dump. **d~ren** *vt*
deposit
deportieren *vt* deport
Depot /de'po:/ *nt* -s,-s depot;
(*Lager*) warehouse; (*Bank-*) safe
deposit
Depression *f* -,-en depression
deprimieren *vt* depress
der, die, das, *pl* **die** *def art* (*acc*
den, die, das, *pl* die; *gen* des, der,
des, *pl* der; *dat* dem, der, dem, *pl*
den) the; **der Mensch** man; **die
Natur** nature; **das Leben** life; **5
Mark das Pfund** 5 marks a pound
□*pron* (*acc* den, die, das, *pl* die;
gen dessen, deren, dessen, *pl*
deren; *dat* dem, der, dem, *pl*
denen) □*dem pron* that; (*pl*)

those; (*substantivisch*) he, she, it;
(*Ding*) it; (*betont*) that; (d~*jenige*)
the one; (*pl*) they, those; (*Dinge*)
those; (*diejenigen*) the ones; **der
und der** such and such; **das waren Zeiten!** those were the days!
□*rel pron* who; (*Ding*) which, that
derb *a* tough; (*kräftig*) strong;
(*grob*) coarse; (*unsanft*) rough
deren *pron s.* der
dergleichen *inv a* such □*pron*
such a thing/such things
der-/die-/dasselbe, *pl* **dieselben**
pron the same; **ein- und dasselbe**
one and the same thing
derzeit *adv* at present
des *def art s.* der
Desert|eur /-'tø:ɐ/ *m* -s,-e deserter.
d~ieren *vi* (sein/haben) desert
desgleichen *adv* likewise □*pron*
the like
deshalb *adv* for this reason; (*also*)
therefore
Desin|fektion /dɛs'ʔnfɛktsjo:n/ *f* -
disinfecting. **D~fektionsmittel** *nt* disinfectant. **d~fizieren**
vt disinfect
dessen *pron s.* der
Destill|ation /-'tsjo:n/ *f* - distillation. **d~ieren** *vt* distil
desto *adv* je mehr, **d~ besser** the
more the better
deswegen *adv* = deshalb
Detektiv *m* -s,-e detective
Deton|ation /-'tsjo:n/ *f* -,-en explosion. **d~ieren** *vi* (sein) explode
deut|en *vt* interpret; predict ⟨*Zukunft*⟩ □*vi* (haben) point (auf
+*acc* at/(*fig*) to). **d~lich** *a* clear;
(*eindeutig*) plain
deutsch *a* German; **auf d~** in
German. **D~** *nt* -[s] (*Lang*) German. **D~e(r)** *m|f* German.
D~land *nt* -s Germany
Deutung *f* -,-en interpretation
Devise *f* -,-n motto. **D~n** *pl* foreign currency *or* exchange *sg*
Dezember *m* -s,- December

dezent a unobtrusive; *(diskret)* discreet

Dezernat nt -[e]s,-e department

Dezimalzahl f decimal

d.h. abbr *(das heißt)* i.e.

Dia nt -s,-s *(Phot)* slide

Diabet|es m - diabetes. **D~iker** m -s,- diabetic

Diadem nt -s,-e tiara

Diagnose f -,-n diagnosis

diagonal a diagonal. **D~e** f -,-n diagonal

Diagramm nt -s,-e diagram; *(Kurven-)* graph

Diakon m -s,-e deacon

Dialekt m -[e]s,-e dialect

Dialog m -[e]s,-e dialogue

Diamant m -en,-en diamond

Diapositiv nt -s,-e *(Phot)* slide

Diaprojektor m slide projector

Diät f -,-en *(Med)* diet

dich pron *(acc of* **du**) you; *(refl)* yourself

dicht a dense; *(dick)* thick; *(undurchlässig)* airtight; *(wasser-)* watertight □adv densely; *(nahe)* close (**bei** to). **D~e** f - density.

d~en[1] vt make watertight

dicht|en[2] vi *(haben)* write poetry. **D~er(in)** m -s,- *(f -,-nen)* poet. **d~erisch** a poetic. **D~ung**[1] f -,-en poetry; *(Gedicht)* poem

Dichtung[2] f -,-en seal; *(Ring)* washer; *(Auto)* gasket

dick a thick; *(beleibt)* fat; *(geschwollen)* swollen; **d~ machen** be fattening. **d~flüssig** a thick; *(Phys)* viscous. **D~kopf** m stubborn person; **einen D~kopf haben** be stubborn

didaktisch a didactic

die def art & pron s. **der**

Dieb(in) m -[e]s,-e *(f -,-nen)* thief. **d~isch** a thieving; *(Freude)* malicious. **D~stahl** m -[e]s,-e theft; *(geistig)* plagiarism

Diele f -,-n floorboard; *(Flur)* hall

dien|en vi *(haben)* serve. **D~er** m -s,- servant; *(Verbeugung)* bow.

D~erin f -,-nen maid, servant

Dienst m -[e]s,-e service; *(Arbeit)* work; *(Amtsausübung)* duty; **außer D~** off duty; *(pensioniert)* retired; **D~ haben** work; *(Soldat, Arzt:)* be on duty

Dienstag m Tuesday. **d~s** adv on Tuesdays

Dienst|bote m servant. **d~frei** a **d~freier Tag** day off; **d~frei haben** have time off; *(Soldat, Arzt:)* be off duty. **D~grad** m rank. **D~leistung** f service. **d~lich** a official □adv **d~lich verreist** away on business. **D~mädchen** nt maid. **D~reise** f business trip. **D~stelle** f office. **D~stunden** fpl office hours. **D~weg** m official channels pl

dies inv pron this. **d~bezüglich** a relevant □adv regarding this matter. **d~e(r,s)** pron this; *(pl)* these; *(substantivisch)* this [one]; *(pl)* these; **d~e Nacht** tonight; *(letzte)* last night

dieselbe pron s. **derselbe**

Dieselkraftstoff m diesel [oil]

diesmal adv this time

Dietrich m -s,-e skeleton key

Differential /-'tsja:l/ nt -s,-e differential

Differenz f -,-en difference. **d~ieren** vt/i *(haben)* differentiate *(zwischen + dat* between)

Digital- pref digital. **D~uhr** f digital clock/watch

Dikt|at nt -[e]s,-e dictation. **D~ator** m -s,-en /-'to:rən/ dictator. **D~atur** f -,-en dictatorship. **d~ieren** vt/i *(haben)* dictate

Dill m -s dill

Dimension f -,-en dimension

Ding nt -[e]s,-e & *(fam)* -er thing; **guter D~e sein** be cheerful; **vor allen D~en** above all

Dinosaurier /-ĭə/ m -s,- dinosaur

Diözese f -,-n diocese

Diphtherie f -diphtheria

Diplom nt -s,-e diploma; (Univ) degree

Diplomat m -en,-en diplomat

dir pron (dat of **du**) [to] you; (refl) yourself; **ein Freund von dir** a friend of yours

direkt a direct □ adv directly; (wirklich) really. **D~ion** /-'tsɪo:n/ f - management; (Vorstand) board of directors. **D~or** m -s,-en /-'to:rən/, **D~orin** f -,-nen director; (Bank-, Theater-) manager; (Sch) head; (Gefängnis) governor. **D~übertragung** f live transmission

Dirigent m -en,-en (Mus) conductor

Dirndl nt -s,- dirndl [dress]

Diskette f -,-n floppy disc

Disko f -,-s (fam) disco. **D~thek** f -,-en discothèque

diskret a discreet

Diskus m -,-se & Disken discus

Diskussion f -,-en discussion. **d~tieren** vt/i (haben) discuss

disponieren vi (haben) make arrangements; **d~ [können] über** (+ acc) have at one's disposal

Disqualifi|**kation** /-'tsɪo:n/ f disqualification. **d~zieren** vt disqualify

Dissident m -en,-en dissident

Distanz f -,-en distance. **d~ieren (sich)** vr dissociate oneself (von from). **d~iert** a aloof

Distel f -,-n thistle

Disziplin f -,-en discipline. **d~arisch** a disciplinary. **d~iert** a disciplined

dito adv ditto

Divid|**ende** f -,-n dividend. **d~ieren** vt divide (durch by)

Division f -,-en division

DJH abbr (Deutsche Jugendherberge) [German] youth hostel

DM abbr (Deutsche Mark) DM

doch conj & adv but; (dennoch) yet; (trotzdem) after all; **wenn d~ . . . !** if only . . . !

Docht m -[e]s,-e wick

Dock nt -s,-s dock. **d~en** vt/i (haben) dock

Dogge f -,-n Great Dane

Dogma nt -s,-men dogma. **d~atisch** a dogmatic, adv -ally

Dohle f -,-n jackdaw

Doktor m -s,-en /-'to:rən/ doctor. **D~arbeit** f [doctoral] thesis

Dokument nt -[e]s,-e document. **D~arbericht** m documentary. **D~arfilm** m documentary film

Dolch m -[e]s,-e dagger

dolmetschen vt/i (haben) interpret. **D~er(in)** m -s,- (f -,-nen) interpreter

Dom m -[e]s,-e cathedral

Domino nt -s,-s dominoes sg. **D~stein** m domino

Dompfaff m -en,-en bullfinch

Donau f - Danube

Donner m -s thunder. **d~n** vi (haben) thunder

Donnerstag m Thursday. **d~s** adv on Thursdays

Donnerwetter nt (fam) telling-off; (Krach) row

doof a (fam) stupid

Doppel nt -s,- duplicate; (Tennis) doubles pl. **D~bett** nt double bed. **d~deutig** a ambiguous. **D~gänger** m -s,- double. **D~kinn** nt double chin. **D~name** m double-barrelled name. **D~punkt** m (Gram) colon. **D~stecker** m two-way adaptor. **d~t** a double; ⟨Boden⟩ false; **in d~ter Ausfertigung** in duplicate; **die d~te Menge** twice the amount □ adv doubly; (zweimal) twice; **d~t so viel** twice as much. **D~zimmer** nt double room

Dorf nt -[e]s,-̈er village. **D~bewohner** m villager

dörflich a rural

Dorn m -[e]s,-en thorn. **d~ig** a thorny

Dorsch m -[e]s,-e cod

dort adv there. **d~ig** a local

Dose f -,-n tin, can; (Schmuck-) box

dösen vi (haben) doze

Dosen|milch f evaporated milk. **D~öffner** m tin or can opener

dosieren vt measure out

Dosis f -, Dosen dose

Dotter m & nt -s,- [egg] yolk

Dozent(in) m -en,-en (f -,-nen) (Univ) lecturer

Dr. abbr (Doktor) Dr

Drache m -n,-n dragon. **D~n** m -s,- kite. **D~nflieger** m hangglider

Draht m -[e]s,-̈e wire; auf D~ (fam) on the ball. **D~seilbahn** f cable railway

Dram|a nt -s,-men drama. **D~atik** f - drama. **D~atiker** m -s,- dramatist. **d~atisch** a dramatic

dran adv (fam) =daran; gut/ schlecht d~ sein be well off/in a bad way; ich bin d~ it's my turn

Drang m -[e]s urge

dräng|eln vt/i (haben) push; (bedrängen) pester. **d~en** vt push; (bedrängen) urge; sich d~en crowd (um round)

dran|halten† (sich) vr sep hurry. **d~kommen†** vi sep (sein) have one's turn

drauf adv (fam) =darauf; d~- und dran sein be on the point (etw zu tun of doing sth). **D~gänger** m -s,- daredevil. **d~gängerisch** a reckless

draus adv (fam) =daraus

draußen adv outside

drechseln vt (Techn) turn

Dreck m -s dirt; (Morast) mud. **d~ig** a dirty; muddy

Dreh m -s (fam) knack; den D~ herausbaben have got the hang of it. **D~bank** f lathe. **D~bleistift** m propelling pencil.

D~buch nt screenplay, script. **d~en** vt turn; (im Kreis) rotate; shoot (Film); **lauter/leiser d~en** turn up/down; sich d~en vi; (im Kreis) rotate; (schnell) spin; sich d~en um revolve around; (sich handeln) be about □vi (haben) turn; (Wind:) change; an etw (dat) d~en turn sth. **D~stuhl** m swivel chair. **D~tür** f revolving door. **D~ung** f -,-en turn; (im Kreis) rotation. **D~zahl** f number of revolutions

drei inv a & f -,-en three; D~ f ≈ pass. **D~eck** nt -[e]s,-e triangle. **d~eckig** a triangular. **d~erlei** inv a three kinds of □pron three things. **d~fach** a triple; in d~facher Ausfertigung in triplicate. **d~mal** adv three times. **D~rad** nt tricycle

dreißig inv a thirty. **d~ste(r,s)** a thirtieth

dreiviertel inv a three-quarter. **D~stunde** f three quarters of an hour

dreizehn inv a thirteen. **d~te(r,s)** a thirteenth

dreschen vt thresh

dress|ieren vt train. **D~ur** f - training

dribbeln vi (haben) dribble

Drill m -[e]s (Mil) drill. **d~en** vt drill

Drillinge mpl triplets

Drink m -[s],-s [alcoholic] drink

drinnen adv inside

dritt adv zu d~ in threes; wir waren zu d~ there were three of us. **d~e(r,s)** a third; ein D~er a third person. **D~el** nt -s,- third. **d~ens** adv thirdly. **d~rangig** a third-rate

Droge f -,-n drug. **D~nabhängige(r)** m/f drug addict. **D~erie** f -,-n chemist's shop. **D~ist** m -en,-en chemist

drohen vi (haben) threaten (jdm s.o.)

dröhnen vi (haben) resound; (tönen) boom

Drohung f -,-en threat

drollig a funny; (seltsam) odd

Drops m -,- [fruit] drop

Drossel f -,-n thrush

drosseln vt (Techn) throttle

drüben adv over there

Druck[1] m -[e]s,-ͤe pressure; **unter D~ setzen** (fig) pressurize

Druck[2] m -[e]s,-e printing; (Schrift, Reproduktion) print. **D~buchstabe** m block letter

drucken vt print

drücken vt/i (haben) press; (aus-)squeeze; (Schuh:) pinch; (umarmen) hug; **Preise d~** force down prices; (an Tür) d~ push; **sich d~vor** (+dat) (fam) shirk; **~d** a heavy; (schwül) oppressive

Drucker m -s,- printer

Druckerei f -,-en printing works

Druck|**knopf** m press-stud. **D~luft** f compressed air. **D~sache** f printed matter. **D~schrift** f type; (Veröffentlichung) publication. **D~stelle** f bruise. **D~taste** f push-button. **D~topf** m pressure-cooker

Drüse f -,-n (Anat) gland

Dschungel m -s,- jungle

du pron (familiar address) you; **auf du und du** on familiar terms

Dübel m -s,- plug

ducken vt duck

Dudelsack m bagpipes pl

Duell nt -s,-e duel

Duett nt -s,-e [vocal] duet

Duft m -[e]s,-ͤe fragrance, scent; (Aroma) aroma. **d~en** vi (haben) smell (nach of)

dumm a stupid; (unklug) foolish; (fam: lästig) awkward; **wie d~!** what a nuisance! **d~erweise** adv stupidly; (leider) unfortunately. **D~heit** f -,-en stupidity; (Torheit) foolishness; (Handlung) folly. **D~kopf** m (fam) fool

dumpf a dull

Düne f -,-n dune

Dung m -s manure

Düng|**emittel** nt fertilizer. **d~en** vt fertilize. **D~er** m -s,- fertilizer

dunk|**el** a dark; (vage) vague; (fragwürdig) shady; **d~les Bier** brown ale; **im D~eln** in the dark

Dunkel|**heit** f - darkness. **D~kammer** f dark-room. **d~n** vi (haben) get dark

dünn a thin; (Buch) slim; (spärlich) sparse; (schwach) weak

Dunst m -es,-ͤe mist, haze; (Dampf) vapour

dünsten vt steam

dunstig a misty, hazy

Duo nt -s,-s [instrumental] duet

Duplikat nt -[e]s,-e duplicate

Dur nt - (Mus) major [key]; **in A-Dur** in A major

durch prep (+acc) through; (mittels) by; [geteilt] **d~** (Math) divided by □adv **die Nacht d~** throughout the night; **d~ und d~** naß wet through

durchaus adv absolutely; **d~nicht** by no means

durchblättern vt sep leaf through

durchblicken vi sep (haben) look through; **d~ lassen** (fig) hint at

Durchblutung f circulation

durchbohren vt insep pierce

durchbrechen[1] vt/i sep (haben) break [in two]

durchbrechen[2]† vt insep break through; break (Schallmauer)

durchbrennen† vi sep (sein) burn through; (Sicherung:) blow; (fam: weglaufen) run away

durchbringen† vt sep get through; (verschwenden) squander; (versorgen) support

Durchbruch m breakthrough

durchdrehen v sep □vt mince □vi (haben/sein) (fam) go crazy

durchdringen† vi sep (sein) penetrate; (sich durchsetzen) get one's way. **d~d** *a* penetrating; 〈Schrei〉 piercing

durcheinander *adv* in a muddle; 〈Person〉 confused. **D~** *nt* **-s** muddle. **d~geraten†** *vi sep* (sein) get mixed up. **d~reden** *vi sep* (haben) all talk at once

durchfahren† *vi sep* (sein) drive through; 〈Zug:〉 go through

Durchfahrt *f* journey/drive through; **auf der D~** passing through; **'D~ verboten'** 'no thoroughfare'

Durchfall *m* diarrhoea. **d~en†** *vi sep* (sein) fall through; (bei Prüfung) fail

durchfliegen† *vi sep* (sein) fly through; (fam: durchfallen) fail

Durchfuhr *f* (Comm) transit

durchführ|bar *a* feasible. **d~en** *vt sep* carry out

Durchgang *m* passage; (Sport) round; **'D~ verboten'** 'no entry'. **D~sverkehr** *m* through traffic

durchgeben† *vt sep* (haben) through; (übermitteln) transmit; (Radio, TV) broadcast

durchgebraten *a* **gut d~** well done

durchgehen† *vi sep* (sein) go through; (davonlaufen) run away; 〈Pferd:〉 bolt; **jdm etw d~ lassen** let s.o. get away with sth. **d~d** *a* continuous; **d~d geöffnet** open all day; **d~der Zug** through train

durchgreifen† *vi sep* (haben) reach through; (vorgehen) take drastic action. **d~d** *a* drastic

durchhalte|n† *v sep* (fig) □ *vi* (haben) hold out □ *vt* keep up. **D~vermögen** *nt* stamina

durchkommen† *vi sep* (sein) come through; (gelangen, am Telefon) get through

durchlassen† *vt sep* let through

durchlässig *a* permeable; (undicht) leaky

Durchlauferhitzer *m* **-s,-** geyser

durchlesen† *vt sep* read through

durchleuchten *vt insep* X-ray

durchlöchert *a* riddled with holes

durchmachen *vt sep* go through; (erleiden) undergo

Durchmesser *m* **-s,-** diameter

durchnäßt *a* wet through

durchnehmen† *vt sep* (Sch) do

durchnumeriert *a* numbered consecutively

durchpausen *vt sep* trace

durchqueren *vt insep* cross

Durchreiche *f* **-,-n** hatch

Durchreise *f* journey through; **auf der D~** passing through. **d~n** *vi sep* (sein) pass through

durchreißen† *vt/i sep* (sein) tear

Durchsage *f* **-,-n** announcement. **d~n** *vt sep* announce

Durchschlag *m* carbon copy; (Culin) colander. **d~en†** *v sep* □ *vt* (Culin) rub through a sieve; **sich d~en** (fig) struggle through □ *vi* (sein) 〈Sicherung:〉 blow

durchschneiden† *vt sep* cut

Durchschnitt *m* average; **im D~** on average. **d~lich** *a* average □ *adv* on average. **D~s-** *pref* average

Durchschrift *f* carbon copy

durchsehen† *v sep* □ *vi* (haben) see through □ *vt* look through

durchsetzen *vt sep* force through; **sich d~** assert oneself; 〈Mode:〉 catch on

Durchsicht *f* check

durchsichtig *a* transparent

durchsickern *vi sep* (sein) seep through; 〈Neuigkeit:〉 leak out

durchstreichen† *vt sep* cross out

durchsuch|en *vt insep* search. **D~ung** *f* **-,-en** search

durchwachsen *a* 〈Speck〉 streaky; (fam: gemischt) mixed

durchwählen *vi sep* (haben) (Teleph) dial direct

durchweg *adv* without exception

durchwühlen *vt insep* rummage through; ransack ⟨*Haus*⟩

Durchzug *m* through draught

dürfen† *vt & v aux* etw [tun] d~ be allowed to do sth; darf ich? may I? ich hätte es nicht tun d~ I ought not to have done it; das dürfte nicht allzu schwer sein that should not be too difficult

dürftig *a* poor; ⟨*Mahlzeit*⟩ scanty

dürr *a* dry; ⟨*Boden*⟩ arid; ⟨*mager*⟩ skinny. **D~e** *f* -,-n drought

Durst *m* -[e]s thirst; **D~ haben** be thirsty. **d~ig** *a* thirsty

Dusche *f* -,-n shower. **d~n** *vi/r* (*haben*) [sich] d~ have a shower

Düse *f* -,-n nozzle. **D~nflugzeug** *nt* jet

Dutzend *nt* -s,-e dozen

duzen *vt* d~ jdn d~ call s.o. 'du'

Dynamik *f* - dynamics *sg*; ⟨*fig*⟩ dynamism. **d~isch** *a* dynamic; ⟨*Rente*⟩ index-linked

Dynamit *nt* -es dynamite

Dynamo *m* -s,-s dynamo

Dynastie *f* -,-n dynasty

D-Zug /ˈdeː-/ *m* express (train)

E

Ebbe *f* -,-n low tide

eben *a* level; ⟨*glatt*⟩ smooth; zu e~er Erde on the ground floor □*adv* just; ⟨*genau*⟩ exactly; **e~ noch** only just; ⟨*gerade vorhin*⟩ just now. **E~bild** *nt* image

Ebene *f* -,-n ⟨*Geog*⟩ plain; ⟨*Geom*⟩ plane; ⟨*fig: Niveau*⟩ level

eben|falls *adv* also; danke, e~falls thank you, [the] same to you. **E~holz** *nt* ebony. **e~so** *adv* just the same; ⟨*ebensosehr*⟩ just as much; **e~so gut** just as good. **e~sosehr** *adv* just as much. **e~soviel** *adv* just as much/many. **e~sowenig** *adv* just as little/few

Eber *m* -s,- boar

ebnen *vt* level; ⟨*fig*⟩ smooth

Echo *nt* -s,-s echo. **e~en** *vt/i* (*haben*) echo

echt *a* genuine, real; authentic □*adv* ⟨*fam*⟩ really; typically. **E~heit** *f* - authenticity

Eck|ball *m* ⟨*Sport*⟩ corner. **E~e** *f* -,-n corner; **um die E~e bringen** ⟨*fam*⟩ bump off. **e~ig** *a* angular; ⟨*Klammern*⟩ square. **E~zahn** *m* canine tooth

Ecu, ECU /eˈkyː/ *m* -[s],-[s] ecu

edel *a* noble; ⟨*wertvoll*⟩ precious; ⟨*fein*⟩ fine. **E~stahl** *m* stainless steel. **E~stein** *m* precious stone

Efeu *m* -s ivy

Effekt *m* -[e]s,-e effect. **E~en** *pl* securities. **e~iv** *a* actual; ⟨*wirksam*⟩ effective

egal *a* das ist mir e~ ⟨*fam*⟩ it's all the same to me □*adv* e~ **wie/wo** no matter how/where

Egge *f* -,-n harrow

Ego|ismus *m* - selfishness. **E~ist(in)** *m* -en,-en ⟨*f* -,-nen⟩ egoist. **e~istisch** *a* selfish

eh *adv* ⟨*Aust fam*⟩ anyway

ehe *conj* before; **ehe nicht** until

Ehe *f* -,-n marriage. **E~bett** *nt* double bed. **E~bruch** *m* adultery. **E~frau** *f* wife. **e~lich** *a* marital; ⟨*Recht*⟩ conjugal; ⟨*Kind*⟩ legitimate

ehemalig *a* former. **e~s** *adv* formerly

Ehe|mann *m* (*pl* -männer) husband. **E~paar** *nt* married couple

eher *adv* earlier, sooner; ⟨*lieber, vielmehr*⟩ rather; ⟨*mehr*⟩ more

Ehering *m* wedding ring

Ehr|e *f* -,-n honour; **e~en** *vt* honour. **e~enamtlich** *a* honorary □*adv* in an honorary capacity. **E~engast** *m* guest of honour. **e~enhaft** *a* honourable. **E~enrunde** *f* lap of honour. **E~ensache** *f* point of honour. **E~enwort** *nt* word of honour. **E~erbietung** *f* deference. **E~furcht**

f reverence; (Scheu) awe.
e~fürchtig a reverent. E~gefühl nt sense of honour. E~geiz m ambition. e~geizig a ambitious. e~lich a honest; e~lich gesagt to be honest. E~lichkeit f - honesty. e~los a dishonourable. e~würdig a venerable; (als Anrede) Reverend

Ei nt -[e]s,-er egg
Eibe f -,-n yew
Eiche f -,-n oak. E~l f -,-n acorn
eichen vt standardize
Eichhörnchen nt -s,- squirrel
Eid m -[e]s,-e oath
Eidechse f -,-n lizard
eidlich a sworn □ adv on oath
Eidotter m & nt egg yolk
Eier|becher m egg-cup. E~kuchen m pancake; (Omelett) omelette. E~schale f eggshell. E~schnee m beaten egg-white. E~stock m ovary
Eifer m -s eagerness. E~sucht f jealousy. e~süchtig a jealous
eifrig a eager
Eigelb nt -[e]s,-e [egg] yolk
eigen a own; (typisch) characteristic (dat of); (genau) particular. E~art f peculiarity. e~artig a peculiar. e~händig a personal; ⟨Unterschrift⟩ own. E~heit f -,-en peculiarity. E~name m proper name. e~nützig a selfish. e~s adv specially. E~schaft f -,-en quality; (Phys) property; (Merkmal) characteristic; (Funktion) capacity. E~schaftswort nt (pl -wörter) adjective. E~sinn m obstinacy. e~sinnig a obstinate
eigentlich a actual, real; (wahr) true □ adv actually, really; (streng genommen) strictly speaking
Eigen|tor nt own goal. E~tum nt -s property. E~tümer(in) m (f -,-nen) owner. E~tumswohnung f freehold flat. e~willig a

self-willed; ⟨Stil⟩ highly individual
eign|en (sich) vr be suitable
Eil|brief m express letter. E~e f - hurry; E~e haben be in a hurry; ⟨Sache:⟩ be urgent. e~en vi (sein) hurry □ (haben) ⟨drängen⟩ be urgent. e~ig a hurried; ⟨dringend⟩ urgent; es e~ig haben be in a hurry. E~zug m semi-fast train
Eimer m -s,- bucket; (Abfall-) bin
ein adj one; mit jdm in einem Zimmer schlafen sleep in the same room as s.o. □ indef art a, (vor Vokal) an; so ein such a; was für ein ⟨Frage⟩ what kind of a? (Ausruf) what a!
einander pron one another
Einäscherung f -,-en cremation
einatmen vt/i sep (haben) inhale, breathe in
Einbahnstraße f one-way street
Einband m binding
Einbau m installation; (Montage) fitting. e~en vt sep install; (montieren) fit. E~küche f fitted kitchen
einbegriffen pred a included
Einberufung f call-up
Einbettzimmer nt single room
einbeulen vt sep dent
einbeziehen† vt sep [mit] e~include; (berücksichtigen) take into account
einbiegen† vi sep (sein) turn
einbild|en vt sep sich (dat) etw e~en imagine sth; sich (dat) viel e~en be conceited. E~ung f imagination; (Dünkel) conceit. E~ungskraft f imagination
einblenden vt sep fade in
Einblick m insight
einbrech|en† vi sep (haben/sein) break in; bei uns ist eingebrochen worden we have been burgled. E~er m burglar
einbring|en† vt sep get in; bring in ⟨Geld⟩

Einbruch m burglary; **bei E~ der Nacht** at nightfall

einbürger|n vt sep naturalize. **E~ung** f naturalization

einchecken /-ʃɛkn/ vt/i sep (haben) check in

eindecken (sich) vr sep stock up

eindeutig a unambiguous; (deutlich) clear

eindicken vt sep (Culin) thicken

eindringen† vi sep (sein) **e~ in** (+ acc) penetrate into; (mit Gewalt) force one's/‹Wasser:› its way into; (Mil) invade

Eindruck m impression

eindrücken vt sep crush

eindrucksvoll a impressive

eine(r,s) pron one; (jemand) someone; (man) one, you

einebnen vt sep level

eineiig a ‹Zwillinge› identical

eineinhalb inv a one and a half; **e~ Stunden** an hour and a half

Einelternfamilie f one-parent family

einengen vt sep restrict

Einer m -s,- (Math) unit. **e~** pron s. **eine(r,s)**. **e~lei** inv a attrib a one kind of □pred a (fam) immaterial; **es ist mir e~lei** it's all the same to me. **e~seits** adv on the one hand

einfach a simple; ‹Essen› plain; ‹Faden, Fahrt› single; **e~er Soldat** private. **E~heit** f simplicity

einfädeln vt sep thread; (fig: arrangieren) arrange; **sich e~** (Auto) filter in

einfahr|en† v sep □vi (sein) arrive; ‹Zug:› pull in □vt (Auto) run in. **E~t** f arrival; (Eingang) entrance, way in; (Auffahrt) drive; (Autobahn) access road; **keine E~t** no entry

Einfall m idea; (Mil) invasion. **e~en†** vi sep (sein) collapse; (eindringen) invade; **jdm e~en** occur to s.o.; **sein Name fällt**

mir nicht ein I can't think of his name

Einfalt f- naïvety

einfarbig a of one colour; ‹Stoff, Kleid› plain

einfass|en vt sep edge; set ‹Edelstein›. **E~ung** f border, edging

einfetten vt sep grease

Einfluß m influence. **e~reich** a influential

einförmig a monotonous. **E~keit** f- monotony

einfrieren vt/i sep (sein) freeze

einfügen vt sep insert; **sich e~ in** fit in

Einfuhr f -,-en import

einführ|en vt sep introduce; (einstecken) insert; (einweisen) initiate; (Comm) import. **e~end** a introductory. **E~ung** f introduction; (Einweisung) initiation

Eingabe f petition; (Computer) input

Eingang m entrance, way in; (Ankunft) arrival

eingebaut a built-in; ‹Schrank› fitted

eingeben† vt sep hand in; (einflößen) give; (jdm s.o.); (Computer) feed in

eingebildet a imaginary; (überheblich) conceited

Eingeborene|r m/f native

eingehen† v sep □vi (sein) come in; (ankommen) arrive; (einlaufen) shrink; (sterben) die; ‹Zeitung, Firma:› fold; **auf etw (acc)** e~ go into sth; (annehmen) agree to sth □vt enter into; contract ‹Ehe›; make ‹Wette›; take ‹Risiko›

eingemacht a (Culin) bottled

eingeschneit a snowbound

eingeschrieben a registered

Einge|ständnis nt admission. **e~stehen†** vt sep admit

eingetragen a registered

Eingeweide pl bowels, entrails

eingewöhnen (sich) *vr sep* settle in

eingießen† *vt sep* pour in; *(ein-schenken)* pour

eingleisig *a* single-track

eingliedern *vt sep* integrate. **E ~ ung** *f* integration

eingravieren *vt sep* engrave

eingreifen† *vi sep (haben)* intervene. **E ~ nt -s** intervention

Eingriff *m* intervention; *(Med)* operation

einhaken *vt/r sep* jdn e ~ *od* sich bei jdm e ~ take s.o.'s arm

einhalten† *v sep □vt* keep; *(befolgen)* observe □*vi (haben)* stop

einhändigen *vt sep* hand in

einhängen *vt sep* hang; put down *⟨Hörer⟩*

einheimisch *a* local; *(eines Landes)* native; *(Comm)* home-produced. **E ~ e(r)** *m/f* local

Einheit *f* -,-en unity; *(Maß-, Mil)* unit. **e ~ lich** *a* uniform. **E ~ spreis** *m* standard price; *(Fahrpreis)* flat fare

einholen *vt sep* catch up with; *(aufholen)* make up for; *(einkaufen)* buy

einhüllen *vt sep* wrap

einhundert *inv a* one hundred

einig *a* united; [sich *(dat)*] e ~ sein be in agreement

einig|e(r,s) *pron* some; *(ziemlich viel)* quite a lot of; *(substantivisch)* e ~ e *pl* some; *(mehrere)* several; e ~ es some; vor e ~ er Zeit some time ago. **e ~ emal** *adv* a few times

einigen *vt* unite; unify *⟨Land⟩*; sich e ~ come to an agreement

einigermaßen *adv* to some extent; *(ziemlich)* fairly; *(ziemlich gut)* fairly well

Einigkeit *f* - unity; *(Übereinstimmung)* agreement

einjährig *a* one-year-old; **e ~ e Pflanze** annual

einkalkulieren *vt sep* take into account

einkassieren *vt sep* collect

Einkauf *m* purchase; *(Einkaufen)* shopping; **Einkäufe machen** do some shopping. **e ~ en** *vt sep* buy; **e ~ en gehen** go shopping. **E ~ s-wagen** *m* shopping trolley

einklammern *vt sep* bracket

Einklang *m* harmony; **in E ~ stehen** be in accord *(mit* with*)*

einkleben *vt sep* stick in

einkleiden *vt sep* fit out

einklemmen *vt sep* clamp

einkochen *v sep □vi (sein)* boil down □*vt* preserve, bottle

Einkommen *nt* -s income. **E ~ [s]steuer** *f* income tax

Einkünfte *pl* income *sg*; *(Einnahmen)* revenue *sg*

einlad|en† *vt sep* load; *(auffordern)* invite; *(bezahlen für)* treat. **E ~ ung** *f* invitation

Einlage *f* enclosure; *(Schuh-)* arch support; *(Programm-)* interlude; *(Comm)* investment; *(Bank-)* deposit; **Suppe mit E ~** soup with noodles/dumplings

Einlaß *m* -sses admittance. **e ~ lassen**† *vt sep* let in; run *⟨Bad, Wasser⟩*

einleben (sich) *vr sep* settle in

Einlege|arbeit *f* inlaid work. **e ~ n** *vt sep* put in; lay in *⟨Vorrat⟩*; lodge *⟨Protest⟩*; *(einfügen)* insert; *(Auto)* engage *⟨Gang⟩*; *(Culin)* pickle; *(marinieren)* marinade; **eine Pause e ~ n** have a break. **E ~ sohle** *f* insole

einleit|en *vt sep* initiate; *(eröffnen)* begin. **E ~ ung** *f* introduction

einleuchten *vi sep (haben)* be clear *(dat* to*)*. **e ~ d** *a* convincing

einliefer|n *vt sep* take *(ins Krankenhaus* to hospital*)*. **E ~ ung** *f* admission

einlösen *vt sep* cash *⟨Scheck⟩*; redeem *⟨Pfand⟩*; *(fig)* keep

einmachen *vt sep* preserve

einmal *adv* once; *(eines Tages)* one or some day; **noch/schon e~** again/before; **noch e~ so teuer** twice as expensive; **auf e~** at the same time; *(plötzlich)* suddenly; **nicht e~** not even. **E~eins** *nt* [multiplication] tables *pl.* **e~ig** *a (einzigartig)* unique; *(fam: großartig)* fantastic

einmarschieren *vi sep (sein)* march in

einmischen (sich) *vr sep* interfere. **E~ung** *f* interference

Einnahme *f* -,-n taking; *(Mil)* capture; **E~n** *pl* income *sg; (Einkünfte)* revenue *sg; (Comm)* receipts; *(eines Ladens)* takings

einnehmen† *vt sep* take; have *⟨Mahlzeit⟩; (Mil)* capture; take up *⟨Platz⟩*

einordnen *vt sep* put in its proper place; *(klassifizieren)* classify; **sich e~** fit in; *(Auto)* get in lane

einpacken *vt sep* pack

einparken *vt sep* park

einpflanzen *vt sep* plant; implant *⟨Organ⟩*

einplanen *vt sep* allow for

einprägen *vt sep* impress **(jdm** [up]on s.o.); **sich** *(dat)* **etw e~** memorize sth

einrahmen *vt sep* frame

einrasten *vi sep (sein)* engage

einräumen *vt sep* put away; *(zugeben)* admit; *(zugestehen)* grant

einrechnen *vt sep* include

einreden *vt sep* **jdm/sich** *(dat)* **etw e~** persuade s.o./oneself of sth

einreiben† *vt sep* rub **(mit** with)

einreichen *vt sep* submit; **die Scheidung e~** file for divorce

Einreih|er *m* -s,- single-breasted suit. **e~ig** *a* single-breasted

Einreise *f* entry. **e~n** *vi sep (sein)* enter *(nach Irland* Ireland)

einreißen† *vt sep* tear; *(abreißen)* pull down *□ vi (sein)* tear; *⟨Sitte:⟩* become a habit

einrenken *vt sep (Med)* set

einricht|en *vt sep* fit out; *(möblieren)* furnish; *(anordnen)* arrange; *(Med)* set *⟨Bruch⟩; (eröffnen)* set up; **sich e~en** furnish one's home. **E~ung** *f* furnishing; *(Möbel)* furnishings *pl; (Techn)* equipment; *(Vorrichtung)* device; *(Eröffnung)* setting up; *(Institution)* institution; *(Gewohnheit)* practice

einrosten *vi sep (sein)* rust; *(fig)* get rusty

eins *inv a & pron* one; **noch e~** one other thing; **mir ist alles e~** *(fam)* it's all the same to me. **E~** *f* -,-en one; *(Sch)* ≈ A

einsam *a* lonely; *(allein)* solitary; *(abgelegen)* isolated. **E~keit** *f* - loneliness; solitude; isolation

einsammeln *vt sep* collect

Einsatz *m* use; *(Mil)* mission; *(Wett-)* stake; *(E~teil)* insert

einschalt|en *vt sep* switch on; *(einschieben)* interpolate; *(fig: beteiligen)* call in; **sich e~en** *(fig)* intervene. **E~quote** *f* *(TV)* viewing figures *pl;* ≈ ratings *pl*

einschätzen *vt sep* assess; *(bewerten)* rate

einschenken *vt sep* pour

einscheren *vi sep (sein)* pull in

einschicken *vt sep* send in

einschiffen (sich) *vr sep* embark. **E~ung** *f* - embarkation

einschlafen† *vi sep (sein)* go to sleep; *(aufhören)* peter out

einschläfern *vt sep* lull to sleep; *(betäuben)* put out; *(töten)* put to sleep. **e~d** *a* soporific

Einschlag *m* impact. **e~en†** *v sep* □ *vt* knock in; *(zerschlagen)* smash; *(drehen)* turn; take *⟨Weg⟩;* take up *⟨Laufbahn⟩* □ *vi (haben)* hit/ *⟨Blitz:⟩* strike *(in* acc sth); *(Erfolg haben)* be a hit

einschleusen *vt sep* infiltrate

einschließen† *vt sep* lock in; *(umgeben)* enclose; *(einkreisen)* surround; *(einbeziehen)* include; **sich**

e~en lock oneself in; **Bedienung eingeschlossen** service included.
e~lich *adv* inclusive □*prep* (+ *gen*) including

Einschnitt *m* cut; (*Med*) incision; (*Lücke*) gap; (*fig*) decisive event

einschränk|en *vt sep* restrict; (*reduzieren*) cut back; **sich e~en** economize. **E~ung** *f* -,-en restriction; (*Reduzierung*) reduction; (*Vorbehalt*) reservation

Einschreib[e]brief *m* registered letter. **e~en†** *vt sep* enter; register ⟨*Brief*⟩; **sich e~en** put one's name down; (*sich anmelden*) enrol. **E~en** *nt* call *od* per **E~en** registered letter/packet; **als** *od* **per E~en** by registered post

einschüchtern *vt sep* intimidate

einsehen† *vt sep* inspect; (*lesen*) consult; (*begreifen*) see

einseitig *a* one-sided; (*Pol*) unilateral □*adv* on one side; (*fig*) one-sidedly; (*Pol*) unilaterally

einsenden† *vt sep* send in

einsetzen *v sep* □*vt* put in; (*einfügen*) insert; (*verwenden*) use; put on ⟨*Zug*⟩; call out ⟨*Truppen*⟩; (*Mil*) deploy; (*ernennen*) appoint; (*wetten*) stake; (*riskieren*) risk □*vi* (*haben*) start; ⟨*Regen:*⟩ set in

Einsicht *f* insight; (*Verständnis*) understanding; (*Vernunft*) reason. **e~ig** *a* understanding

Einsiedler *m* hermit

einsinken† *vi sep* (*sein*) sink in

einspannen *vt sep* harness; **jdn e~** (*fam*) rope s.o. in

einsparen *vt sep* save

einsperren *vt sep* shut/(*im Gefängnis*) lock up

einsprachig *a* monolingual

einspritzen *vt sep* inject

Einspruch *m* objection; **E~ erheben** object; (*Jur*) appeal

einspurig *a* single-track; (*Auto*) single-lane

einst *adv* once; (*Zukunft*) one day

Einstand *m* (*Tennis*) deuce

einstecken *vt sep* put in; post ⟨*Brief*⟩; (*Electr*) plug in; (*fam: behalten*) pocket; (*fam: hinnehmen*) take; suffer ⟨*Niederlage*⟩

einsteigen† *vi sep* (*sein*) get in; (*in Bus/Zug*) get on

einstell|en *vt sep* put in; (*anstellen*) employ; (*aufhören*) stop; (*regulieren*) adjust, set; (*Optik*) focus; tune ⟨*Motor*⟩; tune to ⟨*Sender*⟩; **sich e~en auf** (+ *acc*) adjust to; (*sich vorbereiten*) prepare for. **E~ung** *f* employment; (*Regulierung*) adjustment; (*TV, Auto*) tuning; (*Haltung*) attitude

einstig *a* former

einstimmig *a* unanimous. **E~keit** *f* - unanimity

einstöckig *a* single-storey

einstudieren *vt sep* rehearse

einstufen *vt sep* classify

Einsturz *m* collapse. **e~stürzen** *vi sep* (*sein*) collapse

einstweilen *adv* for the time being; (*inzwischen*) meanwhile

eintasten *vt sep* key in

eintauchen *vt/i sep* (*sein*) dip in

eintauschen *vt sep* exchange

eintausend *inv a* one thousand

einteil|en *vt sep* divide (**in** + *acc* into); **sich** (*dat*) **seine Zeit gut e~en** organize one's time well. **e~ig** *a* one-piece. **E~ung** *f* division

eintönig *a* monotonous. **E~keit** *f* - monotony

Eintopf *m*, **E~gericht** *nt* stew

Eintracht *f* - harmony

Eintrag *m* **-[e]s,-̈e** entry. **e~en†** *vt sep* enter; (*Admin*) register; **sich e~en** put one's name down

einträglich *a* profitable

Eintragung *f* -,-en registration

eintreffen† *vi sep* (*sein*) arrive; (*fig*) come true

eintreiben† *vt sep* drive in; (*einziehen*) collect

eintreten† v sep □vi (sein) enter; (geschehen) occur; e~ für (fig) stand up for □vt kick in

Eintritt m entrance; (zu Veranstaltung) admission; (Beitritt) joining; (Beginn) beginning. E~skarte f [admission] ticket

einüben vt sep practise

einundachtzig inv a eighty-one

Einvernehmen nt understanding; (Übereinstimmung) agreement

einverstanden a e~ sein agree

Einverständnis nt agreement; (Zustimmung) consent

Einwand m -[e]s,-e objection

Einwander|er m immigrant. e~n vi sep (sein) immigrate. E~ung f immigration

einwandfrei a perfect; (untadelig) impeccable

einwärts adv inwards

einwechseln vt sep change

einwecken vt sep preserve, bottle

Einweg- pref non-returnable

einweichen vt sep soak

einweih|en vt sep inaugurate; (Relig) consecrate; (einführen) initiate; in ein Geheimnis e~en let into a secret. E~ung f -,-en inauguration; consecration; initiation

einweisen† vt sep direct; (einführen) initiate; ins Krankenhaus e~ send to hospital

einwerfen† vt sep insert; post ⟨Brief⟩; (Sport) throw in

einwickeln vt sep wrap [up]

einwillig|en vi sep (haben) consent, agree (in + acc to). E~ung f -consent

Einwohner(in) m -s, (f -,-nen) inhabitant. E~zahl f population

Einwurf m interjection; (Einwand) objection; (Sport) throwing; (Münz-) slot

Einzahl f (Gram) singular

einzahlen vt sep pay in. E~ung f payment; (Einlage) deposit

einzäunen vt sep fence in

Einzel nt -s,- (Tennis) singles pl. E~bett nt single bed. E~gänger m -s,- loner. E~haft f solitary confinement. E~handel m retail trade. E~händler m retailer. E~haus nt detached house. E~heit f -,-en detail. E~karte f single ticket. E~kind nt only child

einzeln a single; (individuell) individual; (gesondert) separate; odd ⟨Socken⟩; e~e Fälle some cases. e~e(r,s) pron der/die e~e the individual; im e~en in detail; e~e pl several

Einzel|teil nt [component] part. E~zimmer nt single room

einziehen† v sep □vt pull in; draw in ⟨Atem, Krallen⟩; (Zool, Techn) retract; (aus dem Verkehr ziehen) withdraw; (beschlagnahmen) confiscate; (eintreiben) collect; make ⟨Erkundigungen⟩; (Mil) call up; □vi (sein) enter; (umziehen) move in; (eindringen) penetrate

einzig a only; (einmalig) unique; eine e~e Frage a single question □adv only; e~ und allein solely. e~e(r,s) pron der/die/das e~e the only one; ein/kein e~er a/not a single one; das e~e, was mich stört the only thing that bothers me

Eis nt -es ice; (Speise-) ice-cream; Eis am Stiel ice lolly. E~bahn f ice rink. E~bär m polar bear. E~becher m ice-cream sundae. E~diele f ice-cream parlour

Eisen nt -s,- iron. E~bahn f railway

eisern a iron; (fest) resolute; e~er Vorhang (Theat) safety curtain; (Pol) Iron Curtain

Eis|fach nt freezer compartment. e~gekühlt a chilled. e~ig a icy. e~kaffee m iced coffee. e~lauf m skating. e~laufen†

Eisläufer *vi sep (sein)* skate. **E~läufer(in)** *m(f)* skater. **E~pickel** *m* ice-axe. **E~scholle** *f* ice-floe. **E~würfel** *m* ice-cube. **E~zapfen** *m* icicle. **E~zeit** *f* ice age

eitel *a* vain; *(rein)* pure. **E~keit** *f* vanity

Eiter *m* -s pus. **e~n** *vi (haben)* discharge pus

Eiweiß *nt* -es,-e egg-white

Ekel *m* -s disgust; *(Widerwille)* revulsion. **e~haft** *a* nauseating; *(widerlich)* repulsive. **e~n** *vt/i (haben)* **mich od mir e~t [es] davor** it makes me feel sick □ *vr* sich **e~n vor** (+ *dat*) find repulsive

eklig *a* disgusting, repulsive

Ekzem *nt* -s,-e eczema

elastisch *a* elastic; *(federnd)* springy; *(fig)* flexible. **E~zität** *f* -elasticity; flexibility

Elch *m* -[e]s,-e elk

Elefant *m* -en,-en elephant

elegant *a* elegant. **E~z** *f* -elegance

Elektriker *m* -s,- electrician. **e~sch** *a* electric, *adv* -ally

Elektrizität *f* -electricity. **E~swerk** *nt* power station

Elektroartikel *mpl* electrical appliances. **E~ode** *f* -,-n electrode. **E~oherd** *m* electric cooker. **E~onik** *f* -electronics *sg.* **e~onisch** *a* electronic

Elend *nt* -s misery; *(Armut)* poverty. **e~** *a* miserable; *(krank)* poorly; *(gemein)* contemptible. **E~sviertel** *nt* slum

elf *inv a* f, *m*. **E~** *f* -,-en eleven

Elfe *f* -,-n fairy

Elfenbein *nt* ivory

Elfmeter *m (Fußball)* penalty

elfte(r,s) *a* eleventh

Elite *f* -,-n élite

Ell[en]bogen *m* elbow

Ellipse *f* -,-n ellipse. **e~tisch** *a* elliptical

Elsaß *nt* -Alsace

elsässisch *a* Alsatian

Elster *f* -,-n magpie

elterlich *a* parental. **E~n** *pl* parents. **e~nlos** *a* orphaned. **E~nteil** *m* parent

Email /e'maj/ *nt* -s,-s, **E~le** /e'malja/ *f* -,-n enamel

Emanzipation /-'tsio:n/ *f* -emancipation. **e~piert** *a* emancipated

Embargo *nt* -s,-s embargo

Embryo *m* -s,-s embryo

Emigrant(in) *m* -en,-en *(f* -,-nen) emigrant. **E~ation** /-'tsio:n/ *f* -emigration. **e~ieren** *vi (sein)* emigrate

Empfang *m* -[e]s,-̈e reception; *(Erhalt)* receipt; **in E~ nehmen** receive; *(annehmen)* accept. **e~en†** *vt* receive; *(Biol)* conceive

Empfänger *m* -s,- recipient; *(Post-)* addressee; *(Zahlungs-)* payee; *(Radio, TV)* receiver. **E~nis** *f* -*(Biol)* conception

Empfängnisverhütung *f* contraception. **E~smittel** *nt* contraceptive

Empfangsbestätigung *f* receipt. **E~dame** *f* receptionist. **E~halle** *f* [hotel] foyer

empfehlen† *vt* recommend. **E~ung** *f* -,-en recommendation; *(Gruß)* regards *pl*

empfinden† *vt* feel. **e~lich** *a* sensitive *(gegen* to). **E~lichkeit** *f* -sensitivity; delicacy; tenderness; touchiness. **E~ung** *f* -,-en sensation; *(Regung)* feeling

empor *adv (liter)* up[wards]

empören *vt* incense; **sich e~** be indignant; *(sich auflehnen)* rebel

Emporkömmling *m* -s,-e upstart

empört *a* indignant. **E~ung** *f* -indignation; *(Auflehnung)* rebellion

Ende *nt* -s,-n end; *(eines Films)* ending; **zu E~ sein** be finished; **etw zu E~ schreiben** finish writing sth; **am E~** at the end;

(*schließlich*) in the end; (*fam: erschöpft*) at the end of one's tether

end|en *vi* (*haben*) end. **e~gültig** *a* final; (*bestimmt*) definite

Endivie /-ĭə/ *f* -,-n endive

end|lich *adv* at last, finally; (*schließlich*) in the end. **e~los** *a* endless. **E~station** *f* terminus. **E~ung** *f* -,-en (*Gram*) ending

Energie *f* - energy

energisch *a* resolute; (*nachdrücklich*) vigorous

eng *a* narrow; (*beengt*) cramped; (*anliegend*) tight; (*nah*) close

Engagement /āgažə'mã:/ *nt* -s,-s (*Theat*) engagement; (*fig*) commitment

eng|anliegend *a* tight-fitting. **E~e** *f* - narrowness; **in die E~e treiben** (*fig*) drive into a corner

Engel *m* -s,- angel

England *nt* -s England

Engländer *m* -s,- Englishman; **die E~** the English *pl*. **E~in** *f* -,-nen Englishwoman

englisch *a* English; **auf e~** in English. **E~** *nt* -[s] (*Lang*) English

Engpaß *m* (*fig*) bottle-neck

en gros /ã'gro:/ *adv* wholesale

Enkel *m* -s,- grandson. **E~** *pl* grandchildren. **E~in** *f* -,-nen granddaughter. **E~kind** *nt* grandchild. **E~sohn** *m* grandson. **E~tochter** *f* granddaughter

Ensemble /ã'sã:bəl/ *nt* -s,-s ensemble; (*Theat*) company

entart|en *vi* (*sein*) degenerate. **e~et** *a* degenerate

entbehren *vt* do without; (*vermissen*) miss

entbind|en *vt* release (*von* from); (*Med*) deliver (*von of*)□*vi* (*haben*) give birth. **E~ung** *f* delivery. **E~ungsstation** *f* maternity ward

entdeck|en *vt* discover. **E~er** *m* -s,- discoverer; (*Forscher*) explorer. **E~ung** *f* -,-en discovery

Ente *f* -,-n duck

entehren *vt* dishonour

enteign|en *vt* dispossess; expropriate (*Eigentum*)

enterben *vt* disinherit

Enterich *m* -s,-e drake

entfallen† *vi* not apply; **auf jdn e~** be s.o.'s share

entfern|en *vt* remove; **sich e~en** leave. **e~t** *a* distant; (*schwach*) vague; **2 Kilometer e~t** 2 kilometres away; **e~t verwandt** distantly related. **E~ung** *f* -,-en removal; (*Abstand*) distance; (*Reichweite*) range

entfremden *vt* alienate

entfrosten *vt* defrost

entführ|en *vt* abduct, kidnap; hijack (*Flugzeug*). **E~er** *m* abductor, kidnapper; hijacker. **E~ung** *f* abduction, kidnapping; hijacking

entgegen *adv* towards □*prep* (+ *dat*) contrary to. **e~gehen†** *vi sep* (*sein*) (+ *dat*) go to meet; (*fig*) be heading for. **e~gesetzt** *a* opposite; (*gegensätzlich*) opposing. **e~kommen†** *vi sep* (*sein*) (+ *dat*) come to meet; (*zukommen auf*) come towards; (*fig*) oblige. **E~kommen** *nt* -s helpfulness; (*Zugeständnis*) concession. **e~kommend** *a* approaching; (*Verkehr*) oncoming; (*fig*) obliging. **e~wirken** *vi sep* (*haben*) (+ *dat*) counteract; (*fig*) oppose

entgegn|en *vt/i* reply (**auf** + *acc* to). **E~ung** *f* -,-en reply

entgehen† *vi sep* (*sein*) (+ *dat*) escape; **jdm e~** (*unbemerkt bleiben*) escape s.o.'s notice; **sich** (*dat*) **etw e~ lassen** miss sth

Entgelt *nt* -[e]s payment; **gegen E~** for money

entgleis|en vi (sein) be derailed; (fig) make a gaffe. **E~ung** f -,-en derailment; (fig) gaffe

entgräten vt fillet, bone

Enthaarungsmittel nt depilatory

enthalt|en† vt contain; **in etw** (dat) ~ **sein** be contained/ (eingeschlossen) included in sth; **sich der Stimme e~en** (Pol) abstain. **e~sam** a abstemious. **E~ung** f (Pol) abstention

enthaupten vt behead

entheben† vt **jdn seines Amtes e~** relieve s.o. of his post

Enthusias|mus m - enthusiasm. **E~t** m -en,-en enthusiast

entkernen vt stone; core (Apfel)

entkleid|en vt undress; **sich e~en** undress

entkommen† vi (sein) escape

entkorken vt uncork

entlad|en† vt unload; (Electr) discharge; **sich e~en** discharge; (Gewitter:) break; (Zorn:) explode

entlang adv & prep (+ preceding acc or following dat) along; **die Straße e~** along the road; **an etw** (dat) **e~** along sth. **e~fahren†** vi sep (sein) drive along. **e~gehen†** vi sep (sein) walk along

entlarven vt unmask

entlass|en† vt dismiss; (aus Krankenhaus) discharge; (aus der Haft) release. **E~ung** f -,-en dismissal; discharge; release

entlast|en vt relieve the strain on; ease (Gewissen, Verkehr); relieve (von d); (Jur) exonerate. **E~ung** f - relief; exoneration

entlaufen† vi (sein) run away

entlegen a remote

entleihen† vt borrow (von from)

entlohnen vt pay

entlüft|en vt ventilate. **E~er** m -s,- extractor fan. **E~ung** f ventilation

entmündigen vt declare incapable of managing his own affairs

entmutigen vt discourage

entnehmen† vt take (dat from); (schließen) gather (dat from)

entpuppen (sich) vr (fig) turn out (**als etw** to be sth)

entrahmt a skimmed

entrinnen† vi (sein) escape

entrüst|en vt fill with indignation; **sich e~en** be indignant (**über** + acc at). **e~et** a indignant. **E~ung** f - indignation

entsaft|en vt extract the juice from. **E~er** m -s,- juice extractor

entschädig|en vt compensate. **E~ung** f -,-en compensation

entschärfen vt defuse

entscheid|en† vt/i (haben) decide; **sich e~en** decide; (Sache:) be decided. **e~end** a decisive. **E~ung** f decision

entschließen (sich) vr decide, make up one's mind; **sich anders e~** change one's mind

entschlossen a determined; (energisch) resolute; **kurz e~** without hesitation. **E~heit** f - determination

Entschluß m decision

entschlüsseln vt decode

entschuld|bar a excusable. **e~igen** vt excuse; **sich e~igen** apologize (**bei** to); **e~igen Sie [bitte]!** sorry! (bei Frage) excuse me. **E~igung** f -,-en apology; (Ausrede) excuse

entsetz|en vt horrify. **E~en** nt -s horror. **e~lich** a horrible; (schrecklich) terrible

Entsorgung f - waste disposal

entspann|en vt relax; **sich e~en** relax; (Lage:) ease. **E~ung** f - relaxation; easing; (Pol) détente

entsprech|en† vi (haben) (+ dat) correspond to; (übereinstimmen) agree with. **e~end** a corresponding; (angemessen) appropriate;

entspringen (*zuständig*) relevant □ *adv* correspondingly; appropriately □ *prep* (+ *dat*) in accordance with

entspringen† *vi* (sein) ⟨*Fluß:*⟩ rise; (*fig*) arise, spring (*dat* from)

entstammen *vi* (sein) come/(*abstammen*) be descended (*dat* from)

entstehen|en† *vi* (sein) come into being; (*sich bilden*) form; (*sich entwickeln*) develop; ⟨*Brand:*⟩ start. **E~ung** *f* · origin; formation; development

entstellen *vt* disfigure; (*verzerren*) distort. **E~ung** *f* disfigurement; distortion

entstört *a* (*Electr*) suppressed

enttäuschen *vt* disappoint. **E~ung** *f* disappointment

entwaffnen *vt* disarm

entwässer|n *vt* drain. **E~ung** *f* drainage

entweder *conj & adv* either

entwerfen† *vt* design; (*aufsetzen*) draft; (*skizzieren*) sketch

entwert|en *vt* devalue; (*ungültig machen*) cancel. **E~er** *m* -s,- ticket-cancelling machine. **E~ung** *f* devaluation; cancelling

entwick|eln *vt* develop; **sich e~eln** develop. **E~lung** *f* -,-en development; (*Biol*) evolution. **E~lungsland** *nt* developing country

entwöhnen *vt* wean (*gen* from); cure ⟨*Süchtige*⟩

entwürdigend *a* degrading

Entwurf *m* design; (*Konzept*) draft; (*Skizze*) sketch

entwurzeln *vt* uproot

entzieh|en† *vt* take away (*dat* from); **jdm den Führerschein e~hen** disqualify s.o. from driving. **E~hungskur** *f* treatment for drug/alcohol addiction

entziffern *vt* decipher

Entzug *m* withdrawal; (*Vorenthaltung*) deprivation

entzünd|en *vt* ignite; (*anstecken*) light; (*fig: erregen*) inflame; **sich e~en** ignite; (*Med*) become inflamed. **e~et** *a* (*Med*) inflamed. **e~lich** *a* inflammable. **E~ung** *f* (*Med*) inflammation

entzwei *a* broken

Enzian *m* -s,-e gentian

Enzyklo|pädie *f* -,-en encyclopaedia. **e~pädisch** *a* encyclopaedic

Enzym *nt* -s,-e enzyme

Epidemie *f* -,-n epidemic

Epi|lepsie *f* epilepsy. **E~leptiker(in)** *m* -s,- (*f* -,-nen) epileptic. **e~leptisch** *a* epileptic

Epilog *m* -s,-e epilogue

Episode *f* -,-n episode

Epoche *f* -,-n epoch

Epos *nt* -/Epen epic

er *pron* he; (*Ding, Tier*) it

erachten *vt* consider (**für nötig** necessary). **E~** *nt* -s **meines E~s** is my opinion

erbarmen (sich) *vr* have pity/ ⟨*Gott:*⟩ mercy (*gen* on). **E~** *nt* -s pity; mercy

erbärmlich *a* wretched

erbarmungslos *a* merciless

erbauen *vt* build; **nicht e~t von** (*fam*) not pleased about

Erbe¹ *m* -n,-n heir

Erbe² *nt* -s inheritance; (*fig*) heritage. **e~n** *vt* inherit

erbeuten *vt* get; (*Mil!*) capture

Erbfolge *f* (*Jur*) succession

Erbin *f* -,-nen heiress

erbitten† *vt* ask for

erbittert *a* bitter; (*heftig*) fierce

erblich *a* hereditary

erblicken *vt* catch sight of

erblinden *vi* (sein) go blind

erbrechen† *vt* vomit □ *vi/r* [**sich**] **e~** vomit. **E~** *nt* -s vomiting

Erbschaft *f* -,-en inheritance

Erbse *f* -,-n pea

Erb|stück *nt* heirloom. **E~teil** *nt* inheritance

Erd|apfel m (Aust) potato.
E~beben nt -s,- earthquake.
E~beere f strawberry
Erde f -,-n earth; ground; (Fußboden) floor; **auf der E~** on
earth. **e~n** vt (Electr) earth
erdenklich a imaginable
Erd|gas nt natural gas. **E~ge-
schoß** nt ground floor. **E~kugel**
f globe. **E~kunde** f geography.
E~nuß f peanut. **E~öl** nt [mi-
neral] oil
erdrosseln vt strangle
erdrücken vt crush to death.
e~d a (fig) overwhelming
Erd|rutsch m landslide. **E~teil**
m continent
erdulden vt endure
ereignen (sich) vr happen
Ereignis nt -ses,-se event. **e~los**
a uneventful. **e~reich** a event-
ful
Eremit m -en,-en hermit
erfahr|en† vt learn, hear; (erle-
ben) experience □a experienced.
E~ung f -,-en experience; in
E~ung bringen find out
erfassen vt seize; (begreifen)
grasp; (einbeziehen) include; (aufzeichnen) record
erfind|en† vt invent. **E~er** m -s,-
inventor. **e~erisch** a inventive.
E~ung f -,-en invention
Erfolg m -[e]s,-e success; (Folge)
result. **e~ haben** be successful.
e~en vi (sein) take place; (geschehen) happen. **e~los** a unsuc-
cessful. **e~reich** a successful
erforder|lich a required, neces-
sary. **e~n** vt require, demand
erforschen vt explore; (untersuchen) investigate. **E~ung** f ex-
ploration; investigation
erfreu|en vt please. **e~lich** a
pleasing. **e~licherweise** adv
happily. **e~t** a pleased
erfrier|en† vi (sein) freeze to
death; ⟨Glied:⟩ become frostbit-
ten. **E~ung** f -,-en frostbite

erfrisch|en vt refresh. **E~ung** f
-,-en refreshment
erfüll|en vt fill; (nachkommen)
fulfil; serve ⟨Zweck⟩; discharge
⟨Pflicht⟩; **sich e~en** come true.
E~ung f fulfilment
ergänz|en vt complement; (hinzu-
fügen) add. **E~ung** f complement; supplement; (Zusatz) addition
ergeben† vt produce; (zeigen)
show, establish; **sich e~** result;
⟨Schwierigkeit:⟩ arise; (sich fügen) submit; □a devoted; (resi-
gniert) resigned
Ergebnis nt -ses,-se result.
e~los a fruitless
ergiebig a productive; (fig) rich
ergreifen† vt seize; take ⟨Maß-
nahme, Gelegenheit⟩; take up ⟨Be-
ruf⟩; ⟨rühren⟩ move; **die Flucht
e~** flee. **e~d** a moving
ergriffen a deeply moved.
E~heit f - emotion
ergründen vt (fig) get to the bottom of
erhaben a raised; (fig) sublime
Erhalt m -[e]s receipt. **e~en†** vt
receive, get; (gewinnen) obtain;
(bewahren) preserve, keep; (in-
standhalten) maintain; (unterhalten) support; **am Leben e~en**
keep alive □a **gut/schlecht
e~en** in good/bad condition
erhältlich a obtainable
Erhaltung f - (s. erhalten) preservation; maintenance
erhängen (sich) vr hang oneself
erheben† vt raise; levy ⟨Steuer⟩;
charge ⟨Gebühr⟩; **Anspruch
e~en** lay claim (**auf**+acc to);
Protest e~en protest; **sich
e~en** rise; ⟨Frage:⟩ arise.
e~lich a considerable. **E~ung** f
-,-en elevation; (Anhöhe) rise;
(Aufstand) uprising; (Ermitt-
lung) survey
erheiter|n vt amuse. **E~ung** f -
amusement

erhitzen *vt* heat

erhöh|en *vt* raise; *(fig)* increase; **sich e~en** rise, increase. **E~ung** *f* -,-en increase

erhol|en (sich) *vr* recover (von from); *(nach Krankheit)* convalesce; *(sich ausruhen)* have a rest. **e~sam** *a* restful. **E~ung** *f* - recovery; convalescence; *(Ruhe)* rest

erinner|n *vt* remind (an + *acc* of); **sich e~n** remember (an jdn/etw s.o./sth). **E~ung** *f* -,-en memory; *(Andenken)* souvenir

erkält|en (sich) *vr* catch a cold; **e~et sein** have a cold. **E~ung** *f* -,-en cold

erkenn|bar *a* recognizable; *(sichtbar)* visible. **e~en†** *vt* recognize; *(wahrnehmen)* distinguish. **E~tnis** *f* -,-se recognition; realization; *(Wissen)* knowledge; **die neuesten E~tnisse** the latest findings

Erker *m* -s,- bay

erklär|en *vt* declare; *(erläutern)* explain; **sich bereit e~en** agree (zu to). **e~lich** *a* explicable. *(verständlich)* understandable. **e~licherweise** *adv* understandably. **E~ung** *f* -,-en declaration; explanation; **öffentliche E~ung** public statement

erkrank|en *vi (sein)* fall ill; be taken ill (an + *dat* with). **E~ung** *f* -,-en illness

erkundig|en (sich) *vr* enquire *(nach* jdm/etw after s.o./about sth). **E~ung** *f* -,-en enquiry

Erlaß *m* -sses, -sse *(Admin)* decree; *(Befreiung)* exemption; *(Straf-)* remission

erlass|en† *vt (Admin)* issue; jdm etw **e~** exempt s.o. from sth; let s.o. off *(Strafe)*

erlauben *vt* allow, permit

Erlaubnis *f* -, permission. **E~schein** *m* permit

Erle *f* -,-n alder

erleb|en *vt* experience; *(mit-)* see; have *(Überraschung)*. **E~nis** *nt* -ses,-se *(Erfahrung)* experience

erledigen *vt* do; *(sich befassen mit)* deal with; *(beenden)* finish; *(entscheiden)* settle; *(töten)* kill

erleichter|n *vt* lighten; *(vereinfachen)* make easier; *(befreien)* relieve; *(lindern)* ease. **e~t** *a* relieved. **E~ung** *f* - relief

erleiden† *vt* suffer

erleucht|en *vt* illuminate; **hell e~et** brightly lit

erlogen *a* untrue, false

Erlös *m* -es proceeds *pl*

erlösch|en† *vi (sein)* go out; *(vergehen)* die; *(aussterben)* die out; *(ungültig werden)* expire; **erloschener Vulkan** extinct volcano

erlös|en *vt* save; *(befreien)* release (von from); *(Relig)* redeem. **e~t** *a* relieved. **E~ung** *f* release; *(Erleichterung)* relief; *(Relig)* redemption

ermächtig|en *vt* authorize. **E~ung** *f* -,-en authorization

ermäßig|en *vt* reduce. **E~ung** *f* -,-en reduction

ermessen† *vt* judge; *(begreifen)* appreciate. **E~** *nt* -s discretion; *(Urteil)* judgement; **nach eigenem E~** at one's own discretion

ermittel|n *vt* establish; *(herausfinden)* find out □*vi (haben)* investigate (gegen jdn s.o.). **E~lungen** *fpl* investigations. **E~lungsverfahren** *nt (Jur)* preliminary inquiry

ermöglichen *vt* make possible

ermord|en *vt* murder. **E~ung** *f* -,-en murder

ermüd|en *vt* tire □*vi (sein)* get tired. **E~ung** *f* - tiredness

ermutigen *vt* encourage. **e~d** *a* encouraging

ernähr|en *vt* feed; *(unterhalten)* support, keep; **sich e~en** von live/*(Tier:)* feed on. **E~er** *m* -s,-

breadwinner. **E~ung** f - nourishment; nutrition; (*Kost*) diet

ernennen† vt appoint. **E~ung** f -,-en appointment

erneu|ern vt renew; (*auswechseln*) replace; change (*Verband*); (*renovieren*) renovate. **E~erung** f renewal; replacement; renovation. **e~t** a renewed; (*neu*) new □ *adv* again

ernst a serious; **e~ nehmen** take seriously. **E~** m -es seriousness; **im E~** seriously; **mit einer Drohung E~ machen** carry out a threat; **ist das dein E~?** are you serious? **e~haft** a serious. **e~lich** a serious

Ernte f -,-n harvest; (*Ertrag*) crop. **E~dankfest** nt harvest festival. **e~n** vt harvest; (*fig*) reap, win

ernüchtern vt sober up; (*fig*) bring down to earth. **e~nd** a (*fig*) sobering

Erober|er m -s,- conqueror. **e~n** vt conquer. **E~ung** f -,-en conquest

eröffn|en vt open; **jdm etw e~en** announce sth to s.o. **E~ung** f opening; (*Mitteilung*) announcement

erörter|n vt discuss. **E~ung** f -,-en discussion

Erot|ik f - eroticism. **e~isch** a erotic

Erpel m -s,- drake

erpicht a **e~ auf** (+ *acc*) keen on

erpress|en vt extort; blackmail (*Person*). **E~er** m -s,- blackmailer. **E~ung** f - extortion; blackmail

erproben vt test. **e~t** a proven

erraten† vt guess

erreg|bar a excitable. **e~en** vt excite; (*hervorrufen*) arouse. **e~end** a exciting. **E~er** m -s,- (*Med*) germ. **e~t** a agitated; (*hitzig*) heated. **E~ung** f - excitement

erreich|bar a within reach; (*Ziel*) attainable; (*Person*) available. **e~en** vt reach; catch (*Zug*); live to (*Alter*); (*durchsetzen*) achieve

errichten vt erect

erringen† vt gain, win

erröten vi (*sein*) blush

Errungenschaft f -,-en achievement; (*fam: Anschaffung*) acquisition

Ersatz m -es replacement, substitute; (*Entschädigung*) compensation. **E~reifen** m spare tyre. **E~teil** nt spare part

erschaffen† vt create

erschein|en† vi (*sein*) appear; (*Buch:*) be published. **E~ung** f -,-en appearance; (*Person*) figure; (*Phänomen*) phenomenon; (*Symptom*) symptom; (*Geist*) apparition

erschießen† vt shoot [dead]. **E~ungskommando** nt firing squad

erschlaffen vi (*sein*) go limp

erschlagen† vt beat to death; (*tödlich treffen*) strike dead; **vom Blitz e~ werden** be killed by lightning

erschließen† vt develop; (*zugänglich machen*) open up

erschöpf|en vt exhaust. **e~t** a exhausted. **E~ung** f - exhaustion

erschreck|en† vi (*sein*) get a fright □ vt (*reg*) startle; (*beunruhigen*) alarm; **du hast mich e~t** you gave me a fright

erschrocken a frightened; (*erschreckt*) startled

erschütter|n vt shake; (*ergreifen*) upset deeply. **E~ung** f -,-en shock

erschwinglich a affordable

ersehen† vt (*fig*) see (aus from)

ersetzen vt replace; make good (*Schaden*); refund (*Kosten*); **jdm etw e~** compensate s.o. for sth

ersichtlich a obvious, apparent

erspar|en vt save. **E~nis** f -,-se saving; **E~nisse** savings

erst adv (zuerst) first; (noch nicht mehr als) only; (nicht vor) not until; **e~ dann** only then; **eben e~** [only] just

erstarren vi (sein) solidify; (gefrieren) freeze; (steif werden) go stiff; (vor Schreck) be paralysed

erstatten vt (zurück-) refund; **Bericht e~** report (jdm to s.o.)

Erstaufführung f first performance, première

erstaun|en vt amaze, astonish. **E~en** nt amazement, astonishment. **e~lich** a amazing

Erst|ausgabe f first edition. **e~e(r,s)** a first; (beste) best; **E~e Hilfe** first aid; **als e~es** first of all; **fürs e~e** for the time being. **E~e(r)** m/f/best

erstechen† vt stab to death

ersteigern vt buy at an auction

erst|ens adv firstly, in the first place. **e~ere(r,s)** a the former; **der/die/das e~ere** the former

ersticken vt suffocate; smother ⟨Flammen⟩ ● vi (sein) suffocate. **E~nt** -s suffocation; **zum E~** stifling

erst|klassig a first-class. **e~mals** adv for the first time

ersuchen vt ask, request. **E~nt** -s request

ertappen vt (fam) catch

erteilen vt give (jdm s.o.)

ertönen vi (sein) sound; (erschallen) ring out

Ertrag m -[e]s,-̈e yield. **e~en†** vt bear

erträglich a bearable

ertränken vt drown

ertrinken† vi (sein) drown

erübrigen (sich) vr be unnecessary

erwachsen a grown-up. **E~e(r)** m/f adult, grown-up

erwägen† vt consider. **E~ung** f -,-en consideration; **in E~ung ziehen** consider

erwähnen vt mention

erwärmen vt warm; **sich e~** warm up; (fig) warm (für to)

erwart|en vt expect; (warten auf) wait for. **E~ung** f -,-en expectation. **e~ungsvoll** a expectant

erweisen† vt prove; (bezeigen) do ⟨Gefallen, Dienst, Ehre⟩; **sich e~ als** prove to be

erweiter|n vt widen; dilate ⟨Pupille⟩; (fig) extend, expand

Erwerb m -[e]s acquisition; (Kauf) purchase; (Brot-) livelihood; (Verdienst) earnings pl. **e~en†** vt acquire; (kaufen) purchase. **e~slos** a unemployed. **e~stätig** a employed

erwider|n vt reply; return ⟨Besuch, Gruß⟩. **E~ung** f -,-en reply

erwirken vt obtain

erwürgen vt strangle

Erz nt -es,-e ore

erzähl|en vt tell (jdm s.o.) ● vi (haben) talk (von about). **E~er** m -s,- narrator. **E~ung** f -,-en story, tale

Erzbischof m archbishop

erzeug|en vt produce; (Electr) generate. **E~er** m -s,- producer. **E~nis** nt -ses,-se product; **landwirtschaftliche E~nisse** farm produce sg

Erzfeind m arch-enemy

erzieh|en† vt bring up; (Sch) educate. **E~er** m -s,- [private] tutor. **E~erin** f -,-nen governess. **E~ung** f -upbringing; education

erzielen vt achieve; score ⟨Tor⟩

erzogen a gut/schlecht e~ well/ badly brought up

es pron it; (Mädchen) she; (acc) her; impers es regnet it is raining; **es gibt** there is/(pl) are

Esche f -,-n ash

Esel m -s,- donkey; (fam: Person) ass

Eskimo *m* -[s],-[s] eskimo

Eskort|**e** *f* -,-n (Mil) escort. **e~ieren** *vt* escort

eßbar *a* edible

essen† *vt/i* (haben) eat; **zu Mittag/Abend e~** have lunch/supper; **e~ gehen** eat out. **E~** *nt* -s,- food; (*Mahl*) meal; (*festlich*) dinner

Esser(in) *m* -s,- (*f* -,-nen) eater

Essig *m* -s vinegar. **E~gurke** *f* [pickled] gherkin

Eßlöffel *m* ≈ dessertspoon. **Eßstäbchen** *ntpl* chopsticks. **Eßtisch** *m* dining-table. **Eßwaren** *fpl* food *sg*; (*Vorräte*) provisions. **Eßzimmer** *nt* dining-room

Estland *nt* -s Estonia

Estragon *m* -s tarragon

etablieren (*sich*) *vr* establish oneself/⟨*Geschäft*⟩ itself

Etage /e'ta:ʒə/ *f* -,-n storey. **E~nbett** *nt* bunk-beds *pl*. **E~nwohnung** *f* flat

Etappe *f* -,-n stage

Etat /e'ta:/ *m* -s,-s budget

Eth|**ik** *f* - ethic; (*Sittenlehre*) ethics *sg*. **e~isch** *a* ethical

Etikett *nt* -[e]s,-e[n] label; (*Preis-*) tag. **e~ieren** *vt* label

Etui /e'tvi:/ *nt* -s,-s case

etwa *adv* (*ungefähr*) about; (*zum Beispiel*) for instance; (*womöglich*) perhaps; **nicht e~**, **daß** ... not that ...; **denkt nicht e~** ... don't imagine ...

etwas *pron* something; (*fragend/verneint*) anything; (*ein bißchen*) some, a little; **sonst noch e~?** anything else? **so e~** **Ärgerliches!** what a nuisance! □ *adv* a bit

Etymologie *f* - etymology

euch *pron* (*acc of* **ihr** *pl*) you; (*dat*) [to] you; (*refl*) yourselves; (*einander*) each other

euer *poss pron pl* your. **e~e** = **eure**, **euret-**

Eule *f* -,-n owl

Euphorie *f* - euphoria

eur|**e** *poss pron pl* your. **e~e(r,s)** *poss pron* yours. **e~etwegen** *adv* for your sake; (*wegen euch*) because of you. **e~etwillen** *adv* **um e~etwillen** for your sake. **e~ige** *poss pron* **der/die/das e~ige** yours

Euro- *pref* Euro-

Europa *nt* -s Europe. **E~-** *pref* European

Europä|**er(in)** *m* -s,- (*f* -,-nen) European. **e~isch** *a* European

Euro|**paß** *m* Europassport. **E~scheck** *m* Eurocheque

Euter *nt* -s,- udder

evakuier|**en** *vt* evacuate. **E~ung** *f* - evacuation

evangelisch *a* Protestant. **E~gelium** *nt* -s,-ien gospel

eventuell *a* possible □ *adv* possibly; (*vielleicht*) perhaps

Evolution /-'tsjo:n/ *f* - evolution

ewig *a* eternal. (*endlos*) neverending; **e~ dauern** (*fam*) take ages. **E~keit** *f* - eternity

Examen *nt* -s,- *&* -mina (*Sch*) examination

Exemplar *nt* -s,-e specimen; (*Buch*) copy. **e~isch** *a* exemplary

exerzieren *vt/i* (haben) (Mil) drill; (*üben*) practise

exhumieren *vt* exhume

Exil *nt* -s exile

Existenz *f* -,-en existence; (*Lebensgrundlage*) livelihood

existieren *vi* (haben) exist

exklusiv *a* exclusive. **e~e** *prep* (+ *gen*) excluding

exkommunizieren *vt* excommunicate

Exkremente *npl* excrement *sg*

Expedition /-'tsjo:n/ *f* -,-en expedition

Experiment *nt* -[e]s,-e experiment. **e~ieren** *vi* (haben) experiment

Experte *m* -n,-n expert

explo|dieren vi (sein) explode. **E ~ sion** f -,-en explosion

Export m -[e]s,-e export. **E ~ teur** /-'tø:ɐ/ m -s,-e exporter. **e ~ tieren** vt export

extra adv separately; (zusätzlich) extra; (eigens) specially; (fam: absichtlich) on purpose

extravagant a flamboyant; (übertrieben) extravagant

extravertiert a extrovert

extrem a extreme. **E ~ nt** -s,-e extreme. **E ~ ist** m -en,-en extremist

Exzellenz f - (title) Excellency

Exzentr|iker m -s,- eccentric. **e ~ isch** a eccentric

F

Fabel f -,-n fable. **f ~ haft** a (fam) fantastic

Fabrik f -,-en factory. **F ~ ant** m -en,-en manufacturer. **F ~ at** nt -[e]s,-e product; (Marke) make. **F ~ ation** /-'tsio:n/ f - manufacture

Fach nt -[e]s,-er compartment; (Schub-) drawer; (Gebiet) field; (Sch) subject. **F ~ arbeiter** m skilled worker. **F ~ arzt** m, **F ~ ärztin** f specialist. **F ~ ausdruck** m technical term

Fächer m -s,- fan

Fach|gebiet nt field. **f ~ kundig** a expert. **f ~ lich** a technical; (beruflich) professional. **F ~ mann** m (pl -leute) expert. **F ~ schule** f technical college. **F ~ werkhaus** nt half-timbered house. **F ~ wort** nt (pl -wörter) technical term

Fackel f -,-n torch

Faden m -s, thread; (Bohnen-) string; (Naut) fathom

Fagott nt -[e]s,-e bassoon

fähig a capable (zu/gen of); (tüchtig) able, competent. **F ~ keit** f -,-en ability; competence

fahl a pale

fahnd|en vi (haben) search (nach for). **F ~ ung** f -,-en search

Fahne f -,-n flag; (Druck-) galley [proof]; **eine F ~ haben** (fam) reek of alcohol. **F ~ nflucht** f desertion

Fahr|ausweis m ticket. **F ~ bahn** f carriageway; (Straße) road. **f ~ bar** a mobile

Fähre f -,-n ferry

fahr|en† vi (sein) go, travel; (Fahrer:) drive; (Radfahrer:) ride; (verkehren) run; (ab-) leave; (Schiff:) sail; **mit dem Auto/Zug f ~ en** go by car/train; **was ist in ihn gefahren?** (fam) what has got into him? □vt drive; ride (Fahrrad); take (Kurve). **f ~ end** a moving; (f ~ bar) mobile; (nicht seßhaft) travelling. **F ~ er** m -s,- driver. **F ~ erflucht** f failure to stop after an accident. **F ~ erhaus** nt driver's cab. **F ~ erin** f -,-nen woman driver. **F ~ gast** m passenger; (im Taxi) fare. **F ~ geld** nt fare. **F ~ gestell** nt chassis; (Aviat) undercarriage. **F ~ karte** f ticket. **F ~ kartenausgabe** m ticket office. **F ~ lässigkeit** f -negligence. **F ~ lehrer** m driving instructor. **F ~ plan** m timetable. **f ~ planmäßig** a scheduled □adv according to/(pünktlich) on schedule. **F ~ preis** m fare. **F ~ prüfung** f driving test. **F ~ rad** nt bicycle. **F ~ schein** m ticket. **F ~ schule** f driving school. **F ~ schüler(in)** m(f) learner driver. **F ~ stuhl** m lift

Fahrt f -,-en journey; (Auto) drive; (Ausflug) trip; (Tempo) speed

Fährte f -,-n track; (Witterung) scent

Fahr|tkosten *pl* travelling expenses. **F~werk** *nt* undercarriage. **F~zeug** *nt* -[e]s,-e vehicle; (*Wasser*-) craft, vessel

Fakultät *f* -,-en faculty

Falke *m* -n,-n falcon

Fall *m* -[e]s,-̈e fall; (*Jur, Med, Gram*) case; **im F~ [e]** in case (*gen* of); **auf jeden F~** , **auf alle F~e** in any case; (*bestimmt*) definitely; **für alle F~e** just in case; **auf keinen F~** no no account

Falle *f* -,-n trap

fallen† *vi* (*sein*) fall; (*sinken*) go down; (*im Krieg*) be killed

fällen *vt* fell; (*fig*) pass (*Urteil*)

fallenlassen† *vt sep* (*fig*) drop; make (*Bemerkung*)

fällig *a* due; (*Wechsel*) mature; **längst f~** long overdue. **F~keit** *f* -(*Comm*) maturity

falls *conj* in case; (*wenn*) if

Fallschirm *m* parachute. **F~jäger** *m* paratrooper. **F~springer** *m* parachutist

Falltür *f* trapdoor

falsch *a* wrong; (*nicht echt, unaufrichtig*) false; (*gefälscht*) forged; (*Geld*) counterfeit; (*Schmuck*) fake ☐*adv* wrongly; falsely; (*singen*) out of tune; **f~ gehen** (*Uhr*:) be wrong

fälschen *vt* forge, fake

fälschlich *a* wrong; (*irrtümlich*) mistaken; **f~erweise** *adv* by mistake

Falsch|meldung *f* false report; (*absichtlich*) hoax report. **F~münzer** *m* -s,- counterfeiter

Fälschung *f* -,-en forgery, fake

Falte *f* -,-n fold; (*Rock*-) pleat; (*Knitter*-) crease; (*im Gesicht*) line; (*Runzel*) wrinkle

falten *vt* fold

Falter *m* -s,- butterfly; moth

faltig *a* creased; (*Gesicht*) lined; (*runzlig*) wrinkled

familiär *a* family ...; (*vertraut*) familiar; (*zwanglos*) informal

Familie /-iə/ *f* -,-n family. **F~nforschung** *f* genealogy. **F~nname** *m* surname. **F~nstand** *m* marital status

Fan /fɛn/ *m* -s,-s fan

Fana|tiker *m* -s,- fanatic. **f~tisch** *a* fanatical

Fanfare *f* -,-n trumpet; (*Signal*) fanfare

Fang *m* -[e]s,-̈e capture; (*Beute*) catch; **F~e** (*Krallen*) talons; (*Zähne*) fangs. **F~arm** *m* tentacle. **f~en†** *vt* catch; (*ein-*) capture. **F~en** *nt* -s **F~en spielen** play tag. **F~frage** *f* catch question

Farb|aufnahme *f* colour photograph. **F~band** *nt* (*pl* -bänder) typewriter ribbon. **F~e** *f* -,-n colour; (*Maler*-) paint; (*zum Färben*) dye; (*Karten*) suit. **f~echt** *a* colour-fast

färben *vt* colour; dye (*Textilien*); ☐*vi* (*haben*) not be colour-fast

farben|blind *a* colour-blind. **f~enfroh** *a* colourful. **F~fernsehen** *nt* colour television. **f~ig** *a* coloured ☐*adv* in colour. **F~ige(r)** *m/f* coloured man/woman. **F~kasten** *m* box of paints. **f~los** *a* colourless. **F~stift** *m* crayon. **F~stoff** *m* dye; (*Lebensmittel*-) colouring. **F~ton** *m* shade

Farn *m* -[e]s,-e, **F~kraut** *nt* fern

Färse *f* -,-n heifer

Fasan *m* -[e]s,-e[n] pheasant

Faschierte(s) *nt* (*Aust*) mince

Fasching *m* -s (*SGer*) carnival

Faschis|mus *m* - fascism. **F~t** *m* -en,-en fascist. **f~tisch** *a* fascist

Faser *f* -,-n fibre. **f~n** *vi* (*haben*) fray

Faß *nt* -sses,-̈sser barrel, cask; **Bier vom Faß** draught beer

Fassade *f* -,-n façade

faßbar *a* comprehensible

fassen *vt* take [hold of], grasp; (*ergreifen*) seize; (*fangen*) catch;

(ein-) set; *(enthalten)* hold; *(fig: begreifen)* take in, grasp; conceive ⟨Plan⟩; make ⟨Entschluß⟩; **sich f~** compose oneself; **sich kurz f~** be brief; **nicht zu f~** *(fig)* unbelievable □ *vi (haben)* **f~ an** (+ *acc*) touch

Fassung *f (-,-en* grasp; *(Edelstein-)* setting; *(Electr)* socket; *(Version)* version; *(Beherrschung)* composure; **aus der F~ bringen** disconcert. **f~slos** *a* shaken; *(erstaunt)* flabbergasted

fast *adv* almost, nearly; **f~ nie** hardly ever

fasten *vi (haben)* fast. **F~enzeit** *f* Lent. **F~nacht** *f* Shrovetide; *(Karneval)* carnival. **f~nachtsdienstag** *m* Shrove Tuesday

fatal *a* fatal; *(peinlich)* embarrassing

Fata Morgana *f* --/-- *-nen* mirage

fauchen *vi (haben)* spit, hiss □ *vt* snarl

faul *a* lazy; *(verdorben)* rotten, bad; ⟨Ausrede⟩ lame

faulen *vi (sein)* rot; ⟨Zahn:⟩ decay; *(verwesen)* putrefy. **f~en-zen** *vi (haben)* be lazy. **F~enzer** *m* -s,- lazy-bones *sg.* **F~heit** *f* laziness

Fäulnis *f* decay

Fauna *f* fauna

Faust *f,* **Fäuste** fist; **auf eigene F~** *(fig)* off one's own bat. **F~handschuh** *m* mitten. **F~schlag** *m* punch

Fauxpas /fo'pa/ *m* -,- /-[s],-s/ gaffe

Favorit(in) /favo'ri:t(ɪn)/ *m* -en,-en *(f ~,-nen)* *(Sport)* favourite

Fax *nt* -,-[e] fax. **f~en** *vt* fax

Faxen *fpl (fam)* antics; **F~ machen** fool about

Faxgerät *nt* fax machine

Februar *m* -s,-e February

fechten† *vi (haben)* fence. **F~er** *m* -s,- fencer

Feder *f* -,-n feather; *(Schreib-)* pen; *(Spitze)* nib; *(Techn)* spring. **F~ball** *m* shuttlecock; *(Spiel)* badminton. **F~busch** *m* plume. **f~n** *vi (haben)* be springy; *(nach-geben)* give; *(hoch-)* bounce; **f~nd** springy; *(elastisch)* elastic. **F~ung** *f* - *(Techn)* springs *pl;* *(Auto)* suspension

Fee *f* -,-n fairy

Fegefeuer *nt* purgatory

fegen *vt* sweep

Fehde *f* -,-n feud

fehlen *vi (haben)* **f~ am Platze** out of place. **F~betrag** *m* deficit. **f~en** *vi (haben)* be missing/⟨Sch⟩ absent; *(mangeln)* be lacking; **mir f~t die Zeit** I haven't got the time; **was f~t ihm?** what's the matter with him? **das hat uns noch gefehlt!** that's all we need! **f~end** *a* missing; ⟨Sch⟩ absent

Fehler *m* -s,- mistake, error; *(Sport & fig)* fault; *(Makel)* flaw. **f~frei** *a* faultless. **f~haft** *a* faulty. **f~los** *a* flawless

Fehl|geburt *f* miscarriage. **F~griff** *m* mistake. **F~kalkulation** *f* miscalculation. **F~schlag** *m* failure. **f~schlagen†** *vi sep (sein)* fail. **F~start** *m (Sport)* false start. **F~zündung** *f (Auto)* misfire

Feier *f* -,-n celebration; *(Zeremonie)* ceremony; *(Party)* party. **F~abend** *m* end of the working day; **F~abend machen** stop work. **f~lich** *a* solemn; *(förmlich)* formal. **f~n** *vt* celebrate; hold ⟨Fest⟩ □ *vi (haben)* celebrate. **F~tag** *m* [public] holiday; *(kirchlicher)* feast-day; **erster/zweiter F~tag** Christmas Day/Boxing Day. **F~tags** *adv* on public holidays

feige *a* cowardly; **f~ sein** be a coward □ *adv* in a cowardly way

Feige *f* -,-n fig

Feig|heit f - cowardice. **F~ling** m -s,-e coward

Feile f -,-n file. **f~n** vt/i (haben) file

feilschen vi (haben) haggle

fein a fine; (zart) delicate; ⟨Unterschied⟩ subtle; (vornehm) refined; (prima) great; **sich f~ machen** dress up. **F~arbeit** f precision work

Feind(in) m -es,-e (f -,-nen) enemy. **f~lich** a enemy; (f~selig) hostile. **F~schaft** f -,-en enmity

fein|fühlig a sensitive. **F~gefühl** nt sensitivity; (Takt) delicacy. **F~heit** f -,-en fineness; delicacy; subtlety; refinement. **F~heiten** subtleties. **F~kostgeschäft** nt delicatessen [shop]

feist a fat

Feld nt -[e]s,-er field; (Fläche) ground; (Sport) pitch; (Schach) square; (auf Formular) box. **F~bett** nt camp-bed. **F~forschung** f fieldwork. **F~herr** m commander. **F~stecher** m -s,- field-glasses pl. **F~webel** m (Mil) sergeant. **F~zug** m campaign

Felge f -,-n [wheel] rim

Fell nt -[e]s,-e (Zool) coat; (Pelz) fur; (abgezogen) skin, pelt

Fels m -en,-en rock. **F~block** m boulder. **F~en** m -s,- rock

Femininum nt -s,-na (Gram) feminine

Feminist|in f(m) f m -en,-en (f -,-nen) feminist. **f~isch** a feminist

Fenchel m -s fennel

Fenster nt -s,- window. **F~brett** nt window-sill

Ferien /ˈfeːrjən/ pl holidays; (Univ) vacation sg; **F~ haben** be on holiday. **F~ort** m holiday resort

Ferkel nt -s,- piglet

fern a distant; **der F~e Osten** the Far East □ adv far away; **von f~** from a distance □ prep (+ dat) far

[away] from. **F~bedienung** f remote control. **F~e** f - distance; **in weiter F~e** far away; (zeitlich) in the distant future. **f~er** a further □ adv (außerdem) furthermore; (in Zukunft) in future. **f~gelenkt** a remote-controlled; ⟨Rakete⟩ guided. **F~gespräch** nt long-distance call. **F~glas** nt binoculars pl. **F~kurs[us]** m correspondence course. **F~licht** nt (Auto) full beam. **F~meldewesen** nt telecommunications pl. **F~rohr** nt telescope. **F~schreiben** nt telex. **F~schreiber** m -s,- telex [machine]

Fernseh|apparat m television set. **F~en†** vi sep (haben) watch television. **F~en** nt -s television. **F~er** m -s,- television set

Fernsprech|amt nt telephone exchange. **F~er** m telephone

Fernsteuerung f remote control

Ferse f -,-n heel

fertig a finished; (bereit) ready; (Comm) ready-made; ⟨Gericht⟩ ready-to-serve; **f~ werden mit** finish; (bewältigen) cope with; □ adv **f~ essen/lesen** finish eating/reading. **F~bau** m (pl -bauten) prefabricated building. **f~bringen†** vt sep manage to do; (beenden) finish; **ich bringe es nicht f~** I can't bring myself to do it. **f~en** vt make. **F~gericht** nt ready-to-serve meal. **F~haus** nt prefabricated house. **F~keit** f -,-en skill. **f~machen** vt sep finish; (bereitmachen) get ready; (fam: erschöpfen) wear out; (see-lisch) shatter; **sich f~machen** get ready. **F~stellung** f completion. **F~ung** f - manufacture

fesch a (fam) attractive

Fessel f -,-n ankle

fesseln vt tie up; tie (**an** + acc to); (fig) fascinate

fest a firm; (nicht flüssig) solid; (erstarrt) set; (haltbar) strong;

(*nicht locker*) tight; (*feststehend*) fixed; (*ständig*) steady; (*Anstellung*) permanent; (*Schlaf*) sound; (*Blick*) steady. **F~werden** harden; (*Gelee:*) set; **f~e Nahrung** solids *pl* □*adv* firmly; tightly; steadily; soundly; (*kräftig, tüchtig*) hard; **f~ schlafen** be fast asleep

Fest *nt* -[e]s,-e celebration; (*Party*) party; (*Relig*) festival; **frohes F~!** happy Christmas!

fest|angestellt *a* permanent. **f~binden**† *vt sep* tie (an + *dat* to). **f~bleiben** *vi sep* (*sein*) (*fig*) remain firm. **f~halten**† *v sep* □*vt* hold on to; (*aufzeichnen*) record; **sich f~halten** hold on □*vi* (*haben*) **f~halten an** (+ *dat*) (*fig*) stick to; cling to (*Tradition*). **f~igen** *vt* strengthen. **F~iger** *m* -s,- styling lotion/(*Schaum*-) mousse. **F~igkeit** *f* - firmness; solidity; strength; steadiness. **F~land** *nt* mainland; (*Kontinent*) continent. **f~legen** *vt sep* (*fig*) fix, settle; lay down (*Regeln*); tie up (*Geld*); **sich f~legen** commit oneself

festlich *a* festive. **F~keiten** *fpl* festivities

fest|liegen† *vi sep* (*haben*) be fixed, settled. **f~machen** *v sep* □*vt* fasten/(*binden*) tie (an + *dat* to); (*f~legen*) fix, settle □*vi* (*haben*) (*Naut*) moor. **F~nahme** *f* -,-n arrest. **f~nehmen**† *vt sep* arrest. **f~setzen** *vt sep* fix, settle; (*inhaftieren*) gaol; **sich f~setzen** collect. **f~sitzen**† *vi sep* (*haben*) be firm/(*Schraube:*) tight; (*nicht weiterkommen*) be stuck. **F~spiele** *npl* festival sg. **f~stehen**† *vi sep* (*haben*) be certain. **f~stellen** *vt sep* fix; (*ermitteln*) establish; (*bemerken*) notice; (*sagen*) state. **F~tag** *m* special day

Festung *f* -,-en fortress

Festzug *m* [grand] procession

Fete /ˈfeːtə, ˈfɛːtə/ *f* -,-n party

fett *a* fat; fatty; (*fettig*) greasy; (*üppig*) rich; (*Druck*) bold. **F~** *nt* -[e]s,-e fat; (*flüssig*) grease. **f~arm** *a* low-fat. **f~en** *vt* grease □*vi* (*haben*) be greasy. **F~fleck** *m* grease mark. **f~ig** *a* greasy

Fetzen *m* -s,- scrap; (*Stoff*) rag; **in F~** in shreds

feucht *a* damp, moist; (*Luft*) humid. **F~igkeit** *f* - dampness; (*Nässe*) moisture; (*Luft*) humidity. **F~igkeitscreme** *f* moisturizer

Feuer *nt* -s,- fire; (*für Zigarette*) light; (*Begeisterung*) passion; **F~machen** light a fire. **F~alarm** *m* fire alarm. **F~gefährlich** *a* [in]flammable. **F~leiter** *f* fire-escape. **F~löscher** *m* fire extinguisher. **F~melder** *m* -s,- fire alarm. **F~probe** *f* (*fig*) test. **f~rot** *a* crimson. **F~stein** *m* flint. **F~stelle** *f* hearth. **F~treppe** *f* fire-escape. **F~wache** *f* fire station. **F~waffe** *f* firearm. **F~wehr** *f* -,-en fire brigade. **F~wehrauto** *nt* fire-engine. **F~wehrmann** *m* (*pl* -männer & -leute) fireman. **F~werk** *nt* firework display, fireworks *pl*. **F~zeug** *nt* lighter

feurig *a* fiery; (*fig*) passionate

Fiaker *m* -s,- (*Aust*) horse-drawn cab

Fichte *f* -,-n spruce

Fieber *nt* -s [raised] temperature; **F~ haben** have a temperature. **f~n** *vi* (*haben*) be feverish. **F~thermometer** *nt* thermometer

fiebrig *a* feverish

Figur *f* -,-en figure; (*Roman-, Film-*) character; (*Schach-*) piece

Filet /fiˈleː/ *nt* -s,-s fillet

Filiale *f* -,-n (*Comm*) branch

Filigran *nt* -s filigree

Film m -[e]s,-e film; (Kino-) film; (Schicht) coating. **f~en** vt/i (haben) film. **F~kamera** f cine-/(für Kinofilm) film camera

Filt|er m & (Techn) nt -s,- filter. **f~ern** vt filter. **F~erzigarette** f filter-tipped cigarette. **f~rieren** vt filter

Filz m -es felt. **F~stift** m felt-tipped pen

Fimmel m -s,- (fam) obsession

Finale nt -s,- (Mus) finale; (Sport) final

Finanz f -,-en finance. **F~amt** nt tax office. **f~iell** a financial. **f~ieren** vt finance. **F~minister** m minister of finance

find|en† vt find; (meinen) think; **den Tod f~en** meet one's death; **wie f~est du das?** what do you think of that? **es wird sich f~en** it'll turn up; (fig) it'll be all right □vi (haben) find one's way. **F~er** m -s,- finder. **F~erlohn** m reward. **f~ig** a resourceful

Finesse f -,-n (Kniff) trick; **F~n** (Techn) refinements

Finger m -s,- finger; **die F~ lassen von** (fam) leave alone. **F~abdruck** m finger-mark; (Admin) fingerprint. **F~hut** m thimble. **F~nagel** m finger-nail. **F~spitze** f finger-tip. **F~zeig** m -[e]s,-e hint

Fink m -en,-en finch

Finn|e m -n,-n, **F~in** f -,-nen Finn. **f~isch** a Finnish. **F~land** nt -s Finland

finster a dark; (düster) gloomy; (unheildrohend) sinister. **F~nis** f -,- darkness; (Astr) eclipse

Firma f -,-men firm, company

Firmen|wagen m company car. **F~zeichen** nt trade mark, logo

Firmung f -,-en (Relig) confirmation

Firnis m -ses,-se varnish. **f~sen** vt varnish

First m -[e]s,-e [roof] ridge

Fisch m -[e]s,-e fish; **F~e** (Astr) Pisces. **F~dampfer** m trawler. **f~en** vt/i (haben) fish. **F~er** m -s,- fisherman. **F~erei** f -,- fishing. **F~händler** m fishmonger. **F~reiher** m heron

Fiskus m - der **F~** the Treasury

fit a fit. **F~neß** f -,- fitness

fix a (fam) quick; (geistig) bright; **f~e Idee** obsession; **fix und fertig** all finished; (bereit) all ready; (fam: erschöpft) shattered. **F~er** m -s,- (sl) junkie

fixieren vt stare at; (Phot) fix

Fjord m -[e]s,-e fiord

flach a flat; (eben) level; (niedrig) low; (nicht tief) shallow

Fläche f -,-n area; (Ober-) surface; (Seite) face

Flachs m -es flax. **f~blond** a flaxen-haired; (Haar) flaxen

flackern vi (haben) flicker

Flagge f -,-n flag

Flair /flɛːɐ̯/ nt -s air, aura

Flak f -,-[s] anti-aircraft artillery; (Geschütz) gun

flämisch a Flemish

Flamme f -,-n flame; (Koch-) burner; **in F~n** in flames

Flanell m -s (Tex) flannel

Flasche f -,-n bottle. **F~nbier** nt bottled beer. **F~nöffner** m bottle-opener

flatter|haft a fickle. **f~n** vi (sein/haben) flutter; (Segel:) flap

flau a faint; (Comm) slack

Flaum m -[e]s down

flauschig a fleecy; (Spielzeug) fluffy

Flausen fpl (fam) silly ideas

Flaute f -,-n (Naut) calm; (Comm) slack period; (Schwäche) low

fläzen (sich) vr (fam) sprawl

Flechte f -,-n (Med) eczema; (Bot) lichen; (Zopf) plait. **f~n†** vt plait; weave (Korb)

Fleck m -[e]s,-e[n] spot; (größer) patch; (Schmutz-) stain, mark;

blauer F~ bruise. **f~en** vi (haben) stain. **f~enlos** a spotless.
F~entferner m -s,- stain remover. **f~ig** a stained
Fledermaus f bat
Flegel m -s,- lout. **f~haft** a loutish
flehen vi (haben) beg (**um** for)
Fleisch nt -[e]s flesh; (Culin) meat; (Frucht-) pulp. **F~er** m -s,-, butcher. **f~fressend** a carnivorous. **F~fresser** m -s,- carnivore. **f~ig** a fleshy. **f~lich** a carnal. **F~wolf** m mincer
Fleiß m -es diligence; **mit F~** diligently; (absichtlich) on purpose. **f~ig** a diligent; (arbeitsam) industrious
fletschen vt **die Zähne f~** ⟨Tier:⟩ bare its teeth
flex|ibel a flexible; ⟨Einband⟩ limp. **F~ibilität** f -flexibility
flicken vt mend; (mit Flicken) patch. **F~** m -s,- patch
Flieder m -s lilac
Fliege f -,-n fly; (Schleife) bow-tie. **f~n†** vi (sein) fly; (geworfen werden) be thrown; (fam: fallen) fall; (fam: entlassen werden) be fired; (von der Schule) expelled; **in die Luft f~n** blow up □vt fly. **f~nd** a flying. **F~r** m -s,- airman; (Pilot) pilot; (fam: Flugzeug) plane. **F~rangriff** m air raid
flieh|en† vi (sein) flee (**vor**+dat from); (entweichen) escape □vt shun. **f~end** a fleeing; (Kinn, Stirn) receding
Fliese f -,-n tile
Fließband nt assembly line. **f~en†** vi (sein) flow; (aus Wasserhahn) run. **f~end** a flowing ⟨Wasser⟩ running; ⟨Verkehr⟩ moving; (geläufig) fluent
flimmern vi (haben) shimmer; (TV) flicker
Flinte f -,-n shotgun
Flirt /flœɛt/ m -s,-s flirtation. **f~en** vi (haben) flirt

Flitterwochen fpl honeymoon sg
flitzen vi (sein) (fam) dash
Flocke f -,-n flake; (Wolle) tuft. **f~ig** a fluffy
Floh m -[e]s,ᵉ flea. **F~spiel** nt tiddly-winks sg
Flora f - flora
Florett nt -[e]s,-e foil
florieren vi (haben) flourish
Floskel f -,-n [empty] phrase
Floß nt -es,ᵉ raft
Flosse f -,-n fin; (Seehund-, Gummi-) flipper; (sl: Hand) paw
Flöte f -,-n flute; (Block-) recorder. **f~en** vi (haben) play the flute/recorder; (fam: pfeifen) whistle □vt play on the flute/recorder. **F~ist(in)** m -en,-en (f -,-nen) flautist
flott a quick; (lebhaft) lively; (schick) smart
Flotte f -,-n fleet
flottmachen vt sep wieder f~ (Naut) refloat; get going again ⟨Auto⟩; put back on its feet ⟨Unternehmen⟩
Flöz nt -es,-e [coal] seam
Fluch m -[e]s,ᵉ curse. **f~en** vi (haben) curse, swear
Flucht f - flight; (Entweichen) escape; **die F~ ergreifen** take flight. **f~artig** a hasty
flücht|en vi (sein) flee (**vor**+dat from); (entweichen) escape □vr **sich f~en** take refuge. **f~ig** a fugitive; (kurz) brief; ⟨Blick⟩ fleeting; ⟨Bekanntschaft⟩ passing; (oberflächlich) cursory; (nicht sorgfältig) careless; **f~ig kennen** know slightly. **F~igkeitsfehler** m slip. **F~ling** m -s,-e fugitive; (Pol) refugee
Fluchwort nt (pl -wörter) swearword
Flug m -[e]s,ᵉ flight. **F~abwehr** f anti-aircraft defence
Flügel m -s,- wing; (Fenster-) casement; (Mus) grand piano
Fluggast m [air] passenger

flügge *a* fully-fledged

Flug|gesellschaft *f* airline. **F~hafen** *m* airport. **F~lotse** *m* air-traffic controller. **F~platz** *m* airport; (*klein*) airfield. **F~preis** *m* air fare. **F~schein** *m* air ticket. **F~schneise** *f* flight path. **F~schreiber** *m* -s- flight recorder. **F~schrift** *f* pamphlet. **F~steig** *m* -[e]s,-e gate. **F~zeug** *nt* -[e]s,-e aircraft, plane

Flunder *f* -,-n flounder

Flur *m* -[e]s,-e [entrance] hall; (*Gang*) corridor

Fluß *m* -sses, ̈sse river; (*Fließen*) flow. **f~abwärts** *adv* downstream. **f~aufwärts** *adv* upstream

flüssig *a* liquid; (*Lava*) molten; (*fließend*) fluent; **f~** *adv* freely moving. **F~keit** *f* -,-en liquid; (*Anat*) fluid

Flußpferd *nt* hippopotamus

flüstern *vt/i* (*haben*) whisper

Flut *f* -,-en high tide; (*fig*) flood

Föderation /-'tsio:n/ *f* -,-en federation

Fohlen *nt* -s,- foal

Föhn *m* -s föhn [wind]

Folge *f* -,-n consequence; (*Reihe*) succession; (*Fortsetzung*) instalment; (*Teil*) part. **f~n** *vi* (*sein*) follow (**jdm/etw** s.o./sth); (*zuhören*) listen (*dat* to); **wie f~t** as follows □ (*haben*) (*gehorchen*) obey (**jdm** s.o.). **F~end** *a* following; **f~endes** the following

folgern *vt* conclude (**aus** from). **F~ung** *f* -,-en conclusion

folglich *adv* consequently. **f~sam** *a* obedient

Folie /'fo:liə/ *f* -,-n foil; (*Plastik-*) film

Folklore *f* - folklore

Folter *f* -,-n torture. **f~n** *vt* torture

Fön (**P**) *m* -s,-e hair-drier

Fonds /fõ:/ *m* -,- /-[s],-s/ fund

fönen *vt* [blow-]dry

Förder|band *nt* (*pl* -bänder) conveyor belt. **f~lich** *a* beneficial

fordern *vt* demand; (*beanspruchen*) claim; (*zum Kampf*) challenge

fördern *vt* promote; (*unterstützen*) encourage; (*finanziell*) sponsor; (*gewinnen*) extract

Forderung *f* -,-en demand; (*Anspruch*) claim

Förderung *f* - (*s.* **fördern**) promotion; encouragement; (*Techn*) production

Forelle *f* -,-n trout

Form *f* -,-en form; (*Gestalt*) shape; (*Culin, Techn*) mould; (*Back-*) tin

Formalität *f* -,-en formality

Format *nt* -[e]s,-e format; (*Größe*) size; (*fig: Bedeutung*) stature

Formel *f* -,-n formula

formen *vt* shape, mould; (*bilden*) form; **sich f~** take shape

förmlich *a* formal

form|los *a* shapeless; (*zwanglos*) informal. **F~sache** *f* formality

Formular *nt* -s,-e [printed] form

formulier|en *vt* formulate, word. **F~ung** *f* -,-en wording

forsch|en *vi* (*haben*) search (**nach** for). **F~end** *a* searching. **F~er** *m* -s,- research scientist; (*Reisender*) explorer. **F~ung** *f* -,-en research

Förster *m* -s,- forester

Forstwirtschaft *f* forestry

Fort *nt* -s,-s (*Mil*) fort

fort *adv* away; **f~ sein** be away; (*gegangen/verschwunden*) have gone; **und so f~** and so on; **in einem f~** continuously. **f~bewegung** *f* locomotion. **F~bildung** *f* further education/ training. **f~bleiben†** *vi sep* (*sein*) stay away. **f~bringen†** *vt sep* take away. **f~fallen†** *vi sep* (*sein*) be dropped/(*ausgelassen*) omitted; (*entfallen*) no longer apply; (*aufhören*) cease. **f~führen** *vt sep* continue. **f~gehen†** *vi sep* *(sein)* leave, go away; *(ausgehen)* go out; *(andauern)* go on. **f~geschritten** a advanced; *(spät)* late. **F~geschrittene(r)** f~m/f advanced student. **f~lassen†** vt sep let go; *(auslassen)* omit. **f~laufend** a consecutive. **f~pflanzen (sich)** vr sep reproduce; ⟨Ton, Licht:⟩ travel. **F~pflanzung** f -reproduction. **F~pflanzungsorgan** nt reproductive organ. **f~schicken** vt sep send away; *(abschicken)* send off. **f~schreiten†** vi sep continue; *(Fortschritte machen)* progress, advance. **f~schreitend** a progressive; ⟨Alter:⟩ advancing. **F~schritt** m progress; **F~schritte machen** make progress. **f~schrittlich** a progressive. **f~setzen** vt sep continue; **sich f~setzen** continue. **F~setzung** f -,-en continuation; *(Folge)* instalment; **F~setzung folgt** to be continued. **F~setzungsroman** m serialized novel, serial. **f~während** a constant. **f~ziehen†** v sep ⬦vt pull away ⬦vi *(sein)* move away

Fossil nt -s,-ien /-jən/ fossil

Foto nt -s,-s photo. **F~apparat** m camera. **f~gen** a photogenic

Fotograf(in) m -en,-en (f -,-nen) photographer. **F~ie** f -,-n *(Bild)* photograph. **f~ieren** vt take a photo[graph] of ⬦vi *(haben)* take photographs. **f~isch** a photographic

Fotokopie f photocopy. **F~ren** vt photocopy. **F~rgerät** nt photocopier

Fötus m -,-ten foetus

Foul /faul/ nt -s,-s *(Sport)* foul

Fracht f -,-en freight. **F~er** m -s, freighter. **F~gut** nt freight.

F~schiff nt cargo boat

Frack m -[e]s,¨-e & -s tailcoat

Frage f -,-n question; **etw in F~stellen** question sth; *(ungewiß*

machen) make sth doubtful. **F~bogen** m questionnaire. **f~n** vt/i *(haben)* ask; **sich f~n** wonder *(ob whether)*. **F~nd** a questioning. **F~zeichen** nt question mark

frag|lich a doubtful; ⟨Person, Sache⟩ in question. **f~los** adv undoubtedly

Fragment nt -[e]s,-e fragment

fragwürdig a questionable; *(verdächtig)* dubious

Fraktion /-ˈtsjoːn/ f -,-en parliamentary party

Franken¹ m -s,- *(Swiss)* franc

Franken² nt -s Franconia

frankieren vt stamp, frank

Frankreich nt -s France

Fransen fpl fringe sg

Franz|ose m -n,-n Frenchman; **die F~osen** the French pl. **F~ösin** f -,-nen Frenchwoman. **f~ösisch** a French. **F~ösisch** nt -[s] *(Lang)* French

Fraß m -es feed; *(pej: Essen)* muck

Fratze f -,-n grotesque face; *(Grimasse)* grimace

Frau f -,-en woman; *(Ehe-)* wife; **F~ Thomas** Mrs Thomas; **Unsere Liebe F~** *(Relig)* Our Lady

Frauen|arzt m, **~ärztin** f gynaecologist. **F~rechtlerin** f -,-nen feminist

Fräulein nt -s,- single woman; *(jung)* young lady; *(Anrede)* Miss

frech a cheeky; *(unverschämt)* impudent. **F~heit** f -,-en cheekiness; impudence; *(Äußerung)* impertinence

frei a free; *(freischaffend)* freelance; ⟨Künstler⟩ independent; *(nicht besetzt)* vacant; *(offen)* open; *(bloß)* bare; **f~er Tag** day off; **sich** *(dat)* **f~ nehmen** take time off; **f~ machen** *(räumen)* clear; vacate *(Platz)*; *(befreien)* liberate; *(entkleiden)* bare; **f~lassen** leave free; **ist dieser Platz f~?** is this seat taken?

'Zimmer f~' 'vacancies' □*adv* freely; (*ohne Notizen*) without notes; (*umsonst*) free

Frei|bad *nt* open-air swimming pool. **f~beruflich** *a & adv* freelance. **F~e** *nt* im **F~en** in the open air, out of doors. **f~gabe** *f* release. **f~geben**† *v sep* □*vt* release; (*eröffnen*) open; **jdm einen Tag f~geben** give s.o. a day off□ *vi* (*haben*) **jdm f~geben** give s.o. time off. **f~gebig** *a* generous. **F~gebigkeit** *f* generosity. **f~haben**† *v sep* □*vt* **eine Stunde f~haben** have an hour off; (*Sch*) have a free period □*vi* (*haben*) be off work/(*Sch*) school; (*beurlaubt sein*) have time off. **f~händig** *adv* without holding on

Freiheit *f* -,-en freedom, liberty. **F~sstrafe** *f* prison sentence

Frei|herr *m* baron. **F~körperkultur** *f* naturism. **F~lassung** *f* - release. **F~lauf** *m* free-wheel. **f~legen** *vt sep* expose. **f~lich** *adv* admittedly; (*natürlich*) of course. **F~lichttheater** *nt* open-air theatre. **f~machen** *v sep* □*vt* (*frankieren*) frank □*vi* (*haben*) [**sich**] **f~machen** take time off. **f~schaffend** *a* freelance. **f~schwimmen**† (**sich**) *vr sep* pass one's swimming test. **f~sprechen**† *vt sep* acquit. **F~spruch** *m* acquittal. **f~stehen**† *vi sep* (*haben*) stand empty; **es steht ihm f~** (*fig*) he is free (**zu** to). **f~stellen** *vt sep* exempt (**von** from); **jdm etw f~stellen** leave sth up to s.o. **F~stil** *m* freestyle. **F~stoß** *m* free kick

Freitag *m* Friday. **f~s** *adv* on Fridays

Frei|tod *m* suicide. **F~umschlag** *m* stamped envelope. **f~weg** *adv* freely; (*offen*) openly.

f~willig *a* voluntary. **F~williger(r)** *m/f* volunteer. **F~zeichen** *nt* ringing tone; (*Rufzeichen*) dialling tone. **F~zeit** *f* free or spare time; (*Muße*) leisure. **F~zeit-** *pref* leisure ... **F~zeitbekleidung** *f* casual wear. **f~zügig** *a* unrestricted; (*großzügig*) liberal; (*moralisch*) permissive

fremd *a* foreign; (*unbekannt*) strange; (*nicht das eigene*) other people's; **ein f~er Mann** a stranger; **f~e Leute** strangers; **unter f~em Namen** under an assumed name; **ich bin hier f~** I'm a stranger here. **F~e** *f* - in der **F~e** away from home; (*im Ausland*) in a foreign country. **F~e(r)** *m/f* stranger; (*Ausländer*) foreigner; (*Tourist*) tourist. **F~enführer** *m* [tourist] guide. **F~enverkehr** *m* tourism. **F~enzimmer** *nt* room [to let]; (*Gäste-*) guest room. **f~gehen**† *vi sep* (*sein*) (*fam*) be unfaithful. **F~sprache** *f* foreign language. **F~wort** *nt* (*pl* -wörter) foreign word

Freske *f* -,-n, **Fresko** *nt* -s,-ken fresco

Fresse *f* -,-n (*sl*) (*Mund*) gob; (*Gesicht*) mug. **f~n**† *vt/i* (*haben*) eat. **F~n** *nt* -s feed; (*sl: Essen*) grub

Freßnapf *m* feeding bowl

Freud|e *f* -,-n pleasure; (*innere*) joy; **mit F~en** with pleasure; **jdm eine F~e machen** please s.o. **f~ig** *a* joyful; **f~iges Ereignis** (*fig*) happy event

freuen *vt* please; **sich f~** be pleased (**über**+ *acc* about); **sich f~ auf** (+ *acc*) look forward to; **es freut mich** I'm glad (**daß** that)

Freund *m* -es,-e friend; (*Verehrer*) boyfriend. **F~in** *f* -,-nen friend; (*Liebste*) girlfriend. **f~lich** *a* kind; (*umgänglich*) friendly; (*angenehm*) pleasant. **f~licherweise** *adv* kindly. **F~lichkeit** *f* -,-en kindness; friendliness; pleasantness

Freundschaft *f* -,-en friendship; **F~ schließen** become friends. **f~lich** *a* friendly

Frieden *m* -s peace; **F~ schließen** make peace; **im F~** in peacetime; **laß mich in F~!** leave me alone! **F~svertrag** *m* peace treaty

Fried|hof *m* cemetery. **f~lich** *a* peaceful

frieren† *vi* (haben) ⟨Person:⟩ be cold; *impers* **es friert/hat gefroren** it is freezing/there has been a frost; **frierst du?** are you cold? □ (*sein*) (*gefrieren*) freeze

Fries *m* -es,-e frieze

frisch *a* fresh; (*sauber*) clean; (*leuchtend*) bright; (*munter*) lively; (*rüstig*) fit; **sich f~ machen** freshen up □ *adv* freshly, newly; **ein Bett f~ beziehen** put clean sheets on a bed; **f~ gestrichen!** wet paint! **F~e** *f* - freshness; brightness; liveliness; fitness. **F~haltepackung** *f* vacuum pack

Fri|seur /fri'zø:g/ *m* -s,-e hairdresser; (*Herren-*) barber. **F~seursalon** *m* hairdressing salon. **F~seuse** /-'zø:za/ *f* -,-n hairdresser

frisier|en *vt* **jdn/sich f~en** do s.o.'s/one's hair; **die Bilanz/einen Motor f~en** (*fam*) fiddle the accounts/soup up an engine

Frist *f* -,-en period; (*Termin*) deadline; (*Aufschub*) time; **drei Tage F~** three days' grace. **f~los** *a* instant

Frisur *f* -,-en hairstyle

frivol /fri'vo:l/ *a* frivolous

froh *a* happy; (*freudig*) joyful; (*erleichtert*) glad

fröhlich *a* cheerful; (*vergnügt*) merry. **F~keit** *f* - cheerfulness; merriment

fromm *a* devout; (*gutartig*) docile

Frömmigkeit *f* - devoutness, piety

Fronleichnam *m* Corpus Christi

Front *f* -,-en front. **f~al** *a* frontal; (*Zusammenstoß*) head-on □ *adv* from the front; (*Zusammenstoßen*) head-on. **F~alzusammenstoß** *m* head-on collision

Frosch *m* -[e]s,⸚e frog. **F~laich** *m* frog-spawn. **F~mann** *m* (*pl* -männer) frogman

Frost *m* -[e]s,⸚e frost. **F~beule** *f* chilblain

frösteln *vi* (haben) shiver

frostig *a* frosty. **F~schutzmittel** *nt* antifreeze

Frottee *nt* & *m* -s towelling

frottier|en *vt* rub down. **F~[hand]tuch** *nt* terry towel

Frucht *f* -,⸚e fruit; **F~ tragen** bear fruit. **f~bar** *a* fertile; (*fig*) fruitful. **F~barkeit** *f* - fertility. **f~ig** *a* fruity. **F~saft** *m* fruit juice

früh *a* early □ *adv* early; (*morgens*) in the morning; **heute f~** this morning; **von f~ an** from an early age. **F~aufsteher** *m* -s,-early riser. **F~e** *f* - in aller F~e bright and early; **in der F~e** (*SGer*) in the morning. **f~er** *adv* earlier; (*eher*) sooner; (*ehemals*) formerly; (*vor langer Zeit*) in the old days; **f~er oder später** sooner or later; **ich wohnte f~er in X** I used to live in X. **f~ere(r,s)** *a* earlier; (*ehemalig*) former; (*vorige*) previous. **f~estens** *adv* at the earliest. **F~geburt** *f* premature birth/(*Kind*) baby. **F~jahr** *nt* spring. **F~ling** *m* -s,-e spring. **f~morgens** *adv* early in the morning. **f~reif** *a* precocious

Frühstück *nt* breakfast. **f~en** *vi* (*haben*) have breakfast

frühzeitig *a* & *adv* early; (*vorzeitig*) premature

Frustr|ation /-'tsio:n/ *f* -,-en frustration. **f~ieren** *vt* frustrate; **f~ierend** frustrating

Fuchs *m* -es,-̈e fox; (*Pferd*) chestnut. **f~en** *vt* (*fam*) annoy

Füchsin *f* -,-nen vixen

Fuge¹ *f* -,-n joint

Fuge² *f* -,-n (*Mus*) fugue

fügen *vt* fit (**in** + *acc* into); (*an-*) join (**an** + *acc* on to); (*dazu-*) add (**zu** to); adjoin/(*folgen*) follow (**an etw** *acc* sth); (*fig: gehorchen*) submit (**dat** to). **F~ung** *f* -,-en **die F~ung des Schicksals** a stroke of fate

fühl|bar *a* noticeable. **f~en** *vt/i* (*haben*) feel; **sich f~en** feel (**krank/einsam** ill/lonely); (*fam: stolz sein*) fancy oneself. **F~er** *m* -s,- feeler. **F~ung** *f* - contact

Fuhre *f* -,-n load

führ|en *vt* lead; guide ⟨*Tourist*⟩; (*geleiten*) take; (*leiten*) run; (*befehligen*) command; (*verkaufen*) stock; bear ⟨*Namen, Titel*⟩; keep ⟨*Liste, Bücher, Tagebuch*⟩; **bei od mit sich f~en** carry;□ *vi* (*haben*) lead; (*verlaufen*) go, run; lead (**zu** to). **f~end** *a* leading. **F~er** *m* -s,- leader; (*Fremden-*) guide; (*Buch*) guide[book]. **F~erschein** *m* driving licence; **den F~erschein machen** take one's driving test. **F~erscheinentzug** *m* disqualification from driving. **F~ung** *f* -,-en leadership; (*Leitung*) management; (*Mil*) command; (*Betragen*) conduct; (*Besichtigung*) guided tour; (*Vorsprung*) lead; **in F~ung gehen** go into the lead

Fuhr|unternehmer *m* haulage contractor. **F~werk** *nt* cart

Fülle *f* -,-n abundance, wealth (**an** + *dat* of). **f~n** *vt* fill; (*Culin*) stuff

Füllen *nt* -s,- foal

Fül|er *m* -s,- (*fam*), **F~federhalter** *m* fountain pen. **F~ung** *f* -,-en filling; (*Braten-*) stuffing

fummeln *vi* (*haben*) fumble (**an** + *dat* with)

Fund *m* -[e]s,-e find

Fundament *nt* -[e]s,-e foundations *pl.* **f~al** *a* fundamental

Fundbüro *nt* lost-property office

fünf *inv a*, **F~** *f* -,-en five; (*Sch*) ≈ fail mark. **f~te(r,s)** *a* fifth. **f~zehn** *inv a* fifteen. **f~zehnte(r,s)** *a* fifteenth. **f~zig** *inv a* fifty. **f~zigste(r,s)** *a* fiftieth

fungieren *vi* (*haben*) act (**als** as)

Funk *m* -s radio. **F~e** *m* -n,-n spark. **f~eln** *vi* (*haben*) sparkle; ⟨*Stern:*⟩ twinkle. **F~en** *m* -s,- spark. **f~en** *vt* radio. **F~sprechgerät** *nt* walkie-talkie. **F~spruch** *m* radio message. **F~streife** *f* [police] radio patrol

Funktion /-'tsio:n/ *f* -,-en function; (*Stellung*) position; (*Funktionieren*) working; **außer F~** out of action. **F~är** *m* -s,-e official. **f~ieren** *vi* (*haben*) work

für *prep* (+ *acc*) for; **Schritt für Schritt** step by step; **was für [ein]** what [a]! (*fragend*) what sort of [a]?

Furche *f* -,-n furrow

Furcht *f* - fear (**vor** + *dat* of). **f~bar** *a* terrible, *adv* -bly

fürcht|en *vt/i* (*haben*) fear; **sich f~en** be afraid (**vor** + *dat* of). **f~erlich** *a* dreadful

furcht|erregend *a* terrifying. **f~los** *a* fearless

füreinander *adv* for each other

Furnier nt -s,-e veneer. **f~t** a veneered

Fürsorge f care; (Admin) welfare; (fam: Geld) ≈ social security. **F~er(in)** m -s,- (f -,-nen) social worker. **F~lich** a solicitous

Fürst m -en,-en prince. **F~entum** nt -s,-er principality. **F~in** f -,-nen princess

Furt f -,-en ford

Furunkel m -s,- (Med) boil

Fürwort nt (pl -wörter) pronoun

Furz m -es,-e (vulg) fart

Fusion f -,-en fusion; (Comm) merger

Fuß m -es,-e foot; (Aust: Bein) leg; (Lampen-) base; (von Weinglas) stem; **zu Fuß** on foot; **zu Fuß gehen** walk; **auf freiem Fuß** free. **F~abdruck** m footprint. **F~abtreter** m -s,- doormat. **F~ball** m football. **F~ballspieler** m footballer. **F~balltoto** nt football pools pl. **F~boden** m floor

Fussel f -,-n & m -s,-[n] piece of fluff; **F~n** fluff sg. **f~n** vi (haben) shed fluff

Fußgänger(in) m -s,- (f -,-nen) pedestrian. **F~brücke** f footbridge. **F~zone** f pedestrian precinct

Fuß|geher m -s,- (Aust) = **F~gänger**. **F~gelenk** nt ankle. **F~hebel** m pedal. **F~nagel** m toenail. **F~note** f footnote. **F~pflege** f chiropody. **F~rücken** m instep. **F~sohle** f sole of the foot. **F~tritt** m kick. **F~weg** m footpath; **eine Stunde F~weg** an hour's walk

Futter[1] m -s feed; (Trocken-) fodder

Futter[2] nt -s,- (Kleider-) lining

Futteral nt -s,-e case

füttern[1] vt feed

füttern[2] vt line

G

Gabe f -,-n gift; (Dosis) dose

Gabel f -,-n fork. **g~n (sich)** vr fork. **G~stapler** m -s,- fork-lift truck. **G~ung** f -,-en fork

gackern vi (haben) cackle

gaffen vi (haben) gape, stare

Gage /'ga:ʒə/ f -,-n (Theat) fee

gähnen vi (haben) yawn. **G~** nt -s yawn; (wiederholt) yawning

Gala f - ceremonial dress

Galavorstellung f gala performance

Galerie f -,-n gallery

Galgen m -s,- gallows sg. **G~frist** f (fam) reprieve

Galionsfigur f figurehead

Galle f - bile; (G~nblase) gallbladder. **G~nblase** f gall-bladder. **G~nstein** m gallstone

Galopp m -s gallop; **im G~** at a gallop. **g~ieren** vi (sein) gallop

gammel|n vi (haben) (fam) loaf around. **G~ler(in)** m -s,- (f -,-nen) drop-out

Gams f -,-en (Aust) chamois

Gang m -[e]s,-e walk; (Boten-) errand; (Funktionieren) running; (Verlauf, Culin) course; (Durch-) passage; (Korridor) corridor; (zwischen Sitzreihen) aisle, gangway; (Anat) duct; (Auto) gear; **in G~ bringen** get going; **im G~e sein** be in progress; **Essen mit vier G~en** four-course meal

gängig a common; (Comm) popular

Gangschaltung f gear change

Gangster /'gɛŋstɐ/ m -s,- gangster

Ganove m -n,-n (fam) crook

Gans f -,-e goose

Gänse|blümchen nt -s,- daisy. **G~füßchen** ntpl inverted commas. **G~haut** f goose-pimples pl. **G~rich** m -s,-e gander

ganz *a* whole, entire; (*vollständig*) complete; (*fam: heil*) undamaged, intact; **die g~e Zeit** all the time, the whole time; **eine g~e Weile/Menge** quite a while/ lot; *inv* **g~ Deutschland** the whole of Germany; **wieder g~ machen** (*fam*) mend; **im großen und g~en** on the whole □*adv* quite; (*völlig*) completely, entirely; (*sehr*) very; **nicht g~** not quite; **g~ allein** all on one's own; **g~ wie du willst** just as you like. **g~ und gar** completely, totally; **G~e(s)** *nt* whole. **G~jährig** *adv* all the year round. **g~tägig** *a* & *adv* full-time; (*geöffnet*) all day. **g~tags** *adv* all day; (*arbeiten*) full-time

gar¹ *a* done, cooked

gar² *adv* **gar nicht/nichts/niemand** not/nothing/no one at all

Garage /ga'ra:ʒə/ *f* -,-n garage

Garantie *f* -,-n guarantee. **g~ren** *vt/i* (*haben*) **[für] etw g~ren** guarantee sth. **G~schein** *m* guarantee

Garderobe *f* -,-n (*Kleider*) wardrobe; (*Ablage*) cloakroom. (*Künstler-*) dressing-room. **G~nfrau** *f* cloakroom attendant

Gardine *f* -,-n curtain

garen *vt/i* (*haben*) cook

gären† *vi* (*haben*) ferment

Garn *nt* -[e]s,-e yarn; cotton

Garnele *f* -,-n shrimp; prawn

garnieren *vt* decorate; (*Culin*) garnish

Garnison *f* -,-en garrison

Garnitur *f* -,-en set; (*Möbel-*) suite

garstig *a* nasty

Garten *m* -s,-̈ garden. **G~arbeit** *f* gardening. **G~bau** *m* horticulture. **G~haus** *nt*, **G~laube** *f* summer-house. **G~schere** *f* secateurs *pl*

Gärtner(in) *m* -s,- (*f* -,-nen) gardener. **G~ei** *f* -,-en nursery

Gärung *f* - fermentation

Gas *nt* -es,-e gas; **Gas geben** accelerate. **G~maske** *f* gas mask. **G~pedal** *nt* (*Auto*) accelerator

Gasse *f* -,-n (*Aust*) street

Gast *m* -[e]s,-̈e guest; (*Hotel-*) visitor; (*im Lokal*) patron; **zum Mittag G~e haben** have people to lunch; **bei jdm zu G~ sein** be staying with s.o. **G~arbeiter** *m* foreign worker

Gäste|bett *nt* spare bed. **G~buch** *nt* visitors' book. **G~zimmer** *nt* [hotel] room; (*privat*) spare room

gast|freundlich *a* hospitable. **G~freundschaft** *f* hospitality. **G~geber** *m* -s,- host. **G~geberin** *f* -,-nen hostess. **G~haus** *nt*, **G~hof** *m* inn, hotel

gastlich *a* hospitable

Gastronomie *f* - gastronomy

Gast|spiel *nt* guest performance. **G~spielreise** *f* (*Theat*) tour. **G~stätte** *f* restaurant. **G~wirt** *m* landlord. **G~wirtin** *f* landlady

Gas|werk *nt* gasworks *sg*. **G~zähler** *m* gas-meter

Gatte *m* -n,-n husband

Gattin *f* -,-nen wife

Gattung *f* -,-en kind; (*Biol*) genus; (*Kunst*) genre

Gaudi *f* - (*Aust, fam*) fun

Gaumen *m* -s,- palate

Gauner *m* -s,- crook, swindler. **G~ei** *f* -,-en swindle

Gaze /'ga:zə/ *f* - gauze

Gazelle *f* -,-n gazelle

Gebäck *nt* -s [cakes and] pastries *pl*; (*Kekse*) biscuits *pl*

Gebälk *nt* -s timbers *pl*

geballt *a* (*Faust*) clenched

Gebärde *f* -,-n gesture

gebär|en† *vt* give birth to, bear; **geboren werden** be born. **G~mutter** *f* womb, uterus

Gebäude *nt* -s,- building

Gebeine *ntpl* [mortal] remains

Gebell *nt* -s barking

geben† vt give; (tun, bringen) put; (Karten) deal; (aufführen) perform; (unterrichten) teach; **etw verloren g~** give sth up as lost; **viel/wenig g~ auf** (+acc) set great/little store by; **sich g~** (nachlassen) wear off; (besser werden) get better; **es gibt** there is/are; **was gibt es Neues/zum Mittag/im Kino?** what's the new/s for lunch/on at the cinema? **es wird Regen g~** it's going to rain □vi (haben) (Karten) deal

Gebet nt -[e]s,-e prayer

Gebiet nt -[e]s,-e area; (Hoheits-) territory; (Sach-) field

gebieten† vt command; (erfordern) demand □vi (haben) rule

gebildet a educated; (kultiviert) cultured

Gebirge nt -s,- mountains pl. **g~ig** a mountainous

Gebiß nt -sses, -sse teeth pl; (künstliches) false teeth pl, dentures pl; (des Zaumes) bit

geblümt a floral, flowered

gebogen a curved

geboren a born; **g~er Deutscher** German by birth; **Frau X, g~e Y** Mrs X, née Y

gebraten a fried

Gebrauch m use; (Sprach-) usage; **Gebräuche** customs; **in G~** in use; **G~ machen von** make use of. **g~en** vt use; **zu nichts zu g~en** useless

gebräuchlich a common; (Wort) in common use

Gebrauch|sanleitung, G~san-weisung f directions pl for use. **g~t** a used; (Comm) second-hand. **G~twagen** m used car

gebrechlich a frail, infirm

gebrochen a broken □adv g~ **Englisch sprechen** speak broken English

Gebrüll nt -s roaring

Gebühr f -,-en charge, fee; **über G~** excessively. **g~en** vi be due; (geziemend) proper. **g~enfrei** a free □adv free of charge. **g~en-pflichtig** a & adv subject to a charge; **g~enpflichtige Straße** toll road

Geburt f -,-en birth; **von G~** by birth. **G~enkontrolle, G~en-regelung** f birth-control. **G~en-ziffer** f birth-rate

gebürtig a native (aus of); **g~er Deutscher** German by birth

Geburts|datum nt date of birth. **G~helfer** m obstetrician. **G~hilfe** f obstetrics sg. **G~ort** m place of birth. **G~tag** m birth-day. **G~urkunde** f birth certificate

Gebüsch nt -[e]s,-e bushes pl

Gedächtnis nt -ses memory; **aus dem G~** from memory

Gedanke m -ns,-n thought (an + acc of); (Idee) idea; **sich** (dat) **G~n machen** worry (über + acc about). **g~nlos** a thought-less; (zerstreut) absent-minded. **G~nstrich** m dash

Gedärme ntpl intestines; (Tier-) entrails

Gedeck nt -[e]s,-e place setting; (auf Speisekarte) set meal

gedeihen† vi (sein) thrive

gedenken† vi (haben) propose (etw zu tun to do sth). **G~** nt -s memory

Gedenk|feier f commemoration. **G~gottesdienst** m memorial service

Gedicht nt -[e]s,-e poem

Gedränge nt -s crush, crowd. **g~t** a (knapp) concise

Geduld f - patience; **G~ haben** be patient. **g~en** (sich) vr be patient. **g~ig** a patient.

G~[s]spiel nt puzzle

gedunsen a bloated

geehrt a honoured; **sehr g~er Herr X** dear Mr X

geeignet *a* suitable; **im g~en Moment** at the right moment

Gefahr *f* -,-en danger; **in G~** in danger; **auf eigene G~** at one's own risk; **G~ laufen** run the risk (etw zu tun of doing sth)

gefähr|den *vt* endanger; *(fig)* jeopardize. **g~lich** *a* dangerous

gefahrlos *a* safe

Gefährt *nt* -[e]s,-e vehicle

Gefährte *m* -n,-n, **Gefährtin** *f* -,-nen companion

gefahrvoll *a* dangerous, perilous

Gefälle *nt* -s,- slope; *(Straßen-)* gradient

gefallen† *vi* (haben) **jdm g~** please sb.; **er/es gefällt mir** I like him/it; **sich** *(dat)* **etw g~ lassen** put up with sth

Gefallen¹ *m* -s,- favour

Gefallen² *nt* -s,- pleasure **(an+dat** in); **dir zu G~** to please you

Gefallene(r) *m* soldier killed in the war

gefällig *a* pleasing; *(hübsch)* attractive; *(hilfsbereit)* obliging; **[sonst] noch etwas g~?** will there be anything else? **G~keit** *f* -,-en favour; *(Freundlichkeit)* kindness

Gefangen|e(r) *m/f* prisoner. **g~halten†** *vt sep* hold prisoner, keep in captivity ⟨Tier⟩. **G~nahme** *f* - capture. **g~nehmen†** *vt sep* take prisoner. **G~schaft** *f* - captivity

Gefängnis *nt* -ses,-se prison; *(Strafe)* imprisonment. **G~strafe** *f* imprisonment; *(Urteil)* prison sentence. **G~wärter** *m* [prison] warder

Gefäß *nt* -es,-e container, receptacle; *(Blut-)* vessel

gefaßt *a* composed; *(ruhig)* calm; **g~ sein auf** (+acc) be prepared for

gefedert *a* sprung

gefeiert *a* celebrated

Gefieder *nt* -s plumage. **g~t** *a* feathered

gefleckt *a* spotted

Geflügel *nt* -s poultry. **G~klein** *nt* -s giblets *pl.* **g~t** *a* winged

Geflüster *nt* -s whispering

gefragt *a* popular; **g~ sein** be in demand

Gefreite(r) *m* lance-corporal

gefrier|en† *vi* (sein) freeze. **G~fach** *nt* freezer compartment. **G~punkt** *m* freezing point. **G~schrank** *m* upright freezer. **G~truhe** *f* chest freezer

gefroren *a* frozen

gefügig *a* compliant; *(gehorsam)* obedient

Gefühl *nt* -[e]s,-e feeling; *(Empfindung)* sensation; *(G~sregung)* emotion; **im G~ haben** know instinctively. **g~los** *a* insensitive; *(herzlos)* unfeeling; *(taub)* numb. **g~smäßig** *a* emotional; *(instinktiv)* instinctive. **G~sregung** *f* emotion. **g~voll** *a* sensitive *(sentimental)* sentimental

gefüllt *a* filled; *(voll)* full

gefürchtet *a* feared, dreaded

gefüttert *a* lined

gegeben *a* given; *(bestehend)* present; *(passend)* appropriate. **g~enfalls** *adv* if need be

gegen *prep* (+acc) against; *(Sport)* versus; *(G~über)* to[wards]; *(Vergleich)* compared with; *(Richtung, Zeit)* towards; *(ungefähr)* around; **ein Mittel g~** a remedy for □*adv* **g~ 100 Leute** about 100 people. **G~angriff** *m* counter-attack

Gegend *f* -,-en area, region; *(Umgebung)* neighbourhood

gegeneinander *adv* against/ *(gegenüber)* towards one another

Gegen|fahrbahn *f* opposite carriageway. **G~gift** *nt* antidote. **G~maßnahme** *f* countermeasure. **G~satz** *m* contrast; *(Widerspruch)* contradiction.

(G~ teil) opposite; im G~ satz zu unlike. g~ seitig a mutual; sich g~ seitig hassen hate one another. G~ stand m object; (Gram, Gesprächs-) subject. G~ teil nt opposite, contrary; im G~ teil on the contrary. g~ teilig a opposite

gegenüber prep (+ dat) opposite; (Vergleich) compared with; jdm g~ höflich sein be polite to s.o. □adv opposite. g~ liegend a opposite. g~ stehen† vi sep (haben) (+ dat) face; feindlich g~ stehen (+ dat) be hostile to. g~ stellen vt sep confront; (vergleichen) compare

Gegen|verkehr m oncoming traffic. G~ vorschlag m counter-proposal. G~ wart f present; (Anwesenheit) presence. g~ wärtig a present □adv at present. G~ wehr f resistance. G~ wind m head wind. g~ zeichnen vt sep countersign

geglückt a successful
Gegner|(in) m -s,- (f -,-nen) opponent. g~ isch a opposing
Gehabe nt s affected behaviour
Gehackte(s) nt mince
Gehalt m -[e]s,-er salary. G~ serhöhung f rise

gehässig a spiteful
gehäuft a heaped
Gehäuse nt -s,- case; (TV, Radio) cabinet; (Schnecken-) shell
Gehege nt -s,- enclosure
geheim a secret; im g~ en secretly. G~ dienst m Secret Service. g~ halten† vt sep keep secret. G~ nis nt -ses,-se secret. g~ nisvoll a mysterious
gehemmt a (fig) inhibited
gehen† vi (sein) go; (zu Fuß) walk; (fort-) leave; (funktionieren) work; ⟨Teig:⟩ rise; an die Arbeit g~ set to work; nach Norden g~ ⟨Fenster:⟩ face north; wenn es nach mir ginge if I had my way;

über die Straße g~ cross the road; impers wie geht es [Ihnen]? how are you? es geht mir gut I am well; es geht nicht it's impossible; es geht um it concerns; □vt walk. g~ lassen† (sich) vr sep lose one's self-control; (sich vernachlässigen) let oneself go

Geheul nt -s howling
Gehilfe m -n,-n, Gehilfin f -,-nen trainee; (Helfer) assistant
Gehirn nt -s brain; (Verstand) brains pl. G~ erschütterung f concussion. G~ hautentzündung f meningitis. G~ wäsche f brainwashing

gehoben a (fig) superior
Gehöft nt -[e]s,-e farm
Gehör nt -s hearing
gehorchen vi (haben) (+ dat) obey
gehören vi (haben) belong (dat to); dazu gehört Mut that takes courage; es gehört sich nicht it isn't done
gehörlos a deaf
Gehörn nt -s,-e horns pl; (Geweih) antlers pl
gehorsam a obedient. G~ m -s obedience
Gehsteig m -[e]s,-e pavement
Geier m -s,- vulture
Geige f -,-n violin. g~ en vi (haben) play the violin □vt play on the violin. G~ er(in) m -s,- (f -,-nen) violinist
geil a lecherous; (fam) randy
Geisel f -,-n hostage
Geiß f -,-en (SGer) [nanny-]goat. G~ blatt nt honeysuckle
Geist m -[e]s,-er mind; (Witz) wit; (Gesinnung) spirit; (Gespenst) ghost; der Heilige G~ the Holy Ghost or Spirit
geistes|abwesend a absentminded. G~ blitz m brainwave. g~ gegenwärtig adv with great presence of mind. g~ gestört a

deranged. **g~krank** a mentally ill. **G~krankheit** f mental illness. **G~wissenschaften** fpl arts. **G~zustand** m mental state

geist|ig a mental; (intellektuell) intellectual. **g~lich** a spiritual; (religiös) religious; ⟨Musik⟩ sacred; ⟨Tracht⟩ clerical. **G~liche(r)** m clergyman. **G~lichkeit** f clergy. **g~reich** a clever; (witzig) witty

Geiz m -es meanness. **g~en** vi (haben) be mean (**mit** with). **G~hals** m (fam) miser. **g~ig** a mean, miserly

Gekicher nt -s giggling

gekonnt a accomplished □adv expertly

gekränkt a offended, hurt

Gekritzel nt -s scribble

Gelächter nt -s laughter

geladen a loaded

gelähmt a paralysed

Gelände nt -s,- terrain; (Grundstück) site. **G~lauf** m crosscountry run

Geländer nt -s,- railings pl; (Treppen-) banisters pl

gelangen† vi (sein) reach/(fig) attain (**zu etw/an etw** acc sth)

gelassen a composed; (ruhig) calm. **G~heit** f - equanimity; (Fassung) composure

Gelatine /ʒela-/ f - gelatine

geläufig a common, current; (fließend) fluent; **jdm g~ sein** be familiar to s.o.

gelaunt a **gut/schlecht g~ sein** be in a good/bad mood

gelb a yellow; (bei Ampel) amber. **G~** nt -s,- yellow. **g~lich** a yellowish. **G~sucht** f jaundice

Geld nt -es,-er money; **öffentliche G~er** public funds. **G~beutel** m, **G~börse** f purse. **G~geber** m -s,- backer. **g~lich** a financial. **G~mittel** ntpl funds. **G~schein** m banknote.

G~schrank m safe. **G~strafe** f fine. **G~stück** nt coin

Gelee /ʒe'le:/ nt -s,-s jelly

gelegen a situated; (passend) convenient

Gelegenheit f -,-en opportunity; chance; (Anlaß) occasion; (Comm) bargain; **bei G~** some time. **G~sarbeit** f casual work

gelegentlich a occasional □adv occasionally; (bei Gelegenheit) some time

Gelehrte(r) m/f scholar

Geleit nt -[e]s escort; **freies G~** safe conduct. **g~en** vt escort

Gelenk nt -[e]s,-e joint. **g~ig** a supple; (Techn) flexible

gelernt a skilled

Geliebte(r) m/f lover

gelingen† vi (sein) succeed, be successful. **G~** nt -s success

gellend a shrill

geloben vt promise [solemnly]

Gelöbnis nt -ses,-se vow

gelöst a (fig) relaxed

Geise f -,-n (Aust) mosquito

gelten† vi (haben) be valid; ⟨Regel:⟩ apply; **g~ als** be regarded as; **wenig/viel g~** be worth/(fig) count for little/a lot; **das gilt nicht** that doesn't count. **g~d** a valid; ⟨Preise⟩ current; (Meinung) prevailing; **g~d machen** assert ⟨Recht⟩; **bring to bear** (Einfluß)

Geltung f - validity; (Ansehen) prestige; **zur G~ bringen** set off

Gelübde nt -s,- vow

gelungen a successful

Gelüst nt -[e]s,-e desire

gemächlich a leisurely □adv in a leisurely manner

Gemahl m -s,-e husband. **G~in** f -,-nen wife

Gemälde nt -s,- painting. **G~galerie** f picture gallery

gemäß prep (+ dat) in accordance with

gemäßigt a moderate; ⟨*Klima*⟩ temperate

gemein a common; (*unanständig*) vulgar; (*niederträchtig*) mean; **g~er Soldat** private

Gemeinde f -,-n [local] community; (*Admin*) borough; (*Pfarr~*) parish; (*bei Gottesdienst*) congregation. **G~rat** m local council/ (*Person*) councillor. **G~wahlen** fpl local elections

gemeingefährlich a dangerous. **G~heit** f -,-en (s. gemein) commonness; vulgarity; meanness; (*Bemerkung, Handlung*) mean thing [to say/do]; **so eine G~heit!** how mean! **G~kosten** pl overheads. **g~nützig** a charitable. **g~sam** a common ○ adv together

Gemeinschaft f -,-en community. **g~lich** a joint; (*Besitz*) communal ○ adv jointly; (*zusammen*) together. **G~sarbeit** f team-work

Gemenge nt -s,- mixture

Gemisch nt -[e]s,-e mixture. **g~t** a mixed

Gemme f -,-n engraved gem

Gemse f -,-n chamois

Gemurmel nt -s murmuring

Gemüse nt -s,- vegetable; (*coll*) vegetables pl. **G~händler** m greengrocer

gemustert a patterned

Gemüt nt -[e]s,-er nature, disposition; (*Gefühl*) feelings pl

gemütlich a cosy; (*gemächlich*) leisurely; (*zwanglos*) informal; ⟨*Person*⟩ genial; **es sich** (*dat*) **g~ machen** make oneself comfortable. **G~keit** f cosiness

Gen nt -s,-e gene

genau a exact, precise; (*Messung*) accurate; (*sorgfältig*) meticulous; (*ausführlich*) detailed; **nichts G~es wissen** not know any details; **g~!** exactly! **g~genommen** adv strictly

speaking. **G~igkeit** f - exactitude; precision; accuracy; meticulousness

genauso adv just the same; (*g~sehr*) just as much; **g~gut** just as good. **g~gut** adv just as well. **g~sehr** adv just as much. **g~viel** adv just as much/many. **g~wenig** adv just as little/few; (*noch*) no more

Gendarm /ʒãˈdarm/ m -en,-en (*Aust*) policeman

Genealogie f - genealogy

genehmig|en vt grant; approve ⟨*Plan*⟩. **G~ung** f -,-en permission; (*Schein*) permit

geneigt a sloping, inclined; (*fig*) well-disposed (*dat* towards)

General m -s,-e general. **G~direktor** m managing director. **G~probe** f dress rehearsal. **G~streik** m general strike

Generation /-ˈtsɪoːn/ f -,-en generation

Generator m -s,-en /-ˈtoːrən/ generator

generell a general

genes|en† vi (*sein*) recover. **G~ung** f - recovery; (*Erholung*) convalescence

Genetik f - genetics sg

Genf nt -s Geneva. **G~er** a Geneva ...; **G~er See** see Lake Geneva

genial a brilliant. **G~ität** f - genius

Genick nt -s,-e [back of the] neck; **sich** (*dat*) **das G~ brechen** break one's neck

Genie /ʒeˈniː/ nt -s,-s genius

genieren /ʒeˈniːrən/ vr embarrass; **sich g~** feel or be embarrassed

genieß|bar a fit to eat/drink. **g~en†** vt enjoy; (*verzehren*) eat/ drink. **G~er** m -s,- gourmet

Genitiv m -s,-e genitive

Genosse m -n,-n (*Pol*) comrade. **G~nschaft** f -,-en cooperative

Gentechnologie f genetic engineering

genug inv a & adv enough

Genüge f zur G~ sufficiently. **g~n** vi (haben) be enough. **g~nd** inv a sufficient, enough; (Sch) fair □ adv sufficiently, enough

Genuß m -sses, ¨sse enjoyment; (Vergnügen) pleasure; (Verzehr) consumption

geöffnet a open

Geo|graphie f - geography. **g~graphisch** a geographical. **G~loge** m -n,-n geologist. **G~logie** f- geology. **g~logisch** a geological. **G~meter** m -s,- surveyor. **G~metrie** f - geometry. **g~metrisch** a geometric[al]

geordnet a well-ordered; (stabil) stable; **alphabetisch g~** in alphabetical order

Gepäck nt -s luggage, baggage. **G~ablage** f luggage-rack. **G~aufbewahrung** f left-luggage office. **G~schein** m left-luggage ticket; (Aviat) baggage check. **G~träger** m porter; (Fahrrad-) luggage carrier; (Dach-) roof-rack

Gepard m -s,-e cheetah

gepflegt a well-kept; ⟨Person⟩ well-groomed; ⟨Hotel⟩ first-class

gepunktet a spotted

gerade a straight; (direkt) direct; (aufrecht) upright; (aufrichtig) straightforward; ⟨Zahl⟩ even □ adv straight; directly; (eben) just; (genau) exactly; (besonders) especially; **g~ erst** only just. **G~** f -,-n straight line. **g~aus** adv straight ahead/on

gerade|biegen† vt sep straighten; (fig) straighten out. **g~sitzen†** vi sep (haben) sit [up] straight. **g~so** adv just the same. **g~stehen†** vi sep (haben) stand up

straight; (fig) accept responsibility (**für** for). **g~zu** adv virtually; (wirklich) absolutely

Geranie /-jə/ f -,-n geranium

Gerät nt -[e]s,-e tool; (Acker-) implement; (Küchen-) utensil; (Elektro-) appliance; (Radio-, Fernseh-) set; (Turn-) piece of apparatus; (coll) equipment

geraten† vi (sein) get; **in Brand g~** catch fire; **in Wut g~** get angry; **gut g~** turn out well

Geratewohl nt aufs G~ at random

geräuchert a smoked

geräumig a spacious, roomy

Geräusch nt -[e]s,-e noise. **g~los** a noiseless

gerben vt tan

gerecht a just; (fair) fair. **g~fertigt** a justified. **G~igkeit** f - justice; fairness

Gerede nt -s talk; (Klatsch) gossip

geregelt a regular

gereizt a irritable

Gericht¹ nt -[e]s,-e (Culin) dish

Gericht² nt -[e]s,-e court [of law]; **vor G~** in court; **das Jüngste G~** the Last Judgement. **g~lich** a judicial; ⟨Verfahren⟩ legal □ adv **g~lich vorgehen** take legal action. **G~smedizin** f forensic medicine. **G~ssaal** m courtroom. **G~svollzieher** m -s,- bailiff

gering a small; (niedrig) low; (g~fügig) slight. **g~fügig** a slight. **g~schätzig** a contemptuous; ⟨Bemerkung⟩ disparaging. **g~ste(r,s)** a least

gerinnen† vi (sein) curdle; ⟨Blut:⟩ clot

Gerippe nt -s,- skeleton; (fig) framework

gerissen a (fam) crafty

Germ m -[e]s (Aust) f - yeast

German|e m -n,-n [ancient] German. **g~isch** a Germanic.

G~istik f - German [language and literature]

gern[e] adv gladly; **g~ haben** like; (*lieben*) be fond of; **ich tanze g~** I like dancing; **willst du mit?**—**g~!** do you want to come?—I'd love to!

Gerste f - barley. **G~nkorn** nt (*Med*) stye

Geruch m -[e]s,ᵉ smell (**von**/**nach** of). **g~los** a odourless.

G~ssinn m sense of smell

Gerücht nt -[e]s,-e rumour

gerührt a (*fig*) moved, touched

Gerümpel nt -s lumber, junk

Gerüst nt -[e]s,-e scaffolding; (*fig*) framework

gesamt a entire, whole. **G~ausgabe** f complete edition. **G~heit** f - whole. **G~schule** f comprehensive school. **G~summe** f total

Gesandte(r) m/f envoy

Gesang m -[e]s,ᵉ singing; (*Lied*) song; (*Kirchen-*) hymn. **G~verein** m choral society

Gesäß nt -es buttocks pl.

Geschäft nt -[e]s,-e business; (*Laden*) shop; (*Transaktion*) deal; (*fam: Büro*) office; **ein gutes G~ machen** do very well (**mit** out of); **sein G~ verstehen** know one's job. **g~ehalber** adv on business. **G~igkeit** f - activity. **g~lich** a business ... □adv on business

Geschäfts|brief m business letter. **G~führer** m manager; (*Vereins-*) secretary. **G~mann** m (pl -leute) businessman. **G~stelle** f office; (*Zweigstelle*) branch. **g~tüchtig** a **g~tüchtig sein** be a good businessman/-woman. **G~zeiten** fpl hours of business

geschehen vi (sein) happen (*dat* to); **das geschieht dir recht!** it serves you right! **gern g~!**

you're welcome! **G~** nt -s events pl

gescheit a clever

Geschenk nt -[e]s,-e present, gift

Geschicht|e f -,-n history; (*Erzählung*) story; (*fam: Sache*) business. **g~lich** a historical

Geschick nt -[e]s fate; (*Talent*) skill. **G~lichkeit** f - skilfulness, skill. **g~t** a skilful; (*klug*) clever

geschieden a divorced

Geschirr nt -s,-e (coll) crockery; (*Porzellan*) china; (*Service*) service; (*Pferde-*) harness; **schmutziges G~** dirty dishes pl. **G~spülmaschine** f dishwasher.

G~tuch nt tea-towel

Geschlecht nt -[e]s,-er sex; (*Gram*) gender. **g~lich** a sexual.

G~skrankheit f venereal disease. **G~steile** ntpl genitals.

G~sverkehr m sexual intercourse. **G~swort** nt (pl -wörter) article

geschliffen a (*fig*) polished

Geschmack m -[e]s,ᵉ taste; (*Aroma*) flavour; (*G~ssinn*) sense of taste; **einen guten G~ haben** (*fig*) have good taste. **g~los** a tasteless; **g~los sein** (*fig*) be in bad taste. **g~voll** a (*fig*) tasteful

Geschoß nt -sses,-sse missile; (*Stockwerk*) storey, floor

Geschrei nt -s screaming

Geschütz nt -es,-e gun, cannon

geschützt a protected; ⟨*Stelle*⟩ sheltered

Geschwader nt -s,- squadron

Geschwätz nt -es talk

geschweige conj **g~ denn** let alone

Geschwindigkeit f -,-en speed; (*Phys*) velocity. **G~sbegrenzung**, **G~sbeschränkung** f speed limit

Geschwister pl brother[s] and sister[s]; siblings

geschwollen a swollen; (*fig*) pompous

Geschworene(r) *m/f* juror; **die G~n** the jury *sg*

Geschwulst *f -,-̈e* swelling; (*Tumor*) tumour

geschwungen *a* curved

Geschwür *nt -s,-e* ulcer

gesellig *a* sociable; (*Zool*) gregarious; (*unterhaltsam*) convivial; **g~er Abend** social evening

Gesellschaft *f -,-en* company; (*Veranstaltung*) party; **die G~** society; **jdm G~ leisten** keep s.o. company. **g~lich** *a* social. **G~sspiel** *nt* party game

Gesetz *nt -es,-e* law. **G~entwurf** *m* bill. **g~gebend** *a* legislative. **G~gebung** *f -* legislation. **g~lich** *a* legal. **g~mäßig** *a* lawful; (*gesetzlich*) legal. **g~widrig** *a* illegal

gesichert *a* secure

Gesicht *nt -[e]s,-er* face; (*Aussehen*) appearance. **G~sfarbe** *f* complexion. **G~szüge** *mpl* features

Gesindel *nt -s* riff-raff

gesondert *a* separate

Gespann *nt -[e]s,-e* team; (*Wagen*) horse and cart/carriage

gespannt *a* taut; (*fig*) tense; (*Beziehungen*) strained; (*neugierig*) eager; (*erwartungsvoll*) expectant; **g~ sein, ob** wonder whether; **auf etw g~ sein** look forward eagerly to sth

Gespenst *nt -[e]s,-er* ghost. **g~isch** *a* ghostly; (*unheimlich*) eerie

Gespött *nt -[e]s* mockery; **zum G~ werden** become a laughingstock

Gespräch *nt -[e]s,-e* conversation; (*Telefon-*) call; **ins G~ kommen** get talking; **im G~ sein** be under discussion. **g~ig** *a* talkative. **G~sthema** *nt* topic of conversation

gesprenkelt *a* speckled

Gestalt *f -,-en* figure; (*Form*) shape, form; (*fig*) take shape. **g~en** *vt* shape; (*organisieren*) arrange; (*schaffen*) create; (*entwerfen*) design

Geständnis *nt -ses,-se* confession

Gestank *m -s* stench, [bad] smell

gestatten *vt* allow, permit; **nicht gestattet** prohibited; **g~ Sie?** may I?

Geste /'ge-, 'ge:stə/ *f -,-n* gesture

Gesteck *nt -[e]s,-e* flower arrangement

gestehen† *vt/i* (*haben*) confess; confess to ⟨*Verbrechen*⟩

Gestein *nt -[e]s,-e* rock

Gestell *nt -[e]s,-e* stand; (*Flaschen-*) rack; (*Rahmen*) frame

gesteppt *a* quilted

gestern *adv* yesterday; **g~ nacht** last night

gestrandet *a* stranded

gestreift *a* striped

gestrichelt *a* ⟨*Linie*⟩ dotted

gestrichen *a* **g~er Teelöffel** level teaspoon[ful]

gestrig /'gɛstrɪç/ *a* yesterday's; **am g~en Tag** yesterday

Gestrüpp *nt -s,-e* undergrowth

Gestüt *nt -[e]s,-e* stud [farm]

Gesuch *nt -[e]s,-e* request; (*Admin*) application. **g~t** *a* sought-after; (*gekünstelt*) contrived

gesund *a* healthy; **g~ sein** be in good health; ⟨*Sport, Getränk:*⟩ be good for one; **wieder g~ werden** get well again

Gesundheit *f -* health; **G~!** (*bei Niesen*) bless you! **g~lich** *a* health ...; **g~licher Zustand** state of health □ *adv* **es geht ihm g~lich gut/schlecht** he is in good/poor health. **g~sschädlich** *a* harmful

getäfelt *a* panelled

Getöse *nt -s* racket, din

Getränk *nt -[e]s,-e* drink. **G~ekarte** *f* wine-list

getrauen vt sich (dat) etw g~
dare [to] do sth; sich g~ dare

Getreide nt -s (coll) grain

getrennt a separate; g~ leben
live apart

getreu a faithful g~ prep (+dat)
true to. g~lich adv faithfully

Getriebe nt -s, - bustle; (Techn)
gear; (Auto) transmission; (Gehäuse) gearbox

getrost adv with confidence

Getto nt -s, -s ghetto

Getue nt -s (fam) fuss

Getümmel nt -s tumult

geübt a skilled

Gewächs nt -es, -e plant

gewachsen a jdm/etw g~ sein
be a match for s.o./be equal to sth

Gewächshaus nt greenhouse

gewagt a daring

gewählt a refined

gewahr a g~ werden become
aware (acc/gen of)

Gewähr f guarantee

gewähren vt grant; (geben) offer.
g~leisten vt guarantee

Gewahrsam m -s safekeeping;
(Haft) custody

Gewalt f -,-en power; (Kraft)
force; (Brutalität) violence; mit
G~ by force; G~herrschaft f
tyranny. g~ig a powerful; (fam:
groß) enormous; (stark) tremendous. g~sam a forcible; ⟨Tod⟩
violent. g~tätig a violent.
G~tätigkeit f -,-en violence;
(Handlung) act of violence

Gewand nt -[e]s,-er robe

gewandt a skilful. G~heit f -
skill

Gewebe nt -s, - fabric; (Anat) tissue

Gewehr nt -s,-e rifle, gun

Geweih nt -[e]s,-e antlers pl

Gewerb|e nt -s,- trade. g~lich a
commercial. g~smäßig a professional

Gewerkschaft f -,-en trade union. G~ler(in) m -s,- (f -,-nen)
trade unionist

ewic t nt -[e]s,-e weight; (Bedeutung) importance. G~heben
nt -s weight-lifting

Gewinde nt -s,- [screw] thread

Gewinn m -[e]s,-e profit; (fig)
gain, benefit; (beim Spiel) win-
nings pl; (Preis) prize; (Los) win-
ning ticket. G~beteiligung f
profit-sharing. g~en† vt win; (erlangen) gain; (fördern) extract
□vi (haben) win; g~en an (+
dat) gain in. g~end a engaging.
G~er(in) m -s,- (f -,-nen)
winner

Gewirr nt -s,-e tangle; (Straßen-)
maze

gewiß a certain

Gewissen nt -s,- conscience.
g~haft a conscientious. g~los
a unscrupulous. G~sbisse mpl
pangs of conscience

gewissermaßen adv to a certain
extent; (sozusagen) as it were

Gewißheit f certainty

Gewitt|er nt -s,- thunderstorm.
g~rig a thundery

gewöhnen vt jdn/sich g~ an (+
acc) get s.o. used to/get used to;
[an] jdn/etw gewöhnt sein be
used to s.o./sth

Gewohnheit f -,-en habit.
G~srecht nt common law

gewöhnlich a ordinary; (üblich)
usual; (ordinär) common

gewohnt a customary; (vertraut)
familiar; (üblich) usual; etw (acc)
g~ sein be used to sth

Gewölbe nt -s,- vault

Gewühl nt -[e]s crush

gewunden a winding

Gewürz nt -es,-e spice. G~nelke
f clove

gezackt a serrated

gezähnt a serrated; ⟨Säge⟩
toothed

Gezeiten fpl tides

gezielt a specific; ⟨Frage⟩ pointed

geziert a affected

gezwungen a forced. **g~ermaßen** adv of necessity

Gicht f - gout

Giebel m -s,- gable

Gier f - greed (**nach** for). **g~ig** a greedy

gieß|en† vt pour; water ⟨Blumen, Garten⟩; (Techn) cast □ v impers **es g~t** it is pouring [with rain]. **G~kanne** f watering-can

Gift nt -[e]s,-e poison; ⟨Schlangen-⟩ venom; (Biol, Med) toxin. **g~ig** a poisonous; ⟨Schlange⟩ venomous; (Med, Chem) toxic; ⟨fig⟩ spiteful. **G~müll** m toxic waste. **G~pilz** m toadstool

Gilde f -,-n guild

Gin /dʒɪn/ m -s gin

Ginster m -s (Bot) broom

Gipfel m -s,- summit, top; ⟨fig⟩ peak. **g~n** vi (haben) culminate (**in** + dat in)

Gips m -es plaster. **G~verband** m (Med) plaster cast

Giraffe f -,-n giraffe

Girlande f -,-n garland

Girokonto /'ʒiːro-/ nt current account

Gischt m -[e]s & f - spray

Gitar|re f -,-n guitar. **G~rist(in)** m -en,-en (f -,-nen) guitarist

Gitter nt -s,- bars pl; (Rost) grating, grid; (Gelände, Zaun) railings pl; (Fenster-) grille; (Draht-) wire screen

Glanz m -es shine; (von Farbe, Papier) gloss; (Seiden-) sheen; (Politur) polish; ⟨fig⟩ brilliance; (Pracht) splendour

glänzen vi (haben) shine. **g~d** a shining, bright; ⟨Papier, Haar⟩ glossy; ⟨fig⟩ brilliant

glanz|los a dull. **G~stück** nt masterpiece

Glas nt -es,-̈er glass; (Brillen-) lens; (Fern-) binoculars pl; (Marmeladen-) [glass] jar. **G~er** m -s,- glazier

glasieren vt glaze; ice ⟨Kuchen⟩

glas|ig a glassy; (durchsichtig) transparent. **G~scheibe** f pane

Glasur f -,-en glaze; (Culin) icing

glatt a smooth; (eben) even; ⟨Haar⟩ straight; (rutschig) slippery; (einfach) straightforward; ⟨Absage⟩ flat □ adv smoothly; evenly; (fam: völlig) completely; (gerade) straight; ⟨Lüge⟩ easily; ⟨ablehnen⟩ flatly; **g~ verlaufen** go off smoothly

Glätte f - smoothness; (Rutschigkeit) slipperiness

Glatteis nt [black] ice

glatt|gehen† vi sep (sein) ⟨fig⟩ go off smoothly. **g~weg** adv (fam) outright

Glatz|e f -,-n bald patch; (Voll-) bald head; **eine G~e bekommen** go bald. **g~köpfig** a bald

Glaube m -ns belief (**an** + acc in); (Relig) faith; **G~n schenken** (+ dat) believe. **g~n** vt/i (haben) believe (**an** + acc in); (vermuten) think; **jdm g~n** believe s.o.; **nicht zu g~n** unbelievable, incredible. **G~nsbekenntnis** nt creed

gläubig a religious; (vertrauend) trusting. **G~e(r)** m/f (Relig) believer; **die G~en** the faithful. **G~er** m -s,- (Comm) creditor

glaub|lich a **kaum g~lich** scarcely believable. **g~würdig** a credible; ⟨Person⟩ reliable

gleich a same; (identisch) identical; ⟨g~wertig⟩ equal; **2 mal 5 [ist] g~ 10** two times 5 equals 10; **das ist mir g~** it's all the same to me; **ganz g~,** wo/wer no matter where/who □ adv equally; (übereinstimmend) identically, the same; (sofort) immediately; (in Kürze) in a minute; (fast) nearly;

(direkt) right. **g~altrig** *a* [of] the same age. **g~bedeutend** *a* synonymous. **g~berechtigt** *a* equal. **G~berechtigung** *f* equality

gleichen† *vi (haben)* jdm/etw **g~**; be like*r* or resemble s.o./sth

gleich|ermaßen *adv* equally. **g~falls** *adv* also, likewise; **danke g~falls** thank you, the same to you. **G~gewicht** *nt* balance; *(Phys & fig)* equilibrium. **g~gültig** *a* indifferent; *(unwichtig)* unimportant. **G~gültigkeit** *f* indifference. **g~machen** *vt sep* make equal; **dem Erdboden g~machen** raze to the ground. **g~mäßig** *a* even, regular; *(beständig)* constant. **G~mäßigkeit** *f* · regularity

Gleichnis *nt* -ses, -se parable **Gleich|schritt** *m* im **G~schritt** in step. **g~setzen** *vt sep* equate/ *(g~stellen)* place on a par *(dat/ mit* with). **g~stellen** *vt sep* place on a par *(dat* with). **G~strom** *m* direct current

Gleichung *f* -,-en equation **gleich|wertig** *a* of equal value. **g~zeitig** *a* simultaneous

Gleis *nt* -es,-e track; *(Bahnsteig)* platform; **G~** 5 platform 5

gleiten† *vi (sein)* glide; *(rutschen)* slide. **g~d** *a* gliding; **g~de Arbeitszeit** flexitime

Gleitzeit *f* flexitime

Gletscher *m* -s,- glacier

Glied *nt* -[e]s,-er limb; *(Teil)* part; *(Ketten~)* link; *(Mitglied)* member; *(Mil)* rank. **g~ern** *vt* arrange; *(einteilen)* divide

glitschig *a* slippery

glitzern *vi (haben)* glitter

Globus *m* -(busses), -ben & -busse globe

Glocke *f* -,-n bell

glorreich *a* glorious

Glossar *nt* -s,-e glossary

Glosse *f* -,-n comment

glotzen *vi (haben)* stare

Glück *nt* -[e]s [good] luck; *(Zufriedenheit)* happiness; **g~/kein G~ haben** be lucky/unlucky; **zum G~** luckily, fortunately; **auf gut G~** on the off chance; *(wahllos)* at random. **g~en** *vi (sein)* succeed

gluckern *vi (haben)* gurgle

glücklich *a* lucky, fortunate; *(zufrieden)* happy; *(sicher)* safe □ *adv* happily; safely. **g~erweise** *adv* luckily, fortunately

Glücksspiel *nt* game of chance; *(Spielen)* gambling

Glückwunsch *m* good wishes *pl*; *(Gratulation)* congratulations *pl*; **herzlichen G~!** congratulations! *(zum Geburtstag)* happy birthday! **G~karte** *f* greetings card

Glüh|birne *f* light-bulb. **g~en** *vi (haben)* glow. **g~end** *a* glowing; *(rot~)* red-hot; *(Hitze)* scorching; *(leidenschaftlich)* fervent. **G~faden** *m* filament. **G~wein** *m* mulled wine. **G~würmchen** *nt* -s,- glow-worm

Glukose *f* · glucose

Glut *f* · embers *pl*; *(Röte)* glow; *(Hitze)* heat; *(fig)* ardour

GmbH *abbr* **(Gesellschaft mit beschränkter Haftung)** ≈ plc

Gnade *f* · mercy; *(Gunst)* favour; *(Relig)* grace. **G~nfrist** *f* reprieve

gnädig *a* gracious; *(mild)* lenient; **g~e Frau** Madam

Gnom *m* -en,-en gnome

Gobelin /goba'lɛ̃:/ *m* -s,-s tapestry

Gold *nt* -[e]s gold. **g~en** *a* gold . .; *(g~farben)* golden. **G~fisch** *m* goldfish. **g~ig** *a* sweet, lovely. **G~lack** *m* wallflower. **G~regen** *m* laburnum

Golf¹ *m* -[e]s,-e *(Geog)* gulf

Golf² *nt* -s golf. **G~platz** *m* golf-course. **G~schläger** *m* golf-club. **G~spieler(in)** *m(f)* golfer

Gondel f -,-n gondola; (*Kabine*) cabin

gönnen vt jdm etw g~ not begrudge s.o. sth; **jdm etur nicht g~** begrudge s.o. sth

Gör nt -s,-en, **Göre** f -,-n (*fam*) kid

Gorilla m -s,-s gorilla

Gosse f -,-n gutter

Got|**ik** f - Gothic. **g~isch** a Gothic

Gott m -[e]s,-er God; (*Myth*) god

Götterspeise f jelly

Gottes|**dienst** m service. **G~-lästerung** f blasphemy

Gottheit f -,-en deity

Göttin f -,-nen goddess

göttlich a divine

gottlos a ungodly; (*atheistisch*) godless

Grab nt -[e]s,-er grave

graben† vi (*haben*) dig

Graben m -s,- ditch; (*Mil*) trench

Grabmal nt tomb. **G~stein** m gravestone, tombstone

Grad m -[e]s,-e degree

Graf m -en,-en count

Grafik f -,-en graphics sg; (*Kunst*) graphic arts pl; (*Druck*) print

Gräfin f -,-nen countess

grafisch a graphic; **g~e Darstellung** diagram

Grafschaft f -,-en county

Gram m -s grief

grämen (sich) vr grieve

Gramm nt -s,-e gram

Gramm|**atik** f -,-en grammar. **g~matikalisch** a grammatical

Granat m -[e]s,-e (*Miner*) garnet. **G~e** f -,-n shell; (*Hand-*) grenade

Granit m -s,-e granite

Gras nt -es,-er grass. **g~en** vi (*haben*) graze. **G~hüpfer** m -s,- grasshopper

gräßlich a dreadful

Grat m -[e]s,-e (*mountain*) ridge

Gräte f -,-n fishbone

Gratifikation /-'tsi̯oːn/ f -,-en bonus

gratis adv free [of charge]. **G~probe** f free sample

Gratu|**lant(in)** m -en,-en (f -,-nen) well-wisher. **G~lation** /-'tsi̯oːn/ f -,-en congratulations pl; (*Glückwünsche*) best wishes pl. **g~lieren** vi (*haben*) jdm **g~lieren** congratulate s.o. (zu on); (*zum Geburtstag*) wish s.o. happy birthday

grau a, **G~** nt -s,- grey

grauen v impers **mir graut [es] davor** I dread it. **g~haft** a gruesome; (*gräßlich*) horrible

grausam a cruel. **G~keit** f -,-en cruelty

graus|**en** v impers **mir graust davor** I dread it. **G~en** nt -s horror, dread. **g~ig** a gruesome

gravieren vt engrave. **g~d** a (*fig*) serious

graziös a graceful

greifen† vt take hold of; (*fangen*) catch □vi (*haben*) reach (**nach** for); **um sich g~** (*fig*) spread

Greis m -es,-e old man. **G~in** f -,-nen old woman

grell a glaring; ⟨*Farbe*⟩ garish; (*schrill*) shrill

Gremium nt -s,-ien committee

Grenz|**e** f -,-n border; (*Staats-*) frontier; (*Grundstücks-*) boundary; (*fig*) limit. **g~en** vi (*haben*) border (**an** + acc on). **g~enlos** a boundless; (*maßlos*) infinite

Greuel m -s,- horror

greulich a horrible

Griech|**e** m -n,-n Greek. **G~enland** nt -s Greece. **G~in** f -,-nen Greek woman. **g~isch** a Greek. **G~isch** nt -[s] (*Lang*) Greek

Grieß m -es semolina

Griff m -[e]s,-e grasp, hold; (*Hand-*) movement of the hand; (*Tür-, Messer-*) handle; (*Schwert-*) hilt. **g~bereit** a handy

Grill m -s,-s grill

Grille f -,-n (*Zool*) cricket

grill|en vt grill; (im Freien) barbecue □ vi (haben) have a barbecue. **G~fest** nt barbecue

Grimasse f -,-n grimace; **G~n schneiden** pull faces

grimmig a furious; ⟨Kälte⟩ bitter

grinsen vi (haben) grin

Grippe f -,-n influenza, (fam) flu

grob a coarse; (unsanft, ungefähr) rough; (unhöflich) rude; (schwer) gross; ⟨Fehler⟩ bad; **g~geschätzt** roughly. **G~ian** m -s,-e brute

grölen vt/i (haben) bawl

Groll m -[e]s resentment. **g~en** vi (haben) be angry (dat with); ⟨Donner:⟩ rumble

Grönland nt -s Greenland

Gros nt -ses,- ⟨Maß⟩ gross

Groschen m -s,- (Aust) groschen; (fam) ten-pfennig piece

groß a big; ⟨Anzahl⟩ large; (bedeutend, stark) great; (g~artig) grand; ⟨Buchstabe⟩ capital; **g~e Ferien** summer holidays; **g~e Angst haben** be very frightened; **der größte Teil** the majority; **g~werden** ⟨Person:⟩ grow up; **g~und klein** young and old; **im g~en und ganzen** on the whole □adv ⟨feiern⟩ in style; (fam: viel) much

groß|artig a magnificent. **G~aufnahme** f close-up. **G~britannien** nt -s Great Britain. **G~e(r)** m/f unser **G~er** our eldest; **die G~en** the grown-ups. (fig) the great pl

Größe f -,-n size; (Ausmaß) extent; (Körper-) height; (Bedeutsamkeit) greatness; (Math) quantity; (Person) great figure

Groß|eltern pl grandparents. **G~handel** m wholesale trade. **G~händler** m wholesaler. **G~macht** f superpower. **G~mut** f magnanimity. **G~mutter** f grandmother. **G~schreibung** f capitalization.

g~sprecherisch a boastful. **g~spurig** a pompous; (überheblich) arrogant. **G~stadt** f [large] city. **g~städtisch** a city ... **G~teil** m large proportion; (Hauptteil) bulk

größtenteils adv for the most part

Groß|vater m grandfather. **g~ziehen†** vt sep bring up; rear ⟨Tier⟩. **g~zügig** a generous. **G~zügigkeit** f - generosity

Grotte f -,-n grotto

Grübchen nt -s,- dimple

Grube f -,-n pit

grübeln vi (haben) brood

Gruft f -,·e [burial] vault

grün a green; **im G~en** out in the country; **die G~en** the Greens

Grund m -[e]s,·e ground; (Boden) bottom; (Hinter-) background; (Ursache) reason; **auf G~** + (+ gen) on the strength of; **aus diesem G~e** for this reason; **im G~e [genommen]** basically; **auf G~laufen** (Naut) run aground. **G~besitzer** m landowner

gründ|en vt found, set up; start ⟨Familie⟩; (fig) base (**auf** + acc on); **sich g~en** be based (**auf** + acc on). **G~er(in)** m -s,- (f -,-nen) founder

Grund|farbe f primary colour. **G~form** f (Gram) infinitive. **G~gesetz** nt (Pol) constitution. **G~lage** f basis, foundation

gründlich a thorough. **G~keit** f - thoroughness

Gründonnerstag m Maundy Thursday

Grund|regel f basic rule. **G~riß** m ground-plan; (fig) outline. **g~satz** m principle. **g~sätzlich** a fundamental; (im allgemeinen) in principle; (prinzipiell) on principle. **G~schule** f primary school. **G~stück** nt plot [of land]

Gründung f -,-en foundation

grunzen vi (haben) grunt
Gruppe f -,-n group; (Reise-) party
gruppieren vt group
Grusel|geschichte f horror story. **g~ig** a creepy
Gruß m -es,-¨e greeting; (Mil) salute; **einen schönen G~ an X** give my regards to X; **viele G~e** regards; **Mit freundlichen G~en** Yours sincerely/faithfully
grüßen vt/i (haben) say hallo (jdn to s.o.); (Mil) salute; **g~ Sie X von mir** give my regards to X; **grüß Gott!** (SGer, Aust) good morning/afternoon/ evening!
gucken vi (haben) (fam) look
Guerilla /gɛˈrɪlja/ f - guerilla warfare. **G~kämpfer** m guerilla
Gulasch et & m -s goulash
gültig a valid
Gummi m & nt -s,-[s] rubber; (Harz) gum. **G~band** nt (pl -bänder) elastic or rubber band
gummiert a gummed
Gummi|knüppel m truncheon. **G~stiefel** m gumboot, wellington. **G~zug** m elastic
Gunst f - favour
günstig a favourable; (passend) convenient
Gurgel f -,-n throat. **g~n** vi (haben) gargle
Gurke f -,-n cucumber; (Essig-) gherkin
gurren vi (haben) coo
Gurt m -[e]s,-e strap; (Gürtel) belt; (Auto) safety-belt. **G~band** nt (pl -bänder) waistband
Gürtel m -s,- belt. **G~linie** f waistline. **G~rose** f shingles sg
Guß m -sses,-¨sse (Techn) casting; (Strom) stream; (Regen-) downpour; (Torten-) icing. **G~eisen** nt cast iron
gut a good; (Gewissen) clear; (gütig) kind (zu to); **jdm gut sein** be fond of s.o.; **im g~en** amicably; **schon gut** that's all right □ adv well; (schmecken, riechen) good; (leicht) easily; **gut zu sehen** clearly visible; **gut drei Stunden** a good three hours

Gut nt -[e]s,-¨er possession, property; (Land-) estate; **Gut und Böse** good and evil; **Güter** (Comm) goods
Gutachten nt -s,- expert's report. **G~er** m -s,- expert
gutartig a good-natured; (Med) benign
Güte(s) nt etwas/nichts **G~s** something/nothing good; **G~s tun** do good; **alles G~!** all the best!
Güte f - goodness, kindness; (Qualität) quality
Güterzug m goods train
gut|gehen† vi sep (sein) go well; **es geht mir gut** I am well/(geschäftlich) doing well. **g~gehend** a flourishing, thriving. **g~gemeint** a well-meant. **g~gläubig** a trusting. **g~haben**† vt sep **fünfzig Mark g~haben** have fifty marks credit (with). **G~haben** nt -s,- [credit] balance; (Kredit) credit
gut|machen vt sep make up for; make good (Schaden). **G~mütigkeit** f - good nature. **G~schein** m credit note; (Bon) voucher; (Geschenk-) gift token. **g~schreiben**† vt sep credit. **G~schrift** f credit
Gutshaus nt manor house
gut|situiert a well-to-do. **g~tun**† vi sep (sein) **jdm/etw g~tun** do s.o./sth good
Gymnasium nt -s,-ien ≈ grammar school
Gymnast|ik f - [keep-fit] exercises pl; (Turnen) gymnastics pl

Gynäkologe m -n,-n gynaecologist. **G~logie** f- gynaecology

H

H, h /ha:/ nt -,- (Mus) B, b

Haar nt -[e]s,-e hair; sich (dat) die Haare od das H~ waschen wash one's hair; um ein H~ (fam) very nearly. **H~bürste** f hairbrush. **h~en** vi (haben) shed hairs; ⟨Tier:⟩ moult □or sich h~en moult. **h~ig** a hairy; (fam) tricky. **H~nadelkurve** f hairpin bend. **H~schnitt** m haircut. **H~waschmittel** nt shampoo

Habe f- possessions pl

haben† vt have; Angst/Hunger/ Durst h~ be frightened/hungry/thirsty; ich hätte gern I'd like; sich h~ (fam) make a fuss; es gut/schlecht h~ be well/badly off; was hat er? what's the matter with him? □v aux have; ich habe/hatte geschrieben I have/had written; er hätte ihr geholfen he would have helped her

Habgier f greed. **h~ig** a greedy

Habicht m -[e]s,-e hawk

Hachse f-,-n (Culin) knuckle

Hacke[1] f-,-n hoe; (Spitz-) pick

Hacke[2] f-,-n, **Hacken** m -s,- heel

hack|en vt hoe; ⟨schlagen, zerkleinern⟩ chop; ⟨Vogel:⟩ peck. **H~fleisch** nt mince

Hafen m -s,- harbour; (See-) port. **H~arbeiter** m docker

Hafer m -s oats pl. **H~flocken** fpl [rolled] oats

Haft f - (Jur) custody; (H~strafe) imprisonment. **h~bar** a (Jur) liable. **H~befehl** m warrant

haften vi (haben) cling; (kleben) stick; (bürgen) vouch/(Jur) be liable (für for)

Häftling m -s,-e detainee

Haftpflicht f (Jur) liability. **H~versicherung** f (Auto) third-party insurance

Haftung f- (Jur) liability

Hagebutte f-,-n rose-hip

Hagel m -s hail. **H~korn** nt hailstone. **h~n** vi (haben) hail

hager a gaunt

Hahn m -[e]s,-e cock; (Techn) tap

Hähnchen nt -s,- (Culin) chicken

Hai[fisch] m -[e]s,-e shark

Häkchen nt -s,- tick

häkel|n vt/i (haben) crochet. **H~nadel** f crochet-hook

Haken m -s,- hook, tick; (fam: Schwierigkeit) snag. **h~** vt hook (an + acc to). **H~kreuz** nt swastika

halb a half □adv half; **h~ drei** half past two; **fünf [Minuten] vor/nach h~ vier** twenty-five [minutes] past three/to four. **H~e(r,s)** f/m/nt half (of a litre)

halber prep (+ gen) for the sake of; Geschäfte h~ on business

Halbfinale nt semifinal

halbieren vt halve, divide in half; (Geom) bisect

Halb|insel f peninsula. **H~kreis** m semicircle. **H~kugel** f hemisphere. **h~laut** a low □adv in an undertone. **H~mast** adv at half-mast. **H~mond** m half moon. **H~pension** f half-board. **H~schuh** m [flat] shoe. **h~tags** adv [for] half a day; **h~tags arbeiten** ≈ work part-time. **h~ton** m semitone. **h~wegs** adv half-way; (ziemlich) more or less. **h~wüchsig** a adolescent. **H~zeit** f (Sport) half-time; (Spielzeit) half

Halde f-,-n dump, tip

Hälfte f-,-n half; zur H~ half

Halle f-,-n hall; (Hotel-) lobby; (Bahnhofs-) station concourse

hallen vi (haben) resound; (wider-) echo

Hallen- pref indoor

hallo *int* hallo

Halluzination /-'tsjo:n/ *f* -, -en hallucination

Halm *m* -[e]s, -e stalk; (*Gras-*) blade

Hals *m* -es, -̈e neck; (*Kehle*) throat; **aus vollem H~e** at the top of one's voice; (*lachen*) out loud. **H~band** *nt* (*pl* -bänder) collar. **H~schmerzen** *mpl* sore throat sg.

halt¹ *adv* (*SGer*) just; **es geht h~ nicht** it's just not possible

halt² *int* stop! (*Mil*) halt!

Halt *m* -[e]s, -e hold; (*Stütze*) support; (*innerer*) stability; (*Anhalten*) stop. **h~bar** *a* durable; (*Tex*) hard-wearing; **h~bar bis ...** (*Comm*) use by ...

halten† *vt* hold; make (*Rede*); give (*Vortrag*); (*einhalten, bewahren*) keep; [sich (*dat*)] **etw h~** keep (*Hund*); take (*Zeitung*); **h~ für** regard as; **viel h~ von** think highly of; **sich h~** hold on (**an** + *dat* to); (*Geschäft:*) keep going; (*haltbar sein*) keep; (*Wetter:*) hold; (*Blumen:*) last; **sich links h~** keep left; **sich h~ an** (+ *acc*) (*fig*) keep to □*vi* (*haben*) hold; (*haltbar sein*) keep; (*Blumen:*) last; (*haltmachen*) stop; **auf sich** (*acc*) **h~** take pride in oneself; **zu jdm h~** be loyal to s.o.

Halte|stelle *f* stop. **H~verbot** *nt* waiting restriction; 'H~verbot' 'no waiting'

haltmachen *vi sep* (*haben*) stop

Haltung *f* -, -en (*Körper-*) posture; (*Verhalten*) manner; (*Einstellung*) attitude; (*Fassung*) composure; (*Halten*) keeping

Hammel *m* -s, -̈ ram; (*Culin*) mutton. **H~fleisch** *nt* mutton

Hammer *m* -s, -̈ hammer

Hamster *m* -s, - hamster. **h~n** *vt/i* (*fam*) hoard

Hand *f* -, -̈e hand; **jdm die H~ geben** shake hands with s.o.;

rechter/linker **H~** on the right/ left; **unter der H~** secretly; (*geheim*) secretly; **an H~ von** with the aid of; **H~ und Fuß haben** (*fig*) be sound. **H~arbeit** *f* manual work; (*handwerklich*) handicraft; (*Nadelarbeit*) needlework; (*Gegenstand*) hand-made article. **H~ball** *m* handball. **H~bewegung** *f* gesture. **H~bremse** *f* handbrake. **H~buch** *nt* handbook, manual

Händedruck *m* handshake

Handel *m* -s trade, commerce; (*Unternehmen*) business; (*Geschäft*) deal; **H~ treiben** trade. **h~n** *vi* (*haben*) act; (*Handel treiben*) trade (**mit** in); **von etw** *od* **über etw** (*acc*) **h~n** deal with sth; **sich h~n um** be about, concern. **H~smarine** *f* merchant navy. **H~sschiff** *nt* merchant vessel. **H~sschule** *f* commercial college. **H~sware** *f* merchandise

Hand|feger *m* -s, - brush. **H~fläche** *f* palm. **H~gelenk** *nt* wrist. **H~gemenge** *nt* -s, - scuffle. **H~gepäck** *nt* hand-luggage. **h~greiflich** *a* tangible; **h~greiflich werden** become violent. **H~griff** *m* handle

handhaben *vt insep* (*reg*) handle

Handikap /'hɛndikɛp/ *nt* -s, -s handicap

Handkuß *m* kiss on the hand

Händler *m* -s, - dealer, trader

handlich *a* handy

Handlung *f* -, -en *act*; (*Handeln*) action; (*Roman-*) plot; (*Geschäft*) shop. **H~sweise** *f* conduct

Hand|schellen *fpl* handcuffs. **H~schlag** *m* handshake. **H~schrift** *f* handwriting; (*Text*) manuscript. **H~schuh** *m* glove. **H~stand** *m* handstand. **H~tasche** *f* handbag. **H~tuch** *nt* towel

Handwerk nt craft, trade. **H~er** m -s,-; craftsman; (Arbeiter) workman

Hanf m -[e]s hemp

Hang m -[e]s,ᵉe slope

Hänge|brücke f suspension bridge. **H~lampe** f [light] pendant. **H~matte** f hammock

hängen¹ vt (reg) hang

hängen²†vi (hang) hang; **h~an** (+dat) (fig) be attached to

Hannover nt -s Hanover

hänseln vt tease

hantieren vi (haben) busy oneself

Happen m -s, mouthful; **einen H~ essen** have a bite to eat

Harfe f -,-n harp

Harke f -,-n rake. **h~n** vt/i (haben) rake

harmlos a harmless; (arglos) innocent

Harmonie f -,-n harmony

Harmonika f -,-s accordion; (Mund-) mouth-organ

harmonisch a harmonious

Harn m -[e]s urine. **H~blase** f bladder

Harpune f -,-n harpoon

hart a hard; (heftig) violent; (streng) harsh

Härte f -,-n hardness; (Strenge) harshness; (Not) hardship

Hart|faserplatte f hardboard. **h~gekocht** a hard-boiled. **h~näckig** a stubborn; (ausdauernd) persistent

Harz nt -es,-e resin

Haschee nt -s,-s (Culin) hash

Haschisch nt & m -[s] hashish

Hase m -n,-n hare

Hasel f -,-n hazel. **H~maus** f dormouse. **H~nuß** f hazel-nut

Haß m -sses hatred

hassen vt hate

häßlich a ugly; (unfreundlich) nasty. **H~keit** f- ugliness; nastiness

Hast f - haste. **h~ig** a hasty, hurried

hast, hat, hätte, hätte s. **haben**

Haube f -,-n cap; (Trocken-) drier; (Kühler-) bonnet

Hauch m -[e]s breath; (Luft-) breeze; (Duft) whiff; (Spur) tinge. **h~dünn** a very thin

Haue f -,-n pick; (fam: Prügel) beating. **h~n**† vt beat; (hämmern) knock; (meißeln) hew; **sich h~n** fight □vi (haben) bang (auf+acc on); **jdm ins Gesicht h~n** hit s.o. in the face

Haufen m -s, heap, pile; (Leute) crowd

häufen vt heap or pile [up]; **sich h~** pile up; (zunehmen) increase

häufig a frequent. **H~keit** f - frequency

Haupt nt -[e]s, Häupter head. **H~bahnhof** m main station. **H~fach** nt main subject

Häuptling m -s,-e chief

Haupt|mahlzeit f main meal. **H~mann** m (pl -leute) captain. **H~post** f main post office. **H~quartier** nt headquarters pl. **H~rolle** f lead; (fig) leading role. **H~sache** f main thing; **in der H~sache** in the main. **h~sächlich** a main. **H~satz** m main clause. **H~stadt** f capital. **H~verkehrsstraße** f main road. **H~verkehrszeit** f rush-hour. **H~wort** nt (pl -wörter) noun

Haus nt -es, Häuser house; (Gebäude) building; (Schnecken-) shell; **zu H~e** at home; nach **H~e** home. **H~arbeit** f housework; (Sch) homework. **H~arzt** m family doctor. **H~aufgaben** fpl homework sg. **H~besetzer** m -s, squatter

hausen vi (haben) live; (wüten) wreak havoc

Haus|frau f housewife. **H~halt** m -[e]s,-e household; (Pol) budget. **h~halten**† vi sep (haben) **h~halten mit** manage carefully;

conserve ⟨Kraft⟩. **H~hälterin** f -,-nen housekeeper. **H~halts-geld** nt housekeeping [money]. **H~haltsplan** m budget. **H~herr** m head of the household; ⟨Gastgeber⟩ host

hausieren vi (haben) **h~en mit** hawk. **H~er** m -s,- hawker

Hauslehrer m [private] tutor. **H~in** f governess

häuslich a domestic; ⟨Person⟩ domesticated

Haus|meister m caretaker. **H~ordnung** f house rules pl. **H~putz** m cleaning. **H~rat** m -[e]s household effects pl. **H~schlüssel** m front-door key. **H~schuh** m slipper. **H~su-chungsbefehl** m search-warrant. **H~tier** nt domestic animal; ⟨Hund, Katze⟩ pet. **H~tür** f front door. **H~wirt** m landlord. **H~wirtin** f landlady

Haut f -,Häute skin; ⟨Tier-⟩ hide. **H~arzt** m dermatologist

häuten vt skin; **sich h~** moult

haut|eng a skin-tight. **H~farbe** f colour; ⟨Teint⟩ complexion

Hebamme f -,-n midwife

Hebel m -s,- lever. **H~kraft, H~wirkung** f leverage

heben† vt lift; ⟨hoch-, steigern⟩ raise; **sich h~** rise; ⟨Nebel:⟩ lift; ⟨sich verbessern⟩ improve

hebräisch a Hebrew

hecheln vi (haben) pant

Hecht m -[e]s,-e pike

Heck nt -s,-s ⟨Naut⟩ stern; ⟨Aviat⟩ tail; ⟨Auto⟩ rear

Hecke f -,-n hedge

Heck|fenster nt rear window. **H~tür** f hatchback

Heer nt -[e]s,-e army

Hefe f -,-n yeast

Heft nt -[e]s,-e booklet; ⟨Sch⟩ exercise book; ⟨Zeitschrift⟩ issue. **h~en** vt (nähen) tack; ⟨stecken⟩

pin/(klammern) clip/(mit Heft-maschine) staple (an+acc to). **H~er** m -s,- file

heftig a fierce, violent; ⟨Schlag, Regen⟩ heavy; ⟨Schmerz, Gefühl⟩ intense

Heft|klammer f staple; ⟨Büro-⟩ paper-clip. **H~maschine** f stapler. **H~zwecke** f -,-n drawing-pin

Heide[1] m -n,-n heathen

Heide[2] f -,-n heath; ⟨Bot⟩ heather. **H~kraut** nt heather

Heidelbeere f bilberry

Heidin f -,-nen heathen

heikel a difficult, tricky; ⟨delikat⟩ delicate; ⟨dial⟩ ⟨Person⟩ fussy

heil a undamaged, intact; ⟨Person⟩ unhurt; ⟨gesund⟩ well; **mit h~er Haut** ⟨fam⟩ unscathed

Heil nt -s salvation

Heiland m -s ⟨Relig⟩ Saviour

Heil|anstalt f sanatorium; ⟨Ner-ven-⟩ mental hospital. **H~bad** nt spa. **h~bar** a curable

Heilbutt m -[e]s,-e halibut

heilen vt cure; heal ⟨Wunde⟩ □ vi (sein) heal

Heilgymnastik f physiotherapy

heilig a holy; ⟨geweiht⟩ sacred; **die h~e** Anna Saint Anne. **H~abend** m Christmas Eve. **H~e(r)** m/f saint. **H~enschein** m halo. **H~keit** f- sanctity, holiness. **h~sprechen†** vt sep canonize. **H~tum** nt -s,-ˈer shrine

heil|kräftig a medicinal. **H~kräuter** ntpl medicinal herbs. **H~mittel** nt remedy. **H~praktiker** m -s,- practitioner of alternative medicine. **H~ung** f - cure

Heim m -[e]s,-e home; ⟨Studen-ten-⟩ hostel. **h~** adv home

Heimat f -,-en home; ⟨Land⟩ native land. **H~abend** m folk evening. **h~los** a homeless

heim|begleiten vt sep see home. **H~fahrt** f way home. **h~gehen†** vi sep (sein) go home

heimisch a native, indigenous; (Pol) domestic

Heim|kehr f - return [home]. **h~kehren** vi sep (sein) return home. **h~kommen†** vi sep (sein) come home

heimlich a secret. **H~keit** f -,-en secrecy; **H~keiten** secrets

Heim|reise f journey home. **H~spiel** nt home game. **h~suchen** vt sep afflict. **h~wärts** adv home. **H~weg** m way home. **H~weh** nt -s homesickness; **H~weh haben** be homesick. **H~werker** m -s,- [home] handyman. **h~zahlen** vt sep jdm etw **h~zahlen** (fig) pay s.o. back for sth

Heirat f -,-en marriage. **h~en** vt/i (haben) marry. **H~santrag** m proposal; **jdm einen H~santrag machen** propose to s.o.

heiser a hoarse. **H~keit** f - hoarseness

heiß a hot; (hitzig) heated; (leidenschaftlich) fervent

heißen† vi (haben) be called; (bedeuten) mean; **ich heiße ...** my name is ...; **wie heiße ich? Sie?** what is your name? **wie heißt ... auf englisch?** what's the English for ...? □vt call; **jdn etw tun h~** tell s.o. to do sth

heiter a cheerful; (Wetter) bright; (amüsant) amusing; **aus h~em Himmel** (fig) out of the blue

Heiz|anlage f heating; (Auto) heater. **H~decke** f electric blanket. **h~en** vt heat; (Ofen) □vi (haben) put the heating on; (Ofen:) give out heat. **H~gerät** nt heater. **H~kessel** m boiler. **H~körper** m radiator. **H~lüfter** m -s,- fan heater. **H~material** nt fuel. **H~ung** f -,-en heating; (Heizkörper) radiator

Hektar nt & m -s,- hectare

Held m -en,-en hero. **h~enhaft** a heroic. **H~entum** nt -s heroism. **H~in** f -,-nen heroine

helf|en† vi (haben) help (jdm s.o.); (nützen) be effective; **sich** (dat) **nicht zu h~en wissen** not know what to do; **es hilft nichts** it's no use. **H~er(in)** m -s,- (f -,-nen) helper, assistant

hell a light; (Licht ausstrahlend, klug) bright; (Stimme) clear; (fam: völlig) utter; **h~es Bier** ≈ lager □adv brightly

Hell|igkeit f - brightness. **H~seher(in)** m -s,- (f -,-nen) clairvoyant. **h~wach** a wide awake

Helm m -[e]s,-e helmet

Hemd nt -[e]s,-en vest; (Ober-) shirt

Hemisphäre f -,-n hemisphere

hemm|en vt check; (verzögern) impede; (fig) inhibit. **H~ung** f -,-en (fig) inhibition; (Skrupel) scruple; **H~ungen haben** be inhibited. **h~ungslos** a unrestrained

Hengst nt -s,-[n] (Aust) chicken

Hengst m -[e]s,-e stallion

Henkel m -s,- handle

Henne f -,-n hen

her adv (zeitlich) ago; **her mit ...!** give me ...! **von Norden/weit her** from the north/far away; **vor jdm her** in front of s.o.; **vom Thema her** as far as the subject is concerned

herab adv down [here]; **von oben h~** from above; (fig) condescending

herablass|en† vt sep let down; **sich h~en** condescend (zu to). **H~ung** f - condescension

herab|sehen† vi sep (haben) look down (auf+acc on). **h~setzen** vt sep reduce, cut; (fig) belittle

Heraldik f - heraldry

heran adv near; **[bis] h~ an** (+acc) up to. **h~kommen†** vi *sep* (*sein*) approach; **h~kommen an** (+*acc*) come up to; (*erreichen*) get at; (*fig*) measure up to. **h~machen** (**sich**) *vr sep* sich **h~machen an** (+*acc*) approach; get down to (*Arbeit*). **h~wachsen†** *vi sep* (*sein*) grow up. **h~ziehen†** *vt sep* pull up (**an**+*acc* to); (*züchten*) raise; (*h~bilden*) train; (*hinzuziehen*) call in □*vi* (*sein*) approach

herauf *adv* up [here]; **die Treppe h~** up the stairs. **h~setzen** *vt sep* raise, increase

heraus *adv* out (**aus** of); **h~damit** *od* mit der Sprache! out with it! **h~bekommen†** *vt sep* get out; (*ausfindig machen*) find out; (*lösen*) solve; **Geld h~bekommen** get change. **h~finden†** *v sep* □*vt* find out □*vi* (*haben*) find one's way out. **h~fordern** *vt sep* provoke; challenge (*Person*). **H~forderung** *f* provocation; challenge. **h~geben†** *vt sep* hand over; (*Admin*) issue; (*veröffentlichen*) publish; edit (*Zeitschrift*); **jdm Geld h~geben** give s.o. change □*vi* (*haben*) give change (**auf** +*acc* for). **H~geber** *m* -s,- publisher; editor. **h~halten†** (**sich**) *vr sep* (*fig*) keep out (**aus** of). **h~kommen†** *vi sep* (*sein*) come out; (*aus Schwierigkeit, Takt*) get out; **auf eins** *od* **dasselbe h~kommen** (*fam*) come to the same thing. **h~lassen†** *vt sep* let out. **h~nehmen†** *vt sep* take out; **sich zuviel h~nehmen** (*fig*) take liberties. **h~reden** (**sich**) *vr sep* make excuses. **h~rücken** *v sep* □*vt* move out; (*hergeben*) hand over □*vi* **h~rücken mit** hand over (*fig: sagen*) come out with. **h~schlagen†** *vt sep* knock out; (*fig*) gain. **h~stellen** *vt sep* put out; **sich h~stellen**

turn out (**als** to be; **daß** that). **h~ziehen†** *vt sep* pull out

herb *a* sharp; (*Wein*) dry

herbei *adv* here. **h~führen** *vt sep* (*fig*) bring about. **h~schaffen** *vt sep* get

Herberge *f* -,-n [youth] hostel; (*Unterkunft*) lodging. **H~svater** *m* warden

herbestellen *vt sep* summon

herbitten† *vt sep* ask to come

herbringen† *vt sep* bring [here]

Herbst *m* -[e]s,-e autumn

Herd *m* -[e]s,-e stove, cooker; (*fig*) focus

Herde *f* -,-n herd; (*Schaf-*) flock

herein *adv* in [here]; **h~!** come in! **h~bitten†** *vt sep* ask in. **h~fallen†** *vi sep* (*sein*) (*fam*) be taken in (**auf**+*acc* by). **h~kommen†** *vi sep* (*sein*) come in. **h~lassen†** *vt sep* let in. **h~legen** *vt sep* (*fam*) take for a ride

Herfahrt *f* journey/drive here

hergeben† *vt sep* hand over; (*fig*) give up

hergebracht *a* traditional

hergehen† *vi sep* (*sein*) **h~ vor** (+*dat*) walk along in front of; **es ging lustig her** (*fam*) there was a lot of merriment

herholen *vt sep* fetch; **weit hergeholt** (*fig*) far-fetched

Hering *m* -s,-e herring; (*Zeltpflock*) tent-peg

her|kommen† *vi sep* (*sein*) come here; **wo kommt das her?** where does it come from? **h~kömmlich** *a* traditional. **H~kunft** *f* -origin

herleiten *vt sep* derive

hermachen *vt sep* **viel/wenig h~** be impressive/unimpressive; (*wichtig sehen*) make a lot of/little fuss (**von** of); **sich h~ über** (+*acc*) fall upon; tackle (*Arbeit*)

Hermelin *nt* -s,-e (*Zool*) stoat

Hernie /ˈhɛrniə/ *f* -,-n hernia

Heroin *nt* -s heroin

heroisch a heroic

Herr m -en,-en gentleman; (*Gebieter*) master (**über** + acc of); [Gott,] der H~ the Lord [God]; H~ Meier Mr Meier; **Sehr geehrte H~en** Dear Sirs. H~chen nt -s,- master. H~enhaus nt manor [house]. h~enlos a ownerless; ⟨*Tier*⟩ stray

Herrgott m der H~ the Lord

herrichten vt sep prepare; **wieder h~** renovate

Herrin f -,-nen mistress

herrlich a marvellous; (*großartig*) magnificent

Herrschaft f -,-en rule; (*Macht*) power; (*Kontrolle*) control; **meine H~en!** ladies and gentlemen!

herrsch|en vi (haben) rule; (*verbreitet sein*) prevail; **es h~te Stille** there was silence. H~er(in) m -s,- (f -,-nen) ruler. h~süchtig a domineering

hersein† vi sep (sein) come (**von** from); h~ **hinter** (+ dat) be after; **es ist schon lange her** it was a long time ago

herstammen vi sep (haben) come (**aus/von** from)

herstell|en vt sep establish; (*Comm*) manufacture, make. H~er m -s,- manufacturer, maker. H~ung f - establishment; manufacture

herüber adv over [here]

herum adv im Kreis h~ [round] in a circle; **falsch h~** the wrong way round; **um ...h~** round ...; (*ungefähr*) [round] about ... h~drehen vt sep turn round/ (*wenden*) over; turn ⟨*Schlüssel*⟩; **sich h~drehen** turn round/ over. h~gehen† vi sep (sein) walk around; ⟨*Zeit:*⟩ pass; h~gehen um go round. h~kommen† vi sep (sein) get about; h~kommen um get round; come round ⟨*Ecke*⟩; **um etw [nicht] h~kommen** (fig) [not] get out of sth.

h~sitzen† vi sep (haben) sit around; h~sitzen um sit round. h~sprechen (sich) vr ⟨*Gerücht:*⟩ get about. h~treiben† (sich) vr sep hang around. h~ziehen† vi sep (sein) move around; (*ziellos*) wander about

herunter adv down [here]. h~fallen† vi sep (sein) fall off. h~gekommen a (fig) run-down; ⟨*Gebäude*⟩ dilapidated; ⟨*Person*⟩ down-at-heel. h~kommen† vi sep (sein) come down; (fig) go to rack and ruin; ⟨*Firma, Person:*⟩ go downhill; (*gesundheitlich*) get run down. h~lassen† vt sep let down, lower. h~spielen vt sep (fig) play down. h~ziehen† vt sep pull down

hervor adv out (**aus** of). h~bringen† vt sep produce; utter ⟨*Wort*⟩. h~gehen† vi sep (sein) come/(*sich ergeben*) emerge /(*folgen*) follow (**aus** from). h~heben† vt sep (fig) stress. h~ragend a (fig) outstanding. h~rufen† vt sep (fig) cause. h~stehen† vi sep (haben) protrude. h~treten† vi sep (sein) protrude, bulge; (fig) stand out. h~tun† (sich) vr sep (fig) distinguish oneself; (*angeben*) show off

Herweg m way here

Herz nt -ens,-en heart; (*Kartenspiel*) hearts pl; **sich** (dat) **ein H~ fassen** pluck up courage. H~anfall m heart attack

herzeigen vt sep show

herzhaft a hearty; (*würzig*) savoury

herziehen† v sep □vt **hinter sich** (dat) h~ pull along [behind one] □vi (sein) **hinter jdm h~** follow along behind s.o.; **über jdn h~** (fam) run s.o. down

herzig a sweet, adorable. H~infarkt m heart attack. H~klopfen nt -s palpitations pl

herzlich a cordial; (*warm*) warm; (*aufrichtig*) sincere; **h ~ en Dank!** many thanks! **h ~ e Grüße** kind regards

herzlos a heartless

Herzog m -s,-̈e duke. **H ~ in** f -,-nen duchess. **H ~ tum** nt -s,-̈er duchy

Herzschlag m heartbeat; (*Med*) heart failure

Hessen nt -s Hesse

heterosexuell a heterosexual

Hetze f - rush; (*Kampagne*) virulent campaign (**gegen** against). **h ~ n** vt chase; **sich h ~ n** hurry

Heu nt -s hay

Heuchelei f - hypocrisy

heuch|eln vt feign □vi (*haben*) pretend. **H ~ ler(in)** m -s, (f -,-nen) hypocrite. **h ~ lerisch** a hypocritical

heuer adv (*Aust*) this year

heulen vi (*haben*) howl; (*fam: weinen*) cry; (*Sirene:*) wail

Heu|schnupfen m hay fever. **H ~ schober** m -s, haystack. **H ~ schrecke** f -,-n grasshopper

heut|e adv today; (*heutzutage*) nowadays; **h ~ e früh** od **morgen** this morning; **von h ~ e auf morgen** from one day to the next. **h ~ ig** a today's ...; (*gegenwärtig*) present; **der h ~ ige Tag** today. **h ~ zutage** adv nowadays

Hexe f -,-n witch. **h ~ n** vi (*haben*) work magic. **H ~ nschuß** m lumbago

Hieb m -[e]s,-e blow; (*Peitschen-*) lash; **H ~ e** hiding sg

hier adv here; **h ~ und da** here and there; (*zeitlich*) now and again

hier|auf adv on this/these; (*antworten*) to this; (*zeitlich*) after this. **h ~ aus** adv out of or from this/these. **h ~ bleiben†** vi sep (*sein*) stay here. **h ~ durch** adv through this/these; (*Ursache*) as a result of this. **h ~ her** adv here.

h ~ hin adv here. **h ~ lassen†** vt sep leave here. **h ~ mit** adv with this/ these; (*Comm*) herewith; (*Admin*) hereby. **h ~ nach** adv after this/ these; (*demgemäß*) according to this/these. **h ~ über** adv over/ (*höher*) above this/ these; (*sprechen, streiten*) about this/these. **h ~ von** adv from this/ these; (*h ~ über*) about this/these; (*Menge*) of this/these. **h ~ zu** adv to this/these; (*h ~ für*) for this/ these. **h ~ zulande** adv here

hiesig a local. **H ~ e(r)** m/f local

Hilfe f -,-n help, aid; **um H ~ e rufen** call for help. **h ~ los** a helpless. **H ~ losigkeit** f - helplessness

Hilfs|arbeiter m unskilled labourer. **h ~ bedürftig** a needy; **h ~ bedürftig sein** be in need of help. **h ~ bereit** a helpful. **H ~ kraft** f helper. **H ~ verb** nt auxiliary verb

Himbeere f raspberry

Himmel m -s,- sky; (*Relig & fig*) heaven; (*Bett-*) canopy; **unter freiem H ~** in the open air. **H ~ bett** nt four-poster. **H ~ fahrt** f Ascension

himmlisch a heavenly

hin adv there; **hin und her** to and fro; **hin und zurück** there and back; (*Rail*) return; **hin und wieder** now and again; **auf** (*+ acc*) ... **hin** in reply to (*Brief, Anzeige*); on (*jds Rat*); zu od **nach** ... **hin** towards; **vor sich hin reden** talk to oneself

hinauf adv up [there]. **h ~ gehen†** vi sep (*sein*) go up. **h ~ setzen** vt sep raise

hinaus adv out [there]; (*nach draußen*) outside; **auf Jahre h ~** for years to come; **über etw** (*acc*) **h ~** beyond sth; (*Menge*) [over and] above sth. **h ~ gehen†** vi sep (*sein*) go out; (*Zimmer:*) face

(nach Norden north). **h~lau-**
fen† vi sep (sein) run out; **h~lau-**
fen auf (+acc) (fig) amount to.
h~lehnen (sich) vr sep lean
out. **h~schieben†** vt sep push
out; (fig) put off. **h~sein†** vi sep
(sein) **über etw** (acc) **h~sein**
(fig) be past sth. **h~wollen†** vi
sep (haben) want to go out;
h~wollen auf (+acc) (fig) aim
at; **hoch h~wollen** (fig) be ambitious. **h~ziehen†** v sep □ vt
pull out; (in die Länge ziehen)
drag out; (verzögern) delay; **sich**
h~ziehen drag on; be delayed
□vi (sein) move out. **h~zögern**
vt delay; **sich h~zögern** be delayed

Hinblick m **im H~ auf** (+acc) **in**
view of; (hinsichtlich) regarding
hinder|lich a awkward; **jdm**
h~lich sein hamper s.o. **h~n** vt
hamper; (verhindern) prevent.
H~nis nt **-ses,-se** obstacle.
H~nisrennen nt steeplechase
Hindu m **-s,-s** Hindu. **H~ismus**
m **-** Hinduism
hindurch adv through it/them
hinein adv in [there]; (nach drinnen) inside; **h~** in (+acc) into.
h~gehen† vi sep (sein) go in;
h~gehen in (+acc) go into.
h~reden vi sep (haben) **jdm**
h~reden interrupt s.o.; (sich
einmischen) interfere in s.o.'s affairs. **h~versetzen (sich)** vr
sep **sich in jds Lage h~verset-**
zen put oneself in s.o.'s position.
h~ziehen† vt sep pull in; **h~zie-**
hen in (+acc) pull into; **in etw**
(acc) **h~gezogen werden** (fig)
become involved in sth
hin|fahren† v sep □vi (sein) go/
drive there □vt take/drive there.
H~fahrt f journey/drive there;
(Rail) outward journey. **h~fal-**
len† vi sep (sein) fall. **H~flug** m
flight there; (Admin) outward
flight

Hingeb|ung f - devotion.
h~ungsvoll a devoted
hingehen† vi sep (sein) go/(zu
Fuß) walk there; (vergehen) pass;
h~zu go up to; **wo gehst du hin?**
where are you going?
hingerissen a rapt; **h~ sein** be
carried away (von by)
hinhalten† vt sep hold out; (warten lassen) keep waiting
hinken vi (haben/sein) limp
hin|knien (sich) vr sep kneel
down. **h~kommen†** vi sep
(sein) get there; (fig: hingehören) belong, go; (fam: auskommen) manage (mit with). **h~länglich** a
adequate. **h~laufen†** vi sep
(sein) run/(gehen) walk there.
h~legen vt sep lay or put down;
sich h~legen lie down
hinreichen v sep □vt hand (dat
to) □vi (haben) extend (bis to);
(ausreichen) be adequate. **h~d** a
adequate
Hinreise f journey there; (Rail)
outward journey
hinreißen† vt sep (fig) carry
away; **sich h~ lassen** get carried
away. **h~d** a ravishing
hinrichten vt sep execute.
H~ung f execution
hinschicken vt sep send there
hinschreiben† vt sep write there;
(aufschreiben) write down
hinsehen† vi sep (haben) look
hinsein† vi sep (sein) (fam) be
gone; (kaputt, tot) have had it; **es**
ist noch lange hin it's a long
time yet
hinsetzen vt sep put down; **sich**
h~ sit down
Hinsicht f - **in dieser H~** in this
respect; **in finanzieller H~** financially. **h~lich** prep (+gen)
regarding
hinstrecken vt sep hold out; **sich**
h~ extend
hinten adv at the back; **dort h~**
back there; **nach/von h~** to the

back/from behind. **h~herum**
adv round the back; (*fam*) by
devious means

hinter *prep* (+*dat*/*acc*) behind;
(*nach*) after; **h~jdm/etw her-
laufen** run after s.o./sth; **h~etw**
(*dat*) **stecken** (*fig*) be behind sth;
h~etw (*acc*) **kommen** (*fig*) get
to the bottom of sth; **etw h~sich**
(*acc*) **bringen** get sth over with

Hinterbliebene *pl* (*Admin*) sur-
viving dependants; **die H~n** the
bereaved family *sg*

hintere(r,s) *a* back, rear; **h~s
Ende** far end

hintereinander *adv* one behind/
(*zeitlich*) after the other; **dreimal
h~** three times in succession

Hintergedanke *m* ulterior
motive. **H~grund** *m* background. **H~halt** *m* -[e]s,-e ambush; **aus dem H~halt überfallen** ambush. **h~hältig** *a* under-
hand

hinterher *adv* behind, after; (*zeitlich*) afterwards

Hinterhof *m* back yard. **H~~
kopf** *m* back of the head

hinterlassen† *vt* leave [behind];
(*Jur*) leave, bequeath (*dat* to).
H~schaft *f*-,-en (*Jur*) estate

hinterlegen *vt* deposit

Hinterleib *m* (*Zool*) abdomen.
H~list *f* deceit. **h~listig** *a* de-
ceitful. **H~n** *m* -s,- (*fam*) bottom,
backside. **H~rad** *nt* rear or back
wheel. **h~rücks** *adv* from behind. **h~ste(r,s)** *a* last; **h~ste
Reihe** back row. **H~teil** *nt*
(*fam*) behind. **H~treppe** *f* back
stairs *pl*

hinterziehen† *vt* (*Admin*) evade

hinüber *adv* over or across
[there]. **h~gehen†** *vi sep* (*sein*)
go over or across; **h~gehen über**
(+*acc*) cross

hinunter *adv* down [there].
h~gehen† *vi sep* (*sein*) go down.
h~schlucken *vt sep* swallow

Hinweg *m* way there

hinweg *adv* away, off; **h~über**
(+*acc*) over; **über eine Zeit h~**
over a period. **h~kommen†** *vi
sep* (*sein*) **h~kommen über**
(+*acc*) (*fig*) get over. **h~sehen†**
vi sep (*haben*) **h~sehen über**
(+*acc*) see over; (*fig*) overlook.
h~setzen (sich) *vr sep* sich
h~setzen über (+*acc*) ignore

Hinweis *m* -es,-e reference; (*Andeutung*) hint; (*Anzeichen*) indication; **unter H~auf** (+*acc*)
with reference to. **h~en†** *v sep*
□*vi* (*haben*) point (**auf**+*acc* to)
□*vt* **jdn auf etw** (*acc*) **h~en** point
sth out to s.o.

hinwieder *adv* on the other hand

hinzeigen *vi sep* (*haben*) point
(**auf**+*acc* to). **h~ziehen†** *vt sep*
pull; (*fig: in die Länge ziehen*)
drag out; (*verzögern*) delay; **sich
h~ziehen** drag on

hinzu *adv* in addition. **h~fügen**
vt sep add. **h~kommen†** *vi sep*
(*sein*) be added; (*ankommen*)
arrive [on the scene]; join (**zu**
jdm s.o.)

Hiobsbotschaft *f* bad news *sg*

Hirn *nt* -s brain; (*Culin*) brains *pl*.
H~hautentzündung *f* men-
ingitis

Hirsch *m* -[e]s,-e deer; (*männlich*)
stag; (*Culin*) venison

Hirse *f* - millet

Hirt *m* -en,-en, **Hirte** *m* -n,-n
shepherd

hissen *vt* hoist

Historiker *m* -s,- historian.
h~isch *a* historical; (*bedeutend*)
historic

Hitze *f* - heat. **h~ig** *a* (*fig*)
heated; (*Person*) hot-headed;
(*jähzornig*) hot-tempered.
H~schlag *m* heat-stroke

H-Milch /'haː-/ *f* long-life milk

Hobby *nt* -s,-s hobby

Hobel m -s,- (Techn) plane; (Culin) slicer. **h~n** vt/i (haben)
plane. **H~späne** mpl shavings
hoch a (attrib **hohe(r,s)**) high;
⟨Baum, Mast⟩ tall; ⟨Offizier⟩
high-ranking; ⟨Alter⟩ great;
⟨Summe⟩ large; ⟨Strafe⟩ heavy;
hohe Schuhe ankle boots □ adv
high; (sehr) highly; **die Treppe
h~** up the stairs; **sechs Mann
h~** six of us/them. **H~** nt -s,-s
cheer; (Meteorol) high
Hoch|achtung f high esteem.
H~achtungsvoll adv Yours
faithfully. **h~betrieb** m great
activity. **H~deutsch** nt High
German. **H~druck** m high pressure. **H~ebene**/plateau. **h~ge-
hen†** vi sep (sein) go up; (explodieren) blow up; (aufbrausen)
flare up. **h~gestellt** attrib a
high-ranking; ⟨Zahl⟩ superior.
h~gewachsen a tall. **H~glanz**
m high gloss. **h~gradig** a extreme. **h~hackig** a high-heeled.
h~haus nt high-rise building.
h~heben† vt sep lift up; raise
⟨Kopf, Hand⟩. **h~kant** adv on
end. **h~konjunktur** f boom.
h~krempeln vt sep roll up.
h~leben vi sep (haben) **h~le-
ben lassen** give three cheers for.
H~mut m pride, arrogance.
h~näsig a (fam) snooty. **H~-
ofen** m blast-furnace. **h~ragen**
vi sep rise [up]; ⟨Turm:⟩ soar.
H~ruf m cheer. **H~saison** f
high season. **h~schlagen†** vt
sep turn up ⟨Kragen⟩.
H~schule f university; (Musik-,
Kunst-) academy. **H~sommer**
m midsummer. **H~spannung** f
high/(fig) great tension. **h~-
spielen** vt sep (fig) magnify.
H~sprung m high jump
höchst adv extremely, most
Hochstapler m -s,- confidence
trickster

höchst|e(r,s) a highest; ⟨Baum,
Turm⟩ tallest; (oberste, größte)
top; **es ist h~e Zeit** it is high
time. **h~ens** adv at most; (es sei
denn) except perhaps. **h~ge-
schwindigkeit** f top or maximum speed. **h~maß** nt maximum. **h~persönlich** adv in
person. **H~preis** m top price.
H~temperatur f maximum
temperature
Hoch|verrat m high treason.
H~wasser nt high tide;
(Überschwemmung) floods pl.
H~würden m -s Reverend; (Anrede) Father
Hochzeit f -,-en wedding.
H~sreise f honeymoon.
H~stag m wedding day/(Jahrestag) anniversary
Hocke|f in der **H~ sitzen** squat;
in die H~ gehen squat down.
h~n vi (haben) squat □ vr **sich
h~n** squat down
Hocker m -s,- stool
Höcker m -s,- bump; (Kamel-)
hump
Hockey /'hɔki/ nt -s hockey
Hode f -,-n, **Hoden** m -s,- testicle
Hof m -[e]s,¨e [court]yard;
(Bauern-) farm; ⟨Königs-⟩ court;
(Schul-) playground; (Astr) halo
hoffen vt/i (haben) hope (**auf**+ acc
for). **h~tlich** adv I hope, let us
hope
Hoffnung f -,-en hope. **h~slos** a
hopeless. **h~svoll** a hopeful
höflich a polite. **H~keit** f -,-en
politeness, courtesy
hohe(r,s) a s. **hoch**
Höhe f -,-n height; (Aviat, Geog)
altitude; (Niveau) level; (einer
Summe) size; (An-) hill
Hoheit f -,-en (Staats-) sover-
eignty; (Titel) Highness. **H~sge-
biet** nt [sovereign] territory.
H~szeichen nt national emblem

Höhe|nlinie f contour line.
H~nsonne f sun-lamp. **H~n-zug** m mountain range. **H~-punkt** m (fig) climax, peak. **h~r** a & adv higher; **h~re Schule** secondary school

hohl a hollow; (leer) empty
Höhle f -,-n cave; (Tier-) den; (Hohlraum) cavity; (Augen-) socket

Hohl|maß nt measure of capacity. **H~raum** m cavity
Hohn m -s scorn, derision
höhn|en vt deride
holen vt fetch, get; (kaufen) buy; (nehmen) take (aus from)
Holland nt -s Holland
Hollä|nd|er m -s,- Dutchman; **die H~er** the Dutch pl. **H~erin** f -,-nen Dutchwoman. **h~isch** a Dutch
Hölle f- hell. **h~isch** a infernal
Holunder m -s (Bot) elder
Holz nt -es,"er wood; (Nutz-) timber. **H~blasinstrument** nt woodwind instrument
hölzern a wooden
Holz|hammer m mallet. **H~kohle** f charcoal. **H~schnitt** m woodcut. **H~wolle** f wood shavings pl
Homöopathie f- homoeopathy
homosexuell a homosexual. **H~e(r)** m/f homosexual
Honig m -s honey. **H~wabe** f honeycomb
Hono|rar m -s,-e fee. **h~rieren** vt remunerate; (fig) reward
Hopfen m -s hops pl; (Bot) hop
hopsen vi (sein) jump
horchen vi (haben) listen (auf + acc to); (heimlich) eavesdrop
hören vt hear; (an-) listen to □vi (haben) hear; (horchen) listen; (gehorchen) obey; **h~ auf** (+ acc) listen to
Hör|er m -s,- listener; (Teleph) receiver. **H~funk** m radio. **H~gerät** nt hearing-aid

Horizo|n|t m -[e]s horizon. **h~tal** a horizontal
Hormon nt -s,-e hormone
Horn nt -s,"er horn. **H~haut** f hard skin; (Augen-) cornea
Hornisse f -,-n hornet
Horoskop nt -[e]s,-e horoscope
Hör|saal m (Univ) lecture hall. **H~spiel** nt radio play
Hort m -[e]s,-e (Schatz) hoard; (fig) refuge. **h~en** vt hoard
Hortensie f-|ə| f -,-n hydrangea
Hose f -,-n, **Hosen** pl trousers pl. **H~nschlitz** m fly, flies pl. **H~nträger** mpl braces
Hostess, Hosteß f -,-tessen hostess; (Aviat) air hostess
Hostie /'hostjə/ f -,-n (Relig) host
Hotel nt -s,-s hotel
hübsch a pretty; (nett) nice
Hubschrauber m -s,- helicopter
Huf m -[e]s,-e hoof. **H~eisen** nt horseshoe
Hüfte f -,-n hip
Hügel m -s,- hill. **h~ig** a hilly
Huhn nt -s,"er chicken; (Henne) hen
Hühn|chen nt -s,- chicken. **H~erauge** nt corn
Hülle f -,-n cover; (Verpackung) wrapping; (Platten-) sleeve; in **H~ und Fülle** in abundance. **h~n** vt wrap
Hülse f -,-n (Bot) pod; (Etui) case. **H~nfrüchte** fpl pulses
human a humane. **H~ität** f - humanity
Hummel f -,-n bumble-bee
Hummer m -s,- lobster
Hum|or m -s humour. **h~orvoll** a humorous
humpeln vi (sein/haben) hobble
Humpen m -s,- tankard
Hund m -[e]s,-e dog; (Jagd-) hound
hundert inv a one/a hundred. **H~** nt -s,-e hundred. **H~jahrfeier** f centenary. **h~prozentig** a & adv one hundred per cent. **h~ste(r,s)**

a hundredth. H~**stel** *nt* -s,- hundredth

Hündin *f* -,-**nen** bitch

Hüne *m* -n,-n giant

Hunger *m* -s hunger; H~ **haben** be hungry. **h~n** *vi* (*haben*) starve. H~**snot** *f* famine

hungrig *a* hungry

Hupe *f* -,-n (*Auto*) horn. **h~n** *vi* (*haben*) sound one's horn

hüpfen *vi* (*sein*) skip; ⟨*Frosch:*⟩ hop; ⟨*Grashüpfer:*⟩ jump

Hürde *f* -,-n (*Sport & fig*) hurdle; (*Schaf*) pen, fold

Hure *f* -,-n whore

hurra *int* hurray

husten *vi* (*haben*) cough. **H~** *m* -s cough. H~**saft** *m* cough mixture

Hut[1] *m* -[e]s,-̈e hat; (*Pilz-*) cap

Hut[2] *f* - auf der H~ sein be on one's guard (**vor** + *dat* against)

hüten *vt* watch over; tend ⟨*Tiere*⟩; (*aufpassen*) look after; **das Bett h~ müssen** be confined to bed; **sich h~** be on one's guard (**vor** + *dat* against); **sich h~, etw zu tun** take care not to do sth

Hütte *f* -,-n hut; (*Hunde-*) kennel; (*Techn*) iron and steel works. H~**nkäse** *m* cottage cheese. H~**nkunde** *f* metallurgy

Hyäne *f* -,-n hyena

hydraulisch *a* hydraulic

Hygiene /hy'gie:nə/ *f* - hygiene. **h~isch** *a* hygienic

Hypnose *f* - hypnosis. H~**tiseur** /-'zø:ɐ/ *m* -s,-e hypnotist. **h~tisieren** *vt* hypnotize

Hypothek *f* -,-en mortgage

Hypothese *f* -,-n hypothesis

Hysterie *f* - hysteria. **h~terisch** *a* hysterical

I

ich *pron* I; **ich bin's** it's me. **Ich** *nt* -[s],-[s] self; (*Psych*) ego

IC-Zug /i'tse:-/ *m* inter-city train

ideal *a* ideal. I~ *nt* -s,-e ideal. I~**ismus** *m* - idealism. I~**ist(in)** *m* -en,-en (*f* -,-nen) idealist. **i~istisch** *a* idealistic

Idee *f* -,-n idea; **fixe** I~ obsession

identifizieren *vt* identify

identisch *a* identical

Ideologie *f* -,-n ideology. **i~logisch** *a* ideological

idiomatisch *a* idiomatic

Idiot *m* -en,-en idiot. **i~isch** *a* idiotic

idyllisch /i'dylɪʃ/ *a* idyllic

Igel *m* -s,- hedgehog

ihm *pron* (*dat of* **er**, **es**) [to] him; (*Ding*, *Tier*) [to] it

ihn *pron* (*acc of* **er**) him; (*Ding*, *Tier*) it. i~**en** *pron* (*dat of* **sie** *pl*) [to] them. I~**en** *pron* (*dat of* **Sie**) [to] you

ihr *pron* (2nd pers *pl*) you □ (*dat of* **sie** *sg*) [to] her; (*Ding*, *Tier*) [to] it □ *poss pron* her; (*Ding*, *Tier*) its; (*pl*) their. **Ihr** *poss pron* your. i~**e(r,s)** *poss pron* hers; (*pl*) theirs. I~**e(r,s)** *poss pron* yours. i~**erseits** *adv* for her/(*pl*) their part. i~**etwegen** *adv* for her/(*Ding*, *Tier*) its/(*pl*) their sake; (*wegen*) because of her/it/them, on her/its/their account. I~**etwegen** *adv* for your sake; (*wegen*) because of you, on your account. i~**ige** *poss pron* **der/die/das** i~**ige** hers; (*pl*) theirs. I~**s** *poss pron* yours

Ikone *f* -,-n icon

illegal *a* illegal

Illusion *f* -,-en illusion. i~**orisch** *a* illusory

Illustration *f* -,-en illustration. i~**ieren** *vt* illustrate. I~**ierte** *f* -n,-[n] [illustrated] magazine

Iltis *m* -ses,-se polecat

im *prep*= **in dem**; **im Mai** in May

Imbiß *m* snack

Imitation *f* -,-en imitation. i~**ieren** *vt* imitate

Immatrikul|ation /-'tsio:n/ f - (Univ) enrolment. **i~ieren** vt (Univ) enrol; **sich i~ieren** enrol

immer adv always; **für i~** for ever; (endgültig) for good; **i~ noch** still; **i~ mehr** more and more; **was i~** whatever. **i~hin** adv (wenigstens) at least; (trotzdem) all the same; (schließlich) after all. **i~zu** adv all the time

Immobilien /-jən/ pl real estate sg. **I~makler** m estate agent

immun a immune (**gegen** to)

Imperialismus m - imperialism

impf|en vt vaccinate, inoculate. **I~stoff** m vaccine. **I~ung** f -,-en vaccination, inoculation

imponieren vi (haben) impress (**jdm** s.o.)

Import m -[e]s,-e import. **I~teur** /-'tø:ɐ/ m -s,-e importer. **i~tieren** vt import

impotent a (Med) impotent

imprägnieren vt waterproof

Impressionismus m - impressionism

improvisieren vt/i (haben) improvise

imstande pred a able (**zu** to); capable (**etw zu tun** of doing sth)

in prep (+ dat) in; (+ acc) into, in; (bei Bus, Zug) on; **in der Schule** at school; **in die Schule** to school □ **a in sein be in**

indem conj (während) while; (dadurch) by (+ -ing)

Inder(in) m -s,- (f -,-nen) Indian

indessen conj while □ adv (unterdessen) meanwhile

Indian|er(in) m -s,- (f -,-nen) (American) Indian. **i~isch** a Indian

Indien /'ɪndjən/ nt -s India

indirekt a indirect

indisch a Indian

indiskutabel a out of the question

Individual|ist m -en,-en individualist. **I~alität** f - individuality. **i~ell** a individual

Indizienbeweis /ɪn'di:tsjən-/ m circumstantial evidence

industr|ialisiert a industrialized. **I~ie** f -,-n industry. **i~iell** a industrial

ineinander adv in/into one another

Infanterie f - infantry

Infektion /-'tsio:n/ f -,-en infection. **I~skrankheit** f infectious disease

Infinitiv m -s,-e infinitive

infizieren vt infect; **sich i~** become⟨Person:⟩ be infected

Inflation /-'tsio:n/ f - inflation. **i~är** a inflationary

infolge prep (+ gen) as a result of. **i~dessen** adv consequently

Inform|atik f - information science. **I~ation** /-'tsio:n/ f -,-en information. **i~ieren** vt inform; **sich i~ieren** find out (**über** + acc about)

Ingenieur /ɪnʒe'njø:ɐ/ m -s,-e engineer

Ingwer m -s ginger

Inhaber(in) m -s,- (f -,-nen) holder; (Besitzer) proprietor; (Scheck-) bearer

inhaftieren vt take into custody

inhalieren vt/i (haben) inhale

Inhalt m -[e]s,-e contents pl; (Bedeutung) content; (Geschichte) story

Initiative /initsia'ti:və/ f -,-n initiative

inklusive prep (+ gen) including □ adv inclusive

inkorrekt a incorrect

Inkubationszeit /-'tsio:ns-/ f (Med) incubation period

Inland nt -[e]s home country; (Binnenland) interior. **I~sgespräch** nt inland call

inmitten prep (+ gen) in the middle of; (unter) amongst

innen adv inside; **nach i~** inwards. **I~architekt(in)** m(f) interior designer. **I~minister** m Minister of the Interior; (in UK) Home Secretary. **I~politik** f domestic policy. **I~stadt** f town centre

inner|e(r,s) a inner; (Med, Pol) internal. **I~e(s)** nt interior; (Mitte) centre; (fig: Seele) inner being. **I~eien** fpl (Culin) offal sg. **i~halb** prep (+ gen) inside; (zeitlich & fig) within; (während) during □ adv **i~halb von** within. **i~lich** a internal

innig a sincere

Innung f -,-en guild

inoffiziell a unofficial

Insasse m -n,-n inmate; (im Auto) occupant; (Passagier) passenger

Inschrift f inscription

Insekt nt -[e]s,-en insect. **I~envertilgungsmittel** nt insecticide

Insel f -,-n island

Inser|at nt -[e]s,-e [newspaper] advertisement. **i~ieren** vt/i (haben) advertise

insgeheim adv secretly. **i~samt** adv [all] in all

insofern, insoweit adv /-'zo:-/ in this respect; **i~als** in as much as

Insp|ektion /ɪnspɛk'tsjo:n/ f -,-en inspection. **I~ektor** m -en,-en /-'to:rən/ inspector

Inspiration /ɪnspira'tsjo:n/ f -,-en inspiration. **i~ieren** vt inspire

Install|ateur /ɪnstala'tø:ɐ/ m -s,-e fitter; (Klempner) plumber. **i~ieren** vt install

Instand|haltung f - maintenance, upkeep. **I~setzung** f - repair

Instanz /-st/ f -,-en authority

Instinkt /-st/ m -[e]s,-e instinct. **i~iv** a instinctive

Institut /-st/ nt -[e]s,-e institute

Instrument /-st-/ nt -[e]s,-e instrument. **I~almusik** f instrumental music

Insulin nt -s insulin

inszenieren vt (Theat) produce. **I~ung** f -,-en production

Integr|ation /-'tsjo:n/ f - integration. **i~ieren** vt integrate; **sich i~ieren** integrate

Intellekt m -[e]s intellect. **i~uell** a intellectual

intelligen|t a intelligent. **I~z** f - intelligence

Intendant m -en,-en director

inter|essant a interesting. **I~esse** nt -s,-n interest; **I~esse haben** be interested (**an** + dat in). **I~essengruppe** f pressure group. **I~essent** m -en,-en interested party; (Käufer) prospective buyer. **i~essieren** vt interest; **sich i~essieren** be interested (**für** in)

Inter|nat nt -[e]s,-e boarding school. **i~national** a international. **I~nist** m -en, -en specialist in internal diseases. **I~pretation** /-'tsjo:n/ f -,-en interpretation. **i~pretieren** vt interpret. **I~vall** nt -s,-e interval. **I~vention** /-'tsjo:n/ f -,-en intervention

Interview /'ɪntɐvju:/ nt -s,-s interview. **i~en** /-'vju:ən/ vt interview

intim a intimate

intolerant a intolerant. **I~z** f - intolerance

intravenös a intravenous

Intrige f -,-n intrigue

introvertiert a introverted

Invalidenrente f disability pension

Invasion f - invasion

Inventar nt -s,-e furnishings and fittings pl; (Techn) equipment; (Bestand) stock; (Liste) inventory. **I~tur** f -,-en stock-taking

investieren vt invest

inwie|fern *adv* in what way.
i~weit *adv* how far, to what extent
Inzest *m* -[e]s incest
inzwischen *adv* in the meantime
Irak (der) -[s] Iraq. **i~isch** *a* Iraqi
Iran (der) -[s] Iran. **i~isch** *a* Iranian
irdisch *a* earthly
Ire *m* -n,-n Irishman; **die I~n** the Irish *pl*
irgend *adv* **i~ jemand/etwas** someone/something; (*fragend, verneint*) anyone/anything; **wenn i~ möglich** if at all possible. **i~ein** *indef art* some/any. **i~eine(r,s)** *pron* any one; (*jemand*) someone/anyone. **i~wann** *pron* at some time [or other]/at any time. **i~was** *pron* (*fam*) something [or other]/anything. **i~welche(r,s)** *pron* any. **i~wer** *pron* someone/anyone. **i~wie** *adv* somehow [or other]. **i~wo** *adv* somewhere/anywhere
Irin *f* -,-nen Irishwoman
irisch *a* Irish
Irland *nt* -s Ireland
Ironie *f* - irony
ironisch *a* ironic
irre *a* mad, crazy; (*fam: gewaltig*) incredible; **i~ werden** get confused. **i~(r)** *m/f* lunatic. **i~führen** *vt sep* (*fig*) mislead. **i~machen** *vt sep* confuse. **i~n** *vi/r* (*haben*) [**sich**] **i~n** be mistaken □*vi* (*sein*) wander. **I~nanstalt** *f* lunatic asylum
Irrgarten *m* maze
irritieren *vt* irritate
Irr|sinn *m* madness, lunacy. **i~sinnig** *a* mad; (*fam: gewaltig*) incredible. **I~tum** *m* -s,-er mistake
Ischias *m & nt* - sciatica
Islam (der) -[s] Islam. **islamisch** *a* Islamic
Island *nt* -s Iceland

Isolier|band *nt* insulating tape. **i~en** *vt* isolate; (*Phys, Electr*) insulate; (*gegen Schall*) soundproof. **I~ung** *f* - isolation; insulation; soundproofing
Israel /'ɪsraeːl/ *nt* -s Israel. **I~eli** *m* -[s],-s & *f* -,-[s] Israeli. **i~elisch** *a* Israeli
ist *s.* sein; **er ist** he is
Italien /-jən/ *nt* -s Italy. **I~iener(in)** *m* -s,- (*f* -,-nen) Italian. **i~ienisch** *a* Italian. **I~ienisch** *nt* -[s] (*Lang*) Italian

J

ja *adv* yes; **ich glaube ja** I think so; **'ja nicht!** not on any account! **da seid ihr ja!** there you are!
Jacht *f* -,-en yacht
Jacke *f* -,-n jacket; (*Strick-*) cardigan
Jackett /ʒa'kɛt/ *nt* -s,-s jacket
Jade *m* -[s] & *f* - jade
Jagd *f* -,-en hunt; (*Schießen*) shoot; (*Jagen*) hunting; shooting; (*fig*) pursuit (**nach** of); **auf die J~ gehen** go hunting/shooting. **J~gewehr** *nt* sporting gun. **J~hund** *m* gun-dog; (*Hetzhund*) hound
jagen *vt* hunt; (*schießen*) shoot; (*verfolgen, wegjagen*) chase; (*treiben*) drive; **sich j~** chase each other; **in die Luft j~** blow up □*vi* (*haben*) hunt, go hunting/shooting; (*fig*) chase (**nach** after)
Jäger *m* -s,- hunter
jäh *a* sudden; (*steil*) steep
Jahr *nt* -[e]s,-e year. **j~elang** *adv* for years. **J~eszeit** *f* season. **J~gang** *m* year; (*Wein*) vintage. **J~hundert** *nt* century
jährlich *a* annual, yearly
Jahr|markt *m* fair. **J~tausend** *nt* millennium. **J~zehnt** *nt* -[e]s,-e decade

Jähzorn *m* violent temper. j~ig *a* hot-tempered

Jalousie /ʒalu'zi:/ *f* -,-n venetian blind

Jammer *m* -s misery

jämmerlich *a* miserable; (*mitleiderregend*) pitiful

jammern *vi* (*haben*) lament □*vt* jdn j~ arouse s.o.'s pity

Jänner *m* -s,- (*Aust*) January

Januar *m* -s,-e January

Japan *nt* -s Japan. **J~aner(in)** *m* -s, (*f* -,-nen) Japanese. j~a-nisch *a* Japanese. **J~anisch** *nt* -[s] (*Lang*) Japanese

jäten *vt/i* (*haben*) weed

jaulen *vi* (*haben*) yelp

Jause *f* -,-n (*Aust*) snack

jawohl *adv* yes

Jazz /jats, dʒɛs/ *m* - jazz

je *adv* (*jemals*) ever; (*jeweils*) each; (*pro*) per; je nach according to; **seit eh und je** always; □*conj* je mehr, desto besser the more the better □*prep* (+ *acc*) per

jede(r,s) *pron* every; (*j~ einzelne*) each; (*j~ beliebige*) any; (*substantivisch*) everyone; each one; anyone; **ohne j~en Grund** without any reason. **j~nfalls** *adv* in any case; (*wenigstens*) at least. **j~rmann** *pron* everyone. **j~rzeit** *adv* at any time. **j~smal** *adv* every time

jedoch *adv* & *conj* however

jemals *adv* ever

jemand *pron* someone, somebody

jene(r,s) *pron* that; (*pl*) those; (*substantivisch*) that one; (*pl*) those. **j~seits** *prep* (+ *gen*) [on] the other side of

jetzt *adv* now. **J~zeit** *f* present

jiddisch *a*, **J~** *nt* -[s] Yiddish

Job /dʒɔp/ *m* -s,-s job. **j~ben** *vi* (*haben*) (*fam*) work

Joch *nt* -[e]s,-e yoke

Jockei, Jockey /'dʒɔki/ *m* -s,-s jockey

Jod *nt* -[e]s iodine

jodeln *vi* (*haben*) yodel

Joga *m* & *nt* -[s] yoga

Joghurt *m* & *nt* -[s] yoghurt

Johannisbeere *f* redcurrant

Joker *m* -s,- (*Karte*) joker

Jolle *f* -,-n dinghy

Jongleur /ʒõ'gløːɐ/ *m* -s,-e juggler

Jordanien /-jən/ *nt* -s Jordan

Journal /ʒur'naːl/ *nt* -s,-e journal. **J~ismus** /ʒurna'lɪsmʊs/ *m* - journalism. **J~ist(in)** *m* -en,-en (*f* -,-nen) journalist

Jubel *m* -s rejoicing, jubilation. **j~n** *vi* (*haben*) rejoice

Jubiläum *nt* -s,-äen jubilee; (*Jahrestag*) anniversary

jucken *vi* (*haben*) itch; sich j~ en scratch; **es j~t mich** I have an itch

Jude *m* -n,-n Jew

Jüd|in *f* -,-nen Jewess. **j~isch** *a* Jewish

Judo *nt* -[s] judo

Jugend *f* - youth; (*junge Leute*) young people *pl*. **J~herberge** *f* youth hostel. **J~kriminalität** *f* juvenile delinquency. **j~lich** *a* youthful. **J~liche(r)** *m/f* young man/woman; (*Admin*) juvenile. **J~liche** *pl* young people. **J~stil** *m* art nouveau

Jugoslaw|ien /-jən/ *nt* -s Yugoslavia. **j~isch** *a* Yugoslav

Juli *m* -[s],-s July

jung *a* young; (*Wein*) new □*pron* **j~ und alt** young and old. **J~e** *m* -n,-n boy. **J~e(s)** *nt* young animal; (*Katzen-*) kitten; (*Bären-*) cub; (*Hunde-*) pup; **die J~en** the young *pl*

Jünger *m* -s,- disciple

Jungfrau *f* virgin; (*Astr*) Virgo. **J~geselle** *m* bachelor

Jüngling *m* -s,-e youth

jüngst|e(r,s) *a* youngest; (*neueste*) latest; **in j~er Zeit** recently

Juni *m* -[s],-s June

Jura *pl* law *sg*

Jurist(in) *m* -en,-en (*f* -,-nen) lawyer. **j~isch** *a* legal

Jury /ʒyːriː/ f -,-s jury; (Sport) judges pl

Justiz f - die J~ justice

Juwelier m -s,-e jeweller

Jux m -es,-e (fam) joke; **aus Jux** for fun

K

Kabarett nt -s,-s & -e cabaret

Kabel nt -s,- cable. **K~fernsehen** nt cable television

Kabeljau m -s,-e & -s cod

Kabine f -,-n cabin; (Umkleide-) cubicle; (Telefon-) booth; (einer K~nbahn) car. **K~nbahn** f cable-car

Kabinett nt -s,-e (Pol) Cabinet

Kabriolett nt -s,-s convertible

Kachel f -,-n tile. **k~n** vt tile

Kadenz f -,-en (Mus) cadence

Käfer m -s,- beetle

Kaffee /ˈkafeː, kaˈfeː/ m -s,-s coffee. **K~kanne** f coffee-pot

Käfig m -s,-e cage

kahl a bare; (haarlos) bald

Kahn m -s,ˈe boat; (Last-) barge

Kai m -s,-s quay

Kaiser m -s,- emperor. **K~in** f -,-nen empress. **k~lich** a imperial. **K~reich** nt empire. **K~schnitt** m Caesarean [section]

Kajüte f -,-n (Naut) cabin

Kakao /kaˈkaʊ/ m -s cocoa

Kakerlak m -s & -en,-en cockroach

Kaktus m -,-teen /-ˈteːn/ cactus

Kalb nt -[e]s,ˈer calf. **K~fleisch** nt veal

Kalender m -s,- calendar; (Taschen-, Termin-) diary

Kaliber nt -s,- calibre; (Gewehr-) bore

Kalk m -[e]s,-e lime; (Kalzium) calcium. **k~en** vt whitewash

Kalkul|ation /-ˈtsjoːn/ f -,-en calculation. **k~ieren** vt/i (haben) calculate

Kalorie f -,-n calorie

kalt a cold

Kälte f - cold; **10 Grad K~** 10 degrees below zero

Kalzium nt -s calcium

Kamel nt -s,-e camel

Kamera f -,-s camera

Kamerad(in) m -en,-en (f -,-nen) companion; (Freund) mate; (Mil, Pol) comrade

Kameramann m (pl -männer & -leute) cameraman

Kamille f - camomile

Kamin m -s,-e fireplace; (SGer: Schornstein) chimney. **K~feger** m -s,- (SGer) chimney-sweep

Kamm m -[e]s,ˈe comb; (Berg-) ridge; (Zool, Wellen-) crest

kämmen vt comb; **jdn/sich k~** comb s.o.'s/one's hair

Kammer f -,-n small room; (Techn, Biol, Pol) chamber

Kammgarn nt (Tex) worsted

Kampagne /kamˈpanjə/ f -,-n (Pol, Comm) campaign

Kampf m -es,ˈe fight; (Schlacht) battle; (Wett-) contest; (fig) struggle

kämpf|en vi (haben) fight; **sich k~en durch** fight one's way through. **K~er(in)** m -s,- (f -,-nen) fighter

Kanada nt -s Canada

Kanad|ier(in) /-iɐ, -jərɪn/ m -s,- (f -,-nen) Canadian. **k~isch** a Canadian

Kanal m -s,ˈe canal; (Abfluß-) drain, sewer; (Radio, TV) channel; **der K~** the [English] Channel

Kanalisation /-ˈtsjoːn/ f - sewerage system, drains pl

Kanarienvogel /-jən-/ m canary

Kanarisch a **K~e Inseln** Canaries

Kandidat(in) m -en,-en (f -,-nen) candidate

kandiert a candied

Känguruh nt -s,-s kangaroo

Kaninchen nt -s,- rabbit

Kanister m -s,- canister; (Benzin-) can

Kanne f -,-n jug; (Kaffee-, Tee-) pot; (Öl-) can; (große Milch-) churn

Kannibal|e m -n,-n cannibal. **K ~ ismus** m - cannibalism

Kanone f -,-n cannon, gun

kanonisieren vt canonize

Kantate f -,-n cantata

Kante f -,-n edge

Kanten m -s,- crust [of bread]

Kanter m -s,- canter

kantig a angular

Kantine f -,-n canteen

Kanton m -s,-e (Swiss) canton

Kanu nt -s,-s canoe

Kanzel f -,-n pulpit; (Aviat) cockpit

Kanzler m -s,- chancellor

Kap nt -s,-s (Geog) cape

Kapazität f -,-en capacity

Kapelle f -,-n chapel; (Mus) band

kapern vt (Naut) seize

kapieren vt (fam) understand

Kapital nt -s capital. **K ~ ismus** m - capitalism. **K ~ ist** m -en,-en capitalist. **K ~ istisch** a capitalist

Kapitän m -s,-e captain

Kapitel nt -s,- chapter

Kaplan m -s,-e curate

Kapsel f -,-n capsule; (Flaschen-) top

kaputt a (fam) broken; (zerrissen) torn; (defekt) out of order; (ruiniert) ruined; (erschöpft) worn out. **k ~ gehen†** vi sep (sein) (fam) break; (zerreißen) tear; (defekt werden) pack up; (Ehe, Freundschaft:) break up. **k ~ lachen (sich)** vr sep (fam) be in stitches. **k ~ machen** vt sep (fam) break; (zerreißen) tear; (defekt machen) put out of order; (erschöpfen) wear out

Kapuze f -,-n hood

Kapuzinerkresse f nasturtium

Karamel m -s caramel. **K ~ bonbon** m & nt ≈ toffee

Karat nt -[e]s,-e carat

Karawane f -,-n caravan

Kardinal m -s,-e cardinal

Karfreitag m Good Friday

karg a meagre; (frugal) frugal; (spärlich) sparse; (unfruchtbar) barren; (gering) scant

Karibik f - Caribbean

kariert a check[ed]; (Papier) squared; **schottisch k ~** tartan

Karikatur f -,-en caricature; (Journ) cartoon

karitativ a charitable

Karneval m -s,-e & -s carnival

Kärnten nt -s Carinthia

Karo nt -s, (Raute) diamond; (Viereck) square; (Muster) check; (Kartenspiel) diamonds pl

Karosserie f -,-n bodywork

Karotte f -,-n carrot

Karpfen m -s,- carp

Karree nt -s,-s square; **ums K ~** round the block

Karren m -s,- cart; barrow

Karriere /ka'rie:rə/ f -,-n career; **K ~ machen** get to the top

Karte f -,-n card; (Fahr-) ticket; (Speise-) menu; (Land-) map

Kartei f -,-n card index

Karten|**spiel** nt card-game; (Spielkarten) pack of cards. **K ~ vorverkauf** m advance booking

Kartoffel f -,-n potato. **K ~ brei** m mashed potatoes pl

Karton /kar'tɔŋ/ m -s,-s cardboard; (Schachtel) carton

Karussell nt -s,-s & -e roundabout

Käse m -s,- cheese

Kaserne f -,-n barracks pl

Kasino nt -s,-s casino

Kasperle nt & m -s,- Punch. **K ~ theater** nt Punch and Judy show

Kasse f -,-n till; (Registrier-) cash register; (Zahlstelle) cash desk; (im Supermarkt) check-out; (Theater-) box-office; (Geld) pool

[of money], (*fam*) kitty; (*Kranken-*) health insurance scheme;
knapp bei K~ sein (*fam*) be short of cash. **K~nwart** *m* **-[e]s,-e** treasurer. **K~nzettel** *m* receipt

Kasserolle *f* **-,-n** saucepan [with one handle]

Kassette *f* **-,-n** cassette; (*Film-, Farbband-*) cartridge. **K~nrecorder** /-rəkɔrdɐ/ *m* **-s,-** cassette recorder

kassier|en *vi* (*haben*) collect the money;(*im Bus*) take the fares □*vt* collect. **K~er(in)** *m* **-s,- (** *f* **-,-nen)** cashier

Kastanie /kas'taːnjə/ *f* **-,-n** [horse] chestnut, (*fam*) conker

Kasten *m* **-s,** box; (*Flaschen-*) crate; (*Aust: Schrank*) cupboard

kastrieren *vt* castrate; neuter

Katalog *m* **-[e]s,-e** catalogue

Katalysator *m* **-s,-en** /-'toːrən/ catalyst; (*Auto*) catalytic converter

Katapult *nt* **-[e]s,-e** catapult. **k~ieren** *vt* catapult

Katarrh *m* **-s,-e** catarrh

Katastrophe *f* **-,-n** catastrophe

Katechismus *m* **-** catechism

Kategorie *f* **-,-n** category

Kater *m* **-s,-** tom-cat; (*fam: Katzenjammer*) hangover

Kathedrale *f* **-,-n** cathedral

Kath|olik(in) *m* **-en,-en (** *f* **-,-nen)** Catholic. **k~olisch** *a* Catholic. **K~olizismus** *m* **-** Catholicism

Kätzchen *nt* **-s,-** kitten

Katze *f* **-,-n** cat. **K~njammer** *m* (*fam*) hangover. **K~nsprung** *m* **ein K~nsprung** (*fam*) a stone's throw

Kauderwelsch *nt* **-[s]** gibberish

kauen *vt/i* (*haben*) chew; bite ⟨*Nägel*⟩

Kauf *m* **-[e]s,Käufe** purchase; **guter K~** bargain; **in K~ nehmen** (*fig*) put up with. **k~en** *vt/i* (*haben*) buy; **k~en bei** shop at

Käufer(in) *m* **-s,- (** *f* **-,-nen)** buyer; (*im Geschäft*) shopper

Kauf|haus *nt* department store. **K~laden** *m* shop

käuflich *a* saleable; (*bestechlich*) corruptible; **k~ erwerben** buy

Kauf|mann *m* (*pl* **-leute**) businessman; (*Händler*) dealer; (*dial*) grocer. **K~preis** *m* purchase price

Kaugummi *m* chewing-gum

Kaulquappe *f* **-,-n** tadpole

kaum *adv* hardly

Kaution /-'tsioːn/ *f* **-,-en** surety; (*Jur*) bail; (*Miet-*) deposit

Kautschuk *m* **-s** rubber

Kauz *m* **-es, Käuze** owl

Kavalier *m* **-s,-e** gentleman

Kavallerie *f* **-** cavalry

Kaviar *m* **-s** caviare

keck *a* bold; (*frech*) cheeky

Kegel *m* **-s,-** skittle; (*Geom*) cone. **K~n** *vi* (*haben*) play skittles

Kehle *f* **-,-n** throat; **aus voller K~e** at the top of one's voice. **K~kopf** *m* larynx. **K~kopfentzündung** *f* laryngitis

Kehre *f* **-,-n** [hairpin] bend. **k~en** *vi* (*haben*) (*fegen*) sweep □*vt* sweep; (*wenden*) turn. **K~icht** *m* **-[e]s** sweepings *pl*. **K~reim** *m* refrain. **K~tmachen** *vi sep* (*haben*) turn back; (*sich umdrehen*) turn round

Keil *m* **-[e]s,-e** wedge. **K~riemen** *m* fan belt

Keim *m* **-[e]s,-e** (*Bot*) sprout; (*Med*) germ. **k~en** *vi* (*haben*) germinate; (*austreiben*) sprout. **k~frei** *a* sterile

kein *pron* no; not a; **k~e fünf Minuten** less than five minutes. **k~e(r,s)** *pron* no one, nobody; (*Ding*) none, not one. **k~esfalls** *adv* on no account. **k~mal** *adv* not once. **k~s** *pron* none, not one

Keks *m* **-[es],-[e]** biscuit

Kelch *m* **-[e]s,-e** goblet, cup; (*Relig*) chalice; (*Bot*) calyx

Kelle f -,-n ladle
Keller m -s,- cellar. **K~ei** f -,-en
winery. **K~wohnung** f basement flat
Kellner m -s,- waiter. **K~in** f
-,-nen waitress
keltern vt press
keltisch a Celtic
Kenia nt -s Kenya
kenn|en vt know. **K~enlernen**
vt sep get to know; (treffen) meet.
K~er m -s,-. **K~erin** f -,-nen
connoisseur; (Experte) expert.
k~tlich a recognizable;
k~tlich machen mark. **K~tnis**
f -,-se knowledge; **zur K~tnis
nehmen** take note of; **in K~tnis
setzen** inform (von of). **K~wort**
nt (pl -wörter) reference; (geheimes) password. **K~zeichen**
nt distinguishing mark or
feature; (Merkmal) characteristic; (Markierung) mark, marking; (Auto) registration.
k~zeichnen vt distinguish;
(markieren) mark
kentern vi (sein) capsize
Keramik f -,-en pottery
Kerbe f -,-n notch
Kerker m -s,- dungeon; (Gefängnis) prison
Kerl m -s,-e & -s (fam) fellow
Kern m -s,-e pip; (Kirsch-) stone;
(Nuß-) kernel; (Techn) core;
(Atom-, Zell- & fig) nucleus;
(Stadt-) centre; (einer Sache)
heart. **K~energie** f nuclear
energy. **K~gehäuse** nt core.
k~los a seedless. **K~physik** f
nuclear physics sg
Kerze f -,-n candle. **k~ngerade** a
& adv straight. **K~nhalter** m
-s,- candlestick
keß a pert
Kette f -,-n chain; (Hals-) necklace. **k~n** vt chain (an + acc to)
Ketze|r(in) m -s,- (f -,-nen)
heretic. **K~rei** f -,- heresy

keuch|en vi (haben) pant.
K~husten m whooping cough
Keule f -,-n club; (Culin) leg;
(Hühner-) drumstick
Khaki nt - khaki
kichern vi (haben) giggle
Kiefer[1] f -,-n pine[-tree]
Kiefer[2] m -s,- jaw
Kiel m -s,-e (Naut) keel
Kiemen fpl gills
Kies m -es gravel. **K~el** m -s,-.
K~elstein m pebble
Kilo nt -s,-[s] kilo. **K~gramm** nt
kilogram. **K~hertz** nt kilohertz.
K~meter m kilometre. **K~me-
terstand** m ≈ mileage. **K~watt**
nt kilowatt
Kind nt -es,-er child; **von K~ auf**
from childhood
Kinder|arzt m, **K~ärztin** f paediatrician. **K~bett** nt child's cot.
K~garten m nursery school.
K~geld nt child benefit.
K~lähmung f polio. **k~leicht** a
a very easy. **K~mädchen** nt
nanny. **K~reim** m nursery
rhyme. **K~spiel** nt children's
game. **K~tagesstätte** f day nursery. **K~teller** m children's
menu. **K~wagen** m pram.
K~zimmer nt child's/children's
room; (für Baby) nursery
Kind|heit f - childhood. **k~isch** a
childish. **k~lich** a childlike
kinetisch a kinetic
Kinn nt -[e]s,-e chin. **K~lade** f
jaw
Kino nt -s,-s cinema
Kiosk m -[e]s,-e kiosk
Kippe f -,-n (Müll-) dump; (fam:
Zigaretten-) fag-end. **k~n** vt tilt;
(schütten) tip (in + acc into) □ vi
(sein) topple
Kirch|e f -,-n church. **K~en-
bank** f pew. **K~endiener** m
verger. **K~enlied** nt hymn.
K~enschiff nt nave. **K~hof** m

churchyard. **k~lich** *a* church
... □*adv* **k~lich getraut wer-
den be** married in church.
K~weih *f* -,-en [village] fair
Kirmes *f* -,-sen = **Kirchweih**
Kirsch|e *f* -,-en cherry. **K~-
wasser** *nt* kirsch
Kissen *nt* -s,- cushion; (*Kopf-*) pil-
low
Kiste *f* -,-n crate; (*Zigarren-*) box
Kitsch *m* -es sentimental rubbish;
(*Kunst*) kitsch
Kitt *m* -s [adhesive] cement;
(*Fenster-*) putty
Kittel *m* -s,- overall, smock
Kitz *nt* -es,-e (*Zool*) kid
Kitz|el *m* -s tickle; (*Nerven-*)
thrill. **k~eln** *vt/i* (*haben*) tickle.
k~lig *a* ticklish
kläffen *vi* (*haben*) yap
Klage *f* -,-n lament; (*Beschwerde*)
complaint; (*Jur*) action. **k~n** *vi*
(*haben*) lament; (*sich beklagen*)
complain; (*Jur*) sue
Kläger(in) *m* -s,- (*f* -,-nen) (*Jur*)
plaintiff
klamm *a* cold and damp; (*steif*)
stiff. **K~** *f* -,-en (*Geog*) gorge
Klammer *f* -,-n (*Wäsche-*) peg;
(*Büro-*) paper-clip; (*Heft-*) staple;
(*Haar-*) grip; (*für Zähne*) brace;
(*Techn*) clamp; (*Typ*) bracket.
k~n (sich) *vr* cling (**an**+*acc* to)
Klang *m* -[e]s,-̈e sound;
(*K~farbe*) tone
Klapp|e *f* -,-n flap; (*fam: Mund*)
trap. **k~en** *vt* fold; (*hoch-*) tip up
□*vi* (*haben*) (*fam*) work out
Klapper *f* -,-n rattle. **k~n** *vi* (*haben*) rattle. **K~schlange** rattlesnake
klapprig *a* rickety; decrepit.
K~stuhl *m* folding chair
Klaps *m* -es,-e pat; smack
klar *a* clear; **sich** (*dat*) **k~** *od* **im
k~en sein** realize □*adv* clearly;
(*fam: natürlich*) of course
klären *vt* clarify; **sich k~** clear;
(*fig: sich lösen*) resolve itself
Klarheit *f* - clarity

Klarinette *f* -,-n clarinet
klar|machen *vt sep* make clear
(*dat* to); **sich** (*dat*) **etw k~ma-
chen** understand sth. **K~sicht-
folie** *f* cling film
Klärung *f* - clarification
klarwerden† *vi sep* (*sein*) (*fig*)
become clear (*dat* to); **sich** (*dat*)
k~ make up one's mind
Klasse *f* -,-n class; (*Sch*) class,
form; (*Zimmer*) classroom; **erster K~** first class. **k~** *inv a*
(*fam*) super. **K~nzimmer** *nt*
classroom
Klass|ik *f* - classicism; (*Epoche*)
classical period. **K~iker** *m* -s,-
classical author/(*Mus*) composer. **k~isch** *a* classical; (*typisch*) classic
Klatsch *m* -[e]s gossip. **K~base** *f*
(*fam*) gossip. **k~en** *vt* slap; **Beifall k~en** applaud □*vi* (*haben*)
make a slapping sound; (*im
Wasser*) splash; (*tratschen*) gossip; (*applaudieren*) clap. **k~naß**
a (*fam*) soaking wet
klauben *vt* pick
Klaue *f* -,-n claw; (*fam: Schrift*)
scrawl. **k~n** *vt/i* (*haben*) (*fam*)
steal
Klausel *f* -,-n clause
Klaustrophobie *f* - claustrophobia
Klausur *f* -,-en (*Univ*) paper
Klavier *nt* -s,-e piano. **K~spie-
ler(in)** *m*(*f*) pianist
kleb|en *vt* stick/(*mit Klebstoff*)
glue (**an**+*acc* to) □*vi* (*haben*)
stick (**an**+*dat* to). **k~rig** *a*
sticky. **K~stoff** *m* adhesive,
glue. **K~streifen** *m* adhesive
tape
Klecks *m* -es,-e stain; (*Tinten-*)
blot; (*kleine Menge*) dab. **k~en** *vi*
(*haben*) make a mess
Klee *m* -s clover
Kleid *nt* -[e]s,-er dress; **K~er**
dresses; (*Kleidung*) clothes.
k~en *vt* dress; (*gut stehen*) suit.

K~erbügel *m* coat-hanger.
K~erbürste *f* clothes-brush.
K~erhaken *m* coat-hook.
K~erschrank *m* wardrobe.
k~sam *a* becoming. K~ung *f*-
clothes *pl*, clothing. K~ungs-
stück *nt* garment
Kleie *f*- bran
klein *a* small, little; (*von kleinem
Wuchs*) short; von k~ auf from
childhood. K~arbeit *f* painstaking work. K~bus *m* minibus.
K~e(r,s) *m/f/nt* little one.
K~geld *nt* [small] change.
K~handel *m* retail trade.
K~igkeit *f*-,-en trifle; (*Mahl*)
snack. K~kind *nt* infant.
k~laut *a* subdued. k~lich *a*
petty. K~stadt *f* small town.
k~städtisch *a* provincial
Kleister *m* -s paste. k~n *vt* paste
Klemme *f*-,-n [hair-]grip. k~n *vt*
jam; sich (*dat*) den Finger k~n
get one's finger caught □*vi* (*haben*) jam, stick
Klerus (der) - the clergy
Klette *f*-,-n burr
klettern *vi* (*sein*) climb.
K~pflanze *f* climber
Klettverschluß *m* Velcro (P)
fastening
klicken *vi* (*haben*) click
Klient(in) /kli'ɛnt(ɪn)/ *m* -en,-en
(*f*-,-nen) (*Jur*) client
Kliff *nt* -[e]s,-e cliff
Klima *nt* -s climate. K~anlage *f*
air-conditioning
klimatisch *a* climatic. k~isiert
a air-conditioned
Klinge *f*-,-n blade
Klingel *f*-,-n bell. k~n *vi* (*haben*)
ring; es k~t there's a ring at the
door
klingen† *vi* (*haben*) sound
Klinik *f*-,-en clinic
Klinke *f*-,-n [door] handle
Klippe *f*-,-n (*submerged*) rock
Klips *m* -es,-e clip; (*Ohr-*) clip-on
ear-ring

klirren *vi* (*haben*) rattle
Klischee *nt* -s,-s cliché
Klo *nt* -s,-s (*fam*) loo
klobig *a* clumsy
klopfen *vi* (*haben*) knock; (*leicht*)
tap; (*Herz:*) pound; es k~te there
was a knock at the door
Klops *m* -es,-e meatball
Klosett *nt* -s,-s lavatory
Kloß *m* -es,-e dumpling
Kloster *nt* -s,- monastery; (*Non-
nen-*) convent
klösterlich *a* monastic
Klotz *m* -es,-e block
Klub *m* -s,-s club
Kluft *f*-,-en cleft; (*fig: Gegensatz*)
gulf
klug *a* intelligent; (*schlau*) clever.
K~heit *f*- cleverness
Klumpen *m* -s,- lump
knabbern *vt/i* (*haben*) nibble
Knabe *m* -n,-n boy
Knäckebrot *nt* -[e]s crispbread
knack|en *vt/i* (*haben*) crack.
K~s *m* -es,-e crack
Knall *m* -[e]s,-e bang. K~bon-
bon *m* cracker. k~en *vi* (*haben*)
go bang; (*Peitsche:*) crack □*vt*
jdm eine k~en (*fam*) clout s.o.
K~ig *a* (*fam*) gaudy
knapp *a* (*gering*) scant; (*kurz*)
short; (*mangelnd*) scarce; (*gerade
ausreichend*) bare; (*eng*) tight.
K~heit *f*- scarcity
knarren *vi* (*haben*) creak
Knast *m* -[e]s (*fam*) prison
knattern *vi* (*haben*) crackle;
(*Gewehr:*) stutter
Knäuel *m & nt* -s,- ball
Knauf *m* -[e]s, Knäufe knob
knauserig *a* (*fam*) stingy
knautschen *vt* (*fam*) crumple □
vi (*haben*) crease
Knebel *m* -s,- gag. k~n *vt* gag
Knecht *m* -[e]s,-e farm-hand;
(*fig*) slave
kneifen† *vt* pinch □*vi* (*haben*)
pinch; (*fam: sich drücken*) chick-
en out. K~zange *f* pincers *pl*

Kneipe f -,-n (fam) pub
knet|en vt knead; (formen)
mould. **K~masse** f Plasticine (P)
Knick m -[e]s,-e bend; (Kniff)
crease. **k~en** vt bend; (kniffen)
fold; **geknickt sein** (fam) be dejected
Knicks m -es,-e curtsy. **k~en** vi
(haben) curtsy
Knie nt -s,- /'kni:ə/ knee
knien /'kni:ən/ vi (haben) kneel
□vr **sich k~** kneel [down]
Kniescheibe f kneecap
Kniff m -[e]s,-e pinch; (fam:
Trick) trick. **k~en** vt fold
knipsen vt (lochen) punch; (Phot)
photograph □vi (haben) take a
photograph/photographs
Knirps m -es,-e (fam) little chap;
(P) (Schirm) telescopic umbrella
knirschen vi (haben) grate;
⟨Schnee, Kies:⟩ crunch
knistern vi (haben) crackle; ⟨Papier:⟩ rustle
Knitter|falte f crease. **k~frei** a
crease-resistant. **k~n** vi (haben)
crease
knobeln vi (haben) toss (**um** for)
Knoblauch m -s garlic
Knöchel m -s,- ankle; (Finger-)
knuckle
Knochen m -s,- bone
knochig a bony
Knödel m -s,- (SGer) dumpling
Knolle f -,-n tuber
Knopf m -[e]s,-e button
knöpfen vt button
Knopfloch nt buttonhole
Knorpel m -s gristle; (Anat) cartilage
Knospe f bud
Knoten m -s,- knot; (Med) lump;
(Haar-) bun, chignon. **k~** vt
knot. **K~punkt** m junction
knüll|en vt crumple. **K~er** m -s,-
(fam) sensation
knüpfen vt knot; (verbinden) attach (**an** + acc to)

Knüppel m -s,- club; (Gummi-)
truncheon
knurren vi (haben) growl; ⟨Magen:⟩ rumble
knusprig a crunchy, crisp
knutschen vi (haben) (fam)
smooch
k.o. /ka'?o:/ a **k.o. schlagen** knock
out; **k.o. sein** (fam) be worn out
Koalition /koali'tsjo:n/ f -,-en
coalition
Kobold m -[e]s,-e goblin, imp
Koch m -[e]s,-e cook; (im Restaurant) chef. **K~buch** nt cookery
book. **k~en** vt cook; (sieden)
boil; make (Kaffee, Tee) □vi (haben) cook; (sieden) boil; (fam)
seethe (**vor** + dat with). **K~en** nt
-s cooking; (Sieden) boiling.
k~end a boiling. **K~herd** m
cooker, stove
Köchin f -,-nen (woman) cook
Koch|löffel m wooden spoon.
K~nische f kitchenette.
K~platte f hotplate. **K~topf** m
saucepan
Köder m -s,- bait
Koffein /kɔfe'i:n/ nt -s caffeine.
k~frei a decaffeinated
Koffer m -s,- suitcase. **K~kuli** m
luggage trolley. **K~raum** m
(Auto) boot
Kognak /'kɔnjak/ m -s,-s brandy
Kohl m -[e]s cabbage
Kohle f -,-n coal. **K~[n]hydrat**
nt -[e]s,-e carbohydrate. **K~n-
bergwerk** nt coal-mine, colliery.
K~nsäure f carbon dioxide.
K~nstoff m carbon. **K~papier**
nt carbon paper
Kohlrübe f swede
Koje f -,-n (Naut) bunk
kokett a flirtatious. **k~ieren**
vi (haben) flirt
Kokosnuß f coconut
Koks m -es coke
Kolben m -s,- (Gewehr-) butt;
(Mais-) cob; (Techn) piston;
(Chem) flask

Kolibri *m* -s,-s humming-bird

Kolik *f* -,-en colic

Kollaborateur /-'tø:ɐ̯/ *m* -s,-e collaborator

Kolleg *nt* -s,-s & -ien /-jən/ (*Univ*) course of lectures

Kollege *m* -n,-n, **K ~ in** *f* -,-nen colleague. **K ~ ium** *nt* -s,-ien staff

Kollekte *f* -,-n (*Relig*) collection. **k ~ tiv** *a* collective

Köln *nt* -s Cologne. **K ~ isch-wasser** *nt* eau-de-Cologne

Kolonie *f* -,-n colony

Kolonne *f* -,-n column; (*Mil*) convoy

Koloß *m* -sses,-sse giant

Koma *nt* -s,-s coma

Kombi *m* -s,-s = **K ~ wagen**. **K ~ nation** /-'tsio:n/ *f* -,-en combination; (*Folgerung*) deduction; (*Kleidung*) co-ordinating outfit. **k ~ nieren** *vt* combine; (*fig*) reason; (*folgern*) deduce. **K ~ wagen** *m* estate car

Kombüse *f* -,-n (*Naut*) galley

Komet *m* -en,-en comet

Komfort /kɔm'foːɐ̯/ *m* -s comfort; (*Luxus*) luxury. **k ~ abel** /-'taːbəl/ *a* comfortable; luxurious

Komik *f* - humour. **K ~ er** *m* -s,-comic, comedian

komisch *a* funny; (*sonderbar*) odd, funny. **k ~ erweise** *adv* funnily enough

Komitee *nt* -s,-s committee

Komma *nt* -s,-s & -ta comma; (*Dezimal*) decimal point; **drei K ~ fünf** three point five

Kommando *nt* -s,-s order; (*Befehlsgewalt*) command; (*Einheit*) detachment. **K ~ brücke** *f* bridge

kommen† *vi* (*sein*) come; (*eintreffen*) arrive; (*gelangen*) get (**nach** to); **k ~ lassen** send for; **auf/hinter etw** (*acc*) **k ~** think of/find out about sth; **um/zu etw k ~** lose/acquire sth; **wieder zu sich k ~** come round; **wie**

kommt das? why is that? **k ~ d** *a* coming; **k ~ den Montag** next Monday

Kommentar *m* -s,-e commentary; (*Bemerkung*) comment. **k ~ tieren** *vt* comment on

kommerziell *a* commercial

Kommilitone *m* -n,-n, **K ~ tonin** *f* -,-nen fellow student

Kommiß *m* -sses (*fam*) army

Kommissar *m* -s,-e commissioner; (*Polizei*) superintendent

Kommode *f* -,-n chest of drawers

Kommunalwahlen *fpl* local elections

Kommunion *f* -,-en [Holy] Communion

Kommunismus *m* -s Communism. **K ~ ist(in)** *m* -en,-en (*f* -,-nen) Communist. **k ~ istisch** *a* Communist

kommunizieren *vi* (*haben*) receive [Holy] Communion

Komödie /ko'møːdjə/ *f* -,-n comedy

Kompagnon /'kɔmpanjõ:/ *m* -s,-s (*Comm*) partner

Kompanie *f* -,-n (*Mil*) company

Komparse *m* -n,-n (*Theat*) extra

Kompaß *m* -sses,-sse compass

kompatibel *a* compatible

komplett *a* complete

Komplex *m* -es,-e complex

Komplikation /-'tsio:n/ *f* -,-en complication

Kompliment *nt* -[e]s,-e compliment

Komplize *m* -n,-n accomplice

komplizieren *vt* complicate. **k ~ t** *a* complicated

Komplott *nt* -[e]s,-e plot

komponieren *vt/i* (*haben*) compose. **K ~ nist** *m* -en,-en composer

Kompositum *nt* -s,-ta compound

Kompost *m* -[e]s compost

Kompott *nt* -[e]s,-e stewed fruit

Kompromiß *m* -sses,-sse compromise; **einen K ~ schließen** compromise

Konden|sation /-'tsioːn/ *f* - condensation. **k~sieren** *vt* condense

Kondensmilch *f* evaporated/(*gesüßt*) condensed milk

Kondition /-'tsioːn/ *f* - (*Sport*) fitness; **in K~** in form

Konditor *m* -s,-en /-'toːrən/ confectioner. **K~ei** *f* -,-en patisserie

Kondo|lenzbrief *m* letter of condolence. **k~lieren** *vi* (*haben*) express one's condolences

Kondom *nt & m* -s,-e condom

Konfekt *nt* -[e]s confectionery; (*Pralinen*) chocolates (*pl*)

Konfektion /-'tsioːn/ *f* - ready-to-wear clothes *pl*

Konferenz *f* -,-en conference; (*Besprechung*) meeting

Konfession *f* -,-en [religious] denomination. **k~ell** *a* denominational

Konfetti *nt* -s confetti

Konfirm|and(in) *m* -en,-en (*f* -,-nen) candidate for confirmation. **K~ation** /-'tsioːn/ *f* -,-en (*Relig*) confirmation. **k~ieren** *vt* (*Relig*) confirm

Konfitüre *f* -,-n jam

Konflikt *m* -[e]s,-e conflict

Konföderation /-'tsioːn/ *f* confederation

konfus *a* confused

Kongreß *m* -sses,-sse congress

König *m* -s,-e king. **K~in** *f* -,-nen queen. **k~lich** *a* royal; (*hoheitsvoll*) regal; (*großzügig*) handsome. **K~reich** *nt* kingdom

Konjunktiv *m* -s,-e subjunctive

Konjunktur *f* - economic situation; (*Hoch-*) boom

konkret *a* concrete

Konkurren|t(in) *m* -en,-en (*f* -,-nen) competitor, rival. **K~z** *f* - competition; **jdm K~z machen** compete with s.o. **K~z-kampf** *m* competition, rivalry

konkurrieren *vi* (*haben*) compete

Konkurs *m* -es,-e bankruptcy

können† *vt/i* (*haben*) etw k~ be able to do sth; (*beherrschen*) know sth; **k~ Sie Deutsch?** do you know any German? **für etw nichts k~** not be to blame for sth □*v aux* **lesen k~** be able to read; **er kann/konnte es tun** he can/could do it. **K~** *nt* -s ability; (*Wissen*) knowledge

konsequent *a* consistent; (*logisch*) logical. **K~z** *f* -,-en consequence

konservativ *a* conservative

Konserv|en *fpl* tinned *or* canned food *sg*. **K~endose** *f* tin, can. **K~ierungsmittel** *nt* preservative

Konsonant *m* -en,-en consonant

konsterniert *a* dismayed

Konstitution /-'tsioːn/ *f* -,-en constitution. **k~ell** *a* constitutional

konstruieren *vt* construct; (*entwerfen*) design

Konstruktion /-'tsioːn/ *f* -,-en construction; (*Entwurf*) design

Konsul *m* -s,-n consul. **K~at** *nt* -[e]s,-e consulate

Konsum *m* -s consumption. **K~güter** *npl* consumer goods

Kontakt *m* -[e]s,-e contact. **K~linsen** *fpl* contact lenses. **K~person** *f* contact

kontern *vt/i* (*haben*) counter

Kontinent /'kɔn-, kɔntiˈnɛnt/ *m* -s,-e continent

Kontingent *nt* -[e]s,-e (*Comm*) quota; (*Mil*) contingent

Konto *nt* -s,-s account. **K~aus-zug** *m* [bank] statement. **K~nummer** *f* account number. **K~stand** *m* [bank] balance

Kontrabaß *m* double-bass

Kontroll|abschnitt *m* counterfoil. **K~e** *f* -,-n control; (*Prüfung*) check. **K~eur** /-'løːɡ/ *m* -s,-e [ticket] inspector. **k~ieren** *vt*

check; inspect ⟨*Fahrkarten*⟩; (*beherrschen*) control

Kontroverse f -,-n controversy

Kontur f -,-en contour

Konversationslexikon nt encyclopaedia

konvertieren vi (*haben*) (*Relig*) convert. **K ~ it** m -en,-en convert

Konzentration /-'tsjo:n/ f -,-en concentration. **K ~ slager** nt concentration camp

konzentrieren vt concentrate; **sich k ~** concentrate (**auf** + acc on)

Konzept nt -[e]s,-e [rough] draft; **jdn aus dem K ~ bringen** put s.o. off his stroke

Konzern m -s,-e (*Comm*) group

Konzert nt -[e]s,-e concert; (*Klavier-, Geigen-*) concerto

Konzession /-'tsjo:n/ f -,-en licence; (*Zugeständnis*) concession

Konzil nt -s,-e (*Relig*) council

Kooperation /ko°°pera'tsjo:n/ f co-operation

Koordination /ko°°ordina'tsjo:n/ f -co-ordination. **k ~ ieren** vt co-ordinate

Kopf m -[e]s,ˉe head; **ein K ~ Kohl** a cabbage; **aus dem K ~** from memory; (*auswendig*) by heart; **auf dem K ~** (*verkehrt*) upside down; **sich** (*dat*) **den K ~ waschen** wash one's hair; **sich** (*dat*) **den K ~ zerbrechen** rack one's brains. **K ~ ball** m header

köpfen vt behead; (*Fußball*) head

Kopf ende nt head. **K ~ haut** f scalp. **K ~ hörer** m headphones pl. **K ~ kissen** nt pillow. **k ~ los** a panic-stricken. **K ~ rechnen** nt mental arithmetic. **K ~ salat** m lettuce. **K ~ schmerzen** mpl headache sg. **K ~ sprung** m header, dive. **K ~ stand** m handstand. **K ~ steinpflaster** nt cobblestones pl. **K ~ tuch** nt headscarf. **k ~ über** adv head

first; (*fig*) headlong. **K ~ wäsche** f shampoo. **K ~ weh** nt headache

Kopie f -,-n copy. **k ~ ren** vt copy

Koppel[1 f -,-n enclosure; (*Pferde-*) paddock

Koppel[2 nt -s,- (*Mil*) belt. **k ~ n** vt couple

Koralle f -,-n coral

Korb m -[e]s,ˉe basket; **jdm einen K ~ geben** (*fig*) turn s.o. down. **K ~ ball** m [kind of] netball

Kord m -s (*Tex*) corduroy

Kordel f -,-n cord

Korinthe f -,-n currant

Kork m -s cork. **K ~ en** m -s,- cork. **K ~ enzieher** m -s,- corkscrew

Korn nt -[e]s,ˉer grain; (*Samen-*) seed; (*am Visier*) front sight

Körn chen nt -s,- granule. **k ~ ig** a granular

Körper m -s,- body; (*Geom*) solid. **K ~ bau** m build, physique. **k ~ behindert** a physically disabled. **k ~ lich** a physical; ⟨*Strafe*⟩ corporal. **K ~ pflege** f personal hygiene. **K ~ schaft** f -,-en corporation, body

korpulent a corpulent

korrekt a correct. **K ~ or** m -s,-en /-'to:ran/ proof-reader. **K ~ ur** f -,-en correction. **K ~ urabzug** m proof

Korrespond ent(in) m -en,-en (f -,-nen) correspondent. **K ~ denz** f -,-en correspondence

Korridor m -s,-e corridor

korrigieren vt correct

Korrosion f - corrosion

korrupt a corrupt. **K ~ tion** /-'tsjo:n/ f - corruption

Korsett nt -[e]s,-e corset

Kosename m pet name

Kosmet ik f - beauty culture. **K ~ ika** ntpl cosmetics. **K ~ ikerin** f -,-nen beautician. **k ~ isch** a cosmetic; ⟨*Chirurgie*⟩ plastic

kosm isch a cosmic. **K ~ onaut(in)** m -en,-en (f -,-nen) cosmonaut

Kosmos m - cosmos

Kost f - food; (Ernährung) diet; (Verpflegung) board

kostbar a precious. **K~keit** f -,-en treasure

kosten vt cost; (brauchen) take; **wieviel kostet es?** how much is it? **K~** pl expense sg, cost sg; (Jur) costs; **auf meine K~** at my expense. **K~[vor]anschlag** m estimate. **k~los** a free □ adv free [of charge]

köstlich a delicious; (entzückend) delightful

Kostprobe f taste; (fig) sample

Kostüm nt -s,-e (Theat) costume; (Verkleidung) fancy dress; (Schneider-) suit

Kotelett /kot'let/ nt -s,-s chop, cutlet. **K~en** pl sideburns

Köter m -s,- (pej) dog

Kotflügel m (Auto) wing

kotzen vi (haben) (sl) throw up

Krabbe f -,-n crab; shrimp

krabbeln vi (sein) crawl

Krach m -[e]s,-̈e din, racket; (Knall) crash; (fam: Streit) row; (fam: Ruin) crash. **k~en** vi (haben) crash; **es hat gekracht** there was a bang/(fam: Unfall) a crash □ (sein) break, crack; (auftreffen) crash (**gegen** into)

krächzen vi (haben) croak

Kraft f -,-̈e strength; (Gewalt) force; (Arbeits-) worker; **in/außer K~** in/no longer in force. **k~** prep (+ gen) by virtue of. **K~fahrer** m driver. **K~fahrzeug** nt motor vehicle. **K~fahrzeugbrief** m [vehicle] registration document

kräftig a strong; (gut entwickelt) sturdy; (nahrhaft) nutritious; (heftig) hard □ adv strongly; (heftig) hard. **k~en** vt strengthen

kraftlos a weak. **K~probe** f trial of strength. **K~stoff** m (Auto) fuel. **K~wagen** m motor car. **K~werk** nt power station

Kragen m -s,- collar

Krähe f -,-n crow

krähen vi (haben) crow

Kralle f -,-n claw

Kram m -s (fam) things pl, (fam) stuff; (Angelegenheiten) business. **k~en** vi (haben) rummage about (**in** + dat in; **nach** for). **K~laden** m [small] general store

Krampf m -[e]s,-̈e cramp. **K~adern** fpl varicose veins. **k~haft** a convulsive; (verbissen) desperate

Kran m -[e]s,-̈e (Techn) crane

Kranich m -s,-e (Zool) crane

krank a sick; (Knie, Herz) bad; **k~ sein/werden** be/fall ill; **sich k~ melden** report sick. **K~e(r)** m/f sick man/woman, invalid; **die K~en** the sick pl

kränken vt offend, hurt

Kranken|bett nt sick-bed. **K~geld** nt sickness benefit. **K~gymnast(in)** m -en,-en (f -,-nen) physiotherapist. **K~haus** nt hospital. **K~kasse** f health insurance scheme/(Amt) office. **K~pflege** f nursing. **K~saal** m [hospital] ward. **K~schein** m certificate of entitlement to medical treatment. **K~schwester** f nurse. **K~urlaub** m sick-leave. **K~versicherung** f health insurance. **K~wagen** m ambulance

Krankheit f -,-en illness

kränklich a sickly

Kranz m -es,-̈e wreath

Krapfen m -s,- doughnut

kraß a glaring; (offensichtlich) blatant

Krater m -s,- crater

kratzen vt/i (haben) scratch. **K~er** m -s,- scratch

Kraul nt -s (Sport) crawl. **k~en** vi (haben/sein) (Sport) do the crawl

kraus a wrinkled; (Haar) frizzy; (verworren) muddled

kräuseln vt wrinkle; frizz (Haar); gather (Stoff); **sich k~** wrinkle;

(sich kringeln) curl; *(Haar:)* go frizzy

Kraut *nt* -[e]s, **Kräuter** herb; *(SGer)* cabbage; *(Sauer-)* sauerkraut

Krawall *m* -s,-e riot; *(Lärm)* row

Krawatte *f* -,-n [neck]tie

krea′tiv /krea′ti:f/ *a* creative. **K ~ tur** *f* -,-en creature

Krebs *m* -es,-e crayfish; *(Med)* cancer; *(Astr)* Cancer

Kredit *m* -s,-e credit; *(Darlehen)* loan; **auf K ~** on credit. **K ~ karte** *f* credit card

Kreid|**e** *f* - chalk. **k ~ ig** *a* chalky

kreieren /kreiˈiːrən/ *vt* create

Kreis *m* -es,-e circle; *(Admin)* district

kreischen *vt/i* *(haben)* screech; *(schreien)* shriek

Kreisel *m* -s,- [spinning] top

kreis|**en** *vi* *(haben)* circle; revolve *(um around)*. **k ~ förmig** *a* circular. **K ~ lauf** *m* cycle; *(Med)* circulation. **K ~ säge** *f* circular saw. **K ~ verkehr** *m* [traffic] roundabout

Krem *f* -,-s & *m* -s,-e cream

Krematorium *nt* -s,-ien crematorium

Krempe *f* -,-n [hat] brim

Krempel *m* -s *(fam)* junk

krempeln *vt* turn **(nach oben up)**

Krepp *m* -s,-s & -e crêpe

Kreppapier *nt* crêpe paper

Kresse *f* -,-n cress; nasturtium

Kreta *nt* -s Crete

Kreuz *nt* -es,-e cross; *(Kreuzung)* intersection; *(Mus)* sharp; *(Kartenspiel)* clubs *pl*; *(Anat)* small of the back; **über K ~** crosswise; **das K ~ schlagen** cross oneself. **k ~ en** *vt* cross; **sich k ~ en** cross; *(Straßen:)* intersect; *(Meinungen:)* clash □ *vi* *(haben/sein)* cruise. **K ~ fahrt** *f* *(Naut)* cruise. **K ~ gang** *m* cloister

kreuzig|**en** *vt* crucify. **K ~ ung** *f* -,-en crucifixion

Kreuz|**otter** *f* adder, common viper. **K ~ ung** *f* -,-en intersection; *(Straßen:)* crossroads *sg*; *(Hybride)* cross. **k ~ weise** *adv* crosswise. **K ~ worträtsel** *nt* crossword [puzzle]. **K ~ zug** *m* crusade

kribbel|**ig** *a* *(fam)* edgy. **k ~ n** *vi* *(haben)* tingle; *(kitzeln)* tickle

kriech|**en**† *vi* *(sein)* crawl; *(fig)* grovel **(vor + dat** to). **K ~ spur** *f* *(Auto)* crawler lane. **K ~ tier** *nt* reptile

Krieg *m* -[e]s,-e war

kriegen *vt* *(fam)* get; **ein Kind k ~** have a baby

Kriegs|**beschädigt** *a* war-disabled. **K ~ dienstverweigerer** *m* -s,- conscientious objector. **K ~ gefangene(r)** *m* prisoner of war. **K ~ gefangenschaft** *f* captivity. **K ~ gericht** *nt* court martial. **K ~ list** *f* stratagem. **K ~ rat** *m* council of war. **K ~ recht** *nt* martial law

Krimi *m* -s,-s *(fam)* crime story/film. **K ~ nalität** *f* - crime; *(Vorkommen)* crime rate. **K ~ nalpolizei** *f* criminal investigation department. **K ~ nalroman** *m* crime novel. **k ~ nell** *a* criminal. **K ~ nelle(r)** *m* criminal

Krippe *f* -,-n manger; *(Weihnachts-)* crib; *(Kinder-)* crèche. **K ~ nspiel** *nt* Nativity play

Krise *f* -,-n crisis

Kristall *nt* -s *(Glas)* crystal; *(geschliffen)* cut glass

Kriterium *nt* -s,-ien criterion

Kritik *f* -,-en criticism; *(Rezension)* review; **unter aller K ~** *(fam)* abysmal

Kriti|**ker** *m* -s,- critic; *(Rezensent)* reviewer. **k ~ sch** *a* critical. **k ~ sieren** *vt* criticize; review

kritzeln *vt/i* *(haben)* scribble

Krokette *f* -,-n *(Culin)* croquette

Krokodil *nt* -s,-e crocodile

Krokus *m* -,-[se] crocus

Krone *f* -,-n crown; *(Baum-)* top

krönen *vt* crown

Kronleuchter *m* chandelier

Krönung f -,-en coronation; (fig: Höhepunkt) crowning event

Kropf m -[e]s,⸚e (Zool) crop; (Med) goitre

Kröte f -,-n toad

Krücke f -,-n crutch

Krug m -[e]s,⸚e jug; (Bier-) tankard

Krümel m -s,- crumb. **k∼ig** a crumbly. **k∼n** vt crumble □vi (haben) be crumbly

krumm a crooked; (gebogen) curved; (verbogen) bent. **k∼bei-nig** a bow-legged

krümm|en vt bend; crook ⟨Finger⟩; **sich k∼** bend; (sich winden) writhe. **K∼ung** f -,-en bend; curve

Krüppel m -s,- cripple

Kruste f -,-n crust; (Schorf) scab

Kruzifix nt -es,-e crucifix

Kuba nt -s Cuba. **k∼anisch** a Cuban

Kübel m -s,- tub; (Eimer) bucket; (Techn) skip

Kubik- pref cubic

Küche f -,-n kitchen; (Kochkunst) cooking; **kalte/warme K∼** cold/hot food

Kuchen m -s,- cake

Küchen|herd m cooker, stove. **K∼maschine** f food processor, mixer. **K∼schabe** f -,-n cockroach. **K∼zettel** m menu

Kuckuck m -s,-e cuckoo

Kufe f -,-n [sledge] runner

Kugel f -,-n ball; (Geom) sphere; (Gewehr-) bullet; (Sport) shot. **k∼förmig** a spherical. **K∼-lager** nt ball-bearing. **k∼n** vt/i (haben) roll; **sich k∼n** roll/ (vor Lachen) fall about. **K∼-schreiber** m -s,- ballpoint [pen]. **K∼stoßen** nt -s shot-putting

kühl a cool; (kalt) chilly. **K∼e** f - coolness; chilliness. **k∼en** vt cool; refrigerate ⟨Lebensmittel⟩; chill ⟨Wein⟩. **K∼er** m -s,- (Auto) radiator. **K∼erhaube** f bonnet.

K∼fach nt frozen-food compartment. **K∼raum** m cold store. **K∼schrank** m refrigerator. **K∼truhe** f freezer. **K∼wasser** nt [radiator] water

kühn a bold, daring

Kuhstall m cowshed

Küken nt -s,- chick; (Enten-) duckling

Kulissen fpl (Theat) scenery sg; (seitlich) wings; **hinter den K∼** (fig) behind the scenes

Kult m -[e]s,-e cult

kultivier|en vt cultivate. **k∼t** a cultured

Kultur f -,-en culture. **K∼beutel** m toilet-bag. **k∼ell** a cultural. **K∼film** m documentary film

Kultusminister m Minister of Education and Arts

Kümmel m -s caraway

Kummer m -s sorrow, grief; (Sorge) worry; (Ärger) trouble

kümmer|lich a puny; (dürftig) meagre; (armselig) wretched. **k∼n** vt concern; **sich k∼n um** look after; (sich befassen) concern oneself with; (beachten) take notice of; **ich werde mich darum k∼n** I shall see to it

kummervoll a sorrowful

Kumpel m -s,- (fam) mate

Kunde m -n,-n customer. **K∼n-dienst** m [after-sales] service

Kundgebung f -,-en (Pol) rally

kündig|en vt cancel ⟨Vertrag⟩; give notice of withdrawal for ⟨Geld⟩; give notice to quit ⟨Wohnung⟩; **seine Stellung k∼en** give [in one's] notice □vi (haben) give [in one's] notice. **K∼ung** f -,-en cancellation; notice [of withdrawal/dismissal/to quit]; (Entlassung) dismissal. **K∼ungsfrist** f period of notice

Kund|in f -,-nen [woman] customer. **K∼schaft** f - clientele, customers pl

künftig a future □adv in future

Kunst f -,-e art; (*Können*) skill.
K ~ faser f synthetic fibre. K ~ galerie f art gallery. K ~ geschichte f history of art. K ~ gewerbe nt arts and crafts pl. K ~ griff m trick
Künstler m -s,- artist; (*Könner*) master. K ~ in f -,-nen [woman] artist. k ~ isch a artistic
künstlich a artificial
Kunst|stoff m plastic. K ~ stück nt trick; (*große Leistung*) feat. k ~ voll a artistic; (*geschickt*) skilful
kunterbunt a multicoloured; (*gemischt*) mixed
Kupfer nt -s copper
Kupon /ku'põ:/ m -s,-s voucher; (*Zins-*) coupon; (*Stoff*) length
Kuppe f -,-n [rounded] top
Kuppel f -,-n dome
kupp|eln vt couple (an + acc to) □ vi (haben) (*Auto*) operate the clutch. K ~ lung f -,-en coupling; (*Auto*) clutch
Kur f -,-en course of treatment
Kür f -,-en (*Sport*) free exercise; (*Eislauf*) free programme
Kurbel f -,-n crank. K ~ welle f crankshaft
Kürbis m -ses,-se pumpkin
Kurier m -s,-e courier
kurieren vt cure
kurios a curious, odd. K ~ ität f -,-en oddness; (*Objekt*) curiosity
Kurort m health resort; spa
Kurs m -es,-e course; (*Aktien-*) price. K ~ buch nt timetable
kursieren vi (haben) circulate
kursiv a italic □ adv in italics. K ~ schrift f italics pl
Kursus m -,Kurse course
Kurswagen m through carriage
Kurtaxe f visitors' tax
Kurve f -,-n curve; (*Straßen-*) bend
kurz a short; (*knapp*) brief; (*rasch*) quick; (*schroff*) curt; k ~ e Hosen shorts; vor k ~ em a short time ago; seit k ~ em lately; k ~ vor/ nach (*zeitlich*) shortly before/

after; sich k ~ fassen be brief; k ~ und gut in short; zu k ~ kommen get less than one's fair share. k ~ ärmelig a short-sleeved. k ~ atmig a k ~ atmig sein be short of breath
Kürze f -,- shortness; (*Knappheit*) brevity; in K ~ shortly. k ~ n vt shorten; (*verringern*) cut
kurzfristig a short-term □ adv at short notice
kürzlich adv recently
Kurz|meldung f newsflash. K ~ schluß m short circuit; (*fig*) brainstorm. K ~ schrift f shorthand. k ~ sichtig a shortsighted. K ~ sichtigkeit f -shortsightedness. K ~ streckenrakete f short-range missile
Kürzung f -,-en shortening; (*Verringerung*) cut (gen in)
Kurz|waren fpl haberdashery sg. K ~ welle f short wave
kuscheln (sich) vr snuggle (an + acc up to)
Kusine f -,-n [female] cousin
Kuß m -sses,-sse kiss
küssen vt/i (haben) kiss; sich k ~ kiss
Küste f -,-n coast
Küster m -s,- verger
Kutsch|e f -,-n [horse-drawn] carriage/(geschlossen) coach. K ~ er m -s,- coachman, driver
Kutte f -,-n (*Relig*) habit
Kutter m -s,- (*Naut*) cutter
Kuvert /ku've:ɐ̯/ nt -s,-s envelope

L

Labor nt -s,-s & -e laboratory
Labyrinth nt -[e]s,-e maze, labyrinth
Lache f -,-n puddle; (*Blut-*) pool
lächeln vi (haben) smile. L ~ nt -s smile. l ~ d a smiling
lachen vi (haben) laugh. L ~ nt -s laugh; (*Gelächter*) laughter

lächerlich a ridiculous; **sich l~ machen** make a fool of oneself. **L~keit** f -,-en ridiculousness; (*Kleinigkeit*) triviality

Lachs m -es,-e salmon

Lack m -[e]s,-e varnish; (*Japan-*) lacquer; (*Auto*) paint. **l~en** vt varnish. **l~ieren** vt varnish; (*spritzen*) spray. **L~schuhe** mpl patent-leather shoes

laden† vt load; (*Electr*) charge

Laden m -s,": shop; (*Fenster-*) shutter. **L~dieb** m shop-lifter. **L~schluß** m closing-time. **L~tisch** m counter

Laderaum m (*Naut*) hold

lädieren vt damage

Ladung f -,-en load; (*Naut, Aviat*) cargo; (*elektrische*) charge

Lage f -,-en position; situation; (*Schicht*) layer; **nicht in der L~ sein** not to be in a position (**zu** to)

Lager nt -s,- camp; (*L~haus*) warehouse; (*Vorrat*) stock; (*Techn*) bearing; (*Erz-, Ruhe-*) bed; (*eines Tieres*) lair; **[nicht] auf L~** [not] in stock. **L~haus** nt warehouse. **l~n** vt store; (*legen*) lay; **sich l~n** settle. **L~raum** m store-room. **L~ung** f - storage

Lagune f -,-n lagoon

lahm a lame

lähmen vt paralyse

Lähmung f -,-en paralysis

Laib m -[e]s,-e loaf

Laich m -[e]s (*Zool*) spawn. **l~en** vi (*haben*) spawn

Laie m -n,-n layman; (*Theat*) amateur. **l~nhaft** a amateurish

Laken nt -s,- sheet

Lakritze f - liquorice

lallen vt/i (*haben*) mumble; (*Baby:*) babble

Lametta f -s tinsel

Lamm nt -[e]s,"-er lamb

Lampe f -,-n lamp; (*Decken-, Wand-*) light; (*Glüh-*) bulb. **L~nfieber** nt stage fright

Lampion /lam'pjoŋ/ m -s,-s Chinese lantern

Land nt -[e]s,"-er country; (*Fest-*) land; (*Bundes-*) state, Land; (*Aust*) province; **auf dem L~e** in the country; **an L~ gehen** (*Naut*) go ashore. **L~arbeiter** m agricultural worker. **L~ebahn** f runway. **l~en** vt/i (*sein*) land; (*fam: gelangen*) end up

Länderei|en pl estates

Länderspiel nt international

Landesverrat m treason

Landkarte f map

ländlich a rural

Land|schaft f -,-en scenery; (*Geog, Kunst*) landscape; (*Gegend*) country[side]. **l~schaftlich** a scenic; (*regional*) regional. **L~straße** f country road; (*Admin:*) ≈ B road. **L~streicher** m -s,- tramp. **L~tag** m state/(*Aust*) provincial parliament

Landung f -,-en landing

Land|vermesser m -s,- surveyor. **L~wirt** m farmer. **L~wirtschaft** f agriculture; (*Hof*) farm. **l~wirtschaftlich** a agricultural

lang¹ adv & prep (+ preceding acc or preceding **an** + dat) along

lang² a long; (*groß*) tall; **seit l~em** for a long time □adv eine **Stunde l~** for an hour; **mein Leben l~** all my life. **l~ärmelig** a long-sleeved. **l~atmig** a long-winded. **l~e** adv a long time; (*schlafen*) late; **wie l~e** how long; **l~e nicht** not for a long time; (*bei weitem nicht*) nowhere near

Länge f -,-n length; (*Geog*) longitude; **der L~ nach** lengthways

Läng|engrad m degree of longitude. **l~er** a & adv longer; (*längere Zeit*) [for] some time

Langeweile f - boredom; **L~ haben** be bored

lang|fristig a long-term; ⟨*Vorhersage*⟩ long-range. **l~jährig** a long-standing; ⟨*Erfahrung*⟩ long.
länglich a oblong. **l~rund** a oval
längs adv & prep (+gen/dat) along; ⟨*der Länge nach*⟩ lengthways
lang|sam a slow. **L~samkeit** f slowness
längst adv [schon] **l~** for a long time; ⟨*zurückliegend*⟩ a long time ago; **l~ nicht** nowhere near
Lang|strecken- pref long-distance; ⟨*Mil*⟩ long-range. **l~weilen** vt bore; **sich l~weilen** be bored. **l~weilig** a boring
Lanze f -,-n lance
Lappalie /la'pa:liǝ/ f -,-n trifle
Lappen m -s,- cloth; ⟨*Anat*⟩ lobe
läppisch a silly
Lärche f -,-n larch
Lärm m -s noise
Larve /'larfǝ/ f -,-n larva
lasch a listless; ⟨*schlaff*⟩ limp
Lasche f -,-n tab
Laser /'le:-, 'la:zɐ/ m -s,- laser
lassen† vt leave; ⟨*zulassen*⟩ let; **jdm etw l~** let s.o. keep sth; **sein Leben l~** lose one's life; **etw [sein] l~** not do sth; ⟨*aufhören*⟩ stop [doing] sth; **laß das!** stop it! **jdn warten l~** keep s.o. waiting; **etw machen l~** have sth done; **sich [leicht] öffnen l~** open [easily]; **sich gut waschen l~** wash well
lässig a casual. **L~keit** f - casualness
Lasso nt -s,-s lasso
Last f -,-en load; ⟨*Gewicht*⟩ weight; ⟨*fig*⟩ burden; **L~en** charges; ⟨*Steuern*⟩ taxes. **L~auto** nt lorry. **l~en** vi ⟨*haben*⟩ weigh heavily⟨*liegen*⟩ rest (**auf** + dat on)
Laster[1] m -s,- ⟨*fam*⟩ lorry
Laster[2] nt -s,- vice
läster|n vi ⟨*haben*⟩ make disparaging remarks (**über** + acc about). **L~ung** f -,-en blasphemy

lästig a troublesome; **l~ sein/werden** be/become a nuisance
Last|kahn m barge. **L~[kraft]wagen** m lorry
Latein nt -[s] Latin. **L~amerika** nt Latin America. **l~isch** a Latin
Laterne f -,-n lantern; street lamp. **L~npfahl** m lamppost
Latte f -,-n slat; ⟨*Tor-*⟩ bar
Latz m -es,⸚e bib
Lätzchen f dungarees pl
Laub nt -[e]s leaves pl; ⟨*L~werk*⟩ foliage. **L~baum** m deciduous tree
Laube f -,-n summer-house
Laubsäge f fretsaw
Lauch m -[e]s leeks pl
Lauer f auf der **L~** liegen lie in wait. **l~n** vi ⟨*haben*⟩ lurk
Lauf m -[e]s, **Läufe** run; ⟨*Laufen*⟩ running; ⟨*Verlauf*⟩ course; ⟨*Wett-*⟩ race; ⟨*Sport: Durchgang*⟩ heat; ⟨*Gewehr-*⟩ barrel; **im L~[e]** (+gen) in the course of. **L~bahn** f career. **l~en†** vi ⟨*sein*⟩ run; ⟨*zu Fuß gehen*⟩ walk; ⟨*gelten*⟩ be valid; **Ski l~en** ski. **l~end** a running; ⟨*gegenwärtig*⟩ current; ⟨*regelmäßig*⟩ regular □ adv continually
Läufer m -s,- ⟨*Person, Teppich*⟩ runner; ⟨*Schach*⟩ bishop
Lauf|gitter nt play-pen. **L~masche** f ladder. **L~zettel** m circular
Lauge f -,-n soapy water
Laun|e f -,-n mood; ⟨*Einfall*⟩ whim; **guter L~e sein, gute L~e haben** be in a good mood. **l~isch** a moody
Laus f -,**Läuse** louse; ⟨*Blatt-*⟩ greenfly. **L~bub** m ⟨*fam*⟩ rascal
lauschen vi ⟨*haben*⟩ listen
laut a loud; ⟨*geräuschvoll*⟩ noisy; **l~ lesen** read aloud; **l~er stellen** turn up □ prep (+gen/dat) according to. **L~** m -es,-e sound
Laute f -,-n ⟨*Mus*⟩ lute
läuten vt/i ⟨*haben*⟩ ring

lauter a pure; (ehrlich) honest; ⟨Wahrheit⟩ plain □a inv sheer; (nichts als) nothing but

läutern vt purify

laut|hals adv at the top of one's voice; ⟨lachen⟩ out loud. **l~los** a silent; ⟨Stille⟩ hushed. **L~schrift** f phonetics pl. **L~sprecher** m loudspeaker. **L~stärke** f volume

lauwarm a lukewarm

Lavendel m -s lavender

lavieren vi (haben) manœuvre

Lawine f -,-n avalanche

Lazarett nt -[e]s,-e military hospital

leasen /ˈliːsən/ vt rent

Lebehoch nt cheer

leben vt/i (haben) live (von on); **leb wohl!** farewell! **L~** nt -s, life; (Treiben) bustle; **am L~** alive. **l~d** a living

lebendig a live; (lebhaft) lively; (anschaulich) vivid; **l~ sein** be alive. **L~keit** f liveliness; vividness

Lebens|abend m old age. **L~alter** nt age. **l~fähig** a viable. **L~gefahr** f mortal danger; **in L~gefahr** in mortal danger; ⟨Patient⟩ critically ill. **l~gefährlich** a extremely dangerous; ⟨Verletzung⟩ critical. **L~haltungskosten** pl cost of living sg. **l~länglich** a life ... adv for life. **L~lauf** m curriculum vitae. **L~mittel** ntpl food sg. **L~mittelgeschäft** nt food shop. **L~mittelhändler** m grocer. **L~retter** m rescuer; (beim Schwimmen) life-guard. **L~unterhalt** m livelihood; **seinen L~unterhalt verdienen** earn one's living. **L~versicherung** f life assurance. **L~wandel** m conduct. **l~wichtig** a vital. **L~zeit** f auf **L~zeit** for life

Leber f -,-n liver. **L~fleck** m mole. **L~wurst** f liver sausage

Lebe|wesen nt living being. **L~wohl** nt -s,-s & -e farewell

leb|haft a lively; ⟨Farbe⟩ vivid. **L~kuchen** m gingerbread. **l~los** a lifeless. **L~zeiten** fpl zu jds **L~zeiten** in s.o.'s lifetime

leck a leaking. **L~** nt -s,-s leak

lecken vt/i (haben) lick

lecker a tasty. **L~ei** f -,-en sweet

Leder nt -s,- leather

ledig a single. **l~lich** adv merely

leer a empty; (unbesetzt) vacant; **l~ laufen** (Auto) idle. **l~en** vt empty; **sich l~en** empty. **L~lauf** m (Auto) neutral. **L~ung** f -,-en (Post) collection

legal a legal. **l~isieren** vt legalize. **L~ität** f legality

Legasthenie f - dyslexia. **L~theniker** m -s,- dyslexic

legen vt put; (hin-, ver-) lay; ⟨Haare⟩ set; **sich l~** lie down; (nachlassen) subside

Legende f -,-n legend

leger /leˈʒeːɐ/ a casual

Legierung f -,-en alloy

Legion f -,-en legion

Legislative f - legislature

legitim a legitimate. **L~ität** f - legitimacy

Lehm m -s clay. **l~ig** a clayey

Lehne f -,-n ⟨Rücken-⟩ back; ⟨Arm-⟩ arm. **l~en** vt lean (an + acc against); **sich l~en** lean (an + acc against) □ vi (haben) be leaning (an + acc against)

Lehr|buch nt textbook. **L~e** f -,-n apprenticeship; (Anschauung) doctrine; (Theorie) theory; (Wissenschaft) science; (Erfahrung) lesson. **l~en** vt/i (haben) teach. **L~er** m -s,- teacher; (Fahr-) instructor. **L~erin** f -,-nen teacher. **L~erzimmer** nt staff-room. **L~gang** m course. **L~kraft** f teacher. **L~ling** m -s,-e apprentice; (Auszubildender) trainee. **L~plan** m syllabus. **l~reich** a instructive.

L~stelle f apprenticeship. **L~stuhl** m (Univ) chair. **L~zeit** f apprenticeship.

Leib m -es,-er body; (Bauch) belly. **L~eserziehung** f (Sch) physical education. **L~gericht** nt favourite dish. **L~lich** a physical; (blutsverwandt) real, natural. **L~wächter** m bodyguard

Leiche f -,-n [dead] body; corpse. **L~nbestatter** m -s,- undertaker. **L~nhalle** f mortuary. **L~nwagen** m hearse. **L~nzug** m funeral procession, cortège

Leichnam m -s,-e [dead] body

leicht a light; (Stoff) lightweight; (gering) slight; (mühelos) easy. **L~athletik** f [track and field] athletics sg. **l~fallen†** vi sep (sein) be easy (dat for). **L~gewicht** nt (Boxen) lightweight. **l~gläubig** a gullible. **L~hin** adv casually. **L~igkeit** f lightness; (Mühelosigkeit) ease; (L~sein) easiness; mit L~igkeit with ease. **l~machen** vt sep make easy (dat for); es sich (dat) l~machen take the easy way out. **l~nehmen†** vt sep (fig) take lightly. **L~sinn** m carelessness; recklessness. **l~sinnig** a careless; (unvorsichtig) reckless

Leid nt -[e]s sorrow, grief; (Böses) harm. l~ a jdn/etw l~ sein/ werden be/get tired of s.o./sth; es tut mir l~ I am sorry

Leide|form f passive. **l~n†** vt/i (haben) suffer (an + dat from); jdn [gut] l~n können like s.o. **L~n** nt -s,- suffering; (Med) complaint; (Krankheit) disease. **l~nd** a suffering. **L~nschaft** f -,-en passion. **l~nschaftlich** a passionate

leider adv unfortunately; l~ ja/ nicht I'm afraid so/not

Leier|kasten m barrel-organ. **l~n** vt/i (haben) wind; (herunter) drone out

Leih|e f -,-n loan. l~en† vt lend; sich (dat) etw l~en borrow sth. **L~gabe** f loan. **L~gebühr** f rental; (für Bücher) lending charge. **L~haus** nt pawnshop. **L~wagen** m hire-car. **L~weise** adv on loan

Leim m -s glue. l~en† vt glue

Leine f -,-n rope; (Wäsche-) line; (Hunde-) lead, leash

Lein|en nt -s linen. **L~wand** f linen; (Kunst) canvas; (Film-) screen

leise a quiet; (Stimme, Musik, Berührung) soft; (schwach) faint; l~r stellen turn down

Leiste f -,-n strip; (Holz-) batten; (Zier-) moulding; (Anat) groin

leist|en vt achieve, accomplish; sich (dat) etw l~en treat oneself to sth; ich kann es mir nicht l~en I can't afford it. **L~ung** f -,-en achievement; (Sport, Techn) performance; (Produktion) output; (Zahlung) payment. **l~ungsfähig** a efficient. **L~ungsfähigkeit** f efficiency

Leit|artikel m leader, editorial. **l~en** vt run, manage; (an-/hinführen) lead; (Mus, Techn) conduct; (lenken, schicken) direct

Leiter† f -,-n ladder

Leiter² m -s,- director; (Comm) manager; (Führer) leader. **L~erin** f -,-nen director; manageress; leader. **L~planke** f crash barrier. **L~spruch** m motto. **L~ung** f -,-en (Führung) direction; (Comm) management; (Aufsicht) control; (Electr: Schnur) lead, flex; (Kabel) cable; (Telefon-) line; (Rohr-) pipe; (Haupt-) main. **L~ungswasser** nt tap water

Lektion f -/tsjo:n/-,-en lesson

Lektor m -s,-en /-'to:ran/, **L~orin** f -,-nen (Univ) assistant lecturer; (Verlags-) editor. **L~üre** f -,-n reading matter

Lende f -,-n loin

lenk|bar a steerable; (*fügsam*) tractable. **l~en** vt guide; (*steuern*) steer; (*Aust*) drive; (*regeln*) control; **jds Aufmerksamkeit auf sich** (acc) **l~en** attract s.o.'s attention. **L~rad** nt steering-wheel. **L~stange** f handlebars pl. **L~ung** f -,-en steering

Leopard m -en,-en leopard

Lepra f - leprosy

Lerche f -,-n lark

lernen vt/i (*haben*) learn; (*für die Schule*) study

lesbar a readable

Lesb|ierin ['lɛsbjərɪn] f -,-nen lesbian. **l~isch** a lesbian

les|en vt/i (*haben*) read; (*Univ*) lecture. **L~en** nt -s reading. **L~er(in)** m -s,- (f -,-nen) reader. **l~erlich** a legible. **L~ezeichen** nt bookmark

lethargisch a lethargic

Lettland nt -s Latvia

letzt|e(r,s) a last; (*neueste*) latest; **in l~er Zeit** recently; **l~en Endes** in the end. **l~emal** adv **das l~emal** the last time. **l~ens** adv recently; (*zuletzt*) lastly. **l~ere(r,s)** a the latter

Leucht|e f -,-n light. **l~en** vi (*haben*) shine. **l~end** a shining. **L~er** m -s,- candlestick. **L~feuer** nt beacon. **L~rakete** f flare. **L~reklame** f neon sign. **L~röhre** f fluorescent tube. **L~turm** m lighthouse

leugnen vt deny

Leukämie f - leukaemia

Leumund m -s reputation

Leute pl people; (*Mil*) men; (*Arbeiter*) workers

Leutnant m -s,-s second lieutenant

Lexikon nt -s,-ka encyclopaedia; (*Wörterbuch*) dictionary

Libanon (der) -s Lebanon

Libelle f -,-n dragonfly

liberal a (*Pol*) Liberal

Libyen nt -s Libya

Licht nt -[e]s,-er light; (*Kerze*) candle; **l~ machen** turn on the light. **l~** a bright; (*Med*) lucid; (*spärlich*) sparse. **L~bild** nt [passport] photograph; (*Dia*) slide. **L~blick** m (fig) ray of hope. **l~en** vt thin out; **den Anker l~en** (*Naut*) weigh anchor; **sich l~en** become less dense. **L~hupe** f headlight flasher; **die L~hupe betätigen** flash one's headlights. **L~maschine** f dynamo. **L~ung** f -,-en clearing

Lid nt -[e]s,-er [eye]lid. **L~schatten** m eye-shadow

lieb a dear; (*nett*) nice; (*artig*) good; **es wäre mir l~** I should prefer it (*wenn* if)

Liebe f -,-n love. **l~n** vt love; (*mögen*) like; **sich l~n** love each other; (*körperlich*) make love. **l~nd** a loving. **l~nswert** a lovable. **l~nswürdig** a kind. **l~nswürdigerweise** adv very kindly

lieber adv rather; (*besser*) better; **l~ mögen** like better; **ich trinke l~ Tee** I prefer tea

Liebes|brief m love letter. **L~dienst** m favour. **L~kummer** m heartache. **L~paar** nt [pair of] lovers pl

lieb|evoll a loving; (*zärtlich*) affectionate. **l~haben†** vt sep be fond of; (*lieben*) love. **L~haber** m -s,- lover; (*Sammler*) collector. **L~haberei** f -,-en hobby. **L~kosung** f -,-en caress. **l~lich** a lovely; (*sanft*) gentle; (*süß*) sweet. **L~ling** m -s,-e darling; (*Bevorzugte*) favourite. **L~lings-** pref favourite. **l~los** a loveless; (*Eltern*) uncaring; (*unfreundlich*) unkind. **L~schaft** f -,-en [love] affair. **l~ste(r,s)** a dearest; (*bevorzugt*) favourite □adv **am l~sten** best [of all]; **jdn/etw am l~sten mögen** like s.o./sth best [of all]. **L~ste(r)** m|f beloved; (Schatz) sweetheart

Lied nt -[e]s,-er song

liederlich a slovenly; (unordentlich) untidy. **L~keit** f - slovenliness; untidiness

Lieferant m -en,-en supplier

liefer|bar a (Comm) available. **l~n** vt supply; deliver; (hervorbringen) yield. **L~ung** f -,-en delivery; (Sendung) consignment

Liege f -,-n couch. **l~n†** vi (haben) lie; (gelegen sein) be situated; **l~n an** (+dat) (fig) be due to; (abhängen) depend on; jdm [nicht] l~n [not] suit s.o.; mir liegt viel daran it is very important to me. **l~nbleiben†** vi (sein) remain lying [there]; (Ding:) be left; (Schnee:) remain; (Arbeit:) remain undone. **l~nlassen†** vt sep leave lying [there]; (nicht fortführen) leave undone. **L~stuhl** m deck-chair. **L~stütz** m -es,-e press-up. **L~wagen** m couchette car

Lift m -[e]s,-e & -s lift

Liga f -,-gen league

Likör m -s,-e liqueur

lila inv a mauve; (dunkel) purple

Lilie /'li:liə/ f -,-n lily

Liliputaner(in) m -s,- (f -,-nen) dwarf

Limo f -,-[s] (fam), **L~nade** f -,-n fizzy drink; lemonade

Limousine /limu'zi:nə/ f -,-n saloon; limousine

lind a mild; (sanft) gentle

Linde f -,-n lime tree

linder|n vt relieve, ease. **L~ung** f - relief

Line|al nt -s,-e ruler

Linie /-jə/ f -,-n line; (Zweig) branch; (Bus-) route; **L~ 4** number 4 [bus/tram]. **L~nflug** m scheduled flight

Link|e f -n,-n left side; (Hand) left hand; (Boxen) left; **die L~e** (Pol) the left. **l~e(r,s)** a left; (Pol) leftwing; **l~e Masche** purl

links adv on the left; (bei Stoff) on the wrong side; (verkehrt) inside out; **l~ stricken** purl. **L~händer(in)** m -s,- (f -,-nen) lefthander

Linoleum /-leum/ nt -s lino[leum]

Linse f -,-n lens; (Bot) lentil

Lippe f -,-n lip. **L~nstift** m lipstick

Liquid|ation /-'tsjo:n/ f -,-en liquidation. **l~ieren** vt liquidate

lispeln vi/t (haben) lisp

List f -,-en trick, ruse

Liste f -,-n list

listig a cunning, crafty

Litanei f -,-en litany

Litauen nt -s Lithuania

Liter m & nt -s,- litre

Literatur f - literature

Litfaßsäule f advertising pillar

Liturgie f -,-n liturgy

Lizenz f -,-en licence

Lob nt -[es] praise

Lobby /'lɔbi/ f - (Pol) lobby

loben vt praise

löblich a praiseworthy

Lobrede f eulogy

Loch nt -[e]s,-er hole. **l~en** vt punch a hole/holes in; punch (Fahrkarte). **L~er** m -s,- punch

löcherig a full of holes

Locke f -,-n curl. **l~n†** vt curl

locken² vt lure, entice; (reizen) tempt. **l~d** a tempting

Lockenwickler m -s,- curler

locker a loose; (Seil:) slack; (Erde) light; (zu frei) lax. **l~n** vt loosen; slacken (Seil); break up (Boden); relax (Griff); **sich l~n** become loose; (Seil:) slacken; (sich entspannen) relax

lockig a curly

Lock|mittel nt bait. **L~vogel** m decoy

Loden m -s (Tex) loden

Löffel m -s,- spoon; (L~voll) spoonful. **l~n** vt spoon up

Logarithmus *m* -,-men logarithm

Logbuch *nt* (*Naut*) log-book

Loge /'lo:ʒǝ/ *f* -,-n lodge; (*Theat*) box

Log∣ik *f* - logic. **l∼isch** *a* logical

Logo *nt* -s,-s logo

Lohn *m* -[e]s,˛e wages *pl*, pay; (*fig*) reward. **L∼empfänger** *m* wage-earner. **l∼en** *vi/r* (*haben*) [sich] l∼en be worth it *or* worth while □*vt* be worth. **L∼end** *a* worthwhile; (*befriedigend*) rewarding. **L∼erhöhung** *f* [pay] rise. **L∼steuer** *f* income tax

Lokal *nt* -s,-e restaurant; (*Trink-*) bar. **l∼** *a* local

Lokomotiv∣e *f* -,-n engine, locomotive. **L∼führer** *m* engine driver

London *nt* -s London. **L∼er** *a* London . . . □*m* -s,- Londoner

Lorbeer *m* -s,-en laurel. **L∼blatt** *nt* (*Culin*) bay-leaf

Lore *f* -,-n (*Rail*) truck

Los *nt* -es,-e lot; (*Lotterie-*) ticket; (*Schicksal*) fate

los *pred a* **los sein** be loose; **jdn/etw los sein** be rid of s.o./sth; **was ist [mit ihm] los?** what's the matter [with him]? □*adv* los! go on! **Achtung, fertig, los!** ready, steady, go!

lösbar *a* soluble

losbinden† *vt sep* untie

Lösch∣blatt *nt* sheet of blotting-paper. **l∼en†** *vt* put out, extinguish; quench (*Durst*); blot (*Tinte*); (*tilgen*) cancel

löschen² *vt* (*Naut*) unload

Löschfahrzeug *nt* fire-engine

lose *a* loose

Lösegeld *nt* ransom

losen *vi* (*haben*) draw lots (**um** for)

lösen *vt* undo; (*lockern*) loosen; (*entfernen*) detach; (*klären*) solve; (*auflösen*) dissolve; cancel (*Vertrag*); break off (*Beziehung*);

sich l∼ come off; (*sich trennen*) detach oneself/itself; (*lose werden*) come undone; (*sich klären*) resolve itself; (*sich auflösen*) dissolve

los∣fahren† *vi sep* (*sein*) start; (*Auto:*) drive off; **l∼fahren auf** (+ *acc*) head for. **l∼gehen†** *vi sep* (*sein*) set off; (*fam: anfangen*) start; (*Bombe:*) go off. **l∼kommen†** *vi sep* (*sein*) get away (**von** from). **l∼lassen†** *vt sep* let go of; (*freilassen*) release

löslich *a* soluble

los∣lösen *vt sep* detach; **sich l∼lösen** become detached; (*fig*) break away (**von** from). **l∼reißen†** *vt sep* tear off; **sich l∼reißen** break free; (*fig*) tear oneself away. **l∼schicken** *vt sep* send off. **l∼sprechen†** *vt sep* absolve (**von** from)

Losung *f* -,-en (*Pol*) slogan; (*Mil*) password

Lösung *f* -,-en solution. **L∼smittel** *nt* solvent

loswerden† *vt sep* get rid of

Lot *nt* -[e]s,-e perpendicular; (*Blei-*) plumb[-bob]. **l∼en** *vt* plumb

löt∣en *vt* solder. **L∼lampe** *f* blow-lamp. **L∼metall** *nt* solder

lotrecht *a* perpendicular

Lotse *m* -n,-n (*Naut*) pilot. **l∼n** *vt* (*Naut*) pilot; (*fig*) guide

Lotterie *f* -,-n lottery

Lotto *nt* -s,-s lotto; (*Lotterie*) lottery

Löw∣e *m* -n,-n lion; (*Astr*) Leo. **L∼enzahn** *m* (*Bot*) dandelion

loyal /loa'jaːl/ *a* loyal. **L∼ität** *f* - loyalty

Luchs *m* -es,-e lynx

Lücke *f* -,-n gap. **l∼nhaft** *a* incomplete; (*Wissen*) patchy. **l∼nlos** *a* complete; (*Folge*) unbroken

Luder *nt* -s,- (*sl*) (*Frau*) bitch

Luft f -,÷e air; **in die L~ gehen** explode. **L~angriff** m air raid. **L~aufnahme** f aerial photograph. **L~ballon** m balloon. **L~blase** f air bubble. **l~dicht** a airtight. **L~druck** m atmospheric pressure

lüften vt air; raise ⟨Hut⟩; reveal ⟨Geheimnis⟩

Luft|fahrt f aviation. **L~fahrtgesellschaft** f airline. **L~gewehr** nt airgun. **l~ig** a airy; ⟨Kleid⟩ light. **L~kissenfahrzeug** nt hovercraft. **L~krieg** m aerial warfare. **l~leer** a **l~leerer Raum** vacuum. **L~linie** f 100 km **L~linie** 100 km as the crow flies. **L~matratze** f air-bed, inflatable mattress. **L~pirat** m hijacker. **L~post** f airmail. **L~röhre** f windpipe. **L~schiff** nt airship. **L~schlange** f streamer. **L~schutzbunker** m air-raid shelter

Lüftung f - ventilation

Luft|veränderung f change of air. **L~waffe** f air force. **L~zug** m draught

Lüge f -,-n lie. **l~en†** vt/i (haben) lie. **L~ner(in)** m -s,- (f -,-nen) liar. **l~nerisch** a untrue; ⟨Person⟩ untruthful

Luke f -,-n hatch; ⟨Dach-⟩ skylight

Lümmel m -s,- lout

Lump m -en,-en scoundrel. **L~en** m -s,- rag; **in L~en** in rags. **L~enpack** nt riff-raff. **L~ensammler** m rag-and-bone man. **l~ig** a mean, shabby; ⟨ge-ring⟩ measly

Lunge f -,-n lungs pl; ⟨L~nflügel⟩ lung. **L~nentzündung** f pneumonia

Lupe f -,-n magnifying glass

Lurch m -[e]s,-e amphibian

Lust f -,÷e pleasure; ⟨Verlangen⟩ desire; ⟨sinnliche Begierde⟩ lust; **L~ haben** feel like (**auf etw** acc sth); **ich habe keine L~** I don't feel like it; (will nicht) I don't want to

lustig a jolly; (komisch) funny; **sich ~ machen über** (+ acc) make fun of

Lüstling m -s,-e lecher

lust|los a listless. **L~mörder** m sex killer. **L~spiel** nt comedy

lutsch|en vt/i (haben) suck. **L~er** m -s,- lollipop

Lüttich nt -s Liège

Luv f & nt - **nach Luv** (Naut) to windward

luxuriös a luxurious

Luxus m - luxury

Lymph|drüse f 'lʏmf-/ f, **L~knoten** m lymph gland

lynchen /'lʏnçən/ vt lynch

Lyr|ik f - lyric poetry. **L~iker** m -s,- lyric poet. **l~isch** a lyrical

M

Mach|art f style. **m~en** vt make; get ⟨Mahlzeit⟩; take ⟨Foto⟩; (ausführen, tun, in Ordnung bringen) do; (Math: ergeben) be; (kosten) come to; **sich** (dat) **etw m~en** lassen have sth made; **was m~st du da?** what are you doing? **was m~t die Arbeit?** how is work? **das m~t nichts** it doesn't matter; **sich** (dat) **wenig/nichts m~en aus** care little/nothing for □ vr **sich m~en** do well; **sich an die Arbeit m~en** get down to work □ vi (haben) **ins Bett m~en** (fam) wet the bed; **schnell m~en** hurry

Macht f -,÷e power. **M~haber** m -s,- ruler

mächtig a powerful

machtlos a powerless

Mädchen nt -s,- girl; ⟨Dienst-⟩ maid. **m~haft** a girlish. **M~name** m girl's name; (vor der Ehe) maiden name

Made f -,-n maggot

madig a maggoty

Madonna f -,-nen madonna

Magazin nt -s,-e magazine; (*Lager*) warehouse; store-room

Magd f -,-e maid

Magen m -s,- stomach

mager a thin; ⟨*Fleisch*⟩ lean; ⟨*Boden*⟩ poor; ⟨*dürftig*⟩ meagre. **M~keit** f - thinness; leanness. **M~sucht** f anorexia

Magie f - magic

Magier /'maːgiɐ/ m -s,- magician

Magistrat m -s,-e city council

Magnet m -en & -[e]s, -e magnet. **m~isch** a magnetic

Mahagoni nt -s mahogany

Mäh|drescher m -s,- combine harvester. **m~en** vt/i (haben) mow

Mahl nt -[e]s,-¨er meal

mahlen† vt grind

Mahlzeit f meal; **M~!** enjoy your meal!

Mähne f -,-n mane

mahn|en vt/i (haben) remind (**wegen** about); (*ermahnen*) admonish; (*auffordern*) urge (**zu** to). **M~ung** f -,-en reminder; admonition

Mai m -[e]s,-e May. **M~glöckchen** nt -s,- lily of the valley

Mailand nt -s Milan

Mais m -es maize; (*Culin*) sweet corn

Majestät f -,-en majesty. **m~isch** a majestic

Major m -s,-e major

Majoran m -s marjoram

makaber a macabre

Makkaroni pl macaroni sg

Makler m -s,- (*Comm*) broker

Makrele f -,-n mackerel

Makrone f -,-n macaroon

mal adv (*Math*) times; (*bei Maßen*) by; (*fam: einmal*) once; (*eines Tages*) one day; **nicht mal** not even

Mal¹ nt -[e]s,-e time; **ein für alle Mal** once and for all

Mal|buch nt colouring book. **m~en** vt/i (haben) paint. **M~er** m -s,- painter. **M~erei** f -,-en painting. **M~erin** f -,-nen painter. **m~erisch** a picturesque

Mallorca /maˈlɔrka, -ˈjɔrka/ nt -s Majorca

malnehmen† vt sep multiply (**mit** by)

Malz nt -es malt

Mama /'mama, ma'maː/ f -s,-s mummy

Mammut nt -s,-e & -s mammoth

man pron one, you; (*die Leute*) people, they; **man sagt** they say, it is said

manch|e(r,s) pron many a; [so] **m~es** Mal many a time; **m~e Leute** some people □ (*substantivisch*) **m~er/m~e** many a man/woman; **m~e** pl some; (*Leute*) some people; (*viele*) many some things; (*vieles*) many things. **m~erlei** inv a various □ pron various things

manchmal adv sometimes

Mandant(in) m -en,-en (f -,-nen) (*Jur*) client

Mandarine f -,-n mandarin

Mandat nt -[e]s,-e mandate; (*Jur*) brief; (*Pol*) seat

Mandel f -,-n almond; (*Anat*) tonsil. **M~entzündung** f tonsillitis

Manege /ma'neːʒə/ f -,-n ring; (*Reit-*) arena

Mangel¹ m -s,-¨ lack; (*Knappheit*) shortage; (*Med*) deficiency; (*Fehler*) defect

Mangel² f -,-n mangle

mangel|haft a faulty, defective; (*Sch*) unsatisfactory. **m~n** vi (haben) **es m~t an** (+ dat) there is a lack/(*Knappheit*) shortage of

Mango f -,-s mango

Manie f -,-n mania

Manier f -,-en manner; M~en manners. **m~lich** a well-mannered □ adv properly

Manifest nt -[e]s,-e manifesto

Maniküre f -,-n manicure; (Person) manicurist. **m~n** vt manicure

Manko nt -s disadvantage; (Fehlbetrag) deficit

Mann m -[e]s,ˉer man; (Ehe-) husband

Männchen nt -s,- little man; (Zool) male

Mannequin /ˈmanəkē/ nt -s,-s model

männlich a male; (Gram & fig) masculine; (mannhaft) manly; ⟨Frau⟩ mannish. **M~keit** f masculinity; (fig) manhood

Mannschaft f -,-en team; (Naut) crew. **M~sgeist** m team spirit

Manöver nt -s,- manœuvre; (Winkelzug) trick. **m~rieren** vt/i (haben) manœuvre

Mansarde f -,-n attic room; (Wohnung) attic flat

Manschette f -,-n cuff. **M~nknopf** m cuff-link

Mantel m -s,ˉ coat; (dick) overcoat; (Reifen-) outer tyre

Manuskript nt -[e]s,-e manuscript

Mappe f -,-n folder; (Akten-) briefcase; (Schul-) bag

Märchen nt -s,- fairy-tale

Margarine f - margarine

Marienkäfer /maˈriːən-/ m ladybird

Marinade f -,-n marinade

Marine f marine; (Kriegs-) navy. **m~blau** a navy [blue]. **M~infanterist** m marine

marinieren vt marinade

Marionette f -,-n puppet

Mark[1] f -,- mark

Mark[2] nt -[e]s (Knochen-) marrow; (Bot) pith; (Frucht-) pulp

markant a striking

Marke f -,-n token; (rund) disc; (Erkennungs-) tag; (Brief-) stamp; (Lebensmittel-) coupon; (Spiel-) counter; (Markierung) mark; (Fabrikat) make; (Tabak-) brand. **M~nartikel** m branded article

markieren vt mark; (fam: vortäuschen) fake

Markise f -,-n awning

Markstück nt one-mark piece

Markt m -[e]s, ˉe market; (M~-platz) market-place

Marmelade f -,-n jam; (Orangen-) marmalade

Marmor m -s marble

Marokko nt -s Morocco

Marsch[1] f -,-en marsh

Marsch[2] m -[e]s,ˉe march. **m~int** (Mil) march!

Marschall m -s,ˉe marshal

marschieren vi (sein) march

Marter f -,-n torture

Märtyrer(in) m -s,- (f -,-nen) martyr

Marxismus m - Marxism

März m -,-e March

Marzipan nt -s marzipan

Masche f -,-n stitch; (im Netz) mesh; (fam: Trick) dodge. **M~ndraht** m wire netting

Maschine f -,-n machine; (Flugzeug) plane; (Schreib-) typewriter. **m~egeschrieben** a typed. **m~ell** a machine . . . □ adv by machine. **M~enbau** m mechanical engineering. **M~engewehr** nt machine-gun. **M~ist** m -en,-en machinist; (Naut) engineer

Masern pl measles sg

Maserung f -,-en [wood] grain

Maske f -,-n mask; (Theat) make-up

maskieren vt mask; **sich m~** dress up (als as)

maskulin a masculine

Masochist m -en,-en masochist

Maß[1] nt -es,-e measure; (Abmessung) measurement; (Grad) degree; (Mäßigung) moderation; **in hohem Maße** to a high degree

Maß[2] f -,- (SGer) litre [of beer]

Massage /maˈsaːʒə/ f -,-n massage

Massaker nt -s,- massacre

Maßband nt (pl -bänder) tapemeasure

Masse f -,-n mass; (Menschen-) crowd; **eine M~ Arbeit** (fam) masses of work. **m~nhaft** adv in huge quantities. **M~nproduktion** f mass production. **m~nweise** adv in huge numbers

Masseu|r /maˈsøːr/ m -s,-e masseur. **M~se** /-ˈsøːzə/ f -,-n masseuse

maß|gebend a authoritative; (einflußreich) influential. **m~geblich** a decisive. **m~geschneidert** a made-to-measure

massieren vt massage

massig a massive

mäßig a moderate; (mittelmäßig) indifferent. **m~en** vt moderate; **sich m~en** moderate; (sich beherrschen) restrain oneself. **M~ung** f moderation

massiv a solid; (stark) heavy

Maß|krug m beer mug. **m~los** a excessive; (grenzenlos) boundless; (äußerst) extreme. **M~nahme** f -,-n measure

Maßstab m scale; (Norm & fig) standard. **m~sgetreu** a scale . . . □adv to scale

Mast[1] m -[e]s,-en pole; (Überland-) pylon; (Naut) mast

Mast[2] f - fattening

mästen vt fatten

Material nt -s,-ien /-jən/ material; (coll) materials pl. **M~ismus** m - materialism. **m~istisch** a materialistic

Mathe f - (fam) maths sg.

Mathe|matik f - mathematics sg. **M~matiker** m -s,- mathematician. **m~matisch** a mathematical

Matinee f -,-n (Theat) morning performance

Matratze f -,-n mattress

Matrose m -n,-n sailor

Matsch m -[e]s mud; (Schnee-) slush

matt a weak; (gedämpft) dim; (glanzlos) dull; (Politur, Farbe) matt; **M~** nt -s (Schach) mate

Matte f -,-n mat

Mattglas nt frosted glass

Matura f - (Aust) ≈ A levels pl

Mauer f -,-n wall. **M~werk** nt masonry

Maul nt -[e]s,Mäuler (Zool) mouth; **halt's M~!** (fam) shut up! **M~korb** m muzzle. **M~tier** nt mule. **M~wurf** m mole

Maurer m -s,- bricklayer

Maus f -,Mäuse mouse

Maut f -,-en (Aust) toll. **M~straße** f toll road

maximal a maximum

Maximum nt -s,-ma maximum

Mayonnaise /majɔˈnɛːzə/ f -,-n mayonnaise

Mechan|ik /meˈçaːnɪk/ f - mechanics sg; (Mechanismus) mechanism. **M~iker** m -s,- mechanic. **m~isch** a mechanical. **m~isieren** vt mechanize. **M~ismus** m -,-men mechanism

meckern vi (haben) bleat; (fam: nörgeln) grumble

Medaille /meˈdaljə/ f -,-n medal. **M~on** /-ˈjõː/ nt -s,-s medallion; (Schmuck) locket

Medikament nt -[e]s,-e medicine

Medit|ation /-ˈtsjoːn/ f -,-en meditation. **m~ieren** vi (haben) meditate

Medizin f -,-en medicine. **M~er** m -s,- doctor; (Student) medical student. **m~isch** a medical; (heilkräftig) medicinal

Meer nt -[e]s,-e sea. **M~busen** m gulf. **M~enge** f strait. **M~esspiegel** m sea-level. **M~jungfrau** f mermaid. **M~rettich** m horseradish. **M~schweinchen** nt -s,- guinea-pig

Mehl nt -[e]s flour. **M~schwitze** f (Culin) roux. **M~speise** f (Aust) dessert

mehr pron & adv more; **nichts m~** no more; (nichts weiter) nothing else; **nie m~** never again. **m~ere** pron several. **m~eres** pron several things pl. **m~fach** a multiple; (mehrmalig) repeated □adv several times. **M~fahrtenkarte** f book of tickets. **M~heit** f -,-en majority. **m~malig** a repeated. **m~mals** adv several times. **m~sprachig** a multilingual. **M~wertsteuer** f value-added tax, VAT. **M~zahl** f majority; (Gram) plural. **M~zweck-** pref multi-purpose

meiden† vt avoid, shun

Meile f -,-n mile. **m~nweit** adv [for] miles

mein poss pron my. **m~e(r,s)** poss pron mine; **die M~en** pl my family sg

Meineid m perjury; **einen M~ leisten** perjure oneself

meinen vt mean; (glauben) think; (sagen) say

mein|**erseits** adv for my part. **m~etwegen** adv for my sake; (wegen mir) because of me; (fam: von mir aus) as far as I'm concerned. **m~s** poss pron mine

Meinung f -,-en opinion; **jdm die M~ sagen** give s.o. a piece of one's mind. **M~sumfrage** f opinion poll

Meise f -,-n (Zool) tit

Meißel m -s,- chisel. **m~n** vt/i (haben) chisel

meist adv mostly; (gewöhnlich) usually. **m~e** a der/die/das **m~e** most; **die m~en Leute**

most people; **am m~en** [the] most □ pron **das m~e** most [of it]; **die m~en** most. **m~ens** adv mostly; (gewöhnlich) usually

Meister m -s,- master craftsman; (Könner) master; (Sport) champion. **m~n** vt master. **M~schaft** f -,-en mastery; (Sport) championship

meld|**en** vt report; (anmelden) register; (ankündigen) announce; **sich m~en** report (bei to); (zum Militär) enlist; (Teleph) answer; (Sch) put up one's hand. **M~ung** f -,-en report; (Anmeldung) registration

melken† vt milk

Melodie f -,-n tune, melody

melodisch a melodic; tuneful

Melone f -,-n melon

Membran f -,-en membrane

Memoiren |me'mǫa:rən| pl memoirs

Menge f -,-n amount, quantity; (Menschen-) crowd; (Math) set; **eine M~ Geld** a lot of money. **m~n** vt mix

Mensa f -,-sen (Univ) refectory

Mensch m -en,-en human being; **der M~** man; **die M~en** people; **jeder/kein M~** everybody/nobody. **M~enaffe** m ape. **M~enfresser** m -s,- cannibal. **M~enleben** nt human life; (Lebenszeit) lifetime. **m~enleer** a deserted. **M~enmenge** f crowd. **M~enraub** m kidnapping. **M~enrechte** ntpl human rights. **m~enscheu** a unsociable. **m~enwürdig** a humane. **M~heit** f - die **M~heit** mankind, humanity. **m~lich** a human; (human) humane. **M~lichkeit** f - humanity

Menstru|**ation** |-'tsjo:n| f - menstruation. **m~ieren** vi (haben) menstruate

Mentalität f -,-en mentality

Menü nt -s,-s menu; (festes M~) set meal

Meridian m -s,-e meridian

merk|bar a noticeable. **M~blatt** nt [explanatory] leaflet. **m~en** vt notice; **sich** (dat) **etw m~en** remember sth. **M~mal** nt feature

merkwürdig a odd, strange

Messe[1] f-,-n (Relig) mass; (Comm) [trade] fair

Messe[2] f-,-n (Mil) mess

messen† vt/i (haben) measure; (ansehen) look at; **[bei jdm] Fieber m~** take s.o.'s temperature; **sich m~** compete (mit with)

Messer nt -s,- knife

Messias m - Messiah

Messing nt -s brass

Messung f-,-en measurement

Metabolismus m - metabolism

Metall nt -s,-e metal. **m~isch** a metallic

Metamorphose f-,-n metamorphosis

metaphorisch a metaphorical

Meteor m -s,-e meteor. **M~ologie** f- meteorology

Meter m & nt -s,- metre

Methode f-,-n method. **m~isch** a methodical

Metropole f-,-n metropolis

Metzger m -s,- butcher. **M~ei** f -,-en butcher's shop

Meuterei f-,-en mutiny

meutern vi (haben) mutiny; (fam: schimpfen) grumble

Mexikan|er(in) m -s,- (f -,-nen) Mexican. **m~isch** a Mexican

Mexiko nt -s Mexico

miauen vi (haben) mew, miaow

mich pron (acc of **ich**) me; (refl) myself

Miene f-,-n expression

mies a (fam) lousy

Miet|e f-,-n rent; (Mietgebühr) hire charge; **zur M~e wohnen** live in rented accommodation; **m~en** vt rent ⟨Haus, Zimmer⟩; hire ⟨Auto, Boot⟩. **M~er(in)** m

-s,- (f -,-nen) tenant. **m~frei** a & adv rent-free. **M~vertrag** m lease. **M~wagen** m hire-car. **M~wohnung** f rented flat; (zu vermieten) flat to let

Migräne f-,-n migraine

Mikro|chip m microchip. **M~computer** m microcomputer. **M~film** m microfilm

Mikro|fon, M~phon nt -s,-e microphone. **M~skop** nt -s,-e microscope. **m~skopisch** a microscopic

Mikrowelle f microwave. **M~nherd** m microwave oven

Milbe f-,-n mite

Milch f - milk. **m~ig** a milky. **M~mann** m (pl -männer) milkman. **M~straße** f Milky Way

mild a mild; (nachsichtig) lenient. **M~e** f - mildness; leniency. **m~ern** vt make milder; (mäßigen) moderate; (lindern) ease; **sich m~ern** become milder; (sich mäßigen) moderate; ⟨Schmerz:⟩ ease; **m~ernde Umstände** mitigating circumstances. **m~tätig** a charitable

Milieu /mi'ljø:/ nt -s,-s [social] environment

Militär nt -s army; (Soldaten) troops pl; **beim M~** in the army. **m~isch** a military

Miliz f-,-en militia

Milliarde f -/mr'ljardə/ f-,-n thousand million, billion

Milli|gramm nt milligram. **M~meter** m & nt millimetre. **M~meterpapier** nt graph paper

Million /mr'ljo:n/ f-,-en million. **M~är** m -s,-e millionaire

Milz f- (Anat) spleen

mimen vt (fam: vortäuschen) act

Minderheit f-,-en minority

minderjährig a (Jur) under-age. **M~e(r)** m/f (Jur) minor

minderwertig a inferior. **M~-keit** f · inferiority. **M~keits-komplex** m inferiority complex
Mindest- pref minimum. **m~e** a & pron der/die/das m~e the least. **m~ens** adv at least. **M~maß** nt minimum
Mine f·,-n mine; (Bleistift·) lead; (Kugelschreiber·) refill
Mineral nt ·s,-e & -ien /-jən/ mineral. **m~isch** a mineral. **M~wasser** nt mineral water
Miniatur f·,-en miniature
minimal a minimal
Minimum nt ·s,-ma minimum
Minister m ·s,- minister. **m~steriell** a ministerial. **M~sterium** nt ·s,-ien ministry
minus conj, adv & prep (+gen) minus. **M~** nt· deficit; (Nachteil) disadvantage. **M~zeichen** nt minus [sign]
Minute f·,-n minute
mir pron (dat of ich) [to] me; (refl) myself
Mischehe f mixed marriage. **m~en** vt mix; blend (Tee, Kaffee); toss (Salat); shuffle (Karten); sich m~en mix; (Person:) mingle (unter+acc with); sich m~en in (+acc) join in (Gespräch:) meddle in (Angelegenheit). **M~ling** m ·s,-e half-caste. **M~ung** f·,-en mixture; blend
miserabel a abominable
mißachten vt disregard
Mißachtung f disregard. **M~bildung** f deformity
mißbilligen vt disapprove of
Mißbilligung f disapproval. **M~brauch** m abuse
mißbrauchen vt abuse; (vergewaltigen) rape
Mißerfolg m failure
Missetat f misdeed. **M~täter** m (fam) culprit
mißfallen† vi (haben) displease (jdm s.o.)

Mißfallen nt ·s displeasure; (Mißbilligung) disapproval. **M~geburt** f freak; (fig) monstrosity. **M~geschick** nt mishap; (Unglück) misfortune
mißglücken vi (sein) fail. **m~gönnen** vt begrudge
mißhandeln vt ill-treat
Mißhandlung f ill-treatment
Mission f·,-en mission
Missionar(in) m ·s,-e (f·,-nen) missionary
Mißklang m discord
mißlingen† vi (sein) fail; es mißlang ihr she failed. **M~** nt ·s failure
Mißmut m ill humour. **m~ig** a morose
mißraten† vi (sein) turn out badly
Mißstand m abuse; (Zustand) undesirable state of affairs. **M~stimmung** f discord; (Laune) bad mood
mißtrauen vi (haben) jdm/etw m~ · mistrust s.o./sth; (Argwohn hegen) distrust s.o./sth
Mißtrauen nt ·s mistrust; (Argwohn) distrust. **M~ensvotum** nt vote of no confidence. **m~isch** a distrustful; (argwöhnisch) suspicious
Mißverständnis nt misunderstanding. **m~verstehen†** vt misunderstand. **M~wirtschaft** f mismanagement
Mist m ·[e]s manure; (fam) rubbish
Mistel f·,-n mistletoe
Misthaufen m dungheap
mit prep (+dat) with; (sprechen·) to; (mittels) by; (inklusive) including; (bei) at; **mit Bleistift** in pencil; **mit lauter Stimme** in a loud voice; **mit drei Jahren** at the age of three □adv (auch) as well; **mit anfassen** (fig) lend a hand
Mitarbeit f collaboration. **m~en** vi sep collaborate (an+dat on).

M~er(in) *m(f)* collaborator; (*Kollege*) colleague; (*Betriebsangehörige*) employee

Mitbestimmung *f* co-determination

mitbringen† *vt sep* bring [along]

miteinander *adv* with each other

Mitesser *m* (*Med*) blackhead

mitfahren† *vi sep* (*sein*) go/come along; **mit jdm m~** go with s.o.; (*mitgenommen werden*) be given a lift by s.o.

mitfühlen *vi sep* (*haben*) sympathize

mitgeben† *vt sep* jdm etw m~ give s.o. sth to take with him

Mitgefühl *nt* sympathy

mitgehen† *vi sep* (*sein*) **mit jdm m~** go with s.o.

Mitgift *f* -,-en dowry

Mitglied *nt* member. **M~schaft** *f* - membership

Mithilfe *f* assistance

mitkommen† *vi sep* (*sein*) come [along] too; (*fig: folgen können*) keep up; (*verstehen*) follow

Mitlaut *m* consonant

Mitleid *nt* pity, compassion. **m~erregend** a pitiful. **m~ig** a pitying; (*mitfühlend*) compassionate. **m~slos** a pitiless

mitmachen *v sep* □*vt* take part in; (*erleben*) go through □*vi* (*haben*) join in

Mitmensch *m* fellow man

mitnehmen† *vt sep* take along; (*mitfahren lassen*) give a lift to; (*erschöpfen*) exhaust; '**zum M~**' 'to take away'

mitreden *vi sep* (*haben*) join in [the conversation]; (*mit entscheiden*) have a say (**bei** in)

mitreißen† *vt sep* sweep along; (*fig: begeistern*) carry away; **m~d** rousing

mitsamt *prep* (+*dat*) together with

mitschreiben† *vt sep* (*haben*) take down

Mitschuld *f* partial blame. **m~ig** a m~ ig sein be partly to blame

Mitschüler(in) *m(f)* fellow pupil

mitspielen *vi sep* (*haben*) join in; (*Theat*) be in the cast; (*beitragen*) play a part

Mittag *m* midday, noon; (*Mahlzeit*) lunch; (*Pause*) lunch-break; [**zu**] **M~ essen** have lunch. **m~** *adv* **heute m~** at lunch-time today. **M~essen** *nt* lunch. **m~s** *adv* at noon; (*als Mahlzeit*) for lunch; **um 12 Uhr m~s** at noon. **M~spause** *f* lunch-hour; (*Pause*) lunch-break. **M~schlaf** *m* after-lunch nap

Mittäter(in) *m(f)* accomplice. **M~schaft** *f* - complicity

Mitte *f* -,-n middle; (*Zentrum*) centre; **die goldene M~** the golden mean; **M~ Mai** in mid-May; **in unserer M~** in our midst

mitteilen *vt sep* jdm etw m~en tell s.o. sth; (*amtlich*) inform s.o. of sth. **M~ung** *f* -,-en communication; (*Nachricht*) piece of news

Mittel *nt* -s,- means *sg*; (*Heilremedy*; (*Medikament*) medicine; (*M~wert*) mean; (*Durchschnitt*) average; **M~** *pl* (*Geld-*) funds, resources. **m~** *pred* a medium. **M~alter** *nt* Middle Ages *pl*. **m~alterlich** a medieval. **M~ding** *nt* (*fig*) cross. **m~europäisch** a Central European. **M~finger** *m* middle finger. **m~mäßig** a middling; [**nur**] **m~mäßig** mediocre. **M~meer** *nt* Mediterranean. **M~punkt** *m* centre; (*fig*) centre of attention

mittels *prep* (+*gen*) by means of

Mittelschule *f* = **Realschule**.
M~smann *m* (*pl* -**männer**) intermediary, go-between.
M~stand *m* middle class. **m~ste(r,s)** a middle. **M~streifen** *m* (*Auto*) central reservation.
M~stürmer *m* centre-forward.
M~welle *f* medium wave.

M~wort nt (pl -wörter) participle

mitten adv m~ in/auf (dat/acc) in the middle of. **m~durch** adv [right] through the middle

Mitternacht f midnight

mittler|e(r,s) a middle; (Größe, Qualität) medium; (durchschnittlich) mean, average. **m~weile** adv meanwhile; (seitdem) by now

Mittwoch m ~ Wednesday. **m~s** adv on Wednesdays

mitunter adv now and again

mitwirk|en vi sep (haben) take part; (helfen) contribute. **M~ung** f participation

mix|en vt mix. **M~er** m ~s. (Culin) liquidizer, blender

Möbel pl furniture sg. **M~stück** nt piece of furniture. **M~wagen** m removal van

mobil a mobile; (fam: munter) lively; (nach Krankheit) fit

Mobiliar nt ~ furniture

mobilisieren vt mobilize

Mobilmachung f ~ mobilization

möblier|en vt furnish; **m~tes Zimmer** furnished room

mochte, möchte s. mögen

Mode f ~,-n fashion; **M~ sein** be fashionable

Modell nt -s,-e model. **m~ieren** vt model

Modenschau f fashion show

Modera|tor m -s,-en /-'to:rən/, **M~torin** f -,-nen (TV) presenter

modern a modern; fashionable. **m~isieren** vt modernize

Modeschöpfer m fashion designer

modisch a fashionable

modrig a musty

modulieren vt modulate

Mofa nt -s,-s moped

mogeln vi (haben) (fam) cheat

mögen† vt like; lieber m~ prefer □v aux **ich möchte** I'd like; **möchtest du nach Hause?** do

---

you want to go home? **ich mag mich irren** I may be wrong; **wer/was mag das sein?** whoever/whatever can it be? **[das] mag sein** that may well be

möglich a possible; **alle m~en** all sorts of. **m~erweise** adv possibly. **M~keit** f -,-en possibility. **M~keitsform** f subjunctive. **m~st** adv if possible; **m~st viel** as much as possible

Mohammedan|er(in) m -s,- (f -,-nen) Muslim. **m~isch** a Muslim

Mohn m ~s poppy

Möhre, Mohrrübe f -,-n carrot

Mokka m -s mocha

Molch m -[e]s,-e newt

Mole f -,-n (Naut) mole

Molekül nt -s,-e molecule

Molkerei f -,-en dairy

Moll nt - (Mus) minor

mollig a cosy; (warm) warm; (rundlich) plump

Moment m -s,-e moment; **M~ [mal]!** just a moment! **m~an** a momentary; (gegenwärtig) at the moment

Monarch m -en,-en monarch. **M~ie** f -,-n monarchy

Monat m -s,-e month. **m~elang** adv for months. **m~lich** a & adv monthly

Mönch m -[e]s,-e monk

Mond m -[e]s,-e moon. **M~finsternis** f lunar eclipse. **M~schein** m moonlight

monieren vt criticize

Monitor m -s,-en /-'to:rən/ (Techn) monitor

Monogramm nt -s,-e monogram

Monolog m -s,-e monologue

M~pol nt -s,-e monopoly. **m~ton** a monotonous

Monster nt -s,- monster

Monstrum nt -s,-stren monster

Monsun m -s,-e monsoon

Montag m Monday

Montage /mɔn'ta:ʒə/ f -,-n fitting; (*Zusammenbau*) assembly; (*Film-*) editing; (*Kunst*) montage

montags *adv* on Mondays

Montanindustrie f coal and steel industry

Monteur /mɔn'tø:ɐ/ m -s,-e fitter

montieren *vt* fit; (*zusammenbauen*) assemble

Monument *nt* -[e]s,-e monument. **m~al** *a* monumental

Moor *nt* -[e]s,-e bog; (*Heide-*) moor

Moos *nt* -es,-e moss

Moped *nt* -s,-s moped

Moral f - morals *pl*; (*Selbstvertrauen*) morale; (*Lehre*) moral. **m~isch** *a* moral

Mord *m* -[e]s,-e murder; (*Pol*) assassination. **M~anschlag** *m* murder/assassination attempt. **m~en** *vt/i* (*haben*) murder, kill

Mörder *m* -s,- murderer; (*Pol*) assassin. **M~in** f -,-nen murderess. **m~isch** *a* murderous; (*fam: schlimm*) dreadful

morgen *adv* tomorrow; **m~ früh** tomorrow morning; **heute m~** this morning

Morgen *m* -s,- morning; (*Maß*) ≈ acre. **M~dämmerung** f dawn. **M~grauen** *nt* -s dawn. **M~mantel**, **M~rock** *m* dressinggown. **M~rot** *nt* red sky in the morning. **m~s** *a* in the morning

morgig *a* tomorrow's; **der m~e Tag** tomorrow

Morphium *nt* -s morphine

morsch *a* rotten

Morsealphabet *nt* Morse code

Mörtel *m* -s mortar

Mosaik /moza'i:k/ *nt* -s,-e[n] mosaic

Mosche f -,-n mosque

Mosel f - Moselle

Moskau *nt* -s Moscow

Moskito *m* -s,-s mosquito

Moslem *m* -s,-s Muslim

Motor /'mo:tɔr, mo'to:ɐ/ *m* -s,-en /-'to:rən/ engine; (*Elektro-*) motor. **M~boot** *nt* motor boat

motorisieren *vt* motorize

Motorrad *nt* motor cycle. **M~radfahrer** *m* motor-cyclist. **M~roller** *m* motor scooter

Motte f -,-n moth. **M~nkugel** f mothball

Motto *nt* -s,-s motto

Möwe f -,-n gull

Mücke f -,-n gnat; (*kleine*) midge; (*Stech-*) mosquito

müde *a* tired; **es m~e sein** be tired (**etw zu tun** of doing sth). **M~igkeit** f - tiredness

muffig *a* musty; (*fam: mürrisch*) grumpy

Mühe f -,-n effort; (*Aufwand*) trouble; **sich** (*dat*) **M~ geben** make an effort; (*sich bemühen*) try; **nicht der M~ wert** not worth while; **mit M~ und Not** with great difficulty; (*gerade noch*) only just. **m~los** *a* effortless

muhen *vi* (*haben*) moo

Mühle f -,-n mill; (*Kaffee-*) grinder. **M~stein** *m* millstone

Mühsal f -,-e (*liter*) toil; (*Mühe*) trouble. **m~sam** *a* laborious; (*beschwerlich*) difficult

Mulde f -,-n hollow

Müll *m* -s refuse. **M~abfuhr** f refuse collection

Mullbinde f gauze bandage

Mülleimer *m* waste bin; (*Mülltonne*) dustbin

Müller *m* -s,- miller

Müllhalde f [rubbish] dump. **M~schlucker** *m* refuse chute. **M~tonne** f dustbin

multinational *a* multinational. **M~plikation** /-'tsjo:n/ f -,-en multiplication. **m~plizieren** *vt* multiply

Mumie /'mu:mjə/ f -,-n mummy

Mumm *m* -s (*fam*) energy

Mumps *m* - mumps

Mund m -[e]s,-̈er mouth; **halt den M~!** (sl) shut up! **M~art** f dialect. **m~artlich** a dialect

Mündel nt & m -s,- (Jur) ward. **m~sicher** a gilt-edged

münden vi (sein) flow/⟨Straße:⟩ lead (**in** + acc into)

Mundharmonika f mouth-organ

mündig a **m~ sein/werden** (Jur) be/come of age. **M~keit** f- (Jur) majority

mündlich a verbal; **~e Prüfung** oral

Mündung f -,-en (Fluß-) mouth; (Gewehr-) muzzle

Mund|voll m -,- coin; mouthful. **M~winkel** m corner of the mouth

Munition /·'tsio:n/ f- ammunition

munkeln vt/i (haben) talk (**von** of); **es wird gemunkelt** rumour has it (**daß** that)

Münster nt -s,- cathedral

munter a lively; (heiter) merry; **m~ sein** (wach) be wide awake; **gesund und m~** fit and well □adv [immer] m~ merrily

Münze f -,-n coin; (M~stätte) mint. **m~en** vt mint. **M~fernsprecher** m payphone. **M~wäscherei** f launderette

mürbe a crumbly; ⟨Obst⟩ mellow; ⟨Fleisch⟩ tender. **M~teig** m short pastry

Murmel f -,-n marble

murmeln vt/i (haben) murmur; (undeutlich) mumble. mutter. **M~** nt -s murmur

Murmeltier nt marmot

murren vt/i (haben) grumble

mürrisch a surly

Mus nt -es purée

Muschel f -,-n mussel; [sea] shell

Museum /mu'ze:ʊm/ nt -s,-seen /-'ze:ən/ museum

Musik f - music. **m~alisch** a musical

Musiker(in) m -s,- (f -,-nen) musician

Musik|instrument nt musical instrument. **M~kapelle** f band. **M~pavillon** m bandstand

musisch a artistic

musizieren vi (haben) make music

Muskat m -[e]s nutmeg

Muskel m -s,-n muscle. **M~kater** m stiff and aching muscles pl

muskulös a muscular

Müsli nt -s muesli

muß s. müssen

Muße f - leisure

müssen v aux etw tun m~ have to/⟨fam⟩ have got to do sth; **ich muß jetzt gehen** I have to or must go now

müßte, müßte s. müssen

Muster nt -s,- pattern; (Probe) sample; (Vorbild) model. **M~beispiel** nt typical example; (Vorbild) perfect example. **m~gültig, m~haft** a exemplary. **m~n** vt eye; (inspizieren) inspect. **M~ung** f -,-en inspection; (Mil) medical

Mut m -[e]s courage; **jdm Mut machen** encourage s.o.

mutig a courageous

mutmaßen vt presume; (Vermutungen anstellen) speculate

Mutprobe f test of courage

Mutter¹ f -,-̈ mother

Mutter² f -,-n (Techn) nut

Muttergottes f -,- madonna

Mutterland nt motherland

mütterlich a maternal; (fürsorglich) motherly. **m~erseits** adv on one's/the mother's side

Mutter|mal nt birthmark; (dunkel) mole. **m~seelenallein** a & adv all alone. **M~sprache** f mother tongue. **M~tag** m Mother's Day

Mütze f -,-n cap; **wollene M~** woolly hat

MwSt. abbr (Mehrwertsteuer) VAT

mysteriös _a_ mysterious
Myst|ik /'mʏstɪk/ _f_ - mysticism.
m~isch _a_ mystical
myth|isch _a_ mythical. **M~o-**
logie _f_ - mythology

N

na _int_ well; **na gut** all right then;
na ja oh well; **na und?** so what?
Nabel _m_ -s,- navel. **N~schnur** _f_
umbilical cord
nach _prep_ (+ _dat_) after; (_Uhrzeit_)
past; (_Richtung_) to; (_greifen, ru-_
fen, sich sehnen) for; (_gemäß_) according to; **meiner Meinung n~**
in my opinion; **n~ oben** upwards
□_adv_ **n~ und n~** gradually, bit
by bit; **n~ wie vor** still
nachahm|en _vt sep_ imitate.
N~ung _f_ -,-en imitation
Nachbar(in) _m_ -n,-n (_f_ -,-nen)
neighbour. **N~haus** _nt_ house
next door. **n~lich** _a_ neigh-
bourly; (_Nachbar-_) neighbouring.
N~schaft _f_ - neighbourhood
nachbestell|en _vt sep_ reorder.
N~ung _f_ repeat order
nachbild|en _vt sep_ copy, repro-
duce. **N~ung** _f_ copy, reproduction
nachdatieren _vt sep_ backdate
nachdem _conj_ after; **je n~** it de-
pends
nachdenk|en† _vi sep_ (_haben_)
think (**über** + _acc_ about). **n~lich**
_a_ thoughtful
nachdrücklich _a_ emphatic
nacheinander _adv_ one after the
other
Nachfahre _m_ -n,-n descendant
Nachfolge _f_ succession
nachforsch|en _vi sep_ (_haben_)
make enquiries. **N~ung** _f_ enquiry
Nachfrage _f_ (_Comm_) demand.
n~n _vi sep_ (_haben_) enquire
nachfüllen _vt sep_ refill

nachgeben† _vi sep_ □ _vi_ (_haben_)
give way; (_sich fügen_) give in,
yield □_vt_ **jdm Suppe n~** give s.o.
more soup
Nachgebühr _f_ surcharge
nachgehen† _vi sep_ (_sein_) ⟨_Uhr:_⟩
be slow; **jdm/etw n~** follow
s.o./sth; follow up ⟨_Spur, Angele-_
genheit⟩; pursue ⟨_Angelegenheit_⟩
Nachgeschmack _m_ after-taste
nachgiebig _a_ indulgent; (_gefällig_)
compliant. **N~keit** _f_ - indul-
gence; compliance
nachgrübeln _vi sep_ (_haben_) ponder (**über** + _acc_ on)
nachhaltig _a_ lasting
nachhelfen† _vi sep_ (_haben_) help
nachher _adv_ later; (_danach_) afterwards; **bis n~!** I see you later!
Nachhilfeunterricht _m_ coach-
ing
nachhinein _adv_ **im n~** afterwards
nachholen _vt sep_ (_später holen_)
fetch later; (_mehr holen_) get
more; (_später machen_) do later;
(_aufholen_) catch up on
Nachkomme _m_ -n,-n descendant. **n~n†** _vi sep_ (_sein_) follow
[later], come later; **etw** (_dat_) **n~**
(_fig_) comply with ⟨_Bitte_⟩; carry
out ⟨_Pflicht_⟩. **N~nschaft** _f_ - des-
cendants _pl_, progeny
Nachkriegszeit _f_ post-war
period
Nachlaß _m_ -lasses,-lässe discount; (_Jur_) [deceased's] estate
nachlassen† _v sep_ □ _vi_ (_haben_)
decrease; ⟨_Regen, Hitze:_⟩ let up;
⟨_Schmerz:_⟩ ease; ⟨_Sturm:_⟩ abate;
⟨_Augen, Kräfte, Leistungen:_⟩ deteriorate □_vt_ **vom Preis n~**
take sth off the price
nachlässig _a_ careless; (_leger_) casual; (_unordentlich_) sloppy.
N~keit _f_ - carelessness; sloppi-
ness

nachlöse|n vi sep (haben) pay one's fare on the train/on arrival. **N~schalter** m excess-fare office

nachmachen vt sep (später machen) do later; (imitieren) imitate, copy; (fälschen) forge

Nachmittag m afternoon. **n~** adv heute **n~** this afternoon. **n~s** adv in the afternoon

Nachnahme f etw per **N~ schicken** send sth cash on delivery or COD

Nachname m surname

Nachporto nt excess postage

nachprüfen vt sep check, verify

Nachricht f -,-en [piece of] news sg; **N~en** news sg; **eine N~ hinterlassen** leave a message. **N~endienst** m (Mil) intelligence service

nachrücken vi sep (sein) move up

Nachruf m obituary

nachsagen vt sep repeat (jdm after s.o.); **jdm Schlechtes/ Gutes n~** speak ill/well of s.o.

Nachsaison f late season

nachschicken vt sep (später schicken) send later; (hinterher-) send after (jdm s.o.); send on (Post) (jdm to s.o.)

nachschlagen v sep ▭vt look up ▭vi (haben) **in einem Wörterbuch n~** consult a dictionary

Nachschrift f transcript; (Nachsatz) postscript

Nachschub m (Mil) supplies pl

nachsehen† v sep ▭vt (prüfen) check; (nachschlagen) look up; (hinwegsehen über) overlook ▭vi (haben) have a look; (prüfen) check; **im Wörterbuch n~** consult a dictionary

nachsenden† vt sep forward (Post) (jdm to s.o.); **'bitte n~'** 'please forward'

nachsichtig a forbearing, lenient; indulgent

Nachsilbe f suffix

nachsitzen† vi sep (haben) **n~ müssen** be kept in [after school]; **jdn n~ lassen** give s.o. detention. **N~** nt -s (Sch) detention

Nachspeise f dessert, sweet

nachsprechen† vt sep repeat (jdm after s.o.)

nachspülen vt sep rinse

nächst /-çst/ prep (+ dat) next to. **n~beste(r,s)** a first [available]; (zweitbeste) next best. **n~e(r,s)** a next; (nächstgelegene) nearest; (Verwandte) closest; **in n~er Nähe** close by ▭pron **der/ die/das n~e** the next one; **als n~es** next; **fürs n~e** for the time being. **N~e(r)** m fellow man

nachstehend a following ▭adv below

nächst|emal adv das n~emal [the] next time. **N~enliebe** f charity. **n~ens** adv shortly. **n~gelegen** a nearest

nachsuchen vi sep (haben) search; **n~ um** request

Nacht f -,-ë night; **über/bei N~** overnight/at night. **n~** adv **morgen n~** tomorrow night; **heute n~** tonight; (letzte Nacht) last night; **gestern n~** last night; (vorletzte Nacht) the night before last. **N~dienst** m night duty

Nachteil m disadvantage; **zum N~** to the detriment (gen of)

Nachthemd nt night-dress; (Männer-) night-shirt

Nachtigall f -,-en nightingale

Nachtisch m dessert

Nachtklub m night-club

nächtlich a nocturnal, night ...

Nachtlokal nt night-club

Nachtrag m postscript; (Ergänzung) supplement. **n~en†** vt sep add. **n~end** a vindictive; **n~en sein** bear grudges

nachträglich a subsequent, later; (verspätet) belated ▭adv later; (nachher) afterwards

Nacht|ruhe f night's rest; **angenehme N~ruhe!** sleep well!
n~s adv at night; **2 Uhr n~s** 2 o'clock in the morning.
N~schicht f night-shift.
N~tisch m bedside table.
N~tischlampe f bedside lamp.
N~topf m chamber-pot.
N~wächter m night-watchman. **N~zeit** f night-time
Nachuntersuchung f check-up
Nachwahl f by-election
Nachweis m -es,-e proof. **n~bar** a demonstrable. **n~en†** vt sep prove; (aufzeigen) show; (vermitteln) give details of; **jdm nichts n~en können** have no proof against s.o.
Nachwirkung f after-effect
Nachwuchs m new generation; (fam: Kinder) offspring. **N~~spieler** m young player
nachzahlen vt/i sep (haben) pay extra; (später zahlen) pay later; **Steuern n~** pay tax arrears
Nachzahlung f extra/later payment; (Gehalts-) back-payment
nachzeichnen vt sep copy
Nachzügler m -s,- late-comer; (Zurückgebliebener) straggler
Nacken m -s,- nape or back of the neck
nackt a naked; (bloß, kahl) bare; (Wahrheit) plain. **N~heit** f - nakedness, nudity. **N~kultur** f nudism. **N~schnecke** f slug
Nadel f -,-n needle; (Häkel-) hook; (Schmuck-, Hut-) pin. **N~arbeit** f needlework. **N~baum** m conifer. **N~kissen** n pincushion. **N~stich** m stitch; (fig) pinprick. **N~wald** m coniferous forest
Nagel m -s,- nail. **N~haut** f cuticle. **N~lack** m nail varnish. **n~n** vt nail. **n~neu** a brand-new
nagen vt/i (haben) gnaw (**an+** dat at); **n~d** (fig) nagging
Nagetier n rodent

nah a, adv & prep = **nahe**
Näharbeit f sewing
Nahaufnahme f close-up
nahe a nearby; (zeitlich) imminent; (eng) close; **der N~ Osten** the Middle East; **in n~r Zukunft** in the near future; **von n~m** [from] close to; **n~ sein** be close (dat to) □adv near, close; (verwandt) closely; **n~ an** (+ acc/ dat) near [to], close to; **n~ daran sein, etw zu tun** nearly do sth □prep (+ dat) near [to], close to
Nähe f - nearness, proximity; **aus der N~** [from] close to; **in der N~** near or close by
nahe|legen vt sep recommend (dat to); **jdm n~legen, etw zu tun** urge s.o. to do sth. **n~liegen†** vi sep (haben) (fig) be highly likely. **n~liegend** a obvious
nähen vt/i (haben) sew; (anfertigen) make; (Med) stitch [up]
näher a closer; (Weg) shorter; (Einzelheiten) further □adv closer; (genauer) more closely; **n~ an** (+ acc/dat) nearer [to], closer to □prep (+ dat) nearer [to], closer to. **N~e[s]** nt [further] details pl. **n~kommen†** vi sep (sein) come closer, approach. **n~n (sich)** vr approach
nahestehen† vi sep (haben) (fig) be close (dat to)
nahezu adv almost
Nähgarn nt [sewing] cotton
Nahkampf m close combat
Nähmaschine f sewing machine. **N~nadel** f sewing-needle
nahrhaft a nutritious
Nährstoff m nutrient
Nahrung f - food, nourishment. **N~smittel** nt food
Nährwert m nutritional value
Naht f -,-e seam; (Med) suture. **n~los** a seamless
Nahverkehr m local service

naiv /naːˈiːf/ *a* naïve. **N~ität**
/-viˈtɛːt/ *f* - naïvety

Name *m* -ns,-n name; **im N~** (+
gen) in the name of; ⟨*handeln*⟩ on
behalf of. **n~nlos** *a* nameless;
(*unbekannt*) unknown, anonymous. **N~nstag** *m* name-day.
N~nsvetter *m* 'namesake.
N~nszug *m* signature.
n~ntlich *adv* by name; (*besonders*) especially

namhaft *a* noted; (*ansehnlich*)
considerable; **n~ machen** name

nämlich *adv* (*und zwar*) namely;
(*denn*) because

nanu *int* hallo

Napf *m* -[e]s,ːe bowl

Narbe *f* -,-n scar

Narkose *f* -,-n general anaesthetic. **N~arzt** *m* anaesthetist.
N~mittel *nt* anaesthetic

Narr *m* -en,-en fool; **zum N~en
haben** make a fool of. **n~en** *vt*
fool

Närr|**in** *f* -,-nen fool. **n~isch** *a*
foolish; (*fam: verrückt*) crazy
(**auf**+ *acc* about)

Narzisse *f* -,-n narcissus

nasch|**en** *vt/i* (*haben*) nibble (**an**
+ *dat* at). **n~haft** *a* sweet-toothed

Nase *f* -,-n nose

näseln *vi* (*haben*) speak through
one's nose; **n~d** nasal

Nasen|**bluten** *nt* -s nosebleed.
N~loch *nt* nostril. **N~rücken**
m bridge of the nose

Naseweis *m* -es,-e (*fam*) know-all

Nashorn *nt* rhinoceros

naß *a* wet

Nässe *f* - wet; (*Naßsein*) wetness.
n~n *vt* wet

Nation /natˈsjoːn/ *f* -,-en nation.
n~al *a* national. **N~alhymne** *f*
national anthem. **N~alismus** *m*
- nationalism. **N~alität** *f* -,-en
nationality. **N~alspieler** *m* international

Natrium *nt* -s sodium

Natron *nt* -s doppelkohlen-
saures N~ bicarbonate of soda

Natter *f* -,-n snake; (*Gift-*) viper

Natur *f* -,-en nature; **von N~ aus**
by nature. **n~alisieren**
vt naturalize. **N~alisierung** *f*
-,-en naturalization

Natur|**erscheinung** *f* natural
phenomenon. **N~forscher** *m*
naturalist. **N~kunde** *f* natural
history

natürlich *a* natural □ *adv* naturally; (*selbstverständlich*) of
course. **N~keit** *f* - naturalness

natur|**rein** *a* pure. **N~schutz** *m*
nature conservation; **unter**
N~schutz stehen be protected.
N~schutzgebiet *nt* nature reserve. **N~wissenschaft** *f* [natural] science. **N~wissen-
schaftler** *m* scientist

nautisch *a* nautical

Navigation /-ˈtsjoːn/ *f* - navigation

Nazi *m* -s,-s Nazi

n.Chr. *abbr* (**nach Christus**) AD

Nebel *m* -s,- fog; (*leicht*) mist

neben *prep* (+ *dat*/*acc*) next to,
beside; (+ *dat*) (*außer*) apart
from. **n~an** *adv* next door

Neben|**anschluß** *m* (*Teleph*) extension. **N~ausgaben** *fpl* incidental expenses

nebenbei *adv* in addition; (*beiläufig*) casually

Neben|**bemerkung** *f* passing remark. **N~beruf** *m* second job

nebeneinander *adv* next to each
other, side by side

Neben|**eingang** *m* side entrance.
N~fach *nt* (*Univ*) subsidiary
subject. **N~fluß** *m* tributary.
N~gleis *nt* siding

nebenher *adv* in addition

nebenhin *adv* casually

Neben|**höhle** *f* sinus. **N~kosten**
pl additional costs. **N~produkt**
nt by-product. **N~rolle** *f* supporting role; (*kleine*) minor role.

N~sache f unimportant matter.
n~sächlich a unimportant.
N~satz m subordinate clause.
N~straße f minor road; (Seiten-)
side street. **N~wirkung** f side-
effect.

neblig a foggy; (leicht) misty

Necessaire /nes'sɛːɐ̯/ nt -s,-s toilet bag; (Näh-, Nagel-) set

neck|en vt tease. **N~erei** f - teas-
ing. **n~isch** a teasing

Neffe m -n,-n nephew

negativ a negative. **N~** nt -s,-e
(Phot) negative

Neger m -s,- Negro

nehmen† vt take (dat from); **sich**
(dat) **etw n~** take sth; help oneself to (Essen)

Neid m -[e]s envy, jealousy.
n~isch a envious, jealous
(auf + acc of); **auf jdn n~isch**
sein envy s.o.

neig|en vt incline (zur Seite) tilt;
(beugen) bend; **sich n~en** incline; (Boden-) slope; (Person-)
bend (über + acc over) ○ vi (haben) **n~en zu** (fig) have a tendency towards; be prone to
(Krankheit); incline towards
(Ansicht). **N~ung** f -,-en
inclination; (Gefälle) slope; (fig)
tendency

nein adv, **N~** nt -s no

Nektar m -s nectar

Nelke f -,-n carnation; (Feder-)
pink; (Culin) clove

nenn|en† vt call; (taufen) name;
(angeben) give; (erwähnen) mention; **sich n~en** call oneself.
n~enswert a significant

Neon nt -s neon. **N~beleuch-**
tung f fluorescent lighting

Nerv m -s,-en /-fən/ nerve; **die**
N~en verlieren lose control of
oneself. **n~en** vt (fam) get on
the nerves of. **N~enarzt** m neurologist. **n~enaufreibend** a nerve-
racking. **N~enkitzel** m (fam)
thrill. **N~ensystem** nt nervous

system. **N~enzusammen-**
bruch m nervous breakdown

nervös a nervy, edgy; (Med) nervous; **n~ sein** be on edge

Nervosität f - nerviness, edginess

Nerz m -es,-e mink

Nessel f -,-n nettle

Nest nt -[e]s,-er nest

nett a nice; kind

netto adv net

Netz nt -es,-e net; (Einkaufs-)
string bag; (Spinnen-) web; (auf
Landkarte) grid; (System) network; (Electr) mains pl. **N~haut**
f retina. **N~karte** f area season-
ticket. **N~werk** nt network

neu a new; (modern) modern; **wie**
neu as good as new; **das ist mir**
neu it's news to me; **von n~em**
all over again ○ adv newly; (gerade erst) only just; (erneut)
again. **N~auflage** f new edition;
(unverändert) reprint. **N~bau** m
(pl -ten) new house/building

Neu(e)r m/f new person, new-
comer; (Schüler) new boy/girl.
N~e(s) nt das N~e the new;
etwas N~es something new;
(Neuigkeit) a piece of news; **was**
gibt's N~es? what's the news?

neuerdings adv [just] recently

neuest|e(r,s) a newest; (letzte) la-
test; **seit n~em** just recently.
N~e nt das N~e the latest thing;
(Neuigkeit) the latest news sg

neugeboren a newborn

Neugier, Neugierde f - curiosity;
(Wißbegierde) inquisitiveness

neugierig a curious (auf + acc
about); (wißbegierig) inquisitive

Neuheit f -,-en novelty; newness

Neuigkeit f -,-en piece of news;
N~en news sg

Neujahr nt New Year's Day; **über**
N~ over the New Year

neulich adv the other day

neun inv a, **N~** f -,-en nine.
n~te(r,s) a ninth. **n~zehn** inv
a nineteen. **n~zehnte(r,s)**

nineteenth. **n~zig** *inv a* ninety. **n~zigste(r,s)** *a* ninetieth

Neuralgie *f* -,-n neuralgia

neureich *a* nouveau riche

Neurologe *m* -n,-n neurologist

Neurose *f* -,-n neurosis

Neuseeland *nt* -s New Zealand

neutral *a* neutral. **n~isieren** *vt* neutralize. **N~ität** *f* - neutrality

neu|vermählt *a* **n~vermähltes Paar** newly-weds *pl.* **N~zeit** *f* modern times *pl*

nicht *adv* not; **ich kann n~** I cannot *or* can't; **er ist n~ gekommen** he hasn't come; **bitte n~!** please don't! **n~ berühren!** do not touch! **du kennst ihn doch, n~?** you know him, don't you?

Nichte *f* -,-n niece

Nichtraucher *m* non-smoker. **N~abteil** *nt* non-smoking compartment

nichts *pron a* nothing; **n~mehr** no more. **N~** *nt* - nothingness; *(fig: Leere)* void. **n~ahnend** *a* unsuspecting

Nichtschwimmer *m* non-swimmer

nichts|nutzig *a* a good-for-nothing; *(fam: unartig)* naughty. **n~sagend** *a* meaningless; *(uninteressant)* nondescript. **n~tun** *nt* -s idleness

Nickel *nt* -s nickel

nicken *vi (haben)* nod. **N~** *nt* -s nod

Nickerchen *nt* -s,- *(fam)* nap

nie *adv* never

nieder *a* a low □*adv* down. **n~brennen** *vt/i sep (sein)* burn down. **n~deutsch** *nt* Low German. **n~gedrückt** *a (fig)* depressed. **n~geschlagen** *a* dejected, despondent. **N~kunft** *f* -,̈e confinement. **N~lage** *f* defeat

Niederlande (die) *pl* the Netherlands

Niederländ|er *m* -s,- Dutchman; **die N~er** the Dutch *pl.* **N~e-rin** *f* -,-nen Dutchwoman. **n~isch** *a* Dutch

nieder|lassen *vt sep* let down; **sich n~lassen** settle; *(sich setzen)* sit down. **N~lassung** *f* -,-en settlement; *(Zweigstelle)* branch. **n~legen** *vt sep* put *or* lay down; resign *(Amt)*; **die Arbeit n~legen** go on strike. **n~machen**, **n~metzeln** *vt sep* massacre. **N~sachsen** *nt* Lower Saxony. **N~schlag** *m (Regen)* rainfall; *(radioaktiver)* fall-out. **n~schlagen†** *vt sep* knock down; lower *(Augen)*; *(unterdrücken)* crush. **n~schmettern** *vt sep (fig)* shatter. **n~setzen** *vt sep* put *or* set down; **sich n~setzen** sit down. **n~strecken** *vt sep* fell; *(durch Schuß)* gun down. **n~trächtig** *a* base, vile. **n~walzen** *vt sep* flatten

niedlich *a* pretty; *(goldig)* sweet

niedrig *a* low; *(fig: gemein)* base

niemals *adv* never

niemand *pron* nobody, no one

Niere *f* -,-n kidney; **künstliche N~** kidney machine

niesel|n *vi (haben)* drizzle. **N~regen** *m* drizzle

niesen *vi (haben)* sneeze. **N~** *nt* -s sneezing; *(Nieser)* sneeze

Niet *m & nt* -[e]s,-e, **Niete¹** *f* -,-n rivet; *(an Jeans)* stud

Niete² *f* -,-n blank; *(fam)* failure

nieten *vt* rivet

Nikotin *nt* -s nicotine

Nil *m* -[s] Nile. **N~pferd** *nt* hippopotamus

nimmer *adv (SGer)* not any more; **nie und n~** never

nirgends, **n~wo** *adv* nowhere

Nische *f* -,-n recess, niche

nisten *vi (haben)* nest

Nitrat *nt* -[e]s,-e nitrate

Niveau /ni'vo:/ *nt* -s,-s level; *(geistig, künstlerisch)* standard

nix adv (fam) nothing

Nixe f -,-n mermaid

nobel a noble; ⟨fam: luxuriös⟩ luxurious; ⟨fam: großzügig⟩ generous

noch adv still; (zusätzlich) as well; (mit Komparativ) even; **n~ nicht** not yet; **gerade n~** only just; **n~ immer** od **immer n~** still; **n~ letzte Woche** only last week; **wer/was/wo n~?** who/what/where else? **n~ einmal** again; **n~ ein Bier** another beer; **n~ so sehr** however much □**noch weder ... n~** neither ... nor

nochmal|ig a further. **n~s** adv again

Nomad|e m -n,-n nomad. **n~isch** a nomadic

Nominativ m -s,-e nominative

nominier|en vt nominate. **N~ung** f -,-en nomination

Nonne f -,-n nun. **N~nkloster** nt convent

Nonstopflug m direct flight

Nord m -[e]s north

Norden m -s north

nordisch a Nordic

nördlich a northern; ⟨Richtung⟩ northerly □adv & prep (+gen) **n~ [von] der Stadt** [to the] north of the town

Nordosten m north-east

Nord|pol m North Pole. **N~see** f - North Sea. **N~westen** m north-west

Nörgelei f -,-en grumbling

nörgeln vi (haben) grumble

Norm f -,-en norm; (Techn) standard; (Soll) quota

normal a normal. **n~erweise** adv normally

normen vt standardize

Norwe|gen nt -s Norway. **N~ger(in)** m -s,- (f -,-nen) Norwegian. **n~gisch** a Norwegian

Nost|algie f - nostalgia. **n~algisch** a nostalgic

Not f -,⸚e need; (Notwendigkeit) necessity; (Entbehrung) hardship; (seelisch) trouble; **zur Not** if need be; (äußerstenfalls) in a pinch

Notar m -s,-e notary public

Not|arzt m emergency doctor. **N~ausgang** m emergency exit. **N~behelf** m -[e]s,-e makeshift. **N~bremse** f emergency brake. **N~dienst** m **N~dienst haben** be on call

Note f -,-n note; (Zensur) mark; **ganze/halbe N~** (Mus) semibreve/minim; **N~n lesen** read music; **persönliche N~** personal touch. **N~nblatt** nt sheet of music. **N~nschlüssel** m clef

Notfall m emergency; **für den N~** just in case. **n~s** adv if need be

notieren vt note down; (Comm) quote; **sich** (dat) **etw n~** make a note of sth

nötig a necessary; **n~ haben** need; **das N~ste** the essentials pl □adv urgently. **N~ung** f - coercion

Notiz f -,-en note; (Zeitungs-) item; **[keine] N~ nehmen von** take [no] notice of. **N~buch** nt notebook. **N~kalender** m diary

Not|lage f plight. **n~landen** vi (sein) make a forced landing. **N~landung** f forced landing. **n~leidend** a needy. **N~lösung** f stopgap. **N~lüge** f white lie. **N~ruf** m emergency call; (Naut, Aviat) distress call; (Nummer) emergency services number. **N~signal** nt distress signal. **N~stand** m state of emergency. **N~wehr** f - (Jur) self-defence

notwendig a necessary; (unerläßlich) essential □adv urgently. **N~keit** f -,-en necessity

Notzucht f - (Jur) rape

Nougat /'nu:gat/ m & nt -s nougat

November m -s,- November

Novize m -n,-n, **Novizin** f -,-nen (Relig) novice

Nu m im Nu (fam) in a flash

nüchtern a sober; (sachlich) matter-of-fact; **auf n~en Magen** on an empty stomach

Nudel f -,-n piece of pasta; **N~n** pasta sg; (Band-) noodles. **N~holz** nt rolling-pin

Nudist m -en,-en nudist

nuklear a nuclear

null inv a zero, nought; (Teleph) 0; (Sport) nil; (Tennis) love; **n~ Fehler** no mistakes; **n~ und nichtig** (Jur) null and void. **N~** f -,-en nought, zero; (fig: Person) nonentity. **N~punkt** m zero

numerieren vt number

Nummer f -,-n number; (Ausgabe) issue; (Darbietung) item; (Zirkus-) act; (Größe) size. **N~nschild** nt number-plate

nun adv now; (na) well; (halt) just; **nun gut!** very well then!

nur adv only, just; **wo kann sie nur sein?** wherever can she be? **er soll es nur versuchen!** (drohend) just let him try!

Nürnberg nt -s Nuremberg

nuscheln vt/i (fam) mumble

Nuß f -,Nüsse nut. **N~knacker** m -s,- nutcrackers pl

Nüstern fpl nostrils

Nut f -,-en, **Nute** f -,-n groove

Nutte f -,-n (sl) tart (sl)

nutzbar a usable; **n~bar machen** utilize; cultivate ⟨Boden⟩. **n~bringend** a profitable

nutzen vt use, utilize; (aus-) take advantage of □ vi (haben) = **nützen**. **N~** m -s benefit; (Comm) profit; **N~ ziehen aus** benefit from; **von N~ sein** be useful

nützen vi (haben) be useful or of use (dat to); ⟨Mittel:⟩ be effective; **nichts n~** be useless or no use; **was nützt mir das?** what good is it to me? □ vt = **nutzen**

Nutzholz nt timber

nützlich a useful. **N~keit** f -usefulness

nutzlos a useless; (vergeblich) vain. **N~losigkeit** f - uselessness. **N~ung** f - use, utilization

Nylon /ˈnailɔn/ nt -s nylon

Nymphe /ˈnʏmfə/ f -,-n nymph

O

o int o ja/nein! oh yes/no!

Oase f -,-n oasis

ob conj whether; **ob reich, ob arm** rich or poor; **und ob!** (fam) you bet!

Obacht f O~ **geben** pay attention; O~! look out!

Obdach nt -[e]s shelter. **o~los** a homeless. **O~lose(r)** m/f homeless person; **die O~losen** the homeless pl

Obduktion /-ˈtsjoːn/ f -,-en post-mortem

O-Beine ntpl (fam) bow-legs, bandy legs

oben adv at the top; (auf der Oberseite) on top; (eine Treppe hoch) upstairs; **da o~** up there; **o~ im Norden** up in the north; **siehe o~** see above; **o~ auf** (+ acc/dat) on top of; **nach o~** up[wards]; (die Treppe hinauf) upstairs; **von o~** from above/upstairs; **von o~ bis unten** from top to bottom; ⟨Person:⟩ to toe. **o~drein** on top of that. **o~erwähnt, o~genannt** a above-mentioned

Ober m -s,- waiter

Ober|arm m upper arm. **O~arzt** m ≈ senior registrar. **O~deck** nt upper deck. **o~e(r,s)** a upper; (höhere) higher. **O~fläche** f surface. **o~flächlich** a superficial. **O~geschoß** nt upper storey. **o~halb** adv & prep (+ gen) above. **O~haupt** nt (fig) head. **O~haus** nt (Pol) upper house; (in UK) House of Lords.

O~hemd *nt* [man's] shirt.
o~irdisch *a* surface ... □*adv* above ground. **O~kiefer** *m* upper jaw. **O~körper** *m* upper part of the body. **O~leutnant** *m* lieutenant. **O~lippe** *f* upper lip

Obers *nt* – (Aust) cream
Ober|schenkel *m* thigh. **O~schule** *f* grammar school. **O~seite** *f* upper/(rechte Seite) right side

Oberst *m* -en & -s,-en colonel
oberste(r,s) *a* top; (höchste) highest; (Befehlshaber, Gerichtshof) supreme; (wichtigste) first

Ober|stimme *f* treble. **O~teil** *nt* top. **O~weite** *f* chest/(der Frau) bust size

obgleich *conj* although

obig *a* above

Objekt *nt* -[e]s,-e object; (Haus, Grundstück) property

Objektiv *nt* -s,-e lens. **o~** *a* objective. **O~ität** *f* objectivity

Oblate *f* -,-n (Relig) wafer

obliga|t *a* (fam) inevitable. **O~tion** /ˈts̯ɔːn/ *f* -,-en obligation; (Comm) bond

Obmann *m* (pl -männer) [jury] foreman; (Sport) referee

Oboe /oˈboːə/ *f* -,-n oboe

Obrigkeit *f* - authorities *pl*

obschon *conj* although

Observatorium *nt* -s,-ien observatory

obskur *a* obscure; dubious

Obst *nt* -es (coll) fruit. **O~baum** *m* fruit-tree. **O~garten** *m* orchard. **O~händler** *m* fruiterer

O-Bus *m* trolley bus

obwohl *conj* although

Ochse *m* -n,-n ox

öde *a* desolate; (unfruchtbar) barren; (langweilig) dull. **Öde** *f* - desolation; barrenness; dullness

oder *conj* or; **du kennst ihn doch, o~?** you know him, don't you?

Ofen *m* -s,-̈ stove; (Heiz-) heater; (Back-) oven; (Techn) furnace

offen *a* open; (Haar) loose; (Flamme) naked; (o~herzig) frank; (o~ gezeigt) overt; (unentschieden) unsettled; **o~e Stelle** vacancy; **Wein o~ verkaufen** sell wine by the glass; *adv* **o~ gesagt** od **gestanden** to be honest. **o~bar** *a* obvious □*adv* apparently. **O~barung** *f* -,-en revelation. **o~bleiben†** *vi sep* (sein) remain open. **o~halten†** *vt sep* hold open (Tür); keep open (Mund, Augen). **O~heit** *f* frankness, openness. **o~lassen†** *vt sep* leave open; leave vacant (Stelle). **o~sichtlich** *a* obvious

offenstehen† *vi sep* (haben) be open; (Rechnung:) be outstanding; **jdm o~** *(fig)* be open to s.o.

öffentlich *a* public. **Ö~keit** *f* - public; **in aller Ö~keit** in public, publicly

Offerte *f* -,-n (Comm) offer

offiziell *a* official

Offizier *m* -s,-e (Mil) officer

öffn|en *vt/i* (haben) open; **sich ö~en** open. **O~er** *m* -s,- opener. **O~ung** *f* -,-en opening. **Ö~ungszeiten** *fpl* opening hours

oft *adv* often

öfter *adv* quite often. **ö~e(r,s)** *a* frequent; **des ö~en** frequently. **ö~s** *adv* (fam) quite often

oh *int* oh!

ohne *prep* (+acc) without; **o~ mich!** count me out! **oben o~** topless; □*conj* **o~ zu überlegen** without thinking; **o~ daß ich es merkte** without my noticing it. **o~dies** *adv* anyway. **o~gleichen** *pred* *a* unparalleled. **o~hin** *adv* anyway

Ohn|macht *f* -,-en faint; (fig) powerlessness; **in O~macht fallen** faint. **o~mächtig** *a* unconscious; (fig) powerless; **o~mächtig werden** faint

Ohr *nt* -[e]s,-en ear

Öhr *nt* -[e]s,-e eye

Ohren|schmalz nt ear-wax. **O~-schmerzen** mpl earache sg. **O~sessel** m wing-chair

Ohrfeige f slap in the face. **o~n** vt jdn o~n slap s.o.'s face

Ohr|läppchen nt -s,- ear-lobe. **O~ring** m ear-ring. **O~wurm** m earwig

oje int oh dear!

okay /o'keː/ a & adv (fam) OK

Öko|logie f- ecology. **ö~logisch** a ecological. **ö~nomie** f - economy; (Wissenschaft) economics sg. **ö~nomisch** a economic

Oktave f -,-n octave

Oktober m -s,- October

Öl nt -[e]s,-e oil; **in Öl malen** paint in oils. **Ölbaum** m olivetree. **ölen** vt oil. **Ölfarbe** f oilpaint. **Ölfeld** nt oilfield. **ölig** a oily

Olive f -,-n olive. **O~enöl** nt olive oil

oll a (fam) old; (fam: häßlich) nasty

Ölmeßstab m dip-stick. **Ölstand** m oil-level. **Öltanker** m oil-tanker. **Ölteppich** m oil-slick

Olympiade f -,-n Olympic Games pl, Olympics pl

Olymp|iasieger(in) /o'lʏmpia-/ m(f) Olympic champion. **o~isch** a Olympic; **O~ische Spiele** Olympic Games

Ölzeug nt oilskins pl

Oma f -,-s (fam) granny

Omelett nt -[e]s,-e & -s omelette

Omen nt -s,- omen

Omnibus m bus; (Reise-) coach

onanieren vi (haben) masturbate

Onkel m -s,- uncle

Opa m -s,-s (fam) grandad

Oper f -,-n opera

Operation /-'tsioːn/ f -,-en operation. **O~ssaal** m operating-theatre

Operette f -,-n operetta

operieren vt operate on (Patient, Herz); **sich o~ lassen** have an operation □vi (haben) operate

Opernglas nt opera-glasses pl

Opfer nt -s,- sacrifice; (eines Unglücks) victim; **jdm/ etw zum O~ fallen** fall victim to s.o./sth. **o~n** vt sacrifice

Opium nt -s opium

Opposition /-'tsioːn/ f - opposition. **O~spartei** f opposition party

Optik f - optics sg; (fam: Objektiv) lens. **O~er** m -s,- optician

optimal a optimum

Optimist m -en,-en optimist. **o~tisch** a optimistic

Option /ɔp'tsioːn/ f -,-en option

optisch a optical; (Eindruck) visual

Orakel nt -s,- oracle

Orange /o'rãːʒə/ f -,-n orange. **o~** inv a orange. **O~ade** /orã'ʒaːdə/ f -,-n orangeade. **o~nmarmelade** f [orange] marmalade

Orchester /ɔr'kɛstə/ nt -s,- orchestra. **o~rieren** vt orchestrate

Orchidee /ɔrçi'deːə/ f -,-n orchid

Orden m -s,- (Ritter-, Kloster-) order; (Auszeichnung) medal, decoration

ordentlich a neat, tidy; (anständig) respectable; (ordnungsgemäß, fam: richtig) proper; (Mitglied, Versammlung) ordinary; (fam: gut) decent; (fam: gehörig) good

Order f -,-s & -n order

ordinär a common

Ordination /-'tsioːn/ f -,-en (Relig) ordination; (Aust) surgery

ordnen vt put in order; (aufräumen) tidy; (an-) arrange. **O~er** m -s,- steward; (Akten-) file

Ordnung /-ʊŋ/ f -,-en order; **o~ machen** tidy up; **in O~ bringen** put in order; (aufräumen) tidy; (reparieren) mend; (fig) put right; **in**

O~ sein be in order; (*ordentlich sein*) be tidy; (*fig*) be all right; **[geht] in O~!** OK! **o~gemäß** *a* proper. **O~strafe** *f* (*Jur*) fine. **o~swidrig** *a* improper

Ordonnanz *f* -,-en (*Mil*) orderly

Organ *nt* -s,-e organ; voice

Organisation /'tsio:n/ *f* -,-en organization

organisch *a* organic

organisieren *vt* organize; (*fam: beschaffen*) get [hold of]

Organismus *m* -,-men organism; (*System*) system

Organspenderkarte *f* donor card

Orgasmus *m* -,-men orgasm

Orgel *f* -,-n (*Mus*) organ

Orient /'o:riɛnt/ *m* -s Orient. **o~talisch** *a* Oriental

orientier|en /oriɛn'ti:rən/ *vt* inform (**über** + *acc* about); **sich o~en** get one's bearings, orientate oneself; (*unterrichten*) inform oneself (**über** + *acc* about). **O~ung** *f* - orientation; **die O~ung verlieren** lose one's bearings

original *a* original. **O~** *nt* -s,-e original. **O~übertragung** *f* live transmission

originell *a* original; (*eigenartig*) unusual

Orkan *m* -s,-e hurricane

Ornament *nt* -[e]s,-e ornament

Ort *m* -[e]s,-e place; (*Ortschaft*) [small] town; **am Ort** locally; **am Ort des Verbrechens** at the scene of the crime

ortho|dox *a* orthodox. **O~graphie** *f* -spelling. **o~graphisch** *a* spelling ... **O~päde** *m* -n,-n orthopaedic specialist

örtlich *a* local

Ortschaft *f* -,-en [small] town; (*Dorf*) village; **geschlossene O~** (*Auto*) built-up area

Orts|verkehr *m* local traffic. **O~zeit** *f* local time

Öse *f* -,-n eyelet; (*Schlinge*) loop; **Haken und Öse** hook and eye

Ost *m* -[e]s east

Osten *m* -s east; **nach O~** east

Osteopath *m* -en,-en osteopath

Oster|ei /'o:stə'?aj/ *nt* Easter egg. **O~fest** *nt* Easter. **O~glocke** *f* daffodil. **O~n** *nt* -,- Easter; **frohe O~n!** happy Easter!

Österreich *nt* -s Austria. **Ö~er** *m* -s,-, **Ö~erin** *f* -,-nen Austrian. **ö~isch** *a* Austrian

östlich *a* eastern; (*Richtung*) easterly □ *adv* & *prep* (+*gen*) **ö~ der Stadt** east of the town

Ostsee *f* Baltic [Sea]

Otter[1] *m* -s,- otter

Otter[2] *f* -,-n adder

Ouverture /uver'ty:rə/ *f* -,-n overture

oval *a* oval. **O~** *nt* -s,-e oval

Oxid, Oxyd *nt* -[e]s,-e oxide

Ozean *m* -s,-e ocean

Ozon *nt* -s ozone. **O~loch** *nt* hole in the ozone layer. **O~schicht** *f* ozone layer

P

paar *pron inv* **ein p~** a few; **alle p~ Tage** every few days. **P~** *nt* -[e]s,-e pair; (*Ehe-, Liebes-, Tanz-*) couple. **p~en** *vt* mate; (*verbinden*) combine; **sich p~en** mate. **p~weise** *adv* in pairs, in twos

Pacht *f* -,-en lease; (*P~summe*) rent. **p~en** *vt* lease

Pächter *m* -s,- lessee; (*eines Hofes*) tenant

Pachtvertrag *m* lease

Päckchen *nt* -s,- package

pack|en *vt/i* (*haben*) pack; (*ergreifen*) seize; (*fig: fesseln*) grip. **P~en** *m* -s,- bundle. **P~papier** *nt* [strong] wrapping paper. **P~ung** *f* -,-en packet

Pädagog|e m -n,-n educational-
ist; (*Lehrer*) teacher. **P~ik** f -
educational science

Paddel nt -s,- paddle. **P~boot** nt
canoe. **p~n** vt/i (*haben/sein*)
paddle. **P~sport** m canoeing

Page /'pa:ʒə/ m -n,-n page

Paillette /paj'jetə/ f -,-n sequin

Paket nt -[e]s,-e packet; (*Post*-)
parcel

Pakistan nt -s Pakistan. **P~a-
ner(in)** m -s,- (f -,-nen) Pakistani. **p~anisch** a Pakistani

Palast m -[e]s,-̈e palace

Palästina nt -s Palestine. **P~i-
nenser(in)** m -s,- (f -,-nen) Pal-
estinian. **p~inensisch** a Pales-
tinian

Palette f -,-n palette

Palme f -,-n palm[-tree]

Pampelmuse f -,-n grapefruit

paniert a (*Culin*) breaded

Panik f - panic; **in P~ geraten**
panic

Panne f -,-n breakdown; (*Reifen*-)
flat tyre; (*Mißgeschick*) mishap

Panorama nt -s panorama

Pantine f -,-n [wooden].clog

Pantoffel m -s,-n slipper; mule

Pantomime f -,-n mime

Panzer m -s,- armour; (*Mil*) tank;
(*Zool*) shell. **p~n** vt armour-
plate. **P~schrank** m safe

Papa /'papa, pa'pa:/ m -s,-s daddy

Papagei m -s & -en,-en parrot

Papier nt -s,-e paper. **P~korb**
m waste-paper basket. **P~wa-
ren** fpl stationery sg

Pappe f - cardboard

Pappel f -,-n poplar

pappig a (*fam*) sticky

Papp|karton m, **P~schachtel** f
cardboard box

Paprika m -s,-[s] [sweet] pepper;
(*Gewürz*) paprika

Papst m -[e]s,-̈e pope

päpstlich a papal

Parade f -,-n parade

Paradies nt -es,-e paradise

Paraffin nt -s paraffin

Paragraph m -en,-en section

parallel a & adv parallel. **P~e** f
-,-n parallel

Paranuß f Brazil nut

Parasit m -en,-en parasite

parat a ready

Parcours /par'ku:ɐ̯/ m -,- /-[s],-s/
(*Sport*) course

Parfüm nt -s,-e & -s perfume,
scent. **p~iert** a perfumed,
scented

parieren vi (*haben*) (*fam*) obey

Park m -s,-s park. **p~en** vt/i (*haben*) park. **P~en** nt -s parking;
'**P~en verboten**' 'no parking'

Parkett nt -[e]s,-e parquet floor;
(*Theat*) stalls pl

Park|haus nt multi-storey car
park. **P~lücke** f parking space.
P~platz m car park; (*für ein
Auto*) parking space; (*Autobahn*-)
lay-by. **P~uhr** f parking-meter.
P~verbot nt parking ban;
'**P~verbot**' 'no parking'

Parlament nt -[e]s,-e parliament.
p~arisch a parliamentary

Parodie f -,-n parody

Parole f -,-n slogan; (*Mil*) password

Partei f -,-en (*Pol, Jur*) party;
(*Miet*-) tenant; **für jdn P~ ergreifen** take s.o.'s part. **p~isch**
a biased. **p~los** a independent

Parterre /par'tɛr/ nt -s,-s ground
floor; (*Theat*) rear stalls pl

Partie f -,-n part; (*Tennis, Schach*)
game; (*Golf*) round; (*Comm*)
batch; **eine gute P~ machen**
marry well

Partikel nt -s,- particle

Partitur f -,-en (*Mus*) full score

Partizip nt -s,-ien /-ien/ participle

Partner|(in) m -s,- (f -,-nen)
partner. **P~schaft** f -,-en part-
nership. **P~stadt** f twin town

Party /'pa:ɐ̯ti/ f -,-s party

Parzelle f -,-n plot [of ground]

Paß *m* -sses,̈-sse passport; (*Geog*, *Sport*) pass

Passage /pa'saːʒə/ *f* -,-n passage; (*Einkaufs-*) shopping arcade

Passagier /pasa'ʒiːɐ̯/ *m* -s,-e passenger

Passant(in) *m* -en,-en (*f* -,-nen) passer-by

Passe *f* -,-n yoke

passen *vi* (*haben*) fit; (*geeignet sein*) be right (**für** for); (*Sport*) pass the ball; (*aufgeben*) pass; **p~ zu** go [well] with; (*übereinstimmen*) match; [**ich**] **passe** pass. **p~d** *a* suitable; (*angemessen*) appropriate; (*günstig*) convenient; (*übereinstimmend*) matching

passier|en *vt* pass; cross ⟨*Grenze*⟩; (*Culin*) rub through a sieve □ *vi* (*sein*) happen (**jdm** to s.o.); **es ist ein Unglück p~t** there has been an accident. **P~schein** *m* pass

Passiv *nt* -s,-e (*Gram*) passive

Paste *f* -,-n paste

Pastell *nt* -[e]s,-e pastel

Pastete *f* -,-n pie; (*Gänseleber-*) paté

pasteurisieren /pastøri'ziːrən/ *vt* pasteurize

Pastor *m* -s,-en /-'toːrən/ pastor

Pate *m* -n,-n godfather; (*fig*) sponsor; **P~n,-n** godparents. **P~nkind** *nt* godchild

Patent *nt* -[e]s,-e patent; (*Offiziers-*) commission. **p~** *a* (*fam*) clever. **p~ieren** *vt* patent

Pater *m* -s,- (*Relig*) Father

Pathologe *m* -n,-n pathologist. **p~isch** *a* pathological

Patience /pa'sjãːs/ *f* -,-n patience

Patient(in) /pa'tsjɛnt(ɪn)/ *m* -en,-en (*f* -,-nen) patient

Patin *f* -,-nen godmother

Patriot(in) *m* -en,-en (*f* -,-nen) patriot. **p~isch** *a* patriotic. **P~ismus** *m* - patriotism

Patrone *f* -,-n cartridge

Patrouille /pa'trʊljə/ *f* -,-n patrol

Patsch|e *f* in der **P~e sitzen** (*fam*) be in a jam. **p~naß** *a* (*fam*) soaking wet

Patz|er *m* -s,- (*fam*) slip. **p~ig** *a* (*fam*) insolent

Pauk|e *f* -,-n kettledrum; **auf die P~e hauen** (*fam*) have a good time; (*prahlen*) boast. **p~en** *vt*/*i* (*haben*) (*fam*) swot

pausbäckig *a* chubby-cheeked

pauschal *a* all-inclusive; (*einheitlich*) flat-rate; (*fig*) sweeping ⟨*Urteil*⟩; **p~e Summe** lump sum. **P~e** *f* -,-n lump sum. **P~reise** *f* package tour

Pause¹ *f* -,-n break; (*beim Sprechen*) pause; (*Theat*) interval; (*im Kino*) intermission; (*Mus*) rest; **P~ machen** have a break

Pause² *f* -,-n tracing. **p~n** *vt* trace

pausenlos *a* incessant

pausieren *vi* (*haben*) have a break; (*ausruhen*) rest

Pavian *m* -s,-e baboon

Pavillon /'pavɪljõ/ *m* -s,-s pavilion

Pazifik *m* -s Pacific [Ocean]. **p~sch** *a* Pacific

Pazifist *m* -en,-en pacifist

Pech *nt* -s pitch; (*Unglück*) bad luck; **P~ haben** be unlucky

Pedal *nt* -s,-e pedal

Pedant *m* -en,-en pedant

Pediküre *f* -,-n pedicure

Pegel *m* -s,- level; (*Gerät*) water-level indicator. **P~stand** *m* [water] level

peilen *vt* take a bearing on

peinlich *a* embarrassing, awkward; (*genau*) scrupulous; **es war mir sehr p~** I was very embarrassed

Peitsche *f* -,-n whip. **p~n** *vt* whip; (*fig*) lash □ *vi* (*sein*) lash (**an** + *acc* against). **P~nhieb** *m* lash

Pelikan *m* -s,-e pelican

Pelle *f* -,-n skin. **p~n** *vt* peel; shell ⟨*Ei*⟩; **sich p~n** peel

Pelz *m* -es,-e fur

Pendel

Pendel nt -s,- pendulum. **p ~ n** vi (haben) swing □ vi (sein) commute. **P ~ verkehr** m shuttle-service; (für Pendler) commuter traffic

Pendler m -s,- commuter

penetrant a penetrating; (fig) obtrusive

Penis m -,-se penis

Penne f -,-n (fam) school. **p ~ n** vi (haben) (fam) sleep

Pension /pã'zjoːn/ f -,-en pension; (Hotel) guest-house; **bei voller/halber P ~** with full/half board. **P ~ är(in)** m -s,-e (f -,-nen) pensioner. **P ~ at** nt -[e]s,-e boarding-school. **p ~ ieren** vt retire. **P ~ ierung** f - retirement

Pensum nt -s [allotted] work

Peperoni f -,- chilli

per prep (+ acc) by

Perfekt nt -s (Gram) perfect

Perfektion /-'tsjoːn/ f - perfection

perforiert a perforated

Pergament nt -[e]s,-e parchment. **P ~ papier** nt grease-proof paper

Period|e f -,-n period. **p ~ isch** a periodic

Perl|e f -,-n pearl; (Glas-, Holz-) bead; (Sekt-) bubble; (fam: Hilfe) treasure. **P ~ mutt** nt -s mother-of-pearl

Pers|ien /-jən/ nt -s Persia. **p ~ isch** a Persian

Person f -,-en person; (Theat) character; **für vier P ~ en** for four people

Personal nt -s personnel, staff. **P ~ ausweis** m identity card. **P ~ chef** m personnel manager. **P ~ ien** /-jən/ pl personal particulars. **P ~ mangel** m staff shortage

persönlich a personal □ adv personally, in person

Perücke f -,-n wig

pervers a [sexually] perverted. **P ~ ion** f -,-en perversion

Pfingstrose

Pessimis|mus m - pessimism. **P ~ t** m -en,-en pessimist. **p ~ tisch** a pessimistic

Pest f - plague

Petersilie /-jə/ f - parsley

Petroleum /-leom/ nt -s paraffin

petzen vi (haben) (fam) sneak

Pfad m -[e]s,-e path. **P ~ finder** m -s,- [Boy] Scout. **P ~ finderin** f -,-nen [Girl] Guide

Pfahl m -[e]s,-̈e stake, post

Pfalz (die) - the Palatinate

Pfand nt -[e]s,-̈er pledge; (beim Spiel) forfeit; (Flaschen-) deposit. **p ~ en** vt (Jur) seize. **P ~ er-spiel** nt game of forfeits

Pfandleiher m -s,- pawnbroker

Pfändung f -,-en (Jur) seizure

Pfanne f -,-n [frying-]pan. **P ~ kuchen** m pancake

Pfarr|er m -s,- vicar, parson; (katholischer) priest. **P ~ haus** nt vicarage

Pfau m -s,-en peacock

Pfeffer m -s pepper. **P ~ kuchen** m gingerbread. **P ~ minze** f - (Bot) peppermint. **P ~ n** vt pepper; (fam: schmeißen) chuck

Pfeif|e f -,-n whistle; (Tabak-, Orgel-) pipe. **p ~ en†** vt/i (haben) whistle; (als Signal) blow the whistle

Pfeil m -[e]s,-e arrow

Pfeiler m -s,- pillar; pier

Pfennig m -s,-e pfennig

Pferch m -s,-e [sheep] pen

Pferd nt -es,-e horse; **zu P ~ e** on horseback. **P ~ erennen** nt horse-race; (als Sport) [horse-] racing. **P ~ eschwanz** m horse's tail; (Frisur) pony-tail. **P ~ estall** m stable. **P ~ estärke** f horse-power

Pfiff m -[e]s,-e whistle; **P ~ haben** (fam) have style

Pfifferling m -s,-e chanterelle

pfiffig a smart

Pfingst|en nt -s Whitsun. **P ~ rose** f peony

Pfirsich *m* -s,-e peach
Pflanz|**e** *f* ~,-n plant. **p~en** *vt* plant. **P~enfett** *nt* vegetable fat
Pflaster *nt* -s,- pavement; (*Heft-*) plaster. **p~n** *vt* pave
Pflaume *f* ~,-n plum
Pflege *f* ~ care; (*Kranken-*) nursing; in **P~ nehmen** look after; (*Admin*) foster ⟨*Kind*⟩. **p~be-dürftig** *a* in need of care. **P~el-tern** *pl* foster-parents. **p~leicht** *a* easy-care. **p~n** *vt* look after, care for; nurse ⟨*Kranke*⟩; cultivate ⟨*Künste, Freundschaft*⟩. **P~r(in)** *m* -s,- (*f* -,-nen) nurse; (*Tier-*) keeper
Pflicht *f* -,-en duty; (*Sport*) compulsory exercise/routine. **p~-bewußt** *a* conscientious. **P~ge-fühl** *nt* sense of duty
pflücken *vt* pick
Pflug *m* -[e]s,-̈e plough
pflügen *vt/i* (*haben*) plough
Pforte *f* -,-n gate
Pförtner *m* -s,- porter
Pfosten *m* -s,- post
Pfote *f* -,-n paw
Pfropfen *m* -s,- stopper; (*Korken*) cork. **p~** *vt* graft (**auf**+*acc* on)
pfui *int* ugh
Pfund *nt* -[e]s,-e & - pound
Pfusch |**arbeit** *f* (*fam*) shoddy work. **p~en** *vi* (*haben*) (*fam*) botch one's work
Pfütze *f* -,-n puddle
Phantasie *f* -,-n imagination; **P~n** fantasies; (*Fieber-*) hallucinations. **p~los** *a* unimaginative. **p~ren** *vi* (*haben*) fantasize; (*im Fieber*) be delirious. **p~voll** *a* imaginative
phantastisch *a* fantastic
pharma|**zeutisch** *a* pharmaceutical. **P~zie** *f* ~ pharmacy
Phase *f* -,-n phase
Philolo|**ge** *m* -n,-n teacher/student of language and literature. **P~gie** *f* ~ [study of] language and literature

Philosoph *m* -en,-en philosopher. **P~ie** *f* -,-n philosophy
philosophisch *a* philosophical
Phobie *f* -,-n phobia
Phonet|**ik** *f* ~ phonetics *sg*. **p~isch** *a* phonetic
Phosphor *m* -s phosphorus
Phrase *f* -,-n empty phrase
Physik *f* - physics *sg*. **p~alisch** *a* physical
Physiologie *f* ~ physiology
physisch *a* physical
Pianist(in) *m* -en,-en (*f* -,-nen) pianist
Pickel *m* -s,- pimple, spot; (*Spitz-hacke*) pick. **p~ig** *a* spotty
Picknick *nt* -s,-s picnic
piep|**[s]en** *vi* (*haben*) ⟨*Vogel:*⟩ cheep; ⟨*Maus:*⟩ squeak; (*Techn*) bleep. **P~er** *m* -s,- bleeper
Pier *m* -s,-e [harbour] pier
Pietät /pie'tε:t/ *f* - reverence. **p~los** *a* irreverent
Pigment *nt* -[e]s,-e pigment. **P~ierung** *f* - pigmentation
Pik *nt* -s,-s (*Karten*) spades *pl*
pikant *a* piquant; (*gewagt*) racy
piken *vt* (*fam*) prick
pikiert *a* offended, hurt
piksen *vt* (*fam*) prick
Pilger(in) *m* -s,- (*f* -,-nen) pilgrim. **P~fahrt** *f* pilgrimage
Pille *f* -,-n pill
Pilot *m* -en,-en pilot
Pilz *m* -es,-e fungus; (*eßbarer*) mushroom
Pinguin *m* -s,-e penguin
Pinie /-ịə/ *f* -,-n stone-pine
pinkeln *vi* (*haben*) (*fam*) pee
Pinsel *m* -s,- [paint]brush
Pinzette *f* -,-n tweezers *pl*
Pionier *m* -s,-e (*Mil*) sapper; (*fig*) pioneer
Pirat *m* -en,-en pirate
Piste *f* -,-n (*Ski-*) run, piste; (*Renn-*) track; (*Aviat*) runway
Pistole *f* -,-n pistol
pitschnaß *a* (*fam*) soaking wet
pittoresk *a* picturesque

Pizza f -,-s pizza

Pkw /'pe:kave:/ m -s,-s car

plädieren vi (haben) plead (**für** for); **auf Freispruch p~** (Jur) ask for an acquittal

Plädoyer /plɛdoa'je:/ nt -s,-s (Jur) closing speech; (fig) plea

Plage f -,-n [hard] labour; (Mühe) trouble; (Belästigung) nuisance. **p~n** vt torment, plague; (bedrängen) pester; **sich p~n** struggle

Plakat nt -[e]s,-e poster

Plakette f -,-n badge

Plan m -[e]s,̈e plan

Plane f -,-n tarpaulin; (Boden-) groundsheet

planen vt/i (haben) plan

Planet m -en,-en planet

planieren vt level. **P~raupe** f bulldozer

Planke f -,-n plank

planlos a unsystematic. **p~mäßig** a systematic; ⟨Ankunft⟩ scheduled

Plansch|becken nt paddling pool. **p~en** vi (haben) splash about

Plantage /plan'ta:ʒə/ f -,-n plantation

Planung f - planning

Plapper|maul nt (fam) chatterbox. **p~n** vi (haben) chatter □vt talk ⟨Unsinn⟩

plärren vi (haben) bawl

Plasma nt -s plasma

Plastik[1] f -,-en sculpture

Plast|ik[2] nt -s plastic. **p~isch** a three-dimensional; (formbar) plastic; (anschaulich) graphic

Plateau /pla'to:/ nt -s,-s plateau

Platin nt -s platinum

platonisch a platonic

plätschern vi (haben) splash; ⟨Bach:⟩ babble □vi (sein) ⟨Bach:⟩ babble along

platt a & adv flat. **P~** nt -[s] (Lang) Low German

Plättbrett nt ironing-board

Platte f -,-n slab; (Druck-) plate; (Glas-) sheet; (Fliese) tile; (Tisch-) top; (Schall-) record, disc; (zum Servieren) [flat] dish, platter; **kalte P~** assorted cold meats and cheeses pl

Plätt|eisen nt iron. **p~en** vt/i (haben) iron

Plattenspieler m record-player

Platt|form f -,-en platform. **P~füße** mpl flat feet

Platz m -es,̈e place; (von Häusern umgeben) square; (Sitz-) seat; (Sport-) ground; (Fußball-) pitch; (Tennis-) court; (Golf-) course; (freier Raum) room, space; **P~ nehmen** take a seat; **P~ machen** make room. **P~anweiserin** f -,-nen usherette

Plätzchen nt -s,- spot; (Culin) biscuit

platzen vi (sein) burst; (auf-) split; (fam: scheitern) fall through; ⟨Verlobung:⟩ break off

Platz|karte f seat reservation ticket. **P~konzert** nt open-air concert. **P~mangel** m lack of space. **P~patrone** f blank. **P~verweis** m (Sport) sending off. **P~wunde** f laceration

Plauderei f -,-en chat

plaudern vi (haben) chat

plazieren vt place, put

pleite a (fam) **p~ sein** be broke; ⟨Firma:⟩ be bankrupt; **p~ gehen** go bankrupt. **P~** f -,-n (fam) bankruptcy; (Mißerfolg) flop

plissiert a [finely] pleated

Plombe f -,-n seal; (Zahn-) filling. **p~ieren** vt seal; fill ⟨Zahn⟩

plötzlich a sudden

plump a plump; clumsy

plumpsen vi (sein) (fam) fall

plündern vt/i (haben) loot

Plunderstück nt Danish pastry

Plural m -s,-e plural

plus adv, conj & prep (+ dat) plus. **P~** nt - surplus; (Gewinn) profit; (Vorteil) advantage, plus

Po *m* -s,-s (*fam*) bottom
Pöbel *m* -s mob, rabble
pochen *vi* (*haben*) knock; ⟨*Herz:*⟩ pound
Pocken *pl* smallpox *sg*
Podest *nt* -[e]s,-e rostrum
Podium *nt* -s,-ien /-jan/ platform
Poesie /poe'zi:/ *f* -,-n poetry
poetisch *a* poetic
Pointe /'põɛ:tə/ *f* -,-n point (*of a joke*)
Pokal *m* -s,-e goblet; (*Sport*) cup
pökeln *vt* (*Culin*) salt
Poker *nt* -s poker
Pol *m* -s,-e pole. **p~ar** *a* polar
Polarstern *m* pole-star
Pole *m* -n,-n Pole. **P~n** *nt* -s Poland
Police /po'li:sə/ *f* -,-n policy
Polier *m* -s,-e foreman
polieren *vt* polish
Polin *f* -,-nen Pole
Politesse *f* -,-n traffic warden
Politik *f* - politics *sg*; (*Vorgehen, Maßnahme*) policy
Politiker(in) *m* -s,- (*f* -,-nen) politician. **p~isch** *a* political
Politur *f* -,-en polish
Polizei *f* - police *pl*. **P~beamte(r)** *m* police officer. **p~lich** *a* police ... □ *adv* by the police; ⟨*sich anmelden*⟩ with the police. **P~streife** *f* police patrol. **P~wache** *f* police station
Polizist *m* -en,-en policeman. **P~in** *f* -,-nen policewoman
Pollen *m* -s pollen
polnisch *a* Polish
Polster *nt* -s,- pad; (*Kissen*) cushion; (*Möbel-*) upholstery. **P~möbel** *pl* upholstered furniture *sg*. **p~n** *vt* pad; upholster ⟨*Möbel*⟩. **P~ung** *f* - padding; upholstery
Polter|abend *m* wedding-eve party. **p~n** *vi* (*haben*) thump, bang
Polyäthylen *nt* -s polythene
Polyp *m* -en,-en polyp; (*sl: Polizist*) copper; **P~en** adenoids *pl*

Pommes frites /pɔm'fri:t/ *pl* chips; (*dünner*) French fries
Pomp *m* -s pomp
pompös *a* ostentatious
Pony[1] *nt* -s,-s pony
Pony[2] *m* -s,-s fringe
Pop *m* -[s] pop
Popo *m* -s,-s (*fam*) bottom
populär *a* popular
Porno|graphie *f* - pornography. **p~graphisch** *a* pornographic
Porree *m* -s leeks *pl*
Portemonnaie /pɔrtmɔ'ne:/ *nt* -s,-s purse
Portier /pɔr'tje:/ *m* -s,-s porter
Portion /-'tsjo:n/ *f* -,-en helping
Porto *nt* -s postage. **p~frei** *a* post free, post paid
Porträt /pɔr'trɛ:/ *nt* -s,-s portrait
Portugal *nt* -s Portugal
Portugies|e *m* -n,-n, **P~in** *f* -,-nen Portuguese. **p~isch** *a* Portuguese
Portwein *m* port
Porzellan *nt* -s china, porcelain
Posaune *f* -,-n trombone
Position /-'tsjo:n/ *f* -,-en position
positiv *a* positive. **P~** *nt* -s,-e (*Phot*) positive
Post *f* - post office; (*Briefe*) mail, post; **mit der P~** by post
postalisch *a* postal
Post|amt *nt* post office. **P~anweisung** *f* postal money order. **P~bote** *m* postman
Posten *m* -s,- post; (*Wache*) sentry; (*Waren-*) batch; (*Rechnungs-*) item, entry
Poster *nt* & *m* -s,- poster
Post|fach *nt* post-office *or* PO box. **P~karte** *f* postcard. **p~lagernd** *adv* poste restante. **P~leitzahl** *f* postcode. **P~scheckkonto** *nt* ≈ National Girobank account
postum *a* posthumous
post|wendend *adv* by return of post. **P~wertzeichen** *nt* stamp

Potenz *f* -,-en potency; (*Math & fig*) power

Pracht *f* - magnificence, splendour

prächtig *a* magnificent

prachtvoll *a* magnificent

Prädikat *nt* -[e]s,-e rating; (*Comm*) grade; (*Gram*) predicate

prägen *vt* stamp (**auf**+*acc* on); emboss ⟨*Leder*⟩; mint ⟨*Münze*⟩; coin ⟨*Wort*⟩, (*fig*) shape

prägnant *a* a succinct

prähistorisch *a* prehistoric

prahlen *vi* (*haben*) boast, brag (**mit** about)

Prakti|k *f* -,-en practice. **P~kant(in)** *m* -en,-en (*f* -,-nen) trainee

Prakti|kum *nt* -s,-ka practical training. **p~sch** *a* practical; (*nützlich*) handy; (*tatsächlich*) virtual; **p~scher Arzt** general practitioner □*adv* practically; virtually; (*in der Praxis*) in practice; **p~sch** arbeiten be practical; work. **p~zieren** *vt/i* (*haben*) practise; (*anwenden*) put into practice

Praline *f* -,-n chocolate

prall *a* bulging; (*dick*) plump; ⟨*Sonne*⟩ blazing □*adv* **p~** **gefüllt** full to bursting. **p~en** *vi* (*sein*) **p~** **auf** (+*acc*)/**gegen** collide with, hit; ⟨*Sonne:*⟩ blaze down on

Prämie /-jə/ *f* -,-n premium; (*Preis*) award

prämi[i]eren *vt* award a prize to

Pranger *m* -s,- pillory

Pranke *f* -,-n paw

Präparat *nt* -[e]s,-e preparation

präsentieren *vt* present

Präservativ *nt* -s,-e condom

Präsident(in) *m* -en,-en (*f* -,-nen) president. **P~schaft** *f* - presidency

Präsidium *nt* -s presidency; (*Gremium*) executive committee; (*Polizei-*) headquarters *pl*

prasseln *vi* (*haben*) ⟨*Regen:*⟩ beat down, ⟨*Feuer:*⟩ crackle

Praxis *f* -,-xen practice; (*Erfahrung*) practical experience; (*Arzt-*) surgery; **in der P~** in practice

Präzedenzfall *m* precedent

präzis[e] *a* precise

predig|en *vt/i* (*haben*) preach. **P~t** *f* -,-en sermon

Preis *m* -es,-e price; (*Belohnung*) prize. **P~ausschreiben** *nt* competition

Preiselbeere *f* (*Bot*) cowberry; (*Culin*) ≈ cranberry

preisen *vt* praise

preisgekrönt *a* award-winning. **p~günstig** *a* reasonably priced □*adv* at a reasonable price. **P~lage** *f* price range. **p~lich** *a* price ... □*adv* in price. **P~richter** *m* judge. **P~träger(in)** *m(f)* prize-winner. **p~wert** *a* reasonable; (*billig*) inexpensive

Prell|bock *m* buffers *pl*. **p~en** *vt* bounce; (*verletzen*) bruise. **P~ung** *f* -,-en bruise

Premiere /prə'mje:rə/ *f* -,-n première

Premierminister(in) /prə'mje:-/ *m(f)* Prime Minister

Presse *f* -,-n press. **p~n** *vt* press

Preßluftbohrer *m* pneumatic drill

Preuß|en *nt* -s Prussia. **p~isch** *a* Prussian

prickeln *vi* (*haben*) tingle

Priester *m* -s,- priest

prima *inv* *a* first-class, first-rate; (*fam: toll*) fantastic

primär *a* primary

Primel *f* -,-n primula

primitiv *a* primitive

Prinz *m* -en,-en prince. **P~essin** *f* -,-nen princess

Prinzip *nt* -s,-ien /-jən/ principle. **p~iell** *a* (*Frage*) of principle □*adv* on principle

Prise *f* -,-n **P~ Salz** pinch of salt

Prisma *nt* -s,-men prism

privat *a* private; (*persönlich*) personal. **P~adresse** *f* home address. **p~isieren** *vt* privatize

Privileg *nt* -[e]s,-ien /-jən/ privilege. **p~iert** *a* privileged

pro *prep* (+ *dat*) per. **Pro** *nt* - das Pro und Kontra the pros and cons *pl*

Probe *f* -,-n test, trial; (*Menge, Muster*) sample; (*Theat*) rehearsal; **auf die P~ stellen** put to the test. **p~n** *vt/i* (*haben*) (*Theat*) rehearse. **p~weise** *adv* on a trial basis

probieren *vt/i* (*haben*) try; (*kosten*) taste; (*proben*) rehearse

Problem *nt* -s,-e problem. **p~atisch** *a* problematic

Produkt *nt* -[e]s,-e product

Produktion /-'tsjo:n/ *f* -,-en production. **p~tiv** *a* productive

Produ|zent *m* -en,-en producer. **p~zieren** *vt* produce

professionell *a* professional

Professor *m* -s,-en /-'so:rən/ professor

Profi *m* -s,-s (*Sport*) professional

Profil *nt* -s,-e profile; (*Reifen-*) tread; (*fig*) image

Profit *m* -[e]s,-e profit

Programm *nt* -s,-e programme; (*Computer-*) program; (*TV*) channel; (*Comm: Sortiment*) range. **p~ieren** *vt/i* (*haben*) (*Computer*) program. **P~ierer(in)** *m* -s,- (*f* -,-nen) [computer] programmer

Projekt *nt* -[e]s,-e project

Projektor *m* -s,-en /-'to:rən/ projector

Prolet *m* -en,-en boor. **P~ariat** *nt* -[e]s proletariat

Prolog *m* -s,-e prologue

Promenade *f* -,-n promenade

Promille *pl* (*fam*) alcohol level *sg* in the blood; **zuviel P~ haben** (*fam*) be over the limit

prominen|t *a* prominent. **P~z** *f* - prominent figures *pl*

Promiskuität *f* - promiscuity

promovieren *vi* (*haben*) obtain one's doctorate

prompt *a* prompt

Pronomen *nt* -s,- pronoun

Propaganda *f* - propaganda; (*Reklame*) publicity

Propeller *m* -s,- propeller

Prophet *m* -en,-en prophet

prophezei|en *vt* prophesy. **P~ung** *f* -,-en prophecy

Proportion /-'tsjo:n/ *f* -,-en proportion

Prosa *f* - prose

prosit *int* cheers!

Prospekt *m* -[e]s,-e brochure; (*Comm*) prospectus

prost *int* cheers!

Prostituierte *f*-n,-n prostitute

Protest *m* -[e]s,-e protest

Protestant(in) *m* -en,-en (*f* -,-nen) (*Relig*) Protestant. **p~isch** *a* (*Relig*) Protestant

protestieren *vi* (*haben*) protest

Prothese *f* -,-n artificial limb; (*Zahn-*) denture

Protokoll *nt* -s,-e record; (*Sitzungs-*) minutes *pl*; (*diplomatisches*) protocol

protz|en *vi* (*haben*) show off (**mit etw** sth). **p~ig** *a* ostentatious

Proviant *m* -s provisions *pl*

Provinz *f* -,-en province

Provision *f* -,-en (*Comm*) commission

provisorisch *a* provisional

Provokation /-'tsjo:n/ *f* -,-en provocation

provozieren *vt* provoke

Prozedur *f* -,-en business

Prozent *nt* -[e]s,-e & - per cent. **P~satz** *m* percentage

Prozeß *m* -sses,-sse process; (*Jur*) lawsuit; (*Kriminal-*) trial

prüde *a* prudish

prüfen *vt* test/(*über-*) check (**auf**+*acc* for); audit (*Bücher*); (*Sch*) examine; **p~ender Blick**

searching look. **P~er** m -s,- inspector; (Buch-) auditor; (Sch) examiner. **P~ling** m -s,-e examination candidate. **P~ung** f -,-en examination; (Test) test; (Bücher-) audit; (fig) trial

Prügel m -s,- cudgel; **P~** pl thrashing sg, beating sg. **P~ei** f -,-en brawl, fight. **p~n** vt beat, thrash

Prunk m -[e]s magnificence, splendour

Psalm m -s,-en psalm

Pseudonym nt -s,-e pseudonym

pst int shush!

Psychi|ater m -s,- psychiatrist. **P~atrie** f - psychiatry. **p~atrisch** a psychiatric

psychisch a psychological

Psycho|analyse f psychoanalysis. **P~loge** m -n,-n psychologist. **P~logie** f - psychology. **p~logisch** a psychological

Pubertät f - puberty

Publikum nt -s public; (Zuhörer) audience; (Zuschauer) spectators

Pudding m -s blancmange; (im Wasserbad gekocht) pudding

Pudel m -s,- poodle

Puder m & (fam) nt -s,- powder. **P~n** vt powder. **P~zucker** m icing sugar

Puff m & nt -s,-s (sl) brothel

Puffer m -s,- (Rail) buffer; (Culin) pancake. **P~zone** f buffer zone

Pull|i m -s,-s jumper. **P~over** m -s,- jumper; (Herren-) pullover

Puls m -es pulse. **P~ader** f artery. **p~ieren** vi (haben) pulsate

Pult nt -[e]s,-e desk

Pulver nt -s,- powder. **p~ig** a powdery. **P~kaffee** m instant coffee

pummelig a (fam) chubby

Pumpe f -,-n pump. **p~n** vt/i (haben) pump; (fam: leihen) lend; [sich (dat)] etw **p~n** (fam: borgen) borrow sth

Pumps /pœmps/ pl court shoes

Punkt m -[e]s,-e dot; (Tex) spot; (Geom. Sport & fig) point; (Gram) full stop, period; **P~** **sechs Uhr** at six o'clock sharp

pünktlich a punctual. **P~keit** f punctuality

Pupille f -,-n (Anat) pupil

Puppe f -,-n doll; (Marionette) puppet; (Schaufenster-, Schneider-) dummy; (Zool) chrysalis

pur a pure; (fam: bloß) sheer

Püree nt -s,-s purée

purpurrot a crimson

Purzel|baum m (fam) somersault. **p~n** vi (sein) (fam) tumble

Puste f - (fam) breath. **p~n** vt/i (haben) (fam) blow

Pute f -,-n turkey

Putsch m -[e]s,-e coup

Putz m -es plaster; (Staat) finery. **p~en** vt clean; (Aust) dry-clean; **sich** (dat) **die Zähne/Nase p~en** clean one's teeth/blow one's nose. **P~frau** f cleaner, charwoman. **p~ig** a (fam) amusing, cute; (seltsam) odd

Puzzlespiel /'pazl-/ nt jigsaw

Pyramide f -,-n pyramid

Q

Quadrat nt -[e]s,-e square. **q~isch** a square

quaken vi (haben) quack; (Frosch-) croak

Quäker(in) m -s,- (f -,-nen) Quaker

Qual f -,-en torment

quälen vt torment; (foltern) torture; (bedrängen) pester; (leiden) suffer; (sich mühen) struggle

Quälerei f -,-en torture

Qualifi|kation /-'tsio:n/ f -,-en qualification. **q~ziert** a qualified; (fähig) competent; ⟨Arbeit⟩ skilled

Qualität f -,-en quality

Qualle f -,-n jellyfish

Qualm m -s [thick] smoke. **q~en** vi (haben) smoke

qualvoll a agonizing

Quantum nt -s,-ten quantity; (Anteil) share, quota

Quarantäne f - quarantine

Quark m -s quark, ≈ curd cheese

Quartett nt -[e]s,-e quartet

Quartier nt -s,-e accommodation; (Mil) quarters pl

Quarz m -es quartz

quasseln vi (haben) (fam) jabber

Quatsch m -[e]s (fam) nonsense, rubbish; **Q~ machen** (Unfug machen) fool around; (etw falsch machen) do a silly thing. **q~en** (fam) vi (haben) talk; ⟨Schlamm:⟩ squelch □ vt talk

Quecksilber nt mercury

Quelle f -,-n spring; (Fluß- & fig) source

quellen vi (sein) (fam) whine

quer adv across, crosswise; (schräg) diagonally

Quere f - der **Q~ nach** across, crosswise

quergestreift a horizontally striped. **Q~latte** f crossbar. **Q~schiff** nt transept. **Q~schnitt** m cross-section. **q~schnittsgelähmt** a paraplegic. **Q~straße** f side-street

quetschen vt squash; (drücken) squeeze; (zerdrücken) crush; (Culin) mash; **sich q~ in** (+ acc) squeeze into

Queue /køː/ nt -s,-s cue

quieken vi (haben) squeal; ⟨Maus:⟩ squeak

quietschen vi (haben) squeal; (Tür, Dielen:) creak

Quintett nt -[e]s,-e quintet

Quitte f -,-n quince

quittieren vt receipt ⟨Rechnung⟩; sign for ⟨Geldsumme, Sendung⟩; (reagieren auf) greet (mit with). **den Dienst q~** resign

Quittung f -,-en receipt

Quiz /kvɪs/ nt -,- quiz

Quote f -,-n proportion

R

Rabatt m -[e]s,-e discount

Rabatte f -,-n (Hort) border

Rabattmarke f trading stamp

Rabbiner m -s,- rabbi

Rabe m -n,-n raven

Rache f - revenge, vengeance

Rachen m -s, pharynx

rächen vt avenge; **sich r~** take revenge (**an** + dat on)

Rad nt -[e]s,-̈er wheel; (Fahr-) bicycle, (fam) bike

Radar m & nt -s radar

Radau m -s (fam) din, racket

radeln vi (sein) (fam) cycle

Rädelsführer m ringleader

radfahren† vi sep (sein) cycle. **R~er(in)** m(f) -s,- (f -,-nen) cyclist

radieren vt/i (haben) rub out; (Kunst) etch. **R~gummi** m eraser, rubber. **R~ung** f -,-en etching

Radieschen /-ˈdiːsçən/ nt -s,- radish

radikal a radical; drastic

Radio nt -s,-s radio

radioaktiv a radioactive. **R~ität** f - radioactivity

Radius m -,-ien /-jən/ radius

Radkappe f hub-cap. **R~ler** m -s,- cyclist; ⟨Getränk⟩ shandy

raffen vt grab; (kräuseln) gather; (kürzen) condense

Raffinade f - refined sugar. -**R~erie** f -,-n refinery. **R~esse** f -,-n refinement; (Schlauheit) cunning. **r~iert** a ingenious; (durchtrieben) crafty

ragen vi (haben) rise [up]

Rahm m -s (SGer) cream

rahmen vt frame. **R~** m -s,- frame; (fig) framework; (Grenze) limits pl; (einer Feier) setting

Rakete f -,-n rocket; (Mil) missile

Rallye /'rali/ nt -s,-s rally

rammen vt ram

Rampe f -,-n ramp; (Theat) front of the stage

Ramsch m -es junk

ran adv = **heran**

Rand m -[e]s,ˆ-er edge; (Teller-, Gläser-) rim; (Zier-) border, edging; (Buch-) margin; (Stadt-) outskirts pl; (Ring) ring

randalieren vi (haben) rampage

Rand|**bemerkung** f marginal note. **R~streifen** m (Auto) hard shoulder

Rang m -[e]s,ˆ-e rank; (Theat) tier; **erster/zweiter R~** (Theat) dress/upper circle; **ersten R~es** first-class

rangieren /raŋˈʒiːrən/ vt shunt □vi (haben) rank (vor + dat before)

Rangordnung f order of importance; (Hierarchie) hierarchy

Ranke f -,-n tendril; (Trieb) shoot

ranken (sich) vr (Bot) trail; (in die Höhe) climb

Ranzen m -s,- (Sch) satchel

ranzig a rancid

Rappe m -n,-n black horse

Raps m -es (Bot) rape

rar a rare; **er macht sich rar** (fam) we don't see much of him. **R~ität** f -,-en rarity

rasant a fast; (schick) stylish

rasch a quick

rascheln vi (haben) rustle

Rasen m -s,- lawn

rasen vi (sein) tear [along]; (Puls:) race; (Zeit:) fly; **gegen eine Mauer r~** career into a wall □vi (haben) rave; (Sturm:) rage. **r~d** a furious; (tobend) raving; (Sturm, Durst) raging; (Schmerz) excruciating; (Beifall) tumultuous

Rasenmähe m lawn-mower

Rasier|**apparat** m razor. **r~en** vt shave; **sich r~en** shave. **R~wasser** nt aftershave [lotion]

Raspel f -,-n rasp; (Culin) grater. **r~n** vt grate

Rasse f -,-n race. **R~hund** m pedigree dog

Rassel f -,-n rattle. **r~n** vi (haben) rattle; (Schlüssel:) jangle; (Kette:) clank

Rassendiskriminierung f racial discrimination

rassisch a racial

Rassis|**mus** m - racism. **r~tisch** a racist

Rast f -,-en rest. **r~en** vi (haben) rest. **R~platz** m picnic area. **R~stätte** f motorway restaurant [and services]

Rasur f -,-en shave

Rat m -[e]s [piece of] advice; **zu Rat[e] ziehen** consult

Rate f -,-n instalment

raten† vt guess; (empfehlen) advise □vi (haben) guess; **jdm r~** advise s.o.

Ratenzahlung f payment by instalments

Rat|**geber** m -s,- adviser; (Buch) guide. **R~haus** nt town hall

ratifizier|**en** vt ratify. **R~ung** f -,-en ratification

Ration /raˈtsi̯oːn/ f -,-en ration. **r~ell** a efficient. **r~ieren** vt ration

rat|**los** a helpless; **r~los sein** not know what to do. **r~sam** pred a advisable; (klug) prudent. **R~schlag** m piece of advice

Rätsel nt -s,- riddle; (Kreuzwort-) puzzle; (Geheimnis) mystery. **r~haft** a puzzling, mysterious. **r~n** vi (haben) puzzle

Ratte f -,-n rat

Raub m -[e]s robbery; (Menschen-) abduction; (Beute) loot, booty. **r~en** vt steal; abduct (Menschen)

Räuber m -s,- robber

Raub|mord m robbery with murder. **R~tier** nt predator. **R~vögel** m bird of prey

Rauch m -[e]s smoke. **r~en** vt/i (haben) smoke. **R~en** nt -s smoking; 'R~en verboten' 'no smoking'. **R~er** m -s,- smoker

Räucher|lachs m smoked salmon. **r~n** vt (Culin) smoke

rauf adv = **herauf, hinauf**

raufen vt pull; ⟨□r/i (haben) [sich] r~en fight. **R~erei** f -,-en fight

rauh a rough; (unfreundlich) gruff; ⟨Klima⟩ harsh; (heiser) husky; ⟨Hals⟩ sore

Rauhreif m hoar-frost

Raum m -[e]s, Räume room; (Gebiet) area; (Welt-) space

räumen vt clear; vacate ⟨Wohnung⟩; evacuate ⟨Gebäude, (Mil) Stellung⟩; (bringen) put (in/auf + acc into/on); (holen) get (aus out of)

Raum|fahrer m astronaut. **R~fahrt** f space travel. **R~inhalt** m volume

räumlich a spatial

Raumpflegerin f cleaner

Räumung f - (s. räumen) clearing; vacating; evacuation. **R~sverkauf** m clearance/closing-down sale

Raupe f -,-n caterpillar

raus adv = **heraus, hinaus**

Rausch m -[e]s, Räusche intoxication; (fig) exhilaration; **einen R~ haben** be drunk

rauschen vi (haben) ⟨Wasser, Wind⟩ rush; ⟨Bäume, Blätter⟩ rustle □vi (sein) rush [along]

Rauschgift nt [narcotic] drug; (coll) drugs pl. **R~süchtige[r]** m/f drug addict

räuspern (sich) vr clear one's throat

rausschmeißen† vt sep (fam) throw out; (entlassen) sack

Raute f -,-n diamond

Razzia f -,-ien [-jan] [police] raid

Reagenzglas nt test-tube

reagieren vi (haben) react (auf + acc to)

Reaktion /-'tsjo:n/ f -,-en reaction. **r~är** a reactionary

Reaktor m -s,-en /-'to:rən/ reactor

Realis|mus m - realism. **r~tisch** a realistic

Realität f -,-en reality

Realschule f ≈ secondary modern school

Rebe f -,-n vine

Rebell m -en,-en rebel. **r~ieren** vi (haben) rebel. **R~ion** f -,-en rebellion

rebellisch a rebellious

Rebhuhn nt partridge

Rebstock m vine

Rechen m -s,- rake

Rechen|aufgabe f arithmetical problem; (Sch) sum. **R~maschine** f calculator

recherchieren /reʃɛr'ʃi:rən/ vt/i (haben) investigate; (Journ) research

rechnen vi (haben) do arithmetic; (schätzen) reckon; (zählen) count (zu among; auf + acc on); **r~ mit** reckon with; (erwarten) expect; **gut r~ können** be good at figures. **R~** nt -s arithmetic

Rechner m -s,- calculator; (Computer) computer

Rechnung f -,-en bill; (Comm) invoice; (Berechnung) calculation; **R~ führen über** (+ acc) keep account of. **R~sjahr** nt financial year. **R~sprüfer** m auditor

Recht nt -[e]s,-e law; (Berechtigung) right (auf + acc to); **im R~ sein** be in the right; **mit od zu R~** rightly

recht a right; (wirklich) real; **es jdm r~ machen** please s.o.; **jdm r~ sein** be all right with s.o. □ **r~ haben** be right; **r~ bekommen** be proved right; **jdm r~**

geben agree with s.o. □*adv* correctly; (*ziemlich*) quite; (*sehr*) very

Recht|e *f-n,-[n]* right side; (*Hand*) right hand; (*Boxen*) right; **die R~e** (*Pol*) the right; **zu meiner R~en** on my right. **r~e(r,s)** *a* right; (*Pol*) right-wing; **r~e Masche** plain stitch. **R~e(r)** *m/f* der/die **R~e** the right man/woman. **R~e(s)** *nt* das **R~e** the right thing; **etwas R~es lernen** learn something useful; **nach dem R~en sehen** see that everything is all right

Rechteck *nt* -[e]s,-e rectangle. **r~ig** *a* rectangular

rechtfertigen *vt* justify; **sich r~** justify oneself

recht|lich *a* legal. **r~mäßig** *a* legitimate

rechts *adv* on the right; (*bei Stoff*) on the right side; **von/nach r~** from/to the right; **zwei r~, zwei links stricken** knit two, purl two. **R~anwalt** *m*, **R~anwältin** *f* lawyer

rechtschaffen *a* upright; (*ehrlich*) honest

Rechtschreibung *f-* spelling

Rechts|händer(in) *m* -s,- (*f* -,-nen) right-hander. **r~händig** *a & adv* right-handed. **r~kräftig** *a* legal. **R~streit** *m* law suit. **r~verkehr** *m* driving on the right. **r~widrig** *a* illegal. **R~wissenschaft** *f* jurisprudence

rechtzeitig *a & adv* in time

Reck *nt* -[e]s,-e horizontal bar

recken *vt* stretch

Redakteur /redak'tø:ɐ/ *m* -s,-e editor; (*Radio, TV*) producer

Redaktion /-'tsio:n/ *f* -,-en editing; (*Radio, TV*) production; (*Abteilung*) editorial/production department. **r~ell** *a* editorial

Rede *f-,-n* speech; **zur R~ stellen** demand an explanation from;

nicht der R~ wert not worth mentioning

reden *vi* (*haben*) talk (**von** about; **mit** to); (*eine Rede halten*) speak □*vt* talk; speak ⟨*Wahrheit*⟩. **R~sart** *f* saying

Redewendung *f* idiom

redigieren *vt* edit

Redner *m* -s,- speaker

reduzieren *vt* reduce

Reeder *m* -s,- shipowner. **R~ei** *f* -,-en shipping company

Refer|at *nt* -[e]s,-e report; (*Abhandlung*) paper. **R~ent(in)** *m* -en,-en (*f* -,-nen) speaker; (*Sachbearbeiter*) expert. **R~enz** *f* -,-en reference

Reflex *m* -es,-e reflex; (*Widerschein*) reflection. **R~ion** *f* -,-en reflection. **r~iv** *a* reflexive

Reform *f* -,-en reform. **R~ation** /-'tsio:n/ *f* (*Relig*) Reformation

Reform|haus *nt* health-food shop. **r~ieren** *vt* reform

Refrain /ra'frɛ̃:/ *m* -s,-s refrain

Regal *nt* -s,-e [set of] shelves *pl*

Regatta *f* -,-ten regatta

rege *a* active; (*lebhaft*) lively; (*geistig*) alert; ⟨*Handel*⟩ brisk

Regel *f* -,-n rule; (*Monats-*) period. **r~mäßig** *a* regular. **r~n** *vt* regulate; direct ⟨*Verkehr*⟩; (*erledigen*) settle. **r~recht** *a* real, proper □*adv* really. **R~ung** *f* -,-en regulation; settlement

regen *vt* move; **sich r~** move

Regen *m* -s,- rain. **R~bogen** *m* rainbow. **R~bogenhaut** *f* iris

Regener|ation /-'tsio:n/ *f* - regeneration. **r~ieren** *vt* regenerate

Regen|mantel *m* raincoat. **R~schirm** *m* umbrella. **R~wetter** *nt* wet weather. **R~wurm** *m* earthworm

Regie /re'ʒi:/ *f* - direction; **R~ führen** direct

regier|en *vt/i* (*haben*) govern, rule; ⟨*Monarch:*⟩ reign [over]; (*Gram*) take. **r~end** *a* ruling:

reigning. **R~ung** *f* -,-en government; (*Herrschaft*) rule; (*eines Monarchen*) reign

Regiment *nt* -[e]s,-er regiment

Region *f* -,-en region. **r~al** *a* regional

Regisseur /reʒɪˈsøːɐ̯/ *m* -s,-e director

Register *nt* -s,- register; (*Inhaltsverzeichnis*) index; (*Orgel*) stop

Regler *m* -s,- regulator

reglos *a* & *adv* motionless

regnen *vi* (haben) rain; **es r~et** it is raining. **r~erisch** *a* rainy

regulär *a* normal; (*rechtmäßig*) legitimate. **r~ieren** *vt* regulate

Regung *f* -,-en movement; (*Gefühls*) emotion

Reh *nt* -[e]s,-e roe-deer; (*Culin*) venison

reiben† *vt* rub; (*Culin*) grate □ *vi* (haben) rub. **R~ung** *f* -,- friction. **r~ungslos** *a* (*fig*) smooth

reich *a* rich (**an** + *dat* in)

Reich *nt* -[e]s,-e empire; (*König-*) kingdom; (*Bereich*) realm

Reiche(r) *m/f* rich man/woman; **die R~en** the rich *pl*

reichen *vt* hand; (*anbieten*) offer □ *vi* (haben) be enough; **r~ bis zu** reach [up to]; (*sich erstrecken*) extend to; **mit dem Geld r~** have enough money

reichhaltig *a* extensive, large; (*Mahlzeit*) substantial. **r~lich** *a* ample; (*Vorrat*) abundant. **R~tum** *m* -s,-tümer wealth (**an** + *dat* of). **R~weite** *f* reach; (*Techn, Mil*) range

Reif¹ *m* -[e]s [hoar-]frost

reif² *a* ripe; (*fig*) mature; **r~ für** ready for. **R~en** *vi* (sein) ripen; (*Wein, Käse & fig*) mature

Reifen *m* -s,- hoop; (*Arm-*) bangle; (*Auto-*) tyre. **R~druck** *m* tyre pressure. **R~panne** *f* puncture

Reifeprüfung *f* ≈ A levels *pl*

reiflich *a* careful

Reihe *f* -,-n row; (*Anzahl*) series; **der R~ nach** in turn; **wer ist an der** *od* **kommt an die R~?** whose turn is it? **r~n** (sich) *vr* **sich r~n an** (+ *acc*) follow. **R~nfolge** *f* order. **R~nhaus** *nt* terraced house. **r~nweise** *adv* in rows; (*fam*) in large numbers

Reiher *m* -s,- heron

Reim *m* -[e]s,-e rhyme. **r~en** *vt* rhyme; **sich r~en** rhyme

rein¹ *a* pure; (*sauber*) clean; (*Unsinn*) sheer; **ins r~e schreiben** make a fair copy of; **ins r~e bringen** (*fig*) sort out

rein² *adv* = **herein, hinein**

Reineclaude /rɛːnəˈkloːdə/ *f* -,-n greengage

Reingewinn *m* net profit. **R~heit** *f* - purity

reinigen *vt* clean; (*chemisch*) dry-clean. **R~ung** *f* -,-en cleaning; (*chemische*) dry-cleaning; (*Geschäft*) dry cleaner's

reinlegen *vt* *sep* put in; (*fam*) dupe; (*betrügen*) take for a ride

reinlich *a* clean. **R~keit** *f* - cleanliness

Reis *m* -es rice

Reise *f* -,-n journey; (*See-*) voyage; (*Geschäfts-*) trip. **R~andenken** *nt* souvenir. **R~büro** *nt* travel agency. **R~bus** *m* coach. **R~führer** *m* tourist guide; (*Buch*) guide. **R~leiter(in)** *m(f)* courier. **r~n** *vi* (sein) travel. **R~nde(r)** *m/f* traveller. **R~paß** *m* passport. **R~scheck** *m* traveller's cheque. **R~veranstalter** *m* -s,- tour operator. **R~ziel** *nt* destination

Reißaus *m* **R~ nehmen** (*fam*) run away

Reißbrett *nt* drawing-board

reißen† *vt* tear; (*weg-*) snatch; (*töten*) kill; **Witze r~** crack jokes; **an sich** (*acc*) **r~** snatch; seize (*Macht*); **sich r~ um** (*fam*) fight for; **hin und her gerissen**

sein (fig) be torn □ vi (sein) tear; ⟨Seil, Faden:⟩ break □ vi (haben) **r~ an** (+dat) pull at. **r~d** a raging; ⟨Tier:⟩ ferocious; ⟨Schmerz:⟩ violent

Reißer m -s,- (fam) thriller; (Erfolg) big hit

Reiß|**verschluß** m zip (fastener). **R~wolf** m shredder. **R~zwecke** f -,-n drawing-pin

reit|**en†** vt/i (sein) ride. **R~er(in)** m -s,- (f -,-nen) rider. **R~hose** f riding breeches pl. **R~pferd** nt saddle-horse. **R~weg** m bridle-path

Reiz m -es,-e stimulus; (Anziehungskraft) attraction, appeal; (Charme) charm. **r~bar** a irritable. **R~barkeit** f -irritability. **r~en** vt provoke; (Med) irritate; (interessieren, locken) appeal to, attract; arouse ⟨Neugier⟩; (beim Kartenspiel) bid. **R~ung** f -,-en (Med) irritation. **r~voll** a attractive

rekeln (sich) vr stretch

Reklamation /-'tsjo:n/ f -,-en (Comm) complaint

Reklame f -,-n advertising, publicity; (Anzeige) advertisement; (TV, Radio) commercial; **R~e machen** advertise (für etw sth). **r~ieren** vt complain about; (fordern) claim □ vi (haben) complain

Rekord m -[e]s,-e record

Rekrut m -en,-en recruit

Rek|**tor** m -s,-en /-'to:ran/ (Sch) head[master]; (Univ) vice-chancellor. **R~torin** f -,-nen head[mistress]; vice-chancellor

Relais /rə'lɛ:/ nt -,- /-s,-s/ (Electr) relay

relativ a relative

Religi|**on** f -,-en religion; (Sch) religious education. **r~ös** a religious

Reling f -,-s (Naut) rail

Reliquie /re'li:kvjə/ f -,-n relic

rempeln vt jostle; (stoßen) push

Reneklode f -,-n greengage

Renn|**bahn** f race-track; (Pferde-) racecourse. **R~boot** nt speed-boat. **r~en†** vt/i (sein) run; **um die Wette r~en** have a race. **R~en** nt -s,- race. **R~sport** m racing. **R~wagen** m racing car

renommiert a renowned

renovier|**en** vt renovate; redecorate ⟨Zimmer⟩. **R~ung** f -renovation; redecoration

rentabel a profitable

Rente f -,-n pension; **in R~ gehen** (fam) retire. **R~nversicherung** f pension scheme

Rentier nt reindeer

rentieren (sich) vr be profitable; (sich lohnen) be worth while

Rentner(in) m -s,- (f -,-nen) [old-age] pensioner

Reparatur f -,-en repair. **R~werkstatt** f repair work-shop; (Auto) garage

reparieren vt repair, mend

repatriieren vt repatriate

Reportage /-'ta:ʒə/ f -,-n report

Reporter(in) m -s,- (f -,-nen) reporter

repräsent|**ativ** a representative (für of); (eindrucksvoll) imposing. **r~ieren** vt represent □ vi (haben) perform official duties

Reproduktion /-'tsjo:n/ f -,-en reproduction

Reptil nt -s,-ien /-jən/ reptile

Republik f -,-en republic. **r~anisch** a republican

Requisiten pl (Theat) properties, (fam) props

Reserve f -,-n reserve; (Mil, Sport) reserves pl. **R~rad** nt spare wheel

reservier|**en** vt reserve; **r~en lassen** book. **r~t** a reserved. **R~ung** f -,-en reservation

Reservoir /rezɛr'vɔa:ɐ̯/ nt -s,-s reservoir

Residenz f -,-en residence

Resign|**ation** /ˈtsjoːn/ *f* - resignation. **r ~ iert** *a* resigned

resolut *a* resolute

Resonanz *f* -,-en resonance

Respekt /-sp-, -ʃp-/ *m* -[e]s respect (**vor**+*dat* for). **r ~ ieren** *vt* respect

respektlos *a* disrespectful

Ressort /rɛˈsoːɐ/ *nt* -s,-s department

Rest *m* -[e]s,-e remainder, rest; **R ~ e** remains; (*Stoff*) leftovers

Restaurant /rɛstoˈrãː/ *nt* -s,-s restaurant

Restaur|**ation** /rɛstaʊraˈtsjoːn/ *f* - restoration. **r ~ ieren** *vt* restore

Rest|**betrag** *m* balance. **r ~ lich** *a* remaining. **r ~ los** *a* utter

Resultat *nt* -[e]s,-e result

rett|**en** *vt* save (**vor**+*dat* from); (*aus Gefahr befreien*) rescue. **R ~ er** *m* -s,- rescuer; (*fig*) saviour

Rettich *m* -s,-e white radish

Rettung *f* -,-en rescue; (*fig*) salvation; **jds letzte R ~** s.o.'s last hope. **R ~ sboot** *nt* lifeboat. **R ~ sdienst** *m* rescue service. **R ~ sgürtel** *m* lifebelt. **r ~ slos** *adv* hopelessly. **R ~ sring** *m* lifebelt. **R ~ swagen** *m* ambulance

retuschieren *vt* (*Phot*) retouch

Reue *f* - remorse; (*Relig*) repentance

Revanch|**e** /reˈvãːʃə/ *f* -,-n revenge; **R ~ e fordern** (*Sport*) ask for a return match. **r ~ ieren** (**sich**) *vr* take revenge; (*sich erkenntlich zeigen*) reciprocate (**mit** with)

Revers /reˈvɛːɐ/ *nt* -,- /-[s],-s/ lapel

Revier *nt* -s,-e district; (*Zool & fig*) territory; (*Polizei-*) [police] station

Revision *f* -,-en revision; (*Prüfung*) check; (*Jur*) appeal

Revolution /-ˈtsjoːn/ *f* -,-en revolution. **r ~ är** *a* revolutionary

Revolver *m* -s,- revolver

rezen|**sieren** *vt* review. **R ~ sion** *f* -,-en review

Rezept *nt* -[e]s,-e prescription; (*Culin*) recipe

Rezession *f* -,-en recession

R-Gespräch *nt* reverse-charge call

Rhabarber *m* -s rhubarb

Rhapsodie *f* -,-n rhapsody

Rhein *m* -s Rhine. **R ~ land** *nt* -s Rhineland. **R ~ wein** *m* hock

Rhetorik *f* - rhetoric

Rheum|**a** *nt* -s rheumatism. **r ~ a-tisch** *a* rheumatic. **R ~ atismus** *m* - rheumatism

Rhinozeros *nt* - [ses],-se rhinoceros

rhyth|**misch** /ˈrʏt-/ *a* rhythmic[al]. **R ~ mus** *m* -,-men rhythm

richten *vt* direct (**auf**+*acc* at); address (*Frage*) (**an**+*acc* to); aim (*Waffe*) (**auf**+*acc* at); (*einstellen*) set; (*vorbereiten*) prepare; (*reparieren*) mend; **in die Höhe r ~** raise [up]; **sich r ~** be directed (**auf** + *acc* at; **gegen** against); (*Blick:*) turn (**auf**+*acc* on); **sich r ~ nach** comply with (*Vorschrift*); fit in with (*jds Plänen*); (*abhängen*) depend on

Richter *m* -s,- judge

richtig *a* right, correct; (*wirklich, echt*) real; **das R ~ e** the right thing □*adv* correctly; really; **die Uhr geht r ~** the clock is right

Richtlinien *fpl* guidelines

Richtung *f* -,-en direction

riechen *vt*/*i* (*haben*) smell (**nach** of; **an etw** *dat* sth)

Riegel *m* -s,- bolt; (*Seife*) bar

Riemen *m* -s,- strap; (*Ruder*) oar

Riese *m* -n,-n giant

rieseln *vi* (*sein*) trickle; (*Schnee:*) fall lightly

riesig *a* huge; (*gewaltig*) enormous □*adv* (*fam*) terribly

Riff *nt* -[e]s,-e reef

Rille f -,-n groove

Rind nt -es,-er ox; ⟨Kuh⟩ cow; ⟨Stier⟩ bull; ⟨R~fleisch⟩ beef; **R~er** cattle pl

Rinde f -,-n bark; ⟨Käse-⟩ rind; ⟨Brot-⟩ crust

Rinderbraten m roast beef

Rindfleisch nt beef

Ring m -[e]s,-e ring

ringeln (sich) vr curl

ring|en† vi (haben) wrestle; ⟨fig⟩ struggle (**um/nach** for) □vt wring ⟨Hände⟩. **R~er** m -s,- wrestler. **R~kampf** m wrestling match; ⟨als Sport⟩ wrestling

Rinn|e f -,-n channel; ⟨Dach-⟩ gutter. **r~en†** vi (sein) run; ⟨Sand:⟩ trickle. **R~stein** m gutter

Rippe f -,-n rib. **R~nfellentzündung** f pleurisy

Risiko nt -s,-s & -ken risk

risk|ant a risky. **r~ieren** vt risk

Riß m -sses,-sse tear; ⟨Mauer-⟩ crack; ⟨fig⟩ rift

rissig a cracked; ⟨Haut⟩ chapped

Rist m -[e]s,-e instep

Ritt m -[e]s,-e ride

Ritter m -s,- knight

rittlings adv astride

Ritual nt -s,-e ritual

Ritz m -es,-e scratch. **R~e** f -,-n crack; ⟨Fels-⟩ cleft; ⟨zwischen Betten⟩ gap. **r~en** vt scratch

Rival|e m -n,-n, **R~in** f -,-nen rival. **R~ität** f -,-en rivalry

Robbe f -,-n seal. **R~n** vi (sein) crawl

Robe f -,-n gown; ⟨Talar⟩ robe

Roboter m -s,- robot

robust a robust

Rochen m -s, ⟨Zool⟩ ray

Rock m -[e]s,-̈e skirt

rodel|n vi (sein/haben) toboggan. **R~schlitten** m toboggan

roden vt clear ⟨Land⟩; grub up ⟨Stumpf⟩

Rogen m -s,- [hard] roe

Roggen m -s rye

roh a rough; ⟨ungekocht⟩ raw; ⟨Holz⟩ bare; ⟨brutal⟩ brutal. **R~bau** m -[e]s,-ten shell. **R~kost** f raw [vegetarian] food. **R~ling** m -s,-e brute. **R~öl** nt crude oil

Rohr nt -[e]s,-e pipe; ⟨Geschütz-⟩ barrel; ⟨Bot⟩ reed; ⟨Zucker-⟩ cane

Röhre f -,-n tube; ⟨Radio-⟩ valve; ⟨Back-⟩ oven

Rohstoff m raw material

Rokoko nt -s rococo

Rolladen m roller shutter

Rollbahn f taxiway; ⟨Start-/Landebahn⟩ runway

Rolle f -,-n roll; ⟨Garn-⟩ reel; ⟨Draht-⟩ coil; ⟨Techn⟩ roller; ⟨Lauf-⟩ castor; ⟨Theat⟩ part, role; **das spielt keine R~** ⟨fig⟩ that doesn't matter. **r~n** vt roll; ⟨auf-⟩ roll up; **sich r~n** roll □vi (sein) roll. **R~r** m -s,- scooter

Roll|feld nt airfield. **R~kragen** m polo-neck. **R~mops** m rollmop[s] sg

Rollo nt -s,-s [roller] blind

Roll|schuh m roller-skate; **R~schuh laufen** roller-skate. **R~splitt** m -s loose chippings pl. **R~stuhl** m wheelchair. **R~treppe** f escalator

Rom nt -s Rome

Roman m -s,-e novel. **r~isch** a Romanesque; ⟨Sprache⟩ Romance

Romant|ik f - romanticism. **r~isch** a romantic

Röm|er(in) m -s,- (f -,-nen) Roman. **r~isch** a Roman

Rommé ['rɔme:/ nt -s rummy

röntgen vt X-ray. **R~aufnahme** f, **R~bild** nt X-ray. **R~strahlen** mpl X-rays

rosa inv a, **R~** nt -[s],- pink

Rose f -,-n rose. **R~nkohl** m [Brussels] sprouts pl. **R~nkranz** m ⟨Relig⟩ rosary

Rosette f -,-n rosette

Rosine f -,-n raisin

Rosmarin *m* -s rosemary

Rost[1] *m* -[e]s,-e grating; (*Kamin-*) grate; (*Brat-*) grill

Rost[2] *m* -[e]s rust. **r~en** *vi* (*haben*) rust

rösten *vt* roast; toast (*Brot*)

rostfrei *a* stainless

rostig *a* rusty

rot *a*, **Rot** *nt* -s,- red

Röteln *pl* German measles *sg*

röten *vt* redden; **sich r~** turn red

rothaarig *a* red-haired

rotieren *vi* (*haben*) rotate

Rot|kehlchen *nt* -s,- robin. **R~kohl** *m* red cabbage

rötlich *a* reddish

Rou|lade /ru'la:də/ *f* -,-n beef olive. **R~leau** /-'lo:/ *nt* -s,-s (*roller*) blind

Routine /ru'ti:nə/ *f* -,-n routine; (*Erfahrung*) experience. **r~emäßig** *a* routine ... *adv* routinely. **r~iert** *a* experienced

Rowdy /'raudi/ *m* -s,-s hooligan

Rübe *f* -,-n beet; **rote R~** beetroot

Rubin *m* -s,-e ruby

Ruck *m* -[e]s,-e jerk

ruckartig *a* jerky

rück|bezüglich *a* (*Gram*) reflexive. **R~blende** *f* flashback. **r~blickend** *adv* in retrospect. **r~datieren** *vt* (*inf & pp only*) backdate

Rücken *m* -s,- back; (*Buch-*) spine; (*Berg-*) ridge. **R~lehne** *f* back. **R~mark** *nt* spinal cord. **R~schwimmen** *nt* backstroke. **R~wind** *m* following wind; (*Aviat*) tail wind

rückerstatten *vt* (*inf & pp only*) refund

Rückfahr|karte *f* return ticket. **R~t** *f* return journey

Rück|fall *m* relapse. **R~flug** *m* return flight. **R~frage** *f* [further] query. **R~fragen** *vi* (*haben*) (*inf & pp only*) check (*bei* with). **R~gabe** *f* return. **r~gängig** *a* **r~gängig machen** cancel;

break off (*Verlobung*). **R~grat** *nt* -[e]s,-e spine, backbone. **R~hand** *f* backhand. **R~kehr** *f* return. **R~lagen** *fpl* reserves. **R~licht** *nt* rear-light. **R~reise** *f* return journey

Rucksack *m* rucksack

Rück|schau *f* review. **R~schlag** *m* (*Sport*) return; (*fig*) set-back. **R~seite** *f* back; (*einer Münze*) reverse

Rücksicht *f* -,-en consideration. **R~nahme** *f* - consideration. **r~slos** *a* inconsiderate; (*schonungslos*) ruthless. **r~svoll** *a* considerate

Rück|sitz *m* back seat; (*Sozius*) pillion. **R~spiegel** *m* rear-view mirror. **R~spiel** *nt* return match. **R~stau** *m* (*Auto*) tailback. **R~strahler** *m* -s,- reflector. **R~tritt** *m* resignation; (*Fahrrad*) back pedalling. **r~vergüten** *vt* (*inf & pp only*) refund

rückwärt|ig *a* back ..., rear ... **r~s** *adv* backwards. **R~sgang** *m* reverse [gear]

Rück|weg *m* way back. **r~wirkend** *a* retrospective. **R~wirkung** *f* retrospective force; **mit R~wirkung vom** backdated to. **R~zahlung** *f* repayment

Rüde *m* -n,-n [male] dog

Rudel *nt* -s,- herd; (*Wolfs-*) pack; (*Löwen-*) pride

Ruder *nt* -s,- oar; (*Steuer-*) rudder; **am R~** (*Naut & fig*) at the helm. **R~boot** *nt* rowing boat. **r~n** *vt/i* (*haben/sein*) row

Ruf *m* -[e]s,-e call; (*laut*) shout; (*Telefon*) telephone number; (*Ansehen*) reputation. **r~en†** *vt/i* (*haben*) call (*nach* for); **r~en lassen** send for

Ruf|nummer *f* telephone number. **R~zeichen** *nt* dialling tone

Rüge *f* -,-n reprimand. **r~n** *vt* reprimand; (*kritisieren*) criticize

Ruhe f - rest; (*Stille*) quiet; (*Frieden*) peace; (*innere*) calm; (*Gelassenheit*) composure; **sich zur R ~ setzen** retire; **R ~ [da]!** quiet! **r ~ los** a restless; **R ~ n** vi (*haben*) rest (*auf + dat* on). **R ~ pause** f rest, break. **R ~ stand** m retirement; **im R ~ stand** retired. **R ~ störung** f disturbance of the peace. **R ~ tag** m day of rest; 'Montag **R ~ tag'** 'closed on Mondays'

ruhig a quiet; (*erholsam*) restful; (*friedlich*) peaceful; (*unbewegt, gelassen*) calm; **sehen Sie sich r ~ um** you're welcome to look round; **man kann r ~ darüber sprechen** there's no harm in talking about it

Ruhm m -[e]s fame; (*Ehre*) glory

rühmen vt praise

ruhmreich a glorious

Ruhr f - (*Med*) dysentery

Rühr|ei nt scrambled eggs pl. **r ~ en** vt move; (*Culin*) stir; **sich r ~ en** move □ vi (*haben*) stir; **r ~ en an** (+ *acc*) touch; (*fig*) touch on. **r ~ end** a touching

Rührung f - emotion

Ruin m -s ruin. **R ~ e** f -,-n ruin; ruins pl (*gen* of). **r ~ ieren** vt ruin

rülpsen vi (*haben*) (*fam*) belch

Rum m -s rum

Rumän|**ien** [-jən] *nt* -s Romania. **r ~ isch** a Romanian

Rummel m -s (*fam*) hustle and bustle; (*Jahrmarkt*) funfair

Rumpelkammer f junk-room

Rumpf m -[e]s,ë body, trunk; (*Schiffs-*) hull; (*Aviat*) fuselage

rund a round □ adv approximately. **R ~ blick** m panoramic view

Runde f -,-n round; (*Kreis*) circle; (*eines Polizisten*) beat; (*beim Rennen*) lap; **eine R ~ Bier** a round of beer

Rundfahrt f tour. **R ~ frage** f poll

Rundfunk m radio; **im R ~ on** the radio. **R ~ gerät** nt radio [set]

Rund|**gang** m round; (*Spaziergang*) walk (*durch* round). **r ~ heraus** adv straight out. **r ~ herum** adv all around. **r ~ lich** a rounded; (*mollig*) plump. **R ~ reise** f tour. **R ~ schreiben** nt circular. **R ~ um** adv all round. **R ~ ung** f -,-en curve

runter adv = herunter, hinunter

Runzel f -,-n wrinkle

runzlig a wrinkled

Rüpel m -s,- (*fam*) lout

rupfen vt pull out; pluck

Rüsche f -,-n frill

Ruß m -es soot

Russe m -n,-n Russian

Rüssel m -s,- (*Zool*) trunk

Russ|**in** f -,-nen Russian. **r ~ isch** a Russian. **R ~ isch** nt -[s] (*Lang*) Russian

Rußland nt -s Russia

rüsten vi (*haben*) prepare (**zu/für** for) □ vr refl **sich r ~** get ready

rüstig a sprightly

rustikal a rustic

Rüstung f -,-en armament; (*Harnisch*) armour. **R ~ skontrolle** f arms control

Rute f -,-n twig; (*Angel-, Wünschel-*) rod; (*Schwanz*) tail

Rutsch m -[e]s,-e slide. **R ~ bahn** f slide. **R ~ e** f -,-n chute. **r ~ en** vt slide; (*rücken*) move □ vi (*sein*) slide; (*aus-, ab-*) slip; (*Auto*) skid. **r ~ ig** a slippery

rütteln vt shake □ vi (*haben*) **r ~ an** (+ *dat*) rattle

S

Saal m -[e]s,Säle hall; (*Theat*) auditorium; (*Kranken-*) ward

Saat f -,-en seed; (*Säen*) sowing

sabbern vi (haben) (fam) slobber; ⟨Baby:⟩ dribble; (reden) jabber

Säbel m -s,- sabre

Sabo|tage /zabo'ta:ʒə/ f - sabotage. **S~teur** /-'tø:ɐ̯/ m -s,-e saboteur. **s~tieren** vt sabotage

Sach|bearbeiter m expert. **S~buch** nt non-fiction book

Sache f -,-n matter, business; (Ding) thing; (fig) cause; **zur S~ kommen** come to the point

Sach|gebiet nt (fig) area, field. **s~kundig** a expert. **s~lich** a factual; (nüchtern) matter-of-fact

sächlich a (Gram) neuter

Sachse m -n,-n Saxon. **S~n** nt -s Saxony

sächsisch a Saxon

Sach|verhalt m -[e]s facts pl. **S~verständige(r)** m/f expert

Sack m -[e]s,̈-e sack

Sack|gasse f cul-de-sac; (fig) impasse. **S~leinen** nt sacking

Sadis|mus m - sadism. **S~t** m -en,-en sadist

säen vt/i (haben) sow

Safe /ze:f/ m -s,-s safe

Saft m -[e]s,̈-e juice; (Bot) sap. **s~ig** a juicy

Sage f -,-n legend

Säge f -,-n saw. **S~mehl** nt sawdust

sagen vt say; (mitteilen) tell; (bedeuten) mean

sägen vt/i (haben) saw

sagenhaft a legendary

Säge|späne mpl wood shavings. **S~werk** nt sawmill

Sahne f - cream. **S~ebonbon** m & nt ≈ toffee. **s~ig** a creamy

Saison /zɛ'zõ:/ f -,-s season

Saite f -,-n (Mus, Sport) string

Sakko m & nt -s,-s sports jacket

Sakrament nt -[e]s,-e sacrament

Sakristei f -,-en vestry

Salat m -[e]s,-e salad. **S~soße** f salad-dressing

Salbe f -,-n ointment

Saldo m -s,-dos & -den balance

Salon /za'lõ:/ m -s,-s salon

salopp a casual, adv -ly; ⟨Benehmen⟩ informal

Salto m -s,-s somersault

Salut m -[e]s,-e salute. **s~ieren** vi (haben) salute

Salve f -,-n volley; (Geschütz-) salvo; (von Gelächter) burst

Salz nt -es,-e salt. **s~en†** vt salt. **S~faß** nt salt-cellar. **s~ig** a salty. **S~kartoffeln** fpl boiled potatoes. **S~säure** f hydrochloric acid

Samen m -s,- seed; (Anat) semen, sperm

Sammel|becken nt reservoir. **s~n** vt/i (haben) collect; (suchen, versammeln) gather; **sich s~n** collect; (sich versammeln) gather; (sich fassen) collect oneself. **S~name** m collective noun

Samm|ler(in) m -s,- (f -,-nen) collector. **S~lung** f -,-en collection; (innere) composure

Samstag m -s,-e Saturday. **s~s** adv on Saturdays

samt prep (+ dat) together with

Samt m -[e]s velvet

sämtlich indef pron inv all. **s~e(r,s)** indef pron all the; **s~e Werke** complete works

Sanatorium nt -s,-ien sanatorium

Sand m -[e]s sand

Sandale f -,-n sandal

Sand|bank f sandbank. **s~ig** a sandy. **S~kasten** m sand-pit. **S~kuchen** m Madeira cake

sanft a gentle

Sänger(in) m -s,- (f -,-nen) singer

sanieren vt clean up; redevelop ⟨Gebiet⟩; (modernisieren) modernize; make profitable ⟨Industrie, Firma⟩; **sich s~** become profitable

sanitär a sanitary

Sanität|er m -s,- first-aid man; (Fahrer) ambulance man; (Mil) medical orderly. **S~swagen** *m* ambulance

Sanktion /zaŋk'tsjo:n/ *f* -,-en sanction. **s~ieren** *vt* sanction

Saphir *m* -s,-e sapphire

Sardelle *f* -,-n anchovy

Sardine *f* -,-n sardine

Sarg *m* -[e]s,-e coffin

Satan *m* -s Satan; devil

Satellit *m* -en,-en satellite. **S~enfernsehen** *nt* satellite television

Satire *f* -,-n satire

satt *a* full; ⟨*Farbe*⟩ rich; **s~ sein** have had enough [to eat]; **etw s~ haben** (*fam*) be fed up with sth

Sattel *m* -s,· saddle. **s~n** *vt* saddle. **S~zug** *m* articulated lorry

sättigen *vt* satisfy; (*Chem & fig*) saturate □ *vi* (*haben*) be filling

Satz *m* -es,-e sentence; (*Teil-*) clause; (*These*) proposition; (*Math*) theorem; (*Mus*) movement; (*Tennis, Zusammengehöriges*) set; (*Boden-*) sediment; (*Kaffee-*) grounds *pl*; (*Steuer-, Zins-*) rate; (*Druck-*) setting; (*Schrift-*) type; (*Sprung*) leap, bound. **S~aussage** *f* predicate. **S~gegenstand** *m* subject. **S~zeichen** *nt* punctuation mark

sauber *a* clean; (*ordentlich*) neat; (*anständig*) decent. **S~keit** *f* - cleanliness; neatness

säuberlich *a* neat

säubermachen *vt/i sep* (*haben*) clean

Sauce /'zo:sə/ *f* -,-n sauce

Saudi-Arabien /-jən/ *nt* -s Saudi Arabia

sauer *a* sour; (*Chem*) acid; (*eingelegt*) pickled; (*schwer*) hard; **saurer Regen** acid rain

Sauerkraut *nt* sauerkraut

säuerlich *a* slightly sour

Sauerstoff *m* oxygen

saufen† *vt/i* (*haben*) drink; (*sl*) booze

saugen† *vt/i* (*haben*) suck; (*staub-*) vacuum, hoover; **sich voll Wasser s~** soak up water

säugen *vt* suckle

Sauger *m* -s,· [baby's] dummy

Säugetier *nt* mammal

saugfähig *a* absorbent

Säugling *m* -s,-e infant

Säule *f* -,-n column

Saum *m* -[e]s,-Säume hem

säumen *vt* hem; (*fig*) line

Sauna *f* -,-s & -nen sauna

Säure *f* -,-n acidity; (*Chem*) acid

sausen *vi* (*haben*) rush; ⟨*Ohren:*⟩ buzz □ *vi* (*sein*) rush [along]

Saxophon *nt* -s,-e saxophone

S-Bahn *f* city and suburban railway

sch *int* shush! (*fort*) shoo!

Schabe *f* -,-n cockroach

schaben *vt/i* (*haben*) scrape

schäbig *a* shabby

Schablone *f* -,-n stencil; (*Muster*) pattern; (*fig*) stereotype

Schach *nt* -s chess; **S~!** check! **S~brett** *nt* chessboard. **S~figur** *f* chess-man

schachmatt *a* **s~ setzen** checkmate; **s~!** checkmate!

Schacht *m* -[e]s,-e shaft

Schachtel *f* -,-n box; packet

Schachzug *m* move

schade *a* **s~ sein** be a pity or shame; **zu s~ für** too good for

Schädel *m* -s,· skull. **S~bruch** *m* fractured skull

schaden *vi* (*haben*) (+ *dat*) damage; (*nachteilig sein*) hurt. **S~n** *m* -s,· damage; (*Defekt*) defect; (*Nachteil*) disadvantage. **S~ersatz** *m* damages *pl.* **S~freude** *f* malicious glee. **s~froh** *a* gloating

schädigen *vt* damage, harm. **S~ung** *f* -,-en damage

schädlich *a* harmful

Schädling *m* -s,-e pest. **S~sbekämpfungsmittel** *nt* pesticide

Schaf *nt* -[e]s,-e sheep

Schäfer m -s,- shepherd. **S~hund** m sheepdog; **Deutscher S~hund** alsatian

schaffen¹† vt create; (herstellen) establish; make ⟨Platz⟩

schaffen² v (reg) □vt manage [to do]; pass ⟨Prüfung⟩; catch ⟨Zug⟩ (bringen) take

Schaffner m -s,- conductor; ⟨Zug⟩ ticket-inspector

Schaft m -[e]s,-̈e shaft; ⟨Gewehr-⟩ stock; ⟨Stiefel-⟩ leg

Schal m -s,-s scarf

Schale f -,-n skin; (abgeschält) peel; ⟨Eier-, Nuß-, Muschel-⟩ shell; (Schüssel) dish

schälen vt peel; **sich s~** peel

Schall m -[e]s sound. **S~dämpfer** m silencer. **s~dicht** a soundproof. **s~en** vi (haben) ring out; (nachhallen) resound. **S~mauer** f sound barrier. **S~platte** f record, disc

schalt|en vt switch □vi (haben) switch; ⟨Ampel:⟩ turn (auf + acc to); ⟨Auto⟩ change gear. **S~er** m -s,- switch; ⟨Post-, Bank-⟩ counter; ⟨Fahrkarten-⟩ ticket window. **S~hebel** m switch; ⟨Auto⟩ gear-lever. **S~jahr** nt leap year. **S~ung** f -,-en circuit; ⟨Auto⟩ gear change

schämen (sich) vr be ashamed

scham|haft a modest. **s~los** a shameless

Schampon nt -s shampoo. **s~ieren** vt shampoo

Schande f - disgrace, shame

schändlich a disgraceful

Schanktisch m bar

Schanze f -,-n [ski-]jump

Schar f -,-en crowd; ⟨Vogel-⟩ flock

Scharade f -,-n charade

scharen vt um sich s~ gather round one; **sich s~ um** flock round. **s~weise** adv in droves

scharf a sharp; ⟨stark⟩ strong; (stark gewürzt) hot; ⟨Geruch⟩ pungent; ⟨Frost, Wind, Augen⟩

keen; (streng) harsh; ⟨Galopp, Ritt⟩ hard; ⟨Munition⟩ live; ⟨Hund⟩ fierce; ⟨Phot⟩ focus; **s~ sein** ⟨Phot⟩ be in focus; **s~ sein auf** (+ acc) ⟨fam⟩ be keen on

Schärfe f - (s. scharf) sharpness; strength; hotness; pungency; harshness. **s~n** vt sharpen

Scharfrichter m executioner. **S~schütze** m marksman. **S~sinn** m astuteness

Scharlach m -s scarlet fever

Scharlatan m -s,-e charlatan

Scharnier nt -s,-e hinge

Schärpe f -,-n sash

scharren vi (haben) scrape; ⟨Huhn:⟩ scratch; ⟨Pferd:⟩ paw the ground □vt scrape

Schaschlik m & nt -s,-s kebab

Schatten m -s,- shadow; (schattige Stelle) shade. **S~riß** m silhouette. **S~seite** f shady side; (fig) disadvantage

schattier|en vt shade. **S~ung** f -,-en shading

schattig a shady

Schatz m -es,-̈e treasure; ⟨Freund, Freundin⟩ sweetheart; (Anrede) darling

Schätzchen nt -s,- darling

schätzen vt estimate; (taxieren) value; (achten) esteem; (würdigen) appreciate; (fam: vermuten) reckon

Schätzung f -,-en estimate; (Taxierung) valuation

Schau f -,-en show. **S~bild** nt diagram

Schauder m -s shiver; (vor Abscheu) shudder. **s~haft** a dreadful

schauen vi (haben) ⟨SGer, Aust⟩ look; **s~,** daß make sure that

Schauer m -s,- shower; (Schauder) shiver. **S~geschichte** f horror story. **s~lich** a ghastly. **s~n** vi (haben) shiver

Schaufel f -,-n shovel; (Kehr-) dustpan. **s ~ n** vt shovel; (graben) dig

Schaufenster nt shop-window. **S ~ puppe** f dummy

Schaukel f -,-n swing. **s ~ n** vt rock □ vi (haben) rock; (auf einer Schaukel) swing; (schwanken) sway. **S ~ pferd** nt rocking-horse. **S ~ stuhl** m rocking-chair

Schaum m -[e]s foam; (Seifen-) lather; (auf Bier) froth; (als Frisier-, Rasiermittel) mousse

schäumen vi (haben) foam, froth; ⟨Seife;⟩ lather

Schaum|gummi m foam rubber. **s ~ ig** a frothy; **s ~ ig rühren** (Culin) cream. **S ~ stoff** m [synthetic] foam. **S ~ wein** m sparkling wine

Schauplatz m scene

schaurig a dreadful

Schauspiel nt play; (Anblick) spectacle. **S ~ er** m actor. **S ~ erin** f actress

Scheck m -s,-s cheque. **S ~ buch,** **s ~ heft** nt cheque-book. **S ~ karte** f cheque card

Scheibe f -,-n disc; (Schieß-) target; (Glas-) pane; (Brot-, Wurst-) slice. **S ~ nwaschanlage** f windscreen washer. **S ~ nwischer** m -s, windscreen-wiper

Scheich m -s,-e & -s sheikh

Scheide f -,-n sheath; (Anat) vagina

scheid|en† vt separate; (unterscheiden) distinguish; dissolve ⟨Ehe⟩; **sich s ~ en lassen** get divorced. **S ~ ung** f -,-en divorce

Schein m -[e]s,-e light; (Anschein) appearance; (Bescheinigung) certificate; (Geld-) note. **s ~ en†** vi (haben) shine; (den Anschein haben) seem, appear

scheinheilig a hypocritical

Scheinwerfer m -s, floodlight; (Such-) searchlight; (Auto) headlight; (Theat) spotlight

Scheiße f - (vulg) shit. **s ~ n†** vi (haben) (vulg) shit

Scheitel m -s, parting

scheitern vi (sein) fail

Schelle f -,-n bell. **s ~ n** vi (haben) ring

Schellfisch m haddock

Schelm m -s,-e rogue

Schelte f - scolding

Schema nt -s,-mata model, pattern; (Skizze) diagram

Schenke f -,-n tavern

Schenkel m -s, thigh

schenken vt give [as a present]; **jdm Vertrauen s ~** trust s.o.

Scherbe f -,-n [broken] piece

Schere f -,-n scissors pl; (Techn) shears pl; (Hummer-) claw. **s ~ n†¹** vt shear; crop ⟨Haar⟩

scheren² vt (reg) (sim) bother; **sich nicht s ~ um** not care about

Scherenschnitt m silhouette

Scherereien fpl (fam) trouble sg

Scherz m -es,-e joke; **im/zum S ~** as a joke. **s ~ en** vi (haben) joke

scheu a shy; ⟨Tier⟩ timid; **s ~ werden** ⟨Pferd;⟩ shy

scheuchen vt shoo

scheuen vt be afraid of; (meiden) shun; **keine Mühe/Kosten s ~** spare no effort/expense; **sich s ~** be afraid (vor + dat of); shrink (etw zu tun from doing sth)

scheuern vt scrub; (reiben) rub; [wund] s ~ chafe □ vi (haben) rub, chafe

Scheuklappen fpl blinkers

Scheune f -,-n barn

Scheusal nt -s,-e monster

scheußlich a horrible

Schi m -s,-er ski; **S ~ fahren** od **laufen** ski

Schicht f -,-en layer; (Geol) stratum; (Gesellschafts-) class; (Arbeits-) shift. **S ~ arbeit** f shift work. **S ~ en** vt stack [up]

schick a stylish; ⟨Frau⟩ chic. **S ~ m -[e]s** style

schicken *vt/i (haben)* send; **s~ nach** send for

Schicksal *nt* -s,-e fate. **S~sschlag** *m* misfortune

Schieb|edach *nt (Auto)* sun-roof. **s~en†** *vt* (*geleitend*) slide; (*nicht senkrecht*) slant; **etw s~en auf** (+ *acc*) (*fig*) put sth down to; **shift** (*Schuld*) on to □*vi (haben)* push. **S~etür** *f* sliding door. **S~ung** *f* -,-en (*fam*) illicit deal; (*Betrug*) rigging, fixing

Schieds|gericht *nt* panel of judges; (*Jur*) arbitration tribunal. **S~richter** *m* referee; (*Tennis*) umpire; (*Jur*) arbitrator

schief *a* crooked; (*unsymmetrisch*) lopsided; (*geneigt*) slanting, sloping; (*nicht senkrecht*) leaning; (*Winkel*) oblique; (*fig*) false; (*mißtrauisch*) suspicious

Schiefer *m* -s slate

schielen *vi (haben)* squint

Schienbein *nt* shin; (*Knochen*) shinbone

Schiene *f* -,-n rail; (*Gleit-*) runner; (*Med*) splint. **s~n** *vt (Med)* put in a splint

schießen† *vt* shoot; fire (*Kugel*); score (*Tor*) □*vi (haben)* shoot, fire (**auf** + *acc* at). **S~scheibe** *f* target. **S~stand** *m* shooting-range

Schiffahren *nt* skiing. **S~er(in)** *m(f)* skier

Schiff *nt* -[e]s,-e ship; (*Kirchen-*) nave; (*Seiten-*) aisle

Schiffahrt *f* shipping

schiff|bar *a* navigable. **S~bau** *m* shipbuilding. **S~bruch** *m* shipwreck

Schikan|e *f* -,-n harassment; **mit allen S~en** (*fam*) with every refinement. **s~ieren** *vt* harass

Schi|laufen *nt* = skiing. **S~läufer(in)** *m(f)* skier

Schild¹ *nt* -[e]s,-er sign; (*Namens-, Nummern-*) plate; (*Mützen-*) badge; (*Etikett*) label

Schilddrüse *f* thyroid [gland]

schilder|n *vt* describe. **S~ung** *f* -,-en description

Schild|kröte *f* tortoise; (*See-*) turtle. **S~patt** *nt* -[e]s tortoiseshell

Schilf *nt* -[e]s reeds *pl*

schillern *vi (haben)* shimmer

Schimmel *m* -s,- mould; (*Pferd*) white horse. **s~ig** *a* mouldy. **s~n** *vi (haben/sein)* go mouldy

Schimpanse *m* -n,-n chimpanzee

schimpf|en *vi (haben)* grumble (**mit** at; **über** + *acc* about); scold (**mit jdm** s.o.) □*vt* call. **S~wort** *nt* (*pl* **-wörter**) swear-word

Schinken *m* -s,- ham

Schippe *f* -,-n shovel. **s~n** *vt* shovel

Schirm *m* -[e]s,-e umbrella; (*Sonnen-*) sunshade; (*Lampen-*) shade; (*Augen-*) visor; (*Mützen-*) peak; (*Bild-*) screen; (*fig: Schutz*) shield. **S~herrschaft** *f* patronage. **S~mütze** *f* peaked cap

schizophren *a* schizophrenic. **S~ie** *f* - schizophrenia

Schlacht *f* -,-en battle

schlachten *vt* slaughter, kill

Schlachter, Schlächter *m* -s,- (*NGer*) butcher

Schlacht|feld *nt* battlefield. **S~hof** *m* abattoir

Schlacke *f* -,-n slag

Schlaf *m* -[e]s sleep; **im S~** in one's sleep. **S~anzug** *m* pyjamas *pl*

Schläfe *f* -,-n (*Anat*) temple

schlafen† *vi (haben)* sleep; **s~ gehen** go to bed; **er schläft noch** he is still asleep

Schläfer(in) *m* -s,- (*f* -,-nen) sleeper

schlaff *a* limp; (*Seil*) slack; (*Muskel*) flabby

Schlaf|lied *nt* lullaby. **s~los** *a* sleepless. **S~losigkeit** *f* - insomnia. **S~mittel** *nt* sleeping drug

schläfrig *a* sleepy

Schlaf·saal *m* dormitory. **S~sack** *m* sleeping-bag. **S~tablette** *f* sleeping-pill. **S~wagen** *m* sleeping-car, sleeper. **S~wandeln** *vi* (*haben*/*sein*) sleep-walk. **S~zimmer** *nt* bedroom

Schlag *m* -[e]s,˙-e blow; (*Faust-*) punch; (*Herz-, Trommel-*) beat; (*einer Uhr*) chime; (*Glocken- & Med*) stroke; (*elektrischer*) shock; (*Art*) type; **S~e bekommen** get a beating; **S~ auf S~** in rapid succession. **S~ader** *f* artery. **S~anfall** *m* stroke. **S~baum** *m* barrier

schlagen† *vt* hit, strike; (*fällen*) fell; knock (*Loch, Nagel*) (**in** + *acc* into); (*prügeln, besiegen*) beat; (*Culin*) whisk (*Eiweiß*); whip (*Sahne*); (*legen*) strike; (*wickeln*) wrap; **sich s~** fight; □*vi* (*haben*) beat; (*Uhr:*) strike; (*melodisch*) chime; **mit den Flügeln s~** flap its wings; □*vi* (*sein*) hit s.o. in etw (*acc*) **s~** (*Blitz, Kugel:*) strike sth; **nach jdm s~** (*fig*) take after s.o.

Schlager *m* -s,- popular song; (*Erfolg*) hit

Schläger *m* -s,- racket; (*Tischtennis-*) bat; (*Golf-*) club; (*Hockey-*) stick. **S~ei** *f* -,-en fight

schlag·fertig *a* quick-witted. **S~loch** *nt* pot-hole. **S~sahne** *f* whipped cream; (*ungeschlagen*) whipping cream. **S~seite** *f* (*Naut*) list. **S~stock** *m* truncheon. **S~wort** *nt* (*pl* -worte) slogan. **S~zeile** *f* headline. **S~zeug** *nt* (*Mus*) percussion. **S~zeuger** *m* -s,- percussionist; (*in Band*) drummer

Schlamm *m* -[e]s mud. **S~ig** *a* muddy

Schlampe *f* -,-n (*fam*) slut. **s~ig** *a* slovenly; (*Arbeit*) sloppy

Schlange *f* -,-n snake; (*Menschen-*) queue; **S~ stehen** queue

schlängeln (sich) *vr* wind; (*Person:*) weave (**durch** through)

schlank *a* slim. **S~heitskur** *f* slimming diet

schlapp *a* tired; (*schlaff*) limp

schlau *a* clever; (*gerissen*) crafty; **ich werde nicht s~ daraus** I can't make head or tail of it

Schlauch *m* -[e]s,Schläuche tube; (*Wasser-*) hose[pipe]. **S~boot** *nt* rubber dinghy

Schlaufe *f* -,-n loop

schlecht *a* bad; (*böse*) wicked; (*unzulänglich*) poor; **s~ werden** go bad; (*Wetter:*) turn bad; **mir ist s~** I feel sick. **s~gehen†** *vi sep* (*sn*) (+ *dat*) **es geht ihm s~** he's doing badly; (*gesundheitlich*) he's not well. **s~gelaunt** *attrib a* bad-tempered

schlecken *vt*/*i* (*haben*) lick (**an etw** *dat* sth); (*auf-*) lap up

Schlegel *m* -s,- mallet; (*Trommel-*) stick; (*SGer: Keule*) leg; (*Hühner-*) drumstick

schleichen† *vi* (*sein*) creep; (*langsam gehen*/*fahren*) crawl □*vr* **sich s~** creep. **S~d** *a* creeping; (*Krankheit*) insidious

Schleier *m* -s,- veil; (*fig*) haze

Schleife *f* -,-n bow; (*Fliege*) bow-tie; (*Biegung*) loop

schleifen¹ *v* (*reg*) □*vt* drag □*vi* (*haben*) trail, drag

schleifen²† *vt* grind; (*schärfen*) sharpen; cut (*Edelstein, Glas*)

Schleim *m* -[e]s slime; (*Anat*) mucus; (*Med*) phlegm. **s~ig** *a* slimy

schlemmen *vi* (*haben*) feast

schlendern *vi* (*sein*) stroll

schlenkern *vt*/*i* (*haben*) swing; **mit** swing; dangle (*Beine*)

Schlepp·dampfer *m* tug. **S~e** *f* -,-n train. **s~en** *vt* drag; (*tragen*) carry; (*ziehen*) tow; **sich s~en** drag oneself; (*sich hinziehen*) drag on; **sich s~en mit** carry. **S~er** *m* -s,- tug; (*Traktor*) tractor. **S~kahn** *m* barge. **S~lift** *m* T-bar lift. **S~tau** *nt* tow-rope; **ins S~tau nehmen** take in tow

Schleuder f ˗,-n catapult; (Wäsche-) spin-drier. **s~n** vt hurl; spin (Wäsche); □ vi (sein) skid; **ins S~n geraten** skid. **S~sitz** m ejector seat

Schleuse f ˗,-n lock; (Sperre) sluice(-gate). **s~n** vt steer

Schliche pl tricks

schlicht a plain; simple

Schlichtung f- settlement; (Jur) arbitration

Schließe f-,-n clasp; buckle

schließen† vt close; (ab-) lock; fasten (Kleid, Schluß); (stillegen) close down; (beenden, folgern) conclude; enter into (Vertrag); **sich s~** close; **etw s~ an** (+ acc) connect sth to; **sich s~ an** (+ acc) follow □ vi (haben) close; (den Betrieb einstellen) close down; (enden, folgern) conclude

Schließfach nt locker. **s~lich** adv finally, in the end; (immerhin) after all. **S~ung** f-,-en closure

Schliff m -[e]s cut; (Schleifen) cutting; (fig) polish

schlimm a bad

Schlinge f-,-n loop; (Henkers-) noose; (Med) sling; (Falle) snare

Schlingel m -s,- (fam) rascal

schlingen† vt wind, wrap; tie (Knoten)

Schlips m -es,-e tie

Schlitten m -s,- sledge; (Rodel-) toboggan; (Pferde-) sleigh

schlittern vi (haben/sein) slide

Schlittschuh m skate; **S~ laufen** skate. **S~läufer(in)** m(f) skater

Schlitz m -es,-e slit; (für Münze) slot; (Jacken-) vent; (Hosen-) flies pl. **s~en** vt slit

Schloß nt -sses,-sser lock; (Vorhänge-) padlock; (Verschluß) clasp; (Gebäude) castle; palace

Schlosser m -s,- locksmith; (Auto-) mechanic

Schlucht f-,-en ravine, gorge

schluchzen vi (haben) sob

Schluck m -[e]s,-e mouthful; (klein) sip

Schluckauf m -s hiccups pl

schlucken vt/i (haben) swallow

Schlummer m -s slumber

Schlund m -[e]s [back of the] throat; (fig) mouth

schlüpfen vi (sein) slip; [aus dem Ei] **s~en** hatch. **S~er** m -s,- knickers pl. **s~rig** a slippery

schlürfen vt/i (haben) slurp

Schluß m -sses,̈sse end; (S~folgerung) conclusion; **zum S~** finally; **S~ machen** stop (mit etw sth); finish (mit jdm with s.o.)

Schlüssel m -s,- key; (Schrauben-) spanner; (Geheim-) code; (Mus) clef. **S~bein** nt collar-bone. **S~bund** m & nt bunch of keys. **S~loch** nt keyhole

Schlußfolgerung f conclusion

schlüssig a conclusive

Schluß|licht nt rear light. **S~verkauf** m [end of season] sale

Schmach f- disgrace

schmächtig a slight

schmackhaft a tasty

schmal a narrow; (dünn) thin; (schlank) slender; (karg) meagre

Schmalz¹ nt -es lard; (Ohren-) wax

Schmalz² nt -es (fam) schmaltz

Schmarren m -s,- (Aust) pancake [torn into strips]; (fam: Unsinn) rubbish

schmatzen vi (haben) eat noisily

schmausen vi (haben) feast

schmecken vt/i (haben) taste (nach of); [gut] **s~** taste good □ vt taste

Schmeichelei f -,-en flattery; (Kompliment) compliment

schmeichelhaft a complimentary, flattering

schmeißen† vt/i (haben) **s~ [mit]** (fam) chuck

Schmeißfliege f bluebottle

schmelz|en† *vt/i (sein)* melt; smelt ⟨*Erze*⟩. **S~wasser** *nt* melted snow

Schmerz *m* **-es,-en** pain; (*Kummer*) grief; **S~en haben** be in pain. **s~en** *vt* hurt; (*fig*) grieve □ *vi (haben)* hurt; be painful. **S~ensgeld** *nt* compensation for pain and suffering. **s~los** *a* painless. **s~stillend** *a* pain-killing. **s~stillendes Mittel** analgesic, pain-killer. **S~tablette** *f* pain-killer

Schmetterball *m* (*Tennis*) smash

Schmetterling *m* **-s,-e** butterfly

schmettern *vt* hurl; (*Tennis*) smash; (*singen*) sing; (*spielen*) blare out □ *vi (haben)* resound

Schmied *m* **-[e]s,-e** blacksmith

Schmiede *f* **-,-n** forge. **S~eisen** *nt* wrought iron. **s~n** *vt* forge

Schmier|e *f* **-,-n** grease; (*Schmutz*) mess. **s~en** *vt* lubricate; (*streichen*) spread; (*schlecht schreiben*) scrawl □ *vi (haben*) smudge; (*schreiben*) scrawl. **S~geld** *nt* (*fam*) bribe. **s~ig** *a* greasy; (*schmutzig*) grubby. **S~mittel** *nt* lubricant

Schminke *f* **-,-n** make-up. **s~n** *vt* make up; **sich** (*dat*) **die Lippen s~n** put on lipstick

schmirgel|n *vt* sand down. **S~papier** *nt* emery-paper

schmollen *vi (haben)* sulk

schmor|en *vt/i (haben)* braise. **S~topf** *m* casserole

Schmuck *m* **-[e]s** jewellery; (*Verzierung*) ornament, decoration

schmücken *vt* decorate, adorn

schmuck|los *a* plain. **S~stück** *nt* piece of jewellery; (*fig*) jewel

Schmuggel *m* **-s** smuggling. **s~n** *vt* smuggle. **S~ware** *f* contraband

Schmuggler *m* **-s,-** smuggler

schmunzeln *vi (haben)* smile

schmusen *vi (haben)* cuddle

Schmutz *m* **-es** dirt. **s~ig** *a* dirty

Schnabel *m* **-s,-̈** beak, bill; (*eines Kruges*) lip; (*Tülle*) spout

Schnalle *f* **-,-n** buckle. **s~n** *vt* strap; (*zu-*) buckle

schnapp|en *vi (haben)* **s~en nach** snap at; gasp for ⟨*Luft*⟩ □ *vt* snatch, grab; (*fam: festnehmen*) nab. **S~schloß** *nt* spring lock. **S~schuß** *m* snapshot

Schnaps *m* **-es,-̈e** schnapps

schnarchen *vi (haben)* snore

schnattern *vi (haben)* cackle

schnauben *vi (haben)* snort □ *vt* **sich** (*dat*) **die Nase s~** blow one's nose

schnaufen *vi (haben)* puff, pant

Schnauze *f* **-,-n** muzzle; (*eines Kruges*) lip; (*Tülle*) spout

Schnecke *f* **-,-n** snail; (*Nackt-*) slug; (*Spirale*) scroll. **S~nhaus** *nt* snail-shell

Schnee *m* **-s** snow; (*Eier-*) beaten egg-white. **S~besen** *m* whisk. **S~brille** *f* snow-goggles *pl*. **S~fall** *m* snowfall. **S~flocke** *f* snowflake. **S~glöckchen** *nt* **-s,-** snowdrop. **S~kette** *f* snow chain. **S~mann** *m* (*pl-männer*) snowman. **S~pflug** *m* snowplough. **S~schläger** *m* whisk. **S~sturm** *m* snowstorm, blizzard. **S~wehe** *f* **-,-n** snow-drift

Schneide *f* **-,-n** [cutting] edge; (*Klinge*) blade

schneiden† *vt* cut; (*in Scheiben*) slice; (*kreuzen*) cross; (*nicht beachten*) cut dead; **Gesichter s~** pull faces; **sich s~** cut oneself; (*über-*) intersect

Schneider *m* **-s,-** tailor. **S~in** *f* **-,-nen** dressmaker. **s~n** *vt* make ⟨*Anzug, Kostüm*⟩

Schneidezahn *m* incisor

schneien *vi (haben)* snow

Schneise *f* **-,-n** path; (*Feuer-*) fire-break

schnell *a* quick; ⟨*Auto, Tempo*⟩ fast □ *adv* quickly; (*in s~em Tempo*) fast; (*bald*) soon; **mach s~!**

hurry up! **S~imbiß** m snack-bar. **S~kochtopf** m pressure-cooker. **S~reinigung** f express cleaners. **S~zug** m express (train)

schnetzeln vt cut into thin strips

schneuzen (sich) vr blow one's nose

Schnipsel m & nt -s,- scrap

Schnitt m -[e]s,-e cut; (Film-) cutting; (S~muster) [paper] pattern; **im S~** (durchschnittlich) on average

Schnitte f -,-n slice [of bread]; (belegt) open sandwich

schnittig a stylish; (stromlinien-förmig) streamlined

Schnitt|käse m hard cheese. **S~lauch** m chives pl. **S~mu-ster** nt [paper] pattern. **S~punkt** m [point of] intersection. **S~wunde** f cut

Schnitzel nt -s,- scrap; (Culin) escalope. **s~n** vt shred

schnitzen vt/i (haben) carve

schnodderig a (fam) brash

Schnorchel m -s,- snorkel

Schnörkel m -s,- flourish; (Kunst) scroll. **s~ig** a ornate

schnüffeln vi (haben) sniff (an etw dat sth); (fam: spionieren) snoop [around]

Schnuller m -s,- [baby's] dummy

Schnupf|en m -s,- [head] cold. **S~tabak** m snuff

schnuppern vt/i (haben) sniff (an etw dat sth)

Schnur f -,-̈e string; (Kordel) cord; (Besatz-) braid; (Electr) flex

schnüren vt tie; lace [up] (Schuhe)

schnurgerade a & adv dead straight

Schnurr|bart m moustache. **s~en** vi (haben) hum; (Katze:) purr

Schnürsenkel m [shoe-]lace

schnurstracks adv straight

Schock m -[e]s,-s shock. **s~en** vt (fam) shock. **s~ieren** vt shock; **s~ierend** shocking

Schöffe m -n,-n lay judge

Schokolade f - chocolate

Scholle f -,-n clod [of earth]; (Eis-) [ice-]floe; (Fisch) plaice

schon adv already; (allein) just; (sogar) even; (ohnehin) anyway; **s~einmal** before; (jemals) ever; **s~immer/oft/wieder** always/often/again; **s~der Gedanke daran** the mere thought of it; **s~deshalb** for that reason alone; **das ist s~möglich** that's quite possible; **ja s~,** **aber** well yes, but

schön a beautiful; (Wetter:) fine; (angenehm, nett) nice; (gut) good; (fam: beträchtlich) pretty; **s~en Dank!** thank you very much!

schonen vt spare; (gut behandeln) look after. **s~d** a gentle

Schönheit f -,-en beauty. **S~sfehler** m blemish. **S~skon-kurrenz** f, beauty contest

Schonung f -,-en gentle care; (nach Krankheit) rest; (Baum-) plantation. **s~slos** a ruthless

Schonzeit f close season

schöpf|en vt scoop [up]; ladle (Suppe); **Mut s~en** take heart. **s~erisch** a creative. **S~kelle** f, **S~löffel** m ladle. **S~ung** f -,-en creation

Schoppen m -s,- (SGer) ≈ pint

Schorf m -[e]s scab

Schornstein m chimney. **S~feger** m -s,- chimney-sweep

Schoß m -es,-̈e lap; (Frack-) tail

Schote f -,-n pod; (Erbse) pea

Schotte m -n,-n Scot, Scotsman

Schotter m -s gravel

schott|isch a Scottish, Scots. **S~land** nt -s Scotland

schraffieren vt hatch

schräg a diagonal; (geneigt) sloping; **s~halten** tilt. **S~strich** m oblique stroke

Schramme f -,-n scratch

Schrank m -[e]s,⁻e cupboard; (Kleider-) wardrobe; (Akten-, Glas-) cabinet

Schranke f -,-n barrier

Schraube f -,-n screw; (Schiffs-) propeller. **s~n** vt screw; (ab-) unscrew; (drehen) turn. **S~nschlüssel** m spanner. **S~nzieher** m -s,- screwdriver

Schraubstock m vice

Schrebergarten m ≈ allotment

Schreck m -[e]s,-e fright. **S~en** m -s,- fright; (Entsetzen) horror

Schreck|gespenst nt spectre. **s~haft** a easily frightened; (nervös) jumpy. **s~lich** a terrible. **S~schuß** m warning shot

Schrei m -[e]s,-e cry, shout; (gellend) scream; (fam) der letzte **S~** (fam) the latest thing

schreib|en† vt/i (haben) write; (auf der Maschine) type; falsch **s~en** spell wrong; sich **s~en** ⟨Wort:⟩ be spelt; (korrespondieren) correspond; **sich krank s~en lassen** get a doctor's certificate. **S~en** nt -s,- writing; (Brief) letter. **S~fehler** m spelling mistake. **S~heft** nt exercise book. **S~kraft** f clerical assistant; (für Maschineschreiben) typist. **S~maschine** f typewriter. **S~tisch** m desk. **S~ung** f -,-en spelling. **S~waren** fpl stationery sg

schrei|en† vt/i (haben) cry; (gellend) scream; (rufen, laut sprechen) shout

Schreiner m -s,- joiner

Schrift f -,-en writing; (Druck-) type; (Abhandlung) paper; die Heilige **S~** the Scriptures pl. **S~führer** m secretary. **s~lich** a written □adv in writing. **S~sprache** f written language. **S~steller(in)** m (f -,-nen) writer. **S~stück** nt document. **S~zeichen** nt character

Schritt m -[e]s,-e step; (Entfernung) pace; (Gangart) walk; (der Hose) crotch. **S~macher** m -s,- pace-maker. **s~weise** adv step by step

schroff a precipitous; (abweisend) brusque; (unvermittelt) abrupt; (Gegensatz) stark

Schrot m & nt -[e]s coarse meal; (Blei-) small shot

Schrott m -[e]s scrap[-metal]; **zu S~ fahren** (fam) write off. **S~platz** m scrap-yard

schrubb|en vt/i (haben) scrub. **S~er** m -s,- scrubbing-brush

Schrulle f -,-n whim; **alte S~** (fam) old crone. **s~ig** a cranky

schrumpfen vi (sein) shrink

schrump[e]lig a wrinkled

Schub m -[e]s,⁻e (Phys) thrust; (S~fach) drawer; (Menge) batch. **S~fach** nt drawer. **S~karre** f, **S~karren** m wheelbarrow. **S~lade** f drawer

Schubs m -es,-e push, shove. **s~en** vt push, shove

schüchtern a shy; (zaghaft) tentative. **S~heit** f- shyness

Schuh m -[e]s,-e shoe. **S~anzieher** m -s,- shoehorn. **S~creme** f shoe-polish. **S~löffel** m shoehorn. **S~macher** m -s,- shoemaker

Schul|abgänger m -s,- schoolleaver. **S~arbeiten**, **S~aufgaben** fpl homework sg

Schuld f -,-en guilt; (Verantwortung) blame; (Geld-) debt; **S~en machen** get into debt □**s~ haben** od **sein** to be blame (an + dat for); jdm **s~ geben** blame s.o. **s~en** vt owe

schuldig a guilty (gen of); (gebührend) due; jdm etw **s~ sein** owe s.o. sth. **S~keit** f- duty

schuld|los a innocent. **S~ner** m -s,- debtor

Schule f -,-n school; **in der/die S~** at/to school. **s~n** vt train

Schüler(in) m -s,- (f -,-nen) pupil
schul|frei a wir haben morgen **s~frei** there's no school tomorrow. **S~hof** m [school] playground. **S~jahr** nt school year; (Klasse) form. **S~kind** nt schoolchild. **S~leiter(in)** m(f) head [teacher]. **S~stunde** f lesson
Schulter f -,-n shoulder. **S~blatt** nt shoulder-blade
Schulung f - training
schummeln vi (haben) (fam) cheat
Schund m -[e]s trash
Schuppe f -,-n scale; **S~n** pl dandruff sg. **s~n (sich)** vr flake
Schuppen m -s,- shed
Schür|eisen nt poker. **s~en** vt poke; (fig) stir up
schürfen vt mine. **S~wunde** f abrasion, graze
Schurke m -n,-n villain
Schürze f -,-n apron
Schuß m -sses,-̈sse shot; (kleine Menge) dash
Schüssel f -,-n bowl; (TV) dish
Schuß|fahrt f (Ski) schuss. **S~waffe** f firearm
Schuster m -s,- = Schuhmacher
Schutt m -[e]s rubble. **S~abladeplatz** m rubbish dump
Schüttel|frost m shivering fit. **s~n** vt shake; **sich s~n** shake oneself/itself; (vor Ekel) shudder; **jdm die Hand s~n** shake s.o.'s hand
schütten vt pour; (kippen) tip; (ver-) spill □ vi (haben) **es schüttet** it is pouring [with rain]
Schutz m -es protection; (Zuflucht) shelter; (Techn) guard; **S~** **suchen** take refuge. **S~anzug** m protective suit. **S~blech** nt mudguard. **S~brille** goggles pl
Schütze m -n,-n marksman; (Tor-) scorer; (Astr) Sagittarius

schützen vt protect/(Zuflucht gewähren) shelter (vor + dat from) □ vi (haben) give protection/shelter (vor + dat from)
Schutz|engel m guardian angel. **S~heilige(r)** m/f patron saint
Schützling m -s,-e charge
schutz|los a defenceless, helpless. **S~mann** m (pl -männer & -leute) policeman. **S~umschlag** m dust-jacket
Schwaben nt -s Swabia
schwäbisch a Swabian
schwach a weak; (nicht gut; gering) poor; (leicht) faint
Schwäche f -,-n weakness. **s~n** vt weaken
schwäch|lich a delicate. **S~ling** m -s,-e weakling
Schwachsinn m mental deficiency. **s~ig** a mentally deficient; (fam) idiotic
Schwager m -s,-̈ brother-in-law
Schwägerin f -,-nen sister-in-law
Schwalbe f -,-n swallow
Schwamm m -[e]s,-̈e sponge; (SGer: Pilz) fungus; (eßbar) mushroom. **s~ig** a spongy
Schwan m -[e]s,-̈e swan
schwanger a pregnant
Schwangerschaft f -,-en pregnancy
Schwank m -[e]s,-̈e (Theat) farce
schwanken vi (haben) sway; (Boot:) rock; (sich ändern) fluctuate; (unentschieden sein) be undecided □ (sein) stagger
Schwanz m -es,-̈e tail
schwänzen vt (fam) skip; **die Schule s~** play truant
schwärmen vi (haben) swarm; **s~ für** (fam) adore; (verliebt sein) have a crush on
Schwarte f -,-n (Speck-) rind
schwarz a black; (fam: illegal) illegal; **s~ auf weiß** in black and white; **ins S~e treffen** score a bull's-eye. **S~** nt -[e]s,- black.

S~arbeit f moonlighting. **s~ar-beiten** vi sep (haben) moonlight.
S~e(r) m/f black

Schwärze f - blackness. **s~n** vt blacken

Schwarz|fahrer m fare-dodger.
S~händler m black marketeer.
S~markt m black market.
S~wald m Black Forest.
s~weiß a black and white

schwatzen (SGer) **schwätzen** vi (haben) chat; (klatschen) gossip

Schwebe f - in der **S~** (fig) undecided. **S~bahn** f cable railway.
s~n vi (haben) float; (fig) be undecided; (Verfahren:) be pending; **in Gefahr s~n** be in danger

Schwed|e m -n,-n Swede. **S~en** nt -s Sweden. **S~in** f -,-nen Swede. **s~isch** a Swedish

Schwefel m -s sulphur

schweigen† vi (haben) be silent; **ganz zu s~ von** let alone. **S~** nt -s silence; **zum S~ bringen** silence

schweigsam a silent; (wortkarg) taciturn

Schwein nt -[e]s,-e pig; (Culin) pork; (sl) (Schuft) swine; **S~ haben** (fam) be lucky. **S~ebraten** m roast pork. **S~efleisch** nt pork. **S~erei** f -,-en (sl) (dirty) mess; (Gemeinheit) dirty trick.
S~estall m pigsty. **S~sleder** nt pigskin

Schweiß m -es sweat

schweißen vt weld

Schweiz (die) - Switzerland.
S~er a & m -s,-. **S~erin** f -,-nen Swiss. **s~erisch** a Swiss

Schwelle f -,-n threshold; (Eisenbahn-) sleeper

schwell|en† vi (sein) swell.
S~ung f -,-en swelling

schwer a heavy; (schwierig) difficult; (mühsam) hard; (ernst) serious; (schlimm) bad; **3 Pfund s~ sein** weigh 3 pounds □ adv heavily; with difficulty; (mühsam)

hard; (schlimm, sehr) badly, seriously; **s~ hören** be hard of hearing; **s~ zu sagen** hard to say

Schwere f - heaviness; (Gewicht) weight; (Schwierigkeit) difficulty; (Ernst) gravity. **S~losigkeit** f weightlessness

schwer|fallen† vi sep (sein) be hard (dat for). **S~gewicht** nt heavyweight. **s~hörig** a **s~ hörig sein** be hard of hearing.
S~kraft f (Phys) gravity.
s~krank a seriously ill. **s~machen** vt sep make difficult (dat for). **s~mütig** a melancholic.
s~nehmen† vt sep take seriously. **S~punkt** m centre of gravity

Schwert nt -[e]s,-er sword. **S~lilie** f iris

schwer|tun† (sich) vr sep have difficulty (mit with). **S~verbrecher** m serious offender.
s~verdaulich a indigestible.
s~verletzt a seriously injured

Schwester f -,-n sister; (Kranken-) nurse. **s~lich** a sisterly

Schwieger|eltern pl parents-in-law. **S~mutter** f mother-in-law.
S~sohn m son-in-law.
S~tochter f daughter-in-law.
S~vater m father-in-law

schwierig a difficult. **S~keit** f -,-en difficulty

Schwimm|bad nt swimming-baths pl. **S~becken** nt swimming-pool. **s~en**† vi/t (sein/haben) swim; (auf dem Wasser treiben) float. **S~weste** f life-jacket

Schwindel m -s dizziness, vertigo; (fam: Betrug) fraud; (Lüge) lie. **s~frei** a **s~ frei sein** have a good head for heights. **s~n** vi (haben) (lügen) lie

Schwindler m -s,- liar; (Betrüger) fraud, con-man. **s~ig** a dizzy; **mir ist s~ig** I feel dizzy

schwing|en† vi (haben) swing; (Phys) oscillate; (vibrieren) vibrate □ vt swing; wave ⟨Fahne⟩; (drohend) brandish. **S~ung** f -,-en oscillation; vibration

Schwips m -es,-e einen S~ haben (fam) to be tipsy

schwitzen vi (haben) sweat

schwören† vt/i (haben) swear (auf + acc by)

schwul a (fam: homosexuell) gay

schwül a close. **S~e** f - closeness

Schwung m -[e]s,⸚e swing; (Bogen) sweep; (Schnelligkeit) momentum; (Kraft) vigour; (Feuer) verve. **s~voll** a vigorous; ⟨Linie⟩ sweeping; (mitreißend) spirited

Schwur m -[e]s,⸚e vow; (Eid) oath. **S~gericht** nt jury [court]

sechs inv a & f -,-en six; (Sch) ≈ fail mark. **s~eckig** a hexagonal. **s~te(r,s)** a sixth

sech|zehn inv a sixteen. **s~zehnte(r,s)** a sixteenth. **s~zig** inv a sixty. **s~zigste(r,s)** a sixtieth

See¹ m -s,-n lake

See² f - sea; **an der See** at the seaside; **auf See** at sea. **S~fahrt** f [sea] voyage; (Schiffahrt) navigation. **S~gang** m schwerer S~ rough sea. **S~hund** m seal. **s~krank** a seasick

Seele f -,-n soul

seelisch a psychological; (geistig) mental

See|macht f maritime power. **S~mann** m (pl -leute) seaman, sailor. **S~not** f in S~ not in distress. **S~räuber** m pirate. **S~rose** f water-lily. **S~sack** m kitbag. **S~stern** m starfish. **S~tang** m seaweed. **S~tüchtig** a seaworthy. **S~zunge** f sole

Segel nt -s,- sail. **S~boot** nt sailing-boat. **S~flugzeug** nt glider. **s~n** vt/i (sein/haben) sail. **S~schiff** nt sailing-ship.

S~sport m sailing. **S~tuch** nt canvas

Segen m -s blessing

Segler m -s,- yachtsman

segnen vt bless

sehen† vt see; watch ⟨Fernsehsendung⟩ □ vi (haben) see; (blicken) look (auf + acc at); (ragen) show (aus above); **gut/schlecht** s~ have good/bad eyesight; **vom S~ kennen** know by sight; **s~ nach** keep an eye on; (betreuen) look after; (suchen) look for. **s~swert** a worth seeing. **S~swürdigkeit** f -,-en sight

Sehne f -,-n tendon; (eines Bogens) string

sehnen (sich) vr long (nach for)

Sehn|sucht f -longing (nach for). **s~süchtig** a longing; ⟨Wunsch⟩ dearest

sehr adv very; (mit Verb) very much

seid s. **sein**¹; **ihr s~** you are

Seide f -,-n silk

Seidel nt -s,- beer-mug

seiden a silk … **S~papier** nt tissue paper

seidig a silky

Seife f -,-n soap. **S~npulver** nt soap powder. **S~nschaum** m lather

Seil nt -[e]s,-e rope; (Draht-) cable. **S~bahn** f cable railway. **S~tänzer(in)** m(f) tightrope walker

sein¹† vi (sein) be; **mir ist schlecht** I feel sick; **wie dem auch sei** be that as it may □ v aux have; **angekommen/gestorben s~** have arrived/died; **es ist/war viel zu tun** there is/was a lot to be done

sein² poss pron his; (Ding, Tier) its; (nach man) one's; **sein Glück versuchen** try one's luck. **s~e(r,s)** poss pron his; (nach man) one's own; **das S~ e tun** do one's share. **s~erseits** adv for his part. **s~etwegen** *adv* for his sake; (*wegen ihm*) because of him, on his account. **s~ige** *poss pron* **der/die/das s~ige** his

seinlassen† *vt sep* leave; (*aufhören mit*) stop

seins *poss pron* his; (*nach man*) one's own

seit *conj & prep* (+ *dat*) since; **s~ einiger Zeit** for some time [past]; **ich wohne s~ zehn Jahren hier** I've lived here for ten years. **s~dem** *conj* since □*adv* since then

Seite *f*,-n side; (*Buch-*) page; **zur S~ treten** step aside; **jds starke S~** s.o.'s strong point; **von S~n** (+ *gen*) on the part of; **auf der einen/anderen S~** (*fig*) on the one/other hand

Seiten|schiff *nt* [side] aisle. **S~sprung** *m* infidelity. **S~stechen** *nt* -s (*Med*) stitch. **S~straße** *f* side-street. **S~streifen** *m* verge; (*Autobahn-*) hard shoulder

seither *adv* since then

seitlich *a* side ... □*adv* at/on the side; **s~ von** to one side of □*prep* (+ *gen*) to one side of

Sekret|är *m* -s,-e secretary; (*Schrank*) bureau. **S~ariat** *nt* -[e]s,-e secretary's office. **S~ärin** *f* -,-nen secretary

Sekt *m* -[e]s [German] sparkling wine

Sekte *f* -,-n sect

Sektor *m* -s,-en /-'to:rən/ sector

Sekunde *f* -,-n second

selber *pron* (*fam*) = selbst

selbst *pron* oneself; **ich/du/er/sie s~** I myself /you yourself/ he himself/she herself; **wir/ihr/sie s~** we ourselves/you yourselves/ they themselves; **ich schneide mein Haar s~** I cut my own hair; **von s~** of one's own accord; (*automatisch*) automatically □*adv* even

selbständig *a* independent; self-employed (*Handwerker*); **sich s~ machen** set up on one's own. **S~keit** *f* independence

Selbstbedienung *f* self-service. **S~srestaurant** *nt* self-service restaurant, cafeteria

Selbst|befriedigung *f* masturbation. **s~bewußt** *a* self-confident. **S~bewußtsein** *nt* self-confidence. **S~erhaltung** *f* self-preservation. **s~gemacht** *a* home-made. **s~haftend** *a* self-adhesive. **S~hilfe** *f* self-help. **s~klebend** *a* self-adhesive. **S~kostenpreis** *m* cost price. **S~laut** *m* vowel. **s~los** *a* selfless. **S~mord** *m* suicide. **S~mörder(in)** *m(f)* suicide. **s~mörderisch** *a* suicidal. **S~porträt** *nt* self-portrait. **s~sicher** *a* self-assured. **S~sucht** *f* selfishness. **s~süchtig** *a* selfish. **S~tanken** *nt* self-service (for petrol). **s~tätig** *a* automatic. **S~versorgung** *f* self-catering

selbstverständlich *a* natural; etw für **s~ halten** take sth for granted; **das ist s~** that goes without saying; **s~!** of course!

Selbst|verteidigung *f* self-defence. **S~vertrauen** *nt* self-confidence. **S~verwaltung** *f* self-government

selig *a* blissfully happy; (*Relig*) blessed; (*verstorben*) late. **S~keit** *f* bliss

Sellerie *m* -s,-s & *f* -,- celeriac; (*Stangen-*) celery

selten *a* rare □*adv* rarely, seldom; (*besonders*) exceptionally. **S~heit** *f* -,-en rarity

seltsam *a* odd, strange. **s~erweise** *adv* oddly/strangely enough

Semester *nt* -s,- (*Univ*) semester

Semikolon *nt* -s,-s semicolon

Seminar *nt* -s,-e seminar; (*Institut*) department; (*Priester-*) seminary

Semmel f -,-n [bread] roll

Senat m -[e]s,-e senate. **S~or** m -s,-en /-'to:rən/ senator

senden[1] vt send

sende|n[2] vt (reg) broadcast; (über Funk) transmit, send. **S~r** m -s,- [broadcasting] station; (Anlage) transmitter. **S~reihe** f series

Sendung f -,-en consignment, shipment; (TV) programme

Senf m -s mustard

senil a senile. **S~ität** f - senility

Senior m -s,-en /-'o:rən/ senior; **S~en** senior citizens. **S~enheim** nt old people's home

senken vt lower; bring down ⟨Fieber, Preise⟩; bow ⟨Kopf⟩; **sich s~** come down, fall; (absinken) subside

senkrecht a vertical. **S~e** f -n,-n perpendicular

Sensation /-'tsjo:n/ f -,-en sensation. **s~ell** a sensational

Sense f -,-n scythe

sentimental a sentimental

September m -s,- September

Serie /'ze:rjə/ f -,-n series; (Briefmarken) set; (Comm) range. **S~nnummer** f serial number

Serpentine f -,-n winding road; (Kehre) hairpin bend

Service[1] /zɛr'vi:s/ nt -[s],- /-'vi:s[əs], -'vi:sə/ service, set

Service[2] /'zœ:gvis/ m & nt -s /-vis[əs]/ (Comm, Tennis) service

servier|en vt/i (haben) serve. **S~erin** f -,-nen waitress

Serviette f -,-n napkin, serviette

Servus int (Aust) cheerio; (Begrüßung) hallo

Sessel m -s,- armchair. **S~bahn** f, **S~lift** m chair-lift

setz|en vt put; (abstellen) set down; (hin-) sit down ⟨Kind⟩; move ⟨Spielstein⟩; } (pflanzen) plant; (schreiben, wetten) put; **sich s~en** sit down; (sinken) settle □vi (sein) leap □vi (haben) **s~en auf** (+acc) back

Seuche f -,-n epidemic

seufz|en vi (haben) sigh. **S~er** m -s,- sigh

Sex /zɛks/ m -[es] sex

Sexu|**alität** f - sexuality. **s~ell** a sexual

sezieren vt dissect

Shampoo /ʃam'pu:/ nt -s shampoo

siamesisch a Siamese

sich refl pron oneself; (mit er/sie/es) himself/herself/itself; (mit sie pl) themselves; (mit Sie) yourself; (pl) yourselves; (einander) each other; **s~ kennen** know oneself/(einander) each other; **s~ waschen** have a wash; **s~** (dat) **die Haare kämmen** comb one's hair; **s~ wundern** be surprised

Sichel f -,-n sickle

sicher a safe; (gesichert) secure; (gewiß) certain; (zuverlässig) reliable; sure ⟨Urteil⟩; steady ⟨Hand⟩; (selbstbewußt) self-confident; **bist du s~?** are you sure? □adv safely; securely; certainly; reliably; self-confidently; (wahrscheinlich) most probably; **s~!** certainly!

Sicherheit f - safety; (Pol, Psych) security; (Gewißheit) certainty; (Zuverlässigkeit) reliability; (des Urteils) surety; (Selbstbewußtsein) self-confidence. **S~sgurt** m safety-belt; (Auto) seat-belt. **S~snadel** f safety-pin

sicherlich adv certainly; (wahrscheinlich) most probably

sicher|n vt secure; (garantieren) safeguard; (schützen) protect; put the safety-catch on ⟨Pistole⟩. **S~ung** f -,-en safeguard, protection; (Gewehr-) safety-catch; (Electr) fuse

Sicht f - view; (S~weite) visibility; **auf lange S~** in the long term. **s~bar** a visible. **S~vermerk** m visa. **S~weite** f visibility; **in S~weite** within sight

sie *pron* (*nom*) (*sg*) she; (*Ding, Tier*) it; (*pl*) they; (*acc*) (*sg*) her; (*Ding, Tier*) it; (*pl*) them

Sie *pron* you; **gehen/warten Sie!** go/wait!

Sieb *nt* -[e]s,-e sieve; (*Tee-*) strainer. **s~en**[1] *vt* sieve, sift

sieben[2] *inv a*, **S~** *f* -,-en seven. **s~te(r,s)** *a* seventh

sieb|te(r,s) *a* seventh. **s~zehn** *inv a* seventeen. **s~zehnte(r,s)** *a* seventeenth. **s~zig** *inv a* seventy. **s~zigste(r,s)** *a* seventieth

siede|n† *vt/i* (*haben*) boil. **S~punkt** *m* boiling point

Siedlung *f* -,-en (*housing estate*); (*Niederlassung*) settlement

Sieg *m* -[e]s,-e victory

Siegel *nt* -s,- seal. **S~ring** *m* signet-ring

sieg|en *vi* (*haben*) win. **S~er(in)** *m* -s,- (*f* -,-nen) winner. **s~reich** *a* victorious

siezen *vt jdn* **s~** call s.o. 'Sie'

Signal *nt* -s,-e signal

Silbe *f* -,-n syllable

Silber *nt* -s silver

Silizium *nt* -s silicon

Silo *m* & *nt* -s,-s silo

Silvester *nt* -s New Year's Eve

Sims *m* & *nt* -es,-e ledge

sind *s. sein*[1]; **wir/sie s~** we/they are

Sinfonie *f* -,-n symphony

singen† *vt/i* (*haben*) sing

Singvogel *m* songbird

sinken† *vi* (*sein*) sink; (*niedriger werden*) drop; (*niedriger werden*) go down, fall; **den Mut s~ lassen** lose courage

Sinn *m* -[e]s,-e sense; (*Denken*) mind; (*Zweck*) point; **in gewissem S~e** in a sense; **es hat keinen S~** it is pointless. **S~bild** *nt* symbol

sinnlich *a* sensory; (*sexuell*) sensual; (*Genüsse*) sensuous.

S~keit *f* - sensuality; sensuousness

sinn|los *a* senseless; (*zwecklos*) pointless. **s~voll** *a* meaningful; (*vernünftig*) sensible

Sintflut *f* flood

Sippe *f* -,-n clan

Sirene *f* -,-n siren

Sirup *m* -s,-e syrup

Sitte *f* -,-n custom; **S~n** manners

sittlich *a* moral. **S~keit** *f* - morality. **S~keitsverbrecher** *m* sex offender

Situation /-'tsjo:n/ *f* -,-en situation. **s~iert** *a* **gut/schlecht s~iert** well/badly off

Sitz *m* -es,-e seat; (*Paßform*) fit

sitzen† *vi* (*haben*) sit; (*sich befinden*) be; (*passen*) fit; (*fam: treffen*) hit home; **s~ bleiben** remain seated; **[im Gefängnis] s~** (*fam*) be in jail. **s~bleiben**† *vi sep* (*sein*) (*fam*) (*Sch*) stay or be kept down; (*nicht heiraten*) be left on the shelf; **s~bleiben auf** (+ *dat*) be left with

Sitz|gelegenheit *f* seat. **S~platz** *m* seat. **S~ung** *f* -,-en session

Sizilien /-jan/ *nt* -s Sicily

Skala *f* -,-len scale; (*Reihe*) range

Skalpell *nt* -s,-e scalpel

skalpieren *vt* scalp

Skandal *m* -s,-e scandal. **s~ös** *a* scandalous

Skandinav|ien /-jan/ *nt* -s Scandinavia. **s~isch** *a* Scandinavian

Skat *m* -s skat

Skelett *nt* -[e]s,-e skeleton

Skep|sis *f* - scepticism. **s~tisch** *a* sceptical

Ski /ʃiː/ *m* -s,-er ski; **Ski fahren od laufen** ski. **S~fahrer(in)**, **S~läufer(in)** *m(f)* skier. **S~sport** *m* skiing

Skizze *f* -,-n sketch. **s~ieren** *vt* sketch

Sklav|e *m* -n,-n slave. **S~erei** *f* - slavery. **S~in** *f* -,-nen slave

Skorpion m -s,-e scorpion; (Astr) Scorpio

Skrupel m -s,-. scruple. **s~los** a unscrupulous

Skulptur f -,-en sculpture

Slalom m -s,-s slalom

Slang /slɛŋ/ m -s slang

Slaw|e m -n,-n, **S~in** f -,-nen Slav. **s~isch** a Slav; (Lang) Slavonic

Slip m -s,-s briefs pl

Slowakische Republik f Slovakia

Smaragd m -[e]s,-e emerald

Smoking m -s,-s dinner jacket

Snob m -s,-s snob. **S~ismus** m snobbery. **s~istisch** a snobbish

so adv so; (so sehr) so much; (auf diese Weise) like this/that; (solch) such; (fam: sowieso) anyway; (fam: umsonst) free; (fam: ungefähr) about; **so gut/bald wie** as good/soon as; **so ein Zufall!** what a coincidence! **mir ist so, als ob** I feel as if; **so oder so** in any case; **so um zehn Mark** (fam) about ten marks; **so?** really? **so kommt doch!** come on then! **so** (also) so; (dann) then; **so daß** so that

sobald conj as soon as

Söckchen nt -s,- [ankle] sock

Socke f -,-n sock

Sockel m -s,- plinth, pedestal

Socken m -s,- sock

Sodbrennen nt -s heartburn

soeben adv just [now]

Sofa nt -s,-s settee, sofa

sofern adv provided [that]

sofort adv at once, immediately; (auf der Stelle) instantly

Software /ˈzɔftvɛːɐ̯/ f software

sogar adv even

sogenannt a so-called

Sohle f -,-n sole; (Tal-) bottom

Sohn m -[e]s,-̈e son

Sojabohne f soya bean

solange conj as long as

solch inv pron such; **s~ einer/ eine/eins** one/(Person) someone

like that. **s~e(r,s)** pron such one/(Person) someone like that; **s~ ein/eins** one/(Person) someone like that; **s~e** (pl) those; (Leute) people like that

Soldat m -en,-en soldier

Söldner m -s,- mercenary

Solidarität f -solidarity

solide a solid; (haltbar) sturdy; (sicher) sound, (anständig) respectable

Solist(in) m -en,-en (f -,-nen) soloist

Soll nt -s debit; (Produktions-) quota

sollen† v aux **er soll warten** he is to wait; (möge) let him wait; **was soll ich machen?** what shall I do? **du sollst nicht lügen** you shouldn't tell lies; **ihr sollt jetzt still sein!** will you be quiet now! **ich hätte es nicht tun s~** I ought not to or should not have done it; **er soll sehr nett/reich sein** he is supposed to be very nice/rich; **sollte es regnen, so ...** if it should rain then ...; **soll ich [mal versuchen]?** shall I [try]? **soll er doch!** let him!

Solo nt -s,-los & -li solo

somit adv therefore, so

Sommer m -s,- summer. **s~lich** a summery; (Sommer-) summer ... □adv **s~lich warm** as warm as summer. **S~schlußverkauf** m summer sale. **S~sprossen** fpl freckles

Sonate f -,-n sonata

Sonde f -,-n probe

Sonder|angebot nt special offer. **s~bar** a odd. **S~fahrt** f special excursion. **S~fall** m special case. **S~marke** f special stamp

sondern conj but; **nicht nur ... s~ auch** not only ... but also

Sonderpreis m special price

Sonett nt -[e]s,-e sonnet

Sonnabend m -s,-e Saturday. **s~s** adv on Saturdays

Sonne f -,-n sun. **s~n (sich)** vr sun oneself

Sonnen|aufgang m sunrise. **s~baden** vi (haben) sunbathe. **S~bank** f sun-bed. **S~blume** f sunflower. **S~brand** m sunburn. **S~brille** f sun-glasses pl. **S~energie** f solar energy. **S~finsternis** f solar eclipse. **S~milch** f sun-tan lotion. **S~öl** nt sun-tan oil. **S~schein** m sunshine. **S~schirm** m sunshade. **S~stich** m sunstroke. **S~uhr** f sundial. **S~untergang** m sunset. **S~wende** f solstice

sonnig a sunny

Sonntag m -s,-e Sunday. **s~s** adv on Sundays

sonst adv (gewöhnlich) usually; (im übrigen) apart from that; (andernfalls) otherwise, or [else]; **wer/was/wie/wo s~?** who/what/how/where else? **s~ nichts** nothing else; **s~ noch etwas?** anything else? **s~ noch Fragen?** any more questions? **s~ig** a other. **s~jemand** pron (fam) someone/(fragend, verneint) anyone else. **s~wer** pron = **s~jemand. s~wo** adv (fam) somewhere/anywhere else

sooft conj whenever

Sopran m -s,-e soprano

Sorge f -,-n worry (**um** about); (Fürsorge) care; **sich** (dat) **S~n machen** worry. **S~n** vi (haben) **s~n für** look after, care for; (vorsorgen) provide for; (sich kümmern) see to; **dafür s~n, daß see** [to it] or make sure that □vr **sich s~n** worry. **s~nfrei** a carefree. **s~nvoll** a worried. **s~recht** nt (Jur) custody

Sorg|falt f -,- care. **s~fältig** a careful

Sorte f -,-n kind, sort; (Comm) brand

sort|ieren vt sort [out]; (Comm) grade. **S~iment** nt -[e]s,-e range

sosehr conj however much

Soße f -,-n sauce; (Braten-) gravy; (Salat-) dressing

Souvenir /zuvə'niːɐ̯/ nt -s,-s souvenir

souverän /zuvə'rɛːn/ a sovereign

soviel conj however much; **s~ ich weiß** as far as I know □adv as much (**wie** as)

soweit conj as far as; (insoweit) [in] so far as □adv on the whole; **s~ wie möglich** as far as possible; **s~ sein** be ready

sowenig conj however little □adv no more (**wie** than)

sowie conj as well as; (sobald) as soon as

sowieso adv anyway, in any case

sowjetisch a Soviet

sowohl adv **s~ ... als od wie auch ...** as well as ...

sozial a social; (Beruf) caring. **S~arbeit** f social work. **S~demokrat** m social democrat. **S~hilfe** f social security

Sozialismus m - socialism. **S~t** m -en,-en socialist

Sozial|versicherung f National Insurance. **S~wohnung** f ≈ council flat

Soziologie f - sociology

Sozius m -,-se (Comm) partner; (Beifahrersitz) pillion

Spachtel m -s,- & f -,-n spatula

Spagat m -[e]s,-e (Aust) string; **S~ machen** do the splits pl

Spaghetti pl spaghetti sg

Spalier nt -s,-e trellis; **S~ stehen** line the route

Spalt m -[e]s,-e crack; (Gletscher-) crevasse; (Druck-) column; (Orangen-) segment. **s~en†** vt split. **S~ung** f -,-en splitting; (Kluft) split; (Phys) fission

Span m -[e]s,-e [wood] chip

Spange f -,-n clasp; (Haar-) slide; (Zahn-) brace; (Arm-) bangle

Span|ien /-jən/ *nt* -s Spain. **S~ier**
m -s,-, **S~ierin** *f* -,-nen Spaniard. **s~isch** *a* Spanish. **S~isch**
nt -[s] (*Lang*) Spanish

Spann *m* -[e]s instep

Spanne *f* -,-n span; (*Zeit-*) space;
(*Comm*) margin

spann|en *vt* stretch; put up
⟨*Leine*⟩; (*straffen*) tighten; (*an-*)
harness (**an** + *acc* to) □*vi* (*haben*)
be too tight. **s~end** *a* exciting.
S~ung *f* -,-en tension; (*Erwartung*) suspense; (*Electr*) voltage

Spar|buch *nt* savings -book.
S~büchse *f* money-box. **s~en**
vt/i (*haben*) save; (*sparsam sein*)
economize (**mit/an** + *dat* on).
S~er *m* -s,- saver

Spargel *m* -s,- asparagus

Spar|kasse *f* savings bank.
S~konto *nt* deposit account

sparsam *a* economical; ⟨*Person*⟩
thrifty. **S~keit** *f* - economy;
thrift

Sparschwein *nt* piggy bank

Sparte *f* -,-n branch; (*Zeitungs-*)
section; (*Rubrik*) column

Spaß *m* -es,ꞏe fun; (*Scherz*) joke;
S~ machen be fun; ⟨*Person:*⟩ be
joking; **viel S~!** I have a good
time! **s~en** *vi* (*haben*) joke

Spastiker *m* -s,- spastic

spät *a & adv* late; **wie s~ ist es?**
what time is it? **zu s~ kommen**
be late

Spaten *m* -s,- spade

später *a* later; (*zukünftig*) future

spätestens *adv* at the latest

Spatz *m* -en,-en sparrow

Spätzle *pl* (*Culin*) noodles

spazieren *vi* (*sein*) stroll. **s~-
gehen†** *vi sep* (*sein*) go for a walk

Spazier|gang *m* walk; **einen
S~gang machen** go for a walk.
S~stock *m* walking-stick

Specht *m* -[e]s,-e woodpecker

Speck *m* -s bacon

Spedi|teur /ʃpediˈtøːɐ/ *m* -s,-e
haulage|(*für Umzüge*) removals

contractor. **S~tion** /-ˈtsjoːn/ *f*
-,-en carriage, haulage; (*Firma*)
haulage|(*für Umzüge*) removals
firm

Speer *m* -[e]s,-e spear; (*Sport*)
javelin

Speiche *f* -,-n spoke

Speichel *m* -s saliva

Speicher *m* -s,- warehouse; (*Computer*) memory. **s~n** *vt* store

Speise *f* -,-n food; (*Gericht*) dish.
S~eis *nt* ice-cream. **S~kam-
mer** *f* larder. **S~karte** *f* menu.
s~n *vi* eat □*vt* feed. **S~röhre** *f*
oesophagus. **S~saal** *m* dining-
room. **S~wagen** *m* dining-car

Spektrum *nt* -s,-tra spectrum

Spekul|ant *m* -en,-en speculator.
S~ieren *vi* (*haben*) speculate

Spelze *f* -,-n husk

spendabel *a* generous

Spende *f* -,-n donation. **s~n** *vt*
donate; give ⟨*Blut, Schatten*⟩.
Beifall s~n applaud. **S~r** *m* -s,-
donor; (*Behälter*) dispenser

spendieren *vt* pay for

Sperling *m* -s,-e sparrow

Sperr|e *f* -,-n barrier; (*Verbot*) ban;
(*Comm*) embargo. **s~n** *vt* close;
(*ver-*) block; (*verbieten*) ban; cut
off ⟨*Telefon*⟩; stop ⟨*Scheck*⟩; **s~n**
in (+ *acc*) put in ⟨*Gefängnis*⟩

Sperr|holz *nt* plywood. **S~ig** *a*
bulky. **S~müll** *m* bulky refuse.
S~stunde *f* closing time

Spesen *pl* expenses

spezial|isieren (sich) *vr* special-
ize (**auf** + *acc* in). **S~ist** *m*
-en,-en specialist. **S~ität** *f*-,-en
speciality

spicken *vt* (*Culin*) lard; **gespickt
mit** (*fig*) full of □*vi* (*haben*) (*fam*)
crib (**bei** from)

Spiegel *m* -s,- mirror; (*Wasser-*)
level. **S~bild** *nt* reflection. **S~ei**
nt fried egg. **s~n** *vt* reflect; **sich**
s~n be reflected □*vi* (*haben*) reflect [the light]; (*glänzen*) gleam.
S~ung *f* -,-en reflection

Spiel *nt* -[e]s,-e game; *(Spielen)* playing; *(Glücks-)* gambling; *(Schau-)* play; *(Satz)* set; **auf dem S~ stehen** be at stake; **aufs S~ setzen** risk. **S~automat** *m* fruit machine. **S~bank** *f* casino. **S~dose** *f* musical box. **s~en** *vt/i (haben)* play; *(im Glücksspiel)* gamble; *(vortäuschen)* act; *(Roman:)* be set (**in** + *dat* in); **s~en mit** *(fig)* toy with

Spieler(in) *m* -s,- *(f* -,-nen) player; *(Glücks-)* gambler

Spielfeld *nt* field, pitch. **S~marke** *f* chip. **S~plan** *m* programme. **S~platz** *m* playground. **S~raum** *m (fig)* scope; *(Techn)* clearance. **S~regeln** *fpl* rules [of the game]. **S~sachen** *fpl* toys. **S~verderber** *m* -s,- spoilsport. **S~waren** *fpl* toys. **S~warengeschäft** *nt* toyshop. **S~zeug** *nt* toy; toys *pl*

Spieß *m* -es,-e spear; *(Brat-)* spit; skewer; *(Fleisch-)* kebab. **S~er** *m* -s,- [petit] bourgeois. **s~ig** *a* bourgeois

Spike[s]reifen /'ʃpaɪk[s]-/ *m* studded tyre

Spinat *m* -s spinach

Spindel *f* -,-n spindle

Spinne *f* -,-n spider

spinn|en *vt/i (haben)* spin; **er spinnt** *(fam)* he's crazy. **S~[en]gewebe** *nt*, **S~webe** *f* -,-n cobweb

Spion *m* -s,-e spy

Spionage /ʃpio'naːʒə/ *f* - espionage, spying. **S~abwehr** *f* counter-espionage

spionieren *vi (haben)* spy

Spionin *f* -,-nen [woman] spy

Spiral|**e** *f* -,-n spiral. **s~ig** *a* spiral

Spirituosen *pl* spirits

Spiritus *m* - alcohol; *(Brenn-)* methylated spirits *pl*. **S~kocher** *m* spirit stove

spitz *a* pointed; *(scharf)* sharp; *(schrill)* shrill; *(Winkel)* acute

Spitze *f* -,-n point; *(oberer Teil)* top; *(vorderer Teil)* front; *(Pfeil-, Finger-)* tip; *(Schuh-)* toe; *(Ziga-retten-)* holder; *(Höchstleistung)* maximum; *(Tex)* lace

Spitzel *m* -s,- informer

spitzen *vt* sharpen; purse *(Lip-pen)*; prick up *(Ohren)*. **S~geschwindigkeit** *f* top speed

Spitzname *m* nickname

Spleen /ʃpliːn/ *m* -s,-e obsession

Splitter *m* -s,- splinter. **s~n** *vi (sein)* shatter

sponsern *vt* sponsor

Sporn *m* -[e]s,Sporen spur; **ei-nem Pferd die Sporen geben** spur a horse

Sport *m* -[e]s sport; *(Hobby)* hobby. **S~ler** *m* -s,- sportsman. **S~lerin** *f* -,-nen sportswoman. **s~lich** *a* sports . . . ; *(fair)* sporting; *(flott)* sporty. **S~platz** *m* sports ground. **S~verein** *m* sports club. **S~wagen** *m* sports car; *(Kinder-)* push-chair

Spott *m* -[e]s mockery

spotten *vi (haben)* mock

spöttisch *a* mocking

Sprach|e *f* -,-n language; *(Sprech-fähigkeit)* speech; **zur S~e bringen** bring up. **S~fehler** *m* speech defect. **S~labor** *nt* language laboratory. **s~los** *a* speechless

Spray /ʃpreː/ *nt & m* -s,-s spray

Sprechanlage *f* intercom

sprechen† *vt/i (haben)* speak/*(sich unterhalten)* talk *(über* + *acc* von about/of); **deutsch s~** speak German *vt* speak; *(sagen)* say; pronounce *(Urteil)*; **schuldig s~** find guilty; **Herr X ist nicht zu s~** Mr X is not available

Sprechstunde *f* consulting hours *pl*; *(Med)* surgery. **S~nhilfe** *f* *(Med)* receptionist

Sprechzimmer *nt* consulting room

spreizen vt spread

spreng|en vt blow up; blast ⟨Felsen⟩; ⟨fig⟩ burst; ⟨begießen⟩ water; ⟨mit Sprenger⟩ sprinkle; dampen ⟨Wäsche⟩. **S~er** m -s,- sprinkler. **S~kopf** m warhead. **S~körper** m explosive device. **S~stoff** m explosive

Sprich|wort nt (pl -wörter) proverb. **s~wörtlich** a proverbial

Springbrunnen m fountain

spring|en† vi (sein) jump; ⟨Schwimmsport⟩ dive; ⟨Ball:⟩ bounce; ⟨spritzen⟩ spurt; ⟨zer-⟩ break; ⟨rissig werden⟩ crack; ⟨SGer: laufen⟩ run. **S~er** m -s,- jumper; ⟨Kunst-⟩ diver; ⟨Schach⟩ knight. **S~reiten** nt show-jumping. **S~seil** nt skipping-rope

Sprint m -s,-s sprint

Spritz|e f -,-n syringe; ⟨Injektion⟩ injection; ⟨Feuer-⟩ hose. **s~en** vt spray; ⟨be-, ver-⟩ splash; ⟨Culin⟩ pipe; ⟨Med⟩ inject □vi ⟨haben⟩ splash; ⟨Fett:⟩ spit □vi ⟨sein⟩ splash; ⟨hervor-⟩ spurt. **S~er** m -s,- splash; ⟨Schuß⟩ dash. **s~ig** a lively; ⟨Wein⟩ sparkling

spröde a brittle; ⟨trocken⟩ dry

Sprosse f -,-n rung

Sprotte f -,-n sprat

Spruch m -[e]s,-̈e saying; ⟨Denk-⟩ motto; ⟨Zitat⟩ quotation. **S~band** nt (pl -bänder) banner

Sprudel m -s, sparkling mineral water. **s~n** vi ⟨haben/sein⟩ bubble

Sprüh|dose f aerosol [can]. **s~en** vt spray □vi ⟨sein⟩ ⟨Funken:⟩ fly; ⟨fig⟩ sparkle

Sprung m -[e]s,-̈e jump, leap; ⟨Schwimmsport⟩ dive; ⟨fam: Katzen-⟩ stone's throw; ⟨Riß⟩ crack. **S~brett** nt springboard. **S~schanze** f ski-jump

Spucke f - spit. **s~n** vt/i ⟨haben⟩ spit; ⟨sich übergeben⟩ be sick

Spuk m -[e]s,-e apparition. **s~en** vi ⟨haben⟩ ⟨Geist:⟩ walk

Spülbecken nt sink

Spule f -,-n spool

spulen vt spool

spül|en vt rinse; ⟨schwemmen⟩ wash; **Geschirr s~en** wash up □vi ⟨haben⟩ flush [the toilet]. **S~mittel** nt washing-up liquid

Spur f -,-en track; ⟨Fahr-⟩ lane; ⟨Fährte⟩ trail; ⟨Anzeichen⟩ trace; ⟨Hinweis⟩ lead

spürbar a noticeable

spür|en vt feel; ⟨seelisch⟩ sense. **S~hund** m tracker dog

spurlos adv without trace

spurten vi ⟨sein⟩ put on a spurt

sputen (sich) vr hurry

Staat m -[e]s,-en state; ⟨Land⟩ country. **s~lich** a state ...

Staatsangehörige(r) m/f national. **S~keit** f - nationality

Staats|anwalt m state prosecutor. **S~beamte(r)** m civil servant. **S~besuch** m state visit. **S~bürger(in)** m(f) national. **S~streich** m coup

Stab m -[e]s,-̈e rod; ⟨Gitter-⟩ bar; ⟨Sport⟩ baton; ⟨Mil⟩ staff

Stäbchen ntpl chopsticks

Stabhochsprung m pole-vault

stabil a stable; ⟨gesund⟩ robust; ⟨solide⟩ sturdy

Stachel m -s,- spine; ⟨Gift-⟩ sting; ⟨Spitze⟩ spike. **S~beere** f gooseberry. **S~draht** m barbed wire. **s~ig** a prickly

Stadion nt -s,-ien stadium

Stadium nt -s,-ien stage

Stadt f -,-̈e city ⟨Groß-⟩ city

städtisch a urban; ⟨kommunal⟩ municipal

Stadt|mitte f town centre. **S~plan** m street map. **S~teil** m district

Staffel f -,-n team; ⟨S~lauf⟩ relay; ⟨Mil⟩ squadron

Staffelei f -,-en easel

Staffel|lauf m relay race. **s~n** vt stagger; ⟨abstufen⟩ grade

Stahl m -s steel. **S~beton** m reinforced concrete

Stall m -[e]s,¨e stable; (Kuh-) shed; (Schweine-) sty; (Hühner-) coop; (Kaninchen-) hutch

Stamm m -[e]s,¨e trunk; (Sippe) tribe; (Wort-) stem. **S~baum** m family tree; (eines Tieres) pedigree

stammeln vt/i (haben) stammer

stammen vi (haben) come/(zeitlich) date (von/aus from)

stämmig a sturdy

Stamm|kundschaft f regulars pl. **S~lokal** nt favourite pub

stampfen vi (haben) stamp; (Maschine:) pound; **mit den Füßen s~en** stamp one's feet □vi (sein) tramp □vt pound

Stand m -[e]s,¨e standing position; (Zustand) state; (Spiel-) score; (Höhe) level; (gesellschaftlich) class; (Verkaufs-) stall; (Messe-) stand; (Taxi-) rank; **auf den neuesten S~ bringen** update

Standard m -s,-s standard

Standbild nt statue

Ständer m -s,- stand; (Geschirr-, Platten-) rack; (Kerzen-) holder

Standes|amt nt registry office. **S~beamte(r)** m registrar

ständig a constant; (fest) permanent

Stand|licht nt sidelights pl. **S~ort** m position; (Firmen-) location; (Mil) garrison. **S~punkt** m point of view. **S~spur** f hard shoulder. **S~uhr** f grandfather clock

Stange f -,-n bar; (Holz-) pole; (Gardinen-) rail; (Hühner-) perch; **von der S~** (fam) off the peg. **S~nbohne** f runner bean

Stanniol nt -s tin foil. **S~papier** nt silver paper

stanzen vt stamp; punch (Loch)

Stapel m -s,- stack, pile. **S~lauf** m launch[ing]. **s~n** vt stack or pile up

Star[^1] m -[e]s,-e starling

Star[^2] m -[e]s (Med) [grauer] **S~** cataract; **grüner S~** glaucoma

Star[^3] m -s,-s (Theat, Sport) star

stark a strong; (Motor) powerful; (Verkehr, Regen) heavy; (Hitze) severe; (groß) big; (schlimm) bad; (dick) thick; (korpulent) stout

Stärke f -,-n (s. stark) strength; power; thickness; (Größe) size; (Mais-, Wäsche-) starch. **S~emehl** nt cornflour. **s~n** vt strengthen; starch (Wäsche). **S~ung** f -,-en strengthening; (Erfrischung) refreshment

starr a rigid; (steif) stiff

starren vi (haben) stare

Starrsinn m obstinacy

Start m -s,-s start; (Aviat) take-off. **S~bahn** f runway. **s~en** vi (sein) start; (Aviat) take off; (aufbrechen) set off; (teilnehmen) compete □vt start; (fig) launch

Station /-'tsio:n/ f -,-en station; (Haltestelle) stop; (Abschnitt) stage; (Med) ward; **S~ machen** break one's journey. **s~är** adv as an in-patient. **s~ieren** vt station

statisch a static

Statist(in) m -en,-en (f -,-nen) (Theat) extra

Statistik f -,-en statistics sg; (Aufstellung) statistics pl. **s~sch** a statistical

Stativ nt -s,-e (Phot) tripod

statt prep (+ gen) instead of; **s~dessen** instead

statt|finden† vi sep (haben) take place. **s~haft** a permitted

Statue /'ʃta:tuǝ/ f -,-n statue

Statur f -,- build, stature

Status m -, status

Statut nt -[e]s,-en statute

Stau m -[e]s,-s congestion; (Auto) [traffic] jam; (Rück-) tailback

Staub *m* -[e]s dust; **S~ wischen** dust

Staubecken *nt* reservoir

staub|ig *a* dusty. **s~saugen** *vt/i* (*haben*) vacuum, hoover. **S~sauger** *m* vacuum cleaner, Hoover (P)

Staudamm *m* dam

stauen *vt* dam up; **sich s~** accumulate; ⟨*Autos:*⟩ form a tail-back

staunen *vi* be amazed or astonished. **S~** *nt* -s amazement

Stau|see *m* reservoir. **S~ung** *f* -,-en congestion; [traffic] jam

Steak /ʃteːk, steːk/ *nt* -s,-s steak

stechen† *vt* stick (**in** + *acc*); ⟨*verletzen*⟩ prick; (*mit Messer*) stab; ⟨*Insekt:*⟩ sting; ⟨*Mücke:*⟩ bite; □*vi* (*haben*) prick; ⟨*Insekt:*⟩ sting; ⟨*Mücke:*⟩ bite; (*mit Stechuhr*) clock in/out

Stech|ginster *m* gorse. **S~kahn** *m* punt. **S~palme** *f* holly. **S~uhr** *f* time clock

Steck|brief *m* 'wanted' poster. **S~dose** *f* socket. **s~en** *vt* put; (*mit Nadel, Reißzwecke*) pin; (*pflanzen*) plant □*vi* (*haben*) be; (*fest-*) be stuck

stecken|bleiben† *vi sep* (*sein*) get stuck. **S~pferd** *nt* hobby-horse

Steck|er *m* -s,- (*Electr*) plug. **S~nadel** *f* pin

Steg *m* -[e]s,-e foot-bridge; ⟨*Boots-*⟩ landing-stage; ⟨*Brillen-*⟩ bridge

stehen† *vi* (*haben*) stand; (*sich befinden*) be; (*still-*) be stationary; ⟨*Maschine, Uhr:*⟩ have stopped; **vor dem Ruin s~** face ruin; **zu jdm s~** ⟨*fig*⟩ stand by s.o.; **jdm [gut] s~** suit s.o.; **jdm gut s~** be on good terms; **es steht 3 zu 1** the score is 3 – 1. **s~bleiben†** *vi sep* (*sein*) stop; ⟨*Motor:*⟩ stall; ⟨*Zeit:*⟩ stand still; ⟨*Gebäude:*⟩ be left standing. **s~d** *a* standing; (*sich nicht bewegend*) stationary

⟨*Gewässer*⟩ stagnant. **s~lassen†** *vt sep* leave

Stehlampe *f* standard lamp

stehlen† *vt/i* (*haben*) steal; **sich s~** steal, creep

Steh|platz *m* standing place. **S~vermögen** *nt* stamina

steif *a* stiff

Steig|bügel *m* stirrup. **S~eisen** *nt* crampon

steigen† *vi* (*sein*) climb; ⟨*hochgehen*⟩ rise, go up; ⟨*Schulden, Spannung:*⟩ mount; **s~ auf** (+ *acc*) climb on [to] ⟨*Stuhl*⟩; climb ⟨*Berg*⟩; get on ⟨*Pferd, Fahrrad*⟩; **s~ in** (+ *acc*) climb into; get in ⟨*Auto*⟩; get on ⟨*Bus*⟩; **s~ aus** climb out of; get out of ⟨*Bett, Auto*⟩; get off ⟨*Bus*⟩; **s~de Preise** rising prices

steiger|n *vt* increase; **sich s~n** increase; (*sich verbessern*) improve. **S~ung** *f* -,-en increase; improvement. **S~** (*Gram*) comparison

steil *a* steep. **S~küste** *f* cliffs *pl*

Stein *m* -[e]s,-e stone; ⟨*Ziegel-*⟩ brick; ⟨*Spiel-*⟩ piece. **S~bock** *m* ibex; (*Astr*) Capricorn. **S~bruch** *m* quarry. **S~garten** *m* rockery. **S~gut** *nt* earthenware. **s~ig** *a* stony. **S~schlag** *m* rock fall

Stelle *f* -,-n place; (*Fleck*) spot; (*Abschnitt*) passage; (*Stellung*) job, post; (*Büro*) office; (*Behörde*) authority; **auf der S~** immediately

stellen *vt* put; (*aufrecht*) stand; set ⟨*Wecker, Aufgabe*⟩; ask ⟨*Frage*⟩; make ⟨*Antrag, Diagnose*⟩; **zur Verfügung s~** provide; **lauter/leiser s~** turn up/down; **kalt/warm s~** chill/keep hot; **sich s~** [go and] stand; give oneself up (*der Polizei* to the police); **gut gestellt sein** be well off

Stellen|anzeige f job advertisement. **S~vermittlung** f employment agency. **s~weise** adv in places

Stellung f -,-en position; (Arbeit) job; **S~ nehmen** make a statement (**zu** on). **S~suche** f job-hunting

Stellvertreter m deputy

Stelzen fpl stilts

stemmen vt press; lift ⟨Gewicht⟩

Stempel m -s,- stamp; (Post-) postmark; (Präge-) die; (Feingehalts-) hallmark. **s~n** vt stamp; hallmark ⟨Silber⟩; cancel ⟨Marke⟩

Stengel m -s,- stalk, stem

Steno f - (fam) shorthand

Steno|gramm n -[e]s,-e shorthand text. **S~graphie** f shorthand. **s~graphieren** vt take down in shorthand □vi (haben) do shorthand. **S~typistin** f -,-nen shorthand typist

Steppdecke f quilt

Steptanz m tap-dance

sterben† vi (sein) die (**an**+dat of); **im S~ liegen** be dying

sterblich a mortal. **S~keit** f - mortality

stereo adv in stereo. **S~anlage** f stereo (system)

steril a sterile. **s~isieren** vt sterilize. **S~ität** f - sterility

Stern m -[e]s,-e star. **S~bild** nt constellation. **S~chen** nt -s,- asterisk. **S~kunde** f astronomy. **S~schnuppe** f -,-n shooting star. **S~warte** f -,-n observatory

Steuer[1] nt -s,- steering-wheel; (Naut) helm; **am S~** at the wheel

Steuer[2] f -,-n tax

Steuer|bord nt -[e]s starboard [side]. **S~erklärung** f tax return. **s~frei** a & adv tax-free. **S~mann** m (pl -leute) helmsman; (beim Rudern) cox. **s~n** vt steer; (Aviat) pilot; (Techn) control. **s~pflichtig** a taxable. **s~rad** nt steering-wheel.

S~ruder nt helm. **S~ung** f - steering; (Techn) controls pl. **S~zahler** m -s,- taxpayer

Stewardeß f'stju:ɐdɛs/ f -,-dessen air hostess, stewardess

Stich m -[e]s,-e prick; (Messer-) stab; (S~wunde) stab wound; (Bienen-) sting; (Mücken-) bite; (Schmerz) stabbing pain; (Näh-) stitch; (Kupfer-) engraving; (Kartenspiel) trick

Stichprobe f spot check

stick|en vt/i (haben) embroider. **S~erei** f - embroidery

Stickstoff m nitrogen

Stiefel m -s,- boot

Stief|kind nt stepchild. **S~mutter** f stepmother. **S~mütterchen** nt -s,- pansy. **S~sohn** m stepson. **S~tochter** f stepdaughter. **S~vater** m stepfather

Stiege f -,-n stairs pl

Stiel m -[e]s,-e handle; (Blumen-, Gläser-) stem; (Blatt-) stalk

Stier m -[e]s,-e bull; (Astr) Taurus

Stierkampf m bullfight

Stift[1] m -[e]s,-e pin; (Nagel) tack; (Blei-) pencil; (Farb-) crayon

Stift[2] nt -[e]s [endowed] foundation. **s~en** vt endow; (spenden) donate; create ⟨Unheil⟩; bring about ⟨Frieden⟩. **S~ung** f -,-en foundation; (Spende) donation

Stil m -[e]s,-e style; **in großem S~** in style

still a quiet; (reglos, ohne Kohlensäure) still; (heimlich) secret; **der S~e Ozean** the Pacific

Stilleben nt still life

stilleg|en vt sep close down. **S~ung** f -,-en closure

stillen vt satisfy; quench ⟨Durst⟩; stop ⟨Schmerzen⟩; breast-feed ⟨Kind⟩

stillhalten† vi sep (haben) keep still

Stillschweigen nt silence

Still|stand *m* standstill; **zum S~stand bringen** stop. **S~stehen†** *vi sep* (*haben*) stand still; (*anhalten*) stop; ⟨*Verkehr:*⟩ be at a standstill

Stimm|bänder *ntpl* vocal cords. **s~berechtigt** *a* entitled to vote. **S~bruch** *m* **er ist im S~bruch** his voice is breaking

Stimme *f* -,-n voice; (*Wahl-*) vote

stimmen *vi* (*haben*) be right; (*wählen*) vote □ *vt* tune

Stimmung *f* -,-en mood; (*Atmosphäre*) atmosphere. **s~svoll** *a* full of atmosphere

Stimmzettel *m* ballot-paper

stink|en† *vi* (*haben*) smell/(*stark*) stink (**nach** of). **S~tier** *nt* skunk

Stipendium *nt* -s,-ien scholarship; (*Beihilfe*) grant

Stirn *f* -,-en forehead; **die S~ bieten** (+ *dat*) (*fig*) defy

stochern *vi* (*haben*) **s~ in** (+ *dat*) poke ⟨*Feuer*⟩; pick at ⟨*Essen*⟩

Stock¹ *m* -[e]s,⸚e stick; (*Ski-*) pole; (*Bienen-*) hive; (*Rosen-*) bush; (*Reb-*) vine

Stock² *m* -[e]s,- storey, floor. **S~bett** *nt* bunk-beds *pl*

stock|en *vi* (*haben*) stop; ⟨*Verkehr:*⟩ come to a standstill. **S~ung** *f* -,-en hold-up

Stockwerk *nt* storey, floor

Stoff *m* -[e]s,-e substance; (*Tex*) fabric, material; (*Thema*) subject [matter]; (*Gesprächs-*) topic. **S~wechsel** *m* metabolism

stöhnen *vi* (*haben*) groan, moan

Stola *f* -,-len stole

Stollen *m* -s,- gallery; (*Kuchen*) stollen

stolpern *vi* (*sein*) stumble; **s~ über** (+ *acc*) trip over

stolz *a* proud (**auf** + *acc* of). **S~** *m* -es pride

stopfen *vt* stuff; (*stecken*) put; (*ausbessern*) darn □ *vi* (*haben*) be constipating; (*fam: essen*) guzzle

Stopp *m* -s,-s stop. **s~** *int* stop!

stoppelig *a* stubbly

stopp|en *vt* stop; (*Sport*) time □ *vi* (*haben*) stop. **S~uhr** *f* stopwatch

Stöpsel *m* -s,- plug; (*Flaschen-*) stopper

Storch *m* -[e]s,⸚e stork

Store /ʃtoːɐ/ *m* -s,-s net curtain

stören *vt* disturb; disrupt ⟨*Rede*⟩; jam ⟨*Sender*⟩; (*mißfallen*) bother □ *vi* (*haben*) be a nuisance

stornieren *vt* cancel

Störung *f* -,-en (*s. stören*) disturbance; disruption; (*Med*) trouble; (*Radio*) interference; **technische S~** technical fault

Stoß *m* -es,⸚e push, knock; (*mit Ellbogen*) dig; (*Hörner-*) butt; (*mit Waffe*) thrust; (*Schwimm-*) stroke; (*Erd-*) shock. **S~dämpfer** *m* -s,- shock absorber

stoßen† *vt* push, knock; (*mit Füßen*) kick; (*mit Kopf*) butt; (*anpoke*, nudge; (*treiben*) thrust; **sich** (*dat*) **den Kopf s~** hit one's head □ *vi* (*haben*) push; **s~ an** (+ *acc*) knock against; (*angrenzen*) adjoin □ *vi* (*sein*) **s~ gegen** knock against; bump into ⟨*Tür*⟩; **s~ auf** (+ *acc*) bump into; (*entdecken*) come across; strike ⟨*Öl*⟩

Stoß|stange *f* bumper. **S~verkehr** *m* rush-hour traffic. **S~zeit** *f* rush-hour

stottern *vt/i* (*haben*) stutter, stammer

Str. *abbr* (*Straße*) St

Strafanstalt *f* prison

Strafe *f* -,-n punishment; (*Jur & fig*) penalty; (*Geld-*) fine; (*Freiheits-*) sentence. **s~n** *vt* punish

straff *a* tight, taut

Strafgesetz *nt* criminal law

sträf|lich *a* criminal. **S~ling** *m* -s,-e prisoner

Straf|mandat *nt* (*Auto*) [parking/speeding] ticket. **S~porto** *nt* excess postage. **S~stoß** *m* penalty. **S~tat** *f* crime

Strahl m -[e]s,-en ray; (einer Taschenlampe) beam; (Wasser-) jet. **s~en** vi (haben) shine; (funkeln) sparkle; (lächeln) beam. **S~enbehandlung** f radiotherapy. **S~ung** f radiation

Strähne f -,-n strand

Strampel|höschen nt -s,- rompers pl. **s~n** vi (haben) ⟨Baby:⟩ kick

Strand m -[e]s,-e beach

Strang m -[e]s,-e rope

Strapaz|e f -,-n strain. **s~ieren** vt be hard on; tax ⟨Nerven⟩

Straß m - & -sses paste

Straße f -,-n road; street; (Meeres-) strait. **S~nbahn** f tram. **S~nkarte** f road-map. **S~nsperre** f road-block

Strateg|ie f -,-n strategy. **s~egisch** a strategic

Strauch m -[e]s,Sträucher bush

Strauß[1] m -es, Sträuße bunch [of flowers]; (Bukett) bouquet

Strauß[2] m -es,-e ostrich

streb|en vi (haben) strive (nach for). **S~er** m -s,- (Sch) swot. **s~sam** a industrious

Strecke f -,-n stretch, section; (Entfernung) distance; (Rail) line; (Route) route

strecken vt stretch; (aus-) stretch out; (gerade machen) straighten; **den Kopf aus dem Fenster s~** put one's head out of the window

Streich m -[e]s,-e prank, trick

streicheln vt stroke

streichen† vt spread; (weg-) smooth; (an-) paint; (aus-) delete; (kürzen) cut

Streichholz nt match. **S~schachtel** f matchbox

Streich|instrument nt stringed instrument. **S~käse** m cheese spread. **S~ung** f -,-en deletion; (Kürzung) cut

Streife f -,-n patrol

streifen vt brush against; (berühren) touch; (verletzen) graze; (fig) touch on ⟨Thema⟩

Streifen m -s,- stripe; (Licht-) streak; (auf der Fahrbahn) line; (schmales Stück) strip

Streifenwagen m patrol car

Streik m -s,-s strike; **in den S~ treten** go on strike. **S~brecher** m strike-breaker, (pej) scab. **s~en** vi (haben) strike; (fam) refuse; (versagen) pack up. **S~ende(r)** m striker. **S~posten** m picket

Streit m -[e]s,-e quarrel; (Auseinandersetzung) dispute. **s~en†** vr|i (haben) [sich] s~en quarrel. **S~igkeiten** fpl quarrels. **S~kräfte** fpl armed forces

streng a strict; ⟨Blick, Ton⟩ stern; (rauh) severe; ⟨Geschmack⟩ sharp. **S~e** f - strictness; sternness; severity. **s~genommen** adv strictly speaking

Streß m -sses,-sse stress

streu|en vt spread; (ver-) scatter; sprinkle ⟨Zucker, Salz⟩; **die Straßen s~** grit the roads

streunen vi (sein) roam

Strich m -[e]s,-e line; (Feder-, Pinsel-) stroke; (Gedanken-) dash. **S~kode** m bar code. **S~punkt** m semicolon

Strick m -[e]s,-e cord; (Seil) rope

strick|en vt|i (haben) knit. **S~jacke** f cardigan. **S~leiter** f rope-ladder. **S~waren** fpl knitwear sg. **S~zeug** nt knitting

striegeln vt groom

strittig a contentious

Stroh nt -[e]s straw. **S~blumen** fpl everlasting flowers. **S~dach** nt thatched roof. **S~halm** m straw

Strolch m -[e]s,-e (fam) rascal

Strom m -[e]s,-e river; (Menschen-, Blut-) stream; (Tränen-) flood; (Schwall) torrent; (Electr) current, power; **gegen den S~**

(*fig*) against the tide. **s~ab-wärts** *adv* downstream. **s~auf-wärts** *adv* upstream

strömen *vi* (*sein*) flow; (*Menschen, Blut:*) stream, pour

Strom|kreis *m* circuit. **s~linienförmig** *a* streamlined. **S~sperre** *f* power cut

Strömung *f* -,-en current

Strophe *f* -,-n verse

Strudel *m* -s,- whirlpool; (*SGer Culin*) strudel

Strumpf *m* -[e]s,ẹ stocking; (*Knie-*) sock. **S~bandgürtel** *m* suspender belt. **S~hose** *f* tights *pl*

Strunk *m* -[e]s,ẹ stalk

struppig *a* shaggy

Stube *f* -,-n room. **s~nrein** *a* house-trained

Stuck *m* -s stucco

Stück *nt* -[e]s,-e piece; (*Zucker-*) lump; (*Theater-*) play; (*Gegenstand*) item; (*Exemplar*) specimen. **S~chen** *nt* -s,- [little] bit. **s~weise** *adv* bit by bit; (*einzeln*) singly

Student|(in) *m* -en,-en (*f* -,-nen) student. **s~isch** *a* student ...

Studie *f* -,-n study

studieren *vt/i* (*haben*) study

Studio *nt* -s,-s studio

Studium *nt* -s,-ien studies *pl*

Stufe *f* -,-n step; (*Treppen-*) stair; (*Raketen-*) stage; (*Niveau*) level. **s~n** *vt* terrace; (*staffeln*) grade

Stuhl *m* -[e]s,ẹ chair; (*Med*) stools *pl*. **S~gang** *m* bowel movement

stülpen *vt* put (*über* + *acc* over)

stumm *a* dumb; (*schweigsam*) silent

Stummel *m* -s,- stump; (*Zigaretten-*) butt; (*Bleistift-*) stub

Stümper *m* -s,- bungler. **s~haft** *a* incompetent

stumpf *a* blunt; (*Winkel*) obtuse; (*glanzlos*) dull; (*fig*) apathetic. **S~** *m* -[e]s,ẹ stump

Stunde *f* -,-n hour; (*Sch*) lesson

stunden *vt* **jdm eine Schuld s~** give s.o. time to pay a debt

Stunden|kilometer *mpl* kilometres per hour. **s~lang** *adv* for hours. **S~lohn** *m* hourly rate. **S~plan** *m* timetable. **s~weise** *adv* by the hour

stündlich *a & adv* hourly

stur *a* pigheaded; (*phlegmatisch*) stolid; (*unbeirrbar*) dogged

Sturm *m* -[e]s,ẹ gale; (*schwer*) storm; (*Mil*) assault

stürm|en *vi* (*haben*) (*Wind:*) blow hard □ *vi* (*sein*) rush □ *vt* storm; (*bedrängen*) besiege. **S~er** *m* -s,- forward. **s~isch** *a* stormy; (*Überfahrt*) rough

Sturz *m* -es,ẹ [heavy] fall; (*Preis-*) sharp drop; (*Pol*) overthrow

stürzen *vi* (*sein*) fall [heavily]; (*in die Tiefe*) plunge; (*Preise, Kurse:*) drop sharply; (*Regierung:*) fall; (*eilen*) rush □ *vt* throw; turn out (*Speise*); (*Pol*) overthrow, topple; **sich s~** throw oneself (*aus/in* + *acc* out of/into)

Sturzhelm *m* crash-helmet

Stute *f* -,-n mare

Stütze *f* -,-n support; (*Kopf-*) rest

stutzen *vi* (*haben*) stop short □ *vt* trim; (*Hort*) cut back

stützen *vt* support; (*auf-*) rest; **sich s~ auf** (+ *acc*) lean on

stutzig *a* puzzled

Stützpunkt *m* (*Mil*) base

Substantiv *nt* -s,-e noun

Substanz *f* -,-en substance

Subvention /-/'tsjo:n/ *f* -,-en subsidy. **s~ieren** *vt* subsidize

Suche *f* - search; **auf der S~e nach** looking for. **s~en** *vt* look for; (*intensiv*) search for; seek (*Hilfe, Rat*); '**Zimmer gesucht**' 'room wanted' □ *vi* (*haben*) look, search (**nach** for). **S~er** *m* -s,- (*Phot*) viewfinder

Sucht *f* -,ẹ addiction; (*fig*) mania

süchtig *a* addicted. **S~e(r)** *m/f* addict

Süd *m* -[e]s south. **S~afrika** *nt* South Africa. **S~amerika** *nt* South America. **s~deutsch** *a* South German

Süden *m* -s south; **nach S~** south

Süd|frucht *f* tropical fruit. **s~lich** *a* southern; ⟨*Richtung*⟩ southerly ⟨*adv & prep* (+ *gen*) **s~lich der Stadt** south of the town. **S~pol** *m* South Pole. **s~wärts** *adv* southwards

Sühne *f* -,-n atonement; ⟨*Strafe*⟩ penalty. **s~n** *vt* atone for

Sultanine *f* -,-n sultana

Sülze *f* -,-n [meat] jelly

Summe *f* -,-n sum

summen *vi* (*haben*) hum; ⟨*Biene:*⟩ buzz ⟨*vt* hum

summieren (sich) *vr* add up; ⟨*sich häufen*⟩ increase

Sumpf *m* -[e]s,-e marsh, swamp

Sünde *f* -,-n sin. **S~nbock** *m* scapegoat. **S~er(in)** *m* -s,- (*f* -,-nen) sinner. **s~igen** *vi* (*haben*) sin

super *inv* *a* ⟨*fam*⟩ great. **S~markt** *m* supermarket

Suppe *f* -,-n soup. **S~nlöffel** *m* soup-spoon. **S~nteller** *m* soup-plate. **S~nwürfel** *m* stock cube

Surf|brett /'sø:ɡf-/ *nt* surfboard. **S~en** *nt* -s surfing

surren *vi* (*haben*) whirr

süß *a* sweet. **s~en** *vt* sweeten. **S~igkeit** *f* -,-en sweet. **s~lich** *a* sweetish; ⟨*fig*⟩ sugary. **S~speise** *f* sweet. **S~stoff** *m* sweetener. **S~waren** *fpl* confectionery *sg*, sweets *pl*. **S~wasser-** *pref* freshwater …

Symbol *nt* -s,-e symbol. **S~ik** *f* -symbolism. **s~isch** *a* symbolic

Sym|metrie *f* - symmetry. **s~metrisch** *a* symmetrical

Sympathie *f* -,-n sympathy

sympathisch *a* agreeable; ⟨*Person*⟩ likeable

Symptom *nt* -s,-e symptom. **s~atisch** *a* symptomatic

Synagoge *f* -,-n synagogue

synchronisieren /zʏnkroniˈziː-ran/ *vt* synchronize; dub ⟨*Film*⟩

Syndikat *nt* -[e]s,-e syndicate

Syndrom *nt* -s,-e syndrome

synonym *a* synonymous

Syrien /-iən/ *nt* -s Syria

System *nt* -s,-e system. **s~atisch** *a* systematic

Szene *f* -,-n scene

T

Tabak *m* -s,-e tobacco

Tabelle *f* -,-n table; (*Sport*) league table

Tablett *nt* -[e]s,-s tray

Tablette *f* -,-n tablet

tabu *a* taboo. **T~** *nt* -s,-s taboo

Tacho *m* -s,-s, **Tachometer** *m & nt* speedometer

Tadel *m* -s,- reprimand; (*Kritik*) censure; (*Sch*) black mark. **t~los** *a* impeccable. **t~n** *vt* reprimand; censure

Tafel *f* -,-n (*Tisch, Tabelle*) table; (*Platte*) slab; (*Anschlag-, Hinweis-*) board; (*Gedenk-*) plaque; (*Schiefer-*) slate; (*Wand-*) black-board; (*Bild-*) plate; (*Schokolade*) bar. **t~n** *vi* (*haben*) feast

Täfelung *f* - panelling

Tag *m* -[e]s,-e day; **am T~e** in the daytime; **unter T~e** under-ground; **guten Tag!** good morning/afternoon!

Tage|buch *nt* diary. **t~lang** *adv* for days

Tages|anbruch *m* daybreak. **T~ausflug** *m* day trip. **T~karte** *f* day ticket; (*Speise-*) menu of the day. **T~licht** *nt* daylight. **T~mutter** *f* child-minder. **T~ordnung** *f* agenda. **T~rückfahrkarte** *f* day return [ti-

cket]. **T~zeit** f time of the day.
T~zeitung f daily [news]paper

täglich a & adv daily; **zweimal t~** twice a day

tags adv by day; **t~ zuvor/darauf** the day before/after

tagsüber adv during the day

tag|täglich a daily □adv every single day. **T~ung** f -,-en meeting; (Konferenz) conference

Taill|e /ˈtaljə/ f -,-n waist. **t~iert** /taˈjiːɐ̯t/ a fitted

Takt m -[e]s,-e tact; (Mus) bar; (Tempo) time; (Rhythmus) rhythm; **im T~** in time

Taktik f - tactics pl

takt|los a tactless. **T~losigkeit** f - tactlessness. **T~stock** m baton. **t~voll** a tactful

Tal nt -[e]s,-er valley

Talar m -s,-e robe; (Univ) gown

Talent nt -[e]s,-e talent. **t~iert** a talented

Talg m -s tallow; (Culin) suet

Talsperre f dam

Tampon /tamˈpõː/ m -s,-s tampon

Tank m -s,-s tank. **t~en** vt fill up with ⟨Benzin⟩ vi (haben) fill up with petrol; (Aviat) refuel. **T~er** m -s,- tanker. **T~stelle** f petrol station. **T~wart** m -[e]s,-e petrol-pump attendant

Tanne f -,-n fir [tree]. **T~nbaum** m fir tree; (Weihnachtsbaum) Christmas tree

Tante f -,-n aunt

Tantiemen /tanˈtjeːmən/ pl royalties

Tanz m -es,-e dance. **t~en** vt/i (haben) dance

Tänzer(in) m -s,- (f -,-nen) dancer

Tanzlokal nt dance-hall

Tapete f -,-n wallpaper

tapezieren vt paper

tapfer a brave. **T~keit** f - bravery

Tarif m -s,-e rate; (Verzeichnis) tariff

tarn|en vt disguise; (Mil) camouflage. **T~ung** f - disguise; camouflage

Tasche f -,-n bag; (Hosen-) pocket. **T~nbuch** nt paperback. **T~ndieb** m pickpocket. **T~ngeld** nt pocket-money. **T~nlampe** f torch. **T~nmesser** nt penknife. **T~ntuch** nt handkerchief

Tasse f -,-n cup

Tastatur f -,-en keyboard

Tast|e f -,-n key; (Druck-) pushbutton. **t~en** vi (haben) feel, grope (nach for) □vt key in (Daten)

Tat f -,-en action; (Helden-) deed; (Straf-) crime; **auf frischer Tat ertappt** caught in the act

Täter(in) m -s,- (f -,-nen) culprit; (Jur) offender

tätig a active; **t~ sein** work. **T~keit** f -,-en activity; (Arbeit) work, job

Tatkraft f energy

Tatort m scene of the crime

tätowier|en vt tattoo. **T~ung** f -,-en tattooing; (Bild) tattoo

Tatsache f fact. **T~nbericht** m documentary

tatsächlich a actual

Tatze f -,-n paw

Tau¹ m -[e]s dew

Tau² nt -[e]s,-e rope

taub a deaf; (gefühllos) numb

Taube f -,-n pigeon; (Turtel- & fig) dove. **T~nschlag** m pigeon-loft

Taub|heit f - deafness. **t~stumm** a deaf and dumb

tauch|en vt dip, plunge; (unter-) duck □vi (haben/sein) dive/(ein-) plunge (in+acc into); (auf-) appear (aus out of). **T~er** m -s,- diver. **T~eranzug** m diving-suit

tauen vi (sein) melt, thaw □impers es **taut** it is thawing

Tauf|becken nt font. **T~e** f -,-n christening, baptism. **t~en** vt christen, baptize

taugen vi (haben) etwas/nichts t~ be good/no good

tauglich a suitable; (Mil) fit

Tausch m -[e]s,-e exchange, (fam) swap. t~en vt exchange; (handeln) barter (gegen for) □ vi (haben) swap (mit etw sth; mit jdm with s.o.)

täuschen vt deceive, fool; betray ⟨Vertrauen⟩; sich t~ delude oneself; (sich irren) be mistaken □ vi (haben) be deceptive. t~d a deceptive; ⟨Ähnlichkeit⟩ striking

Täuschung f -,-en deception; (Irrtum) mistake; (Illusion) delusion

tausend inv a one/a thousand. T~ nt -s,-e thousand. T~füßler m -s,- centipede. t~ste(r,s) a thousandth. T~stel nt -s,- thousandsth

Tau|tropfen m dewdrop. T~wetter nt thaw. T~ziehen nt -s tug of war

Taxe f -,-n charge; (Kur-) tax

Taxi nt -s,-s taxi, cab

taxieren vt estimate/(im Wert) value (auf + acc at)

Taxi|fahrer m taxi driver. T~stand m taxi rank

Teakholz /'ti:k-/ nt teak

Team /ti:m/ nt -s,-s team

Techni|k f -,-en technology; (Methode) technique. T~ker m -s,- technician. t~sch a technical; (technologisch) technological; T~sche Hochschule Technical University

Technologie f -,-n technology

Teddybär m teddy bear

Tee m -s,-s tea. T~beutel m teabag. T~kanne f teapot. T~löffel m teaspoon

Teer m -s tar. t~en vt tar

Tee|sieb nt tea-strainer. T~wagen m [tea] trolley

Teich m -[e]s,-e pond

Teig m -[e]s,-e pastry; (Knet-) dough; (Rühr-) mixture; (Pfannkuchen-) batter. T~rolle f, rolling-pin. T~waren fpl pasta sg

Teil m -[e]s,-e part; (Bestand-) component; (Jur) party; zum T~ partly □m & nt -[e]s (Anteil) share; ich für mein[en] T~ for my part □nt -[e]s,-e part; (Ersatz-) spare part; (Anbau-) unit

Teil|chen nt -s,- particle. t~en vt divide; (auf-) share out; (gemeinsam haben) share; (Pol) partition ⟨Land⟩; sich (dat) etw [mit jdm] t~en share sth [with s.o.]; sich t~en divide; (sich gabeln) fork; ⟨Meinungen:⟩ differ □vi (haben) share

Teilhaber m -s,- (Comm) partner

Teilnahme f - participation; (innere) interest; (Mitgefühl) sympathy

teilnehmen† vi sep (haben) t~en an (+ dat) take part in; (mitfühlen) share [in]. T~er(in) m -s,- (f -,-nen) participant; (an Wettbewerb) competitor

teils adv partly. T~ung f -,-en division; (Pol) partition. t~weise a partial □adv. partially, partly. T~zahlung f part-payment; (Rate) instalment

Teint /tɛ̃:/ m -s,-s complexion

Telefax nt fax

Telefon nt -s,-e [tele]phone. T~at nt -[e]s,-e [tele]phone call. T~buch nt [tele]phone book. t~ieren vi (haben) [tele]phone

telefonisch a [tele]phone ... □adv by [tele]phone. T~ist(in) m -en,-en (f -,-nen) telephonist. T~karte f phone card. T~nummer f [tele]phone number. T~zelle f [tele]phone box

Telegraf m -en,-en telegraph. t~ieren vi (haben) send a telegram. t~isch a telegraphic □adv by telegram

Telegramm nt -s,-e telegram
Teleobjektiv nt telephoto lens
Teleskop nt -s,-e telescope
Telex nt -,-[e] telex. t~**en** vt telex
Teller m -s,- plate
Tempel m -s,- temple
Temperament nt -s,-e temperament; (Lebhaftigkeit) vivacity
Temperatur f -,-en temperature
Tempo nt -s,-s speed; (Mus: pl -pi) tempo; T~ [T~]! hurry up!
Tendenz f -,-en trend; (Neigung) tendency
Tennis nt - tennis. T~**schläger** m tennis-racket
Teppich m -s,-e carpet. T~**boden** m fitted carpet
Termin m -s,-e date; (Arzt-) appointment. T~**kalender** m [appointments] diary
Terpentin nt -s turpentine
Terrasse f -,-n terrace
Terrier /'tɛrɪe/ m -s,- terrier
Terrine f -,-n tureen
Territorium nt -s,-ien territory
Terror m -s terror. t~**isieren** vt terrorize. T~**ismus** m - terrorism. T~**ist** m -en,-en terrorist
Tesafilm (P) m ≈ Sellotape (P)
Test m -[e]s,-s & -e test
Testament nt -[e]s,-e will; Altes/Neues T~ Old/New Testament. T~**svollstrecker** m -s,- executor
testen vt test
Tetanus m - tetanus
teuer a expensive; (lieb) dear; wie t~? how much?
Teufel m -s,- devil. T~**skreis** m vicious circle
teuflisch a fiendish
Text m -[e]s,-e text; (Passage) passage. T~**er** m -s,- copy-writer
Textilien /-ʃən/ pl textiles; (Textilwaren) textile goods
Textverarbeitungssystem nt word processor
Theater nt -s,- theatre. T~**kasse** f box-office. T~**stück** nt play

Theke f -,-n bar; (Ladentisch) counter.
Thema nt -s,-men subject
Themse f - Thames
Theologe m -n,-n theologian. T~**gie** f - theology
theoretisch a theoretical. T~**ie** f -,-n theory
Therapeut(in) m -en,-en (f -,-nen) therapist
Therapie f -,-n therapy
Thermalbad nt thermal bath
Thermometer nt -s,- thermometer
Thermosflasche (P) f Thermos flask (P)
Thermostat m -[e]s,-e thermostat
Thrombose f -,-n thrombosis
Thron m -[e]s,-e throne. T~**folge** f succession. T~**folger** m -s,- heir to the throne
Thunfisch m tuna
Thymian m -s thyme
ticken vi (haben) tick
tief a deep; (t~ liegend, niedrig) low; (t~ gründig) profound; t~**er** low; (sehr) deeply, profoundly; (schlafen) soundly. T~ nt -s,-s (Meteorol) depression. T~**bau** m civil engineering. T~**e** f -,-n depth
Tiefgarage f underground car park. t~**gekühlt** a [deep-]frozen
Tiefkühlfach nt freezer compartment. T~**kost** f frozen food. T~**truhe** f deep-freeze
Tiefsttemperatur f minimum temperature
Tier nt -[e]s,-e animal. T~**arzt** m, T~**ärztin** f vet, veterinary surgeon. T~**garten** m zoo. T~**kreis** m zodiac. T~**kreiszeichen** nt sign of the zodiac. T~**kunde** f zoology. T~**quälerei** f cruelty to animals
Tiger m -s,- tiger

tilgen vt pay off ⟨Schuld⟩; (streichen) delete; (fig: auslöschen) wipe out

Tinte f -,-n ink. **T~nfisch** m squid

Tip m -s,-s (fam) tip

tipp|en vt (fam) type ⟨vi (haben) (berühren) touch (auf/an etw acc sth); (fam: maschineschreiben) type; t~en auf (+ acc) (fam: wetten) bet on. **T~schein** m pools/lottery coupon

tipptopp a (fam) immaculate

Tirol nt -s [the] Tyrol

Tisch m -[e]s,-e table; (Schreib-) desk; nach **T~** after the meal. **T~decke** f table-cloth. **T~gebet** nt grace. **T~ler** m -s,- joiner; (Möbel-) cabinet-maker. **T~rede** f after-dinner speech. **T~tennis** nt table tennis

Titel m -s,- title

Toast /to:st/ m -[e]s,-e toast; (Scheibe) piece of toast. **T~er** m -s,- toaster

toben vi (haben) rave; ⟨Sturm:⟩ rage; ⟨Kinder:⟩ play boisterously

Tochter f -,- daughter. **T~gesellschaft** f subsidiary

Tod m -es death

Todes|angst f mortal fear. **T~anzeige** f death announcement; ⟨Zeitungs-⟩ obituary. **T~fall** m death. **T~opfer** nt fatality, casualty. **T~strafe** f death penalty. **T~urteil** nt death sentence

tödlich a fatal; ⟨Gefahr:⟩ mortal; (groß) deadly

Toilette /toa'lɛtə/ f -,-n toilet. **T~npapier** nt toilet paper

toler|ant a tolerant. **T~anz** f - tolerance. **t~ieren** vt tolerate

toll a crazy, mad; (fam: prima) fantastic; (schlimm) awful. **t~kühn** a foolhardy. **T~wut** f rabies. **t~wütig** a rabid

tolpatschig a clumsy

Tölpel m -s,- fool

Tomate f -,-n tomato. **T~nmark** nt tomato purée

Tombola f -,-s raffle

Ton¹ m -[e]s clay

Ton² m -[e]s,-e tone; (Klang) sound; (Note) note; (Betonung) stress; (Farb-) shade; der gute **Ton** (fig) good form. **T~abnehmer** m -s,- pick-up. **t~angebend** a (fig) leading. **T~art** f tone [of voice]; (Mus) key. **T~band** nt (pl -bänder) tape. **T~bandgerät** nt tape recorder

tönen vi (haben) sound ⟨vt tint

Ton|fall m tone. **T~leiter** f scale

Tonne f -,-n barrel, cask; (Müll-) bin; (Maß) tonne, metric ton

Topf m -[e]s,-e pot; (Koch-) pan

Topfen m -s (Aust) ≈ curd cheese

Töpfer|ei f -,-en pottery

Topf|lappen m oven-cloth. **T~pflanze** f potted plant

Tor nt -[e]s,-e gate; (Einfahrt) gateway; (Sport) goal

Torf m -s peat

töricht a foolish

torkeln vi (sein/haben) stagger

Tornister m -s,- knapsack; (Sch) satchel

Torpedo m -s,-s torpedo

Torpfosten m goal-post

Torte f -,-n gâteau; (Obst-) flan

Tortur f -,-en torture

Torwart m -s,-e goalkeeper

tot a dead

total a total. **T~schaden** m ≈ write-off

Tote(r) m/f dead man/woman; ⟨Todesopfer⟩ fatality; die **T~n** the dead pl

Töten vt kill

Toten|kopf m skull. **T~schein** m death certificate

Toto nt u. m -s football pools pl. **T~schein** m pools coupon

tot|schlagen† vt sep shoot dead. **T~schlag** m (Jur) manslaughter. **t~schlagen**† vt sep kill. **t~stellen (sich)** *vr sep* pretend to be dead

Tötung *f* -,-en killing; **fahrlässige T~** (*Jur*) manslaughter

Toupet /tuˈpeː/ *nt* -s,-s toupee. **t~ieren** *vt* back-comb

Tour /tuːɐ̯/ *f* -,-en tour; (*Ausflug*) trip; (*Auto-*) drive; (*Rad-*) ride; (*Strecke*) distance; (*Techn*) revolution; (*fam: Weise*) way

Tourismus /tuˈrɪsmʊs/ *m* - tourism. **T~t** *m* -en,-en tourist

Tournee /tʊrˈneː/ *f* -,-n tour

Trab *m* -[e]s trot

Trabant *m* -en,-en satellite

traben *vi* (*haben/sein*) trot

Tracht *f* -,-en [national] costume; **eine T~ Prügel** a good hiding

Tradition /-ˈtsi̯oːn/ *f* -,-en tradition. **t~ell** *a* traditional

Trafik *f* -,-en (*Aust*) tobacconist's

Tragbahre *f* stretcher. **t~bar** *a* portable; (*Kleidung*) wearable

tragen† *vt* carry; (*an-/aufhaben*) wear; (*fig*) bear □*vi* (*haben*) carry; **gut t~** ⟨*Baum:*⟩ produce a good crop

Träger *m* -s,- porter; (*Inhaber*) bearer; (*eines Ordens*) holder; (*Bau-*) beam; (*Stahl-*) girder; (*Achsel-*) [shoulder] strap

Tragetasche *f* carrier bag. **T~flächenboot,** **T~flügelboot** *nt* hydrofoil

Trägheit *f* - sluggishness; (*Faulheit*) laziness; (*Phys*) inertia

Tragik *f* - tragedy. **t~isch** *a* tragic

Tragödie /-i̯ə/ *f* -,-n tragedy

Trainer /ˈtrɛːnɐ/ *m* -s,- trainer; (*Tennis-*) coach. **t~ieren** *vt/i* (*haben*) train

Training /ˈtrɛːnɪŋ/ *nt* -s training. **T~sanzug** *m* tracksuit. **T~sschuhe** *mpl* trainers

Traktor *m* -s,-en /-ˈtoːrən/ tractor

trampeln *vi* (*haben*) stamp one's feet □*vi* (*sein*) trample (**auf**+*acc* **on**) □*vt* trample

trampen /ˈtrɛmpən/ *vi* (*sein*) (*fam*) hitch-hike

Tranchiermesser /trãˈʃiːɐ̯-/ *nt* carving-knife. **t~en** *vt* carve

Träne *f* -,-n tear. **t~n** *vi* (*haben*) water. **T~ngas** *nt* tear-gas

Tränke *f* -,-n watering-place; (*Trog*) drinking-trough. **t~n** *vt* water (*Pferd*); (*nässen*) soak (**mit with**)

Transfer *m* -s,-s transfer. **T~formator** *m* -s,-en /-ˈtoːrən/ transformer. **T~fusion** *f* -,-en [blood] transfusion

Transit /tranˈziːt/ *m* -s transit

Transparent *nt* -[e]s,-e banner; (*Bild*) transparency

transpirieren *vi* (*haben*) perspire

Transport *m* -[e]s,-e transport; (*Güter-*) consignment. **t~ieren** *vt* transport

Trapez *nt* -es,-e trapeze

Tratsch *m* -[e]s (*fam*) gossip

Tratte *f* -,-n (*Comm*) draft

Traube *f* -,-n bunch of grapes; (*Beere*) grape; (*fig*) cluster. **T~nzucker** *m* glucose

trauen *vi* (*haben* + *dat*) trust □*vt* marry; **sich t~** dare (**etw zu tun** [to] do sth); venture (**in**+*acc*/**aus** into/out of)

Trauer *f* - mourning; (*Schmerz*) grief (**um** for); **T~** tragen be [dressed] in mourning. **T~fall** *m* bereavement. **T~feier** *f* funeral service. **t~n** *vi* (*haben*) grieve; **t~n um** mourn [for]. **T~spiel** *nt* tragedy. **T~weide** *f* weeping willow

Traum *m* -[e]s,**Träume** dream

Trauma *nt* -s,-men trauma

träumen /ˈtrɔʏ-/ *vt/i* (*haben*) dream

traumhaft *a* dreamlike; (*schön*) fabulous

traurig *a* sad; (*erbärmlich*) sorry. **T~keit** *f* - sadness

Trau|ring m wedding-ring. **T~schein** m marriage certificate. **T~ung** f-,-en wedding

Treff nt -s,-s (Karten) spades pl. **treffen**† vt hit; ⟨Blitz:⟩ strike; ⟨fig: verletzen⟩ hurt; ⟨zusammenkommen mit⟩ meet; take ⟨Maßnahme⟩; **sich t~en** meet (mit jdm s.o.); **sich gut t~en** be convenient; **es gut t~en** be lucky □vi (haben) hit the target; **t~en auf** (+ acc) meet; ⟨fig⟩ meet with. **T~en** nt -s,- meeting. **T~er** m -s,- hit; (Los) winner. **T~punkt** m meeting-place

treiben† vt drive; ⟨sich befassen mit⟩ do; carry on ⟨Gewerbe⟩; indulge in ⟨Luxus⟩; get up to ⟨Unfug⟩; **Handel t~** trade □ vi (sein) drift; (schwimmen) float □vi (haben) (Bot) sprout. **T~** nt -s activity

Treib|haus nt hothouse. **T~hauseffekt** m greenhouse effect. **T~holz** nt driftwood. **T~riemen** m transmission belt. **T~sand** m quicksand. **T~stoff** m fuel

trenn|bar a separable. **t~en** tr separate/(abmachen) detach (von from); divide, split ⟨Wort⟩; **sich t~en** separate; (auseinandergehen) part; **sich t~en von** leave; (fortgeben) part with. **T~ung** f-,-en separation; (Silben-) division. **T~ungsstrich** m hyphen. **T~wand** f partition

trepp|ab adv downstairs. **t~auf** adv upstairs

Treppe f-,-n stairs pl; (Außen-) steps pl. **T~nhaus** nt stairwell

Tresor m -s,-e safe

Tresse f-,-n braid

Treteimer m pedal bin

treten† vi (sein/haben) step; (versehentlich) tread; (ausschlagen) kick (nach at) □vt tread; (mit Füßen) kick

treu a faithful; (fest) loyal. **T~e** f- faithfulness; loyalty; (eheliche) fidelity. **T~händer** m -s,- trustee. **t~los** a disloyal; (untreu) unfaithful

Tribüne f-,-n platform; (Zuschauer-) stand

Trichter m -s,- funnel; (Bomben-) crater

Trick m -s,-s trick. **T~film** m cartoon. **t~reich** a clever

Trieb m -[e]s,-e drive, urge; (Instinkt) instinct; (Bot) shoot. **T~täter** m sex offender. **T~werk** nt (Aviat) engine; (Uhr-) mechanism

triefen† vi (haben) drip

triftig a valid

Trigonometrie f- trigonometry

Trikot[1] /tri'ko:/ m -s (Tex) jersey

Trikot[2] nt -s,-s (Sport) jersey; (Fußball-) shirt

Trimester nt -s,- term

Trimm-dich nt -s keep-fit

trimmen vt trim; (fam) train

trink|en† vt/i (haben) drink. **T~er(in)** m -s,- (f -,-nen) alcoholic. **T~geld** nt tip. **T~spruch** m toast

trist a dreary

Tritt m -[e]s,-e step; (Fuß-) kick. **T~brett** nt step

Triumph m -s,-e triumph. **t~ieren** vi (haben) rejoice

trocken a dry. **T~haube** f drier. **T~heit** f -,-en dryness; (Dürre) drought. **t~legen** vt sep change ⟨Baby⟩; drain ⟨Sumpf⟩. **T~milch** f powdered milk

trock|**nen** vt/i (sein) dry. **T~er** m -s,- drier

Trödel m -s (fam) junk. **t~n** vi (haben) dawdle

Trödler m -s,- (fam) slowcoach; (Händler) junk-dealer

Trog m -[e]s,-e trough

Trommel f -,-n drum. **T~fell** nt ear-drum. **t~n** vi (haben) drum

Trommler m -s,- drummer

Trompete f ~,-n trumpet. **T~r** m
-s,- trumpeter

Tropen pl tropics

Tropf m -[e]s,-e ⟨Med⟩ drip

tröpfeln vt/i ⟨sein/haben⟩ drip

tropfen vt/i ⟨sein/haben⟩ drip.
T~ m -s,- drop; ⟨fallend⟩ drip.
t~weise adv drop by drop

Trophäe /tro'fɛːə/ f ~,-n trophy

tropisch a tropical

Trost m -[e]s consolation, comfort

trösten vt console; comfort.
t~lich a comforting

trost|los a desolate; ⟨elend⟩
wretched; ⟨reizlos⟩ dreary.
T~preis m consolation prize

Trott m -[e]s amble; ⟨fig⟩ routine

Trottel m -s,- ⟨fam⟩ idiot

Trottoir /trɔ'toaːɐ/ nt -s,-s pavement

trotz prep (+ gen) despite, in spite
of. **T~** m -es defiance. **t~dem** adv
nevertheless. **t~ig** a defiant;
⟨Kind⟩ stubborn

trübe a dull; ⟨Licht⟩ dim; ⟨Flüssig-
keit⟩ cloudy; ⟨fig⟩ gloomy

Trubel m -s bustle

trüben vt dull; make cloudy ⟨Flüs-
sigkeit⟩; ⟨fig⟩ spoil; strain ⟨Ver-
hältnis⟩; **sich t~** ⟨Flüssigkeit⟩
become cloudy; ⟨Himmel:⟩ cloud
over; ⟨Augen:⟩ dim

Trüb|sal f -,-e misery. **T~sinn** m
melancholy. **t~sinnig** a melancholy

trügen† vt deceive □vi ⟨haben⟩ be
deceptive

Trugschluß m fallacy

Truhe f -,-n chest

Trümmer pl rubble sg; ⟨T~teile⟩
wreckage sg; ⟨fig⟩ ruins

Trumpf m -[e]s,⁀e trump [card].
t~en vt/i ⟨haben⟩ play trumps

Trunk m -[e]s drink. **T~enheit** f
- drunkenness. **T~enheit am
Steuer** drunken driving

Trupp m -s,-s group; ⟨Mil⟩ squad.
T~e f -,-n ⟨Mil⟩ unit; ⟨Theat⟩
troupe; **T~en** troops

Truthahn m turkey

Tscheche m -n,-n, **T~in** f -,-nen
Czech. **t~isch** a Czech;
T~ische Republik f Czech Re-
public

tschüs int bye, cheerio

Tuba f -,-ben ⟨Mus⟩ tuba

Tube f -,-n tube

Tuberkulose f - tuberculosis

Tuch nt -[e]s,⁀er cloth; ⟨Hals-,
Kopf-⟩ scarf; ⟨Schulter-⟩ shawl

tüchtig a competent; ⟨reichlich,
beträchtlich⟩ good; ⟨groß⟩ big.
T~keit f - competence

Tück|e f -,-n malice. **t~isch** a
malicious; ⟨gefährlich⟩ treacher-
ous

Tugend f -,-en virtue. **t~haft** a
virtuous

Tülle f -,-n spout

Tulpe f -,-n tulip

Tumor m -s,-en /-'moːrən/ tumour

Tümpel m -s,- pond

Tumult m -[e]s,-e commotion,
⟨Aufruhr⟩ riot

tun† vt do; take ⟨Schritt, Blick⟩;
work ⟨Wunder⟩; ⟨bringen⟩ put
(in + acc into); **sich t~** happen;
jdm etwas t~ hurt s.o.; **das tut
nichts** it doesn't matter □vi ⟨ha-
ben⟩ act (als ob as if); **er tut nur
so** he's just pretending; **zu tun
haben** have things/work to do;
[es] **zu tun haben mit** have to
deal with. **Tun** nt -s actions pl

Tünche f -,-n whitewash; ⟨fig⟩
veneer. **t~n** vt whitewash

Tunesien /-jan/ nt -s Tunisia

Tunke f -,-n sauce

tunlich st ⟨?⟩... tunnel

tupf|en vt dab □vi ⟨haben⟩ **t~en
an/auf** (+ acc) touch. **T~en** m
-s,- spot. **T~er** m -s,- spot; ⟨Med⟩
swab

Tür f -,-en door

Turban m -s,-e turban

Turbine f -,-n turbine

Türk|e m -n,-n Turk. **T~ei** (die) -
Turkey. **T~in** f -,-nen Turk

türkis inv a turquoise

türkisch *a* Turkish

Turm *m* -[e]s,-e tower; (*Schach*) rook, castle

Türmchen *nt* -s,- turret

Turmspitze *f* spire

turn|en *vi* (*haben*) do gymnastics. **T~en** *nt* -s gymnastics *sg*; (*Sch*) physical education, (*fam*) gym. **T~er(in)** *m* -s,- (*f* -,-nen) gymnast. **T~halle** *f* gymnasium

Turnier *nt* -s,-e tournament; (*Reit-*) show

Turnschuhe *mpl* gym shoes

Tusche *f* -,-n [drawing] ink

tuscheln *vt/i* (*haben*) whisper

Tüte *f* -,-n bag; (*Comm*) packet; (*Eis-*) cornet; **in die T~ blasen** (*fam*) be breathalysed

TÜV *m* - ≈ MOT [test]

Typ *m* -s,-en type; (*fam: Kerl*) bloke. **T~e** *f* -,-n type

Typhus *m* - typhoid

typisch *a* typical (**für** of)

Tyrann *m* -en,-en tyrant. **T~ei** *f* - tyranny. **t~isch** *a* tyrannical. **t~isieren** *vt* tyrannize

U

U-Bahn *f* underground

übel *a* bad; (*häßlich*) nasty; **mir ist/wird ü~** I feel sick. **Ü~** *nt* -s,- evil. **Ü~keit** *f* - nausea

üben *vt/i* (*haben*) practise

über *prep* (+ *dat/acc*) over; (*höher als*) above; (*betreffend*) about; (*Buch, Vortrag*) on; (*Scheck, Rechnung*) for; (*quer ü~*) across; **ü~ Köln fahren** go via Cologne; **ü~ Ostern** over Easter; **die Woche ü~** during the week □*adv* **ü~ und ü~** all over; **jdm ü~ sein** be better/(*stärker*) stronger than s.o. □*a* (*fam*) **ü~ sein** be left over; **etw ü~ sein** be fed up with sth

überall *adv* everywhere

überanstrengen *vt insep* overtax; strain (*Augen*)

überarbeiten *vt insep* revise; **sich ü~** overwork

überbieten† *vt insep* outbid

Überblick *m* overall view; (*Abriß*) summary

überblicken *vt insep* overlook; (*abschätzen*) assess

überbringen† *vt insep* deliver

überbrücken *vt insep* (*fig*) bridge

überdies *adv* moreover

überdimensional *a* oversized

Überdosis *f* overdose

überdrüssig *a* **ü~ sein/werden** be/grow tired (*gen* of)

übereignen *vt insep* transfer

übereilt *a* over-hasty

übereinander *adv* one on top of/above the other; (*sprechen*) about each other

übereinkommen† *vi sep* (*sein*) agree. **Ü~kunft** *f* - agreement. **ü~stimmen** *vi sep* (*haben*) agree; (*Zahlen*;) tally; (*Ansichten*;) coincide; (*Farben*;) match. **Ü~stimmung** *f* agreement

überfahren† *vt insep* run over

Überfahrt *f* crossing

Überfall *m* attack; (*Bank-*) raid

überfallen† *vt insep* attack; raid (*Bank*;); (*bestürmen*) bombard (**mit** with)

überfällig *a* overdue

Überfluß *m* abundance; (*Wohlstand*) affluence

überflüssig *a* superfluous

überfordern *vt insep* overtax

überführen *vt insep* transfer; (*Jur*) convict (*gen* of). **Ü~ung** *f* transfer; (*Straße*) flyover; (*Fußgänger-*) foot-bridge

überfüllt *a* overcrowded

Übergabe *f* (*s.* **übergeben**) handing over; transfer

Übergang *m* crossing; (*Wechsel*) transition

übergeben† *vt insep* hand over; (*übereignen*) transfer; **sich ü ~** be sick

übergehen† *vt insep* (*fig*) pass over; (*nicht beachten*) ignore; (*auslassen*) leave out

Übergewicht *nt* excess weight; (*fig*) predominance; **Ü ~ haben** be overweight

übergreifen† *vi sep* (*haben*) spread (**auf +** *acc* to). **Ü ~ griff** *m* infringement

übergroß *a* outsize; (*übertrieben*) exaggerated. **Ü ~ größe** *f* outsize

überhandnehmen† *vi sep* (*haben*) increase alarmingly

überhäufen *vt insep* inundate (**mit** with)

überhaupt *adv* (*im allgemeinen*) altogether; (*eigentlich*) anyway; (*überdies*) besides; **ü ~ nicht/ nichts** not/nothing at all

überheblich *a* arrogant. **Ü ~ keit** *f* - arrogance

überhol|en *vt insep* overtake; (*reparieren*) overhaul. **ü ~ t** *a* outdated. **Ü ~ ung** *f* -,-en overhaul. **Ü ~ verbot** *nt* 'Ü ~ verbot' 'no overtaking'

überirdisch *a* supernatural

überkochen *vi sep* (*sein*) boil over

überladen† *vt insep* overload □ *a* over-ornate

überlassen† *vt insep* **jdm etw ü ~** leave sth to s.o.; (*geben*) let s.o. have sth; **sich** (*dat*) **selbst ü ~ sein** be left to one's own devices

überlasten *vt insep* overload; overtax ⟨*Person*⟩

Überlauf *m* overflow

überlaufen† *vi sep* (*sein*) overflow; (*Mil, Pol*) defect

Überläufer *m* defector

überleben *vt/i insep* (*haben*) survive. **Ü ~ de(r)** *m/f* survivor

überlegen¹ *v insep* □ *vt* [**sich** *dat*] **ü ~** think over, consider; **es sich**

(*dat*) **anders ü ~** change one's mind □ *vi* (*haben*) think, reflect

überlegen² *a* superior; (*herablassend*) supercilious. **Ü ~ heit** *f* - superiority

Überlegung *f* -,-en reflection

überliefern *vt insep* hand down. **Ü ~ ung** *f* tradition

überlisten *vt insep* outwit

Übermacht *f* superiority

übermäßig *a* excessive

Übermensch *m* superman. **ü ~ lich** *a* superhuman

übermitteln *vt insep* convey; (*senden*) transmit

übermorgen *adv* the day after tomorrow

übermüdet *a* overtired

Über|mut *m* high spirits *pl*. **ü ~ mütig** *a* high-spirited

übernächste(r,s) *a* next ... but one; **ü ~ es Jahr** the year after next

übernacht|en *vi insep* (*haben*) stay overnight. **Ü ~ ung** *f* -,-en overnight stay; **Ü ~ ung und Frühstück** bed and breakfast

Übernahme *f* - taking over; (*Comm*) take-over

übernatürlich *a* supernatural

übernehmen† *vt insep* take over; (*annehmen*) take on; **sich ü ~** overdo things; (*finanziell*) overreach oneself

überqueren *vt insep* cross

überrasch|en *vt insep* surprise. **ü ~ end** *a* surprising; (*unerwartet*) unexpected. **Ü ~ ung** *f* -,-en surprise

überreden *vt insep* persuade

überreste *mpl* remains

Überschall- *pref* supersonic

Überschlag *m* rough estimate; (*Sport*) somersault

überschlagen¹† *vt sep* cross ⟨*Beine*⟩

überschlagen²† *vt insep* estimate roughly; (*auslassen*) skip;

sich ü~ somersault; ⟨*Ereignisse:*⟩ happen fast □ *a* tepid
überschneiden† (**sich**) *vr insep* intersect, cross; (*zusammenfallen*) overlap
überschreiten† *vt insep* cross; (*fig*) exceed
Überschrift *f* heading; (*Zeitungs-*) headline
Über|schuß *m* surplus. **ü~schüssig** *a* surplus
überschwemm|en *vt insep* flood; (*fig*) inundate. **Ü~ung** *f* -,-en flood
Übersee in/nach ü~ overseas.
Ü~dampfer *m* ocean liner.
ü~isch *a* overseas
übersehen† *vt insep* look out over; (*abschätzen*) assess; (*nicht sehen*) overlook, miss; (*ignorieren*) ignore
übersenden† *vt insep* send
übersetzen¹ *vi sep* (*haben/sein*) cross [over]
übersetz|en² *vt insep* translate.
Ü~er(in) *m* -s,- (*f* -,-nen) translator. **Ü~ung** *f* -,-en translation
Übersicht *f* overall view; (*Abriß*) summary; (*Tabelle*) table.
ü~lich *a* clear
Übersiedlung *f* move
überspielen† *vt insep* (*fig*) cover up; **auf Band** ü~ tape
überstehen† *vt insep* come through; get over ⟨*Krankheit*⟩; (*überleben*) survive
übersteigen† *vt insep* climb [over]; (*fig*) exceed
überstimmen *vt insep* outvote
Überstunden *fpl* overtime *sg*;
Ü~ machen work overtime
überstürz|en *vt insep* rush; **sich ü~en** ⟨*Ereignisse:*⟩ happen fast; ⟨*Worte:*⟩ tumble out. **ü~t** *a* hasty
übertönen *vt insep* drown [out]
übertrag|bar *a* transferable; (*Med*) infectious. **ü~en†** *vt insep* transfer; (*übergeben*) assign (*dat*

to); (*Techn, Med*) transmit; (*Radio, TV*) broadcast; (*übersetzen*) translate; (*anwenden*) apply (**auf**+*acc* to) □*a* transferred, figurative. **Ü~ung** *f* -,-en transfer; transmission; broadcast; translation; application
übertreffen† *vt insep* surpass; (*übersteigen*) exceed
übertreib|en† *vt insep* exaggerate; (*zu weit treiben*) overdo.
Ü~ung *f* -,-en exaggeration
übertret|en† *vt insep* infringe; break ⟨*Gesetz*⟩. **Ü~ung** *f* -,-en infringement; breach
übervölkert *a* overpopulated
überwachen *vt insep* supervise; (*kontrollieren*) monitor; (*bespitzeln*) keep under surveillance
überwachsen *a* overgrown
überwältigen *vt insep* overpower; (*fig*) overwhelm
überweis|en† *vt insep* transfer; refer ⟨*Patienten*⟩. **Ü~ung** *f* transfer; (*ärztliche*) referral
überwiegen† *vt insep* □*vi* (*haben*) predominate □*vt* outweigh
überwinden† *vt insep* overcome; **sich ü~en** force oneself.
Ü~ung *f* effort
Über|zahl *f* majority. **ü~zählig** *a* spare
überzeug|en *vt insep* convince; **sich** [**selbst**] **ü~en** satisfy oneself. **ü~end** *a* convincing.
Ü~ung *f* -,-en conviction
überziehen† *vt insep* cover; overdraw ⟨*Konto*⟩
Überzug *m* cover; (*Schicht*) coating
üblich *a* usual; (*gebräuchlich*) customary
U-Boot *nt* submarine
übrig *a* remaining; (*andere*) other; **alles ü~e** [all] the rest; **im ü~en** besides; (*ansonsten*) apart from that; **ü~ sein** be left [over]. **ü~bleiben†** *vi sep* (*sein*) be left [over]; **uns blieb nichts anderes**

ü ~ we had no choice. **ü ~ ens** *adv* by the way

Übung *f* -,-en exercise; *(Üben)* practice; **außer ü ~** *or* **aus der Ü ~** out of practice

Ufer *nt* -s,- shore; *(Fluß-)* bank

Uhr *f* -,-en clock; *(Armband-)* watch; *(Zähler)* meter; **um ein U ~** at one o'clock; **wieviel U ~ ist es?** what's the time? **U ~ armband** *nt* watch-strap. **U ~ macher** *m* -s,- watch and clockmaker. **U ~ werk** *nt* clock/watch mechanism. **U ~ zeiger** *m* [clock-/watch-]hand. **U ~ zeit** *f* time

Uhu *m* -s,-s eagle owl

UKW *abbr* **(Ultrakurzwelle)** VHF

ulkig *a* funny; *(seltsam)* odd

Ulme *f* -,-n elm

Ultrakurzwelle *f* very high frequency

Ultraschall *m* ultrasound

ultraviolett *a* ultraviolet

um *prep (+ acc)* [a]round; *(Uhrzeit)* at; *(bitten)* for; *(streiten)* over; *(betrügen)* out of; *(bei Angabe einer Differenz)* by; **um [... herum]** around, [round] about; **Tag um Tag** day after day □ *adv (ungefähr)* around, about □ *conj* **um zu** to; *(Absicht)* [in order] to; **zu müde, um zu ...** too tired to ...; **um so besser** all the better

umarbeiten *vt sep alter; (bearbeiten)* revise

umarm|en *vt insep* embrace, hug. **U ~ ung** *f* -,-en embrace, hug

Umbau *m* rebuilding; *(Umbauen)* conversion (**zu** into). **u ~ en** *vt sep* rebuild; convert (**zu** into)

Umbildung *f* reorganisation; *(Pol)* reshuffle

umbinden† *vt sep* put on

umblättern *v sep* □ *vt* turn [over] □ *vi (haben)* turn the page

umbringen† *vt sep* kill

umbuchen *v sep* □ *vt* change; *(Comm)* transfer □ *vi* change one's booking

umdrehen *v sep* □ *vt* turn round/ *(wenden)* over; turn *(Schlüssel)*; *(umkrempeln)* turn inside out; **sich u ~** turn round; *(im Liegen)* turn over □ *vi (haben/sein)* turn back

Umdrehung *f* turn; *(Motor-)* revolution

umfahren† *vt sep* run over

umfallen† *vi sep (sein)* fall over; *(Person:)* fall down

Umfang *m* girth; *(Geom)* circumference; *(Größe)* size

umfangreich *a* extensive; *(dick)* big

umfassen *vt insep* consist of, comprise; *(umgeben)* surround. **u ~ d** *a* comprehensive

Umfrage *f* survey, poll

umfüllen *vt sep* transfer

Umgang *m* [social] contact; *(Umgehen)* dealing (**mit** with)

Umgangssprache *f* colloquial language

umgeb|en† *vt/i insep (haben)* surround. **U ~ ung** *f* -,-en surroundings *pl*

umgehen† *vt insep* avoid; *(nicht beachten)* evade; *(Straße:)* bypass

umgehend *a* immediate

Umgehungsstraße *f* bypass

umgekehrt *a* inverse; *(Reihenfolge)* reverse; **es war u ~** it was the other way round

umgraben† *vt sep* dig [over]

Umhang *m* cloak

umhauen† *vt sep* knock down; *(fällen)* chop down

umhören (sich) *vr sep* ask around

Umkehr *f* -turning back. **u ~ en** *v sep* □ *vi (sein)* turn back □ *vt* turn round; turn inside out *(Tasche)*; *(fig)* reverse. **U ~ ung** *f* - reversal

umkippen v sep ⊔vt tip over; (versehentlich) knock over ⊔vi (sein) fall over; ⟨Boot:⟩ capsize

Umkleide|kabine f changing-cubicle. **u ~ n (sich)** vr sep change. **U ~ raum** m changing-room

umknicken v sep ⊔vt bend; (falten) fold ⊔vi (sein) bend; (mit dem Fuß) go over on one's ankle

Umkreis m surroundings pl

umkreisen vt insep circle; ⟨Astr⟩ revolve around; ⟨Satellit:⟩ orbit

umkrempeln vt sep turn up; (von innen nach außen) turn inside out; ⟨ändern⟩ change radically

Umlauf m (circulation; (Astr) revolution. **U ~ bahn** f orbit

Umlaut m umlaut

umlegen vt sep lay or put down; flatten ⟨Getreide:⟩; turn down ⟨Kragen⟩; put on ⟨Schal⟩; throw ⟨Hebel⟩; (verlegen) transfer

umleit|en vt sep divert. **U ~ ung** f diversion

umliegend a surrounding

umpflanzen vt sep transplant

umranden vt insep edge

umräumen vt sep rearrange

umrechn|en vt sep convert. **U ~ ung** f conversion

Umriß m outline

umrühren vt/i sep (haben) stir

ums pron = **um das**

Umsatz m ⟨Comm⟩ turnover

umschalten vt/i sep (haben) switch over; **auf Rot u ~** ⟨Ampel:⟩ change to red

Umschau / U ~ halten nach look out for

Umschlag m cover; ⟨Schutz⟩ jacket; ⟨Brief⟩ envelope; ⟨Med⟩ compress; ⟨Hosen⟩ turn-up. **u ~ en** v sep ⊔vt turn up; turn over ⟨Seite⟩; ⟨fällen⟩ chop down ⊔vi (sein) topple over; ⟨Wetter:⟩ change; ⟨Wind:⟩ veer

umschließen† vt insep enclose

umschreiben† vt insep define; (anders ausdrücken) paraphrase

umschulen vt sep retrain; ⟨Sch⟩ transfer to another school

Umschwung m ⟨fig⟩ change; ⟨Pol⟩ U-turn

umsehen† (sich) vr sep look round; ⟨zurück⟩ look back; **sich u ~ nach** look for

umseitig a & adv overleaf

umsetzen vt sep move; ⟨umpflanzen⟩ transplant; ⟨Comm⟩ sell

umsied|eln v sep ⊔vt resettle ⊔vi (sein) move. **U ~ lung** f resettlement

umsonst adv in vain; ⟨grundlos⟩ without reason; ⟨gratis⟩ free

Umstand m circumstance; ⟨Tatsache⟩ fact; ⟨Aufwand⟩ fuss; ⟨Mühe⟩ trouble; **unter U ~ en** possibly; **U ~ e machen** make a fuss; **in anderen U ~ en** pregnant

umständlich a laborious; (kompliziert) involved

Umstands|kleid nt maternity dress. **U ~ wort** nt (pl -wörter) adverb

Umstehende pl bystanders

umsteigen† vi sep (sein) change

umstellen¹ vt insep surround

umstell|en² vt sep rearrange; (anders einstellen) reset; ⟨Techn⟩ convert; ⟨ändern⟩ change; **sich u ~ en** adjust. **U ~ ung** f rearrangement; resetting; conversion; change; adjustment

umstritten a controversial; (ungeklärt) disputed

umstülpen vt sep turn upside down; (von innen nach außen) turn inside out

Um|sturz m coup. **u ~ stürzen** v sep ⊔vt overturn; ⟨Pol⟩ overthrow ⊔vi (sein) fall over

umtaufen vt sep rename

Umtausch m exchange. **u ~ en** vt sep exchange (**gegen** for)

umwandeln vt sep convert; ⟨fig⟩ transform

umwechseln vt sep change

Umweg m detour; **auf U~en** in a roundabout way

Umwelt f environment. **u~freundlich** a environmentally friendly. **U~schutz** m protection of the environment

umwerfen† vt sep knock over; (fig) upset ⟨Plan⟩

umziehen† v sep □vi (sein) move □vt change; **sich u~** change

Umzug m move; (Prozession) procession

unabänderlich a irrevocable; ⟨Tatsache⟩ unalterable

unabhängig a independent; **u~ davon, ob** irrespective of whether. **U~keit** f - independence

unablässig a incessant

unabsehbar a incalculable

unabsichtlich a unintentional

unachtsam a careless. **U~keit** f - carelessness

unangebracht a inappropriate

unangenehm a unpleasant; (peinlich) embarrassing

Unannehmlichkeiten fpl trouble sg

unansehnlich a shabby

unanständig a indecent

unappetitlich a unappetizing

Unart f -,-en bad habit. **u~ig** a naughty

unauffällig a inconspicuous, unobtrusive

unaufgefordert adv without being asked

unaufhaltsam a inexorable. **u~hörlich** a incessant

unaufmerksam a inattentive

unaufrichtig a insincere

unausbleiblich a inevitable

unbarmherzig a merciless

unbeabsichtigt a unintentional

unbedenklich a harmless □adv without hesitation

unbedeutend a insignificant; (geringfügig) slight

unbedingt a absolute; **nicht u~** not necessarily

unbefriedigend a unsatisfactory. **u~t** a dissatisfied

unbefugt a unauthorized □adv without authorization

unbegreiflich a incomprehensible

unbegrenzt a unlimited □adv indefinitely

unbegründet a unfounded

Unbehagen nt unease; (körperlich) discomfort

unbekannt a unknown; (nicht vertraut) unfamiliar. **U~e(r)** m/f stranger

unbeliebt a unpopular. **U~heit** f unpopularity

unbemannt a unmanned

unbemerkt a & adv unnoticed

unbenutzt a unused

unbequem a uncomfortable; (lästig) awkward

unberechenbar a unpredictable

unberechtigt a unjustified; (unbefugt) unauthorized

unberührt a untouched; (fig) virgin; ⟨Landschaft⟩ unspoilt

unbescheiden a presumptuous

unbeschränkt a unguarded

unbeschränkt a unlimited □adv without limit

unbeschwert a carefree

unbesiegbar a invincible

unbesiegt a undefeated

unbespielt a blank

unbeständig a inconsistent; ⟨Wetter⟩ unsettled

unbestechlich a incorruptible

unbestimmt a indefinite; ⟨Alter⟩ indeterminate; (ungewiß) uncertain; (unklar) vague

unbestritten a undisputed □adv indisputably

unbeteiligt a indifferent; **u~ an** (+ dat) not involved in

unbeweglich a & adv motionless, still

unbewohnt a uninhabited

unbewußt *a* unconscious

unbezahlbar *a* priceless

unbrauchbar *a* useless

und *conj* and; **und so weiter** and so on; **nach und nach** bit by bit

Undank *m* ingratitude. **u ~ bar** *a* ungrateful; *(nicht lohnend)* thankless. **U ~ barkeit** *f* ingratitude

undeutlich *a* indistinct; *(vage)* vague

undicht *a* leaking; **u ~ e Stelle** leak

Unding *nt* absurdity

unduldsam *a* intolerant

undurchdringlich *a* impenetrable; *(Miene)* inscrutable. **u ~ führbar** *a* impracticable

undurchlässig *a* impermeable. **u ~ sichtig** *a* opaque; *(fig)* doubtful

uneben *a* uneven. **U ~ heit** *f* -,-en unevenness; *(Buckel)* bump

unecht *a* false; **u ~ er Schmuck/ Pelz** imitation jewellery/fur

unehelich *a* illegitimate

uneinig *a* *(fig)* divided; [**sich** *(dat)*] **u ~ sein** disagree. **U ~ keit** *f* disagreement; *(Streit)* discord

uneins *a* **u ~ sein** be at odds

unempfindlich *a* insensitive (**gegen** to); *(widerstandsfähig)* tough; *(Med)* immune

unendlich *a* infinite; *(endlos)* endless. **U ~ keit** *f* infinity

unentbehrlich *a* indispensable

unentgeltlich *a* free; *(Arbeit)* unpaid □ *adv* free of charge

unentschieden *a* undecided; *(Sport)* drawn; **u ~ spielen** draw. **U ~ *nt* -s,-** draw

unerfahren *a* inexperienced. **U ~ heit** *f* - inexperience

unerfreulich *a* unpleasant

unergründlich *a* unfathomable

unerhört *a* enormous; *(empörend)* outrageous

unerklärlich *a* inexplicable

unerläßlich *a* essential

unerlaubt *a* unauthorized □ *adv* without permission

unerschwinglich *a* prohibitive

unersetzlich *a* irreplaceable; *(Verlust)* irreparable

unerträglich *a* unbearable

unerwartet *a* unexpected

unerwünscht *a* unwanted; *(Besuch)* unwelcome

unfähig *a* incompetent; **u ~, etw zu tun** incapable of doing sth; *(nicht in der Lage)* unable to do sth. **U ~ keit** *f* incompetence; inability (**zu** to)

unfair *a* unfair

Unfall *m* accident. **U ~ flucht** *f* failure to stop after an accident. **U ~ station** *f* casualty department

unfolgsam *a* disobedient

unförmig *a* shapeless

unfreiwillig *a* involuntary; *(unbeabsichtigt)* unintentional

unfreundlich *a* unfriendly; *(unangenehm)* unpleasant. **U ~ keit** *f* unfriendliness; unpleasantness

Unfriede[n] *m* discord

unfruchtbar *a* infertile; *(fig)* unproductive. **U ~ keit** *f* infertility

Unfug *m* -s mischief; *(Unsinn)* nonsense

Ungar(in) *m* -n,-n *(f* -,-nen) Hungarian. **u ~ isch** *a* Hungarian. **U ~ n** *nt* -s Hungary

ungeachtet *prep* (+ *gen*) in spite of. **ungebraucht** *a* unused. **ungedeckt** *a* uncovered; *(Sport)* unmarked; *(Tisch)* unlaid

Ungeduld *f* impatience. **u ~ ig** *a* impatient

ungeeignet *a* unsuitable

ungefähr *a* approximate

ungefährlich *a* harmless

ungeheuer *a* enormous. **U ~ *nt* -s,-** monster

ungehorsam *a* disobedient. **U ~ *m* disobedience

ungeklärt *a* unsolved; *(Frage)* unsettled; *(Ursache)* unknown

ungelegen *a* inconvenient

ungelernt *a* unskilled

ungemütlich *a* uncomfortable; ⟨*unangenehm*⟩ unpleasant

ungenau *a* inaccurate; ⟨*vage*⟩ vague

ungeniert /'ʊnʒeːniːɐ̯t/ *a* uninhibited □ *adv* openly

ungenießbar *a* inedible; ⟨*Getränk*⟩ undrinkable. **ungenügend** *a* inadequate; ⟨*Sch*⟩ unsatisfactory. **ungepflegt** *a* neglected; ⟨*Person*⟩ unkempt. **ungerade** *a* ⟨*Zahl*⟩ odd

ungerecht *a* unjust. **U~igkeit** *f* -,-en injustice

ungern *adv* reluctantly

ungesalzen *a* unsalted

Ungeschicklichkeit *f* clumsiness. **u~t** *a* clumsy

ungeschminkt *a* without make-up; ⟨*Wahrheit*⟩ unvarnished. **ungesellig** *a* unsociable. **ungesetzlich** *a* illegal. **ungestört** *a* undisturbed. **ungesund** *a* unhealthy. **ungesüßt** *a* unsweetened. **ungetrübt** *a* perfect

Ungetüm *nt* -s,-e monster

ungewiß *a* uncertain; **im ungewissen lassen** leave in the dark. **U~heit** *f* uncertainty

ungewöhnlich *a* unusual. **ungewohnt** *a* unaccustomed; ⟨*nicht vertraut*⟩ unfamiliar

Ungeziefer *nt* -s vermin

ungezogen *a* naughty

ungezwungen *a* informal; ⟨*natürlich*⟩ natural

ungläubig *a* incredulous

unglaublich *a* incredible, unbelievable

ungleich *a* unequal; ⟨*verschieden*⟩ different. **U~heit** *f* inequality. **u~mäßig** *a* uneven

Unglück *nt* -s,-e misfortune; ⟨*Pech*⟩ bad luck; ⟨*Mißgeschick*⟩ mishap; ⟨*Unfall*⟩ accident. **u~lich** *a* unhappy; ⟨*ungünstig*⟩

unfortunate. **u~licherweise** *adv* unfortunately

ungültig *a* invalid; ⟨*Jur*⟩ void

ungünstig *a* unfavourable; ⟨*unpassend*⟩ inconvenient

unhandlich *a* unwieldy

Unheil *nt* -s disaster

unheilbar *a* incurable

unheimlich *a* eerie; ⟨*gruselig*⟩ creepy; ⟨*fam: groß*⟩ terrific □ *adv* eerily; ⟨*fam: sehr*⟩ terribly

unhöflich *a* rude. **U~keit** *f* rudeness

unhygienisch *a* unhygienic

Uni *f* -,-s ⟨*fam*⟩ university

uni /y'niː/ *inv a* plain

Uniform *f* -,-en uniform

uninteressant *a* uninteresting

Union *f* -,-en union

universell *a* universal

Universität *f* -,-en university

Universum *nt* -s universe

unkenntlich *a* unrecognizable. **U~nis** *f* ignorance

unklar *a* unclear; ⟨*ungewiß*⟩ uncertain; ⟨*vage*⟩ vague; **im u~en sein** be in the dark

unkompliziert *a* uncomplicated

Unkosten *pl* expenses

Unkraut *nt* -s weed; ⟨*coll*⟩ weeds *pl*; **U~ jäten** weed. **U~vertilgungsmittel** *nt* weed-killer

unlängst *adv* recently

unlauter *a* dishonest; ⟨*unfair*⟩ unfair

unleserlich *a* illegible

unleugbar *a* undeniable

unlogisch *a* illogical

Unmenge *f* enormous amount/ ⟨*Anzahl*⟩ number

Unmensch *m* ⟨*fam*⟩ brute. **u~lich** *a* inhuman

unmerklich *a* imperceptible

unmittelbar *a* immediate; ⟨*direkt*⟩ direct

unmöbliert *a* unfurnished

unmodern *a* old-fashioned

unmöglich *a* impossible. **U~keit** *f* impossibility

Unmoral f immorality. **u~isch** a immoral

unmündig a under-age

Unmut m displeasure

unnatürlich a unnatural

unnormal a abnormal

unnötig a unnecessary

unord|entlich a untidy; (*nachlässig*) sloppy. **U~nung** f disorder; (*Durcheinander*) muddle

unorthodox a unorthodox □ adv in an unorthodox manner

unparteiisch a impartial

unpassend a inappropriate; (*Moment*) inopportune

unpersönlich a impersonal

unpraktisch a impractical

unpünktlich a unpunctual □ adv late

unrealistisch a unrealistic

unrecht a wrong □ n **u~ haben** be wrong; **jdm u~ tun** do s.o. an injustice; **jdm u~ geben** disagree with s.o. **U~nt** wrong; **zu U~** wrongly

unregelmäßig a irregular

unreif a unripe; (*fig*) immature

unrein a impure; (*Luft*) polluted; (*Haut*) bad; **ins u~e schreiben** make a rough draft of

unrentabel a unprofitable

Unruh|e f -,-n restlessness; (*Erregung*) agitation; (*Besorgnis*) anxiety; **U~en** (*Pol*) unrest sg **u~ig** a restless; (*besorgt*) anxious

uns pron (*acc/dat of* wir) us; (*refl*) ourselves; (*einander*) each other

unsauber a dirty; (*nachlässig*) sloppy; (*unlauter*) dishonest

unschädlich a harmless

unscharf a blurred

unschätzbar a inestimable

unscheinbar a inconspicuous

unschlagbar a unbeatable

unschlüssig a undecided

Unschuld f - innocence; (*Jungfräulichkeit*) virginity. **u~ig** a innocent

unselbständig a dependent □ adv **u~ denken** not think for oneself

unser poss pron our. **u~e(r,s)** poss pron ours. **u~erseits** adv for our part. **u~twegen** adv for our sake; (*wegen uns*) because of us, on our account

unsicher a unsafe; (*ungewiß*) uncertain; (*nicht zuverlässig*) unreliable; (*Schritte, Hand*) unsteady; (*Person*) insecure □ adv unsteadily. **U~heit** f uncertainty; unreliability; insecurity

unsichtbar a invisible

Unsinn m nonsense

Unsitt|e f bad habit. **u~lich** a indecent

unsportlich a not sporty; (*unfair*) unsporting

uns|re(r,s) poss pron = **unsere(r,s)**. **u~rige** poss pron **der/die/das u~rige** ours

unsterblich a immortal. **U~keit** f immortality

Unsumme f vast sum

unsympathisch a unpleasant

untätig a idle

untauglich a unsuitable; (*Mil*) unfit

unten adv at the bottom; (*auf der Unterseite*) underneath; (*eine Treppe tiefer*) downstairs; **hier/da u~** down here/there; **nach u~** down[wards]

unter prep (+ dat/acc) under; (*niedriger als*) below; (*inmitten, zwischen*) among; **u~ der Woche** during the week; **u~ sich** by themselves

Unter|arm m forearm. **U~bewußtsein** nt subconscious

unterbieten† vt insep undercut; beat (*Rekord*)

unterbinden† vt insep stop

unterbrechen† vt insep interrupt; break (*Reise*)

unterbringen† vt sep put; (*beherbergen*) put up

unterdessen *adv* in the meantime

Unterdrückung *f* - suppression; oppression

untere(r,s) *a* lower

untereinander *adv* one below the other; (*miteinander*) among ourselves/yourselves/themselves

unterernährt *a* undernourished. **U~ung** *f* malnutrition

Unterführung *f* underpass; (*Fußgänger-*) subway

Untergang *m* (*Astr*) setting; (*Naut*) sinking; (*Zugrundegehen*) disappearance; (*der Welt*) end

Untergebene(r) *m/f* subordinate

untergehen *vi sep* (*sein*) (*Astr*) set; (*versinken*) go under; ⟨*Schiff:*⟩ go down, sink; (*zugrunde gehen*) disappear; ⟨*Welt:*⟩ come to an end

Untergeschoß *nt* basement

Untergrund *m* foundation; (*Hintergrund*) background. **U~bahn** *f* underground [railway]

unterhaken *vt sep* jdn u~ take s.o.'s arm; **untergehakt** arm in arm

unterhalb *adv & prep* (+ *gen*) below

Unterhalt *m* maintenance

unterhalten† *vt insep* maintain; (*ernähren*) support; (*betreiben*) run; (*erheitern*) entertain; **sich u~en** talk; (*sich vergnügen*) enjoy oneself. **U~ung** *f* -,-en maintenance; (*Gespräch*) conversation; (*Zeitvertreib*) entertainment

Unter|haus *nt* (*Pol*) lower house; (*in UK*) House of Commons. **U~hemd** *nt* vest. **U~hose** *f* underpants *pl.* **u~irdisch** *a & adv* underground

Unterkiefer *m* lower jaw

unterkommen† *vi sep* (*sein*) find accommodation; (*eine Stellung finden*) get a job

Unterkunft *f* -,-künfte accommodation

Unterlage *f* pad; **U~n** papers

Unterlaß *m* ohne U~ incessantly

Unterlassung *f* -,-en omission

unterlaufen† (*sein*) occur; **mir ist ein Fehler u~** I made a mistake

unterlegen *a* inferior; (*Sport*) losing; **zahlenmäßig u~** outnumbered (*dat* by). **U~e(r)** *m/f* loser

Unterleib *m* abdomen

unterliegen† *vi insep* (*sein*) lose (*dat* to); (*unterworfen sein*) be subject (*dat* to)

Unterlippe *f* lower lip

Untermiete *f* zur U~ wohnen be a lodger. **U~r(in)** *m(f)* lodger

unternehmen† *vt insep* undertake; take ⟨*Schritte*⟩; **etw/nichts u~en** do sth/nothing. **U~en** *nt* -s,- undertaking, enterprise; (*Betrieb*) concern. **U~er** *m* -s,- employer; (*Bau-*) contractor; (*Industrieller*) industrialist. **u~ungslustig** *a* enterprising (*abenteuerlustig*) adventurous

Unteroffizier *m* non-commissioned officer

unterordnen *vt sep* subordinate

Unterredung *f* -,-en talk

Unterricht *m* -[e]s teaching; (*Privat-*) tuition; (*U~sstunden*) lessons *pl*

unterrichten *vt/i insep* (*haben*) teach; (*informieren*) inform

Unterrock *m* slip

untersagen *vt insep* forbid

Untersatz *m* mat; (*mit Füßen*) stand; (*Gläser-*) coaster

unterscheiden† *vt/i insep* (*haben*) distinguish; (*auseinanderhalten*) tell apart; **sich u~en** differ. **U~ung** *f* distinction

Unterschied *m* -[e]s,-e difference; (*Unterscheidung*) distinction; **im U~ zu ihm** unlike him

unterschlagen† *vt insep* embezzle; (*verheimlichen*) suppress.

U~ung *f* -,-en embezzlement; suppression

Unterschlupf *m* -[e]s shelter; (*Versteck*) hiding-place

unterschreiben† *vt/i insep* (*haben*) sign

Unter|schrift *f* signature; (*Bild-*) caption. **U~seeboot** *nt* submarine

Unterstand *m* shelter

unterste(r,s) *a* lowest, bottom

unterstehen† *vi insep* (*haben*) be answerable (*dat* to); (*unterliegen*) be subject (*dat* to)

unterstellen¹ *vt sep* put underneath; (*abstellen*) store

unterstellen² *vt insep* place under the control of (*dat* of); (*annehmen*) assume; (*fälschlich zuschreiben*) impute (*dat* to)

unterstreichen† *vt insep* underline

unterstütz|en *vt insep* support; (*helfen*) aid. **U~ung** *f* -,-en support; (*finanziell*) aid; (*regelmäßiger Betrag*) allowance; (*Arbeitslosen-*) benefit

untersuch|en *vt insep* examine; (*Jur*) investigate; (*prüfen*) test; (*überprüfen*) check; (*durchsuchen*) search. **U~ung** *f* -,-en examination; investigation; test; check; search. **U~ungshaft** *f* detention on remand

Untertan *m* -s & -en,-en subject

Untertasse *f* saucer

Unterteil *nt* bottom (part)

Untertitel *m* subtitle

untervermieten *vt/i insep* (*haben*) sublet

Unterwäsche *f* underwear

unterwegs *adv* on the way; (*außer Haus*) out; (*verreist*) away

unterziehen¹† *vt sep* put on underneath; (*Culin*) fold in

unterziehen²† *vt insep etw einer Untersuchung/Überprüfung u~** examine/ check sth;

---

sich einer Operation/Prüfung u~ have an operation/take a test

Untier *nt* monster

untragbar *a* intolerable

untrennbar *a* inseparable

untreu *a* disloyal; (*in der Ehe*) unfaithful. **U~e** *f* disloyalty; infidelity

untröstlich *a* inconsolable

Untugend *f* bad habit

unübersehbar *a* obvious; (*groß*) immense

ununterbrochen *a* incessant

unveränderlich *a* invariable; (*gleichbleibend*) unchanging

unverändert *a* unchanged

unverantwortlich *a* irresponsible

unverbesserlich *a* incorrigible

unverbindlich *a* non-committal; (*Comm*) not binding □ *adv* without obligation

unverdaulich *a* indigestible

unvergeßlich *a* unforgettable

unvergleichlich *a* incomparable

unverheiratet *a* unmarried. **u~käuflich** *a* not for sale; (*Muster*) free

unverkennbar *a* unmistakable

unverletzt *a* unhurt

unvermeidlich *a* inevitable

unvermindert *a & adv* undiminished. **u~mutet** *a* unexpected

Unvernunft *f* folly. **u~nünftig** *a* foolish

unverschämt *a* insolent; (*fam: ungeheuer*) outrageous. **U~heit** *f* -,-en insolence

unversehens *adv* suddenly. **u~sehrt** *a* unhurt; (*unbeschädigt*) intact

unverständlich *a* incomprehensible; (*undeutlich*) indistinct

unverträglich *a* incompatible; (*Person*) quarrelsome; (*unbekömmlich*) indigestible

unverwundbar *a* invulnerable. **u~wüstlich** *a* indestructible;

⟨*Person, Humor*⟩ irrepressible; ⟨*Gesundheit*⟩ robust. **u ~ zeihlich** *a* unforgivable

unverzüglich *a* immediate

unvollendet *a* unfinished

unvollkommen *a* imperfect; (*unvollständig*) incomplete

unvollständig *a* incomplete

unvor|bereitet *a* unprepared. **u ~ eingenommen** *a* unbiased. **u ~ hergesehen** *a* unforeseen

unvorsichtig *a* careless

unvorstellbar *a* unimaginable

unvorteilhaft *a* unfavourable; (*nicht hübsch*) unattractive; ⟨*Kleid, Frisur*⟩ unflattering

unwahr *a* untrue. **U ~ heit** *f*, **-en** untruth. **u ~ scheinlich** *a* unlikely; (*unglaublich*) improbable; (*fam: groß*) incredible

unweit *adv & prep* (+ *gen*) not far

unwesentlich *a* unimportant

Unwetter *nt* **-s,-** storm

unwichtig *a* unimportant

unwider|legbar *a* irrefutable. **u ~ ruflich** *a* irrevocable

Unwill|e *m* displeasure. **u ~ ig** *a* angry; (*widerwillig*) reluctant

unwirklich *a* unreal

unwirksam *a* ineffective

unwirtlich *a* inhospitable

unwirtschaftlich *a* uneconomic

unwissen|d *a* ignorant. **U ~ heit** *f* - ignorance

unwohl *a* unwell; (*unbehaglich*) uneasy

unwürdig *a* unworthy (*gen of*)

Unzahl *f* vast number. **unzählig** *a* innumerable, countless

unzerbrechlich *a* unbreakable

unzerstörbar *a* indestructible

unzertrennlich *a* inseparable

Unzucht *f* sexual offence; **gewerbsmäßige U ~** prostitution

unzüchtig *a* indecent; ⟨*Schriften*⟩ obscene

unzufrieden *a* dissatisfied; (*innerlich*) discontented. **U ~ heit** *f* dissatisfaction; (*Pol*) discontent

unzulässig *a* inadmissible

unzurechnungsfähig *a* insane. **U ~ keit** *f* insanity

unzusammenhängend *a* incoherent

unzutreffend *a* inapplicable; (*falsch*) incorrect

unzuverlässig *a* unreliable

üppig *a* luxuriant; (*überreichlich*) lavish

uralt *a* ancient

Uran *nt* **-s** uranium

Uraufführung *f* first performance

Urenkel *m* great-grandson; (*pl*) great-grandchildren

Urgroß|mutter *f* great-grandmother. **U ~ vater** *m* great-grandfather

Urheber *m* **-s,-** originator; (*Verfasser*) author. **U ~ recht** *nt* copyright

Urin *m* **-s,-e** urine

Urkunde *f* **-,-n** certificate; (*Dokument*) document

Urlaub *m* **-s** holiday; (*Mil, Admin*) leave; **auf U ~** on holiday/ leave; **U ~ haben** be on holiday/ leave. **U ~ er(in)** *m* **-s,-** (*f* **-,-nen**) holiday-maker. **U ~ sort** *m* holiday resort

Urne *f* **-,-n** urn; (*Wahl-*) ballot-box

Ursache *f* cause; (*Grund*) reason; **keine U ~** ! don't mention it!

Ursprung *m* origin

ursprünglich *a* original; (*anfänglich*) initial; (*natürlich*) natural

Urteil *nt* **-s,-e** judgement; (*Meinung*) opinion; (*U ~ sspruch*) verdict; (*Strafe*) sentence. **u ~ en** *vi* (*haben*) judge

Urwald *m* primeval forest; (*tropischer*) jungle

Urzeit *f* primeval times *pl*

USA *pl* USA *sg*

usw. *abbr* (*und so weiter*) etc.

utopisch *a* Utopian

V

Vakuum /'va:kuʊm/ *nt* -s vacuum
Vanille /va'nɪljə/ *f* - vanilla
Vari|ante *f* -,-n variant. **v~ie~ren** *vt/i* (*haben*) vary
Vase /'va:zə/ *f* -,-n vase
Vater *m* -s,"- father. **V~land** *nt* -,-er fatherland
väterlich *a* paternal; (*fürsorglich*) fatherly. **v~erseits** *adv* on one's/the father's side
Vater|schaft *f* - fatherhood; (*Jur*) paternity. **V~unser** *nt* -s,- Lord's Prayer
v. Chr. *abbr* (**vor Christus**) BC
Vegetar|ier(in) /vege'ta:rɪɐ, -jərɪn/ *m(f)* -s,- (*f* -,-nen) vegetarian. **v~isch** *a* vegetarian
Veilchen *nt* -s,- violet
Vene /'ve:nə/ *f* -,-n vein
Venedig /ve'ne:dɪç/ *nt* -s Venice
Ventil /ven'ti:l/ *nt* -s,-e valve. **V~ator** *m* -s,-en /-'to:rən/ fan
verabred|en *vt* arrange; **sich v~en** arrange to meet. **V~ung** *f* -,-en arrangement; (*Treffen*) appointment
verabschieden *vt* say goodbye to; (*aus dem Dienst*) retire; pass (*Gesetz*); **sich v~** say goodbye
verachten *vt* despise
Verachtung *f* - contempt
verallgemeinern *vt/i* (*haben*) generalize
veränder|lich *a* changeable; (*Math*) variable. **V~n** *vt* change; **sich v~n** change; (*beruflich*) change one's job. **V~ung** *f* - change
verängstigt *a* frightened, scared
verankern *vt* anchor
veranlag|t *a* künstlerisch/musikalisch **v~t** sein have an artistic/a musical bent; **praktisch v~t** practically minded. **V~ung**

f -,-en disposition; (*Neigung*) tendency; (*künstlerisch*) bent
veranlassen *vt* (*reg*) arrange for; (*einleiten*) institute; **jdn v~ prompt** s.o. (**zu** to)
veranschlagen *vt* (*reg*) estimate
veranstalt|en *vt* organize; hold, give (*Party*); make (*Lärm*). **V~er** *m* -s,- organizer. **V~ung** *f* -,-en event
verantwort|lich *a* responsible; **v~lich machen** hold responsible. **V~ung** *f* - responsibility. **V~ungslos** *a* irresponsible. **V~ungsvoll** *a* responsible
verarbeiten *vt* use; (*Techn*) process; (*verdauen & fig*) digest
verärgern *vt* annoy
veräußern *vt* sell
Verb /verp/ *nt* -s,-en verb
Verband *m* -[e]s,"-e association; (*Mil*) unit; (*Med*) bandage; (*Wund-*) dressing. **V~szeug** *nt* first-aid kit
verbann|en *vt* exile; (*fig*) banish. **V~ung** *f* - exile
verbergen† *vt* hide; **sich v~** hide
verbesser|n *vt* improve; (*berichtigen*) correct. **V~ung** *f* -,-en improvement; correction
verbeug|en (sich) *vr* bow. **V~ung** *f* bow
verbeulen *vt* dent
verbiegen† *vt* bend
verbiet|en† *vt* forbid; (*Admin*) prohibit, ban
verbilligen *vt* reduce [in price]. **v~t** *a* reduced
verbind|en† *vt* connect (**mit** to); (*zusammenfügen*) join; (*verknüpfen*) combine; (*in Verbindung bringen*) associate; (*Med*) bandage; dress (*Wunde*); **jdm verbunden sein** (*fig*) be obliged to
verbindlich *a* friendly; (*bindend*) binding

Verbindung f connection; (*Verknüpfung*) combination; (*Kontakt*) contact; (*Vereinigung*) association; **chemische V~** chemical compound; **in V~ stehen/in V~ setzen** be/get in touch

verbissen a grim

verbittern vt make bitter. **v~t** a bitter. **V~ung** f - bitterness

verblassen vi (sein) fade

Verbleib m -s whereabouts pl. **v~en†** vi (sein) remain

verbleit a ⟨Benzin⟩ leaded

verblüffen vt amaze, astound. **V~ung** f - amazement

verblühen vi (sein) wither, fade

verbluten vi (sein) bleed to death

verborgen¹ a hidden

verborgen² vt lend

Verbot nt -[e]s,-e ban. **v~en** a forbidden; (*Admin*) prohibited

Verbrauch m -[e]s consumption. **v~en** vt use; consume ⟨Lebensmittel⟩; ⟨erschöpfen⟩ use up, exhaust. **V~er** m -s,- consumer

Verbrechen nt -s,- crime

Verbrecher m -s,- criminal

verbreiten vt spread. **v~et** a widespread. **V~ung** f - spread; (*Verbreiten*) spreading

verbrennen† vt/i (sein) burn; cremate ⟨Leiche⟩. **V~ung** f -,-en burning; cremation; (*Wunde*) burn

verbringen† vt spend

verbrühen vt scald

verbuchen vt enter

verbünden (sich) vr form an alliance. **V~ete(r)** m/f ally

verbürgen vt guarantee; **sich v~ für** vouch for

Verdacht m -[e]s suspicion; **in** or **im V~ haben** suspect

verdächtig a suspicious. **v~en** vt suspect (*gen* of). **V~te(r)** m/f suspect

verdammen vt condemn; (*Relig*) damn. **v~t** a & adv (sl) damned; **v~t!** damn!

verdampfen vt/i (sein) evaporate

verdanken vt owe (dat to)

verdau|en vt digest. **v~lich** a digestible. **V~ung** f - digestion

Verdeck nt -[e]s,-e hood; (*Oberdeck*) top deck

verderb|en† vi (sein) spoil; ⟨Lebensmittel:⟩ go bad □vt spoil; **ich habe mir den Magen verdorben** I have an upset stomach. **V~en** nt -s ruin. **v~lich** a perishable; (*schädlich*) pernicious

verdien|en vt/i (haben) earn; (*fig*) deserve. **V~er** m -s,- wage-earner

Verdienst¹ m -[e]s earnings pl

Verdienst² nt -[e]s,-e merit

verdient a well-deserved

verdoppeln vt double

verdorben a spoilt, ruined; ⟨Magen⟩ upset; (*moralisch*) corrupt; (*verkommen*) depraved

verdrehen vt twist; roll ⟨Augen⟩; (*fig*) distort. **v~t** a (*fam*) crazy

verdreifachen vt treble, triple

verdrücken vt crumple; (*fam: essen*) polish off; **sich v~** (*fam*) slip away

Verdruß m -sses annoyance

verdünnen vt dilute

verdunst|en vi (sein) evaporate. **V~ung** f - evaporation

verdursten vi (sein) die of thirst

veredeln vt refine; (*Hort*) graft

verehr|en vt revere; (*Relig*) worship; (*bewundern*) admire; (*schenken*) give. **V~er(in)** m -s,- (f -,-nen) admirer. **V~ung** f - veneration; worship; admiration

vereidigen vt swear in

Verein m -s,-e society; (*Sport*) club

vereinbar a compatible. **v~en** vt arrange. **V~ung** f -,-en agreement

vereinfachen vt simplify

vereinheitlichen vt standardize

vereinig|en vt unite; merge ⟨Firmen⟩; **sich v~en** unite; **V~te**

Staaten [von Amerika] United States sg [of America]. **V~ung** f -,-en union; (Organisation) organization

vereinzelt a isolated □adv occasionally

vereist a frozen; ⟨Straße⟩ icy

vereitert a septic

verenden vi (sein) die

verengen vt restrict; **sich v~** narrow; ⟨Pupille⟩ contract

vererben vt leave (dat to); (Biol & fig) pass on (dat to)

verfahren† vi (sein) proceed; **v~ mit** deal with □vr **sich v~** lose one's way □a muddled. **V~** nt -s,- procedure; (Techn) process; (Jur) proceedings pl

Verfall m decay; ⟨eines Gebäudes⟩ dilapidation; ⟨körperlich & fig⟩ decline; ⟨Ablauf⟩ expiry. **v~en†** vi (sein) decay; ⟨Person, Sitten⟩ decline; ⟨ablaufen⟩ expire; **v~en in** (+ acc) lapse into

verfärben (sich) vr change colour; ⟨Stoff:⟩ discolour

verfass|en vt write; (Jur) draw up; (entwerfen) draft. **V~er** m -s,- author. **V~ung** f (Pol) constitution; (Zustand) state

verfaulen vi (sein) rot, decay

verfechten† vt advocate

verfehlen vt miss

verfeinde|n (sich) vr become enemies; **v~t sein** be enemies

verfilmen vt film

verfliegen† vi (sein) evaporate; ⟨Zeit:⟩ fly

verflixt a (fam) awkward; (verdammt) blessed; **v~!** damn!

verfluch|en vt curse. **v~t** a & adv (fam) damned; **v~t!** damn!

verfolg|en vt pursue; (folgen) follow; (bedrängen) pester; (Pol) persecute; **strafrechtlich v~en** prosecute. **V~er** m -s,- pursuer. **V~ung** f - pursuit; persecution

verfrachten vt ship

verfrüht a premature

verfügbar a available

verfüg|en vt order; (Jur) decree □vi (haben) **v~en über** (+ acc) have at one's disposal. **V~ung** f -,-en order; (Jur) decree

verführ|en vt seduce; tempt. **V~ung** f seduction; temptation

vergangen a past; (letzte) last. **V~heit** f - past; (Gram) past tense

vergänglich a transitory

Vergas|en vt gas. **V~er** m -s,- carburettor

vergeb|en† vt award (an + dat to); (weggeben) give away; (verzeihen) forgive. **v~lich** a futile □adv in vain. **V~ung** f - forgiveness

vergehen† vi (sein) pass; **sich v~** violate (gegen etw sth). **V~** nt -s,- offence

vergelt|en† vt repay. **V~ung** f - retaliation; (Rache) revenge

vergessen† vt forget; (liegenlassen) leave behind

vergeßlich a forgetful. **V~keit** f - forgetfulness

vergeuden vt waste, squander

vergewaltig|en vt rape. **V~ung** f -,-en rape

vergießen† vt spill; shed ⟨Tränen, Blut⟩

vergift|en vt poison. **V~ung** f -,-en poisoning

Vergißmeinnicht nt -[e]s,-[e] forget-me-not

vergittert a barred

verglasen vt glaze

Vergleich m -[e]s,-e comparison; (Jur) settlement. **v~bar** a comparable. **v~en†** vt compare (mit with/to)

vergnüg|en (sich) vr enjoy oneself. **V~en** nt -s,- pleasure; (Spaß) fun; **viel v~en!** have a good time! **v~t** a cheerful; (zufrieden) happy

vergolden vt gild; (plattieren) gold-plate

vergraben† vt bury

vergriffen a out of print

vergrößer|n vt enlarge; ⟨Linse:⟩ magnify; (vermehren) increase; (erweitern) extend; expand ⟨Geschäft:⟩ **sich v~n** grow bigger; ⟨Firma:⟩ expand; (Phot) enlargement. **V~ungsglas** nt magnifying glass

vergüt|en vt pay for. **V~ung** f -,-en remuneration; (Erstattung) reimbursement

verhaft|en vt arrest. **V~ung** f -,-en arrest

verhalten† (**sich**) vr behave; (handeln) act; (beschaffen sein) be. **V~** nt -s behaviour, conduct

Verhältnis nt -ses,-se relationship; (Liebes-) affair; (Math) ratio; **V~se** circumstances; (Bedingungen) conditions. **v~mäßig** adv comparatively, relatively

verhand|eln vt discuss; (Jur) try ⟨vi (haben) negotiate. **V~lung** f (Jur) trial; **V~lungen** negotiations

Verhängnis nt -ses fate, doom

verhärten vt/i (sein) harden

verhätscheln vt spoil, pamper

verhauen† vt (fam) beat; make a mess of ⟨Prüfung⟩

verheilen vi (sein) heal

verheimlichen vt keep secret

verheirat|en (**sich**) vr get married (**mit** to). **v~et** a married

verhelfen† vi (haben) **jdm zu etw v~** help s.o. get sth

verherrlichen vt glorify

verhexen vt bewitch; **es ist wie verhext** (fam) there is a jinx on it

verhinder|n vt prevent; **v~t sein** be unable to come

verhöhnen vt deride

Verhör nt -s,-e interrogation; **ins V~ nehmen** interrogate. **v~en** vt interrogate; **sich v~en** mishear

verhungern vi (sein) starve

verhüt|en vt prevent. **V~ung** f -,-prevention. **V~ungsmittel** nt contraceptive

verirren (**sich**) vr get lost

verjagen vt chase away

verkalk|t a (fam) senile

verkalkulieren (**sich**) vr miscalculate

Verkauf m sale; **zum V~** for sale. **v~en** vt sell; **zu v~en** for sale

Verkäufer(in) m seller; (im Geschäft) shop assistant

Verkehr m -s traffic; (Kontakt) contact; **aus dem V~ ziehen** take out of circulation. **v~en** vi (haben) operate; ⟨Bus, Zug:⟩ run; (Umgang haben) associate, mix (**mit** with); (Gast sein) visit (**bei jdm** s.o.)

Verkehrs|ampel f traffic lights pl. **V~unfall** m road accident. **V~verein** m tourist office. **V~zeichen** nt traffic sign

verkehrt a wrong. **v~herum** adv the wrong way round; (links) inside out

verklagen vt sue (**auf**+acc for)

verkleid|en vt disguise; (Techn) line; **sich v~en** disguise oneself; (für Kostümfest) dress up. **V~ung** f -,-en disguise; (Kostüm) fancy dress; (Techn) lining

verkleiner|n vt reduce [in size]. **V~ung** f - reduction

verklemmt a jammed; (psychisch) inhibited

verknittern vt/i (sein) crumple

verkomm|en† vi (sein) be neglected; (sittlich) go to the bad; (verfallen) decay; ⟨Haus:⟩ fall into disrepair; ⟨Gegend:⟩ become run-down; ⟨Lebensmittel:⟩ go bad □ a neglected; (sittlich) depraved; ⟨Haus⟩ dilapidated; ⟨Gegend⟩ run-down

verkörpern vt embody, personify

verkraften vt cope with

verkrampft a (fig) tense

verkrümmt a crooked, bent

verkrüppelt a crippled; ⟨*Glied*⟩ deformed

verkühl|en (sich) vr catch a chill. **V~ung** f -,-en chill

verkümmern vi (sein) waste/⟨*Pflanze:*⟩ wither away

verkünden vt announce; pronounce ⟨*Urteil*⟩

verkürzen vt shorten; (*verringern*) reduce; (*abbrechen*) cut short; while away ⟨*Zeit*⟩

Verlag m -[e]s,-e publishing firm

verlangen vt ask for; (*fordern*) demand; (*berechnen*) charge. **V~nt** -s desire; (*Bitte*) request; **auf V~** on demand

verlänger|n vt extend; lengthen ⟨*Kleid*⟩; (*zeitlich*) prolong; renew ⟨*Paß, Vertrag*⟩. **V~ung** f -,-en extension; renewal. **V~ungsschnur** f extension cable

verlassen vt leave; (*im Stich lassen*) desert; **sich v~ auf** (+*acc*) rely or depend on □ a deserted. **V~heit** f - desolation

verläßlich a reliable

Verlauf m course. **v~en†** vi (sein) run; (*ablaufen*) go; **gut v~en** go [off] well □ vr **sich v~en** lose one's way

verleben vt spend

verlegen vt move; (*verschieben*) postpone; (*vor-*) bring forward; (*verlieren*) mislay; (*versperren*) block; (*legen*) lay ⟨*Teppich*⟩; (*veröffentlichen*) publish; **sich v~ auf** (+*acc*) take up ⟨*Beruf*⟩ □ a embarrassed. **V~heit** f embarrassment

Verleger m -s,- publisher

verleih|en† vt lend; (*gegen Gebühr*) hire out; (*überreichen*) award; (*fig*) give

verlernen vt forget

verletz|en vt injure; (*kränken*) hurt; (*verstoßen gegen*) infringe; violate ⟨*Grenze*⟩. **V~te(r)** m/f injured person; (*bei Unfall*)

casualty. **V~ung** f -,-en injury; (*Verstoß*) infringement; violation

verleugnen vt deny; disown ⟨*Freund*⟩

verleumd|en vt slander; (*schriftlich*) libel. **V~ung** f -,-en slander; (*schriftlich*) libel

verlieben (sich) vr fall in love (**in** + *acc* with); **verliebt sein** be in love (**in** + *acc* with)

verlier|en† vt lose; shed ⟨*Laub*⟩ □ vi (haben) lose (**an etw** *dat* sth). **V~er** m -s,- loser

verlob|en (sich) vr get engaged (**mit** to); **v~t sein** be engaged. **V~te** f fiancée. **V~te(r)** m fiancé. **V~ung** f -,-en engagement

verlock|en vt tempt. **V~ung** f -,-en temptation

verloren a lost

verlos|en vt raffle. **V~ung** f -,-en raffle; (*Ziehung*) draw

Verlust m -[e]s,-e loss

vermachen vt leave, bequeath

Vermächtnis nt -ses,-se legacy

vermähl|en (sich) vr marry. **V~ung** f -,-en marriage

vermehren vt increase; propagate ⟨*Pflanzen*⟩; **sich v~** increase; (*sich fortpflanzen*) breed

vermeiden† vt avoid

Vermerk m -[e]s,-e note. **v~en** vt note [down]

vermessen† vt measure; survey ⟨*Gelände*⟩ □ a presumptuous. **V~ung** f measurement; (*Land-*) survey

vermiet|en vt let, rent [out]; hire out ⟨*Boot, Auto*⟩; **zu v~en** to let; ⟨*Boot:*⟩ for hire. **V~er** m landlord. **V~erin** f landlady

vermischen vt mix

vermissen vt miss

vermißt a missing

vermitt|eln vi (haben) mediate □ vt arrange; (*beschaffen*) find; place ⟨*Arbeitskräfte*⟩

Vermittl|er *m* -s,- agent; (*Schlichter*) mediator. **V~ung** *f* -,-en arrangement; (*Agentur*) agency; (*Teleph*) exchange; (*Schlichtung*) mediation

Vermögen *nt* -s,- fortune

vermut|en *vt* suspect; (*glauben*) presume. **v~lich** *a* probable. **V~ung** *f* -,-en supposition; (*Verdacht*) suspicion

vernachlässigen *vt* neglect

vernehm|en† *vt* hear; (*verhören*) question; (*Jur*) examine. **V~ung** *f* -,-en questioning

verneigen (sich) *vr* bow

vernein|en *vt* answer in the negative; (*ablehnen*) reject. **V~ung** *f* -,-en negative answer

vernicht|en *vt* destroy; (*ausrotten*) exterminate. **V~ung** *f* - destruction; extermination

Vernunft *f* - reason; **V~ annehmen** see reason

vernünftig *a* reasonable, sensible; (*fam: ordentlich*) decent

veröffentlichen *vt* publish

verordn|en *vt* prescribe (*dat* for). **V~ung** *f* -,-en prescription; (*Verfügung*) decree

verpachten *vt* lease [out]

verpack|en *vt* pack; (*einwickeln*) wrap. **V~ung** *f* packaging

verpassen *vt* miss

verpfänden *vt* pawn

verpfleg|en *vt* feed; **sich selbst v~en** cater for oneself. **V~ung** *f* - board; (*Essen*) food; **Unterkunft und V~ung** board and lodging

verpflicht|en *vt* oblige; (*einstellen*) engage; (*Sport*) sign; **sich v~en** undertake/(*versprechen*) promise (*zu* to); (*vertraglich*) sign a contract. **V~ung** *f* -,-en obligation, commitment

verprügeln *vt* beat up, thrash

Verputz *m* -es plaster. **v~en** *vt* plaster; (*fam: essen*) polish off

Verrat *m* -[e]s betrayal, treachery. **v~en†** *vt* betray; give away (*Geheimnis*)

Verräter *m* -s,- traitor

verrechn|en *vt* settle; clear (*Scheck*); **sich v~nen** make a mistake; (*fig*) miscalculate. **V~nungsscheck** *m* crossed cheque

verreisen *vi* (*sein*) go away; **verreist sein** be away

verrenken *vt* dislocate

verrichten *vt* perform, do

verriegeln *vt* bolt

verring|ern *vt* reduce; **sich v~n** decrease. **V~ung** *f* - reduction; decrease

verrost|en *vi* (*sein*) rust. **v~et** *a* rusty

verrückt *a* crazy, mad. **V~e(r)** *m/f* lunatic. **V~heit** *f* -,-en madness; (*Torheit*) folly

verrühren *vt* mix

verrunzelt *a* wrinkled

Vers /fers/ *m* -es,-e verse

versag|en *vi* (*haben*) fail. **V~en** *nt* -s,- failure. **V~er** *m* -s,- failure

versalzen† *vt* put too much salt in/on; (*fig*) spoil

versamm|eln *vt* assemble. **V~lung** *f* assembly, meeting

Versand *m* -[e]s dispatch. **V~haus** *nt* mail-order firm

versäum|en *vt* miss; lose (*Zeit*); (*unterlassen*) neglect; **[es] v~, etw zu tun** fail to do sth

verschärfen *vt* intensify; tighten (*Kontrolle*); increase (*Tempo*); aggravate (*Lage*); **sich v~** intensify; increase; (*Lage:*) worsen

verschätzen (sich) *vr* **sich v~ in** (+ *dat*) misjudge

verschenken *vt* give away

verscheuchen *vt* shoo/(*jagen*) chase away

verschicken *vt* send; (*Comm*) dispatch

verschieb|en† *vt* move; (*aufschieben*) put off, postpone; **sich**

v~en move, shift; (verrutschen) slip; (zeitlich) be postponed.
V~ung f shift; postponement

verschieden a different; v~es some things; (dieses und jenes) various things; das ist v~ it varies □adv differently; v~ groß/lang of different sizes/lengths.
v~artig a diverse. v~tlich adv several times

verschimmeln vi (sein) go mouldy. v~t a mouldy

verschlafen† vi (haben) oversleep □vt sleep through ⟨Tag⟩□a sleepy

verschlagen† vt lose ⟨Seite⟩; jdm die Sprache/den Atem v~ leave s.o. speechless/take s.o.'s breath away □a sly

verschlechtern vt make worse; sich v~n get worse, deteriorate.
V~ung f -,-en deterioration

Verschleiß m -es wear and tear

verschleppen vt carry off; (entführen) abduct; spread ⟨Seuche⟩; neglect ⟨Krankheit⟩; (hinausziehen) delay

verschleudern vt sell at a loss

verschließen† vt close; (abschließen) lock; (einschließen) lock up

verschlimmern vt make worse; aggravate ⟨Lage⟩; sich v~n get worse, deteriorate. V~ung f -,-en deterioration

verschlossen a reserved.
V~heit f - reserve

verschlucken vt swallow; sich v~ choke (an+dat on)

Verschluß m -sses,-sse fastener, clasp; (Fenster-, Koffer-) catch; (Flaschen-) top; (luftdicht) seal; (Phot) shutter

verschlüsselt a coded

verschmelzen† vt/i (sein) fuse

verschmerzen vt get over

verschmutzen vt soil; pollute ⟨Luft⟩ □vi (sein) get dirty.
V~ung f - pollution

verschneit a snow-covered

verschnörkelt a ornate

verschnüren vt tie up

verschollen a missing

verschonen vt spare

verschossen a faded

verschränken vt cross

verschreiben† vt prescribe; sich v~ make a slip of the pen

verschrotten vt scrap

verschulden vt be to blame for.
V~ nt -s fault

verschuldet a v~ sein be in debt

verschütten vt spill; (begraben) bury

verschweigen† vt conceal, hide

verschwenden vt waste.
V~ung f - extravagance; (Vergeudung) waste

verschwiegen a discreet

verschwinden† vi (sein) disappear; [mal] v~ (fam) spend a penny

verschwommen a blurred

verschwör|en† (sich) vr conspire. V~ung f -,-en conspiracy

versehen† vt perform; hold ⟨Posten⟩; keep ⟨Haushalt⟩; v~ mit provide with; sich v~ make a mistake. V~ nt -s,- oversight; (Fehler) slip; aus V~ by mistake.
v~tlich adv by mistake

Versehrte(r) m disabled person

versengen vt singe; (stärker) scorch

versessen a keen (auf+acc on)

versetz|en vt move; transfer ⟨Person⟩; (Sch) move up; (verpfänden) pawn; (verkaufen) sell; (vermischen) blend; jdn v~en (fam: warten lassen) stand s.o. up; jdn in Angst/Erstaunen v~ frighten/astonish s.o.; sich in jds Lage v~en put oneself in s.o.'s place. V~ung f -,-en move; transfer; (Sch) move to a higher class

verseuchen vt contaminate

versicher|n vt insure; (bekräftigen) affirm; jdm v~n assure s.o.

(daß that). **V~ung** f-,-en insurance; assurance

versiegeln vt seal

versiert [vɛrˈziːɐt] a experienced

versilbert a silver-plated

versöhn|en vt reconcile; **sich v~en** become reconciled. **v~lich** a conciliatory. **V~ung** f-,-en reconciliation

versorg|en vt provide, supply (**mit** with); provide for ⟨Familie⟩; ⟨betreuen⟩ look after. **V~ung** f- provision, supply; ⟨Betreuung⟩ care

verspät|en (sich) vr be late. **v~et** a late; ⟨Zug⟩ delayed; ⟨Dank⟩ belated. **V~ung** f- lateness; **V~ung haben** be late

versperren vt block; bar ⟨Weg⟩

verspiel|en vt gamble away; **sich v~** play a wrong note

versprech|en† vt promise; **sich v~en** make a slip of the tongue; **sich** (dat) **viel v~en von** have high hopes of: **V~en** nt -s,- promise. **V~ungen** fpl promises

verstaatlich|en vt nationalize. **V~ung** f- nationalization

Verstand m -[e]s mind; ⟨Vernunft⟩ reason; **den V~ verlieren** go out of one's mind

verständig a sensible; ⟨klug⟩ intelligent. **v~en** vt notify, inform; **sich v~en** communicate; ⟨sich verständlich machen⟩ make oneself understood. **V~ung** f- notification; communication; ⟨Einigung⟩ agreement

verständlich a comprehensible; ⟨deutlich⟩ clear; ⟨begreiflich⟩ understandable; **sich v~ machen** make oneself understood. **v~erweise** adv understandably

Verständnis nt -ses understanding

verstärk|en vt strengthen, reinforce; ⟨steigern⟩ intensify, increase; amplify ⟨Ton⟩. **V~er** m

-s,- amplifier. **V~ung** f reinforcement; increase; amplification

verstaubt a dusty

verstauchen vt sprain

Versteck nt -[e]s,-e hiding-place; **V~ spielen** play hide-and-seek. **v~en** vt hide; **sich v~en** hide

verstehen† vt understand; ⟨können⟩ know; **falsch v~** misunderstand; **sich v~** understand one another; ⟨auskommen⟩ get on

versteiger|n vt auction. **V~ung** f auction

versteinert a fossilized

verstell|bar a adjustable. **v~en** vt adjust; ⟨versperren⟩ block; ⟨verändern⟩ disguise; **sich v~en** pretend. **V~ung** f- pretence

versteuern vt pay tax on

verstimm|t a disgruntled; ⟨Magen⟩ upset; ⟨Mus⟩ out of tune. **V~ung** f- ill humour; ⟨Magen-⟩ upset

verstockt a stubborn

verstopf|en vt plug; ⟨versperren⟩ block; **v~t** blocked; ⟨Person⟩ constipated. **V~ung** f -,-en blockage; ⟨Med⟩ constipation

verstorben a late, deceased. **V~e(r)** m/f deceased

Verstoß m infringement. **v~en†** vt disown □vi ⟨haben⟩ **v~en gegen** contravene, infringe

verstreuen vt scatter

verstümmeln vt mutilate; garble ⟨Text⟩

Versuch m -[e]s,-e attempt; ⟨Experiment⟩ experiment. **v~en** vt/i ⟨haben⟩ try; **v~t sein** be tempted (**zu** to). **V~ung** f -,-en temptation

vertagen vt adjourn; ⟨aufschieben⟩ postpone; **sich v~** adjourn

vertauschen vt exchange; ⟨verwechseln⟩ mix up

verteidig|en vt defend. **V~er** m -s,- defender; ⟨Jur⟩ defence counsel. **V~ung** f-,-en defence

verteil|en *vt* distribute; (*zuteilen*) allocate; (*ausgeben*) hand out; (*verstreichen*) spread. **V~ung** *f*- distribution; allocation

vertief|en *vt* deepen. **V~ung** *f*-,-en hollow, depression

vertikal /verti'ka:l/ *a* vertical

vertilgen *vt* exterminate; kill [off] ⟨*Unkraut*⟩

vertippen (sich) *vr* make a typing mistake

vertonen *vt* set to music

Vertrag *m* -[e]s,ᵉe contract; (*Pol*) treaty

vertragen† *vt* tolerate, stand; take ⟨*Kritik, Spaß*⟩; **sich v~** get on

verträglich *a* contractual

verträglich *a* good-natured; (*bekömmlich*) digestible

vertrauen *vi* (*haben*) trust ⟨*jdm/etw* s.o./sth; **auf**+*acc* in). **V~** *nt* -s trust, confidence (**zu** in); **im V~** in confidence. **v~swürdig** *a* trustworthy

vertraulich *a* confidential

vertraut *a* intimate; (*bekannt*) familiar. **V~heit** *f*- intimacy

vertreib|en† *vt* drive away; drive out ⟨*Feind*⟩; (*Comm*) sell; **sich** (*dat*) **die Zeit v~en** pass the time. **V~ung** *f*-,-en expulsion

vertret|en† *vt* represent; (*einspringen für*) stand in *or* deputize for; (*verfechten*) support; hold ⟨*Meinung*⟩; **sich** (*dat*) **den Fuß v~en** twist one's ankle. **V~er** *m* -s,- representative; deputy; (*Arzt-*) locum; (*Verfechter*) supporter. **V~ung** *f* -,-en representation; (*Person*) deputy; (*eines Arztes*) locum; (*Handels-*) agency

Vertrieb *m* -[e]s (*Comm*) sale. **V~ene(r)** *m/f* displaced person

vertrocknen *vi* (*sein*) dry up

verüben *vt* commit

verunglücken *vi* (*sein*) be involved in an accident; (*fam:*

mißglücken) go wrong; **tödlich v~** be killed in an accident

verunreinigen *vt* pollute; (*verseuchen*) contaminate

verursachen *vt* cause

verurteil|en *vt* condemn; (*Jur*) convict (**wegen** of); sentence (**zum Tode** to death). **V~ung** *f*- condemnation; (*Jur*) conviction

vervielfachen *vt* multiply

vervielfältigen *vt* duplicate

vervollständigen *vt* complete

verwählen (sich) *vr* misdial

verwahren *vt* keep; (*verstauen*) put away; **sich v~** (*fig*) protest

verwahrlost *a* neglected

Verwahrung *f* - keeping

verwaist *a* orphaned

verwalt|en *vt* administer; (*leiten*) manage; govern ⟨*Land*⟩. **V~ung** *f* -,-en administration; management; government

verwand|eln *vt* transform, change (**in**+*acc* into); **sich v~eln** change, turn (**in**+*acc* into). **V~lung** *f* transformation

verwandt *a* related (**mit** to). **V~e(r)** *m/f* relative. **V~schaft** *f* - relationship; (*Menschen*) relatives *pl*

verwarn|en *vt* warn, caution. **V~ung** *f* warning, caution

verwechs|eln *vt* mix up, confuse; (*halten für*) mistake (**mit** for). **V~lung** *f* -,-en mix-up

verweiger|n *vt/i* (*haben*) refuse ⟨*jdm etw* s.o sth). **V~ung** *f* refusal

Verweis *m* -es,-e reference (**auf**+*acc* to); (*Tadel*) reprimand. **v~en**† *vt* refer (**auf/an**+*acc* to); (*tadeln*) reprimand; **von der Schule v~en** expel

verwelken *vi* (*sein*) wilt

verwend|en† *vt* use; spend ⟨*Zeit, Mühe*⟩. **V~ung** *f* use

verwerten *vt* utilize, use

verwesen *vi* (*sein*) decompose

verwickeln vt involve (in + acc in); **sich v~eln** get tangled up. **v~elt** a complicated

verwildert a wild; ⟨Garten⟩ overgrown; ⟨Aussehen⟩ unkempt

verwinden† vt get over

verwirklichen vt realize

verwirr|en vt tangle up; ⟨fig⟩ confuse; **sich v~en** get tangled; ⟨fig⟩ become confused. **v~t** a confused. **V~ung** f - confusion

verwischen vt smudge

verwitwet a widowed

verwöhn|en vt spoil. **v~t** a spoilt

verworren a confused

verwund|bar a vulnerable. **v~en** vt wound

verwunder|lich a surprising. **v~n** vt surprise; **sich v~n** be surprised. **V~ung** f - surprise

Verwund|ete(r) m wounded soldier. **V~ung** f -,-en wound

verwüst|en vt devastate, ravage. **V~ung** f -,-en devastation

verzähl|en (sich) vr miscount

verzaubern vt bewitch; ⟨fig⟩ enchant; **v~ in** (+ acc) turn into

Verzehr m -s consumption. **v~en** vt eat

verzeich|nen vt list; ⟨registrieren⟩ register. **V~nis** nt -ses,-se list; ⟨Inhalts⟩ index

verzeih|en† vt forgive; **v~en Sie!** excuse me! **V~ung** f - forgiveness; **um V~ung bitten** apologize; **V~ung!** sorry! ⟨bei Frage⟩ excuse me!

Verzicht m -[e]s renunciation (auf + acc of). **v~en** vi ⟨haben⟩ do without; **v~en auf** (+ acc) give up; renounce ⟨Recht, Erbe⟩

verziehen† vt pull out of shape; ⟨verwöhnen⟩ spoil; ⟨verschwinden⟩ disappear □ vi ⟨sein⟩ move [away]

verzier|en vt decorate. **V~ung** f -,-en decoration

verzinsen vt pay interest on

verzöger|n vt delay; ⟨verlangsamen⟩ slow down. **V~ung** f -,-en delay

verzollen vt pay duty on; **haben Sie etwas zu v~?** have you anything to declare?

verzweif|eln vi ⟨sein⟩ despair. **v~elt** a desperate. **V~lung** f - despair; ⟨Ratlosigkeit⟩ desperation

verzweigen (sich) vr branch [out]

Veto /'ve:to/ nt -s,-s veto

Vetter m -s,-n cousin

vgl. abbr ⟨vergleiche⟩ cf

Viadukt /via'dʊkt/ nt -[e]s,-e viaduct

Video /'vi:deo/ nt -s,-s video. **V~kassette** f video cassette. **V~recorder** /-rəkɔrdə/ m -s,- video recorder

Vieh nt -[e]s livestock; ⟨Rinder⟩ cattle pl; ⟨fam: Tier⟩ creature

viel pron a great deal/⟨fam⟩ a lot of, ⟨pl⟩ many, ⟨fam⟩ a lot of; ⟨substantivisch⟩ **v~[es]** much, ⟨fam⟩ a lot; **nicht/zu v~** not/too much; **v~e** pl many; **das v~e Geld** all that money □adv much, ⟨fam⟩ a lot; **v~ mehr/weniger** much more/less

viel|deutig a ambiguous. **v~fach** a multiple □adv many times; ⟨fam: oft⟩ frequently. **V~falt** f - diversity, [great] variety

vielleicht adv perhaps, maybe; ⟨fam: wirklich⟩ really

vielmals adv very much

vielmehr adv rather; ⟨im Gegenteil⟩ on the contrary

vielseitig a varied; ⟨Person⟩ versatile. **V~keit** f - versatility

vielversprechend a promising

vier inv a, **V~** f -,-en four; ⟨Sch⟩ ≈ fair. **V~eck** nt -[e]s,-e oblong, rectangle; ⟨Quadrat⟩ square. **v~eckig** a oblong, rectangular;

square. **V~linge** *mpl* quadruplets

Viertel /'fɪrtl/ *nt* -s,- quarter; (*Wein*) quarter litre; **V~ nach** [a] quarter past eight; **drei V~ neun** [a] quarter to nine. **V~finale** *nt* quarter-final. **V~jahr** *nt* three months *pl*; (*Comm*) quarter. **v~jährlich** *â & adv* quarterly. **V~stunde** *f* quarter of an hour

vier|zehn /'fɪr-/ *inv a* fourteen. **v~zehnte(r,s)** *a* fourteenth. **v~zig** *inv a* forty. **v~zigste(r,s)** *a* fortieth

Villa /'vɪla/ *f* -,-len villa

violett /vjo'lɛt/ *a* violet

Vio|line /vjo'li:nə/ *f* -,-n violin. **V~linschlüssel** *m* treble clef

Virus /'vi:rʊs/ *nt* -,-ren virus

Visier /vi'zi:ɐ/ *nt* -s,-e visor

Visite /vi'zi:tə/ *f* -,-n round; **V~ machen** do one's round

Visum /'vi:zʊm/ *nt* -s,-sa visa

Vitamin /vita'mi:n/ *nt* -s,-e vitamin

Vitrine /vi'tri:nə/ *f* -,-n display cabinet; (*im Museum*) case

Vizepräsident /'fi:tsə-/ *m* vice president

Vogel *m* -s, ̈ bird; **einen V~ haben** (*fam*) have a screw loose. **V~scheuche** *f* -,-n scarecrow

Vokabeln /vo'ka:bəln/ *fpl* vocabulary *sg*

Vokal /vo'ka:l/ *m* -s,-e vowel

Volant /vo'lã:/ *m* -s,-s flounce

Volk *nt* -[e]s, ̈er people *sg*; (*Bevölkerung*) people *pl*

Völker|kunde *f* ethnology. **V~mord** *m* genocide. **V~recht** *nt* international law

Volks|abstimmung *f* plebiscite. **V~fest** *nt* public festival. **V~hochschule** *f* adult education classes *pl* (*Gebäude*) centre. **V~lied** *nt* folk-song. **v~tümlich** *a* popular. **V~wirt** *m*

economist. **V~wirtschaft** *f* economics *sg*. **V~zählung** *f* [national] census

voll *a* full (**von** *od* **mit** of); (*Haar*) thick; (*Erfolg, Ernst*) complete; (*Wahrheit*) whole; **v~ machen** fill up ▫*adv* (*ganz*) completely; (*arbeiten*) full-time; (*auszahlen*) in full; **v~ und ganz** completely

vollbringen† *vt insep* accomplish; work (*Wunder*)

vollende|n *vt insep* complete. **v~t** *a* perfect

Vollendung *f* completion; (*Vollkommenheit*) perfection

voller *inv a* full of

Volleyball /'vɔli-/ *m* volleyball

vollführen *vt insep* perform

vollfüllen *vt sep* fill up

Vollgas *nt* **V~ geben** put one's foot down; **mit V~** flat out

völlig *a* complete

volljährig *a* **v~ sein** (*Jur*) be of age. **V~keit** *f* -(*Jur*) majority

Vollkaskoversicherung *f* fully comprehensive insurance

vollkommen *a* perfect; (*völlig*) complete

Voll|kornbrot *nt* wholemeal bread. **V~macht** *f* -,-en authority; (*Jur*) power of attorney. **V~pension** *f* full board

vollständig *a* complete

vollstrecken *vt insep* execute; carry out (*Urteil*)

volltanken *vt sep* (*haben*) (*Auto*) fill up [with petrol]

Volltreffer *m* direct hit

vollzählig *a* complete

vollziehen† *vt insep* carry out; perform (*Handlung*); consummate (*Ehe*); **sich v~** take place

Volt /vɔlt/ *nt* -[s]- volt

Volumen /vo'lu:mən/ *nt* -s,- volume

vom *prep* = **von dem**

von *prep* (+ *dat*) of; (*über*) about; (*Ausgangspunkt, Ursache*) from; (*beim Passiv*) by; **einer von euch**

one of you; **von mir aus** I don't mind

voneinander adv from each other; ⟨abhängig⟩ on each other

vor prep (+ dat/acc) in front of; ⟨zeitlich, Reihenfolge⟩ before; (+ dat) ⟨bei Uhrzeit⟩ to; ⟨warnen, sich fürchten/schämen⟩ of; ⟨schützen, davonlaufen⟩ from; ⟨Respekt haben⟩ for; **vor Angst/ Kälte zittern** tremble with fear/ cold; **vor drei Tagen** three days ago; **vor allen Dingen** above all □adv forward; **vor und zurück** backwards and forwards

Vorabend m eve

voran adv at the front; ⟨voraus⟩ ahead; ⟨vorwärts⟩ forward. **v~kommen** vi sep (sein) make progress

Vor|anschlag m estimate. **V~anzeige** f advance notice. **V~arbeit** f preliminary work. **V~arbeiter** m foreman

voraus adv ahead (dat of); ⟨vorn⟩ at the front; ⟨vorwärts⟩ forward **□im voraus** in advance. **v~bezahlen** vt sep pay in advance. **v~gehen**† vi sep (sein) go on ahead; **jdm/etw v~** precede s.o./sth. **V~sage** f **-,-n** prediction. **v~sagen** vt sep predict **voraussetz|en** vt sep take for granted; ⟨erfordern⟩ require; **vorausgesetzt, daß** provided that. **V~ung** f **-,-en** assumption; ⟨Erfordernis⟩ prerequisite

voraussichtlich a anticipated, expected □adv probably

Vorbehalt m **-[e]s,-e** reservation **vorbei** adv past ⟨an jdm/etw s.o./ sth⟩; ⟨zu Ende⟩ over. **v~gehen**† vi sep (sein) go past; ⟨verfehlen⟩ miss; ⟨vergehen⟩ pass; ⟨fam: besuchen⟩ drop in (bei on)

vorbereit|en vt sep prepare; prepare for ⟨Reise⟩; **sich v~en** prepare [oneself] (**auf**+acc for). **V~ung** f **-,-en** preparation

vorbestellen vt sep order/⟨im Theater, Hotel⟩ book in advance

vorbestraft a **v~ sein** have a [criminal] record

Vorbeugung f **-** prevention

Vorbild nt model. **v~lich** a exemplary, model

vordatieren vt sep post-date

Vorder|bein nt foreleg. **v~e(r,s)** a front. **V~grund** m foreground. **V~rad** nt front wheel. **v~ste(r,s)** a front, first. **V~teil** nt front

vor|drängeln (sich) vr sep (fam) jump the queue. **v~drängen (sich)** vr sep push forward. **v~dringen**† vi sep (sein) advance

voreilig a rash

voreingenommen a biased

vorenthalten† vt sep withhold

vorerst adv for the time being

Vorfahr m **-en,-en** ancestor

Vorfahrt f right of way; **'V~ beachten'** 'give way'. **V~s- straße** f major road

Vorfall m incident. **v~en**† vi sep (sein) happen

vorfinden† vt sep find

Vorfreude f ⟨happy⟩ anticipation

vorführ|en vt sep present, show; ⟨demonstrieren⟩ demonstrate; ⟨aufführen⟩ perform. **V~ung** f presentation; demonstration; performance

Vor|gabe f ⟨Sport⟩ handicap. **V~gang** m occurrence; ⟨Techn⟩ process. **V~gänger(in)** m **-s,-** (f **-,-nen**) predecessor. **V~garten** m front garden

vorgehen† vi sep (sein) go forward; ⟨voraus-⟩ go on ahead; ⟨Uhr:⟩ be fast; ⟨wichtig sein⟩ take precedence; ⟨verfahren⟩ act; ⟨geschehen⟩ happen. **V~** nt **-s** action

vor|geschichtlich a prehistoric. **V~geschmack** m foretaste. **V~gesetzte(r)** m/f superior.

v~gestern *adv* the day before yesterday

vorhaben† *vt sep* propose, intend (zu to); **etw v~** have sth planned; **V~ nt -s,-** plan

Vorhand *f* (*Sport*) forehand

vorhanden *a* existing; **v~ sein** exist; be available

Vorhang *m* curtain

Vorhängeschloß *nt* padlock

vorher *adv* before[hand]

vorhergehend *a* previous

Vorher|sage *f* -,-n prediction; (*Wetter-*) forecast. **v~sagen** *vt sep* predict; forecast (*Wetter*). **v~sehen†** *vt sep* foresee

vorhin *adv* just now

vorige(r,s) *a* last, previous

Vor|kehrungen *fpl* precautions. **V~kenntnisse** *fpl* previous knowledge *sg*

vorkommen† *vi sep* (*sein*) happen; (*vorhanden sein*) occur; (*nach vorn kommen*) come forward; (*hervorkommen*) come out; (*zu sehen sein*) show; **jdm bekannt v~** seem familiar to s.o.

Vorkriegszeit *f* pre-war period

vorladen† *vt sep* (*Jur*) summons. **V~ung** *f* summons

Vorlage *f* model; (*Muster*) pattern; (*Gesetzes-*) bill

vorlassen† *vt sep* admit; **jdn v~** (*fam*) let s.o. pass

Vor|lauf *m* (*Sport*) heat. **V~läufer** *m* forerunner. **v~läufig** *a* provisional; (*zunächst*) for the time being. **V~leben** *nt* past

vorleg|en *vt sep* put on (*Kette*); (*unterbreiten*) present; (*vorzeigen*) show. **V~er** *m* -s,- mat

vorles|en† *vt sep* read [out]. **V~ung** *f* lecture

vorletzt|e(r,s) *a* last ... but one; **v~es Jahr** the year before last

Vorliebe *f* preference

vorliegen† *vi sep* (*haben*) be present/(*verfügbar*) available; (*bestehen*) exist, be

vorlügen† *vt sep* lie (*dat* to)

vormachen *vt sep* put up; put on (*Kette*); push (*Riegel*); (*zeigen*) demonstrate; **jdm etwas v~** (*fam:* *täuschen*) kid s.o.

Vormacht *f* supremacy

vormals *adv* formerly

vormerken *vt sep* make a note of; (*reservieren*) reserve

Vormittag *m* morning. **v~** *adv* gestern/heute **v~** yesterday/this morning. **v~s** *adv* in the morning

Vormund *m* -[e]s,-munde & -münder guardian

vorn *adv* at the front; **nach v~** to the front; **von v~** from the front/(*vom Anfang*) beginning

Vorname *m* first name

vorne *adv* = **vorn**

vornehm *a* distinguished

vornehmen† *vt sep* carry out

vornherein *adv* von **v~** from the start

Vor|ort *m* suburb. **V~rang** *m* priority, precedence (**vor**+*dat* over). **V~rat** *m* -[e]s,-e supply, stock (**an**+*dat* of). **v~rätig** *a* available; **v~rätig haben** have in stock. **V~ratskammer** *f* larder. **V~recht** *nt* privilege. **V~richtung** *f* device

Vorrunde *f* qualifying round

vorsagen *vt/i sep* (*haben*) recite; **jdm v~** tell s.o. the answer

Vorsatz *m* resolution. **v~sätzlich** *a* deliberate; (*Jur*) premeditated

Vorschau *f* preview (*Film-*) trailer

Vorschlag *m* suggestion, proposal. **v~en†** *vt sep* suggest, propose

vorschnell *a* rash

vorschreiben† *vt sep* lay down; dictate ⟨*dat* to); **vorgeschriebene Dosis** prescribed dose

Vorschrift *f* regulation; (*Anweisung*) instruction; **jdm V~en machen** tell s.o. what to do. **v~smäßig** *a* correct

Vorschule *f* nursery school

Vorschuß *m* advance

vorseh|en† *vt sep* intend (**für/als** for/as); (*planen*) plan; **sich v~en** be careful (**vor** + *dat* of). **V~ung** *f* - providence

vorsetzen *vt sep* move forward; **jdm etw v~** serve s.o. sth

Vorsicht *f* - care; (*bei Gefahr*) caution; **V~!** careful! (*auf Schild*) 'caution'. **v~ig** *a* careful; cautious. **V~smaßnahme** *f* precaution

Vorsilbe *f* prefix

Vorsitz *m* chairmanship; **den V~ führen** be in the chair. **V~ende(r)** *m/f* chairman

Vorsorge *f* **V~ treffen** take precautions; make provision (**für** for). **v~n** *vi sep* (haben) provide (**für** for)

Vorspeise *f* starter

Vorspiel *nt* prelude. **v~en** *vt sep* perform; (*Mus*) play (**dat** for)

vorsprechen† *v sep* ⟨*vt* recite; (*zum Nachsagen*) say ⟨*dat* to) ⟩*vi* (haben) (*Theat*) audition; **bei jdm v~** call on s.o.

Vor|sprung *m* projection; (*Fels-*) ledge; (*Vorteil*) lead (**vor** + *dat* over). **V~stadt** *f* suburb. **V~stand** *m* board [of directors]; (*Vereins-*) committee; (*Partei-*) executive

vorsteh|en† *vi sep* (haben) project, protrude; **einer Abteilung v~en** be in charge of a department. **V~er** *m* -s,- head; chairman

vorstell|en *vt sep* put forward ⟨*Bein, Uhr*⟩; (*darstellen*) represent; (*bekanntmachen*) introduce;

sich v~en introduce oneself; (*bei Bewerber*) go for an interview; **sich** (*dat*) **etw v~en** imagine sth. **V~ung** *f* introduction; (*bei Bewerbung*) interview; (*Aufführung*) performance; (*Idee*) idea; (*Phantasie*) imagination

Vorstoß *m* advance

Vorstrafe *f* previous conviction

Vortag *m* day before

vortäuschen *vt sep* feign, fake

Vorteil *m* advantage. **v~haft** *a* advantageous; flattering

Vortrag *m* -[e]s,·e talk; (*wissenschaftlich*) lecture. **v~en**† *vt sep* perform; (*aufsagen*) recite; (*singen*) sing; (*darlegen*) present (**dat** to)

Vortritt *m* precedence; **jdm den V~ lassen** let s.o. go first

vorüber *adv* **v~ sein** be over; **an etw** (*dat*) **v~** past sth. **v~gehend** *a* temporary

Vor|urteil *nt* prejudice. **V~verkauf** *m* advance booking

vorverlegen *vt sep* bring forward

Vor|wahl[nummer] *f* dialling code. **V~wand** *m* -[e]s,·e pretext; (*Ausrede*) excuse

vorwärts *adv* forward[s]. **v~kommen** *vi sep* (sein) make progress; (fig) get on

vorwiegend *adv* predominantly

Vorwort *nt* (*pl* -worte) preface

Vorwurf *m* reproach; **jdm Vorwürfe machen** reproach s.o.

Vorzeichen *nt* sign; (fig) omen

vorzeigen *vt sep* show

vorzeitig *a* premature

vorziehen† *vt sep* pull forward; draw ⟨*Vorhang*⟩; (*lieber mögen*) prefer; favour

Vor|zimmer *nt* ante-room; (*Büro*) outer office. **V~zug** *m* preference; (*gute Eigenschaft*) merit, virtue; (*Vorteil*) advantage

vorzüglich *a* excellent

vulgär /vʊlˈgɛːɐ̯/ *a* vulgar

Vulkan /vʊlˈkaːn/ *m* -s,-e volcano

W

Waage *f* -,-n scales *pl*; (*Astr*) Libra. **w~recht** *a* horizontal

Wabe *f* -,-n honeycomb

wach *a* awake; (*aufgeweckt*) alert; **w~ werden** wake up

Wache *f* -,-n guard; (*Posten*) sentry; (*Dienst*) guard duty; (*Naut*) watch; (*Polizei-*) station; **W~ halten** keep watch

Wacholder *m* -s juniper

Wachs *nt* -es wax

wachsam *a* vigilant. **W~keit** *f* - vigilance

wachsen *vi* (sein) grow

wachsen² *vt* (reg) wax. **W~figur** *f* waxwork

Wachstum *nt* -s growth

Wächter *m* -s,- guard; (*Park-*) keeper; (*Parkplatz-*) attendant

Wachtmeister *m* [police] constable. **W~posten** *m* sentry

wackel|ig *a* wobbly; (*Stuhl*) rickety; (*Person*) shaky. **W~kontakt** *m* loose connection. **w~n** *vi* (haben) wobble; (*zittern*) shake

Wade *f* -,-n (*Anat*) calf

Waffe *f* -,-n weapon; **W~n** arms

Waffel *f* -,-n waffle; (*Eis-*) wafer

Waffen|ruhe *f* cease-fire. **W~schein** *m* firearms licence. **W~stillstand** *m* armistice

Wagemut *m* daring

wagen *vt* risk; **es w~, etw zu tun** dare [to] do sth; **sich w~** (*gehen*) venture

Wagen *m* -s,- cart; (*Eisenbahn-*) carriage, coach; (*Güter-*) wagon; (*Kinder-*) pram; (*Auto*) car. **W~heber** *m* -s,- jack

Waggon /va'gõ:/ *m* -s,-s wagon

Wahl *f* -,-en choice; (*Pol, Admin*) election; (*geheime*) ballot; **zweite W~** (*Comm*) seconds *pl*

wähl|en *vt/i* (haben) choose; (*Pol, Admin*) elect; (*stimmen*) vote;

(*Teleph*) dial. **W~er(in)** *m* -s,- (*f* -,-nen) voter. **w~erisch** *a* choosy, fussy

Wahl|fach *nt* optional subject. **w~frei** *a* optional. **W~kampf** *m* election campaign. **W~kreis** *m* constituency. **W~lokal** *nt* polling-station. **W~spruch** *m* motto. **W~urne** *f* ballot-box

Wahn *m* -[e]s delusion; (*Manie*) mania

Wahnsinn *m* madness. **w~ig** *a* mad, insane; (*fam: unsinnig*) crazy; **w~ig werden** go mad. **W~ige(r)** *m/f* maniac

wahr *a* true; (*echt*) real; **du kommst doch, nicht w~?** you are coming, aren't you?

während *prep* (+ *gen*) during □*conj* while; (*wohingegen*) whereas

Wahrheit *f* -,-en truth. **w~sgemäß** *a* truthful

wahrnehm|en† *vt sep* notice; (*nutzen*) take advantage of; exploit (*Vorteil-*); look after (*Interessen*). **W~ung** *f* -,-en perception

Wahrsagerin *f* -,-nen fortune-teller

wahrscheinlich *a* probable. **W~keit** *f* - probability

Währung *f* -,-en currency

Wahrzeichen *nt* symbol

Waise *f* -,-n orphan. **W~nhaus** *nt* orphanage. **W~nkind** *nt* orphan

Wal *m* -[e]s,-e whale

Wald *m* -[e]s,-er wood; (*groß*) forest. **w~ig** *a* wooded

Waliser *m* -s,- Welshman. **w~isch** *a* Welsh

Wall *m* -[e]s,-e mound

Wallfahr|er(in) *m*(*f*) pilgrim. **W~t** *f* pilgrimage

Walnuß *f* walnut

Walze *f* -,-n roller. **w~n** *vt* roll

Walzer *m* -s,- waltz

Wand f -ˌ̈e wall; (Trenn-) partition; (Seite) side; (Fels-) face

Wandel m -s ˌchange. **w~n** vi (sein) stroll □ vr sich **w~n** change

Wander|er m -s,-, f **~in** f -,-nen hiker, rambler. **w~n** vi (sein) hike, ramble; (ziehen) travel. **W~schaft** f - travels pl. **W~ung** f -,-en hike, ramble. **W~weg** m footpath

Wandlung f -,-en change

Wand|malerei f mural. **W~tafel** f blackboard. **W~teppich** m tapestry

Wange f -,-n cheek

wann adv when

Wanne f -,-n bath

Wanze f -,-n bug

Wappen nt -s,- coat of arms. **W~kunde** f heraldry

war, wäre s. sein[1]

Ware f -,-n article; (Comm) commodity; (coll) merchandise; **W~n** goods. **W~nhaus** nt department store. **W~nprobe** f sample. **W~nzeichen** nt trademark

warm a warm; ⟨Mahlzeit⟩ hot; **w~ machen** heat □ adv warmly; **w~ essen** have a hot meal

Wärme f - warmth; (Phys) heat; **10 Grad W~** 10 degrees above zero. **w~en** vt warm; heat ⟨Essen⟩. **W~flasche** f hot-water bottle

Warn|blinkanlage f hazard [warning] lights pl. **w~en** vt/i (haben) warn (vor + dat of). **W~ung** f -,-en warning

Warteliste f waiting list

warten vi (haben) wait (auf+ acc for) □ vt service

Wärter(in) m -s,- (f -,-nen) keeper; (Museums-) attendant; (Gefängnis-) warder

Wartezimmer nt (Med) waiting-room

Wartung f - (Techn) service

warum adv why

was f -,-e wart

was pron what □ rel pron that; **alles, was ich brauche** all [that] I need □ indef pron (fam: etwas) something; (fragend, verneint) anything; **so was Ärgerliches!** what a nuisance! □ adv (fam) (warum) why; (wie) how

wasch|bar a washable. **W~becken** nt wash-basin

Wäsche f - washing; (Unter-) underwear

waschecht a colour-fast

Wäscheklammer f clothes-peg

waschen† vt wash; **sich w~** have a wash □ vi (haben) do the washing

Wäscherei f -,-en laundry

Wäsche|schleuder f spin-drier. **W~trockner** m tumble-drier

Wasch|küche f laundry-room. **W~lappen** m face-flannel. **W~maschine** f washing machine. **W~mittel** nt detergent. **W~pulver** nt washing-powder. **W~salon** m launderette

Wasser nt -s water. **W~ball** m beach-ball; (Spiel) water polo. **w~dicht** a watertight; ⟨Kleidung⟩ waterproof. **W~fall** m waterfall. **W~farbe** f watercolour. **W~hahn** m tap. **W~kraft** f water-power. **W~kraftwerk** nt hydroelectric power-station. **W~leitung** f water-main; **aus der W~leitung** from the tap. **W~mann** m (Astr) Aquarius

wässern vt soak; (begießen) water □ vi (haben) water

Wasser|ski nt -s water-skiing. **W~stoff** m hydrogen. **W~straße** f waterway. **W~waage** f spirit-level. **W~werfer** m -s,- water-cannon

wäßrig a watery

watscheln vi (sein) waddle

Watt nt -s,- (Phys) watt

Watt|e f - cotton wool. **w~iert** a padded; (gesteppt) quilted

WC /ve'tse:/ nt -s,-s WC

web|en vt/i (haben) weave. **W~er** m -s,- weaver. **W~stuhl** m loom

Wechsel m -s,- change; (Tausch) exchange; (Comm) bill of exchange. **W~geld** nt change. **w~haft** a changeable. **W~jahre** npl menopause sg. **W~kurs** m exchange rate. **w~n** vt change; (tauschen) exchange □vi (haben) change. **W~strom** m alternating current. **W~stube** f bureau de change

weck|en vt wake [up]; (fig) awaken □vi (haben) ⟨Wecker:⟩ go off. **W~er** m -s,- alarm [clock]

wedeln vi (haben) wave; **mit dem Schwanz w~** wag its tail

weder conj **w~ ... noch** neither ... nor

Weg m -[e]s,-e way; (Fuß-) path; (Fahr-) track; (Gang) errand; **sich auf den Weg machen** set off

weg adv away, off; (verschwunden) gone; **weg sein** be away; (gegangen/verschwunden) have gone; **Hände weg!** hands off!

wegen prep (+ dat) because of; (um ... willen) for the sake of; (bezüglich) about

weg|fahren† vi sep (sein) go away; (abfahren) leave. **w~fallen†** vi sep (sein) be dropped/(ausgelassen) omitted; (entfallen) no longer apply. **w~gehen†** vi sep (sein) leave, go away. **w~lassen†** vt sep let go; (auslassen) omit. **w~laufen†** vi sep (sein) run away. **w~räumen** vt sep put away; (entfernen) clear away. **w~schicken** vt sep send away; (abschicken) send off. **w~tun†** vt sep put away; (wegwerfen) throw away

Wegweiser m -s,- signpost

wegziehen† v sep □vt pull away □vi (sein) move away

weh a sore; **weh tun** hurt; ⟨Kopf:⟩ ache; **jdm weh tun** hurt s.o.

wehe int alas; **w~ [dir/euch]!** (drohend) don't you dare!

wehen vi (haben) blow; (flattern) flutter □vt blow

Wehen fpl contractions

wehleidig a soft; (weinerlich) whining

Wehr¹ nt -[e]s,-e weir

Wehr² f **sich zur W~ setzen** resist. **W~dienst** m military service. **W~dienstverweigerer** m -s,- conscientious objector

wehren (sich) vr resist; (gegen Anschuldigung) protest; (sich sträuben) refuse

wehrlos a defenceless. **W~macht** f armed forces pl. **W~pflicht** f conscription

Weib nt -[e]s,-er woman. **W~chen** nt -s,- (Zool) female. **w~lich** a feminine; (Biol) female

weich a soft; (gar) done

Weiche f -,-n (Rail) points pl

Weichheit f - softness. **w~lich** a soft; ⟨Charakter⟩ weak. **W~spüler** m -s,- (Tex) conditioner

Weide¹ f -,-n (Bot) willow

Weide² f -,-n pasture. **w~n** vt/i (haben) graze

weigern (sich) vr refuse. **W~ung** f -,-en refusal

Weihe f -,-n consecration; (Priester-) ordination. **w~n** vt consecrate; (zum Priester) ordain

Weiher m -s,- pond

Weihnacht|en nt -s & pl Christmas. **w~lich** a Christmassy. **W~sbaum** m Christmas tree. **W~sfest** nt Christmas. **W~slied** nt Christmas carol. **W~smann** m (pl -männer) Father Christmas. **W~stag** m

erster/zweiter W ~ stag Christmas Day/Boxing Day

Weih|rauch *m* incense. **W ~ wasser** *nt* holy water

weil *conj* because; *(da)* since

Weile *f* ~ while

Wein *m* -[e]s,-e wine; *(Bot)* vines *pl*; *(Trauben)* grapes *pl*. **W ~ bau** *m* wine-growing. **W ~ berg** *m* vineyard. **W ~ brand** *m* -[e]s brandy

weinen *vt/i (haben)* cry, weep

Wein|glas *nt* wineglass. **W ~ karte** *f* wine-list. **W ~ lese** *f* grape harvest. **W ~ probe** *f* wine-tasting. **W ~ rebe** *f*, **W ~ stock** *m* vine. **W ~ stube** *f* wine-bar. **W ~ traube** *f* bunch of grapes; *(W ~ beere)* grape

weise *a* wise

Weise *f* -,-n way; *(Melodie)* tune

Weisheit *f* -,-en wisdom. **W ~ szahn** *m* wisdom tooth

weiß *a*, **W ~ nt** -,- white

weissag|en *vt/i insep (haben)* prophesy. **W ~ ung** *f* -,-en prophecy

Weiß|brot *nt* white bread. **W ~ e(r)** *m/f* white man/woman. **W ~ wein** *m* white wine

Weisung *f* -,-en instruction; *(Befehl)* order

weit *a* wide; *(ausgedehnt)* extensive; *(lang)* long □*adv* widely; *(offen, öffnen)* wide; *(lang)* far; **von w ~ em** from a distance; **bei w ~ em** by far; **w ~ und breit** far and wide; **ist es noch w ~ ?** is it much further? **ich bin so w ~** I'm ready

Weite *f* -,-n expanse; *(Entfernung)* distance; *(Größe)* width. **w ~ n** *vt* widen; stretch *(Schuhe)*

weiter *a* further □*adv* further; *(außerdem)* in addition; *(anschließend)* then; **etw w ~ tun** go on doing sth; **w ~ nichts/niemand** nothing/no one else; **und so w ~** and so on

weiter|e(r,s) *a* further; **im w ~ en Sinne** in a wider sense; **ohne w ~ es** just like that; *(leicht)* easily

weiter|erzählen *vt sep* go on with; *(w ~ sagen)* repeat. **w ~ fahren†** *vi sep (sein)* go on. **w ~ geben†** *vt sep* pass on. **w ~ hin** *adv* *(immer noch)* still; *(in Zukunft)* in future; *(außerdem)* furthermore; **etw w ~ hin tun** go on doing sth. **w ~ machen** *vi sep (haben)* carry on

weit|gehend *a* extensive □*adv* to a large extent. **w ~ reichend** *a* far-reaching. **w ~ sichtig** *a* long-sighted; *(fig)* far-sighted. **W ~ sprung** *m* long jump. **w ~ verbreitet** *a* widespread

Weizen *m* -s wheat

welch *inv pron* what; **w ~ ein(e)** what a. **w ~ e(r,s)** *pron* which; **um w ~ e Zeit?** at what time? □*rel pron* which; *(Person)* who □*indef pron* some; *(fragend)* any; **was für w ~ e?** what sort of?

Welle *f* -,-n wave; *(Techn)* shaft. **W ~ enlänge** *f* wavelength. **W ~ enlinie** *f* wavy line. **W ~ enreiten** *nt* surfing. **W ~ ensittich** *m* -s,-e budgerigar. **w ~ ig** *a* wavy

Welt *f* -,-en world; **auf der W ~** in the world; **auf die od zur W ~ kommen** be born. **W ~ all** *nt* universe. **w ~ fremd** *a* unworldly. **W ~ kugel** *f* globe. **w ~ lich** *a* worldly; *(nicht geistlich)* secular

Weltmeister(in) *m(f)* world champion. **W ~ schaft** *f* world championship

Weltraum *m* space. **W ~ fahrer** *m* astronaut

Weltrekord *m* world record

wem *pron (dat of wer)* to whom

wen *pron (acc of wer)* whom

Wende *f* -,-n change. **W ~ kreis** *m* *(Geog)* tropic

Wendeltreppe *f* spiral staircase

wenden[1] *vt (reg)* turn □ *vi (haben)*
turn [round]

wenden[2]† *(& reg) vt* turn; **sich
w~** turn

Wende|punkt *m (fig)* turning-
point. **W~ung** *f -,-en* turn; *(Biegung)* bend

wenig *pron* little; *(pl)* few; **w~e** *pl*
few □ *adv* little; *(kaum)* not much.
w~er *pron* less; *(pl)* fewer □ *adv
& conj* less. **w~ste(r,s)** least; **am
w~sten** least [of all]. **w~stens**
adv at least

wenn *conj* if; *(sobald)* when; **immer w~** whenever; **w~ nicht**
unless; **w~ auch** even though

wer *pron* who; *(fam: jemand)*
someone; *(fragend)* anyone

Werbe|agentur *f* advertising
agency. **w~n**† *vt* recruit; attract
(Kunden) □ *vi (haben)* **w~n für**
advertise; canvass for *(Partei)*.
W~spot */-sp-/ m -s,-s* commercial

Werbung *f -* advertising

werden† *vi (sein)* become; *(müde,
alt)* get; grow; *(blind, wahnsinnig)* go; **blaß w~** turn pale;
krank w~ fall ill; **es wird warm**
it is getting warm; **mir wurde
schlecht** I felt sick; **er will Lehrer
w~** he wants to be a teacher
□ *v aux (Zukunft)* shall; **es wird
bald regnen** it's going to rain
soon; **würden Sie so nett sein?**
would you be so kind? □ *(Passiv;
pp worden)* be; **geliebt/geboren
w~** be loved/born; **es wurde
gemunkelt** it was rumoured

werfen† *vt* throw; cast *(Blick,
Schatten)*; **sich w~** *(Holz:)* warp

Werft *f -,-en* shipyard

Werk *nt -[e]s,-e* work; *(Fabrik)*
works *sg*, factory; *(Trieb-)*
mechanism. **W~en** *nt -s (Sch)*
handicraft. **W~statt** *f -,-en*
workshop; *(Auto-)* garage.
W~tag *m* weekday. **w~tags**

adv on weekdays. **w~tätig** *a*
working

Werkzeug *nt* tool; *(coll)* tools *pl*

Wermut *m -s* vermouth

wert *a* viel/**50 Mark w~** worth a
lot/50 marks; **nichts w~ sein** be
worthless. **W~ m -[e]s,-e** value;
(Nenn-) denomination; **im W~
von** worth

Wert|gegenstand *m* object of
value. **w~los** *a* worthless.
W~papier *nt (Comm)* security.
W~sachen *fpl* valuables.
w~voll *a* valuable

Wesen *nt -s,-* nature; *(Lebe-)* being; *(Mensch)* creature

wesentlich *a* essential; *(grundlegend)* fundamental

weshalb *adv* why

Wespe *f -,-n* wasp

wessen *pron (gen of* **wer***)* whose

westdeutsch *a* West German

Weste *f -,-n* waistcoat

Westen *m -s* west; **nach W~** west

Western *m -[s],-* western

Westfalen *nt -s* Westphalia

Westindien *nt* West Indies *pl*

west|lich *a* western; *(Richtung)*
westerly □ *adv & prep (+gen)*
w~lich der Stadt west of the
town. **w~wärts** *adv* westwards

weswegen *adv* why

Wettbewerb *m -s,-e* competition

Wette *f -,-n* bet; **um die W~
laufen** race *(mit jdm s.o.)*

wetten *vt/i (haben)* bet *(auf+ acc
on)*

Wetter *nt -s,-* weather; *(Un-)*
storm. **W~bericht** *m* weather
report. **W~warte** *f -,-n* meteoro-
logical station

Wett|kampf *m* contest. **W~
kämpfer(in)** *m(f)* competitor.
W~lauf *m* race. **W~rennen** *nt*
race. **W~streit** *m* contest

Whisky *m -s* whisky

wichtig *a* important; **w~ nehmen** take seriously. **W~keit** *f -*
importance

Wicke f -,-n sweet pea
Wickel m -s,- compress
wickeln vt wind; (ein-) wrap; (bandagieren) bandage; **ein Kind frisch w~** change a baby
Widder m -s,- ram; (Astr) Aries
wider prep (+ acc) against; (entgegen) contrary to
wider|lich a repulsive; (unangenehm) nasty. **W~rede** f contradiction; **keine W~rede!** don't argue!
widerrufen† vt/i insep (haben) retract; revoke (Befehl)
Widersacher m -s,- adversary
widersetzen (sich) vr insep resist (jdm/etw s.o./sth)
widersprechen† vi insep (haben) contradict (jdm/etw s.o./sth)
Wider|spruch m contradiction; (Protest) protest. **w~sprüchlich** a contradictory. **w~spruchslos** adv without protest
Widerstand m resistance; **W~leisten** resist. **w~sfähig** a resistant; (Bot) hardy
widerstehen† vi insep (haben) resist (jdm/etw s.o./sth)
Widerstreben nt -s reluctance
widerwärtig a disagreeable
Widerwill|e m aversion, repugnance. **w~ig** a reluctant
widm|en vt dedicate (dat to); (verwenden) devote (dat to); **sich w~en** (+ dat) devote oneself to. **W~ung** f -,-en dedication
wie adv how; **wie ist Ihr Name?** what is your name? **wie ist das Wetter?** what is the weather like? □conj as; (gleich wie) like; (sowie) as well as; (als) when, as; **so gut/reich wie** as good/rich as; **nichts wie** nothing but; **größer wie ich** (fam) bigger than me
wieder adv again
Wiederaufbau m reconstruction. **w~en** vt sep reconstruct
wieder|bekommen† vt sep get back. **w~beleben** vt sep revive.

W~belebung f - resuscitation.
w~erkennen† vt sep recognize.
W~gabe f (s. w~geben) return; portrayal; rendering; reproduction. **w~geben†** vt sep give back, return; (darstellen) portray; (Techn) reproduce. **W~geburt** f reincarnation
wiedergutmach|en vt sep (fig) make up for; redress (Unrecht); (bezahlen) pay for. **W~ung** f - reparation; (Entschädigung) compensation
wiederherstellen vt sep re-establish; restore (Gebäude); restore to health (Kranke)
wiederhol|en vt insep repeat; (Sch) revise; **sich w~en** recur; (Person:) repeat oneself. **w~t** a repeated. **W~ung** f -,-en repetition; (Sch) revision
Wieder|hören nt **auf W~hören!** goodbye! **W~käuer** m -s,- ruminant. **W~kehr** f - return; (W~holung) recurrence. **w~kommen†** vi sep (sein) come back
wiedersehen† vt sep see again. **W~** nt -s,- reunion; **auf W~!** goodbye!
wiedervereinig|en vt sep reunify (Land). **W~ung** f reunification
wiederverwerten vt sep recycle
Wiege f -,-n cradle
wiegen[1]† vt/i (haben) weigh
wiegen[2] vt (reg) rock. **W~lied** nt lullaby
wiehern vi (haben) neigh
Wien nt -s Vienna. **W~er** a Viennese □m -s,- Viennese □f -,- ≈ frankfurter. **w~erisch** a Viennese
Wiese f -,-n meadow
Wiesel nt -s,- weasel
wieso adv why
wieviel pron how much/(pl) many; **um w~ Uhr?** at what time? **w~te(r,s)** a which; **der**

W ~ te ist heute? what is the date today?

wieweit adv how far

wild a wild; ⟨Stamm⟩ savage; **w ~ er Streik** wildcat strike. **W ~ nt -[e]s game;** ⟨Rot-⟩ deer; ⟨Culin⟩ venison. **W ~ e(r)** m/f savage

Wilder|er m -s,-. poacher. **w ~ n** vt/i (haben) poach

wildfremd a totally strange

Wild|heger, **W ~ hüter** m -s,-. gamekeeper. **W ~ leder** nt suede. **w ~ ledern** a suede. **W ~ nis** f -. wilderness. **W ~ schwein** nt wild boar. **W ~ westfilm** m western

Wille m -ns will; **Letzter W ~** will

Willenskraft f will-power

willig a willing

willkommen a welcome. **W ~** nt -s welcome

willkürlich a arbitrary

wimmern vi (haben) whimper

Wimper f -,-n [eye]lash. **W ~ ntusche** f mascara

Wind m -[e]s,-e wind

Winde f -,-n ⟨Techn⟩ winch

Windel f -,-n nappy

winden† vt wind; make ⟨Kranz⟩; **in die Höhe w ~** winch up; **sich w ~** wind (um round); ⟨sich krümmen⟩ writhe

Wind|hund m greyhound. **W ~ ig** a windy. **W ~ mühle** f windmill. **W ~ pocken** fpl chickenpox sg. **W ~ schutzscheibe** f windscreen. **W ~ stille** f calm. **W ~ surfen** nt windsurfing

Windung f -,-en bend; ⟨Spirale⟩ spiral

Winkel m -s,- angle; ⟨Ecke⟩ corner. **W ~ messer** m -s,- protractor

winken vi (haben) wave

Winter m -s,- winter. **w ~ lich** a wintry; ⟨Winter-⟩ winter ... **W ~ schlaf** m hibernation

Winzer m -s,- winegrower

winzig a tiny, minute

Wipfel m -s,- [tree-]top

Wippe f -,-n see-saw

wir pron we; **wir sind es** it's us

Wirbel m -s,- eddy; ⟨Drehung⟩ whirl; ⟨Anat⟩ vertebra; ⟨Haar-⟩ crown; ⟨Aufsehen⟩ fuss. **w ~ n** vt/i ⟨sein/haben⟩ whirl. **W ~ säule** f spine. **W ~ sturm** m cyclone. **W ~ tier** nt vertebrate. **W ~ wind** m whirlwind

wird s. werden

wirken vi (haben) have an effect (**auf +** acc on); ⟨zur Geltung kommen⟩ be effective; ⟨tätig sein⟩ work; ⟨scheinen⟩ seem

wirklich a real. **W ~ keit** f -,-en reality

wirksam a effective

Wirkung f -,-en effect

wirr a tangled; ⟨Haar⟩ tousled; ⟨verwirrt, verworren⟩ confused

Wirt m -[e]s,-e landlord. **W ~ in** f -,-nen landlady

Wirtschaft f -,-en economy; ⟨Gast-⟩ restaurant; ⟨Kneipe⟩ pub. **w ~ en** vi (haben) manage one's finances. **w ~ lich** a economic; ⟨sparsam⟩ economical. **W ~ sgeld** nt housekeeping [money]. **W ~ prüfer** m auditor

Wirtshaus nt inn; ⟨Kneipe⟩ pub

wischen vt/i (haben) wipe; wash

wissen† vt/i (haben) know; **weißt du noch?** do you remember? **nichts w ~ wollen von** not want anything to do with. **W ~** nt -s knowledge; **meines W ~ s** to my knowledge

Wissenschaft f -,-en science. **W ~ ler** m -s,- academic; ⟨Natur-⟩ scientist. **w ~ lich** a academic; scientific

wissenswert a worth knowing

witter|n vt scent; ⟨ahnen⟩ sense. **W ~ ung** f - scent; ⟨Wetter⟩ weather

Witwe f -,-n widow. **W ~ r** m -s,- widower

Witz *m* -es,-e joke; (*Geist*) wit. **W~bold** *m* -[e]s,-e joker. **W~ig** *a* funny; (*geistreich*) witty

wo *adv* where; (*als*) when; (*irgendwo*) somewhere; **wo immer** wherever □ *conj* seeing that; (*obwohl*) although; (*wenn*) if

woanders *adv* somewhere else

Woche *f* -,-n week. **W~nende** *nt* weekend. **W~nkarte** *f* weekly ticket. **w~nlang** *adv* for weeks. **W~ntag** *m* day of the week; (*Werktag*) weekday. **w~ntags** *adv* on weekdays

wöchentlich *a & adv* weekly

Wodka *m* -s vodka

wofür *adv* what ... for; (*relativ*) for which

woher *adv* where from; **w~ weißt du das?** how do you know that? **wohin** *adv* where [to]; **w~ gehst du?** where are you going?

wohl *adv* well; (*vermutlich*) probably; (*etwa*) about; (*zwar*) perhaps; **w~ kaum** hardly; **sich w~ fühlen** feel well/(*behaglich*) comfortable. **W~** *nt* -[e]s welfare, well-being; **zum W~** (+ *gen*) for the good of; **zum W~~!** cheers!

Wohl|befinden *nt* well-being. **W~ergehen** *nt* -s welfare. **w~erzogen** *a* well brought-up

Wohlfahrt *f* - welfare. **W~sstaat** *m* Welfare State

wohl|habend *a* prosperous, well-to-do. **w~schmeckend** *a* tasty

Wohlstand *m* prosperity. **W~sgesellschaft** *f* affluent society

Wohltat *f* [act of] kindness; (*Annehmlichkeit*) treat; (*Genuß*) bliss. **Wohltät|er** *m* benefactor. **w~ig** *a* charitable

wohl|verdient *a* well-deserved. **w~weislich** *adv* deliberately

Wohlwollen *nt* -s goodwill; (*Gunst*) favour. **w~d** *a* benevolent

Wohn|block *m* block of flats. **w~en** *vi* (*haben*) live; (*vorübergehend*) stay. **W~gegend** *f* residential area. **w~haft** *a* resident. **W~heim** *nt* hostel; (*Alten-*) home. **w~lich** *a* comfortable. **W~mobil** *nt* -s,-e camper. **W~ort** *m* place of residence. **W~sitz** *m* place of residence

Wohnung *f* -,-en flat; (*Unterkunft*) accommodation. **W~snot** *f* housing shortage

Wohn|wagen *m* caravan. **W~zimmer** *nt* living-room

wölben *vt* curve; arch 〈*Rücken*〉. **W~ung** *f* -,-en curve; (*Archit*) vault

Wolf *m* -[e]s,-e wolf; (*Fleisch-*) mincer; (*Reiß-*) shredder

Wolke *f* -,-n cloud. **W~nbruch** *m* cloudburst. **W~nkratzer** *m* skyscraper. **w~nlos** *a* cloudless. **w~ig** *a* cloudy

Woll|decke *f* blanket. **W~e** *f* -,-n wool

wollen *vt|i* (*haben*) & *v aux* want; **etw tun w~** want to do sth; (*beabsichtigen*) be going to do sth; **wir wollten gerade gehen** we were just going

Wollsachen *fpl* woollens

womit *adv* what ... with; (*relativ*) with which. **wonach** *adv* what ... after/〈*suchen*〉 for/〈*riechen*〉 of; (*relativ*) after/for/of which

woran *adv* what ... on/〈*denken, sterben*〉 of; (*relativ*) on/of which; **w~ hast du ihn erkannt?** how did you recognize him? **worauf** *adv* what ... on/〈*warten*〉 for; (*relativ*) on/for which; (*woraufhin*) whereupon. **woraus** *adv* what ... from; (*relativ*) from which

Wort *nt* -[e]s,-er & -e word; **jdm ins W~ fallen** interrupt s.o.

Wörterbuch *nt* dictionary

Wort|führer *m* spokesman. **w~getreu** *a & adv* word-for-word. **w~karg** *a* taciturn

wörtlich a literal; *(wortgetreu)* word-for-word

wort|los a silent □adv without a word. **W~schatz** m vocabulary. **W~spiel** nt pun, play on words

worüber adv what ... over/⟨lachen, sprechen⟩ about; *(relativ)* over/about which. **worum** adv what ... round/⟨bitten, kämpfen⟩ for; *(relativ)* round/for which; **w~ geht es?** what is it about? **wovon** adv what ... from/⟨sprechen⟩ about; *(relativ)* from/about which. **wovor** adv what ... in front of; ⟨sich fürchten⟩ what ... of; *(relativ)* in front of which; of which. **wozu** adv what ... to/ ⟨brauchen, benutzen⟩ for; *(relativ)* to/for which

Wrack nt -s,-s wreck

wringen† vt wring

Wucher|preis m extortionate price. **W~ung** f-,-en growth

Wuchs m -es growth; *(Gestalt)* stature

wühlen vi *(haben)* rummage; *(in der Erde)* burrow □vt dig

Wulst m -[e]s,-e bulge; *(Fett-)* roll

wund a sore; **w~ reiben** chafe. **W~brand** m gangrene

Wunde f-,-n wound

Wunder nt -s,- wonder, marvel; *(übernatürliches)* miracle; **kein W~!** no wonder! **w~bar** a miraculous; *(herrlich)* wonderful. **W~kind** nt infant prodigy. **w~n** vt surprise; **sich w~n** be surprised *(über + acc* at)

Wundstarrkrampf m tetanus

Wunsch m -[e]s,-e wish; *(Verlangen)* desire; *(Bitte)* request

wünschen vt want; **sich** *(dat)* **etw w~** want sth; *(bitten um)* ask for sth; **jdm Glück/gute Nacht w~** wish s.o. luck/good night; **Sie w~?** can I help you? **w~swert** a desirable

wurde, würde s. werden

Würde f-,-n dignity; *(Ehrenrang)* honour. **w~los** a undignified. **W~nträger** m dignitary. **w~voll** a dignified

würdig a dignified; *(wert)* worthy

Wurf m -[e]s,-e throw; *(Junge)* litter

Würfel m -s,- cube; *(Spiel-)* dice; *(Zucker-)* lump. **w~n** vi *(haben)* throw the dice; **w~n um** play dice for □vt throw; *(in Würfel schneiden)* dice. **W~zucker** m cube sugar

würgen vt choke □vi *(haben)* retch; choke **(an+dat** on)

Wurm m -[e]s,-er worm; *(Made)* maggot. **w~en** vi *(haben)* jdn **w~en** *(fam)* rankle [with s.o.]

Wurst f-,-e sausage; **das ist mir W~** *(fam)* I couldn't care less

Würze f-,-n spice; *(Aroma)* aroma

Wurzel f-,-n root; **W~n schlagen** take root

würzen vt season. **w~ig** a tasty; *(aromatisch)* aromatic; *(pikant)* spicy

wüst a chaotic; *(wirr)* tangled; *(wild)* wild; *(schlimm)* terrible

Wüste f-,-n desert

Wut f- rage, fury. **W~anfall** m fit of rage

wüten vi *(haben)* rage. **w~d** a furious; **w~d machen** infuriate

X

x /ɪks/ inv a *(Math)* x; *(fam)* umpteen. **X-Beine** ntpl knock-knees. **x-beinig** a knock-kneed. **x-beliebig** a *(fam)* any. **x-mal** adv *(fam)* umpteen times

Y

Yoga /'jo:ga/ m & nt -[s] yoga

Z

Zack|e *f* -,-n point; (*Berg-*) peak; (*Gabel-*) prong. **z~ig** *a* jagged; (*gezackt*) serrated

zaghaft *a* timid; (*zögernd*) tentative

zäh *a* tough; (*hartnäckig*) tenacious. **z~flüssig** *a* viscous; (*Verkehr*) slow-moving. **Z~igkeit** *f* - toughness; tenacity

Zahl *f* -,-en number; (*Ziffer*, *Betrag*) figure

zahlen *vt/i* (*haben*) pay; (*bezahlen*) pay for; **bitte z~!** the bill please!

zählen *vi* (*haben*) count; **z~ zu** (*fig*) be one/(*pl*) some of □*vt* count; **z~ zu** add to; (*fig*) count among

zahlenmäßig *a* numerical

Zähler *m* -s,- meter

Zahl|grenze *f* fare-stage. **Z~karte** *f* paying-in slip. **z~los** *a* countless. **z~reich** *a* numerous; (*Anzahl, Gruppe*) large. **Z~ung** *f* -,-en payment; **in Z~ung nehmen** take in part-exchange

Zählung *f* -,-en count

Zahlwort *nt* (*pl* -wörter) numeral

zahm *a* tame

zähmen *vt* tame; (*fig*) restrain

Zahn *m* -[e]s,ˮe tooth; (*am Zahnrad*) cog. **Z~arzt** *m*, **Z~ärztin** *f* dentist. **Z~belag** *m* plaque. **Z~fleisch** *nt* gums *pl*. **Z~los** *a* toothless. **Z~pasta** / *s* -, en toothpaste. **Z~rad** *nt* cog-wheel. **Z~schmelz** *m* enamel. **Z~schmerzen** *mpl* toothache *sg*. **Z~spange** *f* brace. **Z~stein** *m* tartar. **Z~stocher** *m* -s,- toothpick

Zange *f* -,-n pliers *pl*; (*Kneif-*) pincers *pl*; (*Kohlen-*) tongs *pl*

Zank *m* -[e]s squabble. **z~en** *vr* **sich z~en** squabble

zänkisch *a* quarrelsome

Zäpfchen *nt* -s,- (*Anat*) uvula; (*Med*) suppository

zapfen *vt* tap, draw. **Z~streich** *m* (*Mil*) tattoo

Zapf|hahn *m* tap. **Z~säule** *f* petrol-pump

zappel|ig *a* fidgety; (*nervös*) jittery. **z~n** *vi* (*haben*) wriggle

zart *a* delicate; (*zärtlich*) tender; (*sanft*) gentle. **Z~gefühl** *nt* tact

zärtlich *a* tender; (*liebevoll*) loving. **Z~keit** *f* -,-en tenderness; (*Liebkosung*) caress

Zauber *m* -s magic; (*Bann*) spell. **Z~er** *m* -s,- magician. **z~haft** *a* enchanting. **Z~künstler** *m* conjurer. **z~n** *vi* (*haben*) do magic; (*Zaubertricks ausführen*) do conjuring tricks □*vt* produce as if by magic. **Z~stab** *m* magic wand. **Z~trick** *m* conjuring trick

Zaum *m* -[e]s,Zäume bridle

Zaun *m* -[e]s,Zäune fence

z.B. *abbr* (*zum Beispiel*) e.g.

Zebra *nt* -s,-s zebra. **Z~streifen** *m* zebra-crossing

Zeche *f* -,-n bill; (*Bergwerk*) pit

Zeder *f* -,-n cedar

Zeh *m* -[e]s,-en toe. **Z~e** *f* -,-n toe; (*Knoblauch-*) clove

zehn *inv a, Z~ f* -,-en ten. **z~te(r,s)** *a* tenth. **Z~tel** *nt* -s,-tenth

Zeichen *nt* -s,- sign; (*Signal*) signal. **Z~setzung** *f* - punctuation

zeichn|en *vt/i* (*haben*) draw. **Z~er** *m* -s,- draughtsman. **Z~ung** *f* -,-en drawing

Zeige|finger *m* index finger. **z~n** *vt* show; **sich z~n** appear; (*sich herausstellen*) become clear □*vi* (*haben*) point (**auf** + *acc* to). **Z~r** *m* -s,- pointer; (*Uhr-*) hand

Zeile *f* -,-n line; (*Reihe*) row

Zeit *f* -,-en time; **sich** (*dat*) **Z~ lassen** take one's time; **es hat Z~**

there's no hurry; **mit der Z~** in time; **in nächster Z~** in the near future; **zur Z~** at present; *(rechtzeitig)* in time

Zeit|alter *nt* age, era. **z~gemäß** *a* modern, up-to-date. **Z~genosse** *m*, **Z~genossin** *f* contemporary. **z~ig** *a* & *adv* early. **Z~lang/eine Z~lang** for a time *or* while

zeitlich *a* ⟨*Dauer*⟩ in time; ⟨*Folge*⟩ chronological □ *adv* **z~begrenzt** for a limited time

zeit|los *a* timeless. **Z~lupe** *f* slow motion. **Z~punkt** *m* time. **z~raubend** *a* time-consuming. **Z~raum** *m* period. **Z~schrift** *f* magazine, periodical

Zeitung *f* -,**-en** newspaper. **Z~spapier** *nt* newspaper

Zeit|verschwendung *f* waste of time. **Z~vertreib** *m* pastime. **z~weise** *adv* at times. **Z~wort** *nt* (*pl* **-wörter**) verb. **Z~zünder** *m* time fuse

Zelle *f* -,**-n** cell; (*Telefon-*) box

Zelt *nt* **-[e]s,-e** tent; (*Fest-*) marquee. **z~en** *vi* (*haben*) camp. **Z~en** *nt* -s camping. **Z~plane** *f* tarpaulin. **Z~platz** *m* campsite

Zement *m* **-[e]s** cement

zen|sieren *vt* (*Sch*) mark; censor ⟨*Presse, Film*⟩. **Z~sur** *f* -,**-en** (*Sch*) mark

Zentimeter *m* & *nt* centimetre. **Z~maß** *nt* tape-measure

Zentner *m* -s,- [metric] hundredweight (*50 kg*)

zentral *a* central. **Z~e** *f* -,**-n** central office; (*Partei-*) headquarters *pl*; (*Teleph*) exchange. **Z~heizung** *f* central heating

Zentrum *nt* -s,**-tren** centre

zerbrech|en† *vt/i* (*sein*) break. **z~lich** *a* fragile

zerdrücken *vt* crush

Zeremonie *f* -,**-n** ceremony

Zerfall *m* disintegration; (*Verfall*) decay. **z~en†** *vi* (*sein*) disintegrate; (*verfallen*) decay

zerkleinern *vt* chop⟨*schneiden*⟩ cut up; ⟨*mahlen*⟩ grind

zerknirscht *a* contrite

zerknüllen *vt* crumple [up]

zerkratzen *vt* scratch

zerlassen† *vt* melt

zerlegen *vt* take to pieces, dismantle; ⟨*zerschneiden*⟩ cut up; ⟨*tranchieren*⟩ carve

zerlumpt *a* ragged

zermalmen *vt* crush

zermürben *vt* (*fig*) wear down

zerquetschen *vt* squash, crush

Zerrbild *nt* caricature

zerreißen† *vt* tear; (*in Stücke*) tear up; break ⟨*Faden, Seil*⟩ □ *vi* (*sein*) tear; break

zerren *vt* drag; pull ⟨*Muskel*⟩ □ *vi* (*haben*) pull (**an** + *dat* at)

zerrissen *a* torn

zerrütten *vt* ruin, wreck; shatter ⟨*Nerven*⟩

zerschlagen† *vt* smash; smash up ⟨*Möbel*⟩; **sich z~** (*fig*) fall through; ⟨*Hoffnung*⟩ be dashed

zerschmettern *vt/i* (*sein*) smash

zerschneiden† *vt* cut; (*in Stücke*) cut up

zersplittern *vi* (*sein*) splinter; ⟨*Glas*⟩ shatter □ *vt* shatter

zerspringen† *vi* (*sein*) shatter; (*bersten*) burst

Zerstäuber *m* -s,- atomizer

zerstör|en *vt* destroy; ⟨*zunichte machen*⟩ wreck. **Z~er** *m* -s,- destroyer. **Z~ung** *f* destruction

zerstreu|en *vt* scatter; disperse ⟨*Menge*⟩; dispel ⟨*Zweifel*⟩; **sich z~en** disperse; ⟨*sich unterhalten*⟩ amuse oneself. **z~t** *a* absent-minded. **Z~ung** *f* -,**-en** (*Unterhaltung*) entertainment

zerstückeln *vt* cut up into pieces

Zertifikat *nt* **-[e]s,-e** certificate

zertrümmern *vt* smash [up]; wreck ⟨*Gebäude, Stadt*⟩

Zettel *m* -s,- piece of paper; (*Notiz*) note; (*Bekanntmachung*) notice

Zeug *nt* -s (*fam*) stuff; (*Sachen*) things *pl*; **dummes Z~** nonsense

Zeuge *m* -n,-n witness. **Z~n** *vi* (*haben*) testify □*vt* father. **Z~naussage** *f* testimony. **Z~nstand** *m* witness box

Zeugin *f* -,-nen witness

Zeugnis *nt* -ses,-se certificate; (*Sch*) report; (*Referenz*) reference; (*fig: Beweis*) evidence

Zickzack *m* -[e]s,-e zigzag

Ziege *f* -,-n goat

Ziegel *m* -s,- brick; (*Dach-*) tile

ziehen† *vt* pull; (*sanfter: zücken*, *zeichnen*) draw; (*heraus-*) pull out; extract (*Zahn*); raise (*Hut*); put on (*Bremse*); move (*Schachfigur*); (*dehnen*) stretch; make (*Grimasse*); (*züchten*) breed; grow (*Rosen*); **nach sich z~** (*fig*) entail □*vr* **sich z~** (*sich erstrecken*) run; (*sich verziehen*) warp □ *vi* (*haben*) pull (**an**+*dat* on/at); (*Tee, Ofen:*) draw; (*Culin*) simmer; **es zieht** there is a draught; **solche Filme z~ nicht mehr** films like that are no longer popular □ *vi* (*sein*) (*um-*) move (**nach** to); (*Menge:*) march; (*Vögel:*) migrate; (*Wolken*) drift

Ziehharmonika *f* accordion

Ziehung *f* -,-en draw

Ziel *nt* -[e]s,-e destination; (*Sport*) finish; (*Z~scheibe & Mil*) target; (*Zweck*) aim, goal. **z~bewußt** *a* purposeful. **z~en** *vi* (*haben*) aim (**auf**+*acc* at). **z~los** *a* aimless. **Z~scheibe** *f* target

ziemlich *a* (*fam*) fair □*adv* rather, fairly

Zierde *f* -,-n ornament

zierlich *a* dainty

Ziffer *f* -,-n figure, digit; (*Zahlzeichen*) numeral. **Z~blatt** *nt* dial

Zigarette *f* -,-n cigarette

Zigarre *f* -,-n cigar

Zigeuner(in) *m* -s,- (*f* -,-nen) gypsy

Zimmer *nt* -s,- room. **Z~mädchen** *nt* chambermaid. **Z~mann** *m* (*pl* -leute) carpenter. **z~n** *vt* make (*zu*+*dat*) do carpentry. **Z~nachweis** *m* accommodation bureau. **Z~pflanze** *f* house plant

Zimt *m* -[e]s cinnamon

Zink *nt* -s zinc

Zinn *nt* -s tin; (*Gefäße*) pewter

Zins *m* (*pl* interest *sg*; **Z~en tragen** earn interest. **Z~eszins** *m* -es,-en compound interest. **Z~fuß, Z~satz** *m* interest rate

Zipfel *m* -s,- corner; (*Spitze*) point

zirka *adv* about

Zirkel *m* -s,- [pair of] compasses *pl*; (*Gruppe*) circle

Zirkulation /-'tsjo:n/ *f* - circulation. **z~ieren** *vi* (*sein*) circulate

Zirkus *m* -,-se circus

zirpen *vi* (*haben*) chirp

zischen *vi* (*haben*) hiss; (*Fett:*) sizzle □*vt* hiss

Zitat *nt* -[e]s,-e quotation. **z~ieren** *vt/i* (*haben*) quote

Zitronat *m* -[e]s candied lemon-peel. **Z~one** *f* -,-n lemon. **Z~onenlimonade** *f* lemonade

zittern *vi* (*haben*) tremble; (*vor Kälte*) shiver; (*beben*) shake

zittrig *a* shaky

Zitze *f* -,-n teat

zivil *a* civilian; (*Ehe, Recht*) civil. **Z~** *nt* -s civilian clothes *pl*. **Z~dienst** *m* community service

Zivilisation /-'tsjo:n/*f* -,-en civilization. **z~siert** *a* civilized

Zivilist *m* -en,-en civilian

zögern *vi* (*haben*) hesitate. **Z~** *nt* -s hesitation. **z~d** *a* hesitant

Zoll¹ *m* -[e]s,- inch

Zoll² *m* -[e]s,-̈e [customs] duty; (*Behörde*) customs *pl*. **Z~abfertigung** *f* customs clearance.

Z~**beamte(r)** *m* customs officer. z~**frei** *a* & *adv* duty-free.
Z~**kontrolle** *f* customs check
Zone *f*-,-n zone
Zoo *m* -s,-s zoo
Zopf *m* -[e]s,⸚e plait
Zorn *m* -[e]s anger. z~**ig** *a* angry
zottig *a* shaggy
zu *prep* (+ *dat*) to; (*dazu*) with;
(*zeitlich*, *preislich*) at; (*Zweck*)
for; (*über*) about; **zu ... hin** towards; **zu Hause** at home; **zu
Fuß** on foot; **zu beiden Seiten** on
both sides; **zu diesem Zweck** for
this purpose; **zu Dutzenden** by
the dozen; **eine Marke zu 60
Pfennig** a 60-pfennig stamp; **wir
waren zu dritt** there were three
of us; **es steht 5 zu 3** the score is
5-3; **zu etw werden** turn into sth
□*adv* (*allzu*) too; (*Richtung*) towards; (*geschlossen*) closed; (*an
Schalter, Hahn*) off; **Augen zu!**
close your eyes! **Tür zu!** shut the
door! **macht zu!** (*fam*) hurry up!
□*conj* to; **etwas zu essen** something to eat; **nicht zu glauben**
unbelievable

zuallererst *adv* first of all.
z~**letzt** *adv* last of all
Zubehör *nt* -s accessories *pl*
zubereit|en *vt sep* prepare.
Z~**ung** *f* - preparation
zubinden† *vt sep* tie [up]
zubring|en† *vt sep* spend. Z~**er**
m -s,- access road; (*Bus*) shuttle
Zucchini /tsu'ki:ni/ *pl* courgettes
Zucht *f* -,-en breeding; (*Pflanzen*-)
cultivation; (*Art, Rasse*) breed;
(*von Pflanzen*) strain; (Z~*farm*)
farm; (*Pferde*-) stud
zücht|en *vt* breed; grow (*Rosen*).
Z~**er** *m* -s,- breeder
Zuchthaus *nt* prison
Züchtung *f* -,-en breeding; (*Pflanzen*-) cultivation; (*Art, Rasse*)
breed; (*von Pflanzen*) strain
zucken *vi* (*haben*) twitch; (*sich
z~d bewegen*) jerk; (*Blitz*:) flash;

(*Flamme*:) flicker □*vt* **die Achseln z~** shrug one's shoulders
Zucker *m* -s sugar. Z~**dose** *f*
sugar basin. Z~**guß** *m* icing.
z~**krank** *a* diabetic. Z~**krankheit** *f* diabetes. z~**n** *vt* sugar.
Z~**rohr** *nt* sugar cane. Z~**rübe**
f sugar beet. Z~**watte** *f* candy-
floss
zudecken *vt sep* cover up; (*im
Bett*) tuck up; cover (*Topf*)
zudringlich *a* pushing
zueinander *adv* to one another;
z~ **passen** go together
zuerkennen† *vt sep* award (*dat*
to)
zuerst *adv* first; (*anfangs*) at first
zufahr|en† *vi sep* (*sein*) z~ **auf**
(+ *acc*) drive towards. Z~**t** *f*
access; (*Einfahrt*) drive
Zufall *m* chance; (*Zusammentref-
fen*) coincidence; **durch** Z~ by
chance/coincidence. z~**en**† *vi
sep* (*sein*) close, shut; **jdm** z~**en**
(*Aufgabe*:) fall/(*Erbe*:) go to s.o.
zufällig *a* chance, accidental
□*adv* by chance
Zuflucht *f* refuge; (*Schutz*) shelter. Z~**sort** *m* refuge
zufolge *prep* (+ *dat*) according to
zufrieden *a* contented; (*befrie-
digt*) satisfied. z~**geben**† (*sich*)
vr sep be satisfied. Z~**heit** *f* -
contentment; satisfaction.
z~**lassen**† *vt sep* leave in peace.
z~**stellend** *a* satisfactory
zufrieren† *vi sep* (*sein*) freeze
over
zufügen *vt sep* inflict (dat on)
Zufuhr *f* - supply
Zug *m* -[e]s,⸚e train; (*Kolonne*) column; (*Um*-) procession; (*Mil*) platoon; (*Vogelschar*) flock; (*Ziehen,
Zugkraft*) pull; (*Wandern, Ziehen*) migration; (*Schluck, Luft*-)
draught; (*Atem*-) breath; (*beim
Rauchen*) puff; (*Schach*-) move;
(*beim Schwimmen, Rudern*)

stroke; (Gesichts-) feature; (Wesens-) trait

Zugabe f (Geschenk) [free] gift; (Mus) encore

Zugang m access

zugänglich a accessible; ⟨Mensch:⟩ approachable

Zugbrücke f drawbridge

zugeben† vt sep add; (gestehen) admit; (erlauben) allow

zugehen† vi sep (sein) close; **jdm z~** be sent to s.o.; **z~ auf** (+acc) go towards; **dem Ende z~** draw to a close; ⟨Vorräte:⟩ run low; **auf der Party ging es lebhaft zu** the party was pretty lively

Zugehörigkeit f - membership

Zügel m -s,- rein

zugelassen a registered

zügel|los a unrestrained. **z~n** vt rein in; (fig) curb

Zuge|ständnis nt concession. **z~stehen**† vt sep grant

zügig a quick

Zugluft f draught

zugreifen† vi sep (haben) grab it/ them; (bei Tisch) help oneself; (bei Angebot) jump at it; (helfen) lend a hand

zugunsten prep (+gen) in favour of; ⟨Sammlung⟩ in aid of

zugute adv **jdm/etw z~ kommen** benefit s.o./sth

Zugvogel m migratory bird

zuhalten† vt sep keep closed; (bedecken) cover; **sich** (dat) **die Nase z~** hold one's nose

Zuhälter m -s,- pimp

Zuhause nt -s, home

zuhör|en vi sep (haben) listen (dat to). **Z~er(in)** m(f) listener

zujubeln vi sep (haben) **jdm z~** cheer s.o.

zukehren vt sep turn (dat to)

zukleben vt sep seal

zuknöpfen vt sep button up

zukommen† vi sep (sein) **z~ auf** (+acc) come towards; (sich nähern) approach; **z~ lassen** send

(jdm s.o.); devote ⟨Pflege⟩ (dat to); **jdm z~** be s.o.'s right

Zukunft f - future. **zukünftig** a future ⟨Frau⟩ adv in future

zulächeln vi sep (haben) smile (dat at)

Zulage f -,-n extra allowance

zulangen vi sep (haben) help oneself; **tüchtig z~** tuck in

zulassen† vt sep allow, permit; (teilnehmen lassen) admit; (Admin) license, register; (geschlossen lassen) leave closed; leave unopened ⟨Brief⟩

Zulassung f -,-en admission; registration; ⟨Lizenz⟩ licence

zuletzt adv last; (schließlich) in the end; **nicht z~** not least

zuliebe adv **jdm/etw z~** for the sake of s.o./sth

zum prep = zu dem; **zum Spaß** for fun; **etw zum Lesen** sth to read

zumachen v sep vt close, shut; do up ⟨Jacke⟩; seal ⟨Umschlag⟩; turn off ⟨Hahn⟩; (stillegen) close down □vi (haben) close, shut; (stillgelegt werden) close down

zumindest adv at least

zumutbar a reasonable

zumute adv **mir ist nicht danach z~** I don't feel like it

zumuten† vt sep **jdm etw z~en** ask or expect sth of s.o.; **sich** (dat) **zuviel z~en** overdo things. **Z~ung** f - imposition

zunächst adv first [of all]; (anfangs) at first; (vorläufig) for the moment □prep (+dat) nearest to

Zunahme f -,-n increase

Zuname m surname

zünd|en vt/i (haben) ignite. **Z~er** m -s,- detonator, fuse. **Z~holz** nt match. **Z~kerze** f sparkingplug. **Z~schlüssel** m ignition key. **Z~schnur** f fuse. **Z~ung** f -,-en ignition

zunehmen† vi sep (haben) increase (**an**+dat in); ⟨Mond:⟩ wax; (an Gewicht) put on weight

Zuneigung *f* - affection
Zunft *f* -,⸗e guild
Zunge *f* -,-n tongue. **Z~nbrecher** *m* tongue-twister
zunutze *a* **sich** (*dat*) **etw z~ machen** make use of sth; (*ausnutzen*) take advantage of sth
zuoberst *adv* right at the top
zuordnen *vt sep* assign (*dat* to)
zupfen *vt/i* (*haben*) pluck (**an** + *dat* at); pull out ⟨*Unkraut*⟩
zur *prep* = **zu der; zur Schule** to school; **zur Zeit** at present
zurechnungsfähig *a* of sound mind
zurecht|finden† **(sich)** *vr sep* find one's way. **z~legen** *vt sep* put out ready; **sich** (*dat*) **eine Ausrede z~legen** have an excuse all ready. **z~machen** *vt sep* get ready. **Z~weisung** *f* reprimand
zureden *vi sep* (*haben*) **jdm z~** try to persuade s.o.
zurichten *vt sep* prepare; (*beschädigen*) damage; (*verletzen*) injure
zuriegeln *vt sep* bolt
zurück *adv* back; **Berlin, hin und z~** return to Berlin. **z~bekommen**† *vt sep* get back. **z~bleiben**† *vi sep* (*sein*) stay behind; (*nicht mithalten*) lag behind. **z~bringen**† *vt sep* bring back; (*wieder hinbringen*) take back. **z~erstatten** *vt sep* refund. **z~finden**† *vi sep* (*haben*) find one's way back. **z~führen** *v sep* □*vt* take back; (*fig*) attribute (**auf** + *acc* to) □*vi* (*haben*) lead back. **z~geblieben** *a* retarded. **z~gehen**† *vi sep* (*sein*) go back, return; (*abnehmen*) go down; **z~gehen auf** (+ *acc*) (*fig*) go back to
zurückgezogen *a* secluded. **Z~heit** *f* - seclusion
zurückhalt|en† *vt sep* hold back; (*abhalten*) stop. **z~end** *a* reserved. **Z~ung** *f* - reserve
zurück|kehren *vi sep* (*sein*) return. **z~kommen**† *vi sep* (*sein*) come back, return; (*ankommen*) get back. **z~lassen**† *vt sep* leave behind; (*z~kehren lassen*) allow back. **z~legen** *vt sep* put back; (*reservieren*) keep; (*sparen*) put by; cover ⟨*Strecke*⟩. **z~liegen**† *vi sep* (*haben*) be in the past; (*Sport*) be behind; **das liegt lange zurück** that was long ago. **z~melden (sich)** *vr sep* report back. **z~schicken** *vt sep* send back. **z~schlagen**† *v sep* □*vi* (*haben*) hit back □*vt* hit back; (*abwehren*) beat back. **z~schrecken**† *vi sep* (*sein*) shrink back, recoil; (*fig*) shrink (**vor** + *dat* from). **z~setzen** *v sep* □*vt* put back; (*Auto*) reverse, back; (*herabsetzen*) reduce; (*fig*) neglect □*vi* (*haben*) reverse, back. **z~stellen** *vt sep* put back; (*reservieren*) keep; (*fig*) put aside; (*aufschieben*) postpone. **z~stoßen**† *v sep* □*vt* push back □*vi* (*sein*) reverse, back. **z~treten**† *vi sep* (*sein*) step back; (*vom Amt*) resign; (*verzichten*) withdraw. **z-weisen**† *vt sep* turn away; (*fig*) reject. **z~zahlen** *vt sep* pay back. **z~ziehen**† *vt sep* draw back; (*fig*) withdraw; **sich z~ziehen** withdraw; (*vom Beruf*) retire
Zuruf *m* shout. **r~en**† *vt sep* shout (*dat* to)
Zusage *f* -,-n acceptance; (*Versprechen*) promise. **z~n** *v sep* □*vt* promise □*vi* (*haben*) accept
zusammen *adv* together; (*insgesamt*) altogether. **Z~arbeit** *f* co-operation. **z~arbeiten** *vi sep* (*haben*) co-operate. **z~bauen** *vt sep* assemble. **z~bleiben**† *vi sep* (*sein*) stay together. **z~brechen**† *vi sep* (*sein*) collapse. **Z~bruch** *m* collapse; (*Nerven- & fig*) breakdown. **z~fallen**† *vi sep*

(sein) collapse; *(zeitlich)* coincide.
z~**fassen** *vt sep* summarize, sum up. Z~**fassung** *f* summary.
z~**fügen** *vt sep* fit together.
z~**gehören** *vi sep (haben)* belong together; *(z~passen)* go together. z~**gesetzt** *a (Gram)* compound. z~**halten**† *v sep □vt* hold together; *(beisammenhalten)* keep together *□vi (haben)* *(fig)* stick together. Z~**hang** *m* connection; *(Kontext)* context.
z~**hanglos** *a* incoherent.
z~**klappen** *v sep □vt* fold up *□vi (sein)* collapse. z~**kommen**† *vi sep (sein)* meet; *(sich sammeln)* accumulate. z~**laufen**† *vi sep (sein)* gather; *(Flüssigkeit:)* collect; *(Linien:)* converge. z~**legen** *v sep □vt* put together; *(vereinigen)* amalgamate; pool *(Geld)* *□vi (haben)* club together. z~**nehmen**† *vt sep* gather up; summon up *(Mut)*; collect *(Gedanken)*; **sich** z~**nehmen** pull oneself together. z~**passen** *vi sep (haben)* go together, match. Z~**prall** *m* collision. z~**rechnen** *vt sep* add up. z~**schlagen**† *vt sep* smash up; *(prügeln)* beat up. z~**schließen**† **(sich)** *vr sep* join together; *(Firmen:)* merge. Z~**schluß** *m* union; *(Comm)* merger
zusammensein† *vi sep* be together. Z~ *nt* -s get-together.
zusammensetz|en *vt sep* put together; *(Techn)* assemble; **sich** z~**en** sit [down] together; *(bestehen)* be made up *(aus* from*)*. Z~**ung** *f* -,-en composition; *(Techn)* assembly; *(Wort)* compound
zusammen|**stellen** *vt sep* put together; *(gestalten)* compile.
Z~**stoß** *m* collision; *(fig)* clash.
z~**stoßen**† *vi sep (sein)* collide.
Z~**treffen** *nt* meeting; coincidence. z~**ziehen**† *v sep □vt* draw together; *(addieren)* add up;

(konzentrieren) mass; **sich** z~**ziehen** contract; *(Gewitter:)* gather *□vi (sein)* move in together; move in *(mit* with*)*
Zusatz *m* addition; *(Jur)* rider; *(Lebensmittel-)* additive. **zusätzlich** *a* additional *□adv* in addition
zuschau|en *vi sep (haben)* watch.
Z~**er(in)** *m* -s,- *(f* -,-nen*)* spectator; *(TV)* viewer
Zuschlag *m* surcharge; *(D-Zug-)* supplement. z~**pflichtig** *a* for which a supplement is payable
zuschließen† *v sep □vt* lock *□vi (haben)* lock up
zuschreiben† *vt sep* attribute *(dat* to*)*; **jdm die Schuld** z~ blame s.o.
Zuschrift *f* letter; *(auf Annonce)* reply
zuschulden *adv* **sich** *(dat)* **etwas** z~ **kommen lassen** do wrong
Zuschuß *m* contribution; *(staatlich)* subsidy
zusehends *adv* visibly
zusein† *vi sep (sein)* be closed
zusenden† *vt sep* send *(dat* to*)*
zusetzen *vt sep* add; *(einbüßen)* lose
zusichern *vt sep* promise.
Z~**ung** *f* promise
zuspielen *vt sep (Sport)* pass
zuspitzen (sich) *vr sep (fig)* become critical
Zustand *m* condition, state
zustande *adv* z~ **bringen/kommen** bring/come about
zuständig *a* competent; *(verantwortlich)* responsible
zustehen† *vi sep (haben)* **jdm** z~ be s.o.'s right; *(Urlaub:)* be due to s.o.
zusteigen† *vi sep (sein)* get on; **noch jemand zugestiegen?** tickets please
zustell|en *vt sep* block; *(bringen)* deliver. Z~**ung** *f* delivery

zusteuern v sep □vi (sein) head (auf + acc for) □vt contribute

zustimm|en vi sep (haben) agree. (billigen) approve (dat of). **Z~ung** f consent; approval

zustoßen† vi sep (sein) happen (dat to)

Zustrom m influx

Zutat f (Culin) ingredient

zuteil|en vt sep allocate; assign ⟨Aufgabe⟩. **Z~ung** f allocation

zutiefst adv deeply

zutragen† vt sep carry/(fig) report (dat to); **sich z~** happen

zutrauen vt sep jdm etw z~ believe s.o. capable of sth. **Z~** nt -s confidence

zutreffen† vi sep (haben) be correct; **z~ auf** (+ acc) apply to

Zutritt m admittance

zuunterst adv right at the bottom

zuverlässig a reliable. **Z~keit** f reliability

Zuversicht f - confidence. **z~lich** a confident

zuviel pron & adv too much; (pl) too many

zuvor adv before; (erst) first

zuvorkommen† vi sep (sein) (+ dat) anticipate

Zuwachs m -es increase

zuwege adv **z~ bringen** achieve

zuweilen adv now and then

zuweisen† vt sep assign

Zuwendung f donation; (Fürsorge) care

zuwenig pron & adv too little; (pl) too few

zuwerfen† vt sep slam ⟨Tür⟩; **jdm etw z~** throw s.o. sth

zuwider adv jdm **z~ sein** be repugnant to s.o. □prep (+ dat) contrary to

zuzahlen vt sep pay extra

zuziehen† vt sep pull tight; draw ⟨Vorhänge⟩; (hinzu-) call in; **sich** ⟨dat⟩ **etw z~** contract ⟨Krankheit⟩; sustain ⟨Verletzung⟩; incur ⟨Zorn⟩

zuzüglich prep (+ gen) plus

Zwang m -[e]s,-e compulsion; (Gewalt) force; (Verpflichtung) obligation

zwängen vt squeeze

zwanglos a informal. **Z~igkeit** f -informality

Zwangsjacke f straitjacket

zwanzig a twenty. **z~ste(r,s)** a twentieth

zwar adv admittedly

Zweck m -[e]s,-e purpose; (Sinn) point. **z~los** a pointless. **z~mäßig** a suitable; (praktisch) functional. **z~s** prep (+ gen) for the purpose of

zwei inv a, **Z~** f -,-en two; (Sch) ≈ B. **Z~bettzimmer** nt twin-bedded room

zweideutig a ambiguous

zweierlei inv a two kinds of □pron two things. **z~fach** a double

Zweifel m -s,- doubt. **z~haft** a doubtful; (fragwürdig) dubious. **z~los** adv undoubtedly. **z~n** vi (haben) doubt (an etw dat sth)

Zweig m -[e]s,-e branch. **Z~stelle** f branch [office]

Zwei|kampf m duel. **z~mal** adv twice. **z~reihig** a double-breasted. **z~sprachig** a bilingual

zweit adv zu **z~** in twos; **wir waren zu z~** there were two of us. **z~beste(r,s)** a second-best. **z~e(r,s)** a second

zweitens adv secondly

Zwerchfell nt diaphragm

Zwerg m -[e]s,-e dwarf

Zwickel m -s,- gusset

zwicken vt/i (haben) pinch

Zwieback m -[e]s,-e rusk

Zwiebel f -,-n onion; bulb

Zwielicht nt half-light; (Dämmerlicht) twilight. **z~ig** a shady

Zwilling m -s,-e twin; **Z~e** (Astr) Gemini

zwingen† *vt* force; **sich z~** force oneself. **z~d** *a* compelling

Zwinger *m* -s,- run; (*Zucht-*) kennels *pl*

zwinkern *vi* (*haben*) blink; (*als Zeichen*) wink

Zwirn *m* -[e]s button thread

zwischen *prep* (+ *dat/acc*) between; (*unter*) among[st]. **Z~bemerkung** *f* interjection. **z~durch** *adv* in between; (*in der Z~zeit*) in the meantime. **Z~fall** *m* incident. **Z~landung** *f* stopover. **Z~raum** *m* gap, space.

Z~wand *f* partition. **Z~zeit** *f* in der **Z~zeit** in the meantime

zwitschern *vi* (*haben*) chirp

zwölf *inv a* twelve. **z~te(r,s)** *a* twelfth

Zylind|er *m* -s,- cylinder; (*Hut*) top hat. **z~risch** *a* cylindrical

Zyn|iker *m* -s,- cynic. **z~isch** *a* cynical. **Z~ismus** *m* - cynicism

Zypern *nt* -s Cyprus

Zypresse *f* -,-n cypress

Zyste /'tsʏsta/ *f* -,-n cyst

z.Zt. *abbr* (**zur Zeit**) at present

A

a (vor einem Vokal **an**) indef art
ein(e); (each) pro; **not a** kein(e)

aback adv **be taken ~** verblüfft
sein

abandon vt verlassen; (give up)
aufgeben □ n Hingabe f

abashed a beschämt, verlegen

abate vi nachlassen

abattoir n Schlachthof m

abbey n Abtei f. **~ot** n Abt m

abbreviate vt abkürzen. **~ion** n
Abkürzung f

abdicate vi abdanken

abdomen n Unterleib m. **~inal** a
Unterleibs-

abduct vt entführen

aberration n Abweichung f;
(mental) Verwirrung f

abet vt **aid and ~** (Jur) Beihilfe
leisten (+ dat)

abeyance n **in ~** [zeitweilig]
außer Kraft

abhor vt verabscheuen. **~rence**
n Abscheu f. **~rent** a abscheulich

abide vt (tolerate) aushalten; ausstehen ⟨person⟩ □ vi **~e by** sich
halten an (+ acc). **~ing** a blei-
bend

ability n Fähigkeit f; (talent) Begabung f

abject a erbärmlich

ablaze a in Flammen

able a fähig; **be ~ to do sth**
etw tun können. **~-bodied**
a körperlich gesund; (Mil)
tauglich

abnormal a anormal; (Med) abnorm. **~ity** n Abnormität f

aboard adv & prep an Bord (+
gen)

abode n Wohnsitz m

abolish vt abschaffen. **~ition** n
Abschaffung f

abominable a abscheulich

abominate vt verabscheuen

aborigines npl Ureinwohner pl

abort vt abtreiben. **~ion** n Ab-
treibung f. **~ive** a vergeblich

abound vi reichlich vorhanden
sein

about adv umher, herum; (approximately) ungefähr; **be ~** (in circulation) umgehen; (in existence) vorhanden sein; **be ~ to
do sth** im Begriff sein, etw zu tun;
there are a lot ~ es gibt viele;
there was no one ~ es war kein
Mensch da; **run/play ~** herum-
laufen/-spielen □ prep um (+ acc)
[. . . herum]; (concerning) über (+
acc); **what is it ~?** worum geht
es? ⟨book:⟩ wovon handelt es? **I
know nothing ~** it ich weiß
nichts davon; **talk/know ~** re-
den/wissen von

about: **~-'face** n, **-'turn** n Kehrtwendung f

above adv oben □ prep über (+
dat/acc); **~ all** vor allem

above: **~-'board** a legal.
~-'mentioned a obenerwähnt

abrasion n Schürfwunde f

abrasive a Scheuer-; (remark)
verletzend □ n Scheuermittel nt

abreast adv nebeneinander; **keep
~ of** Schritt halten mit

abroad adv im Ausland; **go ~** ins
Ausland fahren

abrupt a abrupt; (sudden) plötzlich; (curt) schroff

abscess n Abszeß m

abscond vi entfliehen

absence n Abwesenheit f

absent a abwesend; **be ~** fehlen

absentee n Abwesende(r) m/f

absent-minded a geistesabwesend; (forgetful) zerstreut

absolute a absolut

absolve vt lossprechen

absorb vt absorbieren, aufsaugen; **~ed** in vertieft in (+ acc). **~ent** a saugfähig

absorption n Absorption f

abstain vi sich enthalten (from gen)

abstemious a enthaltsam

abstention n [Stimm]enthaltung f

abstinence n Enthaltsamkeit f

abstract a abstrakt □n (summary) Abriß m

absurd a absurd. **~ity** n Absurdität f

abundan|ce n Fülle f (of an + dat). **~t** a reichlich

abuse¹ vt mißbrauchen; (insult) beschimpfen

abus|e² n Mißbrauch m; (insults) Beschimpfungen pl. **~ive** a ausfallend

abysmal a (fam) katastrophal

abyss n Abgrund m

academic a akademisch □n Akademiker(in) m(f)

academy n Akademie f

accede vi **~ to** zustimmen (+ dat)

accelerat|e vt beschleunigen □vi die Geschwindigkeit erhöhen. **~ion** n Beschleunigung f. **~or** n Gaspedal nt

accent n Akzent m

accentuate vt betonen

accept vt annehmen; (fig) akzeptieren □vi zusagen. **~able** a annehmbar. **~ance** n Annahme f; (of invitation) Zusage f

access n Zugang m; (road) Zufahrt f. **~ible** a zugänglich

accessor|y n (Jur) Mitschuldige(r) m/f; **~ies** pl (fashion) Accessoires pl; (Techn) Zubehör nt

accident n Unfall m; (chance) Zufall m; **by ~** zufällig; (unintentionally) versehentlich. **~al** a zufällig; versehentlich

acclaim n Beifall m □vt feiern

acclimatize vt **become ~d** sich akklimatisieren

accolade n Auszeichnung f

accommodat|e vt unterbringen; (oblige) entgegenkommen (+ dat). **~ion** n Unterkunft f

accompaniment n Begleitung f

accompany vt begleiten

accomplice n Komplize/-zin m/f

accomplish vt erfüllen; (achieve) erreichen. **~ed** a fähig. **~ment** n Fertigkeit f; (achievement) Leistung f

accord n (treaty) Abkommen nt; **of one's own ~** aus eigenem Antrieb □vt gewähren. **~ance** n **in ~ance with** entsprechend (+ dat)

according adv **~ to** nach (+ dat). **~ly** adv entsprechend

accordion n Akkordeon nt

accost vt ansprechen

account n Konto nt; (bill) Rechnung f; (description) Darstellung f; (report) Bericht m; **~s** pl (Comm) Bücher pl; **on ~ of** wegen (+ gen); **on no ~** auf keinen Fall; **on my ~** meinetwegen; **take into ~** in Betracht ziehen □vi **~ for** Rechenschaft ablegen für; (explain) erklären

accountant n Buchhalter(in) m(f); (chartered) Wirtschaftsprüfer m; (for tax) Steuerberater m

accrue vi sich ansammeln

accumulat|e vt ansammeln □vi sich ansammeln. **~ion** n Ansammlung f. **~or** n (Electr) Akkumulator m

accura|cy n Genauigkeit f. **~te** a genau

accusation n Anklage f

accusative a & n ~ [**case**] (Gram) Akkusativ m

accuse vt (Jur) anklagen (**of** gen); ~ **s.o. of doing sth** jdn beschuldigen, etw getan zu haben. ~ **d** n the ~ **d** der/die Angeklagte

accustom vt gewöhnen (**to** an + dat); **grow** or **get** ~ **ed to** sich gewöhnen an (+ acc)

ace n (Cards, Sport) As nt

ache n Schmerzen pl □ vi weh tun, schmerzen

achieve vt leisten; (gain) erzielen; (reach) erreichen. ~ **ment** n (feat) Leistung f

acid a sauer; (fig) beißend □ n Säure f. ~ '**rain** n saurer Regen m

acknowledge vt anerkennen; (admit) zugeben; erwidern ⟨greeting⟩. ~ **ment** n Anerkennung f; (of letter) Empfangsbestätigung f

acorn n Eichel f

acoustic a akustisch. ~ **s** npl Akustik f

acquaint vt ~ **s.o. with** jdn bekannt machen mit; **be** ~ **ed with** kennen; vertraut sein mit ⟨fact⟩. ~ **ance** n Bekanntschaft f; (person) Bekannte(r) m/f; **make s.o.'s** ~ **ance** jdn kennenlernen

acquiesce vi einwilligen (**to** in + acc)

acquire vt erwerben

acquisit|ion n Erwerb m; (thing) Erwerbung f. ~ **ive** a habgierig

acquit vt freisprechen. ~ **tal** n Freispruch m

acre n ≈ Morgen m

acrimon|ious a bitter. ~ **y** n Bitterkeit f

acrobat n Akrobat(in) m(f). ~ **ic** a akrobatisch

across adv hinüber/herüber; (wide) breit; (not lengthwise) quer; (in crossword) waagerecht; **come** ~ **sth** auf etw (acc)

stoßen □ prep über (+ acc); (crosswise) quer über (+ acc/dat); (on the other side of) auf der anderen Seite (+ gen)

act n Tat f; (action) Handlung f; (law) Gesetz nt; (Theat) Akt m; **put on an** ~ (fam) sich verstellen □ vi handeln; (behave) sich verhalten; (Theat) spielen; (pretend) sich verstellen; ~ **as** fungieren als □ vt spielen ⟨role⟩. ~ **ing** a (deputy) stellvertretend

action n Handlung f; (deed) Tat f; (Mil) Einsatz m; (Jur) Klage f; **out of** ~ außer Betrieb; **take** ~ handeln

activate vt betätigen

activ|e|a, aktiv. ~ **ity** n Aktivität f

act|or n Schauspieler m. ~ **ress** n Schauspielerin f

actual a eigentlich; (real) tatsächlich. ~ **ity** n Wirklichkeit f

acumen n Scharfsinn m

acupuncture n Akupunktur f

acute a scharf; ⟨angle⟩ spitz; ⟨illness⟩ akut. ~ **ly** adv sehr

AD abbr (Anno Domini) n.Chr.

adamant a **be** ~ **that** darauf bestehen, daß

adapt vt anpassen; bearbeiten ⟨play⟩ □ vi sich anpassen. ~ **able** a anpassungsfähig

adaptation n Bearbeitung f

adapter, adaptor n Adapter m; (two-way) Doppelstecker m

add vt hinzufügen; (Math) addieren □ vi zusammenzählen, addieren; ~ **to** hinzufügen zu; (fig: increase) steigern; (compound) verschlimmern. ~ **up** vt zusammenzählen; ~ **up to** machen; **it doesn't** ~ **up** (fig) da stimmt etwas nicht

adder n Kreuzotter f

addict n Süchtige(r) m/f

addict|ed a süchtig; ~ **ed to drugs** drogensüchtig. ~ **ion** n Sucht f. ~ **ive** a **be** ~ **ive** zur Süchtigkeit führen

addition n Hinzufügung f; (Math) Addition f; (thing added) Ergänzung f. **~al** a zusätzlich

additive n Zusatz m

address n Adresse f, Anschrift f; (speech) Ansprache f □vt adressieren (**to** an + acc); anreden (person); sprechen vor (+ dat) (meeting). **~ee** n Empfänger m

adenoids npl [Rachen]polypen pl

adept a geschickt (**at** in + dat)

adequate a ausreichend

adhere vi kleben/(fig) festhalten (**to** an + dat)

adhesive a klebend □n Klebstoff m

adjacent a angrenzend

adjective n Adjektiv nt

adjoin vt angrenzen an (+ acc)

adjourn vt vertagen (**until** auf + acc) □vi sich vertagen. **~ment** n Vertagung f

adjudicate vi entscheiden

adjust vt einstellen; (alter) verstellen □vi sich anpassen (**to** dat). **~ment** n Einstellung f; Anpassung f

ad lib adv aus dem Stegreif □vi (fam) improvisieren

administer vt verwalten; verabreichen (medicine)

administrat|ion n Verwaltung f; (Pol) Regierung f. **~or** n Verwaltungsbeamte(r) m /-beamtin f

admirable a bewundernswert

admiral n Admiral m

admiration n Bewunderung f

admire vt bewundern. **~r** n Verehrer(in) m(f)

admissible a zulässig

admission n Eingeständnis nt; (entry) Eintritt m

admit vt hereinlassen; (acknowledge) zugeben; **~ to sth** etw zugeben. **~tance** n Eintritt m. **~tedly** adv zugegebenermaßen

admonish vt ermahnen

ado n **without more ~** ohne weiteres

adolescen|ce n Jugend f, Pubertät f. **~t** a Jugend-; (boy, girl) halbwüchsig □n Jugendliche(r) m/f

adopt vt adoptieren; ergreifen (measure). **~ion** n Adoption f. **~ive** a Adoptiv-

ador|able a bezaubernd. **~ation** n Anbetung f

adore vt anbeten; (fam: like) lieben

adorn vt schmücken

adrenalin n Adrenalin nt

Adriatic a & n ~ [Sea] Adria f

adroit a gewandt, geschickt

adult n Erwachsene(r) m/f

adulterate vt verfälschen

adultery n Ehebruch m

advance n Fortschritt m; (Mil) Vorrücken nt; (payment) Vorschuß m; **in ~** im voraus □vi vorankommen; (Mil) vorrücken; (make progress) Fortschritte machen □vt fördern (cause); vorbringen (idea); vorschießen (money). **~d** a fortgeschritten. **~ment** n Förderung f

advantage n Vorteil m; **take ~ of** ausnutzen. **~ous** a vorteilhaft

advent n Ankunft f; A~ (season) Advent m

adventur|e n Abenteuer nt. **~ous** a abenteuerlich; (person) abenteuerlustig

adverb n Adverb nt

adversary n Widersacher m

advers|e a ungünstig. **~ity** n Not f

advertise vt Reklame machen für; (by small ad) inserieren □vi Reklame machen; inserieren

advertisement n Anzeige f; (publicity) Reklame f; (small ad) Inserat nt

advertis|er n Inserent m. **~ing** n Werbung f

advice n Rat m

advisable a ratsam

advis|e vt raten (s.o. jdm); (counsel) beraten; (inform) benachrichtigen; **~e s.o. against sth** jdm von etw abraten □ vi raten. **~er** n Berater(in) m(f). **~ory** a beratend

advocate[1] n [Rechts]anwalt m/ -anwältin f; (supporter) Befürworter m

advocate[2] vt befürworten

aerial a Luft- □ n Antenne f

aerobics n Aerobic nt

aero|drome n Flugplatz m. **~plane** n Flugzeug nt

aerosol n Spraydose f

aesthetic a ästhetisch

afar adv from ~ aus der Ferne

affair n Angelegenheit f, Sache f; (scandal) Affäre f; **[love-]~** [Liebes]verhältnis nt

affect vt sich auswirken auf (+ acc); (concern) betreffen. **~ed** a affektiert

affection n Liebe f. **~ate** a liebevoll

affinity n Ähnlichkeit f

affirm vt behaupten; (Jur) eidesstattlich erklären

affirmative a bejahend □ n Bejahung f

affix vt anbringen (**to** dat); (stick) aufkleben (**to** auf + acc); setzen (signature) (**to** unter + acc)

afflict vt be **~ed with** behaftet sein mit. **~ion** n Leiden nt

affluen|ce n Reichtum m. **~t** a wohlhabend

afford vt (provide) gewähren; **be able to ~ sth** sich (dat) etw leisten können. **~able** a erschwinglich

affront n Beleidigung f

afield adv **further ~** weiter weg

afloat a be ~ flott sein; **keep ~** ⟨person:⟩ sich über Wasser halten

afoot a im Gange

aforesaid a (Jur) obenerwähnt

afraid a be ~ Angst haben (**of** vor + dat); **I'm ~** not leider nicht; **I'm ~ so** [ja] leider; **I'm ~ I can't help you** ich kann Ihnen leider nicht helfen

Africa n Afrika nt. **~n** a afrikanisch □ n Afrikaner(in) m(f)

after adv danach □ prep nach (+ dat); **~ that** danach; **~ all** schließlich; **the day ~** tomorrow übermorgen □ conj nachdem

after: ~math n Auswirkungen pl. **~'noon** n Nachmittag m; **good ~noon!** guten Tag! **~shave** n Rasierwasser nt. **~thought** n nachträglicher Einfall m. **~wards** adv nachher

again adv wieder; (once more) noch einmal; (besides) außerdem; **~ and ~** immer wieder

against prep gegen (+ acc)

age n Alter nt; (era) Zeitalter nt; **~s** (fam) ewig; **under ~** minderjährig; **of ~** volljährig □ vi altern; (mature) reifen

aged[1] a **~ two** zwei Jahre alt

aged[2] a betagt □ n **the ~** pl die Alten

ageless a ewig jung

agency n Agentur f; (office) Büro nt

agenda n Tagesordnung f; **on the ~** auf dem Programm

agent n Agent(in) m(f); (Comm) Vertreter(in) m(f)

aggravat|e vt verschlimmern; (fam: annoy) ärgern. **~ion** n (fam) Ärger m

aggregate a gesamt □ n Gesamtzahl f

aggress|ion n Aggression f. **~ive** a aggressiv. **~or** n Angreifer(in) m(f)

aghast a entsetzt

agil|e a flink, behende. **~ity** n Flinkheit f, Behendigkeit f

agitat|e vt bewegen; (shake) schütteln □ vi (fig) **~ for** agitieren für. **~ed** a erregt. **~ion** n

Erregung *f*; (*Pol*) Agitation *f*.
~**or** *n* Agitator *m*

agnostic *n* Agnostiker *m*

ago *adv* vor (+ *dat*); **a month ~**
vor einem Monat; **how long ~ is
it?** wie lange ist es her?

agoniz|e *vi* [innerlich] ringen.
~**ing** *a* qualvoll

agony *n* Qual *f*

agree *vt* vereinbaren; (*admit*) zugeben; ~ **to do sth** sich bereit
erklären, etw zu tun □*vi* (*figures:*) übereinstimmen; (*reach
agreement*) sich einigen; (*con-
sent*) einwilligen (**to** in + *acc*); **I**
~ **der Meinung bin ich auch;** ~
with s.o. jdm zustimmen; ⟨*food:*⟩
jdm bekommen; ~ **with sth** (*approve of*) mit etw einverstanden
sein

agreeable *a* angenehm

agreement *n* Übereinstimmung
f; (*consent*) Einwilligung *f*; (*contract*) Abkommen *nt*

agricultur|al *a* landwirtschaft-
lich. ~**e** *n* Landwirtschaft *f*

aground *a* gestrandet; **run ~**
stranden

ahead *adv* **straight ~** geradeaus;
be ~ of s.o.,/sth vor jdm/etw sein;
(*fig*) voraus sein; **go ~!** (*fam*)
bitte! **look/plan ~** voraus-
blicken/-planen

aid *n* Hilfe *f*; (*financial*) Unterstützung *f*; **in ~ of** zugunsten (+
gen) □*vt* helfen (+ *dat*)

aide *n* Berater *m*

Aids *n* Aids *nt*

ailment *n* Leiden *nt*

aim *n* Ziel *nt*; **take ~** zielen □*vt*
richten (**at** auf + *acc*) □*vi* zielen
(**at** auf + *acc*); ~ **to do sth** beabsichtigen, etw zu tun

air *n* Luft *f*; (*tune*) Melodie *f*;
(*expression*) Miene *f*; (*appearance*) Anschein *m*; **put on** ~**s**
vornehm tun; **by** ~ auf dem Luft-
weg; (*airmail*) mit Luftpost □*vt*
lüften; vorbringen ⟨*views*⟩

air: ~**-conditioned** *a* klimati-
siert. ~**-conditioning** *n* Klima-
anlage *f*. ~**craft** *n* Flugzeug *nt*.
~**force** *n* Luftwaffe *f*. ~**gun** *n*
Luftgewehr *nt*. ~**hostess** *n*
Stewardeß *f*. ~**letter** *n* Aero-
gramm *nt*. ~**line** *n* Fluggesell-
schaft *f*. ~**lock** *n* Luftblase *f*.
~**mail** *n* Luftpost *f*. ~**man** *n*
Flieger *m*. ~**port** *n* Flughafen *m*.
~**raid** *n* Luftangriff *m*. ~**ship** *n*
Luftschiff *nt*. ~**ticket** *n* Flugschein *m*. ~**tight** *a* luftdicht. ~**-
traffic controller** *n* Fluglotse
m. ~**worthy** *a* flugtüchtig

aisle *n* Gang *m*

ajar *a* angelehnt

akin *a* ~ **to** verwandt mit; (*similar*) ähnlich (**to** *dat*)

alabaster *n* Alabaster *m*

alacrity *n* Bereitfertigkeit *f*

alarm *n* Alarm *m*; (*device*) Alarmanlage *f*; (*clock*) Wecker *m*; (*fear*)
Unruhe *f* □*vt* erschrecken; alar-
mieren. ~**clock** *n* Wecker *m*

alas *int* ach!

album *n* Album *nt*

alcohol *n* Alkohol *m*. ~**ic** *a* alko-
holisch □*n* Alkoholiker(in) *m(f)*.
~**ism** *n* Alkoholismus *m*

alcove *n* Nische *f*

alert *a* aufmerksam □*vt* alarmie-
ren

algae *npl* Algen *pl*

algebra *n* Algebra *f*

Algeria *n* Algerien *nt*

alias *n* Deckname *m* □*adv* alias

alibi *n* Alibi *nt*

alien *a* fremd □*n* Ausländer(in)
m(f)

alienate *vt* entfremden

alight[1] *vi* aussteigen (**from** aus)

alight[2] *a* **be ~** brennen; **set ~**
anzünden

align *vt* ausrichten. ~**ment** *n*
Ausrichtung *f*

alike *a* & *adv* ähnlich; (*same*)
gleich; **look ~** sich (*dat*) ähnlich
sehen

alive *a* lebendig; **be** ~ leben

alkali *n* Base *f*, Alkali *nt*

all *a* alle *pl*; *(whole)* ganz; ~ **[the] children** alle Kinder; ~ **day** den ganzen Tag; ~ **the wine** der ganze Wein □ *pron* alle *pl*; *(everything)* alles; ~ **of you/them** Sie/sie alle; ~ **of the town** der ganzen Stadt; **not at** ~ gar nicht; **in** ~ insgesamt; **most of** ~ am meisten; **once and for** ~ ein für allemal □ *adv* ganz; ~ **at once** auf einmal; ~ **too soon** viel zu früh; ~ **the better** um so besser; **four** ~ *(Sport)* vier zu vier

allegation *n* Behauptung *f*

allege *vt* behaupten. **~d** *a* angeblich

allegiance *n* Treue *f*

allegor|ical *a* allegorisch. **~y** *n* Allegorie *f*

allerg|ic *a* allergisch (**to** gegen). **~y** *n* Allergie *f*

alleviate *vt* lindern

alley *n* Gasse *f*; *(for bowling)* Bahn *f*

alliance *n* Verbindung *f*; *(Pol)* Bündnis *nt*

allied *a* alliiert; *(fig: related)* verwandt (**to** mit)

alligator *n* Alligator *m*

allocat|e *vt* zuteilen. **~ion** *n* Zuteilung *f*

allot *vt* zuteilen (**s.o.** jdm). **~ment** *n* ≈ Schrebergarten *m*

allow *vt* erlauben; *(give)* geben; *(grant)* gewähren; *(reckon)* rechnen; ~ **s.o. to do sth** jdm erlauben, etw zu tun; **be** ~**ed to do sth** etw tun dürfen

allowance *n* [finanzielle] Unterstützung *f*; ~ **for petrol** Benzingeld *nt*

alloy *n* Legierung *f*

allusion *n* Anspielung *f*

ally[1] *n* Verbündete(r) *m/f*; **the Allies** *pl* die Alliierten

ally[2] *vt* verbinden

almighty *a* allmächtig; *(fam: big)* Riesen- □ *n* **the A~** der Allmächtige

almond *n* *(Bot)* Mandel *f*

almost *adv* fast, beinahe

alone *a* & *adv* allein; **leave me** ~ laß mich in Ruhe; **let** ~ ganz zu schweigen von

along *prep* entlang (+ *acc*); ~ **the river** den Fluß entlang □ *adv* ~ **with** zusammen mit; **all** ~ die ganze Zeit; **I'll bring it** ~ ich bringe es mit

alongside *adv* daneben □ *prep* neben (+ *dat*)

aloud *adv* laut

alphabet *n* Alphabet *nt.* **~ical** *a* alphabetisch

alpine *a* alpin; **A~** Alpen-

Alps *npl* Alpen *pl*

already *adv* schon

Alsace *n* Elsaß *nt*

Alsatian *n* *(dog)* [deutscher] Schäferhund *m*

also *adv* auch

altar *n* Altar *m*

alter *vt* ändern □ *vi* sich verändern. **~ation** *n* Änderung *f*

alternate[1] *vi* [sich] abwechseln □ *vt* abwechseln

alternate[2] *a* abwechselnd

alternating current *n* Wechselstrom *m*

alternative *a* andere(r,s) □ *n* Alternative *f*. **~ly** *adv* oder aber

although *conj* obgleich, obwohl

altitude *n* Höhe *f*

altogether *adv* insgesamt

aluminium *n* Aluminium *nt*

always *adv* immer

a.m. *abbr* *(ante meridiem)* vormittags

amalgamate *vt* vereinigen

amass *vt* anhäufen

amateur *n* Amateur *m* □ *attrib* Amateur-. **~ish** *a* laienhaft

amaze *vt* erstaunen. **~d** *a* erstaunt. **~ment** *n* Erstaunen *nt*

amazing *a* erstaunlich

ambassador n Botschafter m

amber n Bernstein m □ a gelb

ambience n Atmosphäre f

ambigu|ity n Zweideutigkeit f. ~ous a zweideutig

ambition n Ehrgeiz m; (aim) Ambition f. ~ous a ehrgeizig

ambivalent a zwiespältig

amble vi schlendern

ambulance n Krankenwagen m. ~ man n Sanitäter m

ambush n Hinterhalt m □ vt aus dem Hinterhalt überfallen

amen int amen

amend vt ändern. ~ment n Änderung f. ~s npl make ~s for sth etw wiedergutmachen

amenities npl Einrichtungen pl

America n Amerika nt. ~n a amerikanisch □n Amerikaner(in) m(f)

amiable a nett

amicable a freundschaftlich

amid[st] prep inmitten (+ gen)

amiss a be ~ nicht stimmen □ adv not come ~ nicht unangebracht sein; take sth ~ etw übelnehmen

ammonia n Ammoniak nt

ammunition n Munition f

amnesia n Amnesie f

amnesty n Amnestie f

among[st] prep unter (+ dat/acc); ~ yourselves untereinander

amorous a zärtlich

amount n Menge f; (sum of money) Betrag m; (total) Gesamtsumme f □ vi ~ to sich belaufen auf (+ acc); (fig) hinauslaufen auf (+ acc)

amp n Ampere nt

amphibi|an n Amphibie f. ~ous a amphibisch

amphitheatre n Amphitheater nt

ample a reichlich

ampli|fier n Verstärker m. ~y vt weiter ausführen; verstärken ⟨sound⟩

amputate vt amputieren

amuse vt amüsieren, belustigen; (entertain) unterhalten. ~ment n Belustigung f; Unterhaltung f

amusing a amüsant

an see a

anaem|ia n Blutarmut f, Anämie f. ~ic a blutarm

anaesthesia n Betäubung f

anaesthetic n Narkosemittel nt, Betäubungsmittel nt; under [an] ~ in Narkose

anaesthet|ist n Narkosearzt m. ~ize vt betäuben

analogy n Analogie f

analyse vt analysieren

analysis n Analyse f

analyst n Chemiker(in) m(f); (Psych) Analytiker m

analytical a analytisch

anarch|ist n Anarchist m. ~y n Anarchie f

anatom|ical a anatomisch. ~y n Anatomie f

ancest|or n Vorfahr m. ~ry n Abstammung f

anchor n Anker m □ vi ankern □ vt verankern

anchovy n Sardelle f

ancient a alt

and conj und; ~ so on und so weiter; six hundred ~ two sechshundertzwei; nice ~ warm schön warm

anecdote n Anekdote f

angel n Engel m. ~ic a engelhaft

anger n Zorn m

angle n Winkel m; (fig) Standpunkt m; at an ~ schräg

angler n Angler m

Anglican a anglikanisch □n Anglikaner(in) m(f)

Anglo-Saxon a angelsächsich

angry a zornig; be ~ with böse sein auf (+ acc)

anguish n Qual f

animal n Tier nt □ a tierisch

animate[1] a lebendig

animat|e[2] vt beleben. ~ed a lebhaft

animosity n Feindseligkeit f
aniseed n Anis m
ankle n [Fuß]knöchel m
annex[e] n Nebengebäude nt; (extension) Anbau m
annihilat|e vt vernichten. **~ion** n Vernichtung f
anniversary n Jahrestag m
announce vt bekanntgeben; (over loudspeaker) durchsagen; (at reception) ankündigen; (Radio, TV) ansagen; (in newspaper) anzeigen. **~ment** n Bekanntgabe f, Bekanntmachung f; Durchsage f; Ansage f; Anzeige f. **~r** n Ansager(in) m(f)
annoy vt ärgern; (pester) belästigen; **get ~ed** sich ärgern. **~ance** n Ärger m. **~ing** a ärgerlich
annual a jährlich □ n (Bot) einjährige Pflanze f; (book) Jahresalbum nt
annul vt annullieren
anoint vt salben
anomaly n Anomalie f
anonymous a anonym
anorak n Anorak m
anorexia n Magersucht f
another a & pron ein anderer/ eine andere/ein anderes; (additional) noch ein(e); **~ [one]** noch einer/eine/eins; **~ time** ein anderer/ mal; **one ~** einander
answer n Antwort f; (solution) Lösung f □ vt antworten (s.o. jdm); beantworten (question); **~ the door/telephone** an die Tür/ans Telefon gehen □ vi antworten; (Teleph) sich melden; **~ for** verantwortlich sein für. **~ing machine** n (Teleph) Anrufbeantworter m
ant n Ameise f
antagonis|m n Antagonismus m. **~tic** a feindselig
antagonize vt gegen sich aufbringen
Antarctic n Antarktis f
antelope n Antilope f

antenatal a **~ care** Schwangerschaftsfürsorge f
antenna n Fühler m; (aerial) Antenne f
anthem n Hymne f
anthology n Anthologie f
anthropology n Anthropologie f
antibiotic n Antibiotikum nt
antibody n Antikörper m
anticipat|e vt vorhersehen; (forestall) zuvorkommen (+ dat); (expect) erwarten. **~ion** n Erwartung f
anticlimax n Enttäuschung f
anticlockwise a & adv gegen den Uhrzeigersinn
anticyclone n Hochdruckgebiet nt
antidote n Gegengift nt
antifreeze n Frostschutzmittel nt
antipathy n Abneigung f
antiquarian a antiquarisch. **~ bookshop** n Antiquariat nt
antique a antik □ n Antiquität f
antiquity n Altertum nt
anti-Semitic a antisemitisch
antiseptic a antiseptisch □ n Antiseptikum nt
antisocial a asozial; (fam) ungesellig
antlers npl Geweih nt
anus n After m
anvil n Amboß m
anxiety n Sorge f
anxious a ängstlich; (worried) besorgt
any a irgendein(e); pl irgendwelche; (every) jede(r,s); pl alle; (after negative) kein(e); pl keine; **~ colour/number you like** eine beliebige Farbe/Zahl; **have you ~ wine/apples?** haben Sie Wein/ Äpfel? **for ~ reason** aus irgendeinem Grund □ pron [irgend]einer/eine/eins; pl [irgend]welche; (some) welche(r,s); pl welche; (all) alle pl; (negative) keiner/keine/keins; pl keine; **I don't want ~ of it** ich will nichts

davon; **there aren't ~** es gibt keine □*adv* noch; **~ quicker/slower** noch schneller/langsamer; **would you like ~ more?** möchten Sie noch [etwas]?

anybody *pron* [irgend] jemand; *(after negative)* niemand; **~ can do that** das kann jeder

anyhow *adv* jedenfalls; *(nevertheless)* trotzdem

anyone *pron* = **anybody**

anything *pron* [irgend] etwas; *(after negative)* nichts; *(everything)* alles

anyway *adv* jedenfalls; *(in any case)* sowieso

anywhere *adv* irgendwo; *(after negative)* nirgendwo; *(live)* überall

apart *adv* auseinander; **live ~** getrennt leben; **~ from** abgesehen von

apartment *n* Wohnung *f*

ape *n* [Menschen]affe *m*

aperitif *n* Aperitif *m*

aperture *n* Öffnung *f*; *(Phot)* Blende *f*

apex *n* Spitze *f*; *(fig)* Gipfel *m*

apologetic *a* entschuldigend

apologize *vi* sich entschuldigen **(to** bei)

apology *n* Entschuldigung *f*

apostle *n* Apostel *m*

apostrophe *n* Apostroph *m*

appal *vt* entsetzen. **~ling** *a* entsetzlich

apparatus *n* Apparatur *f*; *(Sport)* Geräte *pl*

apparent *a* offenbar; *(seeming)* scheinbar. **~ly** *adv* offenbar, anscheinend

apparition *n* Erscheinung *f*

appeal *n* Appell *m*, Aufruf *m*; *(request)* Bitte *f*; *(attraction)* Reiz *m*; *(Jur)* Berufung *f* □ *vi* appellieren **(to** an + *acc*); *(ask)* bitten **(for** um); *(be attractive)* zusagen **(to** *dat*); *(Jur)* Berufung einlegen. **~ing** *a* ansprechend

appear *vi* erscheinen; *(seem)* scheinen. **~ance** *n* Erscheinen *nt*; *(look)* Aussehen *nt*

appendage *n* Anhängsel *m*

appendicitis *n* Blinddarmentzündung *f*

appendix *n* *(of book)* Anhang *m*; *(Anat)* Blinddarm *m*

appetite *n* Appetit *m*

appetizing *a* appetitlich

applaud *vt/i* Beifall klatschen (+ *dat*). **~se** *n* Beifall *m*

apple *n* Apfel *m*

appliance *n* Gerät *nt*

applicable *a* anwendbar **(to** auf + *acc*); **(on** form) **not ~** nicht zutreffend

applicant *n* Bewerber(in) *m(f)*

application *n* Anwendung *f*; *(request)* Antrag *m*; *(for job)* Bewerbung *f*; *(diligence)* Fleiß *m*

apply *vt* auftragen *(paint)*; anwenden *(force)* □ *vi* zutreffen **(to** auf + *acc*); **~ for** beantragen; sich bewerben um *(job)*

appoint *vt* ernennen; *(fix)* festlegen; **well ~ed** gut ausgestattet. **~ment** *n* Ernennung *f*; *(meeting)* Verabredung *f*; *(at doctor's)* Termin *m*; *(job)* Posten *m*; **make an ~ment** sich anmelden

appreciable *a* merklich; *(considerable)* beträchtlich

appreciate *vt* zu schätzen wissen; *(be grateful for)* dankbar sein für; *(enjoy)* schätzen; *(understand)* verstehen □ *vi (increase in value)* im Wert steigen. **~ion** *n (gratitude)* Dankbarkeit *f*. **~ive** *a* dankbar

apprehend *vt* festnehmen

apprehension *n* Festnahme *f*; *(fear)* Angst *f*. **~ive** *a* ängstlich

apprentice *n* Lehrling *m*. **~ship** *n* Lehre *f*

approach *n* Näherkommen *nt*; *(of time)* Nahen *nt*; *(access)* Zugang *m*; ⟨*road*⟩ Zufahrt *f* □ *vi* sich nähern; ⟨*time*:⟩ nahen □ *vt* sich nähern (+ *dat*); ⟨*with request*⟩ herantreten an (+ *acc*). **~able** *a* zugänglich

appropriate[1] *a* angebracht, angemessen

appropriate[2] *vt* sich (*dat*) aneignen

approval *n* Billigung *f*; **on** ~ zur Ansicht

approve *vt* billigen □ *vi* ~ **of** sth/s.o. mit etw/jdm einverstanden sein

approximate[1] *vi* ~ **to** nahekommen (+ *dat*)

approximate[2] *a* ungefähr. **~ly** *adv* ungefähr, etwa

approximation *n* Schätzung *f*

apricot *n* Aprikose *f*

April *n* April *m*

apron *n* Schürze *f*

apropos *adv* ~ **[of]** betreffs (+ *gen*)

apt *a* passend

aptitude *n* Begabung *f*

aqualung *n* Tauchgerät *nt*

aquarium *n* Aquarium *nt*

Aquarius *n* Wassermann *m*

Arab *a* arabisch □ *n* Araber(in) *m(f)*. **~ian** *a* arabisch

Arabic *a* arabisch

arable *a* ~ **land** Ackerland *nt*

arbitrary *a* willkürlich

arbitrat|e *vi* schlichten. **~ion** *n* Schlichtung *f*

arc *n* Bogen *m*

arcade *n* Laubengang *m*; ⟨*shops*⟩ Einkaufspassage *f*

arch *n* Bogen *m*

archaeological *a* archäologisch

archaeolog|ist *n* Archäologe *m/* -login *f*. **~y** *n* Archäologie *f*

archaic *a* veraltet

archbishop *n* Erzbischof *m*

archenemy *n* Erzfeind *m*

archer *n* Bogenschütze *m*. **~y** *n* Bogenschießen *nt*

architect *n* Architekt(in) *m(f)*. **~ural** *a* architektonisch

architecture *n* Architektur *f*

archives *npl* Archiv *nt*

Arctic *a* arktisch □ *n* **the** ~ die Arktis

ardent *a* leidenschaftlich

arduous *a* mühsam

area *n* ⟨*surface*⟩ Fläche *f*; ⟨*Geom*⟩ Flächeninhalt *m*; ⟨*region*⟩ Gegend *f*; ⟨*fig*⟩ Gebiet *nt*. **~ code** *n* Vorwahlnummer *f*

arena *n* Arena *f*

Argentina *n* Argentinien *nt*

Argentin|e, **~ian** *a* argentinisch

argue *vi* streiten (**about** über + *acc*); ⟨*two people*⟩ sich streiten; ⟨*debate*⟩ diskutieren; **don't** ~ ! keine Widerrede! □ *vt* ⟨*debate*⟩ diskutieren; ⟨*reason*⟩ ~ **that** argumentieren, daß

argument *n* Streit *m*, Auseinandersetzung *f*; ⟨*reasoning*⟩ Argument *nt*. **~ative** *a* streitlustig

aria *n* Arie *f*

arid *a* dürr

Aries *n* ⟨*Astr*⟩ Widder *m*

arise *vi* sich ergeben (**from** aus)

aristocracy *n* Aristokratie *f*

aristocrat *n* Aristokrat(in) *m(f)*. **~ic** *a* aristokratisch

arithmetic *n* Rechnen *nt*

ark *n* Noah's **A** ~ die Arche Noah

arm *n* Arm *m*; ⟨*of chair*⟩ Armlehne *f*; **~s** *pl* ⟨*weapons*⟩ Waffen *pl* □ *vt* bewaffnen

armament *n* Bewaffnung *f*; **~s** *pl* Waffen *pl*

armchair *n* Sessel *m*

armed *a* bewaffnet; ~ **forces** Streitkräfte *pl*

armistice *n* Waffenstillstand *m*

armour *n* Rüstung *f*

armpit *n* Achselhöhle *f*

army *n* Heer *nt*; ⟨*specific*⟩ Armee *f*

aroma *n* Aroma *nt*, Duft *m*. **~tic** *a* aromatisch

around *adv* **[all]** ~ rings herum; **he's not** ~ er ist nicht da; **look/**

turn ~ sich umsehen/umdrehen □*prep* um (+ *acc*) ... herum; (*approximately*) gegen

arouse *vt* aufwecken; (*excite*) erregen

arrange *vt* arrangieren; anordnen ⟨*furniture*⟩; (*settle*) abmachen; **I have ~ d to go there** ich habe abgemacht, daß ich dahingehe. **~ment** *n* Anordnung *f*; (*agreement*) Vereinbarung *f*; (*of flowers*) Gesteck *nt*

arrears *npl* Rückstände *pl*; **in ~** im Rückstand

arrest *n* Verhaftung *f*; **under ~** verhaftet □*vt* verhaften

arrival *n* Ankunft *f*; **new ~s** *pl* Neuankömmlinge *pl*

arrive *vi* ankommen

arrogan|ce *n* Arroganz *f*. **~t** *a* arrogant

arrow *n* Pfeil *m*

arse *n* (*vulg*) Arsch *m*

arsenic *n* Arsen *nt*

arson *n* Brandstiftung *f*

art *n* Kunst *f*; **A~s** *pl* (*Univ*) Geisteswissenschaften *pl*

artery *n* Schlagader *f*, Arterie *f*

arthritis *n* Arthritis *f*

artichoke *n* Artischocke *f*

article *n* Artikel *m*; (*object*) Gegenstand *m*

articulate[1] *a* deutlich; **be ~** sich gut ausdrücken können

articulate[2] *vt* aussprechen. **~d lorry** *n* Sattelzug *m*

artifice *n* Arglist *f*

artificial *a* künstlich

artillery *n* Artillerie *f*

artist *n* Künstler(in) *m(f)*

artiste *n* Artist(in) *m(f)*

artistic *a* künstlerisch

as *conj* (*because*) da; (*when*) als; (*while*) während □*prep* als; **as a child/foreigner** als Kind/Ausländer □*adv* as well auch; **as soon as** sobald; **as much as** soviel wie; **as quick as you** so schnell wie du

asbestos *n* Asbest *m*

ascend *vi* [auf]steigen

Ascension *n* (*Relig*) [Christi] Himmelfahrt *f*

ascent *n* Aufstieg *m*

ascertain *vt* ermitteln

ascribe *vt* zuschreiben (**to** *dat*)

ash[1] *n* (*tree*) Esche *f*

ash[2] *n* Asche *f*

ashamed *a* beschämt; **be ~** sich schämen (**of** über + *acc*)

ashore *adv* an Land

ash: **~tray** *n* Aschenbecher *m.* **A~ Wednesday** *n* Aschermittwoch *m*

Asia *n* Asien *nt*. **~n** *a* asiatisch □*n* Asiat(in) *m(f)*. **~tic** *a* asiatisch

aside *adv* beiseite

ask *vt/i* fragen; stellen ⟨*question*⟩; (*invite*) einladen; **~ for** bitten um; verlangen ⟨*s.o.*⟩; **~ after** sich erkundigen nach; **~ s.o. in** jdn hereinbitten; **~ s.o. to do sth** jdn bitten, etw zu tun

asleep *a* **be ~** schlafen; **fall ~** einschlafen

asparagus *n* Spargel *m*

aspect *n* Aspekt *m*

asphalt *n* Asphalt *m*

asphyxiate *vt/i* ersticken

aspirations *npl* Streben *nt*

aspire *vi* **~ to** streben nach

ass *n* Esel *m*

assailant *n* Angreifer(in) *m(f)*

assassin *n* Mörder(in) *m(f)*. **~ate** *vt* ermorden. **~ation** *n* [politischer] Mord *m*

assault *n* (*Mil*) Angriff *m*; (*Jur*) Körperverletzung *f* □*vt* [tätlich] angreifen

assemble *vi* sich versammeln □*vt* versammeln; (*Techn*) montieren

assembly *n* Versammlung *f*; (*Sch*) Andacht *f*; (*Techn*) Montage *f.* **~ line** *n* Fließband *nt*

assent *n* Zustimmung *f*

assert *vt* behaupten; ~ **oneself** sich durchsetzen. ~**ion** *n* Behauptung *f*. ~**ive** *a* be ~**ive** sich durchsetzen können

assess *vt* bewerten; *(fig & for tax purposes)* einschätzen; schätzen ⟨*value*⟩. ~**ment** *n* Einschätzung *f*; *(of tax)* Steuerbescheid *m*

asset *n* Vorteil *m*; ~ **s** *pl (money)* Vermögen *nt*; *(Comm)* Aktiva *pl*

assign *vt* zuweisen (**to** *dat*). ~**ment** *n (task)* Aufgabe *f*

assimilate *vt* aufnehmen

assist *vt/i* helfen (+ *dat*). ~**ance** *n* Hilfe *f*. ~**ant** *a* Hilfs- □*n* Assistent(in) *m(f)*; *(in shop)* Verkäufer(in) *m(f)*

associate[e[1] *vt* verbinden; *(Psych)* assoziieren □*vi* ~**e with** verkehren mit. ~**ion** *n* Verband *m*

associate[2] *a* assoziiert □*n* Kollege *m/*-gin *f*

assortment *n* Mischung *f*

assum|**e** *vt* annehmen; übernehmen ⟨*office*⟩. ~**ing that** angenommen, daß

assumption *n* Annahme *f*

assurance *n* Versicherung *f*; *(confidence)* Selbstsicherheit *f*

assure *vt* versichern (**s.o.** jdm)

asterisk *n* Sternchen *nt*

asthma *n* Asthma *nt*. ~**tic** *a* asthmatisch

astonish *vt* erstaunen. ~**ing** *a* erstaunlich. ~**ment** *n* Erstaunen *nt*

astound *vt* in Erstaunen setzen

astray *adv* go ~ verlorengehen; ⟨*person:*⟩ sich verlaufen; *(fig)* vom rechten Weg abkommen

astride *adv* rittlings

astrolog|**er** *n* Astrologe *m/*-gin *f*. ~**y** *n* Astrologie *f*

astronaut *n* Astronaut(in) *m(f)*

astronom|**er** *n* Astronom *m*. ~**ical** *a* astronomisch. ~**y** *n* Astronomie *f*

astute *a* scharfsinnig

asylum *n* Asyl *nt*

at *prep* an (+ *dat/acc*); *(with town)* in; *(price)* zu; *(speed)* mit; **at the beginning/end** am Anfang/Ende; **at home** zu Hause; **at John's** bei John; **at work/the hairdresser's** bei der Arbeit/beim Friseur; **at school/the office** in der Schule/im Büro; **at a party/wedding** auf einer Party/Hochzeit; **at one o'clock** um ein Uhr; **at Christmas/Easter** zu Weihnachten/Ostern; **at the age of** im Alter von; **at times** manchmal

atheist *n* Atheist(in) *m(f)*

athlet|**e** *n* Athlet(in) *m(f)*. ~**ic** *a* sportlich. ~**ics** *n* Leichtathletik *f*

Atlantic *a & n* the ~ [Ocean] der Atlantik

atlas *n* Atlas *m*

atmospher|**e** *n* Atmosphäre *f*. ~**ic** *a* atmosphärisch

atom *n* Atom *nt*

atomic *a* Atom-

atone *vi* büßen (**for** für). ~**ment** *n* Buße *f*

atrocious *a* abscheulich

atrocity *n* Greueltat *f*

attach *vt* befestigen (**to** an + *dat*); beimessen ⟨*importance*⟩ (**to** *dat*)

attaché *n* Attaché *m*. ~ **case** *n* Aktenkoffer *m*

attachment *n* Bindung *f*; *(tool)* Zubehörteil *nt*; *(additional)* Zusatzgerät *nt*

attack *n* Angriff *m*; *(Med)* Anfall *m* □*vt/i* angreifen. ~**er** *n* Angreifer *m*

attain *vt* erreichen; *(get)* erlangen. ~**able** *a* erreichbar

attempt *n* Versuch *m* □*vt* versuchen

attend *vt* anwesend sein bei; *(go regularly to)* besuchen; *(take part in)* teilnehmen an (+ *dat*); *(accompany)* begleiten; □*vi* anwesend sein; *(pay attention)* aufpassen; ~ **to** sich kümmern um; *(in shop)* bedienen. ~**ance** *n* Anwesenheit *f*; *(number)* Besucherzahl

f. ~ant n Wärter(in) m(f); (in car park) Wächter m

attention n Aufmerksamkeit f; ~! (Mil) stillgestanden! pay ~ aufpassen; **pay** ~ **to** beachten, achten auf (+ acc); **for the** ~ **of** zu Händen von

attentive a aufmerksam

attic n Dachboden m

attitude n Haltung f

attract vt anziehen; erregen (attention). ~**ion** n Anziehungskraft f; (charm) Reiz m; (thing) Attraktion f. ~**ive** a attraktiv

attribute[1] n Attribut nt

attribute[2] vt zuschreiben (**to** dat)

attrition n **war of** ~ Zermürbungskrieg m

aubergine n Aubergine f

auburn a kastanienbraun

auction n Auktion f, Versteigerung f □vt versteigern. ~**eer** n Auktionator m

audaci|ous a verwegen. ~**ty** n Verwegenheit f

audible a hörbar

audience n Publikum nt; (Theat, TV) Zuschauer pl; (Radio) Zuhörer pl; (meeting) Audienz f

audit n Bücherrevision f □vt (Comm) prüfen

audition n (Theat) Vorsprechen nt; (Mus) Vorspielen nt; (for singer) Vorsingen nt □vi vorsprechen; vorspielen; vorsingen

auditor n Buchprüfer m

auditorium n Zuschauerraum m

augment vt vergrößern

augur vi ~ **well/ill** etwas/nichts Gutes verheißen

August n August m

aunt n Tante f

au pair n ~ **[girl]** Au-pair-Mädchen nt

aura n Fluidum nt

auspicious a günstig

austere a streng; (simple) nüchtern. ~**ity** n Strenge f; (hardship) Entbehrung f

Australia n Australien nt. ~**n** a australisch □n Australier(in) m(f)

Austria n Österreich nt. ~**n** a österreichisch □n Österreicher(in) m(f)

authentic a echt, authentisch. ~**ate** vt beglaubigen. ~**ity** n Echtheit f

author n Schriftsteller m, Autor m; (of document) Verfasser m

authoritarian a autoritär

authoritative a maßgebend

authority n Autorität f; (public) Behörde f

authorize vt ermächtigen (s.o.); genehmigen (sth)

autobiography n Autobiographie f

autocratic a autokratisch

autograph n Autogramm nt

automatic a automatisch □n (car) Fahrzeug nt mit Automatikgetriebe

automation n Automation f

autonom|ous a autonom. ~**y** n Autonomie f

autopsy n Autopsie f

autumn n Herbst m. ~**al** a herbstlich

auxiliary a Hilfs- □n Helfer(in) m(f), Hilfskraft f

avail n **to no** ~ vergeblich □vi ~ **oneself of** Gebrauch machen von

available a verfügbar; (obtainable) erhältlich

avalanche n Lawine f

avarice n Habsucht f. ~**ious** a habgierig, habsüchtig

avenge vt rächen

avenue n Allee f

average a Durchschnitts-, durchschnittlich □n Durchschnitt m; **on** ~ im Durchschnitt, durchschnittlich ○vt durchschnittlich schaffen

avers|e a **not be** ~**e to sth** etw (dat) nicht abgeneigt sein. ~**ion** n Abneigung f (**to** gegen)

avert *vt* abwenden

aviation *n* Luftfahrt *f*

avid *a* gierig (**for** nach)

avocado *n* Avocado *f*

avoid *vt* vermeiden; ~ **s.o.** jdm aus dem Weg gehen. ~**ance** *n* Vermeidung *f*

await *vt* warten auf (+ *acc*)

awake *a* wach; **wide** ~ hellwach □ *vi* erwachen

awaken *vt* wecken □ *vi* erwachen. ~**ing** *n* Erwachen *nt*

award *n* Auszeichnung *f*; (*prize*) Preis *m* □ *vt* zuerkennen (**to s.o.** *dat*); verleihen ⟨*prize*⟩

aware *a* bewußt; **become** ~ gewahr werden (**of** *gen*). ~**ness** *n* Bewußtsein *nt*

away *adv* weg, fort; (*absent*) abwesend; **be** ~ nicht da sein; **four kilometres** ~ vier Kilometer entfernt; **play** ~ (*Sport*) auswärts spielen

awe *n* Ehrfurcht *f*

awful *a* furchtbar

awhile *adv* eine Weile

awkward *a* schwierig; (*clumsy*) ungeschickt; (*embarrassing*) peinlich; (*inconvenient*) ungünstig

awning *n* Markise *f*

awry *adv* schief

axe *n* Axt *f* □ *vt* streichen; (*dismiss*) entlassen

axis *n* Achse *f*

axle *n* (*Techn*) Achse *f*

ay[e] *adv* ja □ *n* Jastimme *f*

B

B *n* (*Mus*) H *nt*

babble *vi* plappern; ⟨*stream:*⟩ plätschern

baboon *n* Pavian *m*

baby *n* Baby *nt*

baby: ~**-minder** *n* Tagesmutter *f*. ~**-sit** *vi* babysitten. ~**-sitter** *n* Babysitter *m*

bachelor *n* Junggeselle *m*; **B**~ **of Arts/Science** Bakkalaureus Artium/Scientium

back *n* Rücken *m*; (*reverse*) Rückseite *f*; (*of chair*) Rückenlehne *f*; (*Sport*) Verteidiger *m*; **at/** (*Auto*) **in the** ~ hinten; **on the** ~ auf der Rückseite; ~ **to front** verkehrt; **at the** ~ **of beyond** am Ende der Welt □ *a* Hinter- □ *adv* zurück □ *vt* (*support*) unterstützen; (*with money*) finanzieren; (*Auto*) zurücksetzen; (*Betting*) [Geld] setzen auf (+ *acc*) □ *vi* (*Auto*) zurücksetzen. ~ **down** *vi* klein beigeben. ~ **out** *vi* rückwärts hinaus-/herausfahren; (*fig*) aussteigen (**of** aus). ~ **up** *vt* unterstützen; (*confirm*) bestätigen □ *vi* (*Auto*) zurücksetzen

back: ~**ache** *n* Rückenschmerzen *pl*. ~**biting** *n* gehässiges Gerede *nt*. ~**bone** *n* Rückgrat *nt*. ~**chat** *n* Widerrede *f*. ~**date** *vt* rückdatieren

backer *n* Geldgeber *m*

back: ~**fire** *vi* (*Auto*) fehlzünden; (*fig*) fehlschlagen. ~**ground** *n* Hintergrund *m*. ~**hand** *n* (*Sport*) Rückhand *f*

backing *n* (*support*) Unterstützung *f*; (*material*) Verstärkung *f*

back: ~**lash** *n* (*fig*) Gegenschlag *m*. ~**log** *n* Rückstand *m* (**of** an + *dat*). ~**side** *n* (*fam*) Hintern *m*. ~**stroke** *n* Rückenschwimmen *nt*. ~**up** *n* Unterstützung *f*

backward *a* zurückgeblieben; ⟨*country*⟩ rückständig □ *adv* rückwärts. ~**s** *adv* rückwärts; ~**s and forwards** hin und her

bacon *n* [Schinken]speck *m*

bacteria *npl* Bakterien *pl*

bad *a* schlecht; (*serious*) schwer, schlimm; (*naughty*) unartig; ~ **language** gemeine Ausdrucksweise *f*; **go** ~ schlecht werden

badge *n* Abzeichen *nt*

badger *n* Dachs *m* □ *vt* plagen

badly adv schlecht; (seriously) schwer; ~ off schlecht gestellt; **want** ~ sich (dat) sehnsüchtig wünschen; **need** ~ dringend brauchen

badminton n Federball m

bad-tempered a schlecht gelaunt

baffle vt verblüffen

bag n Tasche f; (of paper) Tüte f; (pouch) Beutel m; ~**s of** (fam) jede Menge □ vt (fam: reserve) in Beschlag nehmen

baggage n [Reise]gepäck nt

baggy a ausgebeult

bagpipes npl Dudelsack m

bail n Kaution f; **on** ~ gegen Kaution □ vt ~ **s.o. out** jdn gegen Kaution freibekommen; (fig) jdm aus der Patsche helfen

bailiff n Gerichtsvollzieher m; (of estate) Gutsverwalter m

bait n Köder m

bake vt/i backen

baker n Bäcker m; ~'**s [shop]** Bäckerei f. ~**y** n Bäckerei f

baking n Backen nt. ~**-powder** n Backpulver nt. ~**-tin** n Backform f

balance n Gleichgewicht nt, Balance f; (scales) Waage f; (Comm) Saldo m; (outstanding sum) Restbetrag m; **[bank]** ~ Kontostand m □ vt balancieren; (equalize) ausgleichen; (Comm) abschließen ⟨books⟩ □ vi balancieren; (fig & Comm) sich ausgleichen. ~ **sheet** n Bilanz f

balcony n Balkon m

bald a kahl; (person) kahlköpfig; **go** ~ eine Glatze bekommen

bale n Ballen m

balk vt vereiteln □ vi ~ **at** zurückschrecken vor (+ dat)

Balkans npl Balkan m

ball[1] n Ball m; (Billiards) Kugel f; (of yarn) Knäuel m & nt; **on the** ~ (fam) auf Draht

ball[2] n (dance) Ball m

ballad n Ballade f

ballast n Ballast m

ball-bearing n Kugellager nt

ballerina n Ballerina f

ballet n Ballett nt. ~ **dancer** n Balletttänzer(in) m(f)

ballistics n Ballistik f

balloon n Luftballon m; (Aviat) Ballon m

ballot n [geheime] Wahl f. ~**-box** n Wahlurne f. ~**-paper** n Stimmzettel m

ball: ~**-point [pen]** n Kugelschreiber m. ~**room** n Ballsaal m

balm n Balsam m

Baltic a & n the ~ **[Sea]** die Ostsee

balustrade n Balustrade f

bamboo n Bambus m

ban n Verbot nt □ vt verbieten

banal a banal

banana n Banane f

band n Band nt; (stripe) Streifen m; (group) Schar f; (Mus) Kapelle f □ vi ~ **together** sich zusammenschließen

bandage n Verband m; (for support) Bandage f □ vt verbinden; bandagieren ⟨limb⟩

bandit n Bandit m

band: ~**stand** n Musikpavillon m. ~**wagon** n **jump on the** ~ **wagon** (fig) sich einer erfolgreichen Sache anschließen

bandy[1] vt wechseln ⟨words⟩

bandy[2] a **be** ~ O-Beine haben. ~-**legged** a O-beinig

bang n (noise) Knall m; (blow) Schlag m □ adv **go** ~ knallen □ int bums! peng! □ vt knallen; (shut noisily) zuknallen; (strike) schlagen (+ acc) □ vi schlagen; ⟨door:⟩ zuknallen

banger n (firework) Knallfrosch m; **old** ~ (fam: car) Klapperkiste f

bangle n Armreifen m

banish vt verbannen

banisters npl [Treppen]geländer nt

banjo n Banjo m

bank[1] n (of river) Ufer nt; (slope) Hang m □vi (Aviat) in die Kurve gehen

bank[2] n Bank f□vt einzahlen. ~ **on** sich verlassen auf (+ acc)

bank account n Bankkonto nt

banker n Bankier m

bank: ~ **holiday** n gesetzlicher Feiertag m. ~**note** n Banknote f

bankrupt a bankrott; **go** ~ bankrott machen □n Bankrotteur m □vt bankrott machen. ~**cy** n Bankrott m

banner n Banner nt

banns npl (Relig) Aufgebot nt

banquet n Bankett nt

baptism n Taufe f

Baptist n Baptist(in) m(f)

baptize vt taufen

bar n Stange f; (of cage) [Gitter]-stab m; (of gold) Barren m; (of chocolate) Tafel f; (of soap) Stück nt; (long) Riegel m; (café) Bar f; (counter) Theke f; (Mus) Takt m; (fig: obstacle) Hindernis nt □vt versperren ⟨way⟩; ausschließen ⟨person⟩ □prep außer

barbarian n Barbar m

barbaric a barbarisch

barbecue n Grill m; (party) Grillfest nt □vt [im Freien] grillen

barbed a ~ **wire** Stacheldraht m

barber n [Herren]friseur m

bar code n Strichkode m

bare a nackt, bloß; ⟨tree⟩ kahl; (empty) leer; (mere) bloß □vt entblößen; fletschen ⟨teeth⟩

bare: ~**back** adv ohne Sattel. ~**faced** a schamlos. ~**foot** adv barfuß

barely adv kaum

bargain n (agreement) Geschäft nt; (good buy) Gelegenheitskauf m □vi handeln; (haggle) feilschen; ~ **for** (expect) rechnen mit

barge n Lastkahn m □vi ~ **in** (fam) hereinplatzen

baritone n Bariton m

bark[1] n (of tree) Rinde f

bark[2] n Bellen nt □vi bellen

barley n Gerste f

bar: ~**maid** n Schankmädchen nt. ~**man** n Barmann m

barn n Scheune f

barometer n Barometer nt

baron n Baron m. ~**ess** n Baronin f

baroque a barock □n Barock nt

barracks npl Kaserne f

barrage n (in river) Wehr nt; (fig) Hagel m

barrel n Faß nt; (of gun) Lauf m

barren a unfruchtbar; ⟨landscape⟩ öde

barricade n Barrikade f

barrier n Barriere f; (across road) Schranke f; (Rail) Sperre f; (fig) Hindernis nt

barrister n [plädierender] Rechtsanwalt m

barrow n Karre f, Karren m

barter vt tauschen (**for** gegen)

base n Fuß m; (fig) Basis f; (Mil) Stützpunkt m □a gemein; (metal) unedel □vt stützen (**on** auf + acc)

base: ~**ball** n Baseball m. ~**ment** n Kellergeschoß nt

bash n Schlag m □vt hauen

bashful a schüchtern

basic a Grund-; (fundamental) grundlegend; (essential) wesentlich; (unadorned) einfach. ~**ally** adv grundsätzlich

basil n Basilikum nt

basin n Becken nt; (for washing) Waschbecken nt; (for food) Schüssel f

basis n Basis f

bask vi sich sonnen

basket n Korb m. ~**ball** n Basketball m

Basle n Basel nt

bass a Baß- □n Baß m; (person) Bassist m

bassoon n Fagott nt
bastard n (sl) Schuft m
baste vt (Culin) begießen
bastion n Bastion f
bat[1] n Schläger m □ vt schlagen
bat[2] n (Zool) Fledermaus f
batch n Gruppe f; (of papers) Stoß m; (of goods) Sendung f
bated a with ~ **breath** mit angehaltenem Atem
bath n Bad nt; (tub) Badewanne f; ~**s** pl Badeanstalt f; **have a** ~ baden □ vt/i baden
bathe vt Bad nt □ vt/i baden. ~**r** n Badende(r) m/f
bathing: ~-**cap** n Bademütze f. ~-**costume** n Badeanzug m
bath: ~-**room** n Badezimmer nt. ~-**towel** n Badetuch nt
baton n (Mus) Taktstock m; (Mil) Stab m
battalion n Bataillon nt
batten n Latte f
batter n (Culin) flüssiger Teig m □ vt schlagen. ~-**ed** a ⟨car⟩ verbeult; ⟨wife⟩ mißhandelt
battery n Batterie f
battle n Schlacht f; (fig) Kampf m □ vi (fig) kämpfen (for um)
battle: ~-**field** n Schlachtfeld nt. ~**ship** n Schlachtschiff nt
Bavaria n Bayern nt. ~**n** a bayrisch □ n Bayer(in) m(f)
bawl vt/i brüllen
bay[1] n (Geog) Bucht f; (Archit) Erker m
bay[2] n (Bot) [echter] Lorbeer m. ~-**leaf** n Lorbeerblatt nt
bayonet n Bajonett nt
bazaar n Basar m
BC abbr (before Christ) v. Chr.
be vi sein; (lie) liegen; (stand) stehen; (cost) kosten; **he is a teacher** er ist Lehrer; **be quiet!** sei still! **I am cold/hot** mir ist kalt/heiß; **how are you?** wie geht es Ihnen? **I am well** mir geht es gut; **there is/are** es gibt; **it's hot, isn't it?** es ist heiß, nicht [wahr]?

it's yours, is it? das gehört also Ihnen? **three and three are six** drei und drei macht sechs □ v aux ~ **reading/going** lesen/gehen; **I am coming/staying** ich komme/bleibe; **what is he doing?** was macht er? **I am being lazy** ich faulenze; **I was thinking of you** ich dachte an dich □ passive werden; **be attacked/deceived** überfallen/betrogen werden
beach n Strand m
beacon n Leuchtfeuer nt; (Naut, Aviat) Bake f
bead n Perle f
beak n Schnabel m
beaker n Becher m
beam n Balken m; (of light) Strahl m □ vi strahlen
bean n Bohne f
bear[1] n Bär m
bear[2] vt/i tragen; (endure) ertragen; gebären ⟨child⟩; ~ **right** sich rechts halten. ~-**able** a erträglich
beard n Bart m
bearing n Haltung f; (Techn) Lager nt; **have a** ~ **on** von Belang sein für; **get one's** ~**s** sich orientieren
beast n Tier nt; (fam: person) Biest nt
beat n Schlag m; (of policeman) Runde f; (rhythm) Takt m □ vt/i schlagen; (thrash) verprügeln; klopfen ⟨carpet⟩; (hammer) hämmern (**on** an + acc). ~ **up** vt zusammenschlagen
beautician n Kosmetikerin f
beauti|**ful** a schön. ~-**fy** vt verschönern
beauty n Schönheit f. ~ **parlour** n Kosmetiksalon m
beaver n Biber m
because conj weil □ adv ~ **of** wegen (+ gen)
beckon vt/i ~ [**to**] herbeiwinken
become vi/i werden. ~-**ing** a ⟨clothes⟩ kleidsam

bed n Bett nt; (*layer*) Schicht f; (*of flowers*) Beet nt; **in** ~ ins *od* zu Bett gehen; ~ **and breakfast** Zimmer mit Frühstück. ~**clothes** npl, ~**ding** n Bettzeug nt

bedlam n Chaos nt

bed: ~**ridden** a bettlägerig. ~**room** n Schlafzimmer nt. ~**sitter** n, ~-**sitting-room** n Wohnschlafzimmer nt. ~**spread** n Tagesdecke f

bee n Biene f

beech n Buche f

beef n Rindfleisch nt. ~**burger** n Hamburger m

bee: ~**hive** n Bienenstock m. ~-**keeper** n Imker(in) m(f)

beer n Bier nt

beet n [sugar] ~ Zuckerrübe f

beetle n Käfer m

beetroot n rote Bete f

before prep vor (+ dat/acc); **the day** ~ **yesterday** vorgestern; ~ **long** bald □adv vorher; (*already*) schon; **never** ~ noch nie; ~ **that** davor □conj (*time*) ehe, bevor. ~**hand** adv vorher, im voraus

beg v □vi betteln □vt (*entreat*) anflehen; (*ask*) bitten (**for** um)

beggar n Bettler(in) m(f)

begin vt/i anfangen, beginnen; to ~ **with** anfangs. ~**ner** n Anfänger(in) m(f). ~**ning** n Anfang m, Beginn m

begrudge vt mißgönnen

beguile vt betören

behalf n **on** ~ **of** im Namen von; **on my** ~ meinetwegen

behave vi sich verhalten; ~ **oneself** sich benehmen

behaviour n Verhalten nt; **good/bad** ~ gutes/schlechtes Benehmen nt

behead vt enthaupten

behind prep hinter (+ dat/acc); **be** ~ **sth** hinter etw (dat) stecken □adv hinten; (*late*) im Rückstand; **a long way** ~ weit zurück □n

(*fam*) Hintern m. ~**hand** adv im Rückstand

behold vt (*liter*) sehen

beholden a verbunden (**to** dat)

beige a beige

being n Dasein nt; **living** ~ Lebewesen nt

belated a verspätet

belch vi rülpsen □vt ~ **out** ausstoßen ⟨smoke⟩

belfry n Glockenstube f; (*tower*) Glockenturm m

Belgian a belgisch □n Belgier(in) m(f)

Belgium n Belgien nt

belief n Glaube m

believable a glaubhaft

believe vt/i glauben (**s.o.** jdm; **in** an + acc). ~**r** n (*Relig*) Gläubige(r) m/f

bell n Glocke f; (*on door*) Klingel f

belligerent a kriegführend; (*aggressive*) streitlustig

bellow vt/i brüllen

bellows npl Blasebalg m

belly n Bauch m

belong vi gehören (**to** dat); (*be member*) angehören (**to** dat). ~**ings** npl Sachen pl

beloved a geliebt □n Geliebte(r) m/f

below prep unter (+ dat/acc) □adv unten; (*Naut*) unter Deck

belt n Gürtel m; (*area*) Zone f; (*Techn*) [Treib]riemen m □vi (*fam: rush*) rasen □vt (*fam: hit*) hauen

bench n Bank f; (*work-*) Werkbank f

bend n Biegung f; (*in road*) Kurve f □v □vt biegen; beugen ⟨arm⟩ □vi sich biegen; ⟨thing:⟩ sich biegen; ⟨road:⟩ eine Biegung machen. ~**down** vi sich bücken. ~ **over** vi sich vornüberbeugen

beneath prep unter (+ dat/acc); ~ **him** (fig) unter seiner Würde □adv darunter

benediction n (*Relig*) Segen m

benefactor n Wohltäter(in) m(f)
beneficial a nützlich
benefit n Vorteil m; (allowance) Unterstützung f; (insurance) Leistung f; **sickness ~** Krankengeld nt □v □vt nützen (+ dat) □vi profitieren (**from** von)
benevolen|ce n Wohlwollen nt. **~t** a wohlwollend
bent a(u) ⟨person⟩ gebeugt; (distorted) verbogen; (fam: dishonest) korrupt; **be ~ on doing sth** darauf erpicht sein, etw zu tun □n Hang m, Neigung f (**for** zu)
be|queath vt vermachen (**to** dat). **~quest** n Vermächtnis nt
bereave|d n the **~d** pl die Hinterbliebenen. **~ment** n Trauerfall m; (state) Trauer f
bereft a **~ of** beraubt (+ gen)
beret n Baskenmütze f
Berne n Bern nt
berry n Beere f
berserk a **go ~** wild werden
berth n (on ship) [Schlaf]koje f; (ship's anchorage) Liegeplatz m
beseech vt anflehen
beside prep neben (+ dat/acc); **~ oneself** außer sich (dat)
besides prep außer (+ dat) □adv außerdem
besiege vt belagern
best a im beste(r,s); **the ~** der/die/ das Beste; **at ~** bestenfalls; **all the ~!** alles Gute! **do one's ~** sein Bestes tun □adv am besten; **as ~ I could** so gut ich konnte. **~ man** n ≈ Trauzeuge m
bestseller n Bestseller m
bet n Wette f □vt **~ s.o. £5** mit jdm um £5 wetten □vi wetten; **~ on** [Geld] setzen auf (+ acc)
betray vt verraten. **~al** n Verrat m
better a besser; **get ~** sich bessern; (after illness) sich erholen □adv besser; **~ off** besser dran; **~ not** lieber nicht; **all the ~** um so besser; **the sooner the ~** je eher,

desto besser □vt verbessern; (do better than) übertreffen
betting shop n Wettbüro nt
between prep zwischen (+ dat/ acc); **~ you and me** unter uns □adv [in] ~ dazwischen
beverage n Getränk nt
beware vi sich in acht nehmen (**of** vor + dat); **~ of the dog!** Vorsicht, bissiger Hund!
bewilder vt verwirren
beyond prep über (+ acc) ... hinaus; (further) weiter als; **~ reach** außer Reichweite; **~ doubt** ohne jeden Zweifel □adv darüber hinaus
bias n Voreingenommenheit f; (preference) Vorliebe f; (Jur) Befangenheit f □vt (influence) beeinflussen. **~ed** a voreingenommen; (Jur) befangen
bib n Lätzchen nt
Bible n Bibel f
biblical a biblisch
bibliography n Bibliographie f
bicarbonate n **~ of soda** doppeltkohlensaures Natron nt
bicycle n Fahrrad nt
bid¹ n Gebot nt; (attempt) Versuch m □vt/i bieten (**for** auf + acc); (Cards) reizen
bid² vt (liter) heißen; **~ s.o. welcome** jdn willkommen heißen
bide vi **~ one's time** den richtigen Moment abwarten
biennial a zweijährlich; (lasting two years) zweijährig
bier n [Toten]bahre f
bifocals npl [**pair of**] **~** Bifokalbrille f
big a groß □adv talk **~** (fam) angeben
bigam|ist n Bigamist m. **~y** n Bigamie f
bigot n Eiferer m. **~ed** a engstirnig
bigwig n (fam) hohes Tier nt
bike n (fam) [Fahr]rad nt
bikini n Bikini m

bilberry n Heidelbeere f

bile n Galle f

bilingual a zweisprachig

bill[1] n Rechnung f; (poster) Plakat nt; (Pol) Gesetzentwurf m; ~ of exchange Wechsel m □vt eine Rechnung schicken (+ dat)

bill[2] n (beak) Schnabel m

billet n (Mil) Quartier nt □vt einquartieren (on bei)

billiards n Billard nt

billion n (thousand million) Milliarde f; (million million) Billion f

bin n Mülleimer m; (for bread) Kasten m

bind vt binden (to an + acc); (bandage) verbinden; (Jur) verpflichten; (cover the edge of) einfassen. ~**ing** a verbindlich □ n Einband m; (braid) Borte f; (on ski) Bindung f

binge n (fam) go on the ~ eine Sauftour machen

binoculars npl [pair of] ~ Fernglas nt

bio|chemistry n Biochemie f. ~**degradable** a biologisch abbaubar

biography n Biographie f

biological a biologisch

biolog|ist n Biologe m. ~**y** n Biologie f

birch n Birke f; (whip) Rute f

bird n Vogel m; **kill two ~s with one stone** zwei Fliegen mit einer Klappe schlagen

Biro (P) n Kugelschreiber m

birth n Geburt f

birth: ~ **certificate** n Geburtsurkunde f. ~**control** n Geburtenregelung f. ~**day** n Geburtstag m. ~**mark** n Muttermal nt

biscuit n Keks m

bisect vt halbieren

bishop n Bischof m; (Chess) Läufer m

bit[1] n Stückchen nt; (for horse) Gebiß nt; (Techn) Bohreinsatz m;

a ~ ein bißchen; ~ **by** ~ nach und nach

bitch n Hündin f; (sl) Luder nt. ~**y** a gehässig

bite n Biß m; [insect] ~ Stich m; (mouthful) Bissen m □vt/i beißen; ⟨insect:⟩ stechen; kauen ⟨one's nails⟩

bitter a bitter; **cry** ~**ly** bitterlich weinen; ~**ly cold** bitterkalt □n bitteres Bier nt

bizarre a bizarr

black a schwarz; **be** ~ **and blue** grün und blau sein □n Schwarz nt; (person) Schwarze(r) m/f □vt schwärzen; boykottieren ⟨goods⟩

black: ~**berry** n Brombeere f. ~**bird** n Amsel f. ~**board** n (Sch) [Wand]tafel f. ~**currant** n schwarze Johannisbeere f

blacken vt/i schwärzen

black: ~**eye** n blaues Auge nt. **B**~ **Forest** n Schwarzwald m. ~**ice** n Glatteis nt. ~**leg** n Streikbrecher m. ~**list** vt auf die schwarze Liste setzen. ~**mail** n Erpressung f □vt erpressen. ~**market** n schwarzer Markt m. ~**smith** n [Huf]schmied m

bladder n (Anat) Blase f

blade n Klinge f; (of grass) Halm m

blame n Schuld f □vt die Schuld geben (+ dat); **no one is to** ~ keiner ist schuld daran

blanch vi blaß werden □vt (Culin) blanchieren

blancmange n Pudding m

bland a mild

blank a leer; ⟨look⟩ ausdruckslos □n Lücke f; (cartridge) Platzpatrone f. ~ **cheque** n Blankoscheck m

blanket n Decke f

blare vt/i schmettern

blasé a blasiert

blaspheme vi lästern

blasphem|ous a [gottes]lästerlich. ~**y** n [Gottes]lästerung f

blast n (gust) Luftstoß m; (sound) Stoß m □vt sprengen □int (sl) verdammt

blast: ~**-furnace** n Hochofen m. ~**-off** n (of missile) Start m

blatant a offensichtlich

blaze n Feuer nt □vi brennen

blazer n Blazer m

bleach n Bleichmittel n □vt/i bleichen

bleak a öde; (fig) trostlos

bleat vi blöken; ⟨goat:⟩ meckern

bleed vi bluten □vt entlüften ⟨radiator⟩

bleep n Piepton m □vi piepsen □vt mit dem Piepser rufen □ ~**er** n Piepser m

blemish n Makel m

blend n Mischung f □vt mischen □vi sich vermischen. ~**er** n (Culin) Mixer m

bless vt segnen. ~**ed** a heilig; (sl) verflixt. ~**ing** n Segen m

blight n (Bot) Brand m

blind a blind; ⟨corner⟩ unübersichtlich; ~ **man/woman** Blinde(r) m/f □n [roller] ~ Rouleau nt □vt blenden

blind: ~ **alley** n Sackgasse f. ~**fold** a & adv mit verbundenen Augen □n Augenbinde f □vt die Augen verbinden (+ dat). ~**ness** n Blindheit f

blink vi blinzeln; ⟨light:⟩ blinken

blinkers npl Scheuklappen pl

bliss n Glückseligkeit f. ~**ful** a glücklich

blister n (Med) Blase f

blizzard n Schneesturm m

blob n Klecks m

bloc n (Pol) Block m

block n Block m; (of wood) Klotz m; (of flats) [Wohn]block m □vt blockieren. ~ **up** vt zustopfen

blockade n Blockade f □vt blockieren

blockage n Verstopfung f

bloke n (fam) Kerl m

blonde a blond □n Blondine f

blood n Blut nt

blood: ~ **count** n Blutbild nt. ~ **donor** n Blutspender m. ~ **group** n Blutgruppe f. ~**hound** n Bluthund m. ~**-poisoning** n Blutvergiftung f. ~ **pressure** n Blutdruck m. ~**shed** n Blutvergießen nt. ~**shot** a blutunterlaufen. ~**stream** n Blutbahn f. ~**thirsty** a blutdürstig. ~ **transfusion** n Blutübertragung f. ~**-vessel** n Blutgefäß nt

bloody a blutig; (sl) verdammt. ~**-minded** a (sl) stur

bloom n Blüte f □vi blühen

blossom n Blüte f □vi blühen

blot n [Tinten]klecks m; (fig) Fleck m. ~ **out** vt auslöschen

blotch n Fleck m. ~**y** a fleckig

blotting-paper n Löschpapier nt

blouse n Bluse f

blow¹ n Schlag m

blow² vt blasen; (fam: squander) verpulvern; ~ **one's nose** sich (dat) die Nase putzen □vi blasen; ⟨fuse:⟩ durchbrennen. ~ **up** vt (inflate) aufblasen; (enlarge) vergrößern; (shatter by explosion) sprengen □vi explodieren

blow: ~**-dry** vt fönen. ~**-fly** n Schmeißfliege f. ~**-lamp** n Lötlampe f

bludgeon vt (fig) zwingen

blue a blau □n Blau nt; out of the ~ aus heiterem Himmel

blue: ~**bell** n Sternhyazinthe f. ~**berry** n Heidelbeere f. ~**bottle** n Schmeißfliege f. ~**print** n (fig) Entwurf m

bluff n Bluff m □vi bluffen

blunder n Schnitzer m

blunt a stumpf; ⟨person⟩ geradeheraus

blur n it's all a ~ alles ist verschwommen □vt verschwommen machen

blurb n Klappentext m

blurt vt ~ **out** herausplatzen mit

blush vi erröten

boar n Eber m

board n Brett nt; (*for notices*) schwarzes Brett nt; (*committee*) Ausschuß m; (*of directors*) Vorstand m; **on ~** an Bord; **full ~** Vollpension f; **~ and lodging** Unterkunft und Verpflegung pl; **go by the ~** (*fam*) unter den Tisch fallen □vt einsteigen in (+ acc); (*Naut, Aviat*) besteigen □vi an Bord gehen

board: ~-game n Brettspiel nt. **~ing-house** n Pension f. **~ing-school** n Internat nt

boast vt sich rühmen (+ gen) □vi prahlen (about mit). **~ful** a prahlerisch

boat n Boot nt; (*ship*) Schiff nt

bob vi knicksen; **~ up and down** sich auf und ab bewegen

bobbin n Spule f

bob-sleigh n Bob m

bode vi **~ well/ill** etwas/nichts Gutes verheißen

bodice n Mieder nt

body n Körper m; (*corpse*) Leiche f; (*corporation*) Körperschaft f. **~guard** n Leibwächter m. **~work** n (*Auto*) Karosserie f

bog n Sumpf m □vi **get ~ged down** steckenbleiben

bogus a falsch

boil[1] n Furunkel m

boil[2] n bring/come to the ~ zum Kochen bringen/kommen □vt/i kochen; **~ed potatoes** Salzkartoffeln pl

boiler n Heizkessel m. **~suit** n Overall m

boisterous a übermütig

bold a kühn; (*Typ*) fett

bollard n Poller m

bolster n Nackenrolle f □vt **~ up** Mut machen (+ dat)

bolt n Riegel m; (*Techn*) Bolzen m; **nuts and ~s** Schrauben und Muttern pl □vt schrauben (to an + acc); verriegeln 〈*door*〉 □adv **~ upright** adv kerzengerade

bomb n Bombe f □vt bombardieren

bombard vt beschießen; (*fig*) bombardieren

bombastic a bombastisch

bomber n (*Aviat*) Bomber m; (*person*) Bombenleger(in) m(f)

bond n (*fig*) Band nt; (*Comm*) Obligation f

bondage n (*fig*) Sklaverei f

bone n Knochen m; (*of fish*) Gräte f □vt von den Knochen lösen 〈*meat*〉; entgräten 〈*fish*〉. **~-'dry** a knochentrocken

bonfire n Gartenfeuer nt; (*celebratory*) Freudenfeuer nt

bonnet n Haube f

bonus n Prämie f; (*gratuity*) Gratifikation f; (*fig*) Plus nt

bony a knochig; 〈*fish*〉 grätig

boo int buh! □vt ausbuhen □vi buhen

boob n (*fam: mistake*) Schnitzer m

book n Buch nt; (*of tickets*) Heft nt; **keep the ~s** (*Comm*) die Bücher führen □vt/i buchen; (*reserve*) [vor]bestellen; (*for offence*) aufschreiben

book: ~case n Bücherregal nt. **~-ends** npl Buchstützen pl. **~ing-office** n Fahrkartenschalter m. **~-keeping** n Buchführung f. **~let** n Broschüre f. **~maker** n Buchmacher m. **~mark** n Lesezeichen nt. **~shop** n Buchhandlung f

boom n (*Comm*) Hochkonjunktur f; (*upturn*) Aufschwung m □vi dröhnen; (*fig*) blühen

boon n Segen m

boor n Flegel m

boost n Auftrieb m □vt Auftrieb geben (+ dat)

boot n Stiefel m; (*Auto*) Kofferraum m

booth n Bude f; (*cubicle*) Kabine f

booty n Beute f

border n Rand m; (frontier) Grenze f; (in garden) Rabatte f □vi ~ **on** grenzen an (+ acc)

bore[1] vt/i (Techn) bohren

bor|e[2] n (of gun) Kaliber nt; (person) langweiliger Mensch m; (thing) langweilige Sache f □vt langweilen; **be ~ed** sich langweilen. **~edom** n Langeweile f. **~ing** a langweilig

born pp **be ~** geboren werden

borough n Stadtgemeinde f

borrow vt [sich (dat)] borgen od leihen (**from** von)

bosom n Busen m

boss n (fam) Chef m. **~y** a herrschsüchtig

botanical a botanisch

botan|ist n Botaniker(in) m(f). **~y** n Botanik f

botch vt verpfuschen

both a & pron beide; **~ [of] the children** beide Kinder □adv **~ men and women** sowohl Männer als auch Frauen

bother n Mühe f; (minor trouble) Ärger m □vt belästigen; (disturb) stören □vi sich kümmern (**about** um)

bottle n Flasche f □vt auf Flaschen abfüllen; (preserve) einmachen

bottle: ~neck n (fig) Engpaß m. **~-opener** n Flaschenöffner m

bottom a unterste(r,s) □n (of container) Boden m; (of river) Grund m; (of page) Fuß m; (buttocks) Hintern m. **~less** a bodenlos

bough n Ast m

boulder n Felsblock m

bounce vi [auf]springen; (cheque) (fam) nicht gedeckt sein □vt aufspringen lassen (ball)

bouncer n (fam) Rausschmeißer m

bound[1] n Sprung m □vi springen

bound[2] a **be ~ to do sth** etw bestimmt machen; (obliged) verpflichtet sein, etw zu machen

boundary n Grenze f

boundless a grenzenlos

bouquet n [Blumen]strauß m; (of wine) Bukett nt

bourgeois a (pej) spießbürgerlich

bout n (Med) Anfall m; (Sport) Kampf m

bow[1] n (weapon & Mus) Bogen m; (knot) Schleife f

bow[2] n Verbeugung f □vi sich verbeugen □vt neigen (head)

bow[3] n (Naut) Bug m

bowel n Darm m; (pl) movement Stuhlgang m. **~s** pl Eingeweide pl

bowl[1] n Schüssel f; (shallow) Schale f

bowl[2] vt/i werfen. **~ over** vt umwerfen

bow-legged a O-beinig

bowler[1] n (Sport) Werfer m

bowler[2] n **~ [hat]** Melone f

bowling n Kegeln nt. **~-alley** n Kegelbahn f

bowls n Bowlsspiel nt

bow-'tie n Fliege f

box[1] n Schachtel f; (wooden) Kiste f; (cardboard) Karton m; (Theat) Loge f

box[2] vt/i (Sport) boxen

box|er n Boxer m. **~ing** n Boxen nt. **B~ing Day** n zweiter Weihnachtstag m

box: ~-office n (Theat) Kasse f. **~-room** n Abstellraum m

boy n Junge m

boycott n Boykott m □vt boykottieren

boy: ~friend n Freund m. **~ish** a jungenhaft

bra n BH m

brace n Strebe f, Stütze f; (dental) Zahnspange f; **~s** npl Hosenträger mpl □vt **~ oneself** (fig) sich gefaßt machen (**for** auf + acc)

bracelet n Armband nt

bracken n Farnkraut nt

bracket n Konsole f; (group) Gruppe f; (Typ) **round/square**

~s runde/eckige Klammern □*vt* einklammern

brag *vi* prahlen (**about** mit)

braid *n* Borte *f*

braille *n* Blindenschrift *f*

brain *n* Gehirn *nt*; ~s ⟨*fig*⟩ Intelligenz *f*

brain: ~**child** *n* geistiges Produkt *nt*. ~**wash** *vt* einer Gehirnwäsche unterziehen. ~**wave** *n* Geistesblitz *m*

brainy *a* klug

braise *vt* schmoren

brake *n* Bremse *f* □*vt/i* bremsen. ~**light** *n* Bremslicht *nt*

bramble *n* Brombeerstrauch *m*

bran *n* Kleie *f*

branch *n* Ast *m*; ⟨*fig*⟩ Zweig *m*; ⟨*Comm*⟩ Zweigstelle *f*; ⟨*shop*⟩ Filiale *f*. ~ **out** *vi* ~ **out into** sich verlegen auf (+ *acc*)

brand *n* Marke *f* □*vt* ⟨*fig*⟩ brandmarken als

brandish *vt* schwingen

brand-new *a* nagelneu

brandy *n* Weinbrand *m*

brass *n* Messing *nt*; ⟨*Mus*⟩ Blech *nt*; **top** ~ ⟨*fam*⟩ hohe Tiere *pl*. ~ **band** *n* Blaskapelle *f*

brassiere *n* Büstenhalter *m*

brave *a* tapfer □*vt* die Stirn bieten (+ *dat*). ~**ry** *n* Tapferkeit *f*

brawl *n* Schlägerei *f* □*vi* sich schlagen

bray *vi* iahen

brazen *a* unverschämt

brazier *n* Kohlenbecken *nt*

Brazil *n* Brasilien *nt*. ~**ian** *a* brasilianisch. ~ **nut** *n* Paranuß *f*

breach *n* Bruch *m*; ⟨*Mil & fig*⟩ Bresche *f* □*vt* durchbrechen

bread *n* Brot *nt*

bread: ~**crumbs** *npl* Brotkrümel *pl*; ⟨*Culin*⟩ Paniermehl *nt*. ~**line** *n* be on the ~ line gerade genug zum Leben haben

breadth *n* Breite *f*

'bread-winner *n* Brotverdiener *m*

break *n* Bruch *m*; ⟨*interval*⟩ Pause *f*; ⟨*interruption*⟩ Unterbrechung *f*; ⟨*fam: chance*⟩ Chance *f* □*vt* brechen; ⟨*smash*⟩ zerbrechen; ⟨*damage*⟩ kaputtmachen ⟨*fam*⟩; ⟨*interrupt*⟩ unterbrechen; **one's arm** sich ⟨*dat*⟩ den Arm brechen □*vi* brechen; ⟨*day:*⟩ anbrechen; ⟨*storm:*⟩ losbrechen; ⟨*thing:*⟩ kaputtgehen ⟨*fam*⟩; ⟨*rope:*⟩ reißen; ⟨*news:*⟩ bekanntwerden. ~ **down** *vi* zusammenbrechen; ⟨*Techn*⟩ eine Panne haben; ⟨*negotiations:*⟩ scheitern □*vt* aufbrechen ⟨*door*⟩; aufgliedern ⟨*figures*⟩. ~ **in** *vi* einbrechen. ~ **off** *vt/i* abbrechen; lösen ⟨*engagement*⟩

'break|able *a* zerbrechlich. ~ **n** Bruch *m*. ~**down** *n* ⟨*Techn*⟩ Panne *f*; ⟨*Med*⟩ Zusammenbruch *m*; ⟨*of figures*⟩ Aufgliederung *f*

breakfast *n* Frühstück *m*

breakthrough *n* Durchbruch *m*

breast *n* Brust *f*. ~**bone** *n* Brustbein *nt*. ~**feed** *vt* stillen. ~**stroke** *n* Brustschwimmen *nt*

breath *n* Atem *m*; **out of** ~ außer Atem

breathalyse *vt* ins Röhrchen blasen lassen. ~**r (P)** *n* Röhrchen *nt*

breathe *vt/i* atmen

breather *n* Atempause *f*. ~**ing** *n* Atmen *nt*

breath: ~**less** *a* atemlos. ~**taking** *a* atemberaubend. ~ **test** *n* Alcotest (P) *m*

breed *n* Rasse *f* □*vt* züchten; ⟨*give rise to*⟩ erzeugen □*vi* sich vermehren. ~**er** *n* Züchter *m*. ~**ing** *n* Zucht *f*; ⟨*fig*⟩ [gute] Lebensart *f*

breez|e *n* Lüftchen *nt*; ⟨*Naut*⟩ Brise *f*. ~**y** *a* [leicht] windig

brew *n* Gebräu *nt* □*vt* brauen; kochen ⟨*tea*⟩ □*vi* ⟨*fig*⟩ sich zusammenbrauen. ~**er** *n* Brauer *m*. ~**ery** *n* Brauerei *f*

bribe n (money) Bestechungsgeld nt □ vt bestechen. **~ry** n Bestechung f

brick n Ziegelstein m, Backstein m. □ vt ~ **up** zumauern

'bricklayer n Maurer m

bridal a Braut-

bride n Braut f. ~**groom** n Bräutigam m. **~smaid** n Brautjungfer f

bridge[1] n Brücke f; (of nose) Nasenrücken m

bridge[2] n (Cards) Bridge nt

bridle n Zaum m. ~**path** n Reitweg m

brief[1] a kurz

brief[2] n Instruktionen pl; (Jur: case) Mandat nt □ vt Instruktionen geben (+ dat); (Jur) beauftragen. ~**case** n Aktentasche f

briefing n Informationsgespräch nt

briefs npl Slip m

brigad|**e** n Brigade f. ~**ier** n Brigadegeneral m

bright a hell; (day) heiter

bright|**en** v ~**en** [**up**] □ vt aufheitern □ vi sich aufheitern. ~**ness** n Helligkeit f

brilliance n Glanz m; (of person) Genialität f

brilliant a glänzend; (person) genial

brim n Rand m; (of hat) Krempe f

brine n Salzwasser nt; (Culin) [Salz]lake f

bring vt bringen. ~ **about** vt verursachen. ~ **along** vt mitbringen. ~ **off** vt vollbringen. ~ **round** vt vorbeibringen; (persuade) überreden; wieder zum Bewußtsein bringen (unconscious person). ~ **up** vt heraufbringen; (vomit) erbrechen; aufziehen (children); erwähnen (question)

brink n Rand m

brisk a lebhaft; schnell

bristl|**e** n Borste f. ~**ly** a borstig

Brit|**ain** n Großbritannien nt. ~**ish** a britisch; **the ~ish** die Briten pl. ~**on** n Brite m/Britin f

Brittany n die Bretagne

brittle a brüchig, spröde

broach vt anzapfen; anschneiden (subject)

broad a breit; (hint) deutlich; **in daylight** am hellichten Tag. ~ **beans** npl dicke Bohnen pl

'broadcast n Sendung f □ vt/i senden

broad'minded a tolerant

brocade n Brokat m

broccoli n inv Brokkoli pl

brochure n Broschüre f

broke a (fam) pleite

broken a zerbrochen, (fam) kaputt

broker n Makler m

bronchitis n Bronchitis f

bronze n Bronze f

brooch n Brosche f

brood n Brut f □ vi brüten; (fig) grübeln

brook[1] n Bach m

brook[2] vt dulden

broom n Besen m; (Bot) Ginster m. ~**stick** n Besenstiel m

broth n Brühe f

brothel n Bordell nt

brother n Bruder m

brother: ~**in-law** n Schwager m. ~**ly** a brüderlich

brow n Augenbraue f; (forehead) Stirn f; (of hill) [Berg]kuppe f

'browbeat vt einschüchtern

brown a braun □ n Braun nt □ vt bräunen □ vi braun werden

Brownie n Wichtel m

browse vi (read) schmökern; (in shop) sich umsehen

bruise n blauer Fleck m □ vt beschädigen (fruit); ~ **one's arm** sich (dat) den Arm quetschen

brunch n Brunch m

brunette n Brünette f

Brunswick n Braunschweig nt

brunt n **the ~ of** die volle Wucht (+ gen)

brush n Bürste f; (with handle)
Handfeger m; (for paint) Pinsel m
□ vt bürsten; putzen ⟨teeth⟩. ~ **up**
vt/i (fig) ~ **up** [on] auffrischen

brusque a brüsk

Brussels n Brüssel nt. ~ **sprouts**
npl Rosenkohl m

brutal a brutal. ~**ity** n Brutalität
f

brute n Unmensch m. ~ **force** n
rohe Gewalt f

bubble n [Luft]blase f □ vi sprudeln

buck[1] n (deer & Gym) Bock m;
(rabbit) Rammler m □ vi ⟨horse:⟩
bocken. ~ **up** vi (fam) sich aufheitern; (hurry) sich beeilen

buck[2] n pass the ~ die Verantwortung abschieben

bucket n Eimer m

buckle n Schnalle f □ vt zuschnallen □ vi sich verbiegen

bud n Knospe f

Buddhis|**m** n Buddhismus m. ~**t**
a buddhistisch □ n Buddhist(in)
m(f)

budge vt bewegen □ vi sich [von
der Stelle] rühren

budgerigar n Wellensittich m

budget n Budget nt; (Pol) Haushaltsplan m; (money available) Etat m □ vi ~ **for** sth etw
einkalkulieren

buff a sandfarben □ vt polieren

buffalo n Büffel m

buffer n (Rail) Puffer m

buffet[1] n Büfett nt; (on station)
Imbißstube f

buffet[2] vt hin und her werfen

buffoon n Narr m

bug n Wanze f; (fam: virus) Bazillus m; (fam: device) Abhörgerät
nt, (fam) Wanze f □ vt (fam) verwanzen ⟨room⟩; abhören ⟨telephone⟩

buggy n [Kinder]sportwagen m

bugle n Signalhorn m

build n (of person) Körperbau m
□ vt/i bauen

builder n Bauunternehmer m

building n Gebäude nt. ~ **site** n
Baustelle f. ~ **society** n Bausparkasse f

built-in a eingebaut

bulb n [Blumen]zwiebel f; (Electr)
[Glüh]birne f

Bulgaria n Bulgarien nt

bulge n Ausbauchung f □ vi sich
ausbauchen

bulk n Masse f; (greater part)
Hauptteil m; **in** ~ en gros; (loose)
lose. ~**y** a sperrig; (large) massig

bull n Bulle m, Stier m

bulldog n Bulldogge f

bulldozer n Planierraupe f

bullet n Kugel f

bulletin n Bulletin nt

'bullet-proof a kugelsicher

'bullfight n Stierkampf m. ~**er** n
Stierkämpfer m

'bullfinch n Dompfaff m

bullion n **gold** ~ Barrengold nt

bullock n Ochse m

bull: ~**ring** n Stierkampfarena f.
~**'s-eye** n **score a** ~**'s-eye** ins
Schwarze treffen

bully n Tyrann m □ vt tyrannisieren

bum n (sl) Hintern m

bumble-bee n Hummel f

bump n Bums m; (swelling) Beule
f; (in road) holperige Stelle f □ vt
stoßen

bumper n (Auto) Stoßstange f

bumpy a holperig

bun n Milchbrötchen nt; (hair)
[Haar]knoten m

bunch n (of flowers) Strauß m; (of
keys) Bund m; ~ **of grapes**
[ganze] Weintraube f

bundle n Bündel nt □ vt ~ **[up]**
bündeln

bungalow n Bungalow m

bungle vt verpfuschen

bunion n (Med) Ballen m

bunk n [Schlaf]koje f. ~**-beds** npl
Etagenbett nt

bunker n Bunker m

buoy n Boje f. ~ **up** vt ⟨fig⟩ stärken

buoyan|cy n Auftrieb m. ~**t a** be ~**t** schwimmen; ⟨water:⟩ gut tragen

burden n Last f □vt belasten

bureau n ⟨desk⟩ Sekretär m; ⟨office⟩ Büro nt

bureaucracy n Bürokratie f

bureaucrat n Bürokrat m. ~**ic a** bürokratisch

burglar n Einbrecher m. ~**alarm** n Alarmanlage f

burglary n Einbruch m

burgle vt einbrechen in (+ acc); **they have been ~d** bei ihnen ist eingebrochen worden

Burgundy n Burgund nt; **b**~ ⟨wine⟩ Burgunder m

burial n Begräbnis nt

burly a stämmig

Burm|a n Birma nt. ~**ese a** & n burmanisch

burn n Verbrennung f; ⟨on skin⟩ Brandwunde f; ⟨on material⟩ Brandstelle f □vt verbrennen □vi brennen; ⟨food:⟩ anbrennen

burnish vt polieren

burp vi ⟨fam⟩ aufstoßen

burrow n Bau m □vi wühlen

bursar n Rechnungsführer m. ~**y** n Stipendium nt

burst n Bruch m; ⟨surge⟩ Ausbruch m □vt platzen machen □vi platzen

bury vt begraben; ⟨hide⟩ vergraben

bus n [Auto]bus m

bush n Strauch m; ⟨land⟩ Busch m. ~**y** a buschig

business n Angelegenheit f; ⟨Comm⟩ Geschäft nt; **on** ~ geschäftlich; **he has no** ~ **to** er hat kein Recht, zu; **mind one's own** ~ sich um seine eigenen Angelegenheiten kümmern; **that's none of your** ~ das geht Sie nichts an. ~**-like** a geschäftsmäßig. ~**man** n Geschäftsmann m

busker n Straßenmusikant m

'**bus-stop** n Bushaltestelle f

bust[1] n Büste f

bust[2] a ⟨fam⟩ kaputt; **go** ~ pleite machen

bustl|e n Betrieb m, Getriebe nt □vi ~**e about** geschäftig hin und her laufen. ~**ing** a belebt

'**bust-up** n ⟨fam⟩ Streit m

busy a beschäftigt; ⟨day⟩ voll; ⟨street⟩ belebt; ⟨with traffic⟩ stark befahren; **be** ~ zu tun haben □vt ~ **oneself** sich beschäftigen (**with** mit)

'**busybody** n Wichtigtuer(in) m(f)

but conj aber; ⟨after negative⟩ sondern □prep außer (+ dat); ~ **for** ⟨without⟩ ohne (+ acc); **the last** ~ **one** der/die/das vorletzte; **the next** ~ **one** der/die/das übernächste □adv nur

butcher n Fleischer m, Metzger m; ~'**s [shop]** Fleischerei f, Metzgerei f □vt [ab]schlachten

butler n Butler m

butt n ⟨of gun⟩ [Gewehr]kolben m; ⟨fig: target⟩ Zielscheibe f; ⟨of cigarette⟩ Stummel m; ⟨for water⟩ Regentonne f □vt mit dem Kopf stoßen □vi ~ **in** unterbrechen

butter n Butter f □vt mit Butter bestreichen. ~ **up** vt ⟨fam⟩ schmeicheln (+ dat)

butter: ~**cup** n Butterblume f. ~**fly** n Schmetterling m

buttocks npl Gesäß nt

button n Knopf m □vt ~ **[up]** zuknöpfen. ~**hole** n Knopfloch nt

buttress n Strebepfeiler m

buxom a drall

buy n Kauf m □vt kaufen. ~**er** n Käufer(in) m(f)

buzz n Summen nt □vi summen. ~ **off** vi ⟨fam⟩ abhauen

buzzard n Bussard m

buzzer n Summer m

by prep ⟨close to⟩ bei (+ dat); ⟨next to⟩ neben (+ dat/acc); ⟨past⟩ an (+ dat) . . . vorbei; ⟨to the extent of⟩ um (+ acc); ⟨at the latest⟩ bis;

(*by means of*) durch; **by** Mozart/
Dickens von Mozart/Dickens; ~
oneself allein; ~ **the sea** am
Meer; ~ **car/bus** mit dem Auto/
Bus; ~ **sea** mit dem Schiff; ~ **the
hour** pro Stunde; ~ **the metre**
meterweise □*adv* ~ **and** ~ mit
der Zeit; ~ **and large** im großen
und ganzen

bye *int* (*fam*) tschüs

by: ~**-election** *n* Nachwahl *f*.
~**gone** *a* vergangen. ~**-law** *n*
Verordnung *f*. ~**pass** *n* Umgehungsstraße *f*; (*Med*) Bypass *m*
□*vt* umfahren. ~**-product** *n*
Nebenprodukt *nt*. ~**stander** *n*
Zuschauer(in) *m(f)*

C

cab *n* Taxi *nt*; (*of lorry*) Führer-
haus *nt*

cabaret *n* Kabarett *nt*

cabbage *n* Kohl *m*

cabin *n* Kabine *f*; (*hut*) Hütte *f*

cabinet *n* Schrank *m*; **C~** (*Pol*)
Kabinett *nt*

cable *n* Kabel *nt*; (*rope*) Tau *nt*. ~
'**railway** *n* Seilbahn *f*. ~ '**television** *n* Kabelfernsehen *nt*

cache *n* Versteck *nt*; ~ **of arms**
Waffenlager *nt*

cactus *n* Kaktus *m*

caddie *n* Caddie *m*

cadet *n* Kadett *m*

cadge *vt/i* (*fam*) schnorren

Caesarean *a* & *n* ~ [**section**]
Kaiserschnitt *m*

café *n* Café *nt*

cafeteria *n* Selbstbedienungsres-
taurant *nt*

caffeine *n* Koffein *nt*

cage *n* Käfig *m*

cajole *vt* gut zureden (+ *dat*)

cake *n* Kuchen *m*

calamity *n* Katastrophe *f*

calcium *n* Kalzium *nt*

calculate *vt* berechnen; (*estimate*) kalkulieren. ~**ion** *n* Rechnung *f*. ~**or** *n* Rechner *m*

calendar *n* Kalender *m*

calf[1] *n* Kalb *nt*

calf[2] *n* (*Anat*) Wade *f*

calibre *n* Kaliber *nt*

call *n* Ruf *m*; (*Teleph*) Anruf *m*;
(*visit*) Besuch *m*; **be on** ⟨*doctor*:⟩ Bereitschaftsdienst haben
□*vt* rufen; (*Teleph*) anrufen;
(*wake*) wecken; ausrufen (*strike*); (*name*) nennen; **be ~ed** heißen □*vi* rufen; ~ [**in** *or* **round**]
vorbeikommen. ~ **off** *vt* zurückrufen ⟨*dog*⟩; (*cancel*) absagen. ~
on *vt* bitten (**for** um); (*appeal to*)
appellieren an (+ *acc*); (*visit*) besuchen. ~ **out** *vt* rufen; aufrufen
⟨*names*⟩ □*vi* rufen

call: ~**-box** *n* Telefonzelle *f*. ~**er**
n Besucher *m*; (*Teleph*) Anrufer
m. ~**ing** *n* Berufung *f*

callous *a* gefühllos

calm *a* ruhig □*n* Ruhe *f* □*vt* ~
[**down**] beruhigen □*vi* ~ **down**
sich beruhigen. ~**ness** *n* Ruhe *f*;
(*of sea*) Stille *f*

calorie *n* Kalorie *f*

camber *n* Wölbung *f*

camel *n* Kamel *nt*

camera *n* Kamera *f*. ~**man** *n*
Kameramann *m*

camouflage *n* Tarnung *f* □*vt* tar-
nen

camp *n* Lager *nt* □*vi* campen;
(*Mil*) kampieren

campaign *n* (*Comm*, *Pol*) Kampagne *f* □*vi* kämpfen;
(*Pol*) im Wahlkampf arbeiten

camp: ~**-bed** *n* Feldbett *nt*. ~**er** *n*
Camper *m*; (*Auto*) Wohnmobil *nt*.
~**ing** *n* Camping *nt*. ~**site** *n*
Campingplatz *m*

campus *n* (*Univ*) Campus *m*

can[1] *n* (*for petrol*) Kanister *m*;
(*tin*) Dose *f*, Büchse *f*

can[2] *v aux* können; **I cannot**/
can't go ich kann nicht gehen

Canad|a n Kanada nt. **~ian** a
kanadisch □n Kanadier(in) m(f)

canal n Kanal m

Canaries npl Kanarische Inseln
pl

canary n Kanarienvogel m

cancel vt/i absagen; entwerten
⟨stamp⟩; (annul) rückgängig machen; (Comm) stornieren; abbestellen ⟨newspaper⟩ **~lation** n
Absage f

cancer n, & (Astr) **C~** Krebs m

candelabra n Armleuchter m

candid a offen

candidate n Kandidat(in) m(f)

candle n Kerze f. **~stick** n Ker-
zenständer m, Leuchter m

candour n Offenheit f

cane n Rohr nt; (stick) Stock m □ vt
mit dem Stock züchtigen

canine a Hunde-. **~ tooth** n Eck-
zahn m

canister n Blechdose f

cannabis n Haschisch nt

cannibal n Kannibale m. **~ism** n
Kannibalismus m

cannon n inv Kanone f. **~-ball** n
Kanonenkugel f

canoe n Paddelboot nt; (Sport)
Kanu nt □ vi paddeln; (Sport)
Kanu fahren

canon n Kanon m; (person) Kano-
nikus m. **~ize** vt kanonisieren

'can-opener n Dosenöffner m

canopy n Baldachin m

cantankerous a zänkisch

canteen n Kantine f

canter n Kanter m □ vi kantern

canvas n Segeltuch nt; (Art) Leinwand f; (painting) Gemälde nt

canvass vi um Stimmen werben

canyon n Cañon m

cap n Kappe f, Mütze f; (nurse's)
Haube f; (top, lid) Verschluß m
□ vt (fig) übertreffen

capability n Fähigkeit f

capable a fähig; **be ~ of doing
sth** fähig sein, etw zu tun

capacity n Fassungsvermögen nt;
(ability) Fähigkeit f

cape¹ n (cloak) Cape nt

cape² n (Geog) Kap nt

caper n (Culin) Kaper f

capital a (letter) groß □n (town)
Hauptstadt f; (money) Kapital nt;
(letter) Großbuchstabe m

capital|ism n Kapitalismus m.
~ist a kapitalistisch □n Kapita-
list m. **~ize** vi **~ize on** (fig)
Kapital schlagen aus. **~ 'letter** n
Großbuchstabe m. **~ 'punishment** n Todesstrafe f

capitulate vi kapitulieren. **~ion**
n Kapitulation f

capricious a launisch

Capricorn n (Astr) Steinbock m

capsize vi kentern

capsule n Kapsel f

captain n Kapitän m; (Mil)
Hauptmann m □ vt anführen

caption n Überschrift f; (of illustration) Bildtext m

captivate vt bezaubern

captivity n Gefangenschaft f

capture n Gefangennahme f □ vt
gefangennehmen; [ein]fangen
⟨animal⟩

car n Auto nt, Wagen m; **by ~** mit
dem Auto od Wagen f

carafe n Karaffe f

caramel n Karamel m

carat n Karat nt

caravan n Wohnwagen m

carbohydrate n Kohlenhydrat nt

carbon n Kohlenstoff m

carbon: ~ copy n Durchschlag
m. **~ di'oxide** n Kohlendioxid
nt; (in drink) Kohlensäure f. **~
paper** n Kohlepapier nt

carburettor n Vergaser m

carcass n Kadaver m

card n Karte f

'cardboard n Pappe f, Karton m.
~ 'box n Pappschachtel f; (large)
[Papp]karton m

cardigan n Strickjacke f

cardinal a Kardinal-; ~ **number** Kardinalzahl f □ n (Relig) Kardinal m

card 'index n Kartei f

care n Sorgfalt f; (caution) Vorsicht f; (protection) Obhut f; (looking after) Pflege f; (worry) Sorge f; ~ **of** (on letter abbr c/o) bei; **take** ~ vorsichtig sein; **take into** ~ in Pflege nehmen; **take** ~ **of** sich kümmern um □ vi ~ **about** sich kümmern um; ~ **for** (like) mögen; (look after) betreuen; **I don't** ~ das ist mir gleich

career n Laufbahn f; (profession) Beruf m □ vi rasen

care: ~**free** a sorglos. ~**ful** a sorgfältig; (cautious) vorsichtig. ~**less** a nachlässig

caress n Liebkosung f □ vt liebkosen

'caretaker n Hausmeister m

cargo n Ladung f

Caribbean n **the** ~ die Karibik

caricature n Karikatur f □ vt karikieren

caring a (parent) liebevoll; (profession) sozial

carnage n Gemetzel n

carnal a fleischlich

carnation n Nelke f

carnival n Karneval m

carnivorous a fleischfressend

carol n [Christmas] ~ Weihnachtslied n

carp[1] n inv Karpfen m

carp[2] vi nörgeln

'car park n Parkplatz m; (multistorey) Parkhaus nt; (underground) Tiefgarage f

carpent|er n Zimmermann m; (joiner) Tischler m. ~**ry** n Tischlerei f

carpet n Teppich m

carriage n Kutsche f; (Rail) Wagen m; (of goods) Beförderung f; (cost) Frachtkosten pl; (bearing) Haltung f. ~**way** n Fahrbahn f

carrier n Träger(in) m(f); (Comm) Spediteur m. ~ **[-bag]** Tragetasche f

carrot n Möhre f, Karotte f

carry vt/i tragen. ~ **out** vt hinaus-/heraustragen; (perform) ausführen

'carry-cot n Babytragetasche f

cart n Karren m □ vt karren; (fam: carry) schleppen

cartilage n (Anat) Knorpel m

carton n [Papp]karton m; (for drink) Tüte f; (of cream) Becher m

cartoon n Karikatur f; (joke) Witzzeichnung f; (strip) Comic Strips pl; (film) Zeichentrickfilm m; (Art) Karton m. ~**ist** n Karikaturist m

cartridge n Patrone f; (for film) Kassette f

carve vt schnitzen; (in stone) hauen; (Culin) aufschneiden

carving-knife n Tranchiermesser nt

'car wash n Autowäsche f; (place) Autowaschanlage f

case[1] n Fall m; **in any** ~ auf jeden Fall; **just in** ~ für alle Fälle; **in** ~ **he comes** falls er kommt

case[2] n Kasten m; (crate) Kiste f; (for spectacles) Etui nt

cash n Bargeld nt; **pay [in]** ~ in bar bezahlen; ~ **on delivery** per Nachnahme □ vt einlösen (cheque). ~ **desk** n Kasse f

cashier n Kassierer(in) m(f)

'cash register n Registrierkasse f

casino n Kasino nt

cask n Faß nt

casket n Kasten m

casserole n Schmortopf m; (stew) Eintopf m

cassette n Kassette f. ~ **recorder** n Kassettenrecorder m

cast n (throw) Wurf m; (mould) Form f; (model) Abguß m; (Theat) Besetzung f; **[plaster]** (Med) Gipsverband m □ vt (throw) werfen; (*shed*) abwerfen; abgeben (*vote*); gießen (*metal*); (*Theat*) besetzen ⟨*role*⟩

castanets *npl* Kastagnetten *pl*

castaway *n* Schiffbrüchige(r) *m/f*

caste *n* Kaste *f*

cast 'iron *n* Gußeisen *nt*

castle *n* Schloß *nt*; (*fortified*) Burg *f*; (*Chess*) Turm *m*

castor *n* (*wheel*) [Lauf]rolle *f*

'castor sugar *n* Streuzucker *m*

castrate *vt* kastrieren. **~ion** *n* Kastration *f*

casual *a* (*chance*) zufällig; (*offhand*) lässig; (*informal*) zwanglos; (*not permanent*) Gelegenheits-; **~ wear** Freizeitbekleidung *f*

casualty *n* [Todes]opfer *nt*; (*injured person*) Verletzte(r) *m/f*; **~ [department]** Unfallstation *f*

cat *n* Katze *f*

catalogue *n* Katalog *m* □ *vt* katalogisieren

catalyst *n* (*Chem & fig*) Katalysator *m*

catalytic *a* **~ converter** (*Auto*) Katalysator *m*

catapult *n* Katapult *nt* □ *vt* katapultieren

cataract *n* (*Med*) grauer Star *m*

catarrh *n* Katarrh *m*

catastrophe *n* Katastrophe *f*. **~ic** *a* katastrophal

catch *n* (*of fish*) Fang *m*; (*fastener*) Verschluß *m*; (*on door*) Klinke *f*; (*fam: snag*) Haken *m* (*fam*) □ *vt* fangen; (*be in time for*) erreichen; (*travel by*) fahren mit; bekommen ⟨*illness*⟩; **~ a cold** sich erkälten □ *vi* (*burn*) anbrennen; (*get stuck*) klemmen. **~ on** *vi* (*fam*) (*understand*) kapieren; (*become popular*) sich durchsetzen. **~ up** *vt* einholen □ *vi* aufholen

catching *a* ansteckend

catch: **~-phrase** *n*, **~word** *n* Schlagwort *nt*

catchy *a* einprägsam

catechism *n* Katechismus *m*

categor|ical *a* kategorisch. **~y** *n* Kategorie *f*

cater *vi* **~ for** beköstigen; ⟨*firm:*⟩ das Essen liefern für ⟨*party*⟩; (*fig*) eingestellt sein auf (+ *acc*). **~ing** *n* (*trade*) Gaststättengewerbe *nt*

caterpillar *n* Raupe *f*

cathedral *n* Dom *m*, Kathedrale *f*

Catholic *a* katholisch □ *n* Katholik(in) *m(f)*. **C~ism** *n* Katholizismus *m*

catkin *n* (*Bot*) Kätzchen *nt*

cattle *npl* Vieh *nt*

cauldron *n* [großer] Kessel *m*

cauliflower *n* Blumenkohl *m*

cause *n* Ursache *f*; (*reason*) Grund *m*; **good ~** gute Sache *f* □ *vt* verursachen

'causeway *n* [Insel]damm *m*

caustic *a* ätzend; (*fig*) beißend

caution *n* Vorsicht *f*; (*warning*) Verwarnung *f* □ *vt* (*Jur*) verwarnen

cautious *a* vorsichtig

cavalry *n* Kavallerie *f*

cave *n* Höhle *f* □ *vi* **~ in** einstürzen

cavern *n* Höhle *f*

caviare *n* Kaviar *m*

caving *n* Höhlenforschung *f*

cavity *n* Hohlraum *m*; (*in tooth*) Loch *nt*

cease *n* **without ~** unaufhörlich □ *vt/i* aufhören. **~-fire** *n* Waffenruhe *f*. **~less** *a* unaufhörlich

cedar *n* Zeder *f*

cede *vt* abtreten (**to** an + *acc*)

ceiling *n* [Zimmer]decke *f*

celebrat|e *vt/i* feiern. **~ed** *a* berühmt (**for** wegen). **~ion** *n* Feier *f*

celebrity *n* Berühmtheit *f*

celery *n* [Stangen]sellerie *m & f*

celiba|cy *n* Zölibat *nt*. **~te** *a* **~ te** im Zölibat leben

cell *n* Zelle *f*

cellar *n* Keller *m*

cellist n Cellist(in) m(f)

cello n Cello nt

Celsius a Celsius

Celt n Kelte m/ Keltin f. ~**ic** a keltisch

cement n Zement m □ vt zementieren

cemetery n Friedhof m

censor n Zensor m □ vt zensieren. ~**ship** n Zensur f

censure n Tadel m □ vt tadeln

census n Volkszählung f

centenary n Hundertjahrfeier f

centi|grade a Celsius-; 5° ~ 5° Celsius. ~**metre** n Zentimeter m & nt. ~**pede** n Tausendfüßler m

central a zentral. ~ '**heating** n Zentralheizung f. ~**ize** vt zentralisieren. ~ **reser'vation** n (Auto) Mittelstreifen m

centre n Zentrum nt; (middle) Mitte f □ vt zentrieren; ~ on (fig) sich drehen um. ~'**forward** n Mittelstürmer m

centrifugal a ~ **force** Fliehkraft f

century n Jahrhundert nt

ceramic a Keramik-. ~**s** n Keramik f

cereal n Getreide nt; (breakfast food) Frühstücksflocken pl

ceremon|ial a zeremoniell, feierlich □ n Zeremoniell nt. ~**ious** a formell

ceremony n Zeremonie f

certain a sicher; (not named) gewiß; **for** ~ mit Bestimmtheit; **make** ~ (check) sich vergewissern (that daß); (ensure) dafür sorgen (that daß); **he is** ~ **to win** er wird ganz bestimmt siegen. ~**ly** adv bestimmt, sicher; ~**ly not!** auf keinen Fall! ~**ty** n Sicherheit f, Gewißheit f

certificate n Bescheinigung f; (Jur) Urkunde f; (Sch) Zeugnis nt

certify vt bescheinigen

cesspool n Senkgrube f

cf abbr (compare) vgl

chafe vt wund reiben

chaff n Spreu f

chaffinch n Buchfink m

chain n Kette f □ vt ketten (**to** an + acc). ~ **up** vt anketten

chain: ~ re'action n Kettenreaktion f. ~ **store** n Kettenladen m

chair n Stuhl m; (Univ) Lehrstuhl m □ vt den Vorsitz führen bei. ~**lift** n Sessellift m. ~**man** n Vorsitzende(r) m/f

chalet n Chalet nt

chalice n (Relig) Kelch m

chalk n Kreide f. ~**y** a kreidig

challenge n Herausforderung f □ vt herausfordern; (fig) anfechten ⟨statement⟩. ~**er** n Herausforderer m. ~**ing** a herausfordernd; (demanding) anspruchsvoll

chamber n Kammer f; ~ **pl** (Jur) [Anwalts]büro nt; **C**~ **of Commerce** Handelskammer f

chamber: ~ **maid** n Zimmermädchen nt. ~ **music** n Kammermusik f. ~**pot** n Nachttopf m

chamois[1] n inv (animal) Gemse f

chamois[2] n [-leather] Ledertuch nt

champagne n Champagner m

champion n Meister(in) m(f); (of cause) Verfechter m □ vt sich einsetzen für. ~**ship** n Meisterschaft f

chance n Zufall m; (prospect) Chancen pl; (likelihood) Aussicht f; (opportunity) Gelegenheit f; **by** ~ zufällig; **take a** ~ ein Risiko eingehen □ attrib zufällig □ vt ~ **it** es riskieren

chancellor n Kanzler m; (Univ) Rektor m; **C**~ **of the Exchequer** Schatzkanzler m

chandelier n Kronleuchter m

change n Veränderung f; (alteration) Änderung f; (money) Wechselgeld nt; **for a** ~ zur Abwechslung □ vt wechseln; (alter) ändern; (exchange) umtauschen (for gegen); (transform) verwandeln □vi sich verändern; (~ clothes) sich umziehen; (~ trains) umsteigen; all ~! alles aussteigen!

changeable a wechselhaft

'**changing-room** n Umkleideraum m

channel n Rinne f; (TV) Kanal m; (fig) Weg m; the **[English] C~** der Ärmelkanal; the **C~ Islands** die Kanalinseln □vt leiten; (fig) lenken

chant vi singen; (demonstrators:) skandieren

chaos n Chaos nt. ~**tic** a chaotisch

chap n (fam) Kerl m

chapel n Kapelle f

chaperon n Anstandsdame f □vt begleiten

chaplain n Geistliche(r) m

chapter n Kapitel nt

character n Charakter m; (in novel) Gestalt f; (Typ) Schriftzeichen nt; out of ~ uncharakteristisch

characteristic charakteristisch (of für) □n Merkmal nt

charcoal n Holzkohle f

charge n (price) Gebühr f; (Electr) Ladung f; (attack) Angriff m; (Jur) Anklage f; free of ~ kostenlos □vt berechnen (/fee); (Electr) laden; (attack) angreifen; (Jur) anklagen (with gen)

chariot n Wagen m

charisma n Charisma nt. ~**tic** a charismatisch

charitable a wohltätig

charity n Nächstenliebe f; (organization) wohltätige Einrichtung f

charlatan n Scharlatan m

charm n Reiz m; (object) Amulett nt □ Charme f; (object) Amulett nt □ vt bezaubern; ~**ing** a reizend; (person) charmant

chart n Karte f; (table) Tabelle f

charter n ~ **[flight]** Charterflug m □vt chartern; ~**ed accountant** Wirtschaftsprüfer(in) m(f)

chase n Verfolgungsjagd f □vt jagen, verfolgen

chasm n Kluft f

chassis n Chassis nt

chaste a keusch

chastise vt züchtigen

chastity n Keuschheit f

chat n Plauderei f □vi plaudern. ~ **show** n Talk-Show f

chatter n Geschwätz nt □vi schwatzen; (child:) plappern; (teeth:) klappern

chauffeur n Chauffeur m

chauvin|ism n Chauvinismus m. ~**ist** n Chauvinist m; **male ~ist** (fam) Chauvi m

cheap a billig. ~**en** a entwürdigen

cheat n Betrüger(in) m(f); (at games) Mogler m □vt betrügen □vi (at games) mogeln (fam)

check[1] a (squared) kariert □n Karo nt

check[2] n Überprüfung f; (inspection) Kontrolle f; (Chess) Schach nt □vt [über]prüfen; (inspect) kontrollieren □vi [go and] nachsehen. ~ **in** vi sich anmelden; (Aviat) einchecken □vt abfertigen; einchecken. ~ **out** vi sich abmelden. ~ **up** vi prüfen, kontrollieren

checked a kariert

check: ~**mate** int schachmatt! ~**-out** n Kasse f. ~**up** n (Med) [Kontroll]untersuchung f

cheek n Backe f; (impudence) Frechheit f. ~**y** a frech

cheep vi piepen

cheer n Beifallsruf m; **three** ~**s** ein dreifaches Hoch (for auf + acc); ~**s!** prost! □vt zujubeln (+ dat) □vi jubeln. ~ **up** vt aufmuntern □vi munterer werden. ~**ful** a fröhlich

cheerio int (fam) tschüs!

cheese n Käse m. **~cake** n Käsekuchen m

cheetah n Gepard m

chef n Koch m

chemical a chemisch □ n Chemikalie f

chemist n (pharmacist) Apotheker(in) m(f); (scientist) Chemiker(in) m(f); **~'s [shop]** Drogerie f; (dispensing) Apotheke f. **~ry** n Chemie f

cheque n Scheck m. **~-book** n Scheckbuch nt. **~ card** n Scheckkarte f

cherish vt lieben; (fig) hegen

cherry n Kirsche f

cherub n Engelchen nt

chess n Schach nt

chest n Brust f; (box) Truhe f

chestnut n Eßkastanie f, Marone f; (horse-) [Roß]kastanie f

chest of 'drawers n Kommode f

chew vt kauen. **~ing-gum** n Kaugummi m

chic a schick

chick n Küken nt

chicken n Huhn nt □ a (fam) feige □ vi **~ out** (fam) kneifen. **~-pox** n Windpocken pl

chief a Haupt- □ n Chef m; (of tribe) Häuptling m. **~ly** adv hauptsächlich

child n Kind nt

child: ~hood n Kindheit f. **~ish** a kindisch. **~like** a kindlich. **~minder** n Tagesmutter f

Chile n Chile nt

chill n Kälte f; (illness) Erkältung f □ vt kühlen

chilli n Chili m

chilly a kühl

chime vi läuten; ⟨clock:⟩ schlagen

chimney n Schornstein m. **~-sweep** n Schornsteinfeger m

chimpanzee n Schimpanse m

chin n Kinn nt

china n Porzellan nt

China| n China nt. **~ese** a chinesisch □ n (Lang) Chinesisch nt; **the ~ese** pl die Chinesen

chip n (fragment) Span m; (in china) angeschlagene Stelle f; (Computing) Chip m; **~s** pl (Culin) Pommes frites pl □ vt (damage) anschlagen

chiropod|ist n Fußpfleger(in) m(f). **~y** n Fußpflege f

chirp vi zwitschern

chisel n Meißel m

chit n Zettel m

chival|rous a ritterlich. **~ry** n Ritterlichkeit f

chives npl Schnittlauch m

chlorine n Chlor nt

chocolate n Schokolade f

choice n Wahl f; (variety) Auswahl f □ a auserlesen

choir n Chor m

choke n (Auto) Choke m □ vt würgen; (to death) erwürgen □ vi sich verschlucken

cholera n Cholera f

cholesterol n Cholesterin nt

choose vt/i wählen; (select) sich (dat) aussuchen

choos[e]y a (fam) wählerisch

chop n (blow) Hieb m; (Culin) Kotelett nt □ vt hacken

chop|per n Beil nt; (fam) Hubschrauber m. **~py** a kabbelig

'chopsticks npl Eßstäbchen pl

chord n (Mus) Akkord m

chore n lästige Pflicht f

choreography n Choreographie f

chorus n Chor m; (of song) Refrain m

Christ n Christus m

christen vt taufen. **~ing** n Taufe f

Christian a christlich □ n Christ(in) m(f). **~ity** n Christentum nt. **~ name** n Vorname m

Christmas n Weihnachten nt. **~ 'Day** n erster Weihnachtstag m. **~ 'Eve** n Heiligabend m

chrome *n*, **chromium** *n* Chrom *nt*

chromosome *n* Chromosom *nt*

chronic *a* chronisch

chronicle *n* Chronik *f*

chronological *a* chronologisch

chrysalis *n* Puppe *f*

chrysanthemum *n* Chrysantheme *f*

chubby *a* mollig

chuck *vt* (*fam*) schmeißen

chuckle *vi* in sich (*acc*) hineinlachen

church *n* Kirche *f*. ~ **yard** *n* Friedhof *m*

churn *n* Butterfaß *nt*; (*for milk*) Milchkanne *f* □ *vt* ~ **out** am laufenden Band produzieren

chute *n* Rutsche *f*

CID *abbr* (**Criminal Investigation Department**) Kripo *f*

cider *n* Apfelwein *m*

cigar *n* Zigarre *f*

cigarette *n* Zigarette *f*

cinema *n* Kino *nt*

cinnamon *n* Zimt *m*

circle *n* Kreis *m*; (*Theat*) Rang *m* □ *vt* umkreisen □ *vi* kreisen

circuit *n* Runde *f*; (*race-track*) Rennbahn *f*; (*Electr*) Stromkreis *m*

circular *a* kreisförmig □ *n* Rundschreiben *nt*

circulate *vt* in Umlauf setzen □ *vi* zirkulieren. ~**ion** *n* Kreislauf *m*; (*of newspaper*) Auflage *f*

circumcise *vt* beschneiden. ~**ion** *n* Beschneidung *f*

circumference *n* Umfang *m*

circumspect *a* umsichtig

circumstance *n* Umstand *m*; ~**s** *pl* Umstände *pl*

circus *n* Zirkus *m*

CIS *abbr* (**Commonwealth of Independent States**) GUS *f*

cistern *n* (*tank*) Wasserbehälter *m*; (*of WC*) Spülkasten *m*

cite *vt* zitieren

citizen *n* Bürger(in) *m(f)*. ~**ship** *n* Staatsangehörigkeit *f*

citrus *n* ~ [**fruit**] Zitrusfrucht *f*

city *n* [Groß]stadt *f*

civic *a* Bürger-

civil *a* bürgerlich; (*aviation*) zivil; (*polite*) höflich. ~ **engi'neering** *n* Hoch- und Tiefbau *m*

civilian *a* Zivil-. **in ~ clothes** in Zivil □ *n* Zivilist *m*

civiliz|**ation** *n* Zivilisation *f*. ~**e** *vt* zivilisieren

civil: ~'**servant** *n* Beamte(r) *m*/ Beamtin *f*. **C~** '**Service** *n* Staatsdienst *m*

claim *n* Anspruch *m*; (*application*) Antrag *m*; (*demand*) Forderung *f*; (*assertion*) Behauptung *f* □ *vt* beanspruchen; (*apply for*) beantragen; (*demand*) fordern; (*assert*) behaupten; (*collect*) abholen. ~**ant** *n* Antragsteller *m*

clairvoyant *n* Hellseher(in) *m(f)*

clam *n* Klaffmuschel *f*

clamour *n* Geschrei *nt*

clamp *n* Klammer *f* □ *vt* [ein]spannen □ *vi* (*fam*) ~ **down** durchgreifen

clan *n* Clan *m*

clandestine *a* geheim

clap *vt/i* Beifall klatschen (+ *dat*); ~ **one's hands** [in die Hände] klatschen

clarify *vt/i* klären

clarinet *n* Klarinette *f*

clarity *n* Klarheit *f*

clash *n* Geklirr *nt*; (*fig*) Konflikt *m* □ *vi* klirren; (*colours:*) sich beißen; (*events:*) ungünstig zusammenfallen

clasp *n* Verschluß *m* □ *vt* ergreifen

class *n* Klasse *f* □ *vt* einordnen

classic *a* klassisch □ *n* Klassiker *m*; ~**s** *pl* (*Univ*) Altphilologie *f*. ~**al** *a* klassisch

classi|**fication** *n* Klassifikation *f*. ~**fy** *vt* klassifizieren

'classroom *n* Klassenzimmer *nt*

clatter *n* Geklapper *nt* □ *vi* klappern

clause n Klausel f; (*Gram*) Satzteil m

claustrophobia n Klaustrophobie f, (*fam*) Platzangst f

claw n Kralle f, (*of bird & Techn*) Klaue f; (*of crab*) Schere f

clay n Lehm m; (*pottery*) Ton m

clean a sauber □adv glatt □vt saubermachen; putzen (*shoes*)

cleaner n Putzfrau f; [**dry**] n chemische Reinigung f

cleanliness n Sauberkeit f

clear a klar; (*obvious*) eindeutig; (*distinct*) deutlich; (*conscience*) rein; (*without obstacles*) frei; **make sth ~** etw klarmachen (to dat) □adv **stand ~** zurücktreten; **keep ~** of aus dem Wege gehen (+ dat) □vt räumen; abräumen (*table*); (*acquit*) freisprechen; (*authorize*) genehmigen; (*jump over*) überspringen □vi (*fog:*) sich auflösen. **~ away** vt wegräumen. **~ off** vi (*fam*) abhauen. **~ up** vt (tidy) aufräumen; (solve) aufklären □vi (*weather:*) sich aufklären

clearance n Räumung f; (*authorization*) Genehmigung f; (*customs*) [Zoll]abfertigung f; (*Techn*) Spielraum m

clearing n Lichtung f

cleavage n Dekolleté nt

clef n Notenschlüssel m

cleft n Spalte f

clemency n Milde f. **~t** a mild

clench vt **~ one's fist** die Faust ballen; **~ one's teeth** die Zähne zusammenbeißen

clergy npl Geistlichkeit f. **~man** n Geistliche(r) m

cleric n Geistliche(r) m. **~al** a Schreib-; (*Relig*) geistlich

clerk n Büroangestellte(r) m/f

clever a klug

cliché n Klischee nt

click vi klicken

client n Kunde m/ Kundin f; (*Jur*) Klient(in) m(f)

clientele n Kundschaft f

cliff n Kliff nt

climat|e n Klima nt. **~ic** a klimatisch

climax n Höhepunkt m

climb n Aufstieg m □vt besteigen (*mountain*); steigen auf (+ acc) (*ladder*) □vi klettern; (*rise*) steigen; (*road:*) ansteigen

climber n Bergsteiger m

cling vi sich klammern (to an + acc); (stick) haften (to an + acc). **~ film** n Sichtfolie f mit Hafteffekt

clinic n Klinik f. **~al** a klinisch

clip¹ n Klammer f. (*jewellery*) Klipp m □vt anklammern (to an + acc)

clip² n (extract) Ausschnitt m □vt schneiden; knipsen (*ticket*). **~board** n Klemmbrett nt. **~pers** npl Schere f

clique n Clique f

cloak n Umhang m. **~room** n Garderobe f

clock n Uhr f.

clock: **~wise** a & adv im Uhrzeigersinn. **~work** n Uhrwerk nt; (*of toy*) Aufziehmechanismus m

clog n Holzschuh m

cloister n Kreuzgang m

close¹ a nah[e] (to dat); (*friend*) eng; (*weather*) schwül □adv nahe; **~ by** nicht weit weg (+ (*street*) Sackgasse f

close² n Ende nt; **draw to a ~** sich dem Ende nähern □vt zumachen, schließen; (bring to an end) beenden; sperren (*road*) □vi sich schließen; (*shop:*) schließen, zumachen; (end:) enden. **~ down** vt schließen; stillegen (*factory*) □vi schließen; (*factory:*) stillgelegt werden

close-up n Nahaufnahme f

closure n Schließung f; (*of factory*) Stillegung f; (*of road*) Sperrung f

clot n [Blut]gerinnsel nt □vi ⟨blood:⟩ gerinnen

cloth n Tuch nt

clothes npl Kleider pl

clothing n Kleidung f

cloud n Wolke f □vi ~ **over** sich bewölken

cloudy a wolkig; ⟨liquid⟩ trübe

clout n (fam) Schlag m; (influence) Einfluß m □vt (fam) hauen

clove n [Gewürz]nelke f; ~ **of garlic** Knoblauchzehe f

clover n Klee m

clown n Clown m □vi ~ **[about]** herumalbern

club n Klub m; (weapon) Keule f; (Sport) Schläger m; ~**s** pl (Cards) Kreuz nt, Treff nt □vt knüppeln □vi ~ **together** zusammenlegen

clue n Anhaltspunkt m; (in crossword) Frage f; **I haven't a** ~ (fam) ich habe keine Ahnung

clumsy a ungeschickt; (unwieldy) unförmig

cluster n Gruppe f □vi sich scharen (**round** um)

clutch n Griff m; (Auto) Kupplung f; **be in s.o.'s** ~**es** (fam) in jds Klauen sein □vt festhalten; (grab) ergreifen

clutter n Kram m □vt ~ **[up]** vollstopfen

c/o abbr (care of) bei

coach n [Reise]bus m; (Rail) Wagen m; (horse-drawn) Kutsche f; (Sport) Trainer m □vt Nachhilfestunden geben (+ dat); (Sport) trainieren

coagulate vi gerinnen

coal n Kohle f

coalition n Koalition f

coarse a grob

coast n Küste f □vi (free-wheel) im Freilauf fahren; (Auto) im Leerlauf fahren. ~**al** a Küsten-. ~**er** n (mat) Untersatz m

coast: ~**guard** n Küstenwache f. ~**line** n Küste f

coat n Mantel m; (of animal) Fell nt; (of paint) Anstrich m; ~ **of arms** Wappen nt □vt überziehen. ~**-hanger** n Kleiderbügel m

coax vt gut zureden (+ dat)

cob n (of corn) [Mais]kolben m

cobble¹ n Kopfstein m

cobble² vt flicken. ~**r** n Schuster m

cobweb n Spinnengewebe nt

cocaine n Kokain f

cock n Hahn m; (any male bird) Männchen nt □vt ⟨animal:⟩ ~ **its ears** die Ohren spitzen

cockerel n [junger] Hahn m

cockle n Herzmuschel f

cock: ~**pit** n (Aviat) Cockpit nt. ~**roach** n Küchenschabe f. ~**tail** n Cocktail m. ~**-up** n (sl) **make a** ~**-up** Mist bauen (**of** bei)

cocky a (fam) eingebildet

cocoa n Kakao m

coconut n Kokosnuß f

cocoon n Kokon m

cod n inv Kabeljau m

COD abbr (**cash on delivery**) per Nachnahme

code n Kode m; (Computing) Code m; (set of rules) Kodex m

coedu'cational a gemischt. ~ **school** n Koedukationsschule f

coerce vt zwingen. ~**ion** n Zwang m

coe'xist vi koexistieren. ~**ence** n Koexistenz f

coffee n Kaffee m

coffee: ~**-grinder** n Kaffeemühle f. ~**-table** n Couchtisch m

coffin n Sarg m

cog n (Techn) Zahn m

cogent a überzeugend

cohabit vi (Jur) zusammenleben

coherent a zusammenhängig

coil n Rolle f; (Electr) Spule f; (one ring) Windung f □vt ~ **[up]** zusammenrollen

coin n Münze f □vt prägen

coincide vi zusammenfallen

coinciden|ce n Zufall m. ~**tal** a zufällig

coke n Koks m

Coke (P) n (drink) Cola f

colander n (Culin) Durchschlag m

cold a kalt; **I am** or **feel** ~ mir ist kalt □n Kälte f; (Med) Erkältung f

cold: ~-**blooded** a kaltblütig. ~-**'hearted** a kaltherzig

coleslaw n Krautsalat m

colic n Kolik f

collaborat|e vi zusammenarbeiten (with mit); ~**e on sth** mitarbeiten bei etw. ~**ion** n Zusammenarbeit f, Mitarbeit f; (with enemy) Kollaboration f. ~**or** n Mitarbeiter(in) m(f); Kollaborateur m

collapse n Zusammenbruch m; Einsturz m □vi zusammenbrechen; ⟨roof:⟩ einstürzen

collar n Kragen m; (for animal) Halsband nt. ~-**bone** n Schlüsselbein nt

colleague n Kollege m/ Kollegin f

collect vt sammeln; (fetch) abholen; einsammeln ⟨tickets⟩; einziehen ⟨taxes⟩ □vi sich [an]sammeln

collection n Sammlung f; (in church) Kollekte f; (of post) Leerung f; (designer's) Kollektion f

collective a gemeinsam; (Pol) kollektiv

collector n Sammler(in) m(f)

college n College nt

collide vi zusammenstoßen

colliery n Kohlengrube f

collision n Zusammenstoß m

colloquial a umgangssprachlich. ~**ism** n umgangssprachlicher Ausdruck m

Cologne n Köln nt

colon n Doppelpunkt m; (Anat) Dickdarm m

colonel n Oberst m

colonial a Kolonial-

colon|ize vt kolonisieren. ~**y** n Kolonie f

colossal a riesig

colour n Farbe f □vt färben; ~ **[in]** ausmalen

colour: ~-**blind** a farbenblind. ~**ed** a farbig □n (person) Farbige(r) m/f. ~-**fast** a farbecht. ~**ful** a farbenfroh. ~**less** a farblos

colt n junger Hengst m

column n Säule f; (of soldiers) Kolonne f; (Typ) Spalte f; (Journ) Kolumne f. ~**ist** n Kolumnist m

coma n Koma nt

comb n Kamm m □vt kämmen; (search) absuchen

combat n Kampf m □vt bekämpfen

combination n Verbindung f; (for lock) Kombination f

combine[1] vt verbinden □vi sich verbinden; ⟨people:⟩ sich zusammenschließen

combine[2] n (Comm) Konzern m. ~ **[harvester]** n Mähdrescher m

combustion n Verbrennung f

come vi kommen; (reach) reichen (to an + acc); **that** ~s **to £10** das macht £10; **how** ~? (fam) wie das? ~ **about** vi geschehen. ~ **across** vi herüberkommen; (fam) klar werden □vt stoßen auf (+ acc). ~ **by** vi vorbeikommen □vt (obtain) bekommen. ~ **off** vi abgehen; (take place) stattfinden; (succeed) klappen (fam). ~ **round** vi vorbeikommen; (after fainting) [wieder] zu sich kommen; (change one's mind) sich umstimmen lassen. ~ **to** vi [wieder] zu sich kommen

'come-back n Comeback m

comedian n Komiker m

comedy n Komödie f

comet n Komet m

come-uppance n **get one's** ~ (fam) sein Fett abkriegen

comfort n Bequemlichkeit f; (consolation) Trost m □vt trösten

comfortable a bequem

comic a komisch □n Komiker m; (periodical) Comic-Heft nt. ~ **al** a komisch. ~ **strip** n Comic Strips pl

comma n Komma nt

command n Befehl m; (Mil) Kommando nt; (mastery) Beherrschung f □vt befehlen (+ dat); kommandieren

commandeer vt beschlagnahmen

command|er n Befehlshaber m; (of unit) Kommandeur m; (of ship) Kommandant m. ~ **ing officer** n Befehlshaber m. ~ **ment** n Gebot nt

commemorat|e vt gedenken (+ gen). ~ **ion** n Gedenken nt

commence vt/i anfangen, beginnen. ~ **ment** n Anfang m, Beginn m

commend vt loben; (recommend) empfehlen (to dat). ~ **able** a lobenswert. ~ **ation** n Lob nt

commensurate a angemessen

comment n Bemerkung f; **no** ~! kein Kommentar! □vi sich äußern (on zu)

commentary n Kommentar m; [running] ~ (TV) Reportage f

commentator n Kommentator m; (Sport) Reporter m

commerce n Handel m

commercial a kommerziell □n (TV) Werbespot m. ~ **ize** vt kommerzialisieren

commiserate vi sein Mitleid ausdrücken (with dat)

commission n (order for work) Auftrag m; (body of people) Kommission f; (payment) Provision f; (Mil) [Offiziers]patent nt □vt beauftragen ‹s.o.›; in Auftrag geben ‹thing›; (Mil) zum Offizier ernennen

commissionaire n Portier m

commissioner n Kommissar m; ~ **for oaths** Notar m

commit vt begehen; (entrust) anvertrauen (to dat); (consign) einweisen (to in + acc); ~ **oneself** sich festlegen. ~ **ment** n Verpflichtung f; (involvement) Engagement nt. ~ **ted** a engagiert

committee n Ausschuß m, Komitee nt

common a gemeinsam; (frequent) häufig; (ordinary) gewöhnlich; (vulgar) ordinär □n Gemeindeland nt; **House of C~s** Unterhaus nt. ~ **er** n Bürgerliche(r) m/f

common: ~ **'law** n Gewohnheitsrecht nt. **C~ 'Market** n Gemeinsamer Markt m. ~ **place** a häufig. ~ **-room** n Aufenthaltsraum m. ~ **'sense** n gesunder Menschenverstand m

communal a gemeinschaftlich

communicate vt mitteilen (to dat); übertragen ‹disease› □vi sich verständigen; (be in touch) Verbindung haben

communication n Verständigung f; (contact) Verbindung f; (of disease) Übertragung f; (message) Mitteilung f; ~ **s** pl (technology) Nachrichtenwesen nt

Communion n [Holy] ~ das [heilige] Abendmahl; (Roman Catholic) die [heilige] Kommunion

communiqué n Kommuniqué nt

Communis|m n Kommunismus m. ~ **t** a kommunistisch □n Kommunist(in) m(f)

community n Gemeinschaft f; **local** ~ Gemeinde f. ~ **centre** n Gemeinschaftszentrum nt

commute vi pendeln. ~ **r** n Pendler(in) m(f)

compact a kompakt. ~ **disc** n CD f

companion n Begleiter(in) m(f)

company n Gesellschaft f; (firm) Firma f; (Mil) Kompanie f; (fam: guests) Besuch m. ~ **car** n Firmenwagen m

comparable *a* vergleichbar

comparative *a* vergleichend; (*relative*) relativ □ *n* (*Gram*) Komparativ *m*. **~ly** *adv* verhältnismäßig

compare *vt* vergleichen (**with/to** mit) □ *vi* sich vergleichen lassen

comparison *n* Vergleich *m*

compartment *n* Fach *nt*; (*Rail*) Abteil *nt*

compass *n* Kompaß *m*. **~es** *npl* **pair of ~es** Zirkel *m*

compassion *n* Mitleid *nt*. **~ate** *a* mitfühlend

compatible *a* vereinbar; ⟨drugs⟩ verträglich; (*Techn*) kompatibel; **be ~** ⟨people:⟩ [gut] zueinander passen

compatriot *n* Landsmann *m*/ -männin *f*

compel *vt* zwingen

compensat|e *vt* entschädigen □ *vi* **~e for** (*fig*) ausgleichen. **~ion** *n* Entschädigung *f*; (*fig*) Ausgleich *m*

compère *n* Conférencier *m*

compete *vi* konkurrieren

competen|ce *n* Tüchtigkeit *f*; (*ability*) Fähigkeit *f*; (*Jur*) Kompetenz *f*. **~t** *a* tüchtig; fähig; (*Jur*) kompetent

competition *n* Konkurrenz *f*; (*contest*) Wettbewerb *m*; (in *newspaper*) Preisausschreiben *nt*

competitive *a* (*Comm*) konkurrenzfähig

competitor *n* Teilnehmer *m*; (*Comm*) Konkurrent *m*

compile *vt* zusammenstellen

complacent *a* selbstzufrieden

complain *vi* klagen (**about/of** über + *acc*); (*formally*) sich beschweren. **~t** *n* Klage *f*; (*formal*) Beschwerde *f*; (*Med*) Leiden *nt*

complement[1] *n* Ergänzung *f*; **full ~** volle Anzahl *f*

complement[2] *vt* ergänzen

complete *a* vollständig; (*finished*) fertig; (*utter*) völlig □ *vt*

vervollständigen; (*finish*) abschließen; (*fill in*) ausfüllen. **~ly** *adv* völlig

completion *n* Vervollständigung *f*; (*end*) Abschluß *m*

complex *a* komplex □ *n* Komplex *m*

complexion *n* Teint *m*; (*colour*) Gesichtsfarbe *f*; (*fig*) Aspekt *m*

complicat|e *vt* komplizieren. **~ed** *a* kompliziert. **~ion** *n* Komplikation *f*

complicity *n* Mittäterschaft *f*

compliment *n* Kompliment *nt*; **~s** *pl* Grüße *pl* □ *vt* ein Kompliment machen (+ *dat*). **~ary** *a* schmeichelhaft; (*given free*) Frei-

comply *vi* **~ with** nachkommen (+ *dat*)

component *a* & *n* **~ [part]** Bestandteil *m*, Teil *nt*

compose *vt* verfassen; (*Mus*) komponieren; **~oneself** sich fassen. **~d** *a* (*calm*) gefaßt. **~r** *n* Komponist *m*

composition *n* Komposition *f*; (*essay*) Aufsatz *m*

compost *n* Kompost *m*

composure *n* Fassung *f*

compound[1] *vt* verschlimmern

compound[2] *a* zusammengesetzt; ⟨fracture⟩ kompliziert □ *n* (*Chem*) Verbindung *f*; (*Gram*) Kompositum *nt*; (*enclosure*) Einfriedigung *f*. **~ 'interest** *n* Zinseszins *m*

comprehen|d *vt* begreifen. **~sible** *a* verständlich. **~sion** *n* Verständnis *nt*

comprehensive *a* & *n* umfassend; **~ [school]** Gesamtschule *f*. **~ insurance** *n* (*Auto*) Vollkaskoversicherung *f*

compress[1] *n* Kompresse *f*

compress[2] *vt* zusammenpressen; **~ed air** Druckluft *f*

comprise *vt* umfassen

compromise n Kompromiß m □vt kompromittieren ⟨person⟩ □vi einen Kompromiß schließen

compuls|ion n Zwang m. ~ive a zwanghaft; ~ive eating Eßzwang m. ~ory a obligatorisch; ~ory subject Pflichtfach nt

comput|er n Computer m. ~ing n Computertechnik f

comrade n Kamerad m; (Pol) Genosse m/Genossin f. ~ship n Kameradschaft f

con n ⟨fam⟩ Schwindel m □vt ⟨fam⟩ beschwindeln

concave a konkav

conceal vt verstecken

concede vt zugeben

conceit n Einbildung f. ~ed a eingebildet

conceivable a denkbar

conceive vt (Biol) empfangen; ⟨fig⟩ sich (dat) ausdenken □vi schwanger werden. ~ of ⟨fig⟩ sich (dat) vorstellen

concentrat|e vt konzentrieren □vi sich konzentrieren. ~ion n Konzentration f

concept n Begriff m. ~ion n Empfängnis f; (idea) Vorstellung f

concern n Angelegenheit f; (worry) Sorge f; (Comm) Unternehmen nt □vt (be about) betreffen; (worry) kümmern; be ~ed about besorgt sein um. ~ing prep bezüglich (+ gen)

concert n Konzert nt; in ~ im Chor. ~ed a gemeinsam

concertina n Konzertina f

concerto n Konzert nt

concession n Zugeständnis nt; (Comm) Konzession f; (reduction) Ermäßigung f

conciliation n Schlichtung f

concise a kurz

conclude vt/i schließen

conclusion n Schluß m; in ~ abschließend, zum Schluß

conclusive a schlüssig

concoct vt zusammenstellen; ⟨fig⟩ fabrizieren. ~ion n Zusammenstellung f; ⟨drink⟩ Gebräu nt

concourse n Halle f

concrete a konkret □n Beton m □vt betonieren

concurrently adv gleichzeitig

concussion n Gehirnerschütterung f

condemn vt verurteilen; (declare unfit) für untauglich erklären

condensation n Kondensation f

condense vt zusammenfassen; (Phys) kondensieren □vi sich kondensieren. ~d milk n Kondensmilch f

condescend vi sich herablassen (to zu)

condiment n Gewürz nt

condition n Bedingung f; (state) Zustand m; ~s pl Verhältnisse pl; on ~ that unter der Bedingung, daß □vt (Psych) konditionieren. ~al a bedingt; be ~al on abhängen von □n (Gram) Konditional m. ~er n Haarkur f; (for fabrics) Weichspüler m

condolences npl Beileid nt

condom n Kondom nt

condone vt hinwegsehen über (+ acc)

conducive a förderlich (to dat)

conduct¹ n Verhalten nt; (Sch) Betragen nt

conduct² vt führen; (Phys) leiten; (Mus) dirigieren. ~or n Dirigent m; (of bus) Schaffner m; (Phys) Leiter m. ~ress n Schaffnerin f

cone n Kegel m; (Bot) Zapfen m; (for ice-cream) [Eis]tüte f; (Auto) Leitkegel m

confectionery n Süßwaren pl

confederation n Bund m; (Pol) Konföderation f

conference n Konferenz f

confess vt/i gestehen; (Relig) beichten. ~ion n Geständnis nt; (Relig) Beichte f. ~ional n

Beichtstuhl m. ~ **or** n Beichtvater m

confetti n Konfetti nt

confide vi ~ **in** s.o. sich jdm anvertrauen

confidence n (trust) Vertrauen nt; (self-assurance) Selbstvertrauen nt; (secret) Geheimnis nt; **in** ~ im Vertrauen. ~ **trick** n Schwindel m

confident a zuversichtlich; (self-assured) selbstsicher

confidential a vertraulich

confine vt beschränken; (keep shut up) einsperren. ~**ment** n Haft f

confirm vt bestätigen; (Relig) konfirmieren; (Roman Catholic) firmen. ~**ation** n Bestätigung f; Konfirmation f; Firmung f

confiscate vt beschlagnahmen

conflict[1] n Konflikt m

conflict[2] vi im Widerspruch stehen (**with** zu). ~**ing** a widersprüchlich

conform vi (person:) sich anpassen; (thing:) entsprechen (to dat). ~**ist** n Konformist m

confront vt konfrontieren. ~**ation** n Konfrontation f

confus|e vt verwirren; (mistake for) verwechseln (**with** mit). ~**ion** n Verwirrung f

congeal vi fest werden; (blood:) gerinnen

congenital a angeboren

congest|ed a verstopft; (with people) überfüllt. ~**ion** n Verstopfung f; Überfüllung f

congratulate vt gratulieren (+ dat) (**on** zu). ~**ions** npl Glückwünsche pl; ~**ions!** [ich] gratuliere!

congregat|e vi sich versammeln. ~**ion** n (Relig) Gemeinde f

congress n Kongreß m

conical a kegelförmig

conifer n Nadelbaum m

conjecture n Mutmaßung f

conjugal a ehelich

conjugat|e vt konjugieren. ~**ion** n Konjugation f

conjunction n Konjunktion f; **in** ~ **with** zusammen mit

conjunctivitis n Bindehautentzündung f

conjur|e vi zaubern □vt ~ **e up** heraufbeschwören. ~**or** n Zauberkünstler m

conker n (fam) [Roß]kastanie f

'con-man n (fam) Schwindler m

connect vt verbinden (**to** mit); (Electr) anschließen (**to** an + acc) □vi verbunden sein; (train:) Anschluß haben (**with** an + acc)

connection n Verbindung f; (Rail, Electr) Anschluß m; **in** ~ **with** in Zusammenhang mit. ~**s** npl Beziehungen pl

conniv|ance n stillschweigende Duldung f. ~**e** vi ~**e at** stillschweigend dulden

connoisseur n Kenner m

conquer vt erobern; (fig) besiegen. ~**or** n Eroberer m

conquest n Eroberung f

conscience n Gewissen nt

conscientious a gewissenhaft. ~ **objector** n Kriegsdienstverweigerer m

conscious a bewußt; [fully] ~ bei [vollem] Bewußtsein. ~**ness** n Bewußtsein n

conscript[1] n Einberufene(r) m

conscript[2] vt einberufen. ~**ion** n allgemeine Wehrpflicht f

consecrat|e vt weihen. ~**ion** n Weihe f

consecutive a aufeinanderfolgend. ~**ly** adv fortlaufend

consensus n Übereinstimmung f

consent n Einwilligung f □vi einwilligen (**to** in + acc)

consequen|ce n Folge f; (importance) Bedeutung f. ~**tly** adv folglich

conservation *n* Erhaltung *f*, Bewahrung *f*. ~**ist** *n* Umweltschützer *m*

conservative *a* konservativ; ⟨*estimate*⟩ vorsichtig. **C** ~ (*Pol*) *a* konservativ □ *n* Konservative (*r*) *m*/*f*

conservatory *n* Wintergarten *m*

conserve *vt* erhalten, bewahren; sparen ⟨*energy*⟩

consider *vt* erwägen; (*think over*) sich (*dat*) überlegen; (*take into account*) berücksichtigen; (*regard as*) betrachten als. ~**able** *a* erheblich

consider|ate *a* rücksichtsvoll. ~**ation** *n* Erwägung *f*; (*thoughtfulness*) Rücksicht *f*; (*payment*) Entgelt *nt*; **take into** ~**ation** berücksichtigen. ~**ing** *prep* wenn man bedenkt (**that**, daß)

consign *vt* übergeben (**to** *dat*). ~**ment** *n* Lieferung *f*

consist *vi* ~ **of** bestehen aus

consisten|cy *n* Konsequenz *f*; (*density*) Konsistenz *f*. ~**t** *a* konsequent; (*unchanging*) gleichbleibend; **be** ~**t with** entsprechen (+ *dat*)

consolation *n* Trost *m*. ~ **prize** *n* Trostpreis *m*

console *vt* trösten

consolidate *vt* konsolidieren

consonant *n* Konsonant *m*

conspicuous *a* auffällig

conspiracy *n* Verschwörung *f*

conspire *vi* sich verschwören

constant *a* beständig

constellation *n* Sternbild *nt*

consternation *n* Bestürzung *f*

constipat|ed *a* verstopft. ~**ion** *n* Verstopfung *f*

constituency *n* Wahlkreis *m*

constituent *n* Bestandteil *m*; (*Pol*) Wähler(in) *m*(*f*)

constitute *vt* bilden. ~**ion** *n* (*Pol*) Verfassung *f*; (*of person*) Konstitution *f*

constrain *vt* zwingen. ~**t** *n* Zwang *m*; (*restriction*) Beschränkung *f*

constrict *vt* einengen

construct *vt* bauen. ~**ion** *n* Bau *m*

consul *n* Konsul *m*. ~**ate** *n* Konsulat *nt*

consult *vt* [um Rat] fragen; konsultieren ⟨*doctor*⟩; nachschlagen in (+ *dat*) ⟨*book*⟩. ~**ant** *n* Berater *m*; (*Med*) Chefarzt *m*. ~**ation** *n* Beratung *f*; (*Med*) Konsultation *f*

consume *vt* verzehren; (*use*) verbrauchen. ~**r** *n* Verbraucher *m*. ~**r goods** *npl* Konsumgüter *pl*

consummate *vt* vollziehen. ~**ion** *n* Vollzug *m*

consumption *n* Konsum *m*; (*use*) Verbrauch *m*

contact *n* Kontakt *m*; (*person*) Kontaktperson *f* □ *vt* sich in Verbindung setzen mit. ~'**lenses** *npl* Kontaktlinsen *pl*

contagious *a* direkt übertragbar

contain *vt* enthalten; (*control*) beherrschen. ~**er** *n* Behälter *m*; (*Comm*) Container *m*

contaminat|e *vt* verseuchen. ~**ion** *n* Verseuchung *f*

contemplate *vt* betrachten; (*meditate*) nachdenken über (+ *acc*). ~**ion** *n* Betrachtung *f*; Nachdenken *nt*

contemporary *a* zeitgenössisch □ *n* Zeitgenosse *m*/-genossin *f*

contempt *n* Verachtung *f*. ~**ible** *a* verachtenswert. ~**uous** *a* verächtlich

contend *vi* kämpfen (**with** mit) □ *vt* (*assert*) behaupten. ~**er** *n* Bewerber(in) *m*(*f*); (*Sport*) Wettkämpfer(in) *m*(*f*)

content[1] *n* & **contents** *pl* Inhalt *m*

content[2] *a* zufrieden □ *vt* ~ **oneself** sich begnügen (**with** mit). ~**ed** *a* zufrieden

contention 303 convert

contention n Behauptung f

contest[1] n Kampf m; (competition) Wettbewerb m

contest[2] vt (dispute) bestreiten; (Jur) anfechten; (Pol) kandidieren in (+ dat). **~ant** n Teilnehmer m

context n Zusammenhang m

continent n Kontinent m

continental a Kontinental-. **~ breakfast** n kleines Frühstück nt. **~ quilt** n Daunendecke f

contingen|cy n Eventualität f. **~t a** be **~ t upon** abhängen von

continual a dauernd

continuation n Fortsetzung f

continue vt fortsetzen; **to be ~d** Fortsetzung folgt □vi weitergehen; (doing sth) weitermachen; (speaking) fortfahren; ⟨weather:⟩ anhalten

continuity n Kontinuität f

continuous a anhaltend

contour n Kontur f; (line) Höhenlinie f

contraband n Schmuggelware f

contracep|tion n Empfängnisverhütung f. **~tive** a empfängnisverhütend □vi Empfängnisverhütungsmittel nt

contract[1] n Vertrag m

contract[2] vi sich zusammenziehen □vt zusammenziehen; sich (dat) zuziehen (illness). **~ion** n Zusammenziehung f; (abbreviation) Abkürzung f; (in childbirth) Wehe f. **~or** n Unternehmer m

contradict vt widersprechen (+ dat). **~ion** n Widerspruch m. **~ory** a widersprüchlich

contra-flow n Umleitung f [auf die entgegengesetzte Fahrbahn]

contralto n Alt m; (singer) Altistin f

contraption n (fam) Apparat m

contrary a entgegengesetzt; **~ to** entgegen (+ dat) □vi n Gegenteil nt; **on the ~** im Gegenteil

contrast[1] n Kontrast m

contrast[2] vt gegenüberstellen (with dat) □vi einen Kontrast bilden (with zu). **~ing** a gegensätzlich

contraven|e vt verstoßen gegen. **~tion** n Verstoß m (of gegen)

contribut|e vt/i beitragen; beisteuern ⟨money⟩; spenden ⟨donate⟩. **~ion** n Beitrag m; (donation) Spende f. **~or** n Beitragende(r) m/f

contrite a reuig

contrive vt verfertigen; **~ to do sth** es fertigbringen, etw zu tun

control n Kontrolle f; (mastery) Beherrschung f; (Techn) Regler m; **~s** pl (of car) Steuerung f □vt kontrollieren; (restrain) unter Kontrolle halten; **~oneself** sich beherrschen

controvers|ial a umstritten. **~y** n Kontroverse f

conurbation n Ballungsgebiet nt

convalesce vi sich erholen. **~nce** n Erholung f

convene vt einberufen □vi sich versammeln

convenience n Bequemlichkeit f; [public] ~ öffentliche Toilette f; **with all modern ~s** mit allem Komfort

convenient a günstig; be ~ for s.o. jdm gelegen sein od jdm passen

convent n [Nonnen]kloster nt

convention n (custom) Brauch m, Sitte f; (agreement) Konvention f; (assembly) Tagung f. **~al** a konventionell

converge vi zusammenlaufen

conversation n Gespräch nt

converse[1] vi sich unterhalten

converse[2] n Gegenteil nt. **~ly** adv umgekehrt

conversion n Umbau m; (Relig) Bekehrung f; (calculation) Umrechnung f

convert[1] n Bekehrte(r) m/f, vertit m

convert² vt bekehren ⟨person⟩; ⟨change⟩ umwandeln (**into** in + acc); umbauen ⟨building⟩; ⟨calculate⟩ umrechnen □(Techn) umstellen. ~**ible** a verwandelbar □n ⟨Auto⟩ Kabriolett nt

convex a konvex

convey vt befördern; vermitteln ⟨idea⟩. ~**ance** n Beförderung f; ⟨vehicle⟩ Beförderungsmittel nt. ~**or belt** n Förderband nt

convict¹ n Sträfling m

convict² vt verurteilen (**of** wegen). ~**ion** n Verurteilung f; ⟨belief⟩ Überzeugung f

convince vt überzeugen

convoy n Konvoi m

convulsion n Krampf m

cook n Koch m/ Köchin f; □vt/i kochen

cooker n [Koch]herd m; ⟨apple⟩ Kochapfel m. ~**y** n Kochen nt. ~**y book** n Kochbuch nt

cool a kühl □n Kühle f□vt kühlen □vi abkühlen

coop n [Hühner]stall m □vt ~ **up** einsperren

co-operat|e vi zusammenarbeiten. ~**ion** n Kooperation f

co-operative a hilfsbereit □n Genossenschaft f

co-opt vt hinzuwählen

co-ordinate vt koordinieren

cope vi ⟨fam⟩ zurechtkommen; ~ **with** fertig werden mit

copious a reichlich

copper n Kupfer nt □a kupfern

coppice n, **copse** n Gehölz nt

copulate vi sich begatten

copy n Kopie f; ⟨book⟩ Exemplar nt□vt kopieren; ⟨imitate⟩ nachahmen; ⟨Sch⟩ abschreiben

copy: ~right n Copyright nt. ~**-writer** n Texter m

coral n Koralle f

cord n Schnur f

cordial a herzlich □n Fruchtsirup m

cordon n Kordon m □vt ~ **off** absperren

corduroy n Cordsamt m

core n Kern m; ⟨of apple⟩ Kerngehäuse nt

cork n Kork m; ⟨for bottle⟩ Korken m. ~**screw** n Korkenzieher m

corn¹ n Korn nt

corn² n ⟨Med⟩ Hühnerauge nt

cornea n Hornhaut f

corner n Ecke f; ⟨bend⟩ Kurve f; ⟨football⟩ Eckball m □vt ⟨fig⟩ in die Enge treiben; ⟨Comm⟩ monopolisieren ⟨market⟩. ~**stone** n Eckstein m

cornet n ⟨Mus⟩ Kornett nt; ⟨for ice-cream⟩ [Eis]tüte f

cornflour n Stärkemehl nt

corny a ⟨fam⟩ abgedroschen

coronary a & n ~ [**thrombosis**] Koronarthrombose f

coronation n Krönung f

coroner n Beamte(r) m, der verdächtige Todesfälle untersucht

coronet n Adelskrone f

corporal¹ n ⟨Mil⟩ Stabsunteroffizier m

corporal² a körperlich; ~ **punishment** körperliche Züchtigung

corporate a gemeinschaftlich

corporation n Körperschaft f; ⟨of town⟩ Stadtverwaltung f

corps n Korps m

corpse n Leiche f

corpuscle n Blutkörperchen nt

correct a richtig; ⟨proper⟩ korrekt □vt verbessern; ⟨Typ⟩ korrigieren. ~**ion** n Verbesserung f; ⟨Typ⟩ Korrektur f

correspond vi entsprechen (**to** dat); ⟨two things⟩ sich entsprechen; ⟨write⟩ korrespondieren. ~**ence** n Briefwechsel m; ⟨Comm⟩ Korrespondenz f. ~**ent** n Korrespondent(in) m(f). ~**ing** a entsprechend

corridor n Gang m; ⟨Pol, Aviat⟩ Korridor m

corroborate vt bestätigen
corro|de vt zerfressen □ vi rosten. **~ sion** n Korrosion f
corrugated a gewellt. **~ iron** n Wellblech nt
corrupt a korrupt □ vt korrumpieren; (spoil) verderben. **~ion** n Korruption f
corset n & -s pl Korsett nt
Corsica n Korsika nt
cortège n [funeral] **~** Leichenzug m
cosh n Totschläger m
cosmetic a kosmetisch □ n **~s** pl Kosmetika f
cosmic a kosmisch
cosmonaut n Kosmonaut(in) m(f)
cosmopolitan a kosmopolitisch
cosmos n Kosmos m
cost n Kosten pl; **~s** pl (Jur) Kosten; **at all ~s** um jeden Preis □ vt **~ [out]** die Kosten kalkulieren für
costly a teuer
cost: ~ of 'living n Lebenshaltungskosten pl. **~ price** n Selbstkostenpreis m
costume n Kostüm nt; (national) Tracht f. **~ jewellery** n Modeschmuck m
cosy a gemütlich □ n (tea-) Wärmer m
cot n Kinderbett nt
cottage n Häuschen nt. **'cheese** n Hüttenkäse m
cotton n Baumwolle f; (thread) Nähgarn nt □ a baumwollen
cotton 'wool n Watte f
couch n Liege f
couchette n (Rail) Liegeplatz m
cough n Husten m □ vi husten
'cough mixture n Hustensaft m
council n Rat m; (Admin) Stadtverwaltung f; (rural) Gemeindeverwaltung f. **~ house** n ≈ Sozialwohnung f
councillor n Stadtverordnete(r) m|f

'council tax n Gemeindesteuer f
counsel n Rat m; (Jur) Anwalt m □ vt beraten. **~lor** n Berater(in) m(f)
count[1] n Graf m
count[2] vt/i zählen. **~ on** vt rechnen auf (+ acc)
countenance n Gesicht nt □ vt dulden
counter[1] n (in shop) Ladentisch m; (in bank) Schalter m; (in café) Theke f; (Games) Spielmarke f
counter[2] vt/i kontern
counter'act vt entgegenwirken (+ dat)
'counter-attack n Gegenangriff m
'counterfeit a gefälscht □ n Fälschung f □ vt fälschen
'counterfoil n Kontrollabschnitt m
'counterpart n Gegenstück nt
country n Land nt; (native land) Heimat f; (countryside) Landschaft f; **in the ~** auf dem Lande. **~man** n [fellow] **~man** n Landsmann m
county n Grafschaft f
coup n (Pol) Staatsstreich m
couple n Paar nt □ vt verbinden
coupon n Kupon m; (voucher) Gutschein m; (entry form) Schein m
courage n Mut m. **~ous** a mutig
courgettes npl Zucchini pl
courier n Bote m; (diplomatic) Kurier m; (for tourists) Reiseleiter(in) m(f)
course n (Naut, Sch) Kurs m; (Culin) Gang m; (for golf) Platz m; **of ~** natürlich, selbstverständlich
court n Hof m; (Sport) Platz m; (Jur) Gericht nt □ vt werben um; herausfordern (danger)
courteous a höflich
courtesy n Höflichkeit f
court: ~'martial n Militärgericht nt. **~yard** n Hof m

cousin n Vetter m, Cousin m; (female) Kusine f

cove n kleine Bucht f

cover n Decke f; (of cushion) Bezug m; (of umbrella) Hülle f; (of typewriter) Haube f; (of book) Deckel m; (of magazine) Umschlag m; (protection) Deckung f. **take ~** Deckung nehmen; **under separate ~** mit getrennter Post □vt bedecken; beziehen (cushion); decken (costs, needs); zurücklegen (distance); (Journ) berichten über (+ acc); (insure) versichern

cover: ~ charge n Gedeck nt. **~ up** n Vertuschung f

cow n Kuh f

coward n Feigling m. **~ice** n Feigheit f. **~ly** a feige

'cowboy n Cowboy m

cower vi sich [ängstlich] ducken

cox n, **coxswain** n Steuermann m

coy a gespielt schüchtern

crab n Krabbe f. **~-apple** n Holzapfel m

crack n Riß m; (in china) Sprung m; (noise) Knall m; (fam: joke) Witz m; (fam: attempt) Versuch m □a (fam) erstklassig □vt knacken (nut, code); einen Sprung machen in (+ acc) (china); (fam) reißen (joke); (fam) lösen (problem) □vi (china) springen; (whip:) knallen

cracker n (biscuit) Kräcker m; (firework) Knallkörper m. **[Christmas] ~** n Knallbonbon m

crackle vi knistern

cradle n Wiege f

craft¹ n inv (boat) [Wasser]fahrzeug nt

craft² n Handwerk nt; (technique) Fertigkeit f. **~sman** n Handwerker m

crafty a gerissen

crag n Felszacken m. **~gy** a felsig; (face) kantig

cram vt hineinstopfen (into in + acc); vollstopfen (with mit) □vi (for exams) pauken

cramp n Krampf m. **~ed** a eng

crampon n Steigeisen nt

cranberry n (Culin) Preiselbeere f

crane n Kran m; (bird) Kranich m

crank¹ n (fam) Exzentriker m

crank² n (Techn) Kurbel f. **~shaft** n Kurbelwelle f

crash n (noise) Krach m; (Auto) Zusammenstoß m; (Aviat) Absturz m □vi krachen (into gegen); (cars) zusammenstoßen; (plane:) abstürzen □vt einen Unfall haben mit (car)

crash: ~ course n Schnellkurs m. **~-helmet** n Sturzhelm m. **~landing** n Bruchlandung f

crate n Kiste f

crater n Krater m

crave vi **~ for** sich sehnen nach. **~ing** n Gelüst nt

crawl n (Swimming) Kraul nt; **do the ~** kraulen; **at a ~** im Kriechtempo □vi kriechen; (baby:) krabbeln

crayon n Wachsstift m; (pencil) Buntstift m

craze n Mode f

crazy a verrückt

creak vi knarren

cream n Sahne f; (Cosmetic, Med, Culin) Creme f □a (colour) cremefarben □vt (Culin) cremig rühren. **~ 'cheese** n Quark m. **~y** a sahnig; (smooth) cremig

crease n Falte f; (unwanted) Knitterfalte f □vt falten; (accidentally) zerknittern □vi knittern. **~-resistant** a knitterfrei

create vt schaffen. **~ion** n Schöpfung f. **~ive** a schöpferisch. **~or** n Schöpfer m

creature n Geschöpf nt

crèche n Kinderkrippe f

credentials npl Beglaubigungsschreiben nt

credible *a* glaubwürdig

credit *n* Kredit *m*; (*honour*) Ehre *f*
□ *vt* glauben

credit: **~ card** *n* Kreditkarte *f.*
~ or *n* Gläubiger *m*

creed *n* Glaubensbekenntnis *nt*

creep *vi* schleichen □ *n* (*fam*) fieser Kerl *m*; **it gives me the ~s** es ist mir unheimlich. **~y** *a* gruselig

cremat|e *vt* einäschern. **~ion** *n* Einäscherung *f*

crematorium *n* Krematorium *nt*

crêpe *n* Krepp *m*. **~ paper** *n* Kreppapier *nt*

crescent *n* Halbmond *m*

cress *n* Kresse *f*

crest *n* Kamm *m*; (*coat of arms*) Wappen *nt*

Crete *n* Kreta *nt*

crevasse *n* [Gletscher]spalte *f*

crevice *n* Spalte *f*

crew *n* Besatzung *f*; (*gang*) Bande *f*

crib[1] *n* Krippe *f*

crib[2] *vt/i* (*fam*) abschreiben

cricket[1] *n* (*insect*) Grille *f*

cricket[2] *n* Kricket *nt*

crime *n* Verbrechen *nt*

criminal *a* kriminell, verbrecherisch; (*law, court*) Straf- □ *n* Verbrecher *m*

crimson *a* purpurrot

cringe *vi* sich [ängstlich] ducken

cripple *n* Krüppel *m* □ *vt* zum Krüppel machen; (*fig*) lahmlegen. **~d** *a* verkrüppelt

crisis *n* Krise *f*

crisp *a* knusprig. **~bread** *n* Knäckebrot *nt*. **~s** *npl* Chips *pl*

criterion *n* Kriterium *nt*

critic *n* Kritiker *m*. **~al** *a* kritisch

criticism *n* Kritik *f*

criticize *vt* kritisieren

croak *vi* krächzen; (*frog:*) quaken

crochet *n* Häkelarbeit *f* □ *vt/i* häkeln. **~hook** *n* Häkelnadel *f*

crockery *n* Geschirr *nt*

crocodile *n* Krokodil *nt*

crocus *n* Krokus *m*

crook *n* Schwindler *m*, Gauner *m*

crooked *a* schief; (*bent*) krumm

crop *n* Feldfrucht *f*; (*harvest*) Ernte *f*; (*of bird*) Kropf *m*

croquet *n* Krocket *nt* ·

croquette *n* Krokette *f*

cross *a* (*annoyed*) böse (**with** auf + *acc*); **talk at ~ purposes** aneinander vorbeireden □ *n* Kreuz *nt*; (*Bot, Zool*) Kreuzung *f* □ *vt* kreuzen (*cheque, animals*); überqueren (*road*); **~ oneself** sich bekreuzigen; **~ one's arms** die Arme verschränken; **~ one's legs** die Beine übereinanderschlagen; **keep one's fingers ~ed for s.o.** jdm die Daumen drücken □ *vi* (*go across*) hinübergehen/-fahren; (*lines:*) sich kreuzen

cross: **~bar** *n* Querlatte *f*; (*on bicycle*) Stange *f.* **~'country** *n* (*Sport*) Crosslauf *m*. **~examination** *n* Kreuzverhör *nt*. **~ing** *n* Übergang *m*; (*sea journey*) Überfahrt *f.* **~'reference** *n* Querverweis *m*. **~roads** *n* [Straßen]kreuzung *f.* **~'section** *n* Querschnitt *m.* **~word** *n* **~word [puzzle]** Kreuzworträtsel *nt*

crotchet *n* Viertelnote *f*

crouch *vi* kauern

crow *n* Krähe *f*; **as the ~ flies** Luftlinie □ *vi* krähen. **~bar** *n* Brechstange *f*

crowd *n* [Menschen]menge *f* □ *vi* sich drängen

crown *n* Krone *f* □ *vt* krönen

crucial *a* höchst wichtig; (*decisive*) entscheidend (**to** für)

crucifix *n* Kruzifix *nt*

cruci|fixion *n* Kreuzigung *f.* **~fy** *vt* kreuzigen

crude *a* (*raw*) roh

cruel *a* grausam (**to** gegen). **~ty** *n* Grausamkeit *f*; **~ty to animals** Tierquälerei *f*

cruise n Kreuzfahrt f □ vi kreuzen; ⟨car:⟩ fahren. **~er** n (Mil) Kreuzer m; (motor boat) Kajütboot nt

crumb n Krümel m

crumble vt/i krümeln; (collapse) einstürzen

crumple vt zerknittern □ vi knittern

crunch vt mampfen □ vi knirschen

crusade n Kreuzzug m; (fig) Kampagne f. **~r** n Kreuzfahrer m; (fig) Kämpfer m

crush n (crowd) Gedränge nt

crust n Kruste f

crutch n Krücke f

crux n (fig) springender Punkt m

cry n Ruf m; (shout) Schrei m; **a far ~ from** (fig) weit entfernt von □ vi (weep) weinen; (louder) schreien; (call) rufen

crypt n Krypta f. **~ic** a rätselhaft

crystal n Kristall m; (glass) Kristall nt. **~lize** vi [sich] kristallisieren

cub n (Zool) Junge(s) nt; **C~** [Scout] Wölfling m

Cuba n Kuba nt

cube n Würfel m. **~ic** a Kubik-

cubicle n Kabine f

cuckoo n Kuckuck m. **~ clock** n Kuckucksuhr f

cucumber n Gurke f

cuddle vt herzen □ vi **~e up to** sich kuscheln an (+ acc). **~y** a kuschelig

cudgel n Knüppel m

cue[1] n Stichwort nt

cue[2] n (Billiards) Queue nt

cuff n Manschette f; **off the ~** (fam) aus dem Stegreif □ vt ohrfeigen. **~-link** n Manschettenknopf m

cul-de-sac n Sackgasse f

culinary a kulinarisch

culminate vi gipfeln (**in in** + dat). **~ion** n Gipfelpunkt m

culottes npl Hosenrock m

culprit n Täter m

cult n Kult m

cultivate vt anbauen; bebauen ⟨land⟩

cultural a kulturell

culture n Kultur f. **~d** a kultiviert

cumbersome a hinderlich

cumulative a kumulativ

cunning a listig □ n List f

cup n Tasse f; (prize) Pokal m

cupboard n Schrank m

Cupid n Amor m

curate n Vikar m; (Roman Catholic) Kaplan m

curator n Kustos m

curb vt zügeln

curdle vi gerinnen

cure n [Heil]mittel nt □ vt heilen; (salt) pökeln; (smoke) räuchern

curfew n Ausgangssperre f

curiosity n Neugier f; (object) Kuriosität f

curious a neugierig; (strange) merkwürdig

curl n Locke f □ vt locken □ vi sich locken

curler n Lockenwickler m

curly a lockig

currant n (dried) Korinthe f

currency n Geläufigkeit f; (money) Währung f; **foreign ~** Devisen pl

current a augenblicklich, gegenwärtig; (in general use) geläufig, gebräuchlich □ n Strömung f; (Electr) Strom m. **~ affairs** npl Aktuelle(s) nt. **~ly** adv zur Zeit

curriculum n Lehrplan m. **~ vitae** n Lebenslauf m

curry n Curry m & nt; (meal) Currygericht nt □ vt **~ favour** sich einschmeicheln (**with** bei)

curse n Fluch m □ vt verfluchen □ vi fluchen

cursory a flüchtig

curt a barsch

curtain n Vorhang m

curtsy n Knicks m □ vi knicksen

curve n Kurve f □ vi einen Bogen machen

cushion n Kissen nt □ vt dämpfen

custard n Vanillesoße f
custodian n Hüter m
custody n Obhut f; (of child) Sorgerecht nt; (imprisonment) Haft f
custom n Brauch m; (habit) Gewohnheit f; (Comm) Kundschaft f. **~ary** a üblich; (habitual) gewohnt. **~er** n Kunde m/Kundin f
customs npl Zoll m. **~ officer** n Zollbeamte(r) m
cut n Schnitt m; (Med) Schnittwunde f; (reduction) Kürzung f; (in price) Senkung f □vt/i schneiden; (mow) mähen; abheben (cards); (reduce) kürzen; senken (price). **~ back** vt zurückschneiden; (fig) einschränken, kürzen. **~ down** vt fällen; (fig) einschränken
'cut-back n Kürzung f, Einschränkung f
cute a (fam) niedlich
cut 'glass n Kristall nt
cuticle n Nagelhaut f
cutlery n Besteck nt
cutlet n Kotelett nt
cutting a (remark) bissig □n (from newspaper) Ausschnitt m
cycl|e n Zyklus m; (bicycle) [Fahr]rad nt □vi mit dem Rad fahren. **~ist** n Radfahrer(in) m(f)
cyclone n Wirbelsturm m
cylinder n Zylinder m. **~rical** a zylindrisch
cymbals npl Becken nt
cynic n Zyniker m. **~al** a zynisch. **~ism** n Zynismus m
cypress n Zypresse f
Cyprus n Zypern nt
cyst n Zyste f. **~itis** n Blasenentzündung f
Czech a tschechisch □n Tscheche m/ Tschechin f. **~ Republic** n Tschechische Republik f

D

dabble vi **~ in sth** (fig) sich nebenbei mit etw befassen

dachshund n Dackel m
dad(dy) n (fam) Vati m
daddy-'long-legs n [Kohl]schnake f
daffodil n Osterglocke f
daft a dumm
dagger n Dolch m
dahlia n Dahlie f
daily a & adv täglich
dainty a zierlich
dairy n Molkerei f; (shop) Milchgeschäft nt. **~ products** pl Milchprodukte pl
daisy n Gänseblümchen nt
dam n [Stau]damm m □vt eindämmen
damage n Schaden m (**to** an + dat); **~s** pl (Jur) Schadenersatz m □vt beschädigen; (fig) beeinträchtigen
damask n Damast m
damn a, int & adv (fam) verdammt □n **I don't care or give a ~** (fam) ich schere mich einen Dreck darum □vt verdammen. **~ation** n Verdammnis f
damp a feucht □n Feuchtigkeit f
dampen vt anfeuchten; (fig) dämpfen
dance n Tanz m; (function) Tanzveranstaltung f □vt/i tanzen
dancer n Tänzer(in) m(f)
dandelion n Löwenzahn m
dandruff n Schuppen pl
Dane n Däne m/Dänin f; **Great ~** [deutsche] Dogge f
danger n Gefahr f; **in/out of ~** in/außer Gefahr. **~ous** a gefährlich; **~ously ill** schwer erkrankt
dangle vi baumeln □vt baumeln lassen
Danish a dänisch. **~pastry** n Hefeteilchen m
Danube n Donau f
dare □vt/i (challenge) herausfordern (**to** zu); **~ [to] do sth** [es] wagen, etw zu tun. **~devil** n Draufgänger m

daring a verwegen □ n Verwegen-
heit f
dark a dunkel; ~ **horse** (fig)
stilles Wasser nt □ n Dunkelheit f;
after ~ nach Einbruch der Dunkelheit; **in the** ~ im Dunkeln
dark|en vt verdunkeln □ vi dunk-
ler werden. ~**ness** n Dunkelheit f
'**dark-room** n Dunkelkammer f
darling a allerliebst □ n Liebling m
darn vt stopfen
dart n Pfeil m; ~**s** sg (game)
[Wurf]pfeil m □ vi flitzen
dash n (Typ) Gedankenstrich m
□ vi rennen □ vt schleudern; ~ **off**
vi losstürzen □ vt (write quickly)
hinwerfen
'**dashboard** n Armaturenbrett nt
data npl & sg Daten pl. ~ **processing** n Datenverarbeitung f
date[1] n (fruit) Dattel f
date[2] n Datum nt; (fam) Verabredung f; **to** ~ bis heute; **out of** ~
überholt; ⟨expired⟩ ungültig; **be
up to** ~ auf dem laufenden sein
□ vt/i datieren
dated a altmodisch
'**date-line** n Datumsgrenze f
dative a & n (Gram) ~ [**case**]
Dativ m
daughter n Tochter f. ~**-in-law** n
Schwiegertochter f
daunt vt entmutigen; **nothing**
~**ed** unverzagt
dawdle vi trödeln
dawn n Morgendämmerung f; **at**
~ bei Tagesanbruch □ vi anbrechen; **it** ~**ed on me** (fig) es ging
mir auf
day n Tag m; ~ **by** ~ Tag für Tag;
~ **after** ~ Tag um Tag; **these** ~**s**
heutzutage
day: ~**break** n **at** ~**break** bei
Tagesanbruch m. ~**dream** n
Tagtraum m □ vi [mit offenen Au-
gen] träumen
daze n **in a** ~ wie benommen. ~**d**
a benommen
dazzle vt blenden

deacon n Diakon m
dead a tot; ⟨flower⟩ verwelkt;
(numb) taub; ~ **centre** genau in
der Mitte □ adv ~ **tired** todmüde;
~ **slow** sehr langsam □ n **the** ~ pl
die Toten; **in the** ~ **of night**
mitten in der Nacht
deaden vt dämpfen ⟨sound⟩; betäuben ⟨pain⟩
dead: ~ **'end** n Sackgasse f. ~
'**heat** n totes Rennen nt. ~ **line** n
[letzter] Termin m
deadly a tödlich
deaf a taub; ~ **and dumb** taub-
stumm
deaf|en vt betäuben; (permanent-
ly) taub machen. ~**ening** a oh-
renbetäubend. ~**ness** n Taub-
heit f
deal n (transaction) Geschäft nt;
whose ~? (Cards) wer gibt? **a**
good or **great** ~ eine Menge □ n
(Cards) geben; ~ **out** austeilen
□ vi ~ **in** handeln mit; ~ **with** zu
tun haben mit; (handle) sich befassen mit; ⟨cope with⟩ fertig werden mit; (be about) handeln von
deal|er n Händler m. ~**ings** npl
have ~**ings with** zu tun haben
mit
dean n Dekan m
dear a lieb; (expensive) teuer; (in
letter) liebe(r,s)/ (formal) sehr
geehrte(r,s) □ n Liebe(r) m/f
□ int **oh** ~! oje! ~**ly** adv ⟨love⟩
sehr; ⟨pay⟩ teuer
dearth n Mangel m (of an + dat)
death n Tod m; **three** ~**s** drei
Todesfälle. ~ **certificate** n Ster-
beurkunde f. ~ **duty** n Erb-
schaftssteuer f
deathly a ~ **silence** Totenstille f
□ adv ~ **pale** totenblaß
death: ~ **penalty** n Todesstrafe f.
~**-trap** n Todesfalle f
debase vt erniedrigen
debatable a strittig
debate n Debatte f □ vt/i debattie-
ren

debauchery n Ausschweifung f

debit n Schuldbetrag m; ~ **[side]** Soll nt □vt (Comm) belasten; abbuchen ⟨sum⟩

debris n Trümmer pl

debt n Schuld f; **in** ~ verschuldet. ~ **or** n Schuldner m

début n Debüt nt

decade n Jahrzehnt nt

decadent a dekadent

decaffeinated a koffeinfrei

decant vt umfüllen. ~ **er** n Karaffe f

decapitate vt köpfen

decay n Verfall m; (rot) Verwesung f; (of tooth) Zahnfäule f □vi verfallen; (rot) verwesen; ⟨tooth:⟩ schlecht werden

deceased a verstorben □n **the** ~ der/die Verstorbene

deceit n Täuschung f. ~ **ful** a unaufrichtig

deceive vt täuschen; (be unfaithful to) betrügen

December n Dezember m

decency n Anstand m

decent a anständig

decentralize vt dezentralisieren

decept|ion n Täuschung f; (fraud) Betrug m. ~ **ive** a täuschend

decibel n Dezibel nt

decide vt entscheiden □vi sich entscheiden (**on** für)

deciduous a ~ **tree** Laubbaum m

decimal □n Dezimalzahl f. ~ **'point** n Komma nt

decipher vt entziffern

decision n Entscheidung f

decisive a ausschlaggebend; (firm) entschlossen

deck n (Naut) Deck nt; **on** ~ an Deck. ~ **-chair** n Liegestuhl m

declaration n Erklärung f

declare vt erklären; angeben ⟨goods⟩; **anything to** ~? etwas zu verzollen?

decline n Rückgang m; (in health) Verfall m □vt ablehnen; (Gram)

deklinieren □vi ablehnen; (fall) sinken; (decrease) nachlassen

decompose vi sich zersetzen

décor n Ausstattung f

decorat|e vt (adorn) schmücken; verzieren ⟨cake⟩; (paint) streichen; (wallpaper) tapezieren; (award medal to) einen Orden verleihen (+ dat). ~ **ion** n Verzierung f; (medal) Orden m; ~ **ions** pl Schmuck m. ~ **ive** a dekorativ. ~ **or** n **painter and** ~ **or** Maler und Tapezierer m

decorum n Anstand m

decoy n Lockvogel m

decrease[1] n Verringerung f; (in number) Rückgang m; **be on the** ~ zurückgehen

decrease[2] vt verringern; herabsetzen ⟨price⟩ □vi sich verringern; ⟨price:⟩ sinken

decree n Erlaß m □vt verordnen

decrepit a altersschwach

dedicat|e vt widmen; (Relig) weihen. ~ **ed** a hingebungsvoll; ⟨person⟩ aufopfernd. ~ **ion** n Hingabe f; (in book) Widmung f

deduce vt folgern (**from** aus)

deduct vt abziehen

deduction n Abzug m

deed n Tat f; (Jur) Urkunde f

deem vt halten für

deep a tief

deer n inv Hirsch m; (roe) Reh nt

deface vt beschädigen

defamat|ion n Verleumdung f. ~ **ory** a verleumderisch

default n (Jur) Nichtzahlung f; (failure to appear) Nichterscheinen nt; **win by** ~ (Sport) kampflos gewinnen □vi nicht zahlen; nicht erscheinen

defeat n Niederlage f; (defeating) Besiegung f; (rejection) Ablehnung f □vt besiegen; ablehnen; (frustrate) vereiteln

defect[1] vi (Pol) überlaufen

defect² *n* Fehler *m*; (*Techn*) Defekt *m*. ~**ive** *a* fehlerhaft; (*Techn*) defekt

defence *n* Verteidigung *f*. ~**less** *a* wehrlos

defend *vt* verteidigen; (*justify*) rechtfertigen. ~**ant** *n* (*Jur*) Beklagte(r) *m/f*; (*in criminal court*) Angeklagte(r) *m/f*

defensive *a* defensiv □ *n* Defensive *f*

defer *vt* aufschieben; ~ **to s.o.** sich jdm fügen

deference *n* Ehrerbietung *f*

defian|ce *n* Trotz *m*. ~**t** *a* aufsässig

deficien|cy *n* Mangel *m*. ~**t** *a* mangelhaft

deficit *n* Defizit *nt*

define *vt* bestimmen; definieren ⟨*word*⟩

definite *a* bestimmt; (*certain*) sicher

definition *n* Definition *f*; (*Phot*) Schärfe *f*

definitive *a* endgültig

deflat|e *vt* die Luft auslassen aus. ~**ion** *n* (*Comm*) Deflation *f*

deflect *vt* ablenken

deformity *n* Mißbildung *f*

defraud *vt* betrügen (**of** um)

defrost *vt* entfrosten; abtauen ⟨*fridge*⟩; auftauen ⟨*food*⟩

deft *a* geschickt. ~**ness** *n* Geschicklichkeit *f*

defunct *a* aufgelöst

defuse *vt* entschärfen

defy *vt* trotzen (+ *dat*); widerstehen (+ *dat*) ⟨*attempt*⟩

degenerate¹ *vi* degenerieren

degenerate² *a* degeneriert

degree *n* Grad *m*; (*Univ*) akademischer Grad *m*

dehydrate *vt* Wasser entziehen (+ *dat*). ~**d** *a* ausgetrocknet

de-ice *vt* enteisen

deign *vi* ~ **to do sth** sich herablassen, etw zu tun

deity *n* Gottheit *f*

delay *n* Verzögerung *f*; (*of train*) Verspätung *f*; **without** ~ unverzüglich □ *vt* aufhalten; (*postpone*) aufschieben

delegate¹ *n* Delegierte(r) *m/f*

delegat|e² *vt* delegieren. ~**ion** *n* Delegation *f*

delete *vt* streichen

deliberate¹ *a* absichtlich

deliberat|e² *vt/i* überlegen. ~**ion** *n* Überlegung *f*

delicacy *n* Feinheit *f*; Zartheit *f*; ⟨*food*⟩ Delikatesse *f*

delicate *a* fein; ⟨*health*⟩ zart; (*situation*) heikel; ⟨*mechanism*⟩ empfindlich

delicatessen *n* Delikatessengeschäft *nt*

delicious *a* köstlich

delight *n* Freude *f* □ *vt* entzücken □ *vi* ~ **in** sich erfreuen an (+ *dat*). ~**ful** *a* reizend

delinquent *a* straffällig □ *n* Straffällige(r) *m/f*

deli|rious *a* **be** ~**rious** im Delirium sein. ~**rium** *n* Delirium *nt*

deliver *vt* liefern; zustellen ⟨*post*⟩; halten ⟨*speech*⟩; überbringen ⟨*message*⟩; versetzen ⟨*blow*⟩; (*set free*) befreien. ~**ance** *n* Erlösung *f*. ~**y** *n* Lieferung *f*; (*of post*) Zustellung *f*; (*Med*) Entbindung *f*

delta *n* Delta *nt*

delude *vt* täuschen; ~ **oneself** sich (*dat*) Illusionen machen

deluge *n* Flut *f*; (*heavy rain*) schwerer Guß *m*

delusion *n* Täuschung *f*

de luxe *a* Luxus-

delve *vi* hineingreifen (**into** in + *acc*); (*fig*) eingehen (**into** auf + *acc*)

demand *n* Forderung *f*; (*Comm*) Nachfrage *f*; **in** ~ gefragt; **on** ~ auf Verlangen □ *vt* verlangen, fordern (**of/from** von). ~**ing** *a* anspruchsvoll

demarcation *n* Abgrenzung *f*

demeanour n Verhalten nt

demise n Tod m

demister n (Auto) Defroster m

demobilize vt (Mil) entlassen

democracy n Demokratie f

democrat n Demokrat m. ~**ic** a demokratisch

demo|lish vt abbrechen; (destroy) zerstören. ~**lition** n Abbruch m

demon n Dämon m

demonstrat|e vt beweisen; vorführen ⟨appliance⟩ □vi (Pol) demonstrieren. ~**ion** n Vorführung f; (Pol) Demonstration f

demonstrative a (Gram) demonstrativ; be ~ seine Gefühle zeigen

demonstrator n Vorführer m; (Pol) Demonstrant m

demoralize vt demoralisieren

demote vt degradieren

demure a sittsam

den n Höhle f; (room) Bude f

denial n Leugnen nt; official ~ Dementi nt

denigrate vt herabsetzen

denim n Jeansstoff m

Denmark n Dänemark nt

denomination n (Relig) Konfession f; (money) Nennwert m

denote vt bezeichnen

denounce vt denunzieren

dens|e a dicht. ~**ity** n Dichte f

dent n Delle f; (Bild) vt einbeulen

dental a Zahn-; ⟨treatment⟩ zahnärztlich. ~ **floss** n Zahnseide f. ~ **surgeon** n Zahnarzt m

dentist n Zahnarzt m/-ärztin f. ~**ry** n Zahnmedizin f

denture n Zahnprothese f; ~**s** pl künstliches Gebiß nt

denunciation n Denunziation f

deny vt leugnen; (officially) dementieren

deodorant n Deodorant nt

depart vi abfahren; (Aviat) abfliegen; (go away) weggehen/-fahren; (deviate) abweichen (from von)

department n Abteilung f; (Pol) Ministerium nt. ~ **store** n Kaufhaus nt

departure n Abfahrt f; (Aviat) Abflug m; (from rule) Abweichung f

depend vi abhängen (on von); (rely) sich verlassen (on auf + acc); **it all** ~**s** das kommt darauf an. ~**able** a zuverlässig. ~**ant** n Abhängige(r) m/f. ~**ence** n Abhängigkeit f. ~**ent** a abhängig (on von)

depict vt darstellen

depilatory n Enthaarungsmittel nt

deplor|able a bedauerlich. ~**e** vt bedauern

deploy vt einsetzen

depopulate vt entvölkern

deport vt deportieren, ausweisen. ~**ation** n Ausweisung f

deportment n Haltung f

depose vt absetzen

deposit n Anzahlung f; (against damage) Kaution f; (on bottle) Pfand nt; (sediment) Bodensatz m; (Geol) Ablagerung f □ vt legen; (for safety) deponieren; (Geol) ablagern. ~ **account** n Sparkonto nt

depot n Depot nt

deprave vt verderben. ~**d** a verkommen

deprecate vt mißbilligen

depreciat|e vi an Wert verlieren. ~**ion** n Wertminderung f; (Comm) Abschreibung f

depress vt deprimieren; (press down) herunterdrücken. ~**ed** a deprimiert; ~**ed area** Notstandsgebiet nt. ~**ing** a deprimierend. ~**ion** n Vertiefung f; (Med) Depression f; (Meteorol) Tief nt

deprivation n Entbehrung f

deprive vt entziehen. ~**d** a benachteiligt

depth n Tiefe f; **in** ~ gründlich

deputize vi ~ **for** vertreten

deputy n Stellvertreter m □attrib stellvertretend

derailment n Entgleisung f

deranged a geistesgestört

derelict a verfallen

deri|de vt verhöhnen. **~sion** n Hohn m

derisory a höhnisch; ⟨offer⟩ lächerlich

derivation n Ableitung f

derive vt/i ⟨obtain⟩ gewinnen (**from** aus)

dermatologist n Hautarzt m/-ärztin f

derogatory a abfällig

derrick n Bohrturm m

derv n Diesel[kraftstoff] m

descend vt/i hinunter-/heruntergehen; ⟨vehicle, lift:⟩ hinunter-/herunterfahren. **~ant** n Nachkomme m

descent n Abstieg m; ⟨lineage⟩ Abstammung f

describe vt beschreiben

descrip|tion n Beschreibung f. **~tive** a beschreibend; ⟨vivid⟩ anschaulich

desecrat|e vt entweihen. **~ion** n Entweihung f

desert[1] n Wüste f

desert[2] vt verlassen □vi desertieren. **~ed** a verlassen. **~er** n (Mil) Deserteur m. **~ion** n Fahnenflucht f

deserv|e vt verdienen. **~ing** a verdienstvoll

design n Entwurf m; ⟨pattern⟩ Muster nt; ⟨construction⟩ Konstruktion f; ⟨aim⟩ Absicht f □vt entwerfen; ⟨construct⟩ konstruieren

designate vt bezeichnen

designer n Designer m; (Techn) Konstrukteur m; (Theat) Bühnenbildner m

desirable a wünschenswert; ⟨sexually⟩ begehrenswert

desire n Wunsch m; ⟨longing⟩ Verlangen nt (**for** nach); ⟨sexual⟩

Begierde f □vt [sich (dat)] wünschen; ⟨sexually⟩ begehren

desk n Schreibtisch m; (Sch) Pult nt

desolat|e a trostlos. **~ion** n Trostlosigkeit f

despair n Verzweiflung f □vi verzweifeln

desperat|e a verzweifelt; ⟨urgent⟩ dringend. **~ion** n Verzweiflung f

despicable a verachtenswert

despise vt verachten

despite prep trotz (+ gen)

despondent a niedergeschlagen

despot n Despot m

dessert n Dessert nt, Nachtisch m. **~ spoon** n Dessertlöffel m

destination n [Reise]ziel nt; ⟨of goods⟩ Bestimmungsort m

destiny n Schicksal nt

destitute a völlig mittellos

destroy vt zerstören; ⟨totally⟩ vernichten. **~er** n (Naut) Zerstörer m

destruc|tion n Zerstörung f; Vernichtung f. **~tive** a zerstörerisch

detach vt abnehmen; ⟨tear off⟩ abtrennen. **~able** a abnehmbar. **~ed** a ⟨fig⟩ distanziert; **~ed house** Einzelhaus nt

detachment n Distanz f; ⟨objectivity⟩ Abstand m; (Mil) Sonderkommando nt

detail n Einzelheit f, Detail nt; **in ~** ausführlich □vt einzeln aufführen; (Mil) abkommandieren. **~ed** a ausführlich

detain vt aufhalten; ⟨police:⟩ in Haft behalten. **~ee** n Häftling m

detect vt entdecken; ⟨perceive⟩ wahrnehmen. **~ion** n Entdeckung f

detective n Detektiv m

detector n Suchgerät nt; ⟨for metal⟩ Metalldetektor m

detention n Haft f; (Sch) Nachsitzen nt

deter vt abschrecken

detergent n Waschmittel nt

deteriorat|e vi sich verschlechtern. **~ion** n Verschlechterung f

determination n Entschlossenheit f

determine vt bestimmen; **~ to** (resolve) sich entschließen zu. **~d** a entschlossen

deterrent n Abschreckungsmittel nt

detest vt verabscheuen. **~able** a abscheulich

detonat|e vt zünden □ vi explodieren. **~or** n Zünder m

detour n Umweg m; (for traffic) Umleitung f

detract vi **~ from** beeinträchtigen

detriment n **to the ~** zum Schaden (of gen)

deuce n (Tennis) Einstand m

devaluation n Abwertung f

de'value vt abwerten ⟨currency⟩

devastat|e vt verwüsten. **~ion** n Verwüstung f

develop vt entwickeln; erschließen ⟨area⟩ □ vi sich entwickeln (into zu). **~er** n Bodenspekulant m

de'veloping country n Entwicklungsland nt

development n Entwicklung f

deviant a abweichend

deviat|e vi abweichen. **~ion** n Abweichung f

device n Gerät nt; (fig) Mittel nt; **leave s.o. to his own ~s** jdn sich (dat) selbst überlassen

devil n Teufel m. **~ish** a teuflisch

devious a verschlagen

devise vt sich (dat) ausdenken

devoid a **~ of** ohne

devolution n Dezentralisierung f; (of power) Übertragung f

devote vt widmen (to dat). **~d** a ergeben; ⟨care⟩ liebevoll

devotion n Hingabe f. **~s** pl (Relig) Andacht f

devour vt verschlingen

devout a fromm

dew n Tau m

dexterity n Geschicklichkeit f

diabet|es n Zuckerkrankheit f. **~ic** n Zuckerkranke(r) m/f, Diabetiker(in) m(f)

diabolical a teuflisch

diagnose vt diagnostizieren

diagnosis n Diagnose f

diagonal a diagonal

diagram n Diagramm nt

dial n (of clock) Zifferblatt nt; (Techn) Skala f; (Teleph) Wählscheibe f □ vt/i (Teleph) wählen; **~ direct** durchwählen

dialect n Dialekt m

dialling: ~ code n Vorwahlnummer f. **~ tone** n Amtszeichen nt

dialogue n Dialog m

diameter n Durchmesser m

diamond n Diamant m; (cut) Brillant m; (shape) Raute f; **~s** pl (Cards) Karo nt

diaphragm n (Anat) Zwerchfell nt; (Phot) Blende f

diarrhoea n Durchfall m

diary n Tagebuch nt; (for appointments) [Termin]kalender m

dice n inv Würfel m □ vt (Culin) in Würfel schneiden

dictat|e vt/i diktieren. **~ion** n Diktat nt

dictator n Diktator m. **~ial** a diktatorisch. **~ship** n Diktatur f

dictionary n Wörterbuch nt

didactic a didaktisch

die¹ n (Techn) Prägestempel m; (metal mould) Gußform f

die² vi sterben (of an + dat); ⟨plant, animal:⟩ eingehen; ⟨flower:⟩ verwelken; **be dying to do sth** (fam) darauf brennen, etw zu tun; **be dying for sth** (fam) sich nach etw sehnen

diesel n Diesel m. **~ engine** n Dieselmotor m

diet n Kost f; (restricted) Diät f; (for slimming) Schlankheitskur f; **be on a ~** diät leben; **eine Schlankheitskur machen** □ vi diät leben; eine Schlankheitskur machen

dietician n Diätassistent(in) m(f)

differ vi sich unterscheiden; (disagree) verschiedener Meinung sein

differen|ce n Unterschied m; (disagreement) Meinungsverschiedenheit f. ~ **t** a andere(r,s); (various) verschiedene; **be ~ t** anders sein (**from** als)

differential n Unterschied m; (Techn) Differential nt

differentiate vt/i unterscheiden (**between** zwischen + dat)

difficult a schwierig, schwer. ~ **y** n Schwierigkeit f

diffiden|ce n Zaghaftigkeit f. ~ **t** a zaghaft

diffuse[1] a ausgebreitet

diffuse[2] vt (Phys) streuen

dig n (poke) Stoß m; (remark) spitze Bemerkung f; (Archaeol) Ausgrabung f; ~ **s** pl (fam) möbliertes Zimmer nt □ vt/i graben; umgraben ⟨garden⟩

digest[1] n Kurzfassung f

digest[2] vt verdauen. ~ **ion** n Verdauung f

digger n (Techn) Bagger m

digit n Ziffer f; (finger) Finger m; (toe) Zehe f

digital a Digital-

dignified a würdevoll

dignitary n Würdenträger m

dignity n Würde f

digress vi abschweifen. ~ **ion** n Abschweifung f

dike n Deich m; (ditch) Graben m

dilapidated a baufällig

dilate vt erweitern □ vi sich erweitern

dilatory a langsam

dilemma n Dilemma nt

dilettante n Dilettant(in) m(f)

diligen|ce n Fleiß m. ~ **t** a fleißig

dill n Dill m

dilute vt verdünnen

dim a (weak) schwach; (dark) trüb[e]; (indistinct) undeutlich; (fam: stupid) dumm, (fam) doof □ vt dämpfen □ vi schwächer werden

dimension n Dimension f; ~ **s** pl Maße pl

diminish vt verringern □ vi sich verringern

diminutive a winzig □ n Verkleinerungsform f

dimple n Grübchen nt

din n Krach m, Getöse nt

dine vi speisen. ~ **r** n Speisende(r) m/f

dinghy n Dinghi nt; (inflatable) Schlauchboot nt

dingy a trübe

dining: ~ **-car** n Speisewagen m. ~ **-room** n Eßzimmer nt. ~ **-table** n Eßtisch m

dinner n Abendessen nt; (at midday) Mittagessen nt; (formal) Essen nt. ~ **-jacket** n Smoking m

dinosaur n Dinosaurier m

diocese n Diözese f

dip n (in ground) Senke f; (Culin) Dip m □ vt [ein]tauchen; ~ **one's headlights** (Auto) [die Scheinwerfer] abblenden □ vi sich senken

diphtheria n Diphtherie f

diphthong n Diphthong m

diploma n Diplom nt

diplomacy n Diplomatie f

diplomat n Diplomat m. ~ **ic** a diplomatisch

'dip-stick n (Auto) Ölmeßstab m

dire a bitter; ⟨consequences⟩ furchtbar

direct a & adv direkt □ vt (aim) richten (**at** auf / (fig) an + acc); (control) leiten; (order) anweisen; ~ **s.o.** (show the way) jdm den Weg sagen; ~ **a film/play** bei einem Film/Theaterstück Regie führen. ~ **'current** n Gleichstrom m

direction n Richtung f; (control) Leitung f; (of play) Regie f; ~ s pl Anweisungen pl; ~ s for use Gebrauchsanweisung f

directly adv direkt; (at once) sofort

director n (Comm) Direktor m; (of play, film) Regisseur m

directory n Verzeichnis nt; (Teleph) Telefonbuch nt

dirt n Schmutz m; (soil) Erde f; ~ **cheap** (fam) spottbillig

dirty a schmutzig

dis'ability n Behinderung f. ~**abled** a [körper]behindert

disad'vantage n Nachteil m. ~**d** a benachteiligt

disaf'fected a unzufrieden

disa'gree vi nicht übereinstimmen (with mit); I ~ ich bin anderer Meinung; **oysters** ~ **with me** Austern bekommen mir nicht

disa'greeable a unangenehm

disa'greement n Meinungsverschiedenheit f

disap'pear vi verschwinden. ~**ance** n Verschwinden nt

disap'point vt enttäuschen. ~**ment** n Enttäuschung f

disap'proval n Mißbilligung f

disap'prove vi dagegen sein; ~ **of** mißbilligen

dis'arm vt entwaffnen □vi abrüsten. ~**ament** n Abrüstung f

disar'ray n Unordnung f

disast|er n Katastrophe f; (accident) Unglück nt. ~**rous** a katastrophal

disbe'lief n Ungläubigkeit f

disc n Scheibe f; (record) [Schall]platte f; (CD) CD f

discard vt ablegen

discern vt wahrnehmen. ~**ible** a wahrnehmbar. ~**ing** a anspruchsvoll

'discharge[1] n Ausstoßen nt; (Electr) Entladung f; (dismissal) Entlassung f; (Jur) Freispruch m; (Med) Ausfluß m

dis'charge[2] vt ausstoßen; (Electr) entladen; (dismiss) entlassen; (Jur) freisprechen (accused)

disciple n Jünger m; (fig) Schüler m

discipline n Disziplin f □vt Disziplin beibringen (+ dat); (punish) bestrafen

'disc jockey n Diskjockey m

dis'claim vt abstreiten. ~**er** n Verzichterklärung f

dis'close vt enthüllen. ~**ure** n Enthüllung f

disco n (fam) Disko f

dis'colour vt verfärben □vi sich verfärben

dis'comfort n Beschwerden pl

disconcert vt aus der Fassung bringen

discon'nect vt trennen; (Electr) ausschalten; (cut supply) abstellen

discon'tent n Unzufriedenheit f

discon'tinue vt einstellen; (Comm) nicht mehr herstellen

'discord n Zwietracht f; (Mus & fig) Mißklang m

discothèque n Diskothek f

'discount[1] n Rabatt m

dis'count[2] vt außer acht lassen

dis'courage vt entmutigen

dis'courteous a unhöflich

discover vt entdecken. ~**y** n Entdeckung f

discreet a diskret

discrepancy n Diskrepanz f

discretion n Diskretion f

discriminat|e vi unterscheiden (between zwischen + dat); ~**e against** diskriminieren; (fig). ~**ion** n Diskriminierung f

discus n Diskus m

discuss vt besprechen; (examine critically) diskutieren. ~**ion** n Besprechung f; Diskussion f

disdain n Verachtung f □vt verachten. ~**ful** a verächtlich

disease n Krankheit f. ~**d** a krank

disem'bark vi an Land gehen

disen'chant vt ernüchtern

disen'gage vt losmachen; ~ **the clutch** (Auto) auskuppeln

dis'figure vt entstellen

dis'grace n Schande f; **in** ~ **in Ungnade** □vt Schande machen (+ dat). ~**ful** a schändlich

disgruntled a verstimmt

disguise n Verkleidung f; **in** ~ verkleidet □vt verkleiden; verstellen ⟨voice⟩

disgust n Ekel m; **in** ~ empört □vt anekeln; (appal) empören. ~**ing** a eklig

dish n Schüssel f; (shallow) Schale f; (small) Schälchen nt; (food) Gericht nt

'dishcloth n Spültuch nt

dis'hearten vt entmutigen

dishevelled a zerzaust

dis'honest a unehrlich. ~**y** n Unehrlichkeit f

dis'honour n Schande f □vt entehren; nicht honorieren ⟨cheque⟩. ~**able** a unehrenhaft

'dishwasher n Geschirrspülmaschine f

disil'lusion vt ernüchtern

disin'fect vt desinfizieren. ~**ant** n Desinfektionsmittel nt

dis'integrate vi zerfallen

dis'interested a unvoreingenommen

dis'jointed a unzusammenhängend

dis'like n Abneigung f □vt nicht mögen

dislocate vt ausrenken; ~ **one's shoulder** sich (dat) den Arm auskugeln

dis'lodge vt entfernen

dis'loyal a illoyal. ~**ty** n Illoyalität f

dismal a trüb[e]; ⟨person⟩ trübselig

dismantle vt auseinandernehmen

dis'may n Bestürzung f. ~**ed** a bestürzt

dis'miss vt entlassen; (reject) zurückweisen. ~**al** n Entlassung f; Zurückweisung f

dis'mount vi absteigen

diso'bedient a ungehorsam

diso'bey vt/i nicht gehorchen (+ dat); nicht befolgen ⟨rule⟩

dis'order n Unordnung f; (Med) Störung f. ~**ly** a unordentlich

dis'organized a unorganisiert

dis'orientate vt verwirren

dis'own vt verleugnen

disparaging a abschätzig

disparity n Ungleichheit f

dispassionate a gelassen

dispatch n (Comm) Versand m; (Mil) Nachricht f; (report) Bericht m □vt [ab]senden; (deal with) erledigen; (kill) töten

dispel vt vertreiben

dispensable a entbehrlich

dispensary n Apotheke f

dispense vt austeilen; ~ **with** verzichten auf (+ acc). ~**r** n Spender(in) m(f); (device) Automat m

dispers|al n Zerstreuung f. ~**e** vt zerstreuen □vi sich zerstreuen

dis'place vt verschieben; ~**d person** Vertriebene(r) m/f

display n Ausstellung f; (Comm) Auslage f; (performance) Vorführung f □vt zeigen; ausstellen ⟨goods⟩

dis'please vt mißfallen (+ dat)

disposable a Wegwerf-; ⟨income⟩ verfügbar

disposal n Beseitigung f; **be at s.o.'s** ~ jdm zur Verfügung stehen

dispose vi ~ **of** beseitigen

disposition n Veranlagung f; (nature) Wesensart f

disproportionate a unverhältnismäßig

dis'prove vt widerlegen

dispute n Disput m; (quarrel) Streit m □vt bestreiten

dis'qualify vt disqualifizieren; ~ **s.o. from driving** jdm den Führerschein entziehen

disre'gard vt nicht beachten, ignorieren

dis'reputable a verrufen

disre'pute n Verruf m

disre'spect n Respektlosigkeit f. ~**ful** a respektlos

disrupt vt stören. ~**ion** n Störung f

dissatis'faction n Unzufriedenheit f

dis'satisfied a unzufrieden

dissect vt zergliedern; (Med) sezieren. ~**ion** n Zergliederung f; (Med) Sektion f

disseminate vt verbreiten

dissent n Nichtübereinstimmung f

dissertation n Dissertation f

dis'service n schlechter Dienst m

dissident n Dissident m

dis'similar a unähnlich (**to** dat)

dissociate vt trennen; ~ **oneself** sich distanzieren (**from** von)

dissolve vt auflösen □ vi sich auflösen

dissuade vt abbringen (**from** von)

distance n Entfernung f; **in the/from a** ~ in/aus der Ferne

distant a fern; (aloof) kühl; (relative) entfernt

dis'taste n Abneigung f. ~**ful** a unangenehm

distil vt brennen; (Med) destillieren. ~**lery** n Brennerei f

distinct a deutlich; (different) verschieden. ~**ion** n Unterschied m; (Sch) Auszeichnung f. ~**ive** a kennzeichnend; (unmistakable) unverwechselbar

distinguish vt/i unterscheiden; (make out) erkennen; ~ **oneself** sich auszeichnen. ~**ed** a angesehen; (appearance) distinguiert

distort vt verzerren; (fig) verdrehen. ~**ion** n Verzerrung f; (fig) Verdrehung f

distract vt ablenken. ~**ion** n Ablenkung f; (despair) Verzweiflung f

distraught a [völlig] aufgelöst

distress n Kummer m; (pain) Schmerz m; (poverty) Not f □ vt Kummer/Schmerz bereiten (+ dat); (sadden) bekümmern; (shock) erschüttern

distribute vt verteilen; (Comm) vertreiben. ~**ion** n Verteilung f; Vertrieb m. ~**or** n Verteiler m

district n Gegend f; (Admin) Bezirk m. ~ **nurse** n Gemeindeschwester f

dis'trust n Mißtrauen nt

disturb vt stören; (perturb) beunruhigen; (touch) anrühren. ~**ance** n Unruhe f; (interruption) Störung f. ~**ed** a beunruhigt; [mentally] ~**ed** geistig gestört. ~**ing** a beunruhigend

dis'used a stillgelegt; (empty) leer

ditch n Graben m

dither vi zaudern

ditto n dito; (fam) ebenfalls

divan n Polsterbett nt

dive n [Kopf]sprung m; (Aviat) Sturzflug m; (fam: place) Spelunke f □ vi einen Kopfsprung machen; (when in water) tauchen; (Aviat) einen Sturzflug machen; (fam: rush) stürzen

diver n Taucher m; (Sport) [Kunst]springer m

diverge vi auseinandergehen

diverse a verschieden

diversify vt/i variieren; (Comm) diversifizieren

diversion n Umleitung f; (distraction) Ablenkung f

divert vt umleiten; ablenken (attention)

divide vt teilen; (separate) trennen; (Math) dividieren (**by** durch) □ vi sich teilen

dividend n Dividende f

divine a göttlich

diving n (Sport) Kunstspringen nt. ~**board** n Sprungbrett nt

divinity n Göttlichkeit f; (subject) Theologie f

division *n* Teilung *f*; (*separation*) Trennung *f*; (*Math, Mil*) Division *f*; (*Parl*) Hammelsprung *m*; (*line*) Trennlinie *f*; (*group*) Abteilung *f*

divorce *n* Scheidung *f* □ *vt* sich scheiden lassen von. **~d** *a* geschieden; **get ~d** sich scheiden lassen

divorcee *n* Geschiedene(r) *m/f*

divulge *vt* preisgeben

dizzy *a* schwindlig; **I feel ~** mir ist schwindlig

do *n* (*fam*) Veranstaltung *f* □ *vt/i* tun, machen; (*be suitable*) passen; (*be enough*) reichen, genügen; (*cook*) kochen; (*clean*) putzen; (*Sch: study*) durchnehmen; (*fam: cheat*) beschwindeln (**out of** um); **do without** auskommen ohne; **do away with** abschaffen; **well done** gut gemacht! (*Culin*) gut durchgebraten; **are you doing anything today?** haben Sie heute etwas vor? □ *v aux* **do you speak German?** sprechen Sie deutsch? **yes, I do** ja; (*emphatic*) doch; **no, I don't** nein; **I don't smoke** ich rauche nicht; **don't you/doesn't he?** nicht [wahr]? **how do you do?** guten Tag

docile *a* fügsam

dock[1] *n* (*Jur*) Anklagebank *f*

dock[2] *n* Dock *nt* □ *vi* anlegen, docken □ *vt* docken. **~er** *n* Hafenarbeiter *m*. **~yard** *n* Werft *f*

doctor *n* Arzt *m*/ Ärztin *f*; (*Univ*) Doktor *m* □ *vt* kastrieren; (*spay*) sterilisieren. **~ate** *n* Doktorwürde *f*

doctrine *n* Lehre *f*, Doktrin *f*

document *n* Dokument *nt*. **~ary** *a* Dokumentar- □ *n* Dokumentarbericht *m*; (*film*) Dokumentarfilm *m*

dodge *n* (*fam*) Trick *m*, Kniff *m* □ *vt/i* ausweichen (+ *dat*)

dodgems *npl* Autoskooter *pl*

dodgy *a* (*fam*) (*awkward*) knifflig; (*dubious*) zweifelhaft

doe *n* Ricke *f*; (*rabbit*) [Kaninchen]weibchen *nt*

dog *n* Hund *m*

dog: **~-collar** *n* Hundehalsband *nt*; (*Relig, fam*) Kragen *m* eines Geistlichen. **~-eared** *a* be **~-eared** Eselsohren haben

dogged *a* beharrlich

dogma *n* Dogma *nt*. **~tic** *a* dogmatisch

doily *n* Deckchen *nt*

do-it-yourself *n* Heimwerken *nt*. **~ shop** *n* Heimwerkerladen *m*

doldrums *npl* **be in the ~** niedergeschlagen sein; (*business:*) darniederliegen

dole *n* (*fam*) Stempelgeld *nt*; **be on the ~** arbeitslos sein

doll *n* Puppe *f*

dollar *n* Dollar *m*

dolphin *n* Delphin *m*

domain *n* Gebiet *nt*

dome *n* Kuppel *m*

domestic *a* häuslich; (*Pol*) Innen-; (*Comm*) Binnen-

dominant *a* vorherrschend

dominat|e *vt* beherrschen □ *vi* dominieren. **~ion** *n* Vorherrschaft *f*

dominion *n* Herrschaft *f*

domino *n* Dominostein *m*; **~es** *sg* (*game*) Domino *nt*

don *n* [Universitäts]dozent *m*

donate *vt* spenden. **~ion** *n* Spende *f*

donkey *n* Esel *m*; **~'s years** (*fam*) eine Ewigkeit. **~-work** *n* Routinearbeit *f*

donor *n* Spender(in) *m(f)*

doodle *vi* kritzeln

doom *n* Schicksal *nt*; (*ruin*) Verhängnis *nt*

door *n* Tür *f*; **out of ~s** im Freien

door: **~man** *n* Portier *m*. **~mat** *n* [Fuß]abtreter *m*. **~step** *n* Türschwelle *f*

dope *n* (*fam*) Drogen *pl* □ *vt* betäuben; (*Sport*) dopen

dopey *a* (*fam*) benommen

dormant *a* ruhend

dormer *n* ~ **[window]** Mansardenfenster *nt*

dormitory *n* Schlafsaal *m*

dormouse *n* Haselmaus *f*

dosage *n* Dosierung *f*

dose *n* Dosis *f*

dot *n* Punkt *m*; **on the** ~ pünktlich

dote *vi* ~ **on** vernarrt sein in (+ *acc*)

dotted ~ **line** punktierte Linie *f*

double *a* & *adv* doppelt; ⟨bed, chin⟩ Doppel-; ⟨flower⟩ gefüllt □ *n* das Doppelte; ⟨person⟩ Doppelgänger *m*; ~ **s** *pl* ⟨Tennis⟩ Doppel *nt* □ *vt* verdoppeln; ⟨fold⟩ falten □ *vi* sich verdoppeln

double: ~-**'bass** *n* Kontrabaß *m*. ~-**breasted** *a* zweireihig. ~-**'cross** *vt* ein Doppelspiel treiben mit. ~-**'decker** *n* Doppeldecker *m*. ~ **'Dutch** *n* ⟨fam⟩ Kauderwelsch *nt*. ~ **'glazing** *n* Doppelverglasung *f*. ~ **'room** *n* Doppelzimmer *nt*

doubt *n* Zweifel *m* □ *vt* bezweifeln. ~**ful** *a* zweifelhaft; ⟨disbelieving⟩ skeptisch. ~**less** *adv* zweifellos

dough *n* ⟨fester⟩ Teig *m*; ⟨fam: money⟩ Pinke *f*. ~**nut** *n* Berliner ⟨Pfannkuchen⟩ *m*, Krapfen *m*

douse *vt* übergießen; ausgießen ⟨flames⟩

dove *n* Taube *f*. ~-**tail** *n* ⟨Techn⟩ Schwalbenschwanz *m*

down[1] *n* ⟨feathers⟩ Daunen *pl*

down[2] *adv* unten; ⟨with movement⟩ nach unten; **go** ~ hinuntergehen; **come** ~ herunterkommen; ~ **there** da unten; £50 ~ £50 Anzahlung; ~ **!** ⟨to dog⟩ Platz! ~ **with...!** nieder mit...! □ *prep* ~ **the road/stairs** die Straße/ Treppe hinunter; ~ **the river** den Fluß abwärts □ *vt* ⟨fam⟩ ⟨drink⟩ runterkippen; ~ **tools** die Arbeit niederlegen

down: ~-**and-'out** *n* Penner *m*. ~**cast** *a* niedergeschlagen. ~**fall** *n* Sturz *m*; ⟨ruin⟩ Ruin *m*.

'grade *vt* niedriger einstufen. ~-**'hearted** *a* entmutigt. ~-**'hill** *adv* bergab. ~ **payment** *n* Anzahlung *f*. ~**pour** *n* Platzregen *m*. ~**right** *a* & *adv* ausgesprochen. ~-**'stairs** *adv* unten; ⟨go⟩ nach unten □ *a* im Erdgeschoß. ~-**'stream** *adv* stromabwärts. ~-**to-'earth** *a* sachlich. ~-**'trodden** *a* unterdrückt. ~**ward** *a* nach unten; ⟨slope⟩ abfallend □ *adv* & ~**wards** abwärts, nach unten

dowry *n* Mitgift *f*

doze *n* Nickerchen *nt* □ *vi* dösen. ~ **off** *vi* einnicken

dozen *n* Dutzend *nt*

draft *n* Entwurf *m*; ⟨Comm⟩ Tratte *f* □ *vt* entwerfen

drag *n* ⟨fam⟩ Klotz *m* am Bein; **in** ~ ⟨fam⟩ ⟨man⟩ als Frau gekleidet □ *vt* schleppen

dragon *n* Drache *m*. ~-**fly** *n* Libelle *f*

'drag show *n* Transvestitenshow *f*

drain *n* Abfluß *m*; ⟨underground⟩ Kanal *m*; **the** ~ **s** die Kanalisation □ *vt* entwässern ⟨land⟩; ablassen ⟨liquid⟩; das Wasser ablassen aus ⟨tank⟩; abgießen ⟨vegetables⟩; austrinken ⟨glass⟩ □ *vi* ~ **[away]** ablaufen

drain|age *n* Kanalisation *f*; ⟨of land⟩ Dränage *f*. ~**ing board** *n* Abtropfbrett *nt*. ~**pipe** *n* Abflußrohr *nt*

drake *n* Enterich *m*

drama *n* Drama *nt*

dramatic *a* dramatisch

dramat|ist *n* Dramatiker *m*. ~**ize** *vt* für die Bühne bearbeiten; ⟨fig⟩ dramatisieren

drastic *a* drastisch

draught *n* ⟨Luft⟩zug *m*; ~**s** *sg* ⟨game⟩ Damespiel *nt*

draught: ~ **beer** *n* Bier *nt* vom Faß. ~**sman** *n* technischer Zeichner *m*

draughty *a* zugig; **it's** ~ es zieht

draw n Attraktion f; (Sport) Unentschieden nt; (in lottery) Ziehung f □vt ziehen; (attract) anziehen; zeichnen (picture); abheben (money); holen (water); ~ the curtains die Vorhänge zuziehen/ (back) aufziehen □vi (tea:) ziehen; (Sport) unentschieden spielen. ~ in vt einziehen □vi einfahren; (days:) kürzer werden. ~ out vt herausziehen; abheben (money) □vi ausfahren; (days:) länger werden. ~ up vt aufsetzen (document); herrücken (chair)

draw: ~**back** n Nachteil m. ~**bridge** n Zugbrücke f

drawer n Schublade f

drawing n Zeichnung f

drawing: ~**-board** n Reißbrett nt. ~**-pin** n Reißzwecke f. ~**-room** n Wohnzimmer nt

drawl n schleppende Aussprache f

dread n Furcht f (of vor + dat) □vt fürchten

dreadful a fürchterlich

dream n Traum m □vt/i träumen (about/of von)

dreary a trüb[e]

dredge vt/i baggern. ~**r** n [Naß]bagger m

dregs npl Bodensatz m

drench vt durchnässen

dress n Kleid nt; (clothing) Kleidung f □vt anziehen; (decorate) schmücken; (Culin) anmachen; (Med) verbinden; ~ one**self, get** ~ed sich anziehen. ~ **up** vi sich schön anziehen; (in disguise) sich verkleiden (as als)

dress: ~ **circle** n (Theat) erster Rang m. ~**er** n (furniture) Anrichte f

dressing n (Culin) Soße f; (Med) Verband m

dressing: ~**-gown** n Morgenmantel m. ~**-room** n Ankleidezimmer nt; (Theat) [Künstler]garderobe f. ~**-table** n Frisiertisch m

dress: ~**maker** n Schneiderin f. ~ **rehearsal** n Generalprobe f

dribble vi sabbern; (Sport) dribbeln

dried a getrocknet; ~ **fruit** Dörrobst nt

drier n Trockner m

drift n Abtrift f; (of snow) Schneewehe f; (meaning) Sinn m □vi treiben; (off course) abtreiben; (snow:) Wehen bilden; (fig) (person:) sich treiben lassen. ~**wood** n Treibholz nt

drill n Bohrer m; (Mil) Drill m □vt/i bohren (for nach); (Mil) drillen

drink n Getränk nt; (alcoholic) Drink m; (alcohol) Alkohol m; **have a** ~ etwas trinken □vt/i trinken

drinking-water n Trinkwasser nt

drip n Tropfen m; (drop) Tropfen m; (Med) Tropf m; (fam: person) Niete f □vi tropfen. ~**-dry** a bügelfrei. ~**ping** n Schmalz nt

drive n [Auto]fahrt f; (entrance) Einfahrt f; (energy) Elan m; (Psych) Trieb m; (Pol) Aktion f; (Sport) Treibschlag m; (Techn) Antrieb m □vt treiben; fahren (car); (Sport: hit) schlagen; (Techn) antreiben; ~ **s.o. mad** (fam) jdn verrückt machen □vi fahren

drive-in a ~ **cinema** Autokino nt

driver n Fahrer(in) m(f); (of train) Lokführer m

driving a (rain) peitschend; (force) treibend

driving: ~ **licence** n Führerschein m. ~ **school** n Fahrschule f. ~ **test** Fahrprüfung f; **take one's** ~ **test** den Führerschein machen

drizzle n Nieselregen m □vi nieseln

drone n Drohne f; (sound) Brummen nt

droop vi herabhängen; ⟨flowers:⟩ die Köpfe hängen lassen

drop n Tropfen m; (fall) Fall m; (in price, temperature) Rückgang m □vt fallen lassen; abwerfen ⟨bomb⟩; (omit) auslassen; (give up) aufgeben □vi fallen; (fall lower) sinken; ⟨wind:⟩ nachlassen. ~ **in** vi vorbeikommen. ~ **off** vt absetzen ⟨person⟩ □vi abfallen; (fall asleep) einschlafen. ~ **out** vi herausfallen; (give up) aufgeben

drop-out n Aussteiger m

droppings npl Kot m

drought n Dürre f

drown vi ertrinken □vt ertränken; übertönen ⟨noise⟩

drowsy a schläfrig

drug n Droge f □vt betäuben. ~ **addict** n Drogenabhängige(r) m/f

drum n Trommel f; (for oil) Tonne f □vi trommeln □vt ~ **sth into s.o.** (fam) jdm etw einbleuen. ~ **mer** n Trommler m; (in pop-group) Schlagzeuger m

drunk a betrunken; **get** ~ sich betrinken □n Betrunkene(r) m

drunk|ard n Trinker m. ~ **en** a betrunken; ~ **en driving** Trunkenheit f am Steuer

dry a trocken □vt/i trocknen

dry-'clean vt chemisch reinigen. ~ '-**cleaner's** n (shop) chemische Reinigung f

dual a doppelt

dual: ~ '**carriageway** n ≈ Schnellstraße f. ~ '-'**purpose** a zweifach verwendbar

dub vt synchronisieren ⟨film⟩; kopieren ⟨tape⟩; (name) nennen

dubious a zweifelhaft; **be** ~ **about** Zweifel haben über (+ acc)

duchess n Herzogin f

duck n Ente f □vi sich ducken. ~ **ling** n Entchen nt; (Culin) Ente f

duct n Rohr nt; (Anat) Gang m

dud a (fam) nutzlos; ⟨coin⟩ falsch; ⟨cheque⟩ ungedeckt; (forged) gefälscht □n (fam) (banknote) Blüte f; (Mil: shell) Blindgänger m

due a angemessen; **be** ~ fällig sein; ⟨baby:⟩ erwartet werden; ⟨train:⟩ planmäßig ankommen; ~ **to** (owing to) wegen (+ gen); **be** ~ **to** zurückzuführen sein auf (+ acc); **in** ~ **course** im Laufe der Zeit; ⟨write⟩ zu gegebener Zeit □adv ~ **west** genau westlich

duel n Duell nt

duet n Duo m; (vocal) Duett nt

duke n Herzog m

dull a (overcast) trüb[e]; (not shiny) matt; ⟨sound⟩ dumpf; (boring) langweilig; (stupid) schwerfällig □vt betäuben; abstumpfen ⟨mind⟩

duly adv ordnungsgemäß

dumb a stumm; (fam: stupid) dumm. ~ **founded** a sprachlos

dummy n (tailor's) [Schneider]-puppe f; (for baby) Schnuller m; (Comm) Attrappe f

dump n Abfallhaufen m; (for refuse) Müllhalde f, Deponie f; (fam: town) Kaff nt □vt abladen; (fam: put down) hinwerfen (on auf + acc)

dumpling n Kloß m, Knödel m

dune n Düne f

dung n Mist m

dungarees npl Latzhose f

dungeon n Verlies nt

duo n Paar nt; (Mus) Duo nt

duplicate[1] n Doppel nt; (document) Duplikat nt; **in** ~ in doppelter Ausfertigung f

duplicat|e[2] vt kopieren; (do twice) zweimal machen. ~ **or** n Vervielfältigungsapparat m

durable a haltbar

duration n Dauer f

duress n Zwang m

during prep während (+ gen)

dusk n [Abend]dämmerung f

dust n Staub m □vt abstauben; (sprinkle) bestäuben (with mit) □vi Staub wischen

dust: ~**bin** n Mülltonne f. ~**er** n Staubtuch nt. ~**jacket** n Schutzumschlag m. ~**man** n Müllmann m. ~**pan** n Kehrschaufel f

dusty a staubig

Dutch a holländisch; **go** ~ (fam) getrennte Kasse machen □n (Lang) Holländisch nt; **the** ~ pl die Holländer. ~**man** n Holländer m

dutiful a pflichtbewußt

duty n Pflicht f; (task) Aufgabe f; (tax) Zoll m; **be on** ~ Dienst haben. ~**-free** a zollfrei

duvet n Steppdecke f

dwarf n Zwerg m

dwell vi (liter) wohnen; ~ **on** (fig) verweilen bei. ~**ing** n Wohnung f

dwindle vi abnehmen

dye n Farbstoff m □vt färben

dynamic a dynamisch. ~**s** n Dynamik f

dynamite n Dynamit nt

dynamo n Dynamo m

dynasty n Dynastie f

dysentery n Ruhr f

dyslex|ia n Legasthenie f. ~**ic** a legasthenisch; **be** ~**ic** Legastheniker sein

E

each a & pron jede(r,s); (per) je; ~ **other** einander

eager a eifrig. ~**ness** n Eifer m

eagle n Adler m

ear[1] n (of corn) Ähre f

ear[2] n Ohr nt. ~**ache** n Ohrenschmerzen pl. ~**drum** n Trommelfell nt

earl n Graf m

early a & adv früh; (reply) baldig; **be** ~ früh dran sein

earn vt verdienen

earnest a ernsthaft □n in ~ im Ernst

earnings npl Verdienst m

ear: ~**phones** npl Kopfhörer pl. ~**ring** n Ohrring m; (clip-on) Ohrklips m. ~**shot** n within/out of ~**shot** in/außer Hörweite

earth n Erde f; (of fox) Bau m; **where/what on** ~? wo/was in aller Welt? □vt (Electr) erden

earthenware n Tonwaren pl

earthly a irdisch; **be no** ~ **use** (fam) völlig nutzlos sein

'earthquake n Erdbeben nt

earwig n Ohrwurm m

ease n Leichtigkeit f; **at** ~! (Mil) rührt euch! □vt erleichtern; lindern (pain) □vi (pain:) nachlassen; (situation:) sich entspannen

easel n Staffelei f

east n Osten m; **to the** ~ of östlich von □a Ost-, ost- □adv nach Osten

Easter n Ostern nt. ~ **egg** n Osterei f

east|erly a östlich. ~**ern** a östlich. ~**ward[s]** adv nach Osten

easy a leicht; **take it** ~ (fam) sich schonen

easy: ~ **chair** n Sessel m. ~-'**going** a gelassen

eat vt/i essen; (animal:) fressen. ~ **up** vt aufessen

eau-de-Cologne n Kölnisch Wasser nt

eaves npl Dachüberhang m. ~**drop** vi [heimlich] lauschen

ebb n (tide) Ebbe f □vi zurückgehen; (fig) verebben

ebony n Ebenholz nt

ebullient a überschwenglich

eccentric a exzentrisch □n Exzentriker m

ecclesiastical a kirchlich

echo n Echo nt, Widerhall m □vt zurückwerfen; (imitate) nachsagen □vi widerhallen (with von)

eclipse n (Astr) Finsternis f □vt (fig) in den Schatten stellen

ecolog|ical *a* ökologisch. **~y** *n* Ökologie *f*

economic *a* wirtschaftlich. **~al** *a* sparsam. **~s** *n* Volkswirtschaft *f*

economist *n* Volkswirt *m*; ⟨*Univ*⟩ Wirtschaftswissenschaftler *m*

economize *vi* sparen (**on** an + *dat*)

economy *n* Wirtschaft *f*; ⟨*thrift*⟩ Sparsamkeit *f*

ecstasy *n* Ekstase *f*

ecstatic *a* ekstatisch

ecu *n* Ecu *m*

ecumenical *a* ökumenisch

eczema *n* Ekzem *nt*

edge *n* Rand *m*; ⟨*of table*⟩ Kante *f*; ⟨*of knife*⟩ Schneide *f*

edgy *a* ⟨*fam*⟩ nervös

edible *a* eßbar

edict *n* Erlaß *m*

edifice *n* [großes] Gebäude *nt*

edify *vt* erbauen

edit *vt* redigieren; herausgeben ⟨*anthology*⟩; schneiden ⟨*film*⟩

edition *n* Ausgabe *f*; ⟨*impression*⟩ Auflage *f*

editor *n* Redakteur *m*; ⟨*of anthology*⟩ Herausgeber *m*; ⟨*of newspaper*⟩ Chefredakteur *m*; ⟨*of film*⟩ Cutter(in) *m(f)*

editorial *a* redaktionell, Redaktions- □ *n* ⟨*Journ*⟩ Leitartikel *m*

educate *vt* erziehen; ⟨*Univ, Sch*⟩ ausbilden. **~d** *a* gebildet

education *n* Erziehung *f*; ⟨*culture*⟩ Bildung *f*. **~al** *a* pädagogisch; ⟨*visit*⟩ kulturell

eel *n* Aal *m*

eerie *a* unheimlich

effect *n* Wirkung *f*, Effekt *m*; **take ~** in Kraft treten □ *vt* bewirken

effective *a* wirksam, effektiv; ⟨*striking*⟩ wirkungsvoll, effektvoll; ⟨*actual*⟩ tatsächlich. **~ness** *n* Wirksamkeit *f*

effeminate *a* unmännlich

effervescent *a* sprudelnd

efficiency *n* Tüchtigkeit *f*; ⟨*of machine*⟩ Leistungsfähigkeit *f*

efficient *a* tüchtig; ⟨*machine, organization*⟩ leistungsfähig; ⟨*method*⟩ rationell

effigy *n* Bildnis *nt*

effort *n* Anstrengung *f*; **make an ~** sich ⟨*dat*⟩ Mühe geben. **~less** *a* mühelos

effusive *a* überschwenglich

e.g. *abbr* (exempli gratia) z.B.

egalitarian *a* egalitär

egg *n* Ei *nt*. **~-cup** *n* Eierbecher *m*. **~-timer** *n* Eieruhr *f*

ego *n* Ich *nt*. **~centric** *a* egozentrisch. **~ism** *n* Egoismus *m*. **~ist** *n* Egoist *m*. **~tism** *n* Ichbezogenheit *f*. **~tist** *n* ichbezogener Mensch *m*

Egypt *n* Ägypten *nt*. **~ian** *a* ägyptisch □ *n* Ägypter(in) *m(f)*

eiderdown *n* Daunendecke *f*

eight *a* acht □ *n* Acht *f*. **~teen** *a* achtzehn. **~teenth** *a* achtzehnte(r,s)

eighth *a* achte(r,s) □ *n* Achtel *nt*

eightieth *a* achtzigste(r,s)

eighty *a* achtzig

either *a & pron* **~ [of them]** einer von [den] beiden; ⟨*both*⟩ beide; **on ~ side** auf beiden Seiten □ *adv* **I don't ~** ich auch nicht □ *conj* **~ ... or** entweder ... oder

eject *vt* hinauswerfen

eke *vt* **~ out** strecken; ⟨*increase*⟩ ergänzen

elaborate¹ *a* kunstvoll; ⟨*fig*⟩ kompliziert

elaborate² *vi* ausführlicher sein

elapse *vi* vergehen

elastic *a* elastisch □ *n* Gummiband *nt*. **~ 'band** *n* Gummiband *nt*

elated *a* überglücklich

elbow *n* Ellbogen *m*

elder¹ *n* Holunder *m*

eld|er² *a* ältere(r,s) □ *n* **the ~** der/die Ältere. **~erly** *a* alt. **~est** *a* älteste(r,s) □ *n* **the ~est** der/die Älteste

elect *a* the president ~ der designierte Präsident □*vt* wählen.
~**ion** *n* Wahl *f*

elector *n* Wähler(in) *m(f)*. ~**al** *a* Wahl-; ~**al roll** Wählerverzeichnis *nt*. ~**ate** *n* Wählerschaft *f*

electric *a* elektrisch

electrical *a* elektrisch; ~ **engineering** Elektrotechnik *f*

electrician *n* Elektriker *m*

electricity *n* Elektrizität *f*; (*supply*) Strom *m*

electrify *vt* elektrifizieren. ~**ing** *a* (*fig*) elektrisierend

electrocute *vt* durch einen elektrischen Schlag töten

electrode *n* Elektrode *f*

electron *n* Elektron *nt*

electronic *a* elektronisch. ~**s** *n* Elektronik *f*

elegance *n* Eleganz *f*

elegant *a* elegant

elegy *n* Elegie *f*

element *n* Element *nt*. ~**ary** *a* elementar

elephant *n* Elefant *m*

elevat|e *vt* heben; (*fig*) erheben.
~**ion** *n* Erhebung *f*

eleven *a* elf □*n* Elf *f*. ~**th** *a* elfte(r,s)

elf *n* Elfe *f*

elicit *vt* herausbekommen

eligible *a* berechtigt

eliminate *vt* ausschalten

élite *n* Elite *f*

ellip|se *n* Ellipse *f*. ~**tical** *a* elliptisch

elm *n* Ulme *f*

elocution *n* Sprecherziehung *f*

elope *vi* durchbrennen (*fam*)

eloquen|ce *n* Beredsamkeit *f*. ~**t** *a* beredt

else *adv* sonst; **who** ~? wer sonst?
nothing ~ sonst nichts; **or** ~
oder; (*otherwise*) sonst; **someone/somewhere** ~ jemand/
irgendwo anders. ~**where** *adv*
woanders

elusive *a* be ~ schwer zu fassen
sein

emaciated *a* abgezehrt

emanate *vi* ausgehen (**from** von)

emancipat|ed *a* emanzipiert.
~**ion** *n* Emanzipation *f*

embalm *vt* einbalsamieren

embankment *n* Böschung *f*; (*of
railway*) Bahndamm *m*

embargo *n* Embargo *nt*

embark *vi* sich einschiffen; ~ **on**
anfangen mit. ~**ation** *n* Einschiffung *f*

embarrass *vt* in Verlegenheit bringen. ~**ed** *a* verlegen. ~**ing** *a* peinlich. ~**ment** *n* Verlegenheit *f*

embassy *n* Botschaft *f*

embellish *vt* verzieren

embezzle *vt* unterschlagen.
~**ment** *n* Unterschlagung *f*

emblem *n* Emblem *nt*

embody *vt* verkörpern

embrace *n* Umarmung *f* □*vt*
umarmen; (*fig*) umfassen □*vi*
sich umarmen

embroider *vt* besticken; sticken
⟨*design*⟩; (*fig*) ausschmücken □*vi*
sticken. ~**y** *n* Stickerei *f*

embroil *vt* **become** ~**ed in sth** for
etw (*acc*) verwickelt werden

embryo *n* Embryo *m*

emerald *n* Smaragd *m*

emer|ge *vi* auftauchen (**from**
aus); (*become known*) sich herausstellen; (*come into being*) entstehen. ~**gence** *n* Auftauchen
nt; Entstehung *f*

emergency *n* Notfall *m*. ~ **exit** *n*
Notausgang *m*

emigrant *n* Auswanderer *m*

emigrat|e *vi* auswandern. ~**ion**
n Auswanderung *f*

eminent *a* eminent

emission *n* Ausstrahlung *f*; (*of
pollutant*) Emission *f*

emit *vt* ausstrahlen ⟨*light*⟩; ausstoßen ⟨*smoke*⟩

emotion *n* Gefühl *nt*. ~**al** *a* emotional

emotive *a* emotional

empathy *n* Einfühlungsvermögen *nt*

emperor *n* Kaiser *m*

emphasis *n* Betonung *f.*

emphasize *vt* betonen

emphatic *a* nachdrücklich

empire *n* Reich *nt*

empirical *a* empirisch

employ *vt* beschäftigen; *(appoint)* einstellen; *(fig)* anwenden. **~ee** *n* Beschäftigte(r) *m/f;* Arbeitnehmer *m.* **~er** *n* Arbeitgeber *m.* **~ment** *n* Beschäftigung *f; (work)* Arbeit *f.* **~ment agency** *n* Stellenvermittlung *f*

empress *n* Kaiserin *f*

empty *a* leer □ *vt* leeren; ausleeren *⟨container⟩* □ *vi* sich leeren

emulate *vt* nacheifern (+ *dat*)

emulsion *n* Emulsion *f*

enable *vt* – **s.o. to** es jdm möglich machen, zu

enamel *n* Email *nt; (on teeth)* Zahnschmelz *m; (paint)* Lack *m* □ *vt* emaillieren

enchant *vt* bezaubern. **~ing** *a* bezaubernd. **~ment** *n* Zauber *m*

enclave *n* Enklave *f*

enclose *vt* einschließen; *(in letter)* beilegen (**with** *dat*). **~ure** *n (at zoo)* Gehege *nt; (in letter)* Anlage *f*

encore *n* Zugabe *f*

encounter *n* Begegnung *f* □ *vt* begegnen (+ *dat*); *(fig)* stoßen auf (+ *acc*)

encourag|e *vt* ermutigen; *(promote)* fördern. **~ement** *n* Ermutigung *f.* **~ing** *a* ermutigend

encroach *vt* ~ **on** eindringen in (+ *acc*) *⟨land⟩;* beanspruchen *⟨time⟩*

encumbrance *n* Belastung *f*

encyclopaed|ia *n* Lexikon *nt.* **~ic** *a* enzyklopädisch

end *n* Ende *nt; (purpose)* Zweck *m;* **in the** ~ schließlich; **for days on**

~ **tagelang** □ *vt* beenden □ *vi* enden; ~ **up in** *(fam: arrive at)* landen in (+ *dat*)

endanger *vt* gefährden

endeavour *n* Bemühung *f* □ *vi* sich bemühen (**to** *zu*)

ending *n* Schluß *m,* Ende *nt; (Gram)* Endung *f*

endive *n* Endivie *f*

endless *a* endlos

endorse *vt (Comm)* indossieren; *(confirm)* bestätigen. **~ment** *n (Comm)* Indossament *nt; (fig)* Bestätigung *f; (on driving licence)* Strafvermerk *m*

endow *vt* stiften. **~ment** *n* Stiftung *f*

endurance *n* Durchhaltevermögen *nt*

endure *vt* ertragen □ *vi* [lange] bestehen

enemy *n* Feind *m*

energetic *a* tatkräftig

energy *n* Energie *f*

enforce *vt* durchsetzen

engage *vt* einstellen *⟨staff⟩;* *(Theat)* engagieren; *(Auto)* einlegen *⟨gear⟩* □ *vi* sich beteiligen (**in** an + *dat*); *(Techn)* ineinandergreifen. **~d** *a* besetzt; *⟨person⟩* beschäftigt; *(to be married)* verlobt; **get** ~ **d** sich verloben (**to** mit). **~ment** *n* Verlobung *f; (appointment)* Verabredung *f; (Mil)* Gefecht *nt*

engine *n* Motor *m; (Naut)* Maschine *f; (Rail)* Lokomotive *f; (of jet-plane)* Triebwerk *nt.* **~driver** *n* Lokomotivführer *m*

engineer *n* Ingenieur *m; (service)* Techniker *m; (Naut)* Maschinist *m* □ *vt (fig)* organisieren. **~ing** [**mechanical**] **~ing** Maschinenbau *m*

England *n* England *nt*

English *a* englisch; **the** ~ **Channel** der Ärmelkanal □ *n (Lang)* Englisch *nt;* **in** ~ auf englisch; **into** ~ ins Englische; **the** ~ *pl* die

Engländer. **~ man** n Engländer m. **~ woman** n Engländerin f

engrave vt eingravieren. **~ing** n Stich m

engross vt be **~ ed** in vertieft sein in (+ acc)

enhance vt verschönern; (fig) steigern

enigma n Rätsel nt. **~ tic** a rätselhaft

enjoy vt genießen; **~ oneself** sich amüsieren. **~ able** a angenehm, nett. **~ ment** n Vergnügen n

enlarge vt vergrößern □vi **~ upon** sich näher auslassen über (+ acc). **~ ment** n Vergrößerung f

enlighten vt aufklären. **~ ment** n Aufklärung f

enlist vt (Mil) einziehen □vi (Mil) sich melden

enliven vt beleben

enmity n Feindschaft f

enormity n Ungeheuerlichkeit f

enormous a riesig

enough a, adv a be genug; be **~** reichen; **funnily ~** komischerweise; **I've had ~ !** (fam) jetzt reicht's mir aber!

enquire vi sich erkundigen (about nach) □vt sich erkundigen nach. **~ y** n Erkundigung f; (investigation) Untersuchung f

enrich vt bereichern

enrol □vi einschreiben □vi sich einschreiben. **~ ment** n Einschreibung f

ensemble n Ensemble nt

ensign n Flagge f

enslave vt versklaven

ensure vt sicherstellen; **~ that** dafür sorgen, daß

entangle vt get **~ d** sich verfangen (in in + dat); (fig) sich verstricken (in in + acc)

enter vt eintreten/(vehicle:) einfahren in (+ acc); einreisen in (+ acc) (country); (register) eintragen; sich anmelden zu (competition) □vi eintreten; (vehicle:) einfahren; (Theat) auftreten; (register as competitor) sich anmelden; (take part) sich beteiligen (in an + dat)

enterprise n Unternehmen nt; (quality) Unternehmungsgeist m

entertain vt unterhalten; (invite) einladen; (to meal) bewirten (guest); (fig) in Erwägung ziehen □vi unterhalten; (have guests) Gäste haben. **~ er** n Unterhalter m. **~ ment** n Unterhaltung f

enthusias|m n Begeisterung f. **~ t** n Enthusiast m. **~ tic** a begeistert

entice vt locken

entire a ganz. **~ ly** adv ganz, völlig. **~ ty** n in its **~ ty** in seiner Gesamtheit

entitle vt berechtigen; **~ d . . .** mit dem Titel . . . ; be **~ d to sth** das Recht auf etw (acc) haben

entity n Wesen nt

entomology n Entomologie f

entourage n Gefolge nt

entrails npl Eingeweide pl

entrance[1] vt bezaubern

entrance[2] n Eintritt m; (Theat) Auftritt m; (way in) Eingang m; (for vehicle) Einfahrt f

entrant n Teilnehmer(in) m(f)

entreat vt anflehen (for um)

entrust vt **~ s.o. with sth**, **~ sth to s.o.** jdm etw anvertrauen

entry n Eintritt m; (into country) Einreise f; (on list) Eintrag m; no **~** Zutritt/(Auto) Einfahrt verboten. **~ visa** n Einreisevisum nt

enumerate vt aufzählen

enunciate vt [deutlich] aussprechen

envelop vt einhüllen

envelope n [Brief]umschlag m

envious a neidisch (of auf + acc)

environment n Umwelt f

environmental a Umwelt-. ~**ist** n Umweltschützer m. ~**ly** adv ~ly friendly umweltfreundlich

envisage vt sich (dat) vorstellen

envoy n Gesandte(r) m

envy n Neid m □vt ~ s.o. sth jdn um etw beneiden

enzyme n Enzym nt

epic a episch □n Epos nt

epidemic n Epidemie f

epilep|sy n Epilepsie f. ~**tic** a epileptisch □n Epileptiker(in) m(f)

epilogue n Epilog m

episode n Episode f; (instalment) Folge f

epistle n (liter) Brief m

epitaph n Epitaph nt

epitom|e n Inbegriff m. ~**ize** vt verkörpern

epoch n Epoche f

equal a gleich (**to** dat); **be** ~ **to a task** einer Aufgabe gewachsen sein □n Gleichgestellte(r) m(f)□vt gleichen (+ dat); (fig) gleichkommen (+ dat). ~**ity** n Gleichheit f

equalize vt/i ausgleichen

equanimity n Gleichmut f

equat|e vt gleichsetzen (**with** mit). ~**ion** n (Math) Gleichung f

equator n Äquator m. ~**ial** a Äquator-

equestrian a Reit-

equilibrium n Gleichgewicht nt

equinox n Tagundnachtgleiche f

equip vt ausrüsten; (furnish) ausstatten. ~**ment** n Ausrüstung f; Ausstattung f

equity n Gerechtigkeit f

equivalent a gleichwertig; (corresponding) entsprechend □n Äquivalent nt; (value) Gegenwert m; (counterpart) Gegenstück n

equivocal a zweideutig

era n Ära f, Zeitalter nt

eradicate vt ausrotten

erase vt ausradieren; (from tape) löschen; (fig) auslöschen. ~**r** n Radiergummi m

erect a aufrecht □vt errichten. ~**ion** n Errichtung f; (building) Bau m; (Biol) Erektion f

ermine n Hermelin m

erode vt (water:) auswaschen; (acid:) angreifen. ~**sion** n Erosion f

erotic a erotisch. ~**ism** n Erotik f

err vi sich irren

errand n Botengang m

erratic a unregelmäßig; (person) unberechenbar

erroneous a falsch; (belief) irrig

error n Irrtum m; (mistake) Fehler m

erudite a gelehrt

erupt vi ausbrechen. ~**ion** n Ausbruch m

escalat|e vt/i eskalieren. ~**ion** n Eskalation f. ~**or** n Rolltreppe f

escapade n Eskapade f

escape n Flucht f; (from prison) Ausbruch m □vi flüchten; (prisoner:) ausbrechen; entkommen (**from** aus; **from s.o.** jdm); (gas:) entweichen

escapism n Eskapismus m

escort¹ n (of person) Begleiter m

escort² vt begleiten

Eskimo n Eskimo m

esoteric a esoterisch

especial a besondere(r,s). ~**ly** adv besonders

espionage n Spionage f

essay n Aufsatz m

essence n Wesen nt; (Chem, Culin) Essenz f; **in** ~ im wesentlichen

essential a wesentlich; (indispensable) unentbehrlich □n **the** ~**s** das Wesentliche; (items) das Nötigste. ~**ly** adv im wesentlichen

establish vt gründen; (form) bilden; (prove) beweisen. ~**ment** n (firm) Unternehmen nt

estate n Gut nt; (possessions) Besitz m; (after death) Nachlaß m; (housing) [Wohn]siedlung f. ~ **agent** n Immobilienmakler m. ~ **car** n Kombi[wagen] m

esteem n Achtung f

estimate[1] n Schätzung f; (Comm) [Kosten]voranschlag m

estimat|e[2] vt schätzen. ~**ion** n Einschätzung f; (esteem) Achtung f

estuary n Mündung f

etc. abbr (et cetera) und so weiter, usw.

etching n Radierung f

eternal a ewig

eternity n Ewigkeit f

ethic n Ethik f. ~**al** a ethisch; (morally correct) moralisch einwandfrei. ~**s** n Ethik f

Ethiopia n Äthiopien nt

ethnic a ethnisch

etiquette n Etikette f

etymology n Etymologie f

eucalyptus n Eukalyptus m

eulogy n Lobrede f

euphemis|m n Euphemismus m. ~**tic** a verhüllend

euphoria n Euphorie f

Euro-: pref ~**cheque** n Euroscheck m. ~**passport** n Europaß m

Europe n Europa nt

European a europäisch; ~ **Union** n Europäische Union f □ n Europäer(in) m(f)

evacuat|e vt evakuieren; räumen (building). ~**ion** n Evakuierung f; Räumung f

evade vt sich entziehen (+ dat); hinterziehen (taxes)

evaluate vt einschätzen

evange|lical a evangelisch. ~**list** n Evangelist m

evaporat|e vi verdunsten; ~**ed milk** Kondensmilch f, Dosenmilch f. ~**ion** n Verdampfung f

evasion n Ausweichen nt

evasive a ausweichend; **be** ~ ausweichen

eve n (liter) Vorabend m

even a (level) eben; (same, equal) gleich; (regular) gleichmäßig; (number) gerade; **get** ~ **with s.o.** (fam) es jdm heimzahlen □ adv sogar, selbst; ~ **so** trotzdem; **not** ~ nicht einmal □ vt ~ **the score** ausgleichen

evening n Abend m; **this** ~ heute abend; **in the** ~ abends, am Abend

event n Ereignis nt; (function) Veranstaltung f; (Sport) Wettbewerb m; **in the** ~ **of** im Falle (+ gen); **in the** ~ **wie** es sich ergab. ~**ful** a ereignisreich

eventual a **his** ~ **success** der Erfolg, der ihm schließlich zuteil wurde. ~**ity** n Eventualität f, Fall m. ~**ly** adv schließlich

ever adv je[mals]; **not** ~ nie; **for** ~ für immer; **hardly** ~ fast nie; ~ **since** seitdem

'evergreen n immergrüner Strauch m/ (tree) Baum m

ever'lasting a ewig

every a jede(r,s); ~ **one** jede(r,s) einzelne

every: ~**body** pron jeder[mann]; alle pl. ~**day** a alltäglich. ~**one** pron jeder[mann]; alle pl. ~**thing** pron alles. ~**where** adv überall

evict vt [aus der Wohnung] hinausweisen. ~**ion** n Ausweisung f

eviden|ce n Beweise pl; (Jur) Beweismaterial nt; (testimony) Aussage f. ~**t** a offensichtlich

evil a böse □ n Böse nt

evoke vt heraufbeschwören

evolution n Evolution f

evolve vt entwickeln □ vi sich entwickeln

ewe n Schaf nt

exacerbate vt verschlimmern

exact *a* genau; **not ~ly** nicht gerade. □*vt* erzwingen. **~ing** *a* anspruchsvoll

exaggerat|e *vt/i* übertreiben. **~ion** *n* Übertreibung *f*

exalt *vt* erheben

exam *n* (*fam*) Prüfung *f*

examination *n* Untersuchung *f*; (*Sch*) Prüfung *f*

examine *vt* untersuchen; (*Sch*) prüfen; (*Jur*) verhören. **~r** *n* (*Sch*) Prüfer *m*

example *n* Beispiel *nt* (**of** für); **for ~** zum Beispiel

exasperat|e *vt* zur Verzweiflung treiben. **~ion** *n* Verzweiflung *f*

excavat|e *vt* ausschachten; (*Archaeol*) ausgraben. **~ion** *n* Ausgrabung *f*

exceed *vt* übersteigen

excel *vi* sich auszeichnen □*vt* **~ oneself** sich selbst übertreffen

excellen|ce *n* Vorzüglichkeit *f*. **E~cy** *n* (*title*) Exzellenz *f*. **~t** *a* ausgezeichnet

except *prep* außer (+ *dat*); **~ for** abgesehen von □*vt* ausnehmen. **~ing** *prep* außer (+ *dat*)

exception *n* Ausnahme *f*. **~al** *a* außergewöhnlich

excerpt *n* Auszug *m*

excess *n* Übermaß *nt* (**of** an + *dat*); (*surplus*) Überschuß *m*; **~es** *pl* Exzesse *pl*

excessive *a* übermäßig

exchange *n* Austausch *m*; (*Teleph*) Fernsprechamt *nt*; (*Comm*) [Geld]wechsel *m*; **[stock] ~** Börse *f*; **in ~** dafür □ *vt* austauschen (**for** gegen); tauschen (*places*). **~ rate** *n* Wechselkurs *m*

exchequer *n* (*Pol*) Staatskasse *f*

excise[1] *n* **~ duty** Verbrauchssteuer *f*

excit|e *vt* aufregen; (*cause*) erregen. **~ed** *a* aufgeregt; **get ~ed**

sich aufregen. **~ement** *n* Aufregung *f*; Erregung *f*. **~ing** *a* aufregend; (*story*) spannend

exclaim *vt/i* ausrufen

exclamation *n* Ausruf *m*. **~ mark** *n* Ausrufezeichen *nt*

exclu|de *vt* ausschließen. **~ding** *pron* ausschließlich (+ *gen*). **~sion** *n* Ausschluß *m*

exclusive *a* ausschließlich; (*select*) exklusiv

communicate *vt* exkommunizieren

excrement *n* Kot *m*

excrete *vt* ausscheiden

excruciating *a* gräßlich

excursion *n* Ausflug *m*

excuse[1] *n* Entschuldigung *f*; (*pretext*) Ausrede *f*

excuse[2] *vt* entschuldigen; **~ me!** Entschuldigung!

execute *vt* ausführen; (*put to death*) hinrichten

execution *n* Ausführung *f*; Hinrichtung *f*. **~er** *n* Scharfrichter *m*

executive *a* leitend □ *n* leitende(r) Angestellte(r) *m*|*f*; (*Pol*) Exekutive *f*

executor *n* (*Jur*) Testamentsvollstrecker *m*

exemplary *a* beispielhaft

exempt *a* befreit □ *vt* befreien (**from** von). **~ion** *n* Befreiung *f*

exercise *n* Übung *f*; **physical ~** körperliche Bewegung *f* □ *vt* (*use*) ausüben; bewegen (*horse*); spazierenführen (*dog*) □ *vi* sich bewegen. **~ book** *n* [Schul]heft *nt*

exert *vt* ausüben; **~ oneself** sich anstrengen. **~ion** *n* Anstrengung *f*

exhale *vt/i* ausatmen

exhaust *n* (*Auto*) Auspuff *m*; (*pipe*) Auspuffrohr *nt*; (*fumes*) Abgase *pl* □ *vt* erschöpfen. **~ed** *a* erschöpft. **~ing** *a* anstrengend. **~ion** *n* Erschöpfung *f*

exhibit 332 **extensive**

exhibit n Ausstellungsstück nt; (Jur) Beweisstück nt □vt ausstellen; (fig) zeigen

exhibition n Ausstellung f. ~**ist** n Exhibitionist(in) m(f)

exhibitor n Aussteller m

exhilerating a berauschend

exhume vt exhumieren

exile n Exil nt; (person) im Exil Lebende(r) m/f □vt ins Exil schicken

exist vi bestehen, existieren. ~**ence** n Existenz f

exit n Ausgang m; (Auto) Ausfahrt f; (Theat) Abgang m □vi (Theat) abgehen. ~ **visa** n Ausreisevisum nt

exonerate vt entlasten

exorbitant a übermäßig hoch

exorcize vt austreiben

exotic a exotisch

expand vt ausdehnen; (explain better) weiter ausführen □vi sich ausdehnen; (Comm) expandieren

expanse n Weite f. ~**ion** n Ausdehnung f; (Techn, Pol, Comm) Expansion f. ~**ive** a mitteilsam

expect vt erwarten; (suppose) annehmen

expectan|cy n Erwartung f. ~**t** a erwartungsvoll; ~**t mother** werdende Mutter f

expectation n Erwartung f

expedient a zweckdienlich

expedite vt beschleunigen

expedition n Expedition f

expel vt ausweisen (from aus); (from school) von der Schule verweisen

expend vt aufwenden. ~**able** a entbehrlich

expenditure n Ausgaben pl

expense n Kosten pl; business ~**s** pl Spesen pl; **at my** ~ auf meine Kosten

expensive a teuer

experience n Erfahrung f □vt erleben. ~**d** a erfahren

experiment n Versuch m, Experiment nt □vi experimentieren. ~**al** a experimentell

expert a fachmännisch □n Fachmann m, Experte m

expertise n Sachkenntnis f

expire vi ablaufen

expiry n Ablauf m

explain vt erklären

explanation n Erklärung f

expletive n Kraftausdruck m

explicit a deutlich

explode vi explodieren

exploit[1] n [Helden]tat f

exploit[2] vt ausbeuten. ~**ation** n Ausbeutung f

explorat|ion n Erforschung f. ~**tory** a Probe-

explore vt erforschen. ~**r** n Forschungsreisende(r) m

explos|ion n Explosion f. ~**ive** a explosiv □n Sprengstoff m

exponent n Vertreter m

export[1] n Export m, Ausfuhr f

export[2] vt exportieren, ausführen. ~**er** n Exporteur m

expos|e vt freilegen; (to danger) aussetzen (to dat); (reveal) aufdecken; (Phot) belichten. ~**ure** n Aussetzung f; (Med) Unterkühlung f; (Phot) Belichtung f

expound vt erläutern

express a ausdrücklich; (purpose) fest □adv (send) per Eilpost □n (train) Schnellzug m □vt ausdrücken. ~**ion** n Ausdruck m. ~**ive** a ausdrucksvoll

expulsion n Ausweisung f; (Sch) Verweisung f von der Schule

expurgate vt zensieren

exquisite a erlesen

extend vt verlängern; (stretch out) ausstrecken; (enlarge) vergrößern □vi sich ausdehnen; (table:) sich ausziehen lassen

extension n Verlängerung f; (to house) Anbau m; (Teleph) Nebenanschluß m; ~ **7** Apparat 7

extensive a weit; (fig) umfassend

extent n Ausdehnung f; (scope) Ausmaß nt, Umfang m; **to a certain ~** in gewissem Maße

extenuating a mildernd

exterior a äußere(r,s) □ **the ~** das Äußere

exterminate vt ausrotten

external a äußere(r,s); **for ~ use only** (Med) nur äußerlich

extinct a ausgestorben; (volcano) erloschen. **~ion** n Aussterben nt

extinguish vt löschen

extol vt preisen

extortion n Erpressung f

extortionate a übermäßig hoch

extra a zusätzlich □ adv extra; (especially) besonders; **~ strong** extrastark □ n (Theat) Statist(in) m(f); **~s** pl Nebenkosten pl; (Auto) Extras pl

extract[1] n Auszug m; (Culin) Extrakt m

extract[2] vt herausziehen; ziehen ⟨tooth⟩; (fig) erzwingen

extradit|e vt (Jur) ausliefern. **~ion** n (Jur) Auslieferung f

extra'marital a außerehelich

extraordinary a außerordentlich; (strange) seltsam

extravagan|ce n Verschwendung f; **~t** a verschwenderisch; (exaggerated) extravagant

extreme a äußerste(r,s); (fig) extrem □ n Extrem nt; **in the ~** im höchsten Grade. **~ely** adv äußerst. **~ist** n Extremist m

extremit|y n the **~ies** pl die Extremitäten pl

extricate vt befreien

extrovert n extravertierter Mensch m

exuberant a überglücklich

exult vi frohlocken

eye n Auge nt; (of needle) Öhr nt; (for hook) Öse f □ vt ansehen

eye: **~ball** n Augapfel m. **~brow** n Augenbraue f. **~lash** n Wimper f. **~lid** n Augenlid nt. **~shadow** n Lidschatten m.

~sight n Sehkraft f. **~sore** n (fam) Schandfleck m. **~witness** n Augenzeuge m

F

fable n Fabel f

fabric n Stoff m

fabrication n Erfindung f

fabulous a (fam) phantastisch

façade n Fassade f

face n Gesicht nt; (grimace) Grimasse f; (surface) Fläche f; (of clock) Zifferblatt nt □ vt/i gegenüberstehen (+ dat); **~ north** ⟨house:⟩ nach Norden liegen

face: **~less** a anonym. **~-lift** n Gesichtsstraffung f

facet n Facette f; (fig) Aspekt m

facetious a spöttisch

'face value n Nennwert m

facial a Gesichts-

facile a oberflächlich

facilitate vt erleichtern

facilit|y n Leichtigkeit f; (skill) Gewandtheit f; **~ies** pl Einrichtungen pl

facsimile n Faksimile nt

fact n Tatsache f; **in ~** tatsächlich; (actually) eigentlich

faction n Gruppe f

factor n Faktor m

factory n Fabrik f

factual a sachlich

faculty n Fähigkeit f; (Univ) Fakultät f

fad n Fimmel m

fade vi verblassen; ⟨material:⟩ verbleichen; ⟨sound:⟩ abklingen; ⟨flower:⟩ verwelken

Fahrenheit a Fahrenheit

fail n **without ~** unbedingt □ vi ⟨attempt:⟩ scheitern; ⟨grow weak⟩ nachlassen; ⟨break down⟩ versagen; (in exam) durchfallen; **~ to do sth** etw nicht tun; **he ~ed to break the record** es gelang ihm nicht, den Rekord zu brechen □ vt nicht bestehen ⟨exam⟩; durchfallen lassen ⟨candidate⟩ ⟨disappoint⟩ enttäuschen

failing n Fehler m □ prep ~ **that** andernfalls

failure n Mißerfolg m; ⟨breakdown⟩ Versagen nt; ⟨person⟩ Versager m

faint a schwach □ n Ohnmacht f □ vi ohnmächtig werden

faint-'hearted a zaghaft

fair¹ n Jahrmarkt m; ⟨Comm⟩ Messe f

fair² a ⟨hair⟩ blond; ⟨skin⟩ hell; ⟨weather⟩ heiter; ⟨just⟩ gerecht, fair; ⟨quite good⟩ ziemlich gut; ⟨Sch⟩ genügend □ adv **play** ~ fair sein. ~**ly** adv gerecht; ⟨rather⟩ ziemlich. ~**ness** n Blondheit f; Helle f; Gerechtigkeit f; ⟨Sport⟩ Fairneß f

fairy n Elfe f; **good/wicked** ~ gute/böse Fee f. ~**story**, ~**tale** n Märchen nt

faith n Glaube m; ⟨trust⟩ Vertrauen nt (in zu)

faithful a treu; ⟨exact⟩ genau; Yours ~**ly** Hochachtungsvoll. ~**ness** n Treue f; Genauigkeit f

'faith-healer n Gesundbeter(in) m(f)

fake a falsch □ n Fälschung f; ⟨person⟩ Schwindler m □ vt fälschen; ⟨pretend⟩ vortäuschen

falcon n Falke m

fall n Fall m; ⟨heavy⟩ Sturz m; ⟨in prices⟩ Fallen □ vi fallen; ⟨heavily⟩ stürzen; ⟨night:⟩ anbrechen; ~ **in love** sich verlieben; ~ **back on** zurückgreifen auf (+ acc). ~ **in** hineinfallen; ⟨collapse⟩ einfallen; ⟨Mil⟩ antreten; ~ **in with** sich anschließen (+ dat). ~ **out** vi herausfallen; ⟨hair:⟩ ausfallen; ⟨quarrel⟩ sich überwerfen. ~ **through** vi durchfallen; ⟨plan:⟩ ins Wasser fallen

fallacy n Irrtum m

fallible a fehlbar

'fall-out n [radioaktiver] Niederschlag m

false a falsch; ⟨artificial⟩ künstlich; ~ **start** ⟨Sport⟩ Fehlstart m. ~**hood** n Unwahrheit f

false 'teeth npl [künstliches] Gebiß nt

falsify vt fälschen

falter vi zögern

fame n Ruhm m

familiar a vertraut; ⟨known⟩ bekannt; too ~ familiär. ~**ity** n Vertrautheit f. ~**ize** vt vertraut machen (with mit)

family n Familie f

family: ~ **al'lowance** n Kindergeld nt. ~ **'doctor** n Hausarzt m. ~ **'planning** n Familienplanung f. ~ **'tree** n Stammbaum m

famine n Hungersnot f

famished a sehr hungrig

famous a berühmt

fan¹ n Fächer m; ⟨Techn⟩ Ventilator m

fan² n ⟨admirer⟩ Fan m

fanatic n Fanatiker m. ~**al** a fanatisch. ~**ism** n Fanatismus m

'fan belt n Keilriemen m

fanciful a phantastisch

fancy n Phantasie f; **have a** ~ Lust haben, zu; **I have taken a real** ~ **to him** er hat es mir angetan □ a ausgefallen □ vt ⟨believe⟩ meinen; ⟨imagine⟩ sich ⟨dat⟩ einbilden; ⟨fam: want⟩ Lust haben auf (+ acc); ~ **that!** stell dir vor! ~**'dress** n Kostüm nt

fanfare n Fanfare f

fang n Fangzahn m; ⟨of snake⟩ Giftzahn m

fan: ~ **heater** n Heizlüfter m. ~**light** n Oberlicht nt

fantasize vi phantasieren. ~**tic** a phantastisch. ~**y** n Phantasie f

far adv weit; ⟨much⟩ viel; **by** ~ bei weitem; ~ **away** weit weg □ a **at the** ~ **end** am anderen Ende; **the F~ East** der Ferne Osten

farc|e n Farce f. **~ical** a lächerlich

fare n Fahrpreis m; (money) Fahrgeld nt; (food) Kost f; **air ~** Flugpreis m

farewell int (liter) lebe wohl! □n Lebewohl nt

farm n Bauernhof m □vi Landwirtschaft betreiben □vt bewirtschaften (land). **~er** n Landwirt m

farm: ~house n Bauernhaus nt. **~ing** n Landwirtschaft f. **~yard** n Hof m

far: ~-'reaching a weitreichend. **~-'sighted** a (fig) umsichtig

fart vi (vulg) furzen

farther adv weiter; **~off** weiter entfernt □a **at the ~end** am anderen Ende

fascinat|e vt faszinieren. **~ing** a faszinierend. **~ion** n Faszination f

fasci|sm n Faschismus m. **~t** n Faschist m □a faschistisch

fashion n Mode f; (manner) Art f □vt machen; (mould) formen. **~able** a modisch

fast¹ a & adv schnell; (firm) fest; (colour) waschecht; **be ~** (clock:) vorgehen; **be ~ asleep** fest schlafen

fast² n Fasten nt □vi fasten

fasten vt zumachen; (fix) befestigen (**to** an + dat). **~er** n, **~ing** n Verschluß m

fastidious a wählerisch

fat a dick; (meat) fett □n Fett nt

fatal a tödlich; (error) verhängnisvoll. **~ism** n Fatalismus m. **~ist** n Fatalist m. **~ity** n Todesopfer nt

fate n Schicksal nt. **~ful** a verhängnisvoll

father n Vater m; **F~** Christmas der Weihnachtsmann □vt zeugen

father: ~hood n Vaterschaft f. **~-in-law** n Schwiegervater m. **~ly** a väterlich

fathom n (Naut) Faden m □vt verstehen

fatigue n Ermüdung f

fatty a (foods) fetthaltig

fatuous a albern

fault n Fehler m; (Techn) Defekt m; (Geol) Verwerfung f; **find ~ with** etwas auszusetzen haben an (+ dat); **it's your ~** du bist schuld □vt etwas auszusetzen haben an (+ dat). **~less** a fehlerfrei

faulty a fehlerhaft

fauna n Fauna f

favour n Gunst f; **I am in ~** ich bin dafür; **do s.o. a ~** jdm einen Gefallen tun □vt begünstigen; (prefer) bevorzugen. **~able** a günstig

favourite a Lieblings- □n Liebling m; (Sport) Favorit(in) m(f). **~ism** n Bevorzugung f

fawn a rehbraun □n Hirschkalb nt

fax n Fax nt □vt faxen (s.o. jdm). **~ machine** n Faxgerät nt

fear n Furcht f, Angst f (**of** vor + dat); **no ~!** (fam) keine Angst! □vt/i fürchten

fearless a furchtlos. **~some** a furchterregend

feasible a durchführbar; (possible) möglich

feast n Festmahl nt; (Relig) Fest nt □vi **~ [on]** schmausen

feat n Leistung f

feather n Feder f

feature n Gesichtszug m; (quality) Merkmal nt; (Journ) Feature nt □vt darstellen. **~ film** n Hauptfilm m

February n Februar m

feckless a verantwortungslos

fed a **be ~ up** (fam) die Nase voll haben (**with** von)

federal a Bundes-

federation n Föderation f

fee n Gebühr f; (professional) Honorar nt

feeble *a* schwach

feed *n* Futter *nt*; (*for baby*) Essen *nt* □ *vt* füttern; (*support*) ernähren; (*into machine*) eingeben; speisen ⟨*computer*⟩ □ *vi* sich ernähren (**on** von)

'feedback *n* Feedback *nt*

feel *vt* fühlen; (*experience*) empfinden; (*think*) meinen □ *vi* sich fühlen; ~ **soft/hard** sich weich/hart anfühlen; **I ~ hot/ill** mir ist heiß/schlecht. ~**er** *n* Fühler *m*. ~**ing** *n* Gefühl *nt*

feint *n* Finte *f*

feline *a* Katzen-; (*catlike*) katzenartig

fell *vt* fällen

fellow *n* (*of society*) Mitglied *nt*; (*fam: man*) Kerl *m*

fellow: ~**'countryman** *n* Landsmann *m*. ~ **men** *pl* Mitmenschen *pl*. ~**ship** *n* Kameradschaft *f*; (*group*) Gesellschaft *f*

felony *n* Verbrechen *nt*

felt *n* Filz *m*. ~**-[tipped] 'pen** *n* Filzstift *m*

female *a* weiblich □ *nt* Weibchen *nt*; (*pej: woman*) Weib *nt*

femin|ine *a* weiblich □ *n* (*Gram*) Femininum *nt*. ~**inity** *n* Weiblichkeit *f*. ~**ist** *a* feministisch □ *n* Feminist(in) *m(f)*

fenc|e *n* Zaun *m*; (*fam: person*) Hehler *m* □ *vi* (*Sport*) fechten □ *vt* ~ **e in** einzäunen. ~**er** *n* Fechter *m*. ~**ing** *n* (*Sport*) Fechten *nt*

fend *vi* ~ **for oneself** sich allein durchschlagen

fender *n* Kaminvorsetzer *m*; (*Naut*) Fender *m*

fennel *n* Fenchel *m*

ferment *vi* gären □ *vt* gären lassen

fern *n* Farn *m*

feroc|ious *a* wild. ~**ity** *n* Wildheit *f*

ferret *n* Frettchen *nt*

ferry *n* Fähre *f* □ *vt* ~ [**across**] übersetzen

fertile *a* fruchtbar

fertilize *vt* befruchten; düngen ⟨*land*⟩. ~ **r** *n* Dünger *m*

fervent *a* leidenschaftlich

fester *vi* eitern

festival *n* Fest *nt*; (*Mus, Theat*) Festspiele *pl*

festiv|e *a* festlich; ~**e season** Festzeit *f*. ~**ities** *npl* Feierlichkeiten *pl*

fetch *vt* holen; (*collect*) abholen; (*be sold for*) einbringen

fête *n* Fest *nt* □ *vt* feiern

fetish *n* Fetisch *m*

fetter *vt* fesseln

feud *n* Fehde *f*

feudal *a* Feudal-

fever *n* Fieber *nt*. ~**ish** *a* fiebrig; (*fig*) fieberhaft

few *a* wenige; **every ~ days** alle paar Tage □ *n* **a ~** ein paar

fiancé *n* Verlobte(r) *m*. **fiancée** *n* Verlobte *f*

fiasco *n* Fiasko *nt*

fib *n* kleine Lüge *f*

fibre *n* Faser *f*

fickle *a* unbeständig

fiction *n* Erfindung *f*; [**works of**] ~ Erzählungsliteratur *f*. ~**al a** erfunden

fictitious *a* [frei] erfunden

fiddle *n* (*fam*) Geige *f*; (*cheating*) Schwindel *m* □ *vi* herumspielen (**with** mit) □ *vt* (*fam*) frisieren ⟨*accounts*⟩

fidelity *n* Treue *f*

fidget *vi* zappeln

field *n* Feld *nt*; (*meadow*) Wiese *f*; (*subject*) Gebiet *nt*

field: ~ **events** *npl* Sprung- und Wurfdisziplinen *pl*. **F~ 'Marshal** *n* Feldmarschall *m*. ~**work** *n* Feldforschung *f*

fiendish *a* teuflisch

fierce *a* wild; (*fig*) heftig. ~**ness** *n* Wildheit *f*; (*fig*) Heftigkeit *f*

fifteen *a* fünfzehn □ *n* Fünfzehn *f*. ~**th** *a* fünfzehnte(r,s)

fifth *a* fünfte(r,s)

fiftieth *a* fünfzigste(r,s)

fifty a fünfzig

fig n Feige f

fight n Kampf m; (brawl) Schlägerei f; (between children) Rauferei f □vt kämpfen gegen; (fig) bekämpfen □vi kämpfen; (brawl) sich schlagen; (children:) sich raufen. **~er** n Kämpfer m; (Aviat) Jagdflugzeug nt

figment n ~ **of the imagination** Hirngespinst n

figurative a bildlich

figure n (digit) Ziffer f; (number) Zahl f; (sum) Summe f; (sculpture, woman's) Figur f; (form) Gestalt f; (illustration) Abbildung f; ~ **of speech** Redefigur f □vi (appear) erscheinen. ~ **out** vt ausrechnen

figure: ~**head** n (fig) Repräsentationsfigur f. ~ **skating** n Eiskunstlauf m

file[1] n Akte f; (for documents) [Akten]ordner m □vt ablegen (documents); (Jur) einreichen

file[2] n (line) Reihe f; **in single** ~ im Gänsemarsch

file[3] n (Techn) Feile f □vt feilen

filigree n Filigran nt

filings npl Feilspäne pl

fill vt füllen; plombieren (tooth) □vi sich füllen. ~ **in** vt auffüllen; ausfüllen (form). ~ **out** vt ausfüllen (form). ~ **up** vi sich füllen □vt vollfüllen; (Auto) volltanken; ausfüllen (form)

fillet n Filet nt □vt entgräten

filling n Füllung f; (of tooth) Plombe f

filly n junge Stute f

film n Film m; (Culin) **[cling]** ~ Klarsichtfolie f □vt/i filmen; verfilmen (book). ~ **star** n Filmstar m

filter n Filter m □vt filtern

filth n Dreck m. ~**y** a dreckig

fin n Flosse f

final a letzte(r,s); (conclusive) endgültig; ~ **result** Endresultat

nt □n (Sport) Finale nt, Endspiel nt

finale n Finale nt

finalize vt endgültig festlegen. ~**ly** adv schließlich

finance n Finanz f □vt finanzieren

financial a finanziell

finch n Fink m

find n Fund m □vt finden; (establish) feststellen. ~ **out** vt herausfinden; (learn) erfahren □vi (enquire) sich erkundigen

fine[1] n Geldstrafe f □vt zu einer Geldstrafe verurteilen

fine[2] a fein; (weather) schön; he's ~ es geht ihm gut □adv gut; **cut it** ~ (fam) sich (dat) wenig Zeit lassen. ~ **arts** npl schöne Künste pl

finery n Putz m, Staat m

finesse n Gewandtheit f

finger n Finger m

finger: ~**nail** n Fingernagel m. ~**print** n Fingerabdruck m. ~**tip** n Fingerspitze f

finish n Schluß m; (Sport) Finish nt; (line) Ziel nt; (of product) Ausführung f □vt beenden; (use up) aufbrauchen □vi fertig werden; (performance:) zu Ende sein; (runner:) durchs Ziel gehen

finite a begrenzt

Finland n Finnland nt

Finn n Finne m/ Finnin f. ~**ish** a finnisch

fiord n Fjord m

fir n Tanne f

fire n Feuer nt; (forest, house) Brand m □vt brennen (pottery); abfeuern (shot); schießen mit (gun); (fam: dismiss) feuern □vi schießen (**at** auf + acc)

fire: ~ **alarm** n Feueralarm m; (apparatus) Feuermelder m. ~**arm** n Schußwaffe f. ~ **brigade** n Feuerwehr f. ~**engine** n Löschfahrzeug nt. ~~**escape**

n Feuertreppe *f*. ~ **extinguisher** *n* Feuerlöscher *m*. ~ **man** *n* Feuerwehrmann *m*. ~**place** *n* Kamin *m*. ~ **station** *n* Feuerwache *f*. ~**wood** *n* Brennholz *nt*. ~**work** *n* Feuerwerkskörper *m*

'**firing squad** *n* Erschießungskommando *nt*

firm[1] *n* Firma *f*

firm[2] *a* fest; *(resolute)* entschlossen; *(strict)* streng

first *a* & *n* erste(r,s); **at** ~ zuerst □*adv* zuerst; *(firstly)* erstens

first: ~ '**aid** *n* Erste Hilfe. ~ **'aid kit** *n* Verbandkasten *m*. ~**-class** *a* erstklassig; *(Rail)* erster Klasse. ~**ly** *adv* erstens. ~ **name** *n* Vorname *m*. ~**-rate** *a* erstklassig

fish *n* Fisch *m* □*vt/i* fischen; *(with rod)* angeln

fish: ~**bone** *n* Gräte *f*. ~**erman** *n* Fischer *m*. ~**-farm** *n* Fischzucht *f*. ~ '**finger** *n* Fischstäbchen *nt*

fishing *n* Fischerei *f*. ~ **boat** *n* Fischerboot *nt*. ~**-rod** *n* Angel[rute] *f*

fish: ~**monger** *n* Fischhändler *m*. ~**slice** *n* Fischheber *m*. ~ **y** *a* *(fam: suspicious)* verdächtig

fission *n* *(Phys)* Spaltung *f*

fist *n* Faust *f*

fit[1] *n* *(attack)* Anfall *m*

fit[2] *a* *(suitable)* geeignet; *(healthy)* gesund; *(Sport)* fit

fit[3] *n* *(of clothes)* Sitz *m*; **be a good** ~ **gut passen** □*vi* *(be the right size)* passen □*vt* anbringen *(to an* + *dat)*; *(install)* einbauen; *(clothes:)* passen (+ *dat)*

fit|ment *n* Einrichtungsgegenstand *m*. ~**ness** *n* Eignung *f*; **[physical]** ~**ness** *n* Gesundheit *f*; *(Sport)* Fitneß *f*. ~**ted** *a* eingebaut; *(garment)* tailliert

fitted: ~'**carpet** *n* Teppichboden *m*. ~ '**kitchen** *n* Einbauküche *f*

fitter *n* Monteur *m*

fitting *a* passend □*n* *(of clothes)* Anprobe *f*; *(of shoes)* Weite *f*;

(Techn) Zubehörteil *nt*; ~ **s** *pl* Zubehör *nt*

five *a* fünf □*n* Fünf *f*

fix *n* *(sl: drugs)* Fix *m*; **be in a** ~ *(fam)* in der Klemme sitzen □*vt* befestigen *(to an* + *dat)*; *(arrange)* festlegen; *(repair)* reparieren; *(Phot)* fixieren

fixation *n* Fixierung *f*

fixed *a* fest

fixture *n* *(Sport)* Veranstaltung *f*

fizz *vi* sprudeln

fizzy *a* sprudelnd. ~ **drink** *n* Brause[limonade] *f*

flag[1] *n* Fahne *f*; *(Naut)* Flagge *f* □*vt* ~ **down** anhalten

flag[2] *vi* ermüden

flagrant *a* flagrant

'**flagstone** *n* [Pflaster]platte *f*

flair *n* Begabung *f*

flake *n* Flocke *f*

flaky *a* blättrig. ~ **pastry** *n* Blätterteig *m*

flamboyant *a* extravagant

flame *n* Flamme *f*

flammable *a* feuergefährlich

flan *n* [fruit] ~ Obsttorte *f*

flannel *n* Flanell *m*; *(for washing)* Waschlappen *m*

flap *n* Klappe *f*; **in a** ~ *(fam)* aufgeregt □*vi* flattern; *(fam)* aufregen □*vt* ~ **its wings** mit den Flügeln schlagen

flare *n* Leuchtsignal *nt* □*vi* ~ **up** auflodern; *(fam: get angry)* aufbrausen

flash *n* Blitz *m*; **in a** ~ *(fam)* im Nu □*vi* blitzen; *(repeatedly)* blinken

flash: ~**back** *n* Rückblende *f*. ~**light** *n* *(Phot)* Blitzlicht *nt*. ~ *y* auffällig

flask *n* Flasche *f*; *(Chem)* Kolben *m*; *(vacuum* ~ *)* Thermosflasche (P) *f*

flat *a* flach; *(surface)* eben; *(refusal)* glatt; *(beer)* schal; *(battery)* verbraucht; *(Auto)* leer; *(tyre)* platt; *(Mus)* **A** ~ As *nt*; **B** ~ B *nt*

flat feet

□*n* Wohnung *f*; (*Mus*) Erniedrigungszeichen *nt*; (*fam: puncture*) Reifenpanne *f*

flat: ~ **'feet** *npl* Plattfüße *pl*. ~**-fish** *n* Plattfisch *m*. ~**ly** *adv* ⟨*refuse*⟩ glatt

flatter *vt* schmeicheln (+ *dat*). ~**y** *n* Schmeichelei *f*

flat 'tyre *n* Reifenpanne *f*

flatulence *n* Blähungen *pl*

flaunt *vt* prunken mit

flautist *n* Flötist(in) *m(f)*

flavour *n* Geschmack *m* □*vt* abschmecken

flaw *n* Fehler *m*. ~**less** *a* tadellos

flax *n* Flachs *m*

flea *n* Floh *m*. ~ **market** *n* Flohmarkt *m*

fleck *n* Tupfen *m*

flee *vi* fliehen (**from** vor + *dat*) □*vt* flüchten aus

fleec|e *n* Vlies *nt*. ~**y** *a* flauschig

fleet *n* Flotte *f*; (*of cars*) Wagenpark *m*

fleeting *a* flüchtig

Flemish *a* flämisch

flesh *n* Fleisch *nt*

flex[1] *vt* anspannen ⟨*muscle*⟩

flex[2] *n* (*Electr*) Schnur *f*

flexib|ility *n* Biegsamkeit *f*; (*fig*) Flexibilität *f*. ~**le** *a* biegsam; (*fig*) flexibel

'flexitime *n* Gleitzeit *f*

flicker *vi* flackern

flight[1] *n* (*fleeing*) Flucht *f*

flight[2] *n* (*flying*) Flug *m*

flight: ~ **path** *n* Flugschneise *f*. ~ **recorder** *n* Flugschreiber *m*

flimsy *a* dünn; ⟨*excuse*⟩ fadenscheinig

flinch *vi* zurückzucken

fling *vt* schleudern

flint *n* Feuerstein *m*

flippant *a* leichtfertig

flipper *n* Flosse *f*

flirt *vi* flirten

flirtatious *a* kokett

flit *vi* flattern

float *n* Schwimmer *m*; (*in procession*) Festwagen *m*. (*money*) Wechselgeld *nt* □*vi* ⟨*thing:*⟩ schwimmen; ⟨*person:*⟩ sich treiben lassen; (*in air*) schweben; (*Comm*) floaten

flock *n* Herde *f*; (*of birds*) Schwarm *m* □*vi* strömen

flog *vt* auspeitschen; (*fam: sell*) verkloppen

flood *n* Überschwemmung *f*; (*fig*) Flut *f* □*vt* überschwemmen □*vi* ⟨*river:*⟩ über die Ufer treten

'floodlight *n* Flutlicht *nt*

floor *n* Fußboden *m*; (*storey*) Stock *m*

floor: ~**board** *n* Dielenbrett *nt*. ~**-cloth** *n* Scheuertuch *nt*. ~**-polish** *n* Bohnerwachs *nt*. ~ **show** *n* Kabarettvorstellung *f*

flop *n* (*fam*) (*failure*) Reinfall *m*; (*Theat*) Durchfall *m* □*vi* (*fam*) (*fail*) durchfallen

floppy *a* schlapp. ~ **'disc** *n* Diskette *f*

flora *n* Flora *f*

florid *a* ⟨*complexion*⟩ gerötet; ⟨*style*⟩ blumig

florist *n* Blumenhändler(in) *m(f)*

flounder[1] *vi* zappeln

flounder[2] *n* (*fish*) Flunder *f*

flour *n* Mehl *nt*

flourish *vi* gedeihen; (*fig*) blühen

flout *vt* mißachten

flow *n* Fluß *m*; (*of traffic, blood*) Strom *m* □*vi* fließen

flower *n* Blume *f* □*vi* blühen

flower: ~**-bed** *n* Blumenbeet *nt*. ~**ed** *a* geblümt. ~**-pot** *n* Blumentopf *m*. ~**y** *a* blumig

flu *n* (*fam*) Grippe *f*

fluctuate *vi* schwanken

fluent *a* fließend

fluid *a* flüssig; (*fig*) veränderlich □*n* Flüssigkeit *f*

fluke *n* [glücklicher] Zufall *m*

fluorescent *a* fluoreszierend; ~ **lighting** Neonbeleuchtung *f*

fluoride *n* Fluor *nt*

flurry n (snow) Gestöber nt

flush vi rot werden □ vt spülen □ a
in einer Ebene (**with** mit); (fam:
affluent) gut bei Kasse

flustered a nervös

flute n Flöte f

flutter vi flattern

fly[1] n Fliege f

fly[2] vi fliegen; ⟨flag:⟩ wehen;
(rush) sausen □ vt fliegen; führen
⟨flag⟩

fly[3] n & **flies** pl (on trousers)
Hosenschlitz m

flyer n Flieger(in) m(f)

flying: ~ '**buttress** n Strebebo-
gen m. ~ '**saucer** n fliegende
Untertasse f. ~ '**visit** n Stipp-
visite f

fly: ~**leaf** n Vorsatzblatt nt.
~**over** n Überführung f

foal n Fohlen nt

foam n Schaum m; (synthetic)
Schaumstoff m □ vi schäumen. ~'
rubber n Schaumgummi m

fob vt ~ **sth off** etw andrehen (**on**
s.o. jdm); ~ **s.o. off** jdn abspeisen
(**with** mit)

focus n Brennpunkt m; in ~
scharf eingestellt □ vt einstellen
(**on** auf + acc); (fig) konzentrieren (**on** auf + acc) □ vi (fig) sich
konzentrieren (**on** auf + acc)

fodder n Futter nt

foe n Feind m

foetus n Fötus m

fog n Nebel m

foggy a neblig

foible n Eigenart f

foil[1] n Folie f; (Culin) Alufolie f

foil[2] vt (thwart) vereiteln

foil[3] n (Fencing) Florett nt

foist vt andrehen (**on** s.o. jdm)

fold n Falte f; (in paper) Kniff m
□ vt falten; ~ **one's arms** die
Arme verschränken □ vi sich falten lassen; (fail) eingehen

fold|er n Mappe f. ~**ing** a Klapp-

foliage n Blätter pl; (of tree) Laub
nt

folk npl Leute pl

folk: ~**dance** n Volkstanz m.
~**lore** n Folklore f. ~**song** n
Volkslied nt

follow vt/i folgen (+ dat); (pursue) verfolgen; (in vehicle) nach-
fahren (+ dat)

follow|er n Anhänger(in) m(f).
~**ing** a folgend □ n Folgende(s)
nt; (supporters) Anhängerschaft
f □ prep im Anschluß an (+ acc)

folly n Torheit f

fond a liebevoll; **be** ~ **of** gern
haben

fondle vt liebkosen

font n Taufstein m

food n Essen nt; (for animals)
Futter nt; (groceries) Lebensmittel pl

food: ~ **poisoning** n Lebensmit-
telvergiftung f. ~ **processor** n
Küchenmaschine f

fool[1] n (Culin) Fruchtcreme f

fool[2] n Narr m □ vt hereinlegen
□ vi ~ **around** herumalbern

'**fool|hardy** a tollkühn. ~**ish** a
dumm. ~**proof** a narrensicher

foot n Fuß m; (measure) Fuß m
(30,48 cm); (of bed) Fußende nt; **on**
~ zu Fuß

foot: ~-**and**-'**mouth disease** n
Maul- und Klauenseuche f.
~**ball** n Fußball m. ~**baller** n
Fußballspieler m. ~**bridge** n
Fußgängerbrücke f. ~**hills** npl
Vorgebirge nt. ~**hold** n Halt m.
~**ing** n Halt m; (fig) Basis f.
~**lights** npl Rampenlicht nt.
~**note** n Fußnote f. ~**path** n
Fußweg m. ~**print** n Fußab-
druck m. ~**step** n Schritt m;
follow in s.o.'s ~**steps** (fig) in
jds Fußstapfen treten. ~**stool** n
Fußbank f. ~**wear** n Schuhwerk
nt

for prep für (+ acc); ⟨send, long⟩
nach; ⟨ask, fight⟩ um; **what** ~?
wozu? ~ **nothing** umsonst □ conj
denn

forbearance n Nachsicht f
forbid vt verbieten (s.o. jdm)
force n Kraft f; (of blow) Wucht f; (violence) Gewalt f; in ~ gültig; (in large numbers) in großer Zahl; **come into** ~ in Kraft treten; **the** ~**s** pl die Streitkräfte pl □vt zwingen; (break open) aufbrechen
force: ~-'**feed** vt zwangsernähren. ~**ful** a energisch
forceps n im Zange f
forcible a gewaltsam
ford n Furt f
fore a vordere(r,s) □n **to the** ~ im Vordergrund
fore: ~**arm** n Unterarm m. ~**cast** n Voraussage f; (for weather) Vorhersage f □vt voraussagen, ~ vorhersagen. ~**fathers** npl Vorfahren pl. ~**finger** n Zeigefinger m. ~**front** n **be in the** ~ **front** führend sein. ~**gone** a **be a** ~ **gone conclusion** von vornherein feststehen. ~**ground** n Vordergrund m. ~**head** n Stirn f. ~**hand** n Vorhand f
foreign a ausländisch; (country) fremd. ~ **currency** n Devisen pl. ~**er** n Ausländer(in) m(f). ~ **language** n Fremdsprache f
Foreign: ~ **Office** n ≈ Außenministerium nt. ~ '**Secretary** n ≈ Außenminister m
fore: ~**leg** n Vorderbein nt. ~**man** n Vorarbeiter m. ~**most** a führend □adv **first and** ~**most** zuallererst
forensic a ~ **medicine** Gerichtsmedizin f
forerunner n Vorläufer m
fore'see vt voraussehen
foresight n Weitblick m
forest n Wald m
fore'stall vt zuvorkommen (+ dat)
forester n Förster m. ~**ry** n Forstwirtschaft f

foretaste n Vorgeschmack m
fore'tell vt vorhersagen
forever adv für immer
foreword n Vorwort nt
forfeit n (in game) Pfand nt □vt verwirken
forge[1] vi ~ **ahead** (fig) Fortschritte machen
forge[2] n Schmiede f □vt schmieden; (counterfeit) fälschen. ~**r** n Fälscher m. ~**ry** n Fälschung f
forget vt/i vergessen; verlernen (language). ~**ful** a vergeßlich. ~-**me-not** n Vergißmeinnicht nt
forgive vt ~ **s.o. for sth** jdm etw vergeben. ~**ness** n Vergebung f
forgo vt verzichten auf (+ acc)
forgot vt verzichten auf (+ acc)
fork n Gabel f; (in road) Gabelung f □vi (road:) sich gabeln
fork-lift 'truck n Gabelstapler m
forlorn a verlassen
form n Form f; (document) Formular nt; (bench) Bank f; (Sch) Klasse f □vt formen (into zu); (create) bilden □vi sich bilden; (idea:) Gestalt annehmen
formal a formell, förmlich. ~**ity** n Förmlichkeit f
format n Format nt
formative a ~ **years** Entwicklungsjahre pl
former a ehemalig; **the** ~ der/die/das erstere. ~**ly** adv früher
formidable a gewaltig
formula n Formel f
formulate vt formulieren
forsake vt verlassen
fort n (Mil) Fort nt
forte n Stärke f
forth adv **back and** ~ hin und her
forth: ~'**coming** a bevorstehend. ~**right** a direkt. ~'**with** adv umgehend
fortieth a vierzigste(r,s)
fortify vt befestigen; (fig) stärken
fortitude n Standhaftigkeit f

fortnight n vierzehn Tage pl.
~**ly** a vierzehntäglich □adv alle
vierzehn Tage

fortress n Festung f

fortuitous a zufällig

fortunate a glücklich; **be** ~
Glück haben. ~**ly** adv glücklicherweise

fortune n Glück nt; (money) Vermögen nt. ~**-teller** n Wahrsagerin f

forty a vierzig □n Vierzig f

forum n Forum nt

forward adv vorwärts; (to the
front) nach vorn □a Vorwärts-;
(presumptuous) anmaßend □n
(Sport) Stürmer m □vt nachsenden (letter). ~**s** adv vorwärts

fossil n Fossil nt. ~**ized** a versteinert

foster vt fördern; in Pflege nehmen (child). ~**-child** n Pflege-
kind nt. ~**-mother** n Pflegemut-
ter f

foul a widerlich; (language) un-
flätig; ~ **play** (Jur) Mord m □n
(Sport) Foul nt □vt verschmutzen; (obstruct) blockieren;
(Sport) foulen

found vt gründen

foundation n (basis) Grundlage
f; (charitable) Stiftung f; ~**s** pl
Fundament nt

founder[1] n Gründer(in) m(f)

founder[2] vi (fig) scheitern

foundry n Gießerei f

fountain n Brunnen m. ~**-pen** n
Füllfederhalter m

four a vier □n Vier f

four: ~**-'poster** n Himmelbett nt.
~**some** n in a ~ some zu viert.
~**'teen** a vierzehn □n Vierzehn f.
~**'teenth** a vierzehnte(r,s)

fourth a vierte(r,s)

fowl n Geflügel nt

fox n Fuchs m □vt verblüffen

foyer n Foyer nt; (in hotel) Emp-
fangshalle f

fraction n Bruchteil m; (Math)
Bruch m

fracture n Bruch m □vt/i brechen

fragile a zerbrechlich

fragment n Bruchstück nt, Fragment nt

fragran|ce n Duft m. ~**t** a duf-
tend

frail a gebrechlich

frame n Rahmen m; (of spectacles)
Gestell nt; (Anat) Körperbau m.
~ **of mind** Gemütsverfassung f
□vt einrahmen; (fig) formulieren; (sl) ein Verbrechen anhän-
gen (+ dat). ~**work** n Gerüst nt;
(fig) Gerippe nt

franc n (French, Belgian) Franc
m; (Swiss) Franken m

France n Frankreich nt

franchise n (Pol) Wahlrecht nt;
(Comm) Franchise nt

frank[1] vt frankieren

frank[2] a offen

frankfurter n Frankfurter f

frantic a verzweifelt

fraternal a brüderlich

fraud n Betrug m; (person) Betrü-
ger(in) m(f)

fray[1] n Kampf m

fray[2] vi ausfransen

freak n Mißbildung f; (person)
Mißgeburt f; (phenomenon) Aus-
nahmeerscheinung f □a anormal

freckle n Sommersprosse f

free a frei; (ticket, copy) Frei-;
(lavish) freigebig; ~ **[of charge]**
kostenlos. □vt freilassen; (rescue)
befreien; (disentangle) freibekommen

free: ~**dom** n Freiheit f. ~**hold** n
[freier] Grundbesitz m. ~**'kick** n
Freistoß m. ~**lance** a & adv frei-
beruflich. ~**ly** adv frei;
(voluntarily) freiwillig; (gener-
ously) großzügig. **F~mason** n
Freimaurer m. ~**-range** a
~**-range eggs** Landeier pl. ~
'sample n Gratisprobe f. ~**style**

n Freistil *m*. ~·'**wheel** *vi* im Freilauf fahren

freeze *vt* einfrieren; stoppen ⟨wages⟩ □*vi* gefrieren

freez|er *n* Gefriertruhe *f*; (upright) Gefrierschrank *m*. ~**ing** *a* eiskalt

freight *n* Fracht *f*. ~**er** *n* Frachter *m*

French *a* französisch □*n* (Lang) Französisch *nt*; **the** ~ *pl* die Franzosen

French: ~ **beans** *npl* grüne Bohnen *pl*. ~ **bread** *n* Stangenbrot *nt*. ~ **fries** *npl* Pommes frites *pl*. ~**man** *n* Franzose *m*. ~ '**window** *n* Terrassentür *f*. ~**woman** *n* Französin *f*

frenzy *n* Raserei *f*

frequency *n* Häufigkeit *f*; (Phys) Frequenz *f*

frequent¹ *a* häufig

frequent² *vt* regelmäßig besuchen

fresco *n* Fresko *nt*

fresh *a* frisch

'**freshwater** *a* Süßwasser-

fret *vi* sich grämen

'**fretsaw** *n* Laubsäge *f*

friar *n* Mönch *m*

friction *n* Reibung *f*; (fig) Reibereien *pl*

Friday *n* Freitag *m*

fridge *n* Kühlschrank *m*

fried *a* gebraten; ~ **egg** Spiegelei *nt*

friend *n* Freund(in) *m(f)*. ~**li·ness** *n* Freundlichkeit *f*. ~**ly** *a* freundlich. ~**ship** *n* Freundschaft *f*

frieze *n* Fries *m*

fright *n* Schreck *m*

frighten *vt* angst machen (+ dat); (startle) erschrecken; **be** ~**ed** Angst haben (**of** vor + dat). ~**ing** *a* angsterregend

frightful *a* schrecklich

frigid *a* frostig; (Psych) frigide

frill *n* Rüsche *f*; (paper) Manschette *f*. ~**y** *a* rüschenbesetzt

fringe *n* Fransen *pl*; (of hair) Pony *m*; (fig: edge) Rand *m*. ~ **benefits** *npl* zusätzliche Leistungen *pl*

frisk *vt* (search) durchsuchen, (fam) filzen

frisky *a* lebhaft

frivolous *a* frivol, leichtfertig

frizzy *a* kraus

frock *n* Kleid *nt*

frog *n* Frosch *m*

frolic *vi* herumtollen

from *prep* von (+ dat); (out of) aus (+ dat); (according to) nach (+ dat)

front *n* Vorderseite *f*; (fig) Fassade *f*; (of garment) Vorderteil *nt*; (sea-) Strandpromenade *f*; (Mil, Pol, Meteorol) Front *f*; **in** ~ **of** vor; **in** or **at the** ~ vorne □*a* vordere(r,s); ⟨page, row⟩ erste(r,s); ⟨tooth, wheel⟩ Vorder-

front: ~ '**door** *n* Haustür *f*. ~ '**garden** *n* Vorgarten *m*

frontier *n* Grenze *f*

front-wheel '**drive** *n* Vorderradantrieb *m*

frost *n* Frost *m*; (hoar-) Raureif *m*. ~**bite** *n* Erfrierung *f*

frost|ed *a* ~**ed glass** Mattglas *nt*. ~**y** *a* frostig

froth *n* Schaum *m* □*vi* schäumen. ~**y** *a* schaumig

frown *n* Stirnrunzeln *nt* □*vi* die Stirn runzeln

frozen *a* gefroren; (Culin) tiefgekühlt. ~ **food** *n* Tiefkühlkost *f*

frugal *a* sparsam; (meal) frugal

fruit *n* Frucht *f*; (collectively) Obst *nt*. ~ **cake** *n* englischer [Tee]kuchen *m*

fruit|erer *n* Obsthändler *m*. ~**ful** *a* fruchtbar

fruition *n* **come to** ~ sich verwirklichen

fruit: ~ '**juice** *n* Obstsaft *m*. ~ '**salad** *n* Obstsalat *m*

fruity *a* fruchtig

frustrat|e vt vereiteln; (Psych) frustrieren. **~ion** n Frustration f

fry vt/i [in der Pfanne] braten. **~ing-pan** n Bratpfanne f

fudge n weiche Karamellen pl

fuel n Brennstoff m; (for car) Kraftstoff m; (for aircraft) Treibstoff m

fugitive n Flüchtling m

fugue n (Mus) Fuge f

fulfil vt erfüllen

full a voll; (detailed) ausführlich; ⟨skirt⟩ weit; **~ of** voll von (+ dat), voller (+ gen)

full: **~ 'moon** n Vollmond m. **~ 'stop** n Punkt m. **~-time** a ganztägig □ adv ganztags

fully adv völlig; (in detail) ausführlich

fumble vi herumfummeln (with an + dat)

fumes npl Dämpfe pl; (from car) Abgase pl

fumigate vt ausräuchern

fun n Spaß m; **for ~** aus od zum Spaß; **make ~ of** sich lustig machen über (+ acc); **have ~!** viel Spaß!

function n Funktion f; (event) Veranstaltung f; (serve) dienen (as als). **~al** a zweckmäßig

fund n Fonds m; (fig) Vorrat m; **~s** pl Geldmittel pl □ vt finanzieren

fundamental a grundlegend

funeral n Beerdigung f; (cremation) Feuerbestattung f

funeral: **~ directors** pl Bestattungsinstitut nt. **~ march** n Trauermarsch m. **~ service** n Trauergottesdienst m

'funfair n Jahrmarkt m, Kirmes f

fungus n Pilz m

funicular n Seilbahn f

funnel n Trichter m; (on ship, train) Schornstein m

funny a komisch. **~-bone** n (fam) Musikantenknochen m

fur n Fell nt; (for clothing) Pelz m. **~ 'coat** n Pelzmantel m

furious a wütend (with auf + acc)

furnace n (Techn) Ofen m

furnish vt einrichten; (supply) liefern. **~ed** a **~ed room** möbliertes Zimmer nt. **~ings** npl Einrichtungsgegenstände pl

furniture n Möbel pl

furrow n Furche f

further a weitere(r,s); **at the ~ end** am anderen Ende; **until ~ notice** bis auf weiteres □ adv weiter; **~ off** weiter entfernt □ vt fördern

further: **~ edu'cation** n Weiterbildung f. **~'more** adv überdies

furthest a am weitesten entfernt □ adv am weitesten

furtive a verstohlen

fury n Wut f

fuse[1] n (of bomb) Zünder m

fuse[2] n (Electr) Sicherung f □ vt/i verschmelzen; **the lights have ~d** die Sicherung [für das Licht] ist durchgebrannt. **~-box** n Sicherungskasten m

fuselage n (Aviat) Rumpf m

fusion n Verschmelzung f, Fusion f

fuss n Getue nt; **make a ~ of** verwöhnen □ vi Umstände machen

fussy a wählerisch

futile a zwecklos. **~ity** n Zwecklosigkeit f

future a zukünftig □ n Zukunft f; (Gram) [erstes] Futur nt; **~ per'fect** zweites Futur nt

futuristic a futuristisch

fuzzy a ⟨hair⟩ kraus; (blurred) verschwommen

G

gabble vi schnell reden

gable n Giebel m

gadget n [kleines] Gerät nt

Gaelic a Gälisch nt

gaffe n Fauxpas m

gag n Knebel m; (joke) Witz m; (Theat) Gag m □ vt knebeln

gaiety n Fröhlichkeit f

gain n Gewinn m; (increase) Zunahme f □ vt gewinnen; (obtain) erlangen; ~ **weight** zunehmen □ vi ⟨clock:⟩ vorgehen

gait n Gang m

gala n Fest nt; **swimming** ~ Schwimmfest nt

galaxy n Galaxie f

gale n Sturm m

gall n Galle f; (impudence) Frechheit f

gallant a tapfer; (chivalrous) galant. ~**ry** n Tapferkeit f

'gall-bladder n Gallenblase f

gallery n Galerie f

galley n (ship's kitchen) Kombüse f; ~ **[proof]** [Druck]fahne f

gallon n Gallone f (= 4,5 l)

gallop n Galopp m □ vi galoppieren

gallows n Galgen m

'gallstone n Gallenstein m

galore adv in Hülle und Fülle

gambit n Eröffnungsmanöver nt

gamble n (risk) Risiko nt □ vt [um Geld] spielen; ~ **on** (rely) sich verlassen auf (+ acc). ~**r** n Spieler(in) m(f)

game n Spiel nt; (animals) Wild nt; ~**s** (Sch) Sport m. ~**keeper** n Wildhüter m

gammon n [geräucherter] Schinken m

gander n Gänserich m

gang n Bande f; (of workmen) Kolonne f □ vi ~ **up** sich zusammenrotten (**on** gegen)

gangling a schlaksig

gangrene n Wundbrand m

gangster n Gangster m

gangway n Gang m; (Naut, Aviat) Gangway f

gaol n Gefängnis nt □ vt ins Gefängnis sperren. ~**er** n Gefängniswärter m

gap n Lücke f

gape vi gaffen; ~**e at** anstarren. ~**ing** a klaffend

garage n Garage f; (for repairs) Werkstatt f; (for petrol) Tankstelle f

garbled a verworren

garden n Garten m □ vi im Garten arbeiten. ~**er** n Gärtner(in) m(f). ~**ing** n Gartenarbeit f

gargle n (liquid) Gurgelwasser nt □ vi gurgeln

gargoyle n Wasserspeier m

garland n Girlande f

garlic n Knoblauch m

garment n Kleidungsstück nt

garnet n Granat m

garnish n Garnierung f □ vt garnieren

garret n Dachstube f

garrison n Garnison f

garrulous a geschwätzig

garter n Strumpfband nt

gas n Gas nt □ vt vergasen

gash n Schnitt m; (wound) klaffende Wunde f

gasket n (Techn) Dichtung f

gas: ~ **mask** n Gasmaske f. ~**-meter** n Gaszähler m

gasp vi keuchen

gastric a Magen-. ~ **'flu** n Darmgrippe f. ~ **'ulcer** n Magengeschwür nt

gastronomy n Gastronomie f

gate n Tor nt; (to field) Gatter nt; (barrier) Schranke f; (at airport) Flugsteig m

gate: ~**crasher** n ungeladener Gast m. ~**way** n Tor nt

gather vt sammeln; (pick) pflücken; (conclude) folgern (**from** aus) □ vi sich versammeln; ⟨storm:⟩ sich zusammenziehen. ~**ing** n family ~**ing** Familientreffen nt

gaudy a knallig

gauge n Stärke f; (Rail) Spurweite f; (device) Meßinstrument nt
□vt messen; (estimate) schätzen

gaunt a hager

gauntlet n run the ~ Spießruten laufen

gauze n Gaze f

gawp vi (fam) glotzen

gay a fröhlich; (fam) homosexuell, (fam) schwul

gaze n [langer] Blick m □vi sehen

gazelle n Gazelle f

gear n Ausrüstung f; (Techn) Getriebe nt; (Auto) Gang m; **in ~** mit eingelegtem Gang; **change ~** schalten

gear: ~**box** n Getriebe nt. ~**lever** n Schalthebel m

gel n Gel nt

gelatine n Gelatine f

gelignite n Gelatinedynamit nt

gem n Juwel nt

Gemini n (Astr) Zwillinge pl

gender n (Gram) Geschlecht nt

gene n Gen nt

genealogy n Genealogie f

general a allgemein □n General m; **in ~** im allgemeinen. ~ e'**lection** n allgemeine Wahlen pl

generalize vi verallgemeinern

generally adv im allgemeinen

general prac'titioner n praktischer Arzt

generate vt erzeugen

generation n Generation f

generator n Generator m

generic a ~ **term** Oberbegriff m

generosity n Großzügigkeit f

generous a großzügig

genetic a genetisch. ~**engineering** n Gentechnologie f. ~**s** n Genetik f

Geneva n Genf nt

genial a freundlich

genitals pl Geschlechtsteile pl

genitive a & n ~ [**case**] Genitiv m

genius n Genie nt

genocide n Völkermord m

genre n Gattung f, Genre nt

gentle a sanft

gentleman n Herr m; (well-mannered) Gentleman m

genuine a echt; (sincere) aufrichtig

genus n (Biol) Gattung f

geograph|ical a geographisch. ~**y** n Geographie f, Erdkunde f

geological a geologisch

geolog|ist n Geologe m/-gin f. ~**y** n Geologie f

geometric(al) a geometrisch. ~**y** n Geometrie f

geranium n Geranie f

geriatric a geriatrisch. ~**s** n Geriatrie f

germ n Keim m; ~**s** pl (fam) Bazillen pl

German a deutsch □n (person) Deutsche(r) m/f; (Lang) Deutsch nt; **in ~** auf deutsch; **into ~** ins Deutsche

Germanic a germanisch

German: ~ '**measles** n Röteln pl. ~ 'shepherd [dog] n [deutscher] Schäferhund m

Germany n Deutschland nt

germinate vi keimen

gesticulate vi gestikulieren

gesture n Geste f

get vt bekommen, (fam) kriegen; (procure) besorgen; (buy) kaufen; (fetch) holen; (take) bringen; (on telephone) erreichen; (fam: understand) kapieren; ~ **s.o. to do sth** jdn dazu bringen, etw zu tun □vi (become) werden; ~ **to** kommen zu/nach (town); (reach) erreichen; ~ **dressed** sich anziehen; ~ **married** heiraten. ~ **at** vt herankommen an (+ acc); **what are you ~ting at?** worauf willst du hinaus? ~ **by** vi vorbeikommen; (manage) sein Auskommen haben. ~ **off** vi (dismount) absteigen; (from bus) aussteigen; (leave) weggehen; (Jur) freigesprochen werden □vt (remove) abbekommen. ~ **on** vi (mount) aufsteigen; (to bus) einsteigen; (be on good terms) gut auskommen (**with** mit); (make progress) Fortschritte machen; **how are you ~ting on?** wie geht's? ~ **round** vi herumkommen; (avoid) umgehen; **I never ~ round to it** ich komme nie dazu □vt herumkriegen. ~ **up** vi aufstehen

get: ~ **away** n Flucht f. ~**up** n Aufmachung f

geyser n (Geol) Geysir m

ghastly a gräßlich

gherkin n Essiggurke f

ghetto n Getto nt

ghost n Geist m, Gespenst nt. ~**ly** a geisterhaft

ghoulish a makaber

giant n Riese m □a riesig

gibberish n Kauderwelsch nt

gibe n spöttische Bemerkung f

giblets npl Geflügelklein nt

giddy a schwindlig

gift n Geschenk nt; (to charity) Gabe f; (talent) Begabung f. ~**ed** a begabt. ~**wrap** vt als Geschenk einpacken

gig n (fam, Mus) Gig m

gigantic a riesig, riesengroß

giggle n Gekicher □vi kichern

gild vt vergolden

gills npl Kiemen pl

gilt a vergoldet □n Vergoldung f. ~**-edged** a (Comm) mündelsicher

gimmick n Trick m

gin n Gin m

ginger n rotblond; ⟨cat⟩ rot □n Ingwer m. ~**bread** n Pfefferkuchen m

giraffe n Giraffe f

girder n (Techn) Träger m

girdle n Bindegürtel m; (corset) Hüfthalter m

girl n Mädchen nt; (young woman) junge Frau f. ~**friend** n Freundin f

giro n Giro nt; (cheque) Postscheck m

girth n Umfang m; (for horse) Bauchgurt m

gist n the ~ das Wesentliche

give n Elastizität f □v geben/(as present) schenken (**to** dat); (donate) spenden; (lecture) halten; ⟨one's name⟩ angeben □vi geben; (yield) nachgeben. ~ **away** vt verschenken; (betray) verraten; (distribute) verteilen. ~ **in** vt einreichen □vi (yield) nachgeben. ~ **way** vi nachgeben; (Auto) die Vorfahrt beachten

glacier n Gletscher m

glad a froh (**of** über + acc)

glamorous a glanzvoll

glamour n [betörender] Glanz m

glance n [flüchtiger] Blick m □vi ~ **at** einen Blick werfen auf (+ acc)

gland n Drüse f

glare n □vi ~ **at** böse ansehen

glaring a grell; ⟨mistake⟩ kraß

glass n Glas nt; ~**es** pl (spectacles) Brille f. ~**y** a glasig

glaze n Glasur f □vt verglasen; (Culin, Pottery) glasieren

glazier n Glaser m

gleam n Schein m □vi glänzen

glean vi Ähren lesen □vt (learn) erfahren

glee n Frohlocken nt

glib a (pej) gewandt

glide vi gleiten; (through the air) schweben. ~**r** n Segelflugzeug nt

glimmer n Glimmen nt

glimpse n **catch a** ~ **of** flüchtig sehen □vt flüchtig sehen

glint n Blitzen nt □vi blitzen

glisten vi glitzern

glitter vi glitzern

gloat vi schadenfroh sein

global a global

globe n Kugel f; (map) Globus m

gloomy a düster; (fig) pessimistisch

glorify vt verherrlichen

glorious *a* herrlich
glory *n* Ruhm *m*; *(splendour)* Pracht *f* □ *vi* ~ **in** genießen
gloss *n* Glanz *m*
glossary *n* Glossar *nt*
glossy *a* glänzend
glove *n* Handschuh *m*
glow *n* Glut *f*; *(of candle)* Schein *m* □ *vi* glühen; *(candle:)* scheinen
'glow-worm *n* Glühwürmchen *nt*
glucose *n* Traubenzucker *m*, Glukose *f*
glue *n* Klebstoff *m* □ *vt* kleben (**to** an + *acc*)
glum *a* niedergeschlagen
glut *n* Überfluß *m* (**of** an + *dat*)
glutton *n* Vielfraß *m*. ~**ous** *a* gefräßig. ~**y** *n* Gefräßigkeit *f*
gnash *vt* ~ **one's teeth** mit den Zähnen knirschen
gnat *n* Mücke *f*
gnaw *vt/i* nagen (**at** an + *dat*)
gnome *n* Gnom *m*
go *n* Energie *f*; *(attempt)* Versuch *m*; **on the go** auf Trab; **at one go** auf einmal; **it's your go** du bist dran; **make a go of it** Erfolg haben □ *vi* gehen; *(in vehicle)* fahren; *(leave)* weggehen; *(on journey)* abfahren; *(time:)* vergehen *(vanish)* verschwinden; *(fail)* versagen; *(become)* werden; *(belong)* kommen. **go by** vorbeigehen/-fahren; *(time:)* vergehen. **go off** *vi* weggehen/-fahren; *(alarm:)* klingeln; *(gun, bomb:)* losgehen; *(go bad)* schlecht werden; **go off well** gut verlaufen. **go on** *vi* weitergehen/-fahren; *(continue)* weitermachen; *(talking)* fortfahren; *(happen)* vorgehen; **go on at** *(fam)* herumnörgeln an (+ *dat*). **go round** *vi* herumgehen/-fahren; *(visit)* vorbeigehen; *(turn)* sich drehen; *(be enough)* reichen. **go through** *vi* durchgehen/-fahren □ *vt* *(suffer)* durchmachen; *(check)* durchgehen. **go**

without *vt* verzichten auf (+ *acc*) □ *vi* darauf verzichten
goad *vt* anstacheln (**into** zu); *(taunt)* reizen
'go-ahead *a* fortschrittlich; *(enterprising)* unternehmend □ *n* *(fig)* grünes Licht *nt*
goal *n* Ziel *nt*; *(Sport)* Tor *nt*. ~**keeper** *n* Torwart *m*. ~**post** *n* Torpfosten *m*
goat *n* Ziege *f*
gobble *vt* hinunterschlingen
'go-between *n* Vermittler(in) *m(f)*
goblet *n* Pokal *m*; *(glass)* Kelchglas *nt*
goblin *n* Kobold *m*
God, god *n* Gott *m*
god: ~**child** *n* Patenkind *nt*. ~**daughter** *n* Patentochter *f*. ~**dess** *n* Göttin *f*. ~**father** *n* Pate *m*. **G~forsaken** *a* gottverlassen. ~**mother** *n* Patin *f*. ~**parents** *npl* Paten *pl*. ~**send** *n* Segen *m*. ~**son** *n* Patensohn *m*
goggle *vi* (*fam*) ~ **at** anglotzen. ~**s** *npl* Schutzbrille *f*
going *a* *(price)* gängig; *(concern)* gutgehend □ *n* **it is hard** ~ es ist schwierig
gold *n* Gold *nt* □ *a* golden
golden *a* golden. ~ **'handshake** *n* hohe Abfindungssumme *f*. ~ **'wedding** *n* goldene Hochzeit *f*
gold: ~**fish** *n inv* Goldfisch *m*. ~**mine** *n* Goldgrube *f*. ~**plated** *a* vergoldet. ~**smith** *n* Goldschmied *m*
golf *n* Golf *nt*
golf: ~**club** *n* Golfklub *m*; *(implement)* Golfschläger *m*. ~**course** *n* Golfplatz *m*. ~**er** *m* Golfspieler(in) *m(f)*
gondola *n* Gondel *f*. ~**lier** *n* Gondoliere *m*
gong *n* Gong *m*
good *a* gut; *(well-behaved)* brav, artig; ~ **at** gut in (+ *dat*); **a** ~ **deal** ziemlich viel; **as** ~ **so** gut

wie; (*almost*) fast □*n* **the** ~ das Gute; **for** ~ für immer; **do** ~ Gutes tun; **do s.o.** ~ jdm guttun; **it's no** ~ es ist nutzlos; (*hopeless*) da ist nichts zu machen

goodbye *int* auf Wiedersehen; (*Teleph, Radio*) auf Wiederhören

good: ~**-for-nothing** *n* Taugenichts *m*. **G** ~ **'Friday** *n* Karfreitag *m*. ~**-'looking** *a* gutaussehend

goodness *n* Güte *f*; **thank** ~! Gott sei Dank!

goods *npl* Waren *pl*. ~ **train** *n* Güterzug *m*

good'will *n* Wohlwollen *nt*; (*Comm*) Goodwill *m*

goose *n* Gans *f*

gooseberry *n* Stachelbeere *f*

goose ~**-flesh** *n*, ~ **pimples** *npl* Gänsehaut *f*

gore *n* Blut *nt*

gorge *n* (*Geog*) Schlucht *f* □ *vt* ~ **oneself** sich vollessen

gorgeous *a* prachtvoll

gorilla *n* Gorilla *m*

gorse *n* *inv* Stechginster *m*

gory *a* blutig

go-'slow *n* Bummelstreik *m*

gospel *n* Evangelium *nt*

gossip *n* Klatsch *m*; (*person*) Klatschbase *f* □ *vi* klatschen

Gothic *a* gotisch

gouge *vt* ~ **out** aushöhlen

goulash *n* Gulasch *m*

gourmet *n* Feinschmecker *m*

gout *n* Gicht *f*

govern *vt/i* regieren

government *n* Regierung *f*

governor *n* Gouverneur *m*; (*on board*) Vorstandsmitglied *nt*; (*of prison*) Direktor *m*; (*fam: boss*) Chef *m*

gown *n* [elegantes] Kleid *nt*; (*Univ, Jur*) Talar *m*

grab *vt* ergreifen; ~ **[hold of]** packen

grace *n* Anmut *f*; (*before meal*) Tischgebet *nt*; (*Relig*) Gnade *f*;

three **days'** ~ drei Tage Frist. ~**ful** *a* anmutig

gracious *a* gnädig

grade *n* Stufe *f*; (*Comm*) Güteklasse *f*; (*Sch*) Note *f* □ *vt* einstufen; (*Comm*) sortieren

gradient *n* Steigung *f*; (*downward*) Gefälle *nt*

gradual *a* allmählich

graduate[1] *n* Akademiker(in) *m(f)*

graduate^2 *vi* (*Univ*) sein Examen machen

graffiti *npl* Graffiti *pl*

graft *n* (*Bot*) Pfropfreis *nt*; (*Med*) Transplantat *nt*; (*fam: hard work*) Plackerei *f* □ *vt* (*Bot*) aufpfropfen; (*Med*) übertragen

grain *n* Korn *nt*; (*cereals*) Getreide *nt*; (*in wood*) Maserung *f*

gram *n* Gramm *nt*

grammar *n* Grammatik *f*. ~ **school** *n* ≈ Gymnasium *nt*

grammatical *a* grammatisch

granary *n* Getreidespeicher *m*

grand *a* großartig

grandad *n* (*fam*) Opa *m*

grandchild *n* Enkelkind *nt*

granddaughter *n* Enkelin *f*

grandeur *n* Pracht *f*

grandfather *n* Großvater *m*. ~ **clock** *n* Standuhr *f*

grandiose *a* grandios

grand: ~ **mother** *n* Großmutter *f*. ~ **parents** *npl* Großeltern *pl*. ~ **pi'ano** *n* Flügel *m*. ~ **son** *n* Enkel *m*. ~ **stand** *n* Tribüne *f*

granite *n* Granit *m*

granny *n* (*fam*) Oma *f*

grant *n* Subvention *f*; (*Univ*) Studienbeihilfe *f* □ *vt* gewähren; (*admit*) zugeben; **take sth for** ~**ed** etw als selbstverständlich hinnehmen

granulated *a* ~ **sugar** Kristallzucker *m*

granule *n* Körnchen *nt*

grape *n* [Wein]traube *f*; **bunch of** ~ **s** [ganze] Weintraube *f*

grapefruit n inv Grapefruit f, Pampelmuse f

graph n Kurvendiagramm nt

graphic a grafisch; (vivid) anschaulich. **~s** n (design) grafische Gestaltung f

'graph paper n Millimeterpapier nt

grapple vi ringen

grasp vt ergreifen; (understand) begreifen

grass n Gras nt; (lawn) Rasen m. **~hopper** n Heuschrecke f. **~land** n Weideland nt

grate[1] n Feuerrost m

grate[2] vt (Culin) reiben; **~ one's teeth** mit den Zähnen knirschen

grateful a dankbar (**to** dat)

grater n (Culin) Reibe f

gratify vt befriedigen

gratitude n Dankbarkeit f

gratuitous a überflüssig

gratuity n (tip) Trinkgeld nt

grave[1] a ernst; **~ly ill** schwer krank

grave[2] n Grab nt. **~-digger** n Totengräber m

gravel n Kies m

grave: **~stone** n Grabstein m. **~yard** n Friedhof m

gravitate vi gravitieren

gravity n Ernst m; (force) Schwerkraft f

gravy n [Braten]soße f

graze[1] vi (animal:) weiden

graze[2] n Schürfwunde f □vt streifen; (knee) aufschürfen

grease n Fett nt; (lubricant) Schmierfett nt □vt einfetten; (lubricate) schmieren. **~-proof 'paper** n Pergamentpapier nt

greasy a fettig

great a groß; (fam: marvellous) großartig

great: **~-'aunt** n Großtante f. **G~ 'Britain** n Großbritannien nt. **~-'grandchildren** npl Urenkel pl. **~-'grandfather** n Urgroßvater

m. **~-'grandmother** n Urgroßmutter f

greatness n Größe f

great-'uncle n Großonkel m

Greece n Griechenland nt

greed n [Hab]gier f

greedy a gierig

Greek a griechisch □n Grieche m/Griechin f; (Lang) Griechisch nt

green a grün □n Grün nt. **~s** pl Kohl m; the **G~s** pl (Pol) die Grünen pl

'greenfly n Blattlaus f

greengage n Reneklode f

green: **~grocer** n Obst- und Gemüsehändler m. **~house** n Gewächshaus nt. **~house effect** n Treibhauseffekt m

Greenland n Grönland nt

greet vt grüßen; (welcome) begrüßen. **~ing** n Gruß m; (welcome) Begrüßung f

gregarious a gesellig

grenade n Granate f

grey a grau □n Grau nt. **~hound** n Windhund m

grid n Gitter nt; (on map) Gitternetz nt; (Electr) Überlandleitungsnetz nt

grief n Trauer f; **come to ~** scheitern

grievance n Beschwerde f

grieve vt betrüben □vi trauern (**for** um)

grievous a schwer

grill n Gitter nt; (Culin) Grill m; **mixed ~** Gemischtes nt vom Grill □vt/i grillen; (interrogate) [streng] verhören

grille n Gitter nt

grim a ernst

grimace n Grimasse f

grime n Schmutz m

grin n Grinsen nt □vi grinsen

grind vt mahlen; (sharpen) schleifen

grip n Griff m; (bag) Reisetasche f □vt ergreifen; (hold) festhalten; fesseln ⟨interest⟩

grisly a grausig

gristle n Knorpel m

grit n (grober) Sand m; (for roads) Streugut nt □vt streuen ⟨road⟩; **~ one's teeth** die Zähne zusammenbeißen

groan vi stöhnen

grocer n Lebensmittelhändler m; **~'s [shop]** Lebensmittelgeschäft nt. **~ies** npl Lebensmittel pl

groin n (Anat) Leiste f

groom n Bräutigam m; (for horse) Pferdepfleger(in) m(f) □vt striegeln ⟨horse⟩

groove n Rille f

gross a fett; (coarse) derb; ⟨glaring⟩ grob; (Comm) brutto; ⟨salary, weight⟩ Brutto- □n inv Gros nt

grotesque a grotesk

grotto n Grotte f

ground n Boden m; (terrain) Gelände nt; (reason) Grund m; **~s** pl (park) Anlagen pl; (of coffee) Satz m

ground: **~ floor** n Erdgeschoß nt. **~ing** n Grundlage f. **~less** a grundlos. **~'meat** n Hackfleisch nt. **~sheet** n Bodenplane f. **~work** n Vorarbeiten pl

group n Gruppe f □vt gruppieren

grouse n inv schottisches Moorschneehuhn nt

grovel vi kriechen

grow vi wachsen; (become) werden; (increase) zunehmen □vt anbauen. **~ up** vi aufwachsen; ⟨town:⟩ entstehen

growl vi knurren

grown-up a erwachsen □n Erwachsene(r) m/f

growth n Wachstum nt; (increase) Zunahme f; (Med) Gewächs nt

grub n (larva) Made f; (fam: food) Essen nt

grubby a schmuddelig

grudge n Groll m; **bear s.o. a ~** einen Groll gegen jdn hegen □vt **~ s.o. sth** jdm etw mißgönnen

gruesome a grausig

gruff a barsch

grumble vi schimpfen (**at** mit)

grunt vi grunzen

guarantee n Garantie f; (document) Garantieschein m □vt garantieren; garantieren für ⟨quality⟩. **~or** n Bürge m

guard n Wache f; (security) Wächter m; (on train) ≈ Zugführer m; (Techn) Schutz m □vt bewachen; (protect) schützen ⟨+ a⟩ **against** sich hüten vor (+ dat). **~-dog** n Wachhund m

guardian n Vormund m

guerrilla n Guerillakämpfer m. **~ warfare** n Partisanenkrieg m

guess n Vermutung f □vt erraten □vi raten

guest n Gast m. **~-house** n Pension f

guidance n Führung f, Leitung f; (advice) Beratung f

guide n Führer(in) m(f); (book) Führer m; [**Girl**] **G~** Pfadfinderin f □vt führen, leiten. **~-book** n Führer m. **~-dog** n Blindenhund m. **~-lines** npl Richtlinien pl

guild n Gilde f, Zunft f

guile n Arglist f

guillotine n Guillotine f; (for paper) Papierschneidemaschine f

guilt n Schuld f

guilty a schuldig (**of** gen); ⟨look⟩ schuldbewußt; ⟨conscience⟩ schlecht

guinea-pig n Meerschweinchen nt; (person) Versuchskaninchen nt

guitar n Gitarre f. **~ist** n Gitarrist(in) m(f)

gulf n (Geog) Golf m; (fig) Kluft f

gull n Möwe f

gullet n Speiseröhre f; (throat) Kehle f

gullible a leichtgläubig

gully n Schlucht f

gulp vi schlucken □vt ~ **down** hinunterschlucken

gum¹ n & -s pl (Anat) Zahnfleisch nt

gum² n Gummi[harz] nt; (glue) Klebstoff m □vt kleben (**to** an + acc). ~ **boot** n Gummistiefel m

gumption n (fam) Grips m

gun n Schußwaffe f; (pistol) Pistole f; (rifle) Gewehr nt; (cannon) Geschütz nt

gun: ~**fire** n Geschützfeuer nt. ~**man** bewaffneter Bandit m. ~**powder** n Schießpulver nt

gurgle vi gluckern

gusset n Zwickel m

gust n (of wind) Windstoß m; (Naut) Bö f

gusto n **with** ~ mit Schwung

gut n Darm m; ~**s** pl Eingeweide pl; (fam: courage) Schneid m

gutter n Rinnstein m; (fig) Gosse f; (on roof) Dachrinne f

guttural a guttural

guy n (fam) Kerl m

guzzle vt/i schlingen

gymnasium n Turnhalle f

gymnast n Turner(in) m(f). ~**ics** n Turnen nt

gynaecolog|ist n Frauenarzt m/ -ärztin f. ~**y** n Gynäkologie f

gypsy n Zigeuner(in) m(f)

H

haberdashery n Kurzwaren pl

habit n Gewohnheit f; (Relig: costume) Ordenstracht f

habitable a bewohnbar

habitat n Habitat nt

habitual a gewohnt; (inveterate) gewohnheitsmäßig

hack¹ n (writer) Schreiberling m; (hired horse) Mietpferd nt

hack² vt hacken; ~ **to pieces** zerhacken

hackneyed a abgedroschen

hacksaw n Metallsäge f

haddock n inv Schellfisch m

haemorrhage n Blutung f

haemorrhoids npl Hämorrhoiden pl

haggard a abgehärmt

haggle vi feilschen (**over** um)

hail¹ vt begrüßen; herbeirufen (taxi) □vi ~ **from** kommen aus

hail² n Hagel m □vi hageln. ~**stone** n Hagelkorn nt

hair n Haar nt; **wash one's** ~ sich (dat) die Haare waschen

hair: ~**brush** n Haarbürste f. ~**cut** n Haarschnitt m; **have a** ~**cut** sich (dat) die Haare schneiden lassen. ~**dresser** n Friseur m/Friseuse f. ~**drier** n Haartrockner m; (hand-held) Fön (P) m. ~**grip** n [Haar]klemme f. ~**pin** n Haarnadel f. ~**pin 'bend** n Haarnadelkurve f. ~**raising** a haarsträubend. ~**style** n Frisur f

hairy a behaart; (excessively) haarig

hake n inv Seehecht m

half n Hälfte f; **one and a** ~ eineinhalb, anderthalb □a & adv halb; ~ **past two** halb drei

half: ~**board** n Halbpension f. ~**caste** n Mischling m. ~**'hearted** a lustlos. ~**'hourly** a & adv halbstündlich. ~**'mast** n at ~**mast** auf halbmast. ~**measure** n Halbheit f. ~**'term** n schulfreie Tage pl nach dem halben Trimester. ~**'time** n (Sport) Halbzeit f. ~**'way** a the ~**way mark/stage** die Hälfte □adv auf halbem Weg

halibut n inv Heilbutt m

hall n Halle f; (room) Saal m; (Sch) Aula f; (entrance) Flur m; (mansion) Gutshaus nt. ~ **of residence** (Univ) Studentenheim nt

hallmark n [Feingehalts]stempel m

hallo int [guten] Tag! (fam) hallo!

Hallowe'en n der Tag vor Aller-
heiligen

hallucination n Halluzination f

halo n Heiligenschein m; (Astr)
Hof m

halt n Halt m; **come to a** ~ stehenbleiben; ⟨traffic:⟩ zum Stillstand
kommen □vi haltmachen; ~!
halt!

halve vt halbieren

ham n Schinken m

hamburger n Hamburger m

hamlet n Weiler m

hammer n Hammer m □vt/i hämmern (**at** an + acc)

hammock n Hängematte f

hamper[1] n Picknickkorb m;
[gift] ~ Geschenkkorb m

hamper[2] vt behindern

hamster n Hamster m

hand n Hand f; (of clock) Zeiger m;
(writing) Handschrift f; (worker)
Arbeiter(in) m(f); (Cards) Blatt
nt; **on the one/other** ~ einer-/
andererseits; □vt reichen (**to**
dat). ~ **in** vt abgeben. ~ **out** vt
austeilen. ~ **over** vt überreichen

hand: ~**bag** n Handtasche f.
~**book** n Handbuch nt. ~ **brake**
n Handbremse f. ~**cuffs** npl
Handschellen pl

handicap n Behinderung f;
(Sport & fig) Handikap nt. ~**ped**
a **mentally/physically** ~**ped**
geistig/körperlich behindert

handi|craft n Basteln nt; (Sch)
Werken nt. ~**work** n Werk nt

handkerchief n Taschentuch nt

handle n Griff m; (of door) Klinke
f; (of cup) Henkel m; (of broom)
Stiel m □vt handhaben; (treat)
umgehen mit; (touch) anfassen.
~ **bars** npl Lenkstange f

hand: ~**luggage** n Handgepäck
nt. ~**made** a handgemacht.
~**out** n Prospekt m; (money)
Unterstützung f. ~**shake** n Händedruck m

handsome a gutaussehend

hand: ~**stand** n Handstand m.
~**writing** n Handschrift f. ~-
'**written** a handgeschrieben

handy a handlich; ⟨person⟩ geschickt; **have/keep** ~ griffbereit
haben/halten. ~**man** n [home]
~**man** Heimwerker m

hang vt/i hängen; ~**wallpaper**
tapezieren □vt hängen ⟨crim-
inal⟩; ~ **oneself** sich erhängen
□n **get the** ~ **of** it (fam) den Dreh
herauskriegen. ~ **about** vi sich
herumdrücken. ~ **on** vi sich festhalten (**to** an + dat); (fam: wait)
warten

hangar n Flugzeughalle f

hanger n [Kleider]bügel m

hang: ~**glider** n Drachenflieger
m. ~**gliding** n Drachenfliegen
nt. ~**man** n Henker m. ~**over** n
(fam) Kater m (fam). ~-**up** n
(fam) Komplex m

haphazard a planlos

happen vi geschehen, passieren; **I**
~**ed to be there** ich war zufällig
da. ~**ing** n Ereignis nt

happiness n Glück nt

happy a glücklich. ~-**go**-'**lucky** a
sorglos

harass vt schikanieren. ~**ed** a
abgehetzt. ~**ment** n Schikane f;
(sexual) Belästigung f

harbour n Hafen m

hard a hart; (difficult) schwer; ~
of hearing schwerhörig □adv
hart; (work) schwer; ⟨pull⟩ kräftig; ⟨rain, snow⟩ stark; **think** ~!
denk mal nach! **be** ~ **up** (fam)
knapp bei Kasse sein

hard: ~**back** n gebundene Ausgabe f. ~**board** n Hartfaserplatte
f. ~-**boiled** a hartgekocht

hard|ly adv kaum; ~**ly ever**
kaum [jemals]. ~**ship** n Not f

hard: ~ '**shoulder** n (Auto)
Randstreifen m. ~**ware** n Haus-
haltswaren pl; (Computing)
Hardware f. ~-'**working** a
fleißig

hardy *a* abgehärtet; ⟨*plant*⟩ winterhart

hare *n* Hase *m*

harm *n* Schaden *m*; out of ~'s way in Sicherheit; it won't do any~ es kann nichts schaden □ *vt* ~ s.o. jdm etwas antun. ~**ful** *a* schädlich. ~**less** *a* harmlos

harmonica *n* Mundharmonika *f*

harmon|ize *vi* (*fig*) harmonieren. ~**y** *n* Harmonie *f*

harness *n* Geschirr *nt*; (*of parachute*) Gurtwerk *nt*

harp *n* Harfe *f* □ *vi* ~ **on** [about] (*fam*) herumreiten auf (+ *dat*). ~**ist** *n* Harfenist(in) *m(f)*

harpoon *n* Harpune *f*

harpsichord *n* Cembalo *nt*

harrow *n* Egge *f*

harsh *a* hart; ⟨*voice*⟩ rauh; ⟨*light*⟩ grell

harvest *n* Ernte *f*

hashish *n* Haschisch *nt*

hassle *n* (*fam*) Ärger *m* □ *vt* schikanieren

haste *n* Eile *f*

hasten *vi* sich beeilen (to zu); (*go quickly*) eilen □ *vt* beschleunigen

hasty *a* hastig

hat *n* Hut *m*

hatch[1] *n* (*for food*) Durchreiche *f*; (*Naut*) Luke *f*

hatch[2] *vi* ~ [out] ausschlüpfen □ *vt* ausbrüten

hatchback *n* (*Auto*) Modell *nt* mit Hecktür

hatchet *n* Beil *nt*

hate *n* Haß *m* □ *vt* hassen. ~**ful** *a* abscheulich

hatred *n* Haß *m*

haughty *a* hochmütig

haul *n* (*fish*) Fang *m*; (*loot*) Beute *f* □ *vt*/*i* ziehen (on an + *dat*). ~**age** *n* Transport *m*. ~**ier** *n* Spediteur *m*

haunt *n* Lieblingsaufenthalt *m* □ *vt* umgehen in (+ *dat*)

have *vt* haben; bekommen ⟨*baby*⟩; holen ⟨*doctor*⟩; ~ **a meal/**

drink etwas essen/trinken; ~ **lunch** zu Mittag essen; ~ **a walk** spazierengehen; ~ **a dream** träumen; ~ **a rest** sich ausruhen; ~ **to do sth** etw tun müssen; ~ **it out with** zur Rede stellen; so I ~ ! tatsächlich! □ *v aux* haben; (*with verbs of motion & some others*) sein; I ~ **seen him** ich habe ihn gesehen; **he has never been there** er ist nie da gewesen

haven *n* (*fig*) Zuflucht *f*

haversack *n* Rucksack *m*

havoc *n* Verwüstung *f*

hawk[1] *n* Falke *m*

hawk[2] *vt* hausieren mit. ~**er** *n* Hausierer *m*

hawthorn *n* Hagedorn *m*

hay *n* Heu *nt*. ~ **fever** *n* Heuschnupfen *m*. ~**stack** *n* Heuschober *m*

haywire *a* (*fam*) **go** ~ verrückt spielen

hazard *n* Gefahr *f*; (*risk*) Risiko *nt* □ *vt* riskieren. ~**ous** *a* gefährlich; (*risky*) riskant. ~ **[warning] lights** *npl* (*Auto*) Warnblinkanlage *f*

haze *n* Dunst *m*

hazel *n* Haselbusch *m*. ~-**nut** *n* Haselnuß *f*

hazy *a* dunstig

he *pron* er

head *n* Kopf *m*; (*chief*) Oberhaupt *nt*; (*of firm*) Chef(in) *m(f)*; (*of school*) Schulleiter(in) *m(f)*; (*on beer*) Schaumkrone *f*; (*of bed*) Kopfende *nt*; **20** ~ **of cattle** 20 Stück Vieh; ~ **first** kopfüber □ *vt* anführen; (*Sport*) köpfen ⟨*ball*⟩ □ *vi* ~ **for** zusteuern auf (+ *acc*). ~**ache** *n* Kopfschmerzen *pl*

head|er *n* Kopfball *m*. ~**ing** *n* Überschrift *f*

head: ~**land** *n* Landspitze *f*. ~**light** *n* (*Auto*) Scheinwerfer *m*. ~**line** *n* Schlagzeile *f*. ~ **long** *adv* kopfüber. ~**master** *n* Schulleiter *m*. ~**mistress** *n*

Schulleiterin f. ~**-on** a & adv
frontal. ~**phones** npl Kopfhörer
m. ~**quarters** npl Hauptquartier nt; (Pol) Zentrale f. ~**rest** n
Kopfstütze f. ~**strong** a eigenwillig. ~'**waiter** n Oberkellner
m. ~**way** n make ~**way** Fortschritte machen. ~ **wind** n Gegenwind m

heal vt/i heilen

health n Gesundheit f

health: ~ **farm** n Schönheitsfarm f. ~ **foods** npl Reformkost f.
~**-food shop** n Reformhaus nt.
~ **insurance** n Krankenversicherung f

healthy a gesund

heap n Haufen m

hear vt/i hören; ~, ~! hört, hört!

hearing n Gehör nt; (Jur)
Verhandlung f. ~**-aid** n Hörgerät
nt

hearse n Leichenwagen m

heart n Herz nt; (courage) Mut
m; ~**s** pl (Cards) Herz nt;
by ~ auswendig

heart: ~**ache** n Kummer m. ~
attack n Herzanfall m. ~**beat** n
Herzschlag m. ~**break** n Leid
nt. ~**breaking** a herzzerreißend. ~**broken** a untröstlich.
~**burn** n Sodbrennen nt

hearth n Herd m; (fireplace) Kamin m

hearty a herzlich; ⟨meal⟩ groß

heat n Hitze f; (Sport) Vorlauf m
□vt heiß machen; heizen ⟨room⟩.
~**er** n Heizgerät nt; (Auto) Heizanlage f

heath n Heide f

heathen n Heide m/Heidin f

heather n Heidekraut nt

heating n Heizung f

heave vt/i ziehen; (lift) heben

heaven n Himmel m. ~**ly** a
himmlisch

heavy a schwer; ⟨traffic⟩ stark;
⟨sleep⟩ tief. ~**weight** n Schwergewicht nt

Hebrew a hebräisch

heckler n Zwischenrufer m

hectic a hektisch

hedge n Hecke f. ~**hog** n Igel m

heed n beachten

heel n Ferse f; (of shoe) Absatz m

hefty a kräftig

heifer n Färse f

height n Höhe f; (of person)
Größe f. ~**en** vt (fig) steigern

heir n Erbe m. ~**ess** n Erbin f.
~**loom** n Erbstück nt

helicopter n Hubschrauber m

hell n Hölle f; go to ~! (sl) geh
zum Teufel!

hello int [guten] Tag! (fam) hallo!

helm n [Steuer]ruder m

helmet n Helm m

help n Hilfe f □vt/i helfen (s.o.
jdm); ~ **oneself to sth** sich (dat)
etw nehmen; ~ **yourself** (at
table) greif zu; I **could not**
~ **laughing** ich mußte lachen

help|**er** n Helfer(in) m(f). ~**ful** a
hilfsbereit; ⟨advice⟩ nützlich.
~**ing** n Portion f. ~**less** a hilflos

helter-skelter n Rutschbahn f

hem n Saum m

hemisphere n Hemisphäre f

hemp n Hanf m

hen n Henne f; (any female bird)
Weibchen nt

hence adv daher; **five years** ~ in
fünf Jahren. ~**forth** adv von
nun an

her a ihr □pron (acc) sie; (dat) ihr

herald vt verkünden. ~**ry** n Wappenkunde f

herb n Kraut nt

herd n Herde f □ vt (tend) hüten;
(drive) treiben. ~ **together** vt
zusammentreiben

here adv hier; (to this place) hierher; **in** ~ hier drinnen; **come/
bring** ~ herkommen/herbringen. ~'**after** adv im folgenden.
~'**by** adv hiermit

heredit|**ary** a erblich. ~**y** n Vererbung f

here|sy n Ketzerei f. **~tic** n Ketzer(in) m(f)

here'with adv (Comm) beiliegend

heritage n Erbe nt

hermit n Einsiedler m

hernia n Bruch m, Hernie f

hero n Held m

heroic a heldenhaft

heroin n Heroin nt

hero|ine n Heldin f. **~ism** n Heldentum nt

heron n Reiher m

herring n Hering m; **red ~** (fam) falsche Spur f. **~bone** n (pattern) Fischgrätenmuster nt

hers poss pron ihre(r), ihrs; **a friend of ~** ein Freund von ihr; **that is ~** das gehört ihr

her'self pron selbst; (refl) sich; **by ~** allein

hesitat|e vi zögern. **~ion** n Zögern nt

hetero'sexual a heterosexuell

hew vt hauen

hexagonal a sechseckig

'heyday n Glanzzeit f

hi int he! (hallo) Tag!

hiatus n Lücke f

hibernat|e vi Winterschlaf halten. **~ion** n Winterschlaf m

hiccup n Hick m; (fam: hitch) Panne f; **have the ~s** den Schluckauf haben ▫vi hick machen

hide[1] n Haut f; (leather) Leder nt

hide[2] vt verstecken; (keep secret) verheimlichen ▫vi sich verstecken. **~-and-seek** n play **~-and-seek** Versteck spielen

hideous a häßlich; (horrible) gräßlich

'hide-out n Versteck nt

hierarchy n Hierarchie f

hieroglyphics npl Hieroglyphen pl

high a hoch; attrib hohe(r,s); ⟨meat⟩ angegangen; ⟨wind⟩ stark; (on drugs) high; **it's ~ time** es ist höchste Zeit ▫adv

hoch; **~ and low** überall ▫n Hoch nt

high: ~brow a intellektuell. **~ chair** n Kinderhochstuhl m. **~'handed** a selbstherrlich. **~-'heeled** a hochhackig. **~ jump** n Hochsprung m

highlight n (fig) Höhepunkt m; **~s** pl (in hair) helle Strähnen pl ▫vt (emphasize) hervorheben

Highness n Hoheit f

high: ~-rise a **~-rise flats** pl Wohnturm m. **~ season** n Hochsaison f. **~ street** n Hauptstraße f. **~'tide** n Hochwasser nt. **~way** n public **~ way** öffentliche Straße f

hijack vt entführen. **~er** n Entführer m

hike vi wandern. **~r** n Wanderer m

hilarious a sehr komisch

hill n Berg m; (mound) Hügel m; (slope) Hang m

hilt n Griff m; **to the ~** (fam) voll und ganz

him pron (acc) ihn; (dat) ihm. **~'self** pron selbst; (refl) sich; **by ~self** allein

hind|er vt hindern. **~rance** n Hindernis nt

hindsight n **with ~** rückblickend

Hindu n Hindu m ▫a Hindu-. **~ism** n Hinduismus m

hinge n Scharnier nt; (on door) Angel f

hint n Wink m, Andeutung f; (advice) Hinweis m; (trace) Spur f ▫vi **~ at** anspielen auf (+ acc)

hip n Hüfte f

hippopotamus n Nilpferd nt

hire vt mieten ⟨car⟩; leihen ⟨suit⟩; einstellen ⟨person⟩; **~ [out]** vermieten; verleihen. **~-car** n Leihwagen m

his a sein ▫ poss pron seine(r), seins; **a friend of ~** ein Freund

von ihm; **that is** ~ das gehört
ihm

hiss *vt/i* zischen

historian *n* Historiker(in) *m(f)*

historic *a* historisch. ~**al** *a* ge-
schichtlich, historisch

history *n* Geschichte *f*

hit *n* (*blow*) Schlag *m*; (*fam: success*) Erfolg *m*; **direct** ~ Volltreffer *m* □*vt/i* schlagen; (*knock
against*) treffen

hitch *n* Problem *nt*; **technical** ~
Panne *f* □*vt* festmachen (**to** an +
dat); ~ **up** hochziehen. ~**-hike**
vi per Anhalter fahren, (*fam*)
trampen. ~**-hiker** *n* Anhal-
ter(in) *m(f)*

hither *adv* hierher; ~ **and
thither** hin und her. ~**'to** *adv*
bisher

hive *n* Bienenstock *m*

hoard *n* Hort *m* □*vt* horten, ham-
stern

hoarding *n* Bauzaun *m*; (*with ad-
vertisements*) Reklamewand *f*

hoar-frost *n* Rauhreif *m*

hoarse *a* heiser

hoax *n* übler Scherz *m*; (*false
alarm*) blinder Alarm *m*

hob *n* Kochmulde *f*

hobble *vi* humpeln

hobby *n* Hobby *nt*. ~**-horse** *n*
(*fig*) Lieblingsthema *nt*

hockey *n* Hockey *nt*

hoe *n* Hacke *f*

hoist *n* Lastenaufzug *m* □*vt* hochziehen; hissen 〈*flag*〉

hold[^1] *n* (*Naut, Aviat*) Laderaum *m*

hold[^2] *n* Halt *m*; (*Sport*) Griff *m*;
(*fig: influence*) Einfluß *m*; **get** ~
of fassen; (*fam: contact*) erreichen □*vt* halten; (*container:*) fassen; (*believe*) meinen; (*possess*)
haben; anhalten 〈*breath*〉; ~
one's tongue den Mund halten
□*vi* 〈*rope:*〉 halten; 〈*weather:*〉
sich halten. ~ **on** *vi* (*wait*) warten; (*on telephone*) am Apparat
bleiben; ~ **on to** (*keep*) behalten;

(*cling to*) sich festhalten an (+
dat). ~ **out** *vt* hinhalten □*vi*
(*resist*) aushalten

'hold|all *n* Reisetasche *f*. ~**er** *n*
Inhaber(in) *m(f)*; (*container*)
Halter *m*. ~**-up** *n* Verzögerung *f*;
(*attack*) Überfall *m*

hole *n* Loch *nt*

holiday *n* Urlaub *m*; (*Sch*) Ferien
pl; (*public*) Feiertag *m*; (*day off*)
freier Tag *m*. ~**-maker** *n* Ur-
lauber(in) *m(f)*

holiness *n* Heiligkeit *f*

Holland *n* Holland *nt*

hollow *a* hohl

holly *n* Stechpalme *f*

'hollyhock *n* Stockrose *f*

hologram *n* Hologramm *nt*

holster *n* Pistolentasche *f*

holy *a* heilig. **H~ Ghost** *or*
Spirit *n* Heiliger Geist *m*. ~
water *n* Weihwasser *nt*. **H~
Week** *n* Karwoche *f*

homage *n* Huldigung *f*; **pay** ~ **to**
huldigen (+ *dat*)

home *n* Zuhause *nt*; (*house*) Haus
nt; (*institution*) Heim *nt*; (*native
land*) Heimat *f* □*adv* **at** ~ zu
Hause; **come/go** ~ nach Hause
kommen/gehen

home: ~ **ad'dress** *n* Heimatan-
schrift *f*. ~ **com'puter** *n* Heim-
computer *m*. ~ **game** *n* Heim-
spiel *nt*. ~ **help** *n* Haushaltshilfe
f. ~ **land** *n* Heimatland *nt*. ~**less**
a obdachlos

homely *a* gemütlich

home: ~**'made** *a* selbstgemacht.
H~ Office *n* Innenministerium
nt. **H~ 'Secretary** *n* Innenmini-
ster *m*. ~**sick** *a* **be** ~**sick** Heim-
weh haben (**for** nach). ~**work** *n*
(*Sch*) Hausaufgaben *pl*

homoeopathic *a* homöopathisch

homogeneous *a* homogen

homo'sexual *a* homosexuell □*n*
Homosexuelle(r) *m/f*

honest *a* ehrlich. ~**y** *n* Ehr-
lichkeit *f*

honey n Honig m

honey: ~**comb** n Honigwabe f.
~**moon** n Flitterwochen pl;
(journey) Hochzeitsreise f.
~**suckle** n Geißblatt nt

honorary a ehrenamtlich

honour n Ehre f ⊳vt ehren; honorieren ⟨cheque⟩. ~ **able** a ehrenhaft

hood n Kapuze f; (of pram)
[Klapp]verdeck nt; (over cooker)
Abzugshaube f

hoof n Huf m

hook n Haken m; **by ~ or by
crook** mit allen Mitteln

hooligan n Rowdy m. ~**ism** n
Rowdytum nt

hoop n Reifen m

hoot n Ruf m; ~**s of laughter**
schallendes Gelächter nt ⊳vi
⟨owl:⟩ rufen; ⟨car:⟩ hupen; ⟨jeer⟩
johlen. ~**er** n (of factory) Sirene
f; (Auto) Hupe f

hop[1] n, & ~**s** pl Hopfen m

hop[2] n Hüpfer m; **catch s.o. on
the ~** (fam) jdm ungelegen kommen ⊳vi hüpfen

hope n Hoffnung f; (prospect)
Aussicht f (of auf + acc) ⊳vt/i
hoffen (for auf + acc)

hope|**ful** a hoffnungsvoll. ~**fully**
adv hoffnungsvoll; (it is hoped)
hoffentlich. ~**less** a hoffnungslos; (useless) nutzlos

horde n Horde f

horizon n Horizont m

horizontal a horizontal. ~'**bar** n
Reck nt

horn n Horn nt; (Auto) Hupe f

hornet n Hornisse f

horoscope n Horoskop nt

horrible a schrecklich

horrid a gräßlich

horrific a entsetzlich

horrify vt entsetzen

horror n Entsetzen nt. ~ **film** n
Horrorfilm m

hors-d'oeuvre n Vorspeise f

horse n Pferd nt

horse: ~**back** n **on** ~**back** zu
Pferde. ~'**chestnut** n [Roß]kastanie f. ~**power** n Pferdestärke
f. ~**radish** n Meerrettich m.
~**shoe** n Hufeisen nt

horticulture n Gartenbau m

hose n (pipe) Schlauch m ⊳vt ~
down abspritzen

hosiery n Strumpfwaren pl

hospice n Heim nt; (for the
terminally ill) Sterbeklinik f

hospitable a gastfreundlich

hospital n Krankenhaus nt

hospitality n Gastfreundschaft f

host[1] n Gastgeber m

host[2] n (Relig) Hostie f

hostage n Geisel f

hostel n [Wohn]heim nt

hostess n Gastgeberin f

hostile a feindlich

hostil|**ity** n Feindschaft f; ~**ies** pl
Feindseligkeiten pl

hot a heiß; (meal) warm; (spicy)
scharf

hotchpotch n Mischmasch m

hotel n Hotel nt

hot: ~**head** n Hitzkopf m. ~-
'**headed** a hitzköpfig. ~**house** n
Treibhaus nt. ~**plate** n Tellerwärmer m; (of cooker) Kochplatte
f. ~**tempered** a jähzornig. ~-
'**water bottle** n Wärmflasche f

hound n Jagdhund m ⊳vt (fig)
verfolgen

hour n Stunde f. ~**ly** a stündlich.
~**ly rate** Stundenlohn m

house[1] n Haus nt; **at my** ~
bei mir

house[2] vt unterbringen

house: ~**boat** n Hausboot nt.
~**hold** n Haushalt m. ~**keeper**
n Haushälterin f. ~**keeping**
n Haushaltsführung f; (money)
Haushaltsgeld nt. ~**plant** n Zimmerpflanze f. ~**trained** a stubenrein. ~**warming** n **have a ~
warming party** Einstand feiern.
~**wife** n Hausfrau f. ~**work** n
Hausarbeit f

housing n Wohnungen pl. ~
estate n Wohnsiedlung f
hovel n elende Hütte f
hover vi schweben; (be undecided) schwanken; (linger)
herumstehen. ~**craft** n Luftkis-
senfahrzeug nt
how adv wie; ~ **do you do?** guten
Tag! ~ **many** wie viele; ~ **much**
wieviel
how'ever adv (in question) wie;
(nevertheless) jedoch, aber; ~
small wie klein es auch sein mag
howl □ vi heulen; ⟨baby:⟩ brüllen.
~**er** n (fam) Schnitzer m
hub n Nabe f
'**hub-cap** n Radkappe f
hue¹ n Farbe f
hue² n ~ **and cry** Aufruhr m
hug vt umarmen
huge a riesig
hull n (Naut) Rumpf m
hum vt/i summen; ⟨motor:⟩ brummen
human a menschlich □ n Mensch
m. ~ '**being** n Mensch m
humane a human
humanitarian a humanitär
humanit|y n Menschheit f; ~**ies**
pl (Univ) Geisteswissenschaften
pl
humble a demütig □ vt demütigen
humid a feucht. ~**ity** n Feuchtigkeit f
humiliat|e vt demütigen. ~**ion** n
Demütigung f
humility n Demut f
'**humming-bird** n Kolibri m
humorous a humorvoll
humour n Humor m; (mood)
Laune f; **have a sense of** ~
Humor haben □ vt ~ s.o. jdm
seinen Willen lassen
hump n Buckel m; (of camel)
Höcker m
hunch n (idea) Ahnung f
'**hunchback** n Bucklige(r) m/f
hundred a one/a ~ [ein]hundert
□ n Hundert nt; (written figure)

Hundert f. ~**th** a hundertste(r,s)
□ n Hundertstel nt. ~**weight** n
Zentner m
Hungarian a ungarisch □ n Un-
gar(in) m(f)
Hungary n Ungarn nt
hunger n Hunger m. ~**-strike** n
Hungerstreik m
hungry a hungrig; **be** ~ Hunger
haben
hunk n [großes] Stück nt
hunt n Jagd f; (for criminal) Fahndung f □ vt/i jagen; fahnden nach
⟨criminal⟩. ~**er** n Jäger m. ~**ing**
n Jagd f
hurdle n Hürde f
hurl vt schleudern
hurrah, hurray int hurra!
hurricane n Orkan m
hurry n Eile f; **be in a** ~
es eilig haben □ vi sich beeilen;
(go quickly) eilen. ~**up** vi sich
beeilen □ vt antreiben
hurt vt/i (pt/pp **hurt**) weh tun (+ dat); (injure)
verletzen; (offend) kränken.
~**ful** a verletzend
hurtle vi ~ **along** rasen
husband n [Ehe]mann m
hush vt ~ **up** vertuschen
husk n Spelze f
husky a heiser; (burly) stämmig
hustle vt drängen
hut n Hütte f
hutch n [Kaninchen]stall m
hybrid n Hybride f
hydrangea n Hortensie f
hydrant n [fire] ~ Hydrant m
hydraulic a hydraulisch
hydrochloric ~ **acid** Salzsäure
f
hydro'lectric a hydroelek-
trisch. ~ **power station** n Was-
serkraftwerk nt
hydrofoil n Tragflügelboot nt
hydrogen n Wasserstoff m
hyena n Hyäne f
hygien|e n Hygiene f. ~**ic** a hygie-
nisch

hymn n Kirchenlied nt. ~-**book** n Gesangbuch nt

hyphen n Bindestrich m

hypno|sis n Hypnose f. ~ **tic** a hypnotisch

hypno|tism n Hypnotik f. ~ **tist** n Hypnotiseur m. ~ **tize** vt hypnotisieren

hypochondriac n Hypochonder m

hypocrisy n Heuchelei f

hypocrit|e n Heuchler(in) m(f). ~ **ical** a heuchlerisch

hypodermic a & n ~ [syringe] Injektionsspritze f

hypothe|sis n Hypothese f. ~ **tical** a hypothetisch

hyster|ia n Hysterie f. ~ **ical** a hysterisch

I

I pron ich

ice n Eis nt

ice: ~ **age** n Eiszeit f. ~-**axe** n Eispickel m. ~**berg** n Eisberg m. ~-'**cream** n [Speise]eis nt. ~-**cube** n Eiswürfel m

Iceland n Island nt

ice: ~ '**lolly** n Eis nt am Stiel. ~ **rink** n Eisbahn f

icicle n Eiszapfen m

icing n Zuckerguß m. ~ **sugar** n Puderzucker m

icon n Ikone f

icy a eisig; ⟨road⟩ vereist

idea n Idee f; ⟨conception⟩ Vorstellung f; I have no ~! ich habe keine Ahnung!

ideal a ideal □n Ideal nt. ~ **ism** n Idealismus m. ~ **ist** n Idealist(in) m(f). ~ **istic** a idealistisch. ~ **ize** vt idealisieren

identical a identisch; ⟨twins⟩ eineiig

identi|fication n Identifizierung f; ⟨proof of identity⟩ Ausweispapiere pl. ~ **fy** vt identifizieren

identity n Identität f. ~ **card** n [Personal]ausweis m

ideolog|ical a ideologisch. ~ **y** n Ideologie f

idiom n [feste] Redewendung f. ~ **atic** a idiomatisch

idiosyncrasy n Eigenart f.

idiot n Idiot m. ~ **ic** a idiotisch

idle a untätig; ⟨lazy⟩ faul; ⟨empty⟩ leer; ⟨machine⟩ nicht in Betrieb □vi faulenzen; ⟨engine:⟩ leer laufen

idol n Idol nt. ~ **ize** vt vergöttern

idyllic a idyllisch

i.e. abbr (id est) d.h.

if conj wenn; ⟨whether⟩ ob; **as if** als ob

ignite vt entzünden □vi sich entzünden

ignition n (Auto) Zündung f. ~ **key** n Zündschlüssel m

ignorant a unwissend

ignore vt ignorieren

ill a krank; ⟨bad⟩ schlecht; **feel** ~ **at ease** sich unbehaglich fühlen □adv schlecht □n Schlechte(s) nt; ⟨evil⟩ Übel nt. ~-**advised** a unklug. ~-**bred** a schlecht erzogen

illegal a illegal

illegible a unleserlich

illegitimate a unehelich

illicit a illegal

illitera|cy n Analphabetentum nt. ~ **te** a **be** ~ **te** nicht lesen und schreiben können □n Analphabet(in) m(f)

illness n Krankheit f

illogical a unlogisch

ill-treat vt mißhandeln

illuminate vt beleuchten

illusion n Illusion f; **be under the** ~ **that** sich ⟨dat⟩ einbilden, daß

illustrate vt illustrieren. ~ **ion** n Illustration f

image n Bild nt; ⟨statue⟩ Standbild nt; ⟨figure⟩ Figur f; ⟨exact likeness⟩ Ebenbild nt; [public] ~ Image nt

imaginary *a* eingebildet

imaginat|ion *n* Phantasie *f*; (*fancy*) Einbildung *f*. **~ive** *a* phantasievoll; (*full of ideas*) einfallsreich

imagine *vt* sich (*dat*) vorstellen; (*wrongly*) sich (*dat*) einbilden

imbecile *a* Schwachsinnige(r) *m/f*; (*pej*) Idiot *m*

imitat|e *vt* nachahmen, imitieren. **~ion** *n* Nachahmung *f*, Imitation *f*

immaculate *a* tadellos; (*Relig*) unbefleckt

imma'terial *a* (*unimportant*) unwichtig, unwesentlich

imma'ture *a* unreif

immediate *a* sofortig; (*nearest*) nächste(r,s). **~ly** *adv* sofort; **~ly next to** unmittelbar neben □ *conj* sobald

immemorial *a* from time **~** seit Urzeiten

immense *a* riesig

immers|e *vt* untertauchen. **~ion** *n* Untertauchen *nt*. **~ion heater** *n* Heißwasserbereiter *m*

immigrant *n* Einwanderer *m*

immigration *n* Einwanderung *f*

imminent *a* be **~** unmittelbar bevorstehen

immobil|e *a* unbeweglich. **~ize** *vt* (*fig*) lähmen; (*Med*) ruhigstellen

immodest *a* unbescheiden

immoral *a* unmoralisch. **~ity** *n* Unmoral *f*

immortal *a* unsterblich. **~ity** *n* Unsterblichkeit *f*. **~ize** *vt* verewigen

immune *a* immun (to/from gegen). **~ system** *n* Abwehrsystem *nt*

immunity *n* Immunität *f*

immunize *vt* immunisieren

imp *n* Kobold *m*

impact *n* Aufprall *m*

impair *vt* beeinträchtigen

impart *vt* übermitteln (to *dat*); vermitteln ⟨*knowledge*⟩

im'partial *a* unparteiisch

impasse *n* (*fig*) Sackgasse *f*

im'passive *a* unbeweglich

im'patien|ce *n* Ungeduld *f*. **~t** *a* ungeduldig

impeccable *a* tadellos

impede *vt* behindern

impediment *n* Hindernis *nt*; (*in speech*) Sprachfehler *m*

impel *vt* treiben

impending *a* bevorstehend

impenetrable *a* undurchdringlich

imperative *a* be **~** dringend notwendig sein □ *n* (*Gram*) Imperativ *m*, Befehlsform *f*

im'perfect *a* unvollkommen; (*faulty*) fehlerhaft □ *n* (*Gram*) Imperfekt *nt*. **~ion** *n* Unvollkommenheit *f*; (*fault*) Fehler *m*

imperial *a* kaiserlich. **~ism** *n* Imperialismus *m*

imperious *a* herrisch

im'personal *a* unpersönlich

impersonat|e *vt* sich ausgeben als; (*Theat*) nachahmen, imitieren. **~or** *n* Imitator *m*

impertinent *a* frech

impervious *a* **~ to** (*fig*) unempfänglich für

impetuous *a* ungestüm

impetus *n* Schwung *m*

impish *a* schelmisch

im'plant¹ *vt* einpflanzen

implant² *n* Implantat *nt*

implement¹ *n* Gerät *nt*

implement² *vt* ausführen

implicat|e *vt* verwickeln. **~ion** *n* Verwicklung *f*

implicit *a* unausgesprochen

implore *vt* anflehen

imply *vt* andeuten; **what are you ~ing?** was wollen Sie damit sagen?

impo'lite *a* unhöflich

import¹ *n* Import *m*, Einfuhr *f*; (*importance*) Wichtigkeit *f*

import² *vt* importieren, einführen

importan|ce n Wichtigkeit f. ~t a wichtig

importer n Importeur m

impose vt auferlegen (on dat) □ vi sich aufdrängen (on dat)

im'possible a unmöglich

impostor n Betrüger(in) m(f)

impoten|ce n Machtlosigkeit f; (Med) Impotenz f. ~t a machtlos; (Med) impotent

impound vt beschlagnahmen

im'practicable a undurchführbar

im'practical a unpraktisch

impre'cise a ungenau

impregnable a uneinnehmbar

impregnate vt tränken; (Biol) befruchten

im'press vt beeindrucken

impression n Eindruck m; (imitation) Nachahmung f; (imprint) Abdruck m; (edition) Auflage f. ~ism n Impressionismus m

impressive a eindrucksvoll

'imprint[1] n Abdruck m

im'print[2] vt prägen; (fig) einprägen (on dat)

im'prison vt gefangenhalten; (put in prison) ins Gefängnis sperren

im'probable a unwahrscheinlich

impromptu a improvisiert

im'proper a inkorrekt; (indecent) unanständig

impro'priety n Unkorrektheit f

improve vt verbessern; verschönern (appearance) □ vi sich bessern. ~ment n Verbesserung f; (in health) Besserung f

improvise vt/i improvisieren

im'prudent a unklug

impudent a frech

impulse n Impuls m

im'pur|e a unrein. ~ity n Unreinheit f; ~ities pl Verunreinigungen pl

impute vt zuschreiben (to dat)

in prep in (+ dat/(into) + acc); sit in the garden im Garten sitzen;

go in the garden in den Garten gehen; in May im Mai; in the summer/winter im Sommer/Winter; in 1995 [im Jahre] 1995; in this heat bei dieser Hitze; in the evening am Abend; in the sky am Himmel; in the world auf der Welt; in the street auf der Straße; in English/German auf englisch/deutsch □ adv (at home) zu Hause; (indoors) drinnen; he's not in yet er ist noch nicht da; all in alles inbegriffen; (fam: exhausted) kaputt; day in, day out tagaus, tagein □ a (fam: in fashion) in □ n the ins and outs alle Einzelheiten pl

ina'bility n Unfähigkeit f

inac'cessible a unzugänglich

in'accurate a ungenau

in'active a untätig

in'adequate a unzulänglich; feel ~ sich der Situation nicht gewachsen fühlen

inad'missible a unzulässig

inadvertently adv versehentlich

inad'visable a nicht ratsam

in'animate a unbelebt

in'applicable a nicht zutreffend

inap'propriate a unangebracht

inar'ticulate a undeutlich

in'audible a unhörbar

inaugural a Antritts-

inaugurat|e vt [feierlich] in sein Amt einführen. ~ion n Amtseinführung f

inau'spicious a ungünstig

inborn a angeboren

inbred a angeboren

incalculable a nicht berechenbar; (fig) unabsehbar

in'capable a unfähig; be ~ of doing sth nicht fähig sein, etw zu tun

incarcerate vt einkerkern

incarnat|e a the devil ~e der leibhaftige Satan. ~-ion n Inkarnation f

incendiary _a_ & _n_ ~ [bomb] Brandbombe _f_

incense¹ _n_ Weihrauch _m_

incense² _vt_ wütend machen

incentive _n_ Anreiz _m_

incessant _a_ unaufhörlich

incest _n_ Inzest _m_, Blutschande _f_

inch _n_ Zoll _m_ □ _vi_ ~ forward sich ganz langsam vorwärtsschieben

inciden|ce _n_ Vorkommen _nt_. ~ **t** _n_ Zwischenfall _m_

incidental _a_ nebensächlich; ⟨re-mark⟩ beiläufig; ⟨expenses⟩ Ne-ben-. ~**ly** _adv_ übrigens

incinerat|e _vt_ verbrennen. ~ **or** _n_ Verbrennungsofen _m_

incisive _a_ scharfsinnig

incisor _n_ Schneidezahn _m_

incite _vt_ aufhetzen. ~ **ment** _n_ Aufhetzung _f_

in'clement _a_ rauh

inclination _n_ Neigung _f_

incline¹ _vt_ neigen; **be** ~ **d to do sth** dazu neigen, etw zu tun □ _vi_ sich neigen

incline² _n_ Neigung _f_

inclu|de _vt_ einschließen; ⟨contain⟩ enthalten; ⟨incorporate⟩ aufneh-men (**in** in + _acc_). ~ **ding** _a_ ein-schließlich (+ _gen_)

inclusive _a_ Inklusiv-; ~ **of** ein-schließlich (+ _gen_) □ _adv_ inklusive

incognito _adv_ inkognito

inco'herent _a_ zusammenhanglos

income _n_ Einkommen _nt_. ~ **tax** _n_ Einkommensteuer _f_

'incoming _a_ ankommend; ⟨mail⟩ eingehend

in'comparable _a_ unvergleichlich

incom'patible _a_ unvereinbar; **be** ~ nicht zueinander passen

in'competen|ce _n_ Unfähigkeit _f_. ~ **t** _a_ unfähig

incom'plete _a_ unvollständig

incompre'hensible _a_ unver-ständlich

incon'ceivable _a_ undenkbar

incongruous _a_ unpassend

inconsequential _a_ unbedeutend

incon'siderate _a_ rücksichtslos

incon'sistent _a_ widersprüchlich

inconsolable _a_ untröstlich

incon'spicuous _a_ unauffällig

continen|ce _n_ Inkontinenz _f_. ~ **t** _a_ inkontinent

incon'venien|ce _n_ Unannehm-lichkeit _f_; ⟨drawback⟩ Nachteil _m_. ~ **t** _a_ ungünstig

incorporate _vt_ aufnehmen

incor'rect _a_ inkorrekt

incorrigible _a_ unverbesserlich

incorruptible _a_ unbestechlich

increase¹ _n_ Zunahme _f_; ⟨rise⟩ Er-höhung _f_; **be on the** ~ zunehmen

increase² _vt_ vergrößern; ⟨raise⟩ erhöhen □ _vi_ zunehmen; ⟨rise⟩ sich erhöhen

in'credible _a_ unglaublich

incredulous _a_ ungläubig

increment _n_ Gehaltszulage _f_

incriminate _vt_ ⟨Jur⟩ belasten

incubate _vt_ ausbrüten. ~ **ion** _n_ Ausbrüten _nt_. ~ **ion period** _n_ ⟨Med⟩ Inkubationszeit _f_. ~ **or** _n_ ⟨for baby⟩ Brutkasten _m_

incur _vt_ sich ⟨dat⟩ zuziehen; ma-chen ⟨debts⟩

in'curable _a_ unheilbar

indebted _a_ verpflichtet (**to** _dat_)

in'decent _a_ unanständig

inde'cisive _a_ ergebnislos; ⟨per-son⟩ unentschlossen

indeed _adv_ in der Tat, tatsächlich; **yes** ~! allerdings! ~ **I am/do** oh doch!

in'definite _a_ unbestimmt. ~ **ly** _adv_ unbegrenzt; ⟨postpone⟩ auf unbestimmte Zeit

indelible _a_ nicht zu entfernen; ⟨fig⟩ unauslöschlich

indemni|fy _vt_ versichern; ⟨com-pensate⟩ entschädigen. ~ **ty** _n_ Versicherung _f_; Entschädigung _f_

indent _vt_ ⟨Typ⟩ einrücken

inde'penden|ce _n_ Unabhängig-keit _f_; ⟨self-reliance⟩ Selbstän-digkeit _f_. ~ **t** _a_ unabhängig; selb-ständig

indescribable *a* unbeschreiblich

indestructible *a* unzerstörbar

indeterminate *a* unbestimmt

index *n* Register *nt*

index: ~ finger *n* Zeigefinger *m.*
~-linked *a* ⟨*pension*⟩ dynamisch

India *n* Indien *nt.* **~ n** *a* indisch;
⟨*American*⟩ indianisch □*n* Inder(in) *m(f)*; ⟨*American*⟩ Indianer(in) *m(f)*

Indian: ~ ink *n* Tusche *f.* **~ 'summer** *n* Nachsommer *m*

indicate *vt* zeigen; ⟨*point at*⟩ zeigen auf (+ *acc*); ⟨*hint*⟩ andeuten; ⟨*register*⟩ anzeigen □*vi* ⟨*Auto*⟩ blinken. **~ion** *n* Anzeichen *nt*

indicator *n* ⟨*Auto*⟩ Blinker *m*

indict *vt* anklagen. **~ment** *n* Anklage *f*

indifferen|ce *n* Gleichgültigkeit *f.* **~ t** *a* gleichgültig; ⟨*not good*⟩ mittelmäßig

indigenous *a* einheimisch

indi'gest|ible *a* unverdaulich; ⟨*difficult to digest*⟩ schwerverdaulich. **~ion** *n* Magenverstimmung *f*

indigna|nt *a* entrüstet. **~tion** *n* Entrüstung *f*

in'dignity *n* Demütigung *f*

indi'rect *a* indirekt

indi'screet *a* indiskret

indis'cretion *n* Indiskretion *f*

indis'criminate *a* wahllos

indis'pensable *a* unentbehrlich

indis'posed *a* indisponiert

indis'putable *a* unbestreitbar

indis'tinguishable *a* **be ~** nicht zu unterscheiden sein

individual *a* individuell; ⟨*single*⟩ einzeln □*n* Individuum *nt.* **~ity** *n* Individualität *f*

indoctrinate *vt* indoktrinieren

indoor *a* Innen-; ⟨*clothes*⟩ Haus-; ⟨*plant*⟩ Zimmer-; ⟨*Sport*⟩ Hallen-. **~s** *adv* im Haus, drinnen; **go ~s** ins Haus gehen

induce *vt* dazu bewegen (**to** zu); ⟨*produce*⟩ herbeiführen. **~ment** *n* ⟨*incentive*⟩ Anreiz *m*

indulge *vt* frönen (+ *dat*); verwöhnen ⟨*child*⟩ □*vi* **~ in** frönen (+ *dat*). **~nt** *a* [zu] nachgiebig; nachsichtig

industrial *a* Industrie-. **~ist** *n* Industrielle(r) *m.* **~ized** *a* industrialisiert

industr|ious *a* fleißig. **~y** *n* Industrie *f*; ⟨*zeal*⟩ Fleiß *m*

in'edible *a* nicht eßbar

inef'fective *a* unwirksam; ⟨*person*⟩ untauglich

inef'ficient *a* unfähig; ⟨*organization*⟩ nicht leistungsfähig; ⟨*method*⟩ nicht rationell

in'eligible *a* nicht berechtigt

inept *a* ungeschickt

ine'quality *n* Ungleichheit *f*

inert *a* unbeweglich; ⟨*Phys*⟩ träge. **~ia** *n* Trägheit *f*

inescapable *a* unvermeidlich

inestimable *a* unschätzbar

inevitab|le *a* unvermeidlich. **~ly** *adv* zwangsläufig

ine'xact *a* ungenau

inex'cusable *a* unverzeihlich

inexorable *a* unerbittlich

inex'pensive *a* preiswert

inex'perience *n* Unerfahrenheit *f.* **~d** *a* unerfahren

inex'plicable *a* unerklärlich

in'fallible *a* unfehlbar

infam|ous *a* niederträchtig. **~y** *n* Niederträchtigkeit *f*

infan|cy *n* frühe Kindheit *f*; ⟨*fig*⟩ Anfangsstadium *nt.* **~ t** *n* Kleinkind *nt.* **~tile** *a* kindisch

infantry *n* Infanterie *f*

infatuated *a* vernarrt (**with** in + *acc*)

infect *vt* anstecken, infizieren. **~ion** *n* Infektion *f.* **~ious** *a* ansteckend

infer *vt* folgern (**from** aus). **~ence** *n* Folgerung *f*

inferior *a* minderwertig; *(in rank)* untergeordnet □ *n* Untergebene(r) *m/f*

inferiority *n* Minderwertigkeit *f*. **~ complex** *n* Minderwertigkeitskomplex *m*

infern|al *a* höllisch. **~o** *n* flammendes Inferno *nt*

in'fertile *a* unfruchtbar

infest *vt* be **~ed with** befallen sein von

infi'delity *n* Untreue *f*

infiltrate *vt* infiltrieren

infinite *a* unendlich

infinitesimal *a* unendlich klein

infinitive *n* (*Gram*) Infinitiv *m*

infinity *n* Unendlichkeit *f*

infirm *a* gebrechlich. **~ary** *n* Krankenhaus *nt*

inflame *vt* entzünden

in'flammable *a* feuergefährlich

inflammation *n* Entzündung *f*

inflammatory *a* aufrührerisch

inflatable *a* aufblasbar

inflat|e *vt* aufblasen; *(with pump)* aufpumpen. **~ion** *n* Inflation *f*. **~ionary** *a* inflationär

in'flexible *a* starr; *(person)* unbeugsam

inflict *vt* zufügen (**on** *dat*)

influen|ce *n* Einfluß *m* □ *vt* beeinflussen. **~tial** *a* einflußreich

influenza *n* Grippe *f*

influx *n* Zustrom *m*

inform *vt* benachrichtigen; *(officially)* informieren; **~ s.o. of sth** jdm etw mitteilen □ *vi* **~ against** denunzieren

in'formal *a* zwanglos; *(unofficial)* inoffiziell

informant *n* Gewährsmann *m*

informat|ion *n* Auskunft *f*; **a piece of ~ion** eine Auskunft. **~ive** *a* aufschlußreich

informer *n* Spitzel *m*; *(Pol)* Denunziant *m*

infra-red *a* infrarot

infringe *vt/i* **~ [on]** verstoßen gegen. **~ment** *n* Verstoß *m*

infuriat|e *vt* wütend machen. **~ing** *a* ärgerlich

ingenious *a* erfinderisch; *(thing)* raffiniert

ingenuity *n* Geschicklichkeit *f*

ingenuous *a* unschuldig

ingot *n* Barren *m*

ingrained *a* eingefleischt

in'gratitude *n* Undankbarkeit *f*

ingredient *n* (*Culin*) Zutat *f*

ingrowing *a* *(nail)* eingewachsen

inhabit *vt* bewohnen. **~ant** *n* Einwohner(in) *m(f)*

inhale *vt/i* einatmen; *(Med & when smoking)* inhalieren

inherent *a* natürlich

inherit *vt* erben. **~ance** *n* Erbschaft *f*, Erbe *nt*

inhibit *vt* hemmen. **~ion** *n* Hemmung *f*

inho'spitable *a* ungastlich

in'human *a* unmenschlich

iniquitous *a* schändlich

initial *a* anfänglich, Anfangs- □ *n* Anfangsbuchstabe *m*; **my ~s** meine Initialen □ *vt* abzeichnen; *(Pol)* paraphieren. **~ly** *adv* anfangs

initiat|e *vt* einführen. **~ion** *n* Einführung *f*

initiative *n* Initiative *f*

inject *vt* einspritzen, injizieren. **~ion** *n* Spritze *f*, Injektion *f*

injunction *n* gerichtliche Verfügung *f*

injur|e *vt* verletzen. **~y** *n* Verletzung *f*

in'justice *n* Ungerechtigkeit *f*; **do s.o. an ~** jdm unrecht tun

ink *n* Tinte *f*

inland *a* Binnen-. **I~ Revenue** *n* ≈ Finanzamt *nt*

inlet *n* schmale Bucht *f*

inmate *n* Insasse *m*

inn *n* Gasthaus *nt*

innate *a* angeboren

inner *a* innere(r,s). **~most** *a* innerste(r,s)

innocen|ce n Unschuld f. **~t** a unschuldig

innocuous a harmlos

innovation n Neuerung f

innuendo n [versteckte] Anspielung f

innumerable a unzählig

inoculat|e vt impfen. **~ion** n Impfung f

in'operable a nicht operierbar

in'opportune a unpassend

inordinate a übermäßig

inor'ganic a anorganisch

'in-patient n [stationär behandelter] Krankenhauspatient m

input n Input m & nt

inquest n gerichtliche Untersuchung f

inquir|e vi sich erkundigen (**about** nach); **~e into** untersuchen □vt sich erkundigen nach. **~y** n Erkundigung f; (*investigation*) Untersuchung f

inquisitive a neugierig

in'sane a geisteskrank; (*fig*) wahnsinnig

in'sanitary a unhygienisch

in'sanity n Geisteskrankheit f

insatiable a unersättlich

inscri|be vt eingravieren. **~ption** n Inschrift f

inscrutable a unergründlich

insect n Insekt nt. **~icide** n Insektenvertilgungsmittel nt

inse'cur|e a nicht sicher; (*fig*) unsicher. **~ity** n Unsicherheit f

insemination n Besamung f; (*Med*) Befruchtung f

in'sensitive a gefühllos

in'separable a untrennbar; (*people*) unzertrennlich

insert vt einfügen, einsetzen; einstecken ⟨*key*⟩; einwerfen ⟨*coin*⟩. **~ion** n Einsatz m

inside n Innenseite f; **~s** Innere(s) nt □attrib Innen- □adv innen; (*indoors*) drinnen; **~ out** links [herum]; **know sth ~ out** etw in- und auswendig kennen

□prep **~ [of]** in (+ dat/ (*into*) + acc)

insidious a heimtückisch

insight n Einblick m (**into** in + acc)

insignia npl Insignien pl

insig'nificant a unbedeutend

insin'cere a unaufrichtig

insinuat|e vt andeuten. **~ion** n Andeutung f

insipid a fade

insist vi darauf bestehen; **~ on** bestehen auf (+ dat) □vt **~ that** darauf bestehen, daß. **~ent** a beharrlich

'insole n Einlegesohle f

insolen|ce n Unverschämtheit f. **~t** a unverschämt

in'soluble a unlöslich

in'solvent a zahlungsunfähig

insomnia n Schlaflosigkeit f

inspect vt inspizieren; (*test*) prüfen; kontrollieren ⟨*ticket*⟩. **~ion** n Inspektion f. **~or** n Inspektor m; (*of tickets*) Kontrolleur m

inspiration n Inspiration f

inspire vt inspirieren

install vt installieren; [in ein Amt] einführen ⟨*person*⟩. **~ation** n Installation f; Amtseinführung f

instalment n (*Comm*) Rate f; (*of serial*) Fortsetzung f; (*TV*) Folge f

instance n Fall m; (*example*) Beispiel nt; **in the first ~** zunächst; **for ~** zum Beispiel

instant a sofortig; (*Culin*) Instant- □n Augenblick m, Moment m. **~aneous** a unverzüglich, unmittelbar

instant 'coffee n Pulverkaffee m

instead adv statt dessen; **~ of** statt (+ gen), anstelle von; **~ of me** an meiner Stelle

'instep n Spann m, Rist m

instigate vt anstiften; einleiten ⟨*proceedings*⟩

instil vt einprägen (**into s.o.** jdm)

instinct n Instinkt m. **~ive** a instinktiv

institut|e n Institut nt □ vt einführen; einleiten ⟨search⟩. **~ion** n Institution f

instruct vt unterrichten; (order) anweisen. **~ion** n Unterricht m; Anweisung f; **~ions** pl for use Gebrauchsanweisung f. **~or** n Lehrer(in) m(f)

instrument n Instrument nt

insu'bordinate a ungehorsam

in'sufferable a unerträglich

insuf'ficient a nicht genügend

insular a (fig) engstirnig

insulat|e vt isolieren. **~ing tape** n Isolierband nt. **~ion** n Isolierung f

insulin n Insulin nt

insult[1] n Beleidigung f

insult[2] vt beleidigen

insuperable a unüberwindlich

insur|ance n Versicherung f. **~e** vt versichern

insurrection n Aufstand m

intact a unbeschädigt; (complete) vollständig

'intake n Aufnahme f

integral a wesentlich

integrat|e vt integrieren □ vi sich integrieren. **~ion** n Integration f

integrity n Integrität f

intellect n Intellekt m. **~ual** a intellektuell

intelligen|ce n Intelligenz f; (Mil) Nachrichtendienst m; (information) Meldungen pl. **~t** a intelligent

intelligible a verständlich

intend vt beabsichtigen

intense a intensiv; ⟨pain⟩ stark

intensify vt intensivieren □ vi zunehmen

intensity n Intensität f

intensive a intensiv

intent a aufmerksam; **~ on** (absorbed in) vertieft in (+ acc); be **~ on doing sth** fest entschlossen sein, etw zu tun

intention n Absicht f. **~al** a absichtlich

inter vt bestatten

inter'action n Wechselwirkung f

intercede vi Fürsprache einlegen (on behalf of)

intercept vt abfangen

'interchange[1] n Austausch m; (Auto) Autobahnkreuz nt

inter'change[2] vt austauschen

intercom n [Gegen]sprechanlage f

'intercourse n Verkehr m; (sexual) Geschlechtsverkehr m

interest n Interesse nt; (Comm) Zinsen pl □ vt interessieren; be **~ed** sich interessieren (in für). **~ing** a interessant. **~ rate** n Zinssatz m

interfere vi sich einmischen. **~nce** n Einmischung f; (TV) Störung f

interim a Zwischen-; (temporary) vorläufig □ n **in the ~** in der Zwischenzeit

interior a innere(r,s), Innen- □ n Innere(s) nt

interject vt einwerfen

interlude n Pause f; (performance) Zwischenspiel nt

inter'marry vi untereinander heiraten; ⟨different groups:⟩ Mischehen schließen

intermediary n Vermittler(in) m(f)

intermediate a Zwischen-

intermission n Pause f

intermittent a in Abständen auftretend

intern vt internieren

internal a innere(r,s); ⟨dispute⟩ intern

inter'national a international □ n Länderspiel nt

internment n Internierung f

interpret vt interpretieren; auslegen ⟨text⟩; deuten ⟨dream⟩

interpreter **inwards**

(translate) dolmetschen □vi dolmetschen. **~er** n Dolmetscher(in) m(f)

interrogat|e vt verhören. **~ion** n Verhör nt

interrogative a & n ~ [**pronoun**] Interrogativpronomen nt

interrupt vt/i unterbrechen; **don't ~!** red nicht dazwischen! **~ion** n Unterbrechung f

intersect vi sich kreuzen; *(Geom)* sich schneiden. **~ion** n Kreuzung f

interval n Abstand m; *(Theat)* Pause f; *(Mus)* Intervall nt

interven|e vi eingreifen; *(occur)* dazwischenkommen. **~tion** n Eingreifen nt; *(Mil, Pol)* Intervention f

interview n *(Journ)* Interview nt; *(for job)* Vorstellungsgespräch nt; **go for an ~** sich vorstellen □vt interviewen; ein Vorstellungsgespräch führen mit. **~er** n Interviewer(in) m(f)

intestine n Darm m

intimate¹ a vertraut; *⟨friend⟩* eng; *(sexually)* intim

intimate² vt zu verstehen geben

intimidat|e vt einschüchtern. **~ion** n Einschüchterung f

into prep in *(+ acc)*; **go ~ the house** ins Haus [hinein]gehen; **be ~** *(fam)* sich auskennen mit

in'tolerable a unerträglich

in'tolerant a intolerant

intonation n Tonfall m

intoxication n Rausch m

intractable a widerspenstig

intransigent a unnachgiebig

in'transitive a intransitiv

intravenous a intravenös

intrepid a kühn, unerschrocken

intricate a kompliziert

intrigue n Intrige f □vt faszinieren

intrinsic a **~ value** Eigenwert m

introduce vt vorstellen; *(bring in)* einführen

introduction n Einführung f; *(to person)* Vorstellung f; *(to book)* Einleitung f. **~ory** a einleitend

introvert n introvertierter Mensch m

intrude vi stören. **~der** n Eindringling m. **~sion** n Störung f

intuit|ion n Intuition f. **~ive** a intuitiv

inundate vt überschwemmen

invade vt einfallen in *(+ acc)*. **~r** n Angreifer m

invalid¹ n Kranke(r) m/f

invalid² a ungültig. **~ate** vt ungültig machen

in'valuable a unschätzbar

in'variab|le a unveränderlich. **~ly** adv immer

invasion n Invasion f

invent vt erfinden. **~ion** n Erfindung f. **~or** n Erfinder m

inventory n Bestandsliste f

inverse a umgekehrt

invert vt umkehren. **~ed commas** npl Anführungszeichen pl

invest vt investieren, anlegen

investigat|e vt untersuchen. **~ion** n Untersuchung f

invest|ment n Anlage f. **~or** n Kapitalanleger m

invigilate vi *(Sch)* Aufsicht führen

invigorate vt beleben

invincible a unbesiegbar

in'visible a unsichtbar. **~ mending** n Kunststopfen nt

invitation n Einladung f

invite vt einladen

invoice n Rechnung f □ vt **~ s.o.** jdm eine Rechnung schicken

invoke vt anrufen

in'voluntary a unwillkürlich

involve vt beteiligen; *(affect)* betreffen; *(implicate)* verwickeln; *(entail)* mit sich bringen; *(mean)* bedeuten

inward a innere(r,s). **~ly** adv innerlich. **~s** adv nach innen

iodine n Jod nt
iota n Jota nt; (fam) Funke m
IOU abbr (**I owe' you**) Schuldschein m
Iran n der Iran
Iraq n der Irak
irascible a aufbrausend
irate a wütend
Ireland n Irland nt
iris n (Anat) Regenbogenhaut f, Iris f; (Bot) Schwertlilie f
Irish a irisch □n **the ~** pl die Iren. **~man** n Ire m. **~woman** n Irin f
irk vt ärgern
iron a Eisen-; (fig) eisern □n Eisen nt; (appliance) Bügeleisen nt □vt/i bügeln
ironic[al] a ironisch
ironing-board n Bügelbrett nt
ironmonger n **~'s [shop]** Haushaltswarengeschäft nt
irony n Ironie f
irradiate vt bestrahlen
irrational a irrational
irreconcilable a unversöhnlich
irrefutable a unwiderlegbar
irregular a unregelmäßig; (against rules) regelwidrig. **~ity** n Unregelmäßigkeit f; Regelwidrigkeit f
irrelevant a irrelevant
irreparable a unersetzlich
irrepressible a unverwüstlich
irresistible a unwiderstehlich
irrespective a **~ of** ungeachtet (+ gen)
irresponsible a unverantwortlich; (person) verantwortungslos
irreverent a respektlos
irreversible a unwiderruflich; (Med) irreversibel
irrevocable a unwiderruflich
irrigat|e vt bewässern. **~ion** n Bewässerung f
irritable a reizbar
irritat|e vt irritieren; (Med) reizen. **~ion** n Ärger m; (Med) Reizung f

Islam n der Islam. **~ic** a islamisch
island n Insel f
isle n Insel f
isolat|e vt isolieren. **~ion** n Isoliertheit f; (Med) Isolierung f
Israel n Israel nt. **~i** a israelisch □n Israeli m|f
issue n Frage f; (outcome) Ergebnis nt; (of magazine) Ausgabe f; (offspring) Nachkommen pl; **take ~ with s.o.** jdm widersprechen □vt ausgeben; ausstellen (passport); erteilen (order); herausgeben (book)
isthmus n Landenge f
it pron es; (m) er; (f) sie; (as direct object) es; (m) ihn; (f) sie; (as indirect object) ihm; (f) ihr; **it is raining** es regnet; **it's me** ich bin's; **who is it?** wer ist da? **of/from it** davon; **with it** damit; **out of it** daraus
Italian a italienisch □n Italiener(in) m(f); (Lang) Italienisch nt
italic a kursiv. **~s** npl Kursivschrift f; **in ~s** kursiv
Italy n Italien nt
itch n Juckreiz m; **I have an ~** es juckt mich □vi jucken
item n Gegenstand m; (Comm) Artikel m; (on agenda) Punkt m; (on invoice) Posten m; (act) Nummer f. **~ize** vt einzeln aufführen; spezifizieren (bill)
itinerary n [Reise]route f
its poss pron sein; (f) ihr
itself pron selbst; (refl) sich; **by ~** von selbst; (alone) allein
ivory n Elfenbein nt
ivy n Efeu m

J

jab n Stoß m; (fam: injection) Spritze f

jack n (*Auto*) Wagenheber m; (*Cards*) Bube m □vt ~ **up** (*Auto*) aufbocken

jackdaw n Dohle f

jacket n Jacke f; (*of book*) Schutzumschlag m. ~ **po'tato** n in der Schale gebackene Kartoffel f

'jackpot n **hit the ~** das Große Los ziehen

jade n Jade m

jagged a zackig

jail = **gaol**

jam[1] n Marmelade f

jam[2] n Gedränge nt; (*Auto*) Stau m; (*fam: difficulty*) Klemme f □vt klemmen (**in** in + acc); stören 〈*broadcast*〉 □vi klemmen

Jamaica n Jamaika f

jangle vi klimpern

janitor n Hausmeister m

January n Januar m

Japan n Japan nt. ~**ese** a japanisch □n Japaner(in) m(f); (*Lang*) Japanisch nt

jar n Glas nt; (*earthenware*) Topf m

jargon n Jargon m

jaundice n Gelbsucht f

jaunt n Ausflug m

jaunty a keck

javelin n Speer m

jaw n Kiefer m; ~**s** pl Rachen m □vi (*fam*) quatschen

jay n Eichelhäher m. ~**walker** n achtloser Fußgänger m

jazz n Jazz m. ~**y** a knallig

jealous a eifersüchtig (**of** auf + acc). ~**y** n Eifersucht f

jeans npl Jeans pl

jeer vi johlen

jelly n Gelee nt; (*dessert*) Götterspeise f. ~**fish** n Qualle f

jemmy n Brecheisen nt

jeopardize vt gefährden

jerk vt stoßen; (*pull*) reißen □vi rucken; 〈*muscle:*〉 zucken. ~**y** a ruckartig

jersey n Pullover m; (*Sport*) Trikot nt; (*fabric*) Jersey m

jest n Scherz m; **in ~** im Spaß □vi scherzen

jet[1] n (*Miner*) Jett m

jet[2] n (*of water*) [Wasser]strahl m; (*nozzle*) Düse f; (*plane*) Düsenflugzeug nt

jet: ~**'black** a pechschwarz. ~ **lag** n Jet-lag nt. ~**-pro'pelled** a mit Düsenantrieb

jettison vt über Bord werfen

jetty n Landesteg m

Jew n Jude m /Jüdin f

jewel n Edelstein m; (*fig*) Juwel nt. ~**ler** n Juwelier m. ~**ler's** [**shop**] Juweliergeschäft nt. ~**lery** n Schmuck m

Jew|ess n Jüdin f. ~**ish** a jüdisch

jigsaw n ~ [**puzzle**] Puzzlespiel nt

jilt vt sitzenlassen

jingle n (*rhyme*) Verschen nt □vi klimpern

jinx n (*fam*) **it's got a ~ on it** es ist verhext

jittery a (*fam*) nervös

job n Aufgabe f; (*post*) Stelle f, (*fam*) Job m. ~ **centre** n Arbeitsvermittlungsstelle f. ~**less** a arbeitslos

jockey n Jockei m

jocular a spaßhaft

jog vt anstoßen; ~ **s.o.'s memory** jds Gedächtnis nachhelfen □vi (*Sport*) joggen. ~**ging** n Jogging nt

join n Nahtstelle f □vt verbinden (**to** mit); sich anschließen (+ dat) 〈*person*〉; (*become member of*) beitreten (+ dat); eintreten in (+ acc) 〈*firm*〉 □vi 〈*roads:*〉 sich treffen. ~ **in** vi mitmachen

joiner n Tischler m

joint a gemeinsam □n Gelenk nt; (*in wood*) Fuge f; (*Culin*) Braten m; (*fam: bar*) Lokal nt

joist n Dielenbalken m

joke n Scherz m; (*funny story*) Witz m; (*trick*) Streich m □vi scherzen. **~er** n Witzbold m; (Cards) Joker m

jolly a lustig □adv (fam) sehr

jolt n Ruck m □vt einen Ruck versetzen (+ dat) □vi holpern

Jordan n Jordanien nt

jostle vt anrempeln □vi drängeln

jot n Jota nt □vt ~ [down] sich (dat) notieren. **~ter** n Notizblock m

journal n Zeitschrift f; (diary) Tagebuch nt. **~ese** n Zeitungsjargon m. **~ism** n Journalismus m. **~ist** n Journalist(in) m(f)

journey n Reise f

jovial a lustig

joy n Freude f. **~ful** a freudig, froh. **~ride** n (fam) Spritztour f [im gestohlenen Auto]

jubil|ant a überglücklich. **~ation** n Jubel m

jubilee n Jubiläum nt

Judaism n Judentum nt

judge n Richter m; (of competition) Preisrichter m □vt beurteilen; (estimate) [ein]schätzen □vi urteilen (by nach). **~ment** n Beurteilung f; (Jur) Urteil nt; (fig) Urteilsvermögen nt

judic|ial a gerichtlich. **~iary** n Richterstand m. **~ious** a klug

judo n Judo nt

jug n Kanne f; (small) Kännchen nt; (for water) Krug m

juggernaut n (fam) Riesenlaster m

juggle vi jonglieren. **~r** n Jongleur m

juice n Saft m. **~ extractor** n Entsafter m

juicy a saftig

juke-box n Musikbox f

July n Juli m

jumble n Durcheinander nt □vt **~ [up]** durcheinanderbringen. **~ sale** n [Wohltätigkeits]basar m

jumbo n ~ **[jet]** Jumbo[-Jet] m

jump n Sprung m; (in prices) Anstieg m; (in horse racing) Hindernis f □vi springen; (start) zusammenzucken; **make s.o. ~** jdn erschrecken □vt überspringen

jumper n Pullover m, Pulli m

junction n Kreuzung f; (Rail) Knotenpunkt m

June n Juni m

jungle n Dschungel m

junior a jünger; (in rank) untergeordnet; (Sport) Junioren- □n Junior m. **~ school** n Grundschule f

juniper n Wacholder m

junk n Gerümpel nt, Trödel m

junkie n (sl) Fixer m

junk-shop n Trödelladen m

juris|diction n Gerichtsbarkeit f. **~prudence** n Rechtswissenschaft f

juror n Geschworene(r) m/f

jury n **the ~** die Geschworenen pl; (for competition) die Jury

just a gerecht □adv gerade; (only) nur; (simply) einfach; (exactly) genau; **~ as tall** ebenso groß; **I'm ~ going** ich gehe schon

justice n Gerechtigkeit f; **do ~ to** gerecht werden (+ dat); **J~ of the Peace** ≈ Friedensrichter m

justi|fication n Rechtfertigung f. **~fy** vt rechtfertigen

jut vi **~ out** vorstehen

juvenile a jugendlich; (childish) kindisch □n Jugendliche(r) m/f. **~ delinquency** n Jugendkriminalität f

K

kangaroo n Känguruh nt

karate n Karate nt

kebab n Spießchen nt

keel n Kiel m □vi **~ over** umkippen; (Naut) kentern

keen a (sharp) scharf; (intense) groß; (eager) eifrig, begeistert; **~**

keep

on *(fam)* erpicht auf (+ *acc*); ~ on s.o. von jdm sehr angetan

keep n *(maintenance)* Unterhalt m; *(of castle)* Bergfried m; **for ~s** für immer □vt behalten; *(store)* aufbewahren; *(not throw away)* aufheben; *(support)* unterhalten; *(detain)* aufhalten; freihalten ⟨seat⟩; halten ⟨promise⟩; führen, haben ⟨shop⟩; einhalten ⟨law⟩; ~ s.o. waiting jdn warten lassen; ~ sth to oneself etw nicht weitersagen □vi *(remain)* bleiben; ⟨food⟩ sich halten; ~ left/right sich links/rechts halten; ~ doing sth etw weitermachen; ~ on doing sth etw weitermachen. ~ up vi Schritt halten □vt weitermachen

keeper n Wärter(in) m(f). ~sake n Andenken nt

keg n kleines Faß nt

kennel n Hundehütte f

Kenya n Kenia nt

kerb n Bordstein m

kernel n Kern m

ketchup n Ketchup m

kettle n [Wasser]kessel m

key n Schlüssel m; *(Mus)* Tonart f; *(of piano)* Taste f

key: ~**board** n Tastatur f; *(Mus)* Klaviatur f. ~**boarder** n Tastter(in) m(f). ~**hole** n Schlüsselloch nt. ~**-ring** n Schlüsselring m

khaki a khakifarben □n Khaki nt

kick n [Fuß]tritt m; **for ~s** *(fam)* zum Spaß □vt treten; ~**-off** n *(Sport)* Anstoß m

kid n Kitz nt; *(fam: child)* Kind nt □vt *(fam)* ~ s.o. jdm etwas vormachen. ~ **gloves** npl Glacéhandschuhe pl

kidnap vt entführen. ~**per** n Entführer m. ~**ping** n Entführung f

kidney n Niere f. ~ **machine** n künstliche Niere f

kill vt töten; *(fam)* totschlagen ⟨time⟩. ~**er** n Mörder(in) m(f)

killjoy n Spielverderber m

kiln n Brennofen m

kilo n Kilo nt

kilo: ~**gram** n Kilogramm nt. ~**hertz** n Kilohertz nt. ~**metre** n Kilometer m. ~**watt** n Kilowatt nt

kilt n Schottenrock m

kin n Verwandtschaft f; **next of** ~ nächster Verwandter m/nächste Verwandte f

kind[1] n Art f; *(type)* Sorte f; ~ **of** *(fam)* irgendwie

kind[2] a nett

kindergarten n Vorschule f

kindle vt anzünden

kindred a ~ **spirit** Gleichgesinnte(r) m/f

kinetic a kinetisch

king n König m; *(Draughts)* Dame f. ~**dom** n Königreich nt; *(fig & Relig)* Reich nt

king: ~**fisher** n Eisvogel m. ~**-sized** a extragroß

kiosk n Kiosk m

kipper n Räucherhering m

kiss n Kuß m □vt/i küssen

kit n Ausrüstung f; *(tools)* Werkzeug nt; *(construction ~)* Bausatz m □vt ~ **out** ausrüsten. ~**bag** n Seesack m

kitchen n Küche f. ~**ette** n Kochnische f

kitchen: ~ **garden** n Gemüsegarten m. ~ **sink** n Spülbecken nt

kite n Drachen m

kitten n Kätzchen nt

kitty n *(money)* [gemeinsame] Kasse f

kleptomaniac n Kleptomane m/-manin f

knack n Trick m, Dreh m

knapsack n Tornister m

knead vt kneten

knee n Knie nt. ~**cap** n Kniescheibe f

kneel vi knien

knickers npl Schlüpfer m

knife n Messer nt

knight n Ritter m; (Chess) Springer m □vt adeln

knit vt/i stricken; ~ **one, purl one** eine rechts, eine links; ~ **one's brow** die Stirn runzeln. ~**ting** n Stricken nt; (work) Strickzeug nt. ~**ting-needle** n Stricknadel f. ~**wear** n Strickwaren pl

knob n Knopf m; (on door) Knauf m; (small lump) Beule f; (small piece) Stückchen nt

knock n Klopfen nt; (blow) Schlag m; **there was a** ~ **at the door** es klopfte □vt anstoßen; (at door) klopfen an (+ acc); (fam: criticize) heruntermachen. □vi klopfen. ~ **off** vt herunterwerfen; (fam: steal) klauen; (fam: complete quickly) hinhauen □vi (fam: cease work) Feierabend machen. ~ **out** vt ausschlagen; (make unconscious) bewußtlos schlagen; (Boxing) k.o. schlagen. ~ **over** vt umwerfen; (in car) anfahren

knock: ~-**down** a ~-**down prices** Schleuderpreise pl. ~**er** n Türklopfer m. ~-**kneed** a X-beinig. ~-**out** n K.o. m

knot n Knoten m □vt knoten

know vt/i wissen; kennen (person); können (language); **get to** ~ kennenlernen □n **in the** ~ (fam) im Bild

know: ~-**all** n (fam) Alleswisser m. ~-**how** n (fam) (Sach)kenntnis f

knowledge n Kenntnis f (of von/ gen); (general) Wissen nt; (specialized) Kenntnisse pl. ~**able** a be ~**able** viel wissen

knuckle n (Finger)knöchel m; (Culin) Hachse f □vi ~ **under** sich fügen; ~-**down** sich dahinterklemmen

kosher a koscher

kowtow vi Kotau machen (**to vor** + dat)

L

label n Etikett nt □vt etikettieren

laboratory n Labor nt

laborious a mühsam

labour n Arbeit f; (workers) Arbeitskräfte pl; (Med) Wehen pl; **L~** (Pol) die Labourpartei □vi arbeiten □vt (fig) sich lange auslassen über (+ acc). ~**er** n Arbeiter m

'labour-saving a arbeitssparend

laburnum n Goldregen m

labyrinth n Labyrinth nt

lace n Spitze f; (of shoe) Schnürsenkel m □vt schnüren

lack n Mangel m (**of** an + dat)□vt **I** ~ **the time** mir fehlt die Zeit □vi **be** ~**ing** fehlen

lackadaisical a lustlos

laconic a lakonisch ·

lacquer n Lack m; (for hair) [Haar]spray m

lad n Junge m

ladder n Leiter f; (in fabric) Laufmasche f

ladle n [Schöpf]kelle f □vt schöpfen

lady n Dame f; (title) Lady f

lady: ~-**bird** n Marienkäfer m. ~-**like** a damenhaft

lag[1] vi ~ **behind** zurückbleiben

lag[2] vt umwickeln (pipes)

lager n Lagerbier nt

lair n Lager nt

lagoon n Lagune f

lake n See m

lamb n Lamm nt

lame a lahm

lament n Klage f; (song) Klagelied nt □vt beklagen □vi klagen. ~**able** a beklagenswert

laminated a laminiert

lamp n Lampe f; (in street) Laterne f. ~**post** n Laternenpfahl m. ~**shade** n Lampenschirm m

lance n Lanze f □vt (Med) aufschneiden. ~'**corporal** n Gefreite(r) m

land n Land nt; **plot of** ~ Grundstück nt □vt/i landen

landing n Landung f; (top of stairs) Treppenflur m. ~**stage** n Landesteg m

land: ~lady n Wirtin f. ~**locked** a ~**locked country** Binnenstaat m. ~**lord** n Wirt m; (of land) Grundbesitzer m; (of building) Hausbesitzer m. ~**mark** n Erkennungszeichen nt; (fig) Meilenstein m. ~**owner** n Grundbesitzer m. ~**scape** n Landschaft f. ~**slide** n Erdrutsch m

lane n kleine Landstraße f; (Auto) Spur f; (Sport) Bahn f

language n Sprache f. ~ **laboratory** n Sprachlabor nt

languish vi schmachten

lank a ⟨hair⟩ strähnig

lanky a schlaksig

lantern n Laterne f

lap[1] n Schoß m

lap[2] n (Sport) Runde f; (of journey) Etappe f

lapel n Revers nt

lapse n Fehler m; (moral) Fehltritt m; (of time) Zeitspanne f □vi (expire) erlöschen

larceny n Diebstahl m

lard n [Schweine]schmalz m

larder n Speisekammer f

large a groß; **by and** ~ im großen und ganzen. ~**ly** adv großenteils

lark[1] n (bird) Lerche f

lark[2] n (joke) Jux m □vi ~ **about** herumalbern

larva n Larve f

laryngitis n Kehlkopfentzündung f

larynx n Kehlkopf m

lascivious a lüstern

laser n Laser m

lash n Peitschenhieb m; (eyelash) Wimper f □vt peitschen; (tie) festbinden (**to** an + acc). ~ **out** vi sich schlagen; (spend) viel Geld ausgeben (**on** für)

lasso n Lasso nt

last[1] n (for shoe) Leisten m

last[2] a & n letzte(r,s); ~ **night** heute od gestern nacht; (evening) gestern abend; **at** ~ endlich; **the** ~ **time** das letztemal □adv zuletzt; (last time) das letztemal; **do sth** ~ etw zuletzt od als letztes machen □vi dauern; ⟨weather:⟩ sich halten; ⟨relationship:⟩ halten. ~**ing** a dauerhaft. ~**ly** adv schließlich, zum Schluß

latch n [einfache] Klinke f; **on the** ~ nicht verschlossen

late a spät; (delayed) verspätet; (deceased) verstorben; **the** ~**st news** die neuesten Nachrichten; **stay up** ~ bis spät aufbleiben; **arrive** ~ zu spät ankommen; **I am** ~ ich komme zu spät od habe mich verspätet; **the train is** ~ der Zug hat Verspätung. ~**comer** n Zuspätkommende(r) m/f. ~**ly** adv in letzter Zeit

latent a latent

later a später

lateral a seitlich

lathe n Drehbank f

lather n [Seifen]schaum m

Latin a lateinisch □n Latein nt. ~ **A'merica** n Lateinamerika nt

latitude n (Geog) Breite f; (fig) Freiheit f

latter a & n **the** ~ der/die/das letztere

lattice n Gitter nt

Latvia n Lettland nt

laugh n Lachen nt; **with a** ~ lachend □vi lachen (**at/about** über + acc). ~**able** a lachhaft, lächerlich. ~**ing-stock** n Gegenstand m des Spottes

laughter n Gelächter nt

launch[1] n (boat) Barkasse f

launch² *n* Stapellauf *m*; *(of rocket)* Abschuß *m*; *(of product)* Lancierung *f* □ *vt* vom Stapel lassen ⟨ship⟩; zu Wasser lassen ⟨lifeboat⟩; abschießen ⟨rocket⟩; starten ⟨attack⟩; *(Comm)* lancieren ⟨product⟩

launder *vt* waschen. **~ette** *n* Münzwäscherei *f*

laundry *n* Wäscherei *f*; *(clothes)* Wäsche *f*

laurel *n* Lorbeer *m*

lava *n* Lava *f*

lavatory *n* Toilette *f*

lavender *n* Lavendel *m*

lavish *a* großzügig

law *n* Gesetz *nt*; *(system)* Recht *nt*; **~ study** ~ Jura studieren; **~ and order** Recht und Ordnung

law: **~-abiding** *a* gesetzestreu. **~court** *n* Gerichtshof *m*. **~ful** *a* rechtmäßig

lawn *n* Rasen *m*. **~-mower** *n* Rasenmäher *m*

'law suit *n* Prozeß *m*

lawyer *n* Rechtsanwalt *m* /-anwältin *f*

lax *a* lax, locker

laxative *n* Abführmittel *nt*

lay¹ *a* Laien-

lay² *vt* legen; decken ⟨table⟩. **~ down** *vt* hinlegen; festlegen ⟨rules⟩. **~ off** *vt* entlassen ⟨workers⟩ □ *vi* (fam: stop) aufhören

lay: **~about** *n* Faulenzer *m*. **~by** *n* Parkbucht *f*; *(on motorway)* Rastplatz *m*

layer *n* Schicht *f*

layette *n* Babyausstattung *f*

lay: **~man** *n* Laie *m*. **~out** *n* Anordnung *f*; *(design)* Gestaltung *f*; *(Typ)* Layout *nt*

laze *vi* **~ [about]** faulenzen

laziness *n* Faulheit *f*

lazy *a* faul. **~-bones** *n* Faulenzer *m*

lb *abbr* **(pound)** Pfd.

lead¹ *n* Blei *nt*; *(of pencil)* [Bleistift]mine *f*

lead² *n* Führung *f*; *(leash)* Leine *f*; *(flex)* Schnur *f*; *(clue)* Hinweis *m*, Spur *f*; *(Theat)* Hauptrolle *f*; *(distance ahead)* Vorsprung *m*; **be in the ~** in Führung liegen □ *vt/i* führen; leiten ⟨expedition⟩; *(induce)* bringen; *(at cards)* ausspielen

leaded *a* verbleit

leader *n* Führer *m*; *(of group)* Leiter(in) *m(f)*; *(of orchestra)* Konzertmeister *m*; *(in newspaper)* Leitartikel *m*. **~ship** *n* Führung *f*; Leitung *f*

leading *a* führend; **~ lady** Hauptdarstellerin *f*; **~ question** Suggestivfrage *f*

leaf *n* Blatt *nt* □ *vi* **~ through sth** etw durchblättern. **~let** *n* Merkblatt *nt*; *(advertising)* Reklameblatt *nt*; *(political)* Flugblatt *nt*

league *n* Liga *f*

leak *n* *(hole)* undichte Stelle *f*; *(Naut)* Leck *nt*; *(of gas)* Gasausfluß *m* □ *vi* undicht sein; ⟨ship:⟩ leck sein, lecken; ⟨liquid:⟩ auslaufen; ⟨gas:⟩ ausströmen

lean¹ *a* mager

lean² *vt* lehnen **(against/on** an + *acc*) □ *vi* ⟨pers:⟩ sich lehnen **(against/on** an + *acc*); *(not be straight)* sich neigen

leap *n* Sprung *m* □ *vi* springen. **~frog** *n* Bockspringen *nt*. **~ year** *n* Schaltjahr *nt*

learn *vt/i* lernen; *(hear)* erfahren

learn|ed *a* gelehrt. **~er** *n* Anfänger *m*; **~er [driver]** Fahrschüler(in) *m(f)*. **~ing** *n* Gelehrsamkeit *f*

lease *n* Pacht *f*; *(contract)* Mietvertrag *m*; *(Comm)* Pachtvertrag *m* □ *vt* pachten

leash *n* Leine *f*

least *a* geringste(r,s) □ *n* **the ~** das wenigste; **at ~** wenigstens, mindestens; **not in the ~** nicht im geringsten

leather *n* Leder *nt*

leave *n* Erlaubnis *f*; *(holiday)* Urlaub *m*; **on ~** auf Urlaub □*vt* lassen; *(go out of)* verlassen; *(forget)* liegenlassen; *(bequeath)* vermachen **(to** *dat)*; **~ it to me!** überlassen Sie es mir! □*vi* [weg]gehen/-fahren; *(bus:)* abfahren

Lebanon *n* Libanon *m*

lecherous *a* lüstern

lectern *n* [Lese]pult *nt*

lecture *n* Vortrag *m*; *(Univ)* Vorlesung *f*; *(reproof)* Strafpredigt *f* □*vi* einen Vortrag/ eine Vorlesung halten **(on** über + *acc)* □*vt* **~ s.o.** jdm eine Strafpredigt halten. **~r** *n* Vortragende(r) *m/f*; *(Univ)* Dozent(in) *m(f)*

ledge *n* Leiste *f*; *(of window)* Sims *m*; *(in rock)* Vorsprung *m*

ledger *n* Hauptbuch *nt*

leech *n* Blutegel *m*

leek *n* Stange *f* Porree; **~s** *pl* Porree *m*

leer *vi* anzüglich grinsen

leeward *adv* nach Lee. **~way** *n (fig)* Spielraum *m*

left *a* linke(r,s) □*adv* links; *(go)* nach links □*n* linke Seite *f*; **on the ~** links; **from/to the ~** von/ nach links; **the ~** *(Pol)* die Linke

left: **~-handed** *a* linkshändig. **~-luggage [office]** *n* Gepäckaufbewahrung *f*. **~-overs** *npl* Reste *pl.* **~-wing** *a (Pol)* linke(r,s)

leg *n* Bein *nt*; *(Culin)* Keule *f*; *(of journey)* Etappe *f*

legacy *n* Vermächtnis *nt*

legal *a* gesetzlich; *(matters)* rechtlich; *(department, position)* Rechts-

legalize *vt* legalisieren

legend *n* Legende *f.* **~ary** *a* legendär

legible *a* leserlich

legion *n* Legion *f*

legislat|e *vi* Gesetze erlassen. **~ion** *n* Gesetzgebung *f*; *(laws)* Gesetze *pl*

legislat|**ive** *a* gesetzgebend. **~ure** *n* Legislative *f*

legitimate *a* rechtmäßig; *(justifiable)* berechtigt; *(child)* ehelich

leisure *n* Freizeit *f*; **at your ~** wenn Sie Zeit haben. **~ly** *a* gemächlich

lemon *n* Zitrone *f.* **~ade** *n* Zitronenlimonade *f*

lend *vt* leihen. **~ing library** *n* Leihbücherei *f*

length *n* Länge *f*; *(piece)* Stück *nt*; *(of wallpaper)* Bahn *f*; *(of time)* Dauer *f*; **at ~** ausführlich; *(at last)* endlich

length|**en** *vt* länger machen □*vi* länger werden. **~ways** *adv* der Länge nach, längs

lengthy *a* langwierig

lenient *a* nachsichtig

lens *n* Linse *f*; *(Phot)* Objektiv *nt*; *(of spectacles)* Glas *nt*

Lent *n* Fastenzeit *f*

lentil *n (Bot)* Linse *f*

Leo *n (Astr)* Löwe *m*

leopard *n* Leopard *m*

leotard *n* Trikot *nt*

leper *n* Leprakranke(r) *m/f*; *(Bible & fig)* Aussätzige(r) *m/f*

leprosy *n* Lepra *f*

lesbian *a* lesbisch □*n* Lesbierin *f*

lesion *n* Verletzung *f*

less *a, adv, n & prep* weniger

lessen *vt* verringern □*vi* nachlassen

lesser *a* geringere(r,s)

lesson *n* Stunde *f*; *(in textbook)* Lektion *f*; *(Relig)* Lesung *f*

lest *conj (liter)* damit . . . nicht

let *vt* lassen; *(rent)* vermieten; **~ alone** *(not to mention)* geschweige denn; **'to ~'** 'zu vermieten'; **~ us go** gehen wir; **~ me know** sagen Sie mir Bescheid. **~ down** *vt* hinunter-/herunterlassen; *(lengthen)* länger machen; **~ s.o. down** *(fam)* jdn im Stich lassen; *(disappoint)* jdn enttäuschen. **~ off** *vt* abfeuern *(gun)*; hochgehen

lassen ⟨firework, bomb⟩; (emit) ausstoßen; (excuse from) befreien von; (not punish) frei ausgehen lassen

'let-down n Enttäuschung f, (fam) Reinfall m

lethal a tödlich

letharg|ic a lethargisch. **~y** n Lethargie f

letter n Brief m; (of alphabet) Buchstabe m; **by ~** brieflich. **~box** n Briefkasten m. **~head** n Briefkopf m. **~ing** n Beschriftung f

lettuce n [Kopf]salat m

leukaemia n Leukämie f

level a eben; (horizontal) waagerecht; (in height) auf gleicher Höhe; ⟨spoonful⟩ gestrichen □ n Höhe f; (fig) Ebene f, Niveau nt; (stage) Stufe f

level: **~ 'crossing** n Bahnübergang m. **~-'headed** a vernünftig

lever n Hebel m □ vt **~ up** mit einem Hebel anheben. **~age** n Hebelkraft f

levy vt erheben

lewd a anstößig

liabilit|y n Haftung f; **~ies** pl Verbindlichkeiten pl

liable a haftbar

liaison n Verbindung f; (affair) Verhältnis nt

liar n Lügner(in) m(f)

libel n Verleumdung f □ vt verleumden. **~lous** a verleumderisch

liberal a tolerant; (generous) großzügig. **L~** a (Pol) liberal □ n Liberale(r) m(f)

liberate vt befreien. **~ed** a emanzipiert. **~ion** n Befreiung f

liberty n Freiheit f; **take the ~ of doing sth** sich (dat) erlauben, etw zu tun

Libra n (Astr) Waage f

librarian n Bibliothekar(in) m(f)

library n Bibliothek f

Libya n Libyen nt

---

licence n Genehmigung f; (Comm) Lizenz f; (for TV) ≈ Fernsehgebühr f; (for driving) Führerschein m; (for alcohol) Schankkonzession f; (freedom) Freiheit f

license vt eine Genehmigung/ (Comm) Lizenz erteilen (+ dat); **be ~d** ⟨car:⟩ zugelassen sein; ⟨restaurant:⟩ Schankkonzession haben. **~plate** n Nummernschild nt

licentious a lasterhaft

lichen n (Bot) Flechte f

lick vt lecken

lid n Deckel m; (of eye) Lid nt

lie¹ n Lüge f □ vi lügen; **~ to** belügen

lie² vi liegen; **here ~s ...** hier ruht ... **~ down** vi sich hinlegen

Liège n Lüttich nt

lieutenant n Oberleutnant m

life n Leben nt; **lose one's ~** ums Leben kommen

life: **~belt** n Rettungsring m. **~boat** n Rettungsboot nt. **~buoy** n Rettungsring m. **~guard** n Lebensretter m. **~jacket** n Schwimmweste f. **~less** a leblos. **~like** a naturgetreu. **~line** n Rettungsleine f. **~long** a lebenslang. **~size(d)** a ... in Lebensgröße

lift n Aufzug m, Lift m; **give s.o. a ~** jdn mitnehmen □ vt heben; aufheben ⟨restrictions⟩ □ vi ⟨fog:⟩ sich lichten

'lift-off n Abheben nt

ligament n Band nt

light¹ a (not dark) hell; **~ blue** hellblau □ n Licht nt; (lamp) Lampe f; **in the ~ of** (fig) angesichts (+ gen); **have you [got] a ~?** haben Sie Feuer? □ vt anzünden ⟨fire⟩; anmachen ⟨lamp⟩; (illuminate) beleuchten

light² a (not heavy) leicht; **~ sentence** milde Strafe f □ adv **travel ~** mit wenig Gepäck reisen

'light-bulb n Glühbirne f
lighter n Feuerzeug nt
light: ~·'**headed** a benommen.
  ~·'**hearted** a unbekümmert.
  ~ **house** n Leuchtturm m. ~**ing**
  n Beleuchtung f
lightning n Blitz m. ~**-conduc-**
  tor n Blitzableiter m
'lightweight a leicht □ n (Boxing)
  Leichtgewicht nt
like[1] a ähnlich; (same) gleich
  □ prep wie; (similar to) ähnlich
  (+ dat); ~ **this** so; **a man** ~ **that**
  so ein Mann □ conj (fam: as) wie
like[2] vt mögen; **I should/would**
  ~ ich möchte; **I** ~ **the car** das
  Auto gefällt mir; **I** ~ **chocolate**
  ich esse gern Schokolade □ n ~**s**
  and dislikes pl Vorlieben und
  Abneigungen pl
like|able a sympathisch. ~**li-**
  hood n Wahrscheinlichkeit f.
  ~**ly** a wahrscheinlich
'like-minded a gleichgesinnt
liken vt vergleichen (**to** mit)
like|ness n Ähnlichkeit f. ~**wise**
  adv ebenso
lilac n Flieder m □ a fliederfarben
lily n Lilie f. ~ **of the valley** n
  Maiglöckchen nt
limb n Glied nt
lime[1] n (fruit) Limone f; (tree)
  Linde f
lime[2] n Kalk m. ~**light** n **be in**
  the ~**light** im Rampenlicht stehen. ~**stone** n Kalkstein m
limit n Grenze f; (limitation) Beschränkung f; **that's the** ~!
  (fam) das ist doch die Höhe! □ vt
  beschränken (**to** auf + acc).
  ~**ation** n Beschränkung f. ~**ed**
  a beschränkt; ~**ed company** Gesellschaft f mit beschränkter Haftung
limousine n Limousine f
limp[1] n Hinken nt □ vi hinken
limp[2] a schlaff
line[1] n Linie f; (length of rope)
  Leine f; (Teleph) Leitung f; (of

writing) Zeile f; (row) Reihe f;
  (wrinkle) Falte f; (of business)
  Branche f □ vt säumen (street)
line[2] vt füttern (garment);
  (Techn) auskleiden
lineage n Herkunft f
linear a linear
lined[1] a (wrinkled) faltig; (paper)
  liniert
lined[2] a (garment) gefüttert
linen n Leinen nt
linesman n Linienrichter m
linger vi [zurück]bleiben
lingerie n Damenunterwäsche f
linguist n Sprachkundige(r) m/f
linguistic a sprachlich. ~**s** n
  Linguistik f
lining n (of garment) Futter nt;
  (Techn) Auskleidung f
link n (of chain) Glied nt; (fig)
  Verbindung f □ vt verbinden
lint n Verbandstoff m
lion n Löwe m; ~**'s share** (fig)
  Löwenanteil m. ~**ess** n Löwin f
lip n Lippe f; (edge) Rand m; (of
  jug) Schnabel m
lip: ~**-reading** n Lippenlesen nt.
  ~**-service** n **pay** ~**-service** ein
  Lippenbekenntnis ablegen (**to**
  zu). ~**stick** n Lippenstift m
liqueur n Likör m
liquid n Flüssigkeit f □ a flüssig
liquidate vt liquidieren
liquidizer n Mixer m
liquor n Alkohol m
liquorice n Lakritze f
lisp n Lispeln nt □ vt/i lispeln
list[1] n Liste f □ vt aufführen
list[2] vi (Naut) Schlagseite haben
listen vi zuhören (**to** dat); ~ **to**
  the radio Radio hören. ~**er** n
  Zuhörer(in) m(f); (Radio) Hö-
  rer(in) m(f)
litany n Litanei f
literacy n Lese- und Schreibfer-
  tigkeit f
literal a wörtlich. ~**ly** adv
  buchstäblich
literary a literarisch

literate *a* **be ~** lesen und schreiben können

literature *n* Literatur *f*

lithe *a* geschmeidig

Lithuania *n* Litauen *nt*

litigation *n* Rechtsstreit *m*

litre *n* Liter *m* & *nt*

litter *n* Abfall *m*; (*Zool*) Wurf *m* **~bin** *n* Abfalleimer *m*

little *a* klein; (*not much*) wenig □*adv* & *n* wenig; **a ~** ein bißchen/wenig; **~ by ~** nach und nach

liturgy *n* Liturgie *f*

live[1] *a* lebendig; ⟨*ammunition*⟩ scharf; ⟨*broadcast*⟩ Live-Sendung *f*; **be ~** (*Electr*) unter Strom stehen

live[2] *vi* leben; (*reside*) wohnen; **~ up to** gerecht werden (+ *dat*). **~ on** *vt* leben von; (*eat*) sich ernähren von □*vi* weiterleben

livelihood *n* Lebensunterhalt *m*

lively *a* lebhaft, lebendig

liver *n* Leber *f*

livestock *n* Vieh *nt*

living *a* lebend □*n* **earn one's ~** seinen Lebensunterhalt verdienen. **~-room** *n* Wohnzimmer *nt*

lizard *n* Eidechse *f*

load *n* Last *f*; (*quantity*) Ladung *f*; (*Electr*) Belastung *f*. **~s of** (*fam*) jede Menge □*vt* laden ⟨*goods*⟩; beladen ⟨*vehicle*⟩

loaf *n* Brot *nt*

loan *n* Leihgabe *f*; (*money*) Darlehen *nt*; **on ~** geliehen □*vt* leihen (*to s.o.*)

loath *a* **be ~ to do sth** etw ungern tun

loathe *vt* verabscheuen

lobby *n* Foyer *nt*; (*anteroom*) Vorraum *m*; (*Pol*) Lobby *f*

lobe *n* (*of ear*) Ohrläppchen *nt*

lobster *n* Hummer *m*

local *a* hiesig; ⟨*traffic*⟩ Orts-; **under ~ anaesthetic** unter örtlicher Betäubung □*n* Hiesige(r) *m*/*f*; (*fam: pub*) Stammkneipe *f*

~ au'thority *n* Kommunalbehörde *f*. **~ call** *n* (*Teleph*) Ortsgespräch *nt*

locality *n* Gegend *f*

locate *vt* ausfindig machen; **be ~ed** sich befinden. **~ion** *n* Lage *f*; **filmed on ~ion** als Außenaufnahme gedreht

lock *n* (*on door*) Schloß *nt*; (*on canal*) Schleuse *f* □*vt* abschließen □*vi* sich abschließen lassen. **~ up** *vt* abschließen; einsperren ⟨*person*⟩ □*vi* zuschließen

locker *n* Schließfach *nt*

locket *n* Medaillon *nt*

lock: **~-out** *n* Aussperrung *f*. **~smith** *n* Schlosser *m*

locomotion *n* Fortbewegung *f*

locomotive *n* Lokomotive *f*

locum *n* Vertreter(in) *m*(*f*)

locust *n* Heuschrecke *f*

lodge *n* (*porter's*) Pförtnerhaus *nt*; (*masonic*) Loge *f* □*vt* (*submit*) einreichen; (*deposit*) deponieren □*vi* zur Untermiete wohnen (**with** bei); (*become fixed*) steckenbleiben. **~r** *n* Untermieter(in) *m*(*f*)

lodging *n* Unterkunft *f*; **~s** *npl* möbliertes Zimmer *nt*

loft *n* Dachboden *m*

log *n* Baumstamm *m*; (*for fire*) [Holz]scheit *nt*

logarithm *n* Logarithmus *m*

loggerheads *npl* **be at ~** (*fam*) sich in den Haaren liegen

logic *n* Logik *f*. **~al** *a* logisch

logistics *npl* Logistik *f*

logo *n* Symbol *nt*, Logo *nt*

loin *n* (*Culin*) Lende *f*

loiter *vi* herumlungern

lollipop *n* Lutscher *m*

London *n* London *nt* □*attrib* Londoner. **~er** *n* Londoner(in) *m*(*f*)

lone *a* einzeln. **~liness** *n* Einsamkeit *f*

lonely *a* einsam

lone|**r** *n* Einzelgänger *m*. **~some** *a* einsam

long[1] *a* lang; ⟨*journey*⟩ weit; **a ~ time** lange; **a ~ way** weit □*adv* lange; **all day ~** den ganzen Tag; **not ~ ago** vor kurzem; **before ~** bald; **no ~er** nicht mehr; **as** *or* **so ~ as** solange

long[2] *vi* **~ for** sich sehnen nach

long-'distance *a* Fern-; ⟨*Sport*⟩ Langstrecken-

'longhand *n* Langschrift *f*

longing *n* Sehnsucht *f*

longitude *n* (*Geog*) Länge *f*

long: ~ jump *n* Weitsprung *m*. **~-life 'milk** *n* H-Milch *f*. **~-sighted** *a* weitsichtig. **~-sleeved** *a* langärmelig. **~-suffering** *a* langmütig. **~-term** *a* langfristig. **~ wave** *n* Langwelle *f*. **~-winded** *a* langatmig

loo *n* (*fam*) Klo *nt*

look *n* Blick *m*; ⟨*appearance*⟩ Aussehen *nt*; **[good]~s** *pl* [gutes] Aussehen □*vi*: ⟨*search*⟩ nachsehen; ⟨*seem*⟩ aussehen; **don't ~** sieh nicht hin; **~ here!** hören Sie mal! **~ at** ansehen; **for** suchen; **~ forward to** sich freuen auf (+ *acc*). **~ out** *vi* hinaus-/herausschen; ⟨*take care*⟩ aufpassen; **~ out for** Ausschau halten nach; **~ out!** Vorsicht! **~ round** *vi* sich umsehen. **~ up** *vi* aufblicken; **~ up to s.o.** (*fig*) zu jdm aufsehen □*vt* nachschlagen ⟨*word*⟩

'look-out *n* Wache *f*; ⟨*prospect*⟩ Aussicht *f*

loom *n* Webstuhl *m*

loop *n* Schlinge *f*; (*in road*) Schleife *f*; (*on garment*) Aufhänger *m* □*vt* schlingen. **~hole** *n* Hintertürchen *nt*; (*in the law*) Lücke *f*

loose *a* lose; (*not tight enough*) locker; (*inexact*) frei; **be at a ~ end** nichts zu tun haben; **set ~** freilassen. **~ 'chippings** *npl* Rollsplit *m*

loosen *vt* lockern □*vi* sich lockern

loot *n* Beute *f* □*vt/i* plündern. **~er** *n* Plünderer *m*

lop *vt* stutzen. **~ off** *vt* abhacken

lop'sided *a* schief

loquacious *a* redselig

lord *n* Herr *m*; ⟨*title*⟩ Lord *m*; **House of L~s** ≈ Oberhaus *nt*; **the L ~'s Prayer** das Vaterunser

lorry *n* Last[kraft]wagen *m*

lose *vt* verlieren; ⟨*miss*⟩ verpassen □*vi* verlieren; ⟨*clock:*⟩ nachgehen; **get lost** verlorengehen; ⟨*person:*⟩ sich verlaufen. **~r** *n* Verlierer *m*

loss *n* Verlust *m*; **be at a ~** nicht mehr weiter wissen

lost 'property office *n* Fundbüro *nt*

lot[1] *n* Los *nt*; (*at auction*) Posten *m*; **draw ~s** losen (**for un**)

lot[2] *n* **the ~** alle; (*everything*) alles; **a ~ [of]** viel; (*many*) viele; **~s of** (*fam*) eine Menge

lotion *n* Lotion *f*

lottery *n* Lotterie *f*. **~ ticket** *n* Los *nt*

loud *a* laut; ⟨*colours*⟩ grell. **~-'hailer** *n* Megaphon *nt*. **~-'speaker** *n* Lautsprecher *m*

lounge *n* Wohnzimmer *nt*; (*in hotel*) Aufenthaltsraum *m* □*vi* sich lümmeln. **~ suit** *n* Straßenanzug *m*

louse *n* Laus *f*

lout *n* Flegel *m*, Lümmel *m*

lovable *a* liebenswert

love *n* Liebe *f*; ⟨*Tennis*⟩ null; **in ~** verliebt □*vt* lieben; **~ doing sth** etw sehr gerne machen. **~-affair** *n* Liebesverhältnis *nt*. **~ letter** *n* Liebesbrief *m*

lovely *a* schön

lover *n* Liebhaber *m*

low *a* niedrig; ⟨*cloud*⟩ tief; ⟨*voice*⟩ leise; (*depressed*) niedergeschlagen □*adv* niedrig; ⟨*fly*⟩ tief; ⟨*speak*⟩ leise; **feel ~** deprimiert sein □*n* (*Meteorol*) Tief *nt*; (*fig*) Tiefstand *m*

low: ~**brow** a geistig anspruchslos. ~**-cut** a (dress) tief ausgeschnitten

lower vt niedriger machen; (let down) herunterlassen; (reduce) senken

low: ~**-fat** a fettarm. ~**lands** npl Tiefland nt

loyal a treu. ~**ty** n Treue f

lozenge n Pastille f

Ltd abbr (Limited) GmbH

lubricant n Schmiermittel nt

lubricat|e vt schmieren. ~**ion** n Schmierung f

lucid a klar

luck n Glück nt; **bad** ~ Pech nt; **good** ~! viel Glück! ~**ily** adv glücklicherweise, zum Glück

lucky a glücklich; ⟨day⟩ Glücks-; **be** ~ Glück haben; ⟨thing⟩ Glück bringen. ~ '**charm** n Amulett nt

lucrative a einträglich

ludicrous a lächerlich

luggage n Gepäck nt

luggage: ~ **trolley** n Kofferkuli m. ~**-van** n Gepäckwagen m

lukewarm a lauwarm

lullaby n Wiegenlied nt

lumbago n Hexenschuß m

lumber n Gerümpel nt □vt ~ s.o. with sth jdm etw aufhalsen. ~**jack** n Holzfäller m

luminous a leuchtend

lump n Klumpen m; (of sugar) Stück nt; (swelling) Beule f; (in breast) Knoten m; (tumour) Geschwulst f; a ~ in one's throat (fam) ein Kloß im Hals □vt ~ together zusammentun

lump: ~ **sugar** n Würfelzucker m. ~ '**sum** n Pauschalsumme f

lunacy n Wahnsinn m

lunar a Mond-

lunatic n Wahnsinnige(r) m/f

lunch n Mittagessen nt

luncheon n Mittagessen nt. ~ **meat** n Frühstücksfleisch nt. ~ **voucher** n Essensbon m

lunch: ~**-hour** n Mittagspause f. ~**-time** n Mittagszeit f

lung n Lungenflügel m; ~**s** pl Lunge f

lunge vi sich stürzen (at auf + acc)

lure vt locken

lurid a grell; (sensational) reißerisch

luscious a lecker, köstlich

lush a üppig

lust n Begierde f □vi ~ after gieren nach. ~**ful** a lüstern

lustre n Glanz m

lute n Laute f

luxurious a luxuriös

luxury n Luxus m

lynch vt lynchen

lynx n Luchs m

lyric a lyrisch. ~**al** a lyrisch. ~ **poetry** n Lyrik f. ~**s** npl [Lied]text m

M

macabre a makaber

macaroni n Makkaroni pl

macaroon n Makrone f

mace n Amtsstab m

machinations pl Machenschaften pl

machine n Maschine f. ~**-gun** n Maschinengewehr nt

machinery n Maschinerie f

machine tool n Werkzeugmaschine f

machinist n Maschinist m

mackerel n inv Makrele f

mackintosh n Regenmantel m

mad a verrückt; (dog) tollwütig; (fam: angry) böse (at auf + acc)

madam n gnädige Frau f

Madeira cake n Sandkuchen m

madness n Wahnsinn m

madonna n Madonna f

magazine n Zeitschrift f; (Mil, Phot) Magazin nt

maggot n Made f

Magi *npl* the ~ die Heiligen Drei Könige

magic *n* Zauber *m*; *(tricks)* Zauberkunst *f* □*a* magisch; *(word, wand)* Zauber-. ~**al** *a* zauberhaft

magician *n* Zauberer *m*; *(entertainer)* Zauberkünstler *m*

magistrate *n* ≈ Friedensrichter *m*

magnanimous *a* großmütig

magnesia *n* Magnesia *f*

magnet *n* Magnet *m*. ~**ic** *a* magnetisch. ~**ism** *n* Magnetismus *m*

magnification *n* Vergrößerung *f*

magnificent *a* großartig

magnify *vt* vergrößern. ~**ing glass** *n* Vergrößerungsglas *nt*

magnitude *n* Größe *f*; *(importance)* Bedeutung *f*

magpie *n* Elster *f*

mahogany *n* Mahagoni *nt*

maid *n* Dienstmädchen *nt*; *(liter: girl)* Maid *f*; old ~ *(pej)* alte Jungfer *f*

maiden *n* *(liter)* Maid *f* □*a* *(speech, voyage)* Jungfern-. ~**'aunt** *n* unverheiratete Tante *f*. ~ **name** *n* Mädchenname *m*

mail[1] *n* Kettenpanzer *m*

mail[2] *n* Post *f* □*vt* mit der Post schicken

mail: ~**bag** *n* Postsack *m*. ~**ing list** *n* Postversandliste *f*. ~**order firm** *n* Versandhaus *nt*

maim *vt* verstümmeln

main[1] *n* Hauptleitung *f*

main[2] *a* Haupt-. □*n* in the ~ im großen und ganzen

main: ~**land** *n* Festland *nt*. ~**ly** *adv* hauptsächlich

maintain *vt* aufrechterhalten; *(keep in repair)* instand halten; *(support)* unterhalten; *(claim)* behaupten

maintenance *n* Aufrechterhaltung *f*; *(care)* Instandhaltung *f*; *(allowance)* Unterhalt *m*

maisonette *n* Wohnung *f* [auf zwei Etagen]

maize *n* Mais *m*

majestic *a* majestätisch

majesty *n* Majestät *f*

major *a* größer □*n* (*Mil*) Major *m*; (*Mus*) Dur *nt*

Majorca *n* Mallorca *nt*

majority *n* Mehrheit *f*

major road *n* Hauptverkehrsstraße *f*

make *n* *(brand)* Marke *f* □*vt* machen; *(force)* zwingen; *(earn)* verdienen; halten ⟨*speech*⟩ treffen ⟨*decision*⟩; erreichen ⟨*destination*⟩ □*vi* ~ **as if to** Miene machen zu. ~ **do** *vi* zurechtkommen **(with** mit). ~ **out** *vt* *(distinguish)* ausmachen; *(write out)* ausstellen; *(assert)* behaupten. ~ **up** *vt* *(constitute)* bilden; *(invent)* erfinden; *(apply cosmetics to)* schminken; ~ **up one's mind** sich entschließen □*vi* sich versöhnen

'make-believe *n* Phantasie *f*

maker *n* Hersteller *m*

make: ~ **shift** *a* behelfsmäßig. ~-**up** *n* Make-up *nt*

maladjusted *a* verhaltensgestört

malaise *n* Unbehagen *nt*

male *a* männlich □*n* Mann *m*; *(animal)* Männchen *nt*. ~ **nurse** *n* Krankenpfleger *m*

malevolen|ce *n* Bosheit *f*. ~**t** *a* boshaft

malfunction *n* technische Störung *f*; *(Med)* Funktionsstörung *f*

malice *n* Bosheit *f*

malicious *a* böswillig

malign *vt* verleumden

malignant *a* bösartig

malingerer *n* Simulant *m*

malleable *a* formbar

mallet *n* Holzhammer *m*

malnu'trition *n* Unterernährung *f*

mal'practice *n* Berufsvergehen *nt*

malt n Malz nt

mal'treat vt mißhandeln

mammal n Säugetier nt

mammoth n Mammut nt

man n Mann m; ⟨mankind⟩ der Mensch; ⟨chess⟩ Figur f; ⟨draughts⟩ Stein m □vt bemannen ⟨ship⟩; bedienen ⟨pump⟩; besetzen ⟨counter⟩

manage vt leiten; verwalten ⟨estate⟩; ⟨cope with⟩ fertig werden mit; ~ **to do sth** es schaffen, etw zu tun □vi zurechtkommen; ~ **on** auskommen mit. **~able** a ⟨tool⟩ handlich; ⟨person⟩ fügsam. **~ment** n the ~ment die Geschäftsleitung f

manager n Geschäftsführer m; ⟨of bank⟩ Direktor m; ⟨of estate⟩ Verwalter m; ⟨Sport⟩ [Chef-] trainer m. **~ess** n Geschäftsführerin f. **~ial** a ~**ial staff** Führungskräfte pl

managing a ~ **director** Generaldirektor m

mandarin n ~ [orange] Mandarine f

mandate n Mandat nt. **~ory** a obligatorisch

mane n Mähne f

manger n Krippe f

mangle¹ n Wringmaschine f

mangle² vt ⟨damage⟩ verstümmeln

mango n Mango f

man: ~**handle** vt grob behandeln. ~**hole** n Kanalschacht m. ~**hole cover** n Kanaldeckel m. ~**hood** n Mannesalter nt; ⟨quality⟩ Männlichkeit f. ~**-hour** n Arbeitsstunde f. ~**-hunt** n Fahndung f

mania n Manie f. **~iac** n Wahnsinnige(r) m/f

manicure n Maniküre f □vt maniküren. ~**ist** n Maniküre f

manifest a offensichtlich □vt ~ **itself** sich manifestieren

manifesto n Manifest nt

manipulate vt handhaben; ⟨pej⟩ manipulieren. ~**ion** n Manipulation f

man'kind n die Menschheit

manly a männlich

'man-made a künstlich. ~ **fibre** n Kunstfaser f

manner n Weise f; ⟨kind⟩ Art f; **in this** ~ auf diese Weise; [good/bad] ~ **s** [gute/schlechte] Manieren pl. ~**ism** n Angewohnheit f

manœuvre n Manöver nt □vt/i manövrieren

manor n Gutshof m; ⟨house⟩ Gutshaus nt

manpower n Arbeitskräfte pl

mansion n Villa f

'manslaughter n Totschlag m

mantelpiece n Kaminsims m & nt

manual a Hand- □n Handbuch nt

manufacture vt herstellen. ~**r** n Hersteller m

manure n Mist m

manuscript n Manuskript nt

many a viele; ~ **a time** oft □n **a good/great** ~ sehr viele

map n Landkarte f; ⟨of town⟩ Stadtplan m

maple n Ahorn m

marathon n Marathon m

marble n Marmor m; ⟨for game⟩ Murmel f

March n März m

march n Marsch m □vi marschieren

mare n Stute f

margarine n Margarine f

margin n Rand m; ⟨leeway⟩ Spielraum m; ⟨Comm⟩ Spanne f. ~**al** a geringfügig

marigold n Ringelblume f

marijuana n Marihuana f

marina n Jachthafen m

marinade n Marinade f □vt marinieren

marine a Meeres-

marital a ehelich. ~ **status** n Familienstand m

marjoram n Majoran m

mark[1] n (currency) Mark f

mark[2] n Fleck m; (sign) Zeichen nt; (trace) Spur f; (target) Ziel nt; (Sch) Note f □vt markieren; (spoil) beschädigen; (characterize) kennzeichnen; (Sch) korrigieren; (Sport) decken

market n Markt m. ~**ing** n Marketing nt. ~**re'search** n Marktforschung f

marksman n Scharfschütze m

marmalade n Orangenmarmelade f

marmot n Murmeltier nt

maroon a dunkelrot

marquee n Festzelt nt

marquis n Marquis m

marriage n Ehe f; (wedding) Hochzeit f

marrow n (Anat) Mark nt; (vegetable) Kürbis m

marry vt/i heiraten; (unite) trauen

marsh n Sumpf m

marshal n Marschall m; (steward) Ordner m

marsupial n Beuteltier nt

martial a kriegerisch. ~ **'law** n Kriegsrecht nt

martyr n Märtyrer(in) m(f) □vt zum Märtyrer machen. ~**dom** n Martyrium nt

marvel n Wunder nt □vi staunen (at über + acc). ~**lous** a wunderbar

Marxis|m n Marxismus m. ~**t** a marxistisch □n Marxist(in) m(f)

marzipan n Marzipan m

mascara n Wimperntusche f

mascot n Maskottchen nt

masculine a männlich □n (Gram) Maskulinum nt. ~**ity** n Männlichkeit f

mashed potatoes npl Kartoffelpüree nt

mask n Maske f

masochis|m n Masochismus m. ~**t** n Masochist m

mason n Steinmetz m

Mason n Freimaurer m. ~**ic** a freimaurerisch

masonry n Mauerwerk nt

masquerade n (fig) Maskerade f

mass[1] n (Relig) Messe f

mass[2] n Masse f □vi sich sammeln

massacre n Massaker nt □vt niedermetzeln

massage n Massage f □vt massieren

masseu|r n Masseur m. ~**se** n Masseuse f

massive a massiv; (huge) riesig

mass: ~ **media** npl Massenmedien pl. ~**-'pro'duce** vt in Massenproduktion herstellen

mast n Mast m

master n Herr m; (teacher) Lehrer m; (craftsman) Meister m; (of ship) Kapitän m □vt meistern; beherrschen (language)

master: ~**-key** n Hauptschlüssel m. ~**ly** a meisterhaft. ~**mind** n führender Kopf m □vt der führende Kopf sein von. ~**piece** n Meisterwerk nt. ~**y** n (of subject) Beherrschung f

masturbat|e vi masturbieren. ~**ion** n Masturbation f

mat n Matte f

match[1] n Wettkampf m; (in ball games) Spiel nt; (Tennis) Match nt; (marriage) Heirat f □vt (equal) gleichkommen (+ dat); (be like) passen zu; (find sth similar) etwas Passendes finden zu □vi zusammenpassen

match[2] n Streichholz m. ~**box** n Streichholzschachtel f

mate[1] n Kumpel m; (assistant) Gehilfe m; (Naut) Maat m; (Zool) Männchen n; (female) Weibchen nt □vi sich paaren

mate[2] n (Chess) Matt nt

material n Material nt; (fabric) Stoff m

material|ism n Materialismus m.
~**istic** a materialistisch. ~**ize** vi
sich verwirklichen

maternal a mütterlich

maternity n Mutterschaft f. ~
clothes npl Umstandskleidung f.
~ **ward** n Entbindungsstation f

mathematical a mathematisch.
~**ian** n Mathematiker(in) m(f)

mathematics n Mathematik f

maths n (fam) Mathe f

matriculation n Immatrikula-
tion f

matrimony n Ehe f

matron n (of hospital) Oberin f;
(of school) Hausmutter f

matt a matt

matter n (affair) Sache f; (pus)
Eiter m; (Phys: substance) Mate-
rie f; **what is the ~?** was ist los?
□vi wichtig sein; ~ **to s.o.** jdm
etwas ausmachen; **it doesn't ~**
es macht nichts. ~**-of-fact** a
sachlich

mattress n Matratze f

matur|e a reif; (Comm) fällig □vi
reifen; ⟨person:⟩ reifer werden;
(Comm) fällig werden □vt reifen
lassen. ~**ity** n Reife f; (Comm)
Fälligkeit f

Maundy n ~ **Thursday** Gründonnerstag m

mauve a lila

maxim n Maxime f

maximum a maximal □n Maximum nt. ~ **speed** n Höchst-
geschwindigkeit f

may v aux (be allowed to) dürfen;
(be possible) können; **may I
come in?** darf ich reinkommen?
it may be true es könnte wahr
sein

May n Mai m

maybe adv vielleicht

mayonnaise n Mayonnaise f

mayor n Bürgermeister m. ~**ess**
n Bürgermeisterin f; (wife of
mayor) Frau Bürgermeister f

maze n Irrgarten m

me pron (acc) mich; (dat) mir; **it's
~** (fam) ich bin es

meadow n Wiese f

meagre a dürftig

meal n Mahlzeit f; (food) Essen nt

mean[1] a geizig; (unkind) gemein;
(poor) schäbig

mean[2] a mittlere(r,s) □n (average) Durchschnitt m; **the golden
~** die goldene Mitte

mean[3] vt heißen; (signify) bedeuten; (intend) beabsichtigen; **I ~ it**
das ist mein Ernst; ~ **well** es gut
meinen

meander vi sich schlängeln; ⟨per-
son:⟩ schlendern

meaning n Bedeutung f. ~**ful** a
bedeutungsvoll. ~**less** a bedeu-
tungslos

means n Möglichkeit f, Mittel nt;
by all ~! aber natürlich! □npl
(resources) [Geld]mittel pl. ~
test n Bedürftigkeitsnachweis m

'**meantime** n **in the ~** in der
Zwischenzeit □adv inzwischen

'**meanwhile** adv inzwischen

measles n Masern pl

measure n Maß nt; (action) Maßnahme f □vt/i messen. ~**ment**
n Maß nt

meat n Fleisch nt. ~**ball** n Klops
m. ~ **loaf** n falscher Hase m

mechan|ic n Mechaniker m.
~**ical** a mechanisch. ~**ical engineering** n Maschinenbau m.
~**ics** n Mechanik f □n pl Mecha-
nismus m

mechan|ism n Mechanismus m.
~**ize** vt mechanisieren

medal n Orden m; (Sport) Medaille f

medallion n Medaillon nt

medallist n Medaillengewin-
ner(in) m(f)

meddle vi sich einmischen (**in** in
+ acc)

media n pl **the ~** die Medien pl

mediator n Vermittler(in) m(f)

medical a medizinisch; ⟨treatment⟩ ärztlich □n ärztliche Untersuchung f. ~ **insurance** n Krankenversicherung f. ~ **student** n Medizinstudent m
medicated a medizinisch. ~**ion** n Medikamente pl
medicinal a medizinisch; ⟨plant⟩ heilkräftig
medicine n Medizin f; ⟨preparation⟩ Medikament nt
medieval a mittelalterlich
mediocre a mittelmäßig. ~**ity** n Mittelmäßigkeit f
meditate vi nachdenken (on über + acc); ⟨Relig⟩ meditieren. ~**ion** n Meditation f
Mediterranean n Mittelmeer nt
medium a mittlere(r, s); ⟨steak⟩ medium □n Medium nt; ⟨means⟩ Mittel nt □ ⟨person⟩ Medium nt
medium: ~**-sized** a mittelgroß. ~ **wave** n Mittelwelle f
meek a sanftmütig
meet vt treffen; ⟨by chance⟩ begegnen (+ dat); ⟨at station⟩ abholen; ⟨make the acquaintance of⟩ kennenlernen; stoßen auf (+ acc) ⟨problem⟩; bezahlen ⟨bill⟩; erfüllen ⟨requirements⟩ □vi sich treffen; ⟨for the first time⟩ sich kennenlernen
meeting n Treffen nt; ⟨by chance⟩ Begegnung f; ⟨discussion⟩ Besprechung f; ⟨of committee⟩ Sitzung f; ⟨large⟩ Versammlung f
megalomania n Größenwahnsinn m
megaphone n Megaphon nt
melancholy a melancholisch □n Melancholie f
mellow a ⟨fruit⟩ ausgereift; ⟨person⟩ sanft
melodic a melodisch
melodrama n Melodrama nt. ~**tic** a melodramatisch
melody n Melodie f
melon n Melone f
melt vt/i schmelzen

member n Mitglied nt; ⟨of family⟩ Angehörige(r) m|f; **M~ of Parliament** Abgeordnete(r) m|f. ~**ship** n Mitgliedschaft f; ⟨members⟩ Mitgliederzahl f
membrane n Membran f
memento n Andenken nt
memo n Mitteilung f
memoirs n pl Memoiren pl
memorable a denkwürdig
memorandum n Mitteilung f
memorial n Denkmal nt. ~ **service** n Gedenkfeier f
memorize vt sich ⟨dat⟩ einprägen
memory n Gedächtnis nt; ⟨thing remembered⟩ Erinnerung f; ⟨of computer⟩ Speicher m; **from** ~ auswendig
menace n Drohung f; ⟨nuisance⟩ Plage f □vt bedrohen
mend vt reparieren; ⟨patch⟩ flicken; ausbessern ⟨clothes⟩
menial a niedrig
meningitis n Hirnhautentzündung f, Meningitis f
menopause n Wechseljahre pl
menstruate vi menstruieren. ~**ion** n Menstruation f
mental a geistig; ⟨fam: mad⟩ verrückt. ~ **'illness** n Geisteskrankheit f
mentality n Mentalität f
mention n Erwähnung f □vt erwähnen; **don't** ~ **it** keine Ursache; bitte
menu n Speisekarte f
mercenary a geldgierig □n Söldner m
merchandise n Ware f
merchant n Kaufmann m; ⟨dealer⟩ Händler m. ~ **'navy** n Handelsmarine f
merciful a barmherzig. ~**less** a erbarmungslos
mercury n Quecksilber nt
mercy n Barmherzigkeit f, Gnade f; **be at s.o.'s** ~ jdm ausgeliefert sein
mere a bloß

merge vi zusammenlaufen; (Comm) fusionieren □vt (Comm) zusammenschließen

merger n Fusion f

meridian n Meridian m

meringue n Baiser m

merit n Verdienst nt; (advantage) Vorzug m; (worth) Wert m □vt verdienen

mermaid n Meerjungfrau f

merry a fröhlich; ~ Christmas! fröhliche Weihnachten!

merry: ~-go-round n Karussell nt. ~-making n Feiern nt

mesh n Masche f

mesmerize vt hypnotisieren

mess n Durcheinander nt; (trouble) Schwierigkeiten pl; (something spilt) Bescherung f (fam); (Mil) Messe f □vt ~ up in Unordnung bringen; (botch) verpfuschen □vi ~ about herumalbern; (tinker) herumspielen (with mit)

message n Nachricht f; give s.o. a ~ jdm etwas ausrichten

messenger n Bote m

Messiah n Messias m

Messrs (on letter) ~ Smith Firma Smith

messy a schmutzig; (untidy) unordentlich

metabolism n Stoffwechsel m

metal n Metall nt. ~lic a metallisch. ~lurgy n Metallurgie f

metamorphosis n Metamorphose f

metaphor n Metapher f. ~ical a metaphorisch

meteor n Meteor m. ~ic a kometenhaft

meteorolog|ist n Meteorologe m/ -gin f. ~y n Meteorologie f

meter n Zähler m

method n Methode f

methodical a systematisch, methodisch

Methodist n Methodist(in) m(f)

meths n (fam) Brennspiritus m

methylated a ~ spirit[s] Brennspiritus m

meticulous a sehr genau

metre n Meter m & nt; (rhythm) Versmaß nt

metric a metrisch

metropolis n Metropole f

metropolitan a hauptstädtisch; (international) weltstädtisch

Mexican a mexikanisch □n Mexikaner(in) m(f). 'Mexico n Mexiko nt

miaow n Miau nt □vi miauen

microbe n Mikrobe f

micro: ~chip n Mikrochip nt. ~computer n Mikrocomputer m. ~film n Mikrofilm m. ~phone n Mikrophon nt. ~processor n Mikroprozessor m. ~scope n Mikroskop nt. ~scopic a mikroskopisch. ~wave n Mikrowelle f. ~wave [oven] n Mikrowellenherd m

mid a ~ May Mitte Mai; in ~ air in der Luft

midday n Mittag m

middle a mittlere(r, s); the M~ Ages das Mittelalter; the M~ East der Nahe Osten □n Mitte f; in the ~ of the night mitten in der Nacht

middle: ~-aged a mittleren Alters. ~-class a bürgerlich. ~man n (Comm) Zwischenhändler m

midget n Liliputaner(in) m(f)

'midnight n Mitternacht f

midst n in the ~ of mitten in (+ dat); in our ~ unter uns

mid: ~summer n Hochsommer m; (solstice) Sommersonnenwende f. ~way adv auf halbem Wege. ~wife n Hebamme f. ~'winter n Mitte f des Winters

might¹ v aux I ~ vielleicht; it ~ be true es könnte wahr sein; I ~ as well stay am besten bleibe ich hier

might² n Macht f

mighty a mächtig

migraine n Migräne f

migrat|e vi abwandern; ⟨birds:⟩ ziehen. ~**ion** n Wanderung f; (of birds) Zug m

mild a mild

mildew n Schimmel m; (Bot) Mehltau m

mile n Meile f (= 1,6 km); ~**s too big** (fam) viel zu groß

mileage n Meilenzahl f; (of car) Meilenstand m

militant a militant

military a militärisch. ~ **service** n Wehrdienst m

militate vi ~ **against** sprechen gegen

militia n Miliz f

milk n Milch f □vt melken

milkman n Milchmann m

milky a milchig. **M~ Way** n Milchstraße f

mill n Mühle f; (factory) Fabrik f □vt/i mahlen; (Techn) fräsen

millennium n Jahrtausend nt

miller n Müller m

millet n Hirse f

milli|gram n Milligramm nt. ~**metre** n Millimeter m & nt

milliner n Modistin f; (man) Hutmacher m

million n Million f. ~**aire** n Millionär(in) m(f)

'millstone n Mühlstein m

mime n Pantomime f □vt pantomimisch darstellen

mimic n Imitator m □vt nachahmen

mince n Hackfleisch nt □vt (Culin) durchdrehen; not ~ **words** kein Blatt vor den Mund nehmen

mincemeat n Masse f aus Korinthen, Zitronat usw

mincer n Fleischwolf m

mind n Geist m; (sanity) Verstand m; **to my** ~ meiner Meinung nach; **give s.o. a piece of one's** ~ jdm gehörig die Meinung sagen;

make up one's ~ sich entschließen; **be out of one's** ~ nicht bei Verstand sein □vt aufpassen auf (+ acc); **I don't** ~ **the noise** der Lärm stört mich nicht; ~ **the step!** Achtung Stufe! □vi (care) sich kümmern (about um); **I don't** ~ mir macht es nichts aus; **never** ~! macht nichts!

mine[1] poss pron meine(r), meins; **a friend of** ~ ein Freund von mir; **that is** ~ das gehört mir

mine[2] n Bergwerk nt; (explosive) Mine f □vt abbauen; (Mil) verminen. ~ **detector** n Minensuchgerät nt. ~ **field** n Minenfeld nt

miner n Bergarbeiter m

mineral n Mineral nt. ~**ogy** n Mineralogie f. ~ **water** n Mineralwasser nt

minesweeper n Minenräumboot nt

mingle vi ~ **with** sich mischen unter (+ acc)

miniature a Klein-

mini|bus n Kleinbus m. ~**cab** n Taxi nt

minim n (Mus) halbe Note f

minim|al a minimal. ~**ize** vt auf ein Minimum reduzieren. ~**um** n Minimum nt

mining n Bergbau m

minist|er n Minister m; (Relig) Pastor m. ~**erial** a ministeriell

ministry n (Pol) Ministerium nt; **the** ~ (Relig) das geistliche Amt

mink n Nerz m

minor a kleiner; (less important) unbedeutend □n Minderjährige(r) m/f; (Mus) Moll nt

minority n Minderheit f; (age) Minderjährigkeit f

mint[1] n Münzstätte f □ a ⟨stamp⟩ postfrisch; **in** ~ **condition** wie neu □vt prägen

mint[2] n (herb) Minze f; (sweet) Pfefferminzbonbon m & nt

minuet n Menuett nt

minus *prep* minus, weniger; (*fam: without*) ohne □ **n → [sign]** Minuszeichen *nt*

minute[1] *n* Minute *f*; **~s** *pl* (*of meeting*) Protokoll *nt*

minute[2] *a* winzig; (*precise*) genau

miracle *n* Wunder *nt*. **~ulous** *a* wunderbar

mirage *n* Fata Morgana *f*

mirror *n* Spiegel *m* □ *vt* widerspiegeln

mirth *n* Heiterkeit *f*

misanthropist *n* Menschenfeind *m*

misbe'have *vi* sich schlecht benehmen

mis'calculation *n* Fehlkalkulation *f*

'miscarriage *n* Fehlgeburt *f*; **~ of justice** Justizirrtum *m*

miscellaneous *a* vermischt

mischief *n* Unfug *m*

mischievous *a* schelmisch

miscon'ception *n* falsche Vorstellung *f*

mis'conduct *n* unkorrektes Verhalten *nt*; (*adultery*) Ehebruch *m*

miscon'strue *vt* mißdeuten

misde'meanour *n* Missetat *f*

miser *n* Geizhals *m*

miserable *a* unglücklich; (*wretched*) elend

miserly *adv* geizig

misery *n* Elend *nt*

mis'fortune *n* Unglück *nt*

mis'givings *npl* Bedenken *pl*

mishap *n* Mißgeschick *nt*

misin'form *vt* falsch unterrichten

misin'terpret *vt* mißdeuten

mis'lay *vt* verlegen

mis'lead *vt* irreführen

mis'management *n* Mißwirtschaft *f*

misnomer *n* Fehlbezeichnung *f*

'misprint *n* Druckfehler *m*

mis'quote *vt* falsch zitieren

misrepre'sent *vt* falsch darstellen

miss *n* Fehltreffer *m* □ *vt* verpassen; (*fail to hit or find*) verfehlen;

(*fail to attend*) versäumen; (*fail to notice*) übersehen; (*feel the loss of*) vermissen □ *vi* (*fail to hit*) nicht treffen

Miss *n* Fräulein *nt*

missile *n* [Wurf]geschoß *nt*; (*Mil*) Rakete *f*

mission *n* Auftrag *m*; (*Mil*) Einsatz *m*; (*Relig*) Mission *f*

missionary *n* Missionar(in) *m(f)*

mis'spell *vt* falsch schreiben

mist *n* Dunst *m*; (*fog*) Nebel *m*; (*on window*) Beschlag *m* □ *vi* **~ up** beschlagen

mistake *n* Fehler *m*; **by ~** aus Versehen □ *vt* mißverstehen; **~ identity** Verwechslung *f*

mistaken *a* falsch; **be ~** sich irren; **~ly** *adv* irrtümlich

mistletoe *n* Mistel *f*

mistress *n* Herrin *f*; (*teacher*) Lehrerin *f*; (*lover*) Geliebte *f*

mis'trust *n* Mißtrauen *nt* □ *vt* mißtrauen (+ *dat*)

misty *a* dunstig; (*foggy*) neblig; (*fig*) unklar

misunder'stand *vt* mißverstehen. **~ing** *n* Mißverständnis *nt*

misuse[1] *vt* mißbrauchen

misuse[2] *n* Mißbrauch *m*

mite *n* (*Zool*) Milbe *f*

mitigate *vt* mildern

mitten *n* Fausthandschuh *m*

mix *n* Mischung *f* □ *vt* mischen □ *vi* sich mischen; **~ with** (*associate with*) verkehren mit. **~ up** *vt* mischen; (*muddle*) durcheinanderbringen; (*mistake for*) verwechseln (**with** mit)

mixer *n* Mischmaschine *f*; (*Culin*) Küchenmaschine *f*

mixture *n* Mischung *f*; (*medicine*) Mixtur *f*; (*Culin*) Teig *m*

'mix-up *n* Durcheinander *nt*; (*confusion*) Verwirrung *f*; (*mistake*) Verwechslung *f*

moan *n* Stöhnen *nt* □ *vi* stöhnen; (*complain*) jammern

moat *n* Burggraben *m*

mob n Horde f; (rabble) Pöbel m; (fam: gang) Bande f □ vt herfallen über (+ acc); belagern ⟨celebrity⟩

mobile a beweglich □ n Mobile nt. ~ 'home n Wohnwagen m

mobility n Beweglichkeit f

mobilize vt mobilisieren

mock a Schein- □ vt verspotten □ vi spotten. ~ery n Spott m

'mock-up n Modell nt

mode n [Art und] Weise f

model n Modell nt; (example) Vorbild nt; [fashion] ~ Mannequin nt □ a Modell-; (exemplary) Muster- □ vt formen, modellieren; vorführen ⟨clothes⟩ □ vi Mannequin sein; (for artist) Modell stehen

moderate[1] vt mäßigen

moderate[2] a mäßig; (opinion) gemäßigt □ n (Pol) Gemäßigte(r) m|f

moderation n Mäßigung f

modern a modern. ~ize vt modernisieren. ~ languages npl neuere Sprachen pl

modest a bescheiden; (decorous) schamhaft. ~y n Bescheidenheit f

modify vt abändern

moist a feucht

moisten vt befeuchten

moistur|e n Feuchtigkeit f. ~izer n Feuchtigkeitscreme f

molar n Backenzahn m

mole[1] n Leberfleck m

mole[2] n (Zool) Maulwurf m

molecule n Molekül nt

molest vt belästigen

mollusc n Weichtier nt

mollycoddle vt verzärteln

molten a geschmolzen

moment n Moment m, Augenblick m; **at the** ~ im Augenblick, augenblicklich. ~ary a vorübergehend

momentous a bedeutsam

momentum n Schwung m

monarch n Monarch(in) m(f). ~y n Monarchie f

monastery n Kloster nt

Monday n Montag m

money n Geld nt

money: ~-box n Sparbüchse f. ~-lender n Geldverleiher m. ~ order n Zahlungsanweisung f

mongrel n Promenadenmischung f

monitor n (Techn) Monitor m □ vt überwachen

monk n Mönch m

monkey n Affe m. ~-wrench n (Techn) Engländer m

mono n Mono nt

monogram n Monogramm nt

monologue n Monolog m

monopol|ize vt monopolisieren. ~y n Monopol nt

monosyllabic a einsilbig

monoton|ous a eintönig, monoton; (tedious) langweilig. ~y n Eintönigkeit f, Monotonie f

monsoon n Monsun m

monster n Ungeheuer nt; (cruel person) Unmensch m

monstrosity n Monstrosität f

monstrous a ungeheuer

montage n Montage f

month n Monat m. ~ly a & adv monatlich □ n (periodical) Monatszeitschrift f

monument n Denkmal nt. ~al a (fig) monumental

moo vi muhen

mood n Laune f; **be in a good/bad** ~ gute/schlechte Laune haben

moody a launisch

moon n Mond m

moon: ~light n Mondschein m. ~lighting n (fam) ≈ Schwarzarbeit f. ~lit a mondhell

moor[1] n Moor nt

moor[2] vt (Naut) festmachen □ vi anlegen. ~ings npl (chains) Verankerung f; (place) Anlegestelle f

moose n Elch m

moot a it's a ~ point darüber läßt sich streiten

mop n Mop m; ~ **of hair** Wuschelkopf m □vt wischen

moped n Moped nt

moral a moralisch, sittlich; (virtuous) tugendhaft □n Moral f; ~ **s** pl Moral f

morale n Moral f

morality n Sittlichkeit f

moralize vi moralisieren

morbid a krankhaft; (gloomy) trübe

more a, adv & n mehr; (in addition) noch; **a few** ~ noch ein paar; **any** ~ noch etwas; **once** ~ noch einmal; ~ **or less** mehr oder weniger; **some** ~ **tea?** noch etwas Tee? ~ **interesting** interessanter; ~ **[and** ~**] quickly** [immer] schneller

moreover adv außerdem

morgue n Leichenschauhaus nt

morning n Morgen m; **in the** ~ morgens, am Morgen; (tomorrow) morgen früh

Morocco n Marokko nt

morose a mürrisch

morphine n Morphium nt

Morse n ~ **[code]** Morsealphabet nt

morsel n (food) Happen m

mortal a sterblich; (fatal) tödlich □n Sterbliche(r) m/f. ~ **ity** n Sterblichkeit f

mortar n Mörtel m

mortgage n Hypothek f

mortuary n Leichenhalle f; (public) Leichenschauhaus nt

mosaic n Mosaik nt

Moscow n Moskau nt

Moselle n Mosel f

mosque n Moschee f

mosquito n [Stech]mücke f, Schnake f; (tropical) Moskito m

moss n Moos nt

most a der/die/das meiste; (majority) die meisten; **for the** ~ **part** zum größten Teil □adv am meisten; (very) höchst; **the** ~ **interesting day** der interessanteste

Tag; ~ **unlikely** höchst unwahrscheinlich □n das meiste; ~ **of them** die meisten [von ihnen]; **at [the]** ~ höchstens; ~ **of the time** die meiste Zeit. ~ **ly** adv meist

MOT n ≈ TÜV m

motel n Motel nt

moth n Nachtfalter m

moth: ~ **ball** n Mottenkugel f. ~~ **eaten** a mottenzerfressen

mother n Mutter f; **M**~**'s Day** Muttertag m □vt bemuttern

mother: ~ **hood** n Mutterschaft f. ~ **-in-law** n Schwiegermutter f. ~ **land** n Mutterland nt. ~ **ly** a mütterlich. ~ **-of-pearl** n Perlmutter f. ~ **-to-be** n werdende Mutter f. ~ **tongue** n Muttersprache f

motif n Motiv nt

motion n Bewegung f; (proposal) Antrag m

motivate vt motivieren. ~ **ion** n Motivation f

motive n Motiv nt

motor n Motor m

Motorail n Autozug m

motor: ~ **bike** n (fam) Motorrad nt. ~ **boat** n Motorboot nt. ~ **car** n Auto nt, Wagen m. ~ **cycle** n Motorrad nt. ~ **-cyclist** n Motorradfahrer m. ~ **ist** n Autofahrer(in) m(f). ~ **ize** vt motorisieren. ~ **vehicle** n Kraftfahrzeug nt. ~ **way** n Autobahn f

motto n Motto nt

mould[1] n (fungus) Schimmel m

mould[2] n Form f □vt formen (**into** zu)

mouldy a schimmelig

moult vi ⟨bird:⟩ sich mausern; ⟨animal:⟩ sich haaren

mound n Hügel m; (of stones) Haufen m

mount n (animal) Reittier nt; (of jewel) Fassung f; (of picture) Passepartout nt □vt (get on) steigen auf (+ acc); (on pedestal) montieren auf (+ acc); besteigen

⟨*horse*⟩ fassen ⟨*jewel*⟩; aufziehen ⟨*picture*⟩ □*vi* aufsteigen; ⟨*tension:*⟩ steigen

mountain *n* Berg *m*

mountaineer *n* Bergsteiger(in) *m(f)*. ~**ing** *n* Bergsteigen *nt*

mountainous *a* bergig, gebirgig

mourn *vt* betrauern □*vi* trauern (**for** um). ~**er** *n* Trauernde(r) *m/f*. ~**ful** *a* trauervoll. ~**ing** *n* Trauer *f*

mouse *n* Maus *f*. ~**trap** *n* Mausefalle *f*

mousse *n* Schaum *m*; (*Culin*) Mousse *f*

moustache *n* Schnurrbart *m*

mouth *n* Mund *m*; (*of animal*) Maul *nt*; (*of river*) Mündung *f*

mouth: ~**ful** *n* Mundvoll *m*; (*bite*) Bissen *m*. ~**organ** *n* Mundharmonika *f*. ~**piece** *n* Mundstück *nt*; (*fig: person*) Sprachrohr *nt*. ~**wash** *n* Mundwasser *nt*

move *n* Bewegung *f*; (*fig*) Schritt *m*; (*moving house*) Umzug *m*; (*in board-game*) Zug *m*; **on the** ~ unterwegs; **get a** ~ **on** (*fam*) sich beeilen □*vt* bewegen; (*emotionally*) rühren; (*move along*) rücken; (*in board-game*) ziehen; (*take away*) wegnehmen; wegfahren ⟨*car*⟩; (*rearrange*) umstellen; (*transfer*) versetzen ⟨*person*⟩; verlegen ⟨*office*⟩; (*propose*) beantragen; ~ **house** umziehen □*vi* sich bewegen; (*move house*) umziehen; **don't** ~! stillhalten! (*stop*) stillstehen! ~ **in** *vi* einziehen. ~ **out** *vi* ausziehen

movement *n* Bewegung *f*; (*Mus*) Satz *m*

moving *a* beweglich; (*touching*) rührend

mow *vt* mähen

Mr *n* Herr *m*

Mrs *n* Frau *f*

Ms *n* Frau *f*

much *a, adv & n* viel; **as** ~ **as** soviel wie

muck *n* Mist *m*; (*fam: filth*) Dreck *m*. ~ **about** *vi* herumalbern; (*tinker*) herumspielen (**with** mit). ~ **up** *vt* (*fam*) vermasseln

mucus *n* Schleim *m*

mud *n* Schlamm *m*

muddle *n* Durcheinander *nt*; (*confusion*) Verwirrung *f* □*vt* ~ [**up**] durcheinanderbringen

muddy *a* schlammig; ⟨*shoes*⟩ schmutzig

mudguard *n* Kotflügel *m*; (*on bicycle*) Schutzblech *nt*

muesli *n* Müsli *nt*

muffle *vt* dämpfen

muffler *n* Schal *m*

mug[1] *n* Becher *m*; (*for beer*) Bierkrug *m*; (*fam: face*) Visage *f*; (*fam: simpleton*) Trottel *m*

mug[2] *vt* überfallen. ~**ger** *n* Straßenräuber *m*

muggy *a* schwül

mule *n* Maultier *nt*

mull *vt* ~ **over** nachdenken über (+ *acc*)

multi: ~**coloured** *a* vielfarbig, bunt. ~**lingual** *a* mehrsprachig. ~**national** *a* multinational

multiple *a* vielfach; (*with pl*) mehrere □*n* Vielfache(s) *nt*

multiplication *n* Multiplikation *f*

multiply *vt* multiplizieren (**by** mit) □*vi* sich vermehren

multi-storey *a* ~ **car park** Parkhaus *nt*

mum *n* (*fam*) Mutti *f*

mumble *vt/i* murmeln

mummy[1] *n* (*fam*) Mutti *f*

mummy[2] *n* (*Archaeol*) Mumie *f*

mumps *n* Mumps *m*

munch *vt/i* mampfen

mundane *a* banal

municipal *a* städtisch

mural *n* Wandgemälde *nt*

murder *n* Mord *m* □*vt* ermorden. ~**er** *n* Mörder *m*. ~**ess** *n* Mörderin *f*

murmur *vt/i* murmeln

muscle n Muskel m

muscular a Muskel-; (strong) muskulös

muse vi nachsinnen (**on** über + acc)

museum n Museum nt

mush n Brei m

mushroom n [eßbarer] Pilz m, esp Champignon m □vi (fig) wie Pilze aus dem Boden schießen

mushy a breiig

music n Musik f; (written) Noten pl

musical a musikalisch □n Musical nt. ~ **box** n Spieldose f. ~ **instrument** n Musikinstrument nt

'**music-hall** n Varieté nt

musician n Musiker(in) m(f)

Muslim a mohammedanisch □n Mohammedaner(in) m(f)

muslin n Musselin m

mussel n [Mies]muschel f

must v aux müssen; (with negative) dürfen □ n a ~ (fam) ein Muß nt

mustard n Senf m

muster vt versammeln; aufbringen ⟨strength⟩

mutation n Veränderung f; (Biol) Mutation f

mute a stumm

mutilate vt verstümmeln

mutiny n Meuterei f □vi meutern

mutter vt/i murmeln

mutton n Hammelfleisch nt

mutual a gegenseitig; (fam: common) gemeinsam

muzzle n (of animal) Schnauze f; (of firearm) Mündung f; (for dog) Maulkorb m □vt einen Maulkorb anlegen (+ dat)

my a mein

myopic a kurzsichtig

myself pron selbst; (refl) mich; **by ~** allein

mysterious a geheimnisvoll; (puzzling) mysteriös, rätselhaft

mystery n Geheimnis nt; (puzzle) Rätsel nt; ~ [**story**] Krimi m

mystic|[al] a mystisch. ~**cism** n Mystik f

mystique n geheimnisvoller Zauber m

myth n Mythos m ~**ical** a mythisch

mythology n Mythologie f

N

nab vt (fam) erwischen

nag[1] n (horse) Gaul m

nag[2] vt/i herumnörgeln (s.o. an jdm)

nail n Nagel m; **on the ~** (fam) sofort □vt nageln (**to** an + acc)

nail: ~**brush** n Nagelbürste f. ~**file** n Nagelfeile f. ~ **scissors** npl Nagelschere f. ~ **varnish** n Nagellack m

naïve a naiv. ~**ty** n Naivität f

naked a nackt; ⟨flame⟩ offen; **with the ~ eye** mit bloßem Auge

name n Name m; (reputation) Ruf m; **by ~** dem Namen nach; **by the ~ of** namens □vt nennen; (give a name to) einen Namen geben (+ dat); (announce publicly) den Namen bekanntgeben von. ~**ly** adv nämlich

name: ~**plate** n Namensschild nt. ~**sake** n Namensvetter m/ Namensschwester f

nanny n Kindermädchen nt. ~**goat** n Ziege f

nap n Nickerchen nt; **have a ~** ein Nickerchen machen

napkin n Serviette f

nappy n Windel f

narcotic n Narkotikum n

narrat|e vt erzählen. ~**ion** n Erzählung f

narrative n Erzählung f

narrator n Erzähler(in) m(f)

narrow *a* schmal; *(restricted)* eng; *(margin)* knapp; *(fig)* beschränkt. ~'**minded** *a* engstirnig

nasal *a* nasal; *(Med & Anat)* Nasen-

nasturtium *n* Kapuzinerkresse *f*

nasty *a* übel; *(unpleasant)* unangenehm; *(unkind)* boshaft; *(serious)* schlimm; **turn** ~ gemein werden

nation *n* Nation *f*; *(people)* Volk *nt*

national *a* national; *(newspaper)* überregional; *(campaign)* landesweit □ *n* Staatsbürger(in) *m(f)*

national: ~ **'anthem** *n* Nationalhymne *f*. **N**~ **'Health Service** *n* staatlicher Gesundheitsdienst *m*. **N**~ **In'surance** *n* Sozialversicherung *f*

nationalism *n* Nationalismus *m*

nationality *n* Staatsangehörigkeit *f*

national|ization *n* Verstaatlichung *f*. ~**ize** *vt* verstaatlichen

'**nation-wide** *a* landesweit

native *a* einheimisch; *(innate)* angeboren □ *n* Eingeborene(r) *m/f*; *(local inhabitant)* Einheimische(r) *m/f*; **a** ~ **of Vienna** ein gebürtiger Wiener

native: ~'**land** *n* Heimatland *nt*. ~'**language** *n* Muttersprache *f*

Nativity *n* the ~ Christi Geburt *f*. ~ **play** *n* Krippenspiel *nt*

natural *a* natürlich

natural: ~'**gas** *n* Erdgas *nt*. ~'**history** *n* Naturkunde *f*

naturalist *n* Naturforscher *m*

naturalize *vt* einbürgern

nature *n* Natur *f*; *(kind)* Art *f*; **by** ~ von Natur aus. ~ **reserve** *n* Naturschutzgebiet *nt*

naturism *n* Freikörperkultur *f*

naughty *a* unartig; *(slightly indecent)* gewagt

nausea *n* Übelkeit *f*

nauseate *vt* anekeln

nautical *a* nautisch. ~ **mile** *n* Seemeile *f*

naval *a* Marine-

nave *n* Kirchenschiff *nt*

navel *n* Nabel *m*

navigable *a* schiffbar

navigat|e *vi* navigieren □ *vt* befahren *(river)*. ~**ion** *n* Navigation *f*. ~**or** *n* Navigator *m*

navy *n* [Kriegs]marine *f* □ *a* ~ [**blue**] marineblau

near *a* nah[e]; **the** ~ **est bank** die nächste Bank □ *adv* nahe; ~ **by** nicht weit weg; □ *prep* nahe an (+ *dat/acc*); in der Nähe von; ~ **to tears** den Tränen nahe □ *vt* sich nähern (+ *dat*)

near: ~ **by** *a* nahegelegen. ~**ly** *adv* fast, beinahe; **not** ~**ly** bei weitem nicht. ~**side** *n* Beifahrerseite *f*

neat *a* adrett; *(tidy)* ordentlich; *(clever)* geschickt; *(undiluted)* pur

necessarily *adv* notwendigerweise; **not** ~ nicht unbedingt

necessary *a* nötig, notwendig

necessity *n* Notwendigkeit *f*

neck *n* Hals *m*; ~ **and** ~ Kopf an Kopf

necklace *n* Halskette *f*

nectar *n* Nektar *m*

née *a* ~ **Brett** geborene Brett

need *n* Bedürfnis *nt*; *(misfortune)* Not *f*; **be in** ~ Not leiden; **be in** ~ **of** brauchen; **in case of** ~ notfalls; **if** ~ **be** wenn nötig □ *vt* brauchen; **you** ~ **not go** du brauchst nicht zu gehen; ~ **I come?** muß ich kommen? **I** ~ **to know** ich muß es wissen

needle *n* Nadel *f*

needless *a* unnötig; ~ **to say** selbstverständlich

'**needlework** *n* Nadelarbeit *f*

needy *a* bedürftig

negation *n* Verneinung *f*

negative *a* negativ □ *n* Verneinung *f*; *(photo)* Negativ *nt*

neglect n Vernachlässigung f; **state of** ~ verwahrloster Zustand m □vt vernachlässigen; (omit) versäumen (to zu). ~**ed** a verwahrlost. ~**ful** a nachlässig

negligen|ce n Nachlässigkeit f; (Jur) Fahrlässigkeit f. ~**t** a nachlässig; (Jur) fahrlässig

negligible a unbedeutend

negotiable a (road) befahrbar; (Comm) unverbindlich; **not** ~ nicht übertragbar

negotiat|e vt aushandeln; (Auto) nehmen ⟨bend⟩ □vi verhandeln. ~**ion** n Verhandlung f. ~**or** n Unterhändler(in) m(f)

Negro n Neger m

neigh vi wiehern

neighbour n Nachbar(in) m(f). ~**hood** n Nachbarschaft f. ~**ly** a [gut]nachbarlich

neither a & pron keine(r, s) □adv auch nicht □conj weder ... nor weder ... noch □adv □... nor weder ... noch □conj auch nicht

neon n Neon nt. ~ **light** n Neonlicht nt

nephew n Neffe m

nepotism n Vetternwirtschaft f

nerve n Nerv m; (fam: courage) Mut m; (fam: impudence) Frechheit f; **lose one's** ~ den Mut verlieren. ~**racking** a nervenaufreibend

nervous a (afraid) ängstlich; (highly-strung) nervös; (Anat, Med) Nerven-. ~ '**breakdown** n Nervenzusammenbruch m

nest n Nest nt □vi nisten. ~-**egg** n Notgroschen m

net[1] n Netz nt; (curtain) Store m

net[2] a netto; (salary, weight) Netto- □vt netto einnehmen; (yield) einbringen

'netball n Korbball m

Netherlands npl **the** ~ die Niederlande pl

nettle n Nessel f

'network n Netz nt

neuralgia n Neuralgie f

neurolog|ist n Neurologe m/ -gin f. ~**y** n Neurologie f

neur|osis n Neurose f. ~**otic** a neurotisch

neuter a (Gram) sächlich □n (Gram) Neutrum nt □vt kastrieren; (spay) sterilisieren

neutral a neutral □n **in** ~ (Auto) im Leerlauf

never adv nie, niemals; ~ **mind** macht nichts. ~-**ending** a endlos

nevertheless adv dennoch, trotzdem

new a neu

new: ~**born** a neugeboren. ~**comer** n Neuankömmling m. ~ '**moon** n Neumond m

news n Nachricht f; (TV) Nachrichten pl; **piece of** ~ Neuigkeit f

news: ~**agent** n Zeitungshändler m. ~**flash** n Kurzmeldung f. ~**letter** n Mitteilungsblatt nt. ~**paper** n Zeitung f; (material) Zeitungspapier nt. ~**reader** n Nachrichtensprecher(in) m(f)

newt n Molch m

New: ~ **Year's 'Day** n Neujahr nt. ~ **Year's 'Eve** n Silvester nt. ~ **Zealand** n Neuseeland nt

next a & n nächste(r, s); ~ **door** nebenan; **the week after** ~ übernächste Woche □adv als nächstes; ~ **to** neben

nib n Feder f

nibble vt/i knabbern (**at** an + dat)

nice a nett; ⟨day⟩ schön; ⟨food⟩ gut; ⟨distinction⟩ fein

niche n Nische f

nick n einkerben; (steal) klauen; (fam: arrest) schnappen

nickel n Nickel nt

'nickname n Spitzname m

nicotine n Nikotin nt

niece n Nichte f

Nigeria n Nigeria nt. ~**n** a nigerianisch □n Nigerianer(in) m(f)

niggling a gering; (petty) kleinlich; ⟨pain⟩ quälend

night *n* Nacht *f*; *(evening)* Abend *m*; **at ~** nachts; **Monday ~** Montag nacht/abend

night: ~cap *n* Schlafmütze *f*; *(drink)* Schlaftrunk *m*. **~club** *n* Nachtklub *m*. **~dress** *n* Nachthemd *nt*. **~fall** *n* **at ~fall** bei Einbruch der Dunkelheit. **~gown** *n*, *(fam)* **~ie** *n* Nachthemd *nt*

nightingale *n* Nachtigall *f*

night: ~life *n* Nachtleben *nt*. **~ly** *a* nächtlich □*adv* jede Nacht. **~mare** *n* Alptraum *m*. **~-'watchman** *n* Nachtwächter *m*

nil *n* null

nimble *a* flink

nine *a* neun □*n* Neun *f*. **~'teen** *a* neunzehn. **~'teenth** *a* neunzehnte(r, s)

ninetieth *a* neunzigste(r, s)

ninety *a* neunzig

ninth *a* neunte(r, s)

nip *vt* kneifen; *(bite)* beißen; **~ in the bud** *(fig)* im Keim ersticken

nipple *n* Brustwarze *f*

nippy *a* *(fam)* *(cold)* frisch; *(quick)* flink

nitrate *n* Nitrat *nt*

nitrogen *n* Stickstoff *m*

no *adv* nein □*n* Nein *nt* □*a* kein(e); *(pl)* keine; **in no time** [sehr] schnell; **no parking/smoking** Parken/Rauchen verboten; **no one = nobody**

nobility *n* Adel *m*

noble *a* edel; *(aristocratic)* adlig. **~man** *n* Adlige(r) *m*

nobody *pron* niemand, keiner □*n* **a ~** ein Niemand *m*

nocturnal *a* nächtlich; *(animal)* Nacht-

nod *vi* nicken □*vt* **~ one's head** mit dem Kopf nicken

noise *n* Geräusch *nt*; *(loud)* Lärm *m*

noisy *a* laut; *(eater)* geräuschvoll

nomad *n* Nomade *m*. **~ic** *a* nomadisch; *(tribe)* Nomaden-

nominal *a* nominell

nominat|e *vt* nominieren, aufstellen; *(appoint)* ernennen. **~ion** *n* Nominierung *f*; Ernennung *f*

nominative *a* & *n* *(Gram)* **~ [case]** Nominativ *m*

nonchalant *a* nonchalant; *(gesture)* lässig

nondescript *a* unbestimmbar; *(person)* unscheinbar

none *pron* keine(r)/keins; **~ of us** keiner von uns; **~ of it/this** nichts davon □*adv* **too** nicht gerade; **~ too soon** [um] keine Minute zu früh; **~ the wiser** um nichts klüger; **~ the less** dennoch

nonentity *n* Null *f*

non-'fiction *n* Sachliteratur *f*

non-'iron *a* bügelfrei

nonsens|e *n* Unsinn *m*. **~ical** *a* unsinnig

non-'smoker *n* Nichtraucher *m*; *(compartment)* Nichtraucherabteil *nt*

non-'stop *adv* ununterbrochen; *(fly)* nonstop; **~'flight** Nonstopflug *m*

non-'violent *a* gewaltlos

noodles *npl* Bandnudeln *pl*

noon *n* Mittag *m*; **at ~** um 12 Uhr mittags

noose *n* Schlinge *f*

nor *adv* noch □*conj* auch nicht

Nordic *a* nordisch

norm *n* Norm *f*

normal *a* normal. **~ity** *n* Normalität *f*

north *n* Norden *m*; **to the ~ of** nördlich von □*a* Nord-, nord- □*adv* nach Norden

north: N~ America *nt* Nordamerika *m*. **~-east** *a* Nordost- □*n* Nordosten *m*

norther|ly *a* nördlich. **~n** *a* nördlich. **N~n Ireland** *n* Nordirland *nt*

north: N~ 'Pole *n* Nordpol *m*. **N~ 'Sea** *n* Nordsee *f*. **~ward[s**

adv nach Norden. **~-west** *a* Nordwest- □ *n* Nordwesten *m*

Nor|way *n* Norwegen *nt*. **~we-gian** *a* norwegisch □ *n* Norwe-ger(in) *m(f)*

nose *n* Nase *f*

nose: ~ **bleed** *n* Nasenbluten *nt*. ~ **dive** *n* (*Aviat*) Sturzflug *m*

nostalg|ia *n* Nostalgie *f*. **~ic** *a* nostalgisch

nostril *n* Nasenloch *nt*; (*of horse*) Nüster *f*

nosy *a* (*fam*) neugierig

not *adv* nicht; ~ **a** kein(e); **if** ~ wenn nicht; ~ **at all** gar nicht; ~ **a bit** kein bißchen; ~ **even** nicht mal; ~ **yet** noch nicht

notab|le *a* bedeutend; (*remark-able*) bemerkenswert. **~ly** *adv* insbesondere

notary *n* ~ '**public** ≈ Notar *m*

notation *n* Notation *f*; (*Mus*) No-tenschrift *f*

notch *n* Kerbe *f*

note *n* Notiz *f*, Anmerkung *f*; (*short letter*) Briefchen *nt*, Zettel *m*; (*bank~*) Banknote *f*, Schein *m*; (*Mus*) Note *f*; (*sound*) Ton *m*; (*on piano*) Taste *f*; **of** ~ von Bedeutung; **make a** ~ **of** notie-ren □ *vt* beachten; (*notice*) bemer-ken (**that** daß). ~ **down** *vt* notie-ren

'**notebook** *n* Notizbuch *nt*

note: ~ **paper** *n* Briefpapier *nt*. **~worthy** *a* beachtenswert

nothing *n*, *pron* & *adv* nichts; **for** ~ umsonst; ~ **but** nichts als; ~ **much** nicht viel; ~ **interesting** nichts Interessantes

notice *n* Anschlag *m*, Bekannt-machung *f*; (*announcement*) Anzeige *f*; (*review*) Kritik *f*; (*termination of lease, employment*) Kündigung *f*; [**advance**] ~ Bescheid *m*; **give** [**in one's**] ~ kündigen; **give s.o.** ~ jdm kündigen; **take no** ~ **of** keine Notiz nehmen von; **take no** ~! ignoriere es! □ *vt* bemerken.

~**able** *a* merklich. **~-board** *n* Anschlagbrett *nt*

notify *vt* benachrichtigen

notion *n* Idee *f*

notorious *a* berüchtigt

notwith'standing *prep* trotz (+ *gen*) □ *adv* trotzdem, dennoch

nought *n* Null *f*

noun *n* Substantiv *nt*

nourish *vt* nähren

novel *a* neu[artig] □ *n* Roman *m*. ~**ist** *n* Romanschriftsteller(in) *m(f)*. ~**ty** *n* Neuheit *f*

November *n* November *m*

novice *n* Neuling *m*; (*Relig*) No-vize *m*/Novizin *f*

now *adv* & *conj* jetzt; ~ [**that**] jetzt, wo; **just** ~ gerade, eben; **right** ~ sofort; ~ **and again** hin und wieder

'**nowadays** *adv* heutzutage

nowhere *adv* nirgendwo, nir-gends

nozzle *n* Düse *f*

nuance *n* Nuance *f*

nuclear *a* Kern-. ~ **de'terrent** *n* nukleares Abschreckungsmittel *nt*

nucleus *n* Kern *m*

nude *a* nackt □ *n* (*Art*) Akt *m*

nudge *vt* stupsen

nud|ist *n* Nudist *m*. ~ **ity** *n* Nackt-heit *f*

nuisance *n* Ärgernis *nt*; (*pest*) Plage *f*; **be a** ~ ärgerlich sein; ⟨*person:*⟩ lästig sein

null *a* ~ **and void** null und nich-tig

numb *a* gefühllos, taub

number *n* Nummer *f*; (*amount*) Anzahl *f*; (*Math*) Zahl *f* □ *vt* numerieren; (*include*) zählen (**among** zu). ~**plate** *n* Num-mernschild *nt*

numeral *n* Ziffer *f*

numerate *a* **be** ~ rechnen kön-nen

numerical *a* numerisch; **in** ~ **order** zahlenmäßig geordnet

numerous *a* zahlreich

nun *n* Nonne *f*

nuptial *a* Hochzeits-.

nurse *n* [Kranken]schwester *f*; *(male)* Krankenpfleger *m* □ *vt* pflegen. ~**maid** *n* Kindermädchen *nt*

nursery *n* Kinderzimmer *nt*; *(Hort)* Gärtnerei *f*; **[day]** ~ Kindertagesstätte *f*. ~**rhyme** *n* Kinderreim *m*. ~**school** *n* Kindergarten *m*

nursing *n* Krankenpflege *f*. ~**home** *n* Pflegeheim *nt*

nut *n* Nuß *f*; *(Techn)* [Schrauben]mutter *f*. ~**crackers** *npl* Nußknacker *m*. ~**meg** *n* Muskat *m*

nutrition *n* Ernährung *f*. ~**ious** *a* nahrhaft

'**nutshell** *n* Nußschale *f*; **in a** ~ *(fig)* kurz gesagt

nylon *n* Nylon *nt*

nymph *n* Nymphe *f*

O

O *n* *(Teleph)* null

oak *n* Eiche *f*

oar *n* Ruder *nt*. ~**sman** *n* Ruderer *m*

oasis *n* Oase *f*

oath *n* Eid *m*

oatmeal *n* Hafermehl *nt*

oats *npl* Hafer *m*; *(Culin)* **[rolled]** ~ Haferflocken *pl*

obedient *a* gehorsam

obese *a* fettleibig. ~**ity** *n* Fettleibigkeit *f*

obey *vt/i* gehorchen (+ *dat)*; befolgen *(instructions, rules)*

obituary *n* Nachruf *m*; *(notice)* Todesanzeige *f*

object¹ *n* Gegenstand *m*; *(aim)* Zweck *m*; *(intention)* Absicht *f*; *(Gram)* Objekt *nt*; **money is no** ~ Geld spielt keine Rolle

object² *vi* Einspruch erheben **(to** gegen); *(be against)* etwas dagegen haben

objection *n* Einwand *m*; **have no** ~ nichts dagegen haben. ~**able** *a* anstößig; *⟨person⟩* unangenehm

objective *a* objektiv □ *n* Ziel *nt*. ~**ity** *n* Objektivität *f*

obligation *n* Pflicht *f*

obligatory *a* obligatorisch; **be** ~ Vorschrift sein

oblige *vt* verpflichten; *(compel)* zwingen; *(do a small service)* einen Gefallen tun (+ *dat)*. ~**ing** *a* entgegenkommend

oblique *a* schräg; *⟨angle⟩* schief; *(fig)* indirekt. ~ **stroke** *n* Schrägstrich *m*

obliterate *vt* auslöschen

oblivion *n* Vergessenheit *f*

oblivious *a* **be** ~ sich *(dat)* nicht bewußt sein **(of** *or* **to** *gen)*

oblong *a* rechteckig □ *n* Rechteck *nt*

oboe *n* Oboe *f*

obscene *a* obszön; *(atrocious)* abscheulich. ~**ity** *n* Obszönität *f*; Abscheulichkeit *f*

obscure *a* dunkel; *(unknown)* unbekannt □ *vt* verdecken; *(confuse)* verwischen. ~**ity** *n* Dunkelheit *f*; Unbekanntheit *f*

obsequious *a* unterwürfig

observant *a* aufmerksam. ~**tion** *n* Beobachtung *f*; *(remark)* Bemerkung *f*

observatory *n* Sternwarte *f*

observe *vt* beobachten; *(say)* bemerken; *(celebrate)* feiern; *(obey)* einhalten. ~**r** *n* Beobachter *m*

obsess *vt* **be** ~**ed by** besessen sein von. ~**ion** *n* Besessenheit *f*; *(persistent idea)* fixe Idee *f*. ~**ive** *a* zwanghaft

obsolete *a* veraltet

obstacle *n* Hindernis *nt*

obstetrician *n* Geburtshelfer *m*.

obstetrics *n* Geburtshilfe *f*

obstina|cy n Starrsinn m. **~te** a starrsinnig

obstruct vt blockieren; (hinder) behindern. **~ion** n Blockierung f; Behinderung f; (obstacle) Hindernis nt

obtain vt erhalten, bekommen. **~able** a erhältlich

obtrusive a aufdringlich

obtuse a (geom) stumpf; (stupid) begriffsstutzig

obvious a offensichtlich, offenbar

occasion n Gelegenheit f; (time) Mal nt; (event) Ereignis nt; (cause) Anlaß m, Grund m

occasional a gelegentlich; **he has the ~ glass of wine** er trinkt gelegentlich ein Glas Wein. **~ly** adv gelegentlich, hin und wieder

occult a okkult

occupant n Bewohner(in) m(f); (of vehicle) Insasse m

occupation n Beschäftigung f; (job) Beruf m; (Mil) Besetzung f; (period) Besatzung f. **~al** a Berufs-. **~al therapy** n Beschäftigungstherapie f

occupier n Bewohner(in) m(f)

occupy vt besetzen (seat, (Mil) country); einnehmen (space); in Anspruch nehmen (time); (live in) bewohnen; (fig) bekleiden (office); (keep busy) beschäftigen

occur vi vorkommen; (exist) vorkommen, auftreten; **it ~red to me that** es fiel mir ein, daß. **occurrence** n Auftreten nt; (event) Ereignis nt

ocean n Ozean m

o'clock adv [at] **7 ~** [um] 7 Uhr

octagonal a achteckig

octave n (Mus) Oktave f

October n Oktober m

octopus n Tintenfisch m

odd a seltsam, merkwürdig; (number) ungerade; (not of set) einzeln; **forty ~** über vierzig; **~ jobs** Gelegenheitsarbeiten pl; **the ~ one out** die Ausnahme

oddity n Kuriosität f

odds npl (chances) Chancen pl; **at ~** uneinig; **~ and ends** Kleinkram m

ode n Ode f

odour n Geruch m

oesophagus n Speiseröhre f

of prep von (+ dat); (made of) aus (+ dat); **the two of us** wir zwei; **a child of three** ein dreijähriges Kind; **the fourth of January** der vierte Januar; **a pound of butter** ein Pfund Butter

off prep von (+ dat); **£10 ~ the price** £10 Nachlaß; **~ the coast** vor der Küste; **get ~ the ladder/bus** von der Leiter/aus dem Bus steigen □ adv weg; (button, lid, handle) ab; (light) aus; (brake) los; (machine) abgeschaltet; (tap) zu; (on appliance) **'off 'aus'; 2 kilometres ~** 2 Kilometer entfernt; **a long way ~** weit weg; (time) noch lange hin; **~ and on** hin und wieder; **20% ~** 20% Nachlaß; **be ~** (leave) [weg]gehen; (Sport) starten; (food:) schlecht/ (all gone) alle sein; **be better/worse ~** besser/schlechter dran sein; **be well ~** gut dran sein; (financially) wohlhabend sein; **have a day ~** einen freien Tag haben

offal n (Culin) Innereien pl

offence n (illegal act) Vergehen nt; **give/take ~** Anstoß erregen/nehmen (at an + dat)

offend vt beleidigen. **~er** n (Jur) Straftäter m

offensive a beleidigend; (Mil, Sport) offensiv □ n Offensive f

offer n Angebot nt; **on special ~** im Sonderangebot □ vt anbieten (to dat); leisten (resistance); **~ s.o. sth** jdm etw anbieten

offhand a brüsk; (casual) lässig □ adv so ohne weiteres

office n Büro nt; **~ hours** pl Dienststunden pl

officer n Offizier m; (official) Beamte(r) m/ Beamtin f

official a offiziell, amtlich □n Beamte(r) m/ Beamtin f; (Sport) Funktionär m

officiate vi amtieren

officious a übereifrig

'off-licence n Wein- und Spirituosenhandlung f

'offshoot n Schößling m; (fig) Zweig m

'offshore a offshore. ~ **rig** n Bohrinsel f

off side a (Sport) abseits

'offspring n Nachwuchs m

off stage adv hinter den Kulissen

off'white a fast weiß

often adv oft; **every so** ~ von Zeit zu Zeit

ogre n Menschenfresser m

oh int oh! ach! **oh dear!** o weh!

oil n Öl nt; (petroleum) Erdöl nt □vt ölen

oil: ~ **cloth** n Wachstuch nt. ~ **refinery** n [Erd]ölraffinerie f. ~ **skins** npl Ölzeug nt. ~ **slick** n Ölteppich m. ~ **tanker** n Öltanker m. ~ **well** n Ölquelle f

ointment n Salbe f

OK a & int (fam) in Ordnung, okay □adv (well) gut

old a alt; (former) ehemalig

old: ~ **age** n Alter nt. ~ **age 'pensioner** n Rentner(in) m(f). ~ **boy** n ehemaliger Schüler m. ~**'fashioned** a altmodisch. ~ **girl** n ehemalige Schülerin f. ~ **maid** n alte Jungfer f

olive n Olive f; (colour) Oliv nt □a olivgrün. ~ **'oil** n Olivenöl nt

Olympic a olympisch □n the ~s die Olympischen Spiele pl

omelette n Omelett nt

omen n Omen nt

ominous a bedrohlich

omission n Auslassung f

omit vt auslassen

omnipotent a allmächtig

on prep auf (+ dat/(on to) + acc); (on vertical surface) an (+ dat/(on to) + acc); (about) über (+ acc); **on Monday** [am] Montag; **on Mondays** montags; **on the first of May** am ersten Mai; **on arriving** als ich ankam; **on one's finger** an Finger; **on the right/left** rechts/links; **on the Rhine** am Rhein; **on television** im Fernsehen; **on the bus** im Bus; **on me** (with me) bei mir; **it's on me** (fam) das spendiere ich □adv (further on) weiter; (switched on) an; (brake) angezogen; (machine) angeschaltet; (on appliance) 'on' 'ein'; **be on** ⟨film:⟩ laufen; ⟨event:⟩ stattfinden; **be on at** (fam) bedrängen (zu tun); **it's not on** (fam) das geht nicht; **on and on** immer weiter; **on and off** hin und wieder; **and so on** und so weiter

once adv einmal; (formerly) früher; **at** ~ sofort; (at the same time) gleichzeitig; ~ **and for all** ein für allemal □conj wenn; (with past tense) als.

'oncoming a ~ **traffic** Gegenverkehr m

one a ein(e); (only) einzig; **not** ~ kein(e). ~ **day/evening** eines Tages/Abends □n Eins f □pron eine(r)/eins; (impersonal) man; **which** ~ welche(r,s); ~ **another** einander; ~ **by** ~ einzeln; ~ **never knows** man kann nie wissen

one: ~**-parent 'family** n Einelternfamilie f. ~**'self** pron selbst; (refl) sich; **by** ~ **self** allein. ~**way** a ⟨street⟩ Einbahn-; ⟨ticket⟩ einfach

onion n Zwiebel f

'onlooker n Zuschauer(in) m(f)

only a einzig(r,s); an ~ **child** ein Einzelkind nt □adv & conj nur; ~ **just** gerade erst; (barely) gerade noch

'onset n Beginn m; (of winter) Einsetzen nt

onus n the ~ **is on me** es liegt an mir (**to** zu)

onward[s] adv vorwärts; **from then** ~ von der Zeit an

ooze vi sickern

opal n Opal m

opaque a undurchsichtig

open a offen; **be** ~ (shop:) geöffnet sein; **in the** ~ **air** im Freien □n **in the** ~ im Freien □vt öffnen, aufmachen; (start) eröffnen □vi sich öffnen; (flower:) aufgehen; (shop:) öffnen, aufmachen; (be started) eröffnet werden

open: ~**-air 'swimming pool** n Freibad nt. ~**day** n Tag m der offenen Tür

opening n Öffnung f; (beginning) Eröffnung f; (job) Einstiegsmöglichkeit f. ~**hours** npl Öffnungszeiten pl

open: ~**-'minded** a aufgeschlossen. ~**-plan** a ~**-plan office** Großraumbüro nt

opera n Oper f

opera: ~**-glasses** npl Opernglas nt. ~**-singer** n Opernsänger(in) m(f)

operate vt bedienen (machine); betätigen (lever); (fig: run) betreiben □vi (Techn) funktionieren; (be in action) in Betrieb sein; (Mil & fig) operieren; **~** [**on**] (Med) operieren

operation n Bedienung f; Betätigung f; Operation f; **in** ~ (Techn) in Betrieb; **come into** ~ (fig) in Kraft treten; **have an** ~ (Med) operiert werden. ~**al** a **be** ~**al** in Betrieb sein; (law:) in Kraft sein

operator n (user) Bedienungsperson f; (Teleph) Vermittlung f

operetta n Operette f

opinion n Meinung f; **in my** ~ meiner Meinung nach

opium n Opium nt

opponent n Gegner(in) m(f)

opportun|e a günstig. ~**ist** n Opportunist m

opportunity n Gelegenheit f

oppose vt Widerstand leisten (+ dat); (argue against) sprechen gegen; **be** ~**d to sth** gegen etw sein; **as** ~**d to** im Gegensatz zu

opposite a entgegengesetzt; (house, side) gegenüberliegend; ~ **number** (fig) Gegenstück nt; **the** ~ **sex** das andere Geschlecht □n Gegenteil nt □adv gegenüber □prep gegenüber (+ dat)

opposition n Widerstand m; (Pol) Opposition f

oppress vt unterdrücken. ~**ion** n Unterdrückung f. ~**ive** a tyrannisch; (heat) drückend. ~**or** n Unterdrücker m

opt vi ~ **for** sich entscheiden für; ~ **out** ausscheiden (**of** aus)

optical a optisch

optician n Optiker m

optics n Optik f

optimis|m n Optimismus m. ~**t** n Optimist m. ~**tic** a optimistisch

optimum a optimal □n Optimum nt

option n Wahl f; (Comm) Option f. ~**al** a auf Wunsch erhältlich; (subject) wahlfrei

opulent a prunkvoll

or conj oder; (after negative) noch; **or [else]** sonst; **in a year or two** in ein bis zwei Jahren

oracle n Orakel nt

oral a mündlich; (Med) oral □n Mündliche(s) nt

orange n Apfelsine f, Orange f; (colour) Orange nt □a orangefarben

orator n Redner m

oratorio n Oratorium nt

oratory n Redekunst f

orbit n Umlaufbahn f □vt umkreisen. ~**al** a ~**al road** Ringstraße f

orchard n Obstgarten m

orches|tra n Orchester nt. **~tral**
a Orchester-. **~trate** vt orche-
strieren

orchid n Orchidee f

ordain vt bestimmen; (Relig) ordi-
nieren

ordeal n (fig) Qual f

order n Ordnung f; (sequence) Reihenfolge f; (condition) Zustand m;
(command) Befehl m; (in restaurant) Bestellung f; (Comm) Auftrag
m; (Relig, medal) Orden m; out of
~ ⟨machine:⟩ außer Betrieb; in ~
that damit; in ~ to help um zu
helfen; take holy ~s Geistlicher
werden □vt (put in ~) ordnen;
(command) befehlen (+ dat);
(Comm, in restaurant) bestellen;
(prescribe) verordnen

orderly a ordentlich; (not unruly)
friedlich □n Sanitäter m

ordinary a gewöhnlich, normal

ordination n Ordination f

ore n Erz nt

organ n (Biol & fig) Organ nt;
(Mus) Orgel f

organic a organisch; (without
chemicals) biodynamisch; ⟨crop⟩
biologisch angebaut; ⟨food⟩ Bio-;
~ally grown biologisch angebaut. **~ farm** n Biohof m. **~
farming** n biologischer Anbau m

organism n Organismus m

organist n Organist m

organization n Organisation f

organize vt organisieren; veran-
stalten ⟨event⟩. **~r** n Organisator
m; Veranstalter m

orgasm n Orgasmus m

orgy n Orgie f

Orient n Orient m. **o~al** a orien-
talisch □n Orientale m/ Orienta-
lin f

orientation n Orientierung f

orifice n Öffnung f

origin n Ursprung m; (of person,
goods) Herkunft f

original a ursprünglich; (not cop-
ied) (original); (new) originell □n
Original nt. **~ity** n Originalität f

originate vi entstehen □vt hervorbringen

ornament n Ziergegenstand m;
(decoration) Verzierung f. **~al** a
dekorativ

ornithology n Vogelkunde f

orphan n Waisenkind nt, Waise f.
~age n Waisenhaus nt

orthodox a orthodox

orthopaedic a orthopädisch

ostentatious a protzig (fam)

osteopath n Osteopath m

ostracize vt ächten

ostrich n Strauß m

other a, pron & n andere(r,s); the
~ [one] der/das andere; the **~
two** die zwei anderen; **two ~s**
zwei andere; (more) noch zwei; **no
~s** sonst keine □adv anders; **~
than him** außer ihm; **some-
how/somewhere or ~** irgend-
wie/irgendwo

'otherwise adv sonst; (differently)
anders

otter n Otter m

ouch int autsch

ought v aux I/we **~ to stay** ich
sollte/wir sollten eigentlich bleiben; **he ~ not to have done it** er
hätte es nicht machen sollen; **that
~ to be enough** das sollte eigentlich genügen

ounce n Unze f (28,35 g)

our a unser

ours poss pron unsere(r,s); **a
friend of ~** ein Freund von uns;
that is ~ das gehört uns

ourselves pron selbst; (refl) uns;
by ~ allein

out adv (not at home) weg; (outside)
draußen; (not alight) aus; (unconscious) bewußtlos; **be ~**
⟨sun:⟩ scheinen; ⟨flower:⟩ blühen; ⟨workers:⟩ streiken; (calculation:) nicht stimmen; (Sport)
aus sein; (fig: not feasible) nicht in

Frage kommen; ~ **and about** unterwegs; **have it** ~ **with s.o.** (*fam*) jdn zur Rede stellen; **get** ~! (*fam*) raus! **get** ~ **of** aus (+ *dat*); **go** ~ **of the door** zur Tür hinausgehen; **be** ~ **of bed/the room** nicht im Bett/im Zimmer sein; ~ **of breath/danger** außer Atem/Gefahr; ~ **of work** arbeitslos; □ *prep* aus (+ *dat*)

'**outboard** a ~ **motor** Außenbordmotor m

'**outbreak** n Ausbruch m

'**outburst** n Ausbruch m

'**outcast** n Ausgestoßene(r) m/f

'**outcome** n Ergebnis nt

'**outcry** n Aufschrei m

out'**dated** a überholt

'**outdoor** a im Freien

out'**doors** adv draußen

'**outer** a äußere(r,s)

'**outfit** n Ausstattung f; (*clothes*) Ensemble nt; (*fam*: *organization*) Betrieb m; (*fam*) Laden m. ~**ter** n men's ~**ter's** Herrenbekleidungsgeschäft nt

'**outgoing** a ausscheidend; (*mail*) ausgehend; (*sociable*) kontaktfreudig. ~**s** npl Ausgaben pl

'**outing** n Ausflug m

'**outlaw** n Geächtete(r) m/f □ vt ächten

'**outlay** n Auslagen pl

'**outlet** n Abzug m; (*for water*) Abfluß m; (*fig*) Ventil nt; (*Comm*) Absatzmöglichkeit f

'**outline** n Umriß m; (*summary*) kurze Darstellung f □ vt umreißen

'**outlook** n Aussicht f; (*future prospect*) Aussichten pl; (*attitude*) Einstellung f

'**outlying** a entlegen; ~ **areas** pl Außengebiete pl

out'**number** vt zahlenmäßig überlegen sein (+ *dat*)

'**out-patient** n ambulanter Patient m; ~**s' department** Ambulanz f

'**outpost** n Vorposten m

'**output** n Leistung f, Produktion f

'**outrage** n Greueltat f; (*fig*) Skandal m; (*indignation*) Empörung f □ vt empören. ~**ous** a empörend

'**outright¹** a völlig, total; (*refusal*) glatt

out'**right²** adv ganz; (*at once*) sofort; (*frankly*) offen

'**outset** n Anfang m

'**outside¹** a äußere(r,s) □ n Außenseite f

out'**side²** adv außen; (*out of doors*) draußen; □ *prep* außerhalb (+ *gen*); (*in front of*) vor (+ *dat/acc*)

out'**sider** n Außenseiter m

'**outsize** a übergroß

'**outskirts** npl Rand m

'**outstanding** a hervorragend; (*conspicuous*) bemerkenswert; (*not settled*) unerledigt; (*Comm*) ausstehend

'**outward** a äußerlich; ~ **journey** Hinreise f □ adv nach außen

out'**weigh** vt überwiegen

out'**wit** vt überlisten

oval a oval □ n Oval nt

ovary n (*Anat*) Eierstock m

ovation n Ovation f

oven n Backofen m

over prep über (+ *acc/dat*); ~ **dinner** beim Essen; ~ **the weekend** übers Wochenende; ~ **the phone** am Telefon; ~ **the page** auf der nächsten Seite □ adv (*remaining*) übrig; (*ended*) zu Ende; ~ **again** noch einmal; ~ **and** ~ immer wieder; ~ **here/there** hier/da drüben; **all** ~ (*everywhere*) überall; **it's all** ~ es ist vorbei

overall¹ n Kittel m; ~**s** pl Overall m

overall² a gesamt; (*general*) allgemein □ adv insgesamt

over'**awe** vt (*fig*) überwältigen

over'**bearing** a herrisch

'**overboard** adv (*Naut*) über Bord

'**overcast** a bedeckt

'**overcoat** n Mantel m

over'**come** vt überwinden

over'crowded a überfüllt

over'do vt übertreiben; (cook too long) zu lange kochen

'overdose n Überdosis f

'overdraft n [Konto]überziehung f

over'draw vt (Comm) überziehen

over'due a überfällig

'overflow[1] n Überschuß m; (outlet) Überlauf m

over'flow[2] vi überlaufen

over'haul[1] n Überholung f

over'haul[2] vt (Techn) überholen

over'head[1] adv oben

over'head[2] a Ober-; (ceiling) Decken-. **~s** npl allgemeine Unkosten pl

over'hear vt mit anhören

over'joyed a überglücklich

over'lap vt überlappen

over'leaf adv umseitig

over'load vt überladen; (Electr) überlasten

over'look vt überblicken; (fail to see, ignore) übersehen

over'night[1] adv über Nacht; **stay ~** übernachten

'overnight[2] a Nacht-; **~ stay** Übernachtung f

over'populated a übervölkert

over'power vt überwältigen

over'rate vt überschätzen

over'ride vt sich hinwegsetzen über (+ acc)

over'rule vt ablehnen

over'run vt überrennen; überschreiten (time); **be ~ with** überlaufen sein von

over'seas adv in Übersee; **go ~** nach Übersee gehen

over'see vt beaufsichtigen

over'shadow vt überschatten

'oversight n Versehen nt

over'sleep vi [sich] verschlafen

overt a offen

over'take vt/i überholen

over'throw[1] n (Pol) Sturz m

over'throw[2] vt (Pol) stürzen

'overtime n Überstunden pl □adv **work ~** Überstunden machen

'overtone n (fig) Unterton m

overture n (Mus) Ouvertüre f

over'turn vt umstoßen □ vi umkippen

overwhelm vt überwältigen

over'work vi sich überarbeiten

ovulation n Eisprung m

ow|e vt schulden/(fig) verdanken ([to] s.o. jdm); **~ e s.o. sth** jdm etw schuldig sein. **'~ing to** prep wegen (+ gen)

owl n Eule f

own[1] a & pron eigen; **it's my ~ es** gehört mir; **a car of my ~** mein eigenes Auto; **on one's ~** allein

own[2] vt besitzen; (confess) zugeben; **I don't ~ it** es gehört mir nicht. **~ up** vi es zugeben

owner n Eigentümer(in) m(f), Besitzer(in) m(f); (of shop) Inhaber(in) m(f). **~ship** n Besitz m

ox n Ochse m

oxide n Oxyd nt

oxygen n Sauerstoff m

oyster n Auster f

ozone n Ozon nt. **~-'friendly** a ~ ohne FCKW. **~ layer** n Ozonschicht f

P

pace n Schritt m; (speed) Tempo nt; **keep ~ with** Schritt halten mit □ vi **~ up and down** auf und ab gehen. **~-maker** n (Sport & Med) Schrittmacher m

Pacific a & n **the ~ [Ocean]** der Pazifik

pacifist n Pazifist m

pacify vt beruhigen

pack n Packung f; (Mil) Tornister m; (of cards) [Karten]spiel nt; (gang) Bande f; (of hounds) Meute f; (of wolves) Rudel nt; **a ~ of lies** ein Haufen Lügen □ vt/i packen; einpacken (article); **be ~ed** (crowded) [gedrängt] voll sein

package n Paket nt □vt verpacken. ~ **holiday** n Pauschalreise f

packed 'lunch n Lunchpaket nt

packet n Päckchen nt

packing n Verpackung f

pact n Pakt m

pad n Polster nt; (for writing) [Schreib]block m □ vt polstern

paddle[1] n Paddel nt □vt (row) paddeln

paddle[2] vi waten

paddock n Koppel f

padlock n Vorhängeschloß nt

paediatr|ician n Kinderarzt m / -ärztin f

pagan a heidnisch □n Heide m/Heidin f

page[1] n Seite f

page[2] n (boy) Page m □ vt ausrufen ⟨person⟩

pageant n Festzug m

pail n Eimer m

pain n Schmerz m; **be in** ~ Schmerzen haben; **take** ~ s **sich** (dat) Mühe geben

pain: ~ **ful** a schmerzhaft; (fig) schmerzlich. ~ **killer** n schmerzstillendes Mittel nt. ~ **less** a schmerzlos

painstaking a sorgfältig

paint n Farbe f □vt/i streichen; ⟨artist:⟩ malen. ~ **brush** n Pinsel m. ~ **er** n Maler m; (decorator) Anstreicher m. ~ **ing** n Malerei f; (picture) Gemälde nt

pair n Paar nt; ~ **of trousers** Hose f□vt paaren □vi ~ **off** Paare bilden

Pakistan n Pakistan nt. ~ **i** a pakistanisch □n Pakistaner(in) m(f)

palace n Palast m

palate n Gaumen m

pale[1] n (stake) Pfahl m; **beyond the** ~ (fam) unmöglich

pale[2] a blaß

Palestin|e n Palästina nt. ~ **ian** a palästinensisch □n Palästinenser(in) m(f)

palette n Palette f

pall n Sargtuch nt; (fig) Decke f □vi an Reiz verlieren

pallid a bleich. ~ **or** n Blässe f

palm n Handfläche f; (tree) Palme f □vt ~ **sth off on s.o.** jdm etw andrehen. **P** ~ **'Sunday** n Palmsonntag m

palpitate vi klopfen

paltry a armselig

pamper vt verwöhnen

pamphlet n Broschüre f

pan n Pfanne f; (saucepan) Topf m; (of scales) Schale f

panacea n Allheilmittel nt

panache n Schwung m

pancake n Pfannkuchen m

pancreas n Bauchspeicheldrüse f

panda n Panda m. ~ **car** n Streifenwagen m

pandemonium n Höllenlärm m

pander vi ~ **to s.o.** jdm zu sehr nachgeben

pane n [Glas]scheibe f

panel n Tafel f, Platte f

panic n Panik f□vi in Panik geraten. ~ **stricken** a von Panik ergriffen

panoram|a n Panorama nt. ~ **ic** a Panorama-

pansy n Stiefmütterchen nt

pant vi keuchen; ⟨dog:⟩ hecheln

panther n Panther m

panties npl [Damen]slip m

pantomime n [zu Weihnachten aufgeführte] Märchenvorstellung f

pantry n Speisekammer f

pants npl Unterhose f; (woman's) Schlüpfer m; (trousers) Hose f

papal a päpstlich

paper n Papier nt; (newspaper) Zeitung f; (exam ~) Testbogen m;

(exam) Klausur *f*; *(treatise)* Referat *nt*; ~ **s** *pl (documents)* Unterlagen *pl*; *(for identification)* [Ausweis]papiere *pl*; **on** ~ schriftlich
paper: ~ **back** *n* Taschenbuch *nt*.
~-clip *n* Büroklammer *f*.
~-knife *n* Brieföffner *m*.
~ weight *n* Briefbeschwerer *m*.
~ work *n* Schreibarbeit *f*
par *n (Golf)* Par *nt*; **on a** ~ gleichwertig **(with** *dat)*
parable *n* Gleichnis *nt*
parachut|e *n* Fallschirm *m* □ *vi* [mit dem Fallschirm] abspringen. **~ist** *n* Fallschirmspringer *m*.
parade *n* Parade *f*; *(procession)* Festzug *m* □ *vi* marschieren □ *vt (show off)* zur Schau stellen
paradise *n* Paradies *nt*
paradox *n* Paradox *nt*
paraffin *n* Paraffin *nt*
paragon *n* ~ **of virtue** Ausbund *m* der Tugend
paragraph *n* Absatz *m*
parallel *a & adv* parallel □ *n (Geog)* Breitenkreis *m*; *(fig)* Parallele *f*
paralyse *vt* lähmen
paralysis *n* Lähmung *f*
paranoid *a* [krankhaft] mißtrauisch
parapet *n* Brüstung *f*
paraphernalia *n* Kram *m*
paraphrase *vt* umschreiben
paraplegic *a* querschnittsgelähmt □ *n* Querschnittsgelähmte(r) *m/f*
parasite *n* Parasit *m*, Schmarotzer *m*
parasol *n* Sonnenschirm *m*
paratrooper *n* Fallschirmjäger *m*
parcel *n* Paket *nt*
parchment *n* Pergament *nt*
pardon *n* Verzeihung *f*; *(Jur)* Begnadigung *f*; ~? *(fam)* bitte? **I beg**

your ~ wie bitte? *(sorry)* Verzeihung! □ *vt* verzeihen; *(Jur)* begnadigen
parent *n* Elternteil *m*; ~**s** *pl* Eltern *pl*. ~**al** *a* elterlich
parenthesis *n* Klammer *f*
parish *n* Gemeinde *f*
parity *n* Gleichheit *f*
park *n* Park *m* □ *vt/i* parken
parking *n* Parken *nt*; **'no** ~' 'Parken verboten'. **~-meter** *n* Parkuhr *f*
parliament *n* Parlament *nt*. ~**ary** *a* parlamentarisch
parochial *a* Gemeinde-; *(fig)* beschränkt
parody *n* Parodie *f*
parole *n* **on** ~ auf Bewährung
parquet *n* ~ **floor** Parkett *nt*
parrot *n* Papagei *m*
parry *vt* abwehren
parsley *n* Petersilie *f*
parsnip *n* Pastinake *f*
parson *n* Pfarrer *m*
part *n* Teil *m*; *(Techn)* Teil *nt*; *(area)* Gegend *f*; *(Theat)* Rolle *f*; *(Mus)* Part *m*; **spare** ~ Ersatzteil *nt*; **for my** ~ meinerseits; **on the** ~ **of** von Seiten (+ *gen*) □ *vt* trennen; scheiteln ⟨*hair*⟩ □ *vi* ⟨*people*⟩ sich trennen
partake *vt* teilnehmen; ~ **of** zu sich nehmen
partial *a* Teil-; **be** ~ **to** mögen
participant *n* Teilnehmer(in) *m(f)*. ~**ate** *vi* teilnehmen **(in an** + *dat*). ~**ation** *n* Teilnahme *f*
participle *n* Partizip *nt*; **present/past** ~ erstes/zweites Partizip *nt*
particle *n* Körnchen *nt*; *(Phys)* Partikel *nt*; *(Gram)* Partikel *f*
particular *a* besondere(r,s); *(precise)* genau; *(fastidious)* penibel; **in** ~ besonders. **~ly** *adv* besonders. **~s** *npl* nähere Angaben *pl*
parting *n* Abschied *m*; *(in hair)* Scheitel *m*
partition *n* Trennwand *f*; *(Pol)* Teilung *f*

partly *adv* teilweise
partner *n* Partner(in) *m(f);* (Comm) Teilhaber *m.* **~ ship** *n* Partnerschaft *f;* (Comm) Teilhaberschaft *f*
partridge *n* Rebhuhn *nt*
part-'time *a & adv* Teilzeit-; **be at work** ~ Teilzeitarbeit machen
party *n* Party *f*, Fest *nt;* (group) Gruppe *f;* (Pol, Jur) Partei *f*
'party line[1] *n* (Teleph) Gemeinschaftsanschluß *m*
party 'line[2] *n* (Pol) Parteilinie *f*
pass *n* Ausweis *m;* (Geog, Sport) Paß *m;* (Sch) ≈ ausreichend □*vt* vorbeigehen/-fahren an (+ *dat);* (overtake) überholen; (hand) reichen; (Sport) abgeben, abspielen; (approve) annehmen; (exceed) übersteigen; bestehen (exam); machen (remark); fällen (judgement); (Jur) verhängen (sentence); ~ **the time** sich (dat) die Zeit vertreiben □*vi* (go past) vorbeigehen/-fahren; (get by) vorbeikommen; (overtake) überholen; (time:~) vergehen; (in exam) bestehen; **let sth ~** (fig) etw übergehen; **[I]** ~! [ich] passe! **~ away** *vi* sterben. **~ out** *vi* ohnmächtig werden

passage *n* Durchgang *m;* (corridor) Gang *m;* (voyage) Überfahrt *f;* (in book) Passage *f*
passenger *n* Fahrgast *m;* (Naut, Aviat) Passagier *m;* (in car) Mitfahrer *m.* **~ seat** *n* Beifahrersitz *m*

passer-by *n* Passant(in) *m(f)*
passion *n* Leidenschaft *f.* **~ ate** *a* leidenschaftlich
passive *a* passiv □*n* Passiv *nt*
Passover *n* Passah *nt*
pass: **~ port** *n* [Reise]paß *m.* **~ word** *n* Kennwort *nt;* (Mil) Losung *f*
past *a* vergangene(r,s); (former) ehemalig; **in the ~ few days** in den letzten paar Tagen; □*n* Vergangenheit *f* □*prep* an (+

dat) ... vorbei; (after) nach; **at ten ~ two** um zehn nach zwei □*adv* vorbei
pasta *n* Nudeln *pl*
paste *n* Brei *m;* (dough) Teig *m;* (fish-, meat-) Paste *f;* (adhesive) Kleister *m;* (jewellery) Straß *m* □*vt* kleistern
pastel *n* Pastellfarbe *f;* (crayon) Pastellstift *m;* (drawing) Pastell *nt*
pasteurize *vt* pasteurisieren
pastille *n* Pastille *f*
pastime *n* Zeitvertreib *m*
pastoral *a* ländlich; (care) seelsorgerisch
pastr|y *n* Teig *m;* **cakes and ~ ies** Kuchen und Gebäck
pasture *n* Weide *f*
pat *n* Klaps *m;* (of butter) Stückchen *nt* □*adv* **have sth off ~** etw aus dem Effeff können □*vt* tätscheln
patch *n* Flicken *m;* (spot) Fleck *m;* **not a ~ on** (fam) gar nicht zu vergleichen mit □*vt* flicken
pâté *n* Pastete *f*
patent *a* offensichtlich □*n* Patent *nt* □*vt* patentieren. **~ leather** *n* Lackleder *nt*
patern|al *a* väterlich. **~ ity** *n* Vaterschaft *f*
path *n* [Fuß]weg *m*, Pfad *m;* (orbit, track) Bahn *f;* (fig) Weg *m*
pathetic *a* mitleiderregend; (attempt) erbärmlich
patholog|ical *a* pathologisch. **~ ist** *n* Pathologe *m*
pathos *n* Rührseligkeit *f*
patience *n* Geduld *f;* (game) Patience *f*
patient *a* geduldig □*n* Patient(in) *m(f)*
patio *n* Terrasse *f*
patriot *n* Patriot(in) *m(f).* **~ ic** *a* patriotisch. **~ ism** *n* Patriotismus *m*
patrol *n* Patrouille *f* □*vt/i* patrouillieren [in (+ *dat*)]; (police:

auf Streife gehen/fahren [in (+ *dat*)]. ~ **car** n Streifenwagen m

patron n Gönner m; (*of charity*) Schirmherr m; (*of the arts*) Mäzen m; (*customer*) Kunde m/ Kundin f; (*Theat*) Besucher m. ~**age** n Schirmherrschaft f

patroniz|e vt (*fig*) herablassend behandeln. ~**ing** a gönnerhaft

pattern n Muster nt

pauper n Arme(r) m

pause n Pause f ☐vi innehalten

pavement n Bürgersteig m

pavilion n Pavillon m

paw n Pfote f; (*of large animal*) Pranke f, Tatze f

pawn[1] n (*Chess*) Bauer m; (*fig*) Schachfigur f

pawn[2] vt verpfänden ☐**in** ~ verpfändet. ~**broker** n Pfandleiher m. ~**shop** n Pfandhaus nt

pay n Lohn m; (*salary*) Gehalt nt ☐vt bezahlen; zahlen ⟨*money*⟩. ~ **s.o. a compliment** jdm ein Kompliment machen ☐vi zahlen; (*be profitable*) sich bezahlt machen; (*fig*) sich lohnen. ~ **for sth** etw bezahlen

payable a zahlbar; **make** ~ **to** ausstellen auf (+ *acc*)

payee n [Zahlungs]empfänger m

payment n Bezahlung f; (*amount*) Zahlung f

pay: ~ **packet** n Lohntüte f; ~ **phone** n Münzfernsprecher m

pea n Erbse f

peace n Frieden m

peaceful a friedlich

peach n Pfirsich m

peacock n Pfau m

peak n Gipfel m; (*fig*) Höhepunkt m. ~ **hours** npl Hauptbelastungszeit f; (*for traffic*) Hauptverkehrszeit f

peal n (*of bells*) Glockengeläut nt

'peanut n Erdnuß f; **for** ~ **s** (*fam*) für einen Apfel und ein Ei

pear n Birne f

pearl n Perle f

peasant n Bauer m

peat n Torf m

pebble n Kieselstein m

peck vt/i picken/⟨*nip*⟩ hacken (**at** nach). ~**ing order** n Hackordnung f

peculiar a eigenartig, seltsam; ~ **to** eigentümlich (+ *dat*). ~**ity** n Eigenart f

pedal n Pedal nt. ~ **bin** n Treteimer m

pedantic a pedantisch

peddle vt handeln mit

pedestal n Sockel m

pedestrian n Fußgänger(in) m(f) ☐ a (*fig*) prosaisch. ~ **'crossing** n Fußgängerüberweg m. ~ **'precinct** n Fußgängerzone f

pedigree n Stammbaum m

pedlar n Hausierer m

pee vi (*fam*) pinkeln

peek vi (*fam*) gucken

peel n Schale f ☐vt schälen ☐vi ⟨*skin:*⟩ sich schälen; ⟨*paint:*⟩ abblättern

peep vi gucken. ~**-hole** n Guckloch nt. **P~ing 'Tom** n (*fam*) Spanner m

peer[1] vi ~ **at** forschend ansehen

peer[2] n Peer m; **his** ~**s** zu seinesgleichen

peg n (*hook*) Haken m; (*for tent*) Pflock m, Hering m; (*for clothes*) [Wäsche]klammer f; **off the** ~ (*fam*) von der Stange

pejorative a abwertend

pelican n Pelikan m

pellet n Kügelchen nt

pelt[1] n (*skin*) Pelz m, Fell nt

pelt[2] vt bewerfen

pelvis n (*Anat*) Becken nt

pen[1] n (*for animals*) Hürde f

pen[2] n Federhalter m; (*ball-point*) Kugelschreiber m

penalize vt bestrafen

penalty n Strafe f; (*fine*) Geldstrafe f; (*Sport*) Strafstoß m; (*Football*) Elfmeter m

penance n Buße f

pencil n Bleistift m. **~-sharp-ener** n Bleistiftspitzer m

pendant n Anhänger m

pending a unerledigt □ prep bis zu

pendulum n Pendel nt

penetrat|e vt durchdringen; **~ion** n Durchdringen nt

'**penfriend** n Brieffreund(in) m(f)

penguin n Pinguin m

penicillin n Penizillin nt

peninsula n Halbinsel f

penis n Penis m

penitence n Reue f

pen: **~ knife** n Taschenmesser nt. **~-name** n Pseudonym nt

pennant n Wimpel m

penny n Penny m; **the ~'s dropped** (fam) der Groschen ist gefallen

pension n Rente f; (of civil servant) Pension f. **~er** n Rentner(in) m(f); Pensionär(in) m(f)

pensive a nachdenklich

Pentecost n Pfingsten nt

penultimate a vorletzte(r,s)

peony n Pfingstrose f

people npl Leute pl, Menschen pl; (citizens) Bevölkerung f; **the ~** das Volk; **English ~** die Engländer; **~ say** man sagt; **for four ~** für vier Personen □ vt bevölkern

pepper n Pfeffer m; (vegetable) Paprika m

pepper: **~corn** n Pfefferkorn nt. **~mint** n Pfefferminz nt; (Bot) Pfefferminze f. **~pot** n Pfefferstreuer m

per prep pro; **~ cent** Prozent nt

perceive vt wahrnehmen

percentage n Prozentsatz m

percept|ion n Wahrnehmung f. **~ive** a feinsinnig

perch¹ n Stange f □ vi (bird:) sich niederlassen

perch² n inv (fish) Barsch m

percolat|e vi durchsickern. **~or** n Kaffeemaschine f

percussion n Schlagzeug nt. **~ instrument** n Schlaginstrument nt

perennial a (problem) immer wiederkehrend □ n (Bot) mehrjährige Pflanze f

perfect¹ a perfekt, vollkommen; (fam: utter) völlig □ n (Gram) Perfekt nt

perfect² vt vervollkommnen. **~ion** n Vollkommenheit f

perforate vt perforieren; (make a hole in) durchlöchern

perform vt ausführen; erfüllen (duty); (Theat) aufführen (play); spielen (role) □ vi (Theat) auftreten; (Techn) laufen. **~ance** n Aufführung f; (at theatre) Vorstellung f; (Techn) Leistung f. **~er** n Künstler(in) m(f)

perfume n Parfüm nt; (smell) Duft m

perfunctory a flüchtig

perhaps adv vielleicht

peril n Gefahr f. **~ous** a gefährlich

perimeter n [äußere] Grenze f; (Geom) Umfang m

period n Periode f; (Sch) Stunde f; (full stop) Punkt m. **~ic** a periodisch. **~ical** n Zeitschrift f

peripher|al a nebensächlich. **~y** n Peripherie f

periscope n Periskop nt

perish vi (rubber:) verrotten; (food:) verderben; (die) ums Leben kommen

perjur|e vt **~e oneself** einen Meineid leisten. **~y** n Meineid m

perm n Dauerwelle f

permanent a ständig; (job, address) fest. **~ly** adv ständig; (work, live) dauernd, permanent; (employed) fest

permeate vt durchdringen

permissible a erlaubt

permission n Erlaubnis f

permissive a permissiv

permit¹ vt erlauben (s.o. jdm)

permit² n Genehmigung f
perpendicular a senkrecht □n Senkrechte f
perpetrat|e vt begehen. **~or** n Täter m
perpetual a ständig, dauernd
perpetuate vt bewahren
perplex vt verblüffen
persecut|e vt verfolgen. **~ion** n Verfolgung f
perseverance n Ausdauer f
persevere vi beharrlich weitermachen
Persia n Persien nt
Persian a persisch; ⟨cat, carpet⟩ Perser-
persist vi beharrlich weitermachen; ⟨continue⟩ anhalten; ⟨view:⟩ weiter bestehen. **~ent** a beharrlich; ⟨continuous⟩ anhaltend
person n Person f; in **~** persönlich
personal a persönlich. **~ hygiene** n Körperpflege f
personality n Persönlichkeit f
personnel n Personal nt
perspective n Perspektive f
persp|iration n Schweiß m. **~ire** vi schwitzen
persua|de vt überreden; ⟨convince⟩ überzeugen. **~sion** n Überredung f; ⟨powers of ~sion⟩ Überredungskunst f; ⟨belief⟩ Glaubensrichtung f
persuasive a beredsam; ⟨convincing⟩ überzeugend
pertinent a relevant (**to** für)
perturb vt beunruhigen
peruse vt lesen
pervade vt durchdringen
perverse a eigensinnig. **~ion** n Perversion f
pervert¹ vt verdrehen; verführen ⟨person⟩
pervert² n Perverse(r) m
perverted a abartig
pessimis|m n Pessimismus m. **~t** n Pessimist m. **~tic** a pessimistisch

pest n Schädling m; ⟨fam: person⟩ Nervensäge f
pester vt belästigen
pesticide n Schädlingsbekämpfungsmittel nt
pet n Haustier nt
petal n Blütenblatt nt
peter vi **~ out** allmählich aufhören
petition n Bittschrift f □vt eine Bittschrift richten an (+ acc)
pet name n Kosename m
petrif|y vt/i versteinern; **~ied** ⟨frightened⟩ vor Angst wie versteinert
petrol n Benzin nt
petroleum n Petroleum nt
petrol: ~-pump n Zapfsäule f. **~ station** n Tankstelle f. **~ tank** n Benzintank m
'pet shop n Tierhandlung f
petticoat n Unterrock m
petty a kleinlich. **~ 'cash** n Portokasse f
petulant a gekränkt
pew n [Kirchen]bank f
pewter n Zinn nt
phantom n Gespenst nt
pharmaceutical a pharmazeutisch
pharmac|ist n Apotheker(in) m(f). **~y** n Pharmazie f; ⟨shop⟩ Apotheke f
phase n Phase f □vt **~ in/out** allmählich einführen/abbauen
Ph.D. ⟨abbr of **D**octor of **Phi**losophy⟩ Dr. phil.
pheasant n Fasan m
phenomen|al a phänomenal. **~on** n Phänomen nt
philanthropic a menschenfreundlich
philately n Philatelie f, Briefmarkenkunde f
philharmonic n ⟨orchestra⟩ Philharmoniker pl
Philippines npl Philippinen pl
philistine n Banause m

philosopher n Philosoph m.
~ical a philosophisch. **~y** n Philosophie f

phlegm n (Med) Schleim m

phlegmatic a phlegmatisch

phobia n Phobie f

phone n Telefon nt □vt anrufen □vi telefonieren. **~ book** n Telefonbuch nt. **~ box** n Telefonzelle f. **~ card** n Telefonkarte f. **~ -in** n (Radio) Hörersendung f

phonetic a phonetisch. **~s** n Phonetik f

phosphorus n Phosphor m

photo n Foto nt, Aufnahme f. **~copier** n Fotokopiergerät nt. **~copy** n Fotokopie f □vt fotokopieren

photogenic a fotogen

photograph n Fotografie f, Aufnahme f □vt fotografieren

photographer n Fotograf(in) m(f). **~ic** a fotografisch. **~y** n Fotografie f

phrase n Redensart f. **~book** n Sprachführer m

physical a körperlich; ⟨geography, law⟩ physikalisch. **~ edu'cation** n Turnen nt

physician n Arzt m/ Ärztin f

physicist n Physiker(in) m(f). **~s** n Physik f

physiology n Physiologie f

physiotherapist n Physiotherapeut(in) m(f). **~y** n Physiotherapie f

physique n Körperbau m

pianist n Klavierspieler(in) m(f); ⟨professional⟩ Pianist(in) m(f)

piano n Klavier nt

pick¹ n Spitzhacke f

pick² n Auslese f; take one's ~ sich (dat) aussuchen □vt/i ⟨pluck⟩ pflücken; ⟨select⟩ wählen, sich (dat) aussuchen; **~ a quarrel** einen Streit anfangen. **~ on** vt wählen; ⟨fam: find fault with⟩ herumhacken auf (+ dat). **~ up** vt in die Hand nehmen; ⟨off the

ground⟩ aufheben; hochnehmen ⟨baby⟩; ⟨learn⟩ lernen; ⟨acquire⟩ erwerben; ⟨buy⟩ kaufen; ⟨Teleph⟩ abnehmen ⟨receiver⟩; auffangen ⟨signal⟩; ⟨collect⟩ abholen; aufnehmen ⟨passengers; spieler⟩; aufgreifen ⟨criminal⟩; sich holen ⟨illness⟩; ⟨fam⟩ aufgabeln ⟨girl⟩

'pickaxe n Spitzhacke f

picket n Streikposten m □vt Streikposten aufstellen vor (+ dat). **~ line** n Streikpostenkette f

pick: ~pocket n Taschendieb m. **~-up** n ⟨truck⟩ Lieferwagen m

picnic n Picknick nt

picture n Bild nt; ⟨film⟩ Film m; □vt ⟨imagine⟩ sich (dat) vorstellen

picturesque a malerisch

pie n Pastete f; ⟨fruit⟩ Kuchen m

piece n Stück nt; ⟨of set⟩ Teil m; ⟨in game⟩ Stein m; ⟨Journ⟩ Artikel m □vt **~ together** zusammensetzen; ⟨fig⟩ zusammenstückeln. **~meal** adv stückweise. **~work** n Akkordarbeit f

pier n Pier m; ⟨pillar⟩ Pfeiler m

pierce vt durchstechen

pig n Schwein nt

pigeon n Taube f. **~hole** n Fach nt

piggy n ⟨fam⟩ Schweinchen nt. **~back** n give s.o. a **~back** jdn huckepack tragen. **~ bank** n Sparschwein nt

pigment n Pigment nt

pig: ~sty n Schweinestall m. **~tail** n ⟨fam⟩ Zopf m

pike n inv ⟨fish⟩ Hecht m

pilchard n Sardine f

pile n Haufen m □vt **~ sth on to** sth etw auf etw (acc) häufen

piles npl Hämorrhoiden pl

'pile-up n Massenkarambolage f

pilgrim n Pilger(in) f. **~age** n Pilgerfahrt f

pill n Pille f

pillar n Säule f. **~-box** n Briefkasten m

pillion n Sozius[sitz] m

pillory vt anprangern

pillow n Kopfkissen nt. **~ case** n Kopfkissenbezug m

pilot n Pilot m; (Naut) Lotse m □ vt fliegen ⟨plane⟩; lotsen ⟨ship⟩. **~-light** n Zündflamme f

pimp n Zuhälter m

pimple n Pickel m

pin n Stecknadel f; (Techn) Bolzen m, Stift m; (Med) Nagel m; **I have ~s and needles in my leg** (fam) mein Bein ist eingeschlafen □ vt anstecken (to/on an + acc); (sewing) stecken; ⟨hold down⟩ festhalten

pinafore n Schürze f

pincers npl Kneifzange f

pinch n Kniff m; (of salt) Prise f; **at a ~** (fam) zur Not □ vt kneifen, zwicken; (fam: steal) klauen

pincushion n Nadelkissen nt

pine[1] n (tree) Kiefer f

pine[2] vi **~ for** sich sehnen nach; **~ away** sich verzehren

pineapple n Ananas f

ping-pong n Tischtennis nt

pink a rosa

pinnacle n Gipfel m

pint n Pint nt (0,57 l)

pin-up n Pin-up-Girl nt

pioneer n Pionier m

pious a fromm

pip n (seed) Kern m

pipe n Pfeife f; (for water, gas) Rohr nt. **pipe: ~-dream** n Luftschloß nt. **~-line** n Pipeline f; **in the ~ line** (fam) in Vorbereitung

piquant a pikant

pirate n Pirat m

Pisces n (Astr) Fische pl

piss vi (sl) pissen

pistol n Pistole f

piston n (Techn) Kolben m

pit n Grube f; (for orchestra) Orchestergraben m

pitch[1] n (steepness) Schräge f; (of voice) Stimmlage f; (of sound) [Ton]höhe f; (Sport) Feld nt; (of street-trader) Standplatz m; (fig: degree) Grad m □ vt werfen; aufschlagen ⟨tent⟩ □ vi fallen

pitch[2] n (tar) Pech nt. **~-'black** a pechschwarz. **~-'dark** a stockdunkel

pitcher n Krug m

pitchfork n Heugabel f

pitfall n (fig) Falle f

pith n (Bot) Mark nt; (of orange) weiße Haut f; (fig) Wesentliche(s) nt

pithy a prägnant

pitiful a bedauernswert. **~less** a mitleidlos

pittance n Hungerlohn m

pity n Mitleid nt, Erbarmen nt; **[what a] ~!** [wie] schade! **take ~ on** sich erbarmen über (+ acc) □ vt bemitleiden

pivot n Drehzapfen m; (fig) Angelpunkt m □ vi sich drehen (on um)

pizza n Pizza f

placard n Plakat nt

placate vt beschwichtigen

place n Platz m; (spot) Stelle f; (town) Ort m; (fam: house) Haus nt; **out of ~** fehl am Platze; **take ~** stattfinden □ vt setzen; (upright) stellen; (flat) legen; (remember) unterbringen (fam). **~-mat** n Set nt

placid a gelassen

plagiarism n Plagiat nt

plague n Pest f □ vt plagen

plaice n inv Scholle f

plain a klar; (simple) einfach; (not pretty) nicht hübsch; (not patterned) einfarbig; ⟨chocolate⟩ zartbitter □ adv (simply) einfach □ n Ebene f; (Knitting) linke Masche f

plaintiff n (Jur) Kläger(in) m(f)

plaintive a klagend

plait n Zopf m □ vt flechten

plan n Plan m □ vt planen
plane¹ n (tree) Platane f
plane² n Flugzeug nt; (Geom & fig) Ebene f
plane³ n (Techn) Hobel m
planet n Planet m
plank n Brett nt; (thick) Planke f
planning n Planung f. ~ **permission** n Baugenehmigung f
plant n Pflanze f; (Techn) Anlage f; (factory) Werk nt □ vt pflanzen; (place in position) setzen. ~ **ation** n Plantage f
plaque n [Gedenk]tafel f; (on teeth) Zahnbelag m
plasma n Plasma nt
plaster n Verputz m; (sticking ~) Pflaster nt; [of Paris] Gips m □ vt verputzen (wall); (cover) bedecken mit. ~ **er** n Gipser m
plastic n Kunststoff m, Plastik nt □ a Kunststoff-, Plastik-; (malleable) formbar, plastisch
plastic 'surgery n plastische Chirurgie f
plate n Teller m; (flat sheet) Platte f; (with name, number) Schild nt; (gold and silverware) vergoldete/versilberte Ware f; (in book) Tafel f □ vt (with gold) vergolden; (with silver) versilbern
plateau n Hochebene f
platform n Plattform f; (stage) Podium nt; (Rail) Bahnsteig m; ~ **5** Gleis 5
platinum n Platin nt
platitude n Platitüde f
platonic a platonisch
platoon n (Mil) Zug m
plausible a plausibel
play n Spiel nt; [Theater]stück nt; (Radio) Hörspiel nt; (TV) Fernsehspiel nt □ vt/i spielen; ausspielen (card); ~ **safe** sichergehen
play: ~ **boy** n Playboy m. ~ **er** n Spieler(in) m(f). ~ **ful** a verspielt. ~ **ground** n Spielplatz m;

(Sch) Schulhof m. ~ **group** n Kindergarten m
playing: ~ -**card** n Spielkarte f. ~ -**field** n Sportplatz m
play: ~ -**mate** n Spielkamerad m. ~ -**pen** n Laufstall m. ~ **thing** n Spielzeug nt. ~ **wright** n Dramatiker m
plc abbr (public limited company) GmbH
plea n Bitte f
plead vt vorschützen; (Jur) vertreten (case) □ vi flehen (for um); ~ **guilty** sich schuldig bekennen; ~ **with s.o.** jdn anflehen
pleasant a angenehm; (person) nett
please adv bitte □ vt gefallen (+ dat); ~ **s.o.** jdm eine Freude machen. ~ **d** a erfreut; **be ~d with/about sth** sich über etw (acc) freuen
pleasure n Vergnügen nt; (joy) Freude f; **with ~** gern[e]
pleat n Falte f
pledge n Pfand nt; (promise) Versprechen nt □ vt verpfänden; versprechen
plentiful a reichlich
plenty n eine Menge; (enough) reichlich; ~ **of money/people** viel Geld/viele Leute
pleurisy n Rippenfellentzündung f
pliable a biegsam
pliers npl [Flach]zange f
plight n [Not]lage f
plimsolls npl Turnschuhe pl
plod vi trotten
plot n Komplott nt; (of novel) Handlung f; ~ **of land** Stück nt Land □ vt einzeichnen □ vi ein Komplott schmieden
plough n Pflug m □ vt/i pflügen. ~ **back** vt (Comm) wieder investieren
ploy n (fam) Trick m

pluck n zupfen; rupfen ⟨bird⟩; pflücken ⟨flower⟩; ~ **up courage** Mut fassen

plug n Stöpsel m; ⟨wood⟩ Zapfen m; ⟨cotton wool⟩ Bausch m; ⟨Electr⟩ Stecker m; ⟨Auto⟩ Zündkerze f; ⟨fam: advertisement⟩ Schleichwerbung f □vt zustopfen; ⟨fam: advertise⟩ Schleichwerbung machen für

plum n Pflaume f

plumage n Gefieder nt

plumb adv lotrecht □vt loten. ~ **in** vt installieren

plumb|er n Klempner m. ~**ing** n Wasserleitungen pl

'plumb-line n [Blei]lot nt

plume n Feder f

plump a mollig

plunder vt plündern

plunge vt/i tauchen

plu'perfect n Plusquamperfekt nt

plural n Mehrzahl f, Plural m

plus prep plus (+ dat) □a Plus- □n Pluszeichen nt; ⟨advantage⟩ Plus nt

plush[y] a luxuriös

ply vt ausüben ⟨trade⟩; ~ **s.o. with drink** jdm ein Glas nach dem anderen eingießen. ~**wood** n Sperrholz nt

p.m. adv ⟨abbr of post meridiem⟩ nachmittags

pneumatic a pneumatisch. ~ **'drill** n Preßlufthammer m

pneumonia n Lungenentzündung f

poach vt ⟨Culin⟩ pochieren; ⟨steal⟩ wildern. ~**er** n Wilddieb m

pocket n Tasche f □vt einstecken. ~**-money** n Taschengeld nt

pod n Hülse f

poem n Gedicht nt

poet n Dichter(in) m(f). ~**ic** a dichterisch

poetry n Dichtung f

poignant a ergreifend

point n Punkt m; ⟨sharp end⟩ Spitze f; ⟨meaning⟩ Sinn m; ⟨purpose⟩ Zweck m; ⟨Electr⟩ Steckdose f; ~**s** pl ⟨Rail⟩ Weiche f; ~ **of view** Standpunkt m; **good/ bad** ~**s** gute/schlechte Seiten; **what is the ~?** wozu? **the ~ is** es geht darum □vt richten (**at** auf + acc); ausfugen ⟨brickwork⟩ □vi deuten (**at/to** auf + acc); ⟨with finger⟩ mit dem Finger zeigen. ~ **out** vt zeigen auf (+ acc)

point-'blank a aus nächster Entfernung; ⟨fig⟩ rundweg

point|ed a spitz; ⟨question⟩ gezielt. ~**less** a zwecklos, sinnlos

poise n Haltung f. ~**d** a ⟨confident⟩ selbstsicher

poison n Gift nt □vt vergiften. ~**ous** a giftig

poke vt stoßen; schüren ⟨fire⟩; ⟨put⟩ stecken; ~ **fun at** sich lustig machen über (+ acc)

poker[1] n Schüreisen nt

poker[2] n ⟨Cards⟩ Poker nt

Poland n Polen nt

polar a Polar-. ~**'bear** n Eisbär m. ~**ize** vt polarisieren

Pole[1] n Pole m/Polin f

pole[1] n Stange f

pole[2] n ⟨Geog, Electr⟩ Pol m

'polecat n Iltis m

'pole-star n Polarstern m

'pole-vault n Stabhochsprung m

police npl Polizei f

police: ~**man** n Polizist m. ~ **station** n Polizeiwache f. ~**-woman** n Polizistin f

policy[1] n Politik f

policy[2] n ⟨insurance⟩ Police f

polio n Kinderlähmung f

Polish a polnisch

polish n ⟨shine⟩ Glanz m; ⟨for shoes⟩ [Schuh]creme f; ⟨for floor⟩ Bohnerwachs m; ⟨for furniture⟩ Politur f; ⟨for silver⟩ Putzmittel nt; ⟨for nails⟩ Lack m; ⟨fig⟩ Schliff m □vt polieren; bohnern ⟨floor⟩

polite a höflich
politic a ratsam
politic|al a politisch. ~**ian** n Politiker(in) m(f)
politics n Politik f
polka n Polka f
poll n Abstimmung f; (election) Wahl f; [opinion] ~ [Meinungs]-umfrage f□vt erhalten ⟨votes⟩
pollen n Blütenstaub m, Pollen m
polling : ~**-booth** n Wahlkabine f. ~**-station** n Wahllokal nt
'**poll tax** n Kopfsteuer f
pollutant n Schadstoff m
pollut|e vt verschmutzen. ~**ion** n Verschmutzung f
polo n Polo nt. ~**-neck** n Rollkragen m. ~**-shirt** n Polohemd nt
polyester n Polyester m
polystyrene (P) n Polystyrol nt; (for packing) Styropor (P) nt
polytechnic n ≈ technische Hochschule f
polythene n Polyäthylen nt
polyun'saturated a mehrfachungesättigt
pomegranate n Granatapfel m
pompous a großspurig
pond n Teich m
ponder vi nachdenken
ponderous a schwerfällig
pony n Pony nt. ~**-tail** n Pferdeschwanz m. ~**-trekking** n Ponyreiten nt
poodle n Pudel m
pool¹ n [Schwimm]becken nt; (pond) Teich m; (of blood) Lache f
pool² n (common fund) [gemeinsame] Kasse f; ~**s** pl [Fußball]-toto nt
poor a arm; (not good) schlecht □npl the ~ die Armen
pop¹ n Knall m; (drink) Brause f □vt (pp: pop) stecken (**in** in + acc) □vi knallen; (burst) platzen. ~ **in** vi (fam) reinschauen
pop² n (fam) Popmusik f, Pop m
'**popcorn** n Puffmais m
pope n Papst m

poplar n Pappel f
poppy n Mohn m
popular a beliebt, populär; ⟨belief⟩ volkstümlich. ~**ity** n Beliebtheit f, Popularität f
population n Bevölkerung f
porcelain n Porzellan nt
porch n Vorbau m
porcupine n Stachelschwein nt
pore¹ n Pore f
pore² vi ~ **over** studieren
pork n Schweinefleisch nt
pornograph|ic a pornographisch. ~**y** n Pornographie f
porous a porös
porpoise n Tümmler m
porridge n Haferbrei m
port¹ n Hafen m; (town) Hafenstadt f
port² n (Naut) Backbord nt
port³ n (wine) Portwein m
portable a tragbar
porter n Portier m; (for luggage) Gepäckträger m
portfolio n Mappe f; (Comm) Portefeuille nt
'**porthole** n Bullauge nt
portion n Portion f
portrait n Porträt nt
portray vt darstellen
Portugal n Portugal nt. ~**uese** a portugiesisch □n Portugiese m/ -giesin f
pose n Pose f□vt aufwerfen ⟨problem⟩; stellen ⟨question⟩ □vi posieren; (for painter) Modell stehen
posh a (fam) feudal
position n Platz m; (posture) Haltung f; (job) Stelle f; (situation) Lage f, Situation f; (status) Stellung f
positive a positiv; (definite) eindeutig; (real) ausgesprochen □n Positiv nt
possess vt besitzen. ~**ion** n Besitz m; ~**ions** pl Sachen pl
possibility n Möglichkeit f

possib|le *a* möglich. **~ly** *adv* möglicherweise

post[1] *n* (*pole*) Pfosten *m* □*vt* anschlagen ⟨*notice*⟩

post[2] *n* (*place of duty*) Posten *m*; (*job*) Stelle *f* □*vt* postieren; (*transfer*) versetzen

post[3] *n* (*mail*) Post *f*; **by ~** mit der Post □*vt* aufgeben ⟨*letter*⟩; (*send by ~*) mit der Post schicken

postage *n* Porto *nt*. **~ stamp** *n* Briefmarke *f*

postal order *n* ≈ Geldanweisung *f*

post: ~-box *n* Briefkasten *m*. **~card** *n* Postkarte *f*. (*picture*) Ansichtskarte *f*. **~code** *n* Postleitzahl *f*. **~'date** *vt* vordatieren

poster *n* Plakat *nt*

posterity *n* Nachwelt *f*

posthumous *a* postum

post: ~man *n* Briefträger *m*. **~mark** *n* Poststempel *m*

post-mortem *n* Obduktion *f*

'post office *n* Post *f*

postpone *vt* aufschieben; **~ until** verschieben auf (+ *acc*). **~ment** *n* Verschiebung *f*

postscript *n* Nachschrift *f*

posture *n* Haltung *f*

pot *n* Topf *m*; (*for tea, coffee*) Kanne *f*

potassium *n* Kalium *nt*

potato *n* Kartoffel *f*

poten|cy *n* Stärke *f*. **~t** *a* stark

potential *a* potentiell □*n* Potential *nt*

pot: ~hole *n* Höhle *f*; (*in road*) Schlagloch *nt*. **~holer** *n* Höhlenforscher *m*

potter *n* Töpfer(in) *m* (*f*). **~y** *n* Töpferei *f*; (*articles*) Töpferwaren *pl*

pouch *n* Beutel *m*

poultry *n* Geflügel *nt*

pounce *vi* zuschlagen; **~ on** sich stürzen auf (+ *acc*)

pound[1] *n* (*money & 0.454 kg*) Pfund *nt*

pound[2] *vt* hämmern □*vi* ⟨*heart:*⟩ hämmern; (*run heavily*) stampfen

pour *vt* gießen; einschenken ⟨*drink*⟩ □*vi* strömen; (*with rain*) gießen

pout *vi* einen Schmollmund machen

poverty *n* Armut *f*

powder *n* Pulver *nt*; (*cosmetic*) Puder *m* □*vt* pudern

power *n* Macht *f*; (*strength*) Kraft *f*; (*Electr*) Strom *m*; (*nuclear*) Energie *f*; (*Math*) Potenz *f*. **~ cut** *n* Stromsperre *f*. **~ful** *a* mächtig; (*strong*) stark. **~less** *a* machtlos. **~-station** *n* Kraftwerk *nt*

practicable *a* durchführbar

practical *a* praktisch. **~ 'joke** *n* Streich *m*

practice *n* Praxis *f*; (*custom*) Brauch *m*; (*habit*) Gewohnheit *f*; (*exercise*) Übung *f*; (*Sport*) Training *nt*

practise *vt* üben; (*carry out*) praktizieren; ausüben ⟨*profession*⟩ □*vi* üben; ⟨*doctor:*⟩ praktizieren. **~d** *a* geübt

pragmatic *a* pragmatisch

praise *n* Lob *nt* □*vt* loben

pram *n* Kinderwagen *m*

prawn *n* Garnele *f*, Krabbe *f*. **~ 'cocktail** *n* Krabbencocktail *m*

pray *vi* beten. **~er** *n* Gebet *nt*

preach *vt/i* predigen. **~er** *n* Prediger *m*

preamble *n* Einleitung *f*

precarious *a* unsicher

precaution *n* Vorsichtsmaßnahme *f*; **as a ~** zur Vorsicht. **~ary** *a* Vorsichts-

precede *vt* vorangehen (+ *dat*)

precedent *n* Präzedenzfall *m*

preceding *a* vorhergehend

precinct *n* Bereich *m*

precious *a* kostbar

precipice *n* Steilabfall *m*

precipitate[1] *a* voreilig

precipitat|e[2] *vt* schleudern; *(fig: accelerate)* beschleunigen. ~**ion** *n (Meteorol)* Niederschlag *m*

précis *n* Zusammenfassung *f*

precis|e *a* genau. ~**ion** *n* Genauigkeit *f*

preclude *vt* ausschließen

precocious *a* frühreif

precon'ception *n* vorgefaßte Meinung *f*

precursor *n* Vorläufer *m*

predator *n* Raubtier *nt*

predecessor *n* Vorgänger(in) *m(f)*

predicament *n* Zwangslage *f*

predicat|e *(Gram)* Prädikat *nt*. ~**ive** *a* prädikativ

predict *vt* voraussagen. ~**able** *a* voraussehbar; *(person)* berechenbar. ~**ion** *n* Voraussage *f*

pre'domin|**ant** *a* vorherrschend. ~**ate** *vi* vorherrschen

pre-empt *vt* zuvorkommen (+ *dat*)

prefabricated *a* vorgefertigt

preface *n* Vorwort *nt*

prefect *n* Präfekt *m*

prefer *vt* vorziehen; **I ~ to walk** ich gehe lieber zu Fuß

preferen|**ce** *n* Vorzug *m.* ~**tial** *a* bevorzugt

prefix *n* Vorsilbe *f*

pregnan|**cy** *n* Schwangerschaft *f*. ~**t** *a* schwanger; *(animal)* trächtig

prehi'storic *a* prähistorisch

prejudice *n* Vorurteil *nt*; *(bias)* Voreingenommenheit *f* □ *vt* einnehmen (**against** gegen). ~**d** *a* voreingenommen

preliminary *a* Vor-

prelude *n* Vorspiel *nt*

pre-'marital *a* vorehelich

premature *a* vorzeitig; *(birth)* Früh-

pre'meditated *a* vorsätzlich

premier *a* führend □ *n (Pol)* Premier[minister] *m*

première *n* Premiere *f*

premises *npl* Räumlichkeiten *pl*; **on the ~** im Haus

premiss *n* Prämisse *f*

premium *n* Prämie *f*; **be at a ~** hoch im Kurs stehen

preparation *n* Vorbereitung *f*; *(substance)* Präparat *nt*

prepare *vt* vorbereiten; anrichten *(meal)* □ *vi* sich vorbereiten (**for** auf + *acc*)

preposition *n* Präposition *f*

preposterous *a* absurd

prerequisite *n* Voraussetzung *f*

prerogative *n* Vorrecht *nt*

Presbyterian *a* presbyterianisch □ *n* Presbyterianer(in) *m(f)*

prescribe *vt* vorschreiben; *(Med)* verschreiben

prescription *n (Med)* Rezept *nt*

presence *n* Anwesenheit *f*; ~ **of mind** Geistesgegenwart *f*

present[1] *a* gegenwärtig; **be ~** anwesend sein; *(occur)* vorkommen □ *n* Gegenwart *f*; *(Gram)* Präsens *nt*; **at ~** zur Zeit

present[2] *n (gift)* Geschenk *nt*

present[3] *vt* überreichen; *(show)* zeigen; vorlegen *(cheque)*; *(introduce)* vorstellen; ~ **s.o. with sth** jdm etw überreichen

presentation *n* Überreichung *f*. ~ **ceremony** *n* Verleihungszeremonie *f*

presently *adv* nachher

preservation *n* Erhaltung *f*

preservative *n* Konservierungsmittel *nt*

preserve *vt* erhalten; *(Culin)* konservieren; einmachen *(bottle)*

preside *vi* den Vorsitz haben (**over** bei)

presidency *n* Präsidentschaft *f*

president *n* Präsident *m.* ~**ial** *a* Präsidenten-; *(election)* Präsidentschafts-

press *n* Presse *f* □ *vt/i* drücken; drücken auf (+ *acc*) *(button)*; pressen *(flower)*; *(iron)* bügeln;

(urge) bedrängen; ~ **for** drängen auf (+ *acc*)

press: ~ **cutting** *n* Zeitungsausschnitt *m*. ~**ing** *a* dringend. ~**-stud** *n* Druckknopf *m*. ~**-up** *n* Liegestütz *m*

pressure *n* Druck *m*. ~**-cooker** *n* Schnellkochtopf *m*. ~ **group** *n* Interessengruppe *f*

pressurize *vt* Druck ausüben auf (+ *acc*)

prestige *n* Prestige *nt*

presumably *adv* vermutlich

presume *vt* vermuten; ~ **to do sth** sich (*dat*) anmaßen, etw zu tun

presumpt|ion *n* Vermutung *f*; *(boldness)* Anmaßung *f*. ~**uous** *a* anmaßend

presup'pose *vt* voraussetzen

pretence *n* Verstellung *f*

pretend *vt (claim)* vorgeben; ~ **that** so tun, als ob; ~ **to be** sich ausgeben als

pretentious *a* protzig

pretext *n* Vorwand *m*

pretty *a* hübsch □*adv (fam: fairly)* ziemlich

pretzel *n* Brezel *f*

prevail *vi* siegen; *(custom:)* vorherrschen

prevalent *a* vorherrschend

prevent *vt* verhindern, verhüten; ~ **s.o. [from] doing sth** jdn daran hindern, etw zu tun. ~**ion** *n* Verhinderung *f*, Verhütung *f*

preview *n* Voraufführung *f*

previous *a* vorhergehend. ~**ly** *adv* vorher, früher

prey *n* Beute *f*; **bird of** ~ Raubvogel *m*

price *n* Preis *m* □*vt (Comm)* auszeichnen. ~**less** *a* unschätzbar; *(fig)* unbezahlbar

prick *vt/i* stechen; ~ **up one's ears** die Ohren spitzen

prickly *a* stachelig; *(sensation)* stechend

pride *n* Stolz *m*; *(arrogance)* Hochmut *m*; *(of lions)* Rudel *nt* □*vt* ~ **oneself on** stolz sein auf (+ *acc*)

priest *n* Priester *m*

primarily *adv* hauptsächlich

primary *a* Haupt-. ~ **school** *n* Grundschule *f*

prime¹ *a* Haupt-; *(first-rate)* erstklassig □*n* **be in one's** ~ in den besten Jahren sein

prime² *vt* scharf machen *⟨bomb⟩*; grundieren *⟨surface⟩*; *(fig)* instruieren

Prime Minister *n* Premierminister(in) *m(f)*

primeval *a* Ur-

primitive *a* primitiv

primrose *n* gelbe Schlüsselblume *f*

prince *n* Prinz *m*

princess *n* Prinzessin *f*

principal *a* Haupt- □*n (Sch)* Rektor(in) *m(f)*

principality *n* Fürstentum *nt*

principally *adv* hauptsächlich

principle *n* Prinzip *nt*, Grundsatz *m*; **in/on** ~ im/aus Prinzip

print *n* Druck *m*; *(Phot)* Abzug *m*; **in** ~ gedruckt; *(available)* erhältlich; **out of** ~ vergriffen □*vt* drucken; *(write in capitals)* in Druckschrift schreiben; *(Computing)* ausdrucken; *(Phot)* abziehen. ~**ed matter** *n* Drucksache *f*

print|er *n* Drucker *m*. ~**ing** *n* Druck *m*

'printout *n* Ausdruck *m*

prior *a* frühere(r,s); ~ **to** vor (+ *dat*)

priority *n* Priorität *f*, Vorrang *m*; *(matter)* vordringliche Sache *f*

prism *n* Prisma *nt*

prison *n* Gefängnis *nt*. ~**er** *n* Gefangene(r) *m/f*

privacy *n* Privatsphäre *f*; **have no** ~ nie für sich sein

private *a* privat; *(confidential)* vertraulich; *⟨car, secretary⟩* Privat- □*n (Mil)* [einfacher] Soldat *m*

privatize vt privatisieren
privilege n Privileg nt. ~d a privilegiert
prize n Preis m □vt schätzen. ~-**giving** n Preisverleihung f. ~-**winner** n Preisgewinner(in) m(f)
pro n (fam) Profi m; **the ~s and cons** das Für und Wider
probability n Wahrscheinlichkeit f
probable a wahrscheinlich
probation n (Jur) Bewährung f. ~**ary** a Probe-; ~**ary period** Probezeit f
probe vt/i ~ [into] untersuchen
problem n Problem nt; (Math) Textaufgabe f. ~**atic** a problematisch
procedure n Verfahren nt
proceed vi gehen; (in vehicle) fahren; (continue) weitergehen/-fahren; (speaking) fortfahren; (act) verfahren □vt ~ **to do sth** anfangen, etw zu tun
proceedings npl Verfahren nt; (Jur) Prozeß m
proceeds npl Erlös m
process n Prozeß m; (procedure) Verfahren nt □vt verarbeiten; (Admin) bearbeiten; (Phot) entwickeln
procession n Umzug m, Prozession f
proclaim vt ausrufen
procure vt beschaffen
prod vt stoßen; (fig) einen Stoß geben (+ dat)
prodigal a verschwenderisch
prodigious a gewaltig
prodigy n [infant] ~ Wunderkind nt
produce[1] n landwirtschaftliche Erzeugnisse pl
produce[2] vt erzeugen, produzieren; (manufacture) herstellen; (bring out) hervorholen; (cause) hervorrufen; inszenieren ⟨play⟩; (TV) redigieren. ~**r** n Erzeuger

m, Produzent m; Hersteller m; (Theat) Regisseur m; (TV) Redakteur(in) m(f)
product n Erzeugnis nt, Produkt nt. ~**ion** n Produktion f; (Theat) Inszenierung f
productive a produktiv; ⟨talks⟩ fruchtbar. ~**ity** n Produktivität f
profane a weltlich; (blasphemous) [gottes]lästerlich
profess vt behaupten
profession n Beruf m. ~**al** a beruflich; (not amateur) Berufs-; (expert) fachmännisch; (Sport) professionell □n Fachmann m; (Sport) Profi m
professor n Professor m
proficien|cy n Können nt. ~**t** a **be ~t in** beherrschen
profile n Profil nt; (character study) Porträt nt
profit n Gewinn m, Profit m □vi ~ **from** profitieren von. ~**able** a gewinnbringend; (fig) nutzbringend
profound a tief
profuse a üppig; (fig) überschwenglich
program n Programm nt □vt programmieren
programme n Programm nt; (TV) Sendung f. ~**r** n Programmierer(in) m(f)
progress[1] n Vorankommen nt; (fig) Fortschritt m; **in ~** im Gange
progress[2] vi vorankommen; (fig) fortschreiten
progressive a fortschrittlich
prohibit vt verbieten (s.o. jdm)
project[1] n Projekt nt; (Sch) Arbeit f
project[2] vt projizieren ⟨film⟩; (plan) planen □vi (jut out) vorstehen
projectile n Geschoß nt
projector n Projektor m
proletariat n Proletariat nt
prolific a fruchtbar; (fig) produktiv

prologue n Prolog m

prolong vt verlängern

promenade n Promenade f

prominent a vorstehend; (important) prominent; (conspicuous) auffällig; ⟨place⟩ gut sichtbar

promiscuity n Promiskuität f. **~ous** a be **~ous** häufig den Partner wechseln

promise n Versprechen nt ▢vt/i versprechen (s.o. jdm); the P ~ ed Land das Gelobte Land. **~ing** a vielversprechend

promote vt befördern; (advance) fördern; (publicize) Reklame machen für. **~ion** n Beförderung f; (Sport) Aufstieg m; (Comm) Reklame f

prompt a prompt, unverzüglich; (punctual) pünktlich ▢adv pünktlich ▢vt/i veranlassen (to zu); (Theat) soufflieren (+ dat)

pronoun n Fürwort nt, Pronomen nt

pronounce vt aussprechen; (declare) erklären

pronunciation n Aussprache f

proof n Beweis m; (Typ) Korrekturbogen m

prop[1] n Stütze f ▢vt **~ up** stützen; **~ against** ⟨lean⟩ lehnen an (+ acc)

prop[2] n (Theat, fam) Requisit nt

propaganda n Propaganda f

propel vt [an]treiben. **~ler** n Propeller m. **~ling 'pencil** n Drehbleistift m

proper a richtig; (decent) anständig. **~ 'name**, **~ 'noun** n Eigenname m

property n Eigentum nt; (quality) Eigenschaft f; (Theat) Requisit nt; (land) [Grund]besitz m; (house) Haus nt

prophecy n Prophezeiung f

prophesy vt prophezeien

prophet n Prophet m

proportion n Verhältnis nt; (share) Teil m; **~s** pl Proportionen; (dimensions) Maße. **~al** a proportional

proposal n Vorschlag m; (of marriage) [Heirats]antrag m

propose vt vorschlagen; (intend) vorhaben; einbringen ⟨motion⟩; ausbringen ⟨toast⟩ ▢vi einen Heiratsantrag machen

proposition n Vorschlag m

proprietor n Inhaber(in) m(f)

propulsion n Antrieb m

prosaic a prosaisch

prose n Prosa f

prosecute vt strafrechtlich verfolgen. **~ion** n strafrechtliche Verfolgung f; the **~ion** die Anklage. **~or** n [Public] P~or Staatsanwalt m

prospect n Aussicht f

prospective a (future) zukünftig

prospectus n Prospekt m

prosper vi gedeihen, florieren; ⟨person⟩ Erfolg haben. **~ity** n Wohlstand m

prosperous a wohlhabend

prostitute n Prostituierte f. **~ion** n Prostitution f

prostrate a ausgestreckt

protagonist n Kämpfer m; (fig) Protagonist m

protect vt schützen (from vor + dat); beschützen ⟨person⟩. **~ion** n Schutz m

protégé n Schützling m, Protegé m

protein n Eiweiß n

protest[1] n Protest m

protest[2] vi protestieren

Protestant a protestantisch, evangelisch ▢n Protestant(in) m(f), Evangelische(r) m(f)

protester n Protestierende(r) m/f

protocol n Protokoll nt

prototype n Prototyp m

protractor n Winkelmesser m

proud a stolz (of auf + acc)

prove vt beweisen

proverb n Sprichwort nt. **~ial** a sprichwörtlich

provide vt zur Verfügung stellen; spenden ⟨shade⟩; **~ s.o. with sth** jdn mit etw versorgen od versehen □vi **~ for** sorgen für

provided conj **~ [that]** vorausgesetzt [daß]

providence n Vorsehung f

providing conj **=** provided

provinc|e n Provinz f; (fig) Bereich m. **~ial** a provinziell

provision n Versorgung f (of mit); **~s** pl Lebensmittel pl. **~al** a vorläufig

provocat|ion n Provokation f. **~ive** a provozierend; (sexually) aufreizend

provoke vt provozieren

prow n Bug m

prowl vi herumschleichen

proximity n Nähe f

proxy n Stellvertreter(in) m(f); (power) Vollmacht f

prudent a umsichtig; (wise) klug

prudish a prüde

prune[1] n Backpflaume f

prune[2] vt beschneiden

psalm n Psalm m

pseudonym n Pseudonym nt

psychiatric a psychiatrisch

psychiatr|ist n Psychiater(in) m(f). **~y** n Psychiatrie f

psychic a übersinnlich

psychoa'nalysis n Psychoanalyse f

psychological a psychologisch; ⟨illness⟩ psychisch

psycholog|ist n Psychologe m/ -login f. **~y** n Psychologie f

psychopath n Psychopath(in) m(f)

P.T.O. abbr (please turn over) b.w.

pub n (fam) Kneipe f

puberty n Pubertät f

public a öffentlich □n the **~** die Öffentlichkeit

publication n Veröffentlichung f

public: **~ con'venience** n öffentliche Toilette f. **~ 'holiday** n gesetzlicher Feiertag m

publicity n Publicity f

publicize vt Reklame machen für

public: **~ 'school** n Privatschule f. **~-spirited** a be **~-spirited** Gemeinsinn haben. **~ 'transport** n öffentliche Verkehrsmittel pl

publish vt veröffentlichen. **~er** n Verleger(in) m(f); (firm) Verlag m. **~ing** n Verlagswesen nt

pudding n Pudding m; (course) Nachtisch m

puddle n Pfütze f

puff n (of wind) Hauch m; (of smoke) Wölkchen nt; (for powder) Quaste f □vt blasen, pusten. **~ pastry** n Blätterteig m

pull n Zug m; (jerk) Ruck m; (fam: influence) Einfluß m □vt ziehen; ziehen an (+dat) ⟨rope⟩; **~ a muscle** sich (dat) einen Muskel zerren; **~ oneself together** sich zusammennehmen; **~ s.o.'s leg** (fam) jdn auf den Arm nehmen. **~ off** vt abziehen; (fam) schaffen. **~ through** □vi durchziehen □vi (recover) durchkommen

pulley n (Techn) Rolle f

pullover n Pullover m

pulp n Brei m; (of fruit) [Frucht]-fleisch nt

pulpit n Kanzel f

pulse n Puls m

pulses npl Hülsenfrüchte pl

pumice n Bimsstein m

pump n Pumpe f □vt pumpen; (fam) aushorchen. **~ up** vt hochpumpen; (inflate) aufpumpen

pumpkin n Kürbis m

pun n Wortspiel nt

punch[1] n Faustschlag m; (device) Locher m □vt boxen; lochen ⟨ticket⟩; stanzen ⟨hole⟩

punch[2] n (drink) Bowle f

punctual *a* pünktlich. ~**ity** *n* Pünktlichkeit *f*

punctuat|e *vt* mit Satzzeichen versehen. ~**ion** *n* Interpunktion *f*. ~**ion mark** *n* Satzzeichen *nt*

puncture *n* Loch *nt*; (*tyre*) Reifenpanne *f* □*vt* durchstechen

pungent *a* scharf

punish *vt* bestrafen. ~**ment** *n* Strafe *f*

punt *n* (*boat*) Stechkahn *m*

pupil *n* Schüler(in) *m(f)*; (*of eye*) Pupille *f*

puppet *n* Puppe *f*; (*fig*) Marionette *f*

puppy *n* junger Hund *m*

purchase *n* Kauf *m*; (*leverage*) Hebelkraft *f* □*vt* kaufen

pure *a* rein

purée *n* Püree *nt*, Brei *m*

purgatory *n* (*Relig*) Fegefeuer *nt*; (*fig*) Hölle *f*

purge *n* (*Pol*) Säuberungsaktion *f* □*vt* reinigen; (*Pol*) säubern

purify *vt* reinigen

puritanical *a* puritanisch

purity *n* Reinheit *f*

purl *n* (*Knitting*) linke Masche *f*

purple *a* (dunkel)lila

purpose *n* Zweck *m*; (*intention*) Absicht *f*; (*determination*) Entschlossenheit *f*; **on** ~ absichtlich

purr *vi* schnurren

purse *n* Portemonnaie *nt*

pursue *vt* verfolgen; (*fig*) nachgehen (+ *dat*)

pursuit *n* Verfolgung *f*; Jagd *f*; (*pastime*) Beschäftigung *f*

pus *n* Eiter *m*

push *n* Stoß *m*, (*fam*) Schubs *m*; **get the** ~ (*fam*) hinausfliegen □*vt/i* schieben; (*press*) drücken; (*roughly*) stoßen; **be** ~**ed for time** (*fam*) unter Zeitdruck stehen. ~ **off** *vt* hinunterstoßen □*vi* (*fam: leave*) abhauen

push: ~**button** *n* Druckknopf *m*. ~**chair** *n* [Kinder]sportwagen *m*

pussy *n* Mieze *f*

put *vt* tun; (*place*) setzen; (*upright*) stellen; (*flat*) legen; (*express*) ausdrücken; (*say*) sagen; (*estimate*) schätzen (**at** + *acc*); ~ **aside** *or* **by** beiseite legen; ~ **one's foot down** (*fam*) energisch werden; (*Auto*) Gas geben □*vi* ~ **to sea** auslaufen □*a* **stay** ~ dableiben. ~ **down** *vt* hinsetzen/-stellen/-legen; (*suppress*) niederschlagen; (*kill*) töten; (*write*) niederschreiben; (*attribute*) zuschreiben (**to** *dat*). ~ **forward** *vt* vorbringen; vorstellen (*clock*). ~ **in** *vt* hineinsetzen/ -stellen/-legen; (*insert*) stecken; (*submit*) einreichen. ~ **off** *vt* ausmachen; (*postpone*) verschieben; ~ **s.o.** *off* jdn abbestellen; (*disconcert*) jdn aus der Fassung bringen; ~ **s.o.** *off* **sth** jdm etw verleiden. ~ **on** *vt* anziehen (*clothes, brake*); sich aufsetzen (*hat*); (*Culin*) aufsetzen; anmachen (*light*); aufführen (*play*); annehmen (*accent*). ~ **up** *vt* errichten (*building*); aufschlagen (*tent*); aufspannen (*umbrella*); anschlagen (*notice*); erhöhen (*price*); unterbringen (*guest*); ~ **s.o. up to sth** jdn zu etw anstiften □*vi* (*at hotel*) absteigen in (+ *dat*); ~ **up with sth** sich (*dat*) etw bieten lassen

putrid *a* faulig

putty *n* Kitt *m*

puzzle *n* Rätsel *nt*; (*jigsaw*) Puzzlespiel *nt* □*vt* **it** ~**s me** es ist mir rätselhaft □*vi* ~ **over** sich (*dat*) den Kopf zerbrechen über (+ *acc*)

pyjamas *npl* Schlafanzug *m*

pylon *n* Mast *m*

pyramid *n* Pyramide *f*

python *n* Pythonschlange *f*

Q

quack vi quaken
quadrangle n Viereck nt; (court)
Hof m
quadruped n Vierfüßer m
quadruple a vierfach □vt ver-
vierfachen □vi sich vervierfa-
chen. ~ts npl Vierlinge pl
Quaker n Quäker(in) m(f)
qualif|ication n Qualifikation f;
(reservation) Einschränkung f;
~ied a qualifiziert; (trained)
ausgebildet; (limited) bedingt
qualify vt qualifizieren; (entitle)
berechtigen; (limit) einschränken □vi sich qualifizieren
quality n Qualität f; (characteristic) Eigenschaft f
qualm n Bedenken pl
quantity n Quantität f, Menge f
quarantine n Quarantäne f
quarrel n Streit m □vi sich streiten
quarry[1] n (prey) Beute f
quarry[2] n Steinbruch m
quart n Quart nt
quarter n Viertel nt; (of year)
Vierteljahr nt; ~s pl Quartier nt.
~-'final n Viertelfinale nt
quarterly a vierteljährlich
quartet n Quartett nt
quartz n Quarz m
quash vt aufheben
quaver n Achtelnote f
quay n Kai m
queen n Königin f; (Cards, Chess)
Dame f
queer a eigenartig; (dubious)
zweifelhaft; (ill) unwohl
quell vt unterdrücken
quench vt löschen
query n Frage f □vt in Frage
stellen; reklamieren ⟨bill⟩
question n Frage f; (for discussion) Thema nt; out of the ~

ausgeschlossen; **without** ~ ohne
Frage; **the person in** ~ die frag-
liche Person □vt in Frage stellen;
~ **s.o.** jdn ausfragen; ⟨police:⟩
jdn verhören. ~ **mark** n Frage-
zeichen nt
questionnaire n Fragebogen m
queue n Schlange f □vi ~ **[up]**
Schlange stehen, sich anstellen
(for nach)
quick a schnell
quick: ~ **sand** n Treibsand m.
~**-tempered** a aufbrausend
quiet a still; (calm) ruhig; (soft)
leise; **keep** ~ **about** (fam) nichts
sagen von □n Stille f; Ruhe f
quill n Feder f; (spine) Stachel m
quilt n Steppdecke f
quince n Quitte f
quintet n Quintett nt
quintuplets npl Fünflinge pl
quit vt verlassen; (give up) aufgeben; ~ **doing sth** aufhören, etw
zu tun □vi gehen
quite adv ganz; (really) wirklich;
~ **a few** ziemlich viele
quits a quitt
quiver vi zittern
quiz n Quiz nt □vt ausfragen
quorum n **have a** ~ beschlußfä-
hig sein
quota n Anteil m; (Comm) Kontingent nt
quotation n Zitat nt; (price)
Kostenvoranschlag m; (of
shares) Notierung f. ~ **marks**
npl Anführungszeichen pl
quote vt/i zitieren

R

rabbi n Rabbiner m; (title) Rabbi
m
rabbit n Kaninchen nt
rabid a fanatisch; ⟨animal⟩ tollwütig
rabies n Tollwut f
race[1] n Rasse f

race[2] n Rennen nt; (fig) Wettlauf m ◇vi [am Rennen] teilnehmen; ⟨athlete:⟩ laufen; (fam: rush) rasen

race: ~**horse** n Rennpferd nt. ~**track** n Rennbahn f

racial a rassisch; ⟨discrimination, minority⟩ Rassen-

racing n Rennsport m. ~ **car** n Rennwagen m

racis|m n Rassismus m. ~**t** a rassistisch ◇n Rassist m

rack n Ständer m; (for plates) Gestell nt

racket[1] n (Sport) Schläger m

racket[2] n (din) Krach m; (swindle) Schwindelgeschäft nt

radar n Radar m

radiant a strahlend

radiate vt ausstrahlen. ~**ion** f Strahlung f

radiator n Heizkörper m; (Auto) Kühler m

radical a radikal ◇n Radikale(r) m/f

radio n Radio nt; by ~ über Funk ◇vt funken ⟨message⟩

radio'active a radioaktiv. ~**activity** n Radioaktivität f

radiography n Röntgenographie f

radio'therapy n Strahlenbehandlung f

radish n Radieschen nt

radius n Radius m, Halbmesser m

raffle n Tombola f

raft n Floß nt

rafter n Dachsparren m

rag n Lumpen m

rage n Wut f; all the ~ (fam) der letzte Schrei ◇vi rasen; ⟨storm:⟩ toben

ragged a zerlumpt

raid n Überfall m; (Mil) Angriff m; (police) Razzia f ◇vt überfallen; (Mil) angreifen; ⟨police:⟩ eine Razzia durchführen in (+ dat); (break in) eindringen in (+ acc)

rail n Schiene f; (pole) Stange f; (hand~) Handlauf m; (Naut) Reling f; by ~ mit der Bahn

railings npl Geländer nt

railway n [Eisen]bahn f. ~**man** n Eisenbahner m. ~**station** n Bahnhof m

rain n Regen m ◇vi regnen

rain: ~**bow** n Regenbogen m. ~**coat** n Regenmantel m. ~**fall** n Niederschlag m

rainy a regnerisch

raise vt erheben; (upright) aufrichten; (make higher) erhöhen; (lift) [hoch]heben; lüften ⟨hat⟩; [auf]ziehen ⟨children⟩; aufwerfen ⟨question⟩; aufbringen ⟨money⟩

raisin n Rosine f

rake n Harke f, Rechen m ◇vt harken, rechen

rally n Versammlung f; (Auto) Rallye f; (Tennis) Ballwechsel m

ram n Schafbock m; (Astr) Widder m ◇vt rammen

ramble n Wanderung f ◇vi wandern; (in speech) irrereden. ~**er** n Wanderer m

ramp n Rampe f

rampant a weit verbreitet; (in heraldry) aufgerichtet

rampart n Wall m

ranch n Ranch f

rancid a ranzig

random a willkürlich; **a** ~ **sample** eine Stichprobe ◇n at ~ aufs Geratewohl

range n Serie f, Reihe f; (Comm) Auswahl f, Angebot nt (of an + dat); (of mountains) Kette f; (Mus) Umfang m; (distance) Reichweite f; (for shooting) Schießplatz m; (stove) Kohlenherd m ◇vi reichen; ~ **from ... to** gehen von ... bis

rank n (row) Reihe f; (Mil) Rang m; (social position) Stand m

ransack vt durchwühlen; (pillage) plündern

ransom n Lösegeld nt; **hold s.o. to ~** Lösegeld für jdn fordern

rap vt klopfen auf (+ acc)

rape¹ n (Bot) Raps m

rape² n Vergewaltigung f □ vt vergewaltigen

rapid a schnell

rapids npl Stromschnellen pl

rapist n Vergewaltiger m

rapport n (innerer) Kontakt m

raptur|e n Entzücken nt. **~ous** a begeistert

rare¹ a selten

rare² a (Culin) englisch gebraten

rash¹ n (Med) Ausschlag m

rash² a voreilig

rasher n Speckscheibe f

raspberry n Himbeere f

rat n Ratte f

rate n Rate f; (speed) Tempo nt; (of payment) Satz m; (of exchange) Kurs m; **~s** pl (taxes) ≈ Grundsteuer f; **at any ~** auf jeden Fall □ vt einschätzen; **~ among** zählen zu □ vi **~ as** gelten als

rather adv lieber; (willing) ziemlich

ratify vt ratifizieren

ratio n Verhältnis nt

ration n Ration f

rational a rational. **~ize** vt/i rationalisieren

rattle n Rasseln nt; (of china, glass) Klirren nt; (of windows) Klappern nt; (toy) Klapper f □ vi rasseln; klirren; klappern □ vt rasseln mit; (shake) schütteln

'rattlesnake n Klapperschlange f

ravage vt verwüsten

rave vi toben; **~ about** schwärmen von

raven n Rabe m

ravenous a heißhungrig

ravine n Schlucht f

ravishing a hinreißend

raw a roh; (not processed) Roh-; (skin) wund; (weather) naßkalt; (inexperienced) unerfahren; **get a**

~ deal (fam) schlecht wegkommen. **~ ma'terials** npl Rohstoffe pl

ray n Strahl m; **~ of hope** Hoffnungsschimmer m

raze vt **~ to the ground** dem Erdboden gleichmachen

razor n Rasierapparat m. **~ blade** n Rasierklinge f

re prep betreffs (+ gen)

reach n Reichweite f; (of river) Strecke f; **within/out of ~** in/außer Reichweite □ vt erreichen; (arrive at) ankommen in (+ dat); (~ as far as) reichen bis zu; kommen zu (decision, conclusion); (pass) reichen □ vi reichen (to bis)

re'act vi reagieren

re'action n Reaktion f. **~ary** a reaktionär

reactor n Reaktor m

read vt/i lesen; (aloud) vorlesen (to dat); (Univ) studieren; ablesen (meter). **~ out** vt vorlesen

reader n Leser(in) m(f); (book) Lesebuch nt

readiness n Bereitschaft f

ready a fertig; (willing) bereit; (quick) schnell; **get ~** sich fertigmachen; (prepare to) sich bereitmachen

ready: **~-'made** a fertig. **~-to- 'wear** a Konfektions-

real a wirklich; (genuine) echt; (actual) eigentlich. **~ estate** n Immobilien pl

realis|m n Realismus m. **~t** n Realist m. **~tic** a realistisch

reality n Wirklichkeit f, Realität f

realization n Erkenntnis f

realize vt einsehen; (become aware) gewahr werden; verwirklichen (hopes); (Comm) realisieren; einbringen (price)

really adv wirklich; (actually) eigentlich

realm n Reich nt

reap vt ernten

reap'pear vi wiederkommen

rear a Hinter-; (Auto) Heck- □ n the ~ der hintere Teil; **from the** ~ von hinten

'rear-light n Rücklicht nt

re'arm vi wieder aufrüsten

rear-view 'mirror n (Auto) Rückspiegel m

reason n Grund m; (good sense) Vernunft f; (ability to think) Verstand m; **within** ~ in vernünftigen Grenzen □ vi argumentieren; ~ **with** vernünftig reden mit. ~**able** a vernünftig; (not expensive) preiswert. ~**ably** adv (fairly) ziemlich

reas'sure vt beruhigen; ~ **s.o. of sth** jdm etw (gen) versichern

rebate n Rückzahlung f; (discount) Nachlaß m

rebel[1] n Rebell m

rebel[2] vi rebellieren ~**lion** n bellion f. ~**lious** a rebellisch

rebuff vt abweisen; eine Abfuhr erteilen (s.o. jdm)

rebuke vt tadeln

re'call n Erinnerung f; **beyond** ~ unwiderruflich □ vt zurückrufen; abberufen (diplomat); vorzeitig einberufen (parliament); (remember) sich erinnern an (+ acc)

recant vi widerrufen

recapitulate vi/t zusammenfassen; rekapitulieren

rece'de vi zurückgehen. ~**ing** a (forehead, chin) fliehend; ~**ing hair** Stirnglatze f

receipt n Quittung f; (receiving) Empfang m; ~**s** pl (Comm) Einnahmen pl

receive vt erhalten, bekommen; empfangen (guests). ~**r** n (Teleph) Hörer m; (TV) Empfänger m; (of stolen goods) Hehler m

recent a kürzlich erfolgte(r,s). ~**ly** adv in letzter Zeit; (the other day) kürzlich, vor kurzem

receptacle n Behälter m ~ Re-

reception n Empfang m; ~ [**desk**] (in hotel) Rezeption f. ~**ist** n Empfangsdame f

receptive a aufnahmefähig

recess n Nische f; (holiday) Ferien pl

recession n Rezession f

recipe n Rezept nt

recipro|**cal** a gegenseitig. ~**cate** vt erwidern

recital n (of poetry) Vortrag m; (on piano) Konzert nt

recite vt aufsagen; (before audience) vortragen; (list) aufzählen

reckless a leichtsinnig; (careless) rücksichtslos

reckon vt rechnen; (consider) glauben □ vi ~ **on/with** rechnen mit

recline vi liegen. ~**ing seat** n Liegesitz m

recluse n Einsiedler(in) m(f)

recognition n Erkennen nt; (acknowledgement) Anerkennung f

recognize vt erkennen; (know again) wiedererkennen; (acknowledge) anerkennen

recollect vt sich erinnern an (+ acc). ~**ion** n Erinnerung f

recommend vt empfehlen. ~**ation** n Empfehlung f

recompense vt entschädigen

recon|**cile** vt versöhnen; ~**cile oneself to** sich abfinden mit. ~**ciliation** n Versöhnung f

reconnaissance n (Mil) Aufklärung f

reconnoitre vi auf Erkundung ausgehen

recon'sider vt sich (dat) noch einmal überlegen

recon'struction n Wiederaufbau m; Rekonstruktion f

record[1] vt aufzeichnen; (register) registrieren; (on tape) aufnehmen

record[2] n Aufzeichnung f; (Jur) Protokoll nt; (Mus) [Schall]platte *f*; *(Sport)* Rekord *m*; **~s** *pl* Unterlagen *pl*; **keep a ~ of** sich *(dat)* notieren; **off the ~** inoffiziell; **have a [criminal] ~** vorbestraft sein

recorder *n (Mus)* Blockflöte *f*

recording *n* Aufzeichnung *f*, Aufnahme *f*

'record-player *n* Plattenspieler *m*

recount *vt* erzählen

're-count *n (Pol)* Nachzählung *f*

recoup *vt* wiedereinbringen; ausgleichen *⟨losses⟩*

recourse *n* **have ~ to** Zuflucht nehmen zu

recover *vt* zurückbekommen; bergen *⟨wreck⟩* □*vi* sich erholen. **~y** *n* Wiedererlangung *f*; Bergung *f*; *(of health)* Erholung *f*

recreation *n* Erholung *f*; *(hobby)* Hobby *nt*. **~al** *a* Freizeit-

recruit *n (Mil)* Rekrut *m*; **new ~ (member)** neues Mitglied *nt*; *(worker)* neuer Mitarbeiter *m*□*vt* rekrutieren; anwerben *⟨staff⟩*

rectang|le *n* Rechteck *nt*. **~ular** *a* rechteckig

rectify *vt* berichtigen

rector *n* Pfarrer *m*; *(Univ)* Rektor *m*. **~y** *n* Pfarrhaus *nt*

recuperate *vi* sich erholen

recurrence *n* Wiederkehr *f*

recycle *vt* wiederverwerten. **~d paper** *n* Umweltschutzpapier *nt*

red *a* rot □ *n* Rot *nt*. **~'currant** *n* rote Johannisbeere *f*

redeem *vt* einlösen; *(Relig)* erlösen

redemption *n* Erlösung *f*

red: **~-haired** *a* rothaarig. **~-'handed** *a* **catch s.o. ~-handed** jdn auf frischer Tat ertappen. **~ 'herring** *n* falsche Spur *f*. **~-hot** *a* glühend heiß

redi'rect *vt* nachsenden *⟨letter⟩*; umleiten *⟨traffic⟩*

re'double *vt* verdoppeln

redress *vt* wiedergutmachen; wiederherstellen *⟨balance⟩*

red 'tape *n (fam)* Bürokratie *f*

reduce *vt* verringern, vermindern; *(in size)* verkleinern; ermäßigen *⟨costs⟩*; herabsetzen *⟨price⟩*; *(Culin)* einkochen lassen. **~tion** *n* Verringerung *f*; *(in price)* Ermäßigung *f*; *(in size)* Verkleinerung *f*

redundan|cy *n* Beschäftigungslosigkeit *f*; *(payment)* Abfindung *f*. **~t** *a* überflüssig; **make ~t** entlassen; **be made ~t** beschäftigungslos werden

reed *n* [Schilf]rohr *nt*; **~s** *pl* Schilf *nt*

reef *n* Riff *nt*

reel *n* Rolle *f*, Spule *f*□ *vi (stagger)* taumeln

refectory *n* Refektorium *nt*; *(Univ)* Mensa *f*

refer *vt* verweisen **(to** an + *acc)*; übergeben, weiterleiten *⟨matter⟩* **(to** an + *acc)* □*vi* **~ to** sich beziehen auf (+ *acc)*; *(mention)* erwähnen; *(concern)* betreffen; *(consult)* sich wenden an (+ *acc)*; nachschlagen in (+ *dat) ⟨book⟩*

referee *n* Schiedsrichter *m*; *(Boxing)* Ringrichter *m*; *(for job)* Referenz *f*

reference *n* Erwähnung *f*; *(in book)* Verweis *m*; *(for job)* Referenz *f*; *(Comm)* **'your ~** 'Ihr Zeichen'; **with ~ to** in bezug auf (+ *acc)*; *(in letter)* unter Bezugnahme auf (+ *acc)*. **~ book** *n* Nachschlagewerk *nt*

referendum *n* Volksabstimmung *f*

re'fill *vt* nachfüllen

'refill *n (for pen)* Ersatzmine *f*

refine *vt* raffinieren. **~d** *a* fein, vornehm. **~ment** *n* Vornehmheit *f*; *(Techn)* Verfeinerung *f*. **~ry** *n* Raffinerie *f*

reflect *vt* reflektieren; *(mirror:)* [wider]spiegeln □*vi* nachdenken (on über + *acc*). **∼ion** *n* Reflexion *f*; (*image*) Spiegelbild *nt*; on **∼ion** nach nochmaliger Überlegung

reflex *n* Reflex *m*

reflexive *a* reflexiv

reform *vt* reformieren □*vi* sich bessern. **R∼ation** *n* (*Relig*) Reformation *f* ∼**er** *n* Reformer *m*; (*Relig*) Reformator *m*

refract *vt* (*Phys*) brechen

refrain[1] *n* Refrain *m*

refrain[2] *vi* ∼ **from doing sth** etw nicht tun

refresh *vt* erfrischen. **∼ments** *npl* Erfrischungen *pl*

refrigerator *n* Kühlschrank *m*

re'fuel *vt/i* auftanken

refuge *n* Zuflucht *f*

refugee *n* Flüchtling *m*

re'fund *vt* zurückerstatten

refuse[1] *vt* ablehnen; (*not grant*) verweigern; **∼ to do sth** sich weigern, etw zu tun □*vi* ablehnen; sich weigern

refuse[2] *n* Müll, Abfall *m*. **∼ collection** *n* Müllabfuhr *f*

refute *vt* widerlegen

regal *a* königlich

regalia *npl* Insignien *pl*

regard *n* (*heed*) Rücksicht *f*; (*respect*) Achtung *f*; **∼s** *pl* Grüße *pl*; **with ∼ to** in bezug auf (+ *acc*) □*vt* ansehen, betrachten (**as** als); **as ∼s** in bezug auf (+ *acc*). **∼ing** *prep* bezüglich (+ *gen*). **∼less** *adv* ohne Rücksicht (**of** auf + *acc*)

regatta *n* Regatta *f*

regime *n* Regime *nt*

regiment *n* Regiment *nt*. ∼**ation** *n* Reglementierung *f*

region *n* Region *f*; **in the ∼ of** (*fig*) ungefähr. ∼**al** *a* regional

register *n* Register *nt*; (*Sch*) Anwesenheitsliste *f* □*vt* registrieren; (*report*) anmelden; einschreiben 〈*letter*〉; aufgeben 〈*luggage*〉 □*vi* (*report*) sich anmelden

registrar *n* Standesbeamte(r) *m*

registration *n* Registrierung *f*; Anmeldung *f*. ∼ **number** *n* Autonummer *f*

registry office *n* Standesamt *nt*

regret *n* Bedauern *nt* □*vt* bedauern

regrettable *a* bedauerlich

regular *a* regelmäßig; (*usual*) üblich; (*Mil*) Berufs- □*n* Berufssoldat *m*; (*in pub*) Stammgast *m*; (*in shop*) Stammkunde *m*

regulate *vt* regulieren. ∼**ion** *n* (*rule*) Vorschrift *f*

rehabilitation *n* Rehabilitation *f*

rehears|al *n* Probe *f*. ∼**e** *vt* proben

reign *n* Herrschaft *f* □*vi* herrschen, regieren

rein *n* Zügel *m*

reincarnation *n* Reinkarnation *f*, Wiedergeburt *f*

reindeer *n inv* Rentier *nt*

reinforce *vt* verstärken. ∼**ment** *n* Verstärkung *f*

reiterate *vt* wiederholen

reject *vt* ablehnen. ∼**ion** *n* Ablehnung *f*

rejoice *vi* (*liter*) sich freuen

rejuvenate *vt* verjüngen

relapse *n* Rückfall *m*

relate *vt* (*tell*) erzählen; (*connect*) verbinden □*vi* zusammenhängen (**to** mit). ∼**d** *a* verwandt (**to** mit)

relation *n* Beziehung *f*; (*person*) Verwandte(r) *m/f*. ∼**ship** *n* Beziehung *f*; (*link*) Verbindung *f*; (*blood tie*) Verwandtschaft *f*; (*affair*) Verhältnis *nt*

relative *n* Verwandte(r) *m/f* □*a* relativ; (*Gram*) Relativ-. ∼**ly** *adv* relativ, verhältnismäßig

relax *vi* sich lockern, sich entspannen. ∼**ation** *n* Entspannung *f*

relay[1] *vt* weitergeben; (*TV*) übertragen

relay[2] *n* (*Electr*) Relais *nt*. ∼ **[race]** *n* Staffel *f*

release n Freilassung f, Entlassung f; (Techn) Auslöser m □ vt freilassen; (let go of) loslassen; (Techn) auslösen; veröffentlichen ⟨information⟩

relegate vt verbannen; **be ~d** (Sport) absteigen

relent vi nachgeben. **~ less** a erbarmungslos; (unceasing) unaufhörlich

relevan|ce n Relevanz f. **~ t** a relevant (**to** für)

reliable a zuverlässig

reliant a angewiesen (**on** auf + acc)

relic n Überbleibsel nt; (Relig) Reliquie f

relief n Erleichterung f; (assistance) Hilfe f; (distraction) Abwechslung f; (replacement) Ablösung f; (Art) Relief nt. **~ map** n Reliefkarte f

relieve vt erleichtern; (take over from) ablösen; **~ of** entlasten von

religion n Religion f

religious a religiös

relinquish vt loslassen

relish n Genuß □ vt genießen

reluctant a widerstrebend; **be ~** zögern (**to** zu)

rely vi **~ on** sich verlassen auf (+ acc); (be dependent on) angewiesen sein auf (+ acc)

remain vi bleiben; (be left) übrigbleiben. **~der** n Rest m. **~ing** a restlich. **~s** npl Rest pl; [mortal] **~s** [sterbliche] Überreste pl

remand n **on ~** in Untersuchungshaft □ vt **~ in custody** in Untersuchungshaft schicken

remark n Bemerkung f □ vt bemerken. **~able** a bemerkenswert

re'marry vi wieder heiraten

remedial a Hilfs-; (Med) Heil-

remedy n [Heil]mittel nt (**for** gegen); (fig) Abhilfe f

remember vt sich erinnern an (+ acc); **~ to do sth** daran denken, etw zu tun □ vi sich erinnern

remind vt erinnern (**of** an + acc). **~er** n Andenken nt; (warning) Mahnung f

reminisce vi sich seinen Erinnerungen hingeben

remiss a nachlässig

remission n Nachlaß m; (of sentence) [Straf]erlaß m; (Med) Remission f

remnant n Rest m

remonstrate vi protestieren; **~ with s.o.** jdm Vorhaltungen machen

remorse n Reue f

remote a fern; (isolated) abgelegen; (slight) gering. **~ con'trol** n Fernsteuerung f; (for TV) Fernbedienung f. **~-con'trolled** a ferngesteuert; fernbedient

removal n Entfernung f; (from house) Umzug m. **~ van** n Möbelwagen m

remove vt entfernen; (take off) abnehmen; (take out) herausnehmen

remuneration n Bezahlung f

render vt machen; erweisen ⟨service⟩; (translate) wiedergeben; (Mus) vortragen

renew vt erneuern; verlängern ⟨contract⟩

renounce vt verzichten auf (+ acc); (Relig) abschwören (+ dat)

renovate vt renovieren

renowned a berühmt

rent n Miete f □ vt mieten; (hire) leihen; (~ out) vermieten; verleihen. **~al** n Mietgebühr f; Leihgebühr f

renunciation n Verzicht m

re'organize vt reorganisieren

repair n Reparatur f; **in good/bad ~** in gutem/schlechtem Zustand □ vt reparieren

repatriation n Repatriierung f

re'pay vt zurückzahlen

repeal vt aufheben

repeat n Wiederholung f □vt/i wiederholen; ~ **after me** sprechen Sie mir nach

repel vt abwehren; (fig) abstoßen

repent vi Reue zeigen. ~**ance** n Reue f. ~**ant** a reuig

repercussions npl Auswirkungen pl

repertoire n Repertoire nt

repertory n Repertoire nt

repetit|ion n Wiederholung f. ~**ive** a eintönig

re'place vt zurücktun; (take the place of) ersetzen; (exchange) austauschen, auswechseln. ~-**ment** n Ersatz m

'replay n (Sport) Wiederholungsspiel nt; [action] ~ Wiederholung f

replenish vt auffüllen

replica n Nachbildung f

reply n Antwort f (**to** auf + acc) □vt/i antworten

report n Bericht m; (Sch) Zeugnis nt; (rumour) Gerücht nt; (of gun) Knall m □vt berichten; (notify) melden; ~ **s.o. to the police** jdn anzeigen □vi berichten (**on** über + acc); (present oneself) sich melden (**to** bei). ~**er** n Reporter(in) m(f)

reprehensible a tadelnswert

represent vt darstellen; (act for) vertreten, repräsentieren. ~**ation** n Darstellung f

representative a repräsentativ (**of** für) □n Bevollmächtigte(r) m|f; (Comm) Vertreter(in) m(f)

repress vt unterdrücken

reprieve n Begnadigung f; (postponement) Strafaufschub m; (fig) Gnadenfrist f

reprimand n Tadel m □vt tadeln

'reprint[1] n Nachdruck m

re'print[2] vt neu auflegen

reprisal n Vergeltungsmaßnahme f

reproach n Vorwurf m □vt Vorwürfe pl machen (+ dat)

repro'duce vt wiedergeben, reproduzieren □vi sich fortpflanzen. ~**tion** n Reproduktion f; (Biol) Fortpflanzung f

reptile n Reptil nt

republic n Republik f. ~**an** a republikanisch □n Republikaner(in) m(f)

repudiate vt zurückweisen

repugnant a widerlich

repuls|e vt abwehren; (fig) abweisen. ~**ion** n Widerwille m. ~**ive** a abstoßend, widerlich

reputable a von gutem Ruf

reputation n Ruf m

request n Bitte f □vt bitten

require vt (need) brauchen; (demand) erfordern. ~**ment** n Bedürfnis nt; (condition) Erfordernis nt

requisite a erforderlich □n **toilet/travel** ~**s** pl Toiletten-/Reiseartikel pl

rescue n Rettung f □vt retten. ~**r** n Retter m

research n Forschung f □vt erforschen; (Journ) recherchieren □vi ~ **into** erforschen. ~**er** n Forscher m; (Journ) Rechercheur m

resem|blance n Ähnlichkeit f. ~**ble** vt ähneln (+ dat)

resent vt übelnehmen; einen Groll hegen gegen ⟨person⟩

reservation n Reservierung f; (doubt) Vorbehalt m; (enclosure) Reservat nt

reserve n Reserve f; (for animals) Reservat nt; (Sport) Reservespieler(in) m(f) □vt reservieren; ⟨client:⟩ reservieren lassen; (keep) aufheben; sich (dat) vorbehalten ⟨right⟩

reservoir n Reservoir nt

re'shuffle n (Pol) Umbildung f

reside vi wohnen

residence n Wohnsitz m; (official) Residenz f; (stay) Aufenthalt m. ~ **permit** n Aufenthaltsgenehmigung f

resident a ansässig (**in** in + dat); ⟨nurse⟩ im Haus wohnend □ n Bewohner(in) m(f); (of street) Anwohner m

residue n Rest m; (Chem) Rückstand m

resign vt ~ **oneself to** sich abfinden mit □ vi kündigen; (from public office) zurücktreten. ~ **ation** n Resignation f; (from job) Kündigung f; Rücktritt m

resin n Harz nt

resist vt/i sich widersetzen (+ dat); (fig) widerstehen (+ dat). ~**ance** n Widerstand m

resolut|e a entschlossen. ~**ion** n Entschlossenheit f; (intention) Vorsatz m; (Pol) Resolution f

resolve vt beschließen; (solve) lösen

resonance n Resonanz f

resort n (place) Urlaubsort m □ vi ~ **to** (fig) greifen zu

resound vi widerhallen

resource n ~**s** pl Ressourcen pl. ~**ful** a findig

respect n Respekt m, Achtung f (**for** vor + dat); (aspect) Hinsicht f; **with** ~ **to** in bezug auf (+ acc) □ vt respektieren, achten

respectable a ehrbar; (decent) anständig; (considerable) ansehnlich

respective a jeweilig

respiration n Atmung f

respite n [Ruhe]pause f

respond vi antworten; (react) reagieren (**to** auf + acc); ⟨patient:⟩ ansprechen (**to** auf + acc)

response n Antwort f; Reaktion f

responsibility n Verantwortung f; (duty) Verpflichtung f

responsible a verantwortlich; (trustworthy) verantwortungsvoll

rest[1] n Ruhe f; (holiday) Erholung f; (interval & Mus) Pause f; **have a** ~ eine Pause machen; (rest) sich ausruhen □ vt ausruhen; (lean) lehnen (**on** an/auf + acc) □ vi ruhen; (have a rest) sich ausruhen

rest[2] n **the** ~ der Rest; (people) die Übrigen pl

restaurant n Restaurant nt. ~ **car** n Speisewagen m

restful a erholsam

restless a unruhig

restoration n (of building) Restaurierung f

restore vt wiederherstellen; restaurieren ⟨building⟩; (give back) zurückgeben

restrain vt zurückhalten; ~ **oneself** sich beherrschen. ~**t** n Zurückhaltung f

restrict vt einschränken; ~ **to** beschränken auf (+ acc). ~**ion** n Einschränkung f; Beschränkung f

result n Ergebnis nt, Resultat nt; (consequence) Folge f; **as a** ~ als Folge (**of** gen) □ vi sich ergeben (**from** aus)

resume vt wiederaufnehmen; wieder einnehmen ⟨seat⟩ □ vi wieder beginnen

résumé n Zusammenfassung f

resurrect vt (fig) wiederbeleben. ~**ion** n **the R**~**ion** (Relig) die Auferstehung

resuscitate vt wiederbeleben

retail n Einzelhandel m □ a Einzelhandels- □ adv im Einzelhandel □ vt im Einzelhandel verkaufen □ vi ~ **at** im Einzelhandel kosten. ~**er** n Einzelhändler m. ~ **price** n Ladenpreis m

retain vt behalten

retaliation n Vergeltung f

reticent a zurückhaltend

retina n Netzhaut f

retinue n Gefolge nt

retire *vi* in den Ruhestand treten; (*withdraw*) sich zurückziehen. **~d** *a* im Ruhestand. **~ment** *n* Ruhestand *m*

retort *n* scharfe Erwiderung *f*; (*Chem*) Retorte *f*

re'touch *vt* (*Phot*) retuschieren

retract *vt* einziehen; zurücknehmen (*remark*)

re'train *vt* umschulen

retreat *n* Rückzug *m*; (*place*) Zufluchtsort *m* □*vi* sich zurückziehen

re'trial *n* Wiederaufnahmeverfahren *nt*

retribution *n* Verge tung

retrieve *vt* zurückholen; (*from wreckage*) bergen; (*Computing*) wiederauffinden

retrograde *a* rückschrittlich

retrospect *n* in ~ rückblickend. **~ive** *a* rückwirkend; (*looking back*) rückblickend

return *n* Rückkehr *f*; (*giving back*) Rückgabe *f*; (*Comm*) Ertrag *m*; (*ticket*) Rückfahrkarte *f*; (*Aviat*) Rückflugschein *m*; **by ~** [**of post**] postwendend; **many happy ~s!** herzlichen Glückwunsch zum Geburtstag! □*vi* zurückgehen/-fahren; (*come back*) zurückkommen □*vt* zurückgeben; (*put back*) zurückstellen/ -legen; (*send back*) zurückschicken; (*elect*) wählen

return: **~ flight** *n* Rückflug *m*. **~ match** *n* Rückspiel *nt*. **~ ticket** *n* Rückfahrkarte *f*; (*Aviat*) Rückflugschein *m*

reunion *n* Wiedervereinigung *f*; (*social gathering*) Treffen *nt*

re'usable *a* wiederverwendbar

rev *n* (*Auto, fam*) Umdrehung *f* □*vt/i ~* [**up**] den Motor auf Touren bringen

reveal *vt* zum Vorschein bringen; (*fig*) enthüllen

revel *vi* ~ **in sth** etw genießen

revelation *n* Offenbarung *f*, Enthüllung *f*

revenge *n* Rache *f*; (*fig & Sport*) Revanche *f*

revenue *n* [Staats]einnahmen *pl*

reverberate *vi* nachhallen

reverence *n* Ehrfurcht *f*

Reverend *a* the ~ **X** Pfarrer **X**; (*Catholic*) Hochwürden **X**

reverent *a* ehrfürchtig

reversal *n* Umkehrung *f*

reverse *a* umgekehrt □*n* Gegenteil *nt*; (*back*) Rückseite *f*; (*Auto*) Rückwärtsgang *m* □*vt* umkehren; (*Auto*) zurücksetzen; **~ the charges** (*Teleph*) ein R-Gespräch führen □*vi* zurücksetzen

revert *vi* ~ **to** zurückfallen an (+ *acc*); zurückkommen auf (+ *acc*) (*topic*)

review *n* Rückblick *m* (**of** auf + *acc*); (*re-examination*) Überprüfung *f*; (*Mil*) Truppenschau *f*; (*of book*) Kritik *f*, Rezension *f* □*vt* zurückblicken auf (+ *acc*); überprüfen (*situation*); (*Mil*) besichtigen; kritisieren, rezensieren (*book*). **~er** *n* Kritiker *m*, Rezensent *m*

revise *vt* revidieren; (*for exam*) wiederholen. **~ion** *n* Revision *f*; Wiederholung *f*

revival *n* Wiederbelebung *f*

revive *vt* wiederbeleben; (*fig*) wieder aufleben lassen □*vi* wieder aufleben

revoke *vt* aufheben; widerrufen (*command, decision*)

revolt *n* Aufstand *m* □*vi* rebellieren. **~ing** *a* widerlich, eklig

revolution *n* Revolution *f*; (*Auto*) Umdrehung *f*. **~ary** *a* revolutionär. **~ize** *vt* revolutionieren

revolve *vi* sich drehen

revolv|er *n* Revolver *m*. **~ing** *a* Dreh-

revue *n* Revue *f*; (*satirical*) Kabarett *nt*

revulsion *n* Abscheu *m*

reward n Belohnung f □ vt belohnen

rhapsody n Rhapsodie f

rhetoric n Rhetorik f. ~**al** a rhetorisch

rheumatism n Rheumatismus m, Rheuma nt

Rhine n Rhein m

rhinoceros n Nashorn nt, Rhinozeros nt

rhubarb n Rhabarber m

rhyme n Reim m □ vt reimen □ vi sich reimen

rhythm n Rhythmus m. ~**ic[al]** a rhythmisch

rib n Rippe f

ribbon n Band nt; (for typewriter) Farbband nt

rice n Reis m

rich a reich; ⟨food⟩ gehaltvoll; ⟨heavy⟩ schwer □ n the ~ pl die Reichen; ~**es** pl Reichtum m

rickets n Rachitis f

ricochet vi abprallen

rid vt befreien (of von); **get** ~ **of** loswerden

riddance n **good** ~! auf Nimmerwiedersehen!

riddle n Rätsel nt

ride n Ritt m; (in vehicle) Fahrt f □ vt reiten ⟨horse⟩; fahren mit ⟨bicycle⟩ □ vi reiten; (in vehicle) fahren. ~**r** n Reiter(in) m(f); (on bicycle) Fahrer(in) m(f); (in document) Zusatzklausel f

ridge n Erhebung f; (on roof) First m; (of mountain) Grat m, Kamm m; (of high pressure) Hochdruckkeil m

ridicule n Spott m □ vt verspotten, spotten über (+ acc)

ridiculous a lächerlich

rifle n Gewehr nt □ vt plündern; ~ **through** durchwühlen

rift n Spalt m; (fig) Riß m

rig[1] n Ölbohrturm m; (at sea) Bohrinsel f □ vt ~ **out** ausrüsten; ~ **up** aufbauen

right a richtig; (not left) rechte(r,s); **be** ~ ⟨person:⟩ recht haben; ⟨clock:⟩ richtig gehen; **put** ~ wieder in Ordnung bringen; (fig) richtigstellen; **that's** ~! das stimmt! □ adv richtig; (directly) direkt; (completely) ganz; (not left) rechts; ⟨go⟩ nach rechts; ~ **away** sofort □ n Recht nt; (not left) rechte Seite f; **on the** ~ rechts; **the R**~ (Pol) die Rechte. ~ **angle** n rechter Winkel m

righteous a rechtschaffen

rightful a rechtmäßig

right: ~-**handed** a rechtshändig. ~-**hand 'man** n (fig) rechte Hand f. ~ **of way** n Durchgangsrecht nt; (path) öffentlicher Fußweg m; (Auto) Vorfahrt f. ~-**'wing** a (Pol) rechte(r,s)

rigid a starr; (strict) streng

rigorous a streng

rim n Rand m; (of wheel) Felge f

rind n (on fruit) Schale f; (on cheese) Rinde f; (on bacon) Schwarte f

ring[1] n Ring m; (for circus) Manege f □ vt umringen

ring[2] n Klingeln nt; **give s.o. a** ~ (Teleph) jdn anrufen □ vt läuten; ~ **[up]** (Teleph) anrufen □ vi läuten, klingeln

ring: ~**-leader** n Rädelsführer m. ~ **road** n Umgehungsstraße f

rink n Eisbahn f

rinse vt spülen; tönen ⟨hair⟩

riot n Aufruhr m; ~**s** pl Unruhen pl □ vi randalieren. ~**er** n Randalierer m. ~**ous** a aufrührerisch

rip vt/i zerreißen

ripe a reif

'rip-off n (fam) Nepp m

rise n Anstieg m; (fig) Aufstieg m; (increase) Zunahme f; (in wages) Lohnerhöhung f; (in salary) Gehaltserhöhung f; **give** ~ **to** Anlaß geben zu □ vi steigen; ⟨ground:⟩ ansteigen; ⟨sun:⟩ aufgehen; ⟨river:⟩ entspringen; (get

risk _up_) aufstehen; (_fig_) aufsteigen (_to zu_); (_rebel_) sich erheben; (_court:_) sich vertagen

risk _n_ Risiko _nt;_ **at one's own ~** auf eigene Gefahr □_vt_ riskieren

risky _a_ riskant

risqué _a_ gewagt

rissole _n_ Frikadelle _f_

rite _n_ Ritus _m;_ **last ~s** Letzte Ölung _f_

ritual _n_ Ritual _nt_

rival _n_ Rivale _m_/Rivalin _f_ □_vt_ gleichkommen (+ _dat_); (_compete with_) rivalisieren mit. **~ry** _n_ Rivalität _f_

river _n_ Fluß _m._ **~-bed** _n_ Flußbett _nt_

rivet _n_ Niete _f_ □_vt_ [ver]nieten; **~ed by** (_fig_) gefesselt von

road _n_ Straße _f;_ (_fig_) Weg _m._

road: ~-block _n_ Straßensperre_f._ **~-hog** _n_ (_fam_) Straßenschreck _m._ **~-map** _n_ Straßenkarte_f._ **~ safety** _n_ Verkehrssicherheit_f._ **~ sense** _n_ Verkehrssinn _m._ **~-works** _npl_ Straßenarbeiten _pl._ **~worthy** _a_ verkehrssicher

roam _vi_ wandern

roar _n_ Gebrüll _nt_ □_vi_ brüllen; (_with laughter_) schallend lachen

roast _a_ gebraten, Brat-; **~ beef/pork** Rinder-/Schweinebraten _m_ □_n_ Braten _m_ □_vt/i_ braten; rösten (_coffee_)

rob _vt_ berauben (_of gen_); ausrauben (_bank_). **~ber** _n_ Räuber _m._ **~bery** _n_ Raub _m_

robe _n_ Robe _f_

robin _n_ Rotkehlchen _nt_

robot _n_ Roboter _m_

robust _a_ robust

rock[1] _n_ Fels _m;_ **stick of ~** Zuckerstange_f;_ **on the ~s** (_ship_) aufgelaufen; (_marriage_) kaputt; (_drink_) mit Eis

rock[2] _vt/i_ schaukeln

rock[3] _n_ (_Mus_) Rock _m_

rockery _n_ Steingarten _m_

rocket _n_ Rakete _f_

rocking: ~-chair _n_ Schaukelstuhl _m._ **~-horse** _n_ Schaukelpferd _nt_

rod _n_ Stab _m;_ (_stick_) Rute _f;_ (_for fishing_) Angel[rute] _f_

rodent _n_ Nagetier _nt_

roe[1] _n_ Rogen _m;_ (_soft_) Milch _f_

roe[2] _n_ **~-[deer]** Reh _nt_

rogue _n_ Gauner _m_

role _n_ Rolle _f_

roll _n_ Rolle_f;_ (_bread_) Brötchen _nt;_ (_list_) Liste _f;_ (_of drum_) Wirbel _m_ □_vi_ rollen □_vt_ rollen; walzen (_lawn_); ausrollen (_pastry_)

'roll-call _n_ Namensaufruf _m;_ (_Mil_) Appell _m_

roller _n_ Rolle_f;_ (_lawn, road_) Walze_f;_ (_hair_) Lockenwickler _m._ **~-blind** _n_ Rollo _nt._ **~-coaster** _n_ Berg-und-Talbahn _f._ **~-skate** _n_ Rollschuh _m_

'rolling-pin _n_ Teigrolle _f_

Roman _a_ römisch □_n_ Römer(in) _m(f)_

romance _n_ Romantik _f;_ (_love-affair_) Romanze _f;_ (_book_) Liebesgeschichte _f_

Romania _n_ Rumänien _nt._ **~n** _a_ rumänisch □_n_ Rumäne _m_/-nin _f_

romantic _a_ romantisch. **~ism** _n_ Romantik _f_

Rome _n_ Rom _nt_

roof _n_ Dach _nt;_ (_of mouth_) Gaumen _m._ **~-rack** _n_ Dachgepäckträger _m_

rook _n_ Saatkrähe_f;_ (_Chess_) Turm _m_

room _n_ Zimmer _nt;_ (_for functions_) Saal _m;_ (_space_) Platz _m_

roost _n_ Hühnerstange _f_ □_vi_ schlafen

root _n_ Wurzel _f_

rope _n_ Seil _nt_

rope-'ladder _n_ Strickleiter _f_

rosary _n_ Rosenkranz _m_

rose _n_ Rose _f;_ (_of watering-can_) Brause _f_

rosemary _n_ Rosmarin _m_

rosette _n_ Rosette _f_

rostrum n Podest nt, Podium nt

rosy a rosig

rot n Fäulnis f □ vi [ver]faulen

rota n Dienstplan m

rotate vt drehen; im Wechsel anbauen (crops) □ vi sich drehen; (Techn) rotieren. ~ion n Drehung f (of crops) Fruchtfolge

rote n by ~ auswendig

rotten a faul; (fam) mies; (person) fies

rough a rauh; (uneven) uneben; (coarse) grob; (brutal) roh; (turbulent) stürmisch; (approximate) ungefähr □ adv sleep ~ im Freien übernachten □ n do sth in ~ etw ins unreine schreiben □ vt ~ it primitiv leben

roughage n Ballaststoffe pl

'rough paper n Konzeptpapier nt

round a rund □ n Runde f; (slice) Scheibe f; do one's ~s seine Runde machen □ prep um (+ acc); ~ the clock rund um die Uhr □ adv all ~ ringsherum; ~ and ~ im Kreis □ vt biegen um (corner) □ vi ~ on s.o. jdn anfahren

roundabout n Karussell nt; (for traffic) Kreisverkehr m

rouse vt wecken; (fig) erregen

route n Route f; (of bus) Linie f

routine n Routine f; (Theat) Nummer f

row[1] n (line) Reihe f; in a ~ nacheinander

row[2] n □ vi rudern

row[3] n (fam) Krach m □ vi (fam) sich streiten

rowan n Eberesche f

rowing boat n Ruderboot nt

royal a königlich

royalty n Königtum nt; (persons) Mitglieder pl der königlichen Familie; **-ies** pl (payments) Tantiemen pl

rub n vt reiben; (polish) polieren

rubber n Gummi m; (eraser) Radiergummi m. ~ **band** n Gummiband nt

rubbish n Abfall m, Müll m; (fam: nonsense) Quatsch m; (fam: junk) Plunder m, Kram m. ~ **bin** n Mülleimer m, Abfalleimer m. ~ **dump** n Abfallhaufen m; (official) Müllhalde f

rubble n Trümmer pl, Schutt m

ruby n Rubin m

rucksack n Rucksack m

rudder n [Steuer]ruder nt

rude a unhöflich; (improper) unanständig

ruffian n Rüpel m

ruffle vt zerzausen

rug n Vorleger m, [kleiner] Teppich m; (blanket) Decke f

rugged a (coastline) zerklüftet

ruin n Ruine f; (fig) Ruin m □ vt ruinieren

rule n Regel f; (control) Herrschaft f; (government) Regierung f; (for measuring) Lineal nt; as a ~ in der Regel □ vt regieren, herrschen über (+ acc); (fig) beherrschen; (decide) entscheiden; ziehen (line) □ vi regieren, herrschen

ruled a (paper) liniert

ruler n Herrscher(in) m(f); (measure) Lineal nt

rum n Rum m

rumble vi grollen; (stomach:) knurren

ruminant n Wiederkäuer m

rummage vi wühlen

rummy n Rommé nt

rumour n Gerücht nt

rump n Hinterteil m. ~ **steak** n Rumpsteak nt

run n Lauf m; (journey) Fahrt f; (series) Serie f, Reihe f; (Theat) Laufzeit f; (Skiing) Abfahrt f; (enclosure) Auslauf m; ~ **of bad luck** Pechsträhne f; **be on the ~** flüchtig sein; **have the ~ of sth** etw zu seiner freien Verfügung haben; **in the long ~** auf lange Sicht □ vi laufen; (flow) fließen; (eyes:) tränen; (bus:) verkehren;

fahren; ⟨*butter, ink*:⟩ zerfließen; ⟨*colours*:⟩ [ab]färben; ⟨*in election*⟩ kandidieren; ~ **across s.o./sth** auf jdn/etw stoßen □ *vt* laufen lassen; einlaufen lassen ⟨*bath*⟩; ⟨*manage*⟩ führen, leiten; ⟨*drive*⟩ fahren; eingehen ⟨*risk*⟩; ⟨*Journ*⟩ bringen ⟨*article*⟩. ~ **down** *vi* hinunter-/herunterlaufen; ⟨*clockwork*:⟩ ablaufen; ⟨*stocks*:⟩ sich verringern □ *vt* (*run over*) überfahren; ⟨*reduce*⟩ verringern; ⟨*fam: criticize*⟩ heruntermachen. ~ **off** *vi* weglaufen □ *vt* abziehen ⟨*copies*⟩. ~ **out** *vi* hinaus-/herauslaufen; ⟨*supplies, money*:⟩ ausgehen; **I've** ~ **out of sugar** ich habe keinen Zucker mehr. ~ **over** *vt* □ *vi* hinüber-/herüberlaufen; ⟨*overflow*⟩ überlaufen □ *vt* überfahren

'runaway *n* Ausreißer *m*

run-'down *a* ⟨*area*⟩ verkommen

rung *n* ⟨*of ladder*⟩ Sprosse *f*

runner *n* Läufer *m*; ⟨*Bot*⟩ Ausläufer *m*; ⟨*on sledge*⟩ Kufe *f*. ~ **bean** *n* Stangenbohne *f*. ~ **up** *n* Zweite(r) *m/f*

runny *a* flüssig

run: ~ **-of-the-'mill** *a* gewöhnlich. ~ **-up** *n* ⟨*Sport*⟩ Anlauf *m*; ⟨*to election*⟩ Zeit *f* vor der Wahl. ~ **way** *n* Start- und Landebahn *f*, Piste *f*

rupture *n* Bruch *m* □ *vt/i* brechen; ~ **oneself** sich ⟨*dat*⟩ einen Bruch heben

rural *a* ländlich

ruse *n* List *f*

rush¹ *n* ⟨*Bot*⟩ Binse *f*

rush² *n* Hetze *f*; **in a** ~ in Eile □ *vi* sich hetzen; ⟨*run*⟩ rasen; ⟨*water*:⟩ rauschen □ *vt* hetzen, drängen. ~ **hour** *n* Hauptverkehrszeit *f*, Stoßzeit *f*

rusk *n* Zwieback *m*

Russia *n* Rußland *nt*. ~ **n** *a* russisch □ *n* Russe *m*/Russin *f*; ⟨*Lang*⟩ Russisch *nt*

rust *n* Rost *m* □ *vi* rosten

rustic *a* bäuerlich; ⟨*furniture*⟩ rustikal

rustle *vi* rascheln

'rustproof *a* rostfrei

rusty *a* rostig

rut *n* Furche *f*; **be in a** ~ ⟨*fam*⟩ aus dem alten Trott nicht herauskommen

ruthless *a* rücksichtslos

rye *n* Roggen *m*

S

sabbath *n* Sabbat *m*

sabot|age *n* Sabotage *f* □ *vt* sabotieren. ~ **eur** *n* Saboteur *m*

sachet *n* Beutel *m*

sack¹ *vt* ⟨*plunder*⟩ plündern

sack² *n* Sack *m* □ *vt* ⟨*fam*⟩ rausschmeißen

sacrament *n* Sakrament *nt*

sacred *a* heilig

sacrifice *n* Opfer *nt* □ *vt* opfern

sacrilege *n* Sakrileg *nt*

sad *a* traurig; ⟨*loss*⟩ schmerzlich

saddle *n* Sattel *m* □ *vt* satteln

sadis|m *n* Sadismus *m*. ~ **t** *n* Sadist *m*. ~ **tic** *a* sadistisch

sad|ly *adv* traurig; ⟨*unfortunately*⟩ leider. ~ **ness** *n* Traurigkeit *f*

safe *a* sicher; ⟨*journey*⟩ gut □ *n* Safe *m*. ~ **guard** *n* Schutz *m* □ *vt* schützen

safety *n* Sicherheit *f*. ~ **-belt** *n* Sicherheitsgurt *m*. ~ **-pin** *n* Sicherheitsnadel *f*

sag *vi* durchhängen

saga *n* Saga *f*; ⟨*fig*⟩ Geschichte *f*

sage¹ *n* ⟨*Bot*⟩ Salbei *m*

sage² *a* weise □ *n* Weise(r) *m*

Sagittarius *n* ⟨*Astr*⟩ Schütze *m*

sail *n* Segel *nt* □ *vi* segeln; ⟨*on liner*⟩ fahren □ *vt* segeln mit

'sailboard *n* Surfbrett *nt*

sailing *n* Segelsport *m*. ~ **-boat** *n* Segelboot *nt*

sailor *n* Seemann *m*; ⟨*in navy*⟩ Matrose *m*

saint n Heilige(r) m/f

sake n for the ~ of ... um ... (gen) willen; **for my/your** ~ um meinet-/deinetwillen

salad n Salat m

salary n Gehalt nt

sale n Verkauf m; (event) Basar m; (at reduced prices) Schlußverkauf m; **for** ~ zu verkaufen

salesman n Verkäufer m

salient a wichtigste(r,s)

saliva n Speichel m

salmon n Lachs m

saloon n Salon m; (Auto) Limousine f

salt n Salz nt □vt salzen; (cure) pökeln. ~**-cellar** n Salzfaß nt. ~**'water** n Salzwasser nt. ~**y** a salzig

salutary a heilsam

salute n (Mil) Gruß m □vt/i (Mil) grüßen

salvage n (Naut) Bergung f □vt bergen

salvation n Rettung f; (Relig) Heil nt. S~ 'Army n Heilsarmee f

same a & pron the ~ der/die/das gleiche; (pl) die gleichen; (identical) der-/die-/dasselbe; (pl) dieselben □adv the ~ gleich; **all the** ~ trotzdem

sample n Probe f; (Comm) Muster nt □vt probieren

sanatorium n Sanatorium nt

sanctify vt heiligen

sanctimonious a frömmlerisch

sanction n Sanktion f □vt sanktionieren

sanctity n Heiligkeit f

sanctuary n (Relig) Heiligtum nt; (refuge) Zuflucht f

sand n Sand m

sandal n Sandale f

sandpaper n Sandpapier nt □vt [ab]schmirgeln

sandwich n belegtes Brot nt; Sandwich m

sandy a sandig; (beach) Sand-; (hair) rotblond

sane a geistig normal; (sensible) vernünftig

sanitary a hygienisch; (system) sanitär. ~ **towel** n [Damen]binde f

sanitation n Kanalisation und Abfallbeseitigung pl

sanity n [gesunder] Verstand m

sap n (Bot) Saft m □vt schwächen

sapphire n Saphir m

sarcas|m n Sarkasmus m. ~**tic** a sarkastisch

sardine n Sardine f

Sardinia n Sardinien nt

sardonic a höhnisch; (smile) sardonisch

sash n Schärpe f

satanic a satanisch

satchel n Ranzen m

satellite n Satellit m. ~ **dish** n Satellitenschüssel f. ~ **television** n Satellitenfernsehen nt

satin n Satin m

satire n Satire f

satirical a satirisch

satisfaction n Befriedigung f

satisfactory a zufriedenstellend

satisfy vt befriedigen; zufriedenstellen (customer); (convince) überzeugen

saturat|e vt durchtränken; (Chem & fig) sättigen. ~**ed** a durchnäßt; (fat) gesättigt

Saturday n Samstag m, Sonnabend m

sauce n Soße f; (cheek) Frechheit f. ~**pan** n Kochtopf m

saucer n Untertasse f

Saudi Arabia n Saudi-Arabien nt

sauna n Sauna f

saunter vi schlendern

sausage n Wurst f

savage a wild; (fierce) scharf; (brutal) brutal □n Wilde(r) m/f □vt anfallen

save n (Sport) Abwehr f □vt retten (from vor + dat); (keep) aufheben; (not waste) sparen; (collect) sammeln; (avoid) ersparen;

(Sport) verhindern ⟨goal⟩ □ vi ~
[up] sparen □ prep außer (+ dat),
mit Ausnahme (+ gen)

saving n Rettung f; Sparen nt;
Ersparnis f. ~**s** pl (money) Er-
sparnisse pl

saviour n Retter m

savour vt auskosten. ~**y** a herzhaft, würzig

saw n Säge f □ vt/i sägen. ~**dust**
n Sägemehl nt

saxophone n Saxophon nt

say n Mitspracherecht nt; **have
one's** ~ seine Meinung sagen
□ vt/i sagen; sprechen ⟨prayer⟩;
that is to ~ das heißt; **that goes
without** ~**ing** das versteht sich
von selbst. ~**ing** n Redensart f

scab n Schorf m; (pej) Streikbrecher m

scaffold n Schafott nt. ~**ing** n
Gerüst nt

scald vt verbrühen

scale[1] n (of fish) Schuppe f

scale[2] n Skala f; (Mus) Tonleiter f;
(ratio) Maßstab m □ vt (climb) er-
klettern

scales npl (for weighing) Waage f

scalp n Kopfhaut f

scalpel n Skalpell nt

scam n Schwindel m

scamper vi huschen

scan n (Med) Szintigramm nt □ v
□ vt absuchen; (quickly) flüchtig
ansehen; (Med) szintigraphisch
untersuchen □ vi ⟨poetry:⟩ das
richtige Versmaß haben

scandal n Skandal m. ~**ize** vt
schockieren. ~**ous** a skandalös

Scandinavia n Skandinavien n.
~**n** a skandinavisch □ n Skandi-
navier(in) m(f)

scant a wenig

scanty a spärlich

scapegoat n Sündenbock m

scar n Narbe f

scarce a knapp. ~**ely** adv kaum.
~**ity** n Knappheit f

scare n Schreck m; (panic) [allge-
meine] Panik f; (bomb ~) Bom-
bendrohung f □ vt Angst machen
(+ dat); **be** ~**d** Angst haben (of
vor + dat)

'scarecrow n Vogelscheuche f

scarf n Schal m

scarlet a scharlachrot. ~ **'fever**
n Scharlach m

scary a unheimlich

scathing a bissig

scatter vt verstreuen; (disperse)
zerstreuen □ vi sich zerstreuen.
~**-brained** a (fam) schusselig.
~**ed** a verstreut; ⟨showers⟩ vereinzelt

scavenge vi [im Abfall] Nahrung
suchen; ⟨animal:⟩ Aas fressen.
~**r** n Aasfresser m

scenario n Szenario nt

scene n Szene f; (sight) Anblick
m; (place of event) Schauplatz m

scenery n Landschaft f; (Theat)
Szenerie f

scenic a landschaftlich schön;
(Theat) Bühnen-

scent n Duft m; (trail) Fährte f;
(perfume) Parfüm nt

sceptic|al a skeptisch. ~**ism** n
Skepsis f

schedule n Programm nt; (of
work) Zeitplan m; (timetable)
Fahrplan m; **according to** ~
planmäßig □ vt planen. ~**d flight**
n Linienflug m

scheme n Programm nt; (plan)
Plan m; (plot) Komplott m □ vi
Ränke schmieden

schizophren|ia n Schizophrenie
f. ~**ic** a schizophren

scholar n Gelehrte(r) m/f. ~**ly** a
gelehrt. ~**ship** n Gelehrtheit f;
(grant) Stipendium nt

school n Schule f; (Univ) Fakultät
f □ vt schulen; dressieren ⟨an-
imal⟩

school: ~**boy** n Schüler m. ~**girl**
n Schülerin f. ~**teacher** n Leh-
rer(in) m(f)

sciatica n Ischias m

scien|ce n Wissenschaft f. **~ tific** a wissenschaftlich. **~ tist** n Wissenschaftler m

scintillating a sprühend

scissors npl Schere f

scoff[1] vi **~ at** spotten über (+ acc)

scoff[2] vt (fam) verschlingen

scold vt ausschimpfen

scoop n Schaufel f; (Culin) Portionierer m; (Journ) Exklusivmeldung f □ vt **~ out** aushöhlen

scoot vi (fam) rasen. **~ er** n Roller m

scope n Bereich m; (opportunity) Möglichkeiten pl

scorch vt versengen

score n [Spiel]stand m; (individual) Punktzahl f; (Mus) Partitur f; (Cinema) Filmmusik f □ vt erzielen; schießen ⟨goal⟩; (cut) einritzen □ vi Punkte erzielen; (Sport) ein Tor schießen; (keep score) Punkte zählen

scorn n Verachtung f □ vt verachten

Scorpio n (Astr) Skorpion m

scorpion n Skorpion m

Scot n Schotte m/Schottin f

Scotch a schottisch □ n (whisky) Scotch m

scot-'free a get off **~** straffrei ausgehen

Scot|land n Schottland nt. **~s, ~ tish** a schottisch

scour[1] vt (search) absuchen

scour[2] vt (clean) scheuern

scourge n Geißel f

scout n (Mil) Kundschafter m □ vi **~ for** Ausschau halten nach

Scout n [Boy] **~** Pfadfinder m

scowl vi ein böses Gesicht machen

scramble n Gerangel nt □ vi klettern □ vt (Teleph) verschlüsseln. **~d egg[s]** nt[pl] Rührei nt

scrap[1] n (fam: fight) Rauferei f □ vi sich raufen

scrap[2] n Stückchen nt; (metal) Schrott m; **~ s** pl Reste □ vt aufgeben

'scrap-book n Sammelalbum nt

scrape vt schaben; (clean) abkratzen; (damage) [ver]schrammen

scrappy a lückenhaft

'scrap-yard n Schrottplatz m

scratch n Kratzer m; **start from ~** von vorne anfangen; **not be up to ~** zu wünschen übriglassen □ vt/i kratzen

scrawl n Gekrakel nt □ vt/i krakeln

scrawny a (pej) dürr, hager

scream n Schrei m □ vt/i schreien

screech n Kreischen nt □ vt/i kreischen

screen n Schirm m; (Cinema) Leinwand f; (TV) Bildschirm m □ vt schützen; (conceal) verdecken; vorführen ⟨film⟩; (examine) überprüfen; (Med) untersuchen. **~ play** n Drehbuch nt

screw n Schraube f □ vt schrauben. **~ up** vt festschrauben; (crumple) zusammenknüllen; zusammenkneifen ⟨eyes⟩

'screwdriver n Schraubenzieher m

screwy a (fam) verrückt

scribble n Gekritzel nt □ vt/i kritzeln

script n Schrift f; (of speech, play) Text m; (Radio, TV) Skript nt; (of film) Drehbuch nt

Scripture n the **~ s** pl die Heilige Schrift f

scroll n Schriftrolle f

scrounge vt/i schnorren. **~ r** n Schnorrer m

scrub[1] n (land) Buschland nt, Gestrüpp nt

scrub[2] vt/i schrubben

scruff n by the **~** of the neck beim Genick

scruffy a vergammelt

scrum n Gedränge nt

scruple n Skrupel m
scrupulous a gewissenhaft
scrutin|ize vt [genau] ansehen.
~**y** n (look) prüfender Blick m
scuffle n Handgemenge nt
sculpt|or n Bildhauer(in) m(f).
~**ure** n Bildhauerei f; (piece of
work) Skulptur f, Plastik f
scum n Schmutzschicht f
scurrilous a niederträchtig
scuttle[1] vt versenken ⟨ship⟩
scuttle[2] vi schnell krabbeln
scythe n Sense f
sea n Meer nt, See f; **at** ~ auf See;
by ~ mit dem Schiff. ~**food** n
Meeresfrüchte pl. ~**gull** n Möwe
f
seal[1] n (Zool) Seehund m
seal[2] n Siegel nt; (Techn) Dichtung
f ⊔ vt versiegeln; (Techn) abdichten; (fig) besiegeln. ~ **off** vt ab-
riegeln
'**sea-level** n Meeresspiegel m
seam n Naht f
'**seaman** n Seemann m; (sailor)
Matrose m
seance n spiritistische Sitzung f
seaport n Seehafen m
search n Suche f; (official) Durch-
suchung f ⊔ vt durchsuchen; absuchen ⟨area⟩ ⊔ vi suchen (**for**
nach). ~**ing** a prüfend, forschend
search: ~**light** n [Such]schein-
werfer m. ~**party** n Suchmann-
schaft f
seasick a seekrank
season n Jahreszeit f; (sporting)
Saison f ⊔ vt (flavour) würzen.
~**al** a Saison-. ~**ing** n Gewürze
pl
'**season ticket** n Dauerkarte f
seat n Sitz m; (place) Sitzplatz m;
take a ~ Platz nehmen ⊔ vt setzen; (have seats for) Sitzplätze
bieten (+ dat). ~**belt** n Sicherheitsgurt m; **fasten one's** ~**belt**
sich anschnallen
seaweed n [See]tang m

secateurs npl Gartenschere f
seclu|de vt absondern. ~**ded** a
abgelegen. ~**sion** n Zurückgezo-
genheit f
second[1] vt (transfer) [vorüberge-
hend] versetzen
second[2] a zweite(r,s) ⊔ n Sekunde
f; (Sport) Sekundant m ⊔ adv (in a
race) an zweiter Stelle ⊔ vt unterstützen
secondary a zweitrangig. ~
school n höhere Schule f
second: ~**best** a zweitbeste(r,s).
~**class** a zweitklassig
second-hand a gebraucht
secondly adv zweitens
secrecy n Heimlichkeit f
secret a geheim; ⟨agent⟩ Geheim-;
⟨drinker⟩ heimlich ⊔ n Geheimnis nt
secretary n Sekretär(in) m(f)
secret|e vt absondern. ~**ion** n
Absonderung f
secretive a geheimtuerisch.
~**ness** n Heimlichtuerei f
sect n Sekte f
section n Teil m; (of text) Abschnitt m
sector n Sektor m
secular a weltlich
secure a sicher; ⟨firm⟩ fest; (emotionally) geborgen ⊔ vt sichern;
(fasten) festmachen; (obtain)
sich (dat) sichern
securit|y n Sicherheit f; (emo-
tional) Geborgenheit f; ~**ies** pl
Wertpapiere pl; (Fin) Effekten pl
sedate[1] a gesetzt
sedate[2] vt sedieren
sedation n Sedierung f
sedative a beruhigend ⊔ n Beruhigungsmittel nt
sedentary a sitzend
sediment n [Boden]satz m
seduce vt verführen
seduct|ion n Verführung f. ~**ive**
a verführerisch

see *vt* sehen; (*understand*) einsehen; (*imagine*) sich (*dat*) vorstellen □ *vi* sehen; (*check*) nachsehen; ~ **about** sich kümmern um. ~ **off** *vt* verabschieden; (*chase away*) vertreiben. ~ **through** *vt* (*fig*) ~ **through s.o.** jdn durchschauen

seed *n* Samen *m*; (*of grape*) Kern *m*; (*fig*) Saat *f*. ~ed *a* (*Tennis*) gesetzt. ~ling *n* Sämling *m*

seedy *a* schäbig

seek *vt* suchen

seem *vi* scheinen

seemly *a* schicklich

seep *vi* sickern

see-saw *n* Wippe *f*

seethe *vi* ~ **with anger** vor Wut schäumen

'see-through *a* durchsichtig

segment *n* Teil *m*

segregat|e *vt* trennen. ~ion *n* Trennung *f*

seize *vt* ergreifen; (*Jur*) beschlagnahmen

seizure *n* (*Jur*) Beschlagnahme *f*; (*Med*) Anfall *m*

seldom *adv* selten

select *a* ausgewählt; (*exclusive*) exklusiv □ *vt* auswählen; aufstellen (*team*). ~ion *n* Auswahl *f*. ~ive *a* selektiv; (*choosy*) wählerisch

self *n* Ich *nt*

self: ~-ad'dressed *a* adressiert. ~-as'sured *a* selbstsicher. ~-'centred *a* egozentrisch. ~-'confident *a* selbstbewußt. ~-'conscious *a* befangen. ~-con'tained *a* (*flat*) abgeschlossen. ~-de'fence *n* Selbstverteidigung *f*; (*Jur*) Notwehr *f*. ~-em'ployed *a* selbständig. ~-'evident *a* offensichtlich.

self|ish *a* egoistisch, selbstsüchtig. ~less *a* selbstlos

self: ~-'pity *n* Selbstmitleid *nt*. ~-'righteous *a* selbstgerecht

~-'service *n* Selbstbedienung *f*. ~-suf'ficient *a* selbständig

sell *v* □ *vt* verkaufen; **be sold out** ausverkauft sein □ *vi* sich verkaufen

seller *n* Verkäufer *m*

Sellotape (P) *n* ≈ Tesafilm (P) *m*

'sell-out *n* **be a** ~ ausverkauft sein; (*fam: betray*) Verrat sein

semblance *n* Anschein *m*

semen *n* (*Anat*) Samen *m*

semi|breve *n* (*Mus*) ganze Note *f*. ~circle *n* Halbkreis *m*. ~'colon *n* Semikolon *nt*. ~-de'tached *a* & *nt* ~-**detached** [**house**] Doppelhaushälfte *f*. ~'final *n* Halbfinale *nt*

seminar *n* Seminar *nt*

'semitone *n* (*Mus*) Halbton *m*

semolina *n* Grieß *m*

senat|e *n* Senat *m*. ~or *n* Senator *m*

send *vt/i* schicken. ~er *n* Absender *m*

senil|e *a* senil. ~ity *n* Senilität *f*

senior *a* älter; (*in rank*) höher □ *n* Ältere(r) *m/f*; (in rank) Vorgesetzte(r) *m/f*. ~ 'citizen *n* Senior(in) *m(f)*

seniority *n* höheres Alter *nt*; (*in rank*) höherer Rang *m*

sensation *n* Sensation *f*; (*feeling*) Gefühl *nt*. ~al *a* sensationell

sense *n* Sinn *m*; (*feeling*) Gefühl *nt*; (*common*~) Verstand *m*; **in a** ~ in gewisser Hinsicht □ *vt* spüren. ~less *a* sinnlos

sensible *a* vernünftig; (*suitable*) zweckmäßig

sensitiv|e *a* empfindlich; (*understanding*) einfühlsam. ~ity *n* Empfindlichkeit *f*

sensory *a* Sinnes-

sensual *a* sinnlich. ~ity *n* Sinnlichkeit *f*

sensuous *a* sinnlich

sentence n Satz m; (Jur) Urteil nt; (punishment) Strafe f ~vt verurteilen

sentiment n Gefühl nt; (opinion) Meinung f. ~al a sentimental. ~ality n Sentimentalität f

sentry n Wache f

separable a trennbar

separate[1] a getrennt, separat

separat[e2 vt trennen ~vi sich trennen. ~ion n Trennung f

September n September m

septic a vereitert

sequel n Folge f

sequence n Reihenfolge f

sequin n Paillette f

serenade n Ständchen nt

seren[e a gelassen. ~ity n Gelassenheit f

sergeant n (Mil) Feldwebel m; (in police) Polizeimeister m

serial n Fortsetzungsgeschichte f; (Radio, TV) Serie f

series n Serie f

serious a ernst; (illness) schwer. ~ness n Ernst m

sermon n Predigt f

serpent n Schlange f

servant n Diener(in) m(f)

serve n (Tennis) Aufschlag m ~vt dienen (+ dat); bedienen (customer); servieren (food); (Jur) zustellen (on s.o. jdm); verbüßen (sentence) ~vi dienen; (Tennis) aufschlagen

service n Dienst m; (Relig) Gottesdienst m; (in shop, restaurant) Bedienung f; (transport) Verbindung f; (maintenance) Wartung f; (set of crockery) Service nt; (Tennis) Aufschlag m; **be of ~** nützlich sein ~vt (Techn) warten

service: **~ area** n Tankstelle und Raststätte f. **~ charge** n Bedienungszuschlag m

serviette n Serviette f

servile a unterwürfig

session n Sitzung f

set n Satz m; (of crockery) Service f; (of cutlery) Garnitur f; (TV, Radio) Apparat m; (Math) Menge f; (Theat) Bühnenbild nt □ a (ready) fertig, bereit; **be ~ in one's ways** in seinen Gewohnheiten festgefahren sein ~vt setzen; (adjust) einstellen; stellen (task); festsetzen, festlegen (date); aufgeben (homework) ~vi (sun:) untergehen; (become hard:) fest werden. **~ off** vi losgehen; (in vehicle) losfahren ~vt auslösen (alarm); explodieren lassen (bomb). **~ up** vt aufbauen; (fig) gründen

set 'meal n Menü nt

settee n Sofa nt, Couch f

setting n Rahmen m; (surroundings) Umgebung f

settle vt (decide) entscheiden; (agree) regeln; (fix) festsetzen; (calm) beruhigen; (pay) bezahlen ~vi sich niederlassen; (snow:) liegenbleiben. **~ down** vi sich beruhigen; (permanently) seßhaft werden. **~ up** vi abrechnen

settlement n Entscheidung f; Regelung f; Bezahlung f; (Jur) Vergleich m; (colony) Siedlung f

settler n Siedler m

'set-up n System nt

seven a sieben. **~teen** a siebzehn. **~teenth** a siebzehnte(r,s)

seventh a siebte(r,s)

seventieth a siebzigste(r,s)

seventy a siebzig

sever vt durchtrennen; abbrechen (relations)

several a & pron mehrere, einige

sever[e a streng; (pain) stark; (illness) schwer. ~ity n Strenge f; Schwere f

sew vt/i nähen

sewage n Abwasser nt

sewer n Abwasserkanal m

sewing n Nähen nt; (work) Näharbeit f. **~ machine** n Nähmaschine f

sex n Geschlecht nt; (sexuality) Sex m. ~**ist** a sexistisch

sexual a sexuell. ~ **'intercourse** n Geschlechtsverkehr m

sexy a sexy

shabby a schäbig

shack n Hütte f

shade n Schatten m; (of colour) [Farb]ton m; (for lamp) [Lampen]schirm m □vt beschatten; (draw lines on) schattieren

shadow n Schatten m

shady a schattig; (fam: disreputable) zwielichtig

shaft n Schaft m; (Techn) Welle f; (of light) Strahl m

shake vt schütteln; (shock) erschüttern; ~ **hands with s.o.** jdm die Hand geben □vi wackeln; (tremble) zittern

shaky a wackelig; (hand) zittrig

shall v aux **we** ~ **see** wir werden sehen; **what** ~ **I do?** was soll ich machen?

shallow a seicht; (fig) oberflächlich

sham n Heuchelei f; (person) Heuchler(in) m(f) □vt vortäuschen

shambles n Durcheinander nt

shame n Scham f; (disgrace) Schande f; **what a** ~! wie schade! **shame|ful** a schändlich. ~**less** a schamlos

shampoo n Shampoo nt □vt schamponieren

shandy n Radler m

shape n Form f; (figure) Gestalt f; **take** ~ Gestalt annehmen □vt formen (**into** zu)

shapely a wohlgeformt

share n [An]teil m; (Comm) Aktie f □vt/i teilen. ~**holder** n Aktionär(in) m(f)

shark n Hai[fisch] m

sharp a scharf; (pointed) spitz; (severe) heftig; (sudden) steil; (alert) clever; (unscrupulous) gerissen □adv scharf; (Mus) zu

hoch; **at six o'clock** ~ **Punkt** sechs Uhr □n (Mus) Kreuz nt. ~**en** vt schärfen; [an]spitzen (pencil)

shatter vt zertrümmern; (fig) zerstören; **be** ~**ed** (person:) erschüttert sein □vi zersplittern

shave n Rasur f □vt rasieren □vi sich rasieren. ~**r** n Rasierapparat m

shawl n Schultertuch nt

she pron sie

sheaf n Garbe f; (of papers) Bündel nt

shear vt scheren

shears npl (große) Schere f

sheath n Scheide f

shed¹ n Schuppen m

shed² vt verlieren; vergießen (blood); ~ **light on** Licht bringen in (+ acc)

sheen n Glanz m

sheep n inv Schaf nt

sheepish a verlegen

sheer a rein; (steep) steil; (transparent) hauchdünn

sheet n Laken nt, Bettuch nt; (of paper) Blatt nt; (of glass, metal) Platte f

sheikh n Scheich m

shelf n Brett nt, Bord nt

shell n Schale f; (of snail) Haus nt; (of tortoise) Panzer m; (on beach) Muschel f □vt pellen; enthülsen

'shellfish n inv Schalentiere pl; (Culin) Meeresfrüchte pl

shelter n Schutz m □vt schützen (**from** vor + dat) □vi sich unterstellen

shelve vt auf Eis legen

shelving n (shelves) Regale pl

shepherd n Schäfer m

sherry n Sherry m

shield n Schild m; (for eyes) Schirm m; (Techn & fig) Schutz m □vt schützen (**from** vor + dat)

shift n Verschiebung f; (at work) Schicht f □vt rücken

shifty *a* (*pej*) verschlagen

shimmer *vi* schimmern

shin *n* Schienbein *nt*

shine *n* Glanz *m* ◻ *vi* leuchten; (*reflect light*) glänzen; ⟨*sun:*⟩ scheinen

shingle *n* Kiesel *pl*

shingles *n* (*Med*) Gürtelrose *f*

ship: ~**ment** *n* Sendung *f*. ~**per** *n* Spediteur *m*. ~**ping** *n* Versand *m*; (*traffic*) Schiffahrt *f*. ~**wreck** *n* Schiffbruch *m*. ~**yard** *n* Werft *f*

shirk *vt* sich drücken vor (+ *dat*). ~**er** *n* Drückeberger *m*

shirt *n* [Ober]hemd *nt*

shit *n* (*vulg*) Scheiße *f*

shiver *n* Schauder *m* ◻ *vi* zittern

shoal *n* (*of fish*) Schwarm *m*

shock *n* Schock *m*; (*Electr*) Schlag *m*; (*impact*) Erschütterung *f* ◻ *vt* einen Schock versetzen (+ *dat*); (*scandalize*) schockieren. ~**ing** *a* schockierend

shoddy *a* minderwertig

shoe *n* Schuh *m*

shoe: ~**horn** *n* Schuhanzieher *m*. ~**lace** *n* Schnürsenkel *m*

shoo *vt* scheuchen ◻ *int* sch!

shoot *n* (*Bot*) Trieb *m*; (*hunt*) Jagd *f* ◻ *vt* schießen; (*kill*) erschießen; drehen ⟨*film*⟩ ◻ *vi* schießen

shop *n* Laden *m*, Geschäft *nt* ◻ *vi* einkaufen; **go** ~**ping** einkaufen gehen

shop: ~**assistant** *n* Verkäufer(in) *m(f)*. ~**keeper** *n* Ladenbesitzer(in) *m(f)*. ~**lifter** *n* Ladendieb *m*

shopping *n* Einkaufen *nt*; (*articles*) Einkäufe *pl*. ~ **bag** *n* Einkaufstasche *f*. ~ **centre** *n* Einkaufszentrum *nt*. ~ **trolley** *n* Einkaufswagen *m*

shop-steward *n* [gewerkschaftlicher] Vertrauensmann *m*

shore *n* Strand *m*; (*of lake*) Ufer *nt*

short *a* kurz; ⟨*person*⟩ klein; (*curt*) schroff; **a** ~ **time ago** vor kurzem ◻ *adv* kurz; (*abruptly*) plötzlich; (*curtly*) kurz angebunden; **in** ~ kurzum

shortage *n* Mangel *m* (**of** an + *dat*); (*scarcity*) Knappheit *f*

short: ~**bread** *n* ≈ Mürbekekse *pl*. ~ **circuit** *n* Kurzschluß *m*. ~**coming** *n* Fehler *m*. ~ **'cut** *n* Abkürzung *f*

shorten *vt* [ab]kürzen; kürzer machen ⟨*garment*⟩

short: ~**hand** *n* Kurzschrift *f*, Stenographie *f*. ~ **list** *n* engere Auswahl *f*. ~**lived** *a* kurzlebig

shorts *npl* kurze Hose *f*, Shorts *pl*

short: ~**'sighted** *a* kurzsichtig. ~**sleeved** *a* kurzärmelig. ~**'story** *n* Kurzgeschichte *f*. ~**'tempered** *a* aufbrausend. ~**term** *a* kurzfristig. ~ **wave** *n* Kurzwelle *f*

shot *n* Schuß *m*; (*pellets*) Schrot *m*; (*person*) Schütze *m*; (*Phot*) Aufnahme *f*; (*injection*) Spritze *f*; (*fam: attempt*) Versuch *m*; **like a** ~ (*fam*) sofort. ~**gun** *n* Schrotflinte *f*. ~**putting** *n* (*Sport*) Kugelstoßen *nt*

should *v aux* **you** ~ **go** du solltest gehen; **I** ~ **have seen him** ich hätte ihn sehen sollen; **I** ~ **like** ich möchte; **this** ~ **be enough** das müßte eigentlich reichen; **if he** ~ **be there** falls er da sein sollte

shoulder *n* Schulter *f*. ~**blade** *n* Schulterblatt *nt*

shout *vt/i* schreien

shove *vt* stoßen; (*fam*) schubsen; (*fam: put*) tun ◻ *vi* drängeln

shovel *n* Schaufel *f*

show *n* (*display*) Pracht *f*; (*exhibition*) Ausstellung *f*, Schau *f*; (*performance*) Vorstellung *f*; (*Theat, TV*) Show *f*; **on** ~ ausgestellt ◻ *vt* zeigen; (*put on display*) ausstellen; vorführen ⟨*film*⟩ □*vi* sichtbar sein; ⟨*film:*⟩ gezeigt werden. ~ **off** *vi* (*fam*) angeben □*vt* vorführen; (*flaunt*) angeben mit

'show-down *n* Entscheidungskampf *m*

shower *n* Dusche *f*; (*of rain*) Schauer *m*; **have a** ~ duschen □*vt* ~ **with** überschütten mit □*vi* duschen

'show-jumping *n* Springreiten *nt*

show: ~**-off** *n* Angeber(in) *m(f)*. ~**-piece** *n* Paradestück *nt*. ~**room** *n* Ausstellungsraum *m*

shred *n* Fetzen *m*; (*fig*) Spur *f* □*vt* zerkleinern; (*Culin*) schnitzeln. ~**der** *n* Reißwolf *m*; (*Culin*) Schnitzelwerk *nt*

shrewd *a* klug

shriek *vt/i* schreien

shrill *a* schrill

shrimp *n* Garnele *f*, Krabbe *f*

shrine *n* Heiligtum *nt*

shrink *vi* schrumpfen; ⟨*garment:*⟩ einlaufen; (*draw back*) zurückschrecken (**from** vor + *dat*)

shrivel *vi* verschrumpeln

shroud *n* Leichentuch *nt*; (*fig*) Schleier *m*

Shrove *n* ~ **Tuesday** Fastnachtsdienstag *m*

shrub *n* Strauch *m*

shrug *vt/i* ~ **[one's shoulders]** die Achseln zucken

shudder *vi* schaudern

shuffle *vi* schlurfen □*vt* mischen ⟨*cards*⟩

shun *vt* meiden

shut *vt* zumachen, schließen □*vi* sich schließen; ⟨*shop:*⟩ schließen, zumachen. ~ **down** *vt* schließen; stillegen ⟨*factory*⟩ □*vi* schließen; ⟨*factory:*⟩ stillgelegt werden. ~ **up** *vt* abschließen; (*lock in*) einsperren □*vi* (*fam*) den Mund halten

shutter *n* [Fenster]laden *m*; (*Phot*) Verschluß *m*

shuttle: ~**cock** *n* Federball *m*. ~ **service** *n* Pendelverkehr *m*

shy *a* schüchtern; (*timid*) scheu

Siamese *a* siamesisch

siblings *npl* Geschwister *pl*

Sicily *n* Sizilien *nt*

sick *a* krank; ⟨*humour*⟩ makaber; **be** ~ (*vomit*) sich übergeben; **be** ~ **of sth** (*fam*) etw satt haben; **I feel** ~ mir ist schlecht

sicken *vt* anwidern

sickle *n* Sichel *f*

side *n* Seite *f*; **on the** ~ (*as sideline*) nebenbei; ~ **by** ~ nebeneinander; (*fig*) Seite an Seite; **take** ~**s** Partei ergreifen (**with** für) □*vi* ~ **with** Partei ergreifen für

side: ~**board** *n* Anrichte *f*. ~**burns** *npl* Koteletten *pl*. ~**effect** *n* Nebenwirkung *f*. ~**lights** *npl* Standlicht *nt*. ~**line** *n* Nebenbeschäftigung *f*. ~**-show** *n* Nebenattraktion *f*. ~**step** *vt* ausweichen (+ *dat*). ~**ways** *adv* seitwärts

siege *n* Belagerung *f*; (*by police*) Umstellung *f*

sieve *n* Sieb *nt* □*vt* sieben

sift *vt* sieben; (*fig*) durchsehen

sigh *n* Seufzer *m* □*vi* seufzen

sight *n* Sicht *f*; (*faculty*) Sehvermögen *nt*; (*spectacle*) Anblick *m*; (*on gun*) Visier *nt*; ~**s** *pl* Sehenswürdigkeiten *pl*; **at first** ~ auf den ersten Blick □*vt* sichten

'sightseeing *n* **go** ~ die Sehenswürdigkeiten besichtigen

sign *n* Zeichen *nt*; (*notice*) Schild *nt* □*vt/i* unterschreiben; ⟨*artist:*⟩ signieren

signal *n* Signal *nt* □*vt/i* signalisieren; ~ **to s.o.** jdm ein Signal geben (**to zu**). ~**-box** *n* Stellwerk *nt*

signature *n* Unterschrift *f*; (*of artist*) Signatur *f*. ~ **tune** *n* Kennmelodie *f*

signet-ring *n* Siegelring *m*

significan|ce n Bedeutung f. **~t** a bedeutungsvoll

signify vt bedeuten

signpost n Wegweiser m

silence n Stille f; (of person) Schweigen nt □ vt zum Schweigen bringen. **~r** n (on gun) Schalldämpfer m; (Auto) Auspufftopf m

silent a still; (without speaking) schweigend; **remain ~** schweigen. **~ film** n Stummfilm m

silhouette n Silhouette f; (picture) Schattenriß m

silicon n Silizium m

silk n Seide f. **~worm** n Seidenraupe f

sill n Sims m & nt

silly a dumm, albern

silo n Silo m

silt n Schlick m

silver a silbern; (paper) Silber- □ n Silber nt

silver: ~-plated a versilbert. **~ware** n Silber nt. **~'wedding** n Silberhochzeit f

similar a ähnlich. **~ity** n Ähnlichkeit f

simile n Vergleich m

simmer vi leise kochen, ziehen

simple a einfach; (person) einfältig. **~-'minded** a einfältig. **~ton** n Einfaltspinsel m

simplify vt vereinfachen

simulate vt vortäuschen; (Techn) simulieren

simultaneous a gleichzeitig; (interpreting) Simultan-

sin n Sünde f □ vi sündigen

since prep seit (+ dat) □ adv seitdem □ conj seit; (because) da

sincere a aufrichtig; (heartfelt) herzlich. **~ly** adv aufrichtig; **Yours ~ly** Mit freundlichen Grüßen

sincerity n Aufrichtigkeit f

sinew n Sehne f

sing vt/i singen

singe vt versengen

singer n Sänger(in) m(f)

single a einzeln; (one only) einzig; (unmarried) ledig; (ticket) einfach; (room) Einzel- □ n (ticket) einfache Fahrkarte f; (record) Single f; **~s** pl (Tennis) Einzel nt

single: ~-handed a & adv allein. **~-'minded** a zielstrebig. **~ 'parent** n Alleinerziehende(r) m(f)

singular a eigenartig; (Gram) im Singular □ n Singular m. **~ly** adv außerordentlich

sinister a finster

sink n Spülbecken nt □ vi sinken □ vt versenken (ship); senken (shaft)

sinner n Sünder(in) m(f)

sinus n Nebenhöhle f

sip n Schlückchen nt

siphon n (bottle) Siphon m

sir n mein Herr; **S~** (title) Sir; **Dear S~s** Sehr geehrte Herren

siren n Sirene f

sister n Schwester f; (nurse) Oberschwester f. **~-in-law** n Schwägerin f. **~ly** a schwesterlich

sit vi sitzen; (sit down) sich setzen; (committee:) tagen □ vt setzen; machen (exam). **~ down** vi sich setzen. **~ up** vi (aufrecht) sitzen; (rise) sich aufsetzen; (not slouch) gerade sitzen; (stay up) aufbleiben

site n Gelände nt; (for camping) Platz m; (Archaeol) Stätte f

sitting n Sitzung f; (for meals) Schub m

situat|e vt legen; **be ~ed** liegen. **~ion** n Lage f; (circumstances) Situation f; (job) Stelle f

six a sechs. **~teen** a sechzehn. **~teenth** a sechzehnte(r,s)

sixth a sechste(r,s)

sixtieth a sechzigste(r,s)

sixty a sechzig

size n Größe f

sizzle vi brutzeln

skate[1] n inv (fish) Rochen m

skate[2] n Schlittschuh m; (roller-) Rollschuh m □vi Schlittschuh/ Rollschuh laufen. **~r** n Eisläufer(in) m(f); Rollschuhläufer(in) m(f)

skating-rink n Eisbahn f

skeleton n Skelett nt. **~ 'key** n Dietrich m. **~ 'staff** n Minimalbesetzung f

sketch n Skizze f; (Theat) Sketch m □vt skizzieren

skewer n [Brat]spieß m

ski n Ski m □vi Ski fahren or laufen

skid vi schleudern

skier n Skiläufer(in) m(f)

skiing n Skilaufen nt

skilful a geschickt

skill n Geschick nt. **~ed** a geschickt; (trained) ausgebildet

skim vt entrahmen ⟨milk⟩

skin n Haut f; (on fruit) Schale f

skin-diving n Sporttauchen nt

skinny a dünn

skip[1] n Container m

skip[2] vi hüpfen; (with rope) seilspringen □vt überspringen

skipper n Kapitän m

'skipping-rope n Sprungseil nt

skirmish n Gefecht nt

skirt n Rock m

skittle n Kegel m

skull n Schädel m

skunk n Stinktier nt

sky n Himmel m. **~light** n Dachluke f. **~scraper** n Wolkenkratzer m

slab n Platte f

slack a schlaff, locker; ⟨person⟩ nachlässig; (Comm) flau

slacken vi sich lockern; (diminish) nachlassen; ⟨speed:⟩ sich verringern □vt lockern; (diminish) verringern

slacks npl Hose f

slag n Schlacke f

slam vt zuschlagen; (put) knallen (fam); (fam: criticize) verreißen □vi zuschlagen

slander n Verleumdung f □vt verleumden

slang n Slang m

slant n Schräge f

slap vt schlagen; (put) knallen (fam) □adv direkt

slap: **~dash** a (fam) schludrig. **~-up** a (fam) toll

slash vt aufschlitzen; [drastisch] reduzieren ⟨prices⟩

slat n Latte f

slate n Schiefer m

slaughter vt schlachten; abschlachten. **~house** n Schlachthaus nt

Slav a slawisch □n Slawe m/ Slawin f

slave n Sklave m/ Sklavin f □vi **~ [away]** schuften. **~-driver** n Leuteschinder m

slav|ery n Sklaverei f. **~ish** a sklavisch

Slavonic a slawisch

sledge n Schlitten m. **~-hammer** n Vorschlaghammer m

sleek a seidig

sleep n Schlaf m; go to **~** einschlafen □vi schlafen. **~er** n Schläfer(in) m(f); (Rail) Schlafwagen m; (on track) Schwelle f

sleeping: **~-bag** n Schlafsack m. **~-car** n Schlafwagen m. **~-pill** n Schlaftablette f

sleep: **~less** a schlaflos. **~-walking** n Schlafwandeln nt

sleepy a schläfrig

sleet n Schneeregen m

sleeve n Ärmel m; (for record) Hülle f. **~less** a ärmellos

sleigh n [Pferde]schlitten m

slender a schlank; (fig) gering

slice n Scheibe f □vt in Scheiben schneiden; **~d bread** Schnittbrot nt

slick a clever □n (of oil) Ölteppich m

slide n Rutschbahn f; (for hair) Spange f; (Phot) Dia nt □vi rutschen □vt schieben

slight a leicht; ⟨importance⟩ gering; ⟨acquaintance⟩ flüchtig; ⟨slender⟩ schlank; **not in the ~est** nicht im geringsten; **~ly better** ein bißchen besser

slim a schlank; ⟨volume⟩ schmal; ⟨fig⟩ gering □vi eine Schlankheitskur machen

slime n Schleim m. **~y** a schleimig

sling n ⟨Med⟩ Schlinge f □vt ⟨fam⟩ schmeißen

slip n ⟨mistake⟩ Fehler m, ⟨fam⟩ Patzer m; ⟨petticoat⟩ Unterrock m; ⟨for pillow⟩ Bezug m; ⟨paper⟩ Zettel m; **~ of the tongue** Versprecher m □vi rutschen; ⟨fall⟩ ausrutschen; ⟨go quickly⟩ schlüpfen; ⟨decline⟩ nachlassen

slipped 'disc n ⟨Med⟩ Bandscheibenvorfall m

slipper n Hausschuh m

slippery a glitschig

slit n Schlitz m

sliver n Splitter m

slog n [hard] **~** Schinderei f □vi schuften □vt schlagen

slogan n Schlagwort nt; ⟨advertising⟩ Werbespruch m

slope n Hang m; ⟨inclination⟩ Neigung f □vi sich neigen. **~ing** a schräg

sloppy a schludrig; ⟨sentimental⟩ sentimental

slot n Schlitz m; ⟨TV⟩ Sendezeit f □vi sich einfügen (**in** in + acc)

'slot-machine n Münzautomat m; ⟨for gambling⟩ Spielautomat m

slouch vi sich schlecht halten

Slovakia n Slowakische Republik f

slovenly a schlampig

slow a langsam; **be ~** ⟨clock:⟩ nachgehen; **in ~ motion** in Zeitlupe □vt verlangsamen □vi **~ down, ~ up** langsamer werden

slug n Nacktschnecke f

sluice n Schleuse f

slum n ⟨house⟩ Elendsquartier nt; **~s** pl Elendsviertel nt

slumber n Schlummer m

slump n Sturz m □vi fallen; ⟨crumple⟩ zusammensacken; ⟨prices:⟩ stürzen; ⟨sales:⟩ zurückgehen

slur vt undeutlich aussprechen

slurp vt/i schlürfen

slush n [Schnee]matsch m; ⟨fig⟩ Kitsch m

slut n Schlampe f

sly a verschlagen □**on the ~** heimlich

smack[1] vt schlagen; **~ one's lips** mit den Lippen schmatzen

smack[2] vi **~ of** ⟨fig⟩ riechen nach

small a klein; **in the ~ hours** in den frühen Morgenstunden □adv **chop up ~** kleinhacken □n **~ of the back** Kreuz nt

small: ~'change n Kleingeld nt. **~-holding** n landwirtschaftlicher Kleinbetrieb m. **~pox** n Pocken pl. **~ talk** n leichte Konversation f

smart a schick; ⟨clever⟩ schlau, clever; ⟨brisk⟩ flott □vi brennen

smash n Krach m; ⟨collision⟩ Zusammenstoß m; ⟨Tennis⟩ Schmetterball m □vt zerschlagen; ⟨strike⟩ schlagen; ⟨Tennis⟩ schmettern □vi zerschmettern; ⟨crash⟩ krachen (**into** gegen). **~ing** a ⟨fam⟩ toll

smear n verschmierter Fleck m; ⟨Med⟩ Abstrich m; ⟨fig⟩ Verleumdung f □vt schmieren; ⟨coat⟩ beschmieren (**with** mit); ⟨fig⟩ verleumden

smell n Geruch m, ⟨sense⟩ Geruchssinn m □vt riechen; ⟨sniff⟩ riechen an (+ dat) □vi riechen (**of** nach)

smelly a übelriechend

smelt vt schmelzen

smile n Lächeln nt □vi lächeln

smirk vi feixen

smith n Schmied m

smock n Kittel m

smog n Smog m

smoke n Rauch m □vt/i rauchen; (Culin) räuchern; **~less** a rauchfrei; ⟨fuel⟩ rauchlos

'smoke-screen n [künstliche] Nebelwand f

smooth a glatt □vt glätten. **~ out** vt glattstreichen

smother vt ersticken; (cover) bedecken; (suppress) unterdrücken

smoulder vi schwelen

smudge vt verwischen □vi schmieren

smug a selbstgefällig

smuggl|e vt schmuggeln. **~er** n Schmuggler m

smut n Rußflocke f; (mark) Rußfleck m; ⟨fig⟩ Schmutz m

snack n Imbiß m. **~-bar** n Imbißstube f

snail n Schnecke f

snake n Schlange f

snap n Knacken nt; (photo) Schnappschuß m □attrib ⟨decision⟩ plötzlich □vi [entzwei]brechen; **~ at** (bite) schnappen nach; (speak sharply) [scharf] anfahren □vt zerbrechen; (say) fauchen; (Phot) knipsen

'snapshot n Schnappschuß m

snare n Schlinge f

snarl vi [mit gefletschten Zähnen] knurren

snatch vt schnappen; (steal) klauen; entführen ⟨child⟩

sneak n (fam) Petze f □vi schleichen; (fam: tell tales) petzen

sneaky a hinterhältig

sneer vi höhnisch lächeln; (mock) spotten

sneeze vi niesen

sniff vi schnüffeln □vt schnüffeln an (+ dat); ⟨glue⟩

snigger vi [boshaft] kichern

snip n Schnitt m; (fam: bargain) günstiger Kauf m □vt/i **~ [at]** schnippeln an (+ dat)

sniper n Heckenschütze m

snivel vi flennen

snob n Snob m. **~bery** n Snobismus m. **~bish** a snobistisch

snoop vi (fam) schnüffeln

snooze n Nickerchen nt □vi dösen

snore vi schnarchen

snorkel n Schnorchel m

snort vi schnauben

snout n Schnauze f

snow n Schnee m □vi schneien

snow: ~ball n Schneeball m □vi lawinenartig anwachsen. **~-drift** n Schneewehe f. **~drop** n Schneeglöckchen nt. **~flake** n Schneeflocke f. **~man** n Schneemann m. **~-plough** n Schneepflug m. **~storm** n Schneesturm m

snub vt brüskieren

snuff[1] n Schnupftabak m

snuff[2] vt **~ [out]** löschen

snuffle vi schnüffeln

snug a behaglich, gemütlich

snuggle vi sich kuscheln (**up to** an + acc)

so adv so; **not so fast** nicht so schnell; **am I** ich auch; **so I see** das sehe ich; **that is so** das stimmt; **so much the better** um so besser; **if so** wenn ja □pron **I hope so** hoffentlich; **I think so** ich glaube schon; **I told you so** ich hab's dir gleich gesagt; **because I say so** weil ich es sage; **I'm afraid so** leider ja □conj (therefore) also; **so that** damit; **so there!** fertig! **so what!** na und!

soak vt naß machen; (steep) einweichen

soaking a & adv **~ [wet]** patschnaß (fam)

soap n Seife f. **~ opera** n Seifenoper f. **~ powder** n Seifenpulver nt

soar vi aufsteigen; ⟨prices:⟩ in die Höhe schnellen

sob vi schluchzen

sober a nüchtern; (serious) ernst; ⟨colour⟩ gedeckt

'so-called a sogenannt

soccer n (fam) Fußball m

sociable a gesellig

social a gesellschaftlich; (Admin, Pol, Zool) sozial

social|**ism** n Sozialismus m. ~**t** a sozialistisch □n Sozialist m

socialize vi (gesellschaftlich) verkehren

social: ~ **se'curity** n Sozialhilfe f. ~ **work** n Sozialarbeit f. ~ **worker** n Sozialarbeiter(in) m(f)

society n Gesellschaft f; (club) Verein m

sociolog|**ist** n Soziologe m. ~**y** n Soziologie f

sock n Socke f

socket n (of eye) Augenhöhle f; (of joint) Gelenkpfanne f; (wall plug) Steckdose f; (for bulb) Fassung f

soda n Soda nt. ~ **water** n Sodawasser nt

sodium n Natrium nt

sofa n Sofa nt. ~ **bed** n Schlafcouch f

soft a weich; (quiet) leise; (gentle) sanft. ~ **drink** n alkoholfreies Getränk nt

software n Software f

soggy a aufgeweicht

soil[1] n Erde f, Boden m

soil[2] vt verschmutzen

solar a Sonnen-

solder vt löten

soldier n Soldat m □vi ~ **on** [unbeirrbar] weitermachen

sole[1] n Sohle f

sole[2] n (fish) Seezunge f

sole[3] a einzig. ~**ly** adv einzig und allein

solemn a feierlich; (serious) ernst

solicit vt bitten um

solicitor n Rechtsanwalt m/-anwältin f

solicitous a besorgt

solid a fest; (sturdy) stabil; (not hollow) massiv; (unanimous) einstimmig; (complete) ganz □n (Geom) Körper m; ~**s** pl (food) feste Nahrung f

solidarity n Solidarität f

solidify vi fest werden

soliloquy n Selbstgespräch nt

solitary a einsam; (sole) einzig. ~ **con'finement** n Einzelhaft f

solitude n Einsamkeit f

solo n Solo nt □a Solo-; ⟨flight⟩ Allein- □adv solo. ~**ist** n Solist(in) m(f)

solstice n Sonnenwende f

soluble a löslich

solution n Lösung f

solvable a lösbar

solve vt lösen

solvent n Lösungsmittel nt

sombre a dunkel; ⟨mood⟩ düster

some a & pron etwas; (a little) ein bißchen; (with pl noun) einige; (a few) ein paar; (certain) manche(r,s); (one or the other) irgendein; ~ **day** eines Tages; **I want** ~ ich möchte etwas/⟨pl⟩ welche

some: ~**body** pron & n jemand; (emphatic) irgend jemand. ~**how** adv irgendwie. ~**one** pron & n = somebody

somersault n Purzelbaum m; (fam); (Sport) Salto m

something pron & adv etwas; (emphatic) irgend etwas; ~ **different** etwas anderes; ~ **like** so etwas wie

some: ~**time** adv irgendwann □a ehemalig. ~**times** adv manchmal. ~**what** adv ziemlich. ~**where** adv irgendwo; ⟨go⟩ irgendwohin

son n Sohn m

sonata n Sonate f

song n Lied nt. ~ **bird** n Singvogel m

sonic a Schall-. ~ **'boom** n Überschallknall m

'son-in-law n Schwiegersohn m

soon *adv* bald; (*quickly*) schnell; **too** ~ zu früh; **as** ~ **as** sobald; **as** ~ **as possible** so bald wie möglich; ~**er or later** früher oder später; **no** ~**er had I arrived than** ... kaum war ich angekommen, da ...

soot *n* Ruß *m*

soothe *vt* beruhigen; lindern ⟨*pain*⟩

sop *n* Beschwichtigungsmittel *nt*

sophisticated *a* weltgewandt; (*complex*) hochentwickelt

sopping *a* ~**[wet]** durchnäßt

soprano *n* Sopran *m*; (*woman*) Sopranistin *f*

sordid *a* schmutzig

sore *a* wund; (*painful*) schmerzhaft □ *n* wunde Stelle *f*

sorrow *n* Kummer *m*, Leid *nt*

sorry *a* (*sad*) traurig; (*wretched*) erbärmlich; **I am** ~ es tut mir leid; **she is or feels** ~ **for him** er tut ihr leid; **I am** ~ **to say** leider; ~**!** Entschuldigung!

sort *n* Art *f*; (*brand*) Sorte *f*

soul *n* Seele *f*. ~**ful** *a* gefühlvoll

sound[1] *a* gesund; (*sensible*) vernünftig; (*secure*) solide; (*thorough*) gehörig □ *adv* **be** ~ **asleep** fest schlafen

sound[2] *n* Laut *m*; (*noise*) Geräusch *nt*; (*Phys*) Schall *m*; (*TV*) Ton *m*; (*of bells*) Klang *m*; **I don't like the** ~ **of it** (*fam*) das hört sich nicht gut an □ *vi* [er]tönen; (*seem*) sich anhören □ *vt* (*pronounce*) aussprechen; schlagen ⟨*alarm*⟩; (*Med*) abhorchen ⟨*chest*⟩. ~ **barrier** *n* Schallmauer *f*. ~**proof** *a* schalldicht

soup *n* Suppe *f*

sour *a* sauer

source *n* Quelle *f*

south *n* Süden *m*; **to the** ~ **of** südlich von □ *a* Süd-, süd- □ *adv* nach Süden

south: **S~** '**Africa** *n* Südafrika *nt*. **S~** **A'merica** *n* Südamerika *nt*. ~**-'east** *n* Südosten *m*

southerly *a* südlich

southern *a* südlich

South 'Pole *n* Südpol *m*

'**southward[s]** *adv* nach Süden

souvenir *n* Andenken *nt*, Souvenir *nt*

sovereign *n* Souverän *m* □ *a* Souverän *m*. ~**ty** *n* Souveränität *f*

Soviet *a* sowjetisch

sow[1] *n* Sau *f*

sow[2] *vt* säen

soya *n* ~ **bean** Sojabohne *f*

spa *n* Heilbad *nt*

space *n* Raum *m*; (*gap*) Platz *m*; (*Astr*) Weltraum *m*

space: ~**craft** *n* Raumfahrzeug *nt*. ~**ship** *n* Raumschiff *nt*

spacious *a* geräumig

spade *n* Spaten *m*; (*for child*) Schaufel *f*; ~**s** *pl* (*Cards*) Pik *nt*; **call a** ~ **a** ~ das Kind beim rechten Namen nennen. ~**work** *n* Vorarbeit *f*

Spain *n* Spanien *nt*

span *n* Spanne *f*; (*of arch*) Spannweite *f* □ *vt* überspannen

Spaniard *n* Spanier(in) *m(f)*. ~**ish** *a* spanisch □ *n* (*Lang*) Spanisch *nt*; **the** ~**ish** *pl* die Spanier

spank *vt* verhauen

spanner *n* Schraubenschlüssel *m*

spare *a* (*surplus*) übrig; (*additional*) zusätzlich; (*time*) frei; ⟨*room*⟩ Gäste-; ⟨*bed*⟩ Extra- □ *n* (*part*) Ersatzteil *nt* □ *vt* ersparen; (*not hurt*) verschonen; (*do without*) entbehren; (*afford to give*) erübrigen; **to** ~ (*surplus*) übrig. ~ '**wheel** *n* Reserverad *nt*

spark *n* Funke *m* □ *vt* ~ **off** zünden; (*fig*) auslösen. ~**ing-plug** *n* (*Auto*) Zündkerze *f*

sparkl|**e** *vi* funkeln. ~**ing** *a* funkelnd; ⟨*wine*⟩ Schaum-

sparrow *n* Spatz *m*

sparse *a* spärlich

Spartan a spartanisch

spasm n Anfall m; (cramp) Krampf m. ~**odic** a sporadisch

spastic a spastisch [gelähmt]

spate n Flut f; (series) Serie f

spatial a räumlich

spatula n Spachtel m; (Med) Spatel m

spawn n Laich m □vi laichen □vt (fig) hervorbringen

speak vi sprechen (**to** mit); ~**ing!** (Teleph) am Apparat! □vt sprechen; sagen (truth). ~ **up** vi lauter sprechen

speaker n Sprecher(in) m(f); (in public) Redner(in) m(f); (loudspeaker) Lautsprecher m

spear n Speer m □vt aufspießen. ~**head** vt (fig) anführen

special a besondere(r,s), speziell. ~ **ist** n Spezialist m; (Med) Facharzt m/-ärztin f. ~**ity** n Spezialität f

special|ize vi sich spezialisieren (**in** auf + acc). ~**ly** adv speziell; (particularly) besonders

species n Art f

specific a bestimmt; (precise) genau; (Phys) spezifisch. ~**ally** adv ausdrücklich

specification n & ~ **s** pl genaue Angaben pl

specify vt [genau] angeben

specimen n Exemplar nt; (sample) Probe f

speck n Fleck m

speckled a gesprenkelt

spectacle n (show) Schauspiel nt; (sight) Anblick m. ~**s** npl Brille f

spectacular a spektakulär

spectator n Zuschauer(in) m(f)

spectre n Gespenst nt

spectrum n Spektrum nt

speculat|e vi spekulieren. ~**ion** n Spekulation f. ~**or** n Spekulant m

speech n Sprache f; (address) Rede f. ~**less** a sprachlos

speed n Geschwindigkeit f; (rapidity) Schnelligkeit f; (gear) Gang m □vi schnell fahren

speed: ~**boat** n Rennboot nt. ~**ing** n Geschwindigkeitsüberschreitung f. ~ **limit** n Geschwindigkeitsbeschränkung f

speedometer n Tachometer m

spell¹ n Weile f; (of weather) Periode f

spell² vt schreiben; (aloud) buchstabieren; (fig: mean) bedeuten □vi richtig schreiben; (aloud) buchstabieren

spell³ n Zauber m; (words) Zauberspruch m. ~**bound** a wie verzaubert

spelling n Schreibweise f; (orthography) Rechtschreibung f

spend vt/i ausgeben; verbringen (time)

sperm n Samen m

spher|e n Kugel f; (fig) Sphäre f. ~**ical** a kugelförmig

spice n Gewürz nt; (fig) Würze f

spick a ~ **and span** blitzsauber

spicy a würzig, pikant

spider n Spinne f

spike n Spitze f; (Bot, Zool) Stachel m; (on shoe) Spike m

spill vt verschütten; vergießen (blood) □vi überlaufen

spin vt drehen; spinnen (wool); schleudern (washing) □vi sich drehen

spinach n Spinat m

spinal a Rückgrat-. ~ '**cord** n Rückenmark nt

spindle n Spindel f

spin-'drier n Wäscheschleuder f

spine n Rückgrat nt; (of book) [Buch]rücken m; (Bot, Zool) Stachel m. ~**less** a (fig) rückgratlos

spinning-wheel n Spinnrad nt

'**spin-off** n Nebenprodukt nt

spinster n ledige Frau f

spiral a spiralig □n Spirale f □vi sich hochwinden; (smoke:) in

einer Spirale aufsteigen. ~
'staircase n Wendeltreppe f
spire n Turmspitze f
spirit n Geist m; (courage) Mut m;
~ s pl (alcohol) Spirituosen pl; in
high ~s in gehobener Stimmung; in low ~s niedergedrückt
spirit: ~-level n Wasserwaage f.
~ **stove** n Spirituskocher m
spiritual a geistig; (Relig) geistlich. ~**ism** n Spiritismus m.
~**ist** n Spiritist m
spit[1] n (for roasting) [Brat]spieß
m
spit[2] n Spucke f □vt/i spucken;
⟨cat:⟩ fauchen; ⟨fat:⟩ spritzen; **be**
the ~**ting image of s.o.** jdm wie
aus dem Gesicht geschnitten sein
spite n Boshaftigkeit f; **in** ~ **of**
trotz (+ gen) □vt ärgern. ~**ful** a
gehässig
spittle n Spucke f
splash vi spritzen; ~ **s.o. with**
sth jdn mit etw bespritzen □vi
spritzen. ~ **about** vi planschen
spleen n Milz f
splendid a herrlich, großartig
splendour n Pracht f
splint n (Med) Schiene f
splinter n Splitter m
split n Spaltung f; (Pol) Bruch m;
(tear) Riß m □vt spalten; (share)
teilen; (tear) zerreißen □vi sich
spalten; (tear) zerreißen. ~ **on**
s.o. (fam) jdn verpfeifen
splutter vi prusten
spoil n ~s pl Beute f □vt verderben; verwöhnen ⟨person⟩ □vi
verderben. ~**sport** n Spielverderber m
spoke n Speiche f
'spokesman n Sprecher m.
~**bag** n Waschbeutel m. ~
cake n Biskuitkuchen m

sponge n Schwamm m □vt abwaschen □vi ~ **on** schmarotzen bei.

sponsor n Sponsor m; (god-par-
ent) Pate m/Patin f; (for membership) Bürge m □vt sponsern;
bürgen für
spontaneous a spontan
spoof n (fam) Parodie f
spooky a (fam) gespenstisch
spool n Spule f
spoon n Löffel m □vt löffeln. ~
feed vt (fig) alles vorkauen (+
dat). ~**ful** n Löffel m
sporadic a sporadisch
sport n Sport m; (amusement)
Spaß m □vt [stolz] tragen. ~**ing** a
sportlich
sports: ~ **car** n Sportwagen m. ~
coat n, ~ **jacket** n Sakko m. ~
man n Sportler m. ~**woman** n
Sportlerin f
sporty a sportlich
spot n Fleck m; (place) Stelle f;
(dot) Punkt m; (drop) Tropfen m;
(pimple) Pickel m; ~s pl (rash)
Ausschlag m; **on the** ~ auf der
Stelle □vt entdecken
spot: ~ '**check** n Stichprobe f.
~**less** a makellos; (fam: very
clean) blitzsauber. ~**light** n
. Scheinwerfer m; (fig) Rampenlicht nt
spotty a fleckig; (pimply) pickelig
spouse n Gatte m/Gattin f
spout n Schnabel m, Tülle f □vi
schießen (from aus)
sprain vt verstauchen
sprat n Sprotte f
sprawl vi sich ausstrecken
spray n Sprühnebel m; (from sea)
Gischt m; (device) Spritze f; (container) Sprühdose f; (preparation) Spray m □vt spritzen;
(with aerosol) sprühen
spread n Verbreitung f; (paste)
Aufstrich m; (fam: feast) Festes-
sen nt □vt ausbreiten; streichen ⟨butter⟩; bestreichen
⟨bread⟩; streuen ⟨sand⟩; verbreiten ⟨news⟩; verteilen ⟨payments⟩
□vi sich ausbreiten

sprig n Zweig m

spring[1] n Frühling m

spring[2] n (jump) Sprung m; (water) Quelle f; (device) Feder f; (elasticity) Elastizität f □vi springen; (arise) entspringen (from dat) □vt ~ **sth on s.o.** jdn mit etw überfallen

spring: ~**board** n Sprungbrett nt. ~'**cleaning** n Frühjahrsputz m. ~**time** n Frühling m

sprinkl|e vt sprengen; (scatter) streuen; bestreuen (surface). ~**er** n Sprinkler m; (Hort) Sprenger m

sprint n Sprint m □vi rennen; (Sport) sprinten. ~**er** n Kurzstreckenläufer(in) m(f)

sprout n Trieb m; [**Brussels**] ~**s** pl Rosenkohl m □vi sprießen

spruce n Fichte f

spur n Sporn m; (stimulus) Ansporn m; (road) Nebenstraße f; **on the** ~ **of the moment** ganz spontan □vt ~ **[on]** (fig) anspornen

spurious a falsch

spurn vt verschmähen

spurt n Strahl m; (Sport) Spurt m □vi spurten; (Sport) spurten

spy n Spion(in) m(f) □vi spionieren □vt (fam: see) sehen. ~ **on** vt nachspionieren (s.o. jdm)

squabble vi sich zanken

squad n Gruppe f; (Sport) Mannschaft f

squadron n (Mil) Geschwader nt

squalid a schmutzig

squall n Bö f □vi brüllen

squander vt vergeuden

square a quadratisch; ⟨metre⟩ Quadrat-; ⟨meal⟩ anständig; **all** ~ (fam) quitt □ n Quadrat nt; (area) Platz m; (on chessboard) Feld nt □vt (settle) klären; (Math) quadrieren □vi (agree) übereinstimmen

squash n Gedränge nt; (drink) Fruchtsaftgetränk nt; (Sport) Squash nt □vt zerquetschen;

(suppress) niederschlagen. ~**y** a weich

squat vi hocken; ~ **in a house** ein Haus besetzen. ~**ter** n Hausbesetzer m

squawk vi krächzen

squeak vi quieken; quietschen

squeal vi schreien; kreischen

squeamish a empfindlich

squeeze n Druck m; (crush) Gedränge nt □vt drücken; (to get juice) ausdrücken; (force) zwängen; (fam: extort) herauspressen (from aus)

squelch vi quatschen

squid n Tintenfisch m

squint vi schielen

squire n Gutsherr m

squirm vi sich winden

squirrel n Eichhörnchen nt

squirt n/vi spritzen

St abbr (Saint) St.; (Street) Str.

stab n Stich m; (fam: attempt) Versuch m □vt stechen

stability n Stabilität f

stabilize vt stabilisieren □vi sich stabilisieren

stable[1] a stabil

stable[2] n Stall m; (establishment) Reitstall m

stack n Stapel m □vt stapeln

stadium n Stadion nt

staff n (stick & Mil) Stab m □ (& pl) (employees) Personal nt; (Sch) Lehrkräfte pl □vt mit Personal besetzen. ~**-room** n (Sch) Lehrerzimmer nt

stag n Hirsch m

stage n Bühne f; (in journey) Etappe f; (in process) Stadium nt; **by** or **in** ~**s** in Etappen □vt aufführen

stagger vi taumeln □vt staffeln ⟨holidays⟩; versetzt anordnen ⟨seats⟩; **I was** ~**ed** es hat mir die Sprache verschlagen. ~**ing** a unglaublich

stagnant a stehend; (fig) stagnierend

stagnate vi (fig) stagnieren
staid a gesetzt
stain n Fleck m; (for wood) Beize f □vt färben; beizen (wood); (fig) beflecken; ~ed glass farbiges Glas nt. ~less a fleckenlos; (steel) rostfrei. ~ remover n Fleckentferner m
stair n Stufe f; ~s pl Treppe f. ~case n Treppe f
stake n Pfahl m; (wager) Einsatz m; (Comm) Anteil m; be at ~ auf dem Spiel stehen □vt [an einem Pfahl] anbinden; (wager) setzen
stale a alt; (air) verbraucht. ~mate n Patt nt
stalk[1] n Stiel m, Stengel m
stalk[2] vt pirschen auf (+ acc) □vi stolzieren
stall n Stand m; ~s pl (Theat) Parkett nt □vi (engine:) stehenbleiben; (fig) ausweichen □vt abwürgen (engine)
stallion n Hengst m
stamina n Ausdauer f
stammer vt/i stottern
stamp n Stempel m; (postage ~) [Brief]marke f □vt stempeln; (impress) prägen; (put postage on) frankieren □vi stampfen
stampede n wilde Flucht f; (fam) Ansturm m
stand n Stand m; (rack) Ständer m; (pedestal) Sockel m; (Sport) Tribüne f; (fig) Einstellung f □vi stehen; (rise) aufstehen; (be candidate) kandidieren; (stay valid) gültig bleiben; ~ still stillstehen; ~ to reason logisch sein; ~ in for vertreten; ~ for (mean) bedeuten □vt stellen; (withstand) standhalten (+ dat); (endure) ertragen; vertragen (climate); (put up with) aushalten; haben (chance); ~ one's ground nicht nachgeben; I can't ~ her (fam) ich kann sie nicht ausstehen. ~by vi danebenstehen; (be ready) sich bereithalten □vt ~ by s.o.

(fig) zu jdm stehen. ~ down vi (retire) zurücktreten
standard a Normal-; be ~ practice allgemein üblich sein □n Maßstab m; (Techn) Norm f; (level) Niveau nt; (flag) Standarte f; ~s pl (morals) Prinzipien pl; ~ of living Lebensstandard m
'standard lamp n Stehlampe f
'stand-in n Ersatz m
standing a ~ 'order n Dauerauftrag m. ~-room n Stehplätze pl
stand: ~offish a distanziert. ~point n Standpunkt m. ~still n Stillstand m
staple n Heftklammer f □vt heften. ~r n Heftmaschine f
star n Stern m; (asterisk) Sternchen nt; (Theat, Sport) Star m □vi die Hauptrolle spielen
starboard n Steuerbord nt
starch n Stärke f □vt stärken
stare vi starren; ~ at anstarren
'starfish n Seestern m
stark a scharf; (contrast) kraß □adv ~ naked splitternackt
starling n Star m
'starlit a sternhell
start n Anfang m, Beginn m; (departure) Aufbruch m; (Sport) Start m; from the ~ von Anfang an; for a ~ erstens □vi anfangen, beginnen; (set out) aufbrechen; (engine:) anspringen; (Auto, Sport) starten; (jump) aufschrecken; to ~ with zuerst □ vt anfangen, beginnen; (cause) verursachen; (found) gründen; starten (car, race); in Umlauf setzen (rumour). ~er n (Culin) Vorspeise f; (Auto, Sport) Starter m. ~ing-point n Ausgangspunkt m
startle vt erschrecken
starvation n Verhungern nt
starve vi hungern; (to death) verhungern □vt verhungern lassen

state n Zustand m; (grand style) Prunk m; (Pol) Staat m; ~ **of play** Spielstand m; **be in a** ~ (person:) aufgeregt sein; **lie in** ~ feierlich aufgebahrt sein □vt erklären; (specify) angeben

statement n Erklärung f; (Jur) Aussage f; (Banking) Auszug m

'statesman n Staatsmann m

static a statisch

station n Bahnhof m; (police) Wache f; (radio) Sender m; (space, weather) Station f; (Mil) Posten m; (status) Rang m □vt stationieren; (post) postieren. ~ **ary** a stehend

stationer n ~**'s [shop]** Schreibwarengeschäft nt. ~**y** n Briefpapier nt; (writing-materials) Schreibwaren pl

statistic n statistische Tatsache f. ~**al** a statistisch. ~**s** n & pl Statistik f

statue n Statue f

stature n Statur f; (fig) Format nt

status n Status m, Rang m. ~ **symbol** n Statussymbol nt

statute n Statut nt. ~**ory** a gesetzlich

staunch a treu

stay n Aufenthalt m □vi bleiben; (reside) wohnen □vt ~ **the course** durchhalten

stead n **in his** ~ an seiner Stelle; **stand s.o. in good** ~ jdm zustatten kommen. ~ **fast** a standhaft

steady a fest; (not wobbly) stabil; ⟨hand⟩ ruhig; (regular) regelmäßig; (dependable) zuverlässig

steak n Steak nt

steal vt/i stehlen (from dat)

stealthy a heimlich

steam n Dampf m; **under one's own** ~ (fam) aus eigener Kraft □vt (Culin) dämpfen, dünsten □vi dampfen. ~ **up** vi beschlagen

steamer n Dampfer m

'steamroller n Dampfwalze f

steel n Stahl m □vt ~ **oneself** allen Mut zusammennehmen

steep¹ vt (soak) einweichen

steep² a steil; (fam: exorbitant) gesalzen

steeple n Kirchturm m. ~ **chase** n Hindernisrennen nt

steer vt/i steuern. ~ **ing** n (Auto) Steuerung f. ~ **ing-wheel** n Lenkrad nt

stem¹ n Stiel m; (of word) Stamm m □vi ~ **from** zurückzuführen sein auf (+ acc)

stem² vt eindämmen; stillen ⟨bleeding⟩

stench n Gestank m

stencil n Schablone f

step n Schritt m; (stair) Stufe f. ~ **s** pl (ladder) Trittleiter f; **in** ~ im Schritt □vi treten; ~ **in** (fig) eingreifen; ~ **into s.o.'s shoes** an jds Stelle treten

step: ~ **brother** n Stiefbruder m. ~ **child** n Stiefkind nt. ~ **daughter** n Stieftochter f. ~ **father** n Stiefvater m. ~ **ladder** n Trittleiter f. ~ **mother** n Stiefmutter f

'stepping-stone n Trittstein m; (fig) Sprungbrett nt

step: ~ **sister** n Stiefschwester f. ~ **son** n Stiefsohn m

stereo n Stereo nt; (equipment) Stereoanlage f; **in** ~ stereo. ~ **phonic** a stereophon

stereotype n stereotype Figur f

sterile a steril

sterilization n Sterilisation f. ~ **e** vt sterilisieren

sterling n Sterling m

stern¹ a streng

stern² n (of boat) Heck nt

stew n Eintopf m; **in a** ~ (fam) aufgeregt □vt/i schmoren; ~ **ed fruit** Kompott nt

steward n Ordner m; (on ship, aircraft) Steward m. ~ **ess** n Stewardeß f

stick¹ n Stock m; (Sport) Schläger m

stick² vt stecken; ⟨stab⟩ stechen; ⟨glue⟩ kleben; ⟨fam: put⟩ tun; ⟨fam: endure⟩ aushalten □vi stecken; ⟨project⟩ vorstehen, festsitzen; kleben, haften ⟨to an + dat⟩; ⟨jam⟩ klemmen; ~ **to sth** ⟨fig⟩ bei etw bleiben; ~ **at it** ⟨fam⟩ dranbleiben. ~ **out** vi abstehen; ⟨project⟩ vorstehen □vt ⟨fam⟩ hinausstrecken; herausstrecken ⟨tongue⟩

sticker n Aufkleber m

'sticking plaster n Heftpflaster nt

sticky a klebrig

stiff a steif; ⟨brush⟩ hart; ⟨dough⟩ fest; ⟨difficult⟩ schwierig; ⟨penalty⟩ schwer; **be bored** ~ ⟨fam⟩ sich zu Tode langweilen

stifl|e vt ersticken; ⟨fig⟩ unterdrücken. ~**ing** a be ~**ing** zum Ersticken sein

stigma n Stigma nt

stile n Zauntritt m

stiletto n Stilett nt; ⟨heel⟩ Bleistiftabsatz m

still a still; ⟨drink⟩ ohne Kohlensäure; **keep** ~ stillhalten; **stand** ~ stillstehen □n Stille f □adv noch; ⟨emphatic⟩ immer noch; ⟨nevertheless⟩ trotzdem; ~ **not** immer noch nicht

'stillborn a totgeboren

still 'life n Stilleben nt

stilted a gestelzt, geschraubt

stilts npl Stelzen pl

stimulant n Anregungsmittel nt

stimulate vt anregen

stimulus n Reiz m

sting n Stich m; ⟨from nettle, jellyfish⟩ Brennen nt; ⟨organ⟩ Stachel m □vt stechen; ⟨burn⟩ brennen; ⟨insect:⟩ stechen. ~**ing nettle** n Brennessel f

stingy a geizig

stink n Gestank m □vi stinken ⟨of nach⟩

stipulate vt vorschreiben

stir vt rühren □vi sich rühren

stirrup n Steigbügel m

stitch n Stich m; ⟨Knitting⟩ Masche f; ⟨pain⟩ Seitenstechen nt □vt nähen

stoat n Hermelin nt

stock n Vorrat m ⟨of an + dat⟩; ⟨in shop⟩ [Waren]bestand m; ⟨livestock⟩ Vieh nt; ⟨lineage⟩ Abstammung f; ⟨Finance⟩ Wertpapiere pl; ⟨Culin⟩ Brühe f; ⟨plant⟩ Levkoje f; **in/out of** ~ vorrätig/ nicht vorrätig □a Standard- □vt ⟨shop:⟩ führen; auffüllen ⟨shelves⟩

stock: ~ broker n Börsenmakler m. ~ **cube** n Brühwürfel m. **S~ Exchange** n Börse f

stocking n Strumpf m

stock: ~ market n Börse f. ~ **pile** vt horten; anhäufen ⟨weapons⟩. ~**'still** a bewegungslos. ~**taking** n ⟨Comm⟩ Inventur f

stocky a untersetzt

stoical a stoisch

stole n Stola f

stomach n Magen m □vt vertragen. ~**ache** n Magenschmerzen pl

stone n Stein m; ⟨weight⟩ 6,35 kg □a steinern; ⟨wall, Age⟩ Stein- □vt mit Steinen bewerfen; entsteinen ⟨fruit⟩. ~**cold** a eiskalt. ~**'deaf** n ⟨fam⟩ stocktaub

stool n Hocker m

stoop vi sich bücken

stop n Halt m; ⟨break⟩ Pause f; ⟨for bus⟩ Haltestelle f; ⟨for train⟩ Station f; ⟨Gram⟩ Punkt m; ⟨on organ⟩ Register nt □vt anhalten, stoppen; ⟨switch off⟩ abstellen; ⟨plug, block⟩ zustopfen; ⟨prevent⟩ verhindern; ~ **doing sth** aufhören, etw zu tun; □vi anhalten; ⟨cease⟩ aufhören; ⟨clock:⟩ stehenbleiben; ⟨fam: stay⟩ bleiben ⟨with bei⟩ □int halt! stopp!

stop: ~ gap n Notlösung f. ~**over** n Zwischenaufenthalt m; ⟨Aviat⟩ Zwischenlandung f

stoppage n Unterbrechung f; ⟨strike⟩ Streik m; ⟨deduction⟩ Abzug m

stopper n Stöpsel m

stop: ~-**press** n letzte Meldungen pl. ~-**watch** n Stoppuhr f

store n ⟨stock⟩ Vorrat m; ⟨shop⟩ Laden m; ⟨department ~⟩ Kaufhaus nt; ⟨depot⟩ Lager nt; **in** ~ auf Lager; **set great** ~ **by** großen Wert legen auf (+ acc) □vt aufbewahren; ⟨in warehouse⟩ lagern; ⟨Computing⟩ speichern. ~-**room** n Lagerraum m

storey n Stockwerk nt

stork n Storch m

storm n Sturm m; ⟨with thunder⟩ Gewitter nt. ~**y** a stürmisch

story n Geschichte f

stout a beleibt

stove n Ofen m; ⟨for cooking⟩ Herd m

straddle vt rittlings sitzen auf (+ dat)

straight a gerade; ⟨direct⟩ direkt; ⟨clear⟩ klar; ⟨hair⟩ glatt; ⟨drink⟩ pur □adv gerade; ⟨directly⟩ direkt, geradewegs; ⟨clearly⟩ klar; ~ **away** sofort; ~ **on** or **ahead** geradeaus

straighten vt gerademachen; ⟨put straight⟩ geraderichten □vi gerade werden

straight'forward a offen; ⟨simple⟩ einfach

strain n Belastung f; ~**s** pl ⟨of music⟩ Klänge pl □vt belasten; ⟨overexert⟩ überanstrengen; ⟨injure⟩ zerren ⟨muscle⟩; ⟨Culin⟩ durchseihen; abgießen ⟨vegetables⟩ □vi sich anstrengen. ~**er** n Sieb nt

strait n Meerenge f; **in dire** ~**s in** großen Nöten. ~-**jacket** n Zwangsjacke f. ~-**laced** a puritanisch

strand n ⟨of thread⟩ Faden m; ⟨of beads⟩ Kette f; ⟨of hair⟩ Strähne f

strange a fremd; ⟨odd⟩ seltsam, merkwürdig. ~**r** n Fremde(r) m/f

strangle vt erwürgen

strap n Riemen m; ⟨for safety⟩ Gurt m; ⟨to grasp in vehicle⟩ Halteriemen m; ⟨of watch⟩ Armband nt; ⟨shoulder-⟩ Träger m □vt schnallen; ~ **in** or **down** festschnallen

stratagem n Kriegslist f

strategic a strategisch

strategy n Strategie f

stratum n Schicht f

straw n Stroh nt; ⟨single piece, drinking⟩ Strohhalm m; **that's the last** ~ jetzt reicht's aber

strawberry n Erdbeere f

stray vi sich verirren; ⟨deviate⟩ abweichen

streak n Streifen m; ⟨in hair⟩ Strähne f; ⟨fig: trait⟩ Zug m □vi flitzen. ~**y** a streifig; ⟨bacon⟩ durchwachsen

stream n Bach m; ⟨flow⟩ Strom m; ⟨current⟩ Strömung f; ⟨Sch⟩ Parallelzug m □vi strömen

streamer n Luftschlange f

'streamline vt ⟨fig⟩ rationalisieren

street n Straße f

strength n Stärke f; ⟨power⟩ Kraft f; **on the** ~ **of** auf Grund (+ gen). ~**en** vt stärken

strenuous a anstrengend

stress n ⟨emphasis⟩ Betonung f; ⟨strain⟩ Belastung f; ⟨mental⟩ Streß m □vt betonen; ⟨put a strain on⟩ belasten. ~**ful** a stressig ⟨fam⟩

stretch n ⟨of road⟩ Strecke f; ⟨elasticity⟩ Elastizität f; **at a** ~ ohne Unterbrechung; **a long** ~ eine lange Zeit; □vt strecken; ⟨widen⟩ dehnen; ⟨spread⟩ ausbreiten; fordern ⟨person⟩ □vi sich erstrecken; ⟨become wider⟩ sich dehnen; ⟨person:⟩ sich strecken. ~**er** n Tragbahre f

strict *a* streng; **~ly speaking** strenggenommen

stride *n* [großer] Schritt *m*; **take sth in one's ~** mit etw gut fertig werden □*vi* [mit großen Schritten] gehen

strident *a* schrill

strife *n* Streit *m*

strike *n* Streik *m*; (*Mil*) Angriff *m*; **be on ~** streiken □*vt* schlagen; (*knock against*) treffen; prägen ⟨*coin*⟩; anzünden ⟨*match*⟩; stoßen auf (+ *acc*) ⟨*oil*⟩; abbrechen ⟨*camp*⟩; ⟨*delete*⟩ streichen; (*impress*) beeindrucken; (*occur to*) einfallen (+ *dat*); (*Mil*) angreifen □*vi* treffen; ⟨*lightning:*⟩ einschlagen; ⟨*clock:*⟩ schlagen; ⟨*attack*⟩ zuschlagen; ⟨*workers:*⟩ streiken; **~ lucky** Glück haben. **~-breaker** *n* Streikbrecher *m*

striker *n* Streikende(r) *m/f*

string *n* Schnur *f*; (*thin*) Bindfaden *m*; (*of musical instrument, racket*) Saite *f*; (*of bow*) Sehne *f*; (*of pearls*) Kette *f*; **the ~s** (*Mus*) die Streicher *pl* □*vt* (*thread*) aufziehen ⟨*beads*⟩

stringent *a* streng

strip *n* Streifen *m* □*vt* ablösen; ausziehen ⟨*clothes*⟩; abziehen ⟨*bed*⟩; abbeizen ⟨*wood*⟩; auseinandernehmen ⟨*machine*⟩; (*deprive*) berauben (**of** *gen*) □*vi* (*undress*) sich ausziehen

stripe *n* Streifen *m*

'striplight *n* Neonröhre *f*

stripper *n* Stripperin *f*; (*male*) Stripper *m*

strive *vi* sich bemühen (**to** zu); **~ for** streben nach

stroke[1] *n* Schlag *m*; (*of pen*) Strich *m*; (*Swimming*) Zug *m*; (*style*) Stil *m*; (*Med*) Schlaganfall *m*; **~ of luck** Glücksfall *m*

stroke[2] *vt* streicheln

stroll *n* Spaziergang *m*, (*fam*) Bummel *m* □*vi* spazieren, (*fam*) bummeln

strong *a* stark; (*powerful, healthy*) kräftig; (*severe*) streng; (*sturdy*) stabil; (*convincing*) gut

strong: ~-box *n* Geldkassette *f*. **~hold** *n* Festung *f*; (*fig*) Hochburg *f*. **~-'minded** *a* willensstark. **~-room** *n* Tresorraum *m*

structure *n* Struktur *f*; (*building*) Bau *m*

struggle *n* Kampf *m*; **with a ~** mit Mühe □*vi* kämpfen

strum *vt* klimpern auf (+ *dat*)

strut[1] *n* Strebe *f*

strut[2] *vi* stolzieren

stub *n* Stummel *m*; (*counterfoil*) Abschnitt *m* □*vt* **~ one's toe** sich (*dat*) den Zeh stoßen (**on** an + *dat*)

stubble *n* Stoppeln *pl*

stubborn *a* starrsinnig; ⟨*refusal*⟩ hartnäckig

stucco *n* Stuck *m*

stud[1] *n* Nagel *m*; (*on clothes*) Niete *f*; (*for collar*) Kragenknopf *m*; (*for ear*) Ohrstecker *m*

stud[2] *n* (*of horses*) Gestüt *nt*

student *n* Student(in) *m(f)*; (*Sch*) Schüler(in) *m(f)*. **~ nurse** *n* Lernschwester *f*

studio *n* Studio *nt*; (*for artist*) Atelier *nt*

studious *a* lerneifrig

stud|**y** *n* Studie *f*; (*room*) Studierzimmer *nt*; (*investigation*) Untersuchung *f*; **~ies** *pl* Studium *nt* □*vt* studieren; (*examine*) untersuchen □*vi* lernen; (*at university*) studieren

stuff *n* Stoff *m*; (*fam: things*) Zeug *nt* □*vt* vollstopfen; (*with padding, Culin*) füllen; ausstopfen ⟨*animal*⟩. **~ing** *n* Füllung *f*

stuffy *a* stickig

stumble *vi* stolpern. **~ing-block** *n* Hindernis *nt*

stump *n* Stumpf *m*

stun *vt* betäuben

stunning *a* (*fam*) toll

stunt *n* (*fam*) Kunststück *nt*

stupendous *a* enorm

stupid *a* dumm. **~ity** *n* Dummheit *f*

sturdy *a* stämmig; ⟨*furniture*⟩ stabil; ⟨*shoes*⟩ fest

stutter *vt/i* stottern

sty[1] *n* Schweinestall *m*

sty[2], **stye** *n* (*Med*) Gerstenkorn *nt*

style *n* Stil *m*; (*fashion*) Mode *f*; (*sort*) Art *f*

stylish *a* stilvoll

stylist *n* Friseur *m*/ Friseuse *f*. **~ic** *a* stilistisch

stylized *a* stilisiert

suave *a* (*pej*) gewandt

sub·conscious *a* unterbewußt □*n* Unterbewußtsein *nt*

'subdivide *vt* unterteilen

subdue *vt* unterwerfen; (*make quieter*) beruhigen

subject[1] *a* **be ~ to sth** etw (*dat*) unterworfen sein □*n* Staatsbürger(in) *m(f)*; (*of ruler*) Untertan *m*; (*theme*) Thema *nt*; (*of investigation*) Gegenstand *m*; (*Sch*) Fach *nt*; (*Gram*) Subjekt *nt*

subject[2] *vt* unterwerfen (**to** *dat*); (*expose*) aussetzen (**to** *dat*)

subjective *a* subjektiv

subjunctive *n* Konjunktiv *m*

sub'let *vt* untervermieten

sublime *a* erhaben

subliminal *a* unterschwellig

sub-ma'chine-gun *n* Maschinenpistole *f*

submarine *n* Unterseeboot *nt*

submerge *vt* untertauchen

submission *n* Unterwerfung *f*

submit *vt* vorlegen (**to** *dat*); (*hand in*) einreichen □*vi* sich unterwerfen (**to** *dat*)

subordinate[1] *a* untergeordnet □*n* Untergebene(r) *m/f*

subordinate[2] *vt* unterordnen (**to** *dat*)

subscribe *vi* spenden; **~ to** (*fig*) sich anschließen (+ *dat*); abonnieren ⟨*newspaper*⟩. **~r** *n* Spender *m*; Abonnent *m*

subscription *n* (*to club*) [Mitglieds]beitrag *m*; (*to newspaper*) Abonnement *nt*

subsequent *a* folgend; (*later*) später

subservient *a* untergeordnet; (*servile*) unterwürfig

subside *vi* sinken; ⟨*ground:*⟩ sich senken; ⟨*storm:*⟩ nachlassen

subsidiary *a* untergeordnet □*n* Tochtergesellschaft *f*

subsid|ize *vt* subventionieren. **~y** *n* Subvention *f*

substance *n* Substanz *f*

sub'standard *a* unzulänglich; ⟨*goods*⟩ minderwertig

substantial *a* solide; ⟨*meal*⟩ reichhaltig; (*considerable*) beträchtlich

substitute *n* Ersatz *m*; (*Sport*) Ersatzspieler(in) *m(f)* □*vt* **~ A for B** A durch B ersetzen □*vi* **~ for s.o.** jdn vertreten

subterranean *a* unterirdisch

'subtitle *n* Untertitel *m*

subtle *a* fein; (*fig*) subtil

subtract *vt* abziehen, subtrahieren. **~ion** *n* Subtraktion *f*

suburb *n* Vorort *m*; **in the ~s** am Stadtrand. **~an** *a* Vorort-; (*pej*) spießig. **~ia** *n* die Vororte *pl*

subversive *a* subversiv

'subway *n* Unterführung *f*

succeed *vi* Erfolg haben; (*follow*) nachfolgen (+ *dat*); **I ~ed** es ist mir gelungen □*vt* folgen (+ *dat*)

success *n* Erfolg *m*. **~ful** *a* erfolgreich

succession *n* Folge *f*; (*series*) Serie *f*; (*to title*) Nachfolge *f*; (*to throne*) Thronfolge *f*; **in ~** hintereinander

successive *a* aufeinanderfolgend

successor *n* Nachfolger(in) *m(f)*

succinct *a* prägnant

succulent *a* saftig

succumb *vi* erliegen (**to** *dat*)

such a solche(r,s); ~ **a book** ein solches od solch ein Buch; ~ **a thing** so etwas □*pron* **as** ~ als solche(r,s) (*strictly speaking*) an sich; ~ **as** wie [zum Beispiel]

suck *vt/i* saugen; lutschen ⟨*sweet*⟩

suckle *vt* säugen

suction *n* Saugwirkung *f*

sudden a plötzlich; (*abrupt*) jäh □ **n all of a** ~ auf einmal

sue *vt* verklagen (**for** auf + *acc*) □*vi* klagen

suede *n* Wildleder *nt*

suet *n* [Nieren]talg *m*

suffer *vi* leiden (**from** an + *dat*) □*vt* erleiden; (*tolerate*) dulden. ~**ing** *n* Leiden *nt*

suffice *vi* genügen

sufficient a genug, genügend; **be** ~ genügen

suffix *n* Nachsilbe *f*

suffocate *vt/i* ersticken

sugar *n* Zucker *m*. ~ *y* a süß; (*fig*) süßlich

suggest *vt* vorschlagen; (*indicate*) andeuten. ~**ion** *n* Vorschlag *m*; Andeutung *f*; (*trace*) Spur *f*. ~**ive** a anzüglich

suicide *n* Selbstmord *m*

suit *n* Anzug *m*; (*woman's*) Kostüm *nt*; (*Cards*) Farbe *f*; (*Jur*) Prozeß *m*; **follow** ~ (*fig*) das Gleiche tun □*vt* (*adapt*) anpassen (**to** *dat*); (*be convenient for*) passen (+ *dat*); (*go well*) passen zu; ⟨*clothing:*⟩ stehen (**s.o.** jdm)

suitable a geeignet; (*convenient*) passend; (*appropriate*) angemessen; (*for activity*) zweckmäßig

'suitcase *n* Koffer *m*

suite *n* Suite *f*; (*of furniture*) Garnitur *f*

sulk *vi* schmollen

sullen a mürrisch

sulphur *n* Schwefel *m*. ~**ic** a ~**ic acid** Schwefelsäure *f*

sultana *n* Sultanine *f*

sultry a schwül

sum *n* Summe *f*; (*Sch*) Rechenaufgabe *f*

summar|ize *vt* zusammenfassen. ~**y** *n* Zusammenfassung *f*

summer *n* Sommer *m*. ~**house** *n* [Garten]laube *f*. ~**time** *n* Sommer *m*

summit *n* Gipfel *m*. ~ **conference** *n* Gipfelkonferenz *f*

summon *vt* rufen; holen ⟨*help*⟩; (*Jur*) vorladen. ~ **up** *vt* aufbringen

summons *n* (*Jur*) Vorladung *f*□*vt* vorladen

sumptuous a prunkvoll; ⟨*meal*⟩ üppig

sun *n* Sonne *f*

sun: ~**bathe** *vi* sich sonnen. ~**bed** *n* Sonnenbank *f*. ~**burn** *n* Sonnenbrand *m*

Sunday *n* Sonntag *m*

'sundial *n* Sonnenuhr *f*

sundry a verschiedene *pl*; **all and** ~ alle *pl*

'sunflower *n* Sonnenblume *f*

sunny a sonnig

sun: ~**rise** *n* Sonnenaufgang *m*. ~**roof** *n* (*Auto*) Schiebedach *nt*. ~**set** *n* Sonnenuntergang *m*. ~**shine** *n* Sonnenschein *m*. ~**stroke** *n* Sonnenstich *m*. ~**tan** *n* [Sonnen]bräune *f*. ~**tanned** a braun[gebrannt]

super a (*fam*) prima, toll

superb a erstklassig

supercilious a überlegen

superficial a oberflächlich

superfluous a überflüssig

super'human a übermenschlich

superintendent *n* (*of police*) Kommissar *m*

superior a überlegen; (*in rank*) höher *n* Vorgesetzte(r) *m*/*f*. ~**ity** *n* Überlegenheit *f*

superlative a unübertrefflich □*n* Superlativ *m*

'supermarket *n* Supermarkt *m*

super'natural a übernatürlich

'superpower *n* Supermacht *f*

supersede vt ersetzen

super'sonic a Überschall-

superstiti|on n Aberglaube m. ~**ous** a abergläubisch

supervis|e vt beaufsichtigen; überwachen ⟨work⟩. ~**ion** n Aufsicht f; Überwachung f. ~**or** n Aufseher(in) m(f)

supper n Abendessen nt

supple a geschmeidig

supplement n Ergänzung f; (addition) Zusatz m; (to fare) Zuschlag m; (book) Ergänzungsband m; (to newspaper) Beilage f □vt ergänzen. ~**ary** a zusätzlich

supplier n Lieferant m

supply n Vorrat m □vt liefern

support n Stütze f, (fig) Unterstützung f □vt stützen; (bear weight of) tragen; (keep) ernähren; (give money to) unterstützen; (speak in favour of) befürworten; (Sport) Fan sein von. ~**er** n Anhänger(in) m(f); (Sport) Fan m

suppose vt annehmen; (presume) vermuten; (imagine) sich (dat) vorstellen; **be** ~**d to** sollen. ~**dly** adv angeblich

supposition n Vermutung f

suppository n Zäpfchen nt

suppress vt unterdrücken

supremacy n Vorherrschaft f

supreme a höchste(r,s); ⟨court⟩ oberste(r,s)

surcharge n Zuschlag m

sure a sicher; **make** ~ sich vergewissern (of gen); (check) nachprüfen; **be** ~ **to do** sieh zu, daß du es tust. ~**ly** adv sicher; (for emphasis) doch

surety n Bürgschaft f

surf n Brandung f

surface n Oberfläche f □vi (emerge) auftauchen. ~ **mail** n **by** ~ **mail** auf dem Land-/Seeweg

'**surfboard** n Surfbrett nt

surfeit n Übermaß nt

surge vi branden; ~ **forward** nach vorn drängen

surgeon n Chirurg(in) m(f)

surgery n Chirurgie f; (place) Praxis f; (room) Sprechzimmer nt; (hours) Sprechstunde f

surgical a chirurgisch

surly a mürrisch

surmise vt mutmaßen

surmount vt überwinden

surname n Nachname m

surpass vt übertreffen

surplus a überschüssig; **be** ~ **to requirements** nicht benötigt werden

surpris|e n Überraschung f □vt überraschen; **be** ~**ed** sich wundern (at über + acc). ~**ing** a überraschend

surrender n Kapitulation f □vi sich ergeben; (Mil) kapitulieren □vt aufgeben

surreptitious a heimlich

surrogate n Ersatz m. ~ '**mother** n Leihmutter f

surround vt umgeben; (encircle) umzingeln. ~**ings** npl Umgebung f

surveillance n Überwachung f

survey[1] n Überblick m; (poll) Umfrage f; (investigation) Untersuchung f; (of land) Vermessung f; (of house) Gutachten nt

survey[2] vt betrachten; vermessen ⟨land⟩; begutachten ⟨building⟩. ~**or** n Landvermesser m; Gutachter m

survival n Überleben nt; (of tradition) Fortbestand m

surviv|e vt überleben □vi überleben; ⟨tradition⟩ erhalten bleiben. ~**or** n Überlebende(r) m/f

susceptible a empfänglich/ (Med) anfällig ⟨to für⟩

suspect[1] vt verdächtigen; (assume) vermuten

suspect[2] n Verdächtige(r) m/f

suspend vt aufhängen; (stop) [vorläufig] einstellen; (from duty) vorläufig beurlauben.

~er belt n Strumpfbandgürtel m. **~ers** npl Strumpfbänder pl
suspense n Spannung f
suspension n (Auto) Federung f. **~ bridge** n Hängebrücke f
suspici|on n Verdacht m; (mistrust) Mißtrauen nt; (trace) Spur f. **~ous** a mißtrauisch; (arousing suspicion) verdächtig
sustain vt tragen; (fig) aufrechterhalten; erhalten ‹life›; erleiden ‹injury›
swab n (Med) Tupfer m; (specimen) Abstrich m
swagger vi stolzieren
swallow[1] vt/i schlucken
swallow[2] n (bird) Schwalbe f
swamp n Sumpf m
swan n Schwan m
swap vt/i (fam) tauschen (for gegen)
swarm vi schwärmen
swastika n Hakenkreuz nt
swat vt totschlagen
sway vi schwanken; (gently) sich wiegen □vt wiegen; (influence) beeinflussen
swear vt/i schwören □vi schwören (by auf + acc); (curse) fluchen. **~-word** n Kraftausdruck m
sweat n Schweiß m □vi schwitzen
sweater n Pullover m
swede n Kohlrübe f
Swede n Schwede m /-din f. **~en** n Schweden nt. **~ish** a schwedisch
sweep vt fegen, kehren □vi (go swiftly) rauschen; ‹wind:› fegen. **~ up** vt zusammenfegen/-kehren
sweet a süß; **have a ~ tooth** gern Süßes mögen □n Bonbon m & nt; (dessert) Nachtisch m. **~ corn** n [Zucker]mais m
sweetener n Süßstoff m; (fam: bribe) Schmiergeld nt
sweet: ~heart n Schatz m. **~ shop** n Süßwarenladen m
swell vi [an]schwellen; ‹sails:› sich blähen; ‹wood:› aufquellen □vt anschwellen lassen; (increase) vergrößern
swerve vi einen Bogen machen
swift a schnell
swig n (fam) Schluck m, Zug m □vt [herunter]kippen
swill n (for pigs) Schweinefutter nt □vt ~ [out] [aus]spülen
swim vi schwimmen; **my head is ~ming** mir dreht sich der Kopf. **~mer** n Schwimmer(in) m(f)
swimming n Schwimmen nt. **~baths** npl Schwimmbad nt. **~pool** n Schwimmbecken nt; (private) Swimmingpool m
'swim-suit n Badeanzug m
swindle n Schwindel m, Betrug m □vt betrügen. **~r** n Schwindler m
swine n Schwein nt
swing n Schwung m; (shift) Schwenk m; (seat) Schaukel f □vi schwingen; (on swing) schaukeln; (sway) schwanken; (dangle) baumeln; (turn) schwenken □vt schwingen; (influence) beeinflussen. **~-door** n Schwingtür f
swipe n (fam) knallen; (steal) klauen
swirl vt/i wirbeln
Swiss a Schweizer, schweizerisch □n Schweizer(in) m(f); **the ~** pl die Schweizer. **~ 'roll** n Biskuitrolle f
switch n Schalter m; (change) Wechsel m □vt wechseln; (exchange) tauschen □vi wechseln; **~ to** umstellen auf (+ acc). **~ off** vt ausschalten; abschalten ‹engine›. **~ on** vt einschalten; anschalten
switchboard n [Telefon]zentrale f
Switzerland n die Schweiz
swivel vi sich drehen
swoop vi **~ down** herabstoßen
sword n Schwert nt
swot n (fam) Streber m □vt/i (fam) büffeln
syllable n Silbe f

syllabus *n* Lehrplan *m*; (*for exam*) Studienplan *m*

symbol *n* Symbol *nt* (**of** für). **~ic** *a* symbolisch. **~ism** *n* Symbolik *f*. **~ize** *vt* symbolisieren

symmetr|ical *a* symmetrisch. **~y** *n* Symmetrie *f*

sympathetic *a* mitfühlend; (*likeable*) sympathisch

sympathize *vi* mitfühlen

sympathy *n* Mitgefühl *nt*

symphony *n* Sinfonie *f*

symptom *n* Symptom *nt*. **~atic** *a* symptomatisch (**of** für)

synagogue *n* Synagoge *f*

synchronize *vt* synchronisieren

syndicate *n* Syndikat *nt*

syndrome *n* Syndrom *nt*

synonym *n* Synonym *nt*. **~ous** *a* synonym

synopsis *n* Zusammenfassung *f*; (*of opera*) Inhaltsangabe *f*

syntax *n* Syntax *f*

synthesis *n* Synthese *f*

synthetic *a* synthetisch

Syria *n* Syrien *nt*

syringe *n* Spritze *f*

syrup *n* Sirup *m*

system *n* System *nt*. **~atic** *a* systematisch

T

tab *n* (*projecting*) Zunge *f*; (*with name*) Namensschild *nt*; (*loop*) Aufhänger *m*; **keep ~s on** (*fam*) [genau] beobachten

table *n* Tisch *m*; (*list*) Tabelle *f*. **~-cloth** *n* Tischdecke *f*, Tischtuch *nt*. **~spoon** *n* Servierlöffel *m*

tablet *n* Tablette *f*

'table tennis *n* Tischtennis *nt*

tabloid *n* kleinformatige Zeitung *f*; (*pej*) Boulevardzeitung *f*

taboo *a* tabu □*n* Tabu *nt*

tacit *a* stillschweigend

tack *n* (*nail*) Stift *m*; (*stitch*) Heftstich *m*; (*Naut & fig*) Kurs *m* □*vt* festnageln; (*sew*) heften □*vi* (*Naut*) kreuzen

tackle *vt* angehen

tact *n* Takt *m*, Taktgefühl *nt*. **~ful** *a* taktvoll

tactic|al *a* taktisch. **~s** *npl* Taktik *f*

tactless *a* taktlos

tadpole *n* Kaulquappe *f*

tag¹ *n* (*label*) Schild *nt*. **~ along** mitkommen

tag² *n* (*game*) Fangen *nt*

tail *n* Schwanz *m*; **~s** *pl* (*tailcoat*) Frack *m* □*vi* (*fam*: *follow*) beschatten. **heads or ~s?** Kopf oder Zahl?

tail: **~back** *n* Rückstau *m*. **~end** *n* Ende *nt*

tailor *n* Schneider *m*

'tail wind *n* Rückenwind *m*

taint *vt* verderben

take *vt* nehmen; (*with one*) mitnehmen; (*take to a place*) bringen; (*steal*) stehlen; (*win*) gewinnen; (*capture*) einnehmen; (*require*) brauchen; (*last*) dauern; (*teach*) geben; machen (*exam, holiday*); messen (*pulse*) □*vi* (*plant:* grow) angehen; **~ after s.o.** jdm nachschlagen; (*in looks*) jdm ähnlich sehen; **~ to** (*like*) mögen; (*as a habit*) sich (*dat*) angewöhnen. **~ in** *vt* hineinbringen; (*bring indoors*) hereinholen; (*to one's home*) aufnehmen; (*understand*) begreifen; (*deceive*) hereinlegen; (*make smaller*) enger machen. **~ off** *vt* abnehmen; ablegen (*coat*); sich (*dat*) ausziehen (*clothes*); (*deduct*) abziehen; (*mimic*) nachmachen □*vi* (*Aviat*) starten. **~ on** *vt* annehmen; (*undertake*) übernehmen; (*engage*) einstellen; (*as opponent*) antreten gegen. **~ out** *vt* hinausbringen; (*for pleasure*) ausgehen mit; ausführen (*dog*); (*remove*) herausnehmen; (*withdraw*) abheben (*money*); (*from* *library*) ausleihen. ~ **up** *vt* hinaufbringen; annehmen 〈*offer*〉; ergreifen 〈*profession*〉; sich 〈*dat*〉 zulegen 〈*hobby*〉; in Anspruch nehmen 〈*time*〉; einnehmen 〈*space*〉; aufreißen 〈*floorboards*〉; ~ sth up with s.o. mit jdm über etw 〈*acc*〉 sprechen □ *vi* ~ **up with s.o.** sich mit jdm einlassen

take: ~**-away** *n* Essen *nt* zum Mitnehmen; 〈*restaurant*〉 Restaurant *nt* mit Straßenverkauf. ~**-off** *n* 〈*Aviat*〉 Start *m*, Abflug *m*. ~**over** *n* Übernahme *f*

talcum *n* ~ **[powder]** Körperpuder *m*

tale *n* Geschichte *f*

talent *n* Talent *nt*. ~**ed** *a* talentiert

talk *n* Gespräch *nt*; 〈*lecture*〉 Vortrag *m*; **make small** ~ Konversation machen □ *vi* reden, sprechen (**to**/**with** mit)

talkative *a* gesprächig

tall *a* groß; 〈*building, tree*〉 hoch. ~**boy** *n* hohe Kommode *f*. ~'**story** *n* übertriebene Geschichte *f*

talon *n* Klaue *f*

tambourine *n* Tamburin *nt*

tame *a* zahm; 〈*dull*〉 lahm 〈*fam*〉 □ *vt* zähmen. ~**r** *n* Dompteur *m*

tamper *vi* ~ **with** sich 〈*dat*〉 zu schaffen machen an (+ *dat*)

tampon *n* Tampon *m*

tan *a* gelbbraun □ *n* Gelbbraun *nt*; 〈*from sun*〉 Bräune *f* □ *vt* gerben 〈*hide*〉 □ *vi* braun werden

tang *n* herber Geschmack *m*; 〈*smell*〉 herber Geruch *m*

tangent *n* Tangente *f*; **go off at a** ~ 〈*fam*〉 vom Thema abschweifen

tangible *a* greifbar

tangle *vt* ~ **[up]** verheddern □ *vi* sich verheddern

tango *n* Tango *m*

tank *n* Tank *m*; 〈*Mil*〉 Panzer *m*

tankard *n* Krug *m*

tanker *n* Tanker *m*; 〈*lorry*〉 Tank[last]wagen *m*

tantalize *vt* quälen

tantamount *a* **be** ~ **to** gleichbedeutend sein mit

tantrum *n* Wutanfall *m*

tap *n* Hahn *m*; 〈*knock*〉 Klopfen *nt* □ *vt* klopfen an (+ *acc*); anzapfen 〈*barrel*〉; erschließen 〈*resources*〉; abhören 〈*telephone*〉 □ *vi* klopfen. ~**-dance** *n* Step[tanz] *m*

tape *n* Band *nt*; 〈*adhesive*〉 Klebstreifen *m*; 〈*for recording*〉 Tonband *nt* □ *vt* mit Klebstreifen zukleben; 〈*record*〉 auf Band aufnehmen

'**tape-measure** *n* Bandmaß *nt*

taper *vi* sich verjüngen

'**tape recorder** *n* Tonbandgerät *nt*

tapestry *n* Gobelinstickerei *f*

'**tapeworm** *n* Bandwurm *m*

'**tap water** *n* Leitungswasser *nt*

tar *n* Teer *m*

target *n* Ziel *nt*; 〈*board*〉 [Ziel]scheibe *f*

tariff *n* Tarif *m*; 〈*duty*〉 Zoll *m*

tarnish *vi* anlaufen

tarpaulin *n* Plane *f*

tarragon *n* Estragon *m*

tart *a* ≈ Obstkuchen *m*; 〈*individual*〉 Törtchen *nt*; 〈*sl: prostitute*〉 Nutte *f*

tartan *n* Schottenmuster *nt*; 〈*cloth*〉 Schottenstoff *m*

task *n* Aufgabe *f*; **take s.o. to** ~ jdm Vorhaltungen machen. ~ **force** *n* Sonderkommando *nt*

tassel *n* Quaste *f*

taste *n* Geschmack *m*; 〈*sample*〉 Kostprobe *f* □ *vt* kosten, probieren; schmecken 〈*flavour*〉 □ *vi* schmecken (**of** nach). ~**ful** *a* 〈*fig*〉 geschmackvoll

tasty *a* lecker, schmackhaft

tattoo[1] *n* Tätowierung *f*

tattoo[2] *n* 〈*Mil*〉 Zapfenstreich *m*

tatty *a* schäbig

taunt *vt* verhöhnen
Taurus *n* (*Astr*) Stier *m*
taut *a* straff
tavern *n* (*liter*) Schenke *f*
tax *n* Steuer *f* ▢ *vt* besteuern; (*fig*) strapazieren; ~ **with** beschuldigen (+ *gen*). ~**able** *a* steuerpflichtig. ~**ation** *n* Besteuerung *f*. ~**free** *a* steuerfrei
taxi *n* Taxi *nt*. ~ **rank** *n* Taxistand *m*
'taxpayer *n* Steuerzahler *m*
tea *n* Tee *m*. ~**bag** *n* Teebeutel *m*
teach *vt/i* unterrichten; ~ **s.o.** **sth** jdm etw beibringen. ~**er** *n* Lehrer(in) *m(f)*
tea-cloth *n* Geschirrtuch *nt*
teak *n* Teakholz *nt*
team *n* Mannschaft *f*; (*fig*) Team *nt*
'team-work *n* Teamarbeit *f*
teapot *n* Teekanne *f*
tear¹ *n* Riß *m* ▢ *vt* reißen; (*damage*) zerreißen ▢ *vi* [zer]reißen; (*run*) rasen. ~ **up** *vt* zerreißen
tear² *n* Träne *f*. ~**ful** *a* weinend. ~**gas** *n* Tränengas *nt*
tease *vt* necken
tea: ~**set** *n* Teeservice *nt*. ~**spoon** *n* Teelöffel *m*
teat *n* Zitze *f*; (*on bottle*) Sauger *m*
'tea-towel *n* Geschirrtuch *nt*
technical *a* technisch; (*specialized*) fachlich. ~**ity** *n* technisches Detail *nt*; (*Jur*) Formfehler *m*
technician *n* Techniker *m*
technique *n* Technik *f*
technological *a* technologisch
technology *n* Technologie *f*
teddy *n* ~ **[bear]** Teddybär *m*
tedious *a* langweilig
teenager *n* Teenager *m*
teens *npl* the ~ die Teenagerjahre *pl*
teeter *vi* schwanken
teethe *vi* zahnen
teetotaller *n* Abstinenzler *m*

telecommunications *npl* Fernmeldewesen *nt*
telegram *n* Telegramm *nt*
telegraph *n* Telegraf *m*. ~**ic** *a* telegrafisch. ~ **pole** *n* Telegrafenmast *m*
telepathy *n* Telepathie *f*
telephone *n* Telefon *nt* ▢ *vt* anrufen ▢ *vi* telefonieren
telephone: ~ **booth** *n*, ~ **box** *n* Telefonzelle *f*. ~ **directory** *n* Telefonbuch *nt*
telephonist *n* Telefonist(in) *m(f)*
tele'photo *a* ~ **lens** Teleobjektiv *nt*
teleprinter *n* Fernschreiber *m*
telescope *n* Teleskop *nt*, Fernrohr *nt*. ~**ic** *a* teleskopisch; (*collapsible*) ausziehbar
television *n* Fernsehen *nt*; **watch** ~ fernsehen. ~ **set** *n* Fernsehapparat *m*, Fernseher *m*
telex *n* Telex *nt* ▢ *vt* telexen
tell *vt/i* sagen (**s.o.** jdm); (*relate*) erzählen; (*know*) wissen; (*distinguish*) erkennen; **the time** die Uhr lesen; **time will** ~ das wird man erst sehen. ~ **off** *vt* ausschimpfen
temerity *n* Kühnheit *f*
temp *n* (*fam*) Aushilfssekretärin *f*
temper *n* (*disposition*) Naturell *nt*; (*mood*) Laune *f*; (*anger*) Wut *f*; **lose one's** ~ wütend werden
temperament *n* Temperament *nt*. ~**al** *a* temperamentvoll
temperance *n* Mäßigung *f*
temperate *a* gemäßigt
temperature *n* Temperatur *f*; **have** *or* **run a** ~ Fieber haben
tempest *n* Sturm *m*. ~**uous** *a* stürmisch
template *n* Schablone *f*
temple¹ *n* Tempel *m*
temple² *n* (*Anat*) Schläfe *f*
tempo *n* Tempo *nt*
temporary *a* vorübergehend; ⟨*measure*⟩ provisorisch

tempt vt verleiten; (Relig) versuchen; herausfordern ⟨fate⟩; (entice) [ver]locken. **~ation** n Versuchung f

ten a zehn

tenable a (fig) haltbar

tenaci|ous a hartnäckig. **~ty** n Hartnäckigkeit f

tenant n Mieter(in) m(f); (Comm) Pächter(in) m(f)

tend vi **~ to do sth** dazu neigen, etw zu tun

tendency n Tendenz f; (inclination) Neigung f

tender¹ n (Comm) Angebot nt; **legal ~** gesetzliches Zahlungsmittel nt ⟨vt⟩ anbieten; einreichen ⟨resignation⟩

tender² a zart; (loving) zärtlich; (painful) empfindlich. **~ness** n Zartheit f; Zärtlichkeit f

tendon n Sehne f

tenement n Mietshaus nt

tenet n Grundsatz m

tennis n Tennis nt. **~-court** n Tennisplatz m

tenor n Tenor m

tense¹ n (Gram) Zeit f

tense² a gespannt ⟨vt⟩ anspannen ⟨muscle⟩

tension n Spannung f

tent n Zelt nt

tentacle n Fangarm m

tentative a vorläufig; (hesitant) zaghaft

tenth a zehnte(r,s) ⟨n⟩ Zehntel nt

tenuous a (fig) schwach

tepid a lauwarm

term n Zeitraum m; (Sch) ≈ Halbjahr nt; (Univ) ≈ Semester nt; (expression) Ausdruck m; **~s** pl (conditions) Bedingungen pl; **~ of office** Amtszeit f; **in the short/long ~** kurz-/langfristig

terminal a End-; (Med) unheilbar ⟨n⟩ Terminal m; (of bus) Endstation f; (on battery) Pol m; (Computing) Terminal nt

terminate vt beenden; lösen ⟨contract⟩ ⟨vi⟩ unterbrechen ⟨pregnancy⟩ □ vi enden

terminology n Terminologie f

terminus n Endstation f

terrace n Terrasse f; (houses) Häuserreihe f; **the ~s** (Sport) die [Steh]ränge pl. **~d house** n Reihenhaus nt

terrain n Gelände nt

terrible a schrecklich

terrier n Terrier m

terrific a (fam) (excellent) sagenhaft

terri|fy vt angst machen (+ dat); **be ~fied** Angst haben

territory n Gebiet nt

terror n [panische] Angst f; (Pol) Terror m. **~ism** n Terrorismus m. **~ist** n Terrorist m. **~ize** vt terrorisieren

terse a kurz, knapp

test n Test m; (Sch) Klassenarbeit f □ vt prüfen; (examine) untersuchen (for auf + acc)

testament n Old/New T ~ Altes/Neues Testament nt

testicle n Hoden m

testify vt beweisen; **~ that** bezeugen, daß ⟨vi⟩ aussagen; **~ to** bezeugen

testimony n Aussage f

'test-tube n Reagenzglas nt. **~ baby** n (fam) Retortenbaby nt

tetanus n Tetanus m

text n Text m. **~book** n Lehrbuch nt

textile a **~s** pl Textilien pl

texture n Beschaffenheit f; (Tex) Struktur f

Thai a thailändisch. **~land** n Thailand nt

Thames n Themse f

than conj als

thank vt danken (+ dat); **~ you [very much]** danke [schön]. **~ful** a dankbar. **~less** a undankbar

thanks npl Dank m; ~! (fam) danke! ~ **to** dank (+ dat or gen)

that a & pron der/die/das; (pl) die; ~ **one** der/die/das da; **I'll take** ~ ich nehme den/die/das; **I don't like those** die mag ich nicht; ~ **is** das heißt; **is** ~ **you?** bist du es? **who is** ~? wer ist da? **with/after** ~ damit/danach; **like** ~ so; **a man like** ~ so ein Mann □ adv so; ~ **good/hot** so gut/heiß □ conj daß

thatched a strohgedeckt

thaw vt/i auftauen; **it's** ~**ing** es taut

the def art der/die/das; (pl) die; **play** ~ **piano/violin** Klavier/Geige spielen □ adv ~ **more** ~ **better** je mehr, desto besser; **all** ~ **better** um so besser

theatre n Theater nt; (Med) Operationssaal m

theatrical a Theater-; (showy) theatralisch

theft n Diebstahl m

their a ihr

theirs poss pron ihre(r), ihrs; **a friend of** ~ ein Freund von ihnen; **those are** ~ die gehören ihnen

them pron (acc) sie; (dat) ihnen

theme n Thema nt

them'selves pron selbst; (refl) sich; **by** ~ allein

then adv dann; (at that time in past) damals; **by** ~ bis dahin; **since** ~ seitdem; **before** ~ vorher; **from** ~ **on** von da an; **now and** ~ dann und wann; **there and** ~ auf der Stelle □ a damalig

theolog|ian n Theologe m. ~**y** n Theologie f

theorem n Lehrsatz m

theoretical a theoretisch

theory n Theorie f

therapeutic a therapeutisch

therap|ist n Therapeut(in) m(f). ~**y** n Therapie f

there adv da; (with movement) dahin, dorthin; **down/up** ~ da unten/oben; ~ **is/are** da ist/sind; (in existence) es gibt

there: ~**abouts** adv da [in der Nähe]; **or** ~**abouts** (roughly) ungefähr. ~**'after** adv danach. ~**by** adv dadurch. ~**fore** adv deshalb, also

thermal a Thermal-; ~ **'underwear** n Thermowäsche f

thermometer n Thermometer nt

Thermos (P) n ~ [**flask**] Thermosflasche (P) f

thermostat n Thermostat m

thesis n Dissertation f; (proposition) These f

they pron sie; ~ **say** (generalizing) man sagt

thick a dick; (dense) dicht; (liquid) dickflüssig; (fam: stupid) dumm □ adv dick. ~**en** vt dicker machen; eindicken (sauce) □ vi dicker werden; (fog:) dichter werden; (plot:) kompliziert werden. ~**ness** n Dicke f; Dichte f; Dickflüssigkeit f

thick: ~**set** a untersetzt. ~**'skinned** a (fam) dickfellig

thief n Dieb(in) m(f)

thigh n Oberschenkel m

thimble n Fingerhut m

thin a dünn □ adv verdünnen (liquid) □ vi sich lichten. ~ **out** vt ausdünnen

thing n Ding nt; (affair) Sache f; ~**s** pl (belongings) Sachen pl; **for one** ~ erstens; **the right** ~ das Richtige; **just the** ~! genau das Richtige! **how are** ~**s?** wie geht's? **the latest** ~ (fam) der letzte Schrei

think vt/i denken (about/of an + acc); (believe) meinen; (consider) nachdenken; (regard as) halten für; **I** ~ **so** ich glaube schon; **what do you** ~? was meinen Sie? ~ **over** vt sich (dat) überlegen. ~ **up** vt sich (dat) ausdenken

third *a* dritte(r,s) □*n* Drittel *nt.*
~**ly** *adv* drittens

thirst *n* Durst *m.* ~**y** *a* durstig; **be**
~**y** Durst haben

thirteen *a* dreizehn. ~**th** *a* drei-
zehnte(r,s)

thirtieth *a* dreißigste(r,s)

thirty *a* dreißig

this *a* diese(r,s); (*pl*) diese; ~ **one**
diese(r,s) da; **I'll take** ~ ich nehme diesen/dieses; ~ **evening/
morning** heute abend/morgen;
these days heutzutage □*pron*
das, dies[es]; (*pl*) die, diese; ~
and that dies und das; ~ **or that**
dieses oder das; **like** ~ so

thistle *n* Distel *f*

thorn *n* Dorn *m.* ~**y** *a* dornig

thorough *a* gründlich

thorough: ~**bred** *n* reinrassiges
Tier *nt;* ⟨*horse*⟩ Rassepferd *nt.*
~**fare** *n* Durchfahrtsstraße *f;*
'**no** ~**fare**' 'keine Durchfahrt'

thoroughly *adv* gründlich; (*completely*) völlig; (*extremely*) äußerst

though *conj* obgleich, obwohl; **as**
~ als ob □*adv* (*fam*) doch

thought *n* Gedanke *m;* (*thinking*)
Denken *nt.* ~**ful** *a* nachdenklich;
(*considerate*) rücksichtsvoll

thousand *a* **one/a** ~ [ein]tausend
□*n* Tausend *nt.* ~**th** *a* tau-
sendste(r,s) □*n* Tausendstel *nt*

thrash *vt* verprügeln; (*defeat*)
[vernichtend] schlagen. ~
about *vi* sich herumwerfen;
⟨*fish:*⟩ zappeln

thread *n* Faden *m;* (*of screw*)
Gewinde *nt* □*vt* einfädeln; auffä-
deln ⟨*beads*⟩. ~**bare** *a* fadenscheinig

threat *n* Drohung *f;* (*danger*)
Bedrohung *f*

threaten *vt* drohen (+ *dat*);
(*with weapon*) bedrohen □*vi*
drohen. ~**ing** *a* drohend;
(*ominous*) bedrohlich

three *a* drei. ~**fold** *a* dreifach.
~**some** *n* Trio *nt*

thresh *vt* dreschen

threshold *n* Schwelle *f*

thrift *n* Sparsamkeit *f.* ~**y** *a*
sparsam

thrill *n* Erregung *f;* (*fam*) Ner-
venkitzel *m* □*vt* (*excite*) erregen;
be ~**ed with** sich freuen
über (+ *acc*). ~**er** *n* Thriller *m*

thrive *vi* gedeihen (**on** bei);
⟨*business:*⟩ florieren

throat *n* Hals *m*

throb *vi* pochen

throes *npl* **in the** ~ **of**
(*fig*) mitten in (+ *dat*)

thrombosis *n* Thrombose *f*

throne *n* Thron *m*

throttle *vt* erdrosseln

through *prep* durch (+ *acc*);
(*during*) während (+ *gen*) □*adv*
durch; **all** ~ die ganze Zeit; ~
and ~ durch und durch; **wet** ~
durch und durch naß; **read sth**
~ etw durchlesen □*a* ⟨*train*⟩
durchgehend; **be** ~ (*finished*)
fertig sein; (*Teleph*) durch sein

throughout *prep* ~ **the country** im ganzen Land; ~ **the
night** die Nacht durch □*adv*
ganz; (*time*) die ganze Zeit

throw *vt* werfen; schütten ⟨*liquid*⟩; betätigen ⟨*switch*⟩; abwerfen ⟨*rider*⟩; (*fam: disconcert*) aus der Fassung bringen;
(*fam*) geben ⟨*party*⟩. ~ **away** *vt*
wegwerfen. ~ **out** *vt* hinauswerfen; (~ *away*) wegwerfen;
verwerfen ⟨*plan*⟩. ~ **up** *vt* hochwerfen □*vi* (*fam*) sich übergeben

'**throw-away** *a* Wegwerf-

thrush *n* Drossel *f*

thrust *n* Stoß *m;* (*Phys*) Schub *m*
□*vt* stoßen

thug *n* Schläger *m*

thumb *n* Daumen *m;* **rule of** ~
Faustregel *f;* **under s.o.'s** ~
unter jds Fuchtel. ~**-index** *n*
Daumenregister *nt*

thump vt schlagen □ vi hämmern
(**on** an/auf + acc); ⟨heart:⟩ pochen

thunder n Donner m □ vi don-
nern. **~clap** n Donnerschlag m.
~storm n Gewitter nt. **~y** a
gewittrig

Thursday n Donnerstag m

thus adv so

thyme n Thymian m

thyroid n Schilddrüse f

tick n ⟨sound⟩ Ticken nt; ⟨mark⟩
Häkchen nt □ vi ticken □ vt abhaken. **~ off** vt abhaken; ⟨fam⟩
rüffeln

ticket n Karte f; ⟨for bus, train⟩
Fahrschein m; ⟨Aviat⟩ Flugschein
m; ⟨for lottery⟩ Los nt ⟨for article
deposited⟩ Schein m; ⟨label⟩
Schild nt; ⟨for library⟩ Lesekarte
f; ⟨fine⟩ Strafzettel m. **~-collec-
tor** n Fahrkartenkontrolleur m.
~-office n Fahrkartenschalter
m; ⟨for entry⟩ Kasse f

tickle vt/i kitzeln

tidal a Tide-. **~ wave** n Flutwelle
f

tiddly-winks n Flohspiel nt

tide n Gezeiten pl; ⟨of events⟩
Strom m; **the ~ is in/out** es ist
Flut/Ebbe □ vt ~ **s.o. over** jdm
über die Runden helfen

tidy a ordentlich □ vt ~ [**up**] aufräumen

tie n Krawatte f, Schlips m; ⟨cord⟩
Schnur f; ⟨fig: bond⟩ Band nt;
⟨restriction⟩ Bindung f; ⟨Sport⟩
Unentschieden nt; ⟨in competi-
tion⟩ Punktgleichheit f □ vt binden; machen ⟨knot⟩ □ vi ⟨Sport⟩
unentschieden spielen; ⟨have
equal scores⟩ punktgleich sein; **~
in with** passen zu

tier n Stufe f

tiger n Tiger m

tight a fest; ⟨taut⟩ straff; ⟨clothes⟩
eng; ⟨control⟩ streng; ⟨fam:
drunk⟩ blau

tighten vt festerziehen; straffen
⟨rope⟩; anziehen ⟨screw⟩; verschärfen ⟨control⟩ □ vi sich span-
nen

tight: ~-'fisted a knauserig.
~-rope n Hochseil nt

tights npl Strumpfhose f

tile n Fliese f; ⟨on wall⟩ Kachel f;
⟨on roof⟩ [Dach]ziegel m

till[1] prep & conj = **until**

till[2] n Kasse f

tiller n Ruderpinne f

tilt vt kippen; [zur Seite] neigen
⟨head⟩ □ vi sich neigen

timber n [Nutz]holz nt

time n Zeit f; ⟨occasion⟩ Mal nt;
⟨rhythm⟩ Takt m; **~s** ⟨Math⟩ mal;
at any ~ jederzeit; **this ~** dieses
Mal, diesmal; **at ~s** manchmal;
~ and again immer wieder; **two
at a ~** zwei auf einmal; **on ~**
pünktlich; **in ~** rechtzeitig;
⟨eventually⟩ mit der Zeit; **what is
the ~?** wie spät ist es? wieviel
Uhr ist es? □ vt stoppen ⟨race⟩

time: ~ bomb n Zeitbombe f. **~-ly**
a rechtzeitig. **~-table** n Fahrplan
m; ⟨Sch⟩ Stundenplan m

timid a scheu

timing n Wahl f des richtigen
Zeitpunkts; ⟨Sport, Techn⟩ Timing nt

tin n ⟨container⟩ Dose f. **~-
foil** n Stanniol nt; ⟨Culin⟩ Alufolie f

tinge n Hauch m

tingle vi kribbeln

tinker vi herumbasteln (**with** an
+ dat)

tinkle vi klingeln

'tin opener n Dosen-/Büchsenöff-
ner m

tinsel n Lametta nt

tint n Farbton m □ vt tönen

tiny a winzig

tip[1] n Spitze f

tip[2] n ⟨money⟩ Trinkgeld nt; ⟨ad-
vice⟩ Rat m, ⟨fam⟩ Tip m; ⟨for
rubbish⟩ Müllhalde f □ vt ⟨tilt⟩

kippen; (*reward*) Trinkgeld geben (s.o. jdm) □ *vi* kippen. ~ **off** *vt* ~ s.o. off jdm einen Hinweis geben

'tip-off *n* Hinweis *m*

tipsy *a* (*fam*) beschwipst

tiptoe *n* on ~ auf Zehenspitzen

tire *vt/i* ermüden. ~ **d** *a* müde; be ~d of sth etw satt haben; ~d out [völlig] erschöpft. ~**some** *a* lästig

tissue *n* Gewebe *nt*; (*handkerchief*) Papiertaschentuch *nt*. ~~**paper** *n* Seidenpapier *nt*

tit[1] *n* (*bird*) Meise *f*

tit[2] *n* ~ for tat wie du mir, so ich dir

'titbit *n* Leckerbissen *m*

title *n* Titel *m*

to *prep* zu (+ *dat*); (*with place, direction*) nach; (*to cinema, theatre*) in (+ *acc*); (*to wedding, party*) auf (+ *acc*); ⟨*address, send, fasten*⟩ an (+ *acc*); (*per*) pro; (*up to, until*) bis; **to the station** zum Bahnhof; **to Germany/Switzerland** nach Deutschland/in die Schweiz; **to the toilet/one's room** auf die Toilette/sein Zimmer; **to the office/an exhibition** ins Büro/in eine Ausstellung; **to university** auf die Universität; **twenty/quarter to eight** zwanzig/Viertel vor acht; **5 to 6 pounds** 5 bis 6 Pfund; **to the end** bis zum Schluß; **to this day** bis heute; **to the best of my knowledge** nach meinem besten Wissen; **give/say sth to s.o.** jdm etw geben/sagen; **go/come to s.o.** zu jdm gehen/kommen; **I've never been to Berlin** ich war noch nie in Berlin; **there's nothing to it** es ist nichts dabei □*verbal constructions* to go gehen; **want to/ have to go** gehen wollen/müssen; **be easy/difficult to forget** leicht/schwer zu vergessen sein; **too ill/tired to go** zu krank/

müde, um zu gehen; **he did it to annoy me** er tat es, um mich zu ärgern; **you have to** du mußt; **I don't want to** ich will nicht □*pull* to anlehnen; **to and fro** hin und her

toad *n* Kröte *f*. ~**stool** *n* Giftpilz *m*

toast *n* Toast *m* □*vt* toasten ⟨*bread*⟩; ⟨*drink a* ~ *to*⟩ trinken auf (+ *acc*). ~**er** *n* Toaster *m*

tobacco *n* Tabak *m*. ~**nist's** [**shop**] *n* Tabakladen *m*

toboggan *n* Schlitten *m*

today *n* & *adv* heute; ~ **week** heute in einer Woche; ~**'s paper** die heutige Zeitung

toddler *n* Kleinkind *nt*

toe *n* Zeh *m*; (*of footwear*) Spitze *f* □*vt* ~ **the line** spuren. ~**nail** *n* Zehennagel *m*

toffee *n* Karamelbonbon *m* & *nt*

together *adv* zusammen; (*at the same time*) gleichzeitig

toilet *n* Toilette *f*. ~ **bag** *n* Kulturbeutel *m*. ~ **paper** *n* Toilettenpapier *nt*

toiletries *npl* Toilettenartikel *pl*

toilet: ~ **roll** *n* Rolle *f* Toilettenpapier. ~ **water** *n* Toilettenwasser *nt*

token *n* Zeichen *nt*; (*counter*) Marke *f*; (*voucher*) Gutschein *m* □*attrib* symbolisch

tolerable *a* erträglich

tolerance *n* Toleranz *f*. ~**t** *a* tolerant

tolerate *vt* dulden, tolerieren

toll[1] *n* Gebühr *f*; (*for road*) Maut *f* (*Aust*); **death** ~ Zahl *f* der Todesopfer

toll[2] *vi* läuten

tomato *n* Tomate *f*. ~ **purée** *n* Tomatenmark *nt*

tomb *n* Grabmal *nt*

'tomboy *n* Wildfang *m*

'tombstone *n* Grabstein *m*

'tom-cat *n* Kater *m*

tomorrow *n & adv* morgen; ~ **morning** morgen früh; **the day after** ~ übermorgen

ton *n* Tonne *f*

tone *n* Ton *m*; *(colour)* Farbton *m* □ *vt* ~ **down** dämpfen; *(fig)* mäßigen. ~ **up** *vt* kräftigen; straffen *(muscles)*

tongs *npl* Zange *f*

tongue *n* Zunge *f*; ~ **in cheek** *(fam)* nicht ernst. ~-**twister** *n* Zungenbrecher *m*

tonic *n* Tonikum *f*; *(fig)* Wohltat *f*; ~ **[water]** Tonic *nt*

tonight *n & adv* heute nacht; *(evening)* heute abend

tonne *n* Tonne *f*

tonsil *n (Anat)* Mandel *f*. ~**litis** *n* Mandelentzündung *f*

too *adv* zu; *(also)* auch; ~ **much/ little** zuviel/zuwenig

tool *n* Werkzeug *nt*; *(for gardening)* Gerät *nt*

tooth *n* Zahn *m*

tooth: ~**ache** *n* Zahnschmerzen *pl.* ~**brush** *n* Zahnbürste *f*. ~**less** *a* zahnlos. ~**paste** *n* Zahnpasta *f*. ~**pick** *n* Zahnstocher *m*

top¹ *n (toy)* Kreisel *m*

top² *n* oberer Teil *m*; *(apex)* Spitze *f*; *(summit)* Gipfel *m*; *(Sch)* Erste(r) *m/f*; *(top part or half)* Oberteil *nt*; *(head)* Kopfende *nt*; *(of road)* oberes Ende *nt*; *(upper surface)* Oberfläche *f*; *(lid)* Deckel *m*; *(of bottle)* Verschluß *m*; *(garment)* Top *nt* □ *a* oberste(r,s); *(highest)* höchste(r,s); *(best)* beste(r,s) □ *vt* an erster Stelle stehen auf (+ *dat*) *(list)*; *(exceed)* übersteigen; *(remove the* ~ *of)* die Spitze abschneiden. ~ **up** *vt* nachfüllen, auffüllen

top: ~**'hat** *n* Zylinder[hut] *m*. ~-**heavy** *a* kopflastig

topic *n* Thema *nt*. ~**al** *a* aktuell

top: ~**less** *a* oben ohne. ~**most** *a* oberste(r,s)

topple *vt/i* umstürzen

top-'secret *a* streng geheim

topsy-turvy *adv* völlig durcheinander

torch *n* Taschenlampe *f*; *(flaming)* Fackel *f*

torment¹ *n* Qual *f*

torment² *vt* quälen

tornado *n* Wirbelsturm *m*

torpedo *n* Torpedo *m*

torrent *n* reißender Strom *m*. ~**ial** *a* wolkenbruchartig

tortoise *n* Schildkröte *f*. ~**shell** *n* Schildpatt *m*

tortuous *a* verschlungen; *(fig)* umständlich

torture *n* Folter *f*; *(fig)* Qual *f* □ *vt* foltern; *(fig)* quälen

toss *vt* werfen; *(into the air)* hochwerfen; *(shake)* schütteln; *(unseat)* abwerfen; mischen *(salad)*; wenden *(pancake)*; ~ **a coin** mit einer Münze losen *(for)*; ~ **and turn** *(in bed)* sich [schlaflos] im Bett wälzen

total *a* gesamt; *(complete)* völlig, total □ *n* Gesamtzahl *f*; *(sum)* Gesamtsumme *f* □ *vt* zusammenzählen; *(amount to)* sich belaufen auf (+ *acc*)

totalitarian *a* totalitär

totally *adv* völlig, total

touch *n* Berührung *f*; *(sense)* Tastsinn *m*; *(Mus)* Anschlag *m*; *(contact)* Kontakt *m*; *(trace)* Spur *f*; *(fig)* Anflug *m*; **get/be in** ~ sich in Verbindung setzen/in Verbindung stehen **(with** mit) □ *vt* berühren; *(get hold of)* anfassen; *(lightly)* tippen auf/an (+ *acc*); **brush against** streifen [gegen]; *(reach)* erreichen; *(equal)* herankommen an (+ *acc*; *(fig: move)* rühren; anrühren *(food)*

tough *a* zäh; *(severe)* hart; *(difficult)* schwierig; *(durable)* strapazierfähig

tour n Reise f, Tour f; (of building) Besichtigung f; (Theat, Sport) Tournee f; (of duty) Dienstzeit f □vt fahren durch; besichtigen ⟨building⟩ □vi herumreisen

touris|m n Tourismus m, Fremdenverkehr m. **~t** n Tourist(in) m(f) □attrib Touristen-. **~t office** n Fremdenverkehrsbüro nt

tournament n Turnier nt

tout n Anreißer m; (ticket ~) Kartenschwarzhändler m □vt schleppen ziehen ⟨trailer⟩. **~ away** vt abschleppen

toward[s] prep zu (+ dat); (with time) gegen (+ acc); (with respect to) gegenüber (+ dat)

towel n Handtuch nt

tower n Turm m □vi **~ above** überragen. **~ block** n Hochhaus nt

town n Stadt f. **~ hall** n Rathaus nt

tow: ~-path n Treidelpfad m. **~-rope** n Abschleppseil nt

toxic a giftig. **~ 'waste** n Giftmüll m

toxin n Gift nt

toy n Spielzeug nt □vi **~ with** spielen mit; stochern in (+ dat) ⟨food⟩. **~ shop** n Spielwarengeschäft nt

trac|e n Spur f □vt folgen (+ dat); (find) finden; (draw) zeichnen; (with tracing-paper) durchpausen. **~ing-paper** n Pauspapier nt

track n Spur f; (path) (unbefestigter) Weg m; (Sport) Bahn f; (Rail) Gleis nt □vt verfolgen

tracksuit n Trainingsanzug m

tract¹ n (land) Gebiet nt

tract² n (pamphlet) [Flug]schrift f

tractor n Traktor m

trade n Handel m; (line of business) Gewerbe nt; (business) Geschäft nt; (craft) Handwerk nt; by

~ von Beruf □vt tauschen □vi handeln (in mit)

trade: ~ mark n Warenzeichen nt. **~ 'union** n Gewerkschaft f. **'unionist** n Gewerkschaftler(in) m(f)

tradition n Tradition f. **~al** a traditionell

traffic n Verkehr m; (trading) Handel m □vi handeln (in mit)

traffic: ~ jam n [Verkehrs]stau m. **~ lights** npl [Verkehrs]ampel f. **~ warden** n ≈ Hilfspolizist m; (woman) Politesse f

tragedy n Tragödie f

tragic a tragisch

trail n Spur f; (path) Weg m, Pfad m □vi schleifen; ⟨plant:⟩ sich ranken; **~ [behind]** zurückbleiben; (Sport) zurückliegen □vt verfolgen, folgen (+ dat); (drag) schleifen

trailer n (Auto) Anhänger m; (film) Vorschau f

train n Zug m; (of dress) Schleppe f. **~ of thought** Gedankengang m □vt ausbilden; (Sport) trainieren; (aim) richten auf (+ acc); erziehen ⟨child⟩; abrichten/(to do tricks) dressieren ⟨animal⟩; ziehen ⟨plant⟩ □vi eine Ausbildung machen; (Sport) trainieren

trainee n Auszubildende/r m|f; (Techn) Praktikant(in) m(f)

trainer n (Sport) Trainer m; (in circus) Dompteur m; **~s** pl Trainingsschuhe pl

trait n Eigenschaft f

traitor n Verräter m

tram n Straßenbahn f. **~-lines** npl Straßenbahnschienen pl

tramp n Landstreicher m

trample vt/i trampeln (**on** auf + acc)

trampoline n Trampolin nt

trance n Trance f

tranquillity n Ruhe f

tranquillizer n Beruhigungsmittel nt

transaction n Transaktion f

transcend vt übersteigen

transcript n Abschrift f; (of official proceedings) Protokoll nt

transept n Querschiff nt

transfer[1] n Übertragung f; Verlegung f; Versetzung f; Überweisung f; (Sport) Transfer m; (design) Abziehbild nt

transfer[2] vt übertragen; verlegen ⟨firm⟩; versetzen ⟨employee⟩; überweisen ⟨money⟩; (Sport) transferieren □vi [über]wechseln; (when travelling) umsteigen

transform vt verwandeln. **~ation** n Verwandlung f. **~er** n Transformator m

transfusion n Transfusion f

transient a kurzlebig

transistor n Transistor m

transit n **in ~** auf dem Transport

transition n Übergang m

transitive a transitiv

transitory a vergänglich

translat|e vt übersetzen. **~ion** n Übersetzung f. **~or** n Übersetzer(in) m(f)

translucent a durchscheinend

transmission n Übertragung f

transmit vt übertragen. **~ter** n Sender m

transparen|cy n (Phot) Dia nt. **~t** a durchsichtig

transpire vi sich herausstellen; (fam: happen) passieren

transplant[1] n Verpflanzung f; Transplantation f

transplant[2] vt umpflanzen; (Med) verpflanzen

transport[1] n Transport m

transport[2] vt transportieren

transpose vt umstellen

transvestite n Transvestit m

trap n Falle f □vt [mit einer Falle] fangen; (jam) einklemmen. **~'door** n Falltür f

trapeze n Trapez nt

trash n Schund m; (rubbish) Abfall m; (nonsense) Quatsch m

trauma n Trauma nt. **~tic** a traumatisch

travel n Reisen nt □vi reisen; (go in vehicle) fahren; ⟨light, sound:⟩ sich fortpflanzen; (Techn) sich bewegen □vt bereisen; fahren ⟨distance⟩. **~ agency** n Reisebüro nt. **~ agent** n Reisebürokaufmann m

traveller n Reisende(r) m/f; (Comm) Vertreter m; **~s** pl (gypsies) Zigeuner pl. **~'s cheque** n Reisescheck m

trawler n Fischdampfer m

tray n Tablett nt; (for baking) [Back]blech nt; (for documents) Ablagekorb m

treacher|ous a treulos; (dangerous) tückisch. **~y** n Verrat m

treacle n Sirup m

tread n Schritt m; (step) Stufe f; (of tyre) Profil nt □vi (walk) gehen; **~ on/in** treten auf/in (+ acc) □vt treten

treason n Verrat m

treasure n Schatz m □vt in Ehren halten. **~r** n Kassenwart m

treasury n Schatzkammer f; **the T~** das Finanzministerium

treat vt behandeln; **~ s.o. to sth** jdm etw spendieren

treatise n Abhandlung f

treatment n Behandlung f

treaty n Vertrag m

treble a dreifach; **~ the amount** dreimal soviel □n (Mus) Diskant m; (voice) Sopran m □vt verdreifachen

tree n Baum m

trek n Marsch m

trellis n Gitter nt

tremble vi zittern

tremendous a gewaltig; (fam: excellent) großartig

trench n Graben m

trend n Tendenz f; (fashion) Trend m. **~y** a (fam) modisch

trespass vi **~ on** unerlaubt betreten. **~er** n Unbefugte(r) m/f

trial n (*Jur*) [Gerichts]verfahren nt, Prozeß m; (*test*) Probe f; (*ordeal*) Prüfung f; **be on ~** auf Probe sein; (*Jur*) angeklagt sein (**for** wegen)

triang|le n Dreieck nt; (*Mus*) Triangel m. **~ular** a dreieckig

tribe n Stamm m

tribunal n Schiedsgericht nt

tributary n Nebenfluß m

tribute n Tribut m

trick n Trick m; (*joke*) Streich m; (*Cards*) Stich m; (*feat of skill*) Kunststück nt □vt täuschen; (*fam*) hereinlegen

trickle vi rinnen

tricky a schwierig

tricycle n Dreirad nt

trifle n Kleinigkeit f; (*Culin*) Trifle nt

trigger n Abzug m; (*fig*) Auslöser m □vt **~ [off]** auslösen

trigonometry n Trigonometrie f

trim a gepflegt □n (*cut*) Nachschneiden nt; (*decoration*) Verzierung f; (*condition*) Zustand m □vt schneiden; (*decorate*) besetzen; (*Naut*) trimmen

Trinity n **the [Holy] ~** die [Heilige] Dreieinigkeit f

trinket n Schmuckgegenstand m

trio n Trio nt

trip n Reise f; (*excursion*) Ausflug m □vt **~ s.o. up** jdm ein Bein stellen □vi stolpern (**on/over** über + acc)

triple a dreifach □vt verdreifachen

triplets npl Drillinge pl

triplicate n in **~** in dreifacher Ausfertigung

tripod n Stativ nt

trite a banal

triumph n Triumph m □vi triumphieren (**over** über + acc). **~ant** a triumphierend

trivial a belanglos

trolley n (*for serving food*) Servierwagen m; (*for shopping*) Einkaufswagen m; (*for luggage*) Kofferkuli m. **~ bus** n O-Bus m

trombone n Posaune f

troop n Schar f; **~ s** pl Truppen pl

trophy n Trophäe f

tropic n Wendekreis m; **~s** pl Tropen pl. **~al** a tropisch; ⟨fruit⟩ Süd-

trot vi traben

trouble n Ärger m; (*difficulties*) Schwierigkeiten pl; (*inconvenience*) Mühe f; (*conflict*) Unruhe f; (*Med*) Beschwerden pl; (*Techn*) Probleme pl; **get into ~** Ärger bekommen; **take ~** sich (*dat*) Mühe geben □vt (*disturb*) stören; (*worry*) beunruhigen □vi sich bemühen. **~-maker** n Unruhestifter m. **~some** a schwierig; ⟨cough⟩ lästig

trough n Trog m

troupe n Truppe f

trousers npl Hose f

trousseau n Aussteuer f

trout n inv Forelle f

trowel n Kelle f; (*for gardening*) Pflanzkelle f

truant n **play ~** die Schule schwänzen

truce n Waffenstillstand m

truck n Last[kraft]wagen m; (*Rail*) Güterwagen m

true a wahr; (*loyal*) treu; (*genuine*) echt; **come ~** in Erfüllung gehen; **is that ~?** stimmt das?

truism n Binsenwahrheit f

truly adv wirklich; (*faithfully*) treu; **Yours ~** Hochachtungsvoll

trump n (*Cards*) Trumpf m □vt übertrumpfen

trumpet n Trompete f. **~er** n Trompeter m

truncheon n Schlagstock m

trundle vt/i rollen

trunk n [Baum]stamm m; (*body*) Rumpf m; (*of elephant*) Rüssel m; (*for travelling*) [Übersee]koffer

m; (for storage) Truhe f; **~s** pl
Badehose f

trust n Vertrauen nt; (group of
companies) Trust m; (organization) Treuhandgesellschaft f;
(charitable) Stiftung f □vt trauen
(+ dat), vertrauen (+ dat);
(hope) hoffen □vi vertrauen
(in/to auf + acc)

trustee n Treuhänder m

'trustworthy a vertrauenswür-
dig

truth n Wahrheit f. **~ful** a ehrlich

try n Versuch m □vt versuchen;
(sample) probieren; (be a strain
on) anstrengen; (Jur) vor Gericht
stellen; verhandeln (case) □vi
versuchen; (make an effort) sich
bemühen

T-shirt n T-Shirt nt

tub n Kübel m; (carton) Becher m;
(bath) Wanne f

tuba n (Mus) Tuba f

tube n Röhre f; (pipe) Rohr nt;
(flexible) Schlauch m; (of toothpaste) Tube f; (Rail, fam) U-Bahn
f

tuber n Knolle f

tuberculosis n Tuberkulose f

tubular a röhrenförmig

tuck n Saum m; (decorative) Biese
f □vt (put) stecken. **~ in** vt hin-
einstecken; □vi (fam: eat) zulangen.
~ s.o. in jdn zu-
decken □vi (fam: eat) zulangen

Tuesday n Dienstag m

tug n Ruck m; (Naut) Schlepp-
dampfer m □vt ziehen □vi zerren
(at an + dat). **~ of war** n Tauzie-
hen nt

tulip n Tulpe f

tumble vi fallen. **~-drier** n Wä-
schetrockner m

tumbler n Glas nt

tummy n (fam) Magen m; (abdomen) Bauch m

tumour n Geschwulst f, Tumor m

tumultuous a stürmisch

tuna n Thunfisch m

tune n Melodie f; out of ~ (instrument) verstimmt. ~ **up** vi
(Mus) stimmen

Tunisia n Tunesien nt

tunnel n Tunnel m □vi einen Tunnel graben

turban n Turban m

turbine n Turbine f

turbot n Steinbutt m

turbulen|ce n Turbulenz f. **~t** a
stürmisch

tureen n Terrine f

turf n Rasen m; (segment) Rasen-
stück nt

Turk n Türke m/Türkin f

turkey n Pute f, Truthahn m

Turk|ey n die Türkei. **~ish** a
türkisch

turmoil n Aufruhr m

turn n (rotation) Drehung f; (in
road) Kurve f; (change of
direction) Wende f; (short walk)
Runde f; (Theat) Nummer f;
(fam: attack) Anfall m; **do s.o. a
good ~** jdm einen guten Dienst
erweisen; **take ~s** sich abwechseln; **in ~** der Reihe nach; **out of
~** außer der Reihe; **it's your ~**
du bist an der Reihe □vt drehen;
(~ over) wenden; (reverse) umdrehen; (Techn) drechseln
(wood); **~ the page** umblättern;
~ the corner um die Ecke biegen
□vi sich drehen; (~ round) sich
umdrehen; (car:) wenden; (leaves:) sich färben; (weather:) um-
schlagen; (become) werden; ~
right/left nach rechts/links abbiegen. **~ down** vt herunter-
schlagen (collar); herunterdre-
hen (heat); leiser stellen
(sound); (reject) ablehnen; abweisen (person). **~ off** vt zudrehen
(tap); ausschalten (light); abstellen (water, gas) □vi abbiegen. **~
on** vt aufdrehen (tap); einschalten (light); anstellen (water,
gas). **~ out** vt (expel) vertreiben,

(*fam*) hinauswerfen; ausschalten (*light*); abdrehen (*gas*); (*produce*) produzieren; (*empty*) ausleeren; (*gründlich*) aufräumen ⟨*room*⟩ □ *vi* (*go out*) hinausgehen; (*transpire*) sich herausstellen; ~ **out well/badly** gut/schlecht gehen. ~ **up** *vi* hochschlagen ⟨*collar*⟩; aufdrehen ⟨*heat*⟩; lauter stellen ⟨*sound*⟩ □ *vi* auftauchen
turning-point *n* Wendepunkt *m*
turnip *n* weiße Rübe *f*
turn: ~ **over** *n* (*Comm*) Umsatz *m*; (*of staff*) Personalwechsel *m*. ~ **stile** *n* Drehkreuz *nt*. ~ **table** *n* Drehscheibe *f*; (*on record-player*) Plattenteller *m*. ~ **-up** *n* [Hosen]aufschlag *m*
turpentine *n* Terpentin *nt*
turquoise *a* türkis[farben]
turret *n* Türmchen *nt*
turtle *n* Seeschildkröte *f*
tusk *n* Stoßzahn *m*
tutor *n* [Privat]lehrer *m*
tweed *n* Tweed *m*
tweezers *npl* Pinzette *f*
twelfth *a* zwölfte(r,s)
twelve *a* zwölf
twentieth *a* zwanzigste(r,s)
twenty *a* zwanzig
twice *adv* zweimal
twig[1] *n* Zweig *m*
twig[2] *vt/i* (*fam*) kapieren
twilight *n* Dämmerlicht *nt*
twin *n* Zwilling *m*. ~ **beds** *npl* zwei Einzelbetten *pl*
twine *n* Bindfaden *m*
twinkle *vi* funkeln
twin 'town *n* Partnerstadt *f*
twirl *vt/i* herumwirbeln
twist *n* Drehung *f*; (*curve*) Kurve *f*; (*unexpected occurrence*) überraschende Wendung *f* □ *vt* drehen; (*distort*) verdrehen; (*fam: swindle*) beschummeln; ~ **one's ankle** sich (*dat*) den Knöchel verrenken □ *vi* sich drehen; ⟨*road:*⟩ sich winden
twitch *vi* zucken

twitter *vi* zwitschern
two *a* zwei
tycoon *n* Magnat *m*
type *n* Art *f*, Sorte *f*; (*person*) Typ *m*; (*printing*) Type *f* □ *vt* mit der Maschine schreiben, (*fam*) tippen □ *vi* maschineschreiben, (*fam*) tippen. ~ **writer** *n* Schreibmaschine *f*. ~ **written** *a* maschinegeschrieben
typhoid *n* Typhus *m*
typical *a* typisch (*of* für)
typify *vt* typisch sein für
typist *n* Schreibkraft *f*
typography *n* Typographie *f*
tyrannical *a* tyrannisch
tyranny *n* Tyrannei *f*
tyrant *n* Tyrann *m*
tyre *n* Reifen *m*

U

ubiquitous *a* allgegenwärtig; **be** ~ überall zu finden sein
udder *n* Euter *nt*
ugly *a* häßlich; (*nasty*) übel
ulcer *n* Geschwür *nt*
ulterior *a* ~ **motive** Hintergedanke *m*
ultimate *a* letzte(r,s); (*final*) endgültig; (*fundamental*) grundlegend, eigentlich. ~ **ly** *adv* schließlich
ultimatum *n* Ultimatum *nt*
ultrasound *n* (*Med*) Ultraschall *m*
ultra'violet *a* ultraviolett
umbilical *a* ~ **cord** Nabelschnur *f*
umbrella *n* [Regen]schirm *m*
umpire *n* Schiedsrichter *m*
umpteen *a* (*fam*) zig. ~ **th** *a* (*fam*) zigste(r,s)
unac'companied *a* ohne Begleitung; ⟨*luggage*⟩ unbegleitet
unac'customed *a* ungewohnt; **be** ~ **to sth** etw nicht gewohnt sein

lulterated *a* unverfälscht,
rein; (*utter*) völlig
unanimous *a* einmütig; ⟨decision⟩ einstimmig
un'armed *a* unbewaffnet; ~ combat Kampf *m* ohne Waffen
unas'suming *a* bescheiden
unat'tached *a* nicht befestigt; ⟨person⟩ ungebunden
unat'tended *a* unbeaufsichtigt
un'authorized *a* unbefugt
una'voidable *a* unvermeidlich
una'ware *a* be ~ of sth sich (dat) etw (gen) nicht bewußt sein
un'bearable *a* unerträglich
unbe'known *a* (fam) ~ to me ohne mein Wissen
unbe'lievable *a* unglaublich
un'biased *a* unvoreingenommen
un'bolt *vt* aufriegeln
un'breakable *a* unzerbrechlich
un'burden *vt* ~ **oneself** (fig) sich aussprechen
un'button *vt* aufknöpfen
uncalled-for *a* unangebracht
un'canny *a* unheimlich
uncere'monious *a* formlos; (abrupt) brüsk
un'certain *a* (doubtful) ungewiß; ⟨origins⟩ unbestimmt; be ~ nicht sicher sein; in no ~ terms ganz eindeutig. ~ty *n* Ungewißheit *f*
un'changed *a* unverändert
un'charitable *a* lieblos
uncle *n* Onkel *m*
un'comfortable *a* unbequem
un'common *a* ungewöhnlich
un'compromising *a* kompromißlos
uncon'ditional *a* bedingungslos
un'conscious *a* bewußtlos; (unintended) unbewußt
unco'operative *a* nicht hilfsbereit
un'cork *vt* entkorken
uncouth *a* ungehobelt
un'cover *vt* aufdecken

unde'cided *a* unentschlossen; (not settled) nicht entschieden
under *prep* unter (+ dat/acc); ~ it darunter; ~ **there** da drunter; ~ **repair** in Reparatur; ~ **construction** im Bau; ~ **age** minderjährig; ~ **way** unterwegs; (fig) im Gange
'undercarriage *n* (Aviat) Fahrwerk *nt*, Fahrgestell *nt*
'underclothes *npl* Unterwäsche *f*
under'cover *a* geheim
'undercurrent *n* Unterströmung *f*; (fig) Unterton *m*
under'cut *vt* unterbieten
'underdog *n* Unterlegene(r) *m*
under'done *a* nicht gar; (rare) nicht durchgebraten
under'estimate *vt* unterschätzen
under'foot *adv* am Boden
under'go *vt* durchmachen; sich unterziehen (+ dat) ⟨operation⟩
under'graduate *n* Student(in) *m(f)*
under'ground¹ *adv* unter der Erde; (fig) unter Tage
'underground² *a* unterirdisch; (secret) Untergrund-. □*n* (railway) U-Bahn *f*. ~ **car park** *n* Tiefgarage *f*
'undergrowth *n* Unterholz *nt*
under'hand *a* hinterhältig
under'line *vt* unterstreichen
underling *n* (pej) Untergebene(r) *m/f*
under'mine *vt* (fig) unterminieren, untergraben
underneath *prep* unter (+ dat/acc); ~ **it** darunter □*adv* darunter
'underpants *npl* Unterhose *f*
'underpass *n* Unterführung *f*
under'privileged *a* unterprivilegiert
under'rate *vt* unterschätzen
under'stand *vt/i* verstehen; **I** ~ **that** ... (have heard) ich habe gehört, daß ... ~ **able** *a* verständlich

under'standing a verständnisvoll □n Verständnis nt; (agreement) Vereinbarung f

'**understatement** n Untertreibung f

'**understudy** n Ersatzspieler(in) m(f)

under'take vt unternehmen

'**undertaker** n Leichenbestatter m; [firm of] ~s Bestattungsinstitut nt

under'taking n Unternehmen nt; (promise) Versprechen nt

'**undertone** n (fig) Unterton m

under'value vt unterbewerten

'**underwater**[1] a Unterwasser-

under'water[2] adv unter Wasser

'**underwear** n Unterwäsche f

'**underweight** a untergewichtig; be ~ Untergewicht haben

'**underworld** n Unterwelt f

'**underwriter** n Versicherer m

un'do vt aufmachen; (fig) ungeschehen machen; (ruin) zunichte machen

un'doubtedly adv zweifellos

un'dress vt ausziehen □vi sich ausziehen

un'due a übermäßig

un'dying a ewig

un'earth vt ausgraben; (fig) zutage bringen. ~**ly** a unheimlich

un'easy a unbehaglich

uneco'nomic a unwirtschaftlich

uneco'nomical a verschwenderisch

unem'ployed a arbeitslos □npl the ~ die Arbeitslosen

unem'ployment n Arbeitslosigkeit f. ~ benefit n Arbeitslosenunterstützung f

un'ending a endlos

un'equal a unterschiedlich; (struggle) ungleich; be ~ to a task einer Aufgabe nicht gewachsen sein

une'quivocal a eindeutig

un'erring a unfehlbar

un'ethical a unmoralisch

un'even a uneben; (unequal) ungleich; (not regular) ungleichmäßig; (number) ungerade

unex'pected a unerwartet

un'fair a ungerecht, unfair

un'faithful a untreu

unfa'miliar a ungewohnt; (unknown) unbekannt

un'fasten vt aufmachen; (detach) losmachen

un'favourable a ungünstig

un'finished a unvollendet; (business) unerledigt

un'fit a ungeeignet; (incompetent) unfähig; (Sport) nicht fit; ~ for work arbeitsunfähig

un'fold vt auseinanderfalten, entfalten; (spread out) ausbreiten □vi sich entfalten

unfore'seen a unvorhergesehen

unfor'gettable a unvergeßlich

unfor'givable a unverzeihlich

un'fortunate a unglücklich; (unfavourable) ungünstig; (regrettable) bedauerlich. ~**ly** adv leider

un'founded a unbegründet

un'furnished a unmöbliert

un'gainly a unbeholfen

un'godly a gottlos; at an ~ hour (fam) in aller Herrgottsfrühe

un'grateful a undankbar

un'happy a unglücklich; (not content) unzufrieden

un'harmed a unverletzt

un'healthy a ungesund

unhy'gienic a unhygienisch

'**unicorn** n Einhorn nt

unifi'cation n Einigung f

'**uniform** a einheitlich □n Uniform f

'**unify** vt einigen

uni'lateral a einseitig

uni'maginable a unvorstellbar

unim'portant a unwichtig

unin'habited a unbewohnt

unin'tentional a unabsichtlich

'**union** n Vereinigung f; (Pol) Union f; (trade ~) Gewerkschaft f. ~**ist** n (Pol) Unionist m

unique a einzigartig

unison n in ~ einstimmig

unit n Einheit f; (Math) Einer m; (of furniture) Teil nt, Element nt

unite vt vereinigen □ vi sich vereinigen

united a einig. **U~ 'Kingdom** n Vereinigtes Königreich nt. **U~ 'Nations** n Vereinte Nationen pl. **U~ States (of America)** n Vereinigte Staaten pl [von Amerika]

unity n Einheit f; (harmony) Einigkeit f

universal a allgemein

universe n [Welt]all nt, Universum nt

university n Universität f

unjust a ungerecht

unkempt a ungepflegt

unkind a unfreundlich

unknown a unbekannt

unlawful a gesetzwidrig

unleaded a bleifrei

unless conj wenn ... nicht

unlike a nicht ähnlich, unähnlich; (not the same) ungleich □ prep im Gegensatz zu (+ dat)

unlikely a unwahrscheinlich

unlimited a unbegrenzt

unload vt entladen; ausladen (luggage)

unlock vt aufschließen

unlucky a unglücklich; (day, number) Unglücks-; be ~ Pech haben; (thing:) Unglück bringen

unmarried a unverheiratet. ~ 'mother n ledige Mutter f

unmistakable a unverkennbar

unmitigated a vollkommen

unnatural a unnatürlich

unnecessary a unnötig

unobtainable a nicht erhältlich

unobtrusive a unaufdringlich; (thing) unauffällig

unofficial a inoffiziell

unpack vt/i auspacken

unparalleled a beispiellos

unpick vt auftrennen

unplug vt den Stecker herausziehen von

unprecedented a beispiellos

unpredictable a unberechenbar

unprepared a nicht vorbereitet

unpretentious a bescheiden

unprincipled a skrupellos

unprofessional a be ~ gegen das Berufsethos verstoßen; (Sport) unsportlich sein

unprofitable a unrentabel

unqualified a unqualifiziert; (fig: absolute) uneingeschränkt

unquestionable a unbezweifelbar; (right) unbestreitbar

unreal a unwirklich

unreasonable a unvernünftig

unreliable a unzuverlässig

unrequited a unerwidert

unrest n Unruhen pl

unrivalled a unübertroffen

unroll vt aufrollen □ vi sich aufrollen

unruly a ungebärdig

unsafe a nicht sicher

unsalted a ungesalzen

unsatisfactory a unbefriedigend

unsavoury a unangenehm; (fig) unerfreulich

unscathed a unversehrt

unscrew vt abschrauben

unscrupulous a skrupellos

unseemly a unschicklich

unselfish a selbstlos

unsettled a ungeklärt; (weather) unbeständig; (bill) unbezahlt

unsightly a unansehnlich

unskilled a ungelernt; (work) unqualifiziert

unsophisticated a einfach

unsound a krank, nicht gesund; (building) nicht sicher; (advice) unzuverlässig, nicht stichhaltig

unspeakable a unbeschreiblich

unstable a nicht stabil; (mentally) labil

un'stuck *a* **come ~** sich lösen; 〈*fam: fail*〉 scheitern

unsuc'cessful *a* erfolglos

un'suitable *a* ungeeignet; 〈*inappropriate*〉 unpassend; 〈*for weather, activity*〉 unzweckmäßig

unsu'specting *a* ahnungslos

un'thinkable *a* unvorstellbar

un'tidy *a* unordentlich

un'tie *vt* aufbinden; losbinden 〈*person, boat*〉

until *prep* bis (+ *acc*); **not ~** erst; **~ the evening** bis zum Abend; **~ his arrival** bis zu seiner Ankunft □*conj* bis; **not ~** erst wenn; 〈*in past*〉 erst als

un'timely *a* ungelegen; 〈*premature*〉 vorzeitig

un'told *a* unermeßlich

unto'ward *a* ungünstig; 〈*unseemly*〉 ungehörig

un'true *a* unwahr; **that's ~** das ist nicht wahr

unused[1] *a* unbenutzt; 〈*not utilized*〉 ungenutzt

unused[2] *a* **be ~ to sth** etw nicht gewohnt sein

un'usual *a* ungewöhnlich

un'veil *vt* enthüllen

un'warranted *a* ungerechtfertigt

un'welcome *a* unwillkommen

un'well *a* **be** *or* **feel ~** sich nicht wohl fühlen

un'wieldy *a* sperrig

un'wind *vt* abwickeln □*vi* sich abwickeln; 〈*fam: relax*〉 sich entspannen

un'wise *a* unklug

un'witting *a* unwissentlich

un'wrap *vt* auswickeln; auspacken 〈*present*〉

up *adv* oben; 〈*with movement*〉 nach oben; 〈*not in bed*〉 auf; 〈*collar*〉 hochgeklappt; 〈*road*〉 aufgerissen; 〈*price*〉 gestiegen; 〈*curtains*〉 aufgehängt; 〈*shelves*〉 angebracht; 〈*notice*〉 angeschlagen; 〈*tent*〉 aufgebaut; 〈*building*〉 gebaut; **be up for sale** zu verkaufen

sein; **up there** da oben; **up to** 〈*as far as*〉 bis; **time's up** die Zeit ist um; **what's up?** 〈*fam*〉 was ist los? **what's he up to?** 〈*fam*〉 was hat er vor? □*prep* **be up on sth** 〈*oben*〉 auf etw 〈*dat*〉 sein; **up the mountain** oben am Berg; 〈*movement*〉 den Berg hinauf; **be up the tree** oben im Baum sein

'upbringing *n* Erziehung *f*

up'date *vt* auf den neuesten Stand bringen

up'grade *vt* aufstufen

upheaval *n* Unruhe *f*; 〈*Pol*〉 Umbruch *m*

up'hill *a* 〈*fig*〉 mühsam □*adv* bergauf

up'hold *vt* unterstützen; bestätigen 〈*verdict*〉

upholster *vt* polstern. **~er** *n* Polsterer *m*. **~y** *n* Polsterung *f*

'upkeep *n* Unterhalt *m*

up-'market *a* anspruchsvoll

upon *prep* auf (+ *dat/acc*)

upper *a* obere(r,s); 〈*deck, lip*〉 Ober-; **have the ~ hand** die Oberhand haben

upper: **~ circle** *n* zweiter Rang *m*. **~ class** *n* Oberschicht *f*. **~most** *a* oberste(r,s)

upright *a* aufrecht □*n* Pfosten *m*

uprising *n* Aufstand *m*

uproar *n* Aufruhr *m*

up'root *vt* entwurzeln

up'set[1] *vt* umstoßen; 〈*spill*〉 verschütten; durcheinanderbringen 〈*plan*〉; 〈*distress*〉 erschüttern; 〈*food:*〉 nicht bekommen (+ *dat*)

'upset[2] *n* Aufregung *f*; **have a stomach ~** einen verdorbenen Magen haben

'upshot *n* Ergebnis *nt*

upside 'down *adv* verkehrt herum; **turn ~** umdrehen

up'stairs[1] *adv* 〈*go*〉 nach oben

'upstairs[2] *a* im Obergeschoß

'upstart *n* Emporkömmling *m*

up'stream *adv* stromaufwärts

'uptake n slow on the ~ schwer von Begriff; **be quick on the ~** schnell begreifen
up'tight a nervös
'upturn n Aufschwung m
upward a nach oben; ⟨movement⟩ Aufwärts- □adv ~[s] aufwärts, nach oben
uranium n Uran nt
urban a städtisch
urbane a weltmännisch
urge n Trieb m, Drang m □vt drängen
urgent a dringend
urinate vi urinieren
urine n Urin m, Harn m
urn n Urne f
us pron uns; **it's us** wir sind es
US[A] abbr USA pl
usage n Brauch m; ⟨of word⟩ [Sprach]gebrauch m
use¹ n Benutzung f; Verwendung f; Gebrauch m; **be of** ~ nützlich sein; **it is no** ~ es hat keinen Zweck
use² vt benutzen ⟨implement, room⟩; verwenden ⟨ingredient, method⟩; gebrauchen ⟨words⟩; ~ [up] aufbrauchen
used¹ a benutzt; ⟨car⟩ Gebraucht-
used² pt be ~ to sth an etw ⟨acc⟩ gewöhnt sein; **get** ~ to sich gewöhnen an (+ acc); **he** ~ **to say** er hat immer gesagt; **he** ~ **to live here** er hat früher hier gewohnt
useful a nützlich
useless a nutzlos; ⟨not usable⟩ unbrauchbar; ⟨pointless⟩ zwecklos
user-'friendly a benutzerfreundlich
usher n Platzanweiser m; ⟨in court⟩ Gerichtsdiener m
usherette n Platzanweiserin f
usual a üblich; **~ly** adv gewöhnlich
utensil n Gerät nt
uterus n Gebärmutter f
utilize vt nutzen

utmost a äußerste(r,s), größte(r,s) □n **do one's** ~ sein möglichstes tun
utter¹ a völlig
utter² vt von sich geben ⟨sigh, sound⟩; sagen ⟨word⟩
U-turn n ⟨fig⟩ Kehrtwendung f; **'no ~ s'** ⟨Auto⟩ 'Wenden verboten'

V

vacan|cy n ⟨job⟩ freie Stelle f; ⟨room⟩ freies Zimmer nt; **'no ~ cies'** 'belegt'. **~t** a frei; ⟨look⟩ [gedanken]leer
vacate vt räumen
vacation n ⟨Univ⟩ Ferien pl
vaccination n Impfung f
vaccine n Impfstoff m
vacuum n Vakuum nt, luftleerer Raum m. ~ **cleaner** n Staubsauger m. ~ **flask** n Thermosflasche (P) f. ~-**packed** a vakuumverpackt
vagina n ⟨Anat⟩ Scheide f
vagrant n Landstreicher m
vague a vage
vain a eitel; ⟨hope⟩ vergeblich; **in** ~ vergeblich
valet n Kammerdiener m
valiant a tapfer
valid a gültig; ⟨claim⟩ berechtigt; ⟨argument⟩ stichhaltig; ⟨reason⟩ triftig
valley n Tal nt
valuable a wertvoll. **~s** npl Wertsachen pl
valuation n Schätzung f
value n Wert m; ⟨usefulness⟩ Nutzen m □vt schätzen. **~- 'added tax** n Mehrwertsteuer f
valve n Ventil nt; ⟨Anat⟩ Klappe f; ⟨Electr⟩ Röhre f
vampire n Vampir m
van n Lieferwagen m
vandal n Rowdy m. **~ism** n mutwillige Zerstörung f. **~ize** vt demolieren

vanilla n Vanille f

vanish vi verschwinden

vanity n Eitelkeit f. ~ **bag** n Kosmetiktäschchen n

vapour n Dampf m

variable a unbeständig; ⟨Math⟩ variabel

variation n Variation f

varicose a ~ **veins** pl Krampfadern pl

varied a vielseitig; ⟨diet⟩ abwechslungsreich

variety n Abwechslung f; ⟨quantity⟩ Vielfalt f; ⟨Comm⟩ Auswahl f; ⟨type⟩ Art f; ⟨Bot⟩ Abart f; ⟨Theat⟩ Varieté n

various a verschiedene

varnish n Lack m

vary vi sich ändern; (be different) verschieden sein □vt [ver]ändern; (add variety to) abwechslungsreicher gestalten

vase n Vase f

vast a riesig; ⟨expanse⟩ weit

vat n Bottich m

VAT abbr (value added tax) Mehrwertsteuer f, MwST.

vault[1] n ⟨roof⟩ Gewölbe nt; (in bank) Tresor m; (tomb) Gruft f

vault[2] vt/i ~ **[over]** springen über

VDU abbr (visual display unit) Bildschirmgerät nt

veal n Kalbfleisch nt

vegetable n Gemüse nt; ~s pl Gemüse nt

vegetarian n Vegetarier(in) m(f)

vegetat|e vi dahinvegetieren. ~**ion** n Vegetation f

vehement a heftig

vehicle n Fahrzeug nt; ⟨fig: medium⟩ Mittel nt

veil n Schleier m

vein n Ader f; ~s **and arteries** Venen und Arterien

Velcro (P) n ~ **fastening** Klettverschluß m

velocity n Geschwindigkeit f

velvet n Samt m

vending-machine n [Verkaufs]automat m

vendor n Verkäufer(in) m(f)

veneer n Furnier nt; ⟨fig⟩ Tünche f

venerable a ehrwürdig

venereal a ~ **disease** Geschlechtskrankheit f

Venetian a venezianisch. **v**~ **blind** n Jalousie f

vengeance n Rache f

Venice n Venedig nt

venison n ⟨Culin⟩ Wild nt

venom n Gift nt; ⟨fig⟩ Haß m

vent n Öffnung f; ⟨fig⟩ Ventil nt; **give ~ to** Luft machen (+ dat) □vt Luft machen (+ dat)

ventilat|ion n Belüftung f; ⟨installation⟩ Lüftung f. ~**or** n Lüftungsvorrichtung f; ⟨Med⟩ Beatmungsgerät nt

ventriloquist n Bauchredner m

venture n Unternehmung f

venue n Treffpunkt m; (for event) Veranstaltungsort m

veranda n Veranda f

verb n Verb nt. ~**al** a mündlich; ⟨Gram⟩ verbal

verbatim a [wort]wörtlich

verbose a weitschweifig

verdict n Urteil nt

verge n Rand m □vi ~ **on** ⟨fig⟩ grenzen an (+ acc)

verger n Küster m

verify vt überprüfen; (confirm) bestätigen

vermin n Ungeziefer nt

vermouth n Wermut m

versatile a vielseitig

verse n Strophe f; (of Bible) Vers m; (poetry) Lyrik f

version n Version f

versus prep gegen (+ acc)

vertebra n Wirbel m

vertical a senkrecht

vertigo n ⟨Med⟩ Schwindel m

very adv sehr; ~ **much** sehr; (quantity) sehr viel; ~ **little** sehr

vessel   484   viper

wenig; **~ probably** höchstwahrscheinlich; **at the ~ most** allerhöchstens □ *a (mere)* bloß; **the ~ first** der/die/das allererste; **the ~ thing** genau das Richtige; **at the ~ end/beginning** ganz am Ende/Anfang

vessel *n* Schiff *nt*; *(receptacle & Anat)* Gefäß *nt*

vest *n* [Unter]hemd *nt*

vestige *n* Spur *f*

vestry *n* Sakristei *f*

vet *n* Tierarzt *m* /-ärztin *f* □ *vt* überprüfen

veteran *n* Veteran *m*

veterinary *a* tierärztlich

veto *n* Veto *nt* □ *vt* sein Veto einlegen gegen

vexed *a* verärgert; **~ question** vieldiskutierte Frage *f*

VHF *abbr* **(very high frequency)** UKW

via *prep* über (+ *acc*)

viable *a* lebensfähig; *(fig)* realisierbar

viaduct *n* Viadukt *nt*

vibrate *vi* vibrieren

vicar *n* Pfarrer *m*. **~age** *n* Pfarrhaus *nt*

vicarious *a* nachempfunden

vice¹ *n* Laster *nt*

vice² *n (Techn)* Schraubstock *m*

vice 'chairman *n* stellvertretender Vorsitzender *m*

vice 'president *n* Vizepräsident *m*

vice versa *adv* umgekehrt

vicinity *n* Umgebung *f;* **in the ~ of** in der Nähe von

vicious *a* boshaft; *⟨animal⟩* bösartig. **~ 'circle** *n* Teufelskreis *m*

victim *n* Opfer *nt*. **~ize** *vt* schikanieren

victor|ious *a* siegreich. **~y** *n* Sieg *m*

video *n* Video *nt*; *(recorder)* Videorecorder *m* □ *vt* [auf Videoband] aufnehmen

video: ~ cas'sette *n* Videokassette *f*. **~ game** *n* Videospiel *nt*. **~ 'nasty** *n* Horrorvideo *nt*. **~ recorder** *n* Videorecorder *m*

Vienna *n* Wien *nt*. **~ese** *a* Wiener

view *n* Sicht *f*; *(scene)* Aussicht *f*, Blick *m*; *(picture, opinion)* Ansicht *f*; **in my ~** meiner Ansicht nach; **in ~ of** angesichts (+ *gen*) □ *vt* sich *(dat)* ansehen; besichtigen *⟨house⟩*; *(consider)* betrachten □ *vi (TV)* fernsehen. **~er** *n (TV)* Zuschauer(in) *m(f)*; *(Phot)* Diabetrachter *m*

view: ~finder *n (Phot)* Sucher *m*. **~point** *n* Standpunkt *m*

vigil *n* Wache *f*

vigilant *a* wachsam

vigorous *a* kräftig; *(fig)* heftig

vile *a* abscheulich

villa *n (for holidays)* Ferienhaus *nt*

village *n* Dorf *nt*. **~r** *n* Dorfbewohner(in) *m(f)*

villain *n* Schurke *m*; *(in story)* Bösewicht *m*

vindicate *vt* rechtfertigen

vindictive *a* nachtragend

vine *n* Weinrebe *f*

vinegar *n* Essig *m*

vineyard *n* Weinberg *m*

vintage *n (year)* Jahrgang *m*. **~ 'car** *n* Oldtimer *m*

viola *n (Mus)* Bratsche *f*

violate *vt* verletzen; *(break)* brechen; *(disturb)* stören; *(defile)* schänden

violen|ce *n* Gewalt *f*; *(fig)* Heftigkeit *f*. **~t** *a* gewalttätig; *(fig)* heftig

violet *a* violett *□ n (flower)* Veilchen *nt*

violin *n* Geige *f*, Violine *f*. **~ist** *n* Geiger(in) *m(f)*

VIP *abbr* **(very important person)** Prominente(r) *m/f*

viper *n* Kreuzotter *f*

virgin *n* Jungfrau *f.* ~**ity** *n* Unschuld *f*

Virgo *n* (*Astr*) Jungfrau *f*

viril|e *a* männlich. ~**ity** *n* Männlichkeit *f*

virtual *a* a - ...praktisch ein ...

virtue *n* Tugend *f*

virtuous *a* tugendhaft

virulent *a* bösartig

virus *n* Virus *nt*

visa *n* Visum *nt*

vis-à-vis *adv* & *prep* gegenüber (+ *dat*)

viscous *a* dickflüssig

visibility *n* Sichtbarkeit *f*; (*Meteorol*) Sichtweite *f*

visible *a* sichtbar

vision *n* Vision *f*; (*sight*) Sehkraft *f*; (*foresight*) Weitblick *m*

visit *n* Besuch *m* □*vt* besuchen; besichtigen (*town*). ~**ing hours** *npl* Besuchszeiten *pl.* ~**or** *n* Besucher(in) *m(f)*; (*in hotel*) Gast *m*; **have** ~**ors** auf Besuch haben

visor *n* Schirm *m*; (*on helmet*) Visier *nt*; (*Auto*) [Sonnen]blende *f*

visual *a* visuell; ~**ly handicapped** sehbehindert. ~ **aids** *npl* Anschauungsmaterial *nt*

visualize *vt* sich (*dat*) vorstellen

vital *a* unbedingt notwendig; (*essential to life*) lebenswichtig. ~**ity** *n* Vitalität *f*

vitamin *n* Vitamin *nt*

vivacious *a* lebhaft

vivid *a* lebhaft; (*description*) lebendig

vixen *n* Füchsin *f*

vocabulary *n* Wortschatz *m*; (*list*) Vokabelverzeichnis *nt*; **learn** ~ Vokabeln lernen

vocal *a* stimmlich; (*vociferous*) lautstark. ~ **cords** *npl* Stimmbänder *pl*

vocalist *n* Sänger(in) *m (f)*

vocation *n* Berufung *f.* ~**al** *a* Berufs-

vodka *n* Wodka *m*

voice *n* Stimme *f* □*vt* zum Ausdruck bringen

void *a* leer; (*not valid*) ungültig; ~ **of** ohne □*n* Leere *f*

volatile *a* flüchtig; (*person*) sprunghaft

volcanic *a* vulkanisch

volcano *n* Vulkan *m*

volition *n* **of one's own** ~ aus eigenem Willen

volley *n* (*of gunfire*) Salve *f*; (*Tennis*) Volley *m*

volt *n* Volt *nt.* ~**age** *n* (*Electr*) Spannung *f*

volume *n* (*book*) Band *m*; (*Geom*) Rauminhalt *m*; (*amount*) Ausmaß *nt*; (*TV*) Lautstärke *f*

voluntary *a* freiwillig

volunteer *n* Freiwillige(r) *m/f* □ *vt* anbieten; geben (*information*) □*vi* sich freiwillig melden

voluptuous *a* sinnlich

vomit *vi* sich übergeben

voracious *a* gefräßig; (*appetite*) unbändig

vot|e *n* Stimme *f*; (*ballot*) Abstimmung *f*; (*right*) Wahlrecht *nt* □*vi* abstimmen; (*in election*) wählen □*vt* - **e s.o. president** jdn zum Präsidenten wählen. ~**er** *n* Wähler(in) *m(f)*

voucher *n* Gutschein *m*

vow *n* Gelöbnis *nt*; (*Relig*) Gelübde *nt*

vowel *n* Vokal *m*

voyage *n* Seereise *f*; (*in space*) Reise *f*, Flug *m*

vulgar *a* vulgär, ordinär

vulnerable *a* verwundbar

vulture *n* Geier *m*

W

waddle *vi* watscheln

wade *vi* waten

wafer *n* Waffel *f*; (*Relig*) Hostie *f*

waffle [1] *vi* (*fam*) schwafeln

waffle [2] *n* (*Culin*) Waffel *f*

wag vt wedeln mit

wage n, & ~s pl Lohn m

wager n Wette f

waggle vt wackeln mit □vi wackeln

wagon n Wagen m; (Rail) Waggon m

wail vi heulen; (lament) klagen

waist n Taille f. ~coat n Weste f

wait n Wartezeit f; lie in ~ for auflauern (+ dat) □vi warten (for auf + acc); ~ (at table) servieren; ~ on bedienen

waiter n Kellner m; ~! Herr Ober!

waiting: ~-list n Warteliste f. ~-room n Warteraum m; (doctor's) Wartezimmer nt

waitress n Kellnerin f

waive vt verzichten auf (+ acc)

wake[1] n Totenwache f □ vt [auf]wecken □vi aufwachen

wake[2] n (Naut) Kielwasser nt; in the ~ of im Gefolge (+ gen)

waken vt [auf]wecken □vi aufwachen

Wales n Wales nt

walk n Spaziergang m; (gait) Gang m; (path) Weg m; go for a ~ spazierengehen □vi (not ride) laufen, zu Fuß gehen; (ramble) wandern; learn to ~ laufen lernen □vt ausführen □vt/i gehen

walking-stick n Spazierstock m

walk: ~-out n Streik m. ~-over n (fig) leichter Sieg m

wall n Wand f; (external) Mauer f

wallet n Brieftasche f

'wallflower n Goldlack m

wallow vi sich wälzen; (fig) schwelgen

'wallpaper n Tapete f

walnut n Walnuß f

waltz n Walzer m □vi Walzer tanzen

wand n Zauberstab m

wander vi umherwandern, (fam) bummeln; (fig: digress) abschweifen. ~lust n Fernweh nt

wane n be on the ~ schwinden; (moon:) abnehmen □vi schwinden; abnehmen

wangle vt (fam) organisieren

want n Mangel m (of an + dat); (hardship) Not f; (desire) Bedürfnis nt □ vt wollen; (need) brauchen; ~ [to have] sth etw haben wollen; ~ to do sth etw tun wollen; □vi he doesn't ~ for anything ihm fehlt es an nichts. ~ed a gesucht. ~ing a be ~ing fehlen

wanton a mutwillig

war n Krieg m

ward n [Kranken]saal m; (unit) Station f; (of town) Wahlbezirk m; (child) Mündel nt □vt ~ off abwehren

warden n Heimleiter(in) m(f); (of youth hostel) Herbergsvater m; (supervisor) Aufseher(in) m(f)

warder n Wärter(in) m(f)

wardrobe n Kleiderschrank m; (clothes) Garderobe f

warehouse n Lager nt; (building) Lagerhaus nt

wares npl Waren pl

war: ~-head n Sprengkopf m. ~-like a kriegerisch

warm a warm; (welcome) herzlich □vt wärmen. ~ up vt erwärmen □vi warm werden; (Sport) sich aufwärmen

warmth n Wärme f

warn vt warnen (of vor + dat). ~ing n Warnung f; (advance notice) Vorwarnung f; (caution) Verwarnung f

warp vi sich verziehen

warrant n (for arrest) Haftbefehl m; (for search) Durchsuchungsbefehl m □ vt (justify) rechtfertigen; (guarantee) garantieren

warranty n Garantie f

warrior n Krieger m

'warship n Kriegsschiff nt

wart n Warze f

wary *a* vorsichtig; *(suspicious)* mißtrauisch

wash *n* Wäsche *f*; *(Naut)* Wellen *pl*; **have a ~** sich waschen □*vt* waschen; spülen *(dishes)*; aufwischen *(floor)*; *(flow over)* bespülen; **~ one's hands** sich *(dat)* die Hände waschen □*vi* sich waschen; *(fabric)* sich waschen lassen. **~ up** *vt* abwaschen, spülen

washer *n (Techn)* Dichtungsring *m*

washing *n* Wäsche *f*. **~-machine** *n* Waschmaschine *f*. **~-powder** *n* Waschpulver *nt*. **~-'up** *n* Abwasch *m*; **do the ~-'up** abwaschen, spülen. **~-'up liquid** *n* Spülmittel *nt*

wasp *n* Wespe *f*

waste *n* Verschwendung *f*; *(rubbish)* Abfall *m*; **~ s** *pl* Öde *f*; **~ of time** Zeitverschwendung *f* □*vt* verschwenden □*vi* **~ away** immer mehr abmagern

waste: ~-di'sposal unit *n* Müllzerkleinerer *m*. **~-ful** *a* verschwenderisch. **~ land** *n* Ödland *nt*. **~-'paper basket** *n* Papierkorb *m*

watch *n* Wache *f*; *(timepiece)* [Armband]uhr *f* □*vt* beobachten; sich *(dat)* ansehen *(film)*; *(be careful of)* achten auf (+ *acc*); **~ television** fernsehen □*vi* zusehen

watch: ~-dog *n* Wachhund *m*. **~-ful** *a* wachsam. **~-maker** *n* Uhrmacher *m*. **~-strap** *n* Uhrarmband *nt*. **~-tower** *n* Wachturm *m*. **~-word** *n* Parole *f*

water *n* Wasser *nt*; **~ s** *pl* Gewässer *nt* □*vt* gießen *(garden)*; *(dilute)* verdünnen *f*; *(give drink to)* tränken □*vi* *(eyes:)* tränen; **my mouth was ~ing** mir lief das Wasser im Munde zusammen

water: ~-colour *n* Wasserfarbe *f*; *(painting)* Aquarell *nt*. **~-cress**

n Brunnenkresse *f*. **~-fall** *n* Wasserfall *m*

'watering-can *n* Gießkanne *f*

water: ~-logged *a* be **~-logged** *(ground:)* unter Wasser stehen. **~-mark** *n* Wasserzeichen *nt*. **~-polo** *n* Wasserball *m*. **~-proof** *a* wasserdicht. **~-shed** *n* Wasserscheide *f*; *(fig)* Wendepunkt *m*. **~-skiing** *n* Wasserskilaufen *nt*. **~-tight** *a* wasserdicht

watery *a* wäßrig

watt *n* Watt *nt*

wave *n* Welle *f*; *(gesture)* Handbewegung *f*; *(as greeting)* Winken *nt* □*vt* winken mit; *(brandish)* schwingen; *(threateningly)* drohen mit; wellen *(hair)* □*vi* winken **(to** *dat)*; *(flag:)* wehen. **~-length** *n* Wellenlänge *f*

waver *vi* schwanken

wavy *a* wellig

wax[1] *vi (moon:)* zunehmen; *(fig: become)* werden

wax[2] *n* Wachs *nt*; *(in ear)* Schmalz *nt*. **~-works** *n* Wachsfigurenkabinett *nt*

way *n* Weg *m*; *(direction)* Richtung *f*; *(respect)* Hinsicht *f*; *(manner)* Art *f*; *(method)* Art und Weise *f*; **~ s** *pl* Gewohnheiten *pl*; **in the ~** im Weg; **on the ~** auf dem Weg **(to** nach/zu); *(under way)* unterwegs; **a little/long ~** ein kleines/ ganzes Stück; **a long ~ off** weit weg; **this ~** hierher; *(like this)* so; **by the ~** übrigens; **in a ~** in gewisser Weise; **in a bad ~** *(person:)* in schlechter Verfassung; **lead the ~** vorausgehen; **make ~** Platz machen **(for** *dat)*; **'give ~'** *(Auto)* 'Vorfahrt beachten' □*adv* weit; **~ behind** weit zurück. **~ in** *n* Eingang *m*. **~ out** *n* Ausgang *m*; *(fig)* Ausweg *m*.

way-'out *a (fam)* verrückt

wayward *a* eigenwillig

we *pron* wir

weak *a* schwach; *⟨liquid⟩* dünn.
~**en** *vt* schwächen □*vi* schwächer werden. ~**ling** *n* Schwächling *m*. ~**ness** *n* Schwäche *f*

wealth *n* Reichtum *m*; *(fig)* Fülle *f*
(**of** an + *dat*). ~**y** *a* reich

wean *vt* entwöhnen

weapon *n* Waffe *f*

wear *vt* tragen; *(damage)* abnutzen; ~ **a hole in sth** etw durchwetzen; **what shall I** ~ ? was soll ich anziehen? □*vi* sich abnutzen; *(last)* halten

weary *a* müde □*vi* ~ **of sth** etw
(gen) überdrüssig werden

weasel *n* Wiesel *nt*

weather *n* Wetter *nt*

weather: ~**-beaten** *a* verwittert; wettergegerbt *⟨face⟩*. ~ **forecast** *n* Wettervorhersage *f*. ~**-vane** *n* Wetterfahne *f*

weave *vt* weben; *(plait)* flechten; *(fig)* einflechten (**in** in + *acc*). ~**r** *n* Weber *m*

web *n* Netz *nt*. ~**bed feet** *npl* Schwimmfüße *pl*

wedding *n* Hochzeit *f*; *(ceremony)* Trauung *f*

wedding: ~ **day** *n* Hochzeitstag *m*. ~ **dress** *n* Hochzeitskleid *nt*. ~**-ring** *n* Ehering *m*, Trauring *m*

wedge *n* Keil *m*

Wednesday *n* Mittwoch *m*

weed *n* & ~ *s pl* Unkraut *nt*.
'**weed-killer** *n* Unkrautvertilgungsmittel *nt*

week *n* Woche *f*. ~ **day** *n* Wochentag *m*. ~ **end** *n* Wochenende *nt*

weekly *a* & *adv* wöchentlich

weep *vi* weinen. ~**ing 'willow** *n* Trauerweide *f*

weigh *vt/i* wiegen; ~ **anchor** den Anker lichten

weight *n* Gewicht *nt*; **put on/lose** ~ zunehmen/abnehmen

weight: ~**lessness** *n* Schwerelosigkeit *f*. ~**-lifting** *n* Gewichtheben *nt*

weir *n* Wehr *nt*

weird *a* unheimlich; *(bizarre)* bizarr

welcome *a* willkommen; **you're**
~ ! nichts zu danken! **you're** ~ **to have it** das können Sie gerne haben □*n* Willkommen *nt* □*vt* begrüßen

weld *vt* schweißen. ~**er** *n* Schweißer *m*

welfare *n* Wohl *nt*; *(Admin)* Fürsorge *f*. **W**~ **State** *n* Wohlfahrtsstaat *m*

well[1] *n* Brunnen *m*; *(oil* ~*)* Quelle *f*

well[2] *adv* gut; **as** ~ auch; **as** ~ **as**
(in addition) sowohl ... als auch; ~ **done!** gut gemacht! □*a* gesund; **he is not** ~ es geht ihm nicht gut; **get** ~ **soon!** gute Besserung! □*int* nun, na

well: ~**-behaved** *a* artig.
~**-being** *n* Wohl *nt*

wellingtons *npl* Gummistiefel *pl*

well: ~**-known** *a* bekannt.
~**-meaning** *a* wohlmeinend.
~**-meant** *a* gutgemeint. ~**-off** *a* wohlhabend; **be** ~**-off** gut dran sein. ~**-read** *a* belesen. ~**-to-do** *a* wohlhabend

Welsh *a* walisisch □*n* (*Lang*) Walisisch *nt*; **the** ~ *pl* die Waliser. ~**man** *n* Waliser *m*. ~ **rabbit** *n* überbackenes Käsebrot *nt*

west *n* Westen *m*; **to the** ~ **of** westlich von □*a* West-, westlich □*adv* nach Westen; **go** ~ *(fam)* flötengehen. ~**erly** *a* westlich. ~**ern** *a* westlich □*n* Western *m*

West: ~ **'Indian** *a* westindisch □*n* Westinder(in) *m(f)*. ~ **'Indies** *npl* Westindische Inseln *pl*

'**westward[s]** *adv* nach Westen

wet *a* naß; *(fam: person)* weichlich, lasch; ~ **paint** 'frisch gestrichen' □*vt* naß machen.
'**blanket** *n* Spaßverderber *m*

whale *n* Wal *m*

wharf *n* Kai *m*

what *pron & int* was; **~ for?** wozu?; **~ is it like?** wie ist es? **is your name?** wie ist Ihr Name? □*a* welche(r,s); **~ kind of a** was für ein(e)

what'ever *a* [egal] welche(r,s) □*pron* was … auch; **~ is it?** was ist das bloß? **~ he does** was er auch tut; **~ happens** was auch geschieht; **nothing ~** überhaupt nichts

whatso'ever *pron & a* ≈ **whatever**

wheat *n* Weizen *m*

wheel *n* Rad *nt*; *(pottery)* Töpferscheibe *f*; *(steering ~)* Lenkrad *nt*; **at the ~** am Steuer □*vt (push)* schieben

wheel: **~barrow** *n* Schubkarre *f*. **~chair** *n* Rollstuhl *m*. **~clamp** *n* Parkkralle *f*

wheeze *vi* keuchen

when *adv* wann; **the day ~** der Tag, an dem □*conj* wenn; *(in the past)* als; *(although)* wo … doch

whence *adv (liter)* woher

when'ever *conj & adv* [immer] wenn; *(at whatever time)* wann immer; **~ did it happen?** wann ist das bloß passiert?

where *adv & conj* wo; **~ [to]** wohin; **~ [from]** woher

whereabouts¹ *adv* wo

'whereabouts² *n* Verbleib *m*; *(of person)* Aufenthaltsort *m*

where'as *conj* während; *(in contrast)* wohingegen

where'by *adv* wodurch

whereu'pon *adv* worauf[hin]

wher'ever *conj & adv* wo immer; *(to whatever place)* wohin immer; *(from whatever place)* woher immer; *(everywhere)* überall wo; **~ is he?** wo ist er bloß? **~ possible** wenn irgend möglich

whet *vt* wetzen; anregen *(appetite)*

whether *conj* ob

which *a & pron* welche(r,s); **~ one** welche(r,s) □*rel pron* der/die/das, *(pl)* die; *(after clause)* was; **after ~** wonach; **on ~** worauf

which'ever *a & pron* [egal] welche(r, s); **~ it is** was es auch ist

while *n* Weile *f*; **a long ~** lange; **be worth ~** sich lohnen □*conj* während; *(as long as)* solange; *(although)* obgleich □*vt* **~ away** sich (*dat*) vertreiben

whilst *conj* während

whim *n* Laune *f*

whimsical *a* skurril

whine *vi* winseln

whip *n* Peitsche *f*; *(Pol)* Einpeitscher *m* □*vt* peitschen; schlagen; *(snatch)* reißen; *(fam: steal)* klauen. **~ped 'cream** *n* Schlagsahne *f*

whirl *vt/i* wirbeln. **~pool** *n* Strudel *m*. **~wind** *n* Wirbelwind *m*

whisk *n (Culin)* Schneebesen *m* □*vt (Culin)* schlagen

whisker *n* Schnurrhaar *nt*; **~s** *pl (on man's cheek)* Backenbart *m*

whisky *n* Whisky *m*

whisper *n* Flüstern *nt*; *(rumour)* Gerücht *nt*; **in a ~** im Flüsterton □*vt/i* flüstern

whistle *n* Pfiff *m*; *(instrument)* Pfeife *f* □*vt/i* pfeifen

white *a* weiß □*n* Weiß *nt*; *(of egg)* Eiweiß *nt*; *(person)* Weiße(r) *mf*

white: **~ 'coffee** *n* Kaffee *m* mit Milch. **~-'collar worker** *n* Angestellte(r) *m*. **~ 'lie** *n* Notlüge *f*

'whitewash *n* Tünche *f*; *(fig)* Schönfärberei *f* □*vt* tünchen

Whitsun *n* Pfingsten *nt*

whiz[z] *vi* zischen. **~-kid** *n (fam)* Senkrechtstarter *m*

who *pron* wer; *(acc)* wen; *(dat)* wem □*rel pron* der/die/das, *(pl)* die

who'ever *pron* wer [immer]; ~ **he is** wer er auch ist; ~ **is it?** wer ist das bloß?

whole *a* ganz; ⟨*truth*⟩ voll □ *n* Ganze(s) *nt*; **as a** ~ als Ganzes; **on the** ~ im großen und ganzen; **the** ~ **lot** alle; ⟨*everything*⟩ alles; **the** ~ **of Germany** ganz Deutschland

whole: ~**food** *n* Vollwertkost *f*. ~-'**hearted** *a* rückhaltlos. ~**meal** *a* Vollkorn-

'**wholesale** *a* Großhandels- □ *adv* en gros; ⟨*fig*⟩ in Bausch und Bogen. ~**r** *n* Großhändler *m*

wholesome *a* gesund

whom *pron* wen; **to** ~ wem □ *rel pron* den/die/das, ⟨*pl*⟩ die; ⟨*dat*⟩ dem/der/dem, ⟨*pl*⟩ denen

whooping cough *n* Keuchhusten *m*

whore *n* Hure *f*

whose *pron* wessen; ~ **is that?** wem gehört das? □ *rel pron* dessen/deren/dessen, ⟨*pl*⟩ deren

why *adv* warum; ⟨*for what purpose*⟩ wozu; **that's** ~ darum

wick *n* Docht *m*

wicked *a* böse; ⟨*mischievous*⟩ frech, boshaft

wicker *n* Korbgeflecht *nt*

wide *a* weit; ⟨*broad*⟩ breit; ⟨*fig*⟩ groß □ *adv* weit; ⟨*off target*⟩ daneben; ~ **awake** hellwach; **far and** ~ weit und breit

widen *vt* verbreitern; ⟨*fig*⟩ erweitern □ *vi* sich verbreitern

'**widespread** *a* weitverbreitet

widow *n* Witwe *f*. ~**ed** *a* verwitwet. ~**er** *n* Witwer *m*

width *n* Weite *f*; ⟨*breadth*⟩ Breite *f*

wield *vt* schwingen; ausüben ⟨*power*⟩

wife *n* [Ehe]frau *f*

wig *n* Perücke *f*

wild *a* wild; ⟨*animal*⟩ wildlebend; ⟨*flower*⟩ wildwachsend; ⟨*furious*⟩ wütend; **be** ~ **about** ⟨*keen on*⟩ wild sein auf (+ *acc*) □ *adv*

wild; **run** ~ frei herumlaufen □ *n* **in the** ~ wild; **the** ~**s** *pl* die Wildnis *f*

'**wildcat strike** *n* wilder Streik *m*

wilderness *n* Wildnis *f*

wild: ~-'**goose chase** *n* aussichtslose Suche *f*. ~**life** *n* Tierwelt *f*

wilful *a* mutwillig

will[1] *v aux* wollen; ⟨*forming future tense*⟩ werden; **he** ~ **arrive tomorrow** er wird morgen kommen; ~ **you go?** gehst du? **you** ~ **be back soon, won't you?** du kommst doch bald wieder, nicht? ~ **you have some wine?** möchten Sie Wein?

will[2] *n* Wille *m*; ⟨*document*⟩ Testament *nt*

willing *a* willig; ⟨*eager*⟩ bereitwillig; **be** ~ bereit sein. ~**ly** *adv* bereitwillig; ⟨*gladly*⟩ gern

willow *n* Weide *f*

'**will-power** *n* Willenskraft *f*

wilt *vi* welk werden, welken

wily *a* listig

wimp *n* Schwächling *m*

win *vt* gewinnen; bekommen ⟨*scholarship*⟩ □ *vi* gewinnen; ⟨*in battle*⟩ siegen

wince *vi* zusammenzucken

winch *n* Winde *f*

wind[1] *n* Wind *m*; ⟨*breath*⟩ Atem *m*; ⟨*fam: flatulence*⟩ Blähungen *pl*; **have the** ~ **up** ⟨*fam*⟩ Angst haben

wind[2] *vt* ⟨*wrap*⟩ wickeln; ⟨*move by turning*⟩ kurbeln; aufziehen ⟨*clock*⟩ □ *vi* ⟨*road*⟩ sich winden. ~ **up** *vt* aufziehen ⟨*clock*⟩; schließen ⟨*proceedings*⟩

wind: ~**fall** *n* unerwarteter Glücksfall *m*; ~**falls** *pl* ⟨*fruit*⟩ Fallobst *nt*. ~ **instrument** *n* Blasinstrument *nt*. ~**mill** *n* Windmühle *f*

window *n* Fenster *nt*; ⟨*of shop*⟩ Schaufenster *nt*

window: ~-**box** n Blumenkasten m. ~-**cleaner** n Fensterputzer m. ~-**dressing** n Schaufensterdekoration f; (fig) Schönfärberei f. ~-**pane** n Fensterscheibe f. ~-**shopping** n Schaufensterbummel m. ~-**sill** n Fensterbrett m

'windpipe n Luftröhre f

'windscreen n Windschutzscheibe f. ~ **washer** n Scheibenwaschanlage f. ~-**wiper** n Scheibenwischer m

wind: ~-**surfing** n Windsurfen nt. ~-**swept** a windgepeitscht; (person) zersaust

windy a windig

wine n Wein m

wine: ~-**bar** n Weinstube f. ~-**list** n Weinkarte f. ~-**tasting** n Weinprobe f

wing n Flügel m; (Auto) Kotflügel m; ~ s pl (Theat) Kulissen pl

wink vi zwinkern; (light:) blinken

winner n Gewinner(in) m(f); (Sport) Sieger(in) m(f)

wint|er n Winter m. ~**ry** a winterlich

wipe vt abwischen; aufwischen (floor); (dry) abtrocknen. ~ **out** vt (cancel) löschen; (destroy) ausrotten. ~ **up** vt aufwischen; abtrocknen (dishes)

wire n Draht m

wireless n Radio nt

wiring n [elektrische] Leitungen pl

wiry a drahtig

wisdom n Weisheit f. ~ **tooth** n Weisheitszahn m

wise a weise

wish n Wunsch m □vt wünschen; ~ s.o. well jdm alles Gute wünschen □vi ~ **for sth** sich (dat) etw wünschen. ~**ful** a ~**ful thinking** Wunschdenken nt

wisp n Büschel nt; (of hair) Strähne f; (of smoke) Fahne f

wisteria n Glyzinie f

wistful a wehmütig

wit n Geist m, Witz m; (intelligence) Verstand m; (person) geistreicher Mensch m; **be at one's** ~ **s' end** sich (dat) keinen Rat mehr wissen; **scared out of one's** ~ **s** zu Tode erschrocken

witch n Hexe f. ~-**craft** n Hexerei f. ~-**hunt** n Hexenjagd f

with prep mit (+ dat); ~ **fear/cold** vor Angst/Kälte; ~ **it** damit; **I'm going** ~ **you** ich gehe mit

with'draw vt zurückziehen; abheben (money) □vi sich zurückziehen. ~**al** n Zurückziehen nt; (of money) Abhebung f; (of drugs) Entzug m. ~**al symptoms** npl Entzugserscheinungen pl

wither vi [ver]welken

with'hold vt vorenthalten (**from s.o.** jdm)

with'in prep innerhalb (+ gen); ~ **the law** im Rahmen des Gesetzes □adv innen

with'out prep ohne (+ acc); ~ **my noticing it** ohne daß ich es merkte

with'stand vt standhalten (+ dat)

witness n Zeuge m/ Zeugin f; (evidence) Zeugnis nt □vt Zeuge/Zeugin sein (+ gen); bestätigen (signature). ~-**box** n Zeugenstand m

witty a witzig, geistreich

wizard n Zauberer m

wobble vi wackeln

woe n (liter) Jammer m; ~ **is me!** wehe mir!

wolf n Wolf m □vt ~ [**down**] hinunterschlingen

woman n Frau f. ~**izer** n Schürzenjäger m

womb n Gebärmutter f

Women's Liberation n Frauenbewegung f

wonder n Wunder nt; (surprise) Staunen nt □vt/i sich fragen; (be surprised) sich wundern; I ~ da frage ich mich; I ~ **whether she is ill** ob sie wohl krank ist? ~**ful** a wunderbar

wood n Holz nt; (forest) Wald m; **touch** ~! unberufen!

wood: ~**cut** n Holzschnitt m. ~**ed** a bewaldet. ~**en** a Holz-; (fig) hölzern. ~**pecker** n Specht m. ~**wind** n Holzbläser pl. ~**work** n (wooden parts) Holzteile pl; (craft) Tischlerei f. ~**worm** n Holzwurm m

wool n Wolle f ~**len** a wollen **woolly** a wollig; (fig) unklar

word n Wort nt; (news) Nachricht f; **by** ~ **of mouth** mündlich; **have a** ~ **with** sprechen mit; **have** ~**s** einen Wortwechsel haben. ~**ing** n Wortlaut m. ~ **processor** n Textverarbeitungssystem nt

work n Arbeit f; (Art, Literature) Werk nt; ~**s** pl (factory, mechanism) Werk nt; **at** ~ bei der Arbeit; **out of** ~ arbeitslos □vi arbeiten; (machine, system:) funktionieren; (have effect) wirken; (study) lernen; **it won't** ~ (fig) es klappt nicht □vt arbeiten lassen; bedienen (machine); betätigen (lever)

workaholic n arbeitswütiger Mensch m

worker n Arbeiter(in) m(f)

working a berufstätig; (day, clothes) Arbeits-. ~ **class** n Arbeiterklasse f

work: ~**man** n Arbeiter m; (craftsman) Handwerker m. ~**manship** n Arbeit f. ~**out** n [Fitneß]training nt. ~**shop** n Werkstatt f

world n Welt f; **in the** ~ auf der Welt; a ~ **of difference** ein himmelweiter Unterschied; **think the** ~ **of s.o.** große Stücke auf jdn

halten. ~**ly** a weltlich; (person) weltlich gesinnt. ~-**wide** a weltweit

worm n Wurm m

worried a besorgt

worry n Sorge f □vt beunruhigen, Sorgen machen (+ dat); (bother) stören □vi sich beunruhigen, sich (dat) Sorgen machen. ~**ing** a beunruhigend

worse a schlechter, (more serious) schlimmer

worsen vi sich verschlechtern

worship n Anbetung f; (service) Gottesdienst m; **Your/His W**~ Euer/Seine Ehren □vt anbeten □vi am Gottesdienst teilnehmen

worst a schlechteste(r,s) (most serious) schlimmste(r,s)

worsted n Kammgarn m

worth n Wert m; **£10's** ~ **of** petrol Benzin für £10 □a **be** ~ £5 £5 wert sein; **be** ~ **it** (fig) sich lohnen. ~**less** a wertlos. ~**while** a lohnend

worthy a würdig

would v aux I ~ **do it** ich würde es tun, ich täte es; ~ **you go?** würdest du gehen?

wound n Wunde f □vt verwunden

wrap vt ~ [**up**] wickeln; einpacken (present) □vi ~ **up** warmly sich warm einpacken; **be** ~**ped up in** (fig) aufgehen in (+ dat). ~**per** n Hülle f. ~**ping** n Verpackung f. ~**ping paper** n Einwickelpapier nt

wrath n Zorn m

wreak vt ~ **havoc** Verwüstungen anrichten

wreath n Kranz m

wreck n Wrack nt □vt zerstören; zunichte machen (plans); zerrütten (marriage)

wren n Zaunkönig m

wrench n Ruck m; (tool) Schraubenschlüssel m □vt reißen

wrest vt entwinden (**from** s.o. jdm)

wrestl|e vi ringen. ~**er** n Ringer m. ~**ing** n Ringen nt

wretch n Kreatur f. ~**ed** a elend; (very bad) erbärmlich

wriggle vi zappeln; (move forward) sich schlängeln; ~ **out of sth** (fam) sich vor etw (dat) drücken

wring vt wringen; (~ **out**) auswringen; umdrehen (neck); ringen (hands)

wrinkle n Falte f; (on skin) Runzel. ~**d** a runzlig

wrist n Handgelenk nt. ~**watch** n Armbanduhr f

writ n (Jur) Verfügung f

write vt/i schreiben. ~ **down** vt aufschreiben

'**write-off** n ≈ Totalschaden m

writer n Schreiber(in) m(f); (author) Schriftsteller(in) m(f)

'**write-up** n Bericht m; (review) Kritik f

writhe vi sich winden

writing n Schreiben nt; (handwriting) Schrift f; **in** ~ schriftlich. ~**paper** n Schreibpapier nt

wrong a falsch; (morally) unrecht; (not just) ungerecht; **be** ~ nicht stimmen; (person:) unrecht haben; **what's** ~? was ist los? □ adv falsch; **go** ~ (person:) etwas falsch machen; (machine:) kaputtgehen; (plan:) schiefgehen □ n Unrecht nt □ vt Unrecht tun (+ dat). ~**ful** a ungerecht fertigt

wrought 'iron n Schmiedeeisen nt

wry a ironisch; (humour) trocken

X

xerox (P) vt fotokopieren

'**X-ray** n (picture) Röntgenaufnahme f; ~**s** pl Röntgenstrahlen pl □ vt röntgen; durchleuchten (luggage)

Y

yacht n Jacht f; (for racing) Segelboot nt. ~**ing** n Segeln nt

yard[1] n Hof m; (for storage) Lager nt

yard[2] n Yard nt (= 0,91 m). ~**stick** n (fig) Maßstab m

yarn n Garn nt; (fam: tale) Geschichte f

yawn vi gähnen

year n Jahr nt; (of wine) Jahrgang m; **for** ~**s** jahrelang. ~**book** n Jahrbuch nt. ~**ly** a jährlich

yearn vi sich sehnen (**for** nach). ~**ing** n Sehnsucht f

yeast n Hefe f

yell vi schreien

yellow a gelb □ n Gelb nt

yelp vi jaulen

yes adv ja; (contradicting) doch

yesterday n & adv gestern; ~'**s paper** die gestrige Zeitung; **the day before** ~ vorgestern

yet adv noch; (in question) schon; (nevertheless) doch; **as** ~ bisher; **not** ~ noch nicht; **the best** ~ das bisher beste □ conj doch

yew n Eibe f

Yiddish n Jiddisch nt

yield n Ertrag m □ vt bringen; abwerfen (profit) □ vi nachgeben

yodel vi jodeln

yoga n Yoga m

yoghurt n Joghurt m

yoke n Joch nt; (of garment) Passe f

yolk n Dotter m, Eigelb nt

you pron du; (acc) dich; (dat) dir; (pl) ihr; (acc, dat) euch; (formal) (nom & acc, sg & pl) Sie; (dat,

X

Z

& *pl* Ihnen; (*one*) man; (*acc*) einen; (*dat*) einem; **all of** ~ ihr/
Sie alle

young *a* jung □*npl* (*animals*)
Junge *pl*; **the** ~ die Jugend *f*.
~**ster** *n* Jugendliche(r) *m/f*;
(*child*) Kleine(r) *m/f*

your *a* dein; (*pl*) euer; (*formal*)
Ihr

yours *poss pron* deine(r), deins;
(*pl*) eure(r), euers; (*formal, sg &
pl*) Ihre(r), Ihr[e]s; **a friend of** ~
ein Freund von dir/Ihnen/euch;
that is ~ das gehört dir/Ihnen/
euch

your'self *pron* selbst; (*refl*) dich;
(*dat*) dir; (*pl*) euch; (*formal*) sich;
by ~ allein

youth *n* Jugend *f*; (*boy*) Jugendliche(r) *m*. ~ **hostel** *n* Jugendherberge *f*

Yugoslav *a* jugoslawisch. ~**ia** *n*
Jugoslawien *nt*

zany *a* närrisch, verrückt

zeal *n* Eifer *m*

zebra *n* Zebra *nt*. ~'**crossing** *n*
Zebrastreifen *m*

zenith *n* Zenit *m*; (*fig*) Gipfel *m*

zero *n* Null *f*

zest *n* Begeisterung *f*

zigzag *n* Zickzack *m*

zinc *n* Zink *nt*

zip *n* ~ **[fastener]** Reißverschluß
m

zither *n* Zither *f*

zodiac *n* Tierkreis *m*

zone *n* Zone *f*

zoo *n* Zoo *m*

zoological *a* zoologisch

zoolog|ist *n* Zoologe *m* /-gin *f*. ~**y**
Zoologie *f*

zoom *vi* sausen. ~ **lens** *n* Zoomobjektiv *nt*

Pronunciation of the alphabet
Aussprache des Alphabets

English/Englisch		German/Deutsch
eɪ	a	aː
biː	b	beː
siː	c	tseː
diː	d	deː
iː	e	eː
ef	f	ɛf
dʒiː	g	geː
ertʃ	h	haː
aɪ	i	iː
dʒeɪ	j	jɔt
keɪ	k	kaː
el	l	ɛl
em	m	ɛm
en	n	ɛn
əʊ	o	oː
piː	p	peː
kjuː	q	kuː
aː(r)	r	ɛr
es	s	ɛs
tiː	t	teː
juː	u	uː
viː	v	faʊ
'dʌbljuː	w	veː
eks	x	ɪks
waɪ	y	'ypsilɔn
zed	z	tsɛt
eɪ umlaut	ä	ɛː
əʊ umlaut	ö	ø
juː umlaut	ü	yː
es'zed	ß	ɛs'tsɛt

Phonetic symbols used for German words

a	Hand	hant		ŋ	lang	laŋ
aː	Bahn	baːn		o	moral	moˈraːl
ɐ	Ober	ˈoːbɐ		oː	Boot	boːt
ɐ̯	Uhr	uːɐ̯		ǫ	Foyer	fǫaˈjeː
ã	Conférencier	kõferãˈsi̯eː		õ	Konkurs	kõˈkʊrs
ãː	Abonnement	abonəˈmãː		õː	Ballon	baˈlõː
ai̯	weit	vai̯t		ɔ	Post	pɔst
au̯	Haut	hau̯t		ø	Ökonom	økoˈnoːm
b	Ball	bal		øː	Öl	øːl
ç	ich	ɪç		œ	göttlich	ˈɡœtlɪç
d	dann	dan		œy̯	heute	ˈhɔy̯tə
dʒ	Gin	dʒɪn		p	Pakt	pakt
e	Metall	meˈtal		r	Rast	rast
eː	Beet	beːt		s	Hast	hast
ɛ	mästen	ˈmɛstən		ʃ	Schal	ʃaːl
ɛː	wählen	ˈvɛːlən		t	Tal	taːl
ɛ̃ː	Cousin	kuˈzɛ̃ː		ts	Zahl	tsaːl
ə	Nase	ˈnaːzə		tʃ	Couch	kau̯tʃ
f	Faß	fas		u	kulant	kuˈlant
g	Gast	gast		uː	Hut	huːt
h	haben	ˈhaːbən		ʯ	aktuell	akˈtu̯ɛl
i	Rivale	riˈvaːlə		ʊ	Pult	pʊlt
iː	viel	fiːl		v	was	vas
i̯	Aktion	akˈtsi̯oːn		x	Bach	bax
ɪ	Birke	ˈbɪrkə		y	Physik	fyˈziːk
j	ja	jaː		yː	Rübe	ˈryːbə
k	kalt	kalt		ỹ	Nuance	ˈnỹaːsə
l	Last	last		ʏ	Fülle	ˈfʏlə
m	Mast	mast		z	Nase	ˈnaːzə
n	Naht	naːt		ʒ	Regime	reˈʒiːm

ʔ   Glottal stop, e.g. Koordination /koʔɔrdinaˈtsi̯oːn/.
ː   Length sign after a vowel, e.g. Chrom /kroːm/.
ˈ   Stress mark before stressed syllable, e.g. Balkon /balˈkõː/.

Guide to German pronunciation

Consonants are pronounced as in English with the following exceptions:

b	*as*	p	
d	*as*	t	*at the end of a word or syllable*
g	*as*	k	

ch		*as in Scottish* lo*ch after a, o, u, au*
		like an exaggerated h as in huge
		after i, e, ä, ö, ü, eu, ei

-chs	*as*	x	(*as in* bo*x*)
-ig	*as*	-ich /ıç/	*when a suffix*
j	*as*	y	(*as in* yes)

ps		*the p is pronounced*
pn		

qu	*as*	k + v	
s	*as*	z	(*as in* zero) *at the beginning of a word*
	as	s	(*as in* bus) *at the end of a word or syllable, before a consonant, or when doubled*
sch	*as*	sh	

sp	*as*	shp	*at the beginning of a word*
st	*as*	sht	

v	*as*	f	(*as in* for)
	as	v	(*as in* very) *within a word*
w	*as*	v	(*as in* very)
z	*as*	ts	

Vowels are approximately as follows:

a	short	*as*	u	(*as in* b<u>u</u>t)
	long	*as*	a	(*as in* c<u>a</u>r)
e	short	*as*	e	(*as in* p<u>e</u>n)
	long	*as*	a	(*as in* p<u>a</u>per)
i	short	*as*	i	(*as in* b<u>i</u>t)
	long	*as*	ee	(*as in* qu<u>ee</u>n)
o	short	*as*	o	(*as in* h<u>o</u>t)
	long	*as*	o	(*as in* p<u>o</u>pe)
u	short	*as*	oo	(*as in* f<u>oo</u>t)
	long	*as*	oo	(*as in* b<u>oo</u>t)

Vowels are always short before a double consonant, and long when followed by an h or when double

ie	*is pronounced* ee			(*as in* k<u>ee</u>p)

Diphthongs

au		*as*	ow	(*as in* h<u>ow</u>)
ei		*as*	y	(*as in* m<u>y</u>)
ai				
eu		*as*	oy	(*as in* b<u>oy</u>)
äu				

German irregular verbs

1st, 2nd and 3rd person present are given after the infinitive, and past subjunctive after the past indicative, where there is a change of vowel or any other irregularity.

Compound verbs are only given if they do not take the same forms as the corresponding simple verb, e.g. *befehlen*, or if there is no corresponding simple verb, e.g. *bewegen*.

An asterisk (*) indicates a verb which is also conjugated regularly.

Infinitive *Infinitiv*	Past Tense *Präteritum*	Past Participle *2. Partizip*
abwägen	wog (wöge) ab	abgewogen
ausbedingen	bedang (bedänge) aus	ausbedungen
*backen (du bäckst, er bäckt)	buk (büke)	gebacken
befehlen (du befiehlst, er befiehlt)	befahl (beföhle, befähle)	befohlen
beginnen	begann (begänne)	begonnen
beißen (du/er beißt)	biß (bisse)	gebissen
bergen (du birgst, er birgt)	barg (bärge)	geborgen
biegen	bog (böge)	gebogen
bieten	bot (böte)	geboten
binden	band (bände)	gebunden
bitten	bat (bäte)	gebeten
blasen (du/er bläst)	blies	geblasen
bleiben	blieb	geblieben
*bleichen	blich	geblichen
braten (du brätst, er brät)	briet	gebraten
brechen (du brichst, er bricht)	brach (bräche)	gebrochen
brennen	brannte (brennte)	gebrannt
bringen	brachte (brächte)	gebracht
denken	dachte (dächte)	gedacht
dreschen (du drischst, er drischt)	drosch (drösche)	gedroschen

Infinitive *Infinitiv*	Past Tense *Präteritum*	Past Participle *2. Partizip*
dringen	drang (dränge)	gedrungen
dürfen (ich/er darf, du darfst)	durfte (dürfte)	gedurft
empfehlen (du empfiehlst, er empfiehlt)	empfahl (empföhle)	empfohlen
erlöschen (du erlischst, er erlischt)	erlosch (erlösche)	erloschen
*erschrecken (du erschrickst, er erschrickt)	erschrak (erschräke)	erschrocken
erwägen	erwog (erwöge)	erwogen
essen (du/er ißt)	aß (äße)	gegessen
fahren (du fährst, er fährt)	fuhr (führe)	gefahren
fallen (du fällst, er fällt)	fiel	gefallen
fangen (du fängst, er fängt)	fing	gefangen
fechten (du fichtst, er ficht)	focht (föchte)	gefochten
finden	fand (fände)	gefunden
flechten (du flichtst, er flicht)	flocht (flöchte)	geflochten
fliegen	flog (flöge)	geflogen
fliehen	floh (flöhe)	geflohen
fließen (du/er fließt)	floß (flösse)	geflossen
fressen (du/er frißt)	fraß (fräße)	gefressen
frieren	fror (fröre)	gefroren
*gären	gor (göre)	gegoren
gebären (du gebierst, sie gebiert)	gebar (gebäre)	geboren
geben (du gibst, er gibt)	gab (gäbe)	gegeben
gedeihen	gedieh	gediehen
gehen	ging	gegangen
gelingen	gelang (gelänge)	gelungen
gelten (du giltst, er gilt)	galt (gölte, gälte)	gegolten
genesen (du/er genest)	genas (genäse)	genesen
genießen (du/er genießt)	genoß (genösse)	genossen
geschehen (es geschieht)	geschah (geschähe)	geschehen
gewinnen	gewann (gewönne, gewänne)	gewonnen
gießen (du/er gießt)	goß (gösse)	gegossen
gleichen	glich	geglichen

Infinitive *Infinitiv*	Past Tense *Präteritum*	Past Participle *2. Partizip*
gleiten	glitt	geglitten
graben (du gräbst, er gräbt)	grub (grübe)	gegraben
greifen	griff	gegriffen
haben (du hast, er hat)	hatte (hätte)	gehabt
halten (du hältst, er hält)	hielt	gehalten
hängen[2]	hing	gehangen
hauen	haute	gehauen
heben	hob (höbe)	gehoben
heißen (du/er heißt)	hieß	geheißen
helfen (du hilfst, er hilft)	half (hülfe)	geholfen
kennen	kannte (kennte)	gekannt
klingen	klang (klänge)	geklungen
kneifen	kniff	gekniffen
kommen	kam (käme)	gekommen
können (ich/er kann, du kannst)	konnte (könnte)	gekonnt
kriechen	kroch (kröche)	gekrochen
laden (du lädst, er lädt)	lud (lüde)	geladen
lassen (du/er läßt)	ließ	gelassen
laufen (du läufst, er läuft)	lief	gelaufen
leiden	litt	gelitten
leihen	lieh	geliehen
lesen (du/er liest)	las (läse)	gelesen
liegen	lag (läge)	gelegen
lügen	log (löge)	gelogen
mahlen	mahlte	gemahlen
meiden	mied	gemieden
melken	molk (mölke)	gemolken
messen (du/er mißt)	maß (mäße)	gemessen
mißlingen	mißlang (mißlänge)	mißlungen
mögen (ich/er mag, du magst)	mochte (möchte)	gemocht
müssen (ich/er muß, du mußt)	mußte (müßte)	gemußt
nehmen (du nimmst, er nimmt)	nahm (nähme)	genommen
nennen	nannte (nennte)	genannt
pfeifen	pfiff	gepfiffen
preisen (du/er preist)	pries	gepriesen
raten (du rätst, er rät)	riet	geraten

Infinitive *Infinitiv*	Past Tense *Präteritum*	Past Participle *2. Partizip*
reiben	rieb	gerieben
reißen (du/er reißt)	riß	gerissen
reiten	ritt	geritten
rennen	rannte (rennte)	gerannt
riechen	roch (röche)	gerochen
ringen	rang (ränge)	gerungen
rinnen	rann (ränne)	geronnen
rufen	rief	gerufen
*salzen (du/er salzt)	salzte	gesalzen
saufen (du säufst, er säuft)	soff (söffe)	gesoffen
*saugen	sog (söge)	gesogen
schaffen[1]	schuf (schüfe)	geschaffen
scheiden	schied	geschieden
scheinen	schien	geschienen
scheißen (du/er scheißt)	schiß	geschissen
scheren[1]	schor (schöre)	geschoren
schieben	schob (schöbe)	geschoben
schießen (du/er schießt)	schoß (schösse)	geschossen
schlafen (du schläfst, er schläft)	schlief	geschlafen
schlagen (du schlägst, er schlägt)	schlug (schlüge)	geschlagen
schleichen	schlich	geschlichen
schleifen[2]	schliff	geschliffen
schließen (du/er schließt)	schloß (schlösse)	geschlossen
schlingen	schlang (schlänge)	geschlungen
schmeißen (du/er schmeißt)	schmiß (schmisse)	geschmissen
schmelzen (du/er schmilzt)	schmolz (schmölze)	geschmolzen
schneiden	schnitt	geschnitten
*schrecken (du schrickst, er schrickt)	schrak (schräke)	geschreckt
schreiben	schrieb	geschrieben
schreien	schrie	geschrie[e]n
schreiten	schritt	geschritten
schweigen	schwieg	geschwiegen
schwellen (du schwillst, er schwillt)	schwoll (schwölle)	geschwollen
schwimmen	schwamm (schwömme)	geschwommen

Infinitive *Infinitiv*	Past Tense *Präteritum*	Past Participle *2. Partizip*
schwingen	schwang (schwänge)	geschwungen
schwören	schwor (schwüre)	geschworen
sehen (du siehst, er sieht)	sah (sähe)	gesehen
sein (ich bin, du bist, er ist, wir sind, ihr seid, sie sind)	war (wäre)	gewesen
senden[1]	sandte (sendete)	gesandt
sieden	sott (sötte)	gesotten
singen	sang (sänge)	gesungen
sinken	sank (sänke)	gesunken
sitzen (du/er sitzt)	saß (säße)	gesessen
sollen (ich/er soll, du sollst)	sollte	gesollt
*spalten	spaltete	gespalten
spinnen	spann (spönne, spänne)	gesponnen
sprechen (du sprichst, er spricht)	sprach (spräche)	gesprochen
springen	sprang (spränge)	gesprungen
stechen (du stichst, er sticht)	stach (stäche)	gestochen
stehen	stand (stünde, stände)	gestanden
stehlen (du stiehlst, er stiehlt)	stahl (stähle)	gestohlen
steigen	stieg	gestiegen
sterben (du stirbst, er stirbt)	starb (stürbe)	gestorben
stinken	stank (stänke)	gestunken
stoßen (du/er stößt)	stieß	gestoßen
streichen	strich	gestrichen
streiten	stritt	gestritten
tragen (du trägst, er trägt)	trug (trüge)	getragen
treffen (du triffst, er trifft)	traf (träfe)	getroffen
treiben	trieb	getrieben
treten (du trittst, er tritt)	trat (träte)	getreten
*triefen	troff (tröffe)	getroffen
trinken	trank (tränke)	getrunken
trügen	trog (tröge)	getrogen
tun (du tust, er tut)	tat (täte)	getan

Infinitive *Infinitiv*	Past Tense *Präteritum*	Past Participle 2. *Partizip*
verderben (du verdirbst, er verdirbt)	verdarb (verdürbe)	verdorben
vergessen (du/er vergißt)	vergaß (vergäße)	vergessen
verlieren	verlor (verlöre)	verloren
verzeihen	verzieh	verziehen
wachsen[1] (du/er wächst)	wuchs (wüchse)	gewachsen
waschen (du wäschst, er wäscht)	wusch (wüsche)	gewaschen
*wenden[2]	wandte (wendete)	gewandt
werben (du wirbst, er wirbt)	warb (würbe)	geworben
werden (du wirst, er wird)	wurde (würde)	geworden
werfen (du wirfst, er wirft)	warf (würfe)	geworfen
wiegen[1]	wog (wöge)	gewogen
winden	wand (wände)	gewunden
wissen (ich/er weiß, du weißt)	wußte (wüßte)	gewußt
wollen (ich/er will, du willst)	wollte	gewollt
wringen	wrang (wränge)	gewrungen
ziehen	zog (zöge)	gezogen
zwingen	zwang (zwänge)	gezwungen